VOLUME XLVII

SOCIETY
of
ACTUARIES

Transactions

*The work of science is to substitute facts for appearances
and demonstrations for impressions.*—RUSKIN

1995

MANUFACTURED FOR THE SOCIETY BY IPC PUBLISHING
ST. JOSEPH, MICHIGAN

PRINTED IN THE UNITED STATES OF AMERICA

ISBN 0-938959-41-7

FOREWORD

And so, with this volume, the 104-year era of the *Transactions* comes to a close. The book has been transformed over these years from a compilation of the official business of the Actuarial Society of America, to a record of the papers presented at meetings—as well as the ensuing discussions—to a widely respected forum for the presentation of seminal papers in the actuarial profession.

The first *Transactions*, entitled "Papers and Transactions of the Actuarial Society of America for the Years 1889 and 1890," appeared in 1891. That volume comprised a history of the foundation of the Actuarial Society; minutes of the first meeting of the society held in New York City on April 25, 1889 (including the toasts that were given); lists of members; the constitution; papers read at the October 3, 1889 meeting in New York City (including "History of the Dividend System in the United States," by David Parks Fackler); papers read at the April 24, 1890 meeting, again held in New York City; and papers read at the October 23–24, 1890 meeting in Hartford.

Volume I, No. 1 of the *Record* of the American Institute of Actuaries (*RAIA*), also a predecessor of the *TSA*, was published in June 1909 and contained a listing of the Board of Governors, Officers, and Members; the Inaugural Address of the President, Lucius McAdam; the history of the organization of the Institute; the constitution and by-laws; and requirements for admission. Papers read at meetings appeared in No. 2 of Volume I, published in June 1910.

Both publications continued to present papers read at the meetings of their respective organizations and associated discussions through the first half of the twentieth century. Additional materials included at various times were experience studies; examination questions; lists of members; lists of candidates passing the examinations; legal notes; book reviews; minutes of business meetings; obituaries; treasurer's reports; and the presidential addresses.

The last volume of the *Transactions* of the Actuarial Society of America (*TASA*), Volume L published in 1949, reported on the final meeting of that Society, which was held May 19–20, 1949 in New York City. In remarks reprinted therein, Dr. Arthur Hunter, who at the time had been a member for 50 years and admitted to having known all 30 Presidents (having been President himself in 1916–17), reminisced:

iii

"When the organization [the Actuarial Society of America] was first suggested there was considerable opposition on the part of several competitive companies who did not realize that the publication of their experience by a professional group would be of benefit to all. ... A few years later, however, one of the companies which had not favored the formation of the Society had a change of heart, its President stating that the results of all actuarial investigations which would benefit the life insurance business should be made public."

Volume XXXVII[1] of *RAIA,* appearing in 1948, was the last for that publication. It reports on the final joint meeting of the ASA and the AIA, held in French Lick, Indiana, October 27–29, 1948. One of the actions taken by the AIA, in its business meeting after the joint meeting, was the following:

"Authorized the Presidents of the Institute and the Society to appoint a committee to study the questions in connection with the printing of the final copies of the *Transactions* and *The Record* as well as the problems in connection with the *Transactions* of the Society of Actuaries and to report at the next meeting of the Board and Council."

And so, as a result of the merger of the Actuarial Society of America and the American Institute of Actuaries, began the *Transactions* of the Society of Actuaries. Contents of the first volume of the new journal differed rather remarkably from those of the predecessor publications, setting a new direction for actuarial literature on this continent. Space limits us to mentioning only a few of the numerous important contributions here.

In his landmark paper "Pensions—1949" (*TSA* I, 219), Dorrance C. Bronson showed clearly the growing pains being experienced in the pension field and went so far as to include a glossary of technical terms in an effort to standardize pension language. Another major contribution to the pension literature was Charles Trowbridge's[2] "Fundamentals of Pension Funding" (*TSA* IV, 17), in which he undertook to classify the range of funding methods into six classes, from Class I (pay as you go) to Class VI (the theoretical ultimate in heavy advance funding).

---

[1]Note that a paper in that *last* volume of *RAIA*, "Rate Functions and Their Role in Actuarial Mathematics,' was written by C. J. Nesbitt and Marjorie L. Van Eenam. A discussion on a paper in this volume ("Testing Financial Stability of Continuing Care Retirement Communities") was prepared by the same C. (Cecil) J. Nesbitt (see page 349). We couldn't have scripted this occurrence any more fortuitously.

[2]Trowbridge was a prolific contributor to the *TSA*. Discussions or papers with his byline appeared in practically every volume, his latest in Volume XLVI, "Mortality Rates by Marital Status."

Also in that first volume was "A New Mortality Basis for Annuities" (*TSA* I, 369). Authors Wilmer A. Jenkins and Edward A. Lew introduced North American actuaries to the concept of forecast tables based on direct estimates of future mortality decline rather on the crude device of setting back the ages in existing tables. It is indeed fitting that this last volume contains a paper by Robert Johansen ("Review of Adequacy of 1983 Individual Annuity Mortality Table") that deals with the same issue: improving mortality and its effect on annuity valuation tables.

Social Security has been a recurrent topic in the pages of the *TSA*, most notably, the papers by the Social Security Administration's long-time Chief Actuary, Robert J. Myers. His lucid explanations of Social Security Act amendments appeared in every even-numbered year between 1950 and 1960, and also in 1961. In all, 33 papers by Myers appeared in *TASA, RAIA*, and *TSA*. His last paper in the *TSA* was "An Updated Money's-Worth Analysis of Social Security Benefits" (co-authored with Bruce Schobel, Volume XLIV) and dealt with the question "Do workers get their money's worth from the payroll taxes that they pay under the U.S. Social Security program?"—a subject the same authors had first presented in Volume XXXV.

Change in the format of the *TSA* has been inevitable as the profession expanded in new directions. The "Legal Notes" section, started in 1909 in *TASA* and continued in *TSA*, presented authoritative information on important U.S. court decisions affecting actuarial work. The department was largely the work of Wendell M. Strong (from its inception until 1940, except for a hiatus between 1928 and 1935) and Buist M. Anderson (from 1940 until 1964). When Anderson resigned in 1964, the feature was discontinued; possibly actuarial work had expanded into so many areas that it was no longer feasible to cover them all.

A major change occurred in 1975, when the *Record* was created to contain transcripts of presentations and discussions at concurrent sessions, as well as some addresses, lectures, and teaching sessions of Society meetings. Thus, publication of papers and discussions in the *TSA* became independent of the meeting schedule of the Society. The *Record* was in paperback only and would not be published a second time in a clothbound volume, which was then the case for the *TSA* (to allow the insertion of discussions). The *TSA* would print papers, discussions of papers, authors' reviews, and the chronicle of official business of the Society. The *TSA Reports*, containing reports of various Society committees and experience studies, would continue to appear as a separate publication.

In this last volume, we acknowledge with gratitude those editors of this book who worked tirelessly to bring papers of note to the attention of members and to maintain the highest standards of quality in doing so:

John R. Larus	1949
Alden T. Bunyan	1950–1961
Alton O. Groth	1962–1965
Robert T. Jackson	1966–1968
Floyd T. Beasley	1969–1972
K. Arne Eide	1972–1976
Anthony T. Spano	1977–1979
John T. Dillon	1980–1982
Jonathan L. Wooley	1983–1985
Douglas A. Eckley	1986–1988
Jerry F. Enoch	1990–1992
Wilfred L. Thornthwaite	1993–1996

And so now we look to the future. In January 1997, the *North American Actuarial Journal* will make its debut, continuing and enhancing in many ways the spirit and excellence of the *Transactions*. The *Reports* will continue to present mortality and experience studies, task force reports, and industry studies but, beginning in 1997, will add features formerly found in the *Transactions*, such as the Presidential Address, Obituaries, and Financial Report. The *Record* will continue in its current role, offering transcripts of sessions and floor discussions of the Spring and Annual Meetings of the Society, though it will be disseminated in an electronic format.

The Society's intent in developing the *North American Actuarial Journal* is that it will be the premier publication of the Society of Actuaries, serving not only the membership but also the international, scientific, academic, business, and governmental communities. Its content, through feature articles—many of them solicited from widely recognized experts—and regular departments such as research, legislation/regulation, actuarial notes, and book reviews, is intended to scientifically address the domestic and international problems, interests and concerns of actuaries, their customers, related professionals, and public policy decision-makers.

Sam Gutterman
President, Society of Actuaries

The *Transactions* is published annually by the Society of Actuaries, successor to the Actuarial Society of America and the American Institute of Actuaries, in lieu of *Transactions* and the *Record*, respectively, heretofore published by the two former organizations.

NOTICE

The Society assumes no responsibility for statements made or opinions expressed in the articles, criticisms, and discussions published in the *Transactions*.

CONTENTS OF VOLUME XLVII

CONTENTS

Warren Rolland Adams
Lawrence Alpern
Josephine Wakeman Beers
Karen M. Chalk
William Thomas Chambers
Milton F. Chauner
Frank Dominic Cubello
Eugene Frederick Dorfman
Jack M. Elkin
Edmund Dean Forbes
Herbert Symonds Gardner
David Lawrence Gilbert
A. Allan Gruson
Thomas Charles Harding
Richard Fraser Staples Hazlett
James Hunter
William Ward Keffer
Larry Lang

Ben Zijon Lipshitz
Arthur Earl Loadman
Ralph Haynes Maglathlin
Keith Leslie McComb
Alexander Marshall
Laurence Harding Migotti
Morton David Miller
Zehman Irving Mosesson
Charles Edwin Rickards
Alexander Campbell Macintosh Robertson
Joseph F. Saulon
Edward Gladstone Schafer
Philip D. Slater
Anatase Eugene Statius
Terence Norman Towry
Paul Franklin Weber
William Rulon Williamson, Jr.

SOCIETY OF ACTUARIES

475 N. MARTINGALE ROAD, SCHAUMBURG, ILLINOIS 60173

OCTOBER 1995

BOARD OF GOVERNORS

	Term Expires
OFFICERS:	
SAM GUTTERMAN, *President*	1996
DAVID M. HOLLAND, *President-Elect*	1996
HOWARD J. BOLNICK, *Vice-President*	1996
WILLIAM CARROLL, *Secretary/Treasurer*	1996
YUAN CHANG, *Vice-President*	1997
JOHN J. PALMER, *Vice-President*	1997
PATRICIA L. SCAHILL, *Vice-President*	1997
ROBERT W. STEIN, *Vice-President*	1996
PAST PRESIDENTS:	
BARNET N. BERIN, *Immediate Past President*	1996
R. STEPHEN RADCLIFFE, *Penultimate Past President*	1996
ELECTED:	
NANCY A. BEHRENS	1998
WILLIAM F. BLUHM	1997
MORRIS W. CHAMBERS	1997
DONNA R. CLAIRE	1996
SUE ANN COLLINS	1998
DOUGLAS C. DOLL	1996
CINDY L. FORBES	1998
PETER HEPOKOSKI	1997
ANNE M. KATCHER	1997
W. PAUL McCROSSAN	1996
ESTHER H. MILNES	1996
PHILIP K. POLKINGHORN	1998
ANNA M. RAPPAPORT	1996
ALICE ROSENBLATT	1996
RICHARD G. SCHREITMUELLER	1997
ARNOLD F. SHAPIRO	1998
MICHAEL M. C. SZE	1997
MARK A. TULLIS	1998

REVIEWERS FOR PAPERS ACCEPTED FOR PUBLICATION
IN THIS VOLUME

TRANSACTIONS

ADDRESS OF THE PRESIDENT, BARNET N. BERIN

LOOKING FORWARD

During the last two years as President-Elect and now as President, I have tried to act on your behalf and move the Society of Actuaries forward, by changing it from an inward-looking to an outward-looking organization. As this two-year period closes, it seems appropriate to highlight the initiatives undertaken to move in that direction. While self-appraisals can be dangerous, I believe the following significant projects and activities will enhance a broader role for the actuary in the future. Here are some highlights of my involvement.

Macrodemographic Model

The first is the development of a macrodemographic model. This is an area where the actuarial profession can make a significant contribution to society in general and to its own future. A research project will be under way shortly to determine the feasibility of developing a model of the total U.S. population by city, state, and region. This model should include all aspects of demography and reflect the employed, unemployed, and those covered by health insurance or private pensions, in order to answer quantitative questions raised by the government's executive branch, particularly about uncovered groups. This model could be adapted to reflect any local or national series of time payments, such as unemployment, welfare, and so on.

Social Security

Social Security is another area where the actuarial profession can make a major contribution. Too much has been written about Social Security that is misleading to the American public. To help set the record straight, a Social Security education initiative will soon be undertaken by the SOA Foundation.

Its purpose is to provide objective information about the Social Security system—past, present, and future—and what some of the options are to keep it healthy. The Foundation is currently exploring the possibility of working with various corporations on this important project.

Actuarial Circles

Actuarial Circles is another program started last year as a grassroots effort to encourage actuaries to lend their expertise to important issues being discussed in the media. The SOA has held briefings on how to approach and work with the media. To date, almost 300 members have become part of the Circles network. Their activity has focused on writing letters and meeting with reporters on subjects ranging from Social Security to Medicare and tax issues. Circles members benefit personally by gaining communications skills, and the profession benefits by having knowledgeable actuaries step forward to provide an actuarial perspective on appropriate issues.

Matching Resume Service

A fourth program, now about 1½ years old, is a no-fee employment service for unemployed actuaries and students with more than 100 credits. Employers send in job listings with their requirements to the Society of Actuaries. These job listings are then matched against resumes on file. Matched resumes are forwarded to companies for their follow-up.

Right now, we have about 225 positions listed and about 200 resumes on file. To date, 165 members who were listed with the resume service have found positions, with a fair number of those being filled at the Fellowship level. The service is currently receiving about 20 new listings a month, with some listings coming from nontraditional employers in the financial field.

In addition, for our unemployed members, there is a deferment/waiver of dues program, with no repayment required, as well as waived meeting and continuing education fees.

Investment Mathematics

The fifth subject, one I especially wish to emphasize, is the role investment mathematics will play in the actuarial profession. This subject goes to the heart of what an actuary is and touches on several important aspects of the profession.

We all realize that the profession's rate of growth has slowed. Most of it was fueled by the post-World War II increase in consulting firms specializing in employee benefits. This growth flattened about five years ago due, in my opinion, to needlessly complex and costly IRS and accounting rules as well as a slowdown in the economy.

For the first time since the 1930s, our profession has experienced unemployment, even though it's a low 0.7%. Additionally, those entering the profession are finding a difficult job market. I don't know whether these are temporary or permanent circumstances, but I do know we had better act on them.

At the same time that we are experiencing a change in our employment, it has become clear that newly created instruments in the investment field are well-suited to the talents of actuaries. In fact, actuaries have been moving into this field. Today, more than 150 are working for investment bankers and advisors, and one of the leading experts on derivatives in the United States is an actuary.

The investment field presents an opportunity for the actuarial profession, but to capitalize on it, we need to train our students by adding material to the syllabus that is rich in higher investment mathematics and mathematical modeling. This will not be easy, but the E&E Committee is taking the beginning steps, and I support their changes for the future.

And, thanks to the combined efforts of Lincoln National Corporation and the SOA Foundation, an investment mathematics textbook will be published in 1996. We have a top-notch editor and an excellent team of authors. Every member of the Society of Actuaries will receive a complimentary copy of this book, which will fill an important need for actuaries to better understand current problems in finance. This textbook will help actuaries apply this new knowledge in all practice areas and in nontraditional areas as well.

I believe the investment field will open up for actuaries, much as employee benefit consulting did in the past, and provide interesting and rewarding careers. We must, however, increase our ties to the investment community.

Additionally, we must further expand the investment specialty in our E&E syllabus, ensuring that it is rigorous and remains current. What better way to do this than by asking the investment community to review our syllabus and suggest modifications? This would demonstrate our commitment to develop and maintain an excellent knowledge base, and it would also indicate that the actuarial profession is producing competent actuaries who can contribute to their business.

There are those who say the actuary's role is largely managerial and not necessarily quantitative. However, I believe that our roots are technical and that any sustained emphasis on nonquantitative approaches is dangerous to our profession's survival. On any major issue, the actuary should be able to quantify the problem, even if it is no more than a cost/value statement based upon liberal, and then conservative, assumptions. Responding qualitatively to problems can be impressive and may generate much useful material, but in the final analysis, this kind of work need not be done by an actuary. Without quantifying our work, we can lose our place and, most important, our direction. Advanced investment mathematics is an opportunity our profession should not miss.

SOA Foundation

Several times now, I have mentioned the Society of Actuaries Foundation. As its first chairman, I helped define the mission and its direction. Like all of you, I wish the Foundation success, since it will affect the future of the actuarial profession.

Now let me discuss three observations I've made during this two-year term.

SOA Accumulated Goodwill

First, I'm proud to say the SOA has a striking reputation. I have traveled a fair amount these last two years, and I can assure you that the SOA is highly regarded and respected all over the world.

Even so, in the United States, we do not capitalize on our reputation by testifying before the IRS, congressional committees, and so on. While Article X of our Constitution is an impediment, the SOA Sections could be doing more, and they need to be encouraged to tackle such opportunities. We do support the American Academy of Actuaries in its efforts, and as we work together, it's clear that our objectives focus on advancing the profession at large.

The Challenge of Being an International Organization

Second, I've become more aware of the SOA as an international organization. Students are taking our exams in 15 different countries. The largest exam center is in Taiwan, with almost 400 candidates in the last exam cycle. Hong Kong and China also had large turnouts.

However, in the third world countries, access to our education system is frequently difficult. For example, our examination fees are beyond the financial reach of most students; our FSA courses reflect U.S. or Canadian practice so that many students stop at the ASA level, and completion of the

Fellowship Admissions Course requires students to be present at a U.S. or Canadian location. Many are unable to meet the travel expenses. We have an excellent International Committee studying these issues, and I urge it to move forward with recommendations.

Observers at Board of Governors Meetings

"Acting on behalf of the members" has always been important to me. Some years ago, I was responsible for *The Actuary* listing the date and place of the Board meetings to let members know they were welcome to attend as observers. Unfortunately, only a few members have attended these meetings over the years.

I believe that members need to know what transpires at Board meetings beyond the brief published summary of Board actions. We have all made a considerable investment, in years of study, to become members, and I believe we need to position ourselves to better facilitate two-way communications.

To say that Board members are the representatives of the membership at large misses the point. This is no ordinary Board, and we are no ordinary membership.

To help facilitate this communication, I suggest that Section Chairpersons assign Board delegates from their Section. The delegates would rotate, so that two or three Sections would regularly send representatives to each Board of Governors meeting. These delegates can then report on discussions of particular interest to their Sections, through their newsletters, their Section Councils, or Actuaries Online. In addition, a Section delegate may be invited to attend when an agenda item directly affects the Section's special interest.

If we don't do something like this, these meetings in effect become closed to our members, and significant changes may come as surprises. Granted, highlights of the meetings are published, but the debates leading up to Board actions are not.

It is important for members to be aware of the rationale behind decisions as well as individual Board representatives' views on a wide range of subjects, since these representatives frequently become Vice Presidents and Presidents of this organization. The SOA Board is not a typical Board in the conventional sense. Members need to know what transpires, sometimes in considerable detail.

Closing Comments

Now, a few final comments as I end my term as President.

I have met many members these past two years, and the most common question they ask me is, "How are you doing?" The answer has always been, "Just fine." Not only is this job a great honor; it is interesting and responsible, providing a chance to influence the future of the profession.

Two important features make it especially rewarding. First, the SOA staff support is excellent, first-rate by any standard. Second, the SOA, over its history, has built up enormous goodwill that has only been partially tapped. This goodwill, both here and overseas, makes the job of President easier.

We would not be the Society of Actuaries if not for the willingness of members to volunteer for more than 120 committees. Currently, about 1,400 members are on SOA committees. We have never lacked for volunteers, and this has been a tremendous resource. We owe them a lot, but they are us.

Most of us have benefited from involvement in the Society by meeting people with similar interests who also have been willing to contribute to the profession's future. If you have not already done so, I hope you become involved with the SOA and stay involved.

Over the last 12 months, the theme of our meetings has been professional and ethical responsibilities. Beyond the technical challenges we face, there is the wider responsibility of doing the job right and being responsible, through our individual actions, not only to preserve our own personal integrity but also to preserve and enhance the integrity of our profession. I hope I have heightened your awareness of this important issue by repeating this theme.

More than occasionally in actuarial work, we are able to do something that helps an individual or employees or, on a wider scale, contributes to society in general. I have always been grateful for that. Thank you for the opportunity to be your President.

OPERATIONS RESEARCH IN INSURANCE: A REVIEW

PATRICK L. BROCKETT* AND XIAOHUA XIA†

ABSTRACT

Operations research methods have been applied to the modeling and the solution of numerous problems in insurance and actuarial science. This paper reviews the applications of these operations research methods in the insurance industry. The paper is organized according to the categorization of operations research methods. Specifically, various mathematical programming models and their applications are first introduced. Game theory and some new operations research approaches are discussed, along with their applications in insurance and actuarial science. The paper concludes with a general discussion of developments and trends in operations research and insurance.

For the student who has studied specific operations research techniques mandated by the SOA examination system, this paper provides a set of examples of techniques pertinent to actuaries and shows how the expanding field of general quantitative reasoning in risk management can have a positive impact on the insurance industry. For research actuaries, we finally present an updated bibliography of operations research applications in insurance cross-classified by authors, operations research methodologies, and insurance areas of application.

---

1. INTRODUCTION

Operations Research (OR) models have been formulated to solve a wide variety of problems in the insurance industry. In this paper, we review some insurance industry applications of quantitative reasoning techniques, often known as OR methods. Many of these techniques are studied by actuarial students in a non-insurance context (SOA Exam 130), and so a description of actual insurance applications can provide a useful addition and motivation for the educational process.

*Dr. Brockett, not a member of the Society, is Director of the Center for Cybernetic Studies and Gus S. Wortham Chair in Risk Management and Insurance in the Department of Management Science and Information Systems at The University of Texas at Austin.

†Dr. Xia, not a member of the Society, is with AutoBond Acceptance Corp., Austin, Texas.

7

Early overviews of OR in insurance were presented by Zubay [291], who discussed the feasibility of applying OR methods to the insurance industry. Wade et al. [279] presented an excellent annotated bibliography, which was published by the McCahan Foundation. Denenberg [98] provided a review of OR in insurance, and Jewell [151] provided another excellent survey. In addition, early on (in 1960s and 1970s) the Society of Actuaries published a series of insightful discussions on the potential usefulness of OR techniques in actuarial and insurance areas [102]. Since then, Jewell [155] and Shapiro [255] have provided updated surveys. More recently, Haehling von Lanzenauer and Wright [133] presented a very useful overview of the interface of OR and insurance in the broader context of risk management with a unique feature of explicitly dealing with the decision problems by insureds.

Most of the previous review papers were organized according to application in the insurance industry. Shapiro [255], however, presented the material according to specific OR methodologies. This paper is also categorized according to OR areas in an attempt to provide an updated overview of both new and classical OR methodologies and their applications in insurance. This paper is intended to be more technique-oriented, an approach that is consistent with how actuarial students in North America study OR. This survey is thus intended to supplement and motivate the material learned by actuarial students while providing convenient reference for the professional. In particular, actuarial students who have studied OR techniques from non-actuarial textbooks will find herein many applications of OR methods to insurance and finance. Accordingly, the relevance of the OR examination material to actuarial science research and practice is reinforced by the paper.

In addition, the insights gained by using general quantitative reasoning to address problems in risk management will become more apparent to the actuary, who is most responsible for implementing mathematical techniques in the insurance industry. Some mathematical formulations are illustrated, and the connections among various approaches are discussed. In addition, some new OR approaches are explored. Both modeling techniques and computational aspects are briefly considered. Our intent is to deliver a review of deterministic methods in insurance and actuarial science without formally discussing most probabilistic models and stochastic process models such as queuing processes of claim arrivals, and so on.[1]

---

[1]We recognize that uncertainty is the *raison d'etre* of risk and the business of insurance. We have chosen to limit our coverage of stochastic methods primarily to conserve space and to follow more directly the OR methods studied by actuarial students without immediately apparent applications in risk management. Several methodologies presented do, however, have stochastic components and

The paper is organized as follows. Various mathematical programming models and their applications in insurance are presented in the next section. In Section 3, some new OR methods (such as data envelopment analysis, expert systems and neural networks) together with game theory and their applications are illustrated. Next, conclusions and discussions are presented. Finally, a detailed bibliographic reference of OR applications to insurance is given. To make this bibliography useful to both researchers and practicing actuaries, it is cross-referenced in three ways: by author, by OR technique, and by insurance functional area of applications.

2. MATHEMATICAL PROGRAMMING

A major research direction and practical application approach within OR is mathematical programming. Accordingly, the major part of this review paper is dedicated to various mathematical programming models in a variety of risk management and insurance applications. In the following eight subsections, we introduce the developed or promising insurance applications of general linear programming, nonlinear programming, integer programming, and five other special mathematical programming approaches: network optimization, goal programming, dynamic programming, chance-constrained programming, and fuzzy programming.

A general mathematical programming problem can be formulated as[2]:

$$\text{Maximize} \quad f(x, y)$$

$$\text{subject to:} \quad g_i(x, y) = 0, \text{ for } i = l, \ldots, p; \tag{1}$$

$$g_j(x, y) \le 0, \text{ for } j = p, \ldots, p + q,$$

x is a non-negative real-valued n-vector

y is a non-negative integer-valued m-vector.

It is not difficult to show that the non-negativity restriction on the vectors x and y can be made without loss of any generality.[3] Notice also that the

---

statistical content. We also recognize that simulation methods are an important topic for actuaries using quantitative reasoning; however, we do not expand this subject here in the interests of space and because of the availability of other sources for the information.

[2]Throughout we use boldface lowercase letters to represent vectors and non-boldface subscripted letters to represent the components of the vector.

[3]To see this, consider the two cases, that is, negative variables and (upper and lower) bounded variables. If $x \le 0$, then let $y = x$ and substitute $-y$ for x in the various functions to obtain a standard

general formulation above can encompass both minimization and maximization problems, since minimizing an objective function is equivalent to maximizing the negative of the objective function. It is also easy to transform a "greater than or equal" into "less than or equal to" inequality constraint by simply multiplying the inequality by -1. This confirms that Formulation (1) indeed encompasses the most general mathematical programming models. Accordingly, in this paper, we use either maximization or minimization interchangeably without explicit explanation.

In subsequent sections, we see how added restrictions on the objective function or on the constraints and variable domains generate the specific type of mathematical programming problems; this is made clear in the individual subsections. The order of these subsections is as follows. Because LP is the basis of many other mathematical programming approaches, linear programming (LP) is presented first. General nonlinear programming (NLP) is presented next. Finally, integer programming (IP), network optimization (NO), goal programming (GP), dynamic programming (DP), and chance-constrained programming (CCP) are introduced, and last, fuzzy programming (FP) is presented.

2.1 Linear Programming

For the general mathematical formulation (1), a linear programming problem is obtained when the objective function and the constraints are all linear in the unknown variables. Hence, a linear programming problem can be expressed as follows:

$$\text{Maximize } c^T x \tag{2}$$

subject to $Ax \leq b$, and x is a real-valued vector.

where A is an $m \times n$ real-valued matrix, b is an m-dimensional real-valued vector, and c is n-dimensional real-valued vector; that is, we are maximizing a linear function subject to linear inequality constraints.

We now present one illustration of LP in the insurance industry, a linear programming method for measuring the cost of whole life insurance (Schleef

---

formulation. If $x \in [l,u]$, then first, let $x' = x - l$, so that $x' \in [0, u-l]$. The second step is to introduce two non-negative and unbounded variables, y_1 and y_2, and let $x' = y_1 - y_2$. We then obtain two non-negative and unbounded variables and standard formulation by substituting $y_1 - y_2$ for x' and introducing the constraints $y_2 \leq y_1$ and $y_1 \leq u - 1 + y_2$.

[250]).[4] Compared to more traditional methods (the measure of interest adjusted surrender cost method and Linton's rate of return), the linear programming method requires fewer assumptions, because the only input required is the rate of return that is relevant to the policyholder. The method does not attempt to directly separate the protection and savings components of the whole life policy. It assumes that the insured individual requires a given level of protection and is not concerned with how the insurer breaks down the received premium into loading charges, reserves, and so forth. The method also has the additional flexibility of considering the time at which the insured requires protection. The flexibility of varying the year of required protection is the primary characteristic of the LP method that differentiates it from the more traditional methods.

In the LP formulation, the three types of decision variables are the amount w_t lent externally by the insured at the beginning of year t, the amount z_t borrowed externally by the insured at the beginning of year t, and u, the face value of insurance purchased at the time $t=0$. It is assumed that the rate of return, i, or borrowing and lending rate are the same (although this could be relaxed in the LP formulation), so only the net position $(w_t - z_t)$ appears in the formulation. The objective function is to maximize the discounted cash flows associated with a given policy, which is constrained by the amount that the insured is willing to budget for insurance, and the amounts of protection required in each year to the horizon. The linear programming formulation is shown below:

Maximize
$$(1 + i)^{-n} C_n u + \sum_{i=1}^{n} (1 + i)^{-(t-1)} (w_t - z_t)$$

subject to
$$P_t u + w_t - z_t \leq b_t, \text{ for } t = 1, \ldots, n;$$

$$u + \sum_{t=1}^{j} (1 + i)^{-(t-j)} (w_t - z_t) \geq I_j, \text{ for } j = 1, \ldots, n; \text{ and}$$

$$u, w_t, z_t \text{ are non-negative,}$$

where w_t, z_t, and u are decision variables; w_t is the amount lent externally by the insured at the beginning of year t; z_t is the amount borrowed externally by the insured at the beginning of year t; u is the face value of

[4]As Schleef [250] indicated, the LP model can also be applied to other types of life insurance such as term insurance and interest sensitivity products such as universal life.

insurance purchased at the time $t=0$; P_t is the net premium rate in year t; C_t is the cash-value rate at the end of year t; b_t is the amount budgeted by the insured at the beginning of year t; I_t is the insurance protection required at the beginning of year t; and n is the number of years in the planning period.

From this primal linear programming model, the dual linear programming model is obtained.[5] By using the "shadow price" interpretation of the dual parameters corresponding to the constraints in the primal problem, the dual LP model can be used to analyze the marginal discount factors for each year and the marginal discounted cost of increasing the death benefit requirement in each year.

Linear programming is a very general category programming problem. As shown later, many goal programs, integer programs, and network flow models can be formulated as linear programs. Hence, further applications of linear programming are discussed in separate subsections. There are many other interesting applications of LP to insurance. For example, Chan et al. [57], Schuette [253], and Hickman [141] provide theoretical discussion and formulation of LP approaches to graduation.

Financial management is another mature area in insurance and actuarial science in which the LP method has been widely used. Hofflander and Drandell [144], for example, use a linear programming model to discuss profitability, capacity and regulation problems in insurance management. Schleef [249] uses a linear programming model for decision-making in life insurance purchases.

Conwill [79] develops several linear programming models for maximizing policyholder value in problems of making combined decisions of life insurance product purchasing and asset investment. In his long paper, Conwill discusses the techniques used in building linear programming models for insurance problems, the computational issues involved in solving the linear programming problems, and the interpretation of the results produced from computation.

Haehling von Lanzenauer et al. [130] show how to formulate the problem of developing a manpower planning policy as a linear programming problem. Linear programming is also suggested by Jennergren [150] for use as an asset valuation method. Navarro and Nave [211] use linear programming for dynamic investment immunization problems. Indeed, there are many

---

[5]We recommend Hillier and Lieberman [143] for further reading about the definition of dual programming, how a primal linear programming transformed to its dual LP, what the relationship between the optimal solution to the primal and that to the dual is, and how one can interpret the dual (what the economic interpretation is).

applications of LP methods for problems in financial areas such as capital budgeting, portfolio management, duration matching, and immunization. These applications are also of substantial interest to actuaries and to insurance management.

2.2 Nonlinear Programming

In the general mathematical programming Formulation (1), nonlinear programming encompasses the least restrictive set of attributes imposed. In the general nonlinear programming model, the variables are free to be either real-valued or integer-valued, and the objective or the constraints can involve nonlinear functions. Hence, linear programming is actually a special form of nonlinear programming. Compared to linear optimization problems, however, nonlinear programming suffers more serious disadvantages. Nonlinear functions are typically more difficult to specify. In addition, although some special classes of nonlinear programming (such as convex programming) can be optimally solved, in nonlinear optimization there may be a multitude of local optima of the nonlinear objective function. Accordingly, a serious problem in nonlinear optimization is that commonly used solution methods such as Newton-Raphson techniques may find local rather than global optimal solutions. Occasionally, given the search technique used, the global optimum cannot be found within a reasonable time limitation.

In this section, rather than pursuing further discussion on general nonlinear programming, we describe two applications of nonlinear programming in the insurance industry: a quadratic programming model for insurance portfolio analysis (Markle and Hofflander [197]) and an information theoretic approach to mortality table graduation (Brockett [38]).

Among the early efforts at combining underwriting and investment into an integrated portfolio analysis is the work by Markle and Hofflander [197]. As an extension of the Markowitz portfolio model, their combined portfolio analysis indicates an efficient portfolio that may be relevant for insurers' financial decision-making. A similar philosophy is used in Crum and Nye [85], in which generalized network flow models are proposed to obtain optimal insurance and investment portfolios. Other extensions include that of Brockett, Charnes, and Li [40], who consider simultaneously the optimal selection of investment vehicles and insurance lines of business decisions for a casualty insurance company.

Markle and Hofflander's model is a quadratic programming model; that is, the objective function used is quadratic in the unknown decision variables of interest and the constraints involve only linear functions. The objective function involves maximizing the expected portfolio return, and this maximization is done subject to two types of constraints: institutional and regulatory solvency constraints, and accounting types of constraints. The decision variables they use are selected balance sheet variables representing the allocation of assets (including various bonds and stocks) and liabilities (including the premiums written in multiple insurance lines). After all the variance and covariance matrices within and between the asset and liability variables have been estimated, the objective function is written as a quadratic function in the decision variables. All the constraints are linear. With such a formulation, not only can the unique optimal portfolio be found (because the constraint set is convex), but also a sensitivity analysis can be conducted of the effect of changes in the regulatory solvency constraints on the optimal expected portfolio return. Such a quadratic programming formulation for portfolio analysis is widely used in finance and investment literature. In addition, the algorithms for solving quadratic programming problems are also efficient and commercially available for easy use.

We next introduce another application of nonlinear programming of interest to life actuaries, namely, mortality table construction and graduation. The information theoretic methodology (Brockett and Zhang [46], Brockett [38], Brockett et al. [43], and Brockett et al. [45]) can be used for selecting statistical models for analysis when the true underlying distributions are unknown, which is typical of mortality table construction. The graduation of the mortality table using empirical data is a particular problem of interest. A complete discussion of the information theoretic methodology illustrated here can be found in Brockett [38].

Let the vector $\mathbf{u}$ denote the observed series of values $\mathbf{u} = (u_1, u_2, ...)$ that are to be graduated into a mortality table and the vector δ denote the resultant smooth or graduated series of values $\delta = (\delta_1, \delta_2, ...)$. The information distance between the observed series and the graduated series is defined as

$$I(\delta/\mathbf{u}) = \sum_t \delta_i \ln\left[\frac{\delta_i}{u_t}\right].$$

It represents a measure of closeness of the observed and graduated series with $I(\delta/\mathbf{u})=0$ if and only if $\delta=\mathbf{u}$.

The objective of the graduation process is to find a graduated series that is as close as possible to the observed series but satisfies certain constraints. Thus, the objective function is

$$\text{Min}_\delta I(\delta/\mathbf{u}) = \sum_i \delta_i \ln\left[\frac{\delta_i}{u_i}\right].$$

The first constraint is the non-negativity on the graduated series. Other constraints on δ occur because the true underlying pattern of mortality rates is (a) smooth, (b) increasing with age, that is, $\Delta\delta_x = \delta_{x+1} - \delta_x \geq 0$, and (c) more steeply increasing at the higher ends of the range, that is, $\Delta^2\delta_x \geq 0$. Additional constraints in the graduation process are that (d) the graduated number of deaths using δ equals the observed number of deaths using $\mathbf{u}$ and (e) the total of the graduated ages at death equals the total of the observed ages at death. The measure of smoothness is given by $\Sigma(\Delta^3\delta_x)^2 \leq M$, which can be formulated as a quadratic constraint $\delta^T A\delta \leq M$, where the matrix A is:

$$\begin{vmatrix} -1 & 3 & -3 & 1 & 0 & 0 & 0 \\ 0 & -1 & 3 & -3 & 1 & 0 & 0 \\ 0 & 0 & -1 & 3 & -3 & 1 & 0 \\ & & & & & & \\ 0 & 0 & 0 & 0 & 0 & 0 & 1 \end{vmatrix}.$$

The constant M determines the degree of smoothness obtained for the graduated series.

The resulting convex programming model can be solved by using general nonlinear programming codes such as generalized reduced gradient algorithm (GRG2) (Lasdon [173] and Lasdon et al. [174], and [175]).

As mentioned in Brockett [38], other objective functions could be used for graduation, and the quadratic one associated with Whittaker-Henderson graduation provides a case in point. Illustrative of using a mathematical programming approach to the Whittaker-Henderson graduation is the paper of Lowrie [190]. Chan et al. [57] also show that the problem of minimizing the Whittaker-Henderson objective function $F_p(\mathbf{u}) + \lambda S_q(\mathbf{u})$ over $\mathbf{u} \geq 0$, using the fit measure

$$F_p(\mathbf{u}) \equiv \sum w_x |u_x - u_x''|^p$$

and the smoothness measure $S_q(\mathbf{u}) \equiv \Sigma / \Delta^z u_x|^q$, $p \neq q$, can be formulated as a linear programming problem when $p=1$ and $q=\infty$, as a quadratic programming problem when either p or q is 2. These general graduation methods are all amenable to solution by using nonlinear programming methods.

2.3 Integer Programming

An integer program (IP) is obtained from the general mathematical programming Formulation (1), when the decision variables are restricted to being integers. Integer programming problem can involve nonlinear functions in its objective or constraints. For illustrative convenience, we introduce only integer LP.

Integer LP, as a special case of LP, arises in resource allocation or assignment problems, facility location, traveling salesman or vehicle routing problems, and many other combinatorial problems. Graph theory and integer programming are often interrelated. Many graph theory problems are formulated and solved as IP problems, whereas many IP developments are directly related to graph theory study. Because of the integer restriction, the solution obtained by simply rounding the corresponding real-valued LP solutions to integer values is often suboptimal. Accordingly, some other effective algorithms are required to solve integer LP problems.

There are many IP problems known for the NP-complete or NP-hard problem; that is, it is not very likely that polynomial bounded algorithms (in sense of the time required to find the optimal solution) will be found for these classes of problems. In spite of the prevalence of NP-completeness/NP-hardness in IP, many efficient algorithms have recently been developed. Among them are the branch-and-bound search, the Lagrangian relaxation method, the subgradient technique, the decomposition method, and the constraint aggregation method. These algorithms have proven to be computationally successful for complex IP problems, although some of them achieve computation time efficiency by finding the satisfactory, but not necessarily optimal, solution. Several excellent books or papers specializing in integer programming are listed in the bibliography. In particular, for those readers who are interested in the complexity of algorithms in general, we suggest Garey and Johnson [116], while for those who are particularly interested in integer programming modeling, we recommend Nemhauser and Wolsey [212].

Applications of IP models abound in the insurance industry. As discussed in a later section, network flow models can be used in many situations such as financial planning, cash management, and so on. These network flow problems constitute a special case of IP problems under certain reasonable assumptions. In this subsection, we illustrate the application of IP to the problem of reorganizing the sale regions for a life and annuity insurance company (Gelb and Khumawala [118]). The first example in Section 2.5, Goal Programming, provides another integer programming illustration in insurance.

In 1982, a Houston-based company, Variable Annuity Life Insurance Company (VALIC), was interested in reorganization of its sales force of 336 individuals. At that time, there were 16 sales regions, each with a manager and regional office. The regions had evolved as combinations of 57 geographical segments involving states or portions of states. The reorganization plan investigation was specifically undertaken to determine a least-cost solution to determining the number of regions and the geographical configuration of the regions. It was also desirable to compute the cost savings that would be obtained if the suggested sales region configurations were adopted. Three constraints were imposed by the company: (1) the number of regions should not decrease; (2) the number of regions should at most double; and (3) disproportion in market potential should not be exacerbated. The primary task was to improve profitability by either increasing market potential or decreasing the costs incurred. This problem of reorganization of the insurance sales force was formulated by Gelb and Khumawala [118] as follows:

Maximize $\quad \sum_{ij} C_{ij} x_{ij} + \sum_i F_i y_i$

subject to: $\quad \sum_i x_{ij} \geq D_j$, for all j;

$\qquad\qquad \sum_j x_{ij} \leq S_i y_i$, for all i; and

for all i, $y_i = 1$ if $x_{ij} \geq 0$; $y_i = 0$ if $x_{ij} < 0$,

where C_{ij} is the sum of variable costs (operating expenses and cost of lost sales) relating to the i-th regional office and j-th geographical segment; F_i the fixed costs of the i-th potential office; D_j the market potential of the j-th geographic segment; S_i the capacity of the i-th potential office; y_i the integer decision variable indicating the utilization ($y_i=1$) or nonutilization ($y_i=0$) of the i-th regional office; and x_{ij} the integer decision variable denoting the amount of market potential of the j-th segment to be served from the i-th regional office.

This formulation is a typical facility location problem. For an insurance company this model has utility not only for reorganizing existing regional sales force structure geography but also for designing a regional sales office configuration for an insurance company intending to expand its business geographically. Gelb and Khumawala [118] used a branch-and-bound implicit search procedure to solve the problem. The solution showed that if the total number of regional offices was allowed to increase from 16 to 25, the total cost could be reduced from $18,826,000 to $9,993,000, a saving of $8,833,000.

The problem size, however, will expand with the number of potential offices. The branch-and-bound approach may not be able to handle the case of a very large number of potential offices because branch-and-bound techniques basically use an enumerated search approach. Although the search method is wisely designed to potentially reduce the search time substantially, in the worst case, the search time is an exponential function of the problem size (see Garey and Johnson [116] for the precise definition of problem size). For large IP problems, other algorithms such as the Lagrangian relaxation may be required.

Integer programming approaches to problem-solving have also been successfully applied in finance and other business areas. Many portfolio management problems (Faaland [109], and Nauss [209], [210]) and capital budgeting problems (Gonzalez et al. [126], Laughhaunn [176], and Pettway [224]) have been modeled as integer programming problems when assets are indivisible or projects must be adopted or rejected in their entirety. Insurance, in its role as a financial intermediary, has many other potential applications of integer programming. Two such applications of IP in insurance and finance are given in the next section.

2.4 Network Optimization

A network model is denoted by $G(N, A)$, where N is a set of nodes and A is a set of arcs, while G relates the network optimization to graph theory. Each arc $(i, j) \in A$ represents an ordered relationship between two nodes, i, $j \in N$. Thus a network is a directed graph. There are three main types of network flow problems: the shortest path problem (SPP), the maximum flow problem (MFP), and the minimum cost flow problem (MCFP). In fact, both the SPP and MFP are special cases of MCFP; hence, below we give only the general network formulation for a minimum cost flow model. We refer readers to an excellent book by Ahuja, Magnanti, and Orlin [5] for thorough discussion on network flows.

A general network formulation is as follows:

$$\text{Maximize} \quad \sum_{(i,j)\in A} c_{ij} x_{ij}$$

$$\text{subject to} \quad \sum_{\{i:(i,j)\in A\}} x_{ij} - \sum_{\{j:(j,i)\in A\}} p_{ji} x_{ji} = b(i), \text{ for } i \in N; \text{ and}$$

$$0 \le l_{ij} \le x_{ij} \le u_{ij}.$$

where $\{j:(j,i)\in A\}$ denotes the set of nodes j that have an arc leading to node i, while $\{j:(i,j)\in A\}$ denotes the set of nodes j to which an arc originating from node i. For one explanation of the formulation given above, x_{ij} represents the amount of flow from node i to node j; p_{ij} is the transmitting efficient rate of the arc (i, j), which is usually less than or equal to 1; $b(i)$ is the extra demand or excess supply of node i; and c_{ij} represents the benefit of unit flow on arc (i, j) because of the maximization of the objective function.

Networks are pervasive. They arise in numerous application settings and in many forms. Physical networks are perhaps the most common and the most readily identifiable networks. Network flow problems, however, also arise in surprising ways for problems that, on the surface, might not appear to involve networks at all. Sometimes the nodes and arcs have a temporal dimension that model activities that take place over time. Many scheduling applications have this flavor. In any event, network models arise in a wide variety of problems in project management; equipment and crew scheduling (say, claims adjusters or auditors); location layout theory; warehousing and distribution; production planning and control; and social, medical, and financial contexts.

Network flow models have also been used in the insurance industry. In this paper, we present a class of network models applicable to insurance and investment portfolio management.

Our first illustrative application of network flow models is project management. As early as 30 years ago, Zubay [291] suggested potential applications of network models in the insurance industry. In this section, we show three basic models of project management: determination of minimum project duration, just-in-time scheduling, and the time-cost trade-off project scheduling problem.

For an application of network methodology to project scheduling, suppose we are given a set of jobs required to complete a project (for example, a new rate filing or policy filing case). We are also given the order in which the jobs are to be done, as certain jobs must proceed others, while other tasks can be accomplished simultaneously. These constraints on the order in which the jobs can be done are known as the precedence relationships. The objective is to determine the minimum project duration, that is, the least possible amount of time needed to complete the entire project. This problem is a typical shortest path problem. Let $u(i)$ and $u(j)$ denote the earliest possible start times for job i and j. Then the problem has the following formulation:

$$\text{Minimize} \quad u(t) - u(s)$$

$$\text{subject to} \quad u(j) - u(i) \geq c_{ij}, \text{ for } (i, j) \in A; \text{ and}$$

$$u(j) \text{ unrestricted in sign for all } j \in N,$$

where nodes s and t represent the starting point and the finishing point, respectively; A is the set of precedence relationships, and $c_{ij} = u_{ij}$ represents the time duration of job i.

In the previous formulation, there were no restrictions on the variables except for the precedence constraints. In some cases, however, certain jobs in the project might have an absolute time restriction; that is, a job must be started within a specified time limit from the start of some precedent jobs, for example, constraints on the time available after notice of a claim to make payment or the deadlines for rate filing. The objective in this case is still to minimize the entire project duration. The so-called "just-in-time scheduling" problem is an extension of the previous formulation with the additional class of constraints: $u(j) \leq u(i) - \alpha_{ij}$, for all $(i, j) \in A$, where α_{ij} means that job j must start within α_{ij} units of time from the start of job i. The "just-in-time scheduling" problem can also be formulated as a minimum cost flow model.

In some circumstances, the durations of jobs can be reduced by allocating extra resources (manpower, equipment, or money) to them; that is, there are time-resource trade-off curves on certain jobs. If the curves are linear, then the dual program of the primal linear program is the minimum cost flow problem.

As mentioned previously, network flow models are well suited to the situations in which there is a set of entities and flows of some sort between entities. The transportation problem, with minimum cost as the objective, and the traffic light control problem, with maximum flow per unit time as the objective, illustrate classical network flow problems. The best known flow-type problem in insurance involves the flow of cash or funds between suborganizations of an insurance firm and between the insurance firm and other sources or uses of funds. For example, Crum and Nye [85] designed general network flow models for three operations of a multiple-line property-casualty insurance firm: insurance portfolio operations, investment portfolio operations, and the capital acquisition operations. We introduce the first network model and refer readers to Crum and Nye [85] for the other two case studies.

In insurance network flow models, there are four types of nodes: the nodes representing the cash balance, the nodes designating the insurance lines of business, the nodes representing existing claims, and the nodes representing new claims. A network model of the insurance portfolio of an insurance company with two lines of business and spanning three time periods is shown in Figure 1 (see Crum and Nye [85] for the original work).

Corresponding to four types of nodes, there are four cash flow equations balancing dollars in to dollars out of the nodes (these are similar to the equations of balance in asset share calculations and theory of interest). These equations[6] are:

$$\sum_{i=1}^{m} INS_{ij}(1 - UE_{ij}) - \sum_{i=1}^{m} \sum_{k=1}^{j} CP_{ijk} + \sum_{i=1}^{m} PPC_{ij} + CB_{j-1,j} - CB_{i,j+1} = ICB_j,$$

for $j = 1, ..., n + 1$; $k = 1, ..., n$;

$$-INS_{ij} - CR_{ij} = MV_{ij}, \text{ for } i = 1, ..., m, j = 1, ..., n;$$

$$\sum_{j=1}^{n} (1 - LP_{ij})PPC_{ij} = PC_i, \text{ for } i = 1, ..., m; \text{ and}$$

---

[6]In the original paper, the second term of the first equation is: $\sum_{i=1}^{m} \sum_{k=1}^{n} CP_{ijk}$, we think the range for k should be $[1, j]$ instead of $[1, n]$.

FIGURE 1

INSURANCE PORTFOLIO OPERATIONS (TWO LINES AND THREE PERIODS)*

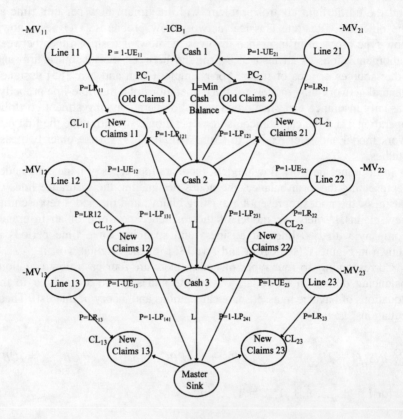

*Reprinted from *Mathematical Programming Study*, Vol. 15, 1981, R.L. Crum and D.J. Nye, "A Network Model for Insurance Company Cash Flow Management," pp. 137–52, 1981 with kind permission of Elsevier Science-NL, Sara Burgerhartstraat 25, 1055 KV Amsterdam, The Netherlands.

$$\sum_{k=1}^{n} (1 - LP_{ijk})CP_{ijk} + LR_{ij}CR_{ij} = CL_{ij},$$

for $i = 1, ..., m$ and $j = 1, ..., n$.

where i is the index of business lines; j the index of time periods; k the index of (time) steps; INS_{ij} the insurance actually sold; UE_{ij} the underwriting expense ratio; CP_{ijk} the dollar amount paid for claims; $CB_{j,j+1}$ the cash balance carried over between periods; MV_{ij} the maximum volume of insurance; CR_{ij} ($=MV_{ij}-INS_{ij}$) the additional insurance that could have been sold; ICB_j the initial cash balance; LP_{ij} the penalty cost incurred from payment delay; LR_{ij} the loss ratio; PC_{ij} the amount of claims; PPC_{ij} the payments' in a period to satisfy claims PC_i; and CL_{ij} the maximum levels of claims, $CL_{ij}=LR_{ij}*MV_{ij}$.

In these four equations, summations preceded by a negative sign represent cash outflows from the node, and positive coefficient terms represent cash inflows to the node. Crum and Nye [85] gave an illustrative example of an insurance portfolio network that contains two lines of business over three time periods. The objective function is expressed to maximize the value of the firm after all incremental capital acquired by the model has been repaid. This can be shown to be equivalent to maximizing the value of the existing equity—the appropriate objective for a public corporation.

The investment portfolio problem can be similarly formulated as a minimum cost flow problem. Combined with the investment portfolio network, the whole network model represents flow of funds over time for the multiple-line insurance company. Given the maximum period premium volume, the initial asset amount, the investment choices, and some other parameters, the network flow model is able to find the optimal portfolios for the company. However, the decision of a major insurance company depends upon how the company acquires external capital such the capital structure (for example, debt-equity composition) and how well the company manages its assets and liabilities. Hence, Crum and Nye used network models to formulate the capital acquisition problem and investment portfolio problem in addition to the above-cited model for the insurance portfolio problem. These three models combined with the objective function form the complete model for a major insurance company. Such an insurer can either be a multiline property and casualty company or a life company including life insurance products and annuities.

To further illustrate the usefulness of network flow models in finance and insurance, we briefly discuss how network optimization might be used to find arbitrage opportunities in currency exchanges for a multinational insurance company. Suppose an American company is the target company and dollar is the target currency; that is, the company has an amount of excess cash that can be used for currency exchange. There exists a set of foreign currencies available for trading. A network model for this problem, as usual, consists of a set of nodes and a set of arcs. The nodes represent currencies, one node for each currency. The arcs represent the possible exchange between the two currencies with an exchange rate attached to the arc. The problem is simply to increment the amount of dollars by finding optimal exchanging paths and amounts. To implement the model, a source node and a sink node are artificially added. The source node has an initial excess of capital (the amount to be invested). An arc connects the source node to the dollar node. Another arc connects the dollar currency node to the sink node. The problem is then transformed into a maximum flow problem (that is, the company is trying to maximize its current dollar holdings by circulating currencies within the market). Clearly, if the exchange rates are spot rates and are fed into the model in real time, the model can be integrated into the company's whole financial management system. Under different specifications, the model can be extended to currency swap or interest swap problems. We refer interested readers to Kornbluth and Salkin [169] for more details.

2.5 Goal Programming

Charnes and Cooper [60] first provided the foundations of goal programming and developed a strategy that is capable of handling multiple, incompatible and/or incommensurable goals. In a typical goal programming model, each goal is formulated as a constraint. There are two variables associated with each goal (each constraint): overachievement deviation and underachievement deviation. The value of these two deviational variables measure how well the corresponding goal is accomplished. For example, if both deviational variables in the final solution to the goal programming model are close or equal to zero, the corresponding goal is well achieved. However, the two deviational variables of each goal cannot be zero at the same time in a feasible solution since it is unusual to have a goal overachieved and underachieved simultaneously. After two deviational variables have been assigned for each goal, the next essential step in setting up a goal programming model is to build an objective function. An objective function in a goal programming formulation is usually a linear function in deviational variables. Specifically, the objective function takes the weighted summation of the deviational variables. The weights assigned to a deviational variable indicate the importance of the corresponding goal in the decision-making process. The objective is thus to minimize the weighted sum of deviations from goal achievement, that is, to accomplish the best overall achievement.

The goal programming method has been extensively applied to problems in management and finance. In the insurance industry, Klock and Lee [164] suggested a goal programming model for an insurance company with profit, current asset returns, and legal bounded goals, while Drandell [103] demonstrated that the goal programming model developed is equivalent to the original linear programming model of optimum allocation of assets. O'Leary and O'Leary [214] also used goal programming to address a problem faced by the financial and personnel departments in many firms: choosing an investment manager.

To further demonstrate the utility of goal programming in the insurance industry, we introduce two applications: capital budgeting in an insurance company (Lawrence and Reeves [179]) and insurance agency management (Gleason and Lilly [123]).

Given a set of projects, such as investment projects for an insurance company and given a set of multiple objectives for these projects (multiple strategies), the capital budgeting problem is to determine which particular projects should be selected in each given time. Specifically, Lawrence and Reeves [179] formulated the above problem utilizing seven objectives or goals that are desired to be met to the extent possible:

(1) Achieve at least a certain minimum level of project rate of return
(2) Do not exceed a certain maximum level of anticipated penalty cost associated with project lateness
(3) Achieve at least a certain minimum level of additional premiums
(4) Achieve at least a certain minimum level of additional agents' earnings
(5) Do not exceed budget
(6) Achieve at least a certain minimum level of social responsibility and
(7) Do not use more than maximum level of resources.

The decision variables, x_{ij}, associated with each potential project are an indicator variable of whether each individual project i is selected in time period j. Accordingly, these decision variables are zero-one (integer) variables. For a three-time-period horizon capital budgeting problem, 21 pairs of deviational variables (d^-, d^+) arise in this seven-goal, three-period setting. The seven types of constraints corresponding to the seven goals are duplicated in order below, followed by certain non-goal (system-characterizing) constraints:

Project rate of return: $\sum_{i=1}^{7} \sum_{j=1}^{3} R_{ij}x_{ij} + d_1^- - d_1^+ = TR;$

Project lateness penalty: $\sum_{i=1}^{7} \sum_{j=1}^{3} PL_{ij}x_{ij} + d_2^- - d_2^+ = TPL;$

Additional premiums: $\sum_{i=1}^{7} AP_{ij}x_{ij} + d_{2-j}^- - d_{2+j}^+ = TAP_j;$

for $j = 1,2,3;$

Additional agents' earnings: $\sum_{i=1}^{7} AE_{ij}x_{ij} + d_{5-j}^- - d_{5+j}^+ = TAE_j;$

for $j = 1,2,3;$

Budget: $\sum_{i=1}^{7} AE_{ij}x_{ij} + d_{8-j}^- - d_{8+j}^+ = TB_j;$

for $j = 1,2,3;$

Social responsibility: $\sum_{i=1}^{7} \sum_{j=1}^{3} B_{ij}SR_{ij}x_{ij} + d_{12}^- - d_{12}^+ = TSR;$

Resources: $\sum_{i=1}^{7} h_{ijk}x_{ij} + d_{9-3j-k}^- - d_{9+3j+k}^- = H_{jk};$

for $j = 1,2,3,$ for all $k,$

Non-goal constraints: $\sum_{i=1}^{3} (x_{1j} + x_{3j}) \geq 1;$ and

$x_{ij+1} - x_{kj} \leq 0.$

where R is the forecast rate of return of project in a certain period; PL the expected penalty cost of project lateness; AP the forecast level of additional premiums that will be written in a period; AE the expected amount of additional agents' earnings associated with the selection of the project in a certain period; B the projected cost of the project in a period; and SR the percentage of the project directly associated with matters of social responsibility and public service (for example, special inserts on household safety, auto care, and so on). Resources include manpower, computer system running time, and so on, and h is the number of work days of a type of resource required to complete the project in a period. Accordingly, the right-hand side of each equation is the target, that is, the goal. For example, TR for the first equation is the target (total) rate of return; TAP_j is the total (target) additional premium in year j; and so on. The subscripts, $9+3j+k$, for some of the deviational variables can be read as follows: when $j=1$ and $k=1$, $9+3 j-k=13$, which is the subscript for the human resource goal in the first period; when $j=3$ and $k=3$, $9+3j+k=21$, which is the subscript for the very last (human resource) goal. It is not surprising to see conceptually that because of the indivisibility of projects, the model is an integer programming formulation.

The first illustrative non-goal constraint represents the dependency between two projects, for example, at least one of project 1 and 3 should be selected over the total time period. The second non-goal constraint specifies that project i cannot begin before project j is complete and is thus able to be used to model multiyear projects. Many other constraints can be added depending upon desired system requirements. The objective function is given below:

$$\text{Maximize} \quad Z = P_1 d_1^- + P_2 d_2^+ + P_3 \sum_{j=3}^{5} d_j^- + P_4 \sum_{j=6}^{8} d_j^-$$
$$+ P_5 \sum_{j=9}^{11} d_j^+ + P_6 d_j^- + P_7 \sum_{j=13}^{21} d_j^-,$$

where $P_k \geq 0$, $k=1, \ldots, 7$, are the preemptive priorities associated with the objectives; that is, those priorities are determined a priori, with higher value meaning greater importance or contribution of a specific goal to the overall decision problem. Obtaining appropriate assignment of weights to the goals is based on the preference of the decision-maker as well as on common sense. For example, since higher rather than lower rate of return is usually favored by financial decision-makers, the reasonable objective is to minimize underachievement in rate of return. That is why the first term appears in the objective (minimization) and the overachievement deviational variable disappears. We leave readers to determine the meaning of other terms in the objective function.

With such a model, the optimal solution is obtainable for each given set of parameters, such as the projected rates for return and expected penalty costs. Also, by adjusting the priorities associated with goals, a sensitivity analysis on the trade-offs between different goals is obtainable.

The above-mentioned goals are neither all-encompassing nor constant among insurance agencies. One goal of an agency might be to increase the amount of premiums written. Income maximization is a concern to an agency in the long run, while growth may be more important in the short run. An agency may have the incentive to represent as many insurers as possible. On the other hand, overdependency on a single insurer might translate into a higher business risk, whereas receiving more services from the insurer reduces business costs. An agency also has the option to specialize in different insurance business lines. For example, independent agencies tend to concentrate in commercial lines of insurance and deemphasize personal lines. In summary, an agency may have multiple business goals, and these goals can be conflicting and compatible. For this reason, Gleason and Lilly [123] modeled the agency operation by using a goal programming problem.

Gleason and Lilly considered six goals grouped into four levels of priorities. The priority 1 goals are: "expand premiums written" and "expand the number of insurers the agency represents." The priority 2 goal is "do not become too dependent upon any single insurer." Two goals are categorized as priority 3 goals: "obtain cost reduction services from the insurers" and "maximize gross income." The lowest priority goal is "to shift from personal to commercial lines."

Each of the six goals is formulated as a goal constraint. Some additional constraints arise from practical agency operation limitations: for example, the annual growth rate is limited to no more than 20%; the business in certain lines might be restricted; and so on. With minimizing the total overachievements and underachievements of the goals as the objective, the goal programming problem is well formulated. The decision variables in this problem are the amount of premiums for each insurance class to be written by the agency using each insurer. In this application then, the decision variable is not required to be integral. Thus, this goal programming can be solved as a linear programming problem.

Goal programming can also be used to model working capital management problems (Satoris and Spreill [247]). Many other risk management problems, such as those involving environmental pollution management (Charnes et al. [63], [65], and [77]) and those involving senior-level decision-making, such as company mergers and acquisitions, can also be modeled and solved as goal programming problems.

In summary, a goal program can be favorably used when there are multiple competing goals involved in the decision-making. Although it is not difficult to set a target for a specific goal and then transform the goal formulation to a constraint, the spirit of goal programming lies in utilizing the deviations from the goals in the objective function formulation, assigning subjective weights to each such deviation, and then minimizing the total weighted deviation. These deviations are essentially treated as decision variables when the resultant linear or nonlinear programming problem is solved computationally. Controversies can arise from the goal weighting strategy, that is, the way that weights are determined and the rationality of the concept that different goals are equalized by assigning quantitatively different weights.

2.6 Dynamic Programming

Dynamic programming is another general approach to problem-solving. In general, the problems that dynamic programming are capable of handling have several basic features. The problem contains a series of stages either physically or conceptually, for example, over time periods or over conceptual stages. In each stage, a prespecified set of states represents the potential outcomes at this stage. A policy decision can cause changes in states from stage to stage. The likelihood of being in any specific state in the next stage is completely determined by the current stage and the policy decisions made within it, but is independent of the states that might have occurred in previous stages. This is the Markov property, which is often assumed to simplify the modeling process. The effects of transitions from state to state over stages are quantified in utility or cost form, and the objective of the problem is to determine a series of (possibly state- or stage-dependent) policy decisions that maximize the total or final utility or that minimize the total or final cost.

Usually, a recursive relationship is developed to solve the dynamic programming problem. The recursive relationship is a formula describing how a state in the subsequent stage is determined from the states in the current stage. If the state in the next stage is determined with certainty by the state in the current stage (together with the adopted policy decision), then the dynamic programming is called deterministic. If the states in the subsequent stage are determined according to some probabilistic distribution (which will generally depend upon the value in the current stage and the adopted policy), then the dynamic programming is called probabilistic. The solution procedure in either case involves first determining the optimal decision strategy in the final stage without recourse to previous stages. From this optimal decision strategy in the final period, the derived recursive relationship is used to derive an optimal solution in the next-to-the-last stage. This backward calculation of optimal decision strategy is continued until the optimal strategy for the current stage is derived.

In this paper, we illustrate this technique with a dynamic model of insurance company management [115]. The model deals only with determining the optimal policy of dividends for a stock insurance company over time. It is assumed that the objective of the company is to maximize the expected utility of the dividend payments, which is calculated according to the distribution of claims. The utility function of dividend payments and the distribution of claim arrivals is not explicitly specified in Frisque, so this dynamic model is a general theoretical construction.

Let $U(d_1, d_2, ..., d_j, ...)$ represent the shareholder's current utility or order of preferences corresponding to the systems of dividend payments $(d_1, d_2, ..., d_j, ...)$, where d_j denotes the payment of dividend made by the company during year j. Also, to account for the time value of consumption in different periods, it is assumed that U is of the following form:

$$U(d_1, d_2, ..., d_j, ...) = u(d_j) - vU(d_2, d_3, ..., d_j, ...),$$

where $u(d_1)$ denotes the shareholders' one-period utility function and v is a factor expressing the shareholders' preferences for an early dividend, $0 < v < 1$. Thus,

$$U(d_1, d_2, ..., d_j, ...) = \Sigma_j v^{j-1} E[u(d_j)],$$

assuming that utility function is time additive. Let S_j denote the expected reserve level of the company at the beginning of year j, and assume the reserve dynamics follows the equations of balance,

$$S_j + 1 = S_j - d_j + k_j \left(P - \int_0^\infty x dF(x) \right),$$

where $F(x)$ is the distribution of claims; k_j is the part of the insurance portfolio retained by the company in a quota reinsurance system; and P is the amount of premiums received during year j. By introducing a function $U_j(S_j)$ as the discounted average utility of the dividends $d_j, d_{j+1}, ...,$

evaluated at decision points $j, j+1, \ldots$ when initial reserve is S_j, an optimal policy is followed with respect to payment of dividends in all subsequent periods. Specifically,

$$U_j(S_j) = \underset{0 \le d_j \le S_j, 0 \le k_j \le 1}{\text{Maximize}} \left[u(d_j) \div v \int_0^\infty U_{j+1}(S_j - d_j + k_j(P - x))dF(x) \right]$$

$$\text{subject to } \int_0^\infty (S_j - d_j + k_j(P - x))dF(x) \ge 0$$

Thus we obtain a dynamic programming model in which the decision variables are the series of dividend payments, d_j, and also the series of reinsurance fractions, k_j. A more practical dynamic model, however, might further examine the effect of introducing additional decision variables (such as insolvency constraints), the soundness of the utility functions used in the calculation, and the sensitivity of the optimal strategy to such parameters of the model as the distribution functions and the discount factor v.

In the previous model, dynamic programming was illustrated with the stages in the decision process being time periods. Bouzaher et al. [33] provided an example of a dynamic programming formulation in which the "stages" are defined differently.

In fact, a deterministic multiple-stage dynamic programming can be equivalently formulated as a one-stage mathematical programming problem (cf., Bellman and Dreyfus [22] and Denardo [97]). We leave readers to verify this claim. This equivalent transformation, however, may not be favored for two main reasons. First, the recursive (multiple-stage) formulation appears more intuitive and straightforward and reveals how the process proceeds from one stage to the next stage. If the underlying process is decision-making, then a decision-maker has certain rules that should be followed to proceed smoothly from stage to stage. Another critical reason may be that the algorithm can be more easily implemented computationally when a recursive equations system is provided. Also, with less variables involved in the recursive formulation, less computer resources (such as memory) are required to solve the problem. We refer readers to Bellman and Dreyfus [22] and Denardo [97] for general discussions about dynamic programming.

2.7 Chance-Constrained Programming

Chance-constrained programming (CCP) (Charnes et al. [68]) is a mathematical programming method dealing with optimization when some of the variables are stochastic. In some circumstances the variables involved in the calculations are only known with uncertainty (for example, are random variables), and it may be impossible to write a constraint that holds deterministically. The main idea of CCP is to allow certain factors, such as risk, to be realization of random variables. The decision variables are then selected such that these random variables are constrained to lie within an acceptable range of values with a pre-specified high probability; that is, the constraint is of the form $Pr(x \geq L) \geq \alpha$, rather than the deterministic equality or inequality of mathematical programming. The objective function may be either maximization or minimization. Among the applications of CCP in insurance are Agnew et al. [4], Pyle and Turnovsky [226], Thompson et al. [270], Kahane [157], McCabe and Witt [203], and Brockett et al. [42]. We use McCabe and Witt [203] for illustration of chance-constrained programming.

According to McCabe and Witt [203], for an insurance firm, the overriding objective is to maximize the profit from underwriting earnings and investment income; however, this objective is constrained by insolvency regulation requirements. A simplified financial model is analyzed for the insurer's behavior under uncertainty for both underwriting and investment income. Since the underwriting earnings and investment income are stochastic, the profits (as a function of underwriting earnings and investment income) are also stochastic. The objective is expressed as the maximization of the expected cash flow, that is, $E(\pi) = E(PQ) + E(I) - E(L) - E_1$, where P is the price per standard exposure unit (SEU), Q is the number of SEU's written, I is the investment income, L is the total losses and loss adjustment expenses, and E_1 is the non-loss or underwriting expenses [see McCabe and Witt [203] for the composition of each category and the definition of SEU]. Along with the profit-maximization objective, the firm should be primarily concerned with the risk of technical insolvency. This insolvency risk is quantified by the probability of insolvency, ϕ. While it is impossible to guarantee with 100% certainty that the firm will not become insolvent in all possible states of the world and economy, the probability of insolvency should be constrained to be below some number, ϕ_1. The model can then be written as:

$$\text{Maximize } E(\pi) \text{ subject to } \phi \leq \phi_1.$$

Given an explicit expression for ϕ and given an admissible risk level, ϕ_1, a Lagrangian multiplier method can be used to solve the (nonlinear) problem after the probabilistic constraint has been transformed into a deterministic equivalent constraint.

As an example, define technical insolvency to be a loss of more than 30% of capital, C. The constraint can be specified in statistical terms as follows: $P(\pi \leq \pi_B) \leq 0.01$, where $\pi B = 0.3C$; that is, the probability of insolvency should be below 1%. Assuming that π follows a normal distribution and using the fact that the 99th percentile of the normal distribution is 2.33, the constraint can be transformed into a deterministic constraint as follows, $P(z \leq (-0.3C - E\pi)/\sigma_\pi) \leq 0.01$ so $E\pi \geq -0.3C + 2.33\sigma_\pi$. The CCP formulation has thus been converted to the deterministic problem as follows:

$$\text{Maximize} \quad E\pi$$
$$\text{subject to} \quad E\pi \geq -0.3C + 2.33\sigma_\pi;$$
$$0 \leq S \leq 1.0: P \geq 0 \text{ and } k \geq 0,$$

where C is the shareholder-supplied capital, P the price per standard exposure unit, k the average number of months elapsing between loss occurrences and loss payments, S the proportion of earning assets that can be invested in stocks, and σ_π the standard deviation of the profit. The variables P, S, and k are the decision variables. Clearly, different optimal solutions are obtained given different insolvency restrictions. Thus, the sensitivity analysis is possible.

Markle and Hofflander, in their quadratic programming portfolio approach, and Crum and Nye [85], in their network flow portfolio approach, both modeled the insurer's behavior at an operational level (as opposed to the more aggregated level used by McCabe and Witt [203]). The work of Brockett, Charnes, and Li [40] extended the McCabe and Witt CCP model to the micro level of analysis utilized by Markle and Hofflander [197] and by Crum and Nye [85].

In insurance, there are many cases in which the chance event can be expressed as a constraint. Events such as "becoming insolvent," "taking certain level of risk in business," "making a certain level (amount) of profit," and so on all involve a degree of uncertainty (randomness). These chance events can be formulated as constraints expressed in probabilistic terms (for example, the probability of being technically insolvent is no greater than

0.05). Techniques such as that illustrated previously can be used to transform the probabilistic constraint into its deterministic equivalent for solving via usual mathematical programming techniques. As mentioned above, sensitivity analysis can readily be conducted by varying the permissible chance levels. We also refer readers to Brockett et al. [42], for the transformation technique illustration.

2.8 Fuzzy Set Theory and Fuzzy Programming

Fuzzy set theory deals with ambiguity and imprecision in linguistic, reasoning, and decision-making. The applications of fuzzy set theory can be found extensively in linguistics, artificial intelligence, robotics, process control, decision analysis, and many other areas. Fuzzy set theory is, however, a rather new methodology to the actuarial and insurance communities. Lemaire [184] provided an introduction of fuzzy set theory and described how it might be used in insurance. Lemaire discussed three problems: the definition of a preferred policyholder in life insurance, the selection of an optimal excess of loss retention, and the computation of the fuzzy premium for a pure endowment policy. Some other applications can be found in Cummins and Derrig [87] and Derrig and Ostaszewski [100]. In addition, the Society of Actuaries has published a book by Ostaszewski [216], entitled *An Investigation into Possible Applications of Fuzzy Set Methods in Actuarial Science*, which further delineates the usefulness of fuzzy set theory to problems in actuarial science and insurance. Here we show how fuzzy set theory can be combined with cluster analysis and applied to risk and claim classification (Derrig and Ostaszewski [100]). We also illustrate a framework of fuzzy programming in insurance decision-making.

In a very fundamental way, there is an intimate relation between the theory of fuzzy sets and the theory of pattern recognition and classification. Acknowledging the fact that the boundaries between most insurance classes are fuzzy in nature (Kandel [160]). Derrig and Ostaszewski [100] applied fuzzy set theory to the clustering of rating territories and also to the classification of insurance claims according to their suspected level of fraud.

The fuzzy cluster method is developed from the so-called c-means cluster analysis method described below. Given n patterns, represented by p-dimensional vectors: x_1, x_2, ..., x_n, the goal of c-means cluster analysis is to divide these n patterns into c, $2 \le c \le n-1$ categorically homogeneous subsets (which are called clusters) such that the variances within clusters are minimized, while the variances between clusters are maximized.

Geometrically, each cluster is characteristically represented by its center point (which is also a p-vector) in the p-dimensional Euclidean space. Hence, the clustering problem is to find the c center points satisfying the above goals.

Clearly, the degree to which a particular pattern vector is believed to belong to a particular cluster is related to the distance between the pattern vector and the cluster mean. If the distance is zero, then clearly that pattern vector belongs to the corresponding cluster, while the degree of belief that the pattern vector belongs to the cluster decreases as the distance from the cluster increases. This degree of belief that the pattern belongs to the cluster, viewed as a function of the pattern vector x, is called the membership function for the cluster. After normalization, each value of the membership function falls continuously between zero and one. When the fuzzy cluster algorithm is applied to classification of rating territories, the clusters are the risk classes, and the degree of belief that each territory belongs to a given cluster (risk class) is quantified as a real-valued number between zero and one. For a given territory, multiple clusters (risk classes) are possible. Such a classification methodology based on a membership function provides decision-makers with more information than does the crisp or nonfuzzy clustering, where the membership function can only take either zero (representing completely not-belonging-to) or one (showing perfectly-belonging-to). As a matter of fact, fuzzy cluster analysis can be transformed into crisp cluster analysis if we assign a pattern to a particular cluster and if the membership function value for that cluster is the largest among those for all the possible clusters. We refer readers to Derrig and Ostaszewski [100] for the details of the fuzzy cluster algorithm.

Fuzziness is to some extent similar to uncertainty, although they are different conceptually. Briefly speaking, fuzziness can arise because of our inability to describe the membership property of an object (ambiguity), whereas uncertainty occurs in situations in which the true membership exists but yet has not been fully revealed. Readers are referred to Zimmermann [289], and [290] for more information about fuzziness and to Dubois and Prade [104] for the foundation of fuzzy set theory and computation.

In the following, we show how a fuzzy linear programming is defined and given as an ordinary linear programming formulation by describing the technique for transforming the fuzzy programming to its crisp or nonfuzzy deterministic equivalent programming. Readers will find a similarity between the development of the deterministic equivalent programming problem in fuzzy programming and in CCP whereby probabilistic constraints are transformed into deterministic equivalent statements.

To make a decision is to achieve a set of goals while simultaneously being constrained by pertinent external and internal restrictions. Often goals and constraints are substitutable. In other words, there are trade-offs among goals and between goals and constraints. The trade-off between costs and benefits is a typical example. For example, an insurance company might be willing to pay higher commissions and increase other expenses to obtain greater premium growth. The decision-maker often prefers knowing how much of a gain on each goal can be obtained without sacrificing too much on other goal(s). Of course, the quantification "how much of a gain" or "sacrificing too much" is not a firm or crisp (nonfuzzy) process. Accordingly, rather than formulating the goal in a strict crisp form, a preferable formulation might be to use fuzzy formulation. The meaning of fuzziness in formulation is made clear in the illustration below.

To develop the notion of fuzzy linear programming, consider first the ordinary linear programming problem:

$$\text{Minimize} \quad C = \sum_{ij} c_{ij} x_{ij}$$

$$\text{subject to} \quad \sum_{j} a_{ij} x_{ij} \geq b_i; \text{ and other constraints}$$

where x_{ij} is the decision variable; (suppose that) C denotes the total cost that is to be minimized; c_{ij} is the cost associated with x_{ij}; b_i the minimum level of some goal; and a_{ij} is the coefficient of x_{ij}.

Now, suppose the decision-maker is willing to be less precise and says that it is acceptable for the bound b_i to be decreased as low as $b_i - \lambda_i$ to achieve a better goal, that is, a lower cost in this case. For this illustration, let all λ_i be equal and denote this common value by λ for convenience. Define a membership function for the i-th constraint as follows:

$$\mu_i(z_i) = 1, \qquad \text{for } z_i \geq b_i;$$

$$\mu_i(z_i) = 1 - \frac{b_i - z_i}{\lambda}, \text{ for } b_i - \lambda \leq z_i < b_i; \text{ and}$$

$$\mu_i(z_i) = 0, \qquad \text{for } z_i < b_i - \lambda, \text{ (where } z_i = \Sigma_j \, a_{ij} x_{ij}).$$

Such a membership function of a constraint can be interpreted as follows: b_i is the perfectly satisfactory value of the constraint, while anything lower than $b_i - \lambda$ is a completely unsatisfactory value of the constraint. Between $b_i - \lambda$ and b_i, the satisfaction level with the constraint increases linearly as the actual value of the constraint increases from $b_i - \lambda$ to b_i. Thus, the membership function value increases continuously from 0 to 1.

When the decision-maker specifies the minimum acceptable satisfaction level θ for each of the constraints, a crisp equivalent programming can be derived as follows. Suppose that θ, $0 \leq \theta \leq 1$, is the minimum acceptable level of satisfaction for each of the constraints. Then we have

$$\mu_i(z_i) = 1 - (b_i - z_i)/\lambda \geq 0,$$

which is equivalent to $z_i - \lambda \theta \geq b_i - \lambda$, for constraint i. Accordingly, the fuzzy constraint $\mu_i(z) \geq \theta$, has been replaced by the deterministic equivalent constraint $z_i - \lambda \theta \geq b_i - \lambda$.

Similarly, if we can determine a target C_0 for the objective function, C (where $C_0 \geq C$ for the relaxation of the objective), then this leads to an inequality,

$$\sum_{ij} c_{ij} x_{ij} \leq C_0,$$

and we can treat the objective as a constraint. The discussion above also applies to the objective function using the membership function μ_0 as before (now linear between C and $C_0 - \lambda$). After inverting this constraint as described above, we obtain the complete crisp programming:

Maximize θ

subject to $\displaystyle\sum_j a_{ij} x_{ij} - \lambda \theta \geq b_i - \lambda;$

$\displaystyle\sum_{ij} c_{ij} x_{ij} + \lambda \theta \leq C + \lambda;$ and

$0 \leq \theta \leq 1.$

The equivalent crisp or deterministic mathematical programming problem is specified once we are given the value of λ (which is the maximum permissible sacrifice level of the constraints and the objective). From the model, we can see that the larger the value of θ, the less the value (cost in this case) of the objective function and the larger the sacrifice value of the constraints. In other words, the crisp equivalent programming problem provides the trade-off between the objective function and the constraints. As previously described, for a multiple-objective optimization problem, some of the objectives can be formulated as constraints and one of them singled out as the objective function in a mathematical programming formulation. It is easy to see that the fuzzy programming method is well suited to the multiple-objective problem, where trade-offs among different objectives are established and the priorities of the various multiple goals are not self-evident.

Using intervals of possibilities to model vague and imprecise situations in insurance and other areas is another closely related approach. Instead of applying probability theory or fuzzy set theory, an interval rather than a single value is used to describe a vague or fuzzy or imprecise concept. Interval analysis as a branch of mathematics has found its applications to insurance issues, specifically to measuring and evaluating financial risk and uncertainty (Babad and Berliner [10], [11], and Berliner and Buehlman [25]).

3. OTHER OPERATIONS RESEARCH METHODS

The field of OR is constantly growing, and the applications of OR techniques in the area of insurance are expanding rapidly. The growing field of OR maintains substantial interactions with computer science, applied mathematics, engineering, finance, economics, and behavioral science. For example, game theory, which was originally developed for use in economics, is now also used in insurance. Portfolio analysis, which is widely used as an investment and risk management technique in finance, has been used in insurance, not only from the traditional investment perspective but also as an insurance composition design technique, by Markle and Hofflander [197], Crum and Nye [85], and others. Utility theory, decision analysis, and many other OR and management science methods have found use in the insurance industry. It is clearly difficult and space-consuming to discuss the numerous branches of OR and to delineate its applications in insurance. In the following sections, we concentrate mainly on game theory and three relatively new OR techniques: data envelopment analysis (DEA), expert systems (ES), and neural networks (NN). As these OR techniques illustrate, the continued expansion of OR methodologies owes greatly to the contributions of and interfaces with economics, applied mathematics, cognitive science, and computer science. Applications of these approaches in insurance is again demonstrated by examples.

3.1. Game Theory

Game theory is a formalized study of a kind of decision-making in which two or more competitors (called players) are involved and the decisions made by one player may affect the outcome of the other players. To achieve a goal, each player chooses a strategy. The final outcome or return from a player's strategic choice depends also on the strategic choice of all the other players. In other words, in such a decision-making context, a player must take this interdependence into account when choosing a strategy (making a decision). We refer readers to *Handbook of Game Theory with Economic Applications* Volume 1 [9] for more detailed formal information.

Game theory was suggested as a useful mathematical modeling technique for investigators involving insurance decision-making as early as the 1960s (Borch [28], Bragg [35], [36], and [264]). Since then game theory has been found useful in many insurance settings, such as cost allocation for an insurance company (Lemaire [183]), negotiation of insurance contracts (Kihlstrom and Roth [162]), optimal insurance purchasing in the presence of compulsory insurance and uninsurable risks (Schulenburg [254]), life insurance underwriting (Lemaire [182]), control of mutual insurance process (Tapiero [268]), out-of-court settlement of liability insurance claims (Fenn and Vlachonikolis [111]), unemployment policy (Zuckerman [292]), and so forth. This brief and incomplete list of applications demonstrates that game theory is applicable to purchasing, underwriting, management, liability claim settlement, and other areas in insurance or reinsurance. Game theory can also be used to explain the underwriting fluctuations as the result of rational behavior among interdependent firms in the industry (as opposed to viewing such underwriting fluctuations as merely irrational aberrations). In this paper, we review two applications: cost allocation and bargaining of liability claims.

Lemaire [183] proposed that a game theory methodology can be applied to the allocation of operating costs among the lines of business for an insurance company. Cost allocation in a large insurance company is extremely complex. For instance, a large Belgian company that operates in three lines of business—life, fire and accident—uses no less than 11 different criteria for cost allocation, including direct imputation; some operating costs are directly assigned to a class, while some costs, such as heating, water, and electricity, are assigned based on the basis of space occupied. Classical cost allocation methods, however, fail to satisfy certain important theoretical properties, as discussed by Lemaire [183]. Two of these properties are individual rationality and collective rationality in case of economies of scale. Lemaire shows that the cost allocation problem is identical to the problem of computing the value of a n-person cooperative game with transferable utilities. In other words, the cost allocation problem can be represented as a pair $[N, c(S)]$, where $N = \{1, 2, \ldots, n\}$ is the set of players and $c(S)$ the characteristic (cost) function of the game. This characteristic or cost function is a super-additive set function that associates a real-valued number $c(S)$ to each coalition (subset) S of players with $c(S)+c(T) \geq c(S \cup T)$ for all S, $T \subset N$ and $S \cap T = \emptyset$. In most of the applications, economies of scale are sufficiently large that the game is convex; that is, $c(S) \div c(T) \geq c(S \cup T) + c(S \cap T)$ for all S, $T \subset N$. The solution space of a convex game is non-void. Further, Lemaire [183] showed that while the classical notions of "solutions of a game," such as the Shapley value, the nucleolus, and the disruptive nucleolus, are not appropriate for the cost allocation problem, the proportional nucleolus is a solution method that satisfies desirable properties for cost allocation and is therefore the best cost allocation method among the four solution methods discussed. The three theoretical properties considered to be desirable by Lemaire are collective rationality, monotonicity in costs, and additivity (see Lemaire [184] for a detailed discussion and justification of these three properties in an insurance cost allocation context).

Formally, let x_i denote a cost allocated to player i. The proportional nucleolus is obtained when the excess is defined by the formula

$$e(\bar{x}, S) = \frac{c(S) - \sum_{i \in S} x_i}{c(S)}.$$

That is, the excess is the proportional gain obtained by players $i \in S$ acting as a coalition S rather than as individuals. Instead of granting the same amount to each proper coalition of N, a subsidy proportional to $c(S)$ is awarded. One has to solve the linear program

Maximize e

subject to $\displaystyle\sum_{i \in S} x_i \leq c(S)(1 - e)$, for $\forall S \subset N$, $S \neq N$, $S \neq \emptyset$;

$\displaystyle\sum_{i \in S} x_i = c(S)$, and

$x_i \geq 0$ for $\forall i$.

It can be shown that the philosophy of the decision expressed in the linear programming is to maximize the minimum excess according to the definition of the excess given above. In fact, many decision-makers take this conservative strategy when they face uncertainty.

Notice that the total number of possible coalitions of N players is $2^N - 1$, which increases exponentially with the size of N. Thus, the number of constraints in the linear programming process should also increase exponentially. The other three solution concepts for theory models (Sharpley value, nucleolus, and disruptive nucleolus) also suffer the same computation-complexity problems. It is, in fact, a disadvantage of the proposed game model for cost allocation. However, for N small, the above computation (and cost allocation) is quite possible.

In yet another insurance application, Fenn and Vlachonikolis [111] model a liability insurance bargaining problem as a game problem. When a liability insurance claim is filed, the lawyers for the defendant are charged with the task of responding to the claim: by persuading the claimant to withdraw, by taking the case to court for adjudication, or by agreeing to an acceptable out-of-court settlement of the claim. This process raises a number of issues. From the insurer's point of view, the predictability of the length of time to settle, as well as the size of the eventual settlement amount, are factors of actuarial importance. However, there is an uncertain relationship between the settlement amount and the actual loss incurred, and this uncertainty may raise questions about the adequacy and equity of the resulting compensation to the plaintiff. If the settlement process is indeterminable and capricious, it may even raise the moral hazard problem.

It is assumed that the lawyer for the insurer is a repeat-playing specialist acting for an insurance company with a large diversified portfolio of risks. The plaintiff, on the other hand, is usually more of a one-time player with a considerable sum at stake relative to his or her wealth and might even possibly be acting with nonspecialized legal advice. The lawyer for the insurer offers an amount for claim compensation based upon an estimate of the minimum "ask value" of the plaintiff. If the offer is greater than the plaintiff's minimum "ask value," the plaintiff will accept the offer. The offer will be rejected in the contrary case. If the offer is rejected, the lawyer for the insurer may either make another greater offer or take the case to court. This process is repeated until either the offer exceeds the minimum "ask value" and the case is settled outside the court, or the minimum "ask value" by the plaintiff is greater than the maximum "willing to be offered" by the insurer and the case has no bargaining outlet. In addition, the insurer's lawyer may not be willing to make too many offers (and risk the loss of reputation as a hard bargainer or incur the multiple fixed costs associated with the offers).

The above bargaining process can be modeled as in a game theoretic manner. Let A denote the minimum ask value of the plaintiff, B the maximum offer value of the insurer, C the amount of costs involved in litigation, and D the amount of damages that would be awarded were the case to be taken to trial. Then: $A=E_p(D)-E_p(C)$, and $B=E_d(D)+E_d(C)$, where E_p and E_d represent the expectation of the plaintiff and defendant (insurer), respectively. Suppose that both parties are risk averse, and let R_p and R_d denote the discount adjustment factors for risk or uncertainty used by the plaintiff and defendant, respectively. Then: $A=E_p(D)-E_p(C)-R_p$, and $B=E_d(D)+E_d(C)+R_d$. To model the bargaining process, the insurer's estimate of the plaintiff's minimum ask value, denoted by A^*, is: $A^*=E^*(D)-E^*(C)-R^*$. Let O denote the offer, then the process is formalized as follows:

Initially, the minimum ask value of the plaintiff is estimated by the defendant (insurer) as the mean of the subjective probability distribution of the minimum ask value. An offer is made at this value if the estimated value obtained by this process is lower than the maximum willing offer level; that is, $O_1=A^*$ if $A^*<B$, and $O_1=0$ otherwise.

The offer is accepted if it exceeds the minimum ask A. If the offer is rejected, the minimum ask should be greater than the estimated value, and the distribution is truncated. The new estimate is based on the truncated distribution: $O_2=O_1+E[\varepsilon|\varepsilon>0]$ if $A>O_1$, and $O_2=0$ otherwise, where ε is a stochastic error, with $\varepsilon\sim N(0,\sigma^2)$. The process is repeated until either the plaintiff accepts the offer at some point or the lawyer cannot or is not willing to offer more. The result of the former is the settlement of the case, whereas that of the latter is the trial at court. More detailed mathematical treatment can be found in Fenn and Vlachonikolis [111].

In this model, the subjective probability distribution should be consistent with the empirical liability settlement data. Whether the truncated distribution retains the identical properties of the original distribution function is another issue. As indicated by Danzon [90], the assumption of not learning by the plaintiff is questionable in that 89% of plaintiffs are represented by a trade union or other solicitor, in which case both parties can act to some extent strategically. In other words, not only does the defendant estimate the minimum ask of its distribution subjectively and also from the previous rejection by the plaintiff, but also the plaintiff adjusts the ask for compensation based on the estimate of the maximum offer of the defendant. In this case the game becomes more complicated and a modified game model is required.

The offer is accepted if it exceeds the minimum ask A. If the offer is rejected, the minimum ask value must be greater than this estimated value, and hence the subjective probability distribution for the minimum ask value can be recalibrated with a lower truncated value equal to the new rejected offer value. The new estimate of the minimum ask value is then based on this newly truncated distribution: $O_2 = O_1 + E[\varepsilon | \varepsilon > 0]$ if $A > O_1$, and $O_2 = 0$ otherwise, where ε is a stochastic error term, which for computational purposes is assigned to be normally distributed with mean zero. The above process is repeated until either the plaintiff accepts the offer at some point or the lawyer for the insurer cannot or is not willing to offer more. The result of the former is the settlement of the case, whereas that of the latter is a court trial. More detailed mathematical treatment can be found in Fenn and Vlachonikolis [111].

In this model, the subjective probability distribution should be consistent with the empirical liability settlement data. Whether the truncated distribution retains the identical properties of the original distribution function is another issue. As indicated by Danzon [90], the assumption that the plaintiff does not learn (and hence change the minimum ask value) is questionable, because 89% of plaintiffs are represented by a trade union or other solicitor, in which case both parties can act to some extent strategically or in a game theoretic method. In other words, not only does the defendant estimate the minimum ask of its distribution subjectively and also from the previous rejection by the plaintiff, but also the plaintiff adjusts the ask price for compensation based on the estimate of the maximum offer of the defendant. In this case the game becomes even more complicated and a modified game theoretic model is required.

3.2 Data Envelopment Analysis (DEA)

Data envelopment analysis (DEA), invented by Charnes et al. [72], is an approach for comparing the relative efficiency of decision-making units (DMU), such as hospitals, schools, insurance agencies, and similar instances, in which there is a relatively homogeneous set of decision-making units with multiple inputs and multiple outputs. In other words, rather than using some absolute norms or standards, DEA evaluates the relative efficiency of each DMU within this homogeneous set or comparable DMUs. Accordingly, DEA does not assume any prespecified production function (such as Cobb-Douglas function) as the norm or standard in an absolute productivity efficiency evaluation. Rather, DEA is a nonparametric methodology.

Similar to the engineering notion of efficiency being the ratio of output to input, the measure of relative efficiency used in DEA models can be simply characterized as:

$$\text{efficiency} = \frac{\text{weighted sum of outputs}}{\text{weighted sum of inputs}}$$

where the technique allows for multiple inputs and multiple outputs. The ability of DEA models to handle multiple outputs is an important and distinctive feature. Indeed, this is an important feature in insurance company efficiency comparisons because different companies may stress different outputs or inputs in their management strategy or business plan. Charnes et al. [72] proposed that the efficiency of a target decision-making unit j_0 can be obtained by solving the following model:

$$\text{Maximize} \quad h_0 = \frac{\sum_{r=1}^{t} u_r y_{r j_0}}{\sum_{i=1}^{m} v_i x_{i j_0}}$$

$$\text{subject to} \quad \frac{\sum_{r=1}^{t} u_r y_{ri}}{\sum_{i=1}^{m} v_i x_{ij}} \leq 1, \text{ for } 1 \leq j \leq n,$$

$$u_r, v_i \geq e, \text{ for all } r \text{ and } i$$

where y_{rj}=amount of output r obtained by DMU j; x_{ij}=amount of input i used by DMU j; u_r=the weight (or virtual multiplier) given to output r; v_i=the weight (or virtual multiplier) given to input i; n, t, m are the number of DMUs, outputs and inputs; and ε is a small positive number.

Essentially the virtual multipliers u_r and v_i are selected by the DMU in such a manner as to frame their own production performance in the best possible (most efficient) light (hence the maximization). The only constraint is that they cannot pick a weighting scheme for inputs and outputs that makes another DMU appear to be "super-efficient" (hence the ≤ 1

constraint). If a DMU is inefficient (has an objective value less than 1) even when it has chosen the virtual multipliers u_r and v_i to put its own efficiency in the best possible light, then it is indeed inefficient since another DMU (or combination of DMU's) using this same "strategic weighting" of inputs and outputs can take the same virtual input x_{ij} and produce higher virtual output y_{ij} than the designated inefficient DMU. Thus, the inefficient DMU is dominated in a Pareto-Koopmans economic efficiency manner.

The above fractional programming problem can be converted into an equivalent linear programming model (termed the CCR model), as follows:

$$\text{Maximize} \quad h_0 = \sum_{r=1}^{t} u_r y_{r j_0}$$

$$\text{subject to} \quad \sum_{i=1}^{m} v_i x_{i j_0} = 1,$$

$$\sum_{r=1}^{t} u_r v_{ri} - \sum_{i=1}^{m} v_i x_{ij} \leq 1, \text{ for } 1 \leq j \leq n,$$

$$u_r, v_i \geq e, \text{ for all } r \text{ and } i,$$

Its dual linear program is:

$$\text{Minimize} \quad Z_0 - \varepsilon \sum_{r=1}^{t} s_r^- - \varepsilon \sum_{i=1}^{m} s_i^-$$

$$\text{subject to} \quad x_{i j_0} Z_0 - s_i^- - \sum_{j=1}^{n} x_{ij} \lambda_j = 0, \ 1 \leq i \leq m;$$

$$- s_r^+ + \sum_{j=1}^{n} y_{rj} \lambda_j = y_{r j_0}, \ 1 \leq r \leq t;$$

$$Z_0 \text{ unrestricted; and } \lambda_j, s_i^-, s_r^+ \geq 0, \text{ for all } j, r, \text{ and } i.$$

From this dual LP (DLP), we can see that DMU j_0 is efficient if and only if all slack variables are equal to zero and Z_0 is equal to one. Conversely, if DMU j_0 is inefficient, then Z_0 is less than one and/or some slacks are positive. The optimal values of λ_j can be used to construct a composite DMU (or a linear combination of DMU's) with exactly the same inputs as the evaluated DMU but with an output that is larger than that obtained by DMU j_0. This then can provide a set of targets for benchmarking purpose by the inefficient DMU j_0 (that is, which utilize the same inputs to produce strictly more outputs). Z_0 represents the maximum proportion of the input levels that DMU j_0 should be expending to secure at least its current output level. See Brockett et al. [44] for a detailed example of this methodology used for benchmarking purpose.

The CCR model assumes constant returns to scale. However, when DMUs vary in returns to scale, the efficiency measure given by the CCR model may be complicated by the varying returns to scale factor. Banker et al. [17] proposed an extension that can decompose the overall or aggregate efficiency given by the CCR model into its technical and scale efficiency components. The modified model, termed the BCC model, is as follows (cf., the dual formulation of the CCR model):

$$\text{Minimize} \quad h - \varepsilon \sum_{r=1}^{t} s_r^+ - \varepsilon \sum_{i=1}^{m} s_i^-$$

$$\text{subject to} \quad x_{ij_0} h - s_i^- - \sum_{j=1}^{n} x_{ij}\lambda_j = 0, \ 1 \le i \le m;$$

$$- s_r^- + \sum_{j=1}^{n} y_{rj}\lambda_j = y_{rj_0}, \ 1 \le r \le t;$$

$$\sum_{j=1}^{n} \lambda_j = 1; \text{ and } \lambda_j, \ s_i^-, \ s_r^+ \ge 0, \text{ for all } j, r, \text{ and } i.$$

The BCC model differs from the CCR model only by the addition of a single constraint on the multipliers, that is, that the summation of all multipliers is equal to unity. This ensures that the BCC model yields a measure of the pure technical efficiency of DMU j_0 (cf., Banker et al. [17]).

Applications of the DEA approach to insurance problems can be found in Bjurek and Hjalmarsson [27b], Rousseau [238], and Mahajan [194]. In this paper, we introduce two of them: a DEA model for assessing the relative efficiency of the insurance-selling function (Mahajan [194]) and a DEA model for detecting troubled or potentially insolvent insurance companies (Rousseau [238]).

Mahajan [194] used the BCC model for assessing the relative efficiency of sales units. The model simultaneously incorporates multiple sales outcomes, controllable and uncontrollable resources, and environmental factors.

The model enables comparisons among a reference set of sales units engaged in selling the same product-service by deriving a single summary measure of relative sales efficiency. Conditions under which the sales unit has additional control over resources are explored, and the effects on relative efficiency are examined. The proposed model is illustrated by applying it to data collected from the branch operations of 33 insurance companies.

Rousseau [238] illustrated the role of DEA in detecting financially troubled insurance companies. The data for this efficiency study came from the National Association of Insurance Commissioners (NAIC) data set on a sample of 111 Texas domestic stock companies for 1987, 1988, and 1989. The DEA analysis was conducted by The Magellan Group, a division of MRCA Information Services. Although DEA can accommodate both financial and nonfinancial variables, only financial variables were selected in the prototype study.

The DEA study can provide the overall performance efficiency rating across all companies, the potential improvement in each input or output factor for an individual company, and the time trend of the overall performance rating of an individual company. If the efficiency rating of a company significantly deteriorates over time, the company is indicated to be in trouble and an early warning for that company is released. In addition, the factor performance analysis (which is unique to the DEA method, as compared to the more widely used regression analysis) provides information on the input or output factors that need to be improved the most to promote the overall efficient performance of the company. These effects are shown in Rousseau [238].

3.3 Expert Systems

An expert system (ES) usually has two components, a knowledge base (facts and rules) and an inference engine (interpreter and scheduler). Domain knowledge comprises the facts and a set of rules that use those facts as the basis for decision-making. The inference engine contains an interpreter that decides how to apply the logical rules to infer new knowledge and a scheduler that decides the order in which the rules should be applied. In an expert system, the knowledge is explicitly represented and accessible. This means that expert system approach is appropriate for those areas in which the knowledge that is to be used in the decision-making can be explicitly expressed. Once built, an expert system provides the high-level expertise to aid in problem-solving and has predictive modeling power; that is, it provides the output when given a situation as the input.

The use of expert systems in the insurance industry is not a new phenomenon. Financial underwriting applications, as well as life insurance applications, have been developed. Both life-health and property-casualty insurers are developing expert systems to aid in the underwriting process. Systems are also being developed to assist in claims management and investment planning. Personal financial planning, loss prevention, risk assessment, and product design are all areas in which expert system development is currently under consideration.

A product of expert systems, called Smart Systems, is becoming a component in insurers' strategic and competitive underwriting and claim systems. For instance, Connecticut Mutual Life Insurance Company expects to realize a 35% productivity gain in underwriting by using image and expert systems. Travelers Insurance Company uses expert systems to detect unusual or illogical patterns in health providers' behavior and claims to thwart fraud, and Erie Insurance Group uses expert systems to combat property and casualty fraud. In this paper, we briefly introduce two applications of expert systems: monitoring health-related expenditures by detecting unusual claims (Martin and Harrison [199]) and auditing workers' compensation insurance premiums (Koster and Raafat [170]).

Firms have often turned to self-insurance to control health care costs. In 1987 nearly 60% of all employees who had health care coverage were enrolled in a plan with some aspect of self-insurance. One reason for the lack of success in controlling health care costs, however, is that most firms do not have the expertise to properly monitor health-related expenditures. This is in fact reason to turn to third-party administers (TPAs) for claims-handling. The claims audit is one method used to monitor the administrator's performance and to help in controlling costs.

Martin and Harrison [199] described an expert system for claim monitoring and fraud detection for such a self-insured company. The expert system monitor's primary task is to review claim payments and identify opportunities for reducing health care expenditures. Cost reduction typically results from recovering improper payments and preventing similar mistakes from occurring in the future. The expert system functions as an initial filter since it reviews claims and identifies potential errors (that is, unjustified payments) by grouping payments according to likely errors and then estimating the likely value of the total error for each group. The production system consists of a set of if-then rules to determine what (if any) error is made on each payment. The knowledge base comprises approximately 50 rules that are mostly independent of each other, and these rules are used to identify 32 different types of errors. For each type of error, there exists a rule that specifies the probability of error, the value of the error, and the time required to further investigate the error (since the database is too large to investigate every claim). The validation experiments demonstrate that the system can screen claims in a manner comparable to human experts in the field (Martin and Harrison [199]).

Koster and Raafat [170] presented another expert system for auditing premium computations for workers compensation insurance. The purpose of premium auditing is to ascertain that the activities of the business are as recorded and to determine whether the employees are complying with the regulations of the insurance governing body in each state. This task is complicated, time-consuming, and error prone. The expert systems described in their paper assist insurance carriers and businesses not only by increasing compliance with statutory requirements but also by improving premium estimation accuracy, reducing auditing errors, and saving auditing time. This system is considered a prototype because it does not encompass all the rules in the workers compensation insurance manual. With this package, however, a user can: (1) solicit advice and justification for a claim, (2) request definitional clarifications, (3) ask for help, (4) request a session trace, and (5) solicit "what if" analysis and improvement suggestions. Koster and Raafat [170] suggested that insurance companies and state insurance agencies would be prime beneficiaries of such a system. The system also could be integrated and could share the same database with other business software.

Qualitative reasoning is often used as the inference mechanism by an expert system. Qualitative reasoning is realized by using logic induction, deduction, comparison, and certain other techniques. Examples of such reasoning includes the mathematical statements, "if A is true then B is true," "A is equivalent to B," and "A implies B," and so on, where A and B are propositions. Hence, the inference rules in expert systems are various rules expressed as "if-then" models. One may well wonder how those reasoning activities are accomplished by a computer since, as we know, computers complete every job by executing a series of binary operations. Below, we introduce a technique that may help elucidate this question. The technique described in the sequel formulates the qualitative reasoning process explicitly and equivalently by discrete mathematical programming.

By using atomic propositions or statements, compound propositions are created by using so-called propositional calculus. The propositional or logical operators (called connectives) include negation, conjunction, disjunction, implication, and equivalence. It is possible to define all propositional connectives in terms of a smaller subset of them so that any given expression can be converted into a "normal form" such as conjunctive normal form (CNF) (the subset of connective includes only negation and conjunction in this case) or disjunctive normal form (DNF) (the subset includes only negation and disjunction in this case). Also, these two normal forms can be converted mutually by using De Morgan's laws. De Morgan's laws, combined with other equivalence transformations, can convert any logical expression to a conjunction or disjunction of clauses by using equivalent statements. This was all shown in Hadjiconstantinou and Mitra [128].

The next step of systematically relating qualitative reasoning to discrete mathematical programming is to express these conjunctive or disjunctive statements as linear constraints involving only binary variables. We illustrate below the variable transformation process in two cases: "A implies B" and "either A or B." Other relationships can be found by referring to Hadjiconstantinou and Mitra [128]. Define x and y as follows: $x=1$ if A is true, 0 otherwise, while $y=1$ if B is true, 0 otherwise. Then, "either A or B" can be equivalently expressed as "$x+y\geq1$." Also, "A implies B" is actually equivalent to "either not A or B," the equivalent inequality is "$x-y\leq0$."

In a manner similar to that illustrated above, each of the rules in an expert system can be numerically formulated as a set of (in)equalities, so that the problem-solving procedure of the expert system is, accordingly, transformed into an integer programming solution process. Since, as discussed previously, integer programming is a rapidly developing area of operations research, such an equivalent transformation provides a promising way for optimally solving qualitative reasoning problems in insurance. In addition, this connection between integer programming and qualitative reasoning provides a bridge connecting qualitative reasoning to quantitative calculation. In addition, this transformation also clearly illustrates what we previously expressed about the expert systems: that expert systems are an alternative modeling technique that utilizes qualitative knowledge rather than explicit numerical computation.

3.4 Neural Networks

In contrast to the expert system, the neural network model is a relatively new methodology for the insurance community. Inspired by the neurophysiological structure of the brain, the neural network model can be structurally represented as a massively parallel interconnection of many simple process-ing units, similar to the interconnection of individual neurons in the brain. Mathematically, the neural network emulates the relationship between inputs and outputs in which outputs are produced as some transformed and weighted composition of the inputs. The formation of proper weights needs a learning process, according to which the neural network is classified as an artificial intelligence approach. The two typical learning strategies (algo-rithms) are supervised learning and unsupervised learning. The difference between the two types results from the characteristics of the patterns in the example or training data set. If each pattern in the example or training set also contains the observed output values, then a supervised learning algo-rithm suffices. In the contrary situation, an unsupervised learning strategy is necessary. The back-propagation algorithm (Rumelhart et al. [239]) is the most widely used supervised training algorithm based on (multiple) layer feed-forward networks. Kohonen's self-organizing feature map (Kohonen [167], [168]) is a very popular unsupervised learning method. The two ap-plications of the neural networks introduced below belong to these two dis-tinct categories. Specifically, one is applied to constructing an index or rank-ing of insurance company insolvency (and thus the creation of an early warning system (Brockett et al. [44]), and the second application is directed towards detecting bodily injury claims fraud (Brockett et al. [48]).

Brockett et al. [47] used a three-layer feed-forward neural network to develop an early warning system for insurers to years prior to insolvency (see Figure 2 for an illustration). The basic building block of the neural network is the mathematical construct known as the single neural-processing unit. This unit takes the multitude of individual inputs, determines (through the learning algorithm) the connection weights that are appropriate (or most effective) for these inputs, and applies a combining or aggregation function to the derived connection weighted inputs to concatenate the multitude of individual inputs into a single value. An activation function, which is then applied, takes the aggregated weighted values for the individual neu-ral unit and produces an individual output for the neural unit. This pro-cess is repeated at the individual neural unit, resulting in the use of as many single neural-processing units as desired, connected in whatever fashion (such as the feed-forward layered structure shown in Figure 2) is needed to produce a well functioning global neural network. The com-bined (weighted aggregate) result, $z = \Sigma w_i x_i$, is then "interpreted" by the network through the use of an activation function. The logistic

FIGURE 2

A THREE-LAYERED FEED-FORWARD NETWORK

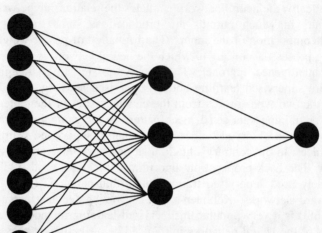

function, $F(z)=1/[1+\exp(-\eta-z)]$, is the usual choice for the activation function because of its desirable properties and its simplicity in analytic representation.

In this particular three-layer network for an early warning model, the eight input units correspond to eight financial input variables that differ significantly between the insolvent and solvent firm. The output of the analysis is the probability of insolvency. Each connection between a unit in a layer output and a unit in the next layer of the neural network is associated with a weight. The learning strategy is the back-propagation algorithm, which is used to find the optimal weights based on minimizing the disparity between the predicted outcome and the observed outcome for the available examples. The data set used in the analysis was 60 U.S. property-casualty insurance companies that became insolvent and 183 companies that remained solvent over the period 1991–93. The data set is divided into three subsets: training sample, stopping rule sample, and testing sample, consisting of 60%, 20%, and 20% of the data, respectively. Their result showed that, for predicting insolvency, the neural network approach outperformed statistical methods such as discriminant analysis and did far better than the A. M. Best ratings and the National Association of Insurance Commissioners IRIS system.

Brockett et al. [48] also applied Kohonen's feature map (Kohonen [167], [168]) to address the problem of uncovering bodily injury claims fraud. Kohonen's feature map is a two-layered and fully connected network, with output units arranged in some topographical form such as squares (as used in the study), rectangles or hexagons. This means that every output unit is associated with a weight vector whose dimensionality is equal to the number of input units or input variables (because of the full connection). As previously mentioned, this technique utilizes an unsupervised learning strategy; in other words, the pattern of each example (bodily injury claim record variables) contains only claims' recorded input variables without presupposing knowledge about the ultimate conclusion on the fraudulence of the claim. The task is to determine whether a claim is fraudulent and to determine the level of suspicion of fraud associated with the claim record file. Rather than using a dichotomous scale, that is, either fraudulent or perfectly valid, an increasing scaled measure of suspicion of fraudulence is used. Hence, the described detection system is designed to provide a fraudulence suspicion level for each claim, and each claim is uniquely classified according to its suspicion level. The Massachusetts Bureau of Automobiles provided a database comprising 127 claims, each of which has 65 objective indicators or input variables about the claim, the accident, and the claimant, such as "were there any witnesses?"

A learning algorithm is used to adjust weights to obtain improved results for classification. The learning process of the feature map can be briefly described as follows.

Each set of prototypical weight vectors is initialized with random numbers before learning begins. Within an epoch or training period, each pattern in the training sample is selected (either randomly or in a fixed order) and fed into the network once as the input vector. The program then computes the distance between this input pattern and each of the prototypical weight vectors and finds an output unit (the best-matching unit), whose prototypical weight vector is the smallest distance to this given input vector (or pattern). The value of the prototypical weight vector is then adjusted to better imitate the current input pattern. This is the "learning" feature. The uniqueness of Kohonen's self-organizing feature map is that updating occurs not only on the weight vector of the best-matching unit but also on the weight vectors of the units "neighboring" the best-matching unit. At the very beginning of the learning process (epoch 1), the neighborhood in which this adjustment takes place is relatively large. The radius of the neighborhood then sequentially decreases to zero, until finally, after a sufficiently large number of epochs or training periods, the neighborhood includes only the best-matching unit. The best-matching unit generally differs across the different input patterns within the training sample and for any particular given pattern may even vary from epoch to epoch. Figure 3 depicts the output units, which are arranged as a square. The figure also captures four snapshots, at t_1, t_2, t_3, and t_4, of the learning process along the time horizon. As shown in the figure, the size of neighborhoods decreases as the learning time proceeds. Kohonen [167], [168] presented a detailed description of the algorithm and the neurophysiological foundation.

FIGURE 3

UPDATING WEIGHTS IN NEIGHBORHOOD SET

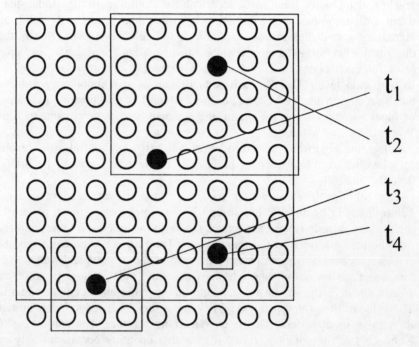

The entire data set of bodily injury fraud claims used in the study was divided into a training sample comprising 77 claims and a testing sample comprising the remaining 50 claims. Each claim, or pattern, was a 65-dimensional binary vector reflecting various claims characteristics.

It is assumed that if two claims have common or similar characteristics (pattern), they should result in approximately equivalent suspicion levels (a continuity assumption). Euclidean geometric distance is used to measure the similarity of two vectors. Consequently, the two input vectors that are close together (have similar claim indicator input variables) should be assigned similar output values (fraud suspicion levels). It is further assumed that each claim indicator is of equal importance in determining the explaining suspicion level for a claim.

As described previously, each claim vector has a corresponding best-matching output unit. Accordingly, when the learning process is terminated, we have obtained a mapping from the input claim vectors to the output space (which in this case is a square). Moreover, because of the topographical arrangement of the output units, the mapping effect can be displayed by a planar map. This planar map shows the correspondence between the claims vectors and the weights vectors (or the output units). By construction and due to the learning process, any two claims that have similar input vectors should be mapped onto geographically close units in the output space. By partitioning the square output space into regions, a topographical division of the map is obtained in which fraudulent claims tend to be mapped onto one area of the square and valid claims tend to be mapped onto a very different area of the square.

In applying this methodology, Brockett et al. [48] found that the feature map learning algorithm outperforms human experts, that is, claims adjusters and investigators, in assessing the suspicion level of bodily injury (BI) claims based on a BI claims sample from Massachusetts. A similar methodology can be used for detecting fraud in Medicare claims as well.

As a final comment, neural network modeling is a nonparametric approach. Without prespecifying any underlying functional form of the relationship between the inputs and the output, a structure is determined and a learning process is applied in order to predict. The described neural network approach can also be related to various statistical methods. In fact, the multilayered feed-forward neural network methodology can be viewed in the context of a constrained nonlinear regression analysis, in which various neural networks differ by the structure and the algorithms. Because of the characteristic of learning intrinsic in algorithms, the neural network approach is better categorized as an artificial intelligence approach.

4. CONCLUSION AND DISCUSSION

Both OR methodologies and insurance industry research are experiencing rapid theoretical and technical developments. In OR, various new algorithms, new modeling techniques, and even new approaches are being developed very rapidly. New methods have been proposed to solve larger and even more complex real-world problems. Moreover, because of rapid advances in computer methodology, operations research techniques are becoming much more easily implemented and on a much larger scale.

For any particular problem, network optimization and their applications are often the cooperative work of scientists and practitioners from various areas such as mathematics, computer science, engineering, and OR. In addition, expert systems and neural network models, which were originally developed by computer scientists, are now found to be useful OR approaches and are being applied in the solution of insurance problems. Because the development of OR depends greatly on algorithmic design and computational implementation, its rapid growth is, to a very large extent, a result of the fast-paced development of the computer industry. Many large-scale problems, which previously could be solved only on supercomputers (or simply not be solved within an acceptable time), can now be solved on desktop PCs.

As mentioned previously, the boundaries between the different OR methods are becoming increasingly blurred. For example, qualitative reasoning processes can be formulated as integer programming models, and this technique also provides a bridge between expert systems and mathematical programming models. Fuzzy programming is, to some extent, similar to robust optimization methods and to CCP in decision-making philosophy. Fuzzy programming is also related to goal programming if certain goals can be treated as constraints in the formulation.

In fact, in the real world, an absolute distinction between various goals often cannot be delineated to determine which goals are to be formulated as belonging to the objective function and which goals are to be formulated as more properly belonging to the constraint set. In practice, of course, these distinctions depend primarily upon the circumstances and the preferences of decision-makers. The fact that a portfolio problem in finance can be formulated as a linear programming problem, a nonlinear programming problem, a network optimization problem, a goal-programming problem, a chance-constrained programming problem, or a dynamic programming problem demonstrates the intrinsic applicability of numerous OR techniques to practical insurance problems.

A further example of asset portfolio-modeling techniques was discussed in Hiller and Schaack [142]. In that paper, four different structured bond portfolio models were presented, although they arise from different situations and need different quantitative considerations in modeling, implementation, and computational solution.

As stated earlier, nonlinear relationships often prevail between variables. Accordingly, one might reasonably look to advances in nonlinear function theory and computation for future OR methods that will be applicable to insurance research. Scientists have developed very efficient algorithms, such as the simplex algorithm, for solving linear programming problems. However, for nonlinear programming problems (except for certain special structured nonlinear programming problems like quadratic programming), conventional algorithms often stop with local optima rather than finding a global optimum. Recently, researchers have been inspired by the knowledge and experience obtained from nonlinear dynamic, neural networks and other classical or new methodologies to further investigate this problem. One highly touted method is called simulated annealing (SA) (Kirkpatrick, Gelatt, and Vecchi [163]). SA algorithms have been theoretically proved to be convergent to the global optimum. Romeo and Sangiovanni-Vincentelli [233] provided a theoretical review on SA algorithms. The solution-searching process, however, is in practice highly dependent on the parameter design (schedule). Many empirical studies, Goffe, Ferrier, and Rogers [125], for instance, confirm that the SA algorithm finds the global optimum with a much higher probability, but it also runs more slowly when compared with various widely used optimization algorithms such as conjugated gradient methods.

Another technique, terminal repeller unconstrained subenergy tunneling (TRUST), which was developed at the Jet Propulsion Laboratory at the California Institute of Technology (Cetin, Barhen, and Burdick [55]), is applied to neural network (back-propagation) training to avoid stopping at local minima.[7] This method seems to perform satisfactorily (Cetin, Burdick, and

---

[7]Finding the optimal weights for a multilayer feed-forward back-propagation network is difficult because of many potential local minima. In other words, it is hard to find the best weights for the neural network to extract as much information as possible from the training sample. Hence, an ad-hoc training schedule very likely ends up with finding suboptimal weights for the network model instead of the optimal weights.

Barhen [55]). One might expect that TRUST can also be used for other situations with a local minima problem.

The genetic algorithms (or evolutionary algorithms) have also been suggested as providing a potential methodology for avoiding local optima. Interestingly, genetic algorithms are currently being used to find models for predicting performance of financial instruments (such as the pricing of stocks and derivatives). We believe, sooner or later, a practical global optimization technique will be developed.

For the insurance industry, as indicated in Haehling von Lanzenauer and Wright [131], a few trends appear to manifest themselves. One trend is the ability to simultaneously consider a variety of problem dimensions and to explicitly model their interactions, often in a dynamic environment. These trends in insurance studies and decision-making practice strive to obtain much more realistic methods for dealing with real-world problems while retaining the ability to actually compute solutions in well specified cases. Decisions by senior management are becoming increasingly dependent on the analytical support from OR or management science. On the other hand, new issues in insurance never stop occurring. These include environmental pollution, the liability insurance crisis, underwriting cycles, regulation and pricing, availability and admissibility, equity and discrimination, and many other legal, financial, economic, and technological issues. These topics should challenge the OR community for some time to come. Globalization of the insurance market also presents new problems. Recent developments also show that financial risks may turn out to be the most dominant cause for risk management techniques (as has already been observed in finance).

Finally, we would like to share our view on optimization software and information technology. For those who have experienced inconvenience in interacting with various software packages such as Lindo, GAMS, GRG2 (Lasdon [173]), Lasdon et al. [174], [175], and other general-purpose optimization software, the good news is that a very user-friendly optimization problem-solver based on the GRG2 algorithm has been available since MS-Excel version 4.0. The solver incorporated in Excel is much easier to use. In addition, as new generations of PCs continue to run faster and faster, the problems of solving large-scale optimization problems will decrease. Another recent advance in developing optimization software is the use of C++ language and object-oriented methodology to build reusable libraries and friendly interfaces, which will likely lower the costs of software development and optimization. The information age is rapidly becoming a reality as more and more people are turning to Internet and other global real-time information superhighways. The impact of information technology on OR and insurance may well be beyond our imagination.

Operations research never stops providing insightful solutions and contributing to the healthy development of the insurance industry. The development of OR methodologies is both challenged and motivated by the complexity of most real-world problems, including those in the insurance industry. Practitioners and students in the insurance industry will quite possibly find that OR techniques can provide a powerful, flexible, accessible, and promising tool for insurance research.

5. ACKNOWLEDGMENT

The support of the Committee on Knowledge Extension Research of the Society of Actuaries is gratefully acknowledged. Helpful comments by Walter Lowrie, Christoph Haehling von Lanzenauer, Elias Shiu, and James Hickman are gratefully acknowledged. Cheryl Enderlein was very helpful in obtaining hard-to-locate references, and we also gratefully acknowledge her efforts on our behalf.

6. BIBLIOGRAPHY

A bibliography is important for a review paper, so we have built three cross-reference lists, each for a particular purpose. These are organized (1) by author, (2) by insurance area involved, and (3) by the OR techniques used. In the first list, all the references are presented in alphabetical order by the last name of the first author. Readers can answer such questions as which author has done what work. Clearly, readers are able to dig deeper in literature through this detailed reference list. The number is then used in the two subsequent reference lists.

In the second list, the references are organized according to the insurance areas that each paper addresses. This insurance area classification scheme was designed so that the references could be distributed into the different areas in a relatively balanced way. Certain areas, such as graduation and environmental risk management, are listed separately rather than embedded in their higher level areas (actuarial science and risk management, respectively). In addition, while we realize that duration-matching and immunization is a very active research in actuarial science and that to insurance companies, it is a vital part of their investment strategy, we still list investment and duration/immunization as separate topics to emphasize that duration matching and immunization in the scheme are more insurance-related, while the references listed under investment are more diversified. Also, duration-matching and immunization can also be considered as a technique used in asset/liability management (ALM). Hence, we have not tried to present a perfect insurance/actuarial science classification. Instead, the scheme is designed to help researchers and practitioners who face a research or practical problem and need to find relevant references and methodologies for solutions.

In the third cross-classification, the references are distributed according to OR method, assuming there are circumstances in which researchers, practitioners, actuarial students, or teachers are studying OR and trying to find relevant applications in insurance and actuarial science.

REFERENCES CLASSIFIED BY AUTHOR

1. AALEN, O.O. "Dynamic Modeling and Casualty," *Scandinavian Actuarial Journal* no. 3–4 (1987): 177–90.
2. AASE, K.K. "Stochastic Equilibrium and Premiums in Insurance," *1st AFIR International Colloquium* (1990): 59–79.
3. AASE, K.K. "Dynamic Equilibrium and the Structure of Premiums in a Reinsurance Market," *The Geneva Papers on Risk and Insurance Theory* 17, no. 2 (1992): 93–136.
4. AGNEW, N.W., AGNEW, R.A., RASMUSSEN, J., AND SMITH, K.R. "Application of Chance Constrained Programming to Portfolio Selection in Casualty Insurance Firm," *Management Science* 15, no. 10 (1969): B512–B520.
5. AHUJA, R.K., MAGNANTI, T.L., AND ORLIN, J.B. *Network Flows, Theory, Algorithms, and Applications.* Englewood Cliffs, N.J.: Prentice Hall, 1993.
6. ALBRECHT, P. "Combining Actuarial and Financial Risk: A Stochastic Corporate Model and its Consequences for Premium Calculation," *1st AFIR International Colloquium* (1990): 129–41.
7. ALEXANDER, A., AND RESNICK, B. "Using Linear and Goal Programming to Immunize Bond Portfolio," *Journal of Banking and Finance* 9, no. 1 (1985): 35–54.
8. ARROW, K.J. "Optimal Insurance and Generalized Deductibles," *Scandinavian Actuarial Journal* 1 (1974): 1–42.
9. AUMANN, R.J., AND HART, S. *Handbook of Game Theory with Economic Applications*, vol. 1. New York, N.Y.: North-Holland, 1992.
10. BABAD, Y.M., AND BERLINER, B. "Intervals of Possibilities and Their Application to Finance and Insurance," working paper, the Center for Research in Information Management, College of Business Administration, University of Illinois at Chicago, Illinois, 1993, and working paper, the M.W. Erhard Center for Higher Studies and Research in Insurance, Faculty of Management, Tel-Aviv University, Tel-Aviv, Israel, 1993.

11. BABAD, Y.M., AND BERLINER, B. "The Use of Intervals of Possibilities to Measure and Evaluate Financial Risk and Uncertainty," *4th AFIR International Colloquium*, 1994: 111–40.
12. BABCOCK, C. "Insurance Tools Developed," *Computerworld* 17 (November 1988): p. 27.
13. BALAS, E., AND MAZZOLA, J.B. "Nonlinear 0-1 Programming: I. Linearization Techniques," *Mathematical Programming* 30 (1984): 1–21.
14. BALAS, E., AND MAZZOLA, J.B. "Nonlinear 0-1 Programming: II. Dominance Relations and Algorithms," *Mathematical Programming* 30 (1984): 22–45.
15. BALCER, Y., AND SAHIN, I. "A Stochastic Theory of Pension Dynamics," *Insurance: Mathematics and Economics* 4 (1983): 179–97.
16. BALCER, Y., AND SAHIN, I. "Dynamics of Pension Reform: The Case of Ontario," *Journal of Risk and Insurance* 51, no. 4 (1984): 652–86.
17. BANKER, R.D., CHARNES, A., AND COOPER, W.W. "Some Models for Estimating Technical and Scale Inefficiencies in Data Envelopment Analysis," *Management Science* 30, no. 9 (1984): 1078–92.
18. BARR, R. "The Multinational Cash Management Problem: A Generalized Network Approach," working paper, The University of Texas at Austin, 1972.
19. BATON, B., AND LEMAIRE, J. "The Bargaining Set of a Reinsurance Market," *ASTIN Bulletin* 12, no. 2 (1981): 101–14.
20. BEEBOWER, G.L., LAWRENCE, K.D., MCINISH, T.H., AND WOOD, R.A. "An Investigation of Compound Portfolio Strategies," in *Advances in Mathematical Programming and Financial Planning*, ed. K.D. Lawrence, J.B. Guerard, Jr., and G.D. Reeves. Greenwich, Conn.: Jai Press Inc., 3 (1993): 3–10.
21. BELLHOUSE, D.R., AND PANJER, H.H. "Stochastic Modeling of Interest Rates with Applications to Life Contingencies—Part II," *Journal of Risk Management and Insurance* (1982): 628–37.
22. BELLMAN, R., AND DREYFUS, S. *Applied Dynamic Programming*, Princeton, N.J.: Princeton University Press, 1962.
23. BELTH, J.M. "Dynamic Life Insurance Programming," *Journal of Risk and Insurance* 31, no. 4 (1964): 539–56.
24. BEN-HORIM, M., AND ZUCKERMAN, D. "Stimulating Job Search Through the Unemployment Insurance System," *Operations Research* 38, no. 2 (1990): 359–61.
25. BERLINER, B., AND BUEHLMAN, N. "A Generalization of the Fuzzy Zooming of Cash Flows," working paper, Tel-Aviv University, Tel-Aviv, Israel, 1993.
26. BERNHARDT, I., AND GERCHAK, Y. "Socially Optimal Job Search and Its Inducement," *Operations Research* 34, no. 6 (1986): 844–50.
27a. BEHZAD, M.H., LEE, P.S., AND VORA, G. "An Exploration of an Individual's Decision-Making Regarding Tax-Deferred Investment Plans," *Journal of Risk and Insurance* 58, no. 2, (1991): 205–26.

27b. BJUREK, H., HJALMARSSON, L., AND FORSUND, F.R. "Deterministic Parametric and Nonparametric Estimation of Efficiency in Service Production: A Comparison," *Journal of Econometrics* 46 (1990): 213–27.

28. BORCH, K.H. "Applications of Game Theory to Some Automobile Insurance," *ASTIN Bulletin* 2 (1962): 208–21.

29. BORCH, K.H. "Recent Developments in Economic Theory and Their Application to Insurance," *ASTIN Bulletin* 2, no. 3 (1963): 322–42.

30. BORCH, K. "Dynamic Decision Problems in an Insurance Company," *ASTIN Bulletin* 5, no. 1 (1968): 118–31.

31. BORCH, K. "Mathematical Models in Insurance," *ASTIN Bulletin* 7, no. 3 (1974): 192–202.

32. BORCH, K. "Optimal Reinsurance Arrangements," *ASTIN Bulletin* 8 (1975): 284–91.

33. BOUZAHER, A., BRADEN, J.B., AND JOHNSON, G.V. "A Dynamic Programming Approach to a Class of Nonpoint Source Pollution Control Problems," *Management Science* 36, no. 1 (1990): 1–15.

34. BRADLEY, S., AND CRANE, D. "A Dynamic Model for Bond Portfolio Management," *Management Science* 19 (1972): 139–51.

35. BRAGG, J.M. "Prices and Commissions Based on the Theory of Games," *Journal of Risk and Insurance* 33 (1966): 169–93.

36. BRAGG, J.M. "Prices and Profits: A New Method for Determining Premium Rates," *IBM Proceedings: Symposium on Operations Research in the Insurance* IBM, Armonk, N.Y.: 1967.

37. BRENNAN, M.J., AND SCHWARTZ, E.S. "The Pricing of Equity Linked Life Insurance Policies with an Asset Value Guarantee," *Journal of Financial Economics* 3 (1976): 195–213.

38. BROCKETT, P.L. "Information Theoretic Approach to Actuarial Science: A Unification and Extension of Relevant Theory and Applications," *Transactions of Society of Actuaries* 43 (1991): 73–114.

39. BROCKETT, P.L., CHARNES, A., COOPER, W.W., KWON, K., AND RUEFLI, T. "Chance Constrained Programming Approach to Empirical Analysis of Mutual Fund Investment Strategies," *Decision Sciences* 23, no. 2 (1992): 385–408.

40. BROCKETT, P.L., CHARNES, A., AND LI, S.X. "Portfolio and Line of Business Selection for a Casualty Insurance Company with Stochastic Assurance," *CCS Research Report 712*, Center for Cybernetic Studies, The University of Texas at Austin, 1992.

41. BROCKETT, P.L., CHARNES, A., AND SUN, L. "A Chance Constrained Programming Approach to Pension Plan Management," *CCS Research Report 701*, The University of Texas at Austin, 1991.

42. BROCKETT, P.L., CHARNES, A., AND SUN, L. "A Chance Constrained Model for Planning and Analyzing the Management of Group Life Insurance," *CCS Research Report 679*, The University of Texas at Austin, 1992.

43. BROCKETT, P.L., COX, S., GOLANY, B., AND PHILLIPS, F.Y. "Actuarial Usage of Grouped Data: An Information Theoretic Approach to Incorporating Secondary Data Information," *TSA* XLVII (1995): 89–114.

44. BROCKETT, P.L., GOLDEN, L.L., GERBERMAN, J., AND SARIN, S. "The Identification of Target Firms and Functional Areas for Strategic Benchmarking," *CCS Research Report 746*, Center for Cybernetic Studies, The University of Texas at Austin, 1994.

45. BROCKETT, P.L., HUANG, Z., LI, H., AND THOMAS, D.A. "Information Theoretic Multivariate Graduation," *Scandinavian Actuarial Journal* 2 (1992): 144–53.

46. BROCKETT, P.L., AND ZHANG, J. "Information Theoretical Mortality Table Graduation," *Scandinavian Actuarial Journal*, no. 3–4 (1986): 131–40.

47. BROCKETT, P.L., COOPER, W.W., GOLDEN, L.L., AND PITAKONG, V. "A Neural Network Method for Obtaining an Early Warning of Insurer Insolvency," *Journal of Risk and Insurance* 61 (1994): 402–24.

48. BROCKETT, P.L., XIA, X., AND DERRIG, R. "Using Neural Networks to Uncover Automobile Bodily Injury Claims Fraud," *CCS Research Report 727*, Center for Cybernetic Studies, The University of Texas at Austin, 1995.

49. BRODT, A.I. "Min-Mad Life: A Multiperiod Optimization Model for Life Insurance Company Investment Decisions," *Insurance: Mathematics and Economics* 2 (1983): 91–102.

50. BUEHLMANN, H., AND JEWELL, W.S. "Optimal Risk Exchange," *ASTIN Bulletin* 10 (1979): 243–62.

51. BYRNES, J.F. "A Survey of the Relationship between Claims Reserves and Solvency Margins," *Insurance: Mathematics and Economics* 5, no. 1 (1986): 3–29.

52. CARIÑO, D.R., KENT, T., MYERS, D.H., STACEY, C., SYLVANUS, M., TURNER, A.L., WATANABE, K., AND ZIEMBA, W.T. "The Russel-Yasuda Kasai Financial Planning Model," working paper, Frank Russel Company, Washington, D.C., 1993.

53. CARIÑO, D.R., KENT, T., MYERS, D.H., STACEY, C., SYLVANUS, M., TURNER, A.L., WATANABE, K., AND ZIEMBA, W.T. "The Russel-Yasuda Kasai Model: An Assets/Liability Model for a Japanese Insurance Company Using Multistage Stochastic Programming," *Interfaces* 24, no. 1 (1994): 29–49.

54. CARSON, J.M. "Financial Distress in the Life Insurance Industry: An Empirical Examination," *4th AFIR International Colloquium* (1994): 1211–40.

55. CETIN, B.C., BARHEN, J., AND BURDICK, J.W. "Terminal Repeller Unconstrained Subenergy Tunneling for Fast Global Optimization," *Journal of Optimization Theory and Applications* 77 (1993).

56. CETIN, B.C., BURDICK, J.W., AND BARHEN, J. "Global Descent Replaces Gradient Descent to Local Minima Problem in Learning with Artificial Neural Networks," *Institute of Electrical and Electronic Engineeers (IEEE)*, (1993): 836–42.

57. CHAN, F.Y., CHAN, L.K., FALKENBERG, J., AND YU, M.H. "Application of Linear and Quadratic Programmings to Some Cases of the Whittaker-Henderson Graduation Method," *Scandinavian Actuarial Journal* no. 3–4 (1986): 141–53.

58. CHARIN, A.C., AND KOSTER, A. "Premium Auditing: An Expert System for Workers Compensation," *CPCU Journal* 40 (1987): 238–45.
59. CHARNES, A., AND COOPER, W.W. "Chance-Constrained Programming," *Management Science* 6, no. 1 (1959): 73–9.
60. CHARNES, A., AND COOPER, W.W. *Management Models and Industrial Applications of Linear Programming*, vol. 1 & 2, New York: Wiley, 1961.
61. CHARNES, A., AND COOPER, W.W. "Goal Programming and Multiple Objective Optimizations: Part I," *European Journal of Operational Research* 1 (1977): 39–54.
62. CHARNES, A., COOPER, W.W., GOLANY, B., SEIFORD, L., AND STUTZ, J. "Foundations of Data Envelopment Analysis for Pareto-Koopmans Efficient Empirical Production Functions," *Journal of Econometrics* 150, no. 1 (1985): 54–78.
63. CHARNES, A., COOPER, W.W., HARRALD, J., KARWAN, K., AND WALLACE, W.A. "Goal Programming Models for Recourse Allocation in a Marine Environmental Protection Program," *Journal of Environmental Economics and Management* 3, no. 4 (1976): 347–62.
64. CHARNES, A., COOPER, W.W., AND IJIRI, Y. "Break-Even Budgeting and Programming to Goals," *Journal of Accounting Research* 1, no. 1 (1963): 16–41.
65. CHARNES, A., COOPER, W.W., KARWAN, K., AND WALLACE, W.A. "A Chance-Constrained Goal Programming Model to Evaluate Response Recourses for Marine Pollution Disasters," *Journal of Environmental Economics and Management* 6, no. 3 (1979): 244–74.
66. CHARNES, A., COOPER, W.W., AND KEANE, M.A. "Application of Linear Programming to Financial Planning," in *Financial Analyst's Handbook*, ed. S. Levine, Homewood, Ill.: Dow-Jones-Irwin, Inc., 1974.
67. CHARNES, A., COOPER, W.W., KOZMETSKY, G., AND STEINMAN, L. "A Multiple-Objective Chance Constrained Approach to Cost Effectiveness," *Proceedings National Aerospace Electronics Conference*, Ohio, (1964): 454–55.
68. CHARNES, A., COOPER, W.W., AND MILLER, M.H. "Application of Linear Programming to Financial Budgeting and the Costing of Funds," *Journal of Business* 32, no. 1 (1959): 20–46.
69. CHARNES, A., COOPER, W.W., AND MILLER, M.H. "Applications of Linear Programming to Financial Budgeting and the Costing of Funds," in *The Theory of Business Finance*, ed. S.H. Archer and C.A. D'Ambrosio, Old Tappin, N.J.: MacMillan, 1967.
70. CHARNES, A., COOPER, W.W., AND MILLER, M.H. "Application of Linear Programming to Financial Budgeting and the Costing of funds," in *Financial Management: Cases and Readings*, ed. P. Hunt and V.L. Andrews. Burr Ridge, Ill.: Richard D. Irwin, 1968, 146–83.
71. CHARNES, A., COOPER, W.W., AND NIEHAUS, R.J. "A Goal Programming Model of Manpower Planning," *Management Science Research Report 115*, Pittsburgh, Pa.: Carnegie-Mellon University, 1967.

72. CHARNES, A., COOPER, W.W., AND RHODES, E. "Measuring the Efficiency of Decision Making Units," *European Journal of Operational Research* 2, no. 6 (1978): 429–44.

73. CHARNES, A., COOPER, W.W., AND SYMONDS, G.H. "Chance-Constrained Programming," in *Mathematical Studies in Management Science*, ed. A.F. Veinott, Jr., New York, N.Y.: MacMillan, 1965, 349–56.

74. CHARNES, A., COOPER, W.W., AND THOMPSON, G.L. "A Survey of Developments in Chance-Constrained Programming," *Journal of the American Statistical Association* 58, no. 302 (1963): 548.

75. CHARNES, A., COOPER, W.W., AND THOMPSON, G.L. "Characteristics of Chance-Constrained Programming," in *Recent Advances in Mathematical Programming*, ed. R.L. Graves and P. Wolfe, New York, N.Y.: McGraw-Hill, 1963, 113–21.

76. CHARNES, A., COOPER, W.W., AND THOMPSON, G.L. "Critical Path Analysis via Chance-Constrained and Stochastic Programming," *Operations Research* 12, no. 3, 1964: 460–70.

77. CHARNES, A., HAYNES, K., HAZLETON, J., AND RYAN, M. "A Hierarchical Goal Programming Approach to Environment-Land Use of Management," *Geographical Analysis* 7 (1975): 121–30.

78. CHRISTOFIDES, N. "Branch and Bound Methods for Integer Programming," in *Combinatorial Optimization*, ed. N. Christofides et al., ch. 1–20, New York, N.Y.: John Wiley & Sons, 1979.

79. CONWILL, M.F. "A Linear Programming Approach to Maximizing Policyholder Value," *Actuarial Research Clearing House* (1991): 1–102.

80. COOPER, M.W. "A Survey of Methods for Pure Nonlinear Integer Programming," *Management Science* 27, no. 3 (1981): 353–61.

81. CORRENTI, S., AND SWEENEY, J.C. "Asset-Liability Management and Asset Allocation for Property and Casualty Companies—the Final Frontier," *4th AFIR International Colloquium* (1994): 907–18.

82. CROWDER, H., JOHNSON, E.L., AND PADBERG, M. "Solving Large-Scale Zero-One Linear Programmings," *Operations Research* 31, no. 5 (1983) 803–33.

83. CRUM, R.L., KLINGMAN, D., AND TRAVIS, L. "An Operational Approach to Integrated Working Capital Planning," *Journal of Economics and Business* 35 (1983a): 345–78.

84. CRUM, R.L., KLINGMAN, D., AND TRAVIS, L. "Strategic Management of Multinational Companies: Network-based Planning Systems," *Applications of Management Science* 3 (1983b): 172–201.

85. CRUM, R.L., AND NYE, D.J. "A Network Model for Insurance Company Cash Flow Management," *Mathematical Programming Study* 15 (1981): 137–52.

86. CUMMINS, J.D. "Asset Pricing Models and Insurance Ratemaking," *ASTIN Bulletin* 20, no. 2 (1990): 125–66.

87. CUMMINS, J.D. AND DERRIG, R.A. "Fuzzy Trends in Property-Liability Insurance Claim Costs," *Journal of Risk and Insurance* 60, no. 3 (1993): 429–65.

88. CUMMINS, J.D. AND NYE, D.J. "Portfolio Optimization Models for Property-Liability Insurance Companies: An Analysis and Some Extensions," *Management Science* 27 (1981): 414–30.

89. DANTZIG, G.B. *Linear Programming and Extensions*, Princeton, N.J.: Princeton University Press, 1963.

90. DANZON, P. "Bargaining Behavior by Defendant Insurers: An Economic Model," *The Geneva Papers on Risk and Insurance Issues and Practice 54*, (1990): 53–4.

91. DARDIS, A., AND HUYNH, V.L. "Application of a Stochastic Asset/Liability Model in Formulating Investment Policy for Long-term Financial Institutions," *4th AFIR International Colloquium* (1994): 919–47.

92. DAVIS, R.E. "Certainty-Equivalent Models for Portfolio Optimization Using Exponential Utility and Gamma-Distributed Returns," in *Advances in Mathematical Programming and Financial Planning*, ed. K.D. Lawrence, J.B. Guerard, Jr., and G.D. Reeves. Greenwich, Conn.: Jai Press Inc., 3 (1993): 69–108.

93. DE DOMINICS, R., MANCE, R., AND GRANATA, L. "The Dynamics of Pension Funds in a Stochastic Environment," *Scandinavian Actuarial Journal* no. 2 (1991): 118–28.

94. DE WIT, G.W. "Underwriting and Uncertainty," *Insurance: Mathematics and Economics* 1 (1982): 277–85.

95. DE VYLDER, F. "An Illustration of the Duality Technique in Semi-Continuous Linear Programming," *ASTIN Bulletin* 11, no. 1 (1980): 17–28.

96. DECKRO, R.F., AND SPAHR, R.W. "A Multiperiod Approach to Investment Portfolio Selection," in *Advances in Mathematical Programming and Financial Planning*, ed. K.D. Lawrence, J.B. Guerard, Jr., and G.D. Reeves. Greenwich, Conn.: Jai Press, Inc., 2 (1990): 217–31.

97. DENARDO, E.V. *Dynamic Programming Models and Applications*, Englewood Cliffs, N.J.: Prentice-Hall, 1982.

98. DENENBERG, H.S. "A Review Article—A Basic Look at Operations Research," *Journal of Risk and Insurance* 35, no. 1 (1968): 159–63.

99. DERRIG, R. "The Development of Property-Liability Insurance Pricing Models in United States 1969–1989," *1st AFIR International Colloquium*, (1990): 237–63.

100. DERRIG, R.A., AND OSTASZEWSKI, K.M. "Fuzzy Techniques of Pattern Recognition in Risk and Claim Classification," unpublished paper, 1993.

101. DOWD, B.E. "The Logic of Moral Hazard: A Game Theoretic Illustration," *Journal of Risk and Insurance* 49, no. 3 (1982): 443–7.

102. Discussions: "Operations Research," *TSA* XVI, Part II (1964): D308–D316; "Operations Research," *TSA* XVII, Part II (1965): D307–D350; "Computer Models and Simulation," *TSA* XXI, Part II (1969): D109–D139; "Utility Theory," *TSA* XXI, Part II (1969): D331–D363; "Computer Models and Simulation," *TSA* XXI, Part II (1969): D445–D457; "Models and Decision Techniques," *TSA* XXII, Part II (1970): D411–D452.

103. DRANDELL, M. "A Resource Association Model for Insurance Management Utilizing Goal Programming," *Journal of Risk and Insurance* 44, vol. 2 (1977): 311–15.

104. DUBOIS, D., AND PRADE, H. *Fuzzy Sets and Systems*, San Diego, Calif.: Academic Press, 1980.

105. D'URSEL, L., AND LAUWERS, M. "Chains of Ruins: Non-Cooperative Equilibrium and Pareto Optimality," *Insurance: Mathematics and Economics* 4, no. 4 (1985): 279–85.

106. EHRHARDT, M.C. "A New Linear Programming Approach to Bond Portfolio Management: A Comment," *The Journal of Financial and Quantitative Analysis* 24 (1989): 533–7.

107. EISENBERG, S., AND KAHANE, Y. "An Analytic Approach to Balance Sheet Optimization and Leverage Problems in a Property-Liability Company," *Scandinavian Actuarial Journal* no. 4 (1978): 205–10.

108. ESSERT, H. "Solvency Risk." *4th AFIR International Colloquium* (1994): 1107–46.

109. FAALAND, B. "An Integer-Programming Algorithm for Portfolio Selection," *Management Science* 20 (1974): 1376–84.

110. FÄRE, R., AND GROSSKOPF, S. "A Nonparametric Cost Approach to Scale Efficiency," *Scandinavian Journal of Economics* 87, no. 4 (1985): 594–604.

111. FENN, P., AND VLACHONIKOLIS, I. "Bargaining Behaviour by Defendant Insurers: An Economic Model," *The Geneva Papers on Risk and Insurance Issues and Practice*, 54 (1990): 41–52.

112. FERRARI, J.R. "A Theoretical Portfolio Selection Approach for Insuring Property and Liability Lines," *Proceedings of the Casualty Actuarial Society* 54 (1967): 33–69.

113. FISHER, M.L. "The Lagrangian Relaxation Method for Solving Integer Programming Problems," *Operations Research* 27 (1981): 1–18.

114. FRANCIS, J.C. "Portfolio Analysis of Asset and Liability Management in Small-, Medium-, and Large-Sized Banks," *Journal of Monetary Economics* 4 (1978): 459–80.

115. FRISQUE, A. "Dynamic Model of Insurance Company's Management," *ASTIN Bulletin* 8, no. 1 (1974): 57–65.

116. GAREY, M.R., AND JOHNSON, D.S. *Computers and Intractability: A Guide to the Theory of NP-Completeness*, New York, N.Y.: Freemen, 1979.

117. GASS, S. *Linear Programming*, 5th ed. New York, N.Y.: McGraw-Hill, 1985.

118. GELB, B.D., AND KHUMAWALA, B.M. "Reconfiguration of an Insurance Company's Sales Regions," *Interfaces* 14 (1984): 87–94.

119. GEOFFRION, A.M. "Lagrangian Relaxation for Integer Programming," *Mathematical Programming Study* 2 (1974): 82–114.

120. GERBER, H.U. "On the Optimal Cancellation of Policies," *ASTIN Bulletin* 9 (1977): 125–38.

121. GERBER, H.U. "Pareto-Optimal Risk Exchanges and Related Decision Problems," *ASTIN Bulletin* 10, no. 1 (1978): 25–33.

122. GIOGARD, M., AND KIM, S. "Lagrangian Decomposition: A Model Yielding Stronger Lagrangian Bounds," *Mathematical Programming* 39 (1987): 215–28.
123. GLEASON, J.M., AND LILLY, C.C. "A Goal Programming Model for Insurance Agency Management," *Decision Sciences* 8, no. 1 (1977): 180–90.
124. GLOVER, F. "Surrogate Constraint Duality in Mathematical Programming," *Operations Research* 23, no. 3 (1976): 434–51.
125. GOFFE, W.L., FERRIER, G.D., AND ROGERS, J. "Global Optimization of Statistical Functions with Simulated Annealing," *Journal of Econometrics* 60 (1994): 65–99.
126. GONZALEZ, J.J., REEVES, G.R., AND FRANZ, L.S. "Capital Budgeting Decision Making: An Interactive Multiple Object Linear Integer Programming Search Procedures," in *Advances in Mathematical Programming and Financial Planning*, ed. K.D. Lawrence, J.B. Geurard, Jr., and G.D. Reeves. Greenwich, Conn.: Jai Press Inc., 1 (1987): 21–44.
127. GUSTAFSON, S.G. "Flexible Income Programming: Comment," *Journal of Risk and Insurance* 49, no. 2 (1982): 290–6.
128. HADJICONSTANTINOU, E., AND MITRA, G. "A Linear and Discrete Programming Framework for Representing Qualitative Knowledge," *Journal of Economic Dynamics and Control* 18 (1994): 273–97.
129. HAEHLING VON LANZENAUER, C. "Optimal Claim Decisions by Policyholders in Automobile Insurance with Merit Rating Structures," *Operations Research* 22 (1974): 979–90.
130. HAEHLING VON LANZENAUER, C., HORWITZ, R., AND WRIGHT, D. "Manpower Planning, Mathematical Programming and the Development of Policies," in *Studies in Operations Management*, ed. A. Hex. New York, N.Y.: North-Holland, 1978.
131. HAEHLING VON LANZENAUER, C., AND WRIGHT, D. "Optimal Claims Fluctuations Reserves," *Management Science* 23 (1977): 1199–207.
132. HAEHLING VON LANZENAUER, C., AND WRIGHT, D. "Multistage Curve Fitting," *ASTIN Bulletin* 9 (1977): 191–202.
133. HAEHLING VON LANZENAUER, C., AND WRIGHT, D. "Operational Research and Insurance," *European Journal of Operational Research* 55, no. 1 (1991): 1–13.
134. HALLAK, B., BENTAMI, S., AND KALLAL, H. "Interest Rates Risk Immunization by Linear Programming," *1st AFIR International Colloquium* (1990): 223–37.
135. HALMSTAD, D.G. "Actuarial Techniques and Their Relations to Noninsurance Models," *Operations Research* 22, no. 5 (1974): 942–53.
136. HARDY, M.R. "Incorporating Individual Life Company Variation in Simulated Equity Returns," *4th AFIR International Colloquium* (1994): 1147–62.
137. HAUGEN, R.A., AND KNONCKE, C.O. "A Portfolio Approach to Optimizing the Structure of Capital Claims and Assets of a Stock Insurance Company," *Journal of Risk and Insurance* 37, no. 1 (1970): 41–8.
138. HAYES-ROTH, F., WATERMAN, D.A., AND LENAT, D.B. *Building Expert Systems*, Reading, Mass.: Addison-Wesley, 1983.

139. HERSHBARGER, R.A., AND DUETT, E.H. "A Cash Flow Model Using Neural Networking to Predict Property/Casualty Insurance Company Insolvency," *The American Risk and Insurance Association Annual Meeting*, San Francisco, Calif.: 1993.

140. HERTZ, J., KROGH, A., AND PALMER, R.G. *Introduction to the Theory of Neural Computation*, Reading, Mass.: Addison-Wesley, 1991.

141. HICKMAN, J.C. Discussion on "A Linear Programming Approach to Graduation," *TSA* (1978): 433–36.

142. HILLER, R.S., AND SCHAACK, C. "A Classification of Structured Bond Portfolio Modeling Techniques," *Journal of Portfolio Management* (Fall 1990): 37–48.

143. HILLIER, F.S., AND LIEBERMAN, G.J. *Introduction to Operations Research*, 5th ed. Oakland, Calif.: Holden-Day, Inc., 1990.

144. HOFFLANDER, A.E., AND DRANDELL, M. "A Linear Programming Model of Profitability, Capacity, and Regulation in Insurance Management," *Journal of Risk and Insurance* 36 (1969): 41–54.

145. HORNIK, K., AND STINCHCOMBE, M. "Multilayer Feedforward Networks Are Universal Approximators," *Neural Networks* 2 (1989): 359–66.

146. HORNIK, K., STINCHCOMBE, M., AND WHITE, H. "Universal Approximation of Unknown Mapping and Its Derivatives Using Multilayer Feedforward Networks," *Neural Networks* 3 (1990): 551–60.

147. HOWARD, E.F. "Strategic Thinking in Insurance," *Long Range Planning* 22 (n.d.): 76–79.

148. HURLIMANN, W. "Negative Claim Amounts, Bessel Functions, Linear Programming, and Miller's Algorithm," *Insurance: Mathematics and Economics* 10, no. 1 (1991): 9–20.

149. JABLONOWSKI, M. "A Game-Theoretic Analysis of Insurer Behavior," *Journal of CPCU* 41, no. 2 (1988): 117–21.

150. JENNERGREN, L.P. "Valuation by Linear Programming—a Pedagogical Note," *Journal of Business Finance and Accounting* 17, no. 5 (1990): 751–6.

151. JEWELL, W.S. "Operations Research in the Insurance Industry: I. A Survey of Application," *Operations Research* 22 (1974): 918–28.

152. JEWELL, W.S. "Operations Research in the Insurance Industry: II. An Application in Claims Operations of Workmens Compensation Insurance," *Operations Research* 22 (1974): 929–41.

153. JEWELL, W.S. "Isotonic Optimization in Tariff Construction," *ASTIN Bulletin* 8, no. 2 (1975): 175–203.

154. JEWELL, W.S. "Approximating the Distribution of a Dynamic Risk Portfolio," *ASTIN Bulletin* 14, no. 2 (1984): 135–48.

155. JEWELL, W.S. "Models in Insurance: Paradigms, Puzzles, Communications, and Revolutions," *Transactions of the 21st International Congress of Actuaries (S)*, Zürich and Lausanne, Switzerland: 1980: 87–141.

156. JONES, N.F. "Linear Programming for Life Insurance Problems," *IBM Proceedings: Symposium on Operations Research in the Insurance*, IBM, Armonk, N.Y.: 1966.

157. KAHANE, Y. "Insurance Exposure and Investment Risks: A Comment on the Use of Chance Constrained Programming," *Operations Research* 25, no. 2 (1977): 330–7.

158. KAHANE, Y. "Determination of the Product Mix and the Business Policy of an Insurance Company—A Portfolio Approach," *Management Science* 23 (1977): 1060–9.

159. KAHANE, Y., AND NYE, D. "A Portfolio Approach to Property-Liability Insurance Industry," *Journal of Risk and Insurance* 42, no. 4 (1975): 578–98.

160. KANDEL, A. *Fuzzy Technique in Pattern Recognition*, New York, N.Y.: John Wiley and Sons, 1982.

161. KEITH, R.J., AND STICKNEY, C.P. "Immunization of Pension Funds and Sensitivity to Actuarial Assumptions," *Journal of Risk and Insurance* 47, no. 2 (1980): 223–39.

162. KIHLSTROM, R.E., AND ROTH, A.E. "Risk Aversion and the Negotiation of Insurance Contracts," *Journal of Risk and Insurance* 49, no. 3 (1982): 372–87.

163. KIRKPATRICK, S., GELATT, JR., C.D., AND VECCHI, M.P. "Optimization by Simulated Annealing," *Science* 220 (1983): 671–80.

164. KLOCK, D.R., AND LEE, S.M. "A Note on Decision Models for Insurers," *Journal of Risk and Insurance* 41, no. 3 (1974): 537–43.

165. KOCHERLAKOTA, R., ROSENBLOOM, E.S., AND SHIU, E.S.W. "Algorithms for Cash-Flow Matching," *TSA* XL (1988): 477–84.

166. KOCHERLAKOTA, R., ROSENBLOOM, E.S., AND SHIU, E.S.W. "Cash-Flow Matching and Linear Programming Duality," *TSA* XLII (1990): 281–93.

167. KOHONEN, T. *Self-Organizing and Associative Memory*, 3rd ed. Berlin, Heidelberg, Germany: Spring-Verlag, 1989.

168. KOHONEN, T. "The Self-Organizing Map," *Proceedings of the IEEE* 78, no. 9 (1990): 1464–80.

169. KORNBLUTH, J.S.H., AND SALKIN, G.R. *The Management of Corporate Financial Assets: Application of Mathematical Programming Models*, Orlando, Fla.: Academic Press, 1987.

170. KOSTER, A., AND RAAFAT, F. "The Application of a Knowledge Based Expert Support System to Workers Compensation Insurance," *Computers and Industrial Engineering* 18, no. 2 (1990): 133–43.

171. KROUSE, C.G. "Portfolio Balancing Corporate Assets and Liabilities with Special Application to Insurance Management," *Journal of Financial and Quantitative Analysis* 5, no. 2 (1970): 77–105.

172. LAMBERT, E.W., JR., AND HOFFLANDER, A.E. "Impact of New Multiple Line Underwriting on Investment Portfolios on Property-Liability Insurers," *Journal of Risk and Insurance* 33, no. 2 (1966): 209–23.

173. LASDON, L.S. *Optimization Theory for Large Systems*, New York, N.Y.: McMillan, 1970.

174. LASDON, L.S., AND WARREN, A.D. *GRG2 User's Guide*. The University of Texas at Austin, School of Business Administration, 1983.

175. LASDON, L.S., WARREN, A.D., AND RATNER, M. "Design and Testing of a Generalized Reduced Gradient Code for Nonlinear Programming," *ACM Transactions on Mathematical Software* (March 1978).
176. LAUGHHAUNN, D.J. "Quadratic Binary Programming with Applications to Capital Budgeting Problems," *Operations Research* 18 (1970): 454–61.
177. LAWRENCE, K.D., LIOTINE, M. "A Model to Plan Capital Expansion Investments," in *Advances in Mathematical Programming and Financial Planning*, ed. K.D. Lawrence, J.B. Guerard, Jr., and G.R. Reeves. Greenwich, Conn.: Jai Press, Inc. 2, (1990): 107–17.
178. LAWRENCE, K.D., AND MAROSE, R.A. "Multi-Decision-Maker, Multicriteria Strategic Planning for the Mutual Life Insurance Company," in *Advances in Mathematical Programming and Financial Planning*, ed. K.D. Lawrence, J.B. Guerard, Jr., and G.R. Reeves. Greenwich, Conn.: Jai Press, Inc., 3, 1993.
179. LAWRENCE, K.D., AND REEVES, G.R. "A Zero-One Goal Programming Model for Capital Budgeting in a Property and Liability Insurance Company," *Computers and Operations Research* 9, no. 4 (1982): 303–9.
180. LEE, S.M., AND LERRO, A.J. "Optimizing the Portfolio Selection for Mutual Funds," *Journal of Finance* 28 (1973): 1087–101.
181. LEMAIRE, J. "A Non Symmetrical Value for Games without Transferable Utilities: Application to Reinsurance," *ASTIN Bulletin* 10, no. 2 (1979): 195–214.
182. LEMAIRE, J. "Game Theory Loot at Life Insurance Underwriting," *ASTIN Bulletin* 11, no. 1 (1980): 1–16.
183. LEMAIRE, J. "An Application of Game Theory: Cost Allocation," *ASTIN Bulletin* 14, no. 1 (1984): 61–82.
184. LEMAIRE, J. "Fuzzy Insurance," *ASTIN Bulletin* 20, no. 1 (1990): 33–56.
185. LEMAIRE, J. "Cooperate Game Theory and Its Insurance Applications," *ASTIN Bulletin* 21, no. 1 (1991): 17–40.
186. LEMAIRE, J. "Three Actuarial Applications of Decision Tree," *MitteiLungen der VSVM*, Heft 2 (1992): 157–79.
187. LI, D.X., AND PANJER, H.H. "Immunization Measures for Life Insurance," *4th AFIR International Colloquium* (1994): 111–40.
188. LILLY, C.C., AND GLEASON, J.M. "Implications of Goal Programming for Insurance Agency Decision Making," *OMEGA* 4, no. 3 (1976): 353–4.
189. LOUBERGÉ, H. "A Portfolio Model of International Reinsurance Operations," *Journal of Risk and Insurance* 50, no. 1 (1983): 44–60.
190. LOWRIE, W.B. "Multidimensional Whittaker-Henderson Graduation with Constraints and Mixed Differences," *TSA* XLV (1994): 27–64.
191. LOWRIE, W.B., DAUER, J., LUCKNER, W., AND OSMAN, M. "An Application of Optimization to Life Insurance Planning," *Proceedings of the Conference of Actuaries in Public Practice (PCAPP)* XXXVI (1990).
192. LUENBERGER, D.G. *Introduction to Linear and Nonlinear Programming*, 3rd ed. Reading, Mass.: Addison-Wesley, 1989.

193. MacDonald, A.S. "Appraising Life Office Valuations," *4th AFIR International Colloquium* (1994): 1163–83.

194. Mahajan, J. "A Data Envelopment Analytic Model for Assessing the Relative Efficiency of the Selling Functions," *European Journal of Operational Research* 53, no. 2 (1991): 189–205.

195. Main, B.G.M. "Some Considerations on the Empirical Research of Goal System of Insurance Companies," *The Geneva Papers on Risk and Insurance Issues and Practice* 24 (1982): 248–63.

196. Manistre, B.J. "The Equivalent Single Scenario in an Arbitrage Free Stochastic Interest Rate Model," *4th AFIR International Colloquium* (1994): 1079–106.

197. Markle, J.L., and Hofflander, A.E. "A Quadratic Programming Model of the Non-Life Insurer," *Journal of Risk and Insurance* 43, no. 1 (1976): 99–118.

198. Markowitz, H.M. "Portfolio Selection," *Journal of Finance* 7 (1952): 77–91.

199. Martin, J.L., and Harrison, T.P. "Design and Implementation of an Expert System for Controlling Health Care Costs," *Operations Research* 41, no. 5 (1993): 819–34.

200. Martin-Löf, A. "A Stochastic Theory of Life Insurance," *Scandinavian Actuarial Journal* 2 (1986): 65–81.

201. Martin-Löf, A. "Entropy, a Useful Concept in Risk Theory," *Scandinavian Actuarial Journal* 3–4 (1986): 223–35.

202. McBride, R.D., and O'Leary, D.E. "A Generalized Network Modeling System for Financial Applications," in *Advances in Mathematical Programming and Financial Planning*, ed. K.D. Lawrence, J.B. Guerard, Jr., and G.D. Reeves. Greenwich, Conn.: Jai Press, Inc., 3, (1993): 119–36.

203. McCabe, G.M., and Witt, R.C. "Insurance Pricing and Regulation under Uncertainty: A Chance Constrained Approach," *Journal of Risk and Insurance* 47, no. 4, (1980): 607–35.

204. Mercer, A. "A Decision Support System for Insurance Marketing," *European Journal of Operational Research* 20 (1985): 10–16.

205. Miller, R.B. "Insurance Contracts as Two-Person Games," *Management Science* 18 (1972): 444–7.

206. Müller, H.H. "Economic Premium Principles in Insurance and the Capital Asset Pricing Model," *ASTIN Bulletin* 17, no. 2 (1987): 141–50.

207. Müller, H.H. "Modern Portfolio Theory: Some Main Results," *ASTIN Bulletin* 18, no. 2 (1988): 127–46.

208. Mulvey, J.M. "Nonlinear Network Models in Finance," in *Advances in Mathematical Programming and Financial Planning*, ed. K.D. Lawrence, J.B. Guerard, Jr., G.R. Reeves. Greenwich, Conn.: Jai Press, Inc. 1, (1987): 253–71.

209. Nauss, R.M. "Bond Portfolio Analysis Using Integer Programming," in *Financial Optimization*, ed. S.A. Zenios. New York, N.Y.: Cambridge University Press, 1993a.

210. Nauss, R.M. "Integer Programming Models for Bond Portfolio Optimization," in *Advances in Mathematical Programming and Financial Planning*, ed. K.D.

Lawrence, J.B. Guerard, Jr., and G.D. Reeves. Greenwich, Conn.: Jai Press, Inc., 3, 1993b.

211. NAVARRO, E., AND NAVE, J. "Dynamic Immunization and Transaction Costs," *4th AFIR International Colloquium* (1994): 397–425.

212. NEMHAUSER, G.L., AND WOLSEY, L.A. *Integer Programming and Combinatorial Optimization*, New York, N.Y.: John Wiley & Sons, 1988.

213. NORRIS, P.D., AND EPSTEIN, S. "Finding the Immunizing Investment for Insurance Liabilities: The Case of the SPDA," *Morgan Stanley Fixed Income Research*, March 1988; in *Fixed-Income Portfolio Strategies*, ed. F.J. Fabozzi. Chicago, Ill.: Probus, 1989, 97–141.

214. O'LEARY, D., AND O'LEARY, J. "A Multiple Goal Approach to the Choice of Pension Fund Management," in *Advances in Mathematical Programming and Financial Planning*, ed. K.D. Lawrence, J.B. Guerard, Jr., and G.R. Reeves. Greenwich, Conn.: Jai Press, Inc., 2, (1987): 187–95.

215. OLSON, D., AND SIMKISS, JR., J.A. "An Overview of Risk Management," *The Geneva Papers on Risk and Insurance Issues and Practice* 23 (1982): 114–28.

216. OSTASZEWSKI, K. *An Investigation into Possible Applications of Fuzzy Set Methods in Actuarial Science*, Schaumburg, Ill.: Society of Actuaries, 1993.

217. PANJER, H.H., AND BELLHOUSE, D.R. "Stochastic Modeling of Interest Rates with Applications to Life Contingencies," *Journal of Risk Management and Insurance* (1980): 91–110.

218. PAROLD, A.F. "Large Scale Portfolio Optimization," *Management Science* 30 (1984): 1143–60.

219. PENTIKÄINEN, T. "A Solvency Testing Model Building Approach for Business Planning," *Scandinavian Actuarial Journal* 1 (1978): 19–37.

220. PENTIKÄINEN, T. "Dynamic Programming, An Approach for Analyzing Competition Strategies," *ASTIN Bulletin* 10, no. 2 (1979): 183–94.

221. PENTIKÄINEN, T. "On Model Building for Insurance Industry," *European Journal of Operational Research* 13 (1983): 310–25.

222. PENTIKÄINEN, T., AND RANTALA, J. "Evaluation of the Capacity of Risk Carriers by Means of Stochastic Dynamic Programming," *ASTIN Bulletin* 12, no. 1 (1981): 1–21.

223. PESANDO, J.E. "The Interest Sensitivity of the Flow of Funds through Life Insurance Companies: An Econometric Analysis," *Journal of Finance* 29, no. 4 (1974): 1105–21.

224. PETTWAY, R.H. "Integer Programming in Capital Budgeting: A Computational Experience," *Journal of Financial and Quantitative Analysis* 8 (1973): 665–72.

225. PRESSACCO, F., AND STUCCHI, P. "Synthetic Portfolio Insurance on the Italian Stock Index: from Theory to Practice," *Insurance: Mathematics and Economics* 9, no. 2/3 (1990): 81–94.

226. PYLE, D.H., AND TURNOVSKY, S.J. "Risk Aversion in Chance Constrained Portfolio Selection," *Management Science* 18 (1971): 218–25.

227. RANTALA, J. "An Approach of Stochastic Control Theory to Insurance Business," *Acta University Tamp. Series A* (1984): 164.

228. RANTALA, J. "Experience Rating of ARIMA Processes by the Kalman Filter," *ASTIN Bulletin* 16, no. 1 (1986): 19–32.

229. REINHARD, J.M. "A Semi-Markovian Game of Economic Survival," *Scandinavian Actuarial Journal* no. 1 (1981): 23–38.

230. REITANO, R.R. "Multivariate Duration Analysis," *TSA* XLIII (1991): 335–75.

231. REITANO, R.R. "Multivariate Immunization Theory," *TSA* XLIII (1991): 393–428.

232. RENSHAW, A.E. "Actuarial Graduation Practice and Generalised Linear and Nonlinear Models," *Journal of the Institute of Actuaries* 118, no. II (1991): 295–312.

233. ROMEO, F., AND SANGIONANNI-VINCENTELLI, A. "A Theoretical Framework for Simulated Annealing," *Algorithmica* 6 (1991): 302–45.

234. RONN, E.L. "A New Linear Programming Approach to Bond Portfolio Management," *Journal of Financial and Quantitative Analysis* 22 (1987): 439–66.

235. ROSE, T., AND MEHR, R.I. "Flexible Income Programming," *Journal of Risk and Insurance* 47, no. 1 (1980): 44–60.

236. ROSE, T., AND MEHR, R.I. "Flexible Income Programming: Authors' Reply," *Journal of Risk and Insurance* 49, no. 2 (1982): 297–9.

237. ROSENBLOOM, E.S., AND SHIU, E.S.W. "The Matching of Assets and Liabilities by Goal Programming Duality," *Managerial Finance* 16, no. 1 (1990): 23–6.

238. ROUSSEAU, J.J. "The Role of DEA in the Development of an Early Warning System for Detecting Troubled Insurance Companies: Report on a Feasibility Study," working report, The Magellan Group, Division of MRCA Information Services, Austin, Tex., 1990.

239. RUMELHART, D.E., HINTON, G.E., AND WILLIAMS, R.J. "Learning Internal Representations by Error Back Propagation," (Chap. 8) in *Parallel Distributed Processing: Explorations in the Microstructure of Cognition* Cambridge, Mass.: MIT Press, 1986.

240. SABER, H.M., AND RAVINDRAN, A. "Nonlinear Goal Programming Theory and Practice: A Survey," *Computers and Operations Research* 20, no. 3 (1993): 275–91.

241. SALCHENBERGER, L.M., CINAR, E.M., AND LASH, N.A. "Neural Networks: A New Tool for Predicting Thrift Failures," *Decision Sciences* 23 (1992): 899–916.

242. SALINELLI, E. "About a Duration Index for Life Insurance," *Scandinavian Actuarial Journal* (1990): 109–21.

243. SAMSON, D. "Corporate Risk Philosophy For Improved Risk Management," *Journal of Business Research* 15 (1987): 107–22.

244. SAMSON, D., AND THOMAS, H. "Decision Tree Structures for a Multistage Reinsurance Decision," working paper, University of Illinois, Urbana, Ill., 1982.

245. SAMSON, D., AND THOMAS, H. "Decision Analysis Models in Reinsurance," *European Journal of Operational Research* 19 (1985): 201–11.

246. SANDERS, A., AND LAVECKY, J. "Some Practical Aspects of Stochastic Asset and Liability Modeling of UK with Profits Business," *4th AFIR International Colloquium* (1994): 949–67.

247. SATORIS, W.L., AND SPREILL, M.L. "Goal Programming and Working Capital Management," *Financial Management* 17 (1974): 67–74.

248. SEIFORD, L.M., AND THRALL, R.M. "Recent Development in DEA. The Mathematical Programming Approach to Frontier Analysis," *Journal of Econometrics* 46 (1990): 7–38.

249. SCHLEEF, H.J. "Using Linear Programming for Planning Life Insurance Purchases," *Decision Sciences* 11, no. 3 (1980): 522–34.

250. SCHLEEF, H.J. "Whole Life Cost Comparison Based upon the Year of Required Protection," *Journal of Risk and Insurance* 56, no. 1 (1989): 83–103.

251. SCHLESINGER, H. "Two-Person Insurance Negotiation," *Insurance: Mathematics and Economics* 3, no. 3 (1984): 147–9.

252. SCHMITTER, H., AND STRAUB, E. "Quadratic Programming in Insurance," *ASTIN Bulletin* 7, no. 3 (1974): 311–22.

253. SCHUETTE, D.R. "A Linear Programming Approach to Graduation," *TSA* XXX (1978): 407–31.

254. SCHULENBURG, J.M. GRAF V.D. "Optimal Insurance and Uninsurable Risks," *The Geneva Papers on Risk and Insurance* 11 (1986): 5–16.

255. SHAPIRO, A.F. "Applications of Operations Research Techniques in Insurance," in *Insurance and Risk Theory*, ed. M. Goovaerts, F. de Vylder, and J. Haezendonck. Norwell, Mass.: Kluwer Academic Publishers, 1986.

256. SHARPE, W.F. "A Linear Programming Model for the Mutual Fund Portfolio Selection," *Management Science* 13 (1967): 499–510.

257. SHARPE, W.F. "A Linear Programming Approximation for the General Portfolio Analysis Problem," *Journal of Financial and Quantitative Analysis* 6 (1971): 1263–75.

258. SHARPE, W.F. *Portfolio Theory and Capital Markets*, New York, N.Y.: McGraw-Hill, 1971.

259. SHIU, E.S.W. Discussion on "Multivariate Duration Analysis," *TSA* XLIII (1991): 377–91.

260. SHIU, E.S.W. Discussion on "Multivariate Immunization Theory," *TSA* XLIII (1991): 429–38.

261. SIEDEL, G.J. "Decision Tree Modeling of Actuarial Liability Litigation," *Accounting Horizons* 5, no. 2 (1991): 80–90.

262. SMITH, M.C. "The Life Insurance Policy as an Option Package," *Journal of Risk and Insurance* 49, no. 4 (1982): 583–601.

263. SMITH, C.W., JR. "On the Convergence of Insurance and Finance Research," *Journal of Risk and Insurance* 53, no. 4 (1986): 693–717.

264. SMITH, V.L. "Optimal Insurance Coverage," *Journal of Political Economy* 76 (1968): 68–77.

265. SPAHR, R.W., DECKRO, R.F., AND HEBERT, J.E. "A Nonlinear (Goal) Programming Approach to Risk Analysis in Capital Budgeting," in *Advances in Mathematical Programming and Financial Planning*, ed. K.D. Lawrence, J.B. Guerard, Jr., and G.R. Reeves. Greenwich, Conn.: Jai Press, Inc. 1, (1987): 45–57.

266. STONE, B.K. "A Linear Programming Formulation of the General Portfolio Revisions," *Journal of Financial and Quantitative Analysis* 8 (1973): 621–36.

267. STOWE, J.D. "Life Insurance Company Portfolio Selection," *Journal of Risk and Insurance* 45, no. 3 (1978): 431–47.

268. TAPIERO, C.S. "The Optimal Control of a Jump Mutual Insurance Process," *ASTIN Bulletin* 13, no. 1 (1982): 13–22.

269. TAPIERO, C.S., ZUCKERMAN, D., AND KAHANE, Y. "Optimal Investment-Dividend Policies of an Insurance Firm under Regulation," *Scandinavian Actuarial Journal* (1983): 65–76.

270. THOMPSON, H.E., MATTHEWS, J.P., AND LI, B.C. "Insurance Exposure and Investment Risk: An Analysis Using Chance Constrained Programming," *Operations Research* 22 (1974): 991–1007.

271. TILLEY, J.A. "The Application of Modern Technologies to the Investment of Insurance and Pension Funds," prepared remarks, International Congress of Actuaries, Helsinki, Finland, July 14, 1988: 301–26.

272. *The Transactions of the 24th International Congress of Actuaries*, 1992 (Volume 2, Topic 2), "Optimization Criteria for the Long Term Surplus Level from a Total Risk Point of View or 'How Much is Enough'."

273. Troutt, M.D. "A Purchasing Timing Model for Life Insurance Decision Support Systems," *Journal of Risk and Insurance* 65 (1988): 628–43.

274. TURBAN, E. *Decision Support and Expert Systems*, New York, N.Y.: MacMillan, 1988.

275. TURNBULL, S.M. "Additional Aspects of Rational Insurance Purchasing," *Journal of Business* 56 (1983): 217–29.

276. VAN KLINKEN, J. "Applications of Methods of Operations Research and Modern Economic Theory: Introduction Report," *ASTIN Bulletin* 5, no. 1 (1968): 51–61.

277. VAN ROY, T.J. "Cross Decomposition for Mixed Integer Programming," *Mathematical Programming* 25 (1983): 46–63.

278. VANDEBROEK, M. "Bonus-Malus System or Partial Coverage to Oppose Moral Hazard Problem," *Insurance: Mathematics and Economics* 13, no. 1 (1993): 1–5.

279. WADE, R.C., ROGOMENTICH, B.C., AND KUNG, E.Y. *Operations Research and Insurance Applications: An Annotated Bibliography*, McCahan Foundation, 1970.

280. WEISS, M.A. "Efficiency in the Property-Liability Insurance Industry," *Journal of Risk and Insurance* 58, no. 3 (1991): 452–79.

281. WEISS, M.A. "Efficiency in the Property-Liability Insurance Industry," *European Journal of Operational Research* 67, no. 3 (1993): 332–43.

282. WINSTON, P.H. *Artificial Intelligence*, 3rd ed. Reading, Mass.: Addison-Wesley, 1992.

283. WISE, A.J. "Matching and Portfolio Selection: Part I," *Journal of Institute of Actuaries* 114, no. I (1987a): 113–34.
284. WISE, A.J. "Matching and Portfolio Selection: Part I," *Journal of Institute of Actuaries* 114, no. III (1987b): 551–68.
285. WITT, R.C. "The Evolution of Risk Management and Insurance: Change and Challenge, Presidential Address," ARIA, *Journal of Risk and Insurance* 53, no. 1 (1986): 9–22.
286. WOOD, R., AND LAWRENCE, K.D. "Application of Linear Programming to Portfolio Formulation," in *Advances in Mathematical Programming and Financial Planning*, ed. K.D. Lawrence, J.B. Guerard, Jr., and G.R. Reeves. Greenwich, Conn.: Jai Press, Inc. 2, (1990): 232–42.
287. YOUNG, V.R. "The Application of Fuzzy Sets to Group Health Underwriting," *TSA* XL (1994): 109–42.
288. YU, G., WEI, C., AND BROCKETT, P.L. "A Generalized Data Envelopment Analysis Model: A Unification and Extension of Existing Methods for Efficiency Analysis of Decision Making Units," working paper, The University of Texas at Austin, 93/94-3-1, 1993.
289. ZIMMERMANN, H.J. *Fuzzy Sets, Decision Making and Expert Systems*, Boston, Mass.: Kluwer Academic Publishers, 1987.
290. ZIMMERMANN, H.J. *Fuzzy Set Theory and its Applications*, 2nd ed. Boston, Mass.: Kluwer Academic Publishers, 1991.
291. ZUBAY, E.A. "Feasibility Study of Operations Research in Insurance," *Journal of Risk and Insurance* 32, no. 3 (1965): 325–36.
292. ZUCKERMAN, D. "Optimal Unemployment Insurance Policy," *Operations Research* 33, no. 2 (1985): 263–76.

REFERENCES CLASSIFIED BY INSURANCE AREAS OF APPLICATION

REFERENCES CLASSIFIED BY OPERATIONS RESEARCH METHODS USED

Economic Theory, Utility Theory, and Others
29, 181, 223, 276
Expert Systems
12, 58, 128, 138, 170, 198, 274, 282
Fuzzy Set Theory and Fuzzy Programming
10, 11, 25, 87, 94, 100, 104, 160, 184, 216, 287, 289, 290
Goal Programming and Multi-Objective Optimization
7, 61, 63, 64, 65, 71, 76, 103, 123, 126, 164, 178, 179, 188, 214, 240, 247, 265
Game Theory
8, 9, 19, 24, 28, 35, 36, 90, 101, 105, 111, 149, 162, 181, 182, 183, 184, 205, 229, 243, 251, 254, 265, 268, 275, 292
Information Theory
38, 43, 45, 46, 200
Integer Programming, and Combinatorial Optimization
13, 14, 78, 80, 82, 113, 116, 118, 119, 122, 124, 126, 176, 209, 210, 212, 224, 277
Linear Programming
20, 27A, 57, 66, 68, 69, 70, 78, 89, 95, 106, 117, 126, 130, 134, 141, 144, 148, 150, 156, 166, 177, 180, 211, 234, 253, 256, 257, 266, 286
Nonlinear Programming
13, 14, 55, 56, 57, 80, 81, 92, 96, 125, 163, 165, 171, 173, 175, 190, 191, 192, 196, 233, 252, 265
Neural Networks, Simulated Annealing, Genetic Algorithm, etc.
47, 48, 56, 125, 139, 140, 145, 146, 163, 167, 168, 233, 239, 241
Network Optimization
5, 18, 83, 84, 85, 153, 169, 202, 208
Portfolio Models
88, 112, 114, 142, 158, 159, 171, 172, 189, 197, 207, 218, 225, 258, 267, 283, 284
Stochastic Processes and Simulation
6, 21, 52, 53, 76, 91, 131, 196, 217, 219, 220, 222, 229, 266, 278
Knowledge, General
195, 215, 263, 285
Miscellaneous Models
2, 32, 34, 50, 54, 99, 107, 120, 121, 127, 132, 136, 152, 161, 187, 193, 213, 228, 230, 231, 232, 235, 236, 242, 259, 260, 262, 269, 271, 272, 280, 281

DISCUSSION OF PRECEDING PAPER

TZONG-HWA WU*:

Dr. Brockett and Dr. Xia are to be congratulated for this excellent review paper listing nearly 300 references. As illustrated in the paper, operations research (OR) models have been formulated to solve a wide variety of problems in the insurance industry. Actuaries and management scientists have constructed stochastic financial models to assist insurers in determining the future financial impact of insured events. As pointed out in the paper, the areas in which these models are applied include determination of insurance premiums, calculation of benefit reserves, estimation of insurance fund solvency, measurement of uncertainty and risk in investments, and asset/liability management (ALM). The purpose of this discussion is to supplement this fine paper by reviewing two ALM models that are perhaps overlooked in the actuarial literature. The first one is due to Bradley and Crane [2], [3], and the second one is developed by Mulvey and his colleagues [5]–[8].

ALM has evolved over the last 20 years in response to the growth of financial markets, the problem of interest rate risk, and the availability of new analytic tools and information systems. The unpredictable path of financial innovation has shaped the development of ALM and poses new challenges for the evolution of current systems. These challenges are not only technical but also organizational. Successful financial institutions need to retain operational flexibility in spite of an ever increasing number of regulatory constraints. This target is especially problematic to achieve for institutions rooted in traditions different from the ones from which current ALM techniques originated.

The Bradley and Crane Model

The stochastic decision tree model depends upon the development of economic scenarios that are intended to include all possible outcomes. The scenarios can be viewed as a tree diagram for which each element (economic conditions) in each path has a set of cash flows and interest rates. The problem is formulated as a linear program whose objective is the maximization of expected terminal wealth of the firm. There are four types of constraints:

---

*Mr. Wu, not a member of the Society, is a Ph.D. student in industrial engineering at the University of Iowa, Iowa City.

(a) Cash flows constraint. The firm cannot purchase more assets than it has funds available.

(b) Inventory balance constraint. This ensures that the firm cannot sell and/or hold more of an asset at the end of a period than it held at the beginning.

(c) Initial holdings constraint. We set the values of the variables $h_{0,0}^k(e_0)$, which refer to the holdings of securities in the initial portfolio, to these amounts.

(d) Non-negativity constraint. The non-negativity of the variables implies that short sales are not permitted.

The basic formulation is

$$\text{maximize} \sum_{e_N \in E_N} p(e_N) \sum_{k=1}^{K} \left\{ \sum_{m=0}^{N-1} [y_m^k(e_m) + v_{m,N}^k(e_N)]h_{mN}^k(e_N) + [y_N^k(e_N) \right.$$

$$\left. + v_{Nn}^k(e_N)]b_N^k(e_N) \right\}$$

subject to

(a) Cash Flows $\displaystyle\sum_{k=1}^{N} b_n^k(e_n) - \sum_{k=1}^{K} \left[\sum_{m=0}^{n-2} y_m^k(e_m)h_{m,n-1}^k(e_{n-1}) \right.$

$$\left. + y_{n-1}^k(e_{n-1})b_{n-1}^k(e_{n-1}) \right] - \sum_{k=1}^{K} \sum_{m=0}^{n-1} [1 + g_{m,n}^k(e_n)]s_{m,n}^k(e_n) = f_n(e_n)$$

(b) Inventory Balance $-h_{m,n-1}^k(e_n - 1) + s_{m,n}^k(e_n) + h_{m,n}^k(e_n) = 0,$

$$m = 0, \ldots, n - 2$$

$$-b_{n-1}^k(e_{n-1}) + s_{n-1,n}^k(e_n) + h_{n-1,n}^k(e_n) = 0,$$

(c) Initial Holdings $h_{0,0}^k(e_0) = h_0^k$

(d) Non-negativity $b_{m,n}^k(e_n) \geq 0, \; s_{m,n}^k(e_n) \geq 0, \; h_{m,n}^k(e_n) \geq 0,$

$$m = 1, \ldots, n - 1$$

where

e_n $\in E_n$, $n = 1, \ldots, N$; $k = 1, \ldots, K$

e_n is an economic scenario from period 1 to n having probability $p(e_n)$

E_n is the set of possible economic scenario from 1 to n

K_i is the number of assets of type i, and K is the total number of assets

N is the number of time periods

$y_m^k(e_m)$ is the income yield per dollar of purchase price in period m of asset of asset k, conditional on e_m

$v_{m,N}^k(e_N)$ is the expected terminal value per dollar of purchase price in period m of asset k held at the horizon (period N), conditional on e_N

$b_n^k(e_n)$ is the dollar amount of asset k purchased in period n, conditional on e_n

$h_{m,n}^k(e_n)$ is the dollar amount of asset k purchased in period m and held in period n, conditional on e_n

$s_{m,n}^k(e_n)$ is the dollar amount of asset k purchased in period m and sold in period n, conditional on e_n

$f_n(e_n)$ is the incremental increase (decrease) of funds available for period n.

The Mulvey Approach

Stochastic programming provides an ideal framework for modeling financial decisions and investment strategies over time. In financial planning via multistage stochastic programs, Mulvey [6] uses the following equations to determine interest rate scenarios:

Short rate: $dr_t = a(r_0 - r_t)dt + b\sqrt{r_t}dZ_1$

Long rate: $dl_t = c(l_0 - l_t)dt + e\sqrt{l_t}dZ_2$

where r_t and l_t represent the short and long interest rates at time t, respectively; a and c are drift coefficients; b and e are instantaneous volatility coefficients; v_0 and l_0 are mean reverting levels. The random coefficients, dZ_1 and dZ_2, depict correlated Wiener terms. These two diffusion equations provide the building blocks for the remaining spot interest rates and then full yield curves.

A fundamental issue in carrying out a financial modeling effort is to settle on the choice of an objective function and the underlying preference structure. There are numerous possibilities. In the basic model, the proposed objective maximizes the investor's wealth at the beginning of period τ, subject to the payout of intermediate cash outflows (liabilities) under each of the $s \in S$ scenarios. The investor's true wealth at the horizon τ equals the following

$$\text{wealth}_\tau^s = \sum_i x_{i,\tau}^s - PV(\text{liab}_{\tau,T}^s) - \text{prin}_\tau^s,$$

where the primary decision variable, $x_{i,\tau}^s$, denotes the amount of investment in asset category i at the beginning of time period τ under scenario s; $\text{liab}_{\tau,T}^s$ is the liability stream from period τ to period T; and prin_τ^s depicts the amount of loans outstanding at time period τ.

There are various alternative objective functions. One possibility is to employ the classical mean-variance function:

$$\max \exp(\text{wealth}_\tau) - \rho \text{ variance }(\text{wealth}_\tau),$$

where ρ indicates the relative importance of variance as compared with the expected value. This objective leads to an efficient frontier of wealth at period τ by varying ρ.

An obvious alternative to mean-variance is the Von Neumann-Morgenstern (VM) expected utility (EU) of wealth at period τ. Here, the objective becomes

$$\max \sum_s \text{prob}_s \text{ utility}(\text{wealth}_\tau^s),$$

where prob_s is the probability of scenario s, and utility(wealth) is the VM utility function as derived via certainty equivalence and risk premium questions. A general objective function for this problem is as follows,

$$\max \sum_s \text{prob}_s \text{ utility}(\text{wealth}_1^s, \text{wealth}_2^s, \ldots, \text{wealth}_\tau^s).$$

In the approach of Mulvey [6], the primary decision variable, $x_{i,t}^s$, denotes the amount of investment in asset category i at the beginning of time period t under scenario s. The x vector depicts the state of the system after the rebalancing decisions have been made in the previous period. At that time the investor's total assets are equal to:

$$\sum_i x_{i,t}^s = \text{assets}_t^s, \ s \in S, t \in T.$$

The uncertain return, $r_{i,t}^s$, for the asset categories—for asset i, time t, and scenario s—are projected by the stochastic modeling subsystem. Each scenario is internally consistent. Thus, $v_{i,t}^s$, the wealth accumulated at the end of the t-th period before rebalancing in asset i, is

$$x_{i,t}^s \left(\frac{1 + r_{i,t}^s}{100} \right) = v_{i,t}^s, \; \forall \; i \in I, \, t \in T, \, s \in S.$$

Rebalancing decisions are rendered at the end of each period. Purchases and sales of assets are accommodated by the variables $ybuys_{i,t}^s$ and $ysells_{i,t}^s$ with transaction costs defined via the coefficients t_s assuring symmetry in the transaction costs.

Using the terminology of robust optimization (Mulvey, Vanderbei, and Zenios [9]), the relationships of the various investment categories are constructed at each period as structural constraints. The flow balance constraint for each asset category and time period is

$$x_{i,t+1}^s = v_{i,t}^s + ybuys_{i,t-1}^s(1 - t_i) - ysells_{i,t-1}^s, \; \forall \; i \in I, \, t \in T, \, s \in S.$$

This equation restricts the cash flows at each period to be consistent. It is assumed that dividends and interest are forthcoming simultaneously with the rebalancing decisions. Thus, the $ysell$ variables consist of two parts corresponding to the involuntary cash outflow—dividend or interest—and a voluntary component for the cash flow—the amount actively sold (*sales*). The requisite equation is

$$ysells_{i,t}^s = div_{i,t}^s + sales_{i,t}^s, \; \forall \; i \in I, \, t \in T, \, s \in S,$$

where $div_{i,t}^s = x_{i,t}^s(divp)_i^s$ and $divp$ is the dividend payout percentage ratio for asset i under scenario s. The cash node at each period t also requires a flow balancing equation

$$cash_t^s = cashin_{t-1}^s + \Sigma_i \, [(sales)_{i,t-1}^s(1 - t_i) + div_{i,t-1}^s]$$

$$- \Sigma_i \, (ybuys_{i,t}^s + bor_{i,t-1}^s) + cash_{t-1}^s - liab_{t-1}^s$$

$$+ bor_{i,t}^s - prin_{t-1}^s, \; \forall \; t \in T, \, s \in S,$$

with two new decision variables: $bor_{i,t}^s$ corresponding to the amount of borrowing in each period t; and $liab_t^s$ corresponding to committed liabilities other than borrowing. The variable $prin_t^s$ represents the reduction in borrowed funds that occurs during period t under scenario s. The liability decisions may be dependent upon the state of the world, as depicted by scenario s.

One assumes that all borrowing is done on a single-period basis. (This assumption can be avoided by adding new decision variables for each category of multiperiod borrowing.) Initial wealth at the end of period 0 equals $v_{i,0}$, for all scenarios s.

In practice, investors restrict their investments in asset categories for a diversity of purposes such as company policy, legal, and historical rules and considerations. These policy constraints may take any form, but we keep the structure to a set of linear restrictions as specified by

$$A^s x^s = b^s, \forall s \in S,$$

where A is an $(m \times n)$ matrix with coefficients that depend upon scenario s.

REFERENCES

1. BARONE-ADESI, GIOVANNI. "ALM in Banks." Working paper 24–94. Philadelphia: The Wharton School, University of Pennsylvania, 1994.
2. BRADLEY, STEPHEN P., AND CRANE, DWIGHT B. "A Dynamic Model for Bond Portfolio Management," *Management Science* 19 (1972): 139–51.
3. BRADLEY, STEPHEN P., AND CRANE, DWIGHT B. *Management of Bank Portfolios.* New York, N.Y.: John Wiley & Sons, 1975.
4. KUSY, M. I., AND ZIEMBA, W. T. "A Bank Asset and Liability Management Model," *Operations Research* 34, no. 3 (May–June 1986): 356–76.
5. LUSTIG, IRVIN J., MULVEY, JOHN M., AND CARPENTER, TAMRA J. "Formulating Two-Stage Stochastic Programs for Interior Point Methods," *Operations Research* 39, no. 5 (September–October 1991): 757–70.
6. MULVEY, JOHN M. "Financial Planning via Multistage Stochastic Programs," *Mathematical Programming: State of the Art 1994,* John Birge and Katta Murty, eds. Published for the Mathematical Programming Society's Symposium at Ann Arbor, Michigan, 1994.
7. MULVEY, JOHN M., AND VLADIMIROU, HERCULES. "Stochastic Network Programming for Financial Planning Problem," *Management Science* 38, no. 11 (November 1992): 1642–64.
8. MULVEY, JOHN M., AND VLADIMIROU, HERCULES. "Stochastic Network Optimization Models for Investment Planning," *Annals of Operations Research* 20 (1989): 187–217.
9. MULVEY, J. M., VANDERBEI, R., AND ZENIOS, S. "Robust Optimization of Large-Scale Systems," *Report SOR-91-13.* Princeton University, 1991.

(AUTHORS' REVIEW OF DISCUSSION)

PATRICK L. BROCKETT AND XIAOHUA XIA:

We thank Mr. Wu for his comments on our article. In the interest of being concise, several applications of OR techniques to actuarial science and insurance were not dealt with fully (or at all in some cases) in our article. Already the paper was quite long. We tried to emphasize techniques learned by SOA students or new techniques that they should learn. In some cases, other articles have provided adequate references and details. We appreciate Mr. Wu providing more applications to asset-liability matching since it touched on a methodology (stochastic optimization) that we did not detail.

Finally, we would like to note also that the Mulvey et al. approach [9] is similar in many ways to that obtained using chance constrained programming as outlined in Brockett, Charnes, and Sun (ref. [41] in the paper). However, the stochastic calculus approach to interest rate term structure was not used and the constraints were not assumed to hold under every conceivable scenario (that is, with probability one) but rather with very high probability. In this sense the chance constrained method gives a "policy" rather than a "hard and fast rule" methodology to asset-liability matching.

ACTUARIAL USAGE OF GROUPED DATA: AN APPROACH TO INCORPORATING SECONDARY DATA

PATRICK L. BROCKETT,* SAMUEL H. COX, BOAZ GOLANY,†
FRED Y. PHILLIPS,‡ AND YUN SONG§

ABSTRACT

This paper addresses some pervasive problems in using secondary data in actuarial research. These problems include:
- Reconciling and matching information from two or more sources
- Estimating the probability and other statistics using banded data
- Reconstructing the distribution function from summarized secondary data
- Incorporating information into derivation of life or loss distributions.

An approach to solving these problems is based on information theory. Explicit mathematical formulas for the probability distributions under study are presented in several specific settings with incomplete or grouped data and concomitant auxiliary information.

---

1. INTRODUCTION

This paper addresses certain pervasive problems in using secondary data in actuarial research. Those problems include the following situations:
- The data are summarized in a histogram or tabular (grouped data) format, perhaps with additional mean or median information (for example, published medical research, demographic data, and so on), which must be incorporated into actuarial analysis.
- Two published sources yield histogram or tabular summaries with the same variable, but the two sources do not group the values of the variable

*Dr. Brockett, not a member of the Society, is Director of the Center for Cybernetic Studies at the University of Texas at Austin.

†Dr. Golany, not a member of the Society, is Associate Professor and Associate Dean, Faculty of Industrial Engineering and Management at the Technion-Israel Institute of Technology, Technion City, Haifa, Israel.

‡Dr. Phillips, not a member of the Society, is Director, Business School, Oregon Graduate Institute of Science and Technology, Portland, Oregon.

§Dr. Song, not a member of the Society, is on the actuarial staff of the National Actuarial Services Group, Ernst & Young, LLP, New York City.

the same way (for example, mortality rates grouped into age intervals can be distinctly different in different medical studies).

• The researcher wishes to answer a question by using information from several distinctly grouped data streams, and the original, detailed data underlying the published summary (which might give a better answer to the question) are unavailable.

Reconciling and matching information from two or more sources is a common analytic problem faced by practicing actuaries. Data reported by magazines, medical journals, or government publications are often given in grouped histogram form. Because these information sources operate independently of one another, their reports usually have incompatibly grouped data. The summary presentation of such information frequently is accompanied by values of some of its moments or the conditional moments with certain subintervals. This data-matching problem is a specific case of the more general question, "How can we make statistical inferences from secondary data and incorporate this information into our actuarial analysis?" In this paper we present a method (a maximum-entropy procedure) that is based on the concepts of statistical information theory and that shows how to use all the information available (and no other) to answer such questions.

Applications with real data often involve conflicting or missing data elements. A publication may provide a histogram along with its overall mean and one conditional mean (that is, the mean of some subinterval), in which the latter two do not agree because of typographical error or because they are a summarization of two different studies.

Situations can also arise in which the data given are insufficient even to apply information theoretic techniques, but a uniform treatment is still needed. Accordingly, the rigorous statistical procedures detailed in Brockett [3] must be supplemented with some heuristics to handle these cases. These heuristic procedures also are discussed.

In this paper we present a procedure for generating maximum-entropy density estimates from data in histogram form with the possibility that additional means and medians may be known. With the computing power now available, completely rigorous maximum-entropy estimates can be obtained for nearly any consistent "information scenario" (combinations of information about moments and conditional moments of the density function that are consistent with at least one probability distribution). This paper provides illustrations of this.

While in general the histograms analyzed are analogous to probability densities, the procedure can also be used in some cases for more general

"$y=f(x)$" variate relationships, where y is a continuous function of x. Graduation of mortality rates by information theoretic methods provides an example (compare Brockett and Zhang [10] and Brockett, Li, et al. [8]). Other applications are risk analysis and individual risk profile analysis.

2. DEFINITION

The early literature on statistical information theory was developed by Kullback and Leibler [16] following the work of Khinchine [14] and grew out of the engineering literature on communication theory. A complete introduction and description as well as applications of information theory to problems in actuarial science can be found in Brockett [3]. To summarize, in information theoretic notation, the expected information for distinguishing between two measures, $\mathbf{p}$ and $\mathbf{q}$, is denoted by $I(\mathbf{p}|\mathbf{q})$. This expected information is mathematically quantified by the expected log-odds ratio; that is,

$$I(\mathbf{p}|\mathbf{q}) = \sum_i p_i \ln\left(\frac{p_i}{q_i}\right) \tag{2.1}$$

where $\mathbf{p}$ and $\mathbf{q}$ are discrete with masses p_i and q_i for each i. Extensive discussion of the information functional (2.1) and its role as a unifying concept for statistics can be extracted from Kullback [15]. Brockett [3] also places the functional in perspective for actuarial science.

By applying Jensen's inequality to the function $h(x)=x-\ln x$, $I(\mathbf{p}|\mathbf{q}) \geq 0$ with $I(\mathbf{p}|\mathbf{q})=0$ if and only if $\mathbf{p}=\mathbf{q}$. As a consequence, the quantity $I(\mathbf{p}|\mathbf{q})$ can be thought of as the (pseudo-) distance or "closeness measure" between $\mathbf{p}$ and $\mathbf{q}$ within the space of all measures having equal total mass. In our case, we want to choose that measure $\mathbf{p}$ that is "as close as possible" to some given measure $\mathbf{q}$ and that satisfies certain additional knowledge we have about $\mathbf{p}$. The measure $\mathbf{q}$ is the benchmark, or beginning measure, and $\mathbf{p}$ is the measure we want to obtain. The additional information about $\mathbf{p}$ is written in the form of constraints that $\mathbf{p}$ must satisfy. Accordingly, our problem becomes one of minimizing $I(\mathbf{p}|\mathbf{q})$ over all possible $\mathbf{p}$, subject to the given constraints on $\mathbf{p}$. The solution $\mathbf{p}^*$ to minimizing (2.1) subject to constraints is referred to as the minimum discrimination information (MDI) estimate.

In many applications, however, there is no such a priori, benchmark, or starting-point measure $\mathbf{q}$ from which to derive $\mathbf{p}$. In this case, we express our ignorance about $\mathbf{q}$ by choosing all values of $\mathbf{q}$ to be equally likely; that is, $q_i=1$ for all i in the discrete measure case or $q(x)=1$ for all x in the continuous density case. Accordingly, our objective function (in the discrete case) is of form

$$\text{Min } I(\mathbf{p}|\mathbf{q}) = \sum_i p_i \ln(p_i) = -\sum_i p_i \ln\left(\frac{1}{p_i}\right),$$

or equivalently

$$\text{Max } \sum_i p_i \ln\left(\frac{1}{p_i}\right) \tag{2.2}$$

The quantity $\sum_i p_i \ln(p_i)$ is called the entropy of $\mathbf{p}$, and the distribution that solves (2.2) is called the maximum-entropy (ME) distribution. The entropy of a distribution conceptually measures the dispersion of the distribution: the maximum-entropy distribution is the uniform distribution (most uniformly dispersed distribution) and the maximum entropy distribution is a point mass distribution with all its mass at a single point (the most concentrated distribution possible).

The principles used in this paper are set forth by Kullback [15], Theil and Feibig [20], Brockett [3], and Brockett, Charnes, et al. [4]. What follows most closely resembles the latter two works, in that inferences are based on data that have already been summarized, rather than on original sample observations. The heuristic that connects with the maximum-entropy choice of probability distribution is that, all the information that is known about the unknown distribution $\mathbf{p}$ is written down. This information constitutes the constraint set that $\mathbf{p}$ must satisfy. The uncertainty (entropy) of $\mathbf{p}$ is then maximized subject to these constraints. In essence, what is known is used, and the uncertainty of what is not known is maximized.

3. SOME MOTIVATING EXAMPLES

To illustrate the problems discussed in Section 1, we examine the medical study by DeVivo et al. [11] on the mortality effects of incomplete and complete paraplegia and quadriplegia resulting in the relative mortality ratio data extracted in Table 1. The age intervals used in the medical study were defined as: 1–24, 25–49, and 50+, and the published reports are based on these intervals.

TABLE 1

RELATIVE MORTALITY RATIOS
FOR 5,131 SPINAL CORD INJURY PATIENTS
INJURED BETWEEN 1973 AND 1980
WHO SURVIVED AT LEAST 24 HOURS
AFTER INJURY; BY NEUROLOGICAL CATEGORY
AND AGE GROUP AT TIME OF INJURY [11]

Neurological Category and Age Group at Injury	Relative Mortality Ratio
Incomplete Paraplegia	
1–24	4.82
25–49	6.59
50+	3.26
Complete Paraplegia	
1–24	4.93
25–49	6.93
50+	3.26
Incomplete Quadriplegia	
1–24	4.22
25–49	6.71
50+	3.95
Complete Quadriplegia	
1–24	12.4
25–49	20.78
50+	14.11

An actuary might attempt to use these data for adjusting a mortality table for use in such cases as wrongful injury damage award compensation calculations and life insurance premium determination for medically impaired lives. A reasonable question is: Is there a statistically rigorous way to estimate, consistent with the data given in Table 1, the mortality rates for, say, incomplete paraplegics that is as close as possible to some presupposed standard table without actually having access to the original detailed data?[1] The answer is "yes." Brockett and Song [9] provide a life table adjustment method based on a constrained information theoretic methodology. This model minimizes the "information theoretic distance" (2.1) between the adjusted mortality rates and the corresponding standard rates subject to constraints that reflect the known characteristics of the individual. An interesting subproblem in their study is how to estimate the exposure level, E_x, that must be used in the calculation. To be most accurate, E_x should be taken as actually exhibited by the patient study population; however, when secondary

---

[1]By "the original detailed data," we mean the original sample observations, including both the sampling frame and the sample size—all the information that would have been available had the actuary done the primary research.

data are used, this detailed information about the precise age distribution of the patient study population is often unavailable. In fact, DeVivo et al. [11] in their report only give partial information on E_x for the three age categories in Table 1. Accordingly, the study of Brockett and Song [9] must develop a method to derive the values E_x for the study population distribution. They show how information theoretic techniques can be used to obtain a set of exposure values, E_x, that are as close as possible to the exposure profile of the standard population but that are consistent with the information about the study patient population profile given in DeVivo et al. [11].

As another example of a situation in which the actuary may be asked to use secondary data to answer questions, consider the loss distribution information presented in Table 2.

TABLE 2

EXPECTED LOSS EXPERIENCE
FOR 1000 CLAIMS

Loss Interval [a, b]	Expected Number of Claims	Average Claim Size in the Interval
0	75	$ 0
1, 1,000	500	900
1,001, 5,000	250	4,000
5,001, 10,000	150	9,000
10,001, 100,000	20	20,000
100,001, 500,000	4	200,000
500,001, 1,000,000	0.8	650,000
1,000,000+	0.2	1,500,000
Total/Average	1,000	$ 4,820

Note that Table 2 gives both the conditional probabilities and conditional means of the loss size subintervals. These may have arisen as summary statistics for a very large data set that has only been saved in "banded" form (compare Reitano [17]) or may have come from a published secondary data source.

The actuary may be asked to determine the probability that a claim will exceed a certain threshold level, say $50,000, and to determine the expected claim size if a policy were issued with this threshold level as a policy limit. Since $50,000 is strictly interior to one of the intervals, the actuary must "interpolate" to find such an answer. The usual actuarial methods of assuming a constant force or a uniform distribution within the individual subinterval will not work, because they would produce probability distributions inconsistent with the known average claim sizes within the subintervals (since the mean of each subinterval is known and is not consistent with the uniform or constant force assumption). For example, the interval [1, 1,000] would have a mean of 500 under the uniform distribution assumption; however, this is incompatible with the fact that the mean for this interval is known to be 900.

The data matching discussed previously can arise when two histograms are incompatible or when the subinterval endpoints on a single histogram are not convenient to the user of the published data. Figure 1 displays data on the use of a particular actuarial software program used in defined-benefit pension plan calculations by consulting actuaries. The marketing actuary for the developer of an improved software that can be used as an adjunct to the original actuarial software has determined the R&D costs of developing the program and ascertained that the purchase is only cost-effective by the consulting actuary who performs this calculation more than 15 times per month. Accordingly, it is desired to know, "How many actuaries perform this calculation more than 15 times per month?" (The fact that usage is not evenly distributed over the 10–30 interval means that a quick proportional calculation based on the histogram data would be unreliable.)

FIGURE 1

PERCENTAGE OF CONSULTING ACTUARIES REPORTING THE NUMBER OF USES
OF DEFINED-BENEFIT CALCULATIONS OF THE GIVEN TYPE PER MONTH
(THE AVAILABLE DATA DESCRIPTION LISTS THE MEAN AS 8.5 AND THE MEDIAN AS 4.5.)

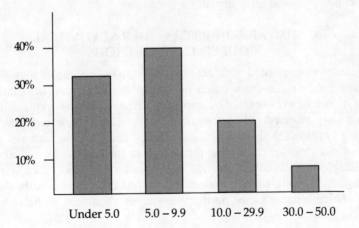

In this paper we propose a technique for addressing all these problems. This technique also shows how to solve a large collection of other problems, such as those that were originally motivated by Reitano's [17] article on banded data but that was actually left unsolved in his paper. This paper can be considered a follow-up to the papers of Reitano [17], Brockett and Cox [6], and Brockett [3].

Why might the primary data be unavailable to the actuary? The original researchers may have lost or discarded the detailed numbers. They may have kept them confidential. The data may have been summarized in the primary data collection in a manner that served the goals of the original investigators, but not those of the actuarial analyst. For example, for questionnaire-type data, rather than asking a respondent to give an age, the respondent might have been asked a categorizing question such as "Is your age under 18, between 18 and 25, or over 25?" Economic or personal questions, such as family income, which might be very pertinent to marketing actuaries, are often presented to the respondent in a categorical manner to increase truthfulness and response rates. Moreover, this sort of "banded" data is often the accessible form of data that is stored by insurance companies (compare Reitano [17]). In addition, even if the specific numbers *could* be provided (perhaps by accessing a much larger, more detailed, and different internal computer tape, or by contacting the authors of the original article and soliciting their time and energy to make available all the original data in a form understandable to the actuarial analyst), the cost and delay in obtaining an answer may be more than the client (or actuary) is willing to bear. The alternative, of course, is to develop and use an estimation technique that uses the secondary data as they actually appear.

4. COMPARISON WITH OTHER STATISTICAL GROUPED DATA METHODS

A researcher presented with data like those in our examples may wish to estimate a density function based on one of the histogram summaries, to match it with other sources. Ordinarily, published histogram representations provide only grouped data rather than the detailed sample data on which they are constructed. In fact, in some cases not even the sample size is reported. Statistical methods that rely solely on the original observations are inapplicable in these situations and one must turn to group data statistical techniques. In many cases maximum likelihood estimates, usually the preferred choice because of the desirable asymptotic behavior of the estimates, cannot be used in their simplest form and a grouped data counterpart is necessary (compare Hogg and Klugman [13]). Other methods of fitting the data to either a polynomial or a specific parametric probability function are least squares (Blum and Rosenblatt [2, pp. 435]), moment matching (Blum and Rosenblatt [2, pp. 323]), or L_1 estimation (Althanari and Dodge [1]). If the underlying density function is presupposed to have a specific parametric form, such as the exponential distribution (the constant force or hazard model), then summary knowledge of sufficient statistics may provide maximum likelihood estimates; for example, the exponential assumption would require only the sample mean to fit the data. These methods still presuppose a parametric model for the data that may not be easily found.

Various nonparametric methods have also been proposed to reconcile data in histogram form. Perhaps the most naive method is the "frequency curve" approach in which the midpoints of the tops of the histogram's bars are connected to create a "frequency polygon" (compare Brockett and Levine [7]). Another method very familiar to actuaries involves fitting a higher-order polynomial (for example, a cubic spline) through the midpoints of the tops of the histogram's bars (Sard and Weintraub [18]). Polynomial fitting is a familiar and fairly obvious strategy that has the advantage that many computer programs are available to execute the procedure. Also, this technique uses the shape of larger sections of the histogram rather than simply treating each interval individually. However, these advantages are often outweighed by the imperfect estimates that result. Moreover, the estimated densities may not satisfy the auxiliary known moment constraints, necessitating some ad-hoc corrective mechanism. Nonparametric kernel density estimates might also be attempted; however, readily available programs to implement this analysis do not apply to grouped data.

In this paper, to make such an estimation in an objective way, we propose using an information theoretic technique involving maximum-entropy estimation. This technique is also a nonparametric approach and is a generalization of Laplace's "Principle of Insufficient Information," which postulates a uniform distribution in situations in which no additional information about the distribution is available. When auxiliary information *is* available, the maximum-entropy method selects the distribution that is "as close to uniform" as possible, subject to the information that is actually known (compare Brockett [3]). This method can be shown to provide a justification for the common uniform distribution of deaths and constant force of mortality assumptions used in the theory of life contingencies (compare Brockett [3]). Moreover, when unimodality of the distribution can be justifiably assumed, this technique can be extended without difficulty to incorporate this additional knowledge (compare Brockett, Charnes et al. [5]).

This technique's minimum discrimination information (MDI) objective function criterion also provides a goodness-of-fit measure with many desirable properties (see Brockett [3, Part IV]). It is often said that the maximum-entropy method provides estimates that are the closest to the observed data (in the sense that it is most difficult to discriminate between the estimated density function and the observed data), subject to the known information that is incorporated as constraint in the model. The estimates are also sometimes said to be maximally unprejudiced in the sense that all available information is used, with the least injection of extraneous assumptions and considerations. See Theil and Feibig [20] for details. To paraphrase Albert Einstein "The model should be as simple as possible, but no simpler." Here the information theoretic approach uses only the data and knowledge constraints and derives the density as a *consequence* of the analysis, rather than presupposing a parametric density before the analysis.

5. MAXIMUM-ENTROPY ESTIMATION APPLIED TO HISTOGRAM DATA

A histogram of a variable X shows frequencies or counts corresponding to n intervals of X. Each such interval is of the form $(a_i, b_i]$, where one or both of a_i and b_i are finite for each $i = 1, \ldots, n$, and $a_{i+1} \leq b_i$ (with the usual case being $a_{i+1} = b_i$) for every i. In graphic form, the height, h_i, of each interval, divided by the total $H = \Sigma_i h_i$ of all interval heights, can be taken to represent the probability mass associated with the interval.

Accordingly, the variable under investigation, X, can be regarded as a random variable and the maximum-entropy algorithm estimates $f(x)$, the density of X, or $F(x)$, the cumulative distribution function of X. When a reallocation of the probability mass to new intervals $(a_i', b_i']$ is desired (as when trying to transform the histogram from one secondary data source into a histogram using intervals $(a_i', b_i']$ so they can be incorporated with a second data source that used the intervals $(a_i', b_i']$), the reallocation can simply be calculated as

$$F(b_i') - F(a_i'), \tag{5.1}$$

where F is the derived distribution function for X.

A naive estimate of the density is a piecewise uniform distribution, if a_1 and b_n are finite, that is,

$$p_i(x) = \frac{h_i}{(b_i - a_i)H} \text{ for } x \in (a_i, b_i]. \tag{5.2}$$

This is, for example, the estimate used in mortality table analysis when the uniform distribution of deaths assumption is used and yields the familiar "bar chart."

When further auxiliary information is available on certain moments (or conditional moments) of $f(x)$, then the ME procedure yields a more desirable estimate $p(x)$ in a manner consistent with maximum-entropy estimation theory.[2] When no such information is given, $p(x)$ becomes the final estimate of $f(x)$.[3]

The conditional moments that might be available are the conditional means $E(X|a_i < X \le b_i) = \mu_i$ and/or the conditional medians $M(X|a_i < X \le b_i) = M_i$ of the individual subintervals $(a_i, b_i]$ (here M denotes the median).

Returning to the general topic of determining a distribution that is close to some distribution $\mathbf{q}$ but that satisfies certain constraints, we define the minimum discrimination information (compare Brockett [3]) estimate of $\mathbf{q}$ to be the distribution $\mathbf{p}$, which solves the extremization problem:

$$\text{Minimize} \quad \int p(x)\ln \frac{p(x)}{q(x)} \, dx \tag{5.3}$$

$$\text{Subject to} \quad \theta_i = \int T_i(x)p(x)dx \quad i = 1, \dots, n.$$

where ln is the natural logarithm, θ_i is a given parameter value; $T_i(x)$ is a given function of X whose known or given expectation defines the i-th constraint; and the distribution $\mathbf{q}$ that is to be estimated may arise from empirical data (as in graduation problems) or from a known distribution (as in adjusting a standard mortality table to reflect certain known mortality ratios at given ages). As previously discussed, the objective function can be construed

---

[2]Since the algorithm used in this paper is concerned only with continuous density functions, we use the notation $p(x)$ and $f(x)$ interchangeably in this discussion.

[3]However, when a_1 or b_n is infinite, different strategies must be used because the uniform distribution is not acceptable in these situations.

as finding the "closest" distribution to q (in the sense that the distribution found is least distinguishable from $\mathbf{q}$; compare Brockett [3]), which is consistent with the known information stated in (5.3).

The analysis given in Brockett [3] implies that the optimal solution of the problem above is a density function $\mathbf{p}^*$ of the form

$$p^*(x) = \frac{q(x)e^{\Sigma_i \beta_i T_i(x)}}{\displaystyle\int q(t)e^{\Sigma_i \beta_i T_i(t)} \, dt} \tag{5.4}$$

(called the minimum discrimination information or MDI density) where β_i are a set of parameters to be estimated in such a way that the constraints are all satisfied. Essentially, the final estimate adjusts the prior estimate q in a multiplicative manner to obtain consistency with the known information constraints.

There are now special cases to consider. First, when the distribution $q(x)$ is a uniform density (like an "ignorance" prior in Bayesian statistics), the optimal solution $\mathbf{p}^*$ for (5.3) is found by solving a maximum-entropy problem

$$\text{Maximize} \quad \int p(x) \ln \frac{1}{p(x)} \, dx$$

Second, when the data or standard distribution $\mathbf{q}$ that is to be estimated is in histogram form, $\mathbf{q}$ can be modeled as a piecewise-uniform density $q(x)$, and the integral

$$\int_{a_1}^{b_n} f(x) \ln \frac{f(x)}{q(x)} \, dx$$

in the objective function of (5.3) can be expressed as

$$\sum_{i=1}^{n} \int_{a_i}^{b_i} p(x) \ln \frac{p(x)}{q_i(x)} \, dx.$$

Each integral in this sum is equivalent (up to a constant) to a corresponding entropy expression over the same interval. We use this equivalency when $f(x)$ must be estimated separately for each interval, rather than "systemwide."

Since the MDI statistic is additive, the estimation of $f(x)$ interval by interval, in fact, provides a global MDI estimate of the entire density, provided that only mass constraints are given (for example, histogram values without auxiliary information). We show below how (5.3) is developed for our piecewise constant choice of $q(x)$ when certain conditional means are also known for each interval in a subset I of the n intervals.

To minimize (5.3) subject to conditional mean constraints of the form

$$\frac{\int\limits_{a_i}^{b_i} xp(x)dx}{\int\limits_{a_i}^{b_i} p(x)dx} = \mu_i \qquad i \in I, \qquad (5.5)$$

for that subset I of indices of subintervals for which this conditional mean type of information is given, we rewrite (5.5) as

$$\int\limits_{a_1}^{b_n} (x - \mu_i)I_{[a_i,\, b_i]}p(x)dx = 0, \qquad (5.6)$$

where $I_{[a_i,\, b_i]}$ denotes the indicator function of the interval $[a_i, b_i]$. This can be written in the global expectation constraint formulation of (5.3) by defining

$$T_i(x) = \begin{cases} x - \mu_i & \text{for } a_i < x \le b_i \\ 0 & \text{otherwise} \end{cases} \qquad i \in I. \qquad (5.7)$$

For intervals $i \notin I$, we know only the mass (or histogram height) information, which can be written as

$$\int\limits_{a_1}^{b_1} p(x)dx = \frac{h_i}{H}, \tag{5.8}$$

which can also be put into the global expectational constraint form of (5.3) by defining

$$T_i(x) = \begin{cases} 1 & \text{for } a_i < x \le b_i \\ 0 & \text{otherwise} \end{cases} \quad i \notin I. \tag{5.9}$$

Note that in the numerator of (5.4), only one of the $T_i(x)$ is nonzero for any given value of x, so that we can reformulate the solution as

$$f^*(x) = \begin{cases} q(x)e^{\beta_i(x-\mu_i)}/C & \text{for } x \in (a_i, b_i], i \in I \\ q(x)e^{\beta_i}/C & \text{for } x \in (a_i, b_i], i \notin I \end{cases}. \tag{5.10}$$

Here the denominator of (5.4), which can be viewed as a normalization constant, is abbreviated by the symbol C. The first expression in (5.10) is a truncated exponential conditional density, and the second expression is a uniform conditional density.

This result also encompasses cases in which (conditional) medians or, more generally, percentiles are known. Using the algebra of densities and expectations, such median knowledge merely translates into additional constraints of the type in (5.3), with $T_i(x)$ again defined by (5.7) or (5.9).

So far, we have shown that the maximum-entropy density over a closed interval $[a, b]$, when no moment information is available, is the uniform density. When a mean for a similar interval is known, the maximum-entropy distribution is the truncated exponential (see Brockett, Charnes, and Paick [5] and Theil and Feibig [20]). Similarly, some other well-known special cases of (5.4) are listed in Table 3 (taken in part from Theil and Feibig [20, pp. 9]).[4]

---

[4]Note the x-axis scaling on the expressions for the exponential and truncated exponential distributions in the table. These density functions are usually applied to intervals with one endpoint at $x=0$. In analyzing histograms, it may be necessary to fit these density functions for individual intervals of x with arbitrary endpoints; for this reason the table displays the most general forms of

TABLE 3

SUMMARY OF MAXIMUM ENTROPY DISTRIBUTION
FOR DIFFERENT KNOWN INFORMATION SCENARIOS

Interval	Moments Known	ME Density
$[a, b]$	None	Uniform: $f(x)=1/(b-a)$
$[a, b]$	Mean μ	Truncated exponential: $f(x)=\alpha\, e^{\alpha x}/(e^{\alpha b}-e^{\alpha a})$ α is an implicit function of μ.
$[a, \infty]$	Mean μ	Exponential: $f(x)=e^{-[x-a/(\mu-a)]}/(\mu-a)$
$[-\infty, b]$	Mean μ	Exponential: $f(x) = e^{-[(b-x)/(b-\mu)]}/(b-\mu)$
$[-\infty, \infty]$	Mean μ and Variance σ^2	Normal: $f(x) = \dfrac{1}{\sqrt{2\pi\sigma^2}}\, e^{-(x-\mu)^2\, 2\sigma^2}$

6. THE HEURISTIC PROCEDURE FOR DENSITY ESTIMATION IN SOME SPECIFIC INFORMATIONAL SETTINGS

In a given information scenario, any combination of the following may be known: the unconditional mean of $f(x)$; the unconditional median of $f(x)$; and conditional (interval) means and/or medians for a number of the intervals $[a_i, b_i]$. The distributional scenarios must be treated differently for the cases of $a_1=-\infty$ and/or $b_n=\infty$. For brevity, in this paper we do not consider moments other than means and quantiles, because such higher-order generalized moments are unlikely to be realized from published secondary data or from subjective estimation methods (although the mathematics for accomplishing their inclusion poses no problems, for example, see Brockett [3]).

The order of precedence for the use of this information in the heuristic algorithm implemented via computer as described in this paper is as follows: If two or more interval means are known, they are used. The unconditional mean, then, is not used, nor are medians for those intervals. Any known medians for the remaining intervals are used. The unconditional median, if it is known and if it does not fall into one of the intervals for which a mean is known, is used. If only one interval mean is known and the overall mean is known, the user can choose which one to use. Any information sets not prohibited by the above rules can be used in their entirety.

the function. Also, the exponential distribution on $(-\infty, b]$ is written to be monotonically increasing. Other combinations of moments and intervals result in ME distributions that can be derived by using the same procedure demonstrated in (5.5)–(5.10).

A restatement may clarify these rules: If a conditional mean and median for the same interval are known, priority is arbitrarily given to the interval mean. Also, a known conditional median simply results in the splitting of an interval into two new subintervals, each with half the probability mass of the original. A known overall median likewise results in the splitting of an interval, although this will usually be an uneven division. Median-only operations always result in a new $q(x)$, which has the same form as (6.2). From the context of the available data, no interval means will be known for these newly created intervals, but the unconditional mean still may be known and used.

The following (not all encompassing set of) illustrations provide estimates for use as building blocks for the inference of the desired but unknown true distribution function $F(x)$. These building blocks can then be composed[5] according to the rules given earlier in this section to obtain the desired global estimates of F. These discussions and those of Brockett [3] show how to include any and all information in the analysis if desired.

A. When the Conditional Mean for a Bounded Interval (a, b] Is Known

The ME conditional distribution for the interval is the truncated exponential. The known mean, μ, is related to the parameter a of the exponential distribution by the equation

$$\mu = \frac{be^{\alpha b} - ae^{\alpha a}}{e^{\alpha b} - e^{\alpha a}} - \alpha^{-1}. \tag{6.1}$$

The segment of the distribution function for $x \in [a, b]$ is then

$$F(x) = F(a) + \frac{e^{\alpha x} - e^{\alpha a}}{e^{\alpha b} - e^{\alpha a}}. \tag{6.2}$$

Now, however, we must adjust the vertical scaling because, as $F(x)$ is written in (6.2), we have $F(b) - F(a) = 1$. To be consistent with the histogram data we started with, this quantity must be scaled upward or downward to reflect the particular interval mass h_i/H (if this is the i-th interval and $a = a_i$ and $b = b_i$), which may not be unity. Accordingly, we revise $F(x)$ to

---

[5]These estimates assume that the user-provided moment information is correct.

$$F^*(x) = F^*(a_i) + \frac{h_i(e^{\alpha x} - e^{\alpha a_i})}{H(e^{\alpha b_i} - e^{\alpha a_i})} \quad \text{for } x \in (a_i, b_i].$$ (6.3)

B. When the Conditional Median of $(a_i, b_i]$ Is Known

The ME conditional distribution is piecewise-uniform in this situation. The "mass" in this interval is h_i according to the histogram data. In this case $(a_i, b_i]$ is split into two subintervals (a_i, M_i) and $(M_i, b_i]$, each of which now is given a mass equal to $h_i/2$. No additional information is available for the newly created intervals, so each such subinterval j is associated with a ME distribution that is uniform on that subinterval. When x belongs to $(a_j, b_j]$,

$$F^*(x) = F^*(a_j) + \frac{h_j(x - a_j)}{[H(b_j - a_j)]}.$$ (6.4)

C. When the Unconditional Mean Is Known and All Subintervals Are Bounded

We apply (5.3) with $q(x) = h_i/[H(b_i - a_i)]$ for $x \in (a_i, b_i]$ and with the constraint set

$$\int_{a_i}^{b_a} xp(x)dx = \mu$$ (6.5)

$$\int_{a_i}^{b_a} p(x)dx = 1$$

The ME distribution is then a piecewise truncated exponential:

$$p(x) = \frac{\dfrac{h_i e^{-\beta x}}{H(b_i - a_i)}}{\displaystyle\int q(t)e^{-\beta t}\, dt} \quad \text{for } x \in (a_i, b_i], \, i = 1, \ldots, n.$$ (6.6)

where the same limits of integration apply. Substituting (6.6) into (6.5) yields

$$\mu = \frac{\sum_i \frac{h_i}{b_i - a_i} \left[\left(a_i + \frac{1}{\beta} \right) e^{-\beta a_i} - \left(b_i + \frac{1}{\beta} \right) e^{-\beta b_i} \right]}{\sum_i \left[\frac{h_i}{b_i - a_i} \right] [e^{-\beta a_i} - e^{-\beta b_i}]} \tag{6.7}$$

While Equation (6.7) is not easily solvable for β in terms of μ, the value of β can easily be obtained by numerical techniques. By integrating (6.6), where $F^*(a_i)=0$, the corresponding distribution function $F^*(x)$ can be written as

$$F^*(x) = F^*(a_i) + \frac{\sum_j \left[\frac{h_j}{b_j - a_j} \right] [e^{-\beta x} - e^{-\beta a_i}]}{\sum_k \left[\frac{h_k}{b_k - a_k} \right] [e^{-\beta b_k} - e^{-\beta a_k}]}, \qquad x \in (a_i, b_i] \tag{6.8}$$

D. When No Subinterval Moment Information Is Available for a Half-Unbounded Interval

This situation must be broken down into two cases: when the overall (unconditional) mean is not known and when this overall mean is known.

(1) When the Unconditional Mean Is Not Known

To be able to use the results of the previous section, the unbounded intervals are closed by means of an ad hoc procedure called the "rule of ten." The total width of the histogram's interior intervals is $b_n - a_1$. An exterior interval that is unbounded is given a width of ten times this quantity. For example, if both exterior intervals of the histogram are half-unbounded, the leftmost interval is given endpoints $[(a_1 - 10(b_n - a_1), a_1]$, and the rightmost is given endpoints $[b_n, b_n + 10(b_n - a_1)]$. These bounded intervals are accorded uniform ME conditional densities, with distribution functions as in (6.4). The rule of ten is justified by the idea that the resulting interval widths would contain 99% of the mass of any monotonically decaying "true" density function. This is a heuristic and may, of course, understate probabilities near the interior endpoint.

(2) When the Unconditional Mean Is Known

The half-unbounded interval must be an exterior interval of the histogram; if $n>2$, it will be adjacent to a bounded interior interval. The rule used in this case is: assign a conditional mean to the half-unbounded interval such that the conditional mean of the two intervals combined is located at their mutual boundary (endpoint).

For example, suppose the histogram's rightmost interval is unbounded on the right. Its endpoints are a_n and $+\infty$. The next-to-rightmost interval is $(a_{n-1}, b_{n-1}]$, where $b_{n-1} = a_n$ and whose conditional mean is μ_{n-1}. We assign a value to μ_n such that

$$\frac{h_{n-1}\,\mu_{n-1} + h_n\,\mu_n}{h_{n-1} + h_n} = a_n \qquad (6.14)$$

that is,

$$\mu_n = \frac{a_n\,(h_{n-1} + h_n) - h_{n-1}\,\mu_{n-1}}{h_n}. \qquad (6.15)$$

The conditional ME density is exponential with mean μ_n. The segment of the distribution function is

$$F^*(x) = F(a_n) + \frac{h_n}{H}\,[1 - e^{(a_n - x)/(\mu_n - a_n)}] \qquad \text{for } x \in (a_n, \infty]. \quad (6.16)$$

For the opposite instance, where the leftmost interval ($i=1$) is unbounded on the left, we assign

$$\mu_1 = \frac{a_2(h_1 + h_2) - h_2\mu_2}{h_1} \qquad (6.17)$$

whence

$$F^*(x) = \frac{h_1}{H}\,e^{(a_2 - x)/(\mu_1 - a_2)} \qquad \text{for } x \in (-\infty, a_2]. \qquad (6.18)$$

7. APPLICATION EXAMPLES

In this section, we apply the formulas derived in Section 6 to solve the problems posed previously.

A. Adjusting the Life Table by Incorporating Medical Study Results

Table 1 contained the relative mortality ratios for 5,131 spinal cord injury patients by neurological category and age group at time of injury. Starting with the 1980 Standard U.S. Life Table, Brockett and Song [9] incorporated the results in Table 1 to derive an adjusted life table for calculating wrongful injury damage award compensation and for determining life insurance premiums for medically impaired lives by minimizing the "information distance" between the adjusted life table and the standard life table subject to the applicable constraints. These constraints are formulated to fulfill the characteristics of a life table as well as the medical study results. Their method provides a way to adjust a standard life table to reflect the known characteristics of the individual while remaining as close as possible to a given standard table. Figure 2 shows the standard and adjusted survival curves for incomplete paraplegia patients.

B. Expected Loss Calculation

Table 2 concerns the expected loss experience for 1,000 claims. We note that when the conditional mean, μ, and probability, p, for a bounded interval $[a, b]$ are known, the ME conditional distribution for the interval is a truncated exponential. Suppose the ME conditional distribution for the interval $[a, b]$ is parametrically expressed as

$$f_L(x) = e^{\alpha + \beta x}.$$

Then the following set of equations must hold for the derived conditional probability and mean to be as given

$$\int_a^b e^{\alpha + \beta x} \, dx = p, \tag{7.1}$$

$$\int_a^b x e^{\alpha + \beta x} \, dx = p\mu.$$

FIGURE 2

ADJUSTED MORTALITY RATES BY INFORMATION THEORETIC APPROACH
FOR INCOMPLETE PARAPLEGIA

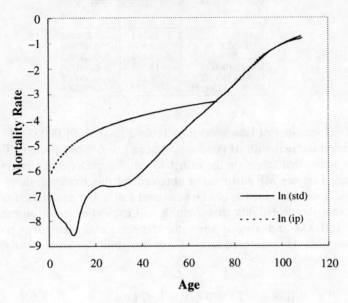

Transforming the equations on the previous page, we obtain

$$\beta = \frac{1}{b-a} \ln \frac{1 + \mu\beta - a\beta}{1 + \mu\beta - b\beta} \tag{7.2a}$$

and

$$\alpha = \ln \frac{p\beta}{e^{b\beta} - e^{a\beta}}. \tag{7.2b}$$

We can then obtain the numerical results, answering any probabilistic questions concerning this example. Because Table 2 shows that the conditional mean for the first interval (loss=\$0) is 0, all the mass (that is, 0.075) is put in one point. The parameters α and β for the next six bounded intervals are presented in Table 4.

TABLE 4

NUMERICAL RESULTS FOR ME CONDITIONAL
PROBABILITY FUNCTION

Loss Interval [a, b]	α	β
1, 1000	−15.294	0.009995
1001, 5000	−12.865	0.000898
5001, 10000	−18.439	0.000960
10001, 100000	−12.124	−0.000100
100001, 500000	−16.215	−0.000009
500001, 1000000	−16.527	−0.000005

Note that the last loss interval in Table 2 (that is, $1,000,000+) is a half-bounded interval with its conditional mean given. The results in Table 3 can then be applied to obtain the distributional function for this interval.

Based on the ME distribution obtained for this example, those questions raised in the introduction can be answered easily. For example, if it is desired to know the probability that a claim will exceed a certain threshold level, say, $50,000, and also to know the expected claim size if a policy were issued with this threshold level as a policy limit, we then calculate

$$P = Pr[\text{Loss} \geq \$50{,}000] = \int_{50{,}000}^{\infty} f_L(x)dx$$

$$= 1 - \int_{0}^{50{,}000} f_L(x)dx$$

$$= 1 - \int_{0}^{10{,}000} f_L(x)dx - \int_{10{,}000}^{50{,}000} f_L(x)dx$$

$$= 1 - 0.975 - \int_{10{,}000}^{50{,}000} e^{-12.124-0.0001x}\, dx$$

$$= 0.0054.$$

Similarly,

E[Claim|claim limit = \$50,000]

$$= \int_0^{50,000} xf_L(x)dx + 50{,}000 \, Pr[\text{Loss} \geq \$50{,}000]$$

$$= (0)(0.075) + (900)(0.5) + (4{,}000)(0.25)$$

$$+ (9{,}000)(0.15)$$

$$+ \int_{10,000}^{50,000} xf_L(x)dx$$

$$+ (50{,}000)(0.0054)$$

$$= 0 + 450 + 1{,}000 + 1{,}350 + 378 + 270$$

$$= \$3{,}448,$$

where the integral from \$10,000 to \$50,000 is easily obtained by calculation using the exponential formula for $f_L(x)$ over the interval.

C. The Actuarial Software Marketer

The percentages corresponding to the bars of Figure 1 were 36%, 39%, 19%, and 5%. The report stated the maximum observed number of uses was 50. It is apparent the median cannot possibly be 4.5; that would make at least 73% of the observations greater than the median. We ran the estimation several times; once without using the untrustworthy median, and also under the assumption that the 4.5 was a typographical error and the true median was 5.5, 6.5, or 7.5. It was also nature to check the feasibility of the mean. Using the endpoints of the published histogram, we can bound the mean:

$$0.36(0) + 0.39(5.0) + 0.19(10.0) + 0.05(30.0) = 5.4 \leq \mu$$

$$\leq 12.1 = 0.36(5.0) + 0.39(9.9) + 0.19(29.9) + 0.05(50.0).$$

A mean of 8.5 appears reasonable, and we can proceed with the estimation. The results are presented in Table 5.

TABLE 5

SENSITIVITY OF THE INFORMATION
THEORETIC DISTRIBUTION ESTIMATE
OF THE PERCENTAGE OF FIRMS
WITH SIXTEEN OR MORE USES
OF THE GIVEN DEFINED-BENEFIT
CALCULATION AS THE SUPPLIED
MEDIAN USE CHANGES

Median	Number of Firms Using	
	0–15 Times	16 or More Times
none	84.6%	15.4%
4.5	84.6	15.4
5.5	83.9	16.1
6.5	84.5	15.5
7.5	85.2	14.8

The insensitivity of the far right column to the choice of median provided some degree of comfort with the initial market estimate for the software product.

8. CONCLUDING REMARKS

The heuristic statistical procedure described in this paper (use what is known and maximize the uncertainty of what is not known) can be categorized as problem-solving for grouped data with auxiliary information. Such problems arise naturally in the actuarial analysis of secondary data. Responding to data interpretation needs that arise in actuarial practice, the algorithmic portion uses available information theoretic techniques when possible. In other cases, when data are missing or in conflict, ad hoc measures (based on practical logic and experience) are taken to facilitate the use of the same techniques. A variety of solved application examples were provided, and further application areas indicated.

ACKNOWLEDGMENT

This paper arose in part from a problem first posed by Edward Lew at the 1984 Actuarial Research Conference in Waterloo, Ontario. The research was funded in part by a grant from the Actuarial Education and Research Fund of the Society of Actuaries. The comments of an anonymous referee are gratefully acknowledged.

REFERENCES

1. ARTHANARI, T.S., AND DODGE, Y. *Mathematical Programming in Statistics*. New York: Wiley, 1981.

2. BLUM, J.R., AND ROSENBLATT, J.I. *Probability and Statistics*. Philadelphia, Pa.: W.B. Saunders Co., 1972.
3. BROCKETT, P.L. "Information Theoretic Approach to Actuarial Science: A Unification and Extension of Relevant Theory and Applications," *TSA* XLIII (1991): 73–114.
4. BROCKETT, P.L., CHARNES, A., GOLDEN, L., AND PAICK, K. "Constructing a Unimodal Bayesian Prior Distribution from Incompletely Assessed Information," *CCS Report #694*, The University of Texas at Austin, 1993.
5. BROCKETT, P.L., CHARNES, A., AND PAICK, K. "Constructing a Unimodal Prior Distribution," Memoria X Congresso Academia Nacional De Ingeneria, Sonora, Mexico, pp. 145–8. Sept. 1984; Dept. of Finance, working paper 83/84-2-26, University of Texas, 1983.
6. BROCKETT, P.L., AND COX, S.H. Discussion of Reitano, "A Statistical Analysis of Banded Data with Applications," *TSA* XLII (1990): 413–5.
7. BROCKETT, P.L., AND LEVINE, A. *Statistics, Probability and Their Applications*, Philadelphia, Pa.: W.B. Saunders Co., 1984.
8. BROCKETT, P.L., LI, H., HUANG, Z., AND THOMAS, D. "Information Theoretic Multivariate Graduation," *SIAM Journal of Applied Mathematics*, no. 2 (1991): 144–53.
9. BROCKETT, P.L., AND SONG, Y. "Obtaining a Life Table for the Spinal Cord Injury Patients Using Medical Results and Information Theory," *Journal of Actuarial Practice*, 3, no. 1 (1995): 77–92.
10. BROCKETT, P.L., AND ZHANG, J. "Information Theoretic Mortality Table Graduation," *Scandinavian Actuarial Journal* (1986): 131–40.
11. DEVIVO, M.J., KARTUS, P.L., STOVER, S.L., RUTT, R.D., AND FINE, P.R. "Seven Year Survival Following Spinal Cord Injury," *Archives of Neurology*, 44 (1987): 872–5.
12. HAITOVSKY, Y. "Grouped Data," in *Encyclopedia of Statistical Sciences* vol. 3, ed. S. Kotz and N.L. Johnson. New York: John Wiley and Sons, 1983, 527–36.
13. HOGG, R., AND KLUGMAN, S. *Loss Distributions*. New York: John Wiley and Sons, 1984.
14. KHINCHINE, A.I. *Mathematical Foundations of Statistical Mechanics*, New York: Dove Publishers, 1948.
15. KULLBACK, S. *Statistical Information Theory*. New York: Wiley, 1959.
16. KULLBACK, S., AND LEIBLER, R.A. "On Information and Sufficiency," *Annals of Mathematical Statistics*, 22 (1951): 79–86.
17. REITANO, R. "A Statistical Analysis of Banded Data with Applications," *TSA* XLII (1990): 375–420.
18. SARD, A., AND WEINTRAUB, S. *A Book of Splines*. New York: Wiley, 1971.
19. SMITH, R.C., JR. ed. *Mergers & Acquisitions Healthcare Sourcebook*, 2nd ed. Philadelphia, Pa.: MLR Publishing Co., 1990.
20. THEIL, H., AND FEIBIG, D.G. *Exploiting Continuity: Maximum Entropy Estimation of Continuous Distributions*, Cambridge, Mass.: Ballinger, 1984.

PAYGO FUNDING STABILITY AND INTERGENERATIONAL EQUITY

ROBERT L. BROWN

ABSTRACT

The paper reviews the demographic shifts, including improved life expectancy and the baby-boom/baby-bust cycle, of the past half-century and discusses their impact on the funding of pay-as-you-go (paygo) social security systems.

The paper draws an analogy between the funding of private pension plans and paygo schemes and discusses the fundamental security of both mechanisms. The paper argues that the true security underlying either funding mechanism is the ability of the economy to transfer wealth. Advantages and disadvantages of both systems are also presented.

The paper then discusses the consequences for social security if the system were based on a defined-contribution approach instead of on a defined-benefit approach. This analysis argues that today's large baby-boom cohort is making relatively small social security contributions and, under a defined-contribution approach, should then expect to receive commensurately small benefits.

The paper shows that the most rapidly aging of the western populations exists in Canada. Hence, Canadian data are used to attempt to formulate a model that brings intergenerational equity to the funding of social security.

The paper argues that by raising the age of eligibility for social security retirement income benefits, only slightly, from age 65 today to age 69 by 2030, intergenerational equity and an acceptable wealth transfer index can be achieved. A series of logical arguments to support that model politically are also presented.

---

1. INTRODUCTION

Most western industrialized nations have in place plans providing significant social security benefits, and virtually all these plans are funded on a pay-as-you-go (paygo) or quasi-paygo basis. At the same time, all these nations have populations that are aging, partly because of enhanced life expectancy, but more importantly because of the decline in birth rates since their peaks in the late 1950s.

115

As will be shown, social security paygo schemes are sensitive to demographic shifts, and an aging population gives rise to pressures for increased social security contribution rates as the ratio of retirees (beneficiaries) to workers (contributors) increases (most sharply after 2015). This pressure in turn raises doubts in the minds of citizens and public-policy-makers about the continued viability of these paygo schemes. Can they survive? Will the next, smaller generation of workers pay the requisite contributions?

This paper explores the true economic security of paygo schemes and, based on that analysis, presents a model for funding stability. The paper argues that this model is also one that creates and provides intergenerational equity and hence will succeed in guaranteeing the future viability of paygo schemes.

2. PAYGO VERSUS INDIVIDUAL ACTUARIAL FUNDING

If an individual wishes to retire at age 65 with an annual income of one unit payable continuously, then an actuary can determine the required level contributions by setting the present value of all contributions equal to the present value of all retirement income benefits at a defined age. Thus, assuming that contributions start at age 20, the formula would be

$$C \int_0^{45} e^{-\delta t} \frac{\ell_{20+t}}{\ell_{20}} dt = e^{-45\delta} \frac{\ell_{65}}{\ell_{20}} \int_0^{\infty} e^{-\delta t} \frac{\ell_{65+t}}{\ell_{65}}, dt$$

which solves for

$$C = e^{-45\delta} \frac{\int_0^{\infty} e^{-\delta t} \ell_{65+t} \, dt}{\int_0^{45} e^{-\delta t} \ell_{20+t} \, dt}$$

$$= \frac{\int_{65}^{\infty} e^{-\delta x} \ell_x \, dx}{\int_{20}^{65} e^{-\delta x} \ell_x \, dx}.$$

The plan is funded by contributions made between ages 20 and 65, contingent on survival; benefits are paid for ages 65 and beyond, also contingent upon survival. Total expected contributions are not as large as total expected benefits because of the discounting effect of the rate of investment return, δ.

For paygo funding, assume a paygo plan wishes to pay an annual income of one unit payable continuously to all citizens alive aged 65 and over. Contributions will be made by all citizens aged 20 to 64 inclusive. Because, in a paygo system, contribution income is immediately distributed as benefit outgo, there is no discounting for investment income. Thus, in a stationary population, the level contribution formula is simply

$$C(T_{20} - T_{65}) = T_{65},$$

or

$$C = \frac{T_{65}}{T_{20} - T_{65}}.$$

For more general applicability, assume the population is stable (rather than stationary) with intrinsic rate of increase, r. Assume it is now time z, and the rate of live births is now $B(z)$. Those now alive aged x were born at time $z-x$ in a birth cohort of size

$$B(z - x) = B(z)e^{-rx}.$$

Thus the paygo funding formula is

$$C \int_{20}^{65} B(z)e^{-rx} s(x)dx = \int_{65}^{\infty} B(z)e^{-rx} s(x)dx,$$

or

$$C = \frac{\int_{65}^{\infty} B(z)e^{-rx} s(x)dx}{\int_{20}^{65} B(z)e^{-rx} s(x)dx}$$

$$= \frac{\int_{65}^{\infty} e^{-rx} \ell_x dx}{\int_{20}^{65} e^{-rx} \ell_x dx}.$$

Hence the formula used to determine the required contribution rate for a paygo social security scheme is analogous to the formula used to determine the required contribution for an individual prefunded retirement scheme. Further, the ability to have total expected paygo benefits that exceed total expected paygo contributions depends on the "discount" rate, r. As presented, this means that the paygo discount rate is the intrinsic growth rate, r, for the stable population.

The funding of social security is normally dependent only on active workers, however. Thus, we need to analyze the intrinsic rate of increase, r, not of the general population, but rather of the active labor force. For example, increasing the labor force participation rate of females, or increasing net immigration of qualified workers, is as helpful to the funding requirements of a paygo system as an increase in the birth rate.

Thus the required contribution rate for a paygo scheme is dependent upon the ratio of beneficiaries to workers. This ratio is dependent upon all the following demographic variables: mortality, fertility, migration, and labor force participation rates. Further, most paygo schemes have a contribution formula such that total contributions increase at the same rate as average wages, whereas benefits after retirement increase at the same rate as inflation. Thus, to the extent that there is real productivity growth (net of inflation), this real productivity growth, as a rate per annum, can be added to the labor force intrinsic growth rate to determine the total paygo discount rate (call it r') for the period between the average contribution date and the average benefit payment date.*

Hence the "discount" rate, r', for the paygo social security system is the total of the growth rate of the labor force and the growth rate of its productivity. In other words, r' is the growth rate in wealth production for society as a whole.

3. DEMOGRAPHIC CONTEXT

As stated earlier, all western industrialized nations currently have aging populations. Population aging here means "growth over time of the proportion of old persons according to some chronological age (usually 65), in the total population" [5].

There are two causes of this population aging. One is enhanced life expectancy; the other is a recent drop in the rate of live births. Statistics for Canada (the choice of Canada as a benchmark is explained later in this section) indicate significant improvement in life expectancy over the past 70 years. Canada has also experienced a falling fertility rate since 1959, as seen in Figure 1.

More important to the analysis of the funding of a paygo scheme is the actual number of live births. Again, Canada experienced a significant drop in the number of live births in the period from 1959 to 1972, as seen in Figure 2.

The U.S. Department of Commerce [21] presented data on the trend in aging for several countries based on medium-variant data generated by the United Nations population division in 1984. Highlights are shown in Table 2. As the publication notes:

---

*It is often argued that retirement benefits should be indexed to average wages versus the cost of living. In this way, retirees would share in the enhanced standard of living produced by the workers. This particular side issue is not explored further in this paper.

For most countries listed, there will be modest increases in the size of the elderly population relative to the size of the working-age population over the first 20 years, but sharp increases from 2005 to 2025.

The statistics underlying Table 2 can also be used to calculate the projected percentage increase in the population aged 65 and over, over the period 1985 to 2025, as in Table 3.

TABLE 1

LIFE EXPECTANCY [20]

Year	At Birth		At Age 65		At Age 75	
	Male	Female	Male	Female	Male	Female
1921	58.8	60.6	13.0	13.6	7.6	8.0
1941	63.0	66.3	12.8	14.1	7.5	8.2
1961	68.4	74.2	13.5	16.1	8.2	9.5
1981	71.9	79.0	14.6	18.9	9.0	11.9
1991	74.6	80.9	15.7	19.9	9.6	12.5

FIGURE 1

FERTILITY RATES (CANADA)*

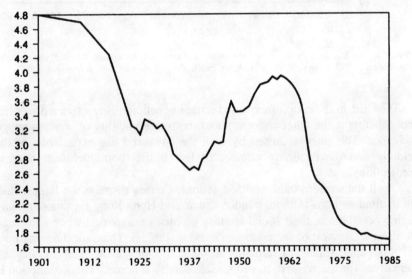

*From STATISTICS CANADA, "Current Demographic Analysis, Fertility in Canada." *Catalogue 91-524E*, 121–122. Ottawa, Ont.: 1984.

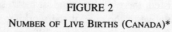

FIGURE 2
NUMBER OF LIVE BIRTHS (CANADA)*

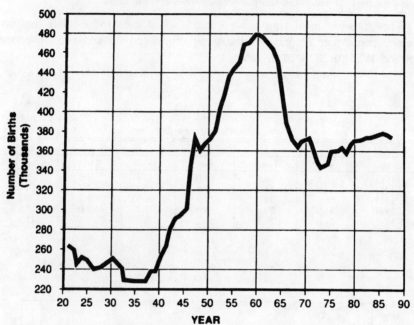

The shift in the ratio of expected retiree-beneficiaries to expected worker-contributors is the chief concern about the future viability of western paygo schemes. The shift is caused by both the enhanced life expectancy of the elderly and the declining number of live births (both included in these projections).

Of all the western industrialized nations, Canada displays the largest shift in its funding ratio. Although India, China, and Hong Kong face more rapidly aging populations, their social security promises are modest when compared to those of the rest of the countries listed in Table 3. Thus, for the remainder of this paper, Canadian statistics are used to analyze the public policy alternatives for the western paygo social security schemes. The assumption is

TABLE 2

AGED POPULATION RATIOS AS PERCENTAGE OF TOTAL POPULATION [20]

Country	1985			2005			2025		
	65+	75+	85+	65+	75+	85+	65+	75+	85+
France	12.4%	6.2%	3.2%	14.8%	6.4%	3.1%	19.3%	7.9%	3.8%
W. Germany	14.5	6.8	3.2	18.9	7.5	3.8	22.5	9.5	5.3
Italy	13.0	5.5	2.5	16.9	7.0	3.4	19.6	8.6	4.3
U.K.	15.1	6.3	3.1	15.3	6.9	3.8	18.7	8.1	4.0
Sweden	16.9	7.2	3.5	17.2	8.2	4.7	22.2	10.5	5.2
U.S.	12.0	4.9	2.6	13.1	6.7	4.1	19.5	8.5	4.8
Canada	10.4	4.0	2.0	12.5	5.6	3.0	18.8	7.5	3.7
Australia	10.1	3.7	1.7	11.4	4.8	2.4	15.9	6.2	2.9
Japan	10.0	3.7	1.7	16.5	6.4	3.0	20.3	10.0	4.9
China	5.1	1.4	0.5	7.4	2.4	1.0	12.8	4.1	1.8
Hong Kong	7.6	2.4	1.0	10.3	4.3	2.1	17.5	5.8	2.6
India	4.3	1.1	0.4	6.1	1.8	0.7	9.7	3.1	1.3
Israel	8.9	3.6	1.5	8.3	3.5	1.8	11.9	4.7	2.1

TABLE 3

PROJECTED PERCENTAGE INCREASE
IN NUMBER AGED 65+ 1985 TO 2025

Country	Percentage Increase
India	264%
China	238
Hong Kong	219
Canada	135
Australia	125
Japan	121
Israel	116
U.S.	105
France	67
Italy	51
W. Germany	36
U.K.	23
Sweden	21

that if a solution can be found that is workable for Canada, it should prove to be acceptable for all the countries listed below Canada in Table 3.

In that regard, the main element of Canada's retirement income paygo system is the Canada/Quebec Pension Plan (C/QPP). As is generally true for most western paygo schemes, C/QPP contributions increase with wages, and retirement benefits increase with inflation. No contributions are made on wages up to 10% of the average industrial wage (AIW). Benefits are a function of the total indexed career wage credits over 40 years on wages up to the AIW.

There are two other smaller sources of government-sponsored retirement income for the elderly in Canada. The first is the Guaranteed Income Supplement (GIS), which is paid only to the poorer elderly based on an income test (assets are ignored). The second is a scheme called Old Age Security (OAS). Until 1989, monthly OAS benefits were paid to all Canadians aged 65 and over who satisfied a residency requirement. Under new legislation however, a special "clawback" has been imposed on these pensions. Individuals with net incomes exceeding a threshold ($53,215 in 1993) must repay 15% of net income over the threshold up to the full OAS pension (this point was achieved at a net income level of $83,800 in 1993). Because the OAS clawback is indexed to inflation less 3%, the OAS scheme will slowly (but surely) degenerate into a second-tier GIS benefit based on need. OAS and GIS benefits are paid from general tax revenues. These plans are not directly analyzed in the remainder of the paper, because they are not true paygo-funded schemes.

The current C/QPP paygo contribution rate is 7.8%. The actual 1994 contribution rate is 5.4% paid 50/50 by employers and workers on wages between 10% of the AIW and the AIW [16]. The C/QPP was initiated in 1966 with the first full retirement pension not paid until 1976 retirements. Thus it was easy to have early contribution rates that were very low and still develop significant C/QPP assets. In fact, from 1966 to 1986, the contribution rate was 3.6% (1.8+1.8). As the C/QPP matures, as the population ages, and as the C/QPP early assets are depleted, these contribution rates must increase. There is already an agreed-upon schedule that will gradually take the combined contribution rate to 10.1% in 2016. However, C/QPP actuarial projections show that the combined contribution rate will have to increase to 14.4% by 2035 [16]. The rate is projected to stabilize thereafter at that level depending, of course, on the realization of the projection assumptions.

These contributions bring a retirement income benefit at age 65 equal to 25% of career earnings over the best 40 years, adjusted for changes in the AIW. Special dropout provisions are allowed for years of disability and for years at home caring for a child under age 7. The C/QPP also pays disability income benefits, death benefits, and benefits to survivors and orphans. The retirement benefit can be taken from age 60 to 70 with an actuarial adjustment (up or down) of ½% per month (which is very close to being actuarially neutral, especially for early retirement [14]).

For a Canadian who consistently earns the AIW, government-sponsored social security will guarantee a 40% replacement ratio at age 65: 25% from the C/QPP, 14% from OAS, and a small payment from GIS. Poorer workers achieve higher replacement ratios from government sources (since OAS is a level dollar benefit and they receive a larger net GIS benefit), and wealthier workers receive lower and lower replacement ratios from government sources as incomes increase.

For example, someone consistently earning three times the AIW will retire and receive no OAS, no GIS, and a C/QPP benefit that provides an 8.3% replacement ratio.

Many commentators in Canada (for example, the Canadian Institute of Actuaries [6]) have raised concerns about whether or not the next generation of workers will agree to contribute 14.4% of their wages up to the AIW to fund the C/QPP retirement benefits now being promised. The Canadian government has now initiated a more formal discussion of this matter. Similar concerns about paygo funding requirements exist in most other western industrialized nations.

4. THE ADVANTAGES OF PAYGO FUNDING

Paygo schemes are under heavy public scrutiny and criticism. It therefore seems worthwhile that, prior to presenting methods that can be used to "save" paygo schemes, we outline reasons why they are worth having.

In general, the following are advantages of government-sponsored paygo schemes:

1. The entire working population can be covered relatively easily.
2. Benefits can be immediately vested and are fully portable, important features for the mobile work force of today.
3. Because contribution income immediately becomes benefit payout, no problem exists with indexation of benefits to wages. A source of "actuarial discounting" for years with real productivity gains exists if benefits are indexed to cost of living and contributions rise with average wages (the norm). On the other hand, negative labor force growth rates will mitigate against this "actuarial discount" factor.
4. Administrative costs are usually very low per unit of cash flow.

Governments can instead sponsor fully funded schemes as opposed to paygo schemes, with several disadvantages, including the following:

1. Fully funded schemes are susceptible to erosion by inflation. This destroyed several fully funded schemes in Europe earlier in the century and is probably the main reason that virtually all government-sponsored social security schemes are funded on a pure or quasi-paygo basis.

2. Government control of the large amounts of capital accumulating under a fully funded scheme is a concern. If this money is "invested" in government bonds, then it provides an easy source of deficit financing and provides an incentive for deficit spending. If invested in the private sector, any fully funded social security scheme would have assets capable of controlling the country's entire available supply of equities. This "backdoor" government control may not be generally supported.
3. Who will decide how to invest this capital and at what administrative expense? How does one avoid political influence?
4. With the large accumulation of assets, continuous pressure will exist to enhance benefits.
5. In any transition from paygo financing to full funding, one generation of workers will have to pay almost double contributions, both to prefund their own benefits and to pay for the paygo benefits not previously funded (equal to the present paygo actuarial liability). This would not likely prove acceptable, making it difficult, now, to switch to a fully funded basis.

Despite this, a switch to full funding of social security has its supporters, including many actuaries, who believe that the method would truly improve security of plan benefits to participants. But is real security enhanced?

5. IS A FULLY FUNDED SCHEME MORE SECURE?

If the assets backing a fully funded social security system are government bonds, then future social security benefits will be financed by a combination of worker contributions, payment of interest on the bonds, and liquidation of bonds as needed. All these funds flow from productive workers. It should make no difference to these workers, in total, whether they pay increased benefits to retirees through increased contributions to a paygo system, or through a combination of contributions, bond interest, and bond liquidation in a "fully funded" scheme. Investing in private sector bonds or other private assets does not change this reality.

The real issue is the balance between production of goods and consumption demands. In his book *The Economics of the Welfare State*, Barr [2] states

> The widely held (but false) view that funded schemes are inherently 'safer' than PAYGO is an example of the fallacy of composition.[a] For *individuals* the economic function of a pension scheme is to transfer consumption over time. But (ruling out the case where current output is stored in holes

in people's gardens) this is not possible for society as a whole; the consumption of pensioners as a group is produced by the next generation of workers. From an *aggregate* viewpoint, the economic function of pension schemes is to divide total production between workers and pensioners, i.e. to reduce the consumption of workers so that sufficient output remains for pensioners. Once this point is understood it becomes clear why PAYGO and funded schemes, which are both simply ways of dividing output between workers and pensioners, should not fare very differently in the face of demographic change.

---

*It is a fallacy of composition to assume that because something is true for an individual it will *necessarily* be true on aggregate. For instance, if I stand on my seat in the theatre I will get a better view, but if everybody does so, nobody will get a better view.

Social security pensions, whether funded on a paygo or fully funded basis, are a means of transferring wealth from workers to retirees. The crucial variable is therefore creation of wealth. The only way that a fully funded social security scheme would enhance the true security of benefits is if two effects were to result. First, there would have to be an overall increase in gross national savings. Second, assuming increased savings, such an increase would have to raise total output or total wealth. While there is extensive literature on this matter (for example, see Barr [2] or Aaron [1]), no conclusive evidence exists to support any enhanced real security by the full funding of social security schemes. In fact, according to Rosa [19, p. 212], the experiences of Sweden and Japan in running state funded schemes:

... offer powerful evidence that this option may only invite squandering capital funds in wasteful, low-yield investments [which] should give pause to anyone proposing similar accumulations elsewhere.

Thus actuarial full funding of social security schemes will not add to their inherent security, even their security in an environment of significant demographic shifts.

The critical factor facing society is the impending shift in the ratio of retiree-consumers to worker-producers. How will we produce enough wealth to supply the consumption demand? This production/consumption equilibrium is the focus of the remainder of the paper.

6. DEFINED-BENEFIT VERSUS DEFINED-CONTRIBUTION PLANS

Although the paper has rejected actuarial full funding as a private pension plan solution to government-funded paygo social security schemes, an analysis of other aspects of private pension funding alternatives does prove to be useful.

Clearly, private pensions can be, and are, formulated on either a defined-benefit or a defined-contribution basis. Government-sponsored paygo social security is almost always formulated on a defined-benefit basis. (This does not include government-mandated employer-sponsored schemes such as in Chile and Australia.) The benefits are defined, and the contributions become the variable. As the population ages, the contribution rates required to fund today's promised defined benefits must increase.

But what would happen if social security schemes were redesigned as defined-contribution plans? That is, each year every worker could make some defined contribution (for example, some percent per dollar of wage). This would create cash flow that would then be divided among the nation's retirees of the day. Note that no fund accrues. The play is purely paygo. The defined contributions from today's workers are immediately divided among today's retirees.

Assume that a transition from defined benefit to defined contribution were to take place today. By definition, for a pure paygo scheme, no change in benefits or contributions would be immediately necessary. As the population ages (that is, as life expectancy improves and as the baby boomers retire), however, the defined paygo contributions would fund smaller and smaller paygo benefits. Is this equitable?

If one studies populations in which birth rates rise and fall cyclically, the following conclusions emerge. A large cohort, in a defined-benefit paygo scheme, will make relatively smaller contributions, but will expect full benefits from the scheme despite these smaller contributions. On the other hand, a small cohort will be forced to make larger contributions with no gain in benefits.

In a defined-contribution paygo scheme, the opposite pattern emerges. Small cohorts make their defined contributions, but then receive retirement benefits well in excess of the actuarial value of their contributions. Similarly, large cohorts make the same defined contribution but receive retirement benefits less than the actuarial value of their contributions.

Neither achieves actuarial equity. Can actuarial equity be achieved? The answer is that it *must* be achieved. Remember that the ability to pay social security benefits has little to do with the funding mechanism. Rather, the ability to pay social security benefits is exactly the ability to transfer wealth from the productive workers to the retirees. The ability to transfer wealth does not rise and fall with the external roller coaster of shifting demographics. In general, it rises slowly in line with real gains in worker productivity, but that is all.

The actuarially equitable solution to the paygo roller coaster is to level off the hills and valleys. In real terms, this means that cohorts of average size will pay "expected" (mean) paygo contributions for "expected" (mean) paygo benefits. Large cohorts can pay below-average contributions but will, in turn, receive below-average benefits. Finally, small cohorts pay above-average contributions but will receive above-average benefits. Thus we achieve actuarial equity. Those who pay average contributions get average benefits. Those who pay below-average contributions receive below-average benefits. And those who pay above-average contributions receive above-average benefits. They are told this; they agree to this; and their expectations are achieved. Add to this the expectation that there will be real worker productivity gains and that all citizens can expect to receive benefits whose expected (nondiscounted) value exceeds the expected value of their contributions.

Having arrived at an actuarially sound process for achieving intergenerational solidarity, can we market the process successfully? One answer is that the citizenry has no choice; there is only so much wealth that can be transferred. To attempt otherwise would create inflation that would achieve the required economic equilibrium by deflating the purchasing power of the benefits.

It should not be difficult to expect average cohorts to accept average benefits for average contributions. Nor should it be difficult to convince large cohorts to make below-average contributions and small cohorts to accept above-average benefits. The problem arises when a large cohort must be convinced to accept below-average benefits or a small cohort to make above-average contributions. But that is exactly the situation today!

Most of the western industrialized nations are now faced with a large birth cohort born in the 1950s and early 1960s that is now approaching normal retirement age. This larger-than-average cohort is currently funding the retirement benefits on a paygo basis of a smaller-than-average cohort (the depression cohort) with smaller-than-average contributions. Unfortunately, what follows the large baby-boom cohort is the smaller-than-average baby-bust cohort.

Thus, the western paygo systems face the following limited alternatives: (a) convince the baby-boom cohort that because they made below-average contributions, they should be happy to receive actuarially equivalent below-average benefits; or (b) convince the baby-bust cohort to make above-average contributions (that is, forego their wealth consumption) so that the baby-boom retirees can receive the full average paygo benefit they have been promised. In return, the baby-bust generation can be promised the expectation of above-average benefits when they retire, if the next generation is larger.

I believe that either sale will prove difficult politically. However, while convincing the baby-boom generation to take smaller benefits will be difficult, the ability to convince the baby-bust generation to dramatically increase their contributions on the basis of a nebulous benefit promise 50 years hence approaches the impossible.

Is there a politically acceptable approach to convincing the baby-boom generation to accept less in real wealth transfer than they are now being promised? I believe that there is.

7. PAYGO STABILITY: AN AGE-OF-ELIGIBILITY MODEL

As stated earlier, the cost per worker of a set of benefits funded on a paygo system is a direct function of the ratio of retiree-beneficiaries to worker-contributors. In turn, this ratio depends upon several demographic variables, including fertility, mortality, immigration, and labor force participation rates. Finally, if contributions are indexed to wages and benefits are indexed to cost of living (that is, inflation), then annual labor force productivity growth can be added to the paygo "discount" factor.

To what extent can the government control or influence these variables in a manner that would prove beneficial to the paygo funding ratios?

7.1 Fertility

Higher fertility rates have a long-term favorable impact on paygo funding ratios. As stated by Myers [15, p. 3]:

> If all other demographic elements are constant, higher fertility rates will have a favorable effect on social insurance systems providing old-age retirement benefits. As long as fertility is above the replacement rate (or the actual fertility plus the effect of net immigration achieves this result), there will be a steadily growing covered work force to provide the contributions necessary to support the retired population. This type of chain-letter effect will show relatively low costs for the social insurance program, although eventually the chain must break (because population size

cannot increase forever), and the cost of the program will become significantly higher.

So while attempts to increase fertility may prove to be marginally beneficial in the short run, in the long run it is a fool's game.

Further, there is no evidence that government can influence fertility rates to any significant extent, if at all. Evidence from countries that have attempted such influence through financial incentives suggests little effect (see, for example, Hohn [11, p. 461]). For example, West Germany offered cash incentives for women to have children and extended mothers' holidays and child-care facilities, but the fertility rate continued to slide. In fact, historically, the countries that have the largest family allowances also have the lowest birth rates [22, p. 21].

Finally, raising fertility rates has a short-term negative impact on the ability to transfer wealth to the elderly, because the increased number of children now compete for some of that wealth transfer.

7.2 Mortality

No government is going to admit to promoting policies that decrease life expectancies. Hence any public policy alternatives must assume continued improvements in life expectancy.

7.3 Immigration

As stated previously by Myers, increased net immigration has the same impact on paygo funding as increased fertility. In terms of wealth-transfer capabilities, immigration may be preferable if workers arrive educated and prepared to joint a productive work force. Increased immigration today is not desirable, however. For most western nations, immigrants over age 28 today only add to the baby-boom cohort, thus exacerbating the paygo funding problem.

In a publication entitled *One in Three*, the Economic Council of Canada states that significant increases in immigration are not desirable until after 2020 and that [8, p. 32]:

> We noted earlier that the retirement income programs would reach just over 7% of GNP by 2031, assuming moderate population growth and maintenance of the present age of eligibility and income-replacement ratio. To reduce this share by only 1 percentage point would necessitate an additional 2.8 million workers in the labour force and no extra retirees by 2031. To accomplish this would require an increase in net immigration in

the decade prior to 2031 from 80,000 to 640,000, assuming, as is now the case, that only half the immigrants would be of workforce ages.

Further, any country presuming to use immigration as a partial solution to the paygo funding problems must prepare the population for the social impact of this significant influx.

7.4 Economic Growth

As stated previously, if paygo contributions are a function of wages, but benefits move only with inflation, then the real productivity gains of the workers can be added to the paygo actuarial discount factor for the time between the average contribution date and the average benefit payment date.

Such real productivity gains are already a part of the actuarial projections calculated for most western paygo systems, and still these projections anticipate significant contribution rate increases over the next 40 years.

For example, for the CPP, the actuarial projections assume an annual 1.0% real productivity growth rate [16]. Despite this, today's total contribution rate of 5.4% (2.7+2.7) is projected to increase 14.4% by 2035.

In a recent publication, the Canadian Institute of Actuaries [6] questioned the acceptability of such a high contribution rate to the next generation of workers, especially given the fact that the actuarial cost of the C/QPP benefits on a fully funded basis is 10.5% based on a real rate of return of 2.5%. Thus, any contribution rate higher than 10.5% corresponds to a real rate of return lower than 2.5%.

However, for the baby-boom generation, because its C/QPP contribution rates to date have been less than 5.4%, a reduction in retirement benefits would not mean a real rate of overall return less than 2.5%. In fact, the CPP Fifteenth Actuarial Report states that someone born in 1948 who starts to contribute to the CPP in 1966, even with the projected contribution rate increases, will realize an internal rate of return of 9.0%, and someone born in 1968 who starts to contribute in 1986 will realize 6.4% per annum. Given that the actuarial projections assume inflation of 3.5% per annum, the corresponding real rates of return are 2.9% and 5.5%, respectively, which are very high net rates of return given the level of security in a government-sponsored system. Thus, benefits to this cohort can be reduced without their experiencing a "bad" deal.

Even assuming that these are convincing arguments to actuaries, the real crux of the matter is still to find a way to decrease the paygo benefits of the baby-boom cohort in a manner that will prove acceptable to *them*. This paper presents an age-of-entitlement formula that satisfies that need.

7.5 Age of Entitlement

Several countries are now reviewing a possible increase in the age of entitlement for social security benefits [12]. For many countries, the first step in this direction is simply bringing the age of entitlement for women up to the same age as that for men. However, some countries have announced the intention to raise the overall age of entitlement to paygo retirement benefits to lessen the projected increase in required contribution rates.

In the U.S., for example, the normal retirement age for OASDI retirement income benefits will be raised gradually from age 65 (the present level) starting in 2003 to age 66 by 2009 and then gradually to age 67 in 2027. By announcing this change in 1983, U.S. public-policy-makers have provided sufficient time for workers and employer-plan-sponsors to modify the retirement planning systems already in place. Such early warning should be a requirement of any such shift in the age of entitlement.

In a recent review of Canada's social security system, the Canadian Institute of Actuaries [6] analyzed a possible shift in the normal retirement age for C/QPP benefits from its present level at age 65 to age 70, over a 20- or 30-year period (both options were presented). The analysis showed that such an increase in the normal retirement age would mean that instead of the ultimate C/QPP contribution rate peaking at 14.4%, it would level out at 11.0% instead.

This analysis assumes that the entire C/QPP funding "problem" must be solved by effectively reducing benefits to the next generation of retirees. However, by remembering that the real issue is not the method of financing but rather the ability to transfer wealth, we can then use the same factors that have created these paygo funding problems to provide a partial solution.

The decline in live births in the 1970s also resulted in a decline in the transfer of wealth required to provide education and health care to the dependent young. Thus, while the number of dependent elderly is increasing, the number of dependent young is decreasing, as indicated in Figure 3, based on Canadian data.

The youth dependency ratio presented is simply the number in the population aged 0 to 17 divided by the population aged 18 to 64. Similarly the aged dependency ratio is the number aged 65 and over to the number aged 18 to 64.

FIGURE 3

YOUTH AND AGED DEPENDENCY RATIOS [18]

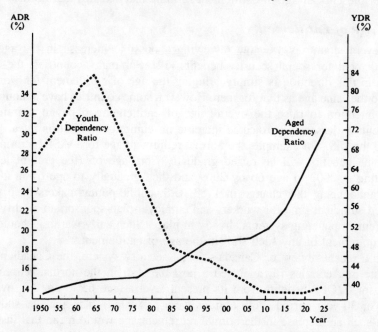

*From "Issues in Pension Policy: Demographic and Economic Aspects of Canada's Ageing Population," *Ontario Treasury Studies 16.* Toronto, Ontario: Ministry of Treasury and Economics, Taxation and Fiscal Policy Branch, October 1979.

If the transfer of wealth required to educate and provide health care to the young were equal to the transfer of wealth required for health care and retirement income security for the elderly, then no problem would exist, since the total dependency ratio (youth plus aged) is no higher in 2025 than it was in 1960.

That is not the case, however.

Analysis for Canada [10] has shown that government expenditures on the elderly are 2.5 times those for the young (per capita). Therefore, any analysis that attempts to derive a shift in the age of entitlement for retirement income security should include the lower demands for wealth by the youth sector and also include the differing transfer factors for the young versus the elderly.

Such an analysis has been done on Canadian data [3]. The authors developed a statistic called the labor force expenditure dependency ratio (LFEDR), which is defined as

$$LFEDR_t = \frac{(1.7 \times Y_t) + (1 \times U_t) + (4.244 \times A_t)}{LF_t}$$

where
  Y = youth, 0–19
  U = those collecting unemployment benefits
  A = aged, 65 and over
  LF = the projected labor force.

The weights of 1.7, 1, and 4.244 were derived by Foot [10, p. 17] and depict relative wealth transfer weights for the young, the unemployed, and the elderly. Statistics Canada population projections were used for the model's projected input variables. The labor force was projected to include trends of increasing female labor force participation, but assumed that male labor force participation rates would remain stationary.

The statistic referred to as $LFEDR_t$ could also be called a wealth transfer index. It is a single statistical indicator of the supply of (denominator) and demand for (numerator) wealth. As shown in Figure 4, this wealth transfer index does not change very much until 2006.

After 2006, it increases rapidly as the population ages and, in particular, as the baby-boom generation retires and the labor force turns to the baby-bust generation for wealth creation. Brown and Iglesias determined an increase in the age of entitlement for wealth transfer to the elderly that would keep the wealth transfer index constant at its 2006 level, as indicated in Figure 4.

This shift in the age of entitlement can be determined by finding K such that

$$LFEDR(2006) = \frac{(1.7 \times Y) + (1 \times U) + (4.244 \times A_{65+K})}{LF_{65+K}}.$$

This model has two assumptions that are not obvious. First, as the age of entitlement increases, the elderly who lose some of their social security retirement income benefits are expected to remain in the labor force, with the same participation rates as those now aged 60 to 64. Second, it is assumed that there will be a slight improvement in health for those aged 65 to 69.

FIGURE 4

WEALTH TRANSFER INDEX*

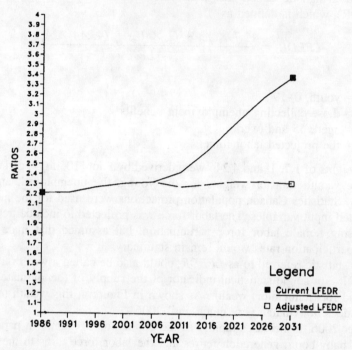

*From BROWN, ROBERT L., AND IGLESIAS, FERDINAND AG. "Social Security Funding Stability: An Age of Eligibility Model," *Research Report 89-01.* Waterloo, Ontario: Institute of Insurance and Pension Research, February 1989. Copyright 1989 by Robert L. Brown and Ferdinand Ag Iglesias. Reprinted with permission.

This latter assumption is not as dramatic as it seems, for several reasons. First, improvement in the health profile of Canadians has occurred with the improvement in life expectancy [22]. Second, the most significant increase in health care costs arises after age 69 [13, p. 555]. Finally, the impact on total wealth transfer from retirement income security is much greater than the impact from health care delivery.

Denton and Spencer [7, p. 14] have shown that between 1980 and 2030 health care costs will rise 69.8%, while social security costs will be three times their 1980 level in 2030 (see Figure 5), solely because of population aging.

FIGURE 5

INDEX OF SOCIAL SECURITY COSTS* (1981 = 100)

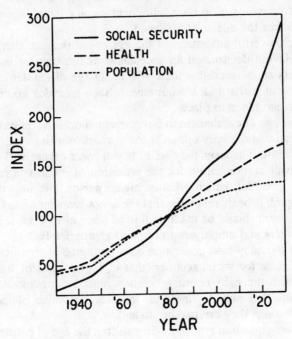

*From DENTON, F.T., AND SPENCER, B.G. "Prospective Changes
in the Population and Their Implications for Government Expenditure," *QSEP Research Report No. 98 (June)*. McMaster University: Program for Quantitative Studies in Economics and Population, 1984.

Given these assumptions, the model developed by Brown and Iglesias
shows that the wealth transfer index will remain level at its 2006 value if
the age of entitlement shifts upward from 65 in 2006 by two months each
year (starting in 2007), until it reaches age 69 in 2030. No further adjustment
is necessary.

This is a remarkable result. As indicated earlier in Table 3, Canada will
have the most rapidly aging population of all western industrialized nations
over the period 1985 to 2025. Thus, if a shift in the age of entitlement from
65 to 69 creates a constant wealth transfer index for Canada, then a smaller
shift would do the same for all other western industrialized nations. Further,

the Brown and Iglesias model does not include the effects of real productivity gains (that is, real growth in wealth creation). Such gains, if not fully transferred to the elderly in their retirement income benefits, could be used to reduce further the age shift indicated.

The other powerful advantage of the age-of-entitlement alternative is its flexibility. Having determined an acceptable wealth transfer index, public-policy-makers are assured that there will be an age-of-entitlement shift that will exactly match that index requirement. Such an index could vary from time to time and place to place.

Raising the age of entitlement to government-sponsored retirement income does not mean that the only option is for workers to wait to retire. They can continue to retire whenever they wish. It just means there will be an extra need for private responsibility for the provision of retirement income prior to the new age of entitlement (that is, higher personal savings rates).

In this regard, it bears repeating that the announcement of any shift in the age of entitlement should be made well in advance of its occurrence to allow time for workers and employers to respond appropriately.

Clearly, if the baby-bust generation does not agree to significantly higher contribution rates for social security (that is, higher rates of foregone consumption), then the baby-boom generation must be convinced to take reduced benefits (but only in line with the actuarial value of the relatively small contributions they are making today).

The following question remains: will a shift in the age of entitlement prove to be a palatable solution to achieving an acceptable wealth transfer equilibrium? There are many reasons to believe that the answer is yes.

For the past 20 years, both government (for example, more flexible retirement within social security) and the private sector have provided incentives for workers to take early retirement. One reason for this was to assist in reducing the high levels of youth unemployment created when the baby boom entered the labor force. Twenty years from now, however, the baby boom will start to retire, and by 2030, the labor force will be dependent on the baby-bust generation for its supply of workers to create wealth. Today's incentives for early retirement will become tomorrow's incentives for later retirement.

Thus an increase in the age of entitlement for social security retirement income will exactly match the goals of all employers (private and public), reason no. 1 that should make it acceptable.

Second, no economy can accommodate a sudden switch of all members of the baby boom (who will reach age 65 between 2015 and 2030) from productive members of the labor force to passive retired consumers. Total production plus imports must equal total consumption plus exports.

A sudden drop in production with no change in consumption would require increased imports, thus eroding the nation's balance of trade. Also, prices for domestic goods would increase. While the productive labor force may be able to achieve wage increases to offset the resulting inflation, the passive retireds will not, and they will see the value of their assets, and their ability to consume, erode, until a new economic equilibrium is achieved. It would be preferable to have some of the baby boomers remain productive members of the labor force for a longer period, to achieve a consumption-production equilibrium without inflation. One cannot avoid the reality that wealth must be created before it can be transferred.

There are also sociological reasons for accepting an increase in the age of entitlement. Many workers today are being forced to retire and would rather be working, at least part time. It is both illogical and unfair to relegate the experience and expertise of capable older workers to empty role structures merely because they have attained a certain chronological age [13, p. 196], [17, p. 65].

There are individual economic reasons to expect a rising age of entitlement to be palatable. While the cohort born between 1946 and 1955 was 30% wealthier than their fathers by age 30, the cohort born between 1956 and 1965 was 10% less well-off than their fathers by age 30 [4]. A great deal of the personal wealth that allows workers today to retire early exists because of the significant real increase in the value of housing that took place in the 1970s and 1980s as the baby boomers bought their first homes. However, that windfall is now history, and there is no reason to expect the real value of housing will rise faster than the GNP for the next 40 years. In fact, if the baby boomers all try to downsize their choice of housing at the time of retirement, capital losses could be expected to occur. Thus, the workers born after 1955 may not be able to accumulate enough wealth to retire early. This is especially true given their enhanced life expectancy. Instead of creating enough wealth to pay for 10 years of retirement income, they may well have to accumulate enough for 20 years.

In fact, it is this improvement in life expectancy that will prove to be the cornerstone in the campaign to sell the concept of a rising age of entitlement.

The cause of the wealth transfer dilemma is the aging population. But the cause of population aging is twofold: first, shifting demographics as the baby bust follows the baby boom, and second, enhanced life expectancy. As life expectancy has continued to improve, each retirement cohort has been the recipient of ever larger wealth transfers from social security (given a constant normal retirement age).

The Canadian data support this contention. The C/QPP was introduced in 1966 with a normal retirement age of 65. Had the criterion for the normal age at retirement for C/QPP been established as the 1966 life expectancy at age 65, then the equivalent ages of retirement, shown in Table 4, would result.

TABLE 4

EQUIVALENT AGE
AT RETIREMENT (CANADA)

Year	Age
1966	65.00
1981	67.30
1991	68.36
2001	69.36
2011	69.86
2021	70.28
2031	70.72

Table 4 shows that, by 2031, a normal retirement age of almost 71 would equate to a 1966 normal retirement age of 65. Remember that the Brown and Iglesias model projects a rise in the age of entitlement from 65 in 2006 to 69 in 2030, without accounting for the productivity gains of workers in that period (because some social security schemes cannot achieve that gain). Thus, a shift in the age of entitlement only slightly more than the equivalent improvement in life expectancy will result in a level wealth transfer index for the country with the fastest aging population. This should be an acceptable alternative for Canadians. All other western nations will experience an easier sales job than that needed in Canada.

Pressure is already mounting in the U.S. for further changes to the OASDI normal retirement age. One example is the Pickle Bill, which would raise the normal retirement age to 70.

More recently, in the U.S., then House Ways and Means Committee Chairman Dan Rostenkowski proposed an acceleration of the shift in the age of entitlement for OASDI benefits from age 65 to age 67, as presented earlier in this paper. The following is part of the editorial reaction carried in *USA Today*, Monday, April 25, 1994:

Speeding up that process saves billions while bowing to the reality that
as people live longer—about six years longer than at Social Security's
birth—they must work longer too....
And it's fair.
Current beneficiaries get two to three times more from Social Security
than they contributed; future generations can't even get their contributions
back.

8. BEWARE DEMANDS TO EXPAND PAYGO SOCIAL SECURITY

It may be surprising that there could be a demand for an expanded paygo
system at a time when the present viability of these schemes is being questioned. However, this is possible given the realities of the initial years of
any paygo system, when it is possible to have all workers contribute immediately, but it could take more than a generation before all retirees draw
full benefits. Hence, early paygo contributions can be far less than the contributions required to fund the mature paygo scheme.

Any new extended layer of benefits can be designed with the same properties (that is, contributions that, actuarially, are much smaller in value than
the new benefits that are promised to be paid in the future). In this way, the
total contributions for the combined new system could appear to be
acceptable.

It is now apparent that paygo systems have two perverse characteristics.
First, once a paygo system is accepted, it is almost impossible to return to
a fully funded system because one generation would have to make double
contributions to pay off the actuarial liability of the paygo system while also
prefunding the fully funded system. Second, one apparent short-term solution to the funding problem with a paygo scheme is an expansion of that
scheme!

However, there exists only a short-term appearance of equity, with the
new expanded cost being added to the chain-letter commitment of the next
generation.

9. CONCLUSION

A paygo security scheme derives much of its apparent security from an
assurance of its permanence. This paper has presented a politically acceptable solution to the funding problems now facing most social security systems in the western industrialized nations that can guarantee that permanence. Having determined that the real issue is not the method of funding

such systems (that is, paygo versus fully funded), the paper analyzes the ability of these western nations to find an acceptable wealth transfer equilibrium given their aging populations. Because Canada has the most rapidly aging population among these western nations, Canadian data were used in the analysis.

The paper presents an age-of-entitlement model that can be used to achieve *any* acceptable wealth transfer ratio. The Canadian data show that the maximum age shift that would be required to solve the problems projected over the next half-century is a shift in the normal retirement age from 65 to only 69 (a proposed graded shift starting in 2007 and being finally achieved in 2030). No western nation should require a shift more dramatic than that.

I hope that this model will prove helpful in the public policy analysis that all western industrialized nations will pursue in the quest for a new wealth transfer equilibrium and for intergenerational solidarity.

10. BIBLIOGRAPHY

1. AARON, HENRY J. *Economic Effects of Social Security.* Washington, D.C.: The Brookings Institute, 1982.
2. BARR, NICHOLAS. *The Economics of the Welfare State.* Stanford, Calif.: Stanford University Press, 1987.
3. BROWN, ROBERT L., AND IGLESIAS, FERDINAND A. "Social Security Funding Stability: An Age of Eligibility Model," *Research Report 89-01.* Waterloo, Ont.: University of Waterloo, Institute of Insurance and Pension Research, 1989.
4. BROWN, ROBERT L. "Economic Security in an Aging Population: Implications to the Design and Marketing of Group Products," *TSA* XLVI (1994): 9–44.
5. CHEN, YUNG-PING. "Making Assets out of Tomorrow's Elderly," *The Gerontologist* 27, no. 4 (1987): 410–16.
6. CIA TASK FORCE ON SOCIAL SECURITY FINANCING. *Canadian Retirement Income Social Security Programs.* Ottawa, Ont.: Canadian Institute of Actuaries, November 1993.
7. DENTON, F.T., AND SPENCER, B.G. "Prospective Changes in the Population and Their Implications for Government Expenditure," *QSEP Research Report No. 98 (June).* Hamilton, Ont.: McMaster University, Program for Quantitative Studies in Economics and Population, 1984.
8. ECONOMIC COUNCIL OF CANADA. *One in Three—Pensions for Canadians to 2030.* Ottawa, Ont: 1979.
9. FELLEGI, IVAN P. "Can We Afford an Aging Society?" *Canadian Economic Observer* (October 1988).

10. FOOT, DAVID K. *Public Expenditures, Population Aging and Economic Dependency in Canada.* University of Toronto: Institute for Policy Analysis, 1982.

11. HOHN, CHARLOTTE. "Population Policies in Advanced Societies: Pronatalist and Migration Strategies," *European Journal of Population* 3 (1987): 459–81.

12. LATULIPPE, DENIS. "Retirement Policy—An International Perspective," *TSA* XLV (1993): 187–214.

13. MARSHALL, VICTOR W. *Aging in Canada, Social Perspectives,* 2nd ed. Markham, Ont.: Fitzhenry and Whiteside, 1987.

14. MÉNARD, JEAN-CLAUDE, AND POTVIN, SONIA. *Actuarial Adjustment Factors: Methodology and Considerations Applicable to a Social Insurance Plan.* Ottawa, Ont.: Canadian Institute of Actuaries, October 1992.

15. MYERS, ROBERT J. "Implications of Population Change on Social Insurance Systems Providing Old-Age Benefits," *Insurance: Mathematics and Economics* 4, no. 1 (January 1985): 3–22.

16. OFFICE OF THE SUPERINTENDENT OF FINANCIAL INSTITUTIONS. *Canada Pension Plan Fifteenth Actuarial Report as at December 31, 1993.* Ottawa, Ont.

17. PIFER, ALAN, AND BRONTE, LYDIA. *Our Aging Society: Paradox and Promise.* New York: W.W. Norton and Company, 1986.

18. PROVINCE OF ONTARIO. "Issues in Pension Policy," *Ontario Treasury Studies No. 16.* Ottawa, Ont.: Ministry of Treasury and Economics, 1979.

19. ROSA, JEAN-JACQUES. *The World Crises in Social Security.* New Brunswick, N.J.: Transaction Publications, 1982.

20. STATISTICS CANADA (NAGNUR, DHRUVA). *Longevity and Historical Life Tables 1921–1981 (Abridged), Canada and the Provinces.* Ottawa, Ont.: Ministry of Supply and Services, 1986.

21. U.S. DEPARTMENT OF COMMERCE. "An Aging World," *International Population Report Series P-95:78.* Washington, D.C.: Bureau of the Census, September 1987.

22. WEITZ, HENRY. *The Foreign Experience with Income Maintenance for the Elderly.* Ottawa, Ont.: Economic Council of Canada, 1979.

23. WILKINS, RUSSELL, AND ADAMS, OWEN. "Health Expectancy in Canada, Late 1970s. Demographic, Regional and Social Dimensions," *American Journal of Public Health* 73 (1983): 1073–80.

DISCUSSION OF PRECEDING PAPER

G.N. WATSON:

This discussion is written from the standpoint of a Canadian who participated in the consultation process at the inception of the Canada Pension Plan (CPP) and is one of only a few actuaries who did so. No position was taken or opinion expressed by the Canadian Institute of Actuaries, and the plan was completely opposed by the life insurance industry, not because it was a pay-as-you-go plan, but because it was not self-supporting based on the contribution rate required at the outset. It was generally assumed that because it was supported by an actuarial report and was certified as sound by the Government Actuary of the day, it was therefore fully supported by the contributions required.

Now, 30 years later, we read in the newspapers that we have a very serious problem, which most actuaries and pension specialists knew all along.

This problem did not arise because it was a pay-as-you-go plan but primarily because there was a built-in deficiency at the start. This was largely due to granting to those residents over 55 the right to start full benefits after making only 10 years of contributions. Other major enhancements were made later without changing the original contribution rate, which was, in total, originally 3.6% and stood unchanged for more than 20 years. There were several enhancements during this period, the most important being the introduction of full CPI indexation for members already retired and the removal of the requirement for complete retirement from the work force for benefits to be payable from ages 65 to 70.

Buried in the original actuarial report was the statement (then seemingly ignored by most writers and speakers on the subject) that, based on the original actuarial assumptions, contribution rates should be increased from the original 3.6% to 5.5%, starting in 1985. This increase was to pay for the considerable gift involved at the inception giving full benefits after 10 years of contributions had been made, as already stated.

In this paper, the author shows that if contributions are made to a pay-as-you-go plan over the full working lifetime, a funded plan contribution rate is the same as the rate for a pay-as-you-go plan, provided that there is a sufficient increase in the active members and in the average wage rate. But no mention is made of what is generally called the past-service benefit, which a funded plan would certainly have to make provision for. It was

143

estimated that the fund required at the inception of the CPP to cover this item was approximately $20 billion dollars.

Thus, there was in this plan a substantial deficit at the outset, which was one of the chief causes for the substantial increase actually required in 1985. No increase was made in 1985 as originally projected, but in 1986 a continuous annual increase in the contribution rate was commenced, to soften the blow. This increase was less than originally projected, whereas conditions and the level of benefit payments had, in the meantime, changed. As a result, a much larger increase was in fact needed. Now, 11 years later, the matter has become a matter of public concern.

This discussion is written to avoid the pitfall of assuming that the CPP and other social security plans in the western world have a problem merely because of a changing birth rate and an aging population. If that was all it was, I agree with the author: there are various solutions that come to mind. The Canadian Institute of Actuaries has listed these, and the authorities understand such alternatives. The magnitude of the problem 30 years later has been caused chiefly by neglect not by demography.

Therefore, let us as actuaries not delude ourselves and, because of our expertise, give comfort to those who must now bear responsibility for the sins and the unsupported promises of the past.

This is a very valuable paper because it analyzes how a pay-as-you-go plan can be self-supporting and shows how it can be compared to a fully funded plan and particularly how the growth rate of contributions compares to the earned interest rate of the fund of the latter. That is an important point because it does indicate certain necessary assumptions implicit in the valuation. This discussion is intended to go further and to point out that there must be in all of this certain additional assumptions if the pay-as-you-go plan is to survive, as follows:

(1) The liability for past employment existing at the inception of the plan must be taken into account in setting the initial contribution rate.

(2) If the terms of the plan are changed, the contribution rates must be changed accordingly.

(3) If there are demographic changes, these must be examined at intervals of five to ten years and changes recommended by the Government Actuary in the required contribution rates and acted on as a matter of law.

(4) To the extent that the plan accumulates a fund because of (1), these funds should be invested at a rate of interest sufficient to meet the valuation assumptions, but not necessarily invested only in government

bonds. Bank stocks should be a good secure investment because of the considerable support banks receive from the federal government. This type of investment would give comfort to the average citizen (and all members of the NDP party), who would rejoice to read of the profits earned by the banks that would, under these circumstances, be used, in part, to pay for his/her pension.

(5) Whenever the administration rules are relaxed so as to increase the rate of claim for benefits, this must be accompanied by a change in the required rate of contribution.

My submission to the special committee that was appointed to consider and report on the proposed CPP, consisting of Senators and Members of Parliament, was made January 13, 1965 in Ottawa. At one point I stated (quoting exactly from the printed record),

> ... it would seem to me that the pension plan should be self-supporting and I deplore the fact that the rate of contribution specified in the Act will not provide a plan which is self-supporting. In fact, from 1985 and on, it will require a higher rate of contribution if we are to rely on the estimates of the chief actuary.

I went on to say,

> ... I would like to see a plan, if this is the action that will be taken, that will stand on its own feet, considering the present population as a group.

That was my principal recommendation. At the conclusion, they smiled, asked questions, and complimented me on the charts and illustrations I had shown them. One member even suggested they should be published in the *Ottawa Citizen*, but otherwise in their report they ignored everything I had to say. Later, the Government Actuary told me privately that he did not agree with the point I was making.

Now, 30 years later, we have a problem that any actuary can perceive, but let us not sugarcoat it. The government of the day ignored the actuarial imperatives and will again unless we clearly tell the truth of the matter. The problem is not pay-as-you-go versus fully funded. It is rather a matter of adhering to proper valuation standards, which all actuaries are required to do, except when it is really a matter of national importance.

Forgive me for writing of the past at such length, but those others who know the truth of what I have said are for the most part dead or suffering from one dread disease or another. The members of the committee who were charged to report on the matter to Parliament are also no longer with us; only the written record survives.

Those younger actuaries who must now advise government may benefit in some small way by reading this discussion, to better understand how we Canadians managed to get in this position and what must now be done to cure it and, further, to prevent recurrence.

BERNARD DUSSAULT:

I commend Rob Brown on a profoundly professional and scientifically rigorous treatment of the economic, social, and political aspects of the issues stemming from social retirement programs run on a pay-as-you go basis in a demographic environment of an aging population. The paper should prove to be a useful reference to aid in the understanding of the complex factors affecting the administration of social insurance and pension programs. I do, however, question one aspect of the solution proposed in the paper for resolving the intergenerational equity issue brought about with the population aging process, and I also submit a comment on the discussion of financing approaches.

Increasing the Normal Retirement Age

Raising the normal retirement age would be consistent with that part of the aging process caused by improved longevity. However, I question whether its permanent implementation would and/or could resolve the intergenerational inequity caused by that part of the aging process resulting from the sustained shift to lower fertility since the mid-1960s. I suggest that increasing the normal retirement age would achieve financial equilibrium temporarily for baby boomers, who would thereby receive reduced benefits consistent with the lower contribution rates resulting from the pay-as-you go approach for relatively larger cohorts of contributors. However,
- If implemented permanently, would the increased retirement age not exacerbate rather than resolve the inequity issue for subsequent "buster" generations, because they would be expected to contribute at higher rates than boomer generations for equivalent benefit amounts?
- Consistent with the sensible, suggested, actuarially equitable solution to the paygo roller coaster whereby smaller cohorts (for example, the buster generations following the boomer generations) paying above-average contributions should receive about-average benefits, would the normal retirement age not have to be accordingly set back to age 65 (or even

below) for the subsequent buster generations, which are projected to contribute at rates higher than any previous generations? In this context, it is not surprising that the model developed by Brown and Iglesias shows that the wealth transfer index will remain level until 2030 at its 2006 value if the retirement age is gradually shifted from 65 to 69. As stated in the paper, this is a remarkable result. But the paper is silent on what this model would produce from 2030 and later. Maintaining the retirement age at its increased level of 69 after 2030 should cause the wealth transfer index to start decreasing after 2030 as dramatically as it increases, as shown in Figure 4 of the paper for 2006 to 2030 under a no-retirement-age-increase scenario.

Discussion of Financing Approaches

My comments here deal with the discussion of the relative merits of paygo and full funding as financing approaches for social retirement programs. Although the paper states that the full-funding approach, as compared to the pay-as-you-go approach, does not add to the inherent security of promised benefits, it fails to disclose the following two important attributes of full funding:

(a) It is generally recognized as the most cost-equitable self-adjusting approach.

(b) It produces lower costs than the paygo approach if and when investment rates of return are higher than increases in total employment earnings. For example, assuming a long-term real rate of return of 2.5% (consistent with the existing CPP investment policy), the CPP full cost contribution rate would, at 10.5%, be about 25% less than the ultimate pay-as-you-go rate of about 14.3% for 2030 and later years projected using an internal rate of return of about 1.5%, as assumed in the fifteenth actuarial report on the CPP. Assuming a real rate of return of 4% (which would normally be considered appropriate for a diversified portfolio investment policy like that applying for the Québec Pension Plan), the CPP full-cost contribution rate would, at about 6.75%, be about 50% less than the above ultimate pay-as-you-go rate.

KENNETH A. STEINER:

In his paper, Mr. Brown develops a wealth transfer index model "for funding stability." According to Mr. Brown, this model "creates and provides intergenerational equity and hence will succeed in guaranteeing the future viability of paygo schemes." I question whether application of Mr. Brown's model would, in fact, achieve either funding stability or intergenerational equity in Canada or elsewhere. Further, I take issue with Mr. Brown's preference for paygo financing over actuarial advance funding of social security benefits.

Funding Stability

According to Mr. Brown, "the actual 1994 contribution rate [for C/QPP] is 5.4% paid 50/50 by employers and workers. ..." This rate is projected by C/QPP actuaries to be 14.4% by 2035. Presumably, this expected increase in contribution rates is the problem Mr. Brown wishes to address with his model. However, the increases in the normal retirement age he proposes would still result in an ultimate contribution for C/QPP in excess of 11%, or more than double the current rate. It seems to me that future generations of taxpayers may still have much the same reluctance to contribute in excess of 11% as they might with a 14.4% rate. A doubling of the contribution rate and possible reluctance of future taxpayers to make required contributions does not seem to reflect a stable funding environment.

Mr. Brown does not specify how his model will work if actual experience deviates from projected experience, if actuarial assumptions for future projections are changed or if C/QPP benefit provisions are changed. Will there be some mechanism in Mr. Brown's model that automatically adjusts the normal retirement age for these changes? It seems somewhat unrealistic that the Canadian government will entrust the provisions of its national retirement program to one or more actuaries and their somewhat arbitrary "LFEDR" calculations. Again, it is difficult to see how funding stability would be achieved under the proposed model.

Intergenerational Equity

Despite Mr. Brown's arguments, I remain unconvinced that the LFEDR model will "create" or even "provide" intergenerational equity. I do not find the ratio to be a particularly good measure of intergenerational equity for several reasons, including the following:
- Because the support of the nation's youth is not borne solely by the working population (at least in the U.S.), it should be eliminated from the numerator.
- The use of the labor force in the denominator favors those generations that did not (or do not) participate as fully in the labor force.

- The numerator fails to reflect transfer of wealth related to other government-sponsored programs such as national defense, servicing of the national debt, and so on.

I agree with Mr. Brown that intergenerational equity can be achieved through actuarial equity. However, I believe that most taxpayers look to "money's-worth" comparisons as the best measure of individual or intergenerational equity (that is, this generation can expect to receive benefits of $x\%$ of accumulated contributions paid versus $y\%$ expected by the preceding generation and $z\%$ expected from the following generation). Under most money's-worth analyses that I have seen, Mr. Brown's solution might introduce more equity between baby-boom and baby-bust generations, but it would doubtless provide less equity between these two generations and preceding generations.

Paygo versus Actuarial Advance Funding

I was disappointed that Mr. Brown felt obligated to attack the "actuarial full funding" straw man that he created. I believe the real question is not whether one approach provides more security than another, but whether actuarial advance funding (note: this is not the same as "full funding") can better accomplish a reasonable funding objective (such as keeping the tax rate nearly level in the future when measured as a percentage of taxable payroll or as a percentage of gross national product or as a percentage of some other reasonable measure). I believe the answer is, "Yes, it can."

Certainly, there are some advantages of paygo financing: initial program costs are usually lower and there is no need to worry about how program assets are to be invested. The advantages of actuarial advance funding for social security programs include the opportunity to level out the tax rate and impose financial discipline in the form of automatic adjustment of gains and losses, changes in assumptions, changes in plan provisions, and so on.

Many individuals favor paygo financing, and many individuals would like to see some type of advance funding of baby-boomer social security retirement benefits with assets either invested by the government or privately invested. If our policymakers choose to finance baby-boomer benefits on a paygo basis, then Mr. Brown's approach is as reasonable an approach as any for determining possible future benefit reductions. If advance funding is desired by our policymakers, we should offer actuarial solutions to ensure that the desired levels of asset accumulations are accomplished. In either event, we should help our policymakers by substituting facts for appearances and demonstrations for impressions. I believe those facts and demonstrations should include graphs of expected future tax rates and individual money's worth comparisons for the various alternatives considered.

JOHN C. MAYNARD:

The Canada Pension Plan faces immediate and critical decisions in financing and structure. The finding of solutions to the underlying problems will be of actuarial and general interest in Canada and in other countries in which similar problems are looming. I thank Robert Brown for writing the paper.

In the following discussion, issue is taken with several of the author's opinions. His suggested method of financing is then examined. Finally, an alternative method of financing is described and recommended.

The advantages of present-day government paygo schemes are important: nearly universal coverage, immediate vesting, and low administrative costs. These advantages will still be there if the government scheme has some funding. In the paper the disadvantages of government-funded schemes are much overstated, and their advantages in relation to paygo are not brought out clearly. The door is therefore open for considering as the best alternative a continuation of the present plan with the injection of some funding.

The destruction of several government fully funded pension schemes in the early part of the century is attributed to inflation. However, in recent times there have been public service plans and some private plans, with benefits indexed to cost-of-living, and they have come through the inflation of 1960 to 1990 very well. My TSA paper[1] bears on the funding of private plans with indexed benefits.

In the paper serious doubts are expressed that the assets of a government-funded scheme can be held securely and invested properly. Rosa, writing in 1982, goes so far as to warn that an attempt to do this "invites squandering capital funds in wasteful low yield investments." These opinions do not allow for the many changes that have occurred in investment systems in the past 15 years or so.

In fact the worldwide demand for capital has expanded enormously, and widening markets have brought buyers and sellers together. Thanks to much improved communications these markets are now international in scope and activity. Along with this growth has come the required knowledge, the skills,

[1]MAYNARD, J.C. "Financing Defined-Benefit Pension Plans with Indexed Benefits." *TSA* XLIV (1992): 193–246.

and the definition of responsibilities required by a professional person, the investment manager.

Speaking of pension fund investments, Keith Ambachstsheer states in a recent article[2]

> The motivations of pension fund managers proceed logically from understanding that it is in the common interest of employers and employees to create pension funds. Such funds secure pension promises and, by earning superior returns, also help create the wealth needed to make the promises economically viable. Legislation supports these arrangements, providing tax deferrals and requiring fund managers to act as fiduciaries solely in the best interests of the beneficiaries.

These remarks apply to public service pension funds as well as private pension funds. In Ontario about six years ago, two new investment systems were set up for two public service pension funds: the Ontario Teachers' Fund and the Ontario Pension Board. The purpose of these changes was to diversify from investments of the Ontario government to a broader range of investments, thereby improving both security and rate of return. The last few years have been kind to investors, and these two funds and others like them have been doing well.

It is estimated that the Public Sector Pension Funds in Canada amount to $225,000,000, while the fund for a partially funded Canada Pension Plan is estimated to have an average of about this amount in the next 25 years.

Is a fully funded scheme more secure than paygo? Authority Barr replies "No," because in both cases it is the transfer of consumption from workers to pensioners that counts and the two methods of funding should not fare very differently. But this reasoning does not allow for differences in timing. Under paygo the current contributions are paid directly to pensioners. Under full funding the contributions are saved up for a generation and then with investment income are paid to pensioners. At any one time the pension payments are supported by the fund and by current contributions, not by current contributions alone. Suppose we had a prolonged economic depression in which incomes were reduced and contributions were much reduced or cut off. Under full funding, earned pensions could continue unabated without a strain on other resources. Under paygo this could not happen. Other examples can be given. Surely it can be accepted that funding, even partial funding, is more secure than paygo.

---

[2] "In defence of pension funds," *Toronto Globe and Mail*, March 6, 1996.

Paygo funding is subject to an inherent instability, and the history and experience of the Canada Pension Plan reveal this. In the early 1960s the federal government of the day asked Dr. Robert M. Clark to study and report on the field of government schemes. His report stated the need for a universal federal scheme with contributions and benefits based on earned income. The government was influenced by schemes of this kind that were in operation in the U.S. and Sweden and decided to proceed. The contribution rates were set to provide for a small fund and for benefits as they fell due. The rates were thus low but above paygo rates, which were initially very low. The actuarial literature of the time is full of warnings that under this system the contribution rates were bound to increase and this would be unfair to future contributors. However, the actual experience has been worse than expected. Projections, which were made every few years, always confirmed that contribution rates had to increase, but the contribution rate for a given year was always going to be higher than the rate for that year in the previous projection. It is not surprising that contributors are disturbed, fearing that contribution rates will increase indefinitely and without limit, and that the Canada Pension Plan is headed for cancellation or major change. As this discussion is being written, press reports appear monthly in favor of cancellation.

The main cause of increasing contribution rates is clearly stated in the paper. It is a characteristic of paygo schemes that when a benefit is introduced "all workers contribute immediately, but it could take more than a generation before all retirees draw full benefits." This characteristic not only explains why rates increase in a paygo system, but also guarantees that this will happen. This characteristic is therefore an inherent flaw.

But there is another flaw. If paygo continues, there is the need each year to balance the equation between cash contributions from current workers and cash payments to current retirees. This is difficult if the ratio of worker population to retiree population varies because birth rates have varied down and up and down in the last 60 years, or for any other reason. Author Brown attempts to bring stability to the "paygo roller coaster" by defining a change in contribution rates, but finds this unsatisfactory. He then attempts to define a change in benefits, concluding that an increase might be made in the retirement age because of improved and improving mortality. This is understandable. But then he requires a further increase in the retirement age for the baby-boom cohort, to be followed presumably by a reduction in retirement age for the following cohort. This amounts to gradual changes in retirement age up and down according to year of birth. In the opinion of this writer the public would not understand or support changes of this kind.

There has been another weakness in the present system. In the past four years the cost of disability claims in the CPP has doubled, while there has been no change in the definition of disability. This situation certainly calls for investigation and correction.

The experience of the first 30 years under CPP/QPP has shown that paygo funding leads to contribution rates that increase unpredictably and that vary according to year of birth and economic factors. On the other hand, there are advocates of full funding, that is, a system in which contributions from individuals provide for their own benefits in retirement. These contributions are made in advance of payments and lead to a large fund that needs to be invested and managed well.

A move from paygo to full funding can be made, but if earned benefits for existing retired persons are to be continued, the contributions will be heavy for a generation of contributors. These contributors will have to pay for the benefits of the retired while paying for their own benefits in advance.

Is there any method of funding other than paygo or a move to full funding? Yes, there is a family of partial funding methods. This is the family for which contribution rates are expected to remain level for a period. This is a good family because if a level contribution rate can be determined and accepted, confidence in the plan will be restored.

For a given year of commencement, the determination of the level contribution rate will depend on: the benefits, the assumptions about the future, the initial fund, the period, and the fund at the end of the period. The technique for determining present and future contribution rates has been highly developed by the Chief Actuary in the last few years and uses the facility for making projections of the fund for many years. In other contexts this process would be risky, even foolhardy. In the present situation the fund is anchored to an aging and well-known population. The economic factors may well differ from the assumptions, but their differences are likely to be offsetting in the projections. The projections are credible and useful, particularly for the shorter periods.

A period of 35 years from 1996 is long enough to include most of the benefit payments to the baby-boom cohort. For this period and with present benefits and an interest rate assumption of 7%, the level annual contribution rate is estimated at 11%. All contribution rates apply to only a portion of earned income. The comparison with paygo is as follows:

Year	Paygo Rate	Estimated Level Rate
1997	8.00%	11.0%
2001	8.36	11.0
2011	10.08	11.0
2021	12.53	11.0
2030	14.22	11.0

With this level rate the fund account is expected to grow at $15 billion per year, reaching $400 billion (five to six times annual benefit payments) in 2016 to 2021. In the following years the growth rate of the fund account is expected to reduce to a level that equals two times annual benefit payments in 2030. This level is large but comparable to the level of public sector funds in Canada and low in relation to the growing level of the world market for capital.

In time there will be periodic reviews of experience, assumptions, benefits, and expected level contribution rates. The original projections will serve as the initial objective for fund assets. If assets exceed the initial objective, as will happen if the actual rate of return exceeds the assumed rate of interest, it would be proper to make a refund of contributions, perhaps over the following five year period. Conversely, if assets are lower than the objective, there should be an increase in contribution rate.

If there is a reduction in benefits, there should be a new calculation of the expected level contribution rate, which should be lower than the current rate. Normally this should be adopted immediately. A possible increase in retirement age is an important example of reduction in benefits.

If there is an increase in benefits or any liberalization in the administration of disability or other claims, there should be a new calculation of the expected level contribution rate at the new level of benefits. The new and higher contribution rate should be adopted on the effective date of the new level of benefits.

The CPP/QPP is a plan in which the benefits and contributions are based on earned income. It has the advantages of universality, portability, low expense. Together with OAS, GIS (the public plans with flat rate benefits), and private savings, the CPP/QPP makes up the three-way structure for the provision of retirement income in Canada.

In public the CPP/QPP has been criticized for continuously increasing contributions and consequent lack of stability. In this discussion, in answer to these criticisms, a practical and stable funding method has been outlined that depends on contribution rates that are expected to be level or nonincreasing for 35 years.

The method outlined requires a jump in contribution rates to a level higher than current paygo. Will the baby-boom generation who makes the contributions be agreeable to this?

Several inducements will help to make them feel agreeable:

1. They will be providing additional security for members of their own generation.
2. Interest rates today are historically high.
3. They get tax credit for the increase in contributions, and investment income is sheltered from tax.

The funding method will require some basic changes in the operation of CPP/QPP:

1. A new structure will be needed for investment management, so that investment policy is left to professionally trained persons. Periodically, public statements on the fund should be available, permitting comparisons with other funds.
2. A board and staff will be responsible for administration of payments, expenses, claims, and decisions on funding based on a commitment to maintain level contribution rates.

KRZYSZTOF M. OSTASZEWSKI:

The issue of stability of pay-as-you-go social insurance systems has gained worldwide attention recently. The book *Averting the Old Age Crisis* [4] illustrates that the security of social security systems has become a central public policy issue throughout the world. The publication of Mr. Brown's work is a welcome addition to this important debate.

There are several important points that should be raised in relation to Mr. Brown's paper.

1. "Pay-As-You-Go" Is Not Properly Defined by Its Name, as the So-called "Funded Plans" Also Pay as They Go

The most fascinating aspect of social security systems is the pretense of those systems of being something completely new in their respective national economies. Social security schemes are presented as transferring cash from the working to the nonworking (for example, retired, disabled, and so on). Alas, if the nonworking group holds a portfolio of claims to cash flows of firms employing the working group, the same kind of transfer is ensured.

When the nonworking want to consume, they collect their interest, dividends, and possibly capital from their portfolio, and cash flows from the working to the nonworking. Then (or actually simultaneously) the cash flows in the opposite direction to ensure the more important transfer of goods and services. Interestingly enough, as much cash flows out of the firms to the nonworking as then flows into purchases of goods and services, and the system pays as it goes.

The above illustrates one purpose of capital markets. We tend to think of modern, efficient markets with numerous intermediaries facilitating the flow. This is beneficial but not necessary for the function described here. Inefficient, monopolistic markets that existed in the nineteenth century, and dominated the economic scene before that, were capital markets nevertheless and allowed for imperfect accumulation of capital assets. We in fact believe that paygo schemes are simply an extension of nineteenth-century government perpetuities used for retirement. Capital assets are merely claims to future cash flows of enterprises, and they are generally prioritized into the following groups:

- Claims to riskless cash flows generated by taxing power (government securities)
- Claims to cash flows guaranteed by an enterprise's existence (bonds)
- Claims to discretionary cash flows generated by an enterprise (stocks).

A paygo scheme is a sophisticated method to hide the true nature of social insurance schemes. What is the true nature? To answer that, let us now engage in a reverse of the exercise presented above. If private markets for retirement (and disability) indeed function on a pay-as-you-go basis, private financial security systems look like social security. Is the opposite true—are social security schemes just like capital markets? Are rights accrued within social security systems a security? One might be tempted to say "no" because the legislature can change them at any session. Alas, the value of a marketable security, even in an efficient market, can be changed by any session of the legislature by a simple twist of the tax code. In fact, participation in a social or private pension scheme is a security, because it is a claim to future cash flows. If the future cash flows become more uncertain, they are discounted at a higher rate and valued less.

Where is that security hiding in social security systems? Social security systems are equivalent to:

- Initial-beneficiaries generation receiving welfare transfer payments
- Government issuing special private placement bonds in return for payroll tax contributions

- Benefits termed "contributions plus interest"
- Special tax/transfer payment instituted for beneficiaries to achieve the prescribed benefit levels.

This is fully described, and presented in an appropriate mathematical model, by Kotlikoff in the "social security" entry in *The New Palgrave Dictionary of Money and Finance* [3]. It is quite common to perceive the social insurance payroll premium as either tax or an insurance premium. If it a premium, it is much closer to an annuity premium—the participants expect a return of it. If it is a tax, we should recall one of the most fascinating claims of classical economics, recently revived by the rational expectations school (represented by last year's Nobel Prize winner, Robert Lucas, or Robert Barro, and numerous others): the Ricardian equivalence. In its simplest form, it proclaims that how government finances itself—taxes or bonds—does not matter, because all of it will become taxes one day anyway. Yes, this is a debatable proposition, especially in view of the Keynesian and supply-side schools of thought, but it deserves attention. Let us observe that one of the heated debates about social security systems is their effect on the savings rate. Many critics of social insurance proclaim that it hampers savings. Ricardian equivalence holds that social security cannot have any effect on the savings rate. In my opinion, however, the main problem with social security systems lies in an entirely different area.

2. Demographics Is Not the Problem, but Centralized Demographical Models Are

There is now nearly a "call to arms" among public-policy scholars about the state of the pay-as-you-go systems in relation to the coming "tsunami" of baby-boomer retirements. If the retirement systems were in the private sector (as they properly should be), we would instead talk of a secular (although precedented) bull ride in the financial markets (which should be followed by a secular bear market, sometime after 2020). In the mixed North American economies, we are blessed with the opportunity to talk about both. Mr. Brown's paper gives demographic projections that imply the issues facing paygo systems. Yet the problem is not demographics, but the concentration of the response to demographics in the hands of government actuaries and the legislature. Are private capital markets efficient enough to price the demographic tsunami into the interest rates? All scholarly work in modern finance indicates that the answer is "Yes." Anecdotal evidence often points to a "no." We must honestly ask: What is the more efficient way to price capital assets?

The problem is that over the next several decades there is going to be an increasing demand for the social insurance benefits paid to the elderly, while the supply of such benefits may not rise to the level demanded. If the benefits were demanded in a private market, price would undoubtedly rise. Alas, they are provided by the government and the price is already set, and even if it is not set yet, it will be set by the government. The actuaries will perform all necessary calculations and arrive at the level of funding that is needed. This will translate into the appropriate payroll tax level, be it 60% or 70% (no, we do not believe we will get to that level, but we do need to get your attention), and then the system will return to equilibrium. There may be temporary shortages and there may be some rationing, but speculators will be punished by law, and the needs of the population will be met.

The production of shoes in the command economy was guided by similar principles. Projected demand for shoes was carefully evaluated by a team of government experts. Then the national economy's capacity to produce and import shoes was analyzed in view of current social priorities. The results of such expert analysis were then brought to the executive of the ruling party. The party then brought the resolution adopted to the legislature, which voted upon it and thus provided for relief from acute shortages of shoes that developed in the marketplace. However, despite repeated efforts of the experts, the party, and the legislature, the acute shortages of shoes persisted and even deepened.

Let us then recall what happened when price controls on consumer goods were removed on January 1, 1990 in Poland. It took less than a week to fill the stores. Yes, there were complaints about prices, but what we need to ask is which of the two sets of prices was the real one: the prices set by the government experts, or the prices set by private speculators hassling refrigerators across the German border. In the U.S., the wealthiest quintile now saves less than an average Korean or an average German. If the purpose of retirement insurance is to provide income replacement, shock therapy may be necessary for such behavior.

I am convinced that the baby boomers will respond to the real incentives soon, and we will see a savings rate of more than 20% in the U.S. economy within a decade, as well as a price/earnings ratio of 50 in the U.S. stock markets.

But the problem is not demographics; the problem is that centralized demographic models of social security systems hide true incentives from economic decision-makers. In a rational economy, prices must be real. This means that demographic projections should be decentralized, and many competing private firms should be struggling with the problem of income replacement for the retired baby boomers. For example, How serious would the overpopulation problem be if every person had the capacity and the commitment to "pay for his/her own space"?

The intergenerational equity issue raised by Mr. Brown is addressed in depth in the recent works on intergenerational accounting, such as Kotlikoff, [2], and we believe that Mr. Brown's analysis would be enhanced by incorporation of that framework.

3. Asset/Liability Management Matters

The entire demographic section assumes static analysis, ignoring the value of embedded options. Yet as the experience of Medicare in the U.S. indicates, the option value for Medicare between 1965 and 1990 turned out to be 900% of the value of the static contract (1990 expenditures were ten times the 1965 projections for 1990 expenditures; this does include Congress' option to raise benefits, but at least 300% is due to participants and providers skillfully adjusting their behavior to maximize cash flows from the system). All proposed ratios in Mr. Brown's analysis depend on the design of the system itself and will self-adjust as the system evolves. The static model assumes that there are no negative feedbacks in the system, an assumption that is a reasonable approximation for small tax levels but that becomes very inaccurate for large tax levels, as the experience of other countries clearly indicates. Thus long-term projections must be considered as standard asset/liability management projects, assuming intricate interactions of the factors.

What interactions would those be? Let us begin with the discount rate. Clearly, there is no single discount rate for premiums and benefits, as Mr. Brown's paper assumes. Benefits generally grow with an index of consumer prices, while contributions grow with wages. The spread of the two was precisely the reason why legislators for the longest time felt unrestrained in increasing benefits levels. If the Ricardian equivalence is incorrect, this is precisely where it may fail—increasing levels of explicit and implicit government debt cause returns to financial capital to rise on a relative basis and cause returns to human capital (that is, labor) to fall on a relative basis. As a result, the taxable wage base for social insurance does not grow as expected, thus forcing an even greater increase in implicit government debt.

The economy is, again, similar to a patient after a morphine shot—no pain is felt (that is, no signals are given to economic decision-makers). But there is no greater disease that needs to be cured to justify the morphine shot. In fact, this addiction to economic painkillers may be the disease that hinders economic growth. If we can get just an additional 3% of growth over the next generation's work life, we will more than double the final gross domestic product.

The labor force expenditure dependency ratio model is particularly troubling. It is simply impossible that the factors of youth and elderly dependency will remain constant at their proposed levels of 1.7 and 4.244, respectively. What Mr. Brown calculates is merely a first-order approximation—it is undoubtedly useful but cannot and should not be used as a basis for public policy. Further study is needed.

Finally, there are incentives. Paygo participants face amazingly twisted incentives. They are often penalized for working while in retirement. They benefit from a relatively short work life with high earnings (it makes even more sense to obtain a professional degree in a country with a paygo system). Social support structures are needed less. Family structure is needed less. Incentives to save and to control one's one destiny are lessened.

4. The Specter of Privatization and the False Dichotomies

Mr. Brown's paper contains an extensive list of disadvantages of privatization and advantages of paygo schemes. This intricate reasoning is, however, built on a central false premise: that there is a dichotomy between fully funding and paygo. As we have stated above, such dichotomy is mythical. The defining characteristic of a paygo scheme is: *Paygo is a nationalized enterprise involved in the retirement and disability provision business.* Privatization, among others, does not involve prefunding because paygo is prefunded—with implicit (off balance sheet) private placement government bonds, backed by government's ability to collect future payroll taxes. Neither is any "fallacious composition" proposed in privatization. The main claim of privatization is not that fully funded schemes are more secure; it is rather that efficient delivery of price signals in a private system ensures more robust economic growth. No more, no less. Mr. Brown debates an illusory opponent.

The list of advantages of paygo is flawed. Let us discuss that:

- "The entire working population can be covered relatively easily." A mandatory private system ensures just that. Clearly, universal coverage is a major public policy issue, but this does not justify nationalization.
- "Benefits can be immediately vested and are fully portable." This problem of private systems actually indicates lack of imagination on the part of legislatures and public-policy scholars. Most certainly, personal defined-contribution schemes have this property, and to extend it to defined-benefit plans requires just that—innovative scholarly and legislative work. Alas, high government debt levels have caused returns to labor to fall so much that we are too busy making ends meet instead of thinking our way out of the box.
- "Administrative costs are usually very low per unit of cash flow." They are in the same range as private defined-benefit plans in Canada (as claimed by Ken Ambachsteer at the recent Fraser Institute conference). In addition, government-run system costs are low because governments do not count costs that private institutions must count, such as:
  — Management costs, which are bundled into the costs of legislature work, elections, and related items
  — Advertisement costs, which are bundled into various government programs, public policy debate, and same as management
  — Marketing costs, which are transferred onto employers and judicial system.
  The question of whether these costs are higher than the opportunity lost because of capital misallocation is of course a different story. Finally, the burden of increasing implicit government debt created by paygo is passed onto labor, resulting in the current "economically anxious society."
- "Fully funded schemes are susceptible to erosion by inflation." This is an amazing argument: you should entrust the provision of retirement to the government because if you use the private sector, the government may confiscate your benefits. Inflation is not a random phenomenon, but entirely a product of irresponsible monetary policy. Are we really to believe that a government that promotes irresponsible monetary policy will be responsible when running a paygo scheme? The experience of Latin American countries clearly indicates the opposite. On the other hand, capital markets *must* deliver long-term returns above inflation; they really do not have a choice in that matter.
- "Government control of the large amounts of capital accumulating under a fully funded scheme is a concern." Naturally it is. This is why

government moves that capital off balance sheet in a paygo scheme. This is not an argument against privatization but for it.

- "Who will decide how to invest this capital?" Who decides how a private defined-benefit plan invests its capital? Who decides how mutual funds invest their capital?

- "With a large accumulation of assets, continuous pressure will exist to enhance benefits." Not in a private system. Mr. Brown apparently envisions something that simply does not exist and should never exist—a government-run national "pension plan" valued on a closed-group basis. This has nothing to do with privatization, is highly recessionary, and should be firmly opposed (as Mr. Brown rightfully does). Again, the position of Mr. Brown's opponents is misrepresented.

- "In any transition from paygo financing to full funding, one generation of workers will have to pay almost double contributions. ..." This is the most persistent myth among proponents of paygo; it is entirely false. The liabilities are already issued (off balance sheet). Thus privatization cannot add to their cost; it merely reallocates capital. Nobody is asking one generation to both prefund its benefits in full and also pay, for example, the $550 billion C/QPP unfunded liability. The only time a double payment happens is at the onset of paygo. In the investment terminology, Mr. Brown confuses earnings with cash flows. In privatization, one cash flow (savings of the working group) will achieve both purposes: funding of the future retirement of the current working group and financing of the current retirees. Or are we to believe that a mutual fund receiving contributions from its shareholders puts the money in a vault instead of using it for its current cash flows? Are banks warehouses of cash? Are pension plans warehouses of cash?

5. Conclusions

As much as I find disagreement with Mr. Brown's analysis, I do find myself in strong agreement with some of his conclusions. He says: "Beware demands to expand paygo social security." As I have indicated above, the paygo scheme is an analogue of price controls in capital markets. Let us examine the consequences of price controls. If the government decides that the price of oil is not allowed to exceed $25 per barrel, such control would probably have very little effect on our lives. If, however, this was followed by an event similar to the 1990 Iraqi invasion of Kuwait and prices rising to $40 per barrel in the open market, our ability to transport people and goods would diminish very rapidly, and the whole country might be brought to a serious recession—without any real reason for that to happen! All we would need would be a removal of price controls, or at least raising of the ceiling to $50. The last thing we would need would be an expansion of price controls!

Similarly, the economy is expected to deliver large amounts of benefits to future retired baby boomers. But those baby boomers do not think that they need to save appropriate amounts of capital to be used in funding productive capacities that will deliver goods and services in the future to them. In other words, baby boomers want to buy oil for $10 a barrel when the market price is $15, and if they can't, the government must help them! This is a dream world and it cannot last. Mr. Brown says we should tell the boomers to retire later. Of course this is a good idea, but what if they vote against it? Precisely because retirement provision is partly nationalized, they can. What they should be doing instead is projecting returns on their retirement portfolios in the range of 3%–5% annually, then really worrying, driving their BMWs for at least ten years, and saving.

We do believe they eventually will. But the longer we wait before delivering true economic signals to them, the more likely that they will need shock therapy.

By the way, Mr. Brown's claim that "once paygo is introduced, it is almost impossible to return to a funded scheme" (I presume this means private enterprise system) is not true. This was easily accomplished in one day: May 1, 1981, in Chile.

REFERENCES

1. BROWN, WILLIAM S. *Principles of Economics*, West Publishing Company, St. Paul, Minn., 1995.
2. KOTLIKOFF, LAURENCE J. *Generational Accounting: Knowing Who Pays, & When, for What We Spend.* New York, N.Y.: The Free Press, 1992.
3. KOTLIKOFF, LAURENCE J. "Social Security." In *The New Palgrave Dictionary of Money and Finance.* London: Macmillan Press and New York, N.Y.: Stockton Press 1992, pp. 479–84.
4. WORLD BANK. *Averting the Old Age Crisis.* Cambridge: Oxford University Press, 1994.

DAVID J. MERKEL:

Mr. Brown's paper succinctly answers a tough problem: how to fund social security when the baby boomers retire. He highlights two often ignored factors:

(1) Retired people are always supported by people who are working. How to get the money from the workers to the retirees, the funding mechanism, is a secondary question. On that question, paygo funding has a few advantages, ably pointed out in the article, and some disadvantages.

(2) The most politically feasible way of funding retirement benefits in a world with fewer workers and more retirees is to correct the imbalance by raising the retirement age. It's common sense. No matter what the leadership of the AARP and their confederates in other nations may say, we all know that we are living longer, so working longer makes sense.

By ranging beyond the usual grazing grounds of actuaries into the field of politics, Mr. Brown has made a significant contribution. He needs to be even more adventuresome and chew on the meaning of "equitable" and the role of families in intergenerational support.

A basic purpose of families for centuries was to care for their aged members. Parents raised children in the expectation that their children would support them in their old age. Over the past 100 years support of children for their parents has been socialized and nationalized, in private pension programs, in group health insurance, and in social security plans. The price for collective security has been weakened families, held together today only by affective ties. Parents have no economic incentive to bear children. Children are national economic assets, but they are family economic liabilities. Families making rational economic decisions have fewer and fewer children, so funding for social security becomes a problem. In fact, only if families continue to act in ways that are economically irrational will there continue to be workers to support retirees. Social security is on a collision course with itself.

Collective safety nets, including social security, weaken families in a second way. They reduce the rational economic incentive for marriage and thus contribute to the increase in one-parent families. Children, however, need two parents to thrive. Our society has a growing number of children so neglected at home that the schools can do little with them. Unskilled and unmotivated workers will not support retirees. Social security is on a collision course with itself.

Now the issue of "equitable." Does any generation in aggregate have an intergenerational equity right? Why should parents who took the time and trouble and expense to raise children share the fruits of their (children's) labor with other old people who had no children of their own? Without grounding in a general system of ethics, the notion of "equity" is a manipulable quantity. What a temptation for politicians to use the idea of "equity" to garner votes from a huge baby-boomer voting block when the time comes, to demand "equal" support to what a previous generation got.

Consideration of the need to give parents the economic incentive to marry and bear children and of the slippery nature of "equity" in collective and intergenerational matters suggests that more serious attention should be given to individualizing retirement plans. Any new plan must satisfy three constraints. First, it must be a system that can work in good and bad economic times. Second, it must recognize and encourage the abiding importance of families to society. Third, the transition to the new system must be slow.

Because any aggregate social insurance system ruins familial economic incentives, thus harming society and ultimately the social insurance systems, the ideal social insurance system is entirely private. Beyond eliminating government social programs, this also would involve eliminating distortions in the tax code encouraging employer-sponsored health and pension plans.

In this new system, the elderly would live off their savings, pensions, and continued labor. To the extent that those are inadequate, their children, churches, and private charities would care for them. Laws would have to be placed on the books entitling parents to a reasonable share of the productivity of their children, if they needed it. This would be an incentive for parents to help their children become productive. Some people, due to negative providence or lack of planning will not fare well under such a system. It is not possible for any social system to be perfect; some people fall through the cracks in any system. This system leads to healthier families and therefore a better long-term economy than any other; that should be enough to urge its adoption.

A system like this takes time to implement. One cannot spring it overnight on unprepared people. Old promises must be kept, while phasing in the ability to keep new ones. It would have to be graded in over time. Here is an example, admittedly oversimplified, of how a transition might work:

From the time the new system is adopted, children born would be exempt from paying taxes into the system. Taxes would continue on all others. The new system would look like the old system for the first 35 years because tax losses would be small. During the second 35 years, taxes would cover those who had not had children in the first 35 years, while those who had children would gain residual support from them. As taxes waned in the second period, benefits would be focused on those who are poor, with no children. Most of those who were children when the system was changed would have children to aid them. The rest would have saved the money they would have spent on children, if they were provident. After 70 years, the system would effectively be private.[1] This could terminate a paygo system without any additional cost.

Finally, we have to confront the fact that total economic security is not achievable. As people have lost their faith in God, they have placed it in the largest entity that they can envision for their support: the government. As the Eastern bloc and Latin America have learned, the ability of the state to provide a safety net is no better than the economies of their nations (which, in turn, depend upon God and His blessing). Various nations in the West are now staring the same problem in the face. The question is, "Will we learn from their collectivist mistakes?" In the short term, we can if we use the smaller institutions of our society—families, churches, and private charities—to a fuller extent. In the long term, I believe we can only if we as a society return to faith in God.[2]

GREGORY SAVORD:

I commend the author on such an intriguing paper on the funding of social security pensions. This topic is of intense interest to the general public. We need intelligent discussion and public education. This paper is a fine addition to this discussion.

The author has made clear that the pensions of retirees are a transfer of income from current workers—even if the system is fully funded. Pension benefits of retirees are only as secure as the creation of economic wealth and increasing economic output. As frightening as it may be, this also applies to private pensions. The public must be educated on this fact so that public debate on social security and pensions addresses the fundamental problem. If a large portion of the population is retired and the remaining workers do not substantially increase their real economic output, the

---

[1]As an innovative alternative to this system, I would recommend John S. Agatston's paper, *"A Promising Future; A Proposal for Avoiding the Coming Crisis in Social Security,"* 1988, available from him at his *Directory* address.

[2]To avoid ambiguity, by "God" I mean the God described by the Bible—the Father, the Son, and the Holy Spirit.

economy cannot support the expected standard of living for both retirees and workers. Even if the fundamental issue is not addressed, symptoms of the problem will continue to appear. Actuaries should be on the forefront in the public analysis and discussion of this issue.

The author states that, currently, a relatively large number of workers are supporting a relatively small number of retirees. Consequently, the workers make a modest contribution to provide generous pension benefits. When the number of retirees becomes relatively larger, the workers would need to make larger contributions or the retirees would receive lower benefits. The author proposes to have workers, who make a modest contribution supporting a small number of retirees, receive a smaller pension benefit when they are supported by a smaller number of workers. The smaller pension benefits would be consistent with the actual contributions made by these retirees when they were working. The smaller number of future workers would contribute more to support the large cohort of retirees, but in turn these future workers would receive larger pension benefits in return for their greater contributions. This suggests that the work force would have to expand to support these distant-future retirees. The author's proposal implies that the population distributions will continue to be cyclic. However, if the population distribution continues to decline into the distant future, as many expect it will, this proposal will fail. Readers should thus be aware that this proposal is not guaranteed to work.

The author correctly states that we are beginning to see the implementation of his proposal in the political arena. The pension benefits of future retirees are being reduced, notably by delaying the retirement age. We will continue to see this adjustment activity, even if the author's proposal is never formally adopted or even recognized.

Again, I congratulate the author on his fine addition to the actuarial literature.

ROBERT J. MYERS:

Mr. Brown has contributed a monumental paper to the field of social-insurance-financing literature. One reason that I say this is that I agree so thoroughly that paygo funding is, by far, the best route for social insurance programs. I also agree that the solution to any long-range financing problems that are due to demographic causes (aging of the population and increasing longevity) should be solved by demographic means (raising the minimum age at which unreduced benefits are first payable). Yet another reason for paygo funding is that any problems on how to invest properly the mammoth sums developing under partial or full funding are thereby avoided.

In Figure 3, Mr. Brown shows the aged dependency ratios for Canada over the years on the basis of the ratio of the population aged 65 and over to that aged 18–64. It would be interesting—and perhaps even more significant—to present such ratios on a dynamic basis, as well as on a static basis, for the minimum retirement age, that is, to use for each future year the equivalent age at retirement as shown in Table 4 (or, alternatively, that from the age-at-entitlement model described in the Conclusions) as the "border" instead of age 65 in all years.

(AUTHOR'S REVIEW OF DISCUSSIONS)

ROBERT L. BROWN:

I am very pleased with the extent of the response to my paygo paper, both in terms of the number of discussants and in terms of the wide variety of content of their discussions.

Any student of social security who thought that this was a dull or straight-forward area of study would know better after reading the diversity of responses. Issues surrounding the funding of social security are subtle and extremely difficult to grasp. Further, because any social security system is economically massive by nature, any proposed modifications have to be analyzed allowing for behavioural response (or the rational expectation school of Nobel Prize-winner Robert Lucas). This is extremely difficult, especially, I believe, for actuaries.

That being said, there are some fundamental truths that can be used as building blocks.

Social security is a means to transfer wealth from workers to retirees (ignoring ancillary benefits for the disabled, orphans, and so on). The wealth that is transferred must be created by someone (that is, workers) and it must be created (with very few exceptions) just prior to consumption.

Thus, whether called pay-as-you-go or fully funded or anything in between, *any* social security plan is dependent on the wealth that the economy creates at the time the system wishes to divide up that wealth.

Therefore, the whole discussion about the advantages and disadvantages of funding is often inappropriate. Funded systems are no more stable or unstable than paygo (which would you rather predict: interest rates, fertility rates, or growth in productivity rates?).

Funded systems are not demographically immune. They will suffer from shifting demographics as much as paygo plans.

Finally, it is inappropriate to say: "Right now we have high real interest rates and low productivity growth rates, so paygo looks bad while funding looks wise. So let's create social security funds of some several trillions of dollars, invest them wisely, and live happily ever after."

Why is this inappropriate?

If you truly create several trillions of dollars of new national savings and invest the money prudently, two things must inevitably result. First, real rates of return will fall, and second, productivity growth rates will rise. By the end of the process, you could easily be arguing for paygo funding once again.

Now to answer some specific points raised in the discussion.

George Watson gives us his personal view of the implementation of the Canada/Quebec Pension Plans in 1966. While there was a significant gift to Mr. Watson's generation by the government of the day in granting full pensions after only 10 years, there was nothing inherently wrong with the adoption of paygo financing. In fact, the rates of growth of the labor force and productivity versus the real rates of interest of the day made it a clear winner versus prefunding. I do not believe that the C/QPP has suffered from neglect. It has suffered from severe and unpredictable changes in fertility rates and productivity growth rates. I agree that we must control the cost of the disability income benefits, and there is early evidence of some success on that front. I would also add that the work done by the valuation actuary is of the highest quality and has always provided us with indications of problems at least 25 years in advance.

Next is Bernard Dussault, who is that high-quality CPP valuation actuary. The funding ratios for paygo plans result from fertility, mortality and productivity. If life expectancy improves, there are ways to get funding stability—increased contributions or an increased retirement age. Sweden has now made its social security system immune to life expectancy by saying that the social security dollar benefits will (rise and) fall exactly with life expectancy.

Were that provision to exist in the CPP, then the normal retirement age from my model would rise for the baby boomers and fall for the baby busters. The fact that the age of eligibility is not expected to fall very much (if at all) for the baby busters is because of their enhanced life expectancy. That is fair.

Mr. Dussault goes on to say that a funded system is recognized as the "most cost-equitable self-adjusting approach." By whom? Why? He further states that a funded CPP would cost less than a paygo CPP. But that is only if his other static assumptions (for example, 4% real return and low productivity growth) hold constant. As I have said, that assumption is virtually impossible.

Kenneth Steiner proposes that the best way to achieve intergenerational equity is to make sure every generation gets the same rate of return on contributions. That may appear a laudable goal. However, social security is not a bank account; it is a wealth transfer scheme. What must be stabilized therefore is the ratio of wealth created and wealth transfered. My model does exactly that.

Finally Mr. Steiner says that I "felt obligated to attack the actuarial full funding straw man that I created." At first I thought that Mr. Steiner referred to funding as a straw man because he realized that funding does not avoid the demographic problems facing social security at all. But no, that is not the case. Mr. Steiner says advance funding can be used to level out the tax rate. Why would this happen? Wouldn't shifting the normal retirement age appropriately in a fully mature social security system (which the CPP is not) level out tax rates more effectively than advance funding? There is no explanation for Mr. Steiner's claim.

Finally, if prefunding of social security is just a straw man of my creation, why is it on the public policy agenda in both Washington and Ottawa?

Jock Maynard makes similar unsupported claims that advance funding, in and of itself, will lead to more stable contribution rates. Of course, anyone could jack up the C/QPP contribution rate well above the necessary paygo rate and then keep that higher rate constant for an extended period. That forced stability of high contribution rates results in advance funding. However, advance funding does not create stable contribution rates. These rates vary with real interest rates, which can be as variable as fertility and/or productivity.

Mr. Maynard claims that if there were a prolonged economic depression in which incomes were reduced (lowering contributions to social security), a fully funded social security pension could continue unabated without strain on other resources. That is just not true. Whether funded or not, social security is a transfer of national product—today's national product. If there is no national product, there will be no social security benefits (whether funded or paygo). If there is a healthy economy, there will be healthy social security benefits (whether funded or paygo). Social security is not a large private pension scheme. Advance funded social security is no more secure from demographic changes than is a paygo plan. Nor is it inherently any more stable, as discussed previously. In social security, individuals do not provide for their own benefits. That is impossible unless we can find a way to store restaurant meals and similar services for several decades.

Krzysztof Ostaszewski has again challenged me with his capital-market arguments. At least we agree that there is little fundamental difference between paygo and funded plans, even if our reasons are different. Krzys (and Laurence Kotlikoff to whom Krzys refers) argues that capital markets would have priced the actuarial liability of social security into interest rates on the day of its enactment. However, between 1958 and 1967 Canada enacted universal health care, the Canada/Quebec Pension Plans, the Guaranteed Income Supplement, the Spousal Pension Allowance, the significant increases to the Old Age Security without a tick of a change in interest rates. How is that explained?

Krzys is correct that there will be a behavioral response to any public policy initiative and that many of the ratios that I hold constant cannot be assumed to stay constant. I acknowledge that, but I do not have a way to do it better. If I wish to see the impact of a change in variable x, I am prone to do the analysis holding everything else constant, even though I know that cannot be true. However, I will stand by my one-variable analysis any day if compared to the "57"-variable economic models that are often created in an attempt to solve this very real stochastic problem.

In closing, Krzys states that Chile's social security system was privatized on one day, May 1, 1981. I disagree. Chilean retirees are still dependent on the taxpayer/worker for the unfunded actuarial liability of social security as at May 1, 1981 which is a significant percentage of their benefit cash flow. Second, more than one-third of the new "privatized" system is "invested" in government bonds. So more than one-third of the new system is not private at all, but dependent on the worker/taxpayer as surely as before. It will take several decades before Chile's system can be called private, if ever.

David Merkel tells us that social security has harmed society through weakened families who now have fewer children. How do the lower birth rates of the pre-social-security 1930s fit into this thesis?

Mr. Merkel says people should be totally dependent on what they make by themselves (including children) and charity. Some will suffer, but so be it.

My personal religious beliefs do not coincide with a wealthy society that does not share. I like a little collectivism, if it means that everyone can be fed, housed, clothed, and educated. A caring society is also a peaceful society, as Canadian and Scandinavian experience indicates to me. So I will continue to support the collectivism inherent in social security.

Gregory Savord says that if fertility rates continue to drop, the baby-bust generation will never see the larger benefits my model promises them. He is correct. However, we cannot continue forever with fertility rates below replacement ratios. Either through a turnaround in fertility (already apparent in the U.S.) or immigration or increased worker productivity, I believe the baby-bust generation can expect a fair deal from social security. Unfortunately, Mr. Savord and I will probably not live long enough to know the final outcome.

I greatly appreciated the kind words of Bob Myers, one of the actuarial architects of OASDI. Mr. Myers has been a supportive ally in much of my work.

He suggests redoing the aged dependency ratios of Figure 3 by using my suggested age-of-entitlement model. I believe the result is highly predictable. The important matter to me is that wealth transfer remain constant. I derived my future age of entitlement by determining the age that produced a constant wealth transfer. In the population models, for years beyond 2006, the fertility variable and the unemployment variable are held constant. Thus, I would predict a new "aged" dependency ratio that would be very nearly flat as its 2006 level. Of course "aged" would not be defined by age 65, but by the new age of entitlement. If time premits I will attempt this analysis for Mr. Myers, but that is what I would expect.

As I stated at the outset, the study of social security funding is complex and subtle. Large-pension-plan truths are often social-security-plan fallacies. I have been studying these matters for 25 years now and am still on the upward slope of the learning curve. The discussion from the eight authors has greatly enhanced my knowledge as I hope it has yours. I thank the discussants most sincerely.

GRADUATION BY KERNEL
AND ADAPTIVE KERNEL METHODS
WITH A BOUNDARY CORRECTION*

JOHN GAVIN[†], STEVEN HABERMAN, AND RICHARD VERRALL[‡]

ABSTRACT

This paper explores the flexibility of kernel estimation as a means of nonparametric graduation and relates it to moving-weighted-average graduation. Our primary objective is to focus attention on a model that makes explicit allowance for the variation in exposure over age. We also consider various transformations of the data, cross-validation as an objective method for choosing the smoothing parameter, and diagnostic methods for checking assumptions. A kernel function for improving the estimate at a boundary is discussed, and the results are applied to two mortality tables.

---

1. INTRODUCTION

Sets of mortality rates, in the form of mortality tables, are widely used by actuaries to calculate life insurance premiums, annuities, reserves, and so on. Producing these tables from a suitable set of crude (or raw) mortality rates is called graduation, and this subject has been extensively discussed in the actuarial literature. To be specific, given a set of crude mortality rates, $\mathring{q}_i$, for each age x_i, we wish to systematically revise these initial estimates to produce smoother estimates, $\hat{q}_i$, of the true but unknown mortality rates, q_i, where $i = 1, \ldots, n$. The crude rate at age x_i is typically based on the number of deaths recorded, d_i, relative to the number of policy-years or person-years initially exposed to the risk of death, e_i, for a homogeneous cohort over a certain time interval. By reducing the unit of time from a year, we could alternatively consider the instantaneous rate of mortality, which is called the force of mortality, also known as the hazard or intensity rate in survival analysis. Intuition and practical convenience lead us to believe that a smooth sequence of graduated rates will more closely reflect the variation

*Supported by the U.K. Engineering and Physical Sciences Research Council.

†John Gavin, not a member of the Society, is a research student, School of Mathematics, University of Bath, England.

‡Richard Verrall, not a member of the Society, is a Senior Lecturer in the Department of Actuarial Science and Statistics at City University, London, England.

due to age in the unknown, true rates of mortality compared to the crude rates. Some nonparametric models reflect this belief by allowing the amount of smoothing to vary over a continuous range.

There are a variety of possible uses of nonparametric methods. A larger class of possible regression surfaces can be considered, reflecting the possibility that the graduated rates may not follow a neat parametric formula. We can use a nonparametric approach to choose the simplest suitable parametric model, to provide a diagnostic check of a parametric model, or to simply explore the data. The power of modern computers and software has made nonparametric smoothing more feasible and consequently more popular. Some of the more popular statistical methods are nearest-neighbor smoothing [12], spline-smoothing [26], [56], and kernel-smoothing, which is discussed in this paper. Kernel-smoothing is not new. For a scatter plot of bivariate data, X and Y, Watson [59] suggests estimating the conditional mean $E(Y|X)$ from nonparametric kernel estimates of the joint density of X and Y and the marginal density of X. Kernel smoothers are also suggested by Nadaraya [47]. Scott [54] offers an introduction to kernel density estimation and regression.

A mortality table can be viewed as a bivariate scatter plot of mortality against age, in which the true mortality rates can be estimated from the mean regression function by using kernel estimators. Although age is a continuous variable, it is typically truncated in some way, such as age last birthday. Thus, the data consist of e_i observations at age x_i, of which d_i die and $e_i - d_i$ survive. Given the discretized nature of a mortality table, it is natural to pool the data by using the average d_i / e_i at each age. This reduces the computational burden and leads to a fixed design model, in which we have a single observed mortality rate at equally spaced ages. In later sections of this paper, we consider how to adjust the model to reflect the amount of exposure at each age. Because the data may not have a constant variance, we may need to consider transforming it to satisfy the model, which is

$$\dot{q}_i^t = q_i^t + r_i, \qquad \text{for } i = 1, \ldots, n, \tag{1}$$

where t denotes some transformation and the residuals r_i are assumed to be independently, identically distributed random variables, with zero mean and a constant, finite variance. We need to ensure that these assumptions are reflected in the data and, if not, to make appropriate adjustments. Although $\dot{q}_i^t$ is treated as a random variable, we adopt the standard actuarial notation for mortality by using a lowercase letter. Once the graduation process is complete, the transformation is reversed to obtain the graduated rates on the original scale.

The Nadaraya-Watson kernel estimator of the true mortality rate is

$$\hat{q}_i^t = \frac{\sum_{j=1}^{n} \dot{q}_j^t \, K_b(x_i - x_j)}{\sum_{j=1}^{n} K_b(x_i - x_j)}, \qquad \text{for } i = 1, \ldots, n. \tag{2}$$

For convenience, $K_b(x) \equiv b^{-1} K(x/b)$ is used throughout. The function K, called a kernel function, is any function for which $\int_{-\infty}^{\infty} K(x)dx = 1$; thus, any probability density function is a kernel function. Frequently, but not always, kernel functions are non-negative, $K(x) \geq 0$. A common example is the standardized normal or Gaussian kernel

$$K^N(x) = (2\pi)^{-1/2} \exp\{-x^2/2\} = \phi(x), \qquad \text{for } -\infty < x < \infty. \tag{3}$$

The bandwidth b acts as a smoothing parameter. Choosing a small bandwidth means that only nearby points are influential; choosing a large bandwidth means that information is averaged over a larger region, and consequently individual points have less influence on our estimate. At the point at which estimation is to take place, x_i, we first use the kernel function, K, and the bandwidth, b, to decide which of our n observations lie nearby; then we fit a constant to these points by averaging. This is our estimate of the curve at x_i.

Ramlau-Hansen [49] discusses the motivation for using this estimator to calculate mortality rates, and its advantages over a related estimator used by Copas and Haberman [16] and by Bloomfield and Haberman [4] are discussed by Gavin, Haberman, and Verrall [25]. It is also the estimator used in this paper, but there are other well-known kernel regression estimators in the statistical literature [43]. A well-known rival to the Nadaraya-Watson estimator is an integral-based estimator due to Gasser and Müller [23]. All kernel estimators have their relative advantages, and which is more suitable for graduation is currently an open question. The recent paper by Chu and Marron [11] comparing the Nadaraya-Watson and Gasser-Müller estimators is highly recommended. We provide a detailed list of references with the aim of generating a greater interest in the application of kernel estimation, and nonparametric methods in general, in actuarial science. However, this has been an active area of research in recent years, so our bibliography is not complete.

Kernel graduation is very similar to moving- (or local) weighted-average graduation (MWA), which is applied to equally spaced observations such as mortality rates or time series. The traditional problem with MWA is that it does not produce smoothed values at the ends of the table. However, in recent years this problem has been addressed in a series of papers by Greville [28], [29], [30] and also by Hoem and Linnemann [39]. In addition, London [45] and Ramsay [50] consider relaxing the assumption of constant variance in an MWA graduation. The kernel estimator in Equation (2) can be viewed as a continuous form of MWA graduation by expressing it as

$$\hat{q}_i^t = \sum_{j=1}^n S_{ij} \, \dot{q}_j^t, \qquad \text{where} \qquad S_{ij} = \frac{K_b(x_i - x_j)}{\sum_{j=1}^n K_b(x_i - x_j)}, \qquad (4)$$

so that $\sum_{j=1}^n S_{ij} = 1$. This suggests that kernel graduation is very similar to MWA graduation. Although Equation (4) produces graduated rates at the ends of the table, we need to consider the properties of the estimator in those regions. Also, kernel graduation is not restricted to equally spaced crude rates, and it can be used to interpolate the mortality rate between the ages for which we have crude rates. In this way, it reflects the fact that age is a continuous variable, whereas MWA treats age as being discrete. However, unequally spaced observations may result in an increase in bias in the Nadaraya-Watson estimator, depending on the distribution of the observed data and on the curvature of the true mortality curve (Chu and Marron [11], Gavin et al [25]). Another contrast with MWA is that the bandwidth parameter in kernel graduation can be varied continuously, whereas the range of a MWA graduation is varied discretely.

It can be shown that the Nadaraya-Watson estimator leads to biased estimates of the true mortality rate [54]. However, the increase in bias leads to a reduction in variance, and so a trade-off between the two can be made through the bandwidth. This governs the amount of smoothing in the graduation process, in a continuous manner. The value for b may be a subjective choice, or it may be chosen as a function of the data. Too large a value for the bandwidth produces a smooth set of graduated rates at a cost of a lack of fidelity to the data. If the bandwidth is too small, then the converse is true. Cross-validation is one method for choosing an objective value for the bandwidth, and it is defined in Section 2.3. In the related problem of density estimation, Scott [54] discusses various other ways of selecting a value for the bandwidth. One disadvantage of Equation (2) is that the bias increases near the ends of the mortality table. This problem is addressed in Section 3. Notice that the bandwidth in Equation (2) is fixed across the entire age range. A more general approach is to allow the bandwidth to vary with age. For example, the bandwidth could be inversely related to the sample size for that age; this leads to a variable or adaptive kernel estimator, which is the main topic of this paper.

The paper is set out as follows: Section 2 discusses the basic ideas needed for kernel graduation; Section 3 describes a method for improving the Nadaraya-Watson estimator near a boundary; Section 4 defines and discusses more general adaptive kernel estimators that allow the bandwidth to vary with age; two mortality tables are considered in Section 5; and finally we summarize our conclusions in Section 6.

2. KERNEL GRADUATION

We start by considering transformations of the data. Thereafter the graduation process is carried out on the transformed scale before back-transforming is used to obtain the graduated rates. In Section 2.2, we discuss the graduation process in detail and in Section 2.4 provide an illustration. Also in this section, we briefly consider the use of diagnostic tests, standard tables, duplicate policies, and measures of smoothness.

2.1 Transforming Mortality Data

Before the model is applied, a key part of any data analysis is to consider transforming the data into a more tractable form that reflects the strengths of the model or that more clearly reveals the structure of the data. In parametric graduation, for example, it may be easier to transform the data and work with a linear model than to graduate the raw rates using a more mathematically demanding nonlinear model. The same philosophy applies in nonparametric graduation. In this section, we consider transforming the crude rates before graduating and then back-transforming to obtain our estimate of the true rates.

Several transformations were considered, such as taking logs of the mortality rates and ages separately and combined and using the logit, Weibull, Gompertz, and $\sin^{-1} (\sqrt{\dot{q}_i})$ transformations. For example, if the transformed crude rates broadly follow a straight line, then this may lead to reduced bias over much of the age range, if the data are also evenly spaced. We consider this effect in more detail in Section 3. Because of the relatively large differences in mortality rates across the age range, the transformed data also result in a more evenly spread scatter plot. In this case, we are aiming to ensure that the residuals in Equation (1) have a constant variance. Nielsen [48] offers a decision theoretic approach to bias reduction via transformations.

From Equation (1), $E(\dot{q}_i|x_i)$ is the expected proportion of lives aged x_i who died during the period of investigation. A commonly used transformation, t, in binary analysis is the logit (or log-odds) transformation. For our application, we have

$$\dot{q}_i^t = \ln \frac{\dot{q}_i}{(1 - \dot{q}_i)}$$

with back-transform

$$\hat{q}_i = \frac{\exp\left\{\sum_{j=1}^{n} S_{ij}\, \dot{q}_j^t\right\}}{1 + \exp\left\{\sum_{j=1}^{n} S_{ij}\, \dot{q}_j^t\right\}},$$

for $i=1, \ldots, n$. By smoothing on a logistic scale and then back-transforming, we are guaranteed that $0 \leq \hat{q}_i \leq 1$. This transformation also reflects the fact that small changes when the mortality rate is near zero are as important as larger changes when the mortality rate is much higher. Renshaw [51] provides further motivation for this transformation, based on the theory of generalized linear models. Note that binary data are often assumed to be independent, but this may not be the case for mortality data due to migration between ages during the period of investigation. This leads us to look for smooth relations between neighboring rates by merging information from individuals with similar ages.

For the Gompertz transformation, we fit $\ln(-\ln(1-\dot{q}_i))$ to x_i, and for the Weibull, we fit $\ln(-\ln(1-\dot{q}_i))$ to $\ln(x_i)$, where $i=1, \ldots, n$. Now the x-axis no longer has evenly spaced observations, but this does not present any computational problem for the kernel method, unlike the related MWA graduation. However, this transformation will induce some bias when we fit a local constant because more of the observations will now lie in the interval (x_i, x_i+b) than in (x_i-b, x_i) [25].

Many other transformations are possible ([9], [17], [18]), but their relative merits are beyond the scope of this paper. Overall, the choice of transformation remains subjective, and the relative success of a particular transformation seems to depend on the data set. For the examples in Section 5, we have chosen the logit transformation.

2.1.1 Crude Rates with No Deaths

One potential problem with transformations that involve taking logs is that the transformed crude rate is not defined for ages at which no deaths are recorded, $d_i=0$. This often happens at older ages, with small data sets. A solution applicable to any transformation is to group together ages for which there are relatively few deaths. The cumulative number of deaths and amount of exposure for the group could be attributed to the midpoint of the group [4].

2.2 Building a Smoother

One way of implementing the Nadaraya-Watson estimator, given in Equation (2), is to place a kernel function at the point for which we wish to estimate the true rate of mortality and then form a weighted average over all the crude rates, where the weight attached to each crude rate is the value of the kernel function at that age.

The kernel has the same basic shape at each age x_i. Let the weight attached to the point x_j to estimate the true curve at x_i be denoted by $S_{ij}=cK_b(x_i-x_j)$, where $c^{-1}=\Sigma_{j=1}^n K_b(x_i-x_j)$ is a normalizing constant. This gives the $1 \times n$ matrix of weights needed to estimate the true value of the curve at x_i. By sliding the kernel function along the x-axis and centering it at every point for which we wish to estimate the mortality curve, we can build up a matrix $S=\{S_{ij}; j=1, ..., n\}$. The i-th row of the matrix contains the n weights allocated to the transformed crude rates, to estimate the true mortality rate at that age. The matrix has a row for every point at which we wish to estimate the true curve. Without loss of generality, we constrain the set of estimated ages to be the same as the set of observed ages, because this is often the case for mortality data. This gives an $n \times n$ matrix of weights that we call a *smoother* matrix (or a *hat* matrix). To help produce smooth graduated rates, we use weights that decrease smoothly towards zero as $|x_i-x_j|$ increases. So if we let $\dot{q}'$ be the n-dimensional vector of transformed crude rates and $\hat{q}'$ be the vector of transformed graduated rates, then the smoother S defines the relationship between them as

$$\hat{q}' = S\dot{q}',$$

where S has been renormalized as in Equation (4), so that $\Sigma_{j=1}^n S_{ij}=1$, for $i=1, ..., n$. Thus, the transformation from the crude to the estimated rates is achieved by filtering the crude rates through the smoother. This equation succinctly summarizes kernel graduation. In particular, for the i-th element of $\hat{\mathbf{q}}'$, we get Equation (2). Notice that the kernel smoother is linear (or distributive); that is, $\mathbf{S}(a\mathbf{v}_1 + b\mathbf{v}_2) = a\mathbf{S}\mathbf{v}_1 + b\mathbf{S}\mathbf{v}_2$, for constants a and b and vectors $\mathbf{v}_1$ and $\mathbf{v}_2$. So from Equation (1), if we believe that the transformed crude rates consist of the transformed, unknown true rates $\mathbf{q}$ plus a vector of residuals $\mathbf{r}$, we arrive at $\hat{\mathbf{q}}' = \mathbf{S}\dot{\mathbf{q}}' = \mathbf{S}(\mathbf{q}' + \mathbf{r}) = \mathbf{S}\mathbf{q}' + \mathbf{S}\mathbf{r}$. We believe that by graduating the error term $\mathbf{S}\mathbf{r}$, we reduce it in a way that more than compensates for any induced bias, which we define as the difference between the true and estimated mortality rates on the transformed scale.

Many other nonparametric smoothers are also linear such as the running-mean, running-line, cubic smoothing spline (Whittaker graduation), regression spline, and locally weighted running line, but there are also nonlinear smoothers such as the running median smoother. Hastie and Tibshirani [38, chapters 2 and 3] offers an excellent introduction to nonparametric smoothers, drawing out the similarity between these methods. Verrall [58] views Whittaker graduation as a dynamic generalized linear model.

2.2.1 Choice of Kernel Function

Some kernel functions such as the Epanechnikov kernel [19],

$$K(x) = \begin{cases} 3(1 - x^2)/4, & \text{for } |x| \leq 1; \\ 0 & \text{otherwise,} \end{cases}$$

have greater theoretical justification than others. This particular kernel minimizes the mean squared error asymptotically. Another potential kernel is one that minimizes the variance of the estimated curve, in some sense, and one such kernel is explored in Gavin, Haberman, and Verrall [24]. The current literature indicates that the choice of kernel function is not as influential as the value of the bandwidth. So for convenience, we use the standardized normal kernel defined in Equation (3) throughout this paper. In general, it would be computationally cheaper to use a truncated kernel such as the Epanechnikov kernel.

2.3 Bandwidth Selection

The choice of bandwidth in Equation (2) is important. Although it is informative to choose the bandwidth by trial and error, it is also convenient to have an objective, risk-based method for selecting the best value for b. The literature on data-driven methods for selecting the optimal bandwidth is vast and continues to grow. Cross-validation [57] is just one such method that is commonly used and simple to understand. This technique has been used by Brooks, Stone, Chan, and Chan [7] to smooth some mortality tables using Whittaker graduation, and Gregoire [27] offers a more rigorous approach.

Working on the transformed scale, cross-validation simultaneously fits and smooths the data by removing one data point at a time, estimating the value of the curve at that missing point, and then comparing the estimate to the omitted, observed value. So our cross-validation statistic or score, $CV(b)$, is

$$CV(b) = n^{-1}(\dot{\mathbf{q}}^t - (\hat{\mathbf{q}}^t)^{(-i)})^T (\dot{\mathbf{q}}^t - (\hat{\mathbf{q}}^t)^{(-i)}) = n^{-1} \sum_{i=1}^{n} (\dot{q}_i^t - (\hat{q}_i^t)^{(-i)})^2, \quad (5)$$

where $(\hat{q}_i^t)^{(-i)}$ is the estimated value at age x_i computed by removing the crude rate at that age on the transformed scale. It is sometimes called the jackknifed fit at x_i. It is easy to calculate $(\hat{q}_i^t)^{(-i)}$: set the i-th weight in the i-th row of $\mathbf{S}$ to zero and renormalize the weights. That is,

$$(\hat{q}_i^t)^{(-i)} = \frac{\displaystyle\sum_{\substack{j=1 \\ j \neq i}}^{n} S_{ij}\, \dot{q}_j^t}{(1 - S_{ii})} = \frac{\displaystyle\sum_{\substack{j=1 \\ j \neq i}}^{n} \dot{q}_j^t\, K_b(x_i - x_j)}{\displaystyle\sum_{\substack{j=1 \\ j \neq i}}^{n} K_b(x_i - x_j)}. \quad (6)$$

To further speed computation, we can use the relation $\dot{q}_i^t - (\hat{q}_i^t)^{(-i)} = (\dot{q}_i^t - \hat{q}_i^t)/(1 - S_{ii})$. The bandwidth that minimizes $CV(b)$ is referred to as the cross-validation bandwidth, b_{cv}, and we find it by systematically searching across a suitable bandwidth region. So we need to balance the benefit of getting close to the optimal bandwidth against the cost of a detailed search. Scott [54] suggests that getting to within ± 15 percent often suffices. For convenience, the bandwidth is always selected by cross-validation in this paper, although some evidence suggests that it may undersmooth the data ([32], [34], [53], [54]).

2.4 Example 1

The techniques outlined in Sections 2.2 and 2.3 are illustrated in Figure 1b, which shows a scatter plot of 20 evenly spaced points where $Y \sim \sin(X) + N(0, 0.05)$. No transformation is needed in this simple example.

FIGURE 1

A CURVE IS FITTED TO SOME RAW DATA, USING CROSS-VALIDATION TO SELECT THE SMOOTHING
PARAMETER. THE CROSS-VALIDATION SCORE IS SHOWN IN PLOT A). PLOT B) SHOWS THE RAW DATA,
THE TRUE CURVE AND THE FITTED CURVE. THE WEIGHTS IN THE SMOOTHER MATRIX, S, ARE SHOWN
IN PLOT C).

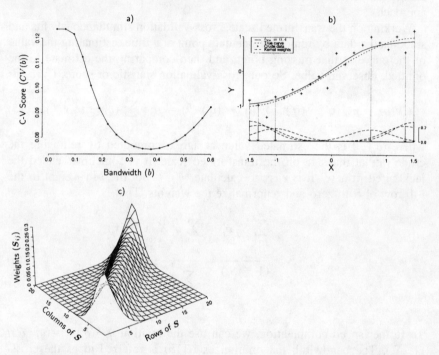

The bandwidth used in Figures 1b and 1c is chosen by cross-validation.
Figure 1a shows the cross-validation scores for about 20 evenly spaced bandwidth values. The optimal cross-validation bandwidth is about $b_{cv}=0.4$. In
Figure 1b, the true curve and the best fit using a normal kernel and the best
cross-validation bandwidth are shown. Six normal kernel functions have
been superimposed on the bottom of this plot to show the relative weights
attached to each of the observed values when estimating the true curve at
the six points indicated by arrows. Each arrow is connected to its corresponding kernel and observed data point. At both ends, the normal kernel
overlaps the boundary, but the denominator in Equation (2) is now summed
over fewer data points, forcing the kernel to rise slightly. This reflects the
fact that we have less information at the boundaries.

The kernel function associated with the i-th point is used to calculate the weights in the i-th row of the 20×20 smoother and is shown in Figure 1c. The weights are shown as the height along the i-th row of the surface. For values in the central region the weights form a normal kernel, but as the point at which we are estimating the true curve moves towards the boundaries the kernel overlaps the boundary. This causes the height of the kernel to increase because fewer observations are available. Notice that all the weights in the smoother are non-negative. For evenly spaced data and a kernel with bounded support, there can be computational savings when the data in the center of the table are estimated, because the denominator in Equation (2) is constant.

2.5 Diagnostic Checks

Having produced graduated rates on the transformed scale, we now consider diagnostic plots of the results to help confirm that the assumptions made by the model, in Equation (1), are valid.

We need to check that the estimator is unbiased with a constant variance. The former assumption means that we require the residuals to have a mean of zero. Plotting the residuals from Equation (1) against the estimated mortality rates on the transformed scale and against age should reveal no clear pattern. One way to check this is to smooth the residuals and get a fairly flat line about zero.

Alternatively, after graduating the crude rates and back-transforming, we can use the mean and variance of the binomial distribution to calculate the standardized deviation between actual and expected deaths,

$$\frac{(d_i - e_i\hat{q}_i)}{\sqrt{e_i\hat{q}_i(1 - \hat{q}_i)}}, \qquad \text{for } i = 1, ..., n, \tag{7}$$

on the grounds that most of the samples at each age are large. We expect this statistic to have a mean of zero and most of the values to be less than two. Note that the distribution may not be normal. If a suitable standard mortality table is available, then we might use that in the denominator of (7).

We also require independent crude rates. One diagnostic check is to examine plots of the estimated autocorrelation of the residuals. To do this, we need equally spaced residuals, so the transformation of the data must be restricted to the mortality rate and not age as well.

Several other diagnostic plots and nonparametric tests could be considered ([2], [13], [21]).

2.6 Reference to a Standard Mortality Table

We may wish to standardize the data relative to a suitable graduated mortality table so that the standard table acts as a prior assumption. This information can be incorporated into a Whittaker or a Bayesian graduation ([44], [46]). One simple way to use this prior knowledge in a kernel graduation is to subtract the crude rates from the standard rates, smooth the residuals, and add the smoothed residuals to the standard table to get the kernel graduated rates, all on the transformed scale ([4], [16]). Subtracting the standard table rates from the crude rates may filter out much of the curvature in the true rates, assuming that the standard table rates are similar in shape to the true rates. This may mean that the residuals are scattered about a simple curve, such as a constant or a straight line. When we investigate the bias of the Nadaraya-Watson estimator, in Section 3, we see that it has a relatively small bias in such situations.

Using a standard table is one way of ensuring that the graduated results reflect known theoretical or empirical models. For example, a small company might want to adjust a standard table to reflect the company's own particular circumstances, such as underwriting practices or geographical location. It is also possible to ensure that monotonicity in the standard table is reflected in the graduated rates by choosing a large enough bandwidth. Unfortunately this is a rather trivial case, because we would simply be adding a constant to the standard table. However, imposing a monotonicity constraint on a relatively simple nonparametric method and expecting good results is being rather optimistic. In Section 5, we consider using a standard table when measuring the relative difference between select and ultimate mortality rates.

2.7 Duplicate Policies

For duplicate policies, an additional complication may arise if the data are based on policy-years rather than person-years. This occurs when a policyholder buys multiple policies, perhaps from different life offices at different times, and consequently is counted more than once in the investigation. As a result, the residuals in Equation (1) may not be independent. This area presents considerable difficulty, because there is little information available that can be justifiably used to filter this undesirable effect from the data. For ultimate data, it could have a potentially significant influence on the number of observed deaths. One possible approach ([14], [40]) is to adjust the data by age, using a variance ratio to reduce the amount of exposure, and Renshaw [51] provides a more recent discussion of this topic. Another possible problem is that correlated observations can affect the cross-validation score. Hart and Wehrly [36] and Altman [1] offer some adjustments to the score statistic for resolving this problem. The issue is not pursued further in this paper, partly for simplicity but also because the adaptive bandwidth, used in Section 4, does not depend heavily on the choice of global bandwidth. However, in Section 4, we briefly mention an adjustment that might be made to one of the adaptive kernel models to help compensate for duplicate policies.

2.8 Choice of Smoothness Criterion

Smooth graduated rates are a primary objective. There are various ways of measuring this criterion, but ultimately it is a subjective choice that depends on the context in which the results are to be used. With the original scale, a traditional actuarial approach is to repeatedly calculate differences of the graduated rates and confirm that the third or fourth differences are random and small by using standard statistical tests. Bloomfield and Haberman [4] define a relative measure of smoothness, which expresses the k-th difference of the graduated rates relative to the graduated rates, as $D^k = (\hat{q}_i/|\Delta^k \hat{q}_i|)^{1/k}$, where Δ^k is the usual forward differencing operator applied repeatedly k times. Other measures of smoothness ([5], [8]) require monotonically increasing or increasing-convex rates over some region of the age range. The former measure requires that

$$\{\hat{q}_i \leq \hat{q}_{i+1} \text{ for } i = 1, ..., n - 1\},$$

and the more stringent, latter measure requires graduated rates that satisfy

$$\hat{q}_i - \hat{q}_{i-1} \leq \hat{q}_{i+1} - \hat{q}_i \qquad \text{for } i = 2, ..., n - 1, \tag{8}$$

excluding the first year of life and males in their 20s. In general, a kernel graduation cannot be guaranteed to preserve monotonicity, unless this prior information is built into the kernel model. Referring to a standard mortality table may be one way of doing this.

3. EXPLICIT ALLOWANCE FOR THE BOUNDARIES

3.1 A Boundary-Correcting Kernel

Figure 1b shows that values in the middle of the age range enjoy full support, for all practical calculations. However, as the normal kernel slides towards young or old ages, it increasingly overlaps the ends of the table and the resulting truncated kernel leads to an increase in bias. For example, at the youngest and oldest ages, half the kernel function will extend beyond the ends of the table.

To consider this problem further, we need to calculate the bias of our estimator. We start with a Taylor series expansion of the Nadaraya-Watson estimator in Equation (2),

$$E(\hat{q}_i^t) = q_i^t + \frac{\sum_{j=1}^n (x_j - x_i) K_b(x_j - x_i)}{\sum_{j=1}^n K_b(x_j - x_i)} (q_i^t)' + R, \qquad (9)$$

where $(q_i^t)'$ denotes the slope of the transformed true curve at age x_i and R is a remainder term consisting of higher-order derivatives. For an age x_i in the middle of the table, the coefficient of the $(q_i^t)'$ term is zero if the crude rates are evenly spaced. However, when estimating rates at the youngest and oldest ages, all the other crude rates will lie to the right and to the left, respectively. As a result, the $x_j - x_i$ term in the coefficient of $(q_i^t)'$ has the same sign for $j = 1, \ldots, n$, so that this coefficient is non-zero. This means that there is increased bias near the ends of the table. A comparison between the bias in the Nadaraya-Watson and the related Copas-Haberman kernel estimator is considered in Gavin, Haberman, and Verrall [25].

To improve the estimate at the boundaries, Hall and Wehrly [33] suggest reflecting the data so that the original data lie in the interior of an enlarged data set. In this way, the original data are less influenced by boundary effects.

We use an alternative method suggested by Rice [52]. Rice's extrapolation method is based on a linear combination of two different kernels with different bandwidths to eliminate the first-order bias. Suppose our two estimates are $\hat{q}_i^1$ and $\hat{q}_i^2$; then from Equation (9), we get

$$E(\hat{q}_i^1) = q_i + C_1 q_i' + R_1$$

$$E(\hat{q}_i^2) = q_i + C_2 q_i' + R_2,$$

where C_1 and C_2 are the coefficients of the first-order terms and R_1 and R_2 are the remainder terms for $\hat{q}_i^1$ and $\hat{q}_i^2$, respectively. Notice that C_1 and C_2 depend on age and not on the true mortality curve, so by a suitable linear combination of the two estimates, we can eliminate the q_i' term. This means that the bias of our estimator at the boundary does not depend on the slope of the mortality curve but only on higher-order terms such as curvature. In the same spirit but in the context of density estimation, Jones [42] suggests redefining the kernel function to be a linear combination of $K(x)$ and $xK(x)$. This leads to a kernel function for the right-hand boundary

$$K_b^R(x) = \frac{[a_2(p) - a_1(p)x]K_b(x)}{a_0(p)a_2(p) - a_1^2(p)}, \tag{10}$$

where $a_t(p) = \int_{-\infty}^{p} u^t K_b(u)du$ and $p = x/b$, which can be used to reduce the bias near the upper boundary. The variable p measures the distance from the point at which we are calculating the mortality rate to the right-hand boundary in units of bandwidth. The variable x measures the distance from the point at which we are calculating the mortality rate to each of the n crude rates, again in units of bandwidth. Substituting the normal kernel from Equation (3) for K_b in Equation (10), we get

$$K_b^R(x) = \frac{[\Phi(p) + (x - p)\phi(p)]\phi(x)}{\Phi(p)[\Phi(p) - p\phi(p)] - \phi^2(p)}, \tag{11}$$

where $\Phi(x) = \int_{-\infty}^{x}\phi(y)dy$ and $\phi(y)$ is as defined in Equation (3). For ages that are closer to the left-hand boundary, that is, younger ages, some obvious adjustments to the formula yield

$$K_b^L(x) = \frac{\{[1 - \Phi(p)] + (p - x)\phi(p)\}\phi(x)}{[1 - \Phi(p)]\{[1 - \Phi(p)] + p\phi(p)\} - \phi^2(p)}. \tag{12}$$

The transformed kernel functions, K_b^L and K_b^R, both behave like the standard Gaussian kernel in the middle of the age range. That is, if $p > 2$, then $a_0(p) \to 1$ and $a_1(p) \to 0$, so $K_b^L \approx K_b^N$ and $K_b^R \approx K_b^N$. As the age at which we are estimating the curve moves closer to the boundary, the weights change shape, becoming asymmetric and negative over some regions, as is shown in Example 2.

3.2 Implementing the Boundary-Correcting Kernel

It is possible to combine the two kernel functions, K_b^L and K_b^R, into a single smoother by first deciding which boundary is closest to the point at which we are estimating the curve. This approach worked satisfactorily for several data sets. However, if the distance from the center of the data to the boundaries is roughly two bandwidths or less, then a kink develops in the graduated rates as the smoother switches from using K_b^L to K_b^R, moving from left to right across the age range. Example 3 in Section 5.1 has a small age range, and cross-validation chooses a large global bandwidth. This results in a noticeable jump in the graduated rates at the central ages.

An ad hoc solution to this large boundary problem is to smooth the data using the left-hand and right-hand kernels, K_b^L and K_b^R, separately. This gives two sets of graduated rates that are blended linearly. So at the left-hand boundary, weights of 1 and 0 are given to the left-hand and right-hand boundaries, respectively. The weights change linearly across the age range to become 0 and 1, respectively, at the right-hand boundary. Benjamin and Pollard [3] mention other ways of blending the data, but this simple linear approach is adequate for our purposes. However, a referee has drawn our attention to a recent paper by Hart and Wehrly [36], which describes kernels that deal with large boundary regions, and these models may be more suitable in this context.

3.3 Example 2

Figure 2a shows the data from Figure 1b fitted by using a linear combination of K_b^L and K_b^R, instead of just K_b^N. The cross-validation curve arising from the boundary-correcting smoother is similar in shape to that given in Figure 1a, so it is not shown. It results in $b_{cv}=0.5$. However, the fitted values and the kernel functions superimposed on the bottom of Figure 2a are quite different from those in Figure 1. The kernel functions shown are those used to estimate the curve at the same six points as in example 1. For x_{15}, the kernel is almost the same as that of a normal kernel, but at x_2, x_3 and x_{19} the function becomes more truncated and its mode increases. When estimating the curve at both boundaries, x_1 and x_{20}, and moving towards the interior, we see that the weights attached to the other observations decrease rapidly, becoming negative and then gradually increasing back towards zero. So the smoother can take negative values.

If we consider the value of the weights in the smoother matrix **S** to be the height of a surface above a plane, then we can plot the surface using a mesh, and this is shown in Figure 2b. The view in Figure 2b has S_{11} as the closest point on the surface and S_{nn} as the furthest away point. The weights needed to estimate the i-th age come from the i-th row of the smoother. For example, the last row of the matrix in Figure 2b contains the weights needed to estimate x_{20}, and these weights are drawn in the bottom-right corner of Figure 2a. For values in the central region, the weights form a normal kernel, but as the point at which we are estimating the true curve moves towards the boundaries, the kernel becomes asymmetric and some of the weights are negative. From Equation (10), we can see that p measures the distance between a given point and the boundary in units of bandwidth, so ages for which $p \geq 2$ have kernel functions that are almost the same as a standardized normal, with asymptotic equality as $p \to \infty$.

FIGURE 2

PLOT A) HAS THE SAME DATA AS IN FIGURE 1B), BUT HERE THE DATA ARE SMOOTHED USING A LINEAR COMBINATION OF K_b^L AND K_b^R. PLOT B) IS A SURFACE PLOT OF THE BOUNDARY-CORRECTING SMOOTHER. PLOTS C) AND D) SHOW THE BENEFITS OF REDUCING FIRST-ORDER BIAS IN THE NADARAYA-WATSON ESTIMATOR BY USING A BOUNDARY ADJUSTMENT.

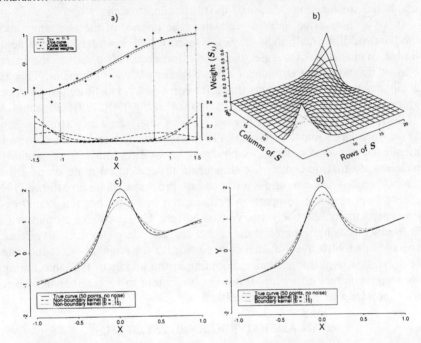

The benefit of allowing the kernel to take negative values at the boundary is that we can reduce the first-order bias term in Equation (9) by building a kernel from Equations (11) and (12). So if the transformed, true curve is approximately a straight line, we can produce better estimates even at the boundary. Figures 2c and 2d show a true curve, which is a straight line at the boundaries. The data are observed without noise, so any error in estimation is due to bias. Fifty evenly spaced observations (not shown) are used, so we might expect any reasonable estimator to do well under these ideal conditions. Both estimated curves use the Nadaraya-Watson estimator from Equation (2). Without adjustment the Nadaraya-Watson estimator is noticeably biased at the boundary in Figure 2c, and this bias increases as the bandwidth increases. The boundary-correcting kernel in Figure 2d can correctly estimate the straight line part of the true curve, even at the boundary. From Equation (9), we know that both estimators have second-order bias terms, so they both incorrectly estimate the curvature in the middle of the graph, underestimating peaks and overestimating troughs.

If we are interested only in graduating the interior of the age range and the bandwidth is small, then the bias caused by the boundary may be negligible. If this is not the case, then the effort required to reduce the extra bias at the boundary complicates the Nadaraya-Watson estimator. This is analogous to the complications that arise when MWA is adjusted to produce graduated rates at the ends of the table ([28], [29], [30], [39]). Example 3 in Section 5.1 suggests that if the age range is small, then the extra bias due to the boundaries may be serious. In such cases, using one of the techniques mentioned above to reduce this bias may be well rewarded. Some authors have argued that other kernel estimators can be adjusted more easily than the Nadaraya-Watson to allow for boundary problems. Chu and Marron [11] offer a very readable comparison between the two most popular kernel estimators, namely, the Nadaraya-Watson and the Gasser-Müller estimators.

Another possible complication is that the boundary problem may force cross-validation to select a smaller bandwidth at the boundary to reduce the bias, but this may lead to undersmoothing in the middle of the table. Using an adaptive kernel estimator allows the bandwidth to vary across the table, so it may help to alleviate this problem.

4. AN ADAPTIVE KERNEL ESTIMATOR

In previous sections, the kernel functions have always had a fixed or global bandwidth, so once b is chosen, it remains constant. Rather than restricting the bandwidth to a fixed value, a more flexible approach is to allow the bandwidth to vary according to the reliability of the data. Thus, for regions in which the amount of exposure (sample size) is large, a low value for b results in an estimate that more closely reflects the crude rates. For regions in which the exposure is small, such as at old ages, a higher value for the bandwidth allows the estimate of the true rates of mortality to progress more smoothly. This means that at older ages we are calculating local averages over a greater number of observations, which reduces the variance of the graduated rates but at a cost of potentially greater bias. This technique is often referred to as a variable or adaptive kernel estimator.

4.1 Some Adaptive Models

We can build our knowledge of the amount of exposure into the basic model in Equation (2) in a number of ways:

- We can calculate a different bandwidth for each age at which the curve is to be estimated. Using that bandwidth, we then measure the distance from the age at which the curve is to be estimated to each of the observed ages. For example, assuming that the age to be estimated is x_i, we measure the distance from x_i to x_j using b_i, for $j=1, \ldots, n$. So the model is

$$\hat{q}_i^t = \sum_{j=1}^{n} S_{ij}\, \dot{q}_j^t, \qquad \text{where} \qquad S_{ij} = \frac{K_{b_i}(x_i - x_j)}{\sum_{j=1}^{n} K_{b_i}(x_i - x_j)} \tag{13}$$

for $i=1, \ldots, n$. If the age to be estimated is not one of the observed ages, then we could smooth the empirical probability density estimate of age,

$$\hat{f}_i = \frac{e_i}{\sum_{j=1}^{n} e_j} \qquad \text{for } i = 1, \ldots, n. \tag{14}$$

- Alternatively, we can calculate a different bandwidth, b_j, for each observed age x_j, for $j=1, \ldots, n$. Then for each observed age, use the corresponding bandwidth to measure the distance from that observed age to the age at which the curve is to be estimated. For example, assuming that the age to be estimated is x_i, we measure the distance from x_i to x_j using b_j, for $j=1, \ldots, n$. This results in a new smoother

$$\hat{q}_i^t = \sum_{j=1}^{n} S_{ij}\, \dot{q}_j^t \qquad \text{where} \qquad S_{ij} = \frac{K_{b_j}(x_i - x_j)}{\sum_{j=1}^{n} K_{b_j}(x_i - x_j)} \tag{15}$$

for $i=1, \ldots, n$.

The local bandwidth at each age is simply the global bandwidth multiplied by a local bandwidth factor, $b_i = b l_i^s$ for $i=1, \ldots, n$. The variation in exposure between different tables and between young and old ages within a table can be enormous. To dampen the effect of this variation, we have chosen

$$l_i^s \propto \hat{f}_i^{-s} \qquad \text{for } i = 1, \ldots, n \quad \text{and} \quad 0 \le s \le 1, \tag{16}$$

where s is a sensitivity parameter. Choosing $s=0$ reduces both models to the fixed bandwidth case, while $s=1$ may result in very large bandwidth variation, depending on the particular table. For convenience, we have chosen the inverse of $\max\{f_i^{-s} : i=1, \ldots, n\}$ as the constant of proportionality in Equation (16), so that $0 < l_i^s \le 1$, for $i=1, \ldots, n$. If there is a small amount of exposure at age x_i, then l_i^s is large. This increases the size of the effective bandwidth, which in turn reduces the weight attached to the crude rate for that age. This allows us to apply more smoothing at those ages. The converse is true if the amount of exposure is large. The first example in Section 5 uses the model defined in Equation (13), and the second uses Equation (15) to graduate some mortality tables.

Once the local bandwidth factors are chosen, they remain fixed in both models, regardless of the location of the age that we are trying to estimate. So another possibility is to choose

$$l_{ij}^s = (e_j/e_i)^s, \qquad \text{for } i, j = 1, \ldots, n. \tag{17}$$

The sensitivity parameter is still necessary to dampen the extreme variations that can arise. In this case, the relative exposure is used to adjust the global bandwidth when a weight is attached to the j-th crude rate to estimate the true rate at the i-th age. This leads to

$$\hat{q}_i^t = \sum_{j=1}^n S_{ij}\, \dot{q}_j^t, \qquad \text{where} \qquad S_{ij} = \frac{K_{b_{ij}}(x_i - x_j)}{\sum_{j=1}^n K_{b_{ij}}(x_i - x_j)}, \tag{18}$$

where $b_{ij} = b l_{ij}^s$ and $i, j = 1, \ldots, n$. This model also offers the possibility of building in a variance ratio to allow for duplicate policies [15].

Clearly there is room for other models to be developed. In theory, we could try taking account of the shape of the true curve by using

$$l_i^s = (|(q_i^t)''|f_i)^{-s}. \tag{19}$$

Consider the true curve in Figures 2c and 2d to provide some motivation for this model. A formula such as $l_i^s = (|(q_i^t)''|f_i)^{-s}$ is saying that to improve the estimate in the center of Figure 2c, we should decrease the bandwidth as the amount of curvature in the true mortality curve increases, provided that the crude rates in that region are reliable. The true mortality rate, q_i, is unknown, so an initial estimate is required. We can use $\hat{f}_i$, as defined in Equation (14), as an estimate of f_i. Second differences could be used to approximate curvature, and we do not distinguish between positive or negative curvature.

We expect explicit allowance for exposure to be a beneficial feature in the models, because this factor directly influences the variability of the crude rates and exposure may vary enormously across the age range. It is worth asking whether models that allow for the shape of the true mortality curve as well as the amount of exposure are worthwhile. This would seem to depend on the purpose of the graduation. If we are merely exploring the data, then the additional information derived might not justify the effort. However, if we wish to use a kernel estimator to check on a parametric graduation [2], then a more detailed model may be worth the effort. This is especially so for large tables where considerable time and effort have been invested in gathering and validating the data.

We do not consider models like Equation (19) further in this paper. Nor do we derive the properties of an adaptive kernel estimator that are more complicated than those of the fixed-bandwidth estimator [31]. Jones [41] considers an alternative approach using a model of the form

$$\hat{q}_i^t = \frac{\sum_{j=1}^{n} w_j \, \hat{q}_j^t \, K_b(x_i - x_j)}{\sum_{j=1}^{n} w_j \, K_b(x_i - x_j)},$$

where w_j are weights that could depend on the amount of exposure.

4.2 Choice of Parameter Values

For each of the models in the previous section, two parameters need to be considered: sensitivity, s, and global bandwidth, b.

The sensitivity parameter could be chosen by cross-validation. However, as s increases from zero, the adaptive kernel becomes more sensitive to the variation in exposure. The amount of variation in exposure can be very large for some mortality data sets, ranging from thousands of person-years at younger ages down to single figures at the oldest ages. In such cases, a large value for s may be unreasonable, because it might result in bandwidths for some ages being several times the age interval covered by the data. Therefore, this parameter is chosen subjectively. Once s has been chosen, cross-validation is still used to choose b.

5. SOME PRACTICAL EXAMPLES

In this section we illustrate how the adaptive kernel model might be used to graduate two mortality tables. These two tables were chosen because the first has relatively little variation in exposure over the age range, while the second has a much greater variation. For both tables, we consider letting the bandwidth vary across the age range. Trial and error indicates that a doubling of the bandwidth, from a minimum at ages with high exposure to a maximum for ages with the lowest exposure, gives reasonable results.

5.1 Example 3

Figure 3a shows a bar plot of the amount of exposure for the crude mortality rates taken from Broffitt [6]. Broffitt adopts a Bayesian approach to graduation. The same data set has subsequently been considered by Carlin [8] using the Gibbs sampler to implement a Bayesian model. The data cover only a small age range, for which it might be expected that the true mortality rates are monotonically increasing. The decrease in exposure with age is typical of mortality tables reflecting the fact that there are relatively fewer older people and that whole-of-life and endowment policies are less likely to be sold to older people, in the case of the females table (Figure 3b). In comparison to the second table, the first has a relatively small amount of exposure and the variation in exposure over age is relatively small. The boundary-correcting kernel discussed in Section 3 along with the adaptive kernel defined in Equation (13) are used to graduate this table.

FIGURE 3

BAR PLOTS OF A) THE AMOUNT OF EXPOSURE FOR THE DURATION SIXTEEN-OR-MORE, MALE ULTIMATE DATA TAKEN FROM BROFFITT [6] AND B) THE AMOUNT OF EXPOSURE FOR THE DURATION TWO-OR-MORE, FEMALE ASSURED LIVES 1975–78 TABLE [14].

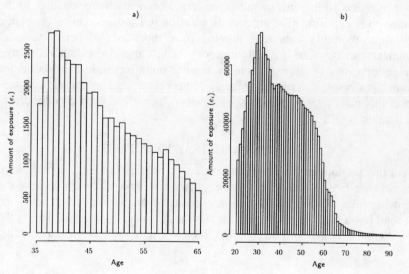

The exposure in Figure 3a decreases with age, though in a less dramatic fashion than is often the case with mortality tables. The resulting local bandwidth parameter values, l_i^s, for various values of the sensitivity parameter, s, are shown in Figure 4a. The observed exposures decide the shape of the local bandwidth curves, but the sensitivity parameter, s, determines the magnification of that shape, becoming more pronounced as $s \rightarrow 1$. Notice that for $s=0$ the local bandwidth curve has a constant value of 1. In this case we are ignoring the variation in exposure, which gives a fixed-width estimator. From Figure 4a, where $s=0.5$, the minimum local bandwidth factor is about 0.5, at age 40. This means that the bandwidth at the oldest ages is about double that at the younger ages. A bandwidth that approximately doubles across the age range produces reasonable results.

After the data have been transformed using the logit transformation, discussed in Section 2.1, cross-validation is then applied to select the optimal bandwidth, b_{cv}. For $s=0$ and $s=0.5$, the cross-validation score, from Equation (5), is calculated for a range of global bandwidths, using the smoother defined in Equation (13). The results are shown in Figure 4b. The cross-validation curve for $s=0$ suggests that there is little to choose between bandwidth values up to about 6. This provides some support for using a subjective choice in or about this value, if desired. By using $s=0.5$, the cross-validation bandwidth is larger. Because we have already obtained the shape and magnification of the local bandwidth factors, this process of cross-validation decides the global value at which the bandwidth curve, from Figure 4a, is located.

The smoother for the case $s=0.5$ is shown in Figure 4c. The basic shape is the same as that of Figure 2. However, row 1 has a smaller effective bandwidth than row 30. So in row 1 the weights decrease rapidly to zero but in row 30 the weights decrease more slowly in order to smooth the older ages more. Rows in the middle of the smoother correspond to ages in the middle of the table and are approximately normal in shape. For example, for element S_{11} of the smoother, we have $b_{cv} l_{35}^{s=.5} \approx 8 \times 0.6$, but for $S_{30\,30}$, we have $b_{cv} l_{64}^{s=.5} \approx 8 \times 1$, giving weights of 0.34 and 0.19, respectively. So the weights in row 1 decrease more slowly than the weights in row 30, because each row is standardized to sum to one. As a second example, consider the center of the surface where $S_{15\,15} \approx 0.08$. This is the weight attached to the crude rate at age 50 when the true rate at age 50 is estimated. It can be calculated from a global bandwidth of about 8 and a local bandwidth factor of about 0.6 for age 50, giving a weight equal to a normal density with mean 0 and a standard deviation of 8×0.6 evaluated at 0.

FIGURE 4

A MORTALITY TABLE TAKEN FROM BROFFITT [6] IS GRADUATED USING EQUATION (13). PLOT A) SHOWS THE LOCAL BANDWIDTH FACTORS l_i^s FOR DIFFERENT VALUES OF THE SENSITIVITY PARAMETER. PLOT B) SHOWS CROSS-VALIDATION SCORES FOR EACH OF THE CASES $s=0$ AND $s = 0.5$. THE SMOOTHER FOR THE CASE $s=0.5$ IS SHOWN IN PLOT C). PLOTS D) AND E) SHOW THREE SETS OF KERNEL GRADUATED RATES ON THE LOGIT AND ORIGINAL SCALES, RESPECTIVELY. FINALLY, PLOT F) SHOWS THE RESIDUALS FROM FITTING A STRAIGHT LINE TO THE TRANSFORMED CRUDE RATES IN D) AND SMOOTHED RESIDUALS USING EQUATION (13).

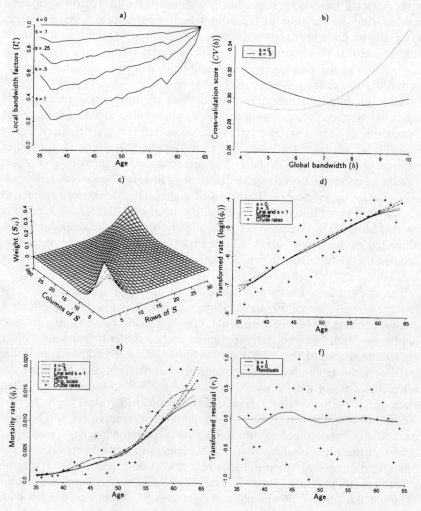

This data set is unusual in that b_{cv} is relatively large compared to other data sets that were tested, especially considering that the age range is quite small. As a result, the distance from age 49 to the left-hand boundary and from age 50 to the right-hand boundary is approximately twice b_{cv}, when $s=0.5$. Consequently, many of the kernels in the center of the table are not quite normal in shape. This gives a notable discontinuity in the fitted values unless the graduated rates are blended in some way. An ad hoc solution is explained in Section 3.2.

The results of the two graduations, using $s=0$ and $s=0.5$, are shown on the transformed scale (logit) in Figure 4d and on the original scale in Figure 4e. For comparison, a natural, cubic, smoothing spline graduation is shown. It also has a smoothing parameter chosen by cross-validation. The curve labeled "orig. scale" in Figure 4e is from the adaptive kernel model but fitted *without* first transforming the data. With $s=0$, the graduated rates are smooth, meeting the increasing convex condition in Equation (8), except at the oldest ages. For $s=0.5$, the graduated rates are lower than those for $s=0$, at the youngest ages. This appears to be due to greater weight being attached to the crude rates for ages 37 to 39, where the exposure is greatest. At the oldest ages, the graduated rates for $s=0.5$ lie below those for $s=0$, due to the larger bandwidth under $s=0.5$ at those ages.

The possibility of building in prior knowledge is discussed in Section 2.6. In the absence of a suitable prior table, we have fitted a straight line by least squares to the crude rates, on a logit scale. This requires the additional assumption of normally distributed residuals. In Figure 4f, the residuals from fitting the straight line are smoothed by using Equation (13) with $s=0$ and $s=1$. The smoothed residuals for $s=1$ are then added to the straight line to get the graduated rates labeled "line and $s=1$" in Figures 4d and 4e. Diagnostic plots of the residuals are satisfactory except that the quantile-quantile plot [10] suggests that the residuals are too scattered in the middle of the table. This might indicate the need for further investigation of the normality assumption. Otherwise, we might conclude that fitting a straight line by least squares on the logit scale gives a satisfactory graduation without any kernel adjustment, because the smoothed residuals in Figure 4e are almost zero at all ages. Azzalini and Bowman [2] offer a more formal approach to this problem by using a ratio test to measure the distance between a parametric and a nonparametric model. In this case, we have used a kernel smoother simply as a way of exploring the data before using a parametric model to estimate the mortality rates.

For comparison with the kernel graduations, another nonparametric graduation is also shown in Figures 4d and 4e. This curve is fitted using a well-known statistical method called natural cubic smoothing splines ([26], [56]). It produces results similar to Whittaker graduation [44, chapter 5], but it uses a slightly different smoothness penalty. We refer to this method as the spline graduation, and it is the set of graduated rates that minimizes the function

$$\sum_{i=1}^{n} (\hat{q}_i^t - \dot{q}_i^t)^2 + b \int_{x_1}^{x_n} ((\hat{q}_x^t)'')^2 \, dx, \qquad (20)$$

where $(\hat{q}_x^t)''$ is the second derivative of the graduated, transformed rates and b is again chosen by cross-validation. So as $b \to \infty$, we fit a straight line by least squares and as $b \to 0$, we fit an interpolating, twice differentiable function. A spline graduation has been chosen for comparison, because Silverman [55] calculates an asymptotically equivalent kernel for this smoother, and he also shows that it is an adaptive as opposed to a fixed-width smoother, so the two methods are consistent in this respect. As can be seen from Figure 4d, the spline graduation is very smooth. After Figure 4e has been back-transformed, this graduation is increasingly convex at all ages.

In plot Figure 4e, the curve labeled "orig. scale" is from the adaptive kernel model fitted *without* first transforming the data. The spline graduation fitted without transforming the data produces a similar result (not shown). This illustrates the importance of a good transformation before a nonparametric method is applied.

5.2 Example 4

The data are taken from a report by the Continuous Mortality Investigation Bureau [14], which contains the crude rates for all causes of death for durations 0, 1, and 2 or more of the Female Assured Lives 1975–78 Table. This mortality table arose from the experience of contributing U.K. life offices from whole-of-life and endowment policies on female lives during the years 1975 to 1978. The boundary-correcting kernel discussed in Section 3 along with the adaptive kernel defined in Equation (15) are used to graduate this table. The results for the adaptive kernel defined in Equation (13) were similar.

Figure 3b shows the exposure for this data set. The overall shape is similar to that of Example 3 in Section 5.1, but the range of exposures is much greater. The small exposures for the oldest ages are likely to result in large variations in the crude rates. The model incorporates these variations using the local bandwidth factors that are shown in Figure 5a, for various values of the sensitivity parameter. The variation in exposures is dampened by reducing the sensitivity parameter to $s=0.1$ in this case. The minimum local bandwidth factor at $s=0.1$ is about 0.5, so the bandwidth at age 94 is about double that at age 30. Thus, the variation in bandwidth is similar to that of the previous example.

After transformation, cross-validation results for a range of global bandwidth values are shown in Figure 5b. For clarity and comparison with Figure 4c, we only show a surface plot of the last 30 ages in Figure 5c. Despite appearances, the maximum weight over this part of the smoother is $S_{64\,64} \approx 0.2$, which is the weight attached to the crude rate at age 64 when the true rate at age 64 is estimated. $S_{64\,64}$ is the point on the surface that is closest to the viewer. This can be calculated from a global bandwidth of 3.3 and a local bandwidth factor of about 0.6 for age 64, giving a weight equal to a normal density with mean 0 and a standard deviation of 3.5×0.6 evaluated at 0, which is approximately 0.2.

Because we are now using Equation (15), the smoother in Figure 5c has a different shape from that in the previous example. To estimate $\hat{q}_i^t$, the i-th row of the smoother shows the weights attached to the crude rates, where each weight is a function of the bandwidth b_j associated with that crude rate $\hat{q}_j^t$ for $j=1, \ldots, n$. One effect of this is that none of the weights are negative.

The calculations for Figure 5d are carried out after the logit transformation has been used. However, so we can see the graduated rates at the younger ages in greater detail, the results are presented by using a log transformation of the x-axis. Using a logit transformation in Figure 5d, a sensitivity value of $s=0.1$ allows the graduated rates to follow the crude rates more closely at younger ages while smoothing more heavily over the older ages, relative to the fixed-bandwidth graduation. Again, for comparison, a natural, cubic, smoothing spline graduation is fitted with the cross-validation used to choose the smoothing parameter. The spline and the $s=0.1$ graduations are both very similar at the youngest ages, but both kernel graduations are less smooth than the spline graduation at the very oldest ages. The published rates, which were produced using a parametric graduation, are also shown.

An interesting aside is that both the adaptive kernel with $s=0.1$ and the spline graduation indicate a fall in mortality rates with increasing age, for females in their 20s (see Figure 5d and 6e). This suggests that like males, females also suffer from an "accidental hump" but at later ages and to a

FIGURE 5

DATA FROM THE FEMALE ASSURED LIVES 1975–78 TABLE ARE ANALYZED IN A MANNER SIMILAR TO THAT SHOWN IN FIGURE 4, BUT USING THE MODEL DEFINED IN EQUATION (15) WITH $s=0$ AND $s=0.1$. PLOT B) SHOWS THE CROSS-VALIDATION SCORES FOR $s=0$ AND $s=0.1$. PLOT C) SHOWS THE SMOOTHER FOR $s=0.1$ FOR THE OLDEST THIRTY AGES, 64–94. THE FITS ON THE TRANSFORMED SCALE ARE SHOWN IN PLOT D) ALONG WITH A SPLINE GRADUATION AND THE PUBLISHED RATES. PLOT E) SHOWS THE RESULTS FROM PLOT D) AFTER BACK-TRANSFORMING. THE STANDARDIZED RESIDUALS FOR $s = 0.1$ ARE SHOWN IN PLOT F).

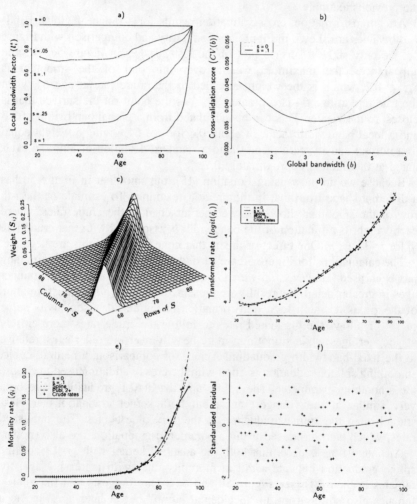

much lesser extent [4]. This feature is not present in the published tables, which are fitted by using a parametric method [14].

Much of this detail is lost when the rates are redrawn on the original scale in Figure 5e, which is one of the reasons for transforming the crude rates. On the original scale, the differences between the spline graduation and the crude rates at the oldest ages are magnified. Figure 5f shows that the standardized residuals, defined in Equation (7), for $s = 0.1$ are well scattered. The residuals can also be smoothed by using a kernel approach, in which case we expect to see a fairly flat line about zero.

5.3 Example 5

Next we consider using the published table for duration two-or-more to graduate the crude rates for duration 1.

In effect, the duration 2 or more table acts as a prior assumption and thus influences the shape and level of the graduated kernel rates for duration 1. This approach is motivated by the fact that both tables are based on the same population, but the duration two-or-more table has a total of 4,616 deaths out of a total of 2,042,853 policyholders exposed to risk during the period of investigation. The corresponding figures for duration 1 are much less at 334 and 459,068, respectively. So having graduated the larger table, we might want to incorporate that knowledge into the graduation of the smaller table.

The procedure is the same as in Figures 4d–4f: subtract the crude rates from the standard table, smooth the residuals using the smoother defined in Equation (13), and then add the smoothed residuals to the standard table. By approaching the problem in this way, we are emphasizing the relative differences in mortality rates among the durations rather than the absolute mortality rates.

Figure 6a shows the crude rates for duration 1 and the published rates for durations two-or-more. The residuals, shown on a logit scale in Figure 6b, are the differences between these two sets of rates. The residuals are smoothed in a similar manner to that in Example 3. In the middle of the age range, both kernels in Figure 6b are fairly constant. This suggests that mortality rates are consistently lower for the lower-duration table, in that part of the table. At both ends of the table, the fixed-bandwidth kernel is affected by the high residuals. However, the adaptive kernel ignores the high residuals at the oldest ages because the exposure is low, but the relatively high exposures at the youngest ages suggest that the upward trend is real, at that end of the table. For example, the exposures at the two youngest ages are 18,018 and 19,408 and the exposures at the two oldest ages are 61 and 48. To ensure a monotonically increasing table, the actuary might decide to ignore this feature. In fact, the published rates for durations 0 and 1 are based on an adjustment to the published rates for durations two-or-more. Adding the smoothed kernels to the durations two-or-more published rates gives the two kernel graduations shown in Figure 6a. For $s=0.3$, the smoothness of the graduated rates at the oldest ages is partly due to the large bandwidth, but it is also due to the smoothness of the standard table. The published rates for duration 1 are also shown in Figure 6a.

This example shows how a nonparametric approach to graduation can provide qualitative information about the bias present in subsequent parametric graduations.

5.4 Example 6

As a final application, we consider using the model defined by Equation (18) to smooth the crude rates of the duration two-or-more table.

For this model, we have a vector of local bandwidth factors for each crude age, which results in a matrix, $\{l_{ij}\}$ where $l_{ij}=e_j/e_i$, for $i, j=1, \ldots, n$. Figure 6c shows this matrix as a surface plot. For $s=0.05$, the local bandwidth factors vary from 0.7 to 1.42. This results in a doubling of the bandwidth across the age range, which like the previous examples gives reasonable results. The diagonal from the nearest to the furthest point in Figure 6c has $l_{ii}=1$, for $i=1, \ldots, n$, and the shape of any row is similar to each of the lines in Figure 5a. The last 30 rows and columns of the resulting smoother are shown in Figure 6d. The shape of this smoother is similar to that in Figure 4c. Notice that the far corner of the smoother is more peaked; this results in graduated rates that rise more sharply at the oldest ages. Figure 6e also shows the results from example 4 in Section 5.2 based on Equation (15), for $s=0.1$. For clarity, the crude and published rates are not shown. At the youngest ages, the graduated rates from Equation (18) are as smooth as the results from Equation (15) with $s=0$, while at the oldest ages the graduated rates are similar to those of the spline graduation. For the duration two-or-more mortality table, the graduated rates from Equation (18) give the smoothest of the three kernel models that we consider, but further work is needed to test these results on other tables. The standardized residuals, in Figure 6f, show no clear pattern.

FIGURE 6

PLOT A) SHOWS THE CRUDE AND PUBLISHED RATES FOR DURATION ONE, THE PUBLISHED RATES FOR DURATION TWO-OR-MORE AND TWO KERNEL GRADUATIONS OF THE DURATION-ONE CRUDE RATES. THE RESIDUALS IN PLOT B) ARE THE DIFFERENCE BETWEEN THE CRUDE RATES FOR DURATION ONE AND THE PUBLISHED RATES FOR DURATION TWO-OR-MORE. THE SMOOTHED RESIDUALS USING EQUATION (13), WITH $s=0$ AND $s=0.3$, ARE ALSO SHOWN. PLOT C) SHOWS THE SURFACE GENERATED FROM EQUATION (17) FOR $s=0.05$ AND THE LAST 30 ROWS AND COLUMNS OF THE CORRESPONDING SMOOTHER FROM EQUATION (18) ARE SHOWN IN PLOT D). PLOT E) SHOWS THE RESULTS FROM EXAMPLE 4 IN SECTION 5.2 BASED ON EQUATION (15), FOR $s=0.1$. THE STANDARDIZED RESIDUALS ARE SMOOTHED IN PLOT F).

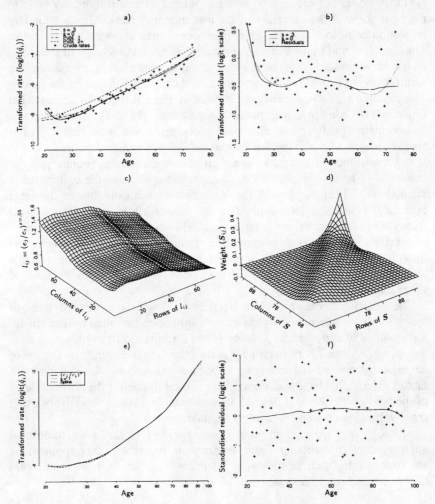

6. DISCUSSION

We start with a bivariate scatterplot of age against mortality, but as the data are grouped by age, we simply average within each group to produce a set of equally spaced observations. This eliminates the first-order bias of the Nadaraya-Watson estimator in the interior of the table. Transforming the data helps to stabilize the variance and to reduce the curvature. This means that the second-order bias, due to curvature, is reduced. The second-order bias may be further reduced by using a suitable, standard mortality table to filter out some of the curvature of the true mortality rates. Also, a boundary correction helps to reduce the extra bias encountered at the ends of the table. Thus, pooling and transforming the data, using prior knowledge of the shape of the curve and an adjustment at the extreme ages all help to validate the assumptions of residuals with zero mean and constant variance in the model. The requirement of independent residuals is more difficult to achieve, but Equation (18) combined with possible adjustments [15] may help to alleviate this problem. Finally, some diagnostic plots, discussed in Section 2.5, offer an easy means of assessing the validity of the assumptions made.

A kernel function that makes explicit allowance for the boundary is defined and illustrated in Section 3. Complications such as the extrapolation method ([42], [52]) applied to the Nadaraya-Watson estimator or the large boundary adjustment [36] applied to the Gasser-Müller estimator subtract from the intuitive appeal of kernel models. However, the extra effort required to specify the kernel does improve the results in the examples shown and for other mortality tables not reported here. This is because the variable bandwidth in our estimators usually increases for older ages because of lower exposures at those ages.

The adaptive kernel model in Section 4 allows the estimated rates of mortality to include explicitly the extra information provided by the changing amounts of exposure, in addition to the information from the crude rates themselves. A sensitivity parameter allows the user to control the degree of emphasis placed on the changing exposures through the local bandwidth factors. The global bandwidth parameter is used to control the absolute level of the bandwidth curve. If desired, its value can be chosen objectively using cross-validation or some equivalent method.

Although our applications have been restricted to the more traditional application of constructing a single-decrement life table, other applications are conceivable, such as transition intensities or probabilities in multiple-decrement and multiple-state models.

Throughout this paper, we have adopted a heuristic approach to kernel graduation, but a more theoretical perspective may offer deeper insight into the connection between this method and MWA graduation. Because of the adaptive bandwidth, both the number of crude rates and the corresponding weights vary in the estimation of the transformed, true rate at each age. In contrast, the range of a MWA is often kept fixed and only the weights are allowed to vary. In this respect, kernel models may offer a more flexible approach to local smoothing. In addition, this paper has concentrated on the Nadaraya-Watson kernel estimator only, but there are many others [43]. Further work is needed to assess their relative merits for graduation.

An alternative model that is closely related to kernel-smoothing is to fit low-order polynomials locally. So instead of fitting a constant, we now fit a straight line or a quadratic using least squares. This approach was popularized by Cleveland [12]. Hastie and Loader [37] review the recent statistical literature on this subject and argue that higher-order models result in a lower order of bias without a corresponding increase in variance. Fan and Marron [22] have pointed out that fast implementations of kernel and local polynomial methods have recently emerged, and they claim speeds comparable to those of smoothing splines. For mortality applications, this model has the advantages of automatically adjusting at the boundaries to reduce the bias. It also provides more reliable estimates of the derivatives of the mortality curve than the Nadaraya-Watson estimator. In the actuarial literature, Renshaw [51] considers generalized linear and nonlinear graduation.

Another area of future interest is robustness. Some of the examples in Section 5 appear to be influenced by outliers, because the Nadaraya-Watson estimator offers no explicit resistance to unusual observations. An influential point may also affect the choice of bandwidth when an automatic selection method is used, such as cross-validation. Cleveland [12] extends his model to include robust iterative estimation. In fact, any smoother can be made robust by using more resistant local averaging, such as the mode or median [54].

The potential uses of a nonparametric approach, listed in the introduction, suggest that they have much to offer as part of the actuarial toolkit. Note that we are not advocating that a nonparametric model should always be used instead of a parametric one. A nonparametric model should be viewed as an exploratory step towards the final model choice, which may be parametric because of its inherent smoothness. Differences between the best parametric and nonparametric graduations will highlight the extent of the actuary's desire for smoothness, at a cost of lack of fit to the data.

ACKNOWLEDGMENT

We thank the panel of referees for their many helpful comments, which led to a much improved paper.

We are grateful to Chris Jones, William Schucany, and David Scott for making available preprints of their work. We would also like to thank Glenn Stone for the use of his dynamic spline fitting program. It was used to produce some of the results in Section 5.

REFERENCES

1. ALTMAN, N.S. "Kernel Smoothing of Data with Correlated Errors," *Journal of the American Statistical Association* 85 (1990): 749–59.
2. AZZALINI, A., AND BOWMAN, A. "On the Use of Nonparametric Regression for Checking Linear Relationships," *Journal of the Royal Statistical Society B* 55, (1993): 549–57.
3. BENJAMIN, B., AND POLLARD, J.H. *The Analysis of Mortality and Other Actuarial Statistics*. London: Heinemann, 1980.
4. BLOOMFIELD, D.S.F., AND HABERMAN, S. "Graduation: Some Experiments with Kernel Methods," *Journal of the Institute of Actuaries* 114 (1987): 339–69.
5. BROCKETT, P.L. "Information Theoretic Approach to Actuarial Science: A Unification and Extension of Relevant Theory and Applications," *TSA* 43 (1991): 73–135.
6. BROFFITT, J.D. "Increasing and Increasing Convex Bayesian Graduation," *TSA* 40 (1988): 115–48.
7. BROOKS, R.J., STONE, M., CHAN, F.Y., AND CHAN, L.Y. "Cross Validatory Graduation," *Insurance: Mathematics and Economics* 7 (1988): 59–66.
8. CARLIN, B.P. "A Simple Monte Carlo Based Approach to Bayesian Graduation," *TSA* 44 (1992): 1–22.
9. CARROLL, R.J., AND RUPPERT, D. *Transformation and Weighting in Regression*. New York: Chapman and Hall, 1988.
10. CHAMBERS, J.M., CLEVELAND, W.S., KLEINER, B., AND TUKEY, P.A. *Graphical Methods for Data Analysis*. Belmont, Calif: Wadsworth, 1983.
11. CHU, C.K., AND MARRON, J.S. "Choosing a Kernel Regression Estimator," *Statistical Science* 6, no. 4 (1991): 404–36.
12. CLEVELAND, W.S. "Robust Locally-Weighted Regression and Smoothing Scatterplots," *Journal of the American Statistical Association* 74 (1979): 829–36.
13. CLEVELAND, W.S., DEVLIN, S.J., AND GROOSE, E. "Regression by Local Fitting," *Journal of Econometrics* 37 (1988): 87–114.
14. CONTINUOUS MORTALITY INVESTIGATION BUREAU. "Graduation of the Mortality Experience of Female Assured Lives: 1975–78," *Report Number 6*. London: Institute and Faculty of Actuaries, 1983.

15. CONTINUOUS MORTALITY INVESTIGATION BUREAU. "An Investigation into the Distribution of Policies Per Life Assured in the Cause of Death Investigation Data," *Report Number 8*. London: Institute and Faculty of Actuaries, 1986.

16. COPAS, J.B., AND HABERMAN, S. "Non-parametric Graduation Using Kernel Methods," *Journal of the Institute of Actuaries* 110 (1983): 135–56.

17. COX, D.R., AND SNELL, E.J. *Analysis of Binary Data*. 2nd ed. New York: Chapman and Hall, 1989.

18. ELANDT-JOHNSON, R.C., AND JOHNSON, N.L. *Survival Models and Data Analysis*. New York: John Wiley & Sons, 1980.

19. EPANECHNIKOV, V.A. "Non-parametric Estimation of a Multivariate Probability Density," *Theory of Probability and Its Applications* 14 (1969): 153–58.

20. SCHUCANY, W.R. "Adaptive Bandwidth Choice for Kernel Regression," *Journal of the American Statistical Association* 90, no. 430 (1995): 535.

21. EUBANK, R.L., AND THOMAS, W. "Detecting Heteroscedasticity in Nonparametric Regression," *Journal of the Royal Statistical Society B* 55 (1993): 145–55.

22. FAN, J., AND MARRON, J.S. "Comment on Hastie & Loader's Paper—Local Regression: Automatic Kernel Carpentry," *Statistical Science* 8, no. 2 (1993): 129–34.

23. GASSER, T., AND MÜLLER, H.G. "Estimating Regression Functions and Their Derivatives by the Kernel Method," *Scandinavian Journal of Statistics* 11 (1984): 171–85.

24. GAVIN, J.B., HABERMAN, S., AND VERRALL, R.J. "Moving Weighted Average Graduation Using Kernel Estimation," *Insurance: Mathematics and Economics* 12 (1993): 113–26.

25. GAVIN, J.B., HABERMAN, S., AND VERRALL, R.J. "On the Choice of Bandwidth for Kernel Graduation," *Journal of the Institute of Actuaries* 121 (1994): 119–34.

26. GREEN, P.J., AND SILVERMAN, B.W. *Nonparametric Regression and Generalised Linear Models*. London: Chapman and Hall, 1994.

27. GREGOIRE, G. "Least Square Cross Validation for Counting Processes Intensities," *Scandinavian Journal of Statistics* 20, no. 4 (1993): 343–60.

28. GREVILLE, T.N.E. "Moving-Weighted-Average Smoothing Extended to the Extremities of the Data. I. Theory," *Scandinavian Actuarial Journal* (1981): 38–55.

29. GREVILLE, T.N.E. "Moving-Weighted-Average Smoothing Extended to the Extremities of the Data. II. Methods," *Scandinavian Actuarial Journal* (1981): 65–81.

30. GREVILLE, T.N.E. "Moving-Weighted-Average Smoothing Extended to the Extremities of the Data. III. Stability and Optimal Properties," *Journal of Approximation Theory* 33 (1981): 43–58.

31. HALL, P. "On the Bias of Variable Bandwidth Curve Estimators," *Biometrika* 77, no. 3 (1990): 529–35.

32. HALL, P., AND JOHNSTONE, I.M. "Empirical Functionals and Efficient Smoothing Parameter Selection," *Journal of the Royal Statistical Society B* 54 (1992): 475–530.

33. HALL, P., AND WEHRLY, T.E. "A Geometrical Method for Removing Edge Effects from Kernel-Type Nonparametric Regression Estimates," *Journal of the American Statistical Association* 86 (1991): 665–72.

34. HÄRDLE, W., HALL, P., AND MARRON, J.S. "How Far Are Automatically Chosen Regression Smoothing Parameters from Their Optimum?" *Journal of the American Statistical Association* 83 (1988): 86–101.

35. HART, J.D., AND WEHRLY, T.E. "Kernel Regression Estimation Using Repeated Measurement Data," *Journal of the American Statistical Association* 81 (1986): 1080–88.

36. HART, J.D., AND WEHRLY, T.E. "Kernel Regression When the Boundary Region is Large, with an Application to Testing the Adequacy of Polynomial Models," *Journal of the American Statistical Association* 87 (1992): 1018–24.

37. HASTIE, T., AND LOADER, C. "Local Regression: Automatic Kernel Carpentry," *Statistical Science* 8, no. 2 (1993): 120–43.

38. HASTIE, T.J., AND TIBSHIRANI, R.J. *Generalized Additive Models.* London: Chapman and Hall, 1990.

39. HOEM, J.M., AND LINNEMANN, P. "The Tails in Moving Average Graduation," *Scandinavian Actuarial Journal* (1988): 193–229.

40. JOINT MORTALITY INVESTIGATION COMMITTEE. "Continuous Investigation into the Mortality of Assured Lives: Memorandum on a Special Inquiry into the Distribution of Duplicate Policies," *Journal of the Institute of Actuaries* 83 (1957): 34–36.

41. JONES, M.C. "Do Not Weight for Heteroscedasticity in Nonparametric Regression," *Australian Journal of Statistics* 35, no. 1 (1993): 89–92.

42. JONES, M.C. "Simple Boundary Correction for Kernel Density Estimation," *Statistics and Computing* (1993): 135–46.

43. JONES, M.C., DAVIES, S.J., AND PARK, B.U. "Versions of Kernel-Type Regression Estimators," *Journal of the American Statistical Association* 89 (1994): 825–32.

44. LONDON, D. *Graduation: The Revision of Estimates.* Winsted and Abington, Conn.: ACTEX Publications, 1985.

45. LONDON, R.L. "In Defence of Minimum-r_0 Linear Compound Graduation and a Simple Modification for Its Improvement," *ARCH* (1981.2): 75–78.

46. LOWRIE, W.B. "An Extension of the Whittaker-Henderson Method of Graduation," *TSA* 34 (1982): 329–72.

47. NADARAYA, E.A. "On Estimating Regression," *Theory of Probability and Its Applications* 9 (1964): 141–42.

48. NIELSEN, J.P. "A Transformation Approach to Bias Correction in Kernel Hazard Estimation," *Research Report Number 115.* University of Copenhagen: Laboratory of Actuarial Mathematics, 1992.

49. RAMLAU-HANSEN, H. "The Choice of a Kernel Function in the Graduation of Counting Process Intensities," *Scandinavian Actuarial Journal* (1983): 165–82.

50. RAMSAY, C.M. "Minimum Variance Moving-Weighted-Average Graduation," *TSA* 43 (1991): 305–33.

51. RENSHAW, A.E. "Actuarial Graduation Practice and Generalised Linear and Nonlinear Models," *Journal of the Institute of Actuaries* 118 (1991): 295.
52. RICE, J.A. "Boundary Modification for Kernel Regression," *Communications in Statistics. Theory and Methods* 13 (1984): 893–900.
53. SCOTT, D.W. "Constrained Oversmoothing and Upper Bounds on Smoothing Parameters in Regression and Density Estimation," *Technical Report 92-8.* Rice University: Department of Statistics, 1992.
54. SCOTT, D.W. *Multivariate Density Estimation; Theory, Practice and Visualisation.* New York: John Wiley & Sons, 1992.
55. SILVERMAN, B.W. "Spline Smoothing: The Equivalent Variable Kernel Method," *Annals of Statistics* 12 (1984): 898–916.
56. SILVERMAN, B.W. "Some Aspects of Spline Smoothing Approaches to Non-parametric Regression Curve Fitting," *Journal of the Royal Statistical Society B* 47 (1985): 1–52.
57. STONE, M. "Cross-Validatory Choice and Assessment of Statistical Predictions," *Journal of the Royal Statistical Society B* 36 (1974): 111–47.
58. VERRALL, R.J. "Whittaker Graduation Viewed as Dynamic Generalised Linear Models," *Insurance: Mathematics and Economics* 13 (1994): 7–14.
59. WATSON, G.S. "Smooth Regression Analysis," *Sankhya A* 26 (1964): 359–72.

REVIEW OF ADEQUACY OF 1983 INDIVIDUAL ANNUITY MORTALITY TABLE

ROBERT J. JOHANSEN

ABSTRACT

The paper analyzes recent individual annuity mortality experience, derives comparative annual mortality improvement rates and, in particular, examines in detail the 1976–86 experience in the most recent Report of the Individual Annuity Experience Committee. Some anomalies in the 1976–86 experience are pointed out, and some attempts to explain them are offered. Finally, the paper suggests that the 1983 Table a should be replaced as soon as possible—that it will not be viable for the second half of the 1990s.

After discussing some special tests of the 1976–86 annuity experience, the paper concludes that instead of constructing a new table from the 1976–86 experience, Improvement Scale G should be used to derive an interim table from the 1983 Table a. The 1996 IAM Table in the paper is intended to be used for valuation until a larger, more detailed study of annuitant mortality can be compiled and analyzed—a task that might not be completed until the early 2000s. The new study would examine the comparative mortality of different classes of individual annuity business. It would also study the use of mortality improvement rates as an integral part of the valuation system similar to that adopted for group annuity valuation.

INTRODUCTION

Improving mortality is a sign of advances in medical diagnostics and treatments, advances in public health, and improvements in socioeconomic factors generally. However, improving mortality creates problems for systems that must pay for medical and custodial care for the aged, and it threatens the solidity of old age income programs in Canada and the U.S.

Improving mortality widens mortality margins in life insurance valuation but reduces the safety in annuity valuation tables. In fact, improving mortality has rendered obsolete not only the 1949 and earlier tables but also the more recent 1971 Individual Annuity Table. The 1983 Group Annuity Table is being replaced by the 1994 Group Annuity Table. This paper examines the 1983 Table a in light of the results of the 1976–86 individual annuity mortality study and recent population data and proposes a replacement.

211

The paper also proposes a cooperative effort by life insurers issuing individual annuities to contribute to a large and detailed study of annuitant mortality. Such a study is needed to keep the annuity business growing and profitable with adequate safety margins over the longer term.

DISCUSSION OF 1976–86 INDIVIDUAL ANNUITY MORTALITY EXPERIENCE

The 1976–86 Individual Annuity Mortality Study

The Individual Annuity Experience Committee well deserves the gratitude of the actuarial profession for producing the first individual annuity study since the 1971–76 study was published nearly 20 years ago [1]. Unfortunately, the new 1976–86 study [2] included only eight companies versus fifteen in the earlier study [3]. In its report, the 1976–86 study committee (the Annuity Committee) expressed the hope that publication of the study would encourage other companies to contribute to future studies. I join with the Annuity Committee in appealing to companies to contribute their experiences to future studies. The importance of additional contributors cannot be stressed too much. Because improving mortality causes annuity valuation tables to become inadequate, it is vital to have up-to-date, representative annuity mortality data to keep annuity valuation standards current.

While the Annuity Committee called attention to "significant differences in percentages of exposures from the various companies for different annuity types," the individual company percentages of contributed exposures in the new study were mostly less than the largest percentages in the 1971–76 study [4], where five companies each contributed 10% or more to the various sections of the mortality experience: two to nonrefund life income settlements (with one contributing more than half) and four to refund; three to matured deferred annuities, with one company contributing half to two-thirds of the nonrefund experience and one-third to half of the refund. As compared with the 1971–76 study, the 1976–86 experience did not have a worse distribution by company despite the smaller number of companies. Nevertheless, the 1976–86 experiences must be viewed with caution considering (1) the small number of companies in the study, (2) the fact that no one company contributed for all ten years, and (3) the wide dispersion of mortality ratios by company, as shown in Appendix Tables C-1 and C-2 of the 1976–86 study [2].

Analysis of the 1976–1986 Mortality Experience

The Annuity Committee noted that the mortality ratios under refund business were generally lower than those under nonrefund business, a finding that was "counter to expectations and prior trends." The self-selection exercised by annuitants has long been recognized—historically it has been evident in low mortality in the early contract years and in higher mortality on refund annuities than on nonrefund. Nonrefund annuities were traditionally considered more likely to be purchased by only the healthiest lives. Possibly the environment (which I will not attempt to define) has changed. I have pursued several avenues, which are described below, to explain the apparent anomaly, but none held the answer.

The report on the derivation of the 1983 Table a [5] made use of a table in the 1971–76 study comparing historical mortality ratios over the period 1948–76 to construct a table of trends in selection. A summary of that table, extended to include the 1976–86 study, appears as Table 1. It presents selection trends over the periods 1948–63, 1963–76, and 1976–86. Comparison of 1963–76 with 1948–63 shows that the effects of selection decreased for male nonrefund and increased for female nonrefund and both refund groups. Comparing 1976–86 with 1963–76 shows that selection has increased in both nonrefund groups and for female refund. While the analysis fails to explain the shift of lower mortality from nonrefund to refund, it at least indicates that the 1976–86 experience is not out of line with prior studies.

Using some data kindly supplied by the Annuity Committee, I was able to analyze nonrefund mortality versus refund separately for nonpension trust and pension trust business. Analyses by experience year (all companies combined) and by company code (all years combined) showed general consistency in refund mortality being lower than nonrefund. An unnumbered table early in the 1976–86 report [6] compares average amounts of annual income based on first-contract-year exposures for the current study and the five preceding studies for male and female refund and nonrefund business—the nonrefund business consistently shows the larger amounts of average income. Considering that the current study shows mortality is lower for larger amounts of income, the larger income of nonrefund annuitants does not explain anything.

Table 2 compares mortality for contract years 11 and over in the 1976–86 study with that for years 6 and over in the 1971–76 study—essentially successive experiences of the same groups of annuitants (differences in

TABLE 1

TRENDS IN SELECTION
BASED ON RATIOS OF MORTALITY IN CONTRACT YEARS 1–5
TO MORTALITY IN CONTRACT YEARS 6 AND OVER

	Attained Age Group	Average 1948–63[a]	Average 1963–76[a]	1976–86[b]
Immediate Nonrefund Annuities				
Males	Under 60	—[c]	—	—
	60–69	83%	79%	64%
	70–79	72	91	53
	80 & up	74	79	79
	All	76	88	74
Females	Under 60	—	—	—
	60–69	76	62	28
	70–79	72	60	53
	80 & up	68	71	62
	All	72	67	62
Immediate Refund Annuities				
Males	Under 60	126%[d]	131%[d]	222%
	60–69	87	79	82
	70–79	88	86	84
	80 & up	93	78	88
	All	96	85	90
Females	Under 60	54	78	46
	60–69	91	103	49
	70–79	93	87	84
	80 & up	87	79	68
	All	91	87	75

[a]Expected deaths on 1949 Annuity Table.
[b]Expected deaths on 1971 IAM.
[c]Indicates numerator and/or denominator based on small number of deaths.
[d]Excludes pension trust business.

constituent companies aside) during two different time periods. We would not expect a shift of lower mortality from nonrefund to refund in this comparison. However, Table 2 indicates that there has been such a shift.

The problem is to determine why the shift occurred. Is it due to a shift in sales emphasis? The exposures indicate that refund products have been more popular than nonrefund, at least among clients of the companies in the study. But this does not answer the question, Why are refund annuitants healthier than nonrefund? Or the corollary question, Why do the less healthy apparently choose nonrefund over refund? On the face of it, the results do not make sense; at least general reasoning does not explain the results. Further, any hypothesis based on sales or other factors affecting selection at issue does not explain the shift (see Table 2) from the 1971–76 experience

TABLE 2

COMPARISON OF 1971–76 VERSUS 1976–86 EXPERIENCE
BY AMOUNTS OF ANNUAL INCOME
EXPECTED DEATHS BASED ON 1971 IAM

	Attained Age Group	Experience Years 1971–76[a] Contract Years 6 and Over		Experience Years 1976–86 Contract Years 11 and Over	
		Nonrefund	Refund	Nonrefund	Refund
Male	60–90	208%	160%	238%[b]	122%
	70–79	136	112	214	92
	80–89	107	111	122	99
	90 & over	83	102	85	94
Female	60–69	179	136	251[b]	164
	70–79	129	107	173	89
	80–89	95	101	99	83
	90 & over	90	104	90	87

[a]Excludes pension trust business.
[b]May not be reliable because of small number of deaths.

for contract years 6 and over to that of 1976–86 for contract years 11 and over.

A hint to a possible explanation can be garnered from Table 40 in the 1971–76 Report [7], which, for refund life income settlements arising from maturities and surrenders and for matured deferred annuities, compares mortality under (a) pension trust issues, (b) qualified nonpension trust issues, and (c) nonqualified business. The qualified nonpension trust mortality ratios were markedly lower than those of the other two groups. A significant increase in the proportion of such qualified business in the refund annuity experience might account for the shift. Qualified nonpension trust business probably includes a substantial amount of 403(b) contracts issued to teachers, an occupation group known for low mortality. The next annuity mortality study should examine qualified nonpension trust business as a separate class to test this hypothesis. The use of special adjustments for valuation of such business could also be explored.

In any case, the nonrefund-to-refund shift bears out the wisdom of the respective committees that constructed the 1971 IAM Table and the 1983 Table *a* in deciding to combine refund and nonrefund immediate annuities, settlement options, and matured deferred annuities in building tables for valuation of all kinds of annuities.

ADEQUACY OF 1983 TABLE *a*

Was the 1983 Table a Adequate in 1983?

Availability of the 1976–86 annuity mortality study permitted completion of the second part of a test of the adequacy of the 1983 Table *a*. Starting in 1984, several members of the National Association of Insurance Commissioners (NAIC) Life and Health Actuarial Task Force (LHATF) expressed misgivings about the adequacy and continued safety of the 1983 IAM tables. The tables had been projected to 1983 from the 1973 Experience Tables constructed [8] from the Society of Actuaries study of annuitant mortality from 1971 to 1976 contract anniversaries. The 1983 Table *a* Committee proposed two tests of the adequacy of the table [9]. Both tests would compare actual mortality improvement rates with those used to project the 1983 Basic Tables from the 1973 Experience Tables.

One test was to compare the 1973 to 1983 improvement rates with those experienced from the 1969–71 U.S. Population Life Tables to the 1979–81 Tables. Results of the population test were described in a discussion of the Myers and Bayo paper on the 1979–81 U.S. Life Tables [10]. The test indicated that the 1983 tables were "adequate" for males and "probably adequate" for females.

The second test was to compare the mortality improvement between the 1971–76 annuity experience and the next Society of Actuaries annuity study, at that time assumed to cover the period 1976–81. The "next" Society annuity mortality study is now available; it covers the experience from 1976 to 1986 contract anniversaries [2]. In the section, "Adequacy of 1983 IAM Table," the Annuity Committee concluded that the 1983 table was adequate in 1983, the average year of the study.

Is the 1983 Table a Adequate for 1996 and Beyond?

There is no quarrel about the 1983 Table *a* being adequate in 1983—the immediate question is whether, taking improving mortality into account, the 1983 tables are still adequate for valuation in 1996 and later. In the absence of up-to-date annuity mortality experience, it is necessary to rely on available past mortality improvement rates and trends to draw a conclusion. Two approaches, one based on annuity experience, the other based on population data, may provide some answers.

Two sets of annual mortality improvement rates based on annuity experience are shown in Table 3: one from 1969 (the 1967–71 study [11]) to

1973 (the 1971–76 study [1]) and one from 1973 to 1983 (the 1976–86 study [2]). (A negative number indicates an increase in mortality.) The table compares them with the improvement rates used to derive the 1983 Basic Table from the 1973 Experience Table and with Projection Scale G [5]. The 1973 to 1983 projection factors are the same for males and females; Scale G has separate improvement rates for males and females. Note that the 1973 to 1983 nonrefund improvement rates are not consistent with those for the other kinds of contracts in Table 3, nor are they consistent with the population improvement rates in Table 4.

Table 4 compares U.S. 1980 population mortality (based on the 1979–81 Life Tables) for white males and white females with corresponding estimated mortality rates for the year 1990 constructed by averaging interpolated abridged tables for 1989, 1990, and 1991. (The 1989–91 Life Tables will not be available until 1996.) Shown for comparison are the annual improvement rates of Projection Scale G. We might expect population mortality improvement to be somewhat different from that of annuitants because of self-selection and socioeconomic factors. Appendix A contains a discussion of a *MetLife Statistical Bulletin* article on the effects of socioeconomic status on population mortality, which may be helpful in evaluating Table 4.

It is likely that annuitants in general represent the higher-income, more highly educated segment of the population. Even so, differences in socioeconomic class may be the reason why annuitant mortality for amounts of annual income of $2,500 and over is somewhat lower than that for all income amounts in both the 1971–76 study and the 1976–86 study for males and females, refund and nonrefund annuities. Unfortunately, the threshold of $2,500 is low, and incompatibilities in the tabular presentations of the two studies discouraged more detailed comparisons.

Allowing for the effects of socioeconomic class on population mortality, it seems reasonable to state that both the annuity experience and the population data indicate that the 1973–83 annuity projection factors used to derive the 1983 Basic Table from the 1973 Experience Table are close to the observed improvement rates. This means that for an improvement rate of 1.5%, mortality will have decreased by about 18% during the 13 years from 1983 to 1996, suggesting that a new table will be needed for 1996.

The 10% loading in 1983 Table *a* was not intended to provide a margin for future mortality improvement; rather, it provides a margin for companies that experience lower-than-average annuitant mortality. The 1983 Table *a* Committee tested the 10% loading using data from the 1971–76 annuity study and noted that it covered all but three of the companies tested and

TABLE 3

COMPARISON OF ANNUITANT MORTALITY ANNUAL IMPROVEMENT RATES EXPERIENCE
BY AMOUNTS OF ANNUAL INCOME—ALL CONTRACT YEARS

Attained Age Groups	Annual Improvement Rates, %				1973 to 1983 Projection Factors,[a] %	Projection Scale G,[e] %	
	Male Lives		Female Lives			Male	Female
	1969 to 1973	1973 to 1983	1969 to 1973	1973 to 1983			
Nonrefund Annuities							
<60		3.49*		1.47*	2.25[b]	1.60	1.85
60–69	−0.24	1.79	0.25	1.13	2.25	1.50	1.75
70–79	1.05	−0.86	−0.42	−2.52	2.125	1.25	1.60
80 and up	0.60	−0.22	1.66	−0.12	1.625[c]	1.25	1.50
All	0.63	0.10	1.17	0	—	—	—
Refund Annuities							
<60		−0.06		1.42	2.25[b]	1.60	1.85
60–69	1.50	2.44	−2.53	2.41	2.25	1.50	1.75
70–79	1.15	2.40	0.67	1.97	2.125	1.25	1.60
80 and up	0.82	1.65	−0.32	2.21	1.625[c]	1.25	1.50
All	1.07	1.98	−0.10	2.10	—	—	—
Settlements from Maturities and Surrenders (Excluding Pension Trust)—Refund							
50–59		4.55		2.89*	2.25[b]	1.60	1.85
60–69		0.84		1.22	2.25	1.50	1.75
70–79		1.67		0.81	2.125	1.25	1.60
80–89		1.68		1.97	1.625[c]	1.25	1.50
90 and up		1.32		2.84	1.50[d]	1.00	1.25
All		1.57		1.71	—	—	—
Matured Deferred Annuities (Excluding Pension Trust)—Refund							
60–69		0.84		0.83	2.25	1.60	1.85
70–79		2.26		1.24	2.125	1.50	1.75
80–89		0.79		1.00	1.625	1.25	1.60
90 and up		1.02		0	1.50[d]	1.25	1.50
All		1.30		0.82	—	—	—
Matured Deferred Annuities (Excluding Pension Trust)—Nonrefund							
60–69		0.65		—	2.25	1.60	1.85
70–79		−2.31		1.29	2.125	1.50	1.75
80–89		0.81		2.28	1.625	1.25	1.60
90 and up		2.05		1.87	1.50[d]	1.25	1.50
All		0.91		2.14	—	—	—

*Indicates 10–49 deaths in numerator or denominator or both.
[a]The 1973 to 1983 projection factors were the same for males and females.
[b]Ages 37–62.
[c]Ages 82–87.
[d]Ages 92–97.
[e] Ages 55, 65, 75, 85, 95.

that the mortality of only one fell much below the 10% corridor. A review of Table C-2 of the 1976–86 annuity mortality study indicates that for some companies in the 1976–86 study, the 10% margin might fall short. However, with only eight companies in the study, there is reason not to accept the results as definitive. The use of 10% as a margin is retained in the derivation of the new annuity table described below.

TABLE 4

COMPARISON OF ANNUAL RATES OF MORTALITY IMPROVEMENT

| Attained Ages | U.S. White Population Annual Improvement Rates | | | | Projection Scale G | |
| | Male Lives | | Female Lives | | | |
	1970–80	1980–90	1970–80	1980–90	Male	Female
57	2.62%	1.82%	1.83%	0.78%	1.50%	1.75%
62	2.24	1.66	1.19	0.66	1.50	1.75
67	2.10	1.82	1.65	0.55	1.50	1.75
72	1.42	1.70	1.90	0.60	1.25	1.75
77	1.64	1.30	2.67	0.71	1.25	1.50
82	1.21	0.98	2.22	1.13	1.25	1.50
87	1.18	N.A.	1.88	N.A.	1.25	1.50
92	0.99	N.A.	1.51	N.A.	1.00	1.25

The Need for a New Individual Annuity Valuation Table

While the 1983 annuity tables seem to have been adequate for the period around 1983, the recent annuity and population mortality improvement rates suggest that the tables are probably now (1995) no longer adequate and almost certainly not adequate for the remainder of this century. If an inadequate table is used for annuity valuation, then unassigned surplus will be overstated and margins that should be retained may be paid out. The situation may be more serious for companies issuing variable annuities because investment margins are not available to make up for mortality losses, although the usual charge for mortality guarantees provides some offset. A test of adequacy of the mortality guarantee charge appears later in this paper.

To construct new, adequate individual annuity valuation tables, a new annuity study should be compiled with at least 20 contributing companies and with a breakout of experience on qualified nonpension trust business. In addition, a suitable source of mortality rates at ages below 60 must be found and evaluated. The 1949 individual annuity tables used group annuity active life experience on persons in clerical occupations; the 1971 IAM Table made use of the 1966 GAM Table at ages under 60. For the 1973 Experience Table from which the 1983 tables were derived, the unloaded 1971 IAM mortality rates were used. The study will also have to focus on the shape of the mortality curve at very high ages; the methods used for the 1994 GAM Tables could be considered.

A set of mortality improvement factors should be included as part of the valuation standard, as was done for the 1994 GAM Table; use of improvement rates on a continuing basis is the only way to keep annuity mortality tables reasonably current, although indefinite extension of mortality improvement is debatable. The use of generation mortality tables as an integral part of the valuation process should be explored in depth: it can affect not only annuity pricing, design, and valuation but also life insurance settlement options.

The long-range effects of reduced smoking, healthier diet, new prescription drugs, and new diagnostic and surgical procedures will have to be evaluated, while changes in Medicare policy in the U.S. may adversely affect mortality improvement, leaving mainly the "flywheel" effects of extended vaccination of children, effective treatment of infections such as rheumatic fever in young people and the reduction in smoking. All the necessary studies will take considerable time to complete and a date of no earlier than 2000 seems likely for collection of data and for the development of a totally new individual annuity valuation system. Meanwhile we need a replacement table for the 1983 Table a.

CONSTRUCTION OF AN INTERIM INDIVIDUAL ANNUITY VALUATION MORTALITY TABLE

We should immediately proceed to construct a new table for, say, the year 1996. Tables 3 and 4 suggest that Scale G, which was developed along with the 1983 Table a to "keep the 1983 Table a (with projection) reasonably up to date during the remainder of the century but not cause it to become unduly conservative" [5], is appropriate for updating the table. Consequently, my recommendation is to apply Scale G to update the 1983 Basic Table to 1996, graduate the resulting table to form a 1996 Basic Table, and then subtract a 10% loading. This method is suggested to quickly derive an updated table whose antecedents are known and which reasonably reflects annuitant mortality improvement from 1983 to 1996.

A set of computer procedures was developed that exactly reproduced the 1983 Basic tables and the 1983 Table a from the 1973 Experience Tables. (See Appendix B for a detailed description. Interpolated values of Scale G appear in Appendix C.) A set of 1996 basic (unloaded) tables was constructed by applying Scale G improvement rates to the 1983 Basic Tables; then a Jenkins osculatory graduation formula and a cubic curve at the high ages were used to obtain the 1996 Basic Tables. A 10% loading was deducted and the tables regraduated to produce the final 1996 IAM Tables. The new table could be referred to, if necessary, as a modification of the 1983 Table a.

Like the 1983 Table a, the age basis for the 1996 IAM is Age Nearest Birthday because the ages used in submissions to the Society of Actuaries annuity mortality studies (on which the tables are based) are age nearest birthday.

The 1996 Individual Annuity Basic tables and the 1996 IAM Tables appear in Appendixes D and E, respectively. Table 5 compares the 1983 and 1996 annuity mortality rates for every fifth age from 50 to 90. Table 6 is similar to Table 17 in the report on the derivation of the 1983 Table a [12]. It shows illustrative values of life annuities on both the 1983 and 1996 tables calculated at 5%, 7% and 9% interest and ratios of annuity values on the 1996 table to those on the 1983 table.

TABLE 5

COMPARISON OF MORTALITY RATES PER 1,000—1983 TABLE a VERSUS 1996 IAM

Age	Male			Female		
	1983 Table a	1996 IAM	1996/1983	1983 Table a	1996 IAM	1996/1983
50	4.057	3.213	79.20%	1.830	1.403	76.67%
55	5.994	4.833	80.63	2.891	2.260	78.17
60	8.338	6.834	81.96	4.467	3.566	79.83
65	12.851	10.564	82.20	7.336	5.762	78.54
70	21.371	17.913	83.82	11.697	9.256	79.13
75	35.046	29.761	84.92	20.127	16.345	81.21
80	57.026	48.449	84.96	36.395	29.786	81.84
85	90.987	77.080	84.72	65.518	54.057	82.51
90	134.887	117.140	86.84	113.605	95.846	84.37

Comparison with 1994 Group Annuity Static Tables

Two comparisons have been made with the new 1994 GAM Static Tables [13]. The first comparison, in Table 7, shows, for every fifth age from 50 to 90, 1996 IAM mortality rates and 1994 GAM Static Table rates projected to 1996 using Improvement Scale AA.

The second comparison updates Graphs 1 and 2 from the report, "Development of the 1983 Group Annuity Mortality Table" [14, p. 879], which compared 1966 and 1983 group and individual basic (unloaded) tables. The updated graphs (Appendix F), tracing ratios of group to individual mortality rates, include comparisons of the 1996 IAM Basic Tables with the 1994 GAM Basic Table projected to 1996 by Scale AA. Values are graphed every

TABLE 6

COMPARISON OF ANNUITY RESERVES:
1996 IAM VERSUS 1983 TABLE a IMMEDIATE ANNUITY—$1 PER ANNUM

Age	5% Interest			7% Interest			9% Interest		
	1983 Table a	1996 IAM	Ratio 1996 to 1983	1983 Table a	1996 IAM	Ratio 1996 to 1983	1983 Table a	1996 IAM	Ratio 1996 to 1983
	Male								
55	13.601	14.050	1.03	11.105	11.397	1.03	9.304	9.503	1.02
60	12.355	12.845	1.04	10.279	10.614	1.03	8.736	8.974	1.03
65	10.918	11.446	1.05	9.265	9.644	1.04	7.999	8.280	1.04
70	9.362	9.909	1.06	8.106	8.519	1.05	7.115	7.433	1.04
75	7.775	8.330	1.07	6.867	7.306	1.06	6.130	6.481	1.06
80	6.237	6.779	1.09	5.613	6.060	1.08	5.092	5.465	1.07
85	4.861	5.351	1.10	4.450	4.869	1.09	4.097	4.459	1.09
90	3.722	4.121	1.11	3.459	3.810	1.10	3.228	3.538	1.10
	Female								
55	14.772	15.188	1.03	11.874	12.129	1.02	9.831	9.995	1.02
60	13.613	14.091	1.04	11.148	11.459	1.03	9.356	9.567	1.02
65	12.262	12.799	1.04	10.246	10.616	1.04	8.734	8.997	1.03
70	10.728	11.305	1.05	9.158	9.577	1.05	7.941	8.253	1.04
75	9.016	9.621	1.07	7.868	8.331	1.06	6.948	7.310	1.05
80	7.239	7.850	1.08	6.455	6.946	1.08	5.807	6.208	1.07
85	5.543	6.118	1.10	5.041	5.524	1.10	4.615	5.024	1.09
90	4.100	4.608	1.12	3.793	4.234	1.12	3.525	3.912	1.11

TABLE 7

COMPARISON OF MORTALITY RATES PER 1,000
1996 IAM VERSUS 1994 GAM STATIC PROJECTED TO 1996

Age	Male			Female		
	1994 GAM Static Projected to 1996	1996 IAM	Ratio GAM/IAM	1994 GAM Static Projected to 1996	1996 IAM	Ratio GAM/IAM
50	2.487	3.213	0.77	1.380	1.403	0.98
55	4.258	4.833	0.88	2.257	2.260	1.00
60	7.723	6.834	1.13	4.395	3.566	1.23
65	14.131	10.564	1.34	8.550	5.762	1.48
70	23.023	17.913	1.29	13.593	9.256	1.47
75	36.176	29.761	1.22	22.324	16.345	1.37
80	60.793	48.449	1.25	38.846	29.786	1.30
85	95.883	77.080	1.24	66.928	54.057	1.24
90	151.710	117.140	1.30	115.568	95.846	1.21

fifth age from 50 to 80. The 1983 Group Annuity Table report identified the 1966 rates as the 1966 Group Annuity Experience Table and the 1963 (individual annuity) Experience Table projected to 1966. The graph shows remarkable consistency over the three decades from 1966 to 1996.

Financial Tests

To test the effect on liabilities (reserves) of adopting the 1996 IAM Tables, a model office was constructed using life table methods assuming that the same amount of immediate life annuity premium was issued at each of ages 60 through 85 over 10 years. At interest rates of 5%, 7%, and 9%, aggregate reserves on the 1996 table were 6.8%, 6.1%, and 5.5%, respectively, higher than reserves on the 1983 tables at the end of 10 years. There was little change when the model office was extended to 20 years. To put the test in perspective, the ratio of capital stock and surplus (excluding Asset Valuation Reserves) to total assets for all U.S. life insurance companies was 8.6% at the end of 1994. The life table functions used in constructing the model office were based on the 1996 IAM.

Since one of the reasons for adopting an up-to-date annuity mortality table is to avoid future mortality losses on variable annuities where interest gains cannot be used to make up such losses, a simple test was made of the adequacy of the usual 0.5% of funds charge for mortality guarantees. Assuming a contract is issued with annual payments of $1,000 consideration accumulated for 13 years from 1983 to 1996 when it matures at age 65, would the accumulated charges be sufficient to make up the difference between the amount of a single premium at 7% on the 1983 Table and one on the 1996 Table?

Two tests were made. In one test the variable annuity fund was accumulated at 10% over the period and in the other, at 15%. In both tests, the mortality guarantee charges were accumulated at 7% assuming they were not carried in a separate account. A 0.5% annual expense guarantee charge was also deducted. No other charges were deducted.

Under the 10% accumulation rate, there is a small profit for both male and female contracts (0.15% and 0.63% of the fund, respectively). If the separate account fund does very well, as illustrated by a 15% accumulation rate, then there is a small loss (0.42%) for male contracts and a small gain (0.06%) for female contracts.

CONCLUSION

This paper was written (1) to call attention to the increasing inadequacy of the 1983 Table a as a valuation standard, (2) to call for a much enlarged study of annuity mortality including an evaluation of qualified nonpension trust business, further study of refund versus nonrefund mortality experience and investigation of possible sources of mortality rates at ages under 60, and (3) to propose adoption of an interim table such as the 1996 IAM Table as a valuation standard. I believe that the paper provides food for thought on each of these points. If the 1996 table is adopted, I will make available a set of blended mortality tables [15, 16] corresponding to those on the 1983 Table a.

END NOTES

1. COMMITTEE ON ORDINARY INSURANCE AND ANNUITIES. "Mortality under Individual Annuities, Life Income Settlements, and Matured Deferred Annuities between 1971 and 1976 Anniversaries," *TSA 1979 Reports of Mortality and Morbidity Experience* (1980): 65–219.

2. INDIVIDUAL ANNUITY EXPERIENCE COMMITTEE. "Mortality under Individual Immediate Annuities, Life Income Settlements, and Matured Deferred Annuities between 1976 and 1986 Anniversaries," *TSA 1991–92 Reports of Mortality, Morbidity and Other Experience* (1993): 65–116.

3. There were 21 companies in the 1967–71 study.

4. See Appendix Table A in both the 1971–76 [1] and 1976–86 [2] studies.

5. "Report of the Committee to Recommend a New Mortality Basis for Individual Annuity Valuation (Derivation of the 1983 Table a)," *TSA* XXXIII (1981): 675–751.

6. See page 70 of the 1976–86 study [1].

7. See Table 40 on page 119 of the 1971–76 study [1].

8. See the 1971–76 study [1] and "Report of the Committee to Recommend a New Mortality Basis for Annuity Valuation (Derivation of the 1983 Table a)" [5].

9. JOHANSEN, R.J. "NAIC Adopts Annuity Table Test," *The Actuary* 19, no. 5 (May 1985): 1, 4.

10. JOHANSEN, R.J. Discussion of "United States Life Tables for 1979–81," by R.J. Myers and F.R. Bayo, *TSA* XXXVII (1985): 345.

11. COMMITTEE ON ORDINARY INSURANCE AND ANNUITIES. "Mortality under Individual Immediate Annuities between 1967 and 1971 Contract Anniversaries," *TSA 1973 Reports of Mortality and Morbidity Experience* (1974): 59–126.

12. See Table 17, "Report of the Committee to Recommend a New Mortality Basis for Annuity Valuation (Derivation of the 1983 Table a) [5].

13. SOCIETY OF ACTUARIES GROUP ANNUITY VALUATION TABLE TASK FORCE. "1994 Group Annuity Mortality Table and 1994 Group Annuity Reserving Table," *TSA* XLVII (1995): 865–920.

14. COMMITTEE ON ANNUITIES. "Development of the 1983 Group Annuity Mortality Table," *TSA* XXXV (1983): 879.
15. SOCIETY OF ACTUARIES COMMITTEE ON NONFORFEITURE AND VALUATION MORTALITY PROBLEMS—INDIVIDUAL LIFE INSURANCE AND ANNUITIES. "Blended 1980 CSO and CET Mortality Tables," *TSA* XXXVII (1985): 393–448.
16. JOHANSEN, ROBERT J. "Blended Mortality Tables—Life Insurance and Annuities," *TSA* XXXIV (1987): 41–105.

APPENDIX A

DISCUSSION ON "THE WIDENING GAP BETWEEN SOCIOECONOMIC STATUS AND MORTALITY"

The April–June 1994 edition of the *MetLife Statistical Bulletin* included an article on "The Widening Gap Between Socioeconomic Status and Mortality."* The article, attributed to several authors at the National Center for Health Statistics, compared 1986 data with a similar 1960 study by Kitagawa and Hauser. The authors stated that their studies "showed that the disparity in U.S. mortality rates according to income and education has increased over the years for men and women and for whites and blacks." Further, the studies showed that mortality over the period 1960 to 1986 improved more among persons with higher levels of education and income for both men and women. The table below shows some of the results for which numerical values were provided in the article—unfortunately only the published results from the 1960 study were available to the authors; backup material had not been archived.

AGE-ADJUSTED MORTALITY RATES—U.S. WHITE POPULATION, AGES 25–64*

		Low Education	High Education	Low Income	High Income
Male	1960	9.0	5.8	NA	NA
	1986	7.6	2.8	16.0	2.4
Female	1960	5.3	3.4	NA	NA
	1986	3.4	1.8	6.5	1.6

*Rates per 1,000 adjusted on 1940 U.S. total population.
NA: Rates were not provided in the article.

The *Statistical Bulletin* article showed that mortality for white men with low education decreased 16% from 1960 to 1986, while that for men with high

*QUEEN, S., PAPPAS, G., HADDEN, W., AND FISHER, G. (all at the National Center for Health Statistics). "The Widening Gap Between Socioeconomic Status and Mortality," *MetLife Statistical Bulletin* (April–June 1994): 31–5; based on data from the 1986 National Mortality Followback Survey, the 1986 National Health Interview Survey, and the 1960 Matched Record Study.

education decreased 52%. Mortality for white women with low education decreased 36% from 1960 to 1986, while that for women with high education decreased 40%. Note that in 1986 mortality for white men with high education was lower than that for women with low education; the same was true in the comparison by income for 1986.

APPENDIX B

SUMMARY OF CALCULATION METHOD FOR 1996 INDIVIDUAL ANNUITY MORTALITY TABLES

The method outlined here was briefly described in the Report of the Committee to Recommend a New Mortality Basis for Individual Annuity Valuation.* The computer programs that implemented this method were tested by reproducing from the 1973 Experience Tables both the 1983 Basic Table and the 1983 Table a appearing in the report.

If s_x is the annual improvement rate percentage at age x, then multiply $1000q_x$ by $(1-s_x/100)^{13}$ at each age to produce an ungraduated 1996 mortality table. Selecting values of q_x at every fifth age from 7 to 97, the table was graduated by a Jenkins fifth difference osculatory formula. A cubic interpolation formula was fitted to values of q_x at ages 95, 96, and 97 and a value of unity at the limiting age, 115. Mortality rates at ages 5 and 6 were obtained by applying the ratio of $q_7^{1996 \ \text{Basic}}/q_7^{1983 \ \text{Basic}}$ to $q_5^{1983 \ \text{Basic}}$ and $q_6^{1983 \ \text{Basic}}$, respectively. This is the same calculation that was used to derive values of q_5 and q_6 in the 1983 Table a. The resulting tables are referred to as 1996 Basic Tables.

A loading of 10%, the same loading percentage as that used for the 1983 tables, was deducted from the graduated 1996 Basic Tables to produce ungraduated, loaded tables. Proceeding in the same way as for the 1996 Basic Tables, I applied the Jenkins graduation formula and the cubic curve to produce the graduated 1996 Individual Annuity Mortality Table. Values of q_5 and q_6 were obtained as above for the 1996 Basic Tables except that the numerator of the ratio was the mortality rate for age 7 on the graduated 1996 Annuity Table.

---

*"Report of the Committee to Recommend a New Mortality Basis for Individual Annuity Valuation (Derivation of the 1983 Table a)," *TSA* XXXIII (1981): 694–704.

APPENDIX C

ANNUITY IMPROVEMENT SCALE G

Age Nearest Birthday	Annual Improvement Rate	Age Nearest Birthday	Annual Improvement Rate	Age Nearest Birthday	Annual Improvement Rate
		Male			
5	1.50%	45	1.85%	85	1.25%
6	1.50	46	1.80	86	1.25
7	1.50	47	1.75	87	1.25
8	1.25	48	1.75	88	1.20
9	1.00	49	1.75	89	1.15
10	0.75	50	1.75	90	1.10
11	0.50	51	1.75	91	1.05
12	0.25	52	1.75	92	1.00
13	0.24	53	1.70	93	1.00
14	0.23	54	1.65	94	1.00
15	0.22	55	1.60	95	1.00
16	0.21	56	1.55	96	1.00
17	0.20	57	1.50	97	1.00
18	0.18	58	1.50	98	0.80
19	0.16	59	1.50	99	0.60
20	0.14	60	1.50	100	0.40
21	0.12	61	1.50	101	0.20
22	0.10	62	1.50	102	0.00
23	0.10	63	1.50	103	0.00
24	0.10	64	1.50	104	0.00
25	0.10	65	1.50	105	0.00
26	0.10	66	1.50	106	0.00
27	0.10	67	1.50	107	0.00
28	0.23	68	1.45	108	0.00
29	0.36	69	1.40	109	0.00
30	0.49	70	1.35	110	0.00
31	0.62	71	1.30	111	0.00
32	0.75	72	1.25	112	0.00
33	1.00	73	1.25	113	0.00
34	1.25	74	1.25	114	0.00
35	1.50	75	1.25	115	0.00
36	1.75	76	1.25		
37	2.00	77	1.25		
38	2.00	78	1.25		
39	2.00	79	1.25		
40	2.00	80	1.25		
41	2.00	81	1.25		
42	2.00	82	1.25		
43	1.95	83	1.25		
44	1.90	84	1.25		

Sum = 109.50

APPENDIX C—*Continued*

Age Nearest Birthday	Annual Improvement Rate	Age Nearest Birthday	Annual Improvement Rate	Age Nearest Birthday	Annual Improvement Rate
		Female			
5	1.50	45	2.10%	85	1.50%
6	1.50	46	2.05	86	1.50
7	1.50	47	2.00	87	1.50
8	1.40	48	2.00	88	1.45
9	1.30	49	2.00	89	1.40
10	1.20	50	2.00	90	1.35
11	1.10	51	2.00	91	1.30
12	1.00	52	2.00	92	1.25
13	0.90	53	1.95	93	1.25
14	0.80	54	1.90	94	1.25
15	0.70	55	1.85	95	1.25
16	0.60	56	1.80	96	1.25
17	0.50	57	1.75	97	1.25
18	0.50	58	1.75	98	1.00
19	0.50	59	1.75	99	0.75
20	0.50	60	1.75	100	0.50
21	0.50	61	1.75	101	0.25
22	0.50	62	1.75	102	0.00
23	0.55	63	1.75	103	0.00
24	0.60	64	1.75	104	0.00
25	0.65	65	1.75	105	0.00
26	0.70	66	1.75	106	0.00
27	0.75	67	1.75	107	0.00
28	0.85	68	1.75	108	0.00
29	0.95	69	1.75	109	0.00
30	1.05	70	1.75	110	0.00
31	1.15	71	1.75	111	0.00
32	1.25	72	1.75	112	0.00
33	1.45	73	1.70	113	0.00
34	1.65	74	1.65	114	0.00
35	1.85	75	1.60	115	0.00
36	2.05	76	1.55		
37	2.25	77	1.50		
38	2.25	78	1.50		
39	2.25	79	1.50		
40	2.25	80	1.50		
41	2.25	81	1.50		
42	2.25	82	1.50		
43	2.20	83	1.50		
44	2.15	84	1.50		

Sum = 140.00

APPENDIX D

1996 INDIVIDUAL ANNUITY BASIC TABLE

Age Nearest Birthday	1000 q_x	Age Nearest Birthday	1000 q_x	Age Nearest Birthday	1000 q_x
			Male		
5	0.344	45	2.097	85	85.600
6	0.320	46	2.363	86	93.466
7	0.304	47	2.647	87	101.851
8	0.342	48	2.943	88	110.762
9	0.373	49	3.253	89	120.192
10	0.398	50	3.576	90	130.139
11	0.419	51	3.914	91	140.593
12	0.436	52	4.266	92	151.547
13	0.450	53	4.634	93	162.997
14	0.462	54	5.017	94	174.935
15	0.473	55	5.411	95	187.361
16	0.485	56	5.816	96	200.266
17	0.498	57	6.230	97	213.647
18	0.513	58	6.655	98	227.911
19	0.531	59	7.109	99	243.465
20	0.552	60	7.616	100	260.717
21	0.575	61	8.196	101	280.073
22	0.600	62	8.874	102	301.940
23	0.628	63	9.670	103	326.726
24	0.658	64	10.603	104	354.838
25	0.687	65	11.691	105	386.683
26	0.716	66	12.951	106	422.667
27	0.742	67	14.402	107	463.199
28	0.764	68	16.055	108	508.685
29	0.783	69	17.910	109	559.532
30	0.798	70	19.958	110	616.148
31	0.808	71	22.194	111	678.939
32	0.815	72	24.609	112	748.312
33	0.818	73	27.206	113	824.676
34	0.822	74	30.019	114	908.436
35	0.831	75	33.093	115	1,000.000
36	0.852	76	36.470		
37	0.889	77	40.194		
38	0.947	78	44.305		
39	1.028	79	48.825		
40	1.134	80	53.775		
41	1.268	81	59.175		
42	1.432	82	65.042		
43	1.627	83	71.396		
44	1.850	84	78.246		

Sum = 11853.681

APPENDIX D—*Continued*

Age Nearest Birthday	1000 q_x	Age Nearest Birthday	1000 q_x	Age Nearest Birthday	1000 q_x
			Female		
5	0.176	45	0.948	85	59.601
6	0.146	46	1.045	86	67.043
7	0.122	47	1.154	87	75.446
8	0.123	48	1.276	88	84.869
9	0.126	49	1.411	89	95.169
10	0.132	50	1.560	90	106.162
11	0.140	51	1.723	91	117.658
12	0.151	52	1.900	92	129.468
13	0.163	53	2.093	93	141.412
14	0.177	54	2.301	94	153.330
15	0.192	55	2.526	95	165.074
16	0.207	56	2.767	96	176.488
17	0.223	57	3.025	97	187.422
18	0.239	58	3.303	98	198.488
19	0.255	59	3.607	99	210.299
20	0.271	60	3.949	100	223.465
21	0.288	61	4.338	101	238.601
22	0.305	62	4.783	102	256.317
23	0.322	63	5.291	103	277.226
24	0.340	64	5.858	104	301.940
25	0.357	65	6.475	105	331.072
26	0.374	66	7.135	106	365.232
27	0.390	67	7.829	107	405.034
28	0.404	68	8.560	108	451.090
29	0.418	69	9.365	109	504.011
30	0.429	70	10.291	110	564.410
31	0.440	71	11.385	111	632.900
32	0.448	72	12.694	112	710.091
33	0.455	73	14.258	113	796.597
34	0.463	74	16.089	114	893.029
35	0.472	75	18.194	115	1,000.000
36	0.486	76	20.578		
37	0.505	77	23.247		
38	0.531	78	26.215		
39	0.566	79	29.523		
40	0.608	80	33.224		
41	0.659	81	37.366		
42	0.718	82	41.999		
43	0.785	83	47.185		
44	0.861	84	53.016		

Sum = 10422.897

APPENDIX E

1996 INDIVIDUAL ANNUITY MORTALITY TABLE

Age Nearest Birthday	1000 q_x	Age Nearest Birthday	1000 q_x	Age Nearest Birthday	1000 q_x
		Male			
5	0.310	45	1.887	85	77.080
6	0.288	46	2.124	86	84.158
7	0.274	47	2.377	87	91.701
8	0.307	48	2.643	88	99.715
9	0.335	49	2.922	89	108.196
10	0.358	50	3.213	90	117.140
11	0.376	51	3.516	91	126.540
12	0.392	52	3.829	92	136.392
13	0.405	53	4.153	93	146.691
14	0.417	54	4.487	94	157.432
15	0.427	55	4.833	95	168.615
16	0.438	56	5.190	96	180.232
17	0.451	57	5.560	97	192.282
18	0.465	58	5.947	98	205.218
19	0.481	59	6.365	99	219.494
20	0.500	60	6.834	100	235.563
21	0.520	61	7.372	101	253.878
22	0.543	62	7.997	102	274.893
23	0.567	63	8.728	103	299.061
24	0.593	64	9.579	104	326.834
25	0.618	65	10.564	105	358.668
26	0.642	66	11.696	106	395.014
27	0.664	67	12.989	107	436.326
28	0.682	68	14.456	108	483.057
29	0.697	69	16.096	109	535.662
30	0.709	70	17.913	110	594.592
31	0.718	71	19.903	111	660.302
32	0.724	72	22.068	112	733.244
33	0.729	73	24.414	113	813.872
34	0.735	74	26.967	114	902.640
35	0.747	75	29.761	115	1,000.000
36	0.770	76	32.829		
37	0.807	77	36.205		
38	0.862	78	39.919		
39	0.937	79	43.993		
40	1.034	80	48.449		
41	1.155	81	53.305		
42	1.301	82	58.582		
43	1.473	83	64.299		
44	1.669	84	70.462		

Sum = 11195.038

APPENDIX E—*Continued*

Age Nearest Birthday	$1000\,q_x$	Age Nearest Birthday	$1000\,q_x$	Age Nearest Birthday	$1000\,q_x$
			Female		
5	0.159	45	0.853	85	54.057
6	0.131	46	0.941	86	60.857
7	0.110	47	1.039	87	68.464
8	0.111	48	1.149	88	76.911
9	0.114	49	1.270	89	86.087
10	0.119	50	1.403	90	95.846
11	0.127	51	1.548	91	106.039
12	0.136	52	1.705	92	116.521
13	0.147	53	1.876	93	127.149
14	0.159	54	2.060	94	137.798
15	0.172	55	2.260	95	148.351
16	0.186	56	2.477	96	158.684
17	0.200	57	2.713	97	168.680
18	0.215	58	2.970	98	178.961
19	0.230	59	3.252	99	190.149
20	0.245	60	3.566	100	202.865
21	0.260	61	3.916	101	217.733
22	0.276	62	4.308	102	235.373
23	0.291	63	4.746	103	256.408
24	0.307	64	5.231	104	281.459
25	0.322	65	5.762	105	311.150
26	0.336	66	6.339	106	346.100
27	0.350	67	6.963	107	386.933
28	0.362	68	7.637	108	434.271
29	0.373	69	8.390	109	488.734
30	0.383	70	9.256	110	550.947
31	0.392	71	10.268	111	621.529
32	0.400	72	11.459	112	701.104
33	0.407	73	12.859	113	790.292
34	0.415	74	14.484	114	889.717
35	0.426	75	16.345	115	1,000.000
36	0.439	76	18.454		
37	0.457	77	20.822		
38	0.481	78	23.469		
39	0.512	79	26.439		
40	0.549	80	29.786		
41	0.593	81	33.560		
42	0.646	82	37.814		
43	0.706	83	42.605		
44	0.775	84	47.995		

Sum = 9942.177

APPENDIX F

RATIOS OF GROUP ANNUITY MORTALITY
TO INDIVIDUAL ANNUITY MORTALITY

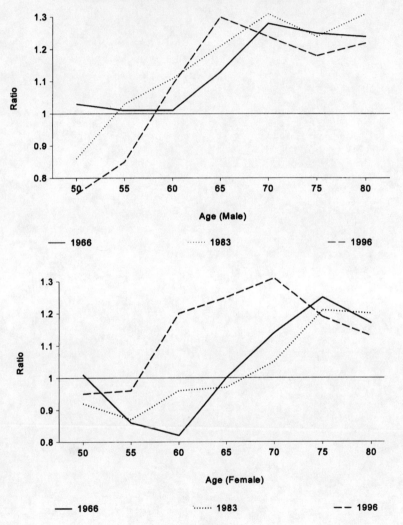

DISCUSSION OF PRECEDING PAPER

JOHN M. BRAGG:

Mr. Johansen is to be congratulated for producing this fine paper, which includes a badly needed new valuation table, the 1996 Individual Annuity Mortality Table.

I very much agree with Mr. Johansen that a new annuity study should be compiled. I hope that it could be completed before the year 2000.

It is unfortunate that the 1996 Individual Annuity Basic Table again had to be projected from an earlier table; the original data were for contract anniversaries 1971–1976, which is a long way back. However, that is all that could be done in the absence of new data.

In 1993, Bragg Associates created the 1993 Bragg Old Age Aggregate Tables from insured-life records. The exposure period was 1985–1991; total exposure was $50.5 billion. The tables are "aggregate" for smoking and for duration but not for sex. The only policy durations included were 6 and up, so that much of the effect of initial selection would have worn off. (This is the basis used in the past to create CSO Basic Tables.)

This is individual insured-life experience, not annuitant experience. However, it *is* fairly recent, centering in 1989. A comparison with 1996 Individual Annuitant Basic is shown below.

	$1000q_x$			
	Male		Female	
Age Nearest Birthday	1996 IA Basic	1993 Bragg Old Age Aggregate	1996 IA Basic	1993 Bragg Old Age Aggregate
55	5.411	4.82	2.526	3.67
65	11.691	12.20	6.475	7.64
75	33.093	30.73	18.194	19.02
85	85.600	87.30	59.601	66.78
95	187.361	214.69	165.074	210.86

In general, these values are quite similar except at the high age 95. Marginally, the annuitant numbers are perhaps lower than the Bragg Aggregate numbers (as preconceived expectations would expect for annuitant business). I concluded from the above that Improvement Scale G, used by

235

Mr. Johansen, had done an adequate job. However, Bragg Old Age Aggregate values, centered in 1996 rather than 1989, might be lower than those shown above.

The 10% margin taken off, to arrive at the 1996 IAM Table itself, gives considerable comfort.

Mr. Johansen discusses the question: "Why are mortality ratios under refund business generally lower than those under nonrefund business, a finding that was counter to expectations and prior trends?" I have no magic answers to this question. However, it does occur to me that people who opt for nonrefund annuities are perhaps straining for maximum annuity payments, at all costs, because of economic necessity; economic necessity could go along with higher mortality. We may be entering a period when many preconceived expectations will prove faulty.

(AUTHOR'S REVIEW OF DISCUSSION)

ROBERT J. JOHANSEN:

First let me express my thanks to John M. Bragg for his discussion of my paper. I especially appreciate his seconding of my appeal for a substantial new annuity experience study. The need was illustrated by the effort to develop the interim Annuity 2000 valuation tables described later in this review.

Mr. Bragg's recent insurance mortality rates add some additional foundation to the construction of an annuity table from improvement factors. He may also have come up with the most reasonable argument yet that accounts for higher mortality among nonrefund than among refund annuitants—that nonrefund annuitants are likely to have sought additional income because of economic necessity and that such persons are also likely to experience somewhat higher mortality.

Subsequent to publication of my paper in preprint form, the National Association of Insurance Commissioners (NAIC) Life and Health Actuarial Task Force Annuity Working Group (AWG) decided that a new individual annuity table was needed. However, the working group wanted a more conservative table than the 1996 IAM included in my paper. Initially the AWG wanted a generation table but agreed to an interim static table to be constructed by projecting the 1983 Table a for 17 years to the year 2000 using Improvement Scale G. I agreed to produce a set of projected basic and loaded mortality tables. The Society of Actuaries Committee on Life Insurance Research (COLIFER) appointed a Project Oversight Group* (POG) to review the new tables.

The POG examined recent U.S. population and Social Security improvement rates and also took into consideration the annuitant mortality experience of the company of one of the POG members. This annuity experience indicated that female mortality improvement since 1983 had been only about half that of male annuitants. The POG suggested using only half the female Scale G improvement rates. The new Annuity 2000 Basic and (loaded) Mortality Tables (included with this discussion) reflect this modification. The loading consisted of a deduction of 10% of the Basic Table rates. The resulting rates were then graduated. An adjustment was made to the male table to remove a small dip in the 30s.

The Society of Actuaries Board of Governors authorized COLIFER to make a statement of opinion accepting the table. The opinion states:

> The attached Annuity 2000 *Basic* Table represents the Committee on Life Insurance Research's best estimate of the mortality pattern that has resulted from the mortality improvement experienced since 1983. The Committee believes that the Annuity 2000 *Mortality* Table is a suitable basis for the statutory valuation of individual annuity business written on lives in the United States.
>
> Note that this recommendation does not apply to structured settlements.

The following table compares Mr. Bragg's insurance mortality rates with the Annuity 2000 Basic mortality rates. The male and female ratios are quite comparable.

COMPARISON OF 1993 BRAGG OLD AGE AGGREGATE TABLES
WITH ANNUITY 2000 BASIC TABLES

Age Nearest Birthday	Male			Female		
	Annuity 2000 Basic	1993 Bragg Old Age Aggregate	Ratio % 2000 to 1993	Annuity 2000 Basic	1993 Bragg Old Age Aggregate	Ratio % 2000 to 1993
55	5.077	4.82	105.3	2.746	3.67	74.8
65	10.993	12.20	90.1	7.017	7.64	91.8
75	31.477	30.73	102.4	19.551	19.02	102.8
85	81.326	87.30	93.2	63.907	66.78	95.7
95	180.245	214.69	84.0	174.492	210.86	82.8

*Harry Klaristenfeld, Chair, Steve Garavaglia, John Paddon, Mark Peavy, and Jonathan Wooley.

The following tables were attached to my August 21, 1996 report on annuity valuation to the Society's Individual Annuity Mortality Table Project Oversight Group.

- Table 1 is the Annuity 2000 Basic (unloaded) Table.
- Table 2 is the Annuity 2000 (loaded) Mortality Table.
- Table 3 compares the Annuity 2000 Mortality Table with the 1983 Table *a*.
- Table 4 compares immediate annuity single premiums on the 1983 Table *a* and Annuity 2000 Basic Table at 5%, 7%, and 9% interest.
- Tables 5, 6, and 7 summarize pertinent data on annuitant mortality.
- Table 8 provides some annual improvement rates based on U.S. population mortality.
- Table 9 shows a test of smoothness of the Annuity 2000 Mortality Table using first and second differences.

TABLE 1

ANNUITY 2000 BASIC TABLE

Age Nearest Birthday (x)	$1000q_x$		Age Nearest Birthday (x)	$1000q_x$	
	Male	Female*		Male	Female*
5	0.324	0.189	61	7.714	4.699
6	0.301	0.156	62	8.348	5.181
7	0.286	0.131	63	9.093	5.732
8	0.328	0.131	64	9.968	6.347
9	0.362	0.134	65	10.993	7.017
10	0.390	0.140	66	12.188	7.734
11	0.413	0.148	67	13.572	8.491
12	0.431	0.158	68	15.160	9.288
13	0.446	0.170	69	16.946	10.163
14	0.458	0.183	70	18.920	11.165
15	0.470	0.197	71	21.071	12.339
16	0.481	0.212	72	23.388	13.734
17	0.495	0.228	73	25.871	15.391
18	0.510	0.244	74	28.552	17.326
19	0.528	0.260	75	31.477	19.551
20	0.549	0.277	76	34.686	22.075
21	0.573	0.294	77	38.225	24.910
22	0.599	0.312	78	42.132	28.074
23	0.627	0.330	79	46.427	31.612
24	0.657	0.349	80	51.128	35.580
25	0.686	0.367	81	56.250	40.030
26	0.714	0.385	82	61.809	45.017
27	0.738	0.403	83	67.826	50.600
28	0.758	0.419	84	74.322	56.865
29	0.774	0.435	85	81.326	63.907
30	0.784	0.450	86	88.863	71.815
31	0.789	0.463	87	96.958	80.682
32	0.789	0.476	88	105.631	90.557
33	0.790	0.488	89	114.858	101.307
34	0.791	0.500	90	124.612	112.759
35	0.792	0.515	91	134.861	124.733
36	0.794	0.534	92	145.575	137.054
37	0.823	0.558	93	156.727	149.552
38	0.872	0.590	94	168.290	162.079
39	0.945	0.630	95	180.245	174.492
40	1.043	0.677	96	192.565	186.647
41	1.168	0.732	97	205.229	198.403
42	1.322	0.796	98	218.683	210.337
43	1.505	0.868	99	233.371	223.027
44	1.715	0.950	100	249.741	237.051
45	1.948	1.043	101	268.237	252.985
46	2.198	1.148	102	289.305	271.406
47	2.463	1.267	103	313.391	292.893
48	2.740	1.400	104	340.940	318.023
49	3.028	1.548	105	372.398	347.373
50	3.330	1.710	106	408.210	381.520
51	3.647	1.888	107	448.823	421.042
52	3.980	2.079	108	494.681	466.516
53	4.331	2.286	109	546.231	518.520
54	4.698	2.507	110	603.917	577.631
55	5.077	2.746	111	668.186	644.427
56	5.465	3.003	112	739.483	719.484
57	5.861	3.280	113	818.254	803.380
58	6.265	3.578	114	904.945	896.693
59	6.694	3.907	115	1000.000	1000.000
60	7.170	4.277			

*Based on 50% of Female Improvement Scale G.

TABLE 2

ANNUITY 2000 MORTALITY TABLE

Age Nearest Birthday (x)	$1000q_x$		Age Nearest Birthday (x)	$1000q_x$	
	Male	Female*		Male	Female*
5	0.291	0.171	61	6.933	4.242
6	0.270	0.141	62	7.520	4.668
7	0.257	0.118	63	8.207	5.144
8	0.294	0.118	64	9.008	5.671
9	0.325	0.121	65	9.940	6.250
10	0.350	0.126	66	11.016	6.878
11	0.371	0.133	67	12.251	7.555
12	0.388	0.142	68	13.657	8.287
13	0.402	0.152	69	15.233	9.102
14	0.414	0.164	70	16.979	10.034
15	0.425	0.177	71	18.891	11.117
16	0.437	0.190	72	20.967	12.386
17	0.449	0.204	73	23.209	13.871
18	0.463	0.219	74	25.644	15.592
19	0.480	0.234	75	28.304	17.564
20	0.499	0.250	76	31.220	19.805
21	0.519	0.265	77	34.425	22.328
22	0.542	0.281	78	37.948	25.158
23	0.566	0.298	79	41.812	28.341
24	0.592	0.314	80	46.037	31.933
25	0.616	0.331	81	50.643	35.985
26	0.639	0.347	82	55.651	40.552
27	0.659	0.362	83	61.080	45.690
28	0.675	0.376	84	66.948	51.456
29	0.687	0.389	85	73.275	57.913
30	0.694	0.402	86	80.076	65.119
31	0.699	0.414	87	87.370	73.136
32	0.700	0.425	88	95.169	81.991
33	0.701	0.436	89	103.455	91.577
34	0.702	0.449	90	112.208	101.758
35	0.704	0.463	91	121.402	112.395
36	0.719	0.481	92	131.017	123.349
37	0.749	0.504	93	141.030	134.486
38	0.796	0.532	94	151.422	145.689
39	0.864	0.567	95	162.179	156.846
40	0.953	0.609	96	173.279	167.841
41	1.065	0.658	97	184.706	178.563
42	1.201	0.715	98	196.946	189.604
43	1.362	0.781	99	210.484	201.557
44	1.547	0.855	100	225.806	215.013
45	1.752	0.939	101	243.398	230.565
46	1.974	1.035	102	263.745	248.805
47	2.211	1.141	103	287.334	270.326
48	2.460	1.261	104	314.649	295.719
49	2.721	1.393	105	346.177	325.576
50	2.994	1.538	106	382.403	360.491
51	3.279	1.695	107	423.813	401.054
52	3.576	1.864	108	470.893	447.860
53	3.884	2.047	109	524.128	501.498
54	4.203	2.244	110	584.004	562.563
55	4.534	2.457	111	651.007	631.645
56	4.876	2.689	112	725.622	709.338
57	5.228	2.942	113	808.336	796.233
58	5.593	3.218	114	899.633	892.923
59	5.988	3.523	115	1000.000	1000.000
60	6.428	3.863			

*Based on 50% of Female Improvement Scale G.

TABLE 3

COMPARISON OF ANNUITY 2000 MORTALITY TABLE WITH 1983 TABLE a

Age Nearest Birthday (x)	1983 Mortality Table a	Annuity 2000 Mortality Table	Ratio 2000/1983	Age Nearest Birthday (x)	1983 Mortality Table a	Annuity 2000 Mortality Table	Ratio 2000/1983
	$1000q_x$				$1000q_x$		
	Male				Male		
5	0.377	0.291	77.19	61	8.983	6.933	77.18
6	0.350	0.270	77.14	62	9.740	7.520	77.21
7	0.333	0.257	77.18	63	10.630	8.207	77.21
8	0.352	0.294	83.52	64	11.664	9.008	77.23
9	0.368	0.325	88.32	65	12.851	9.940	77.35
10	0.382	0.350	91.62	66	14.199	11.016	77.58
11	0.394	0.371	94.16	67	15.717	12.251	77.95
12	0.405	0.388	95.80	68	17.414	13.657	78.43
13	0.415	0.402	96.87	69	19.296	15.233	78.94
14	0.425	0.414	97.41	70	21.371	16.979	79.45
15	0.435	0.425	97.70	71	23.647	18.891	79.89
16	0.446	0.437	97.98	72	26.131	20.967	80.24
17	0.458	0.449	98.03	73	28.835	23.209	80.49
18	0.472	0.463	98.09	74	31.794	25.644	80.66
19	0.488	0.480	98.36	75	35.046	28.304	80.76
20	0.505	0.499	98.81	76	38.631	31.220	80.82
21	0.525	0.519	98.86	77	42.587	34.425	80.83
22	0.546	0.542	99.27	78	46.951	37.948	80.82
23	0.570	0.566	99.30	79	51.755	41.812	80.79
24	0.596	0.592	99.33	80	57.026	46.037	80.73
25	0.622	0.616	99.04	81	62.791	50.643	80.65
26	0.650	0.639	98.31	82	69.081	55.651	80.56
27	0.677	0.659	97.34	83	75.908	61.080	80.47
28	0.704	0.675	95.88	84	83.230	66.948	80.44
29	0.731	0.687	93.98	85	90.987	73.275	80.53
30	0.759	0.694	91.44	86	99.122	80.076	80.79
31	0.786	0.699	88.93	87	107.577	87.370	81.22
32	0.814	0.700	86.00	88	116.316	95.169	81.82
33	0.843	0.701	83.16	89	125.394	103.455	82.50
34	0.876	0.702	80.14	90	134.887	112.208	83.19
35	0.917	0.704	76.77	91	144.873	121.402	83.80
36	0.968	0.719	74.28	92	155.429	131.017	84.29
37	1.032	0.749	72.58	93	166.629	141.030	84.64
38	1.114	0.796	71.45	94	178.537	151.422	84.81
39	1.216	0.864	71.05	95	191.214	162.179	84.82
40	1.341	0.953	71.07	96	204.721	173.279	84.64
41	1.492	1.065	71.38	97	219.120	184.706	84.29
42	1.673	1.201	71.79	98	234.735	196.946	83.90
43	1.886	1.362	72.22	99	251.889	210.484	83.56
44	2.129	1.547	72.66	100	270.906	225.806	83.35
45	2.399	1.752	73.03	101	292.111	243.398	83.32
46	2.693	1.974	73.30	102	315.826	263.745	83.51
47	3.009	2.211	73.48	103	342.377	287.334	83.92
48	3.343	2.460	73.59	103	372.086	314.649	84.56
49	3.694	2.721	73.66	105	405.278	346.177	85.42
50	4.057	2.994	73.80	106	442.277	382.403	86.46
51	4.431	3.279	74.00	107	483.406	423.813	87.67
52	4.812	3.576	74.31	108	528.989	470.893	89.02
53	5.198	3.884	74.72	109	579.351	524.128	90.47
54	5.591	4.203	75.17	110	634.814	584.004	92.00
55	5.994	4.534	75.64	111	695.704	651.007	93.58
56	6.409	4.876	76.08	112	762.343	725.622	95.18
57	6.839	5.228	76.44	113	835.056	808.336	96.80
58	7.290	5.593	76.72	114	914.167	899.633	98.41
59	7.782	5.988	76.95	115	1000.000	1000.000	100.00
60	8.338	6.428	77.09				

TABLE 3—*Continued*

Age Nearest Birthday (x)	$1000q_x$ 1983 Mortality Table a	Annuity 2000 Mortality Table	Ratio 2000/1983	Age Nearest Birthday (x)	$1000q_x$ 1983 Mortality Table a	Annuity 2000 Mortality Table	Ratio 2000/1983
	Female*				Female*		
5	0.194	0.171	88.14	61	4.908	4.242	86.43
6	0.160	0.141	88.13	62	5.413	4.668	86.24
7	0.134	0.118	88.06	63	5.990	5.144	85.88
8	0.134	0.118	88.06	64	6.633	5.671	85.50
9	0.136	0.121	88.97	65	7.336	6.250	85.20
10	0.141	0.126	89.36	66	8.090	6.878	85.02
11	0.147	0.133	90.48	67	8.888	7.555	85.00
12	0.155	0.142	91.61	68	9.731	8.287	85.16
13	0.165	0.152	92.12	69	10.653	9.102	85.44
14	0.175	0.164	93.71	70	11.697	10.034	85.78
15	0.188	0.177	94.15	71	12.905	11.117	86.14
16	0.201	0.190	94.53	72	14.319	12.386	86.50
17	0.214	0.204	95.33	73	15.980	13.871	86.80
18	0.229	0.219	95.63	74	17.909	15.592	87.06
19	0.244	0.234	95.90	75	20.127	17.564	87.27
20	0.260	0.250	96.15	76	22.654	19.805	87.42
21	0.276	0.265	96.01	77	25.509	22.328	87.53
22	0.293	0.281	95.90	78	28.717	25.158	87.61
23	0.311	0.298	95.82	79	32.328	28.341	87.67
24	0.330	0.314	95.15	80	36.395	31.933	87.74
25	0.349	0.331	94.84	81	40.975	35.985	87.82
26	0.368	0.347	94.29	82	46.121	40.552	87.93
27	0.387	0.362	93.54	83	51.889	45.690	88.05
28	0.405	0.376	92.84	84	58.336	51.456	88.21
29	0.423	0.389	91.96	85	65.518	57.913	88.39
30	0.441	0.402	91.16	86	73.493	65.119	88.61
31	0.460	0.414	90.00	87	82.318	73.136	88.85
32	0.479	0.425	88.73	88	92.017	81.991	89.10
33	0.499	0.436	87.37	89	102.491	91.577	89.35
34	0.521	0.449	86.18	90	113.605	101.758	89.57
35	0.545	0.463	84.95	91	125.227	112.395	89.75
36	0.574	0.481	83.80	92	137.222	123.349	89.89
37	0.607	0.504	83.03	93	149.462	134.486	89.98
38	0.646	0.532	82.35	94	161.834	145.689	90.02
39	0.691	0.567	82.05	95	174.228	156.846	90.02
40	0.742	0.609	82.08	96	186.535	167.841	89.98
41	0.801	0.658	82.15	97	198.646	178.563	89.89
42	0.867	0.715	82.47	98	211.102	189.604	89.82
43	0.942	0.781	82.91	99	224.445	201.557	89.80
44	1.026	0.855	83.33	100	239.215	215.013	89.88
45	1.122	0.939	83.69	101	255.953	230.565	90.08
46	1.231	1.035	84.08	102	275.201	248.805	90.41
47	1.356	1.141	84.14	103	297.500	270.326	90.87
48	1.499	1.261	84.12	103	323.390	295.719	91.44
49	1.657	1.393	84.07	105	353.414	325.576	92.12
50	1.830	1.538	84.04	106	388.111	360.491	92.88
51	2.016	1.695	84.08	107	428.023	401.054	93.70
52	2.215	1.864	84.15	108	473.692	447.860	94.55
53	2.426	2.047	84.38	109	525.658	501.498	95.40
54	2.650	2.244	84.68	110	584.462	562.563	96.25
55	2.891	2.457	84.99	111	650.646	631.645	97.08
56	3.151	2.689	85.34	112	724.750	709.338	97.87
57	3.432	2.942	85.72	113	807.316	796.233	98.63
58	3.739	3.218	86.07	114	898.885	892.923	99.34
59	4.081	3.523	86.33	115	1000.000	1000.000	100.00
60	4.467	3.863	86.48				

*Based on 50% of Female Improvement Scale G.

TABLE 4

COMPARISON OF ANNUITY SINGLE PREMIUMS
1983 TABLE *a* VERSUS ANNUITY 2000 MORTALITY TABLE
IMMEDIATE ANNUITY $1 PER ANNUM

Age	5% Interest			7% Interest			9% Interest		
	1983 Table *a*	Annuity 2000 Table	Ratio 2000/1983	1983 Table *a*	Annuity 2000 Table	Ratio 2000/1983	1983 Table *a*	Annuity 2000 Table	Ratio 2000/1983
Male									
60	12.355	12.991	1.051	10.279	10.712	1.042	8.736	9.042	1.035
65	10.918	11.603	1.063	9.265	9.756	1.053	7.999	8.362	1.045
70	9.362	10.075	1.076	8.106	8.643	1.066	7.115	7.528	1.058
75	7.775	8.501	1.093	6.867	7.439	1.083	6.130	6.588	1.075
80	6.237	6.946	1.114	5.613	6.197	1.104	5.092	5.578	1.095
85	4.861	5.502	1.132	4.450	4.996	1.123	4.097	4.568	1.115
90	3.722	4.247	1.141	3.459	3.919	1.133	3.228	3.634	1.126
95	2.757	3.208	1.164	2.598	3.004	1.156	2.455	2.822	1.149
Female									
60	13.613	13.929	1.023	11.148	11.354	1.018	9.356	9.497	1.015
65	12.262	12.617	1.029	10.246	10.491	1.024	8.734	8.909	1.020
70	10.728	11.107	1.035	9.158	9.434	1.030	7.941	8.147	1.026
75	9.016	9.411	1.044	7.868	8.171	1.039	6.948	7.186	1.034
80	7.239	7.635	1.055	6.455	6.774	1.049	5.807	6.068	1.045
85	5.543	5.913	1.067	5.041	5.353	1.062	4.615	4.880	1.057
90	4.100	4.429	1.080	3.793	4.079	1.075	3.525	3.776	1.071
95	3.033	3.318	1.094	2.845	3.101	1.090	2.677	2.908	1.086
Ratio of Female to Male Annuity Single Premiums									
60	1.102	1.072		1.085	1.060		1.071	1.050	
65	1.123	1.087		1.106	1.075		1.092	1.065	
70	1.146	1.102		1.130	1.092		1.116	1.082	
75	1.160	1.107		1.146	1.098		1.133	1.091	
80	1.161	1.099		1.150	1.093		1.140	1.088	
85	1.140	1.075		1.133	1.071		1.126	1.068	
90	1.102	1.043		1.097	1.041		1.092	1.039	
95	1.100	1.034		1.095	1.032		1.090	1.030	

TABLE 5

RATIOS OF ACTUAL TO EXPECTED MORTALITY ON VARIOUS TABLES FROM 1971–76, 1976–86, AND 1987–91[a] ANNUITY MORTALITY STUDIES BY AMOUNTS OF ANNUAL INCOME FOR ALL CONTRACT YEARS (EXPECTED DEATHS BASED ON TABLE INDICATED)

	A/E Ratio for Male Lives (%)					A/E Ratio for Female Lives (%)				
	Based on 1983 Table *a*			Based on 1996 Table	Based on 2000 Table	Based on 1983 Table *a*			Based on 1996 Table	Based on 2000 Table
Age Group	1971–76[b]	1976–86	1987–91	1987–91[b]	1987–91[b]	1971–76[b]	1976–86	1987–91	1987–91[b]	1987–91[b]
Nonrefund Annuities										
<50	c	c	c	c	c	c	c	c	c	c
50–59	93[d]	84[d]	c	c	c	308[d]	338[d]	c	c	c
60–69	129	138	82[d]	99[d]	106[d]	107	131	84[d]	107[d]	99
70–79	104	151	92	108	114	91	156	82	101	94
80–89	81	114	83	98	103	93	115	90	109	102
90 and Up	102	112	137	155	162	92	114	77	90	86
All	94	121	98			94	120	82		
Refund Annuities										
<50	352[d]	508[d]	c	c	c	354[d]	442[d]	c	c	c
50–59	174	158[d]	c	c	c	264	242[d]	c	c	c
60–69	108	105	93	112	120	129	129	174	222	204
70–79	100	99	88	104	109	94	105	109	134	125
80–89	96	101	80	94	99	105	98	98	119	111
90 and Up	107	119	86	98	101	102	96	92	108	102
All	102	104	86			104	103	102		
Settlements from Maturities and Surrenders (Excluding Pension Trust)—Refund										
<50	c	c	c	c	c	c	1,891[a]	c	c	c
50–59	239	105	c	c	c	154[d]	103	c	c	c
60–69	135	123	108	130	140	126	110	110	140	129
70–79	143	117	87	102	108	132	121	102	126	117
80–89	144	118	111	131	138	134	105	93	113	105
90 and Up	136	117	127	144	150	133	90	109	128	121
All	142	118	106			132	108	101		
Matured Deferred Annuities (Excluding Pension Trust)—Refund										
<50	c	c	c	c	c	c	c	c	c	c
50–59	c	c	c	c	c	c	389[d]	c	c	c
60–69	147	134	c	c	c	141	129	c	c	c
70–79	132	99	88	104	109	132	115	124	153	142
80–89	139	128	96	113	119	137	123	110	133	124
90 and Up	141	126	107	121	126	129	130	118	139	131
All	138	119	102			136	124	115		
Matured Deferred Annuities (Excluding Pension Trust)—Nonrefund										
<50	c	c	c	c	c	c	c	c	c	c
50–59	c	c	c	c	c	c	c	c	c	c
60–69	117	109[d]	c	c	c	131	c	c	c	c
70–79	141	167	c	c	c	147	127	81[d]	100[d]	93
80–89	161	124	90	106	112	140	105	95	115	107
90 and Up	138	107	131	149	154	138	110	100	117	111
All	139	126	111			143	109	97		

[a]Based on unpublished data.
[b]Estimated.
[c]Less than 10 deaths.
[d]10–49 deaths.
[e]Annuity 2000 using 50% of Scale G.
Note: The 1987–91 Study contains contributions from only five companies.

TABLE 6

ANNUAL MORTALITY IMPROVEMENT RATES 1973 TO 1989
1971–76 ANNUITY MORTALITY STUDY AND 1987–91 ANNUITY MORTALITY STUDY[a]
BY AMOUNTS OF ANNUAL INCOME FOR ALL CONTRACT YEARS
(EXPECTED DEATHS BASED ON 1983 TABLE a;
1971–76 ACT/EXP ADJUSTED TO 1983 TABLE a)

	Male Lives			Female Lives		
Age Group	1971–76 A/E Ratio (%)	1987–91 A/E Ratio (%)	Annual Improvement Rate (%)	1971–76 A/E Ratio (%)	1987–91 A/E Ratio (%)	Annual Improvement Rate (%)
Nonrefund Annuities						
<50	b	b	b	b	b	b
50–59	93[c]	b	b	308[c]	b	b
60–69	129	82[c]	2.78[c]	107	84[c]	1.51[c]
70–79	104	92	0.75	91	82	0.66
80–89	81	83	−0.16	93	90	0.17
90 and Up	102	137	−1.84	92	77	1.12
All Ages	94	98	−0.24	94	82	0.84
Refund Annuities						
<50	352[c]	b	b	354[c]	b	b
50–59	174	b	b	264	b	b
60–69	108	93	0.91	129	174	−1.89
70–79	100	88	0.81	94	109	−0.95
80–89	96	80	1.16	105	98	0.40
90 and Up	107	86	1.34	102	92	0.67
All Ages	102	86	1.04	104	102	0.14
Settlements from Maturities and Surrenders (Excluding Pension Trust)—Refund						
<50	b	b	b	b	b	b
50–59	239	b	b	154[c]	b	b
60–69	135	108	1.37	126	110	0.86
70–79	143	87	3.05	132	102	1.60
80–89	144	111	1.62	134	93	2.25
90 and Up	136	127	0.43	133	109	1.24
All Ages	142	106	1.80	132	101	1.68
Matured Deferred Annuities (Excluding Pension Trust)—Refund						
<50	b	b	b	b	b	b
50–59	b	b	b	b	b	b
60–69	147	b	b	141	b	b
70–79	132	88	2.50	132	124	0.40
80–89	139	96	2.31	137	110	1.38
90 and Up	141	107	1.71	129	118	0.56
All Ages	138	102	1.87	136	115	1.02
Matured Deferred Annuities (Excluding Pension Trust)—Nonrefund						
<50	b	b	b	b	b	b
50–59	b	b	b	b	b	b
60–69	117	b	b	131	b	b
70–79	141	b	b	147	81[c]	3.66[c]
80–89	161	90	3.58	140	95	2.41
90 and Up	138	131	0.33	138	100	2.00
All Ages	139	111	1.40	143	97	2.39

[a]Based on unpublished data.
[b]Less than 10 deaths in 1971–76 and/or 1987–91 Study.
[c]10–49 deaths in 1976–86 and/or 1987–91.
Note: The 1987–91 Study contains contributions from only five companies.

TABLE 7

ANNUAL MORTALITY IMPROVEMENT RATES 1983 TO 1989
1976–86 ANNUITY MORTALITY STUDY AND 1987–91 ANNUITY MORTALITY STUDY[a]
BY AMOUNTS OF ANNUAL INCOME FOR ALL CONTRACT YEARS
(EXPECTED DEATHS BASED ON 1983 TABLE a)

	Male Lives			Female Lives		
Age Group	1976–86 A/E Ratio (%)	1987–91 A/E Ratio (%)	Annual Improvement Rate (%)	1976–86 A/E Ratio (%)	1987–91 A/E Ratio (%)	Annual Improvement Rate (%)
Nonrefund Annuities						
<50	b	b	b	b	b	b
50–59	84[c]	b	b	338[c]	b	b
60–69	138	82[c]	8.31[c]	131	84[c]	7.14[c]
70–79	151	92	7.93	156	82	10.16
80–89	114	83	5.15	115	90	4.00
90 and Up	112	137	−3.42	114	77	6.33
All Ages	121	98	3.45	120	82	6.15
Refund Annuities						
<50	508[c]	b	b	442[c]	b	b
50–59	158[c]	b	b	242[c]	b	b
60–69	105	93	2.00	129	174	−5.11
70–79	99	88	1.94	105	109	−0.63
80–89	101	80	3.81	98	98	0.00
90 and Up	119	86	5.27	96	92	0.71
All Ages	104	86	3.12	103	102	0.16
Settlements from Maturities and Surrenders (Excluding Pension Trust)—Refund						
<50	b	b	b	1,891	b	b
50–59	105	b	b	103	b	b
60–69	123	108	2.14	110	110	0.00
70–79	117	87	4.82	121	102	2.81
80–89	118	111	1.01	105	93	2.00
90 and Up	117	127	−1.38	90	109	−3.24
All Ages	118	106	1.77	108	101	1.11
Matured Deferred Annuities (Excluding Pension Trust)—Refund						
<50	b	b	b	b	b	b
50–59	b	b	b	389[c]	b	b
60–69	134	b	b	129	b	b
70–79	99	88	1.94	115	124	−1.26
80–89	128	96	4.68	123	110	1.84
90 and Up	126	107	2.69	130	118	1.60
All Ages	119	102	2.54	124	115	1.25
Matured Deferred Annuities (Excluding Pension Trust)—Nonrefund						
<50	b	b	b	b	b	b
50–59	b	b	b	b	b	b
60–69	109[c]	b	b	b	b	b
70–79	167	b	b	127	81[c]	7.22[c]
80–89	124	90	5.20	105	95	1.65
90 and Up	107	131	−3.43	110	100	1.58
All Ages	126	111	2.09	109	97	1.93

[a]Based on unpublished data.
[b]Less than 10 deaths in 1976–86 and/or 1987–91.
[c]10–49 deaths in 1976–86 and/or 1987–91.
Note: The 1987–91 Study contains contributions from only five companies.

TABLE 8

ANNUAL MORTALITY IMPROVEMENT RATES 1985 TO 1995
FOR THE U.S. WHITE POPULATION

Sex and Age Group	Mortality Rates per 100,000				Improvement Rates (%)			
	1985	1993[b]	1994[b]	1995[a,b]	1985–93	1993–94	1994–95	1985–95
Male Lives								
5–14	30.1	26.1	22.8	23.3	1.77	12.64	−2.19	2.53
14–24	134.2	121.7	129.9	127.1	1.21	−6.74	2.16	0.54
25–34	158.8	186.2	179.1	181.0	−2.01	3.81	−1.06	−1.32
35–44	243.1	282.2	288.6	285.5	−1.88	−2.27	1.07	−1.62
45–54	611.7	540.7	523.1	533.6	1.53	3.26	−2.01	1.36
55–64	1625.8	1391.3	1382.4	1314.8	1.93	0.64	4.89	2.10
65–74	3770.7	3334.7	3260.7	3188.8	1.52	2.22	2.21	1.66
75–84	8486.1	7672.1	7433.9	7354.5	1.25	3.10	1.07	1.42
85 and Up	18980.1	18229.2	18126.6	17962.8	0.50	0.56	0.90	0.55
Female Lives								
5–14	19.5	17.6	17.2	16.1	1.27	2.27	6.40	1.90
15–24	48.1	44.9	43.2	42.8	0.86	3.79	0.93	1.16
25–34	59.4	62.9	62.8	64.6	−0.72	0.16	−2.87	−0.84
35–44	121.9	117.1	119.9	122.5	0.50	−2.39	−2.17	−0.05
45–54	341.7	295.7	291.2	297.5	1.79	1.52	−2.16	1.38
55–64	869.1	810.1	788.7	785.5	0.87	2.64	0.41	1.01
65–74	2027.1	1929.2	1928.7	1909.7	0.62	0.03	0.99	0.59
75–84	5111.6	4787.9	4878.4	4823.8	0.81	−1.89	1.12	0.58
85 and Up	14745.4	14669.1	14460.4	14496.0	0.06	1.42	−0.25	0.17

[a]12 months ending November.
[b]Rates for 1993, 1994 and 1995 are provisional.
Source: *Monthly Vital Statistics Report* (NCHS) Vol. 43, no. 13 (October 23, 1995); Vol. 44, no. 12 (July 24, 1996).

TABLE 9

VALUES OF $1000q_x$ AND FIRST AND SECOND DIFFERENCES
ANNUITY 2000 MORTALITY TABLE

Age (x)	Annuity 2000 Mortality Table $1000q_x$	First Difference	Second Difference	Age (x)	Annuity 2000 Mortality Table $1000q_x$	First Difference	Second Difference
	Male				Male		
5	0.291	−0.021	0.008	61	6.933	0.587	0.100
6	0.270	−0.013	0.050	62	7.520	0.687	0.114
7	0.257	0.037	−0.006	63	8.207	0.801	0.131
8	0.294	0.031	−0.006	64	9.008	0.932	0.144
9	0.325	0.025	−0.004	65	9.940	1.076	0.159
10	0.350	0.021	−0.004	66	11.016	1.235	0.171
11	0.371	0.017	−0.003	67	12.251	1.406	0.170
12	0.388	0.014	−0.002	68	13.657	1.576	0.170
13	0.402	0.012	−0.001	69	15.233	1.746	0.166
14	0.414	0.011	0.001	70	16.979	1.912	0.164
15	0.425	0.012	0.000	71	18.891	2.076	0.166
16	0.437	0.012	0.002	72	20.967	2.242	0.193
17	0.449	0.014	0.003	73	23.209	2.435	0.225
18	0.463	0.017	0.002	74	25.644	2.660	0.256
19	0.480	0.019	0.001	75	28.304	2.916	0.289
20	0.499	0.020	0.003	76	31.220	3.205	0.318
21	0.519	0.023	0.001	77	34.425	3.523	0.341
22	0.542	0.024	0.002	78	37.948	3.864	0.361
23	0.566	0.026	−0.002	79	41.812	4.225	0.381
24	0.592	0.024	−0.001	80	46.037	4.606	0.402
25	0.616	0.023	−0.003	81	50.643	5.008	0.421
26	0.639	0.020	−0.004	82	55.651	5.429	0.439
27	0.659	0.016	−0.004	83	61.080	5.868	0.459
28	0.675	0.012	−0.005	84	66.948	6.327	0.474
29	0.687	0.007	−0.002	85	73.275	6.801	0.493
30	0.694	0.005	−0.004	86	80.076	7.294	0.505
31	0.699	0.001	0.000	87	87.370	7.799	0.487
32	0.700	0.001	0.000	88	95.169	8.286	0.467
33	0.701	0.001	0.001	89	103.455	8.753	0.441
34	0.702	0.002	0.013	90	112.208	9.194	0.421
35	0.704	0.015	0.015	91	121.402	9.615	0.398
36	0.719	0.030	0.017	92	131.017	10.013	0.379
37	0.749	0.047	0.021	93	141.030	10.392	0.365
38	0.796	0.068	0.021	94	151.422	10.757	0.343
39	0.864	0.089	0.023	95	162.179	11.100	0.327
40	0.953	0.112	0.024	96	173.279	11.427	0.813
41	1.065	0.136	0.025	97	184.706	12.240	1.298
42	1.201	0.161	0.024	98	196.946	13.538	1.784
43	1.362	0.185	0.020	99	210.484	15.322	2.270
44	1.547	0.205	0.017	100	225.806	17.592	2.755
45	1.752	0.222	0.015	101	243.398	20.347	3.242
46	1.974	0.237	0.012	102	263.745	23.589	3.726
47	2.211	0.249	0.012	103	287.334	27.315	4.213
48	2.460	0.261	0.012	104	314.649	31.528	4.698
49	2.721	0.273	0.012	105	346.177	36.226	5.184
50	2.994	0.285	0.012	106	382.403	41.410	5.670
51	3.279	0.297	0.011	107	423.813	47.080	6.155
52	3.576	0.308	0.011	108	470.893	53.235	6.641
53	3.884	0.319	0.012	109	524.128	59.876	7.127
54	4.203	0.331	0.011	110	584.004	67.003	7.612
55	4.534	0.342	0.010	111	651.007	74.615	8.099
56	4.876	0.352	0.013	112	725.622	82.714	8.583
57	5.228	0.365	0.030	113	808.336	91.297	9.070
58	5.593	0.395	0.045	114	899.633	100.367	
59	5.988	0.440	0.065	115	1000.000		
60	6.428	0.505	0.082				

TABLE 9—Continued

Age (x)	Annuity 2000 Mortality Table $1000q_x$	First Difference	Second Difference	Age (x)	Annuity 2000 Mortality Table $1000q_x$	First Difference	Second Difference
	Female*				Female*		
5	0.171	−0.030	0.007	61	4.242	0.426	0.050
6	0.141	−0.023	0.023	62	4.668	0.476	0.051
7	0.118	0.000	0.003	63	5.144	0.527	0.052
8	0.118	0.003	0.002	64	5.671	0.579	0.049
9	0.121	0.005	0.002	65	6.250	0.628	0.049
10	0.126	0.007	0.002	66	6.878	0.677	0.055
11	0.133	0.009	0.001	67	7.555	0.732	0.083
12	0.142	0.010	0.002	68	8.287	0.815	0.117
13	0.152	0.012	0.001	69	9.102	0.932	0.151
14	0.164	0.013	0.000	70	10.034	1.083	0.186
15	0.177	0.013	0.001	71	11.117	1.269	0.216
16	0.190	0.014	0.001	72	12.386	1.485	0.236
17	0.204	0.015	0.000	73	13.871	1.721	0.251
18	0.219	0.015	0.001	74	15.592	1.972	0.269
19	0.234	0.016	−0.001	75	17.564	2.241	0.282
20	0.250	0.015	0.001	76	19.805	2.523	0.307
21	0.265	0.016	0.001	77	22.328	2.830	0.353
22	0.281	0.017	−0.001	78	25.158	3.183	0.409
23	0.298	0.016	0.001	79	28.341	3.592	0.460
24	0.314	0.017	−0.001	80	31.933	4.052	0.515
25	0.331	0.016	−0.001	81	35.985	4.567	0.571
26	0.347	0.015	−0.001	82	40.552	5.138	0.628
27	0.362	0.014	−0.001	83	45.690	5.766	0.691
28	0.376	0.013	0.000	84	51.456	6.457	0.749
29	0.389	0.013	−0.001	85	57.913	7.206	0.811
30	0.402	0.012	−0.001	86	65.119	8.017	0.838
31	0.414	0.011	0.000	87	73.136	8.855	0.731
32	0.425	0.011	0.002	88	81.991	9.586	0.595
33	0.436	0.013	0.001	89	91.577	10.181	0.456
34	0.449	0.014	0.004	90	101.758	10.637	0.317
35	0.463	0.018	0.005	91	112.395	10.954	0.183
36	0.481	0.023	0.005	92	123.349	11.137	0.066
37	0.504	0.028	0.007	93	134.486	11.203	−0.046
38	0.532	0.035	0.007	94	145.689	11.157	−0.162
39	0.567	0.042	0.007	95	156.846	10.995	−0.273
40	0.609	0.049	0.008	96	167.841	10.722	0.319
41	0.658	0.057	0.009	97	178.563	11.041	0.912
42	0.715	0.066	0.008	98	189.604	11.953	1.503
43	0.781	0.074	0.010	99	201.557	13.456	2.096
44	0.855	0.084	0.012	100	215.013	15.552	2.688
45	0.939	0.096	0.010	101	230.565	18.240	3.281
46	1.035	0.106	0.014	102	248.805	21.521	3.872
47	1.141	0.120	0.012	103	270.326	25.393	4.464
48	1.261	0.132	0.013	104	295.719	29.857	5.058
49	1.393	0.145	0.012	105	325.576	34.915	5.648
50	1.538	0.157	0.012	106	360.491	40.563	6.243
51	1.695	0.169	0.014	107	401.054	46.806	6.832
52	1.864	0.183	0.014	108	447.860	53.638	7.427
53	2.047	0.197	0.016	109	501.498	61.065	8.017
54	2.244	0.213	0.019	110	562.563	69.082	8.611
55	2.457	0.232	0.021	111	631.645	77.693	9.202
56	2.689	0.253	0.023	112	709.338	86.895	9.795
57	2.942	0.276	0.029	113	796.233	96.690	10.387
58	3.218	0.305	0.035	114	892.923	107.077	
59	3.523	0.340	0.039	115	1000.000		
60	3.863	0.379	0.047				

*Based on 50% of Female Improvement Scale G.

ORPHANHOOD IN THE UNITED STATES

BERTRAM M. KESTENBAUM

ABSTRACT

Several improvements and modifications to the methodology for the indirect measurement of child orphanhood are incorporated in estimates of the recent prevalence and incidence of orphanhood. Comparisons are drawn between the situation today and the situations 25 and 50 years ago, and selected characteristics of orphans are discussed.

I. INTRODUCTION

The measurement by indirect methods of the phenomenon of orphanhood among children under age 18 was a significant component of actuarial endeavor before soaring divorce and illegitimacy rates, in combination with falling mortality rates, ended the predominance of orphanhood among the social problems besetting children. Methodology developed in the seminal work by Lotka [3] was applied in papers by Spiegelman [8], Woofter [10], Shudde [6, 7], and Epstein and Skolnik [1] to measure orphanhood in the mid-1900s.

The last four papers cited were authored by actuaries and statisticians in the Social Security Administration who were evaluating the agency's survivors insurance program. The agency, in fact, sponsored in October 1949 an unsuccessful attempt to *count* the orphan population in the Current Population Survey, the only attempt ever at direct measurement of orphanhood in the U.S.

This paper presents estimates of the size and characteristics at the beginning of 1990 of both the orphan population and the subpopulation of orphan Social Security beneficiaries, and a comparison with a quarter-century ago and a half-century ago. Estimates of the annual incidence of orphanhood, as well as of the average age at orphanhood and of the average age of parent at death, are also given.

Several modifications to Lotka's method were made in deriving these estimates, as described below.

251

II. METHODOLOGY

In this section, I discuss (1) the basis for measuring the prevalence of orphanhood, (2) the extension to the measurement of full orphanhood, (3) the progression from relative numbers to absolute numbers, (4) the adaptation of the method to the measurement of incidence, and (5) the specificity of the life table.

In Lotka's method, the proportion of children age X (last birthday) who are maternal orphans is equated to the probability of mother's death in the $\{X+1/2\}$ years after birth. Similarly, the proportion who are paternal orphans is equated to the probability of father's death in the $\{X+5/4\}$ years after conception. These probabilities are calculated, separately by race when possible, from the mean age of mother/father at birth of child and a life table for females/males.

Instead of the mean age alone, a distribution of mothers' ages in five-year intervals was used by Goodman, Keyfitz, and Pullum [2] in their computations on maternal orphanhood. I take this one step further and use a single-age distribution.

Age detail is important because analyses based on averages can easily be misinterpreted. For example, after calculating that paternal orphans were age 10 on average at the death of their fathers, Woofter concluded that their fathers died at age 42 on average, the sum of 10 and the mean age of father at birth of child of 32. He bemoaned the circumstance that the decedent typically has not had the opportunity to accumulate wealth adequate for the support of his survivors. This preoccupation with averages misled Woofter from recognizing that surely fathers survived by minor children were older, as a group, at the birth of those children than were other fathers at the birth of their children.

The proportion of children age X who are *full* orphans (both parents deceased) is derived easily from the proportions orphaned from each parent if mortality of father is independent of mortality of mother. Lotka [3] found evidence to the contrary, however, in data for England and Wales for 1921. He attributed this observed dependence to the contagion of disease in the home and to the stress from the spousal illness and death. Shudde [7] accordingly argued that, in view of the diminished importance of contagious disease among causes of death during the mid-1900s, the independence assumption becomes justifiable.

However, this debate, focused as it is on causal factors of contagion and stress, misses the point that some correlation in mortality must be expected from *the correlation in spouses' ages*. A parent deceased during the offspring's childhood is likely to be an older parent; the spouse is probably also an older parent and hence more likely to become deceased than the average parent.

As an illustration, consider a hypothetical population in which (a) half of all births occur when both parents are age 25 and half when both parents are age 40, and (b) the probabilities of surviving 18 years are 0.9 for any person age 25, male or female, and 0.7 for any person age 40. Then the probability of either paternal orphanhood or maternal orphanhood is 0.2, but the probability of full orphanhood is 0.05, not the square of 0.2.

Accordingly, the estimate given in this paper of the number of full orphans in 1990 is derived from a *joint* distribution of mothers' and fathers' ages.

The *numbers* of paternal, maternal, and full orphans, by age of orphan and race, are then obtained by applying the appropriate proportions to the distribution of children by age and race, from a census or intercensal/postcensal estimate.

The method can be adapted to measure an annual incidence of orphanhood (although Lotka himself offered a different approach to the measurement of incidence). The proportion of children age X who are orphans now but not one year ago is equated to the probability of the parent's death between $\{X-1/2\}$ and $\{X+1/2\}$ years following the child's birth. An upwards adjustment is needed to include children orphaned during the year who later in the year reach adulthood or become deceased.

In their separate preparations of estimates of the number of paternal orphans in 1940, Spiegelman [8] and Woofter [10] disagreed about the appropriateness of total-population life tables for describing the mortality of *parents*. Spiegelman required life tables for married persons, because it was uncommon then for parents to be unmarried, while Woofter argued insightfully that the marital status differential in mortality could well be largely offset by a socioeconomic differential in the other direction, because a more-than-proportionate share of children are born to parents in lower socioeconomic strata, where mortality is higher.

For recent years, as the proportion of births occurring outside marriage surpasses 25%, there might be consensus on the adequacy of total-population life tables for computations of orphanhood.

III. SOCIAL SECURITY CHILD SURVIVOR BENEFITS

The natural child under age 18 of a deceased parent who had sufficient employment to be insured for survivorship is eligible to receive monthly Social Security benefits in an amount related to the average lifetime earnings of the decedent—if the child is not working, is not married, and (more significantly) meets the statutory definition of "child." In general, illegitimacy is not a factor when the decedent is the child's mother, but *is* when the decedent is the child's father. Then benefits are payable only if paternity was acknowledged in writing by the father or established in a court of law, or if there was a combination of oral evidence and the circumstance of the father living with the child or contributing to the child's support.

Social Security benefits are capped by a "family maximum," which might dissuade the children's surviving parent or representative from filing applications for all the children when the family size makes the cap operative. Because of the cap, a family of four receives no more in total survivor benefits than a family of three, and sometimes, depending on the level of benefits, a family of three receives no more in total survivor benefits than a family of two. However, agency officials encourage the filing of an application for each family member eligible for benefits.

Under certain circumstances benefits are also payable to children surviving a stepparent or an adoptive parent, and these few children will unavoidably be included in the beneficiary data presented later.

IV. ORPHANHOOD IN 1940 AND 1965

For 1940, Spiegelman estimated there were 2,472,000 paternal orphans and 1,374,000 maternal orphans in the U.S. and among them 293,000 full orphans (see Table 1). According to this estimate, nearly 10% of the nation's 40 million children were orphaned from at least one parent. For the same year, Woofter estimated there were more than 3.3 million paternal orphans alone. Most, but not all, of the discrepancy between the two estimates derives from whether or not the mortality schedule used was specific to marital status, as discussed earlier.

The first study of orphan recipiency of Social Security benefits is for 1953 [6]. At that time, almost half of paternal orphans were program beneficiaries. The oldest orphans, ages 15 to 17, were only half as likely to be beneficiaries as the youngest, ages 0 to 4, a phenomenon the study's author attributed to the program's immaturity. That is, the greater average duration of orphanhood among older children translates to a greater likelihood that much of

TABLE 1

ESTIMATES OF THE NUMBER OF ORPHANS IN THE U.S. (IN THOUSANDS)

	Paternal	Maternal	Full
1940			
Spiegelman [8]	2,472	1,374	293
Woofter [10]	3,331	N/A	N/A
1965 (Epstein and Skolnik) [1]	2,400	1,000	70
1990 (this study)	1,675	554	28

the employment of the deceased parent did not count towards achievement of insured status, having preceded the inception of the Social Security program in 1937 or its expansion in 1951. Also, black children were only half as likely to be beneficiaries as white children, which the author attributed to the weaker work records of black adults.

In 1965 there were, according to estimates by Epstein and Skolnik [1] and using methods seemingly similar to Spiegelman's, about 2.4 million paternal orphans and about 1.0 million maternal orphans, including about 70,000 full orphans. The drop over the 25-year period in the relative number of orphans, unlike the drop in absolute number, is rather dramatic, because in 1965 there were 70 million children in the U.S., a reflection of the postwar baby boom.

Approximately 1.7 million among the 2.4 million paternal orphans in 1965, or about 70%, were Social Security beneficiaries. No age or race information was provided for this group.

V. DATA FOR 1990 ESTIMATES

My objective is to estimate the prevalence of orphanhood at the beginning of 1990 and the incidence of orphanhood during the preceding year (1989). Because of the much higher adult mortality of blacks, calculations are done separately for blacks and for all other races combined.

All children under age 18 at the beginning of 1990 were born between 1972 and 1989. The incidence estimate requires the number of children born in 1971 who were orphaned in 1989 before their 18th birthday. Accordingly I begin with the age-of-parent distributions for each year from 1971 to 1989 published in the annual compendia of vital registration data [5].

While the published age-of-mother distributions are complete and in single-age detail, the published age-of-father and joint-age distributions contain a large "father's age unknown" component and are presented in five-year age intervals. First, following the practice of the National Center for Health

Statistics, I allocated the fathers with unknown age according to the distribution of fathers with known age within each joint age category of mother. Then, the National Center kindly provided an unpublished joint-age distribution of parents with single-age detail for one year in the observation period, which I used to disaggregate the published data to single-age detail for each year.

The 1979–81 decennial life tables [4], whose reference years are in the middle of the observation period, are used to describe adult mortality by sex and race. Because there is no decennial life table for the category "other than black," I substituted the table for whites. In view of Woofter's argument about counterbalancing socioeconomic differentials and considering that many births now occur outside marriage, the life tables were not adjusted for mortality differentials by marital status.

The combination of age-of-parent distributions and life-table probabilities yields estimates of the relative prevalence and incidence of orphanhood. These are then applied to the Census Bureau's adjusted counts of children in the 1990 census [9] to obtain estimates in absolute terms. The three-month difference between the beginning of 1990 and census day is ignored.

Data on receipt of Social Security survivor benefits come from a 1-in-100 sample of Social Security Administration administrative records. A small but unknown fraction of child beneficiaries are survivors of an adoptive parent or stepparent, rather than a natural parent.

VI. ORPHANHOOD IN 1990

At the beginning of 1990 there were an estimated 1,675,000 paternal orphans and 554,000 maternal orphans, hence a major improvement since 1965. Included in both counts are an estimated 28,000 full orphans. The latter number, derived from the joint distribution of father's age and mother's age, is significantly larger than the estimate of 23,000 produced by the (unsatisfactory) independence assumption.

The number of children counted in the 1990 census is 63,924,000. Thus, 2.62% of children are paternal orphans; 0.87% are maternal orphans; 0.04% are full orphans; and 3.44% are orphaned from at least one parent.

Among 9,833,000 black children, 475,000 (4.83%) are paternal orphans, 142,000 (1.44%) are maternal orphans, and 12,000 (0.12%) are full orphans.

During 1989 an estimated 223,000 children became paternal orphans and an estimated 81,000 became maternal orphans. An estimated 7,000 children became full orphans upon the death of a parent in 1989.

Among children orphaned in 1989, the average age of the child upon the father's death was 10.0, upon the mother's death was 10.6, and upon becoming a full orphan was 13.5.

The father's age at death on average in 1989 was 41.9, and the mother's age at death on average was 38.5. These compare with mean ages over the 1972–1989 period at birth of child of 28.6 and 25.8, respectively, among all fathers and mothers.

Social Security benefits were paid at the beginning of 1990 to 1,082,000 paternal orphans—about 65% of the total—and to 253,000 maternal orphans—about 46% of the total (see Table 2). These percentages are not directly comparable to those for 1965 because the size of the denominator—the total orphaned population—was calculated differently for 1965 and 1990, once with mortality schedules for married persons and once with mortality schedules for all persons.

TABLE 2

RECEIPT OF SOCIAL SECURITY SURVIVOR BENEFITS BY ORPHANS, BEGINNING OF 1990

Characteristics	Paternal Orphans			Maternal Orphans		
	Total (000s)	Beneficiaries (000s)	Percentage	Total (000s)	Beneficiaries (000s)	Percentage
Total, all races and ages	1,675	1,082	65	554	253	46
Race						
White and other	1,200	819	68	412	196	48
Black	475	263	55	142	57	40
Age						
0–4	139	62	45	36	13	36
5–9	365	220	60	115	54	47
10–14	620	411	66	210	98	47
15–17	551	389	71	194	88	45

Among blacks, benefits were paid to 55% of paternal orphans and 40% of maternal orphans. Even considering differences in methodology, it is apparent that the proportion of black orphans receiving Social Security benefits is now much closer to that for the total population than it was several decades earlier.

In contrast to the findings for the earlier period, younger orphans are now less likely to be beneficiaries than older orphans. A partial explanation is that the parents of younger orphans are younger at death, as a group, and hence less likely to have satisfied the requirement for insured status.

Data I have examined on denied claims suggest that while the lack of insured status of the decedent is the most likely reason for nonpayment of benefits, the illegitimacy of the child is a frequent reason for nonpayment to paternal orphans.

VII. CONCLUSION

The extent and parameters of orphanhood are measured by indirect methods, using data on parental age at birth of child, adult mortality schedules, and census-based counts of children by age and race. Here I used single-age distributions of age of father, age of mother, and ages of both parents jointly, 1979–81 decennial life tables, and adjusted 1990 census counts of children.

The numbers of both paternal and maternal orphans have fallen substantially from 1965 to 1990 in both relative and absolute terms. The decreases from 1940 to 1965 were large in relative, but not absolute, terms.

About 35% of paternal orphans in 1990 were not receiving Social Security benefits, largely because either the deceased parent was not insured or the orphan did not meet the statutory definition of child.

REFERENCES

1. EPSTEIN, LENORE A., AND SKOLNIK, ALFRED M. "Social Security Protection after Thirty Years," *Social Security Bulletin* 28 (August 1965): 5–17.
2. GOODMAN, LEO A., KEYFITZ, NATHAN, AND PULLUM, THOMAS W. "Family Formation and the Frequency of Various Kinship Relationships," *Theoretical Population Biology* 5, no. 1 (1974): 1–27.
3. LOTKA, ALFRED J. "Orphanhood in Relation to Demographic Factors," *Metron* 9, no. 2 (1931): 37–109.
4. NATIONAL CENTER FOR HEALTH STATISTICS. *United States Life Tables. U.S. Decennial Life Tables for 1979–81*, Vol. 1, no. 1. Washington, D.C.: U.S. Government Printing Office, 1985.
5. NATIONAL CENTER FOR HEALTH STATISTICS. *Vital Statistics of the United States 19--*, Vol. 1. Washington, D.C.: U.S. Government Printing Office, annual.
6. SHUDDE, LOUIS O. "Orphans in the United States, July 1, 1953," *Social Security Bulletin* 17 (July 1954): 16–18.
7. SHUDDE, LOUIS O. "Orphanhood—A Diminishing Problem," *Social Security Bulletin* 18 (March 1955): 17–19.
8. SPIEGELMAN, MORTIMER. "The American Family," *RAIA* 33, no. 2 (1944): 394–410.

9. U.S. BUREAU OF THE CENSUS. *Age, Sex, Race, and Hispanic Origin Information from the 1990 Census: A Comparison of Census Results with Results Where Age and Race Have Been Modified.* Unpublished report available from the Population Division of the Bureau of the Census. August 1991.
10. WOOFTER, THOMAS J., JR. "Paternal Orphans," *Social Security Bulletin* 9 (October 1945): 5–6.

EXCHANGE RATE DYNAMICS IN MIXED-CURRENCY MEDICAL INSURANCE PLAN ENVIRONMENTS

KEVIN M. LAW

ABSTRACT

This paper examines the financial dynamics resulting from the currency exchange rate for medical insurance products that are denominated in a currency different from that in which covered medical expenses are incurred. Circumstances that can generate this type of coverage are described, and the basic assumptions of the model for analyzing the financial results are presented. A key assumption is that the morbidity of the block of business is precisely projected in the currency of the insured's country of residence, and the exchange rate between the currency of the medical expenses and that of the policies is the only component that varies. Several comments are presented about life insurance products in a mixed-currency setting, which are immunized to a much greater extent against exchange-rate swings.

Five distinct medical plan designs are defined, as well as five currency exchange rate patterns, which combine to produce a total of 25 scenarios of financial results for analysis. Four of the five plans cover medical expenses on a reasonable-and-customary-charge level basis, while the fifth is a scheduled, per-unit-of-benefit product. The first four plans are differentiated by the manner in which conversions are made between the two legal tenders for premium and for claim payments. Several key summary financial parameters for the model block of business are defined, and the variations in these quantities due to differences between actual and expected currency exchange rates are presented and interpreted. The four reasonable-and-customary-charge basis plan designs are compared to determine their relative stability in producing target financial results under different exchange rates. The conclusion is that the mixed-currency environment for medical plans introduces a significant additional risk element as well as potential administrative complications. The specific types of financial distortions that can result from the currency exchange rate influence and their relative severity vary substantially according to plan design.

261

I. INTRODUCTION

Any medical insurance plan that provides coverage regardless of the location of the medical services is subject to the possibility that some expenses will be incurred outside of the insureds' country of residence in a foreign currency. Usually these mixed-currency situations, in which the expenses are denominated in a medium different than that of the policy, are infrequent and are due to unexpected medical problems during business or vacation travel.

However, there are policies for which currency differences are more frequent; that is, a significant portion of the expenses covered under the policy are expected to be incurred in a currency other than that in which the policy is denominated. Several sources tend to generate policies of this type:

(1) An international company may wish to cover some or all of its employees in foreign countries under the identical health benefits program that is used for employees at the company's corporate headquarters.

(2) A company with employees in a number of countries may desire to supplement a relatively skimpy plan in each country's legal tender with a uniform medical plan in one common currency.

(3) The upper-income strata in a particular country may find it attractive to purchase an individual health policy that provides coverage in another country with a more advanced health care system. Such a policy may also cover expenses incurred in the insured's country of residence. Often a policy of this nature is denominated in the medium of exchange of the country with the technologically superior health care delivery system.

A typical example of this type of plan is a dollar-denominated individual health plan sold to the high-middle and upper economic classes in Latin America. The idea is to provide access to the advanced health care system in the U.S. and protection against catastrophic medical expenses that may be incurred in this country. In addition, the policy may reimburse medical expenses incurred in the country of residence for conditions that are not sufficiently serious to warrant a trip to the U.S. These polices appeal to the upper-income echelon who are able to afford the hard currency dollar premiums, plus additional related costs not covered by the policy, such as travel expenses to the U.S. to receive the treatment.

Insurance companies in recent years have tended to expand their geographical spheres of operation across international boundaries, thus increasing the availability of different forms of mixed-currency coverage.

The paper examines, via a simplified modeling technique in a controlled environment, the dynamics of several key policy parameters and their effect on financial results for mixed-currency medical plans. The model consists of a hypothetical block of business studied over a one-year period. Five policy designs are analyzed: four that cover medical expenses on a reasonable-and-customary-charge level basis and one that is a fully scheduled, per-unit-of-benefit product. These five plans are combined with five different assumptions for the progression of currency exchange rates throughout the year, producing a total of 25 distinct scenarios.

Although the model is constructed in the context of a dollar-denominated policy sold outside of the U.S., the same concepts apply to any mixed-currency plan, regardless of the specific countries and legal tenders. To illustrate the full impact of the dual currencies, all the covered medical expenses in the model are assumed to be in a medium of exchange different than the policy's premium and schedule of benefits. The same influences of the exchange rate described in the model are present, but to a lesser degree, for products in which a portion of the incurred expenses involve mixed currencies, with the balance of the expenses denominated in the same currency as the policy.

The starting point for the model is morbidity experience projected for a block of covered lives assuming a plan written directly in the currency of the country in which the insureds reside. The dynamics of writing several types of dollar-denominated plans that are intended to be equivalent, on an expected basis, are then analyzed. This process illustrates the potential effect of the currency exchange rate, the focus of this paper. The process does not imply that in practice the mixed-currency plan is necessarily based upon a rigorous review of expected morbidity experience in the native currency of the country, followed by the creation of an expected equivalent plan in dollars. In the real world such dollar plans might be defined and priced in a less disciplined manner by making relatively crude adjustments to a dollar plan design and rate level that would be appropriate for a U.S. location. To the extent that this actually occurs, the risk of uncertain morbidity results is quite substantial and is in addition to the influence of the currency exchange rate.

As shown in this paper, these mixed-currency products present significant additional risk elements and/or administrative complications, compared to a straightforward single-currency environment. This answer is certainly not welcome news to actuaries who have been or will be involved with these types of medical plans as the international focus of their respective companies increases. Given the spotty record of health insurance financial results on an industry-wide basis over the last quarter-century, the standard loss ratio risk alone has been difficult to accurately project, control, and price for via the development of consistently adequate rate levels. The existence of an additional risk element in mixed-currency plans makes the attainment of desired financial results even more difficult.

To provide a contrast and a comparison for the results of the medical model, several observations are made in the next section about the operation of life insurance products in the mixed-currency environment.

II. LIFE INSURANCE PRODUCTS

Coverages denominated in a medium of exchange other than the legal tender of the insureds' country of residence are more common for life insurance than for medical plans.

Life products that are structured similarly to the medical plans analyzed in this paper—in the sense that the premiums and policy benefits are denominated in the same medium of exchange—are not subject to the same currency risks. These life products internally operate on a completely unitized basis independent of the legal tender in the insureds' country of residence. Premium rates are expressed per unit of policy benefit, and all payments generated by the life policies, such as premiums, death benefits, and surrender benefits, are in the same currency. Investments supporting the reserve liabilities of the life block of business are usually also denominated in the same medium of exchange. That the policy may be sold to persons living in a country with a different medium of exchange is essentially immaterial. It is the insured's responsibility to convert funds to the proper currency in which the policy is denominated to pay the premiums. From that point forward, the life policy functions in a manner identical to that of a product sold to persons living in the country on whose currency the policy is based.

However, there actually is an area of susceptibility for life plans in a mixed-currency environment. A large swing in the exchange rate between the two currencies can either make the life policy too expensive, at one extreme, or render the existing coverage level insufficient, at the other extreme, thereby affecting lapse rates and increasing the variability of the financial results of the block of business. Nevertheless, this potential vulnerability appears to be relatively marginal and much less of a concern than the susceptibility of medical products to shifts in exchange rates. Furthermore, this possible problem for life plans is external, in the sense that all the internal policy values and relationships are not distorted by the currency exchange swing.

These comments do not apply to certain types of life insurance products with premiums and policy benefits denominated in different monetary units. For example, recently in both Mexico and Chile there has been interest in life coverages with local currency premiums in conjunction with benefits indexed to the U.S. dollar. There can be substantial exchange rate risk in these arrangements that would be a function of the specific structure of these products.

Finally, in the dual-currency mode that we are analyzing, it might be theorized, based upon the "unitized life plan" concept, that a fully scheduled medical product would essentially offer the same immunization against currency exchange rate swings as a life insurance product. This question is addressed in Section VIII, which contains model results for a hospital indemnity plan that provides a fixed reimbursement per day of hospital confinement on a per-unit-of-benefit basis.

III. UNDERLYING INCURRED MEDICAL EXPERIENCE IN LOCAL CURRENCY

Table 1 contains a projection of basic financial data for a block of medical policies that forms the hypothetical model in this analysis for the first four policy designs. Because the purpose of this study is to examine the impact of changes in currency exchange rates on financial results, morbidity is assumed to be accurately and precisely projected for medical services received in the insureds' country of residence. In other words, if the medical product were to be written directly in the country's currency, the Table 1 projected morbidity results would be exactly achieved for the portfolio. For convenience, that currency will be called "local currency" (LC).

In Table 1 the projected financial results assume a block of 1,000 lives covered for a calendar year under a reasonable-and-customary-expense basis medical plan, with a deductible of LC 100,000 per person per disability and 80% coinsurance. For simplicity, because variation in currency exchange rates and not morbidity is the focus, 25 claims are presumed to be incurred each month, each representing a new disability. Each claimant in January

TABLE 1

LOCAL CURRENCY MORBIDITY AND FINANCIAL DATA FOR POLICY DESIGNS A–D

(1)	(2)	(3) Lives Insured	(4) Number of Claimants	(5) Trend Factor	(6) Per Claimant Expense Incurred	(7) Per Claimant Benefit Payable	(8) Total Block Expense Incurred	(9) Total Block Benefits Payable
1	January	1,000	25	1	1,000,000	720,000	25,000,000	18,000,000
2	February	1,000	25	1.0221	1,022,104	737,684	25,552,611	18,442,089
3	March	1,000	25	1.0447	1,044,698	755,758	26,117,438	18,893,950
4	April	1,000	25	1.06779	1,067,790	774,232	26,694,749	19,355,799
5	May	1,000	25	1.09139	1,091,393	793,114	27,284,822	19,827,858
6	June	1,000	25	1.11552	1,115,518	812,414	27,887,938	20,310,350
7	July	1,000	25	1.14018	1,140,175	832,140	28,504,386	20,803,509
8	August	1,000	25	1.16538	1,165,378	852,303	29,134,459	21,307,568
9	September	1,000	25	1.19114	1,191,138	872,911	29,778,461	21,822,769
10	October	1,000	25	1.21747	1,217,468	893,974	30,436,697	22,349,358
11	November	1,000	25	1.24438	1,244,379	915,503	31,109,484	22,887,587
12	December	1,000	25	1.27189	1,271,886	937,509	31,797,142	23,437,713
Total			300		13,571,927	9,897,542	339,298,187	247,438,549

Premium per insured per month: 27493.17213
Premium for the total block: 329,918,066
Loss ratio: 0.75
Ratio of benefits paid to expenses incurred: 0.7293

generates a medical expense covered under the policy of LC 1,000,000, while the expense per claimant in subsequent months during the year is assumed to increase at an annual trend rate of 30% in the local currency. Column (5) of Table 1 displays the trend factor applicable to each month, and the resulting per claimant expense is shown in column (6).

The per-claimant benefit payable in column (7) of Table 1 reflects the application of the benefit formula to the column (6) expense, that is, the deductible of LC 100,000 and the 80% coinsurance.

Columns (8) and (9) contain the expenses incurred and the benefits payable for the entire block and are equal to columns (6) and (7), respectively, multiplied by the total of 25 claimants each month.

Several key summary financial results for this assumed portfolio are shown at the bottom of the table. In particular, the loss ratio and the ratio of benefits paid to covered medical expenses incurred are of primary importance:

$$\text{Loss Ratio} = \frac{247,438,549}{329,918,066} = 0.7500$$

$$\text{Benefits Paid/(Expenses Incurred)} = \frac{247,438,549}{339,298,187} = 0.7293$$

The premise is that given the specified plan design written directly in local currency, the experience can be accurately projected as in Table 1 such that the aggregate benefits payable will equal 72.93% of the total expenses incurred and the target incurred loss ratio of 75% will be achieved. What is the effect on these key parameters if we interject into the environment a medical plan denominated in another currency that on an expected basis is intended to be equivalent to the specified local currency plan?

IV. DOLLAR POLICY PLAN DESIGNS

For this block of 1,000 covered lives, the medical plan is not to be defined in the local currency, but rather in dollars, at an expected currency exchange rate for the forthcoming calendar year of $1.00=LC 200. Therefore, the expected equivalent dollar medical plan that will be written to cover these individuals during the calendar year will feature a $500 per person per disability deductible and 80% coinsurance.

In the administration of this dollar plan throughout the year, there are several possibilities for collecting dollar premiums and paying dollar claims, four of which are described as policy designs A to D below. For the premium quantity in these descriptions, the community rate in local currency that is appropriate for the underlying morbidity is shown in Table 1 as LC 27,493.17 per person per month.

Policy Design A

- *Premiums.* Converted at the expected exchange rate throughout the policy year, so that the monthly rate per person is LC 27,493.17/200=$137.47.
- *Claims.* Local currency covered medical expenses are converted to dollars by the expected exchange rate factor of 1/200 for all claims incurred during the year.

Policy Design B

- *Premiums.* The dollar premium payable each month is determined by dividing LC 27,493.17 by the market currency exchange rate for that month.
- *Claims.* Local currency covered medical expenses are converted to dollars for application of the policy's benefit formula via multiplication by the market currency exchange rate for the month in which the claims are incurred.

Policy Design C

- *Premiums.* Converted at the expected exchange rate throughout the policy year, so that the monthly rate per person is LC 27,493.17/200=$137.47 (same as policy design A).
- *Claims.* Converted at the market currency exchange rate each month throughout the policy year (same as policy design B).

Policy Design D

- *Premiums.* Converted at the market currency exchange rate each month throughout the policy year (same as policy design B).
- *Claims.* Converted by the expected exchange rate factor of 1/200 throughout the year (same as policy design A).

Each dollar policy design contains inherent advantages and disadvantages that may influence its selection from among the four alternatives. Several general considerations that may be involved in evaluating, on a surface level, the relative attractiveness of each policy design are described below.

Policy design A is appealing from several perspectives. Because both the premiums and claims are converted by the same expected exchange rate factor of 1/200 during the year, the conversion of these two quantities is "matched," regardless of market exchange rates during the one-year term period. Administration is simplified with the application of the same 1/200 factor throughout, and the insureds should better understand how their policies function. They pay the same dollar premium each month, and any claims incurred during the year are converted by a constant factor.

Policy design B appears even more attractive than A from a financial perspective. Not only are the premium and claim conversions matched at the same exchange rates during the policy year, but the conversion is at the market rate for each month, so the dollar quantities stay completely synchronized with the changing value of the dollar relative to the local currency. This plan is not so kind to the insured or to the administrative process, however, because the premium payable in dollars fluctuates each month, as does the rate of conversion to effect claim payments in dollars. In addition, there may be significant legal and regulatory obstacles to receiving approval from the proper authorities to sell this style of plan design in some countries.

Policy design C can be considered an appropriate compromise to the relative advantages and disadvantages of B. The complexities of the plan to the insured can be substantially reduced by specifying a constant dollar monthly premium payable, rather than the possibility of varying and unknown installments each month. On the claims side, the use of the market exchange rate can be considered a means of keeping the claims payment current with the changing relativity of the two currencies.

For policy design D, it is a little more difficult to identify a compelling rationale for its use. Perhaps it could be argued that the insureds would be willing to let their premiums float according to the market currency exchange rate during the year, but would want to "know what they are buying" by having the claim conversion fixed at issue for the year.

V. CURRENCY EXCHANGE RATES

Five distinct currency exchange rate outcomes are studied in this model, as shown in columns (1) through (5) of Table 2.

Each of the five sets of exchange rate progressions begins with an actual rate of $1.00=LC 178 in January, under the supposition that when the column (1) expected scale of exchange rates was postulated, the timing was sufficiently close to the first month of the policy year so that the actual result in each outcome equals the expected value for January. Thereafter, the monthly actual market exchange rates in the other four outcomes diverge from the expected values.

TABLE 2

CURRENCY EXCHANGE RATE OUTCOMES

		Actual Market Exchange Rates				
		(1) Expected (E)	(2) Moderately High (MH)	(3) Substantially High (SH)	(4) Moderately Low (ML)	(5) Substantially Low (SL)
1	January	178	178	178	178	178
2	February	182	186	190	179	176
3	March	186	194	202	180	174
4	April	190	202	214	181	172
5	May	194	210	226	182	170
6	June	198	218	238	183	168
7	July	202	226	250	184	166
8	August	206	234	262	185	164
9	September	210	242	274	186	162
10	October	214	250	286	187	160
11	November	218	258	298	188	158
12	December	222	266	310	189	156
Average exchange rate		200	222	244	183.5	167

The moderately high (MH) and substantially high (SH) outcomes involve monthly devaluations of $+8$ and $+12$, respectively, compared to the expected monthly devaluation in the exchange rate of $+4$. The moderately low (ML) progression incorporates a monthly increase of $+1$, while the substantially low (SL) series includes a reversal of direction in the exchange rate, with a monthly change of -2.

The linear functions selected for the exchange rate scenarios are not meant to suggest that these normally follow this type of pattern, with the possible exception of countries whose currency is managed by the governmental authorities to produce a steady, programmed devaluation over time. Rather, the linear progression simplifies the model and is an appropriate assumption because the primary purpose of this paper is to study the effects on certain financial parameters of a block of medical policies, given that a divergence between the levels of actual and expected exchange rates occurs during an experience year. The focus is not on the dynamics of currency exchange rates themselves; the theoretical and statistical considerations of projecting actual currency exchange rate relationships are not intended to be addressed by this analysis.

Note that the average currency exchange rate applicable to the calendar year is 200 for the expected set of values, which is the constant factor for the policy year in those policy designs that involve conversions of the premiums or the claims at the expected exchange rate.

Throughout this paper the assumption is made that a free market exists for the legal and convenient exchange of currencies at these exchange rates.

VI. PORTFOLIO FINANCIAL RESULTS

Combining the four policy designs (described in Section IV) with the five currency exchange rate outcomes (in Section V) produces a total of 20 scenarios of financial results for the dollar medical plans during the calendar year. Table 3 displays detailed month-by-month premium and claim figures for the first of these 20 outcomes in the model. The plan analyzed in this scenario is policy design A, and the actual currency exchange rate progression for the year is the expected set of values.

To reduce the bulk of this paper, detailed results in the Table 3 format are not shown for scenarios 2–20. However, key summary statistics from the entire set of 20 tables in the Table 3 format have been extracted and are displayed in Table 4.

Column (4) of Table 3 contains the actual dollar premiums paid by the block of 1,000 lives during the year, which in each scenario is a function of the policy design and the exchange rate outcome. Note that in Table 3, due to the number of significant digits carried internally by the computer, this monthly premium of $137,465.85 differs very slightly from the premium quantity based upon the dollar rate specified in Section IV, which is: $(1,000)(137.47)=\$137,470.00$. There may be other minor rounding differences, which have no bearing on the analysis in this paper. Column (5), the local currency total expense incurred, is taken directly from column (8) of Table 1.

The imputed dollar total expense incurred in column (6) is obtained from multiplying column (5) by the appropriate currency exchange rate, according to the policy design and exchange rate outcome under consideration in each scenario.

Dollar total benefits payable in column (7) are derived from column (6) by application of the dollar benefit formula, which consists of a $500 deductible per person per disability, with 80% coinsurance.

TABLE 3

Financial Results for Policy Design A
Currency Exchange Rate Outcome: Expected
Premiums Converted At: Expected
Claims Converted At: Expected

(1)	(2)	(3) Market Currency Exchange Rate	(4) Total Block Dollar Premium Payable	(5) Local Currency Total Expense Incurred	(6) Imputed Dollar Total Expense Incurred	(7) Dollar Total Benefits Payable	(8) Benefits Converted at Market to Local Currency	(9) Premium Converted at Market to Local Currency
1	January	178	137,465.85	25,000,000	125,000	90,000	16,020,000	24,468,921
2	February	182	137,465.85	25,552,611	127,763	92,210	16,782,301	25,018,785
3	March	186	137,465.85	26,117,438	130,587	94,470	17,571,374	25,568,648
4	April	190	137,465.85	26,694,749	133,474	96,779	18,388,009	26,118,512
5	May	194	137,465.85	27,284,822	136,424	99,139	19,233,022	26,668,375
6	June	198	137,465.85	27,887,938	139,440	101,552	20,107,247	27,218,238
7	July	202	137,465.85	28,504,386	142,522	104,018	21,011,544	27,768,102
8	August	206	137,465.85	29,134,459	145,672	106,538	21,946,795	28,317,965
9	September	210	137,465.85	29,778,461	148,892	109,114	22,913,907	28,867,829
10	October	214	137,465.85	30,436,697	152,183	111,747	23,913,813	29,417,692
11	November	218	137,465.85	31,109,484	155,547	114,438	24,947,470	29,967,555
12	December	222	137,465.85	31,797,142	158,986	117,189	26,015,862	30,517,419
Total			1,649,590	339,298,187	1,696,491	1,237,193	248,851,342	329,918,040

Dollar loss ratio: 0.7500
Local currency benefits paid/expenses incurred: 0.7334
Dollar benefits paid/expenses incurred: 0.7293
Local currency benefits paid/premium: 0.7543

272

Columns (8) and (9) represent columns (7) and (4), respectively, multiplied month by month by the market currency exchange rates displayed in column (3). These are the dollar benefits and dollar premiums generated by this block of business in the model converted back to local currency according to the monthly market exchange rate.

Since the plan is actually denominated in dollars, what is the value of including in Table 3 the premium and claim quantities converted back to local currency? This question is addressed shortly, as part of the description in subsequent paragraphs of the remaining table entries, which consist of summary financial ratios for the policy year displayed in the bottom left portion of the table. These ratios, which represent key policy parameters consisting of comparisons for the entire year of claims to premiums and of benefits paid to expenses incurred, are shown in the last four columns of Table 4 for all 20 outcomes, along with the expected target values for these quantities. Table 4 also specifies the currency exchange rate outcome and the policy design that correspond to each scenario.

TABLE 4

RESULTS OF DEVIATIONS IN ACTUAL TO EXPECTED CURRENCY EXCHANGE RATES
FOR THE POLICY DESIGN AND EXCHANGE RATE SCENARIOS

Scenario Number	Currency Exchange Rate Outcome	Policy Design	Target Loss Ratio	Target Benefits Paid / Expenses Incurred	Dollar Loss Ratio	Local Currency Benefits Paid / Expenses Incurred	Dollar Benefits Paid / Expenses Incurred	Local Currency Benefits Paid / Premium
1	E	A	0.75	0.7293	0.7500	0.7334	0.7293	0.7543
2	E	B	0.75	0.7293	0.7461	0.7293	0.7292	0.7500
3	E	C	0.75	0.7293	0.7496	0.7293	0.7292	0.7500
4	E	D	0.75	0.7293	0.7464	0.7334	0.7293	0.7543
5	MH	A	0.75	0.7293	0.7500	0.8178	0.7293	0.7577
6	MH	B	0.75	0.7293	0.7355	0.7215	0.7220	0.7420
7	MH	C	0.75	0.7293	0.6731	0.7215	0.7220	0.6685
8	MH	D	0.75	0.7293	0.8195	0.8178	0.7293	0.8411
9	ML	A	0.75	0.7293	0.7500	0.6701	0.7293	0.7512
10	ML	B	0.75	0.7293	0.7549	0.7351	0.7350	0.7560
11	ML	C	0.75	0.7293	0.8230	0.7351	0.7350	0.8240
12	ML	D	0.75	0.7293	0.6879	0.6701	0.7293	0.6892
13	SH	A	0.75	0.7293	0.7500	0.9022	0.7293	0.7605
14	SH	B	0.75	0.7293	0.7259	0.7137	0.7151	0.7340
15	SH	C	0.75	0.7293	0.6131	0.7137	0.7151	0.6016
16	SH	D	0.75	0.7293	0.8880	0.9022	0.7293	0.9278
17	SL	A	0.75	0.7293	0.7500	0.6069	0.7293	0.7474
18	SL	B	0.75	0.7293	0.7647	0.7409	0.7412	0.7620
19	SL	C	0.75	0.7293	0.9174	0.7409	0.7412	0.9126
20	SL	D	0.75	0.7293	0.6252	0.6069	0.7293	0.6241

The most important summary quantity is the dollar loss ratio. Defined as the dollar claims payable divided by the dollar premiums received, it is a direct barometer of the financial success, or lack thereof, of the insurance company responsible for this hypothetical block of business.

Recall that our target loss ratio is 75% and that the underlying morbidity level for the plan design in local currency (Table 1) produces exactly this desired result. The only aspects of the portfolio scenarios shown in Table 4 that differ compared to Table 1 are:

(1) The utilization of a dollar plan design that is intended to have an equivalent deductible on an expected currency exchange rate basis
(2) A specific methodology for converting currencies at either market or expected rates (policy designs A–D)
(3) Actual variation in the market exchange rate throughout the year compared to the expected progression.

Table 5, column (4), displays the differences between actual and target results for the dollar loss ratio, revealing that 11 of the 20 scenarios have actual values that vary from the 75% target by more than ± 1.0%. Eight of these deviate by more than ± 5.0%, with a minimum dollar loss ratio of 61.31% and a maximum level of 91.74%. This deviation in the actual versus the expected financial results is due entirely to the effect of the exchange rates in the mixed-currency medical plan environment, as the underlying morbidity in local currency remains unchanged.

The ratio, in local currency, of benefits paid to expenses incurred in Table 3 is column (8) divided by column (5). This ratio is significant, and the derivation of this quantity is one reason that the conversions of the dollar premiums and claims back into local currency are given in the last two columns of the table.

To appreciate the significance of this statistic, the practical mechanics of the disposition of the policy benefits must be considered. The insured will receive a dollar benefit under the medical plan according to the application of the exchange rate to the covered expenses incurred in local currency and the benefit formula of the $500 deductible, 80% coinsurance. To pay the suppliers of medical services, whose bills are in local currency, the claimant must convert the dollar plan benefits back to local currency. This is accomplished at the prevailing, available market currency exchange rate. Effectively, therefore, the percentage of the total local currency expenses reimbursed by the insurance program is determined by comparing the dollar reimbursement converted back into local currency to the original expenses incurred in that same medium of exchange.

TABLE 5

DIFFERENCE BETWEEN TABLE 4 ACTUAL
AND TARGET FINANCIAL RATIOS

Scenario Number	Currency Exchange Rate Outcome	Policy Design	Dollar Loss Ratio	Local Currency Benefits Paid / Expenses Incurred	Local Currency Benefits Paid / Premium
1	E	A	0.0000	0.0041	0.0043
2	E	B	−0.0039	0.0000	0.0000
3	E	C	−0.0004	0.0000	0.0000
4	E	D	−0.0036	0.0041	0.0043
5	MH	A	0.0000	0.0885	0.0077
6	MH	B	−0.0145	−0.0078	−0.0080
7	MH	C	−0.0769	−0.0078	−0.0815
8	MH	D	0.0695	0.0885	0.0911
9	ML	A	0.0000	−0.0592	0.0012
10	ML	B	0.0049	0.0058	0.0060
11	ML	C	0.0730	0.0058	0.0740
12	ML	D	−0.0621	−0.0592	−0.0608
13	SH	A	0.0000	0.1729	0.0105
14	SH	B	−0.0241	−0.0156	−0.0160
15	SH	C	−0.1369	−0.0156	−0.1484
16	SH	D	0.1380	0.1729	0.1778
17	SL	A	0.0000	−0.1224	−0.0026
18	SL	B	0.0147	0.0116	0.0120
19	SL	C	0.1674	0.0116	0.1626
20	SL	D	−0.1248	−0.1224	−0.1259

The local currency plan in Table 1 generated an expected value for the benefits paid to expenses incurred ratio of 72.93%. The corresponding column in Table 5 reveals, however, that 12 of the 20 scenarios have reimbursement ratios that vary from the target by more than ±1.0%. Eight of these 12 differ by more than ±5.0%, with a minimum ratio of 60.69% and a maximum level of 90.22%.

There is a direct link between the percentage of expenses reimbursed by a medical plan and the morbidity level. The model contains the assumption that, given the local currency plan with the deductible of LC 100,000 and 80% coinsurance, the morbidity results in Table 1 will be generated. This plan operates to reimburse an aggregate percentage of 72.93% of the total expenses incurred. To the extent that the application of the currency exchange rates in the dollar plan that is intended to be equivalent function to change that expense reimbursement ratio, the underlying morbidity level will be affected. For those scenarios in the model whose ratios of local currency benefits paid to expenses incurred are substantially greater than

72.93%, the dollar loss ratio shown is actually understated, because the model assumption of unchanged morbidity would no longer be valid and the total of incurred expenses would be higher. Conversely, for those scenarios with reimbursement ratios substantially less than the target of 72.93%, the dollar loss ratio shown is overstated.

Note that scenario 16 appears to be a particularly dangerous situation, because it combines an 88.8% dollar loss ratio with a reimbursement level of 90.22% of local currency expenses incurred. At the other extreme, scenario 20 produces a dollar loss ratio of 62.52% along with a local currency expense reimbursement ratio of 60.69%.

The third summary financial statistic to be discussed is the local currency ratio of benefits paid to premiums. In Table 3, this is the quotient of column (8) and column (9). This statistic measures the value, from a total block of business perspective, that the insureds receive for their premium. As previously described, the insureds will likely convert at a market exchange rate the dollar reimbursement received from the plan to a local currency quantity to fund the amounts due to the providers of the medical services. On the premium side, although dollar amounts are payable to the insurance company, the dollars used to pay these premiums are often obtained via a conversion of the insureds' local currency funds at the available market rate of exchange. This comparison, at market exchange rates, of the benefits converted to local currency to the local currency annual equivalent of the premiums indicates the return that the insureds receive in the form of benefit payments for their funds utilized to pay the premiums.

In the Table 1 results for the equivalent plan written directly in the local legal tender, the loss ratio achieved is 75%. In the Table 4 display of summary statistics by scenario, 11 of the 20 scenarios produce a result that differs from the 75% target by more than ±1%. Eight of these deviations are by more than ±5%, with a minimum ratio of 60.16% and a maximum value of 92.78%.

Although the simplified model does not incorporate a lapse rate assumption, it could be theorized that the effect of changing relationships between local currency benefits paid and premiums would influence the persistency of the block of insured lives and be a further destabilizing influence on the portfolio's financial results. As this ratio decreases throughout the year in certain scenarios due to the currency exchange rate dynamics, the policy would appear less attractive in general and insureds would begin to drop out of the program at an accelerated rate. Conversely, as this ratio increases in other scenarios, fewer people than expected would lapse their coverage.

The fourth summary statistic shown in Table 3 is the dollar comparison of benefits paid to expenses incurred, computed as column (7) divided by column (6). This is the least interesting of the set of four summary ratios. It varies much less than the other indices, ranging in Table 4 from a low of 71.51% to a high of 74.12%. Furthermore, it does not appear to have a meaningful interpretation with respect to its effect, if any, on the results of the portfolio. While the numerator is significant in that it represents the actual dollar claims paid, the denominator is only a converted currency figure that is utilized to apply the benefit formula of the $500 deductible, 80% coinsurance. This quantity does not appear worthy of further comment or analysis and has been omitted from the Table 5 display of differences between actual and target values.

It is also revealing to examine the combined effect of the key financial ratios for each scenario. This is efficiently accomplished via a review of the Table 5 differences between actual and target results.

For the first four scenarios, in which the actual market currency exchange rates are accurately projected in advance of the policy year, all the Table 5 differences are less than 0.50%. This indicates that in an environment in which the currency exchange rates are correctly predicted, all four policy designs produce results that are perfectly consistent with those expected according to the underlying morbidity.

Of the remaining 16 scenarios that involve deviations between the actual and expected market currency exchange rates, all but one feature ratio differences in Table 5 that are all in the same direction. In other words, for scenarios 5–20, except for cells with a zero difference, the values are either all positive or all negative. The one exception is scenario 9, in which the positive difference is so small that it is essentially zero.

This indicates that the deviations in the first two financial ratios (that is, the dollar loss ratio and the local currency ratio of benefits paid to expenses incurred) are always compounded, such that there are never any offsets and both of the deviations combine to force the financial results in the same direction. For example, any scenario with a dollar loss ratio higher than expected will also experience a local currency ratio of benefits paid to expenses incurred that equals or exceeds the target. Positive deviations in this latter ratio will result in increased utilization of medical services, which will, in turn, further force the dollar loss ratio in an upward direction. In addition, this type of scenario will produce a local currency ratio of benefits to premium that exceeds the target level. In a more realistic and sophisticated model, this would tend to increase the persistency of the portfolio and, therefore, generate a greater total volume of losses, because the aggregate financial results would not be diluted to the extent that would be expected due to lapsation.

Conversely, any scenario with a Table 4 dollar loss ratio less than expected should, in reality, experience an actual dollar loss ratio that is even further depressed than the Table 4 value. This is due to reduced utilization caused by the influence of the local currency ratio of benefits to expenses being lower than the target. Furthermore, because of the downward distortion in the comparison of local currency benefits to premiums, the increased lapsation that would result should serve to dilute the exceptionally high profits that would otherwise accrue as a result of the low dollar loss ratio.

VII. POLICY DESIGN ANALYSIS

The model has indicated that a medical plan in a mixed-currency environment is subject to several destabilizing influences and that a significant currency exchange rate risk can be superimposed upon the usual loss ratio, or morbidity, risk of this type of product. However, is any of the four policy designs superior to the others for maintenance of the original intended financial parameters under shifting currency exchange rate circumstances?

This question is addressed in Tables 6, 7, and 8, which revisit in a modified format the 20 scenario values for the three key summary financial ratios—the dollar loss ratio, the ratio of benefits paid to expenses incurred, and ratio of benefits paid to premium, respectively—for the model portfolio. A standard deviation statistic is developed for the ratios shown in each table for each policy design, computed via the typical formula:

$$\text{Std. Dev.} = \left(\frac{\sum_{n=1}^{n=5} (r_n - \text{target})^2}{5} \right)^{1/2}$$

The symbol r above signifies the financial ratio for which the standard deviation is being calculated.

In Table 6, the dollar loss ratios that reflect the actual currency exchange rate pattern matching the expected series all appear consistent with the target loss ratio. This indicates that all four policy designs function well in this environment. However, the dollar loss ratio stability produced by policy designs A and B is clearly superior to that for C and D for the other four currency exchange rate outcomes. For policy design A, there is no change in the dollar loss ratio resulting from exchange rate swings, while the effect on policy design B is minimal. Policy designs C and D display financial results that are quite sensitive to currency exchange fluctuations, having standard deviations equal to 7.4 times and 6.4 times, respectively, the standard deviation of policy design B.

Note also that policy designs C and D react in opposite directions to fluctuations in the currency exchange rates. For upward deviations in the exchange rates, policy design D produces poorer financial results, while policy design C generates more favorable dollar loss ratios. For downward deviations in the exchange rates, the loss ratio movement is reversed for the two types of plans. These dynamics are not surprising given the opposite methods that these two policy designs employ for converting premiums and claims.

TABLE 6

DOLLAR LOSS RATIOS FOR THE POLICY DESIGN
AND EXCHANGE RATE SCENARIOS

Currency Exchange Rate Outcome	Target Loss Ratio	Policy Design*	Dollar Loss Ratio
1. Expected	0.75	A	0.7500
		B	0.7461
		C	0.7496
		D	0.7464
2. Moderately High (MH)	0.75	A	0.7500
		B	0.7355
		C	0.6731
		D	0.8195
3. Substantially High (SH)	0.75	A	0.7500
		B	0.7259
		C	0.6131
		D	0.8880
4. Moderately Low (ML)	0.75	A	0.7500
		B	0.7549
		C	0.8230
		D	0.6879
5. Substantially Low (SL)	0.75	A	0.7500
		B	0.7647
		C	0.9174
		D	0.6252
6. Standard Deviation		A	0.0000
		B	0.0145
		C	0.1077
		D	0.0931

*A = Premiums, expected; claims, expected
B = Premiums, market; claims, market
C = Premiums, expected; claims, market
D = Premiums, market; claims, expected

Table 7 contains interesting results for the effectiveness of the plan designs in maintaining the ideal 72.93% relationship between the benefits paid, converted back to local currency, and the original expenses incurred. In this category, policy designs B and C, both of which use market exchange rates to convert the covered medical expenses incurred to dollars for the application of the benefit formula, do a good job of maintaining the target reimbursement ratio in spite of exchange rate fluctuations. Policy designs A and D, however, which use the expected exchange rate for the application of the benefit formula, do a relatively poor job of maintaining a stable relationship. The standard deviation of policy designs A and D is 10.9 times as great as that of policy designs B and C.

TABLE 7

LOCAL CURRENCY RATIO OF BENEFITS PAID TO EXPENSES INCURRED FOR THE POLICY DESIGN AND EXCHANGE RATE SCENARIOS

Currency Exchange Rate Outcome	Target Benefit/Expense Ratio	Policy Design*	Ratio of Benefits Paid to Expenses Incurred
1. Expected	0.7293	A	0.7334
		B	0.7293
		C	0.7293
		D	0.7334
2. Moderately High (MH)	0.7293	A	0.8178
		B	0.7215
		C	0.7215
		D	0.8178
3. Substantially High (SH)	0.7293	A	0.9022
		B	0.7137
		C	0.7137
		D	0.9022
4. Moderately Low (ML)	0.7293	A	0.6701
		B	0.7351
		C	0.7351
		D	0.6701
5. Substantially Low (SL)	0.7293	A	0.6069
		B	0.7409
		C	0.7409
		D	0.6069
6. Standard Deviation		A	0.1061
		B	0.0097
		C	0.0097
		D	0.1061

*A = Premiums, expected; claims, expected
B = Premiums, market; claims, market
C = Premiums, expected; claims, market
D = Premiums, market; claims, expected

In Table 8, which displays the ratios of local currency benefits paid to premium, the relative effectiveness of each plan follows the same order as for the dollar loss ratio in Table 6, although essentially in this last table policy designs C and D are just about equally poor. Policy designs A and B both are relatively stable with respect to the 75% target loss ratio.

TABLE 8

LOCAL CURRENCY RATIO OF BENEFITS PAID TO PREMIUM
FOR THE POLICY DESIGN AND EXCHANGE RATE SCENARIOS

Currency Exchange Rate Outcome	Target Loss Ratio	Policy Design*	Ratio of Benefits Paid to Premium
1. Expected	0.75	A	0.7543
		B	0.7500
		C	0.7500
		D	0.7543
2. Moderately High (MH)	0.75	A	0.7577
		B	0.7420
		C	0.6685
		D	0.8411
3. Substantially High (SH)	0.75	A	0.7605
		B	0.7340
		C	0.6016
		D	0.9278
4. Moderately Low (ML)	0.75	A	0.7512
		B	0.7560
		C	0.8240
		D	0.6892
5. Substantially Low (SL)	0.75	A	0.7474
		B	0.7620
		C	0.9126
		D	0.6241
6. Standard Deviation		A	0.0063
		B	0.0100
		C	0.1101
		D	0.1091

*A = Premiums, expected; claims, expected
B = Premiums, market; claims, market
C = Premiums, expected; claims, market
D = Premiums, market; claims, expected

So how should these plan designs be ranked for their overall desirability in maintaining stability in the financial parameters in the face of fluctuating exchange rates, or in other terms, in minimizing the currency exchange risk?

If each plan design is graded 1 through 4 from best to worst in each category, recognizing the ties in Table 7, we have the following tabulation:

POLICY DESIGN RANKING

	A	B	C	D
Dollar Loss Ratio	1	2	4	3
LC Benefits Paid/Expenses Incurred	2	1	1	2
LC Benefits Paid/Premium	1	2	4	3

Interestingly, no one policy design is consistently the best or worst across the three financial ratio tests. Policy designs C and D appear to be clearly inferior to A and B. Policy design A is the best in the two loss ratio categories and experiences no fluctuation in the critical dollar loss ratio statistic. However, its performance in maintaining a stable local currency benefits paid to expenses incurred ratio is poor, leaving it subject to changes in underlying utilization patterns if the exchange rates shift. Policy design B performs relatively well in all categories, as none of the three financial parameters become significantly distorted as a result of the exchange rate influence. However, as mentioned in Section IV, a market-exchange-rate-based policy design that is subject to monthly changes in the factor for converting premiums and claims is the most difficult to administer. It also presents uncertainties and inconveniences to the insureds, as well as potential legal and regulatory problems in some countries.

VIII. SCHEDULED MEDICAL PLAN

In Section II, general considerations and comments were made about life insurance products with premiums and policy benefits denominated in a currency other than the medium of exchange of the insureds' country of residence. It was asserted that the life products, as a result of their completely unitized structure, internally function independently of the particular currency of the country in which the policy is sold. The question was: does a medical plan structured on a completely scheduled, per-unit basis afford the same immunity against currency exchange rate fluctuations as a life insurance product?

To address this question, a fifth policy design, E, was established. In contrast to policy designs A–D, policy design E is a fully scheduled plan that provides a benefit of $800.00 per day of confinement as an inpatient in a hospital.

A similar methodology was utilized to examine the results for this scheduled plan. Table 9 is analogous to Table 1 in that it contains a display of the underlying morbidity experience. Once again the model tracks the results of 1,000 insured lives for a policy year equal to the calendar year. In this simple environment, 27 inpatient hospital days are generated each month by the block of insured lives. In local currency, the average hospital charge per day starts in January at LC 180,000 and then increases at an annual trend rate of 25%.

Column (7) in Table 9 displays the total local currency hospital charges generated by the claimants each month and is equal to the product of the number of hospital days in column (4) and the trended hospital charge per day in column (6).

The monthly community rate per 1.00 of benefit per day of hospital confinement, with a 75% target loss ratio and regardless of the currency in which the hospital plan is denominated, is computed as:

$$\frac{(27 \times 12)}{(1000)(12)(0.75)} = 0.036$$

Since our hospital indemnity product provides a benefit of $800 per day, the premiums are as follows:

Per person per month	($800)(0.036)	= $28.80
Total block per month	(1000)($28.80)	= $28,800
Total block, annual	(12)($28,800)	= $345,600

Total claims paid for the year will be: ($800)(27)(12)=$259,200. The calculation below confirms that the desired loss ratio is in fact achieved:

$$\frac{\$259,200}{\$345,600} = 0.75$$

Note that in the administration of this policy design for both premiums and claims, no currency conversions are required. The unit rate, as mentioned previously, is independent of currency. This rate is multiplied by the desired daily benefit amount in any currency to produce the proper premium payable.

For claim payments, the amount due for any confinement is determined as the contractual daily benefit in the currency of the policy multiplied by the number of days of the hospital stay.

Since policy design E involves no explicit currency conversions, it would appear to be protected against currency exchange rate changes in the same manner that a life product is immunized. To test this hypothesis, policy

TABLE 9
Morbidity and Financial Data for Scheduled Plan (Policy Design E)

(1)	(2)	(3) Number of Insured Lives	(4) Number of Hospital Inpatient Days	(5) Trend Factor	(6) Local Currency Hospital Charges per Day	(7) Total Local Currency Hospital Charges	(8) Dollar Benefits Payable at $800 per Day	(9) Dollar Premiums for $800 per Day Benefit
1	January	1000	27	1.00000	180,000	4,860,000	21,600	28,800
2	February	1000	27	1.01877	183,378	4,951,219	21,600	28,800
3	March	1000	27	1.03789	186,820	5,044,149	21,600	28,800
4	April	1000	27	1.05737	190,327	5,138,824	21,600	28,800
5	May	1000	27	1.07722	193,899	5,235,276	21,600	28,800
6	June	1000	27	1.09744	197,538	5,333,539	21,600	28,800
7	July	1000	27	1.11803	201,246	5,433,645	21,600	28,800
8	August	1000	27	1.13902	205,023	5,535,631	21,600	28,800
9	September	1000	27	1.16040	208,871	5,639,530	21,600	28,800
10	October	1000	27	1.18218	212,792	5,745,380	21,600	28,800
11	November	1000	27	1.20437	216,786	5,853,217	21,600	28,800
12	December	1000	27	1.22697	220,855	5,963,077	21,600	28,800
Total			324			64,733,488	259,200	345,600

Monthly rate per 1.00 unit of daily benefit: 0.036
Dollar benefit per day: $800
Total dollar monthly premium: $28,800
Loss ratio for dollar hospital product: 0.75

design E was analyzed in the context of five scenarios defined by the five currency exchange rate outcomes specified in Section V. Table 10 displays detailed month-by-month financial information for the first scenario, in which the actual market exchange rates experienced conform to the expected pattern.

Columns (3), (4), and (5) in Table 10 are taken directly from Table 9. The assumed series of market currency exchange rates appears in column (6). Columns (7) and (8) contain the actual dollar benefits and premiums, respectively, generated by this portfolio during the year converted to local currency at the market currency exchange rates. Therefore, column (7) is equal to the product of columns (4) and (6), while column (8) is determined by multiplying columns (5) and (6).

Summary financial ratios similar to those developed in the review of policy designs A–D are shown in the bottom left corner of Table 10 and are summarized in the last two columns of Table 11 for the five currency exchange rate outcomes.

In contrast to the prior analysis, there are only two summary statistics, which are the local currency ratios of the benefits paid to the expenses incurred and the benefits paid to the premium. The first of these quantities is computed in Table 10 as the ratio of columns (7) and (3), while the second is derived via the quotient of column (7) and column (8). The two dollar ratios that were included in the study of policy designs A through D do not exist for policy design E, since the dollar results shown in Table 9 do not vary according to the currency exchange rate outcome.

The relationship of the local currency benefits paid to premium is not influenced by the varying currency exchange rate outcomes, as Table 11, column (5) demonstrates that the target 75% relativity of claims to premium is always maintained in local currency.

Unfortunately, the results displayed in Table 11, column (6) are not as encouraging. The local currency ratio of benefits paid to expenses incurred is quite sensitive to the influence of the currency exchange rate. When the actual market currency exchange rates conform to the expected pattern, the local currency benefit is about 80% of the charges, which represents a reasonable and typical benefit level. However, this reimbursement ratio fluctuates upward to 97.7% for the "substantially high" exchange rate outcome and plummets to 66.87% in the "substantially low" exchange rate environment.

Under typical circumstances, when the medical policy's dollar benefit is received by the claimant, it must be converted into local currency to

TABLE 10

FINANCIAL RESULTS FOR POLICY DESIGN E
CURRENCY EXCHANGE RATE OUTCOME: EXPECTED

(1)	(2)	(3) Total Local Currency Hospital Charges	(4) Dollar Benefits Payable at $800 per Day	(5) Dollar Premiums for $800 per Day Benefit	(6) Market Exchange Rate	(7) Benefits Converted to Local Currency at Market Rate	(8) Premiums Converted to Local Currency at Market Rate
1	January	4,860,000	21,600	28,800	178	3,844,800	5,126,400
2	February	4,951,219	21,600	28,800	182	3,931,200	5,241,600
3	March	5,044,149	21,600	28,800	186	4,017,600	5,356,800
4	April	5,138,824	21,600	28,800	190	4,104,000	5,472,000
5	May	5,235,276	21,600	28,800	194	4,190,400	5,587,200
6	June	5,333,539	21,600	28,800	198	4,276,800	5,702,400
7	July	5,433,645	21,600	28,800	202	4,363,200	5,817,600
8	August	5,535,631	21,600	28,800	206	4,449,600	5,932,800
9	September	5,639,530	21,600	28,800	210	4,536,000	6,048,000
10	October	5,745,380	21,600	28,800	214	4,622,400	6,163,200
11	November	5,853,217	21,600	28,800	218	4,708,800	6,278,400
12	December	5,963,077	21,600	28,800	222	4,795,200	6,393,600
Total		64,733,488	259,200	345,600		51,840,000	69,120,000

Converted Local Currency Comparisons:
Benefits paid/expenses incurred: 0.8008
Benefits paid/premiums: 0.7500

286

TABLE 11
SUMMARY OF FINANCIAL RATIOS FOR POLICY DESIGN E
FOR CURRENCY EXCHANGE RATE OUTCOMES

(1) Currency Exchange Rate Outcome	(2) Outcome Number	(3) Target Loss Ratio	(4) Target Benefits Paid / Expenses Incurred	(5) Actual Benefits Paid / Premium	(6) Actual Benefits Paid / Expenses Incurred
Expected (E)	1	0.75	0.8008	0.75	0.8008
Moderately High (MH)	2	0.75	0.8008	0.75	0.8889
Substantially High (SH)	3	0.75	0.8008	0.75	0.977
Moderately Low (ML)	4	0.75	0.8008	0.75	0.7348
Substantially Low (SL)	5	0.75	0.8008	0.75	0.6687

reimburse the providers of medical care. In this specific example, it is the hospital bills denominated in the local medium of exchange that must be paid.

Due only to changes in the currency exchange rate outcome, this model produces hospital expense reimbursement levels ranging from about 67% to 98%. Such a range would be expected to influence the underlying morbidity, such that the projection of 27 inpatient days per 1,000 per month, which may have been a perfectly accurate assumption at 80% reimbursement in the expected exchange rate situation, would not be an accurate morbidity projection at reimbursement percentages substantially deviating from this level. A 98% hospital expense reimbursement would produce a greater number of inpatient days per month, making the 0.036 unit rate insufficient, while a 67% reimbursement ratio would generate fewer than 27 inpatient days per month, resulting in an excessive unit rate.

Thus it appears that even the fully scheduled hospital plan's internal financial components are not immune to changes in currency exchange rates. Apart from the standard morbidity risk, there is a definite exchange rate risk that adds additional uncertainty to the financial results.

Note that this scheduled plan reacts in a similar manner as policy design A, in that both are sensitive and vulnerable to the effect on utilization of the expense reimbursement ratio in local currency, but are quite stable with respect to the other currency-generated sources of financial instability.

IX. EFFECT OF INTRODUCING ADDITIONAL VARIABLES AND CHANGES IN POLICY DESIGNS

Sections VI and VII present the financial results of the model portfolio and an analysis of the characteristics of policy designs A–D, given the specific model and plan definitions described in earlier sections.

This section contains an analysis of the effects on the key financial ratios of injecting specific changes into the definition of the policy designs and into certain aspects of the operation of the model.

A. Variation in Deductible Level

The underlying local-currency model claim costs in Table 1 were developed by utilizing a medical plan with a per-cause deductible of LC 100,000. The equivalent dollar plan deductible was $500 at the expected exchange rate of LC 200=$1.00 for the policy year.

Two additional sets of tables corresponding to Table 1 and Table 2 (for all 20 scenarios) were generated for deductibles that were equal to one-half and double the original plan specifications, that is, deductibles equal to LC 50,000 ($250) and LC 200,000 ($1,000). The differences between actual and target ratios are summarized in the following tables for the three deductible levels:

Table 12: Dollar Loss Ratios

Table 13: Local-Currency Benefits Paid/Expenses Incurred

Table 14: Local-Currency Benefits Paid/Premium

In each of these tables, the column of differences between actual and target ratios for the $500 deductible plan is taken directly from Table 5.

There are no surprises in these results: similar influences of the currency exchange rate are present for all three deductibles. The magnitude of the deviations changed somewhat in several of the scenarios for the alternative deductibles, and there are interesting patterns by currency exchange rate outcome and policy design combination in each table.

In Table 12, the analysis of dollar loss ratios, regardless of the deductible level, the target 0.75 value is always achieved for scenarios 1, 5, 9, 13, and 17. This is not surprising because policy design A converts both covered expenses and premiums to dollars throughout the policy year at the expected exchange rate and therefore maintains the same dollar loss ratio of 0.75 inherent in the local currency results.

For policy design D there also is no effect on the dollar loss ratios due to varying the plan deductible. For B and C, however, the deviation between the actual and expected ratios is influenced by the deductible level, because it generally increases with the size of the deductible.

TABLE 12

DIFFERENCE BETWEEN ACTUAL AND TARGET DOLLAR LOSS RATIOS
FOR PLANS WITH VARIOUS DEDUCTIBLES

Scenario Number	Currency Exchange Rate Outcome	Policy Design	Dollar Loss Ratio		
			$250 Deductible Plan	$500 Deductible Plan	$1,000 Deductible Plan
1	E	A	0.0000	0.0000	0.0000
2	E	B	−0.0039	−0.0039	−0.0040
3	E	C	−0.0003	−0.0004	−0.0004
4	E	D	−0.0036	−0.0036	−0.0036
5	MH	A	0.0000	0.0000	0.0000
6	MH	B	−0.0106	−0.0145	−0.0235
7	MH	C	−0.0733	−0.0769	−0.0851
8	MH	D	0.0695	0.0695	0.0695
9	ML	A	0.0000	0.0000	0.0000
10	ML	B	0.0018	0.0049	0.0121
11	ML	C	0.0696	0.0730	0.0809
12	ML	D	−0.0621	−0.0621	−0.0621
13	SH	A	0.0000	0.0000	0.0000
14	SH	B	−0.0166	−0.0241	−0.0415
15	SH	C	−0.1306	−0.1369	−0.1516
16	SH	D	0.1380	0.1380	0.1380
17	SL	A	0.0000	0.0000	0.0000
18	SL	B	0.0082	0.0147	0.0297
19	SL	C	0.1596	0.1674	0.1853
20	SL	D	−0.1248	−0.1248	−0.1248

Table 13 differs from 12 and 14 in that the target for the quotient of the converted local-currency benefits paid and expenses incurred varies by deductible level:

Deductible	Target Ratio of Local Currency Benefits Paid to Expenses Incurred
$ 250	0.7646
$ 500	0.7293
$1,000	0.6585

Identical patterns by scenario number are exhibited for each of the three deductibles. The ratios for policy designs A and D are always equal for each currency exchange rate outcome, because both plans convert covered expenses in the claim adjudication process at the expected exchange rate. Similarly, the policy design B and C ratios are identical because both plans convert covered expenses at the market exchange rate.

TABLE 13

DIFFERENCE BETWEEN ACTUAL AND TARGET RATIOS
OF LOCAL-CURRENCY BENEFITS PAID TO EXPENSES INCURRED
FOR PLANS WITH VARIOUS DEDUCTIBLES

Scenario Number	Currency Exchange Rate Outcome	Policy Design	Ratio of Local Currency Benefits Paid to Expenses Incurred		
			$250 Deductible Plan	$500 Deductible Plan	$1,000 Deductible Plan
1	E	A	0.0042	0.0041	0.0040
2	E	B	0.0000	0.0000	0.0000
3	E	C	0.0000	0.0000	0.0000
4	E	D	0.0042	0.0041	0.0040
5	MH	A	0.0925	0.0885	0.0808
6	MH	B	−0.0039	−0.0078	−0.0155
7	MH	C	−0.0039	−0.0078	−0.0155
8	MH	D	0.0925	0.0885	0.0808
9	ML	A	−0.0620	−0.0592	−0.0533
10	ML	B	0.0030	0.0058	0.0117
11	ML	C	0.0030	0.0058	0.0117
12	ML	D	−0.0620	−0.0592	−0.0533
13	SH	A	0.1807	0.1729	0.1574
14	SH	B	−0.0077	−0.0156	−0.0311
15	SH	C	−0.0077	−0.0156	−0.0311
16	SH	D	0.1807	0.1729	0.1574
17	SL	A	−0.1282	−0.1224	−0.1107
18	SL	B	0.0059	0.0116	0.0234
19	SL	C	0.0059	0.0116	0.0234
20	SL	D	−0.1282	−0.1224	−0.1107

There is some sensitivity by deductible level in the difference between actual and target values for the ratio of benefits paid to expenses incurred. Interestingly, as the deductible increases, the deviation for policy designs A and D decreases. Conversely, for policy designs B and C the ratio differences either remain at zero or increase as the deductible grows in magnitude.

Like Table 12, the Table 14 target ratio, 0.75, is identical for all deductible levels for the comparison of the local-currency benefits paid to the premiums. For all four plan designs, the deviation in the actual compared to the target value either is unaffected or increases as the deductible becomes larger. The effect is minimal on policy designs A and D, because the change in the differences by deductible level is very slight. There is a more substantial impact on policy designs B and C, except for scenarios 2 and 3 in which the actual result achieved is the target ratio for all deductible levels.

TABLE 14

DIFFERENCE BETWEEN ACTUAL AND TARGET RATIOS
OF LOCAL-CURRENCY BENEFITS PAID TO PREMIUM
FOR PLANS WITH VARIOUS DEDUCTIBLES

Scenario Number	Currency Exchange Rate Outcome	Policy Design	Ratio of Local-Currency Benefits Paid to Premium		
			$250 Deductible Plan	$500 Deductible Plan	$1,000 Deductible Plan
1	E	A	0.0041	0.0043	0.0047
2	E	B	0.0000	0.0000	0.0000
3	E	C	0.0000	0.0000	0.0000
4	E	D	0.0041	0.0043	0.0047
5	MH	A	0.0074	0.0077	0.0085
6	MH	B	−0.0038	−0.0080	−0.0177
7	MH	C	−0.0778	−0.0815	−0.0903
8	MH	D	0.0907	0.0911	0.0920
9	ML	A	0.0011	0.0012	0.0013
10	ML	B	0.0029	0.0060	0.0133
11	ML	C	0.0706	0.0740	0.0819
12	ML	D	−0.0607	−0.0608	−0.0609
13	SH	A	0.0100	0.0105	0.0117
14	SH	B	−0.0076	−0.0160	−0.0354
15	SH	C	−0.1415	−0.1484	−0.1643
16	SH	D	0.1773	0.1778	0.1792
17	SL	A	−0.0024	−0.0026	−0.0028
18	SL	B	0.0057	0.0120	0.0266
19	SL	C	0.1551	0.1626	0.1800
20	SL	D	−0.1258	−0.1259	−0.1261

In summary, while the deductible level does exert some influence in the actual key financial ratios generated by the portfolio, the same underlying distorting effects of the exchange rates are present for plans with various deductibles. Depending upon the particular currency exchange rate outcome, policy design, and financial quantity, a difference in plan deductible level may cause the portfolio's financial performance to be affected moderately, but the financial ratios generated will be generally consistent by deductible level.

B. Per-Cause Versus Per-Calendar-Year Deductible Policies

The medical plan utilized in the model incorporates a deductible defined on a per-cause basis. What is the effect, if any, of changing the policy specifications to a per-calendar-year deductible?

Maintaining the deductible amount at the same quantity but changing the basis from per cause to per calendar year would have the same effect on the model as retaining the per-cause basis and lowering the deductible amount. Both types of changes would increase incurred claims and therefore also the required premiums for a given universe of covered medical expenses. In theory, the claim cost generated by any per-cause deductible should correspond to that produced by a specific per-calendar-year deductible of greater magnitude.

Therefore, the results shown in the prior discussion of varying per-cause deductible amounts would also be pertinent to the effect on the model of changing the policy specifications from a per-cause to a per-calendar-year deductible.

C. Lag between Claim Incurral and Paid Dates

It is interesting to consider the effect of claim payment lags, and variations in the lag patterns, in the analyses. Claim runout has not yet been addressed, because the model results to this point ideally assume that claims are paid in the same month as incurred.

1. Dollar Loss Ratios

According to the policy design definitions in Section IV, for both the expected and market exchange rate bases for converting covered expenses to dollars for claim adjudication, the conversion is a function of the incurral date of the medical expense. Therefore, with this definition, the dollar loss ratios displayed in Table 6 would be unaffected by claim lags. Regardless of the time between the incurral and payment dates, the dollar benefit payable would be unchanged.

2. Local-Currency Ratios of Benefits Paid to Expenses Incurred and of Benefits Paid to Premiums

As previously explained in the analyses of the two local-currency ratios of benefits paid to expenses incurred and of benefits paid to premium, these quantities are significant as a result of the insured's conversion of the dollar policy's benefit payment into the local currency to pay the suppliers of medical services. This conversion would be at market exchange rates and, when claim payment lags are incorporated into the process, would logically occur during the month of claim payment.

In this situation, the Table 7 and 8 local-currency ratios would be affected by the payment lag. The exchange rate applied to produce local-currency benefit payments would, on average, be that for a date several months after the incurral month instead of for the incurral month as shown in the tables. Given that the uncertainty in future exchange rates increases as the time lengthens from the present, the application of market exchange rates determined by claim payment dates to generate these local-currency ratios would serve to increase the fluctuations and distortions in policy values that may result.

Longer claim payment lag patterns would tend to intensify the effect described in the prior paragraph, while faster runout would diminish this influence. In the limiting case for shorter lags, in which the payment date approaches the incurral date, the model values displayed in Tables 7 and 8 would be applicable.

To gain further insight into how the specific policy design determines the effect of the exchange rates on the financial parameters, the claim runout influence can be examined in the context of changing the policy design B and C methods for converting local-currency expenses to dollars in the claim adjudication process. These modified products would apply a market exchange rate based upon the paid month, rather than the incurral month, to produce dollar expenses for application of the benefit formula.

In this situation the Table 6 dollar loss ratios would be affected by the application of market exchange rates that would tend to be for later times than those defined by incurral months. If the local currency were devaluating against the dollar, the dollar loss ratios would decrease in comparison to the original values, while an appreciation in the local currency would result in higher dollar loss ratios.

Of course, the longer the claim lags and the greater the rate of change of the relative currency values, the more pronounced the effect on the financial results.

Interestingly, for the modified policy designs B and C, the local currency statistics in Tables 7 and 8 will not be significantly affected because the exchange rate effectively cancels out in the double currency conversion process. This results from the fact that, regardless of whether the local-currency incurred medical expenses are expressed in dollars via multiplications by market rates defined by incurral or paid months, following the application of the plan benefit formula the identical exchange rate is used to convert the dollar benefit back into the local currency. In fact, if it were not for the leveraging effect of the $500 deductible, the dollar benefit paid converted back to local currency would be independent of the exchange rate utilized in the claim calculation process.

D. Experience Rated Versus Manually Rated Products

What is the impact of deviations in actual compared to expected currency exchange rates for insurance products that have been experience-rated (for example, group cases), versus those with a manual or tabular rating foundation?

The potential for exchange rate deviations to distort financial results and internal expected product relationships exists equally for medical plans with both techniques of rate development. A key concept in this analysis is that the morbidity results for the group of covered lives have been accurately projected for the experience year in local currency. The dollar premiums charged are equal to the theoretically correct local premiums converted at either the expected rate for the entire year or the actual market exchange rate each month depending upon the policy design. Whether these exact local premiums were derived via an experience evaluation or a tabular rating basis is immaterial with respect to the currency exchange rate influence demonstrated in this paper.

E. HMO and Other Managed Care Products

From a practical perspective, the mixed-currency scenarios addressed in this paper are applicable to indemnity-style medical products and not to managed care programs featuring negotiated arrangements with providers. The currency influences arise from a medical plan that reimburses insureds on an expense incurred basis for covered charges generated in a different monetary unit. For a medical product to be subject to this situation, it almost by definition would have to be a wide open indemnity-style plan designed to reimburse expenses regardless of incurral location and without an emphasis on the provision of medical care in a limited geographical location close to the insured's residence.

Conversely, HMO and other managed care products with networks of participating providers are structured for medical care services in a limited area with convenient access for the covered population. In order for the same types of currency mismatches reviewed in this paper to occur in a managed care, fee-for-service arrangement outside of the U.S., the following financial arrangements would have to exist:

(a) Contracted providers would have fees negotiated in their native currency
(b) The actual plan reimbursement would be payable in dollars, with the amount determined by converting the fee at either the market or a fixed exchange rate
(c) Dollar premiums would be payable by the enrolled group for the coverage.

Obviously, such a managed care program would not exist in practice. The local care orientation of these network-focused products would always involve a single-currency environment.

X. CONCLUSION

This paper has attempted to analyze via a simplified, hypothetical model the dynamics of medical insurance coverage that is denominated in a currency other than that in which the medical expenses are incurred.

Three key summary financial ratios for the model portfolio were studied to determine their level of stability for five distinct potential policy designs in an environment in which the basic morbidity was accurately projected, but the currency exchange rates varied from the expected progression during the policy year. Four of the five policy designs displayed a lack of stability in one or more of these financial parameters and therefore demonstrated a vulnerability to fluctuations in currency exchange rates. Because this instability in these financial parameters either directly affects the financial performance of the portfolio or would be expected to significantly alter the underlying morbidity, these policy designs inherently contain an additional risk element of currency exchange rate fluctuation in addition to the typical medical insurance morbidity risk.

Policy design B, which involves monthly currency conversions at market exchange rates for both premium payments and claim computations, was the only plan structure for which all three financial ratios remained relatively stable for the various exchange rate scenarios. While none of the three ratios for policy design B was unaffected by the shifting currency relativities, the variation in the financial parameters was not nearly as substantial as for the most sensitive policy designs for each ratio, and none of the financial values was significantly distorted.

However, as previously pointed out, policy design B is the most difficult to administer, and it is less convenient and more difficult for the insured to understand due to currency conversion factors that are subject to change on a monthly basis. Also, this policy design with dynamic values pegged to a foreign currency may face legal and regulatory barriers in some countries.

Following are several comments about the model used to study these scenarios:

(1) The analysis was presented in the context of a dollar-denominated plan operating in a country outside of the U.S. Actually, the same dynamics and considerations would apply in any mixed-currency situation, regardless of the specific countries and legal tenders involved.

(2) Substantial variations in the key financial parameters were shown to exist for four of the five policy designs due solely to the exchange rate influence. When this effect is combined with the potential differences that may occur in reality between the actual morbidity experienced and the expected morbidity level projected prior to the policy year, the financial results are subject to much greater fluctuation and uncertainty. Variations in morbidity may occur independently of, or be induced by, the exchange rate outcomes.

Additional analysis could be performed to study the compound effects of deviations of the actual compared to the expected experience with respect to both the exchange rates and the underlying morbidity.

(3) The model could be additionally refined by varying the trend rate assumed in the local currency charges according to the exchange rate patterns. It would be reasonable to expect that a country's internal rate of trend (that is, inflation) can be affected by differing relationships of its currency to that of other countries. In effect, recognition of this dynamic in the model would be one form of introducing changes into the underlying assumed morbidity.

(4) Other potential enhancements include lapse rates that vary according to changes in the financial ratios, and varying morbidity levels of the lapsing policyholders compared to those that persist in the portfolio.

(5) A fundamental assumption in the approach to the mixed-currency medical policy environment discussed in this paper is that the starting point for pricing one of these policies is a projection of the expected morbidity in the underlying local currency.

However, to the extent that these policies are priced in practice directly in a foreign currency, without good information regarding the actual local currency expected morbidity, the level of risk and uncertainty of the eventual financial performance of the portfolio is greatly magnified.

(6) To focus on the destabilizing influence of dual currencies, all the covered medical expenses in the model were assumed to be incurred in a

different medium of exchange than the policy. In practice, medical products designed for the international market are typically structured to pay benefits for covered expenses incurred both in dollars and in local currencies, depending upon the location at which the medical services are received. The same currency influences will occur for these products, but to a lesser degree than demonstrated in the model as the dollar portion of the covered expenses is matched with the currency in which the policy is denominated.

Given that a market exists for comprehensive medical insurance to cover expenses with significant portions incurred in more than one currency, what options and strategies might be available to an insurer to reduce the vulnerability of the financial results to swings in the relative values of the monetary units? Several possibilities along with potential advantages and disadvantages are briefly presented below.

Use of the shortest possible period over which policy values are fixed as a result of projected currency exchange rates reduces the risk of actual experience differing from expected due to the exchange rate influence. The longer the period for which currency exchange rates (as well as other pricing assumptions, of course) must be projected to determine expected values, the higher the probability of deviations within the projection interval and the greater the magnitude of the deviations.

Note that according to the financial ratios for policy designs A, C, and D in Tables 6, 7, and 8 and for policy design E in Table 11, the results differ only slightly from the targets when the progression of actual currency exchange rates is consistent with the expected values for the projection period.

Policy design B, which maintains all its internal financial relativities for all exchange rate outcomes, is a special case in which the plan is structured so that there is, in effect, no projection period with a fixed, expected exchange rate. Its premium and claim quantities self-adjust each month according to the actual market exchange rate patterns.

Administrative complexities and possibly regulatory restrictions may provide a lower bound for the interval over which a projected currency exchange rate must be utilized, forcing the insurer to accept the exchange rate risk for this period.

In situations in which there is a significant level of uncertainty about fluctuations in both directions of currency exchange rates, the pricing development could include a conservative assumption for the exchange rate progression during the projection interval, plus perhaps an extra explicit margin in the rates. Certainly this would provide additional protection against deterioration in the financial performance of the portfolio resulting from unfavorable swings in the currency relativities.

To make such a conservatively priced product more salable and to avoid excessive lapsation, it could be offered on a participating basis such that dividends or refunds are distributed to policyholders if favorable financial results are realized. To the extent, however, that other companies may be willing to offer a lower-priced similar product on a nonparticipating basis, it could be difficult to market.

A natural issue in the context of international, multi-currency insurance coverages is the medium of exchange in which to invest the assets backing the portfolio's liabilities, and whether switching assets from one legal tender to another should form part of the company's investment strategy.

For the types of policies reviewed in this paper, the insurer is not required to convert the funds it handles from one currency to another, because all premiums are received in dollars and all claims are paid in dollars. The currency exchange risk borne by the insurer in these examples results from the medical expenses reimbursed by these policies being denominated in a non-dollar legal tender. In this environment, it would appear that the most straightforward approach would be to invest the assets supporting the reserves and surplus for this line of business in dollar instruments.

However, if periods can be accurately predicted during which a local currency will strengthen against the dollar and the expected internal rate of return on local currency assets plus the currency appreciation would produce significantly higher total returns than dollar-denominated assets, then it would be advantageous to convert dollar investments into local currency instruments. Such investment actions could entail significant risk and might prudently be limited to temporary periods under special circumstances. The dollar denomination of the policies studied in this paper would seem to require that, over the long term, the portfolio's liabilities and surplus be backed by dollar assets.

The most direct and probably the best technique for eliminating the types of currency exchange risk described herein is simply to avoid mixing currencies by structuring the policy or policies, so that coverage is explicitly and separately denominated in the major currencies in which expenses are expected to be incurred.

In a situation involving two principal mediums of exchange, dollars and a specific local currency, there would be a separate schedule of insurance and distinct premiums payable in both dollars and the local currency.

Although this might involve some administrative complications, there would never be a currency mismatch, because regardless of the locations in which the expenses were incurred, the schedule of insurance in the correct currency would generate a benefit with the proper relativity to the medical expenses. Furthermore, the rate level development in each currency would involve only the usual morbidity projection risk and not the additional uncertainty inherent in projecting the exchange rate throughout the guarantee period during which rates and other policy parameters are fixed.

DISCUSSION OF PRECEDING PAPER

FRANK E. FINKENBERG:

I would like to extend Kevin Law's consideration of mixed-currency medical plans into two areas: hedging and rate-making.

Currency Hedging

The currency risk analyzed in Mr. Law's paper is of limited duration. It is the risk that the exchange rate between the currency in which medical expenses are incurred (local currency, or LC in Mr. Law's analysis) and the currency in which the plan is denominated (U.S. dollars in Mr. Law's paper) will be different at the time claims are incurred from the exchange rate in effect at the time premiums are set. In countries with reasonably developed financial markets, this risk can be greatly reduced. It is not necessary that a futures market exist for the local currency, as long as relatively safe short-term debt instruments (bills or notes of a government, central bank, or other high-grade issuer) are available. The method is outlined below.

Under Mr. Law's assumption that the medical expenses in LC are accurately predicted, the insurer knows the benefits that would be payable month by month if the plan were denominated in LC. Under plan designs B and C, however, benefits in dollars are obtained by converting medical expenses from LC to dollars at the exchange rate at the time claims are incurred, and then applying a dollar deductible and coinsurance. To avoid currency gains or losses in this type of plan, the insurer could purchase notes denominated in LC, matched in amount and maturity to the expected monthly benefit outflow at today's exchange rate. At each note's maturity, its proceeds would be converted back to dollars at the then-current exchange rate. If LC appreciates against the dollar during the term of the note, more dollars will be obtained at maturity than the initial investment plus the expected interest; this offsets the additional dollar benefits payable that month resulting from the exchange rate shift. If LC depreciates, the loss on the hedging investment is offset by the exchange rate gain on the claims.

In a plan without a deductible or with a deductible in LC, the hedge described above would be perfect; the direct currency risk is eliminated. (As Mr. Law notes, an indirect currency risk exists under some designs: the adverse effect on morbidity of a high replacement ratio measured in LC. The above hedge does not remove this.) A hedged plan with a dollar deductible will still experience some currency gains or losses due to the

301

deductible's nonlinear effect on claims, although the fluctuations will be much smaller than an unhedged plan. In a rich medical plan with a reasonable calendar-year deductible, the remaining currency gains or losses are probably *de minimis*.

In practice a hedge is not needed for every month or every currency; restricting hedging to the currencies most important to the plan and grouping expected claims by quarter will likely yield quite an acceptable reduction of risk. The insurer should model various currency and hedging scenarios to determine the residual risk, and structure the hedge accordingly.

The above method involves committing capital to investments in LC. The insurer is compensated for this, of course, by interest received. In some currencies, as short-term interest rates tend to be higher than those in dollars, the hedge actually makes money for the insurer while reducing currency risk.

If there is a futures market in LC, advance commitment of assets is not needed; the insurer merely contracts to purchase the desired amounts of LC for delivery in the appropriate months. The futures contract is sold before the delivery date, so the insurer never actually holds LC. If there is an efficient market, the gain or loss on the transaction will be the same as if a direct investment had been made. The price paid for the futures contract must reflect any interest differential between the currencies; otherwise, one party would be better off using the direct investment method described above, and arbitrage would bring the futures price back into line.

The above discussion of hedging shows that direct or derivative investments in the currency in which claims are incurred reduces risk. I therefore disagree with Mr. Law's conclusion that plan assets should be invested in dollars. Not just plan assets, but an amount equivalent to the remaining claims of the policy term, should in effect be invested in LC, either directly or through futures contracts.

Mr. Law makes an exception to dollar investments where the local currency "can be accurately predicted" to strengthen. This is pure currency speculation, which is extraordinarily risky. The last 15 years have seen extreme volatility in currency markets, with sharp moves having little to do with underlying economic strength or purchasing power parity. The beauty of hedging is that it frees the insurer from any need to forecast currency values during the policy term.

Experience-Rated Premiums for Mixed-Currency Plans

Mr. Law stresses the "fundamental assumption" of his model that morbidity in local currency is accurately projected; he properly adds a strong caveat that, absent good data, risk is greatly magnified. The problem is that, in a plan with medical expenses incurred in a number of currencies, it is not practical to maintain and use local currency morbidity experience in the annual experience rating process. To do so would require, in effect, re-adjudicating all claims during the whole experience period each year, based on the latest exchange rates. If, on the other hand, premiums are based on experience kept in the plan's currency of account, out-of-date exchange rates will introduce distortions. Claims incurred when local currencies were stronger than now will artificially inflate the premium, and vice versa.

As consulting actuary for a worldwide group medical plan, I have addressed this problem by building a weighted index of historical exchange rates between the 15 currencies with the largest claim volume (comprising more than 82% of claims) and the plan currency (the dollar). This plan is large enough and stable enough that the simplifying assumption of a uniform distribution of claims in each currency over the year can be used. The weights, which can change each year, are the ratios of the dollar volume of claims in each currency in the index to the total dollar claims for the 15 currencies. The index is called the claim purchasing power index (CPPI), because it shows the relative strength of the dollar against the currencies in which medical expenses are incurred. If today's CPPI is 105 and that at time t was 100, it means the dollar "buys" 5% more in claims today than at time t.

For experience rating purposes, historical claims paid in dollars are adjusted to the latest available exchange rates by applying the ratio of the CPPI at the time claims were paid to the current CPPI. In the example of the last paragraph, the dollar claims of time t are multiplied by $100 \div 105$. The result closely approximates the effect of maintaining experience in each claim currency and readjudicating claims at current exchange rates.

The importance of this adjustment can be seen in the historical range of the CPPI for the plan. Just from 1990 through 1994, annual average CPPI values ranged from 82.8 to 101.3 (January 1995=100). The use of unadjusted experience from this period, during which the dollar was on balance much weaker than at its end point, would greatly overstate the premium required to meet the plan's expected claims based on today's exchange rates. Conversely, using unadjusted experience from a period in which the dollar was stronger than at its end point would understate the needed premium. The CPPI minimizes these errors without the need to maintain experience in many currencies and without overly complicating the rate-setting process.

(AUTHOR'S REVIEW OF DISCUSSION)

KEVIN M. LAW:

I thank Frank Finkenberg for his contribution to the subject of mixed-currency medical plans.

The currency-hedging technique described by Mr. Finkenberg would eliminate the direct dollar loss ratio risk for policy designs B and C, as he points out. This is particularly important for policy design C, since the structure of plan B effectively provides protection against all the types of distortions in the portfolio's financial parameters that are addressed in the paper.

The hedging strategy does not correct the indirect currency exchange rate risks resulting from the local currency comparisons of benefits paid to medical expenses incurred or of benefits paid to premium. These ratios would continue to experience deviations in actual results compared to expected values, potentially affecting the underlying morbidity level and the persistency of the portfolio.

The direct investment-hedging method (that is, without using futures contracts) would function best if the medical policies' premiums were paid annually in advance, rather than monthly. This would allow the premiums for the coverage to directly fund the claims payments, instead of initially using the company's surplus and later repaying it as the premium installments are paid during the year.

The hedging technique in effect substantially reduces the degree of currency mismatches in policy design C. This is consistent with my recommendation in the next to last paragraph of the paper for the "most direct and probably the best technique for eliminating the types of currency exchange risk described herein," which is to structure the policy directly in the major monetary unit(s) in which the medical expenses are expected to be incurred.

Mr. Finkenberg disagrees with my conclusion that plan assets are more appropriately invested in dollar instruments. I believe that this issue is more of a difference in context, than a divergence of opinion on the proper medium of exchange for the investments.

In the context of an insurer attempting to better match currencies via the hedging technique, I concur with Mr. Finkenberg's assertion that the assets required to fund the policies' remaining liabilities for the policy term be invested in LC-denominated assets. My analysis in the paper was in the context of an insurer that was not directly attempting to match currencies to reduce an exchange rate risk, but rather considering switching assets from one legal tender to another as part of an investment strategy. In the absence of a currency-matching plan, the prudent approach, in general, would be to maintain the portfolio assets in dollars, which is the currency in which the policy is denominated.

However, I am not certain that swapping currencies should be completely ruled out, although I do agree with Mr. Finkenberg that this can be extremely risky. Any endeavors of this nature should be limited and considered with extreme caution.

Mr. Finkenberg mentions at the beginning of the discussion that the currency risk analyzed in the paper is that the exchange rate between the currencies at the time claims are incurred will be different from that when the premiums are established. I would state this in a slightly different manner; the risk involves the actual market currency exchange rate deviating from the expected pattern as of the beginning of the period. Note that all the policy designs studied in the paper produce undistorted financial parameters for the expected progression of currency exchange rates during the interval, although the exchange rates at the end of the year differ by 25% from those at the beginning.

Finally, Mr. Finkenberg describes a workable, practical CPPI index method for adjusting prior claim experience from multiple currencies to a constant set of exchange rates: "historical claims paid in dollars are adjusted to the latest available exchange rates by applying the ratio of the CPPI at the time claims are paid to the current CPPI." I suggest that for prospective experience rating purposes, an additional step be incorporated to restate the claims according to a projected CPPI that corresponds to the expected exchange rates for the future period for which the new rate level will apply.

Once again, I thank Mr. Finkenberg for his comments and observations.

TESTING FINANCIAL STABILITY
OF CONTINUING CARE RETIREMENT COMMUNITIES

ERNEST J. MOORHEAD AND NIELS H. FISCHER

ABSTRACT

This paper introduces continuing care retirement communities (CCRCs) to the *Transactions*. It outlines the major recent developments in financing procedures and regulatory requirements aimed at keeping these entities solvent. In particular, it describes the Actuarially Based Financial Management System (ABFM) created in 1990 by the American Academy of Actuaries and the *Statement of Position 90-8* promulgated by the American Institute of Certified Public Accountants (AICPA).

The paper aims to guide the actuary in making sound judgments of the differing results that arise from these professional requirements and naturally stresses the merits of a comprehensive actuarial approach.

I. INTRODUCTION

The growing senior population and the steadily increasing segment of this population residing in CCRCs have focused ever-increasing attention of operators and regulators upon meeting the financial guarantees to their residents.

The lankmark work of Winklevoss and Powell, published by the Pension Research Council in 1984 [11],* introduced actuaries to this world of CCRCs: senior housing arrangements that bring with them actuarial concepts of selection of risks, health insurance, life insurance, and pensions all rolled into one—plus the additional fascination of real property valuations and the delivery of health care services. Literature published by the Society of Actuaries and other actuarial bodies, however, is sparse. Much of actuaries' work is recorded only in committee minutes of the American Academy of Actuaries, actuarial meeting seminars and open forums, and occasional articles in actuarial newsletters.

The Academy's Committee on CCRCs, with Jarvis Farley as primary drafter, published its Statement of Standards in 1987, which became

---

*It is noteworthy that this extremely important book was never reviewed in the *Transactions*. A brief review by David L. Hewitt appeared in *The Actuary*, May 1984 [7].

Actuarial Standard of Practice (ASOP) No. 3 in 1990. In 1994 that ASOP underwent a revision in principles and reformatting.

The period 1990–1994 saw creation of *Statement of Position 90-8* on the Generally Accepted Accounting Principles (SOP-GAAP) of the American Institute of Certified Public Accountants on CCRCs; this SOP was the first exclusively on CCRCs. A number of new state regulations and changes to the National Association of Insurance Commissioners' (NAIC) accounting manual were also issued during this period. This paper describes the methodologies and the effects of inconsistencies between them.

The paper is organized into the following sections:

II.   Evolution of Today's CCRC Financial Statements and Regulation
III. Definitions and Summaries of Standards of Practice
IV.   Resident Contracts and Their Actuarial Implications
V.   Differences between Standards of Practice Set by Accounting and Actuarial Professional Bodies and Their Implications for Budgeting and Pricing
VI.   Regulatory Accounting Requirements
VII. Conclusion.

The paper provides analyses of the differing results obtained by alternative accounting and actuarial standards to help actuaries understand their consequences, including their impact upon the emergence of earnings.

The authors acknowledge personal debt to the late Jarvis Farley, a friend who identified the importance of actuarial involvement to ensure the financial stability of these facilities. This paper is dedicated to his memory.

II. EVOLUTION OF TODAY'S CCRC FINANCIAL STATEMENTS AND REGULATION

The early CCRCs, copied from European originals, were sponsored by religious bodies that depended upon charitable contributions to cover costs not funded by the residents. So there was no role for regulators to perform other than to monitor the good faith of the organizers. We believe it was not until the 1970s that any North American actuary began to advise these communities on their prospects for making good on their promises to the residents.

As recently as the early 1980s, only a handful of state authorities required CCRCs to demonstrate their financial viability. The state-by-state history is beyond this paper's scope, but we note that the State of New York's Insurance Department prohibited formation of CCRCs until 1991, when the department issued comprehensive financial accounting methods and standards.

It was not until 1988 that the NAIC formed a working group to provide guidance to state insurance departments. The work of that group was completed in 1994, and details on its final report are described in Section VI.

III. DEFINITIONS AND SUMMARIES OF STANDARDS OF PRACTICE

A. Actuarial Definitions

Actuarial Standard of Practice No. 3 (ASOP No. 3) [2] defines essential terms. Those of most importance to an understanding of this paper are defined below. A knowledge of all terms and practices in *ASOP No. 3* is recommended.

Continuing Care Retirement Community. A residential facility for retired people that provides stated housekeeping, social, and health care services in return for some combination of an advance fee, periodic fees, and additional fees.

Residency Agreement. The contract between a CCRC and the resident(s) of a living unit (apartment, cottage, villa, health center unit, and the like) in the community.

Advance Fee. An amount payable by the resident at the inception of a residency agreement, also known as endowment fee, entry fee, or founder's fee.

Nonrefundable Advance Fee. The portion of an advance fee to which the CCRC is unconditionally entitled under the terms of the residency agreement.

Periodic Fees. Amounts payable periodically (usually monthly) during the existence of a residency agreement.

Refundable Advance Fee. The portion of an advance fee, designated in the residency agreement, that is to be returned to the resident or the resident's estate either upon termination of the agreement or upon resale of the unit.

Additional Fees. Amounts that may be payable in accordance with a residency agreement for services made available but not covered by the advance fee and the periodic fees.

Health Center. A place associated with a CCRC where health care (primarily bed nursing care) is provided to residents in accordance with a residency agreement.

Actuarial Balance Sheet. A cumulative measure of the CCRC's assets and liabilities, as of the valuation date. The values of some asset and liability items, such as cash, receivables, accruals, and deposits in escrow, are taken directly from the accounting balance sheet. The values of future periodic fees, operating expenses and refunds are measured as actuarial present values for the closed group.

Actuarial Present Values (APV). The calculation of APVs requires the use of assumptions of mortality, transfers, withdrawal, interest, inflation, changes in periodic fees, changes in advance fees, revenues, expenses, and other pertinent contingencies.

Closed Group. The resident population of the CCRC as of the valuation date.

Permanent Transfer. A resident's move from one level of care to another without expectation of returning to the former level.

Temporary Transfer. A resident's move from one level of care to another with the expectation of returning to the former level.

Physical Property. Physical assets such as land, building, furniture, fixtures, and equipment that belong to the community. These assets (excluding land) are assumed to depreciate over their respective lifetimes.

Other terms are defined when introduced.

B. Actuarial Standards of Practice

ASOP No. 3 provides as follows:

Assets. The values of some items, including *cash* and *receivables*, are taken directly from the accounting balance sheet. *Future periodic fees* are determined by projecting the fees payable by surviving members of the closed group in each future year and discounting the result back to the valuation date. The estimate of future fees usually reflects current rates adjusted for projected future fee increases. Projected fee inflation should reflect appropriate practical, competitive, contractual, and economic considerations.

Value of Physical Property for Assets Currently in Service. The part of the value of assets in service on the valuation date appropriately allocated to current residents is calculated as follows:

a. Each item of property is assigned an assumed useful lifetime and an appropriate rate of inflation.

b. The annual capital expense for the use of an asset is developed for each year using its useful lifetime and is calculated as one of a series of annual amounts. The present value of this series, discounted to the time of acquisition, equals the cost of the asset. This series may be decreasing, level, or increasing. The discounted value of the asset at any later measurement date equals the discounted value of the remaining expense stream.

Liabilities. The values of some items, including *accruals* and *deposits in escrow*, are taken directly from the accounting balance sheet. The actuarial value of long-term debt is the discounted value of the principal and interest stream as of the valuation date.

The value of *future operating expenses* in question for each future year should be developed by allocating the portion of the expenses represented by the appropriate closed-group population projection (or other allocation base) and discounting the result back to the valuation date. The estimate should reflect future cost inflation, and the allocation should reflect underlying expense consumption patterns. For example, certain health center expenses may be allocated in proportion to the number of occupied beds.

The actuarial present value of *the future use of physical property* is the discounted value of the expense for the physical property and its replacement. The expense stream as of the valuation date is described in item b of the list above. The development of the annual capital expense stream and allocation to the survivorship group is described below:

a. It is assumed that each asset will be replaced at the end of its useful lifetime with a new asset. The cost of the new asset is assumed to equal the original cost indexed for inflation. The asset is continually replaced at the end of successive useful lifetimes. A calculation is made as follows for each such replacement during the survivorship of the closed group:

   i. The part of each future year's capital expense that relates to a specific closed group is determined by estimating the ratio of closed-group use to total community use. The ratio may be in proportion to the population, to the number of community occupied beds or units, to square footage, or to some other appropriate measure. For years during fill-up or material change in population, it may be appropriate to substitute a target or ultimate level of use for the actual estimated level of total use.

   ii. The current actuarial liability for the promised future use of a physical asset (and its replacements) with respect to a specific closed group is the sum (for all years) of the part of such capital expense in each future year related to the group or cohort of residents, as determined in (i), discounted to the valuation date.

The actuarial present value of *future refunds* is obtained from an estimate of the amounts and timing of refunds, which are then discounted back to the valuation date.

C. AICPA Statement of Position [11]

As a basis for comparison of this standard to *ASOP No. 3*, the actuary should understand important terms in the AICPA Guide and their treatments and applications.

Refundable Advance Fees. This is the estimated amount of advance fees that is expected to be refunded to current residents under the terms of the contracts; it should be accounted for and reported as a liability. The estimated amount should be based on the individual facility's own experience or, if records are not available, on the experience of comparable facilities. The remaining amount of advance fees should be accounted for as deferred revenue within the liability section of the balance sheet.

The deferred revenue should be amortized to income over future periods based on the estimated life of the resident or contract term, if shorter. The period of amortization should be adjusted annually based on the actuarially determined estimated remaining life expectancy of each individual or joint-and-last-survivor life expectancy of each pair of residents occupying the same unit.

Fees Refundable to Residents Only from Reoccupancy Proceeds of a Contract-Holder's Unit. That portion of fees that will be paid to current residents or their designees only to the extent of the proceeds of reoccupancy of a contract-holder's unit should be accounted for as deferred revenue. Similar amounts received from new residents in excess of the amount to be paid to previous residents or their designees should also be deferred. The deferred revenue should be amortized to income over future periods based on the remaining useful life of the facility.

Nonrefundable Advance Fees. These fees represent payment for future services and should be accounted for as deferred revenue. If a CCRC has sufficient historical experience and relevant statistical data about life expectancies, then it should consider that information when determining the remaining life of residents. A CCRC with insufficient historical experience or reliable actuarial data may use relevant other data. The deferred revenue should be amortized to income over future periods based on the estimated life of the resident or contract term, if shorter. The period of amortization should be adjusted annually based on the actuarially determined estimated remaining life expectancy of each individual or joint-and-last-survivor life expectancy of each pair of residents occupying the same unit.

The Obligation to Provide Future Services and the Use of Facilities to Current Residents. The liability, called the *future service obligation (FSO)*, is the present value of future net cash flows, minus the balance of unamortized deferred revenue, plus depreciation of facilities to be charged related to the contracts, plus unamortized costs of acquiring the related initial continuing care contracts, if applicable.

This future service obligation, a new requirement introduced by SOP-GAAP, has had the effect of bringing actuarial and accounting standards into essential agreement with each other. Previously the tendency was to dismiss the need for this liability item because of the CCRC's presumed unlimited ability to raise fees or to conclude that any loss on a contract is irrelevant because fees of new residents can offset losses on old contracts [4]. However, as pointed out in Section V, the actuarial and accounting approaches still differ substantially in contracts that provide for holding advance fee refunds until living units have been reoccupied.

Cash inflows include revenue contractually committed to support the residents and inflows resulting from periodic fees including anticipated increases in accordance with contract terms. Cash outflows comprise operating expenses, including interest expense and excluding selling and general and administrative expenses. Anticipated cost increases affecting these operating expenses should be considered in determining cash outflows. The expected inflation rate as well as other factors should be considered in determining the discount rate. The period of amortization should be adjusted annually based on the actuarially determined estimated remaining life expectancy of each individual or joint-and-last-survivor life expectancy of each pair of residents occupying the same unit.

Deferred Revenue. AICPA guidelines recognize that a liability called deferred revenue be held for payments of various types that have been made to provide future goods and services. Deferred revenue items are taken into income in future years as their amounts are reduced according to appropriate schedules.

IV. RESIDENT CONTRACTS AND THEIR ACTUARIAL IMPLICATIONS

CCRC contracts with their residents contain a variety of agreements about health services, apartment services, social services, meals, and the like. From an actuarial standpoint, however, the most important agreements concern advance fees (sometimes called endowments), periodic charges and the CCRC's ability to raise them, and the provision of health centers for temporary or permanent skilled nursing care needs.

Under ABFM, the projections used to produce a balance sheet as of a given time are based on the closed group of residents at that time. These projections implicitly assume that new entrants will fill vacancies arising from the deaths and withdrawals among the members of the closed group. Even though revenue and expenses associated with those new entrants are not reflected in the balance sheet, the implicit assumption is necessary because, in the absence of new entrants, the CCRC would inevitably fail.

The contracts usually have no limitations on annual increases in periodic fees. As a result, potential conflict between operators and residents arises about required services and need for surplus funds. Fee increases are frequently limited in fact by fees at competitor facilities nearby and by the facility's need to be able to attract new entrants.

The financial system resembles a combination of a single-premium and a (variable) monthly premium insurance policy. Marketing the plan can be aided by offering a low single premium at the expense of high periodic fees (or plans to raise them). Increases planned for advance fees, however, do not directly affect the balance sheet because they apply only to those not yet members of the existing resident group.

We now examine the types of advance fees, mortality, morbidity and transfer rates, nursing care provisions, periodic fees, and asset liquidity considerations.

A. Advance Fees

The advance fee, perhaps the unique aspect of CCRCs, is usually a component of the resident contract. The origin of the advance fee and its perpetuation today result from several factors:

- Early religiously based facilities frequently required that entrants convey all or most of their assets to the facility in exchange for lifetime care.
- New facilities frequently need to guarantee payment of construction loans by getting major dollar commitments from their first cadres of residents.
- Advance fees help to ensure low turnover of residents and, for those who do withdraw, a financial return commensurate with fixed expenses the CCRC has incurred for marketing, construction costs, and the like.

Advance fees vary today generally between $100,000 and $500,000 depending upon building costs, unit size, single or double occupancy, and the advance fee refund provision. The advance fee refund may decrease rapidly to zero at a rate of, say, 1% per month of residence, or it may remain as high as 95%. Nonrefundable advance fees should be, and usually are, substantially lower than those of the refundable types.

A few CCRCs vary advance fees by age. It seems that greater equity would result if more CCRCs were to vary advance fees according to age at admission and sex.

- In CCRCs that provide substantial refunds, of perhaps 75% to 95%, older entrants clearly are treated more favorably than younger ones; those with longer prospective longevity subsidize those with shorter longevity by having their fees tied up longer and generating more investment income to the facility.
- In CCRCs that provide small or no refunds, the situation is of course reversed. This arrangement would be expected to make the facility especially attractive to healthy young residents.
- There is perhaps a middle-ground schedule of refund percentages by period of residence and by age and sex that would substantially reduce such inequities.

B. Mortality, Morbidity, and Transfer Rates

The actuarial basis for calculating present values of a community's income and outgo streams is of course rooted in the expected experience of each facility. The decrements include the death rates by age and sex for residents in independent living units (ILU), in personal care units (PC), and in skilled nursing (SN). In addition, for each resident in any level of care, experience rates of transfer to any other level of care, and costs associated therewith, must be established.

Supervisory bodies have not so far undertaken to legislate "safe harbor" values for these decrements. One concern is that legitimizing an "industry" table might lead to unsound projections. For newly organized facilities, the assumption is usually made that experience will be the same as that at similar facilities with similar medical and financial underwriting standards for admitting new entrants. If these same assumptions were used for a facility with more lenient qualification standards, severe financial problems might result from, in particular, excessive personal care and nursing expenses. The 1983 Table a [10] is commonly used as a basis for the decrements, a different percentage factor being applied to the table's rates for each different decrement. Winklevoss and Powell [11] shows actual experience, circa 1983, of several CCRCs relative to that table. The Society's CCRC Experience Project Oversight Group has developed a plan for collecting and analyzing the combined experience of many communities and is seeking to bring it into use. Regardless of the source of original assumptions, actuarial analyses and revision of the assumptions are necessary as experience develops.

This paper does not intend to suggest what the decrements and transfer rates are, or the mechanics of estimating transfer and death rates. Table 1 is illustrative only. It shows the age 80–100 values of the decrement table in the Model for Studying the Actuarial Aspects of CCRCs released in 1991 [3] by the Society of Actuaries Research Management Committee. That model produces, inter alia, closed group projections upon which present values are based.

The ILU death rates are low in relation to familiar population and annuitant tables because residents in poor health have been transferred to the PC and SN categories. Speculation about the overall mortality experience of CCRC residents relative to the 1983a Table can be resolved by combining the experience segments. The results for ages 80–100 derived from entry age 80 are shown in Table 2.

The 1983a Table experience was derived from the experience among holders of individual annuity policies and is therefore very low. The overall 87.3% ratio for men and the 87.5% ratio for women of mortality experience to that of the 1983a Table indicate that the selection techniques, living conditions and residents' sense of security produce the excellent mortality experience of many CCRCs.

C. Nursing Care Provisions

An essential CCRC ingredient is the promise to cover some or all nursing care expenses, the health center often being on the CCRC's premises. This benefit may be self-funded or commercially insured through an insurance vehicle, first marketed during the last several years, patterned after group long-term-care coverage.

CCRCs historically have provided complete life care by providing nursing care or long-term care on site funded by a component of advance fees and periodic fees. Self-funding is the most widely used alternative today; the insurance vehicle, however, has grown in popularity among recently opened facilities.

TABLE 1

Illustrative CCRC Mortality and Transfer Factors

| Age | Mortality Rates | | | | | | Transfer to PC | | Transfer to SN | | | | Withdrawals |
| | ILU | | PC | | SN | | ILU | | ILU | | PC | | |
	Male	Female	Male	Female	Male	Female	Male	Female	Male	Female	Male	Female	
80	0.0329	0.0182	0.0578	0.0445	0.1445	0.0714	0.0118	0.0200	0.0136	0.0136	0.0630	0.0706	0.0050
81	0.0362	0.0205	0.0636	0.0499	0.1553	0.0801	0.0125	0.0228	0.0146	0.0146	0.0675	0.0754	0.0050
82	0.0399	0.0232	0.0697	0.0559	0.1673	0.0898	0.0134	0.0260	0.0158	0.0158	0.0719	0.0803	0.0050
83	0.0438	0.0262	0.0764	0.0626	0.1806	0.0996	0.0143	0.0296	0.0175	0.0175	0.0763	0.0857	0.0050
84	0.0482	0.0297	0.0835	0.0699	0.1954	0.1092	0.0151	0.0336	0.0198	0.0198	0.0808	0.0900	0.0050
85	0.0530	0.0335	0.0910	0.0780	0.2118	0.1186	0.0161	0.0380	0.0224	0.0224	0.0861	0.0951	0.0050
86	0.0582	0.0378	0.0989	0.0867	0.2300	0.1280	0.0170	0.0428	0.0256	0.0256	0.0914	0.1024	0.0050
87	0.0639	0.0426	0.1071	0.0961	0.2499	0.1374	0.0181	0.0479	0.0292	0.0292	0.0969	0.1087	0.0050
88	0.0701	0.0479	0.1158	0.1060	0.2718	0.1481	0.0191	0.0534	0.0329	0.0329	0.1022	0.1149	0.0050
89	0.0769	0.0539	0.1248	0.1165	0.2957	0.1602	0.0201	0.0593	0.0365	0.0365	0.1075	0.1212	0.0050
90	0.0842	0.0604	0.1342	0.1274	0.3217	0.1741	0.0213	0.0656	0.0402	0.0402	0.1139	0.1287	0.0050
91	0.0922	0.0677	0.1441	0.1386	0.3500	0.1900	0.0224	0.0722	0.0439	0.0439	0.1202	0.1363	0.0050
92	0.1008	0.0753	0.1546	0.1501	0.3805	0.2080	0.0237	0.0779	0.0475	0.0475	0.1267	0.1439	0.0050
93	0.1102	0.0834	0.1656	0.1619	0.4136	0.2283	0.0249	0.0827	0.0516	0.0516	0.1331	0.1515	0.0050
94	0.1204	0.0917	0.1773	0.1739	0.4412	0.2510	0.0261	0.0865	0.0563	0.0563	0.1394	0.1592	0.0050
95	0.1312	0.1003	0.1898	0.1862	0.4630	0.2764	0.0275	0.0893	0.0614	0.0614	0.1467	0.1681	0.0050
96	0.1427	0.1090	0.2032	0.1992	0.4785	0.3044	0.0288	0.0912	0.0670	0.0670	0.1541	0.1771	0.0050
97	0.1550	0.1177	0.2176	0.2129	0.4874	0.3353	0.0301	0.0927	0.0731	0.0731	0.1613	0.1861	0.0050
98	0.1679	0.1265	0.2332	0.2278	0.4891	0.3693	0.0315	0.0939	0.0837	0.0837	0.1687	0.1952	0.0050
99	0.1814	0.1355	0.2504	0.2441	0.4912	0.4065	0.0330	0.0946	0.0988	0.0988	0.1761	0.2042	0.0050
100	0.1956	0.1446	0.2692	0.2623	0.4939	0.4381	0.0345	0.0950	0.1185	0.1185	0.1844	0.2145	0.0050

TABLE 2

COMBINED ILU, PC AND SN MORTALITY RATES COMPARED TO 1983*a* RATES BY SEX ("MODEL" TABLE BASIS)

Age	Male			Female		
	1983*a* Table	Table 1	Ratio	1983*a* Table	Table 1	Ratio
80	0.0570	0.0371	65.1%	0.0364	0.0226	62.1%
81	0.0628	0.0420	66.9	0.0410	0.0260	63.5
82	0.0691	0.0475	68.7	0.0461	0.0302	65.4
83	0.0759	0.0544	71.7	0.0519	0.0351	67.7
84	0.0832	0.0607	73.0	0.0583	0.0407	69.8
85	0.0910	0.0681	74.8	0.0655	0.0474	72.4
86	0.0991	0.0781	78.8	0.0735	0.0551	74.9
87	0.1076	0.0863	80.2	0.0823	0.0633	76.9
88	0.1163	0.0983	84.5	0.0920	0.0727	79.0
89	0.1254	0.1096	87.4	0.1025	0.0838	81.8
90	0.1349	0.1225	90.8	0.1136	0.0964	84.8
91	0.1449	0.1359	93.8	0.1252	0.1093	87.3
92	0.1554	0.1520	97.8	0.1372	0.1245	90.7
93	0.1666	0.1646	98.9	0.1495	0.1410	94.3
94	0.1785	0.1833	102.7	0.1618	0.1593	98.4
95	0.1912	0.1953	102.1	0.1742	0.1782	102.3
96	0.2047	0.2121	103.6	0.1865	0.1997	107.0
97	0.2191	0.2206	100.7	0.1982	0.2218	111.9
98	0.2347	0.2425	103.3	0.2111	0.2467	116.9
99	0.2519	0.2498	99.2	0.2244	0.2718	121.1
Average*			87.3%			87.5%

*Based on 1983 Table *a* Exposed-to-Risk.

Under a self-funded arrangement, the facility's actuary can measure and project nursing care costs within the framework of his or her comprehensive review of fees and expenses.

The actuary's recommendation to the community about whether to self-fund or to insure should include a stochastic analysis of long-term potential for self-insured nursing care costs being higher than projected, compared to the essentially certain additional costs of the insurance company's expense and profit charges.

Despite its probable higher cost, long-term-care insurance may add to a facility's attractiveness because of the recognized security of a prestigious insurance company and by easing sponsors' concerns about early financial hazards.

D. Periodic Fees

It is common to expect increases in periodic residence fees at rates similar to the consumer price index or elements thereof based on hotel-type (restaurant, housekeeping, refurbishing) costs. Provided the community makes reasonably appropriate provision for inflation and interest rate increases and decreases, the size of the fee increase percentage is limited only by the ability and willingness of residents to accept it.

Periodic fees may be independent of the size of the unit or may vary moderately. The second occupant of a unit is usually charged an extra fee related to the additional food and use of general facilities available to residents.

One complex actuarial task is projecting future income and outgo streams as doubly occupied units of the closed group inevitably become singly occupied. Computer software such as the Society's model [3] assists with these calculations.

E. Asset Liquidity Considerations

The NAIC, in the Appendix to its 1994 accounting manual [9], focused attention on having adequate cash and other liquid assets available to meet cash needs—whether predictable or not. ABFM and SOP-GAAP emphasize cash-flow testing and maintaining adequate contingency margins. *ASOP No. 3* and the NAIC instructions emphasize that the possibility of cash deficiencies should be carefully monitored and safeguards taken to avoid the necessity of borrowing and to immunize investments appropriately.

The cash-flow analysis must recognize all elements of the ABFM balance sheet: physical asset replacement at replacement prices, inflation, interest, and fee increases. The term of the analysis should be related to the expected useful lifetime of the buildings, representing both the longest lifetimes and the largest proportion of assets' value. In addition (and some practitioners may wish to include this analysis within the basic cash-flow analysis), the cash flow of new debt and equity investments, and their redemptions, must be analyzed. This testing will reveal the availability of liquid funds to meet cash needs for physical plant replacements. In the absence of such a cash-flow analysis, avoidable borrowing or disposing of assets in possibly depressed financial markets before their maturity might become necessary.

Cash-flow projections are performed using open-group methods, whereby the financial effects of new residents replacing existing residents are taken into account. Open-group cash-flow projections are necessary at start-up and also if there are plans to enlarge the facility, and to predict whether additional health center facilities will be needed as the population matures. Predictions of health center bed needs may be made through software such as the Society's model [3].

V. DIFFERENCES BETWEEN STANDARDS OF PRACTICE SET BY ACCOUNTING AND ACTUARIAL PROFESSIONAL BODIES AND THEIR IMPLICATIONS FOR BUDGETING AND PRICING

In 1990, Jarvis Farley provided the NAIC working group with a discussion draft [5] on the differences between SOP-GAAP and *ASOP No. 3* standards from which we have borrowed liberally in composing this analysis.

Perhaps the fundamental difference between the two methods described in Section IV is that the AICPA standard undertakes to measure the present while the AAA standard peers into the future. Actuaries recognize that this distinction is at the heart of the difference between the balance sheet of an insurance company and that of a manufacturing company. The CCRC is the insurance company, receiving income from contract-holders to help pay for future services, future use of facilities, and future health care. The comprehensive approach of ABFM provides essential tools for estimating a CCRC's financial ability to meet the promises in its current contracts, to test the adequancy of its fee structure, to set aside adequate reserves, to provide for replacement of components of its physical plant as they reach the ends of their useful lifetimes, and to provide early warning of impending financial difficulties.

At the intellectual foundation for ABFM is the concept that a CCRC be regarded as a permanently going concern; it cannot successfully be operated for a period of years and then closed down, and so must fill vacancies with new residents who pay adequate fees. To attract enough new residents, the facility—its financial condition, its physical appearance, and its general social ambiance—must be continuously maintained in a competitively appealing condition.

Specifically, the plant must be kept up. Elements of the plant—painting, carpets, furnishings, equipment (for apartments, health care, kitchen, housekeeping, groundskeeping, heating, elevators, roofs, and so on)—must all be replaced at the ends of their useful lifetimes. Funds must be provided to pay for such replacements.

ABFM lays a foundation for such funding by using replacement cost as the basis for valuing plant and calculating depreciation.† For the open group, depreciation expense related to any fixed plant category can be accumulated at projected interest and inflation rates to provide ultimate replacement funds. For the closed group, survivorship must also be taken into account to project future depreciation expenses to be reflected in the ABFM balance sheet.

Actuaries and others have taken issue with replacement cost accounting, because it implies mathematically that the same residents who "paid" for the plant and equipment at their original costs must also "pay" for their replacement—a concept antithetical to concepts of intergenerational equity. This does of course happen. On the other hand, and curiously enough, industry committees such as the NAIC Working Group on CCRCs (see Section VI) have established strong requirements for funding replacements with earmarked liquid assets. This has the same effect on the costs passed on to current residents as funding directly for replacement cost.

Actually, the more important difference between results of the methods of calculating net asset value is frequently the result of taking inflation into account in calculating depreciation costs rather than a constant periodic cost. One valuable advantage of using current asset values is that they present a realistic picture of year-by-year cash needed to fund replacements.

A. The Objectives of a Comprehensive Basis of Accounting

SOP-GAAP and ABFM both purport to constitute a "comprehensive basis of accounting." In actuality, SOP-GAAP makes no claim of satisfying all objectives that management would find essential. The AICPA presentation of SOP-GAAP holds that management must use other tools for purposes that SOP-GAAP does not satisfy. Table 3 shows Farley's analysis of those other purposes.

B. Sources of Earnings (or Changes in Surplus)

Tables 4–7 present balance sheets incorporating both SOP-GAAP and ABFM requirements.

Table 4 illustrates the actuarial assets and liabilities, in addition to items from the accountant's balance sheet, that constitute an ABFM balance sheet for a facility that refunds a large portion of advance fees; the last column

---

†Despite the positive features of replacement cost accounting, *ASOP No. 3* (1994) now recognizes only original cost accounting for physical facilities.

TABLE 3

DIFFERENCES BETWEEN SOP-GAAP AND ABFM [5]

Objective	Does SOP-GAAP Do So?	Does ABFM Do So?
1. To test long-term financial ability to carry out promises to residents	No	Yes
2. To test adequacy of fee structure	No	Yes
3. To provide fully for replacement of fixed assets	No	Yes
4. To avoid inadequate cash positions	Yes	Yes
5. To provide early warning of impending difficulties	To some extent	Yes

shows the difference between actual and expected earnings by source. It is prepared in accordance with *ASOP No. 3*, except that fixed assets are valued at replacement costs rather than acquisition costs. Note that the physical property is owned by a nonprofit corporation and carries no mortgage debt.

Lines 1, 2 and 7 are analyzed together with cash-flow data to obtain the gain from investment results relative to prior budget assumptions.

Fixed asset values in line 3 are based on historical costs adjusted by replacement cost indexes obtained from building industry publications. Each asset is assigned a probable useful lifetime. Line 4 shows accumulated depreciation based on the inflation-related method (each year's charge for depreciation being a function of the change in replacement values between year-ends and adjustments for interest and survivorship). Year-by-year changes in building cost inflation, even reductions sometimes, may cause significant fluctuations in values, making isolation of this source of gain or loss important.

Actuarial present values (APVs) are shown in lines 8–14. Each is the result of a present value formula that reflects estimated interest, inflation, rate increases, resident transfers to assisted living and nursing care, and an allocation of future depreciation expense to the present residents. Several practitioners have developed software to derive estimates of the future composition of closed groups: number, single and double residency, and location—apartment and health center—distributions year after year, for example, the program developed for the Society by Milliman & Robertson's team [3].

The "deemed" earning assets item referred to in line 13 means fixed assets and other invested assets less the sum of the APVs (including the APV of deemed earning assets itself) and the depreciation reserve. This is the portion

TABLE 4

ACTUARIALLY BASED (AUTHORS' FORMAT)*

(DOLLAR AMOUNTS IN THOUSANDS)

Line		12/31 This Year	12/31 Last Year	Actual Change	Expected Change	Source of Earnings
	Assets					
1	Liquid, inventory and receivables	$4,289	$4,196	$93	$93	$0
2	Securities	25,061	24,708	353	284	69
	Fixed assets					
3	Replacement cost	53,397	50,209	3,188		
4	Less depreciation reserve	13,050	11,839	1,211		
5	Net value	40,347	38,370	1,977	2,230	(253)
6	Total Assets	$69,697	$67,274			
	Liabilities					
7	Accruals, deposits and amounts payable	$1,665	$1,872	($207)	($207)	
	Discounted Values for the Closed Group					
8	Refundable entrance fees	$37,604	$36,400	$1,204	$923	($281)
9	Residence services	29,920	29,630	290	247	(43)
10	Health care services	17,094	16,994	100	131	31
11	Assistance-in-living	1,872	1,703	169	117	(52)
12	Depreciation expense	9,534	9,172	362	287	(75)
13	Return on "deemed" earning assets	4,754	4,738	16	16	0
14	Monthly fees	(36,154)	(35,549)	(605)	(572)	33
15	Total	$64,624	$63,088			
16	Total Liabilities	$66,289	$64,960			
17	*Surplus*	$3,408	$2,314			
18	Change in Surplus			$1,094		
19	Experience adjustments, total					($571)
20	Gain from expenses vs. budget					$125
21	Gain from changes in assumptions					0
22	Inherent earnings of operations					1,343
23	Earnings on surplus					197
24	Change in surplus					$1,094

*The depreciation reserve and the discounted values are actuarially based. The other items, in accordance with *ASOP No. 3*, 5.4.1, come directly from the accounting balance sheet without the use of actuarial techniques.

of these reserves that is invested in bricks and mortar, for which a "rental" charge must be made.

Actual-to-expected ratios are obtained by usual actuarial techniques. Although somewhat conservative actuarial assumptions may later result in a small net gain being realized, longer-term experience will usually necessitate changes in assumptions, which will be recognized in line 21 as they are made.

The change in surplus (line 24) shows not just the result of a budgeting or inflation assumption change on one year's results, but the effect of that change projected to all future years through which any present residents remain in residence. Thus, the effect of, say, a staffing reduction in a current year reduces projected costs as well, a leveraging effect. Unless these one-time events are identified separately, the leveraged gain may tempt management to modify or reverse a sound decision already made. Line 20 reflects operating economies, and line 23 earnings on surplus funds.

Line 22 is the result that management should watch most closely. It displays the present value of future earnings generated from the pricing of its products and services less its expenses. This result's validity depends upon whether projected schedules of annual fee increases can be achieved, upon the validity of estimates of annual inflation and investment earnings, and upon demographic results. It is calculated by analyzing all sources of earnings.

C. Detailed Comparison of SOP-GAAP and Actuarial Approaches

Tables 5 and 6 illustrate differing accounting treatments of two CCRCs, which are assumed to be identical except for the conditions surrounding refunds. The essential differences are:

- *The treatment of advance fees.* While there is essential agreement in accounting treatment if these fees are unconditionally refundable, large differences are possible when refunds are conditional on reoccupancy. ABFM discounts the liability for advance fee refunds for interest and survivorship.

- *The treatment of physical plant values.* SOP-GAAP requires straight-line amortization of acquisition costs rather than the alternative of taking inflation into account, as is permitted by *ASOP No. 3*.

The following paragraphs contrast accounting treatments of refundable advance fees not conditional on reoccupancy with those so conditioned and with nonrefundable fees.

SOP-GAAP provides, as illustrated in Table 5, for dividing the advance fee paid by a resident in Lines 8–9 between the refundable amount, if any, and the nonrefundable amount remaining. If the contract provides for decreasing amounts of refund, it is necessary to estimate the timing to estimate the amount that will be needed. SOP-GAAP rules, however, require that such amount be held without discount for interest.

ABFM is similar to SOP-GAAP in that the estimated amounts of future advance fee refunds to present residents are projected. However, in ABFM, such amounts are determined by discounting for mortality and interest as in

TABLE 5

SOP-GAAP FOR A CCRC WHICH DOES NOT CONDITION ENTRANCE FEE REFUNDS
ON REOCCUPANCY
(DOLLAR AMOUNTS IN THOUSANDS)

Line		12/31 This Year	12/31 Last Year	Change
	Assets			
1	Liquid, inventory and receivables	$4,289	$4,196	$93
2	Securities	25,061	24,708	353
	Fixed assets			
3	Historical cost	39,217	37,053	2,164
4	Less depreciation reserve	11,607	10,308	1,299
5	Net value	27,610	26,745	865
6	Total Assets	$56,960	$55,649	
	Liabilities			
7	Accruals, deposits and amounts payable	$1,665	$1,872	($207)
	Discounted Values for the Closed Group			
8	Refundable entrance fees	$50,328	$50,193	135
9	Nonrefundable entrance fees	3,556	3,663	(107)
10	Residence services	29,920	29,630	290
1	Health care services	17,094	16,994	100
12	Assistance-in-living	1,872	1,703	169
13	Depreciation expense	9,534	9,172	362
14	Return on "deemed" earning assets	0	0	0
15	Monthly fees	(36,154)	(35,549)	(605)
16	Total	$76,150	$75,806	344
17	Total Liabilities	$77,815	$77,678	
18	*Surplus*	($20,855)	($22,029)	
19	Change in surplus			$1,174

reserving for a single-premium last-survivor life insurance policy. This produces a material difference between the two methods. The difference is largest, of course, when amounts to be refunded reduce slowly or have a small maximum reduction.

SOP-GAAP makes an important distinction between refunds made unconditionally and those that are subject to reoccupancy. As illustrated in Table 6, the portion of fees that will be paid to current residents or their designees when the unit has been reoccupied is accounted for as deferred revenue. Usually, the new residents' advance fees will exceed the refund, in which case that excess is also taken into income over the remaining useful life of the facility. This seems to imply that no liability need be held for refundable fees to the last generation of residents at the end of the CCRC's useful lifetime. *ASOP No. 3* recognizes that this approach has been used and notes that: "This approach may introduce inequities between generations of community residents, and may understate the fees required from future

TABLE 6

SOP-GAAP for a CCRC Which Conditions Entrance Fee Refunds on Reoccupancy
(Dollar Amounts in Thousands)

Line		12/31 This Year	12/31 Last Year	Change
	Assets			
1	Liquid, inventory and receivables	$4,289	$4,196	$93
2	Securities	25,061	24,708	353
	Fixed assets			
3	Historical cost	39,217	37,053	2,164
4	Less depreciation reserve	11,607	10,308	1,299
5	Net value	27,610	26,745	865
6	Total Assets	$56,960	$55,649	
	Liabilities			
7	Accruals, deposits and amounts payable	$1,665	$1,872	($207)
	Discounted Values for the Closed Group			
8	Refundable entrance fees	$50,328	$50,193	135
9	Nonrefundable entrance fees	3,556	3,663	(107)
10	Residence services	SOP-GAAP provides		
11	Health care services	that these "future		
12	Assistance-in-living	service obligations"		
13	Depreciation expense	are not held if they are		
14	Return on "deemed" earning assets	less than deferred		
15	Monthly fees	revenue (lines 8–9),		
16	Total	$53,884	$53,856	28
17	Total Liabilities	$55,549	$55,728	
18	*Surplus*	$1,411	($79)	
19	Change in surplus			$1,490

residents, leading to cash flow problems in future years." In this paper, we show as the ABFM system the conservative approach of setting an actuarially discounted liability for each resident or pair of residents, on the assumption that at some time during the facility's finite existence advance fee refunds must become unconditional. We therefore assume that each unit will be reoccupied and that the liability is the same as for a nonconditional refund agreement.

SOP-GAAP is silent about the accounting treatment in the event of change from a conditional to a nonconditional contract.

D. Treatment of Nonrefundable Advance Fees

For nonrefundable advance fees, SOP-GAAP holds that these represent payment for future services and should be accounted for as deferred revenue and amortized to income over the estimated years of residence (for all residents combined) or contract term, if shorter. It also permits other than straight-line amortization if costs are expected to be significantly higher in the later years of residence [4].

E. Advance Fee Amortization—An Outmoded Approach

It was understood long ago that nonrefundable advance fee income had to be protected from inadvertently being spent before the resident who paid it had died. Somebody introduced the idea of furnishing that protection by spreading the sum more or less evenly over the resident's lifetime.

Unfortunately the notion spread among managements and their advisors that expectation of life and resident's lifetime meant substantially the same thing. This error exists today; actuaries may have been at fault in failing to point out that resident deaths are not bunched closely around the so-called life expectancy calculated at time of entry. A discussion of this matter by David L. Hewitt appears in the *Proceedings of the Conference of Actuaries in Public Practice* [8].

As time went on, various amortization procedures were adopted. None of them, even the adjustment from expectation at entry to expectations altered yearly as residents survive [4], accomplishes the desired purpose of matching income with expense even roughly.

Now that the Academy of Actuaries has produced ABFM, it seems incumbent upon our profession to give the cumbersome and inaccurate amortization system in all its forms its quietus. This will require acceptance of balance sheets incorporating the ABFM system as illustrated in this paper.

F. The Future Service Obligation

The future service obligation (FSO) is equal to the present value of future net cash flows, which are lines 10–13 and 15 less unamortized deferred revenue, all adjusted for unamortized acquisition costs, ignoring any negative result.

As illustrated in Table 6, unamortized deferred revenue usually far more than offsets the universally negative cash flows, depreciation and unamortized costs. As a result, CCRC management can increase cash outflow (by adding to staff, for example) or can reduce cash inflow (by reducing or eliminating annual increases in periodic fees, for example) without affecting the SOP-GAAP balance sheet. It is only after future (negative) net cash flows exceed deferred revenue that the full damage of the imbalance becomes evident.

G. Development Expenses

SOP-GAAP requires capitalization of the direct and indirect costs of developing the facility to the point of housing its first residents (for example, staff expenses and consultants' fees in actuarial, accounting, architecture, food service, marketing, and medical specialties) and direct costs of acquiring subsequent contracts (for example, advertising) that are expected to be paid for from future advance fees and periodic fees. These costs are to be amortized on a straight-line basis over a period of years estimated to be the average number of years of residence for that first group of residents. Indirect costs of acquiring subsequent continuing care contracts are treated as regular operating expenses.

ASOP No. 3 is silent on this issue, but the practicing actuary will recognize that the principles set forth for amortization of expenses attributable to any closed group are applicable to these initial expenses.

Table 4 shows fixed asset values based on replacement cost; the amortization method is inflation-related as permitted in *ASOP No. 3*. SOP-GAAP does not address the valuation basis of assets—replacement cost or acquisition cost. However, basic GAAP prescribes straight-line amortization, which is consisitent with valuing assets at their fixed acquisition costs.

The discussion of the effects of differing accounting standards has concentrated on the high-refund situation, in which the greatest differences occur in balance sheet surplus between ABFM and SOP-GAAP.

Table 7 depicts SOP-GAAP treatment when no refund is offered. Here, because actuarial liabilities, called by SOP-GAAP the future service obligation, exceed deferred revenue in lines 8–9, that FSO must be established as a liability in lieu of the deferred income liability. Line 8 is now zero. Because of the absence of refunds, we have assigned a token $15,000 to that income source. It is, however, to be expected that management would have set lower advance and periodic fees.

An ABFM statement for the same situation would be quite close to, if not identical with, the SOP-GAAP profit picture. The only possible difference between the two would arise if inflation-related depreciation were used under ABFM.

VI. REGULATORY ACCOUNTING REQUIREMENTS

Existing state regulations vary widely, many of these differences depending on the nature of the regulating agency (that is, whether social welfare,

TABLE 7

SOP-GAAP FOR A CCRC WHICH DOES NOT PROVIDE ENTRANCE FEE REFUNDS
(DOLLAR AMOUNTS IN THOUSANDS)

Line		12/31 This Year	12/31 Last Year	Change
	Assets			
1	Liquid, inventory and receivables	$4,289	$4,196	$93
2	Securities	25,061	24,708	353
	Fixed assets			
3	Historical cost	39,217	37,053	2,164
4	Less depreciation reserve	11,607	10,308	1,299
5	Net value	27,610	26,745	865
6	Total Assets	$56,960	$55,649	
	Liabilities			
7	Accruals, deposits and amounts payable	$1,665	$1,872	($207)
	Discounted Values for the Closed Group			
8	Refundable entrance fees	Not included —		
9	Nonrefundable entrance fees	less than FSO.		
10	Residence services	29,920	29,630	(290)
11	Health care services	17,094	16,994	(100)
12	Assistance-in-living	1,872	1,703	(169)
13	Depreciation expense	9,534	9,172	(362)
14	Return on "deemed" earning assets	0	0	0
15	Monthly fees	(15,000)	(15,000)	0
16	Total	$43,420	$42,499	($921)
17	Total Liabilities	$45,085	$44,371	
18	*Surplus*	$11,875	$11,278	
19	Change in Surplus			$597

hospital, insurance, or other state department). The authors welcome discussion from regulators about the principles underlying their approaches.

In early 1990 the NAIC Working Group on CCRCs began preparing an advisory on the numerous differences between *ASOP No. 3* and the AICPA's *Statement of Position 90-8*. The result was a clarifying addendum to NAIC's accounting practices manual for insurance companies. This material reflected recognition that CCRCs "have significant risk characteristics that embody elements of life insurance, annuities, and health benefit programs." The requirements recommended therein cover principally asset liquidity and future service obligations.

The NAIC ruled that assets for debt service and operations must be at least the sum of stipulated principal payments due in the next 12 months (with provision for balloon payments) plus 20% of the facility's anticipated operating expenses of the current year. Liquid asets for asset repair and replacement must be accumulated annually at a rate of 1/60th of the cost of buildings and related fixtures plus 1/15th of the cost of furniture and equipment, and in each case the annual accrual must be increased proportionately to the rise in the Consumer Price Index. Reserve reductions are permitted as replacements are made.

The NAIC text comments:

> These provisions reflect the fact that CCRCs are highly sensitive to swings in cash flow and should be positioned to meet future obligations without undue reliance upon borrowing. . . . .it is strongly urged that CCRC's use actuarial forecasting to favorably influence rate setting and future stability.

With respect to the major differences between the accountants' and the actuaries' pronouncements on future service obligation, the NAIC says this:

> At this time, facilities report on both methods. The variances produced under these methods are focused toward somewhat differing goals. Both rely heavily upon assumptions regarding future cash flows and occupancy rates. Other assumptions respecting mortality, morbidity, population flows and amortization of deferred revenues from subscribers all leverage the resources of a CCRC when considering ultimate espected costs. No generally accepted actuarial tables are available to quantify expected mortality and morbidity. Turnover of living units is often keyed to economic forces peculiar to a specific facility and the nature of the continuing care contract, e.g., a return of capital model; a fee for service model. Differing contracts obligate for varying degrees of health care. Finally, inflation's effect must be also factored to determine the need for subscriber revenues.
>
> Based upon the foregoing there is a need for periodic actuarial review of the propriety of assumptions and an assessment of the need for a contingency margin respecting adverse deviation from expected results. Maintenance of such a margin will dampen the effects of inflation rate fluctuations and variability experienced regarding cost elements that are influenced by economics and survivorship.
>
> Therefore, the use of either method is allowed provided that reasonable assumptions are utilized and adequate margins are maintained. An actuarial certification not less frequently than once every three years is in order.

Actuaries naturally look forward to a revision in SOP-GAAP that will make it more, if not completely, compatible with ABFM. Such an event will of course greatly ease the tasks of insurance department regulators.

VII. CONCLUSION

Quite remarkable progress has been made in the last decade, and especially in the last five years, in the rules and procedures for measuring a CCRC's financial strength and the likelihood that it will be able to redeem its promises to its residents for many years ahead. One can rather confidently predict that the number of failures among these institutions will be smaller from now on than it has been in the past.

And progress has also been made in the respect and understanding between the two professions—accounting and actuarial—that are responsible for advising CCRC managements. More must yet be done in this direction, but there is full acceptance of the principle that neither profession can afford to ignore or denigrate the other.

We think that within the actuarial profession the biggest opportunity that has not yet been fully grasped is a willingness to pool the data about CCRCs that only actuaries are equipped to gather and disseminate. Our profession on this continent became convinced more than a century ago that effectiveness of our labors depends upon exchange of information and of ideas. It would be a sad step backward if this conviction were to weaken.

REFERENCES

1. ACCOUNTING STANDARDS DIVISION, AMERICAN INSTITUTE OF CERTIFIED PUBLIC ACCOUNTANTS. *Financial Accounting and Reporting by Continuing Care Retirement Communities.* New York, N.Y.: AICPA, 1990.
2. ACTUARIAL STANDARDS BOARD. "Practices Related to Continuing Care Retirement Communities," *Actuarial Standard of Practice No. 3.* Washington, D.C.: American Academy of Actuaries, July 1994.
3. BLUHM, WILLIAM F., CUMMING, ROBERT B., AND ROBERTS, STANLEY A. *CCRC Population and Financial Model* (pamphlet and program disk). Itasca, Ill.: Society of Actuaries, 1991.
4. ERNST & YOUNG. *Continuing Care Retirement Communities: Implementing New Accounting and Reporting Guidance.* Dallas, Tex.: November 1991.
5. FARLEY, JARVIS. "Differences between GAAP and ABFA," discussion draft to the NAIC Working Group on CCRC Accounting. Kansas City, Mo.: 1990.
6. FARLEY, JARVIS, AND SILLESKY, J. DARRISON. "Actuarially Based Financial Statements for Living Care Villages of Massachusetts, Inc., D/B/A North Hill, 1986–1990."
7. HEWITT, DAVID L. "Retirement Communities" (review of *Continuing Care Retirement Communities: An Empirical, Financial and Legal Analysis*), *The Actuary* 18, no. 5 (May 1984): 1, 6–7.

8. HEWITT, DAVID L. "Actuarial Amortization of Entry Fees for Life Care Communities," *Proceedings, Conference of Actuaries in Public Practice* XXXI (1981–92): 506–23.
9. NATIONAL ASSOCIATION OF INSURANCE COMMISSIONERS. "Continuing Care Retirement Communities," Appendix in *Accounting Practices and Procedures Manual for Life, Accident and Health Insurance Companies.* Kansas City, Mo.: 1994.
10. "Report of the Committee to Recommend a New Mortality Basis for Individual Annuity Valuation (Derivation of the 1983 Table *a*)," *TSA* XXXIII (1981): 675–751.
11. WINKLEVOSS, HOWARD E., AND POWELL, ALWYN V. *Continuing Care Retirement Communities: An Empirical, Financial, and Legal Analysis.* Homewood, Ill.: Richard D. Irwin, Inc., 1984.

DISCUSSION OF PRECEDING PAPER

J. DARRISON SILLESKY:

Jarvis Farley would have been very pleased with this excellent extension of the principles set forth in *Actuarial Standard of Practice (ASOP) No. 3.* The paper provides details and practical applications of what he originally called ABFA (but is now known as ABFM). I only wish to comment on the nursing care and financing sections of the paper, based on my own experience as recorded in the paper's reference [6].

The nonprofit CCRCs that dominate the current scene have had little incentive to insure this risk, from at least two standpoints, (a) financial stability and (b) residential relations.

Financial Stability

The most important factor to a CCRC's survival is not demographic or other financial risks, but its ability to keep its units *fully occupied.* To stay fully occupied, the CCRC must *compete on the basis of price* with local competition. We compare ourselves with diverse competitors, some of whom group-insure their nursing care. We estimate that their residents pay about 13% more in aggregate monthly fees merely to pay insurance company expense and profit charges. (Based on our studies, the roughly 42% net cost loading in the premiums applies to the assumed 30% of fees related to nursing care.) This cost advantage is most important to our competitive posture—thus to our occupancy rate—and thus to our financial stability.

At our facility we have never regretted carrying our own risks. Tests of the possibility that buying insurance could be a benefit to us have shown that stochastically the possibility is "off the chart." The tests made were the more complete sensitivity tests called for by the Academy's ASOP, and they test all our assumptions, both alone and in combinations [6]. These tests provide meaningful data about *all* possible contingencies, not just nursing care excesses. With these data we can make *prudent decisions about pricing, budgets, and needed surplus.*

Resident Relations

One must also consider the fact that insurance for groups, as usually written, does not have guaranteed premiums and will ultimately, through experience-rating, be cost-plus insurance for all but small facilities. Where a facility assumes its own risks, close monitoring of resident morbidity facilitates smooth adjustment of resident charges, *as trends develop*, in contrast with situations in which there may be large unexpected and therefore *unbudgeted* increases in insurance rates. Thus, in the absence of an unlikely short-term catastrophic experience (and then cancellation of the insurance), we are talking dollar-swapping even if there were no loading.

We have always used our health center with some *flexibility*, in the best interests of our residents, regardless of insurance-type definitions of eligibility for nursing care transfer. Our medical and social staff, in cooperation with residents' families, can make more humane decisions about transfers among different types of nursing care than could an insurance company's claim adjuster.

I have talked about *financial stability* as a thing apart from *resident relations*, but in actuality you cannot have one without the other. This brings us full circle to the reason we retain the nursing care risk.

GARY L. BRACE:

Messrs. Moorhead and Fischer should be commended on the fine paper discussing financial solvency measures of CCRCs. There is very little published information on the subject, and this paper certainly fills a badly needed void.

My comments on the paper cover the five following areas:
1. Effect of competitive pressures on CCRCs
2. Appropriate mortality tables for CCRC residents
3. The use of long-term-care insurance coverage
4. Differences between ABFM and the ASOP
5. Interest earned on fixed assets.

Competitive Pressures

The authors mention that the competitive environment may sometimes prevent building adequate contingency amounts into the fee schedule. This limitation may come about due to prevalent fee levels in the market or pressure to keep fee increases to a minimum. Residents are, for the most part, on a fixed income and are sensitive to increases in fees. CCRC financial managers must always keep residents appraised of any proposed increases in monthly fee levels to get "buy-in" from the residents.

In addition, there are at least two other examples of the effect of the competitive environment on the practices of a CCRC financial manager. First is the determination of the relative split between monthly and entry fees. Second is the relationship between the entry fee for a declining refund contract and a refundable contract.

The facility can establish any relationship between the monthly fees and entry fees as long as the total revenue equals total expenses plus contingencies. Depending upon both the competitive environment and housing market, some parts of the country may have slightly different relationships between the entry and monthly fees. For instance, in a "slow" housing market, prospective residents may prefer a "rental" fee structure with a low or non-existent entry fee. Some facilities have developed the capacity for residents to "buydown" their monthly fee by paying an additional entry fee amount that reduces their monthly fee by an actuarially equivalent amount.

Many facilities price refundable entry fees based on fixed relationships with a declining refund contract entry fee. These relationships are sometimes based on shadow pricing of a competing facility or outdated rules of thumb specifying the relationship between the two types of entry fees. Some of the relationships used in the industry between the two types of entry fees were derived in a period of high interest rates. Since a refundable entry fee is essentially a single-premium endowment policy, this means that the refundable entry fee will be underpriced. Shadow pricing, or using these old entry fee relationships, is fortunately becoming less common.

Mortality Tables

The mortality tables presented by the authors are based on ratios to the 1983 Table *a*. Using multiples of the 1983 Table *a* may be appropriate for a certain distribution of ages within a certain level of care. However, the shape of the actual mortality curve of a CCRC resident population may not conform to the shape of the 1983 Table *a*. This is especially true in projecting the mortality pattern of residents in higher levels of care. In this case, the mortality patterns are affected more by the disability (or dependence) than the aging curve. Therefore, one might deduce that the shape of the mortality curve for residents in assisted and skilled care would be "flatter" than that for residents in independent living.

Long-Term-Care Insurance Coverage

I disagree with the authors' premise that the use of long-term-care (LTC) insurance coverage is growing. During the 1980s and early 1990s, there was a push by many carriers to market this coverage to facilities. The coverage was mainly offered on a group basis with certain mandatory medical screening criteria. CCRCs found this coverage to be expensive due to the necessary expense and contingency loading by the carriers. In addition, many facilities do not feel the need for LTC insurance. This lack of need and perceived insulation from risk may be a result of the large amount of assets held by the facility and the close financial relationship with the facility sponsor.

There is some anecdotal evidence suggesting that for-profit facilities might find the LTC coverage more attractive than not-for-profit facilities. This may possibly be due to a for-profit's heightened awareness of the health center utilization risk and financial ramifications.

ABFM Versus SOP

The authors do a good job discussing differences between the GAAP Standard of Practice (SOP) and ABFM. The authors are exactly right; the SOP does not provide an accurate measure of financial solvency. Unfortunately, since the SOP is the first "mandated" reported measure of financial solvency, many facilities misinterpret the SOP to provide a complete measure of financial solvency.

In addition, the Future Service Obligation (FSO) defined in the SOP can be viewed as a contract termination liability that determines the direct cost of providing care to the group of existing residents. In addition to not providing for asset replacement costs, other costs outside the direct cost of providing care to the residents (for example, marketing) are not included in the calculation. Therefore, the FSO is indeed a liberal indicator of the financial solvency.

Interest Earned on Fixed Assets

The line in the actuarially based balance sheet on Table 4, "Return on 'Deemed' Interest Earnings," is typically a difficult concept for actuaries new to the industry. The item is the outcome of the present-value techniques utilized in the ABFM process. The item can be thought of as the interest amount that would be earned on the entry fee had it been invested. Instead, the entry fee is "traded" for the purchase of fixed assets, and a rental fee, which represents foregone interest, is implicitly included in the fee schedule.

Again, thank you to the authors for a fine article on CCRC financial solvency.

DANIEL W. PETTENGILL:

The Society is indebted to Messrs. Moorhead and Fischer for so ably bringing to its attention the need for actuaries both to be involved with CCRCs and to know the important differences between the Academy's excellent Actuarially Based Financial Management System (ABFM) and AICPA's *Statement of Position 90-8.* I concur with the authors that the ABFM is preferable.

At the risk of being a broken record, I would remind everyone that many, if not most, CCRCs are relatively small. Hence they can and often do experience marked fluctuations in their morbidity experience from year to year. An effort should be made to insure the nursing home benefit with a reputable insurance company, provided the cost thereof will not make the CCRC's rates noncompetitive. The CCRC that builds its own nursing home and is located in a community with a shortage of nursing home beds might for a while be able to loan out its excess beds to the community.

Another factor to keep in mind is that in some areas an oversupply of CCRC units and/or plain retirement community units either already exists or soon will exist. Such competition can make it very difficult to keep a CCRC's occupancy rate at a financially satisfactory level.

JOHN M. BRAGG:

Messrs. Moorhead and Fischer are to be thanked and congratulated for this landmark paper. I hope it will lead to increased and better regulation of CCRCs and greatly increased awareness among CCRC managers (and even residents) of the need for sound financial stability based on proper actuarial principles.

I am one of those in the actuarial profession who, over the last ten years, has developed data and methodology for second-to-die products, living-benefit products, viatical settlements, and long-term-care products (including nursing home and home care products). Much of this knowhow could be directly applicable to CCRC evaluations. It could be used to create provisional actuarial tables for such purposes. It will be a long time before CCRC data are available in sufficiently credible volume to permit direct measurement. (Thousands of deaths are needed to make a mortality study credible.) Such CCRC data as are available could be used to modify provisional tables.

Assisted living and nursing wing evaluations can probably be treated (as two separate matters) from the viewpoint of traditional health insurance actuarial methodology. That methodology makes use of the functions S, H, and K. Once tables are established, it is possible to calculate active and disabled life reserves as well as net premiums (which would enter the CCRC's pricing policies). Active life reserves are applicable to those in living units and exist because of the likelihood that these people will eventually enter other statuses.

Values of S are already available for nursing home confinement (for purposes of long-term-care policies) and for living-benefit provisions in life insurance policies. Much work has been done on viatical settlements; the incidence and mortality patterns are known (by age and sex) for heart, stroke, and various cancer disablements. This information could be used to establish refined disabled life reserves, on a seriatim basis, for permanent residents of the nursing home wing.

A very large proportion of CCRC residents appear to be couples; the subject of last-survivor mortality therefore appears to be very important. CCRC actuaries should have access to computer generators that can calculate last survivorship mortality. Such generators should take into account special adjustments for the common disaster hazard and the heartbreak hazard (which deals with the likelihood that a surviving spouse will become substandard). For these and other reasons, second-to-die generators are tricky; the mortality curve is extremely steep and life expectancies are surprisingly long. (These facts are of importance in evaluating CCRC reoccupancy rates and refund arrangements, for example.)

Life expectancies should not be used in CCRC evaluations; rather, the underlying string of mortality rates should be employed to create commutation functions for use. (Modern personal computers are capable of producing commutation functions very rapidly on a custom-tailored basis.)

I should comment about the 1983 Individual Annuity Table,* which is apparently used for CCRC calculations. Bragg Associates has derived 1993 Aggregate Older Age Life Tables, based upon life insurance data for 1985–91 (excluding business for policy durations 1–5). A comparison follows:

---

*"Report of the Committee to Recommend a New Mortality Basis for Individual Annuity Valuation (Derivation of the 1983 Table a)," *TSA* XXXIII (1981): 695.

Age	$1000q_x$	
	1993 Bragg Aggregate	1983 IAM Basic
Male		
75	30.73	38.986
85	87.30	101.261
95	214.69	212.291
Female		
75	19.02	22.383
85	66.78	72.368
95	210.86	193.795

The 1983 IAM table appears to be inadequately high, especially for males. Annuitant mortality could be even lower than the 1993 Bragg Aggregate, and further improvement may have taken place since 1991. The implications for CCRC evaluations could be severe.

It is my hope that the Moorhead-Fischer paper will stimulate much further research on the important subject of CCRC financing.

THOMAS S. BURKE*:

I enjoyed reading "Testing Financial Stability of Continuing Care Retirement Communities." I believe the paper accurately describes the need for further work on financial presentation in the area of CCRCs to allow accountants and actuaries to assess the likelihood that a CCRC will be able to meet its promises to residents. This need *cannot be understated.*

I also believe that the actuarial profession holds the key to finding a more meaningful financial statement presentation, and I agree with the authors' statement "that within the actuarial profession the biggest opportunity that has not yet been fully grasped is a willingness to pool the data about CCRCs that only actuaries are equipped to gather and disseminate."

I hope that your efforts are rewarded by the stimulation of further work on this topic by the actuarial profession.

ROBERT J. CALLAHAN:

I was first introduced to continuing care retirement communities about 1984 or 1985 while the State of New York was considering legislation to

---

*Mr. Burke, not a member of the Society, is Chief Examiner of the New Hampshire Insurance Department, Concord, and chaired the NAIC Committee on CCRCs, which prepared the report contained in the NAIC Accounting Practices and Procedures Manual [9].

permit the development and operation of CCRCs. While the paper notes that the State of New York Insurance Department prohibited formation of CCRCs until 1991, there were various agencies concerned, such as the Division of the Budget, Social Services, the office of the Aging, and the Health Department. The Health Department had the responsibility for regulating nursing homes. The enabling legislation created a Life Care Council composed of representatives of various interested state departments and representatives of the public, primarily those with interests in the aging, nursing homes and life care for the elderly. The Health Department was made the lead regulatory agency, and the Insurance Department was given the responsibility for reviewing and approving the life care contract and the financial condition of the life care community.

There were various practical considerations. Most of the CCRCs were using high advance or entrance fees. Many of the applications would be expected to sell their homes to raise the entrance fees. Public officials wanted some assurance that the developers would remain in the life care community business and not be primarily real estate developers likely to pull out once they have their money for constructing the facility. Since most of the fee arrangements consisted of a combination of a high advance fee and variable monthly fees, there was an attitude, as the authors note, that reserves need not be maintained since the CCRC had the right to increase the monthly fees. In New York reserves were set as the higher of reserves calculated retrospectively and of reserves calculated prospectively. An educational process was required to sell this dual requirement and adjustments were made to provide for release of excess amounts accumulated.

In New York, perhaps the great majority of individuals in nursing homes are on Medicaid. While Medicaid was originally intended for the financial indigents, many of the rich have found ways to qualify by divesting themselves of their assets when they became terminal and had to go into a nursing home. While assets have to be divested by a year or two before entering the home, in a maintenance of the buildings, they should last far longer than even 60 years, especially in light of the clientele. I can point to numerous buildings more than 60 years old that are still in good condition. The house my parents had built about 65 years ago is probably worth 30 times what they originally paid for it. If a building becomes depreciated to zero but is still in good condition, what is to prevent the operator from selling the buildings and keeping the proceeds even though it builds a completely new facility out of the replacement fund accumulated? Should the capital gains stay with the facility? When we start talking about something that may happen 60 years hence, it is time for me to conclude my remarks.

DAVID L. HEWITT:

This paper analyzes the development of actuarial standards for CCRCs, from 1984 to 1994, and contrasts them with the 1990 accounting position. It also discusses the important tie-in with state regulators through the NAIC. The authors have an established reputation for careful documentation. Their paper is likely to be viewed as a basic source record.

Most of this paper uses the expressions *ASOP No. 3* and actuarially based financial management system (ABFM) interchangeably. But in their mention of replacement cost accounting, the authors make a distinction. They identify ABFM with the earlier, 1987–90 version of the ASOP—and would like to retain its replacement-cost approach to expensing physical facilities. They interpret it as asking that residents pay: (a) for using current facilities, (b) for using any replacements during their lifetimes, and (c) to help finance the first replacement occurring after their deaths—no matter how long after. By contrast, they criticize the current (1994) version of the ASOP as limiting itself to original cost accounting. In fact, the current ASOP provides a detailed method of allocating expenses for the use of current and replacement facilities during residents' lifetimes. And it spells out a method of valuing facilities that is consistent with this expense allocation. Furthermore, we have demonstrated that the value of facilities under this method is mathematically equal to current replacement cost less accumulated provision for replacement.* The real question raised by the authors' views is whether it is valid to charge residents both for their actual use of facilities now and in the future and for financing facilities they will never see.

I would dissent from the authors' general observation that the *SOP 90-8* accounting position brings "actuarial and accounting standards into essential agreement." To me, the weight of their analysis leans in the other direction: They point out that the accountants' "obligation to provide future services" omits certain elements, such as administrative expenses; that its amount is reduced by a large item of unamortized deferred revenue (which is stated as a separate liability); and that if the calculated result would be negative, it will be ignored. They go on to discuss some of the problems this can present.

---

*HEWITT, DAVID L., AND TORRANCE, H. SELWYN, "Actuarial Accounting for the Physical Assets of a CCRC," *Proceedings, Conference of Consulting Actuaries* XLIII (1993): 412–20.

I agree with the paper's helpful discussion of advance fee amortization as prescribed by the accountants.

The authors acknowledge the important contributions of Jarvis Farley in shaping the 1987 actuarial standard and in communicating it to the NAIC. They also cite the pioneering Winklevoss-Powell book published in 1984. Alwyn V. Powell, coauthor of that book, chaired the Academy CCRC committee that wrote the actuarial standard and mediated decisions as to its content; in my opinion he was the leading source of its ideas. Farley added an eloquent voice, drawing on his own experience; he also prepared a timely first draft of the standard for the committee's use, enabling us to get it completed in 1987.

I would note for the record that the Interim Actuarial Standards Board was publisher of the original standard in 1987. The permanent ASB reissued it without change as *ASOP No. 3* in 1990 and published the current version of *ASOP No. 3* in 1994 (based on the content of its exposure draft called 1993 Revision).

The actuarial profession has come a long way in codifying its CCRC standards. This paper offers a detailed overview. It diplomatically alludes to the need for more understanding between accountants and actuaries. The CCRC industry and its regulators are still bedeviled by the fact that the accountants—who hold a controlling grip on financial reporting—have been unwilling to work with the actuaries to reach a goal of complementary and consistent standards, in an area relying on actuarial expertise.

JOHN H. COOK:

My own CCRC is only one of about 1,000 CRCCs throughout the U.S. At this time more than a quarter of a million senior citizens in the U.S. have joined with a community of others with the expectation of living out their lifetimes together. The experience shows that typically only about 2% of the residents who join a CCRC ever withdraw, and very few ever leave after more than five years of residence.

In spite of its current large volume, the CCRC industry is relatively new, at least in the state of New Jersey. We have 17 communities operating now, and before my own was opened six years ago, there were only five. Throughout the country there have been more than 100 of them for some 30 years. Most of those have been in the north central and western states, and there has been relatively little effective state regulation of their operations and financial statements. The state of New York, with the second-largest population of senior citizens, did not have even one, until a year ago. There had been regulation until recently prohibiting residential health care facilities from accepting prepayment for basic services for more than a three-month period.*

Now that increasing numbers of our senior citizens are investing substantial portions of their life savings in prepaying for their care during their final years, it becomes even more important to protect them from the financial chaos they would experience if their facility should become unable to live up to its promises. I feel indebted to the authors of this paper for focusing attention on this.

The Pension Research Council for years had been concerned with the security of those mechanisms designed to provide the financial resources needed for a secure old age. About 15 years ago the council added to its concern the security of arrangements that seek to provide old age security and health care in kind. Now it is time for the regulatory bodies to look to the security of the CCRC industry, much as they have directed their attention in the past to the insurance business and the banking industry.

I am limiting my remarks to a few topics addressed by Fischer and Moorhead and to a few more that they did not address.

Fischer and Moorhead refer to the advisability of CCRCs throughout our country pooling their experience data for the purpose of an "intercompany" study of mortality and morbidity experience. This has been a common practice in the life insurance business for the last century, and it can prove of equal value to the continuing care retirement business. Those who will benefit the most from such a cooperative effort are the residents in the CCRCs themselves.

The financial stability of a CCRC depends heavily on a reasonable expectation of the level of mortality and morbidity that will be experienced by its residents. Pricing of the product, meaning entry fees and monthly service fees, are nothing more than rolls of the dice, unless they are based on reliable projections of future experience. The only reliable projection depends on valid studies of past experience.

Because of the limited amount of data in a single CCRC, it is necessary to consolidate data from many institutions to produce experience representative of future experience. I cannot emphasize that too strongly. In line with

---

*See also Mr. Callahan's discussion of the New York State Insurance Department's regulations.

that, I stress the need for careful inspection of the data and proper classification to avoid falling victim to misleading conclusions. This is especially true when a substantial portion of data comes from CCRCs with a relatively short history.

We are well aware of the differing experience rates under life insurance products when the selection procedures are casual or severe. The same is true for CCRC residents, probably to an even greater degree. I have observed morbidity experience within the first 12 months of operation of a CCRC that is many times the level of experience after a year or two of operation. An experience study that does not recognize this possibility can produce experience rates that are totally inappropriate for use in future pricing.

I am happy to recognize that an industry study of CCRC experience has already been initiated, sponsored by the American Association of Homes and Services for the Aged, and funded by the National Institute on Aging.

It is typical that the only liability item on the balance sheet for a CCRC that exceeds unamortized entry fees is bonded indebtedness. The fact that unamortized entry fees are a liability item declares that there exists an obligation. In spite of this, the only method of amortization approved by the AICPA in *SOP 90-8* fails to recognize any real relationship between the obligation (whatever it is) and the amount of the unamortized entry fee.

When an entry fee is charged upon admittance to residence in a CCRC, the contract does not distinguish obligations that are paid for by the entry fee. What is clear from first principles is that the sum of the entry fee and the present value of future monthly services fees is equal to the present value of all future resident services. The contract does not distinguish between those that are prepaid and those that will be paid for later. Philosophies differ on what is prepaid by the entry fee. What is almost universally accepted is that the entry fee is not all earned income at the time of its receipt, hence the liability item.

As I said at the beginning of my remarks, I am indebted to the authors for addressing the financial stability of CCRCs. I have three other interrelated concerns: the financial stability of the individual residents in a CCRC, financial screening of applications, and benevolent funds to assist those who may later be unable to pay fees in their entirety.

I can cite the experience of the 1980s when the real estate market was at its height, CD rates were double digit, and before the stock market crash of 1987. And it must be remembered that CCRCs, either explicitly or implicitly, guarantee lifetime care. Many applicants were approved for entry based on an apparently sound financial condition. Many were soon in a precarious financial situation. Some CCRCs maintain a benevolent fund, most of which comes from bequests from decreased residents, and this fund provides the subsidy necessary to maintain a needy resident. Newer CCRCs have not been able in short time to accrue such substantial funds. My own CCRC, six years old, has been developing such a fund for the last three or four years. The endowment fund committee, of which I am chairperson, conducted a confidential anonymous survey of our residents two years ago, and the results were a surprise and shock to us. I recommend that other CCRCs develop projections of future needs and provide adequately for these costs.

NORMA L. EDWARDS AND RALPH E. EDWARDS:

As we, two actuaries, face the last final major decision of our lifetimes, selecting a CCRC, how fortunate we are for this paper and its guidance on the financial aspects. When we were younger, there was always the ability to adjust or recoup from any change in our circumstances. At this stage of life, with no children to call upon, our selection of lifestyle and monetary commitment can hardly be revoked. At last we have guidance from Moorhead and Fischer.

Still, the problems are not all solved. The paper gives detail on how and why ABFM and SOP-GAAP financial reports produce markedly different results. We also understand that the SOP-GAAP report is required to be published annually as part of a CCRC's audit. We thus have three related questions for the authors. First, how do CCRC residents respond to seeing two sets of figures, each of which purports to present the true financial position? Second, what if there is no actuarial report at all? Third, how can actuaries employed by accounting firms operate in this environment?

THOMAS K. HARTMAN:

CCRCs are quite fascinating to study from an actuarial point of view. There are just two areas I would like to comment on.

First, I like to think that the capital expenses for the physical plant consist of three pieces: depreciation charges, loan interest, and imputed income. Because of the interaction of these pieces, it might be useful for the paper to make specific mention of the treatment of loan interest.

The paper's development of the annual charge of an asset is similar to a loan amortization schedule in which the annual charge is the annual payment, the loan interest rate is the discount rate used, and the depreciation is the change in the value of the asset over the year.

In the absence of any debt, I would then consider my imputed income to be the annual charge minus the depreciation. However, because it is likely that a community will have some debt, at least when first established, I follow a modified procedure. A net asset value is calculated as the asset value during the year minus the debt during the year. The discount interest rate is then applied to this amount, and the result is the imputed income.

The sum of the depreciation, the imputed income, and the loan interest is then an expense.

A couple of minor comments might be useful here:

- The imputed income described above can be negative.
- In the case in which annual charges are increasing, the charges should not increase faster than the assumed inflation rate.
- In the case in which annual charges are increasing, this methodology can produce assets that initially increase in value instead of decreasing.
- In doing these calculations, care should be used in considering the timing during the year when depreciation, the annual charges, and loan payments occur along with when they are assumed to occur for purposes of calculating the actuarial reserve.

Another equivalent approach would be to have a charge in addition to the annual charge that reflects the difference between the loan interest rate and the discount rate. This could be positive or negative.

A simplified example might be useful. We will assume the following:

Beginning Asset	20,000,000
Current Year's Annual Charge	1,250,000
Discount Rate	5.50%
Beginning Loan	15,000,000
Loan Payment	1,400,000
Loan Interest Rate	8.00%

All payments and charges occur at the end of the year. (For purposes of calculation, the actuarial reserve for these would likely need to be adjusted to mid-year.)

Under the imputed income approach

$$\text{Net Asset} = 20,000,000 - 15,000,000 = 5,000,000$$
$$\text{Imputed Income} = 0.055 \times 5,000,000 = 275,000$$

The end assets value would be:

Beginning Asset Value	$20,000,000
Times Discount Rate	× 1.055
	$21,100,000
	−1,250,000
Ending Asset Value	$19,850,000

Please note the $19,850,000 would also be equal to the discounted value of the remaining annual charges. Depreciation for the year would be:

Beginning Value	$20,000,000
Minus Ending Value	−19,850,000
Depreciation =	$ 150,000

The charge for capital expense would be:

Depreciation	$ 150,000
Loan Interest $15,000,000 × .08 =	1,200,000
Imputed Income	275,000
	$1,625,000

An alternative calculation would consider the difference in the loan interest rate and the discount rate; in this case $8.00\% - 5.50\% = 2.50\%$

Modified Loan Interest = $15,000,000 × 0.025 = $375,000.

Under this approach the charge for capital expenses becomes:

$$\$1,250,000 + \$375,000 = \$1,625,000.$$

As can be seen, the two approaches are actuarially equivalent.

Because of the special calculations needed, some comment concerning the handling of the loan interest seems warranted.

Second, for valuation purposes actuaries have traditionally thought in terms of net premiums. It may be useful to suggest a similar concept here. Consider a life care contract in which there is a $110,000 entrance fee, the present value of the periodic fees is also $110,000, and the present value of the expenses is $200,000. This was essentially designed with a 10% margin in the fee structure for contingencies, profit and contribution to surplus. If the gross premiums are used in calculating reserves, then the balance sheet looks like:

Assets	= Entrance Fee	$110,000
Liability	= PVFB − PVFF = $200,000 − $110,000 =	90,000
Surplus	= Assets − Liabilities	$ 20,000

This means that the present value of all the assumed margins is released immediately. An established concept in valuation is that profits should not be recognized until the emerging experience has borne out their existence.

This suggests the use of a net premium in the present value of future fees calculation. It is also well established for valuation purposes that when premium (or in this case, fees) varies over time, the net premium is a constant percentage of each gross premium and the present value of such net premium equals the present value of benefits.

This example was designed to be easy, so that it can quickly be seen that the net entrance fee is $100,000 and the present value of the net periodic fees is $100,000. The balance sheet now becomes:

Assets	$110,000
Liabilities PVFB − PVFNPF = $200,000 − $100,000 =	100,000
Surplus	$ 10,000

The appropriate amount of the 10% margin in the entrance fee received is released to surplus.

ROBERT F. LINK:

Operations of a typical CCRC involve significant elements of insurance risk. It is therefore good that we have them under the actuarial microscope, and this paper is a good beginning. This discussion is more personal than professional.

My wife and I have considered the CCRC option and have so far resisted for our own reasons. However, we have done some checking and gotten some information. One CCRC gave us a brochure including a table of its monthly charges over time. It appeared that these charges had been increasing for some years at a compound annual rate just under 7%. I think some of the residents may have been a little testy about this.

Asking why these increases should so far outstrip increases in the CPI, I was told the following. When the CCRC opened for business, the health center was not immediately needed for the residents and so was opened to the public. This generated significant revenues. These were applied as an offset to the expenses covered by the monthly charges. As time passed and residents moved into the health center, this revenue declined, and the monthly charges had to pick up the slack. (There were of course other factors in this pie, but the one I have described was a large one.)

This process produced in effect a kind of (I presume innocent) "lowballing" for people who considered this CCRC at its opening. They had every reason to expect charges to follow some reasonable index of costs, which shouldn't be very far from the CPI.

It seems to me that these revenues, to the extent that they were expected to disappear with time, should have been taken out of the operating budget covered by monthly charges. I would prefer to see them "capitalized" in some way and used either to reduce the going-in charges for residents or to create a contingency fund for unexpected problems.

Perhaps the authors will find within their framework some way of dealing with this kind of problem. And in any event, we thank them for the framework.

CECIL J. NESBITT:

The topic of the paper is one of which I have no special knowledge, and so I appreciate the thorough overview given by Messrs. Moorhead and Fischer. They have provided much information and insight into a complex subject that in one way or another we shall all have to address.

While I have some knowledge of pension funding mathematics and some insights into social security financing, I have had little experience with the complexities of a CCRC. My comments therefore are mercifully brief and emerge from limited experience.

One experience has been a public lecture by Rev. Dr. Hans Kung, who is here at Michigan as a Visiting Professor of Religious Thought. His lecture was entitled "Euthanasia: New Theological Perspective in Assisted Dying." In the lecture, he stressed each individual's responsibility for achieving a dignified death. This is a specially current topic in Michigan now because a number of assisted suicides have occurred, including that of a friend suffering from advanced symptoms of Lou Gehrig's disease. I cannot resist quoting another line from the lecture, namely, "Doctors are scared of lawyers; the lawyers are scared of judges; and the judges are scared of theologians."

Through biweekly visits over a four-year period to a local nursing home that another friend has entered, we have observed the deterioration of many individuals, including that of our friend. One wonders what public benefit is emerging from such prolongation of subdued life.

On the other hand, many individuals wish to remain living independently in their own homes as long as possible. Others may be better served by relief from the responsibilities of home and daily care. We are in an age of transition where each family will have to decide the best course for the family to pursue. For single persons, the choice may be clearer.

Turning back to the paper, I note that in the earlier part there is reference to the *closed group* of CCRC members as of the valuation date. This is the usual approach of individual life insurance and annuities and of private pension funding. Later in the paper, there is reference to the *open group* of CCRC members. This may be appropriate if the CCRC is considered to be a permanent institution, as is usually the case for Old-Age Survivors and Disability Insurance (OASDI) and other large public benefit systems. The closed group analysis may be appropriate if the CCRC is considered to exist for only one term until the need for replacement develops. The open group analysis may apply if the CCRC is considered to exist for an indefinite number of years. There then appears a spectrum of financing methods depending on the proposed length of existence.

For OASDI and other large public benefit systems, we have developed at Michigan a theory of n-year roll-forward reserve financing or, even more simple, a theory of m-year ($m>n$) of stepwise level percent financing. For a CCRC that proposes to develop as a permanent institution, an open group analysis may be required but would increase the difference from the accounting approach.

The authors' paper provides careful comparison of an ABFM system with the SOP-GAAP approach of the accounting profession. The authors' analysis is enlightening for this transition period while experience develops. I am grateful for the authors' introduction to the complex questions of CCRCs.

MARK PEAVY:

Mr. Moorhead and Mr. Fischer have done an excellent job of providing an overview of the financial reporting aspects applicable to CCRCs. As they point out in their introduction, CCRCs are amazingly complex entities, combining aspects of life insurance, health insurance in a managed-care setting, and pensions, as well as property management. The authors included the proper amount of detail to enable the reader to understand the broad concepts being illustrated.

They have done a particularly good job of highlighting the differences between GAAP and actuarially based methods. As mentioned in the section on regulatory accounting requirements, "actuaries naturally look forward to a revision in SOP-GAAP that will make it more, if not completely, compatible with ABFM." I certainly share this desire, although I am not sure that this will happen anytime soon.

My skepticism stems from two concerns. First, having been involved in several meetings between accountants and actuaries involving financial reporting for CCRCs, it continually struck me how challenging it was for the two groups to communicate with one another. Each profession has its own fundamental principles on how things should be done. Trying to convince the other that a change is appropriate runs into two obstacles: (a) the professionals who are being asked to change don't have the training to immediately grasp all the implications of the proposed change, and (b) the proposals may run counter to practices that are deeply embedded in the other profession and seem to work adequately.

Second, assuming the challenge of clearly communicating the fundamental principles of each profession can be overcome, the possibility remains that the professionals may not agree with what they hear. I once asked a prominent accountant why he had such a reluctance to accept the methods suggested by ABFM.

His response was that, while the theory may be fine, he did not feel comfortable with what he perceived to be a lack of standard practice among actuaries in setting the assumptions underlying the APVs. He expressed the specific concern that two otherwise identical CCRCs might produce significantly dissimilar financial statements solely because their retained actuaries interpreted past experience differently or had differing perceptions of the future. It was his contention that GAAP, as implemented by the SOP, provided more objective standards that produced a greater consistency in financial statements. To the extent that his opinions are widely shared, achieving greater compatibility between ABFM and GAAP will prove difficult. Although the creation of standardized mortality and morbidity tables might ease his concerns, reaching a consensus on what those tables should be and how much variance from the tables would be permitted is clearly a long-term project.

H. SELWYN TORRANCE:

Those actuaries working with CCRCs owe a debt of gratitude to the authors of this fine paper. By commenting on some details I hope to add to its value.

Mortality, Morbidity, and Transfer Rates

There is a statement that "The 1983 a Table is commonly used as a basis for decrements, a different percentage factor being applied to the table's rates for each different decrement." I think that any implied blessing of this method is inappropriate. Actual rates may be found to be "shaped" quite differently from this table.

Even if an improved method is as simple as fitting observed data with one factor for higher ages and a different factor for lower ages, the difference between the factors may be quite significant.

Further, there is conjecture that some rates may be quite independent of age over a wide range of ages or even decrease over a range of ages. The method described will always force rates to increase as age increases, thus prejudging the outcome. The method should be modified to produce a table not inconsistent with the data.

Amortization of Entry Fees

There is a statement that (under the AICPA SOP on nonrefundable advance fees), "The deferred revenue should be amortized to income over future periods based on the estimated life of the resident or contract term, if shorter." The authors also note that it "permits other than straight-line amortization if costs are expected to be significantly higher in the later years of residence." However, it is necessary to highlight a very significant requirement, namely, that "Unamortized deferred revenue from nonrefundable advance fees should be recorded as revenue upon a resident's death or termination of the contract."

This immediate recognition upon death is a worrying feature of the AICPA SOP that conflicts with past practice of some communities that have spread the release on death, for example in accordance with the basis described in David Hewitt's paper (the paper's ref. [8]). Immediate recognition can be criticized as undesirable because of the volatility that it introduces and because a major element of the community's income remains unknown until the conclusion of its fiscal year. However, protests by the actuarial community have at best been muted.

Some feel that the SOP need not supplant what are essentially sound practices. However, state regulatory authorities are requesting certification of compliance with the AICPA SOP. To add to the confusion, some actuaries are implementing the SOP in a very literal manner (which is actuarially unsound), simply continuing to amortize without modifying the basis to recognize the release on death, but then also recognizing income on death. It is my view that compliance on a sound actuarial basis calls for amortization over life expectancy, taking into account the release upon death in such a way that the expected income follows the desired pattern. Thus, for example, for a resident in skilled nursing with remaining unamortized fee $F\{x\}$ at age x, probability of death $q\{x\}$, and expected income $E\{x\}$, we have:

$$F\{x\} = E\{x\} + (1.0 - q\{x\}) F\{x + 1\}$$

that is, the unamortized fee provides the expected income plus the following year's unamortized fee upon survival. In the simplest design, $E\{x\}$ is defined as 1 unit at all ages, although other definitions can be considered. The corresponding $F\{x\}$ can then be found at all ages by recursion.

If the corresponding income recognized in the year from age x to $(x+1)$ upon survival to $(x+1)$ is $J\{x\}$, then:

$$E\{x\} = q\{x\} F\{x\} + (1.0 - q\{x\}) J\{x\}$$

This can then be solved for $J\{x\}$ at all ages. The values may be found to follow no consistent trend, but, no matter, $E\{x\}$ will follow the desired pattern. Similar (but more complex) equations may be formulated for those in lower level nursing care or independent living, and for couples.

Other Comments

There is a true statement that "*ASOP No. 3* provides ... each item of property is assigned an assumed useful lifetime." However, it may be necessary to treat the property as a composite of assets with different useful lifetimes. This becomes particularly important when projecting future cash flow, which, for example, may need to provide for a series of major repairs before ultimate replacement.

There is a true statement that "*ASOP No. 3* provides ... the values of some items ... are taken directly from the accounting balance sheet." However, the items specified are not all short term. Specifically, deposits in escrow may be held on average for as long as ten years in some communities, and assumed earnings on those deposits may differ materially from contractual earnings that constitute the obligation. In that case it may be appropriate to value the difference.

(AUTHORS' REVIEW OF DISCUSSIONS)

ERNEST J. MOORHEAD AND NIELS H. FISCHER:

The contributors have added much value to this paper. We are grateful.

Three discussions deal in part with self-insuring nursing case costs rather than buying commercial insurance. Mr. Sillesky strongly supports self-insurance; the authors second his reasoning. The $17-million health care services liability in line 10 of our Table 4 illustrates the importance of this matter. That figure would have been about $7 million larger (using Mr. Sillesky's gross premium assumption) if commercial insurance had been used. Whether the insurance premiums are paid by the community or by the resident is not an issue; in either case the resident presumably ends up paying it all. Mr. Brace corrects the authors' presumption that commercial carriers have made inroads with LTC insurance sales; we assume that sound, independent actuarial advice is accountable. Mr. Pettengill suggests that small CCRCs examine the advantages of commercial insurance, but wisely with the proviso that competitiveness of their fee scale be a major consideration.

Mr. Brace, former chair of the Academy CCRC committee, adds a valuable dimension to the paper by exploring the competitive element and available pricing strategies, one of which may indeed be at the heart of the answer to Mr. Link's reference to the ill effects of starting with too low a fee scale and attempting to remedy this error later on. Doubtless both these gentlemen concur that full early occupancy backed by a long waiting list of reasonably committed people is an essential short-term objective. Mr. Brace also draws attention to deficiencies in the SOP's future services obligation definition and the background of the item "return on deemed interest earnings." We look forward with Mr. Brace and Mr. Torrance to development, now under way, of new industry-wide mortality and morbidity tables.

Regulatory authorities need to heed Mr. Pettengill's warning that oversupply of CCRCs in any area is a threat to all. And interested actuaries must make it our business to find out how much effective supervision of this kind is being exerted.

Mr. Bragg likens CCRC pricing and reserving to traditional health insurance and last-to-die mortality methodology, a valuable bridging of actuarial techniques. We believe that the Society's forthcoming experience study of CCRCs will provide data he would need. A longitudinal study of transfer rates and mortality rates in each residency category according to health conditions that arise during the journey, which he suggests, would be a valuable area for research. However, permanent nursing care residents are primarily victims of strokes, Alzheimer's, senility, or simply inability to dress or eat independently; rather few of them become victims of heart or cancer conditions about which, along with stroke-related conditions, most mortality data are concerned.

While we concur that the research Mr. Bragg suggests would be valuable, we doubt that an individual CCRC would benefit enough from seriatim valuations to warrant the additional data collection and analysis expense.

Mr. Burke speaks from the vantage point of one who chaired the NAIC CCRC committee that successfully fashioned a coherent Addendum to the *Accounting Practices and Procedures Manual* during its final year of 1994. We appreciate his view on actuarial involvement.

Mr. Callahan identifies the concerns of his state's insurance department and other regulatory agencies, the problem areas they address, and their resulting unique requirement that reserves be set at the higher of the prospective and retrospective levels. He raises a question that has always plagued accountants about the probable life span of a building. The authors acknowledge that any accounting system can only roughly approximate real estate depreciation.

Mr. Callahan and Mr. Hewitt dissent from the authors' view that SOP's future service obligation (FSO) "brings actuarial and accounting standards into essential agreement." We do stand by what we say, however. We grant that FSO seldom applies; entry fee refunds are usually conditional (Table 6); we later describe the accounting distortions that result. Nevertheless, the FSO is important because AICPA now recognizes in CCRC work the concept of computing actuarial present values from data on future fee increases, inflation, mortality, transfers, and interest; we liken adoption of the FSO to AICPA's acceptance of actuarial concepts for GAAP work with life companies.

Mr. Hewitt holds that the net asset item, line 5 of Table 4, is unaffected by whether original cost or replacement cost accounting is used. We agree, but the asset item is not at issue here. He makes the excellent observation that the 1994 *ASOP* recognizes replacement costs in some respects.

At issue is the difference between original cost and replacement cost accounting as it occurs in the liability item on line 12; here replacement cost accounting calls for making depreciation charges to the closed group for the replacement cost of each asset in service, and each of its replacements, until the last survivor of the closed group dies. As a result, each depreciation charge is higher than permitted by *ASOP No. 3.* Section 5.6.2(b) therein provides that "The present value of this series (of depreciation charges) discounted to the time of acquisition, equals the cost of the asset." The inflation index that Mr. Hewitt refers to has no mathematical impact; the intent of *ASOP No. 3*, to maintain intergenerational equity through original cost accounting, is accomplished. Thus, relating to Mr. Hewitt's second paragraph, *ASOP No. 3* requires the closed group to pay for an asset at its last purchase price, and replacement cost accounting makes them to pay for it as its next replacement price.

Mr. Cook warns that young CCRCs may find their own initially adverse morbidity experience discouraging. Contributing causes, perhaps not yet statistically measured, may include resident trauma arising from abrupt lifestyle change upon moving from one's home into a community, and the necessarily long period (often two years or even longer) between appraisal of a prospective entrant's health and welcoming that person into residence.

Another of Mr. Cook's concerns—that of finding an appropriate amortization for entry fees—fortunately does not arise under the actuarial approach. It seems unlikely that a good solution will be found for use with the accounting approach. Long-range projections seem to offer the sole opportunity for testing fee structure adequacy when that approach is relied upon.

Mr. and Mrs. Edwards ask questions that many actuaries, particularly CCRC residents and prospective residents, have posed. The regrettable fact is that in many CCRCs, the SOP-GAAP report is the only one made available to residents; usually only members of the residents' finance committees are privy to the ABFM statements—if an actuarial report is produced at all. A necessary exception, as in New York, reported by Mr. Callahan, is where legislation or regulation requires such disclosure.

As to how actuaries and accountants in the same accounting firm work together, it should be remembered that *ASOP No. 3* now does not permit the "component approach," which can be interpreted not to permit the actuary to provide an accountant with a piece of the SOP-GAAP report—such as assumptions or methodology for calculating the FSO. This can strain relationships. The "component approach" largely relates to having the actuary provide advice on health care costs, the underlying assumption being that other costs are under control.

Mr. Hartman contributes welcome generalized analysis of physical plant through recognition of loan interest. His net premium concept is key to understanding otherwise bewildering aspects of the ABFM balance sheet so that full benefit may be derived from its role as predictor of things to come.

Dr. Nesbitt's insight into closed versus open group accounting is thought-provoking. The former often projects expenses based on 100% apartment reoccupancy, using unit costs derived from such an optimum-sized group. Of overriding concern to CCRC management, however, is CCRC perpetuation, for which open group analysis is needed. This involves sensitivity testing of unfavorable competitive and environmental factors, a process now described as dynamic financial condition analysis.[1]

Mr. Peavy, from his perspective as NAIC actuary and a participant in the committee work involving actuaries and accountants from the nonregulatory sector, provides a perceptive look into communications between actuaries and accountants. His doubt about imminent improvement in SOP-GAAP at any time soon is echoed by Mr. Hewitt, who reflects on his own committee experience.

Mr. Torrance provides valuable additional detail about shortcomings of the AICPA approach to amortizing entry fees. State regulatory authorities should be aware that the AICPA approach is actuarially unsound. His algebraic development of a sounder approach seems indisputable. Academy members know *ASOP No. 3,* which does not recognize entry fee amortization, as the rational approach—a source of frustration, indeed. Mr. Torrance also provides illuminating comments on difficulties in accounting for fixed assets under *ASOP No. 3.*

The gratifying response to this paper—the wide range of points well covered by so many knowledgeable people[2]—augurs well for the much needed increases in CCRC managements' reliance upon the actuarial approach to income statements and balance sheets, and likewise for timely emergence of more and better pooled statistics on mortality and morbidity data upon which managements can rely for sound planning and for preservation of equities between present and future generations of residents.

---

[1]The authors plan to prepare a paper on open group concerns for submission to the 1998 International Association of Actuaries meeting in Birmingham, England.

[2]The paper has 14 discussions and is, in fact, the second most discussed paper in the *Transactions'* 47-year history. The most discussions, 16, are of: LECKIE, ROBIN B. "Some Actuarial Considerations for Mutual Companies," *TSA* XXXI (1979): 187–259.

CASH VALUE LIFE INSURANCE FOR THE TWENTY-FIRST CENTURY: SEGREGATED LIFE AND THE INDIVIDUAL DEATH BENEFIT ACCOUNT

STEPHEN D. REDDY

ABSTRACT

At present, the life insurance industry is going through a difficult period. Several companies have failed, while many others have seen their capital positions eroded significantly. Competition has become stiffer, and sales targets have become more difficult to achieve. Even where sales have been good, they generally have been at reduced profit margins. Virtually all companies are tightening their belts, including some head-count reduction, to boost profitability and replenish capital. At the same time, regulators are becoming more vigilant and Congress is continually knocking on the door looking for more tax dollars.

Many of these and related difficulties can be traced to problems that have plagued the industry's long-standing bread-and-butter product, cash value life insurance (CVLI). The events of the 1980s and early 1990s are enough to make one question whether the evolution of CVLI is keeping pace with the rapidly changing environment in which it is sold. Many new products have been spawned during this period; however, upon closer examination, one might well conclude that the changes introduced during this period have provided more camouflage than real solutions. In this paper, I describe a new form of CVLI better suited for today's environment and the years ahead. This description is followed by a discussion comparing this new product form with the present form of CVLI. Finally, the paper concludes with a brief discussion of the effect of such a new product form on the key constituents.

I. CASH VALUE LIFE INSURANCE—THE NEXT GENERATION

The Product Defined

A new form of CVLI can be created by legislation that allows two new interrelated products. The first new generic product, which I refer to as segregated life[1] (SL), is defined as follows: An SL policy is any fixed-premium CVLI policy whose loan provisions are worded such that loans are forced upon the policyholder at the maximum level at each premium due date. In other words, an SL policy is any fixed-premium cash value policy that contractually is always fully leveraged by the policyholder. The second new generic product, directly related to the first, is referred to as an individual death benefit account (IDBA). This is defined as is any investment account in any qualified financial institution that is held on behalf of the policyholder and is funded solely by policy loans derived from the policyholder's SL policy or policies.[2]

In other words, the IDBA provides a receptacle for the borrowed SL funds, the earnings on which receive essentially the same tax-deferred treatment at surrender and tax-free treatment at death that they now receive in a conventional cash value policy (part of the new legislation would grant this tax treatment of IDBA funds). The net effect of the introduction of an SL policy and its companion IDBA product is the literal segregation of the investment component of the cash value product from its mortality/expense component. That is, the portion of premium that normally accrues to the cash value is instead withheld, to be invested and accrued outside the contract. Universal life (UL) is often referred to as the "unbundled" product, but the UL policy is really unbundled in appearance only. The SL concept takes the next logical step and unbundles the product in substance.

In the event of surrender or death, proceeds from both SL and IDBA contracts are available to the policyholder. At surrender, the policyholder is entitled to the cash surrender value of both the SL and IDBA contracts. Normally, the bulk of the surrender proceeds comes from the IDBA contract, while the SL contract provides some nominal amount (that is, total cash value, less loan balance, less accrued loan interest). At death, each of the two contracts provides a material part of the death benefit. The SL contract provides something akin to the net amount at risk, based on the SL contract's cash value schedule. The actual proceeds are the SL policy face amount, plus the face amount of any paid-up additions, plus any current dividend

---

[1]While I have chosen the name segregated life, at least for the purpose of this paper, the name integrated life also has appeal, particularly from a marketing standpoint. As the reader will see, the product described herein has elements of both segregation and integration. I chose the former name because much of the discussion in the paper focuses on the product in its segregated state.

[2]In this paper, SL and IDBA products are discussed in the present tense as if they already existed in order to avoid continuous use of the subjunctive mood. Use of the subjunctive mood or future tense has been limited to discussions of uncertain aspects of these new products and their potential ramifications.

accrued, less the loan balance, less accrued loan interest. The IDBA account balance constitutes the remainder of the death benefit. Therefore, the performance of the IDBA account affects the total death benefit, and underperformance could cause the total death benefit to be less than the SL face amount. The SL contract could guarantee that the total death benefit would never be less than the face amount, although some restrictions on the length of the guarantee or the types of IDBA funds that enable such a guarantee may be necessary.

For income and estate tax purposes, both contributions to and distributions from the SL and IDBA contracts are aggregated. The policyholder's net taxable income in the year of surrender is defined as follows:

taxable income = SL proceeds (including loans forgiven)

+ IDBA proceeds (including loans forgiven)

+ SL dividends received

+ IDBA dividends received

− SL gross premiums paid

− IDBA gross premiums paid,

where gross premiums paid include those paid via loan. This can be rewritten as:

taxable income = (SL cash proceeds + final SL loan balance)

+ (IDBA cash proceeds + final IDBA loan balance)

− (SL gross premiums paid − SL dividends received)

− (final SL loan balance − accrued SL loan interest

− IDBA dividends received),

which reduces to:

taxable income = total cash proceeds + final IDBA loan balance

+ accrued SL loan interest + total dividends received

− SL premiums paid.

Interest charged on the required policy loans is not tax-deductible, because this interest is essentially offsetting the tax-deferred earnings inside the SL product. However, as with a traditional CVLI policy, the cost of borrowing (that is, loan interest) effectively becomes deductible at death or surrender because the taxable amount is lower than it otherwise would have been by the cumulative cost of such borrowing.

I anticipate that the administration and tax reporting of the SL/IDBA products would be as follows: The life company selling the SL policy provides the policyholder a form with each bill stating the amount of forgone premium payments (that is, borrowed cash values) associated with that bill. The policyholder then invests the borrowed cash value in the IDBA(s) of his/her choice and forwards copies of such forms to the administrator(s) of those accounts. The policyholder also notifies the SL company of his/her IDBA selection(s). Once invested, monies can be withdrawn or borrowed from an IDBA, subject to the account's specific withdrawal provisions. Monies can be transferred from one IDBA to another, again subject to particular or perhaps generic IDBA restrictions.

Withdrawals of money from IDBAs work much the same as withdrawals from IRAs. A grace period is allowed to accommodate a rollover into another IDBA. Upon a transfer or rollover of funds from one IDBA to another, the policyholder's basis also is transferred, thereby allowing the continued deferral of income-reporting by the new IDBA administrator. The SL company coordinates and records any movement of funds from one IDBA to another, while the SL policy may set limits on the maximum number and minimum size of associated IDBAs, the minimum amount of any contributions to them, and the frequency of rollovers to and from IDBAs.

Upon surrender of the SL policy, the burden is on the SL company to notify the IDBA administrator(s) on record. The IDBA administrator(s) then sends a 1099 form to the policyholder, indicating the taxable "distributions" during the year of surrender of the policy. (The policyholder does not necessarily have to cash in his/her IDBA accounts, but they must be subject to a gains tax as if all the IDBA account proceeds were distributed.) Another possibility is for the SL company to do all the reporting to the policyholder, who receives one form indicating his/her consolidated SL and IDBA results. Perhaps an annual report to the policyholder summarizing his/her holdings would also be desirable.

A 1035 exchange is triggered when one SL policy is exchanged for another. No change in IDBAs is necessary or even relevant to a 1035 exchange. When a 1035 exchange occurs, notification of the IDBAs' administrator is necessary only to note the identity of the new SL company. Deferred tax treatment of current inside buildup continues.

Finally, SL policyholders have a continuous option, exercisable at any time, to repay the SL policy loans in full, thereby opting out of the SL contract and converting the policy back to a standard CVLI contract. This allows the policyholder to shift the responsibility for investing the cash value to the SL company. Normally this is done by closing out the IDBA to repay the policy loans. Any excess earnings could also be poured into the CVLI contract as paid-up additions or dividend accumulations. Any interest earned in any remaining IDBAs from that date forward would become currently taxable.

The legislation required to get the SL/IDBA concept up and running may be confined to the tax code. In other words, it may be sufficient to just change provisions in the federal tax code so that the above-described tax treatment and reporting for SL/IDBA packages could take effect. No change in nonforfeiture laws, IRS definition of life insurance, or Securities and Exchange Commission (SEC) regulation of securities would be necessary, except for perhaps some technical language defining SL as a subset of traditional CVLI. Perhaps some state regulations need slight amendments pertaining to policyholder loans and solicitation requirements for SL products, but some state insurance departments might permit SL products to be sold without any new regulation, as was the case when UL was first introduced.

The Product Mechanics

Now that all the relevant components and rules have been defined, let us examine the mechanics of the SL/IDBA concept. The following are the key steps in the sale, administration and reporting of SL and IDBA products.

1. Agent explains SL/IDBA product concept to prospective buyer and provides illustrations of a company's SL product, either alone or in combination with a generic IDBA product.
2. Policyholder, as part of the application, signs form acknowledging that he or she understands the SL/IDBA product concept.
3. The initial premium due to the SL company is the first-year premium, less any initial loan value.
4. The SL company provides the policyholder with a form indicating the amount of loan value to be currently invested in IDBA(s) and general instructions on investment procedures and limitations. There does not need to be any time limit within which the insured must invest the loaned values—failure to invest in an IDBA simply results in lost income, loss of income tax deferral, or both.

5. The policyholder invests the borrowed cash value in one or more IDBAs. The investments must be registered as IDBAs to obtain the preferential tax treatment.

6. Each IDBA company, after receiving IDBA investment premium, registers the investment with the SL-writing company. The SL company records the IDBA company and product, and verifies that the total amount invested in IDBAs to date does not exceed the total cash value loaned to the policyholder to date.

7. At the end of each calendar year, IDBA companies exclude from any 1099 forms any income produced from registered IDBA accounts.

8. Before the end of each contract year, a premium notice is sent to the policyholder, indicating the gross premium due, the net premium due, and the increase in loan value to be invested in IDBAs. The notice also indicates the total loan balance required to be repaid to opt out of the SL contract and convert it to a conventional CVLI contract.

Steps 4–8 are repeated each contract year, except that the premium due and the IDBA investible amount in renewal years are based upon that year's premium and increase in loan value.

Upon a rollover of funds from one IDBA to another, the previous IDBA company notifies the SL company of the transfer, and the new IDBA company records the basis transferred. Upon a surrender of IDBA funds not associated with an SL policy surrender, the IDBA company reports the distributions, as any company reports withdrawals from CVLI policies. Upon a 1035 exchange of one SL policy for another, the previous SL company transfers all its IDBA data to the new SL company and notifies the IDBA company(ies) of the change so records can be updated.

Upon termination of an SL policy by surrender or death, the SL company ascertains IDBA fund values as of the termination date and provides a report to the policyholder. The report indicates the total net proceeds to the policyholder, broken down by face amount, cash values and policy loan balances for both the SL and the IDBA(s). The report also includes the amount of taxable gain in the policy, if any, reported at year-end. Each IDBA company also provides a notice, as of the SL termination date, indicating the account balance and alerting the policyholder that the tax preference treatment ceases as of that date.

The Product Illustrated

Tables 1–3 present product illustrations of the SL/IDBA concept. To enable this, a hypothetical participating whole life (WL) product was first designed for a nonsmoking male, age 45, with a dividend scale based upon a new investment return assumption of 10% per annum. Table 1 contains an illustration of this product's values under the assumption that dividends purchase paid-up additions. Table 2 contains a comparable illustration for the combination of an SL product with a variable policy loan rate and an IDBA rate of return assumed equal to 10%. Not surprisingly, the total cash values and death benefits equal those from the previous WL illustration. Finally, an SL product with an 8% fixed loan rate was developed by dropping the dividend credited rate by 200 basis points on both the base policy and paid-up additions. The same 10% IDBA return was again assumed. Table 3 contains an illustration of these products' combined results. In this case, some clear differences in the WL illustration are readily observable. The total cash values in the SL/IDBA package track fairly closely with their WL counterparts, but are slightly lower initially and somewhat higher after many years. The death benefits start out in tandem, but the WL values become quite a bit higher after several years.

These differences can be readily explained. The smaller death benefit under the SL/IDBA package results when a cash value is borrowed and then invested outside the contract to achieve a return greater than that of the policy loan rate. This extra return is not being used to purchase additional coverage as it would have in the WL contract via paid-up additions. The result is an increase in net cash value without a corresponding proportionate increase in the death benefit. While this could be considered a problem, it occurs under similar circumstances with a leveraged version of today's WL products. Of course, this occurs only when the loan rate is less than the rate that could be earned in the IDBA contract.

The higher death benefit under the WL policy causes a drain on the cash value, particularly in later years when the net amount at risk difference and the mortality rate are highest. This unintended side effect can be removed, at least for comparison, by adding a one-year term rider to the SL/IDBA package for the amount of coverage shortfall.

The slightly higher initial cash values for the WL policy are seemingly attributable to the fact that SL/IDBA dividends and cash value increases do not begin to earn the market rate of 10% until the end of the year when they are paid (one year later than the WL counterpart). The impact of this

TABLE 1

WHOLE LIFE ILLUSTRATION; FACE AMOUNT = $140,000

Year	(1) Gross Premium	(2) Guaranteed Cash Value	(3) Total Dividends	(4) Paid-Up Additions	(5) PUA Cash Value	(6)* Total Cash Value	(7)† Total Death Benefits
1	2,678	0	0	0	0	0	140,000
2	2,678	0	0	0	0	0	140,000
3	2,678	2,311	126	0	0	2,437	140,126
4	2,678	4,823	255	448	131	5,209	140,703
5	2,678	7,388	441	1,321	402	8,230	141,762
6	2,678	10,009	634	2,771	876	11,518	143,405
7	2,678	12,681	843	4,778	1,568	15,093	145,621
8	2,678	15,400	1,068	7,347	2,504	18,972	148,415
9	2,678	17,833	1,307	10,481	3,707	22,848	151,788
10	2,678	20,318	1,563	14,177	5,201	27,082	155,740
11	2,678	22,851	1,829	18,436	7,010	31,690	160,265
12	2,678	25,432	2,007	23,245	9,156	36,596	165,252
13	2,678	28,066	2,193	28,340	11,558	41,817	170,533
14	2,678	30,751	2,393	33,718	14,230	47,374	176,111
15	2,678	33,489	2,606	39,387	17,194	53,289	181,993
16	2,678	36,277	2,842	45,357	20,469	59,587	188,199
17	2,678	39,109	3,095	51,655	24,084	66,289	194,750
18	2,678	41,976	3,370	58,293	28,064	73,410	201,663
19	2,678	44,869	3,665	65,294	32,434	80,967	208,959
20	2,678	47,781	3,979	72,673	37,218	88,978	216,652
21	2,678	50,704	4,316	80,443	42,442	97,461	224,759
22	2,678	53,640	4,671	88,623	48,134	106,445	233,294
23	2,678	56,591	5,047	97,223	54,323	115,961	242,270
24	2,678	59,559	5,449	106,257	61,039	126,047	251,706
25	2,678	62,544	5,886	115,742	68,315	136,744	261,628
26	2,678	65,534	6,362	125,714	76,190	148,086	272,076
27	2,678	68,516	6,866	136,212	84,701	160,084	283,078
28	2,678	71,470	7,412	147,254	93,868	172,751	294,666
29	2,678	74,372	8,018	158,882	103,720	186,110	306,900
30	2,678	77,204	8,667	171,165	114,303	200,175	319,832

*Column (6) = (2) + (3) + (5)
†Column (7) = 140,000 + (3) + (4)

could be measured and/or removed by allowing the SL policyholder to borrow against the projected year-end dividend at the beginning of the year. Again, this is normally an issue only for fixed policy loan rates, where there might be an appreciable difference between the loan rate and the current market rate.

The remaining differences in total cash values are attributable to subtle differences in the interest crediting mechanics involved, the analysis of which is beyond the scope of this paper. Still, one should not be fooled or discouraged by the lack of a perfect equality between the consolidated values

TABLE 2

Segregated Life/IDBA Illustration; Face Amount = $140,000; Policy Loan Rate = 10%

Year	(1) Gross Premium	(2) Guaranteed Cash Value	(3) Total Dividends	(4) Paid-Up Additions	(5) PUA Cash Value	(6)* Annual Loan	(7)† End-Year Loan Balance	(8)‡ End-Year IDBA Balance	(9)§ Total Cash Value	(10)‖ Total Death Benefit
1	2,678	0	0	0	0	0	0	0	0	140,000
2	2,678	0	0	0	0	0	0	0	0	140,000
3	2,678	2,311	126	0	0	2,101	2,311	2,311	2,437	140,126
4	2,678	4,823	255	448	131	2,192	4,954	4,954	5,209	140,703
5	2,678	7,388	441	1,321	402	2,127	7,789	7,789	8,230	141,762
6	2,678	10,009	634	2,771	876	2,105	10,884	10,884	11,518	143,405
7	2,678	12,681	843	4,778	1,578	2,070	14,250	14,250	15,093	145,621
8	2,678	15,400	1,068	7,347	2,504	2,027	17,904	17,904	18,972	148,415
9	2,678	17,833	1,307	10,481	3,707	1,678	21,540	21,540	22,848	151,788
10	2,678	20,318	1,563	14,177	5,201	1,659	25,519	25,519	27,082	155,740
11	2,678	22,851	1,829	18,436	7,010	1,627	29,861	29,861	31,690	160,265
12	2,678	25,432	2,007	23,245	9,156	1,583	34,589	34,589	36,596	165,252
13	2,678	28,066	2,193	28,340	11,558	1,433	39,624	39,624	41,817	170,533
14	2,678	30,751	2,393	33,718	14,230	1,268	44,981	44,981	47,374	176,111
15	2,678	33,489	2,606	39,387	17,194	1,094	50,683	50,683	53,289	181,993
16	2,678	36,277	2,842	45,357	20,469	904	56,745	56,745	59,587	188,199
17	2,678	39,109	3,095	51,655	24,084	703	63,193	63,193	66,289	194,750
18	2,678	41,976	3,370	58,293	28,064	479	70,040	70,040	73,410	201,663
19	2,678	44,869	3,665	65,294	32,434	235	77,302	77,302	80,967	208,959
20	2,678	47,781	3,979	72,673	37,218	−31	84,999	84,999	88,978	216,652
21	2,678	50,704	4,316	80,443	42,442	−321	93,145	93,145	97,461	224,759
22	2,678	53,640	4,671	88,623	48,134	−624	101,774	101,774	106,445	233,294
23	2,678	56,591	5,047	97,223	54,323	−943	110,914	110,914	115,961	242,270
24	2,678	59,559	5,449	106,257	61,039	−1,279	120,598	120,598	126,047	251,706
25	2,678	62,544	5,886	115,742	68,315	−1,636	130,858	130,858	136,744	261,628
26	2,678	65,534	6,362	125,714	76,190	−2,019	141,724	141,724	148,086	272,076
27	2,678	68,516	6,866	136,212	84,701	−2,435	153,217	153,217	160,084	283,078
28	2,678	71,470	7,412	147,254	93,868	−2,909	165,338	165,338	172,751	294,666
29	2,678	74,372	8,018	158,882	103,720	−3,437	178,092	178,092	186,110	306,900
30	2,678	77,204	8,667	171,165	114,303	−3,994	191,508	191,508	200,175	319,832

*Column (6) = $[(7)_t/1.1] - (7)_{t-1}$

†Column (7) = (2) + (5)

‡Column (8) = $[(8)_{t-1} + (6)_t] \times 1.1$

§Column (9) = (8) + (3)

‖Column (10) = 140,000 + (4) + (8) + (3) − (7)

TABLE 3

SEGREGATED LIFE/IDBA ILLUSTRATION; FACE AMOUNT = $140,000; POLICY LOAN RATE = 8%

Year	(1) Gross Premium	(2) Guaranteed Cash Value	(3) Total Dividends	(4) Paid-Up Additions	(5) PUA Cash Value	(6)* Annual Loan	(7)† End-Year Loan Balance	(8)‡ End-Year IDBA Balance	(9)§ Total Cash Value	(10)‖ Total Death Benefit
1	2,678	0	0	0	0	0	0	0	0	140,000
2	2,678	0	0	0	0	0	0	0	0	140,000
3	2,678	2,311	60	0	0	2,140	2,311	2,354	2,414	140,103
4	2,678	4,823	121	214	63	2,212	4,886	5,023	5,145	140,473
5	2,678	7,388	254	629	191	2,132	7,579	7,871	8,124	141,174
6	2,678	10,009	391	1,463	462	2,116	10,471	10,986	11,376	142,369
7	2,678	12,681	536	2,701	887	2,092	13,568	14,385	14,921	144,055
8	2,678	15,400	691	4,334	1,477	2,059	16,877	18,089	18,780	146,237
9	2,678	17,833	854	6,362	2,250	1,719	20,083	21,788	22,642	148,921
10	2,678	20,318	1,023	8,776	3,219	1,711	23,538	25,849	26,872	152,110
11	2,678	22,851	1,192	11,564	4,397	1,692	27,248	30,295	31,487	155,803
12	2,678	25,432	1,266	14,700	5,790	1,662	31,223	35,153	36,419	159,896
13	2,678	28,066	1,339	17,915	7,306	1,529	35,372	40,350	41,689	164,232
14	2,678	30,751	1,416	21,199	8,947	1,385	39,698	45,909	47,325	168,826
15	2,678	33,489	1,500	24,555	10,719	1,236	44,208	51,859	53,359	173,705
16	2,678	36,277	1,593	27,991	12,632	1,077	48,908	58,230	59,822	178,905
17	2,678	39,109	1,693	31,520	14,696	911	53,805	65,055	66,748	184,463
18	2,678	41,976	1,802	35,151	16,923	731	58,899	72,364	74,166	190,418
19	2,678	44,869	1,916	38,893	19,319	535	64,188	80,189	82,104	196,810
20	2,678	47,781	2,037	42,750	21,894	325	69,674	88,565	90,602	203,678
21	2,678	50,704	2,167	46,726	24,653	100	75,356	97,532	99,699	211,068
22	2,678	53,640	2,298	50,833	27,609	−126	81,249	107,146	109,445	219,029
23	2,678	56,591	2,436	55,065	30,767	−362	87,358	117,463	119,899	227,606
24	2,678	59,559	2,580	59,424	34,136	−604	93,695	128,546	131,125	236,855
25	2,678	62,544	2,738	63,915	37,725	−854	100,268	140,461	143,199	246,846
26	2,678	65,534	2,915	68,554	41,547	−1,119	107,081	153,277	156,192	257,664
27	2,678	68,516	3,097	73,364	45,620	−1,400	114,136	167,064	170,161	269,389
28	2,678	71,470	3,294	78,343	49,941	−1,719	121,411	181,880	185,174	282,106
29	2,678	74,372	3,520	83,511	54,517	−2,069	128,889	197,792	201,312	295,934
30	2,678	77,204	3,762	88,903	59,369	−2,432	136,574	214,896	218,659	310,988

*Column (6) = $[(7)_t/1.08] - (7)_{t-1}$

†Column (7) = (2) + (5)

‡Column (8) = $[(8)_{t-1} + (6)_t] \times 1.1$

§Column (9) = (8) + (3)

‖Column (10) = 140,000 + (4) + (8) + (3) − (7)

368

of WL and SL/IDBA under the same assumptions. Many of these differences are confined to fixed policy loan rates, while others are either trivial or can be designed away in one fashion or another. In any event, these differences should not have any significance in the marketplace.

II. WHERE TODAY'S CVLI PRODUCT FALLS SHORT

What follows is an itemization of 13 problems with the present form of CVLI. Each problem is briefly discussed, including how or why the proposed form of CVLI may be better equipped to deal with it.

Certain Fundamental Trends in CVLI Sales and In Force Are Disturbing

This statement is based on (1) recent declines in the growth rate of new ordinary insurance volume written, (2) the growth in ordinary life premium relative to the growth in ordinary life insurance in force, and (3) the growth in ordinary life reserves relative to the growth in ordinary life insurance in force.

From 1980 to 1985 the amount of ordinary life purchased grew at an annual rate of 18.8%. This growth rate contrasts sharply with the six-year period from 1985 to 1991, when the annual rate of growth averaged only 2.3%.[3] The high interest rates of the early 1980s combined with the early popularity of UL clearly drove the flurry of sales in the first half of the decade. Also, many of the sales in the early 1980s constituted replacement sales, both external and internal, which helped inflate the growth rate.

Not only did the sales growth rate slow down dramatically, but so did the growth of ordinary premium in force relative to the amount of ordinary insurance in force. The amount of ordinary insurance in force increased by a factor of 2.87 ($1.98 trillion to $5.68 trillion) for the 10-year period ending in 1991, while the corresponding premium in force increased by a factor of only 1.82 ($34.5 to $62.8 billion).[4] This is consistent with the fact that more term, flexible-premium UL, and low-premium WL are being written in place of the traditional high-premium WL contract. In fact, the slower growth in in-force premium has occurred despite the fact that first-year premium *has*

---

[3] AMERICAN COUNCIL OF LIFE INSURANCE. *1992 Life Insurance Fact Book*. Washington, D.C., 1992.
[4] Ibid.

kept pace with the volume of business written. This could well be attribut-able to the fact that premium payments for UL tend to be both greater in the first year and less over the long run than those for traditional WL.

Finally, ordinary life insurance reserves have increased by a factor of only 1.87 ($184 billion to $344 billion) for the same ten years, compared with the 2.87 factor increase in the amount of ordinary life in force. This means the average reserve per face amount declined from 9.3% to 6.1% in just 10 years. While this is consistent with the trend towards lower-premium term insurance, it also suggests that the average age of policies might have short-ened due to replacement activity during the period. One problem with re-placements, of course, is that, even though premium income may be main-tained, a large portion of existing cash values can exit insurance companies in the process.

What will be the impact of SL/IDBA on these CVLI sales and premium trends? While the total impact is impossible to predict with any certainty, a few general observations can be made with some confidence.

First, it is likely that SL/IDBA will also appeal to those who might oth-erwise favor variable life (VL) or variable universal life (VUL). Of course, SL/IDBA goes a step further by offering a virtually unlimited universe of investment choices, while VL and VUL only offer a few. Perhaps more significant than that, however, is that SL takes advantage of a much larger distribution system than VL and VUL, because any licensed insurance agent can sell SL, while only a National Association of Securities Dealers (NASD) registered representative can sell variable products. (It is unlikely that the NASD will claim jurisdiction over the SL product, because SL is really just a narrower form of traditional CVLI with policy loans as their primary in-vestments. Furthermore, there is no need or justification for the NASD or SEC to govern any IDBA products that do not already fall within their control, because it is not those products that are changing, but rather the context within which they are being purchased, such context having new tax ramifications.) An SL product is also much simpler to bring to market than SEC-registered products because of the substantial time and expense asso-ciated with an SEC filing. Therefore, at least in theory, SL/IDBA will out-perform VL or VUL, perhaps even making them somewhat obsolete, by virtue of its unlimited investment choice, wider distribution channel, and lower cost.

When sales of CVLI are being measured, it is important to distinguish between volume and premium. Ever since the advent of UL and VUL, pre-mium income and profits for future years have become less certain. The trends are clear, however: premiums are typically dropping off dramatically and continually in renewal years. The result of offering this extra freedom to policyholders is that permanent UL coverage is being replaced by quasi-term, quasi-permanent, low-cash-value coverage. SL presents life companies with an opportunity to reverse that trend, *by giving the policyholder more investment freedom in exchange for less premium freedom.*

The potential demand for SL/IDBA does not come solely from its value as an alternative to today's variable life products. Several other factors make this product more attractive to the insurance public and perhaps to life companies and regulators as well. The separation of mortality and investment components, both from a purchase and replacement perspective, should increase competition and benefit the consumer. The possibility of lower net insurance costs for a contract held until death or at least for several years, in exchange for higher charges in the event of early surrender, may appeal to many insurance consumers who view their coverage as a long-term commitment anyway. SL/IDBA packages may also have either lower or deferred acquisition costs, making the SL product or the SL/IDBA package more competitive than the present-day WL. Perhaps the ability to diversify the equity in a WL policy among two or more companies will appeal to a public that has been stung with some unexpected company failures.

Profit Margins Are Smaller Than Historical Margins

This fact has been hurting the industry for more than a decade now. Several factors have contributed. In the late 1970s, a Federal Trade Commission (FTC) report highlighted the low historical returns of a typical WL policy. This came at a time when interest rates were escalating to historical highs. More and more savings dollars were funneled into mutual funds and annuities over the next several years, reducing the amount that might otherwise have gone into CVLI. At the same time, UL made an impressive debut, but again at the expense of traditional WL dollars. This happened in three ways: the redirecting of new premium dollars into UL, the funding of new UL policies by leveraging or cashing in existing CVLI policies, and the cutting back of future renewal premiums due to UL's flexible premium structure.

UL, interest-sensitive life, traditional life, and annuities now all competed against one another in a crowded playing field, fueled by high credited rates that were also highly visible for the first time. Even some traditional life products began advertising the underlying interest rates in their dividend scales. Nonsmoker pricing was another innovation that helped squeeze margins. Companies were also aggressively pricing policies by projecting a reduction in unit expenses through future growth. Many of these companies did not achieve their targeted sales, and this resulted in lower realized margins than the original pricing implied.

In short, the life insurance industry became much more competitive in the 1980s. A product revolution in a period of high interest rates spawned massive, and often justifiable, replacement activity, and companies were pressured to price aggressively to maintain market shares. Lower margins in products were a natural by-product of such an environment.

The precise impact of SL/IDBA upon profitability, or sales, is difficult to gauge with any certainty. Part of the difficulty in assessing this is that the sale of an SL policy is accompanied by an IDBA sale that may or may not be generated from the same company. Therefore, from an insurance company's perspective, it may appear more appropriate to compare the present-day CVLI product directly with the SL product alone. From the vantage point of all financial institutions that may be writing SL and IDBA contracts, however, the proper comparison is SL versus the combined SL/IDBA package. That being said, what is the expected impact on profitability?

Long-term persistency should be better in two respects. First, to the extent that SL displaces a flexible-premium sale, premium income will be higher. Second, segregation of the mortality and investment components allows replacement of only the SL contract or the IDBA, without requiring the replacement of both. Since many present-day replacements are rooted in policyholder dissatisfaction with the investment performance of the current contract, or expectations of better returns elsewhere, SL contracts may well be spared the bulk of future replacement activity. Though differences may still exist in the interest components of different companies' SL products, such differences will likely be smaller and less apt to be misunderstood or misrepresented in policy illustrations. The credited rates for SL products will hinge directly on the SL policy loan rates, which are clearly visible and, in many cases, the same from one company to the next. (In theory, the credited rate embedded in an SL dividend scale would equal the SL policy loan rate, whether it is fixed or variable, less an interest margin.) In addition, once an SL policy and IDBA policy are issued, virtually all the investment "action" will be in the IDBA, keeping most of the policyholder's attention focused away from the largely predetermined investment performance of the SL product. However, for those SL policies that do eventually get replaced, whether internally or externally, there is a good probability that the policy will be in less of a deficit position, if in one at all, by virtue of having incurred lower acquisition costs than its present-day counterpart (the likelihood of this occurring is discussed later in this paper).

Now consider the expected profitability of an SL product vis-à-vis a traditional WL product. Suppose that SL acquisition costs become lower than those of WLs, because some of the pressure to pay compensation is absorbed by the IDBAs. Therefore, we have an up-front cost savings. What is not clear, however, is how the interest margins will be affected. Nominal spreads expected on a WL policy may be subject to fluctuation because of the particular investment strategy and the methodology for resetting dividend scales, especially the degree to which new money rates are taken into account. SL interest margins should be more stable, although perhaps somewhat lower, since SL investment income (policy loan interest) is riskless and very predictable. (Note that the SL policy need not be participating. It could be participating in the traditional sense, that is, through dividends, participating through excess interest credits, or simply not participating at all.)

How much lower SL interest margins will be is an interesting question. One argument that lower spreads will prevail is that the IDBA will also earn spreads and that competition will keep the total spreads between the SL and IDBA commensurate with present WL margins. An argument against that is that the SL product, with its lower acquisition costs and riskless assets, will be competitive enough with WL even with the same interest margins as WL (after adjusting for credit risk in the WL assets). After all, the IDBAs cannot exist unless the SL policy is sold first, which may allow the SL product to command a premium margin. Another argument against lower SL margins is that policy loans currently command a higher spread than nonloaned reserves, even though their proceeds generally cannot be invested on a tax-deferred basis.

Even with the uncertainty on SL acquisition costs and interest margins, the competitiveness of the SL product seems to hold promise. Even if acquisition costs and interest margins end up on the high side, that is, commensurate with WL, the product will still be competitive with WL, and agents will have the additional incentive of associated IDBA sales. If either compensation or interest margins come down, then from the policyholder's viewpoint the SL looks even better next to traditional WL. The total impact on profitability for insurance companies that sell SL products is indeed difficult to predict because of the many moving parts. One plausible result is that *SL products* will have lower interest margins, which are partially offset by lower compensation. The lower profit margins may or may not be overcome by greater sales or better persistency. Of course, all this ignores the impact of IDBA sales in the same company.

To better understand all the potential factors influencing profitability, let us consider some formulaic expressions, albeit somewhat simplified, for both traditional WL and SL/IDBA. The formulas are not time-specific, but simply reflect the main components of profitability. The periodic profits for a WL product with face amount F can be expressed as the sum of the following four components:

$$WL \text{ Profits} = F \times (1000 - TV) \times \Delta q \quad \text{(mortality)}$$
$$+ F \times TV \times \Delta i \quad \text{(interest)}$$
$$+ F \times (GP - NP - Exp) \text{ (loading)}$$
$$+ F \times (TV - CV) \times w \quad \text{(surrender)}.$$

Similarly,

$$SL \text{ Profits} = F \times (1000 - TV') \times \Delta q'$$
$$+ F \times TV' \times \Delta i'$$
$$+ F \times (GP' - NP' - Exp')$$
$$+ F \times (TV' - CV') \times w',$$

where all primed symbols represent the corresponding SL parameters.

To facilitate the comparison, consider an SL product derived directly from a WL product, so that all product values remain unchanged; that is, $TV'=TV$, $GP'=GP$, $NP'=NP$, and $CV'=CV$. If we then assume that experience is the same with respect to mortality rates (q) and lapse rates (w), then the excess of SL profits over WL profits reduces to:

$$SL \text{ profits} - WL \text{ profits} = F \times TV \times (\Delta i' - \Delta i)$$
$$- F \times (Exp' - Exp).$$

IDBA profits can be expressed in a similar form:

$$IDBA \text{ profits} = F \times TV'' \times \Delta i''$$
$$- F \times TV'' \times Exp''$$
$$+ F \times (TV'' - CV'') \times w'',$$

where all double-primed symbols refer to IDBA parameters, and TV'' and Exp'' are expressed per \$1000 of SL face amount.

The term $(F \times TV'')$ should approximate $(F \times TV')$, and we can define IDBA surrender charges as:

$$SC'' = F \times (TV'' - CV'').$$

Then, by making these substitutions, the excess of the sum of SL and corresponding IDBA profits over WL profits can be expressed as follows:

$$(SL + IDBA) \text{ profits } - WL \text{ profits } = F \times TV \times [(\Delta i' + \Delta i'') - \Delta i]$$
$$- F \times [(Exp' + Exp'') - Exp]$$
$$+ SC'' \times w''.$$

These somewhat simplified formulas suggest that the interplay between interest margins and expenses (including compensation) may be the key to the relative profitability picture. If an even further simplifying assumption is made that $\Delta i'' \approx \Delta i$, then it could be argued that SL interest margins and IDBA surrender charges will be available to fund the *excess* of total $(SL+IDBA)$ expenses over WL expenses, while keeping absolute profits the same. Of course, if any of the simplifying assumptions is eliminated, the potential change in profitability becomes more difficult to quantify. Unfortunately, the mere presence of so many variables in the profitability equation, as illustrated in the above expressions, will make it difficult to reduce the expected change in profitability to a simple expression.

The overall impact on insurance company profits is perhaps most difficult to predict because of the likely redistribution of investment funds among insurance companies, banks, mutual fund companies, and other investment institutions. First, it seems almost certain that the flow of funds into insurance companies will increase, because many sales of fixed-premium SL products will likely be displacing term and flexible-premium insurance product sales. There will also be new incentive for money that is currently invested outside the insurance industry to be redeployed as part of an SL/IDBA package to gain tax-preferenced treatment. Meeting the net amount at risk requirements may suddenly seem like less of an obstacle because of the greatly expanded choice of IDBA investment vehicles.

What is much less clear, though, is what will happen to the money after the SL policies are sold. Insurance companies will no longer have captive funds to invest, but instead will have to compete for the funds with mutual fund companies, banks, and other institutions that can now offer tax-deferred accumulation products in the form of IDBAs. Figure 1 helps illustrate the general redistribution of funds that will occur. The arrows at the top of the chart indicate the current general drift of funds away from fixed-premium permanent insurance products towards flexible-premium and term insurance products and noninsurance products.

FIGURE 1

REDISTRIBUTION OF FUNDS AMONG INSURANCE/SAVINGS PRODUCTS

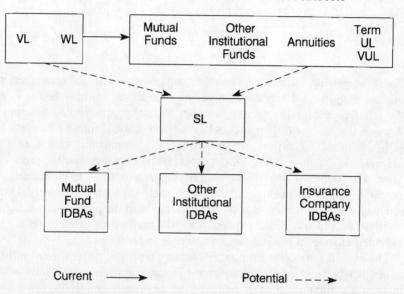

In trying to assess the impact of this redirection of funds attributable to IDBAs, any analysis should take into account that a redistribution has already been and is still taking place today (away from WL and VL, as illustrated in the top portion of the figure). This trend, and efforts to thwart it, have been manifesting themselves through risky investments, aggressive and misleading sales tactics, and excessive unit costs.

Insurance companies will have the first crack at selling IDBA products. Effective marketing or packaging of IDBAs with SLs, perhaps with package discounts, may enable them to achieve a large market share and bring more money under management. A marketing strategy that pays different compensation on IDBA sales funded by the same company's SL product than for "independent" IDBA sales has interesting possibilities. Paying lower compensation on internal IDBA sales can be successful if the company has enough investment vehicles to attract the policyholder (and the agent) and sales become easier because of a packaged approach. An alternative strategy is to pay equal compensation for internal and external IDBA sales, but offer a more competitive product inside. Still another strategy is one in which higher compensation is paid on internal IDBA sales because the company believes that targeting packaged sales will be more profitable.

The challenge for insurance companies is to optimize total profits from SL, internal IDBA and external IDBA sales, given that the unit profits can vary widely from each other and from traditional WL, and that the sales volume of each depends on how well positioned the company is, from both a distribution and product perspective, to capture market share in each product area. Even assuming that insurance companies wind up managing less money than now, by losing funds to outside IDBA contracts, they will still command premium margins on SL policy loans. In short, they may earn less from managing money, but more from renting it out.

In summary, SLs may enhance profitability through greater sales (both volume and premium), greater persistency, lower acquisition costs, and margins for rental of IDBA funds. However, insurers will also have to successfully negotiate their way through a new environment in which they face new competition in their roles as money managers. Companies that can attract equal or larger shares of investment funds then they do now will enjoy a considerably stronger profit outlook in this new environment. Companies that are unable to attract investment funds or that desire to focus on the SL business may need to reorganize their cost structures so that their SL profit margins adequately cover fixed expenses and capital requirements.

The Assets Backing CVLI Policies Have a Low Common Stock Component, Holding Down Long-Term Returns

It is well documented that stocks outperform bonds over the long haul with greater volatility in the short run. Insurance companies, under the burden of nonforfeiture laws and statutory accounting, have usually backed general account CVLI policies with a high proportion of fixed-income assets (that is, bonds and mortgages). The book values of these assets are much more stable than those of common stock, and therefore they do not expose the insurer to as much short-term risk. However, this added safety for the insurance companies comes at a price to the policyholders. Their life insurance purchase generally is based on a long-term need that might be better funded by common stocks, just as retirement funds for people 20 or more years from retirement are heavily stock weighted.

The SL/IDBA package allows the insured to cure this problem, just as does VL, but SL/IDBA offers many more investment choices and potentially unlimited flexibility in moving from one to another. Of course, heavier investing in common stock brings with it the risk that the IDBA's value at the time of the insured's death will be less that the outstanding SL policy loan balance, resulting in a net death benefit that is less than the face amount. Perhaps an SL rider can cover any such shortfall, just as VL policies typically guarantee a minimum death benefit equaling the face amount.

The tremendous growth of mutual funds, combined with the greater historical returns of common stocks relative to bonds, suggests that stocks should somehow play a greater role in the CVLI business. The SL/IDBA product allows this to happen to a greater extent than VL and VUL, which thus far have commanded only a small share.

The Asset Portfolios Backing CVLI Policies Sometimes Are Laden with Undue Risks

To attain yields necessary to support dividend scales, many investment managers have been or are under pressure to take credit risk in the form of junk bond investments. Lack of diversification sometimes prevails with larger than prudent exposure to any one credit or class of investment. Liquidity and refinancing risks have hurt some insurers that were heavily weighted in commercial mortgages. Prepayment risk is the newest kind of investment risk that is common in pass-through securities and exotic collateralized mortgage obligations (CMOs), both of which might be material components of an insurer's portfolio.

Some risk-taking is necessary to achieve returns in excess of Treasury returns. However, the opportunity for imprudent risk-taking certainly exists and unfortunately has been exercised in many instances. Without control of the policy's underlying investments, the policyholder is at the mercy of the insurance company's investment policy and performance. SL gives the insured control over cash value funds; thus the insured has the capability to achieve great diversification and liquidity and avoid undue concentration in certain asset classes that have proved to be the undoing of some insurers. If by no other means, *the insured achieves greater diversification by spreading cash values among two or more institutions.*

Of course, SL may be a double-edged sword that allows the insured to make imprudent investments inherently riskier than a CVLI policy would have allowed. Diversification of investment funds is not automatic and requires some initiative and prudence on the part of the policyholder and/or the writing agent. Even a well-thought-out, diversified investment portfolio does not assure the policyholder better returns than he or she might have had with a WL policy. Consequently, the SL product is appropriate only for those who understand the contractual differences, the ongoing policyholder responsibilities, the investment risks, and all the potential tax effects. Some safeguards will probably be necessary to prevent an unsophisticated prospect from being led into a contract without knowing that investment responsibilities have been shifted to him or her. At a minimum, a signed statement acknowledging the policyholder's duties and the general consequences of failure to invest the funds or poor investment performance will probably be necessary.

Cash Surrender and Policy Loan Rights Expose Companies to Liquidity and Run Risk

The ability of a policyholder to literally cash in a CVLI policy at any time or, alternatively, to borrow against it creates a burden for the writing company. These policyholder options make the timing of policy payouts difficult to project, but at the very least payouts will be accelerated. Both the greater uncertainty and acceleration of benefit payments create a greater need for liquidity in insurance companies' investment portfolios. However, the virtually unlimited access that a policyholder has to the policy's equity, whether through cash surrender or policy loans, cannot be fully hedged by the writing company without forgoing desirable investment opportunities that may be somewhat illiquid. In extreme situations, these policyholder options can cause a run on the bank, where policyholder surrenders become contagious and snowball until either illiquid assets have to be disposed of, possibly at fire sale prices, or regulators step in to help stop the bleeding.

With the SL/IDBA package, the policyholders give up some of those privileges, although the extent of the forfeiture varies from none at all to complete. Because the SL contract itself is always fully leveraged, the SL writing company is fully protected from any run risk. Furthermore, the company benefits because mostly risk-free assets back the contracts, which appropriately carry a zero C-1 factor for risk-based capital requirements (policy loans will be entirely risk-free and constitute most of the SL policy's assets).

The IDBA writers, on the other hand, can offer a variety of products, some of which may grant policyholders full and immediate access to their funds, and others that may impose restrictions, perhaps going so far as permitting no withdrawals prior to death. All the IDBA products will be backed by invested assets (except for IDBA policy loans), which expose the writer to asset and interest rate risk. However, IDBA interest rate and run risk will be more controllable through product provisions, greater diversification of policyholders and associated SL contracts, and greater diversification by the writing agent.

For example, if company X has written SL business and runs into financial difficulty, the IDBA contract-holders who are associated with company X's SL policies, but who have invested away from company X, need not panic because (1) their money is not held by company X, and (2) a potential remedy, if necessary, is to replace the SL policy, which need not affect the associated IDBA(s). Of course, company X's IDBA policyholders may be under pressure to pull their money out. Company X, in this case, can benefit by having written IDBA business through more agents, or perhaps by placing some IDBA business directly through the home office, which leaves it less exposed to agent-induced replacement. The interest rate risk and run risk for IDBAs will be further mitigated by restrictions in fund transfers or early withdrawal or surrender. IDBA penalties will come on top of penalties already built into the cash value scales of the underlying SL products, so the combination will provide more protection to the IDBA writer. Of course, such IDBA products will have to compete with other IDBA products that are virtually penalty-free, have various degrees of interest rate risk, and pay various amounts of compensation, so any one IDBA product will look quite different from the next.

In a nutshell, writers of SL and IDBA products can place themselves virtually anywhere on the risk spectrum they choose to be. Some companies may choose to focus on SL business alone; some, including noninsurers, may focus on IDBAs; the rest may pursue both markets. However, a competitive marketplace and risk-based capital constraints may prevent some insurers from achieving a desired IDBA presence.

Policy Illustrations Are Not Standardized, Are Often Misleading, and Are Viewed by Many As Not Credible

As interest rates hit new highs in the early 1980s and UL joined the fray, competition for new premium heated up. During this period, illustration development sometimes became more important to companies than product development. At the heart of the matter was the illustration of values based upon current dividend scales, which themselves were often based upon the assumption of high interest rates continuing indefinitely. Vanishing-premium payment schemes both capitalized on and were highly dependent upon such dividend scales for this period remaining intact. Now that several years have passed, the original projections of most dividend scales have been lowered, and projected vanish years for such illustrations are not being realized. Many policyholders who did not really understand the vanish concept are now receiving nasty surprises as premiums do not vanish or perhaps do so only temporarily only to reappear at some later date.

Illustrations have been and continue to be a problem, because companies sometimes gain unfair advantage over one another, and policyholders are being misled in the sales process. Many discussions and proposals have left these tough problems largely unsolved.

SL policies go to the heart of the problem and *eliminate the primary cause of the policy illustration problem, that is, questionable interest rate assumptions behind the illustrations.* SL policies short-circuit the inherent difficulty in setting dividend scales by eliminating a key unknown, the policy's gross investment earnings rate for all years. (Actually, this is strictly true only for policies with fixed loan rates. But for both fixed and variable-loan-rate policies, the net dividend credited rate can be clearly defined as the policy loan rate less some specified spread.) For an unbundled form of SL, the excess interest component, rather than the dividend scale, takes on a more predictable form.

The important point is that policy illustrations, or at least their interest components, may become more standardized because they will most likely be defined as a strict function of the policy loan rate and a spread. Perhaps the spread incorporated in the scale will be required to be level to avoid manipulation and facilitate policy comparisons. Furthermore, illustrations that combine the SL product with a potential IDBA, if permitted, can be standardized by requiring that the IDBA be illustrated only with industry standard assumptions (similar to VL illustration requirements). While this does not provide the prospective policyholder with enough information to properly evaluate his or her choice of IDBAs, it allows the choice of an SL product to be more focused and less biased by an investment earnings assumption. These illustrations can be supplemented by IDBA-specific illustrations, which will continue to be governed by existing regulations on the various products that fill the IDBA role.

SL/IDBA will by no means eliminate all illustration problems. The challenge of determining appropriate illustration assumptions may simply be shifted to IDBA products, rather than eliminated. Still, it appears that breaking up CVLI into *simpler* components (that is, SL/IDBA) will enhance the prospects of acceptable illustration solutions. In fact, the introduction of SL/IDBA will no doubt provide further impetus to address the current lack of uniformity in illustrating various noninsurance products that may fill the IDBA role.

Dividend Scales Are Incomprehensible to the Public

Regardless of how a company's scale is derived, the policyholder usually is not aware of the company's gross earned rate, retained interest spread, and net credited rate. UL has improved this situation somewhat by featuring a visible credited rate as a major component of the fund accumulation process. However, traditional life dividend scales are more difficult to understand, due to their bundled structure, and companies generally do not advertise their underlying credited interest rate, even though they could. Changes in the dividend scale can occur without a policyholder even being aware of the changes or the new credited rate. In many cases, such credited rates are nonlevel by policy year, which makes them more difficult to quote and compare with other dividend scales.

In any event, the lack of a visible credited rate increases the probability of greater inequities among blocks of policies. Such inequities may be completely unintentional, but nevertheless can arise because maintaining equity among such blocks can be a complex process and because a policyholder can neither easily assess nor intelligently react to his or her policy's performance. In short, competitive forces alone are not sufficient to ensure equity among traditional WL blocks.

The dividend scales for SL products should be somewhat easier to comprehend than their WL counterparts for much the same reason that illustration difficulties should ease. The net credited interest rate embedded in the scale can be clearly defined in terms of the policy loan rate less a spread.

The spread itself can even be contractually guaranteed. Therefore, the component of the scale that is likely to fluctuate the most for a WL policy and cause the most surrender activity will be much easier to follow for an SL policy. In fact, there may be little or no interest change in an SL dividend scale over the life of the policy with a fixed policy loan rate.

This is not to say that the derivation of SL dividends will become crystal clear to the policyholders. If the SL product has the traditional bundled structure, the components of the total dividend will still be unclear, even though the interest component will be easier to understand. If the SL product takes on an unbundled form, then the product will give the policyholder the advantage of clearly identifiable product components, as well as greater insight into the future performance of the interest component.

Nonforfeiture Requirements Constrain Product Development and Investment Strategies

It might help to first revisit the reasons that cash surrender values exist today. The combination of level premiums, increasing mortality, and an endowment provision at some high age results in equity building up in the contract. This equity rightfully belongs to the policyowner, who is responsible for paying premiums each year. But exactly how should this equity be determined? Current nonforfeiture laws allow companies to withhold from cash values an amount that crudely approximates unamortized acquisition costs. Some laws allow additional market value adjustments that approximate the gain or loss in specific fixed rate bonds that would be attributable to changes in interest rates. Aside from that, however, the nonforfeiture laws effectively shield the policyholder from principal risk by guaranteeing a minimum rate that must be credited to net premiums paid into the contract, even though investments backing the policy could well be subject to principal risk.

While the existence of nonforfeiture laws has much merit generally, the presence of cash surrender values can add significant cost to the product. Having to provide cash surrender benefits normally affects both the required liquidity and maturity targets of an insurer's corresponding investment strategy. A company either has to invest in shorter term securities or else subject itself to greater interest rate risk from policyholder disintermediation. The reduction or elimination of cash surrender benefits, while possibly leaving intact reduced paid-up or extended term, could reduce the long-term cost significantly and open up the door for new product designs.

So how will an SL/IDBA environment facilitate new product development and the relaxation of investment constraints? SL products, for the most part, will not provide the answer, because SL products essentially already exist (except for their unique policy loan provisions) and would be governed by today's nonforfeiture requirements. The complimentary IDBA products, on the other hand, are another story. The total surrender and loan provisions for an SL/IDBA package will be determined by the corresponding provisions of both the SL and the IDBA contracts.

Various degrees of investment risk can be passed on to the policyholder through different IDBA structures. Some IDBAs may be supported by fixed-income assets and offer specific interest rate guarantees. Some may be equity-oriented without any guarantees, while others may have some equity exposure and principal guarantees. A family of IDBA funds could be marketed with periodic penalty-free transfers allowed between funds, perhaps with surrender penalties imposed only on external surrenders. Some may make surrender penalties contingent upon whether the SL product is being surrendered (as opposed to an IDBA exchange). An extreme product may forbid surrenders entirely, or perhaps allow only loans with 401(k)-type requirements.

All these potential contractual arrangements will allow wide latitude to the IDBA writers in developing products and investment strategies. While no changes in life product nonforfeiture laws are necessary for SLs, some potential IDBA products may require changes in nonforfeiture laws governing them. Such a product environment represents a compromise, of sorts, on cash surrender benefits. The SL issuing company will be required to provide the same minimum level of benefits as it does today, but policyholders could voluntarily give up some of those benefits through their choice of the IDBA vehicle. The SL/IDBA environment will therefore encompass elements of both traditional CVLI and VL products, while allowing much freedom in specific product characteristics and investment strategies.

Front-Loaded Commission Structures and Levels Have Been Difficult to Change

CVLI commissions have always been heavily loaded in the first contract year. Attempts to levelize commissions, to both lower surplus strain and provide greater incentive to the agent for long-term policy persistency, have been greatly resisted by agent groups. UL's flexible premium structure has also created problems because many companies have paid out first-year commissions that were close to WL commission levels, only to have premium persistency drop considerably after the first year or two, which effectively turned the policies into little more than prefunded term insurance.

The continued use of front-loaded commission scales may be hurting life insurance products in their competition for savings dollars. Mutual funds and annuities often have level asset-based sales charges and commissions. These lower front-end compensation schemes also create less incentive for churning. In the early 1980s, many life insurance companies felt compelled to pay almost full first-year commissions on internally replaced business (policyholders switching over to new nonsmoker policies or UL policies) even though no new premium resulted for fear of external replacements that paid full first-year commissions. Such actions helped weakened life insurers' capital positions in the 1980s and artificially boosted sales levels.

The implementation of the SL/IDBA concept may succeed in restructuring agent compensation on WL sales where previous efforts have failed. Breaking the WL sale into two sales will certainly force some compensation restructuring, but the exact degree and nature of the restructuring are debatable. Because the same premium dollars (as WL) will be split between two contracts, one might initially expect that:

- The total compensation for the SL/IDBA will be commensurate with WL compensation.
- SL compensation will be somewhat lower than WL compensation.

Certain factors, however, may tend to keep SL compensation close to WL levels and push the total (SL + IDBA) compensation above that for WL:

- SL may be able to compete quite well with WL even with WL's acquisition costs.
- Better SL persistency (versus WL) is expected because IDBAs will bear much of the replacement risk.
- SL's priority status over the IDBA (that is, the IDBA cannot exist without the SL contract) may allow agents to command higher compensation. Stated another way, the SL sale assures the IDBA sale, so the SL agent should be compensated accordingly.
- Two sales presumably will require more time and effort than one, justifying greater *total* compensation than WL.

On the other hand, the fact that SL will compete with WL for premium dollars, and that IDBAs will face stiff competition on their own crowded playing field, will put downward pressure on compensation within each product line. At the very least, SL compensation alone will not exceed WL compensation because interest margins will not support it, and the potential for IDBA compensation makes that unnecessary.

Regardless of the levels, some structural change is inevitable. IDBAs, both new designs and existing products, will have to compete for funds and pay compensation that both fits the product and appropriately complements SL compensation. In other words, compensation on IDBAs will be affected by what other similar IDBA products are paying (even in a non-IDBA role), as well as by how the total SL/IDBA compensation compares with WL compensation. It is unlikely that total compensation on an SL and IDBA sale would exceed the total compensation on two present-day sales, one being WL and the other being an IDBA-like product. Also, asset-based compensation for IDBAs will be easier to justify and implement, since front-loading probably will already exist on the SL contract and deposits into the IDBAs should grow over time (as SL cash value increases grow).

A significant advantage of an SL/IDBA environment is that costly wholesale replacement scenarios are less likely. When widespread systematic replacement occurred in the 1980s, brought on by the introduction of nonsmoker dividend scales and UL policies, many companies paid full, or close to full, first-year commissions on these new policies, even though they were often funded by an existing policy and no new premium. (In the case of external replacements, the new premium came at the expense of the company that wrote the original policy.) Companies in many cases may have felt they were held hostage by agents who made the case that first-year commissions were available across the street and that replacements were easily justified. The agent's leverage has proven to be powerful and arguably forced more compensation during the 1980s than justified by the volume of new premium.

Replacement activity associated with SLs and IDBAs will, at least in theory, be less driven by agents' compensation, and writing companies will be better protected from potential abuses. For example, a replacement of one IDBA fund with another, which will probably be the most common replacement, need not affect the existing SL policy in any way. If IDBA compensation is strictly asset-based, there will also be less agent motivation for such replacements and complete protection for IDBA writers from the cost of internal replacements.

In the event that an SL policy is replaced by another SL policy (a 1035 exchange), the existing SL company may still benefit from lower unamortized acquisition costs than with WL. But an SL replacement will face the hurdle of imposing new surrender charges on the policyholder (buried in the cash value schedules) on a product that is not giving the policyholder any additional investment advantages. This impediment may induce insurers to offer a higher early cash value SL product for replacement situations only, possibly coupled with lower agent compensation. In addition, the new SL company probably will not feel pressured to pay commissions on rollovers of existing cash values into the SL, because those funds will already reside in IDBAs and have generated commissions (and possibly continue to generate commissions).

In summary, it appears likely that breaking up the WL product will facilitate the breakup of the traditional WL commission structure and practices, and that competing market forces will determine where SL and IDBA compensation ultimately settles.

The Underlying Components of CVLI Are Inseparable

The insurance-buying public understands that a CVLI policy has underlying investment and mortality components. This understanding was heightened during the 1980s when UL flourished with its unbundled, high-interest component. For the first time policyholders clearly saw how much interest the policy was earning and how much they were being charged for mortality coverage and expenses.

This unbundling, however, is all appearance and no substance. UL is still a package deal—if you buy a company's product, you get the interest, mortality, and expense charges that the product packages together. You cannot buy the individual components alone. VL and VUL offer some choice on the investment component, but the policyholder is still tied to a company's mortality and expense charges. Similarly, once a policy has been bought, a 1035 exchange can be made only on the entire policy and not on the individual components.

The SL/IDBA package takes the next logical step, the physical unbundling of the interest component of CVLI. This true unbundling benefits the consumer in four clearly identifiable ways:

- Increased competition within each component will put downward pressure on the total cost of insurance.
- SL policies will have virtually no asset or interest rate risk associated with them; that is, SL companies will be selling lower risk policies.
- Wide latitude in the choice of IDBAs, each of which will have its own risk-return profile, will enable consumers to pursue greater long-term returns subject to their own risk tolerance.

- Selective replacement of "bad" components will prevail, instead of today's wasteful practice of total replacement.

Blocks of Whole Life Are Not Easily Sold

There may be several reasons for this. Valuation is made more difficult because of the uncertainty surrounding future dividend scales and policyholder behavior in different interest rate environments. On the asset side, there are probably more illiquid assets such as commercial mortgages, real estate, and certain private placements unattractive to a potential buyer. Another reason may be that annuity blocks, with their simpler asset and liability components, have lent themselves more readily to such transactions. Finally, all acquisitions will be more difficult to transact in the future, given the impending model legislation (and potential federal legislation) that will make it easier for policyholders to opt out of the transfer. While the lack of movement of WL blocks may not have been considered much of a problem to date, it may become more of a problem as many companies attempt to improve their balance sheets through block sales and acquisitions.

Blocks of SL policies will more readily lend themselves to acquisition by another company. Problem assets, which often pose a big obstacle for potential deals, will not be involved. The acquiring company will also avoid the due diligence normally required to assess the selling company's asset portfolio. The liabilities can also be analyzed with more precision because of a more predictable dividend scale for any given interest rate scenario. In fact, there may even be less uncertainty in evaluating SL blocks than annuity blocks, which are often involved in transactions today and which have a lot of disintermediation risk and uncertain credited rate formulas. Furthermore, SL acquisitions will allow companies to take more mortality risk and increase their base of insured lives, without simultaneously increasing their interest rate risk. In short, the SL product will be more of a commodity than WL.

Once SL blocks have reached a critical mass within the industry, they will become attractive acquisition candidates for companies that wish to lower their overall risk profile. Given this, some companies may originate SL policies with the intent of unloading them. However, any sale of a block of SL policies will be subject to each policyholder's consent. Consequently, this transfer of mortality and expense risk may be difficult to execute with sufficient policyholder consent unless the acquiring company has a superior rating. On the other hand, policyholders may find transfers of SL blocks less objectionable than annuity blocks, because no investment risk is being transferred and they may view the event as relatively low risk.

The Life Insurance Industry Has Been under Seemingly Constant Attack from Federal Regulators

Among the revenue-raising measures that passed over the last decade were the tightening of the definition of life insurance, lower reserves for tax purposes, greater taxes on certain distributions from life contracts, and the DAC tax. Other initiatives that have thus far failed include the elimination or restriction of deferred taxes on the inside buildup of both CVLI and deferred annuities. The attacks are likely to continue as federal officials scramble to raise revenue. The net effect is that these taxes can and already have hurt the competitiveness of life insurance products, both in an absolute sense and relative to other investment alternatives.

The security of the tax-deferred inside buildup remains debatable. There are, however, at least three reasons why the blessing of the SL/IDBA concept by Congress could further secure the tax-deferred inside buildup:

(1) Congress would be giving a vote of confidence to the tax-deferred inside buildup principle by opening it up to other financial institutions. To then turn around and attack it anytime soon would appear illogical and unlikely.

(2) Any subsequent attempts by Congress to tax the inside buildup would then likely face a united front comprising insurance, bank, and mutual fund institutions, whereas today these institutions are not allies on this issue. The insurance lobby is already powerful today. The introduction of SL/IDBA would, at least in theory, increase the strength of the opposition that Congress would run into if it decided to go after the inside buildup.

(3) Congress does not need to go after the inside buildup to increase tax revenue. Congress has been very successful over the past decade raiding the back of the fort, while most of the industry's defenses protect the front.

A counterargument to this is that, once Congress has leveled the playing field, it can more easily attack the inside buildup because it would not be extracting tax revenue excessively from any one industry in relation to others. Such a move would hurt life insurers more heavily because their exclusive SL products and traditional WL policies would take the hit as well.

No one knows how a current change will affect Congressional actions well into the future; yet it seems quite likely that any future attacks will at least be deferred for several years.

Confidence in the Life Insurance Industry Is Low

The recent string of life company failures and state takeovers, including some high-profile companies, has tarnished the industry's reputation for financial strength and cast a new light on the meaning of the "guarantees" in their contracts. Such concerns, combined with the failure of illustrated payment schemes and the continued explosion of mutual funds and annuities, will probably continue to depress the growth in new sales of CVLI.

The new National Association of Insurance Commissioners (NAIC) risk-based-capital (RBC) requirements and recently imposed junk bond limitations are important steps in preventing companies from undue risk-taking and should help restore the industry's reputation over time. Unfortunately, it may take more than this to heal the present wounds. The industry needs to be more proactive in reversing the flow of funds away from the industry and in reinforcing the continued importance of permanent life insurance as part of an individual's total financial plan. Embracing SL/IDBA could be such a step. The increased competition will accelerate the current industry shakeout, resulting in healthier companies with cost structures and risk profiles more appropriate for the volume and types of business they generate.

Confidence in life insurance companies is lacking not only with consumers but also with regulators, Congress, and even some of its own agents. State regulators continue to clamp down with new laws, such as RBC and the Investments of Insurers Model Act, to limit undue risk-taking, and Congress continues to peck away at any industry advantages perceived as unfair. Many agents are assisting consumers with the flight to quality, either because they or their clients have been associated with a financially troubled company or because prudence and a sense of responsibility dictate that they deal only with the strongest companies.

SL/IDBA could potentially make contributions on all these fronts. Its separate components allow product design that is more RBC efficient, starting with the low-risk SL product. The greater availability of equity returns may help to counteract the unintended consequence of the present flight to quality, which is higher net cost of insurance to the consumer. SL/IDBA could also go a long way toward minimizing policy illustration problems.

Finally, SL/IDBA could spur a new wave of product development, or perhaps even greater magnitude than the introduction of UL and VUL, which would be quite timely given the public's current appetite for other savings vehicles.

III. TO CHANGE OR NOT TO CHANGE

That is the question facing the key players in the life insurance arena. The following is a brief discussion of the likely reaction of regulators, insurance companies, policyholders, and agents to the proposal and introduction of the SL/IDBA concept.

Will Federal and State Regulators Allow It?

To answer this question, first ask whether the concept is, in theory, defensible. A quick reaction is that this idea is nothing more than "buying term insurance and investing the difference." The truth, however, is that the consumer is buying WL and investing the difference. The purchase of an SL policy represents the same long-term commitment to pay for permanent insurance with level premiums over a long time as traditional CVLI. The segregration of investment funds does not in any way alter that commitment.

The legitimacy of the policy loans may be questioned because they are forced and as such are really just paper assets. I believe the policyholder option to fully repay the loans (thereby opting out of the SL contract) preserves their full integrity as loans and that the states will simply need to permit contracts that contain the appropriate loan provisions. Even though the policyholders' loan options are restricted, there is no reason that these loans could not be treated in all ways like policy loans are today.

Of course, Congress will closely examine the potential impact on tax revenue. If a straight comparison between WL and SL/IDBA is made, where the IDBA and WL investment assumptions are consistent, a case can be made that tax revenue will not be affected. Compare the amount of tax-deferred revenue under a present-day product with that under an SL/IDBA package.

For the sake of simplicity, assume that 10% is the available new money rate, 8% is the fixed policy loan rate, and 0.75% is the spread between earned rate and credited rate for the issuing company. The net credited rate on the traditional product then is 9.25% (10.00 − 0.75), all of which is tax-deferred. In the SL product, 7.25% is credited (8.00 − 0.75) and 8.0% is charged to the policyholder, for a net nondeductible loss of 0.75%. When that is combined with the 10% tax-deferred earnings in the IDBA product, the net result is also a 9.25% tax-deferred earnings rate. Therefore, the SL/IDBA combination results in tax deferrals and tax revenues equal to those found in a present-day cash value product from which no policy loans are taken. In addition, IDBA policy loans, withdrawals from IDBAs, and the resulting investment income from IDBA policy loan proceeds could all be taxed exactly as loans and withdrawals from WL policies are today.

If these tax rules were adopted, only an absolute increase in CVLI business would increase tax-deferred income and reduce tax revenue. Of course, any deferral of income that comes at the expense of annuities, IRAs, or other qualified retirement plans will not affect tax revenue. But a term insurance policy combined with mutual fund contributions could be replaced by an SL/IDBA package, which would reduce current and/or future tax revenue by some amount. Would Congress tolerate such a loss of revenue? It is not clear, especially considering that it could just as easily occur under today's tax law if there was an increase in the market share of VL and VUL. Nevertheless, any loss in current revenue would often be just deferral of revenue, possibly of some higher amount, because the amount ultimately taxed will have grown at a faster rate. If necessary, perhaps some tightening of certain miscellaneous provisions, such as taxation of IDBA withdrawals or policy loans, could satisfy Congressional concerns over tax revenue.

State regulators have less reason to balk. The concept is consistent with new RBC requirements, which are intended to help keep companies financially healthy. While SL/IDBA does transfer more risk to the policyholder, it would arguably do so to no greater degree than VL already does. Furthermore, it offers some built-in advantages for dividend disclosure and illustrations. While SL policy forms may be a simple variation of today's WL forms, new IDBA regulations will be necessary to clarify what is and is not permissible (that is, for cash surrenders and illustrations). Aside from a possible hesitation to increase the workload of already strained staffs, state regulators probably would not stand in the way of such a new product form.

Will SL/IDBA Be Suicide, a Big Gamble, or a Necessary Step for the Life Insurance Industry?

This question is highly debatable. One camp will undoubtedly argue that to voluntarily give up exclusive rights to a tax-advantaged product, if not suicidal for the industry, is certainly a death blow to many of its members.

They will argue that banks and mutual funds have their own unique advantages and that the life industry must protect its own. Of course, the fear is that the life insurers' role as money managers will dwindle, because much of their investment funds will no longer be captive.

While such a consequence is certainly possible, those who fear the results of such competition should assess the present consequences of failure to compete with outside institutions. The life insurance industry instead competes with itself and this has fostered problems that hurt its profitability and plague its image. Dubious sales illustrations have allowed marginal companies to gain sizable market shares and have established unreasonable policyholder expectations. Large front-end commissions have prevailed, even with little new or sustainable premium. Excessive expense structures have been allowed to persist even though the growth in premium and volume have not been sufficient to support them; meanwhile, profit margins have weakened and surplus ratios have shrunk throughout the 1980s. Aside from the limited presence of VL and VUL, the life insurance industry has retained most of the CVLI investment control and charges the policyholder for it. One could make a case that the industry has done more to serve its employees and agents than its customers.

But while the industry maintains its monopoly over CVLI, it does not have a monopoly on retirement savings, for which CVLI is only one vehicle. The diminishing role of CVLI in securing retirement savings suggests that this product needs to be improved and that the life insurance industry needs to provide more vehicles that are in the public's favor (for example, mutual funds). If the public is funneling more and more money into mutual funds, then the life industry should offer more of these.

The greater competition that an SL/IDBA environment would stimulate would quickly diminish the roles of many insurers, particularly among the smaller ones. But this is already occurring, with the tightening of rating agencies' criteria, RBC requirements, and agents' and customers' flight to quality. Perhaps the new environment would accelerate forces already under way. At the same time, a great opportunity would exist for companies to market their investment capabilities and develop new products that could revitalize the public's interest in CVLI. Those companies that are successful may be much better off in the future than they would have been with the status quo. Therefore, a redistribution of wealth would be expected within the industry, with greater speed and perhaps to greater extent than is already occurring. Such redistribution of wealth, while painful for some, is inevitable to some extent and probably necessary for the vitality of the industry.

In summary, the life insurance industry should take a close look at its navigational equipment and determine whether its ship is on course, off course, or lost at sea and perhaps taking on water.

Will Agents Sell It? and Will the Public Buy It?

The public certainly accepted UL quickly, and it has earned its place alongside traditional WL. UL brought to policyholders the indisputable advantages of premium flexibility and the open display of its policy components. All this happened even though agents, and companies underwriting the products, were somewhat less than thrilled. For the agents, UL commissions have not quite stacked up to traditional commissions, either in first or renewal years. For the companies, UL's uncertain premium and agents' traditional commission structure presented pricing problems. Still, in light of the product's unique advantages to policyholders, resisting UL would have required a great deal of courage and conviction, especially because its sale became so widespread. Most companies that offer WL today also offer UL or, if not, some form of interest-sensitive WL with an "unbundled" structure.

Does SL/IDBA also offer the public clear advantages over the present universe of products? If greater freedom of choice and greater control over how a portion of long-term savings are invested mean anything, then the answer should be a resounding "yes." SL/IDBA may be the key that unlocks the full potential of policyholder investment control that VL has brought in a limited form. VL and VUL have been shackled with too few funds, too narrow a distribution channel, and too much administrative and filing time and expense to have the impact that we might have expected. With the tremendous growth in mutual funds over the past decade, it is quite surprising that variable life sales have remained relatively flat at about 5% of all ordinary life purchases. Does it make any sense that most CVLI policies are less than 5% backed by common stocks, while the corresponding figure for private pension plans is roughly 50%?[5] Is the life insurance industry missing the beat by focusing on short-term equity rather than long-term value?

Of course, only an open market can determine the real demand for a currently unavailable product. But does there have to be a minimum threshold of market demand to justify the products' availability in the first place? The regulatory framework required to launch such a product is already in place, so the real risk, if any, is with companies that make product development, marketing, and administrative investments in this new product

[5]Ibid.

arena. Therefore, the question of whether agents will sell it and the public will buy it is best left for the market to answer.

There is probably little that the industry's agents can do to successfully stop the products' introduction or advancement, assuming some measurable demand surfaces. I think that this will be the case, in spite of the agents' powerful lobby, simply because such a position is indefensible. What would their argument be? That too much investment freedom hurts the policyholder? Or that they will have to work harder just to earn the same compensation? Those are hardly the foundations of a strong case, especially when many new selling opportunities will become available to agents in such an environment.

While they may not be able to stop it, agents could do a great deal to incorporate the new product form into their sales repertoire. Agents should be able to refocus their sales pitches to emphasize the generic advantages of CVLI and then select from a greater array of vehicles to suit a particular client's needs and desires, with less reliance on a single page of numbers that may be largely dependent on one particular company's assumptions. Compensation will undoubtedly settle wherever the market takes it, that is, at whatever levels insurers, agents, and customers can peacefully coexist. But because the SL and IDBA products can each be sold by different agents and because each product is somewhat unique compared to existing products, traditional commission structures are more likely to be replaced by new ones.

IV. SUMMARY AND CONCLUDING THOUGHTS

Numerous potential ramifications of SL/IDBA have been touched upon throughout this paper. The key points, both pro and con, are restated below.

Pros

1. Traditional WL sales are down; SL/IDBA should rekindle sales of CVLI through diverse new product offerings and wider distribution of VL types of products.
2. Profitability is down, and risky investments persist. SL products may boost profitability through less risky policy loans, lower acquisition costs, better premium persistency, and better policy persistency due to less policyholder incentive to replace them.
3. SL/IDBA will facilitate more investment of policyholder funds in common stocks, equity funds, or other investments more suited to or preferred by a particular policyholder.

4. SL/IDBA allows policyholders to diversify their equity among two or more companies, reducing the risk that they won't have access to their funds.
5. SL products are not exposed to run or liquidity risk.
6. SL products will have more predictable dividend scales, which should lead to more credible illustration assumptions.
7. SL/IDBA will provide a mechanism for relaxing CVLI nonforfeiture requirements, but only at the option of the policyholder.
8. Compensation restructuring is likely, possibly resulting in less compensation per sale, more asset-based compensation, and less agent incentive to replace IDBAs.
9. Separating the mortality and investment components will promote more competition within the two areas, allow selective packaging of the components by both company and policyholder, and allow selective unpackaging (replacement) of unwanted components.
10. The SL product will facilitate assumption reinsurance transactions and provide a tool for RBC repositioning.
11. SL/IDBA may help secure an untaxed future for the inside buildup of CVLI by letting banks and mutual fund companies participate in its benefits, thereby increasing the base of its defense.
12. The insurance industry may regain the confidence of its many publics by endorsing a new product line that benefits them more directly than itself.
13. Most of the pieces (that is, the products and related laws) necessary for launching the SL/IDBA product concept are already in place.

Cons

1. The product concept is more complicated than traditional CVLI or UL, because the responsibility of investment falls on the policyholders' shoulders. Therefore, it is not appropriate for everyone.
2. Administration will be complex; recordkeeping, billing, and reporting requirements must be split and shared between the SL and IDBA writers.
3. Too much investment freedom for the policyholder may result in imprudent investments and reduced surrender and death benefits for many policyholders.
4. Even though the SL product may be more immune to replacement, IDBA policyholders may be targets of agents who focus on replacement activity or push more speculative investment funds.

5. The product will require a significant, though singular, change in the tax code and therefore must be viewed by Congress as having generic advantages and being, at worst, revenue-neutral.
6. The insurance industry may be more vulnerable to having the inside buildup taxed sometime in the future if this buildup no longer exclusively lies within the insurance domain.
7. Insurance companies will no longer be assured the investment component of a WL contract, and many companies will lose money under management to outside institutions. Such companies will likely have to downsize their operations to remain profitable.
8. Agents may resist the product because it threatens to reduce their compensation or refuse to sell it because of perceived compensation inequities relative to other products.

The potential impact of SL/IDBA can be summarized in the following way: Pure competition among insurance companies and insurance products will increase, benefiting the consumer. However, such increased competition may, for various reasons, be unwelcomed by the providers of CVLI insurance, namely, insurance companies and their agents. This reaction raises a fundamental question: Should any new product that offers to the public some clear and unique inherent advantages over existing products be withheld because current insurance providers fear the long-term ramifications of the new product? I believe the answer is "no," because insurance providers exist to serve the insurance public, not the other way around.

The history of UL provides a useful case in point. There is no question that life was easier for insurance companies and agents before UL. The transition has been difficult in the areas of pricing, administration, compensation, and regulation. But with the benefit of hindsight, we can now ask, "Are these or any other problems that UL has brought with it so severe that its path should have been blocked?" Perhaps those who would answer affirmatively are also those who would oppose the SL/IDBA concept.

Many of the claims or opinions I have presented in this paper about potential SL/IDBA profit margins, persistency, sales volume, and compensation can be substantiated only up to a point. All the research in the world will not conclusively answer any of these questions; only an open market can provide real answers. But how much harm will that open market bring? No company will be forced to provide it, no agent forced to sell it, and no consumer forced to buy it. But if many end up doing so, then it would indicate that there is indeed something in it for all of them.

The twenty-first century is rapidly approaching, and the world all around us is changing quickly and dramatically. Computer power and ingenuity have spawned many new, arcane financial products for which there has been great demand. The technological revolution has made complex electronic equipment commonplace, even in the household. Even simple television-watching threatens to enter another dimension. In light of our rapidly changing environment, the life insurance industry should insure that its flagship product, CVLI, is fit to compete in the years ahead. If not, the product and all those embracing it may be left behind. The process of overhauling it may not be simple or pleasant, but it may be necessary for long-term survival.

By way of analogy, consider a nation whose electronic stores sell combination TV/VCR units and stand-alone TVs and VCRs, but no jacks or any way of connecting them together. Given the relative complexity of VCRs and TVs, the addition of jacks and cables would appear to be a simple change that could unleash a whole new market. In fact, this enhanced scenario in the U.S. today has proven that combination TV/VCR units simply do not appeal to the public nearly as much as separate component systems that are easy to integrate. In fact, it is hard to imagine a market in which separate component systems would not be available.

Yet that is precisely where the life insurance industry stands today with its CVLI product. Could today's prepackaged CVLI be in the same relative position as the combination TV/VCR units in our hypothetical scenario, in sharp contrast to its ultimate, inferior position in the era of integrated components? In this age of booming information technology, is there not an opportunity here to create a better CVLI product?

DISCUSSION OF PRECEDING PAPER

GERARD G. SMEDINGHOFF:

Within the confines of the ivory towers of the insurance industry, Steven Reddy's concept of "Cash Value Life Insurance for the Twenty-First Century" sounds like the magic bullet that will allow the industry to make a great leap forward in the financial services arena. The SL/IDBA concept is most certainly clever, sophisticated, and even elegant. But to quote the guru of design engineers, Donald Norman, "If you think something is clever and sophisticated, beware—it's probably self-indulgence" [3]. Not self-indulgence on the author's part, but on behalf of the life insurance industry in general, which is still trying to push a product, CVLI, that should have gone the way of the eight-track tape player.

To his credit, Mr. Reddy conceived and wrote his paper from the proper starting point, that is, *tabula rosa*, by asking himself how he would design a new life insurance product without any of the current legal and industry constraints. But his new product design falls far short of what customers want because he accepts, almost by default, the CVLI paradigm that has dominated the industry for most of this century. This makes about as much sense as trying to strengthen the French military after World War II by restoring the Maginot Line.

The life insurance industry's future does not lie in (yet another) line extension of its outdated flagship product of whole life insurance. The next major innovation to transform the industry will not be a "new-and-improved whole life" or "whole life lite," but a dramatic paradigm shift along the lines of what Thomas Kuhn cataloged in *The Structure of Scientific Revolutions* [2]. And, if history is any guide, it most likely will not come from within the industry (just as IBM, with its army of R&D engineers, did not invent the personal computer), but from a deconstructionist mind in the spirit of Jacques Derrida or a corporate raider such as Michael Milken.

Mr. Reddy provides an excellent and detailed analysis of the gradual decline and the current state of the life insurance industry. But the conclusion he draws deserves further examination. Is the fact that the industry is in decline and on the verge of a dramatic consolidation (such as what occurred in the auto industry in the 1920s and in banking today) necessarily bad? Is the purpose of the life insurance industry to create value from the services it provides to its policyholders or to single-mindedly increase the total volume of CVLI sales?

As with so many other industries in the U.S. economy (such as the railroads), the recent decline in the life insurance industry—however unsettling it may be to those employed within it—represents a windfall to its customers. Just as customers benefited when the rise of the airlines was coupled with the decline of the railroads, customers are also now benefiting as the decline of the life insurance industry is coupled with the rise of the discount brokerage and mutual fund industries.

People do not need CVLI any more than they need buggy whips or record players. What they do need is the value they derive from these products and services. Rather than asking, "How can the life insurance industry increase the sales of CVLI products?" one should ask, "What services do life insurers provide that are of value to their customers and how can this value be increased?" Why did people buy CVLI during the 1950s and 1960s? What *value* did they derive from the purchase of these policies?

- There was little competition and innovation in the financial services industry in general and the life insurance industry in particular.
- Few investment options were available to the middle class, such as mutual funds, money market funds, discount brokers, and IRAs.
- Inflation was not a factor.
- People expected to work at the same job, stay married to the same person, and live in the same house for the rest of their lives.
- Many people held a cultural bias against wives working outside the home, and purchasing large amounts of life insurance was a means to protect against that possibility.
- Few companies had stable pension plans in place and the cash value in their life insurance policy was the only means of retirement savings for many people.

Now consider how many of these conditions hold in today's economy. Given the vast array of financial products and services available to consumers, why would any rational person purchase CVLI? The only possible incentive is the tax deferral of interest on the policy's accumulating cash value. And even this is an overrated feature because the tax will have to be paid eventually. Bundling a fixed long-term investment program with basic life insurance protection makes as much economic sense as the auto dealership that gives away a free TV with the purchase of a new car. Lots of people need new cars and lots of people need new TVs, but very few need both of them simultaneously. If it makes sense to couple long-term savings with insurance, why don't we have cash value auto insurance and cash value homeowner's insurance?

In fact, why would anyone pay more than the current value received from a product during the period of one's lower-income-earning years for the privilege of paying less than the value received during one's high-income-earning years? People buy cars, houses, and college educations on exactly the opposite premise. They reason: "I can't afford this right now, but if I borrow the money, I can gain the full use of it immediately while paying for it over time."

Why would any young person say, "I don't need to pay for all this life insurance right now. But if I divert funds from some things I could really use now, and pay more than necessary for this policy in advance, I won't have to pay as much when I'm older, my income is much higher and I can afford it much more easily."

Life insurance companies offer two basic services to the public: (1) protection against the loss of one's future earnings via the basic life insurance policy and (2) a guaranteed return on invested funds via an annuity's or life insurance policy's cash value accumulation. The cost of the insurance portion of the policy premium is essentially the same, regardless of whether one buys term or CVLI. The only difference is in internal policyholder accounting.

The investment service offered by life insurers via CVLI requires further examination. Essentially there are four categories on the personal investment scale, starting with the highest risk-reward balance and proceeding to the lowest:

- Invest in oneself or one's own business.
- Use the advantages of size and proven market acceptance to reduce the risk by investing in a larger business that has proven itself in the marketplace by buying shares of its stock.
- Further reduce investment risk via diversification—for example, buying shares in a mutual fund, which spreads the investment risk over many different companies.
- The lowest risk-reward trade-off is the domain of life insurance companies. It involves forgoing most of the rewards of the expanding economy in exchange for a guaranteed return on funds invested. This is the service life insurance companies provide to the investing public, but only via the bundled and convoluted product of CVLI.

Is there any reason that, for an insurance company to provide this valuable service in the domain of the fourth category of personal investing, it must be bundled with a life insurance policy? Banks already offer this service as a stand-alone product. Once the Glass-Steagall Act is finally laid to rest, why can't life insurance companies do the same? This is where insurance companies should ultimately concentrate their product development efforts.

This is another point at which Mr. Reddy's proposal departs from the value principle. When designing changes to the obsolete legislation regulating the life insurance industry, he implicitly asks the question, "How can Congress best rewrite the laws so the life insurance industry can sell more CVLI at higher profit margins and return to its glory days of the past?" [No one wants Congress to regulate the telecommunications industry on that basis.] Instead he should be asking questions such as, What is the ultimate purpose of insurance regulation? Why isn't the current regulation serving that purpose? And if all the current legislation were immediately discarded, how should the life insurance industry be regulated?

No matter how one wants to redefine the life insurance industry, there are two facts that cannot be ignored when envisioning possible future scenarios: (1) information costs—the cost of comparing product offerings from different companies—will ultimately be driven to near zero and (2) transaction costs—the basic cost of exchanging money for products and services—will ultimately be driven to near zero. To predict the future of the life insurance agent, one need only look at its close relative, the travel agent, who is already on the endangered species list.

Why call a travel agent to find the best flight from city A to city B when you're carrying a copy of the *Official Airline Guide* in your travel bag? And why book a flight through a travel agent when you can buy your tickets online and bypass the agent's commission? By now many people are aware that Mother's Day no longer holds the record for peak phone usage. This honor belongs to random weekdays during the summer months when airline fare wars break out and computers, programmed to arbitrage airline tickets, dominate the phone lines [1]. The evolution—or more accurately, the decay—of commissions of travel agents has closely mirrored that of life insurance agents. And there's no reason to believe that the course of their fates will diverge in the future.

Ignoring, for the moment, the past, present and potential future of the life insurance industry, the SL/IDBA concept immediately triggers an alarm from a generic design perspective. Again, to his credit, Mr. Reddy draws an appropriate and timely analogy of TVs and VCRs. But from a marketing and customer perspective, two sentences in particular signal that the SL/IDBA product is too complicated for most consumers and needs to be redesigned:

- The author admits that "The SL product is appropriate only for those who understand the contractual differences, the ongoing policyholder responsibilities, the investment risks and all the potential tax effects." Not only does this restrict the potential market for this product to a minuscule percentage of the population, but one wonders how many actuaries can be qualified as potential responsible prospects. How many VCRs would have been sold if all potential buyers had to prove that they were capable of setting the clock and pre-recording programs in advance?
- In an effort to unload as much responsibility from the insurer onto the buyer, Mr. Reddy advises that, "At a minimum, a signed statement acknowledging the policyholder's duties and the general consequences of failure to invest the funds or poor investment performance will probably be necessary." Wouldn't any investor who was that knowledgeable and sophisticated have many more attractive investment alternatives than a newfangled CVLI product? And how much CVLI would have been sold in the past if all customers had to sign a statement saying they completely understood the dividend illustrations and the risk that their "vanishing premiums" might end up as "vanishing promises?"

The potential market for any new product or service can quickly be judged by a simple test developed by Jack Welch, the CEO of General Electric, who says of any idea, "If you can't explain it to a stranger at a cocktail party, forget it!" One suspects that most people would find the eight steps of the SL/IDBA sale listed under "The Product Mechanics" to be more intimidating than resetting the clock on their VCR to daylight savings time and impossible to explain at a cocktail party without running the risk of destroying a long-term relationship.

Finally, one last case study emphasizes the hard lesson that the life insurance industry is about to learn—unfortunately, the hard way. Throughout the 1980s, IBM marketed the personal computer with the goal of keeping it separate from and protecting its dominance of the mainframe computer market. Back in the mid-1980s, while IBM was posting record profits, Bill Gates is rumored to have said that IBM would cease to exist in seven years.

While IBM hasn't gone out of business, in 1992 its CEO was fired, its stock lost more than half its value, and it now employs about half as many people as it did ten years ago. Should the life insurance industry cling to the archaic concept of CVLI, it will one day wake up to find that start-up competitors have grabbed its customers and have created a new market that shuts them out and turns the most valuable assets on their balance sheets into waste that will have to be dumped into a landfill.

REFERENCES

1. DYSON, ESTHER. "Fare Games," *Forbes*, 25 May 1992, 258.
2. KUHN, THOMAS S. *The Structure of Scientific Revolution.* 2nd ed. Chicago, Ill.: University of Chicago Press, 1970.
3. NORMAN, DONALD. *The Design of Everyday Things.* New York, N.Y.: Doubleday, 1990, p. ix.

(AUTHOR'S REVIEW OF DISCUSSION)

STEPHEN D. REDDY:

I thank Mr. Smedinghoff for taking the time and effort to critique this paper. In his discussion he makes several interesting observations. However, I have to take issue with several statements he makes and objections he raises, which I do in the following paragraphs, generally in the order that they appear in his discussion.

Mr. Smedinghoff gave me credit for writing the paper "tabula rosa ... without any of the current legal and industry constraints." I don't deserve that credit, because I did quite the opposite. I tried to envision a new generation of products that could easily spring to life within the existing insurance and tax legislative framework. Rather than examining all the issues tangent to CVLI, such as the justification of tax-deferred treatment or the desirability of minimum nonforfeiture values, I attempted to pursue a pragmatic improvement to the generic CVLI product *given* its surrounding environment. I discussed those tangential issues only to the extent necessary to explore the product idea itself and to assess the likelihood of surviving the environment to which it would be exposed. Take for example, the tax-deferred treatment of the cash value buildup. My mission was not to justify its continued existence, but rather to put forth reasoning that tax-deferred treatment is as justifiable and probable for the new product form as it is for current forms.

Mr. Smedinghoff states that the "new product design" falls far short of what customers want and that the next major innovation to transform the industry will be a "dramatic paradigm shift." I'm not sure what Mr. Smedinghoff has in mind in either case, but I would argue that SL/IDBA gives consumers more of what they want, that is, much greater investment freedom within the CVLI package, and that it does represent a dramatic paradigm shift. It would certainly be as dramatic a change as variable life and universal life were, if not more so. I also doubt that many would characterize SL/IDBA as another "line extension" of CVLI, and I would expect some challenges from lawmakers that the separate SL and IDBA products cannot be considered as CVLI for tax purposes.

Mr. Smedinghoff then states that "the conclusion he draws deserves further examination." I did not draw any conclusion. I simply suggested a product change that has the potential to remedy many specific problems with CVLI today.

Mr. Smedinghoff has apparently inferred that my primary objective was to propose a product that would "single-mindedly increase the total volume of CVLI sales." Increasing sales was only one of 13 benefits that I suggested could result from the introduction of SL/IDBA. While Mr. Smedinghoff may not think that increased sales alone is a worthy objective, I would still like to know what he, and others, think about the other potential benefits I have discussed.

Then Mr. Smedinghoff poses a fundamental question. "Why would any rational person purchase CVLI?" He responds with: "The only possible incentive is the tax deferral of interest on the policy's accumulating cash value. And even this is an overrated feature since the tax will have to be paid eventually." This response to his own question perhaps sums up his dim view of what CVLI has to offer and furthers the idea that CVLI is not worth saving.

In my view, Mr. Smedinghoff is grossly underestimating or misunderstanding, or both, the value that CVLI brings to consumers. First, the statement that the only possible incentive is the tax deferral is completely false simply because there are several other incentives, some of which I mention below. Unfortunately, Mr. Smedinghoff compounds his error with his next statement, that the tax deferral is overrated because the tax must eventually be paid. Most people would agree that tax deferral is a significant advantage worth seeking. In fact, the whole 401(k) and IRA markets are built around that tax advantage, even though the tax must eventually be paid. However, CVLI offers a further advantage that those other vehicles do not, namely, that the tax *doesn't* ever have to be paid if the policy is held to death. That's right! Life income proceeds are federal income tax free at death! The fact that death benefit proceeds are subject to estate taxes is irrelevant—so are all other assets held at death, including any 401(k) and IRA funds that would have been previously taxed upon distribution.

Also, consider the fact that upon surrender of the policy the taxable gain is calculated using the entire CVLI premium, including the term portion, as the basis of the policy. Contrast this with a "buy term and invest the difference" strategy. Try deducting your term insurance premiums from the gains in your side fund and see how far you get with the IRS! With CVLI, the tax benefit at surrender could be like getting a third of the (term) insurance premiums back!

Another significant advantage of CVLI is the ability to tap the policy's equity, via policy loans, without negative tax consequences. With loans, a policyholder can effectively get at the inside buildup, including the tax-deferred excess interest, without any tax consequences. Furthermore the loan advances once again become tax free if the policy is held to death. Loan capacity in 401(k), IRA, or other investment vehicles is much more limited, if permitted at all, and not as tax advantaged.

Mr. Smedinghoff then argues that young people would be foolish to overpay for CVLI when at the same time they stretch out their payments for cars, houses, and college education. Actually the sellers of those three items all require full and immediate payment, even though the items' value is realized over time, whereas life insurers at least offer the flexibility of spreading payments out over the life of the policy. Borrowing is simply a means for people to solve their cash-flow problems, and it is certainly as applicable to purchases of CVLI as other tangible items. In fact, the built-in policy loan provisions of a CVLI contract make the borrowing process a lot simpler than buying a house or a car.

Mr. Smedinghoff makes the assertion that insurance companies should concentrate their product development efforts on offering investment products on a stand-alone basis, like banks. This paper essentially proposes that, but within the context of an unbundled CVLI product in which IDBA products could take on many different forms. For all the reasons mentioned above, the IDBA products sold in this context would represent more value than those sold on a stand-alone basis.

Mr. Smedinghoff stated that I "should be asking such questions as: What is the ultimate purpose of insurance regulation? Why isn't the current regulation serving that purpose? ... How should the life insurance industry be regulated?" Quite frankly, I have no interest in addressing those questions. Someone else who does have an interest, perhaps Mr. Smedinghoff, can tackle those issues.

I believe Mr. Smedinghoff's comments about information costs and transactions costs being driven to near zero are right on the money. However, while this may present problems for the life insurance agent, it should work to the advantage of the SL/IDBA products because the commission and administrative costs of each should come down over time, including the cost of administering the integration of the two products.

Mr. Smedinghoff states that the product may be too complicated for most prospective buyers and that requiring a signed statement acknowledging policyholder duties is evidence of that. I disagree. There is no question that some will not be able to grasp the essentials of the concept. However, for most, the concept of SL/IDBA should be as easy to grasp as the integration of TVs and VCRs, even if certain details, such as setting the clock, still prove troublesome. Other financial instruments such as mutual funds, variable life products and annuities, and IRAs all have complexities and features that can and do get misunderstood. My suggestion to require a signed statement was not an attempt to shift responsibility from insurer to the buyer, but rather a simple attempt to eliminate some sales that should never take place.

Then Mr. Smedinghoff argues that those who are knowledgeable and sophisticated enough would have many more investment alternatives than a "newfangled CVLI product." To say this is to miss the whole point of the paper, which was to make many more attractive investments available within the purchase of a life insurance product!

I agree with Mr. Smedinghoff's assertion that a new idea must be simple enough to explain at a cocktail party. Fortunately, it passes that test, because I already have (one could sum it up as simply "buying whole life and investing the difference"), but the reader must realize that a cocktail party and the SOA *Transactions* are two different forums and thus require different levels of detail. My original draft did not include the section on the "The Product Mechanics," but the Papers Committee required that I dot the 'i's and cross the 't's in describing the concept, which increased the paper's length by more than 50%. Hopefully, the length of the paper does not discourage many readers from giving the paper a look and the concept some consideration.

Mr. Smedinghoff concludes with a dire prediction of what will happen if the life insurance industry clings to the "archaic concept of CVLI." I wouldn't go quite so far. However, my paper addresses a myriad of problems with the present form of CVLI, which are perhaps strong evidence that such present form is somewhat outdated or in need of an overhaul. I believe the

SL/IDBA concept goes a long way in remedying some of the present problems and offering a more suitable CVLI product for the present times.

I thank Mr. Smedinghoff for his time and thoughts. While I share some of his sentiments about the condition of the life industry, I think he incorrectly dismisses CVLI as either beyond repair or not worth fixing. I would have preferred to have seen more comments on the likely impact of SL/IDBA should it be implemented.

That will have to be left for the actuarial community at large. While critiquing the paper is not that important, critiquing the product concept is, because there are too many problems and too much change around us to rest with the status quo. I just hope that the actuarial community will be proactive in its judgment and not wait for momentum to gather before it gets involved.

SIMULATING RANDOM VARIATES FROM MAKEHAM'S DISTRIBUTION AND FROM OTHERS WITH EXACT OR NEARLY LOG-CONCAVE DENSITIES

DAVID P.M. SCOLLNIK

ABSTRACT

This paper describes how Markov chain Monte Carlo and related methods recently presented in the statistical literature can be used to quickly and efficiently simulate random draws from distributions with log-concave or nearly log-concave densities. These methods should be useful in many actuarial computer simulations, because a number of distributions in actuarial contexts have log-concave or nearly log-concave densities. To illustrate their application, the paper examines how they can be used to simulate realizations of life contingent functions under Makeham's law and certain other patterns of mortality when the distribution of the future lifetime random variable either has a log-concave density or possesses one that is nearly so. These simulation methods allow a variety of previously inaccessible inferences to be made routinely and easily. Several examples are included.

---

1. INTRODUCTION

The analytical laws of mortality devised by Gompertz [16] and Makeham [24] are well-known to actuaries and are also known to be very good representations of the mortality process at adult ages. Unfortunately, neither law lends itself to convenient mathematical analysis. As noted by London [23, p. 18–19] and Anderson [1, p. 124], among others, even evaluating characteristics like the mean or variance of their respective survival distributions is somewhat difficult. Computing the expected value of the life contingent functions defining annuities or insurances under either Gompertz's or Makeham's law is even more burdensome, as is the calculation of any of the associated higher moments or tail probabilities. Fortunately, a number of authors, including Mereu [25], Moore [28], and Carriere [6], have studied and facilitated the application of these laws, thus making them far more palatable to the practicing actuary. Nevertheless, some of these analytical results have been rather limited and yet have typically involved reasonably sophisticated mathematical analyses, often requiring the numerical evaluation of the incomplete or left-truncated gamma function, for instance, Moore [28] and Carrier [6]. Further, none of these references has considered simulating random variates from either Gompertz's or Makeham's survival distribution.

In this paper I take a different approach and describe how Markov chain Monte Carlo (MCMC) methods, related to some of those recently appearing in the *Transactions* [5], can be used to quickly and efficiently simulate realizations of life contingent functions under Makeham's law and certain other patterns of mortality when the distribution of the future lifetime random variable either has a log-concave density or possesses one that is nearly so. For this purpose, a density function $f(t)$ is said to be log-concave if the logarithm of this function is concave with respect to the argument t (that is, the first derivative of $\ln[f(t)]$ is a monotonically decreasing function of t). If the second derivative of $\ln[f(t)]$ exists, then the density $f(t)$ will be log-concave, provided that

$$\frac{d^2}{dt^2} \ln [f(t)] \leq 0$$

for all values of t in the domain $D = \{t \mid f(t) > 0\}$ of the density function. The MCMC methodology described allows a variety of previously inaccessible inferences to be made routinely and easily, for example, in studying the distribution of a prospective loss random variable associated with some insurance contract to determine the necessary reserve under one of the patterns of mortality described above. However, the MCMC methods discussed here are very general and actuarial practitioners should find many other uses for them (see Section 5). The mortality laws of Gompertz and Makeham provide a context for the main examples.

2. THE MORTALITY LAWS OF GOMPERTZ AND MAKEHAM

The force of mortality for a life age x under Gompertz's law is given by

$$\mu_x = BC^x, B > 0, C \geq 1, x \geq 0,$$

and by

$$\mu_x = A + BC^x, A > - B, B > 0, C \geq 1, x \geq 0$$

under Makeham's (London [23] and Bowers et al. [3]). Gompertz's law is obviously a special case of Makeham's. Makeham intended the extra parameter A to capture that part of the hazard that is independent of age

[23, p. 19]. Although negative values of the parameter A may have little practical application, the case $-B<A<0$ is included for completeness. Henceforth, reference is made only to Makeham's law, with the understanding that Gompertz's law is a special instance of it.

As in Chapter 3 of Bowers et al. [3], let X denote the age-at-death random variable for a newborn life, let the symbol (x) denote a life age x, and let $T(x)$ denote the future lifetime random variable for (x). Then the survival function for a newborn life under Makeham's law is given by

$$s(x) = \Pr[X > x]$$

$$= \exp\left[-Ax - \frac{B}{\ln C}(C^x - 1)\right], x \geq 0;$$

the survival function for (x) is given by

$$_tp_x = \Pr[T(x) > t] = \frac{s(x + t)}{s(x)}, t \geq 0;$$

and the probability density function of the random variable $T(x)$ is given by

$$f(t) = {}_tp_x\mu_{x+t}$$

$$= \exp\left[-At - \frac{BC^x}{\ln C}(C^t - 1)\right](A + BC^{x+t}), t \geq 0.$$

The most interesting observation is that

$$\frac{d^2}{dt^2}\ln[f(t)] = -BC^{x+t}\left[1 - \frac{A\ln C}{(A + BC^{x+t})^2}\right]\ln C.$$

When this expression is non-positive for all values of t, the continuous density $f(t)$ is log-concave with respect to its argument. Inspection of the expression above indicates that log-concavity will always be obtained provided that $-B<A\leq 0$. On the other hand, log-concavity may not be obtained when $A>0$. However, the Makeham parameters are usually confined to the ranges

$$0.001 < A < 0.003, \quad 0.000001 < B < 0.001, \quad 1.08 < C < 1.12$$

when describing human mortality [21, p. 24], and so the value of the second derivative of the log-density will still be very close to zero in this case even when $A>0$. Consequently, the distribution of the future lifetime random variable $T(x)$ has a density function that is either concave on the logarithmic scale (that is, log-concave) or else very nearly so in the case of human mortality under Makeham's law. The significance of this result becomes apparent in the following sections.

3. A NUMBER OF USEFUL MCMC-RELATED METHODS

Recently, Carlin [5] showed that a random draw from a complicated k-variate distribution with density $f(x_1, x_2, ..., x_k)$ can be generated by iteratively and repeatedly sampling from each of the associated univariate full conditional distributions $f(x_1|x_2, ..., x_k)$, $f(x_2|x_1, x_3, ..., x_k)$, ..., $f(x_k|x_1, ..., x_{k-1})$ in turn. This algorithm describes a very simple implementation of the so-called Gibbs sampler, a type of MCMC method. A MCMC method is a sampling-based procedure that is used to generate a sequence of dependent random draws from a distribution of interest on a fast computer. Over the last six or seven years, MCMC methods have become very popular within the statistical sciences (for example, Gelfand and Smith [11], Smith and Roberts [33], Tanner [34], and Tierney [35]), and a great deal of effort has been expended to develop efficient and general-purpose random number generators to implement the necessary draws from the full conditional distributions described above (for example, Wakefield et al. [36], Gilks and Wild [13], Gilks [12], and Wild and Gilks [37]). MCMC methods have also recently begun to be applied to actuarial problems. The Gibbs sampler was utilized by Carlin [4] to conduct the Bayesian state space modeling of non-standard actuarial time series, by Carlin [5] and Klugman and Carlin [22] in the context of Bayesian graduation, by Scollnik [31] to implement a Bayesian analysis of a simultaneous equations model for insurance rate-making, and by Scollnik [32] to conduct the Bayesian analysis of some generalized Poisson models. The Gibbs sampler is not used in this paper, but two methods that have recently appeared in the related MCMC literature are used: adaptive rejection sampling (ARS) and adaptive rejection Metropolis sampling (ARMS). These methods are introduced below along with some background material.

A. The Rejection Sampling Method

The rejection sampling method allows one to obtain a random draw from a distribution with a continuous density $f(x)$. It requires that a proposal distribution with density $g(x)$ be available such that random draws from this distribution are easily obtained and also such that there exists a finite constant $M>0$ with $f(x) \leq Mg(x)$ for all values of x in the domain of $f(x)$. Then the following algorithm is known to yield a random draw from the distribution with density $f(x)$:

Step 1. Generate a uniform random variate U on the unit interval.

Step 2. Generate a random variate X from the distribution with density $g(x)$.

Step 3. Determine whether $U < f(X)/Mg(X)$. When this inequality is *false*, return to *Step 1*. When this inequality is *true*, accept the current value of X and stop the algorithm.

The value of X finally accepted will be a random draw from the distribution with density $f(x)$. The rejection sampling method may be applied as many times as necessary in the case that a random sample of size greater than one is required from the distribution with density $f(x)$. The number of iterations of this algorithm required in order to generate each accepted draw is known to be geometriclaly distributed with a mean of M, so this algorithm may be inefficient unless a good proposal distribution is available so that the value of M is close to 1. Rejection sampling and its properties are discussed in more detail by Devroye [10, p. 40–43] and Ross [30, p. 478–83]. These authors also present proofs that the algorithm performs as claimed. The rejection sampling method is included in the course of reading for Associateship Course 130, Operations Research [18, p. 871–2].

The rejection sampling method can also be described pictorially as in Figure 1. In this figure, the bimodal distribution with density $f(x)$ is the one from which we desire a random draw. The density $f(x)$ is plotted with a solid (——) line. The proposal distribution has a density $g(x)$, and some constant M is presumed to be known such that $f(x) \leq Mg(x)$ for all values of x in the domain of $f(x)$. The curve $Mg(x)$ is plotted with a dashed (———) line. We assume that a method is available that permits us to implement random draws from the proposal distribution. Then any value X sampled from the proposal distribution will be accepted with a probability equal to the ratio of the height $f(X)$ to the height $Mg(X)$. These heights are indicated on the figure for the value $X=5$. Rejected values are discarded. This procedure can be repeated as many times as necessary in the case in which a random sample of size greater than one is required from the distribution with density $f(x)$, and the final collection of accepted values constitutes a random sample from the distrubition with density $f(x)$.

FIGURE 1
AN ILLUSTRATION OF THE REJECTION SAMPLING METHOD

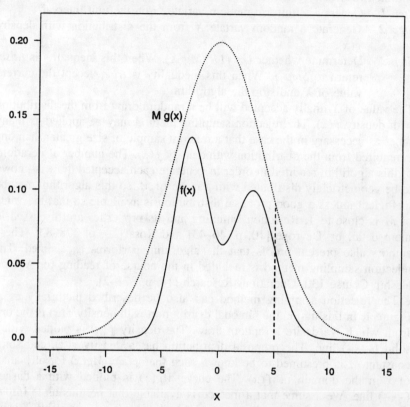

B. Numerical Example 1

The following simple example illustrates the rejection sampling method. Imagine that we want to generate a random variate from the beta distribution (with parameters 3 and 5) having the density function

$$f(x) = 105 \, x^2 \, (1 - x)^4, \, 0 < x < 1.$$

Since the random variable is concentrated on the unit interval, we use the rejection sampling method together with the uniform proposal distribution

$$g(x) = 1, \, 0 < x < 1.$$

To determine the constant M such that $f(x) \leq Mg(x)$, we need to determine the maximum value of the ratio

$$\frac{f(x)}{g(x)} = 105 \, x^2 \, (1 - x)^4,$$

when $0 < x < 1$. Differentiation of this ratio yields

$$\frac{d}{dx}\left[\frac{f(x)}{g(x)}\right] = 210 \, x \, (1 - x)^4 - 420 \, x^2 \, (1 - x)^3.$$

Setting this expression equal to zero and solving for x shows that the maximal value of the ratio is obtained when $x = 1/3$, so that

$$\frac{f(x)}{g(x)} \leq 105 \left(\frac{1}{3}\right)^2 \left(\frac{2}{3}\right)^4 = \frac{560}{243} \equiv M$$

and

$$\frac{f(x)}{Mg(x)} = \frac{729}{16} \, x^2 \, (1 - x)^4.$$

When this last expression is substituted into the rejection sampling algorithm, we find that to generate a random variate from the original beta distribution $f(x)$ of interest, we should perform the following procedure:

Step 1. Generate a uniform random variate U on the unit interval.

Step 2. Generate a random variate X from the uniform proposal distribution with density $g(x)$.

Step 3. Determine whether $U < f(X)/Mg(X) = (729/16) \, X^2 \, (1-X)^4$. If this inequality is *false*, return to *Step 1* and start over. If this inequality is *true*, then accept the current value of X and stop the algorithm.

The value of X finally accepted will be a random draw from the desired beta distribution with density $f(x)$. This example is described pictorially in Figure 2. As mentioned previously, the number of iterations required to generate an accepted draw is known to be geometrically distributed with a mean of M, so for this simple example approximately 2.3 iterations of the algorithm are required. In a sense this is an atypical result, since many applications of the rejection sampling method require dozens or even hundreds of iterations on average to generate a single accepted draw.

FIGURE 2
A SECOND ILLUSTRATION OF THE REJECTION SAMPLING METHOD

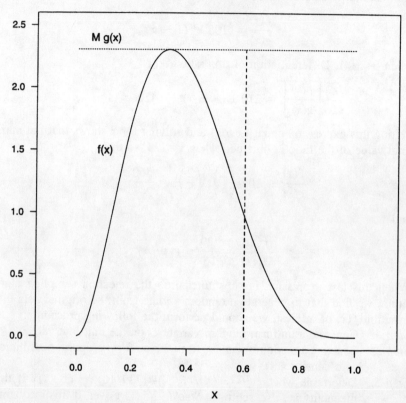

C. The Adaptive Rejection Sampling Method

Two difficulties are associated with this rejection sampling method. First, the practitioner must be able to specify a proposal distribution with a density $g(x)$ satisfying the relation $f(x) \leq Mg(x)$ for some constant M. Second, since M is the average number of iterations required to generate an accepted draw, the practitioner must be able to deduce a small value of M, so that the implementation of the rejection sampling method will be efficient. Gilks and Wild [13] and Gilks [12] have designed ARS methods that remove the difficulties associated with, and improve upon, straightforward rejection sampling when the random draw is required from a distribution with a log-concave density function $f(x)$. Specifically, their ARS methods construct the proposal distribution automatically and cleverly update it periodically, so that the probability of rejecting a candidate draw from the proposal distribution decreases monotonically from iteration to iteration. ARS can be used to obtain an independent random sample of any size from a distribution with a log-concave density. The following paragraphs describe the main idea of ARS, specify the formal algorithm, clearly state the conditions necessary for its successful utilization, and indicate how programming code implementing ARS can be obtained.

Briefly, ARS proceeds by using the fact that a concave function can be squeezed between two bounds or hulls with piece-wise linear structures. The original formulation of ARS given by Gilks and Wild [13] constructs the upper hull by joining tangent lines evaluated at points along the function's domain and the lower hull by joining chords between these same points. This notion of bounding a log-concave function is illustrated in Figure 3. When this construction is applied to the logarithm of a log-concave density, the exponentiated upper hull defines a distribution with a piece-wise exponential form. This is the proposal distribution from which random draws are initially generated. A random draw from the proposal distribution is then accepted with a probability related to how closely the true density is squeezed between the upper and lower hulls at the value of the random draw. Furthermore, if the draw fails a certain test condition, then the upper and lower hulls are updated to incorporate the value of this draw. As the hulls are updated, the proposal distribution comes to more closely resemble the distribution from which random draws are sought, and the probability of rejecting a candidate draw from the proposal distribution monotonically decreases. By carefully tailoring the rejection step and test condition, accepted draws are independently generated realizations from the distribution of interest with the original log-concave density function.

The ARS method of Gilks and Wild [13] can be thought of as a black-box technique for sampling from any univariate log-concave probability density function $f(x)$. The density need only be specified up to a constant of integration, so that rejection sampling can be performed by using $g(x)$ instead of $f(x)$, where $g(x) = cf(x)$ for some possibly unknown value of c (this is not the same $g(x)$ as in the previous section). This is useful when the form of the density is available, but the normalizing constant $c = \int g(x)dx$ is difficult to compute. To use ARS to sample from a density function $f(x)$, it is necessary to check that the domain $D = \{x | f(x) > 0\}$ is a connected set, that $g(x)$

FIGURE 3

BONDING A LOG-CONCAVE DENSITY FUNCTION

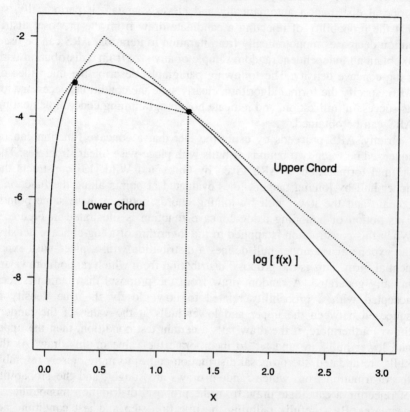

is continuous and differentiable everywhere in D, and that $h(x)=\ln[g(x)]$ is concave everywhere in D (that is, the first derivative of $h(x)$ decreases monotonically with increasing x in D). If the second derivative of $\ln[f(x)]$ exists, then it suffices to check that

$$\frac{d^2}{dx^2} \ln [f(x)] \le 0,$$

for all values of x in the domain of the density function, to ensure that $h(x)$ is concave as required.

A formal description of the ARS algorithm of Gilks and Wild [13] begins by supposing that $h(x)$ and $h'(x)$ have been evaluated at k points $x_1 \leq x_2 \leq ... \leq x_k$ in the domain of $f(x)$. Let $T_k = \{x_i; i=1, ..., k\}$ and let $u_k(x)$ and $l_k(x)$ denote the piece-wise linear upper hull formed by connecting the tangents to $h(x)$ at the points in T_k, and the piece-wise linear lower hull formed by connecting the chords between the adjacent points in T_k, respectively (in the spirit of Figure 3). Define the sampling density

$$S_k(x) = \frac{\exp[u_k(x)]}{\int \exp[u_k(x)]dx}.$$

The following ARS algorithm allows as many independent random draws as desired to be made from the distribution with density proportional to $f(x)$.

Step 1. Select and order the values in T_k. If the domain of $f(x)$ is unbounded on the left, then select x_1 so that $h'(x_1) > 0$. If the domain of $f(x)$ is unbounded on the right, then select x_k so that $h'(x_k) < 0$.

Step 2. Generate a uniform random variate U on the unit interval.

Step 3. Generate a random variate X from the sampling density $S_k(x)$.

Step 4. Determine whether $U < \exp[l_k(X) - u_k(X)]$. When this inequality is *true*, accept the current value of X. When this inequality is *false*, determine whether $U < \exp[h(X) - u_k(X)]$. If this second inequality is *true*, then accept the current value of X; otherwise reject it.

Step 5. If the first inequality in Step 4 is *false*, then insert X into the set T_k, increment k, relabel and reorder the values in T_k, and redefine the functions $u_k(x)$, $l_k(x)$, and $S_k(x)$.

Step 6. Return to Step 2 and iterate this procedure until as many values of X have been accepted as required. The final collection of accepted values constitutes a random sample from the distribution with density proportional to $f(x)$.

Although the ARS algorithm of Gilks and Wild [13] is fairly simply stated, designing and then programming an efficient implementation of it might prove to be a daunting task. Fortunately, this is not required. Wild and Gilks [37] discuss an implementation of the ARS method, which appears as Algorithm AS 287 in *Applied Statistics* [37], and Fortran code implementing ARS is freely available on the computer Internet in the StatLib archive site* maintained at Carnegie Mellon University. Gilks [12] describes

*Send an electronic mail message containing only the two words *send index* to statlib @lib.stat.cmu.edu to receive a message describing the contents of this archive site and how to

a *derivative-free* variant of ARS, which neither assumes continuity in the derivatives of $f(x)$ nor requires the evaluation of these derivatives.

TABLE 1

DENSITIES USEFUL IN ACTUARIAL APPLICATIONS
AND THEIR LOG-CONCAVITY PROPERTIES

Name of Density	Parameters	Log-Concave wrt:
Exponential	λ	x, ln x, λ
Gamma	α, β	ln x, x (if $\alpha \geq 1$), α, β
Lognormal	μ, σ^2	ln x, μ, $1/\sigma$, log σ
Normal	μ, σ^2	x, μ, $1/\sigma$, log σ
Pareto	α, λ	ln x, α
Weibull	c, τ	x (if $\tau \geq 1$), ln x, c, τ
Bernoulli	p	p, logit p
Binomial	n, p	p, logit p
Poisson	λ	λ
Negative Binomial	r, p	p, logit p

Random variate generation techniques for distributions with log-concave density functions should be of interest to the actuarial practitioner precisely because so many of the distributions in practical actuarial applications share this property. A number of these densities, along with their log-concavity properties, are listed in Table 1. These densities are parameterized as in Hogg and Klugman [20]. When a density is indicated as being concave on the logarithmic scale with respect to a transformation of its random variable (for example, ln x) in Table 1, this means that the density for the transformed random variable is log-concave with respect to its argument. As shown in Table 1, a number of these densities are also log-concave with respect to one or more of their continuous parameters, which can prove useful in the context of a Bayesian analysis (for an example, see Gilks and Wild [13]). Of course, many distributions besides those listed in Table 1 also possess log-concave densities. In fact, for the general location-scale family of distributions with densities of form

$$f(x|\theta, \sigma) \propto \frac{1}{\sigma} \phi \left(\frac{x - \theta}{\sigma} \right)$$

retrieve selections from it. Send an electronic mail message containing only the four words *send index from apstat* to statlib@lib.stat.cmu.edu to obtain an index of all the *Applied Statistics* algorithms currently archived in StatLib. Finally, send an electronic mail message containing only the four words *send 287 from apstat* to statlib@lib.stat.cmu.edu to obtain Fortran code implementing Algorithm AS 287.

the logarithm of the density will be concave with respect to x, θ, and $\tau = 1/\sigma$, provided that the function $\phi(z)$ is log-concave with respect to z ([13, p. 343]).

D. The Metropolis-Hastings Algorithm

Rejection sampling and ARS each allow generation of a sequence of independent draws from a distribution of interest. On the other hand, a MCMC method generates a sequence of dependent draws from some distribution. Good discussions of these methods are provided by Smith and Roberts [33], Tanner [34], and Tierney [35]. The Metropolis algorithm (Metropolis et al. [26]) is a form of MCMC method. Hastings [17] proposed a generalization of this method, which has become known as the Metropolis-Hastings (MH) algorithm. The MH algorithm allows a dependent sequence of random draws to be sampled from a distribution with density proportional to $f(x)$, provided that a proposal distribution with density $g(x|z)$ is available such that a random draw is easily obtained from it for any value of z in the domain of $f(x)$. Then the MH algorithm proceeds as follows:

Step 1. Select a starting value X_0 and set i equal to 0.

Step 2. Generate a uniform random variate U on the unit interval.

Step 3. Generate a random variate X from $g(x|X_i)$.

Step 4. Determine whether

$$U < \min\left(1, \frac{f(X)\, g(X_i|X)}{f(X_i)\, g(X|X_i)}\right).$$

When this inequality is *true*, accept the current value of X and set X_{i+1} equal to X. When this inequality is *false*, reject the current value of X and set X_{i+1} equal to X_i.

Step 5. Increment i to $i+1$ and return to Step 2.

After a suitably large number of iterations, relevant asymptotic theory (for example, Smith and Roberts [33] and Tierney [35]) states that the sequence $X_1, X_2, \ldots$, can be considered to be a dependent random sample from $f(x)$ in the sense that

$$X_t \xrightarrow{d} X \sim f(x) \text{ as } t \to \infty$$

and

$$\frac{1}{t}\sum_{i=1}^{t} h(X_i) \to E_f[h(X)] \text{ as } t \to \infty,$$

almost surely.

In plain English, the first result says that as t becomes moderately large, the value X_t is very nearly a random draw from $f(x)$. In practice, a value of $t \approx 10$ to 15 is typically more than sufficient. This result also allows an approximately independent random sample to be generated from the distribution with density $f(x)$ by using only every k-th value appearing in the sequence. The value of k should be taken to be large enough so that the sample autocorrelation function coefficients for the values appearing in the subsequence are reminiscent of those for a purely random process or stochastically independent sequence, that is, until there are no significant autocorrelations at non-zero lags. An illustration is provided below. Autocorrelation functions are covered in some depth in the course of reading for Associateship Course 120, Applied Statistical Methods (also see Miller and Wichern [27, 333–7, 356–65]). The second result says that if h is an arbitrary f-integrable function of X, then the average of the function h taken over the sampled values X_t (the ergodic average of the function) converges (almost surely, as $t \to \infty$) to its expected value under the distribution with density $f(x)$.

Note that the proposal distribution $g(x|z)$ must satisfy some mild regularity conditions to guarantee that the MH algorithm converges in the sense described above. Basically, if u and v are two values in the domain of $f(x)$, then the proposal distribution utilized must permit it to be possible to move from u to v in a finite number of iterations of the MH algorithm with non-zero probability. Further, the number of iterations required to move from u to v should not have to be a multiple of some number. These conditions are usually satisfied if $g(x|z)$ has a positive density on the domain of $f(x)$, or else has a positive density over a restricted domain (for example, $g(x|z)$ corresponds to a uniform distribution around z with finite width) [8], [9]. In short, the practitioner has considerable freedom when selecting the proposal distribution. A popular choice is for the proposal distribution $g(x|z)$ to correspond to a normal distribution with mean z, or perhaps a heavier tailed student t distribution.

Another common selection is to let $g(x|z)$ correspond to a fixed distribution, independent of z, that is, $g(x|z) \equiv g(x)$. An example of this is a normal distribution with zero mean. In practice, the proposal distribution should be selected so that the autocorrelations in the sequence of simulated values generated by the MH algorithm are not too high, and this is often the case if the proposal distribution is selected in such a way that the average number of times the acceptance check in Step 4 of the MH algorithm rejects a candidate draw is about 50% [8], [9].

E. Numerical Example 2

The MH algorithm is illustrated with a trivial yet illuminating example. Consider the distribution with density

$$f(x) = 2\,x,\ 0 \le x \le 1.$$

The MH algorithm is applied with a uniform proposal distribution on the unit interval, so that

$$g(x|z) \equiv g(x) = 1,\ 0 \le x \le 1.$$

In this case, the acceptance probability appearing in Step 4 of the MH algorithm becomes

$$\min\!\left(1, \frac{f(X)\,g(X_i|X)}{f(X_i)\,g(X|X_i)}\right) \equiv \min\!\left(1, \frac{X}{X_i}\right).$$

To initialize the MH algorithm, the starting value X_0 was arbitrarily set equal to 0.5. The $(i+1)$-st iteration was entered with the value X_i; a candidate value X was sampled from the uniform proposal distribution on the unit interval; and the iteration was exited with the value of X_{i+1} set equal to X with a probability equal to $\min(1, X/X_i)$. Otherwise, X_{i+1} was assigned the iteration's entering value X_i. A total of 3,000 iterations of this algorithm was performed, and the first 75 values of X are plotted in Figure 4a. The dependent nature of this sequence is immediately perceptible.

This observation can be confirmed by examining the sample autocorrelation function for this sequence of 3,000 simulated values. This sample autocorrelation function appears as Figure 5a. The heights of the 20 different spikes in this plot represent the values of the sample autocorrelation coefficients at lags 0 through 19. If the sequence of 3,000 sampled values is truly independent, then all the sample autocorrelations at non-zero lags should be close to zero. Spikes crossing either of the two horizontal dashed lines identify autocorrelation coefficients that are significantly different from zero (at the 95% level of significance). For the sequence of 3,000 sampled values, significant autocorrelations are identified at the non-zero lags 1 through 4, reinforcing the original impression that this sequence was

FIGURE 4

PLOTS FOR NUMERICAL EXAMPLE 2

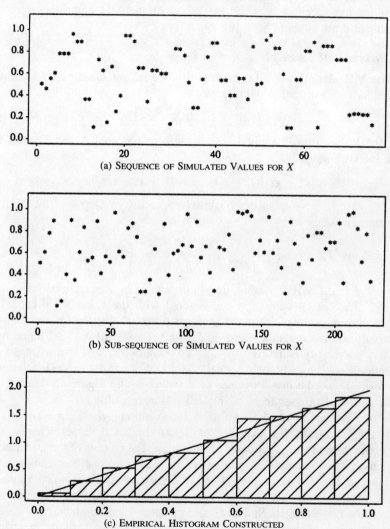

(a) SEQUENCE OF SIMULATED VALUES FOR X

(b) SUB-SEQUENCE OF SIMULATED VALUES FOR X

(c) EMPIRICAL HISTOGRAM CONSTRUCTED
USING THE SUB-SEQUENCE OF SIMULATED VALUES FOR X

dependent. Even so, the empirical mean (0.66121) and variance (0.05520) of these 3,000 sampled values are each very close to the exact theoretical values associated with the random variable with distribution $f(x)$ (0.66667 and 0.05556, respectively).

FIGURE 5

SAMPLE AUTOCORRELATION FUNCTION PLOTS FOR NUMERICAL EXAMPLE 2

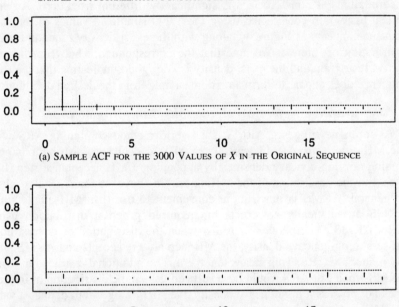

(a) SAMPLE ACF FOR THE 3000 VALUES OF X IN THE ORIGINAL SEQUENCE

(b) SAMPLE ACF FOR THE 1000 VALUES OF X IN THE SUB-SEQUENCE

Incidentally, the implementation of the MH algorithm for this example was monitored as it ran on a fast computer, and the acceptance check in Step 4 of the algorithm rejected 978 of the 3,000 candidate draws from the proposal distribution. Thus, the observed rejection rate was 32.6%. The rejection rate is sometimes referred to as the "staying rate," since when a candidate draw X from the proposal distribution is rejected in Step 4 of the MH algorithm, the value of X_{i+1} stays the same as that of X_i. Obviously, this accounts for the dependence observed in the sequence of 3,000 simulated values.

To recover an approximately independent random sample from this sequence, the sub-sequence of 1,000 values was formed by keeping only every third value in the original sequence of 3,000 (that is, $k=3$ in the discussion above). The first 75 values of this sub-sequence constitute Figure 4b. The sample autocorrelation function for this sub-sequence of 1,000 values appears as Figure 5b. This sample autocorrelation function is reminiscent of what we would expect for a purely random process, since none of the autocorrelations at non-zero lags is significantly different from zero. An empirical histogram constructed using the 1,000 simulated values of the sub-sequence appears as Figure 4c, along with the exact density function for the distribution of interest. We note that the correspondence between the empirical histogram and the exact density is very good, indicating that the sub-sequence does appear to form a random sample from the desired distribution.

F. The Adaptive Rejection Metropolis Sampling Method

As its name suggests, ARMS is a hybrid method combining ARS with the MH algorithm. ARMS generalizes ARS to deal with distributions possessing non-log-concave densities by appending a MH acceptance step (like Step 4 in the description of the MH algorithm above) to the ARS algorithm. In general, ARMS is much more convenient to use than MH alone, since ARMS automatically constructs the required proposal distribution using ARS. ARMS also operates such that when the distribution of interest does possess a log-concave density, the MH step always accepts and ARMS simply reduces to ARS. This means that there is no additional overhead in using ARMS when just ARS would have sufficed. When the distribution of interest does not possess a log-concave density, the ARMS algorithm defines a valid MCMC method and generates a dependent sequence of random draws from the distribution of interest. A detailed description of ARMS can be found in Gilks et al. [14], [15]. Those two papers also announce the free availability of C code implementing ARMS, utilizing a derivative-free version of ARS, and indicate that it may be obtained from the authors on request (e-mail wally.gilks@mrc-bsu.cam.ac.uk). This C code was utilized to perform the simulations discussed in the next section. I will gladly provide interested readers with the main calling program used in conjunction with the ARMS code to implement the random draws from the Makeham survival distribution described in the next section.

4. APPLYING ARS AND ARMS IN THE MAKEHAM CONTEXT

When operating under Makeham's law, as noted at the end of Section 2, the distribution of the future lifetime random variable $T(x)$ either has a log-concave density or possesses one that is nearly so for all practical selections of the Makeham constants. The discussion in Section 3 states that a very efficient and fast random number generator now exists, which can be used to simulate a sequence of (possibly dependent) random draws from the distribution of $T(x)$, in these cases. By utilizing well-known Monte Carlo simulation methods (for example, Ross [29], Tanner [34]), it will also be possible to easily infer a variety of characteristics related to the distribution of various life contingent functions under the assumption of Makeham's law. The remainder of this section provides a few examples illustrating some of the applications of this method.

A. Numerical Example 3

Consider a life age 50 whose future lifetime random variable $T(50)$ is assumed to follow the Makeham distribution, as in Section 2, with parameters

$$A = 0.001, \ B = 0.0000070848535, \ C = 1.1194379,$$

as found in Mereu [25] and Moore [28]. ARMS was utilized to generate 5,000 dependent realizations of $T(50)$ from this Makeham distribution. This simulation took a second or two to run on a desktop UNIX workstation (that is, a SUN Sparcstation LX operating at 50 MHz).† The MH acceptance step in the ARMS algorithm rejected none of the 5,000 candidate draws from the proposal distribution, indicating that the ARS part of ARMS was doing a very good job at constructing and updating an efficient proposal distribution. This comes as no great surprise, since in Section 2 the density of the Makeham survival distribution was very nearly log-concave, so that the ARS algorithm should be able to construct a proposal distribution that closely matches the Makeham survival distribution of interest. As in Example 2, the sample autocorrelation function was examined for the dependent sequence of 5,000 simulated values, and it was reminiscent of that for a purely random process (that is, none of the autocorrelations at non-zero

---

†This simulation time, along with those reported below, should be comparable to that using a fast PC (for example, 486 or Pentium operating at 50 Mhz or faster). In fact, since my Sparcstation is circa 1992 with no upgrades, I would expect even better simulation times using a fast Pentium-based PC.

lags was significantly different from zero). Thus, the 5,000 dependent realizations were treated as independent draws for all practical intents and purposes. The empirical histogram for these sampled values is plotted against the exact density for the random variable $T(50)$ in Figure 6a to demonstrate that they do appear to constitute a random sample from the desired distribution. Recall that the exact density function $f(t)$ for the future lifetime random variable $T(x)$ under Makeham's law was previously derived in Section 2.

For this same life, consider a newly issued unit whole life insurance with benefit payable at the moment of death, so that the present value of the benefit is described by the random variable

$$Z = v^{T(50)} = \exp[-\delta T(50)], \ T(50) \geq 0,$$

in which $\delta \geq 0$ denotes the force of interest. Also, consider a continuous whole life annuity with the random variable

$$Y = \bar{a}_{\overline{T(50)}|} = \frac{1 - \exp[-\delta T(50)]}{\delta}, \ T(50) \geq 0,$$

describing the present value of the annuity payments. Both of these random variables are typical of the sort found in Bowers et al. [3]. We applied these two transformations to the 5,000 previously sampled values of $T(50)$ to generate (effectively independent) random samples from the distributions of Z and Y, taking the force of interest to be equal to $\delta = \ln(1.025)$ for illustrative purposes. In Figures 6b and 6c the empirical histograms of these transformed values have been plotted against the exact density functions for Z and Y to demonstrate that they essentially constitute random samples from the distributions we claim. The exact density functions for the random variables Z and Y were obtained by applying the standard transformation of variable technique to the density function of $T(50)$ (for example, Hogg and Craig [19, p. 132–3]).

At this time ARMS once again was utilized to generate 250,000 realizations of $T(50)$ from the same Makeham distribution as before; these sampled values were also transformed into realizations of Z and Y. This simulation took less than 2 minutes of real time on the same desktop SUN Sparcstation LX. The empirical mean, variance, skewness, kurtosis, and 95th percentile of these sampled values were used to estimate the corresponding population quantities. These empirical values are presented in the third column of Table 2. Estimated approximate Monte Carlo standard errors [34, p. 30] are also

FIGURE 6
EXACT DENSITIES AND EMPIRICAL HISTOGRAMS FOR NUMERICAL EXAMPLE 3

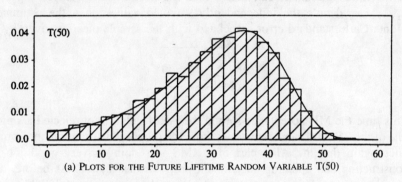

(a) PLOTS FOR THE FUTURE LIFETIME RANDOM VARIABLE $T(50)$

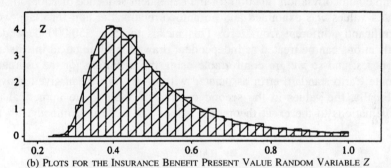

(b) PLOTS FOR THE INSURANCE BENEFIT PRESENT VALUE RANDOM VARIABLE Z

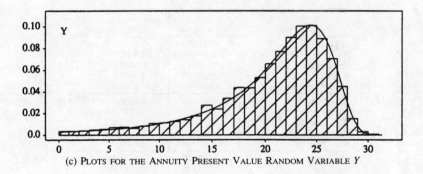

(c) PLOTS FOR THE ANNUITY PRESENT VALUE RANDOM VARIABLE Y

included for the three empirical means in brackets beside these entries in the third column. Recall that if n is the Monte Carlo sample size and $x_1, \ldots, x_n$ denote the independently sampled values, then the estimated Monte Carlo standard error associated with the sample mean is given by

$$\sqrt{\frac{\sum_{i=1}^{n} (x_i - \bar{x})^2}{n(n - 1)}}.$$

This time the MH acceptance step in the ARMS algorithm rejected a single one of the 250,000 candidate draws from the proposal distribution, indicating once again that the ARS part of ARMS was doing a very good job at constructing and updating an efficient proposal distribution. As before, the sample autocorrelation function for the dependent sequence of 250,000 simulated values was examined and no autocorrelations at non-zero lags were significantly different from zero. This means that the 250,000 dependent realizations can be treated as independent draws for all practical intents and purposes, and so we are comfortable using the definition for the estimated Monte Carlo standard error associated with the sample mean given above.

Finally, the values in the second column of Table 2 are numerical approximations to the exact theoretical values and were determined with the

TABLE 2

NUMERICAL APPROXIMATIONS AND EMPIRICAL VALUES
FOR NUMERICAL EXAMPLE 3

Quantity of Interest	Numerical Approximation	Empirical Value
E [T(50)]	30.81125	30.79607 (0.02086)
Variance [T(50)]	108.87118	108.80472
Skewness [T(50)]	−0.60911	−0.61111
Kurtosis [T(50)]	2.96685	2.96872
95th Percentile (T(50))	45.39895	45.35621
E [$v^{T(50)}$]	0.48388	0.48406 (0.00027)
Variance [$v^{T(50)}$]	0.01851	0.01852
Skewness [$v^{T(50)}$]	1.26008	1.26134
Kurtosis [$v^{T(50)}$]	4.50669	4.50692
95th Percentile ($v^{T(50)}$)	0.77004	0.77025
E [$\bar{a}_{\overline{T(50)}}$]	20.90160	20.89457 (0.01102)
Variance [$\bar{a}_{\overline{T(50)}}$]	30.36526	30.38141
Skewness [$\bar{a}_{\overline{T(50)}}$]	−1.26008	−1.26134
Kurtosis [$\bar{a}_{\overline{T(50)}}$]	4.50669	4.50692
95th Percentile ($\bar{a}_{\overline{T(50)}}$)	27.29774	27.2838

aid of a symbolic mathematics computer package (namely, Maple V Release 3). A symbolic mathematics package represents another means by which simple characteristics like moments or tail probabilities associated with the Makeham survival distribution can be determined. Unfortunately, these packages are not always well-suited for more sophisticated problems (for example, like numerical example 4 below), and they are not as commonplace as Fortran or C compilers (Fortran and C being two languages for which programming code implementing ARS and ARMS is freely and readily available). Further, symbolic mathematics packages are usually not designed for simulation applications, so that they may not be very convenient computing environments in which to implement simulation methods such as ARS or ARMS.

B. Numerical Example 4

Now consider a whole life insurance issued to a life age 30 with a 10,000 benefit payable at the moment of death and with a premium of an amount equal to π payable at the beginning of each year. For this policy, the random variable describing the present value of the loss faced by the insurer is defined by

$$L = 10,000 \, v^{T(30)} - \pi \, \ddot{a}_{\overline{K(30)+1}}, \, T(30) \geq 0,$$

where $K(x)$ is used to denote the curtate future lifetime random variable for (x). The value of π is determined according to some premium principle as in Chapter 6 of Bowers et al. [3]. The equivalence principle, for example, selects π such that the insurer's expected loss is equal to zero (that is, $E[L]=0$). For the present numerical illustration, we set π as small as possible such that the insurer faces a positive loss on this single insurance contract with a probability no greater than 5% (that is, $Pr[L>0]\leq0.05$). Unfortunately, the distribution of L is somewhat awkward to study analytically since L is a function of the continuous random variable $T(30)$ along with its discrete valued part $K(30)$. This would also complicate the application of a symbolic mathematics package. Nevertheless, we may easily estimate the value of π on the basis of a Monte Carlo simulation.

Specifically, if the future lifetime random variable $T(30)$ is assumed to follow a Makeham distribution as in Section 2, then it is a simple matter to simulate a large number of realizations of $T(30)$ using ARMS and, for a given value of π, then transform these sampled values into realizations of L. On the basis of just such a Monte Carlo simulation, assuming that the

Makeham parameters remained as in numerical example 3, taking the force of interest δ to be equal to $\ln(1.075)$, and utilizing 250,000 sampled values of $T(30)$, we determined that for a value of π equal to 143.20, the probability $Pr[L>0]$ is approximately equal to 0.05. Incidentally, during this simulation the MH acceptance step in the ARMS algorithm rejected 1,796 of the 250,000 candidate draws from the proposal distribution, thus yielding a rejection rate of 0.7184%. This rejection rate is very small and indicates that the ARS part of ARMS is doing a good job at constructing and updating an efficient proposal distribution. Note that this rejection rate is considerably larger than the one encountered in the previous example, possibly indicating that the Makeham survival distribution for a life age 30 is not quite as log-concave as it is for a life age 50.

To test the value of π determined above, another 250,000 realizations of $T(30)$ were sampled. The empirical histogram of these values is presented in Figure 7a along with a plot of the exact density curve. Taking π equal to 143.20, we transformed these values into realizations of L. The proportion of these realizations exceeding zero was 5.082% (that is, the observed value of L exceeded zero 12,705 times out of 250,000). The empirical histogram for these sampled values of L is also presented in Figure 7b. Note that this second histogram is plotted on a square root scale, so that the proportion of realizations of L observed between $-2,000$ and $-1,500$ is approximately equal to $500 \times 0.039 \times 0.039 = 0.7605$, for example. A square root scale was adopted for the vertical axis of this histogram to better illustrate the long tail of the distribution on the right-hand side. Table 3 presents the empirical mean, variance, skewness, kurtosis, and 95th percentile of the sampled values of L.

Finally, assume that the life under study survives to age 50 and that we are interested in studying the adequacy of the reserve at that time. Using ideas found in Chapter 7 of Bowers et al. [3], the insurer's prospective loss random variable at that time is defined by

$$_{20}L = 10,000 \, v^{T(50)} - 143.20 \, \ddot{a}_{\overline{K(50)+1}|}.$$

By now, it should be apparent that we can simulate random draws from the distribution of $_{20}L$ by sampling values of $T(50)$ using ARMS and then applying the appropriate transformation to them. We simulated 250,000 realizations of $_{20}L$ in this manner and plotted the empirical histogram for the sampled values in Figure 7c. As before and for the same reason, this histogram is plotted on a square root scale. Table 3 presents the empirical mean,

FIGURE 7

EXACT DENSITY AND EMPIRICAL HISTOGRAMS FOR NUMERICAL EXAMPLE 4

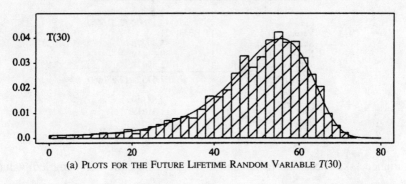

(a) PLOTS FOR THE FUTURE LIFETIME RANDOM VARIABLE $T(30)$

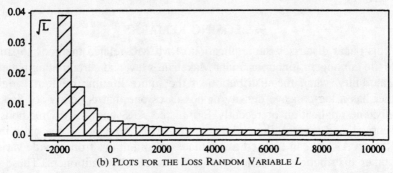

(b) PLOTS FOR THE LOSS RANDOM VARIABLE L

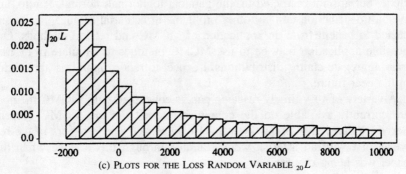

(c) PLOTS FOR THE LOSS RANDOM VARIABLE $_{20}L$

TABLE 3
EMPIRICAL VALUES FOR NUMERICAL EXAMPLE 4

Quantity of Interest	Empirical Value
$E[L]$	$-1,444.17600$ (2.31665)
Variance $[L]$	1,341,721
Skewness $[L]$	5.49276
Kurtosis $[L]$	39.11419
95th Percentile $[L]$	12.89028
$E[_{20}L]$	-267.6755 (3.57699)
Variance $[_{20}L]$	3,198,709
Skewness $[_{20}L]$	2.68140
Kurtosis $[_{20}L]$	11.31819
95th Percentile $[_{20}L]$	3,529.356

variance, skewness, kurtosis, and 95th percentile of the sampled values of $_{20}L$.

5. CLOSING REMARKS

This paper discusses the application of MCMC-related methods to simulate life contingent functions under Makeham's law and certain other patterns of mortality, when the distribution of the future lifetime random variable either has a log-concave density or possesses one that is nearly so. Specifically, the application of recently formulated ARS and ARMS methods is discussed, and several illustrations are provided. As noted in the main text, ARS and ARMS can be used to simulate random draws from a wide variety of other distributions commonly used by actuarial practitioners. These include, but are not restricted to, the gamma, lognormal, normal, Pareto, and Weibull distributions. Many other problems in actuarial science can be expected to benefit from an application of MCMC and related methods. One possible application may be to use MCMC methods to simulate from arbitrary aggregate claims distributions. I expect to report upon this application in the near future.

A variety of very timely research papers concerned with MCMC methods are currently available on the computer Internet via the MCMC Preprint Service located at http://www.statslab.cam.ac.uk/. Those papers in the reference list with an asterisk were available through this service when this paper was being prepared.

REFERENCES

1. ANDERSON, A.W. *Pension Mathematics for Actuaries.* 2nd ed. Wellesley, Ma.: Arthur W. Anderson, 1990.

2. BECKER, R.A., CHAMBERS, J.M., AND WILKS, A.R. *The New S Language.* Pacific Grove, Calif.: Wadsworth & Brooks, 1988.

3. BOWERS, N.L., GERBER, H.U., HICKMAN, J.C., JONES, D.A., AND NESBITT, C.J. *Actuarial Mathematics.* Itasca, Ill.: Society of Actuaries, 1986.

4. CARLIN, B.P. "State Space Modeling of Non-Standard Actuarial Time Series," *Insurance: Mathematics and Economics* 11 (1992): 209–22.

5. CARLIN, B.P. "A Simple Monte Carlo Approach to Bayesian Graduation," *TSA* XLIV (1992): 55–76.

6. CARRIERE, J.F. "An Investigation of the Gompertz Law of Mortality," *ARCH* 1994.2 (1994): 161–77.

7. CASELLA, G., AND GEORGE, E.I. "Explaining the Gibbs Sampler," *The American Statistician* 46 (1992): 167–74.

*8. CHIB, S., AND GREENBERG, E. "Understanding the Metropolis-Hastings Algorithm," Olin School of Business, University of Washington, 1994. Also available via anonymous ftp from *wublib.wustl.edu* in pub/chib/cg_mh.ps.

9. CHIB, S., AND GREENBERG, E. "Understanding the Metropolis-Hastings Algorithm," *The American Statistician* 49 (1995): 327–35.

10. DEVROYE, L. *Non-Uniform Random Variate Generation.* New York: Springer-Verlag, 1986.

11. GELFAND, A.E., AND SMITH, A.F.M. "Sampling Based Approaches to Calculating Marginal Densities," *Journal of the American Statistical Association* 85 (1990): 398–409.

12. GILKS, W.R. "Derivative-Free Adaptive Rejection Sampling for Gibbs Sampling," in *Bayesian Statistics 4*, ed. J.M. Bernardo, J.O. Berger, A.P. Dawid, and A.F.M. Smith. Oxford: University Press, 1992, 641–9.

13. GILKS, W.R., AND WILD, P. "Adaptive Rejection Sampling for Gibbs Sampling," *Applied Statistics* 41, no. 2 (1992): 337–48.

14. GILKS, W.R., BEST, N.G., AND TAN, K.K.C. "Adaptive Rejection Metropolis Sampling for Gibbs Sampling," Technical Report, Medical Research Council Biostatistics Unit, Cambridge, U.K., 1992.

*15. GILKS, W.R., BEST, N.G., AND TAN, K.K.C. "Adaptive Rejection Metropolis Sampling within Gibbs Sampling," Technical Report, Medical Research Council Biostatistics Unit, Cambridge, U.K., 1994.

16. GOMPERTZ, B. "On the Nature of a Function Expressive of the Law of Human Mortality, and On a New Mode of Determining the Value of Life Contingencies," *Philosophical Transactions of the Royal Society* 115 (1825): 513–85.

*Available via MCMC Preprint Service.

17. HASTINGS, W.K. "Monte Carlo Sampling Methods Using Markov Chains and Their Applications," *Biometrika* 57 (1970): 97–109.

18. HILLIER, F.S., AND LIEBERMAN, G.J. *Introduction to Operations Research.* 5th ed. New York: McGraw Hill Publishing Company, 1990.

19. HOGG, R.V., AND CRAIG, A.T. *Introduction to Mathematical Statistics.* 4th ed. New York: Macmillan Publishing Co., Inc., 1978.

20. HOGG, R.V., AND KLUGMAN, S.A. *Loss Distributions.* New York: John Wiley & Sons, 1984.

21. JORDAN, C.W. *Life Contingencies.* 2nd ed. Chicago, Ill.: Society of Actuaries, 1982.

22. KLUGMAN, S.A., AND CARLIN, B.P. "Hierarchical Bayesian Whittaker Graduation," *Scandinavian Actuarial Journal* 2 (1993): 183–96.

23. LONDON, D. *Survival Models and Their Estimation.* 2nd ed. Winsted and Avon, Conn.: Actex Publications, 1988.

24. MAKEHAM, W.M. "On the Law of Mortality, and the Construction of Annuity Tables," *The Assurance Magazine and Journal of the Institute of Actuaries* VIII (1860): 301–10.

25. MEREU, J.A. "Annuity Values Directly from Makeham Constants," *TSA* XIV (1962): 269–86.

26. METROPOLIS, N., ROSENBLUTH, A.W., ROSENBLUTH, M.N., TELLER, A.H., AND TELLER, E. "Equations of State Calculations by Fast Computing Machines," *Journal of Chemical Physics* 21 (1953): 1087–92.

27. MILLER, R.B., AND WICHERN, D.W. *Intermediate Business Statistics: Analysis of Variance, Regression, and Time Series.* New York: Holt, Rinehart and Winston, 1977.

28. MOORE, M.H. "Derivatives of the Annuity Function Assuming Makeham-Gompertz Mortality; and the N-Ages Method," *Communications in Statistics: Computation and Simulation* (1981): 359–67.

29. ROSS, S.M. *A Course in Simulation.* New York: Macmillan Publishing Company, 1990.

30. ROSS, S.M. *Introduction to Probability Models.* 4th ed. San Diego: Academic Press Inc., 1989.

31. SCOLLNIK, D.P.M. "A Bayesian Analysis of a Simultaneous Equations Model for Insurance Rate-making," *Insurance: Mathematics and Economics* 12 (1993): 265–86.

32. SCOLLNIK, D.P.M. "The Bayesian Analysis of Generalized Poisson Models for Claim Frequence Data Utilising Markov Chain Monte Carlo Methods," *ARCH* 1995.1, 339–56.

33. SMITH, A.F.M., AND ROBERTS, G.O. "Bayesian Computation via the Gibbs Sampler and Related Markov Chain Monte Carlo Methods," *Journal of the Royal Statistical Society Series B* 55 (1993): 3–23.

34. TANNER, M.A. *Tools for Statistical Inference, Methods for the Exploration of Posterior Distributions and Likelihood Functions.* 2nd ed. New York: Springer-Verlag, 1993.
35. TIERNEY, L. "Markov Chains for Exploring Posterior Distributions," *The Annals of Statistics* 22, no. 4 (1994): 1701–28.
36. WAKEFIELD, J.C., GELFAND, A.E., AND SMITH, A.F.M. "Efficient Generation of Random Variates via the Ratio-of-uniforms Method," *Statistics and Computing* 1 (1991): 129–33.
37. WILD, P., AND GILKS, W.R. "Adaptive Rejection Sampling from Log-concave Density Functions," *Applied Statistics* 42 (1993): 701–9.

DISCUSSION OF PRECEDING PAPER

JACQUES F. CARRIERE:

Dr. Scollnik's paper presents MCMC-related methods to simulate random variables from densities that are nearly or exactly log-concave. The purpose of this discussion is to argue that these simulations can be done with simple and standard methods.

Let us suppose that we have generated a sequence of independent and identically distributed random variables, denoted as $X_1, \ldots, X_n$, from a common cumulative distribution function (cdf), denoted as $F(x)$. It is well-known that this sequence can be used to construct an empirical function

$$\hat{F}(x) = \frac{1}{n} \sum_{k=1}^{n} 1 \ (X_k \leq x),$$

which can be used to approximate any property of $F(x)$. The paper states that these "simulation methods allow a variety of previously inaccessible inferences to be made routinely and easily." To suggest that this paper solves problems that were "previously inaccessible" is too strong a statement, because these problems are easily solved with standard techniques. Moreover, it is not the simulation methods that allow these inferences to be made easily; rather, it is the empirical function $\hat{F}(x)$. For example, to approximate $\bar{A}_{50}$, we would use the formula

$$\int_0^\infty v^x \, d\hat{F}(x) = \frac{1}{n} \sum_{k=1}^{n} v^{X_k},$$

assuming that $T(50) \sim F(x)$. Again, the more complicated Numerical Example 4 is easily solved, as long as $\hat{F}(x)$ is known.

The paper also states that "none of these references has considered simulating random variates from either Gompertz's or Makeham's survival distribution," possibly implying that these simulations are difficult to implement, thus requiring a sophisticated MCMC-related method. Actually, generating random variables from these distributions is quite simple. Let U be a random variable from a uniform distribution on the interval $(0,1)$. Also, let $F^{-1}(u) = \inf\{x \in \mathcal{R} : F(x) \geq u\}$ be an inverse function of $F(x)$. It is well-known that if $F(x)$ is a continuous function in x, then $F^{-1}(U)$ is a random variable with a cdf equal to $F(x)$. The key to using this result is calculating the inverse function $F^{-1}(u)$. This is a trivial exercise for the Gompertz

439

distribution. For Makeham's law, no explicit expression exists for the inverse function, but the problem of finding the value X such that $F(X)=U$ is easy. In this case the Newton-Raphson method is used, a technique that all actuaries know.

The paper also states that the MCMC-related methods "can be used to quickly and efficiently simulate random draws," possibly implying that these methods are quicker than others. As evidence, the paper states that 250,000 realizations from a Makeham distribution "took less than two minutes of real time" on a SUN Sparcstation LX. Using the GAUSS programming language and the Newton-Raphson method, it took me about six minutes to generate 250,000 observations from the Makeham distribution. These calculations were done on a 66 MHz Pentium processor, and so it is not clear to me that the MCMC-related methods are much faster.

In conclusion, the MCMC-related simulation methods are very interesting and they may be useful under certain situations, but I am not convinced that they are practical enough for simply simulating a Makeham random variable or any other univariate distribution that actuaries may use.

GORDON E. KLEIN:

Dr. Scollnik presents a method for simulating random draws from distributions such as Makeham's. The methods he presents are interesting, and they provide a nice addition to the acceptance-rejection method as covered in the syllabus for Examination 130 [18, p. 871–2]. (Note that my references are to Dr. Scollnik's bibliography.) In particular, the method as presented on the 130 Syllabus can be used only for random variables that are bounded on both sides. The rejection sampling method described by Dr. Scollnik overcomes this problem.

My criticisms of the paper can be stated as follows: (1) This is a method in search of an actuarial problem to solve. I can think of no real problem that is solved by this method, and this paper certainly does not provide one. The illustrations in the paper (particularly Numerical Example 4) are simply artificial problems designed to illustrate the method. I can think of no actuarial application for generating large numbers of random draws from Makeham's distribution. (2) Even if this were not the case, there are ways to simulate Makeham-distributed random variables that are more generally useful. I address the second criticism first.

Other Methods for Simulating Draws from Makeham's Distribution

What if one didn't have the methods of this paper and it were necessary to generate a large number of random draws for a future-lifetime random variable that had the Makeham distribution? One method that comes to mind is to invert the cdf of the future-lifetime random variable and to apply this to random draws from the uniform distribution. Actually, it is a little easier to do this with the survival distribution, of a life currently age (x), instead of the cdf. For a life subject to Makeham's law of mortality, we have

$$_tp_x = s^t g^{c^x(c^t-1)},$$

using the notation of [21], where

$$\ln s = -A,$$

and

$$\ln g = -\frac{B}{\ln c}.$$

Now, let's say that you have a random draw u from the uniform distribution on the unit interval. Setting $_tp_x$ equal to u and solving for t will result in a random draw, t, from the Makeham-distributed random variable, $T(x)$.

The equation

$$u = {}_tp_x = s^t g^{c^x(c^t-1)}$$

cannot be solved explicitly for t, but this presents no real problem. Taking the natural logarithm of each side, we have:

$$\ln u = t \ln s + c^x(c^t - 1) \ln g,$$

which, in terms of the original parameters, is

$$\ln u = -At - \frac{Bc^x}{\ln c}(c^t - 1).$$

Moving all the terms to the left, we have a function whose root we need. Applying the Newton-Raphson Method, we find t as the limit of the quadratically convergent sequence (for an appropriate initial value)

$$t_{k+1} = t_k - \frac{At_k + \dfrac{Bc^x}{\ln c}(c^{t_k} - 1) + \ln u}{A + Bc^{x+t_k}}.$$

This routine required about seven minutes on a 486-66 computer using BASIC to generate 250,000 draws (and calculate the loss random variable for each draw). This compares with less than two minutes for Dr. Scollnik's routine using a SUN Sparcstation and a C-language routine. This does not seem to me to be a significant difference given the infrequency with which one needs to generate 250,000 random draws from a Makeham distribution.

Another method for generating random draws is to simply create a table of the cdf and to search it for each random draw from the uniform distribution on the unit interval. That is, create a table of $_{k|}q_x$ for non-negative integral values of k, and then, for each random draw from the uniform distribution, find the integers that surround that number in the table. This method requires some type of interpolation between the surrounding integers (if you are interested in the exact time of death instead of the number of complete years lived) and an upper bound on the table (even though the Makeham distribution is unbounded). Neither of these problems is very serious. One advantage of this "table lookup" method is that it can be used for *any* distribution of mortality. I think that the method of Dr. Scollnik's paper is more complicated and less general than the method of this paragraph.

A Solution in Search of an Actuarial Problem

My other criticism is that I don't think that the methods of Dr. Scollnik's paper solve any actuarial problem. Numerical Example 4 purports to be a "more sophisticated problem" than can be handled by symbolic mathematics packages. This problem is a variation of one that is common on Examination 150 ("Actuarial Mathematics") and that is easily solved by hand. The random variable L is a continuous (except at the integers), monotonically decreasing function of the remaining-future-lifetime random variable, $T(30)$, which is subsequently referred to as T. Thus, if we find the number t^* such that $\Pr[T < t^*] = 0.05$, then the premium calculated as

$$\pi = \frac{10,000\, v^{t^*}}{\ddot{a}_{\overline{\lfloor t^* \rfloor + 1}}}$$

(where $\lfloor t^* \rfloor$ indicates the greatest integer) will be such that

$$\Pr[L(\pi) > 0] = 0.05$$

(where we have indicated that the loss random variable is a function of the premium).

For the problem considered in Numerical Example 4, t^* is the solution of $_{t^*}q_{30}=0.05$. This is easily found to be 24.323001. Substituting this into the expression for the premium, we have

$$\pi = \frac{10{,}000 \, v^{24.323001}}{\ddot{a}_{\overline{25}|}} \doteq 143.7102.$$

This is exact to the number of places show, but just to demonstrate, I generated 250,000 random draws of the loss random variable using this premium. Of these, 12,603 turned out negative, which is about 5.04%. (Note that this method does not require the generation of any random draws. This was done merely to parallel the "demonstration," actually also the estimation of the answer, in Dr. Scollnik's paper.)

I am interested in Dr. Scollnik's explanation of the discrepancy between this and his answer of 143.20. It appears to me that his method is much more complicated, *requiring* the generation of a huge number of random draws. Yet it gives an answer that is subject to a random error whose range is unbounded. That is, one cannot determine an interval in which the answer lies with probability 1 using Dr. Skollnik's method.

The second part of Numerical Example 4 likewise complicates the process of finding the distribution of the loss random variable 20 years after issue. For example, the 95th percentile of this random variable can easily be found by evaluating the random variable at the value of t^* where $_{t^*}q_{50}=0.05$. It is easily shown that $t^*=10.58276$, so that the 95th percentile of the loss random variable is

$$_{20}L(10.58276) = 10{,}000 \, v^{10.58276} - 143.20 \, \ddot{a}_{\overline{11}|} \doteq 3{,}525.56,$$

(using Dr. Scollnik's premium for comparison). This is exact to the number of places shown. It compares with his "empirical value" of 3,529.356.

The estimation of the x-th percentile of a random variable using the Monte Carlo method (with a given degree of precision) requires a larger sample as x approaches 0 or 100. For example, to estimate the value of the loss random variable, $_{20}L$, that has a one-in-a-million chance of not being exceeded, we could use an estimate between the 10th and 11th order statistics out of a sample of 10 million. This estimate would be unbiased, but its variance would be large. A larger sample would reduce the variance of the estimate.

(The sample of 250,000 from the paper would be useless for this problem.) A better method, when it can be done, is to approach the problem directly. In this particular case, we can find that

$$_{59.002996}p_{50} = 0.000001,$$

so that the 0.0001th percentile of the loss random variable is

$$_{20}L(59.002996) = 10,000 \ v^{59.002996} - 143.20 \ \ddot{a}_{\overline{60|}} = -1,885.536.$$

Conclusion

Despite my two criticisms of this paper, I find the methods interesting. It will be interesting to see what actuarial problems they can be applied to. I look forward to seeing Dr. Skollnik's work applying the methods to aggregate claims distributions.

JEFFREY S. PAI:

Markov chain Monte Carlo methods have become very popular in recent years as a way of generating a sample from a complicated probability distribution. Dr. Scollnik has applied some of these techniques successfully on Makeham's distribution and other distributions. The author has also shown how to easily estimate the distribution of the present value of the benefit as well as the distribution of the present value of the annuity payments using sampling methods. The estimations can be made as accurate as desired by increasing the length of the MCMC simulations.

The problem of the computer generation of random variates with a given force of mortality can be done easily by applying the connection between the cumulative distribution function, F, and the cumulative force of mortality, M:

$$F(t) = 1 - \exp\left[-M(t)\right], \qquad M(t) = \int_0^t \mu(s)ds.$$

For generating a random variate with cumulative mortality M, it suffices to invert an exponential random variate E [Scollnik's ref. 10, p. 260]. If the solution t of $M(t)=E$ is not explicitly known, such as the Makeham's law, we can incorporate Newton-Raphson iterations, the thinning algorithm, or the composition method (see Pai [2]).

The Metropolis algorithm is a method of constructing a reversible Markov transition kernel with a specified invariant distribution. I would like to suggest the applications of the Metropolis algorithm in the optimization procedure and the Bayesian analysis.

The Metropolis algorithm can be used in the simulated annealing method [1], which has attracted significant attention in finding a desired global extremum among many local extrema. Programs coded in C and Fortran are available from Press et al. [3].

Bayesian inference proceeds by obtaining marginal posterior distributions of the components of the model parameters as well as features of these distributions. For instance, suppose we use the data of size 200, say $T = (t_1, \ldots, t_{200})'$, sampled from the Makeham's distribution with

$$\mu(t) = A + BC^{x+t}, \qquad x = 50,$$

where

$A = 0.001$

$B = 0.0000070848535$

$C = 1.1194379.$

If we assume the priors of these parameters are

$$\pi(A) = 1/0.003, \qquad 0 < A < 0.003,$$

$$\pi(B) = 1/0.001, \qquad 0 < B < 0.001,$$

$$\pi(C) = 1/0.2, \qquad 1 < C < 1.2,$$

then the posterior is proportional to the product of the priors and the likelihood function:

$$\pi(A, B, C | T) \propto \prod_{i=1}^{n} (A + BC^{x+t_i}) \exp\left[-A \sum_{i=1}^{n} t_i - \frac{BC^x}{\ln C} \sum_{i=1}^{n} (C^{t_i} - 1) \right].$$

Using the uniform priors stated above, this is essentially the likelihood approach. The ARMS-within-Gibbs method or the Metropolis-within-Gibbs method can be utilized to sample from the full conditional densities. The results of using the Metropolis-within-Gibbs method and the estimated marginal posterior densities are shown in Figure 1 and Figure 2 with 2000 iterations.

As Dr. Scollnik stated, many problems in actuarial science can be expected to benefit from an application of MCMC methods. The attractiveness of the sampling methods is their conceptual simplicity and ease of implementation

FIGURE 1

MCMC OUTPUT FROM THE METROPOLIS-WITHIN-GIBBS ALGORITHM

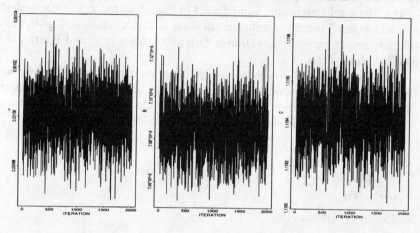

FIGURE 2

ESTIMATED MARGINAL POSTERIOR DENSITIES

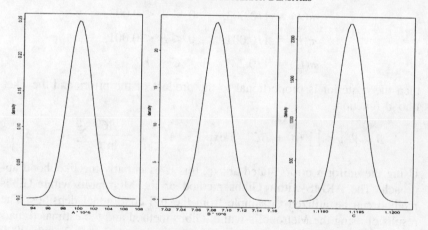

for users with available computing resources but without numerical analytic expertise. I believe that actuarial students will soon gain more insight and understanding in the classroom by using MCMC methods.

REFERENCES

1. KIRKPATRICK, S. "Optimization by Simulated Annealing: Quantitative Studies," *Journal of Statistical Physics* 34 (1984): 975–86.
2. PAI, J.S. *Generating Random Variates with a Given Force of Mortality and Finding a Suitable Force of Mortality by Theoretical Quantile-Quantile Plots.* Manual. University of Manitoba, 1996.
3. PRESS, W.H., TEUKOLSKY, S.A., VETTERLING, W.T., AND FLANNERY, B.P. *Numerical Recipes.* Cambridge: Cambridge University Press, 1992.

JOHN A. MEREU:

Dr. Scollnik has written an interesting paper showing how some new techniques for generating random variables can be used to efficiently solve problems in which mortality follows Makeham's law.

This discussion presents an alternative to Monte Carlo methods referred to as a *grid* approach. The *grid* approach also takes advantage of the computational power of today's personal computers. It calls for the generation of values of a probability density function (pdf) over a broad and dense spectrum of the independent variable.

Let T be the future lifetime random variable for a person aged x. The expected value of T is given by the integral

$$E[T] = \int_0^\infty t \, {}_tp_x \, \mu_{x+t} \, dt.$$

The integral is the limit of the following sum as n approaches infinity and h approaches zero.

$$E[T] = \lim_{\substack{n \to \infty \\ h \to 0}} \sum_{k=0}^n \int_{Kh}^{(K+1)h} t \, {}_tp_x \, \mu_{x+t} \, dt \doteq \sum_{K=0}^n Kh \, {}_{Kh}p_x \, \mu_{x+Kh}.$$

Setting n to 6000 and h to 0.01, I computed the following values given in Table 2 of the paper with an APL program using 1.87 seconds of CPU time:

Quantity of Interest $T(50)$	Numerical Approximation	Empirical Value (Monte Carlo)	Empirical Value (Grid Method)
Mean	30.81125	30.79607	30.80711
Variance	108.87118	108.80472	108.84535
Skewness	−0.60911	−0.61111	−0.60872
Kurtosis	2.96685	2.96872	2.96621
95th Percentile	45.39895	45.35621	45.39

Let Z be the discounted benefit random variable for 1 payable at the moment of death. The expected value of Z is given either of the two integrals, one based on the pdf of Z and the other based on the pdf of T. The grid method can be used to approximate the quantities of interest for either integral. The results are approximately the same and also conform to those given by the Dr. Scollnik in Table 2. If the pdf of T is used, the histograms require a mapping of the pdf values to histogram segments of Z and a totaling of the probabilities by segment. If the pdf of Z is used, the mapping is more straightforward, but some calculus is required to determine the pdf of Z, given by

$$\text{pdf}(Z) = \frac{1}{\delta Z}\left\{(A + Bc^{x+s})\exp\left[-\frac{Bc^x}{\ln c}(c^s - 1)\right]\exp(-As)\right\}$$

where $s = -(1/\delta)\ln Z$. Similar comments apply to Y, the discounted benefit random variable for a continuous annuity to the moment of death.

In Table 3 and Figure 7 Dr. Scollnik provides an analysis of the semi-continuous loss function random variable, L, assuming the premium charged is large enough to reduce the probability of positive loss to 5%. Because it does not seem feasible to derive a probability density function for L, the *grid* method was applied using the pdf of T. The results obtained were consistent with those published by Dr. Scollnik. The premium itself can be obtained by solving $_tp_{30}=0.95$ using the *grid* method to get t and then solving $L(t)=0$ to find the premium. I found the premium to be $143.76.

(AUTHOR'S REVIEW OF DISCUSSIONS)

DAVID P.M. SCOLLNIK:

I thank the discussants for their valuable comments and for the interest that they have shown in this paper.

One goal of this paper was to introduce *Transactions* readers to some of the new and very generally applicable techniques for random number generation and stochastic simulation that have attracted much interest in recent statistical literature. ARS was introduced as an example of an adaptive random variate generation method, and the MH and ARMS algorithms served as two examples of MCMC methods for generating sequences of dependent random variates from a target distribution of interest. These techniques complement, but do not entirely replace, the few tried and true simulation methods currently appearing in the Associateship syllabus.

Another goal of the paper was to demonstrate the application of these MCMC methods in a simple and easily understood actuarial context and to illustrate some of the characteristics of these methods. However, emphasizing the univariate Makeham distributional setting as I did may have obscured the fact that the methods have a much wider field of application. Klein goes so far as to suggest that in this paper I have described a "solution looking for an actuarial problem." Notwithstanding Klein's comment, at the start of Section 3 I did supply a short list of references to a number of problems in actuarial settings with MCMC-driven solutions that have recently appeared in the literature (that is, [4], [5], [22], [31], [32] in the paper). This may be an opportune time to add to this list.

Towards this end, note that: Rosenberg [4] used MCMC to implement the Bayesian analysis of a hierarchical model for the rate of nonacceptable in-patient hospital utilization; Scollnik [5] considers an application of the Gibbs sampler to three hierarchical credibility models for classification rate making and involves the Bayesian prediction of frequency counts in workers compensation insurance; Shephard and Pitt [6] apply MCMC methods to a number of problems arising in the context of parameter-driven exponential family models, notably including the estimation of actuarial death rates and the estimation of the parameters appearing in several stochastic volatility models for financial returns. Professor Pai describes several other applications of MCMC methods in his discussion of my paper. MCMC is certainly not the only tool for stochastic simulation present in the modern actuary's toolbox, but it is another tool that is now available and is also one that more actuaries should be made aware of.

Carriere's first comment addresses the fact that the expected value of a function of a random variable can be estimated by averaging that function with respect to the empirical distribution for an independent sample from the distribution of the random variable in question. This is simply a restatement of my own comments in the second paragraph of Section 3-D regarding the ergodic average of an f-integrable function $h(x)$, in the less general and trivial instance that $g(x|z)=f(x)$. When this is the case, it is obvious that every draw is independent and no draws are rejected, thus yielding the context of Carriere's observation.

Both Carriere and Klein suggest that a brute force method of random variate generation, direct inversion either of the cumulative distribution function (cdf) or of the survival function using the Newton-Raphson method, can be used to generate draws of the Makeham-distributed future lifetime random variable $T(x)$. Whereas I agree that this is technically the case, it must be pointed out that the efficiency of this brute force method is extremely dependent upon the choice of the Makeham parameters, the assumed age x of the life in question, and the selection of the starting value plugged into the Newton-Raphson algorithm. In order to partially illustrate this fact, I implemented the Newton-Raphson algorithm exactly as described by Klein, taking the Makeham parameters equal to the values appearing in my Numerical Example 3 and arbitrarily setting t_0 equal to 75. The algorithm was allowed to iterate until the absolute difference between t_k and t_{k+1} was no larger than a modest 0.01. In this manner, I generated 100 draws of $T(x)$ for each of six different values of x (that is, $x=0, 10, 20, 30, 40,$ and 50). The observed average number of iterations required to generate a single draw of $T(x)$ for the six different values of x is tabulated below. Examining these numbers, it is evident that direct inversion of the cdf using Newton-Raphson's method is not always particularly efficient. In fact, for a newborn life ($x=0$) and under the conditions described above, it required in excess of 200 iterations to generate a single realization of $T(0)$ on seven of the 100 attempts. Please note that these simulation results are only illustrative and are certainly not definitive.

Age x	Average Number of Iterations
0	67.95
10	34.30
20	14.56
30	7.08
40	3.91
50	3.62

Klein also suggests that random draws from an arbitrary univariate distribution can be generated by simply creating a table of the cdf and then searching it for each random draw from the uniform distribution on the unit interval. However, and as noted by Klein, this method requires some type of interpolation and the table must be bounded above and below, even though the distribution itself may be unbounded. Consequently, the sampled values are only approximately from the distribution desired. In Section 2.3.6 of [35], Tierney describes how the MH algorithm can be used to correct for this failing of Klein's suggested "table lookup and interpolation" procedure, so that the values generated actually form a dependent sequence from the exact distribution of interest. This is an excellent example of how a MCMC method can be used to augment a traditional random variate generation procedure. For the convenience of the reader, I have summarized the MCMC method described in [35] immediately below using the terminology and notation previously adopted in Section 3-D of my paper.

Assume that we want to generate a dependent sequence of random draws from a distribution with a density proportional to $f(x)$ on the real line. Candidate draws will be generated from a proposed distribution by means of a two-step procedure, requiring the availability of another distribution $h(x)$ on the real line from which random draws are easily accomplished. To begin with, let $x_1^*, \ldots, x_m^*$ be a fixed set of points, and let X_i be the value of the draw generated in the i-th iteration of the MH sampling algorithm. At the start of the next iteration, select a point X^* from $x_1^*, \ldots, x_m^*$ according to a discrete distribution that is proportional to the density values $f(x_1^*), \ldots, f(x_m^*)$ at these points. Then generate a value Z from $h(x)$ and add this number to X^* in order to obtain $X = X^* + Z$. This process defines a proposal distribution with density

$$g(x|X_i) = \frac{\sum_{j=1}^{m} f(x_j^*) h(x - x_j^*)}{\sum_{j=1}^{m} f(x_j^*)}.$$

According to the MH algorithm, the value of X is accepted with a probability equal to

$$\min \left[1, \frac{f(X) \sum_{j=1}^{m} f(x_j^*) h(X_i - x_j^*)}{f(X_i) \sum_{j=1}^{m} f(x_j^*) h(X - x_j^*)} \right]. \tag{1}$$

In the case that X is accepted, X_{i+1} is set equal to X; otherwise, X_{i+1} is set equal to X_i. This algorithm is iterated until the required number of random variates has been generated.

This algorithm was very simple to program using S-Plus, and I used it to simulate 500 dependent values of the Makeham-distributed future lifetime random variable $T(50)$ for the life in Numerical Example 3. I took $m=100$, and set the fixed points $t_1^*, \ldots, t_{100}^*$ equal to the integers from 1 to 100. For $h(t)$, I simply used the density for a normal distribution with a mean of 0 and a standard deviation of 10. Although this permits an occasional candidate draw from the proposed distribution to take on a negative value, such draws are never accepted because the MH acceptance probability (1) is always equal to 0 in these instances by construction. The simulation results were as follows: the observed staying rate (Section 3-E) for this example was 25.4%; the 500 simulated values of $T(50)$ had a sample mean equal to 30.90; and the empirical histogram of the simulated values appeared to be in agreement with the exact density function for $T(50)$ appearing in Figure 6(a). Unlike the "table lookup and interpolation" procedure suggested by Klein, the MCMC method I described is exact, requires no artificial bounds to be imposed, and requires no interpolation.

Klein describes a simple and elegant exact alternative to my simulation-driven analysis in Numerical Examples 3 and 4, and it is one that I should have presented for comparison. Concerning the value of π, the discrepancy between Klein's answer and my own is almost certainly due to a combination of simulation error and numerical rounding error. In any case, the relative error inherent in my simulation-based answer is approximately equal to $(143.2-143.7102)/143.7102 \approx -0.0035502$, which is not excessive. To correct a minor technical point made by Klein, note that the range of the random error inherent in my estimate of π is not unbounded in the context of Numerical Example 3, because the value of the estimate is restricted to the interval between 0 and 10,000 by construction.

Professor Pai describes how MCMC methods can be used to implement Bayesian posterior parameter estimation when a vector of survival times, $\mathbf{T}$, has been observed from a Makeham distribution with parameters A, B, and C (compare estimation of the Gompertz parameters in [1]). It is a simple matter to extend Pai's discussion to implement Bayesian predictive inference with respect to the future lifetime $T(y)$ for a new life age y as well. Let the values A_i, B_i, and C_i, for $i=1, \ldots, N$, be the dependent sequence simulated from the posterior distribution $p(A, B, C|\mathbf{T})$ using the method described by Pai. According to the discussion in the second paragraph of Section 3-D concerning the ergodic average of a function, we have

$$f(T(y) = t | \mathbf{T})$$

$$= \iiint f(T(y) = t | A, B, C) \, p(A, B, C | \mathbf{T}) \, dA \, dB \, dC$$

$$\approx \frac{1}{N} \sum_{i=1}^{N} f(T(y) = t | A_i, B_i, C_i).$$

The last expression is an estimate of the predictive density at the point t. A sample from the predictive distribution can be obtained by simulating a single draw of $T(y)$ from each Makeham distribution with density $f(T(y)=t | A_i, B_i, C_i)$, for $i=1, \ldots, N$.

The recent text by Gelman, Carlin, Stern, and Rubin [3] provides a comprehensive treatment of the statistical analysis of data from a Bayesian perspective. In particular, a very readable account of posterior integration and Markov chain simulation strategies is given in Chapters 10 and 11.

In his discussion, Professor Pai also mentions that MCMC methods like MH and ARMS can be used in conjunction with Gibbs sampling, thus yielding the so-called MH-within-Gibbs and ARMS-within-Gibbs variants of MCMC. Although the references I cited for ARMS discuss these variants, it appears that I failed to mention this fact explicitly in my paper. See [14] and [15] in the original paper or Section 11.3 of [3] for details. I am thankful to Dr. Pai for bringing this omission to my attention.

I was a student of Professor Mereu's at the University of Western Ontario in 1986–87, and so it was a distinct pleasure to receive his discussion of my paper. His "grid" approach to integration describes a version of numerical quadrature, akin to some of these covered in the Course 135 "Numerical Methods" syllabus. Although these methods are competitive for evaluating univariate or low-dimensional integrals, they may not be quite as successful in high dimensions. Bayesian analyses of actuarial data typically require the evaluation of high-dimensional integrals to obtain posterior and predictive densities, means, variances, and so forth. As indicated at the start of Section 3 and earlier in this discussion, MCMC methods have proven to be very useful in these contexts.

Since my paper was written, Evans and Swartz [2] have developed a class of adaptive rejection algorithms for generating independent random variates for a wide assortment of families of densities. These generators depend on the concavity structure of a transformation of the density. Makeham's distribution is included as one of the examples. Interested readers can obtain a copy of this technical report from the authors.

REFERENCES

1. AMANDA, M.M., DALPATADU, R.J., AND SINGH, A.K. "Estimating the Parameters of the Force of Mortality in Actuarial Studies," *ARCH* 1993.1:129–141.
2. EVANS, M., AND SWARTZ, T. "Random Variable Generation Using Concavity Properties of Transformed Densities," *Technical Report No. 9606*, Department of Statistics, University of Toronto, 1996.
3. GELMAN, A., CARLIN, J.B., STERN, H.S., AND RUBIN, D.B. *Bayesian Data Analysis*. London: Chapman and Hall, 1995.
4. ROSENBERG, M. "A Hierarchical Bayesian Model of the Rate of Non-Acceptable In-Patient Hospital Utilization," doctoral thesis, University of Michigan, 1994.
5. SCOLLNIK, D.P.M. "An Introduction to Markov Chain Monte Carlo Methods and Their Actuarial Applications," *Proceedings of the Casualty Actuarial Society*, in press.
6. SHEPHARD, N., AND PITT, M.K. "Parameter-Driven Exponential Family Models," Nuffield College, Oxford, 1995. Available on the World Wide Web via the MCMC Preprint Service located at *http://www.statslab.cam.ac.uk/*.

EQUIVALENCE OF RESERVE METHODOLOGIES

KEITH P. SHARP

ABSTRACT

The paper considers policies with annual premiums and discusses four types of life insurance reserves calculations: curtate, fully continuous, discounted continuous, and semicontinuous. It is shown that when appropriate corrections are made, each method gives the same reserve; this is as expected in view of the equality of the actual cash flows. The paper concludes with consideration of the methods used in making a practical year-end valuation.

1. INTRODUCTION

Actuaries can use several alternative reserving methodologies in valuing the same life insurance policy. The text by Tullis and Polkinghorn [4] lists in tables on pages 47 and 48 four types of reserves:
(1) Curtate
(2) Fully continuous
(3) Discounted continuous
(4) Semicontinuous.
Also indicated are five items that need to be considered in calculating a reserve:
(a) Refund of unearned premium on death
(b) Nondeduction of deferred premium on death
(c) Immediate payment of claims reserve
(d) Deferred premium asset
(e) Unearned premium liability.
In this paper only annual premium policies are considered, so (b) and (d) are not relevant.

The actuary also has a choice between using midterminal reserves and mean reserves. Thus a reserve can be calculated in many ways. However, the actual timing and amount of benefits and premiums are fixed by the terms of the policy. Thus if all appropriate corrections are taken into account, then the reserve calculated under all methods should be the same. Indeed reserves could be calculated directly, taking into account all benefits and premiums and the exact days on which they are paid with appropriate probabilities.

455

Some of the methods and reserve items listed above exist because in previous decades actuaries needed to simplify calculations and to use labor-saving grouping or "binning" techniques. Very common is the technique whereby policies are binned by policy year and then assumed to have the average policy issue date for that bin. The following examples assume a December 31, 1997 valuation date:

Issue Date	Policy Year at Dec. 31, 1997	Assumed Issue Date
November 18, 1997	1	June 30/July 1, 1997
January 19, 1997	1	June 30/July 1, 1997
August 3, 1995	3	June 30/July 1, 1995
October 9, 1993	5	June 30/July 1, 1993

If the valuation date is December 31, then the binning by policy year is equivalent to binning by calendar year of issue. For the above valuation date of December 31, 1997, all policies issued in calendar year 1996 will be allocated to the bin of policies in policy year 2 at valuation. Then they may for some purposes be assumed to have been issued on June 30, 1996 or July 1, 1996 with probability 0.5 for each of the two dates. For nonannual premiums, this may be an approximation that adequately allows for the mid-policy year premium. Half of the policies are assumed at valuation to be about to pay a premium, and half are assumed to have just paid a premium. This amounts to an approximation to the integration of quantities with use of a uniform distribution of issue dates. A more accurate technique would be to perform seriatim valuations using actual premium due dates.

2. TERMINAL RESERVES

Consider an annual premium whole life insurance policy with the following benefits at the moment of death a fraction s of a year since the last policy anniversary:
(a) $1, plus
(b) a refund of unearned premium, calculated as

$$\bar{P}(\bar{A}_x)\bar{a}_{\overline{1-s}|}.$$

The average refund of unearned premium can be approximated as half the gross premium, but here it is assumed, following Boermeester [1] and Scher [3], that the above theoretically accurate refund is paid. It will be shown that if this refund is assumed, then each of the three types of reserves (1), (3), and (4) above can be adjusted to produce the same terminal reserve $_t\bar{V}(\bar{A}_x)$, for the annual premium policy defined above. Here "terminal reserve" means, as usual, that calculated immediately before the annual premium due date.

The policy considered in the fully continuous case (2) is different in that only benefit (a) above is paid.

A. Discontinued Continuous Type

In verifying that the terminal reserves all equal $_t\bar{V}(\bar{A}_x)$, we first study the discounted continuous type (Table 1).

Let us consider the amount of annual net valuation premium in the discounted continuous case for the policy with benefits (a) and (b) defined above. A direct approach to determination of this premium is the same as that used in deriving Equation (2.8) below in the curtate case; logically if the same benefits are paid, then the same annual premium must result.

A somewhat different argument is used here to derive the annual net valuation premium for benefits (a) and (b) in the discounted continuous case. Let us postulate that the annual premium under the discounted continuous case is $\bar{P}(\bar{A}_x)\bar{a}_{\overline{1}|}$. Then in each policy year (except the year of death), the value at the policy anniversary of that year's premium equals the discounted value $\bar{P}(\bar{A}_x)\bar{a}_{\overline{1}|}$ of the continuous premium for benefit (a) in the fully continuous case. At the policy anniversary preceding death, the discounted value of the fully continuous premium for benefit (a) is $\bar{P}(\bar{A}_x)\bar{a}_{\overline{s}|}$. But we have

$$\bar{P}(\bar{A}_x)\bar{a}_{\overline{1}|} - (1 + i)^{-s}\,\bar{P}(\bar{A}_x)\bar{a}_{\overline{1-s}|} = \bar{P}(\bar{A}_x)\bar{a}_{\overline{s}|}. \tag{2.1}$$

Thus we have equality at each policy anniversary of
- The discounted value of the year's premiums paid for benefit (a) in the fully continuous case
- The discounted value of the excess of the postulated discounted continuous premium over the required benefit (b).

Thus we have verified our postulated annual premium, $\bar{P}(\bar{A}_x)\bar{a}_{\overline{1}|}$, which can now be used as the valuation net premium for a policy with benefits (a) and (b) under the discounted continuous case.

The choice of refund benefit, $\bar{P}(\bar{A}_x)\bar{a}_{\overline{1-s}|}$ (Scher [3]), is confirmed by its leading to the desirable premium $\bar{P}(\bar{A}_x)\bar{a}_{\overline{1}|}$.

In determining the reserve corresponding to the refund, we consider the values of continuous payments of $\bar{P}(\bar{A}_x)$ per annum:

TABLE 1
ADJUSTMENTS TO NET PREMIUMS

Type	Net Premium				Refer To
	Basic	Refund on Death	Immediate Payment of Claims	Corrected	
(1) Curtate	$\dfrac{A_x}{\ddot{a}_x}$	$+\dfrac{\bar{P}(\bar{A}_x)(\bar{A}_x - A_x)}{\delta \ddot{a}_x}$	$+\dfrac{\bar{A}_x - A_x}{\ddot{a}_x}$	$= \bar{P}(\bar{A}_x)\ddot{a}_{\overline{n}|}$	Equation (2.8)
(2) Fully Continuous	$\dfrac{\bar{A}_x}{\bar{a}_x}$	$+0$	$+0$	$= \bar{P}(\bar{A}_x)$	
(3) Discounted Continuous	$\dfrac{\bar{A}_x}{\bar{a}_x}\,\ddot{a}_{\overline{n}|}$	$+0$	$+0$	$= \bar{P}(\bar{A}_x)\ddot{a}_{\overline{n}|}$	
(4) Semicontinuous	$\dfrac{\bar{A}_x}{\ddot{a}_x}$	$+\dfrac{\bar{P}(\bar{A}_x)(\bar{A}_x - A_x)}{\delta \ddot{a}_x}$	$+0$	$= \bar{P}(\bar{A}_x)\ddot{a}_{\overline{n}|}$	Equation (2.4)

Origin for Discounting	Commencement of Payments	Termination of Payments	Discounted Value
Age $x + t$	Age $x + t$	∞	$\dfrac{\bar{P}(\bar{A}_x)}{\delta}$
Age $x + t$	Death	∞	$\dfrac{\bar{P}(\bar{A}_x)}{\delta} \bar{A}_{x+t}$
Age $x + t$	End of year of death	∞	$\dfrac{\bar{P}(\bar{A}_x)}{\delta} A_{x+t}$
Age $x + t$	Death	End of year of death	$\dfrac{\bar{P}(\bar{A}_x)}{\delta} (\bar{A}_{x+t} - A_{x+t})$

Thus the value of this premium refund feature is $\bar{P}(\bar{A}_x)(\bar{A}_{x+t} - A_{x+t})/\delta$, as indicated in the above table (see also Scher [3]).

Then the terminal reserve, $_tV_x^{DC}$, under the discounted continuous method is the reserve considering the value of the main \$1 benefit, the annual premiums and the refund benefit:

$$_tV_x^{DC} = \bar{A}_{x+t} - \ddot{a}_{x+t}\bar{P}(\bar{A}_x)\bar{a}_{\overline{1}|} + \frac{\bar{P}(\bar{A}_x)}{\delta}[\bar{A}_{x+t} - A_{x+t}]$$

$$= \bar{A}_{x+t} - \ddot{a}_{x+t}\bar{P}(\bar{A}_x)\bar{a}_{\overline{1}|} + \frac{\bar{P}(\bar{A}_x)}{\delta}[1 - \delta\bar{a}_{x+t} - 1 + d\ddot{a}_{x+t}]$$

$$= \bar{A}_{x+t} - \bar{P}(\bar{A}_x)\bar{a}_{x+t}$$

$$= {}_t\bar{V}(\bar{A}_x). \tag{2.2}$$

Thus with the "correct" choice of refund of unearned premium on death, the terminal reserve at a policy anniversary under the discounted continuous method equals that under the fully continuous method.

The relevant abbreviations used in this paper are:

DC = discounted continuous
SC = semicontinuous
PR = (unearned) premium refund
IM = immediate payment of claims
CU = curtate
ACC = accurate.

B. Semicontinuous Type

For a whole life insurance, the semicontinuous annual premium is given by $P(\bar{A}_x) = \bar{A}_x/\ddot{a}_x$. Assume that, again, the refund of unearned premium on death a period s after the policy anniversary is $\bar{P}(\bar{A}_x)\bar{a}_{\overline{1-s}|}$. The net annual premium required to pay for the refund benefit is, using the analysis of Table 2 and of Scher [3],

$$P(\bar{A}^{PR}) = \frac{1}{\delta} \frac{\bar{P}(\bar{A}_x)(\bar{A}_x - A_x)}{\ddot{a}_x}. \tag{2.3}$$

Hence the total annual premium is

$$P_x^{SC} = \frac{\bar{A}_x}{\ddot{a}_x^{(m)}} + P(\bar{A}^{PR})$$

$$= \bar{A}_x \left[\frac{1}{\ddot{a}_x} \right] + \frac{\bar{P}(\bar{A}_x)(\bar{A}_x - A_x)}{\delta \ddot{a}_x}$$

$$= \bar{A}_x \left[\frac{\delta \ddot{a}_x + 1 - \delta \bar{a}_x - 1 + d\ddot{a}_x}{\delta \ddot{a}_x \bar{a}_x} \right]$$

$$= \bar{P}(\bar{A}_x)\bar{a}_{\overline{1}|}. \tag{2.4}$$

Thus the total premium under the semicontinuous method is the same as that under the discounted continuous method. This is reasonable since the benefits are the same and equality of the present value of the premiums is satisfied in view of the premium refund feature. Thus the addition to the reserve in respect of the premium refund feature is

$$V(\bar{A}^{PR}) = \frac{1}{\delta} \bar{P}(\bar{A}_x)(\bar{A}_{x+t} - A_{x+t}) - P(\bar{A}^{PR})\ddot{a}_{x+t}$$

$$= \frac{1}{\delta} \bar{P}(\bar{A}_x) \left[\bar{A}_{x+t} - A_{x+t} - \frac{\ddot{a}_{x+t}}{\ddot{a}_x} (\bar{A}_x - A_x) \right]$$

$$= \frac{1}{\delta} \bar{P}(\bar{A}_x) \left[{}_tV(\bar{A}_x) - {}_tV_x \right] \tag{2.5}$$

The total terminal reserve under the semicontinuous case is then given by

$$
\begin{aligned}
{}_tV_x^{SC} &= \bar{A}_{x+t} - P(\bar{A}_x)\ddot{a}_{x+t} + \frac{1}{\delta}\,\bar{P}(\bar{A}_x)\,[{}_tV(\bar{A}_x) - {}_tV_x] \\[2mm]
&= \bar{A}_{x+t} - \frac{\bar{A}_x}{\ddot{a}_x}\,\ddot{a}_{x+t} + \frac{\bar{A}_x}{\delta\bar{a}_x}\left[\bar{A}_{x+t} - \frac{\bar{A}_x}{\ddot{a}_x}\,\ddot{a}_{x+t} - A_{x+t} + \frac{A_x}{\ddot{a}_x}\,\ddot{a}_{x+t}\right] \\[2mm]
&= \bar{A}_{x+t} - \frac{\bar{A}_x}{\bar{a}_x}\,\bar{a}_{x+t} + \bar{A}_x\left[-\frac{\ddot{a}_{x+t}}{\ddot{a}_x} + \frac{1}{\delta\bar{a}_x} - \frac{\ddot{a}_{x+t}}{\delta\bar{a}_x\ddot{a}_x}\right. \\[2mm]
&\qquad \left. + \frac{\ddot{a}_{x+t}}{\ddot{a}_x} - \frac{1 - d\ddot{a}_{x+t}}{\delta\bar{a}_x} + \frac{\ddot{a}_{x+t}}{\delta\bar{a}_x\ddot{a}_x} - \frac{d\ddot{a}_{x+t}}{\delta\bar{a}_x}\right] \\[2mm]
&= {}_t\bar{V}(\bar{A}_x) \tag{2.6}
\end{aligned}
$$

That the terminal reserve under the semicontinuous case equals that under the fully continuous case is intuitively reasonable. The benefits have equal value $\bar{A}_x$, and the annual premiums are set up so that, including the refund benefit, they are level and equal in present value.

C. Curtate Type

The curtate premium is the standard $P_x = A_x/\ddot{a}_x$. Again assume that the refund of unearned premium on death is made of amount $\bar{P}(\bar{A}_x)\bar{a}_{\overline{1-s}|}$. The premium for the refund benefit is again $P(\bar{A}^{PR})$, given by Equation (2.3). For the curtate type only, since A_x is used rather than $\bar{A}_x$, an additional premium is required for the immediate rather than end of year payment of claims, of amount

$$
P_x^{IM} = \frac{\bar{A}_x - A_x}{\ddot{a}_x}. \tag{2.7}
$$

Thus, taking into account also the premium for the refund of unearned premium on death, the total net annual premium is:

$$
\begin{aligned}
P_x^{CU} &= \frac{A_x}{\ddot{a}_x} + P(\bar{A}^{PR}) + \frac{\bar{A}_x - A_x}{\ddot{a}_x} \\[2mm]
&= \frac{\bar{A}_x}{\ddot{a}_x} + \frac{\bar{P}(\bar{A}_x)(\bar{A}_x - A_x)}{\delta\ddot{a}_x} \\[2mm]
&= \bar{P}(\bar{A}_x)\bar{a}_{\overline{1}|}, \tag{2.8}
\end{aligned}
$$

where use has been made of Equations (2.3) and (2.4). There is an associated additional reserve:

$$_tV_x^{IM} = \bar{A}_{x+t} - A_{x+t} - P_x^{IM}\,\ddot{a}_{x+t}$$

$$= {}_tV(\bar{A}_x) - {}_tV_x. \qquad (2.9)$$

Hence the total curtate reserve is

$$_tV_x^{CU} = A_{x+t} - P_x\,\ddot{a}_{x+t} + \frac{\bar{P}(\bar{A}_x)}{\delta}\,[{}_tV(\bar{A}_x) - {}_tV_x]$$

$$+ [{}_tV(\bar{A}_x) - {}_tV_x]$$

$$= {}_tV(\bar{A}_x) + \frac{\bar{P}(\bar{A}_x)}{\delta}\,[{}_tV(\bar{A}_x) - {}_tV_x]$$

$$= {}_t\bar{V}(\bar{A}_x), \qquad (2.10)$$

where the curtate has been reduced to the semicontinuous case and then Equation (2.6) has been used.

D. Summary Tables and Numerical Examples

Table 1 summarizes the calculation of the annual premium when there is immediate payment of claims and a refund of unearned premium $\bar{P}(\bar{A}_x)\bar{a}_{\overline{1-s|}}$ on death. As would be expected, the premium produced under all the methods considered is the same: $\bar{P}(\bar{A}_x)\bar{a}_{\overline{1|}}$ annually in advance, or $\bar{P}(\bar{A}_x)$ continuously. This equality is seen to be a consequence of the equality of the cash flows and assumptions under all the methods.

Table 2 summarizes the calculation of the terminal reserve. Again, under all four methods the terminal reserve taking account of the immediate payment of claims and of the refund benefit is $_t\bar{V}(\bar{A}_x)$.

"Basic" net premiums and "basic" terminal reserves are mentioned in Tables 1 and 2, respectively. These are for "basic" policies, which differ between the four methods as follows:
(1) Curtate: benefit of \$1 at the end of the year of death
(2) Fully continuous: benefit of \$1 immediately on death
(3) Discounted continuous: benefit of \$1 and premium refund of $\bar{P}(\bar{A})\bar{a}_{\overline{1-s|}}$, both immediately on death
(4) Semicontinuous: benefit of \$1 at the end of the year of death.
Tables 3 and 4 give a numerical example of the calculation of the terminal reserve at duration 10 of a whole life policy issued at age 40. Mortality is

TABLE 2
ADJUSTMENTS TO TERMINAL RESERVES

Type		Terminal Reserve			Refer to
	Basic	Refund on Death	Immediate Payment of Claims	Corrected	
(1) Curtate	$A_{x+t} - P_x \ddot{a}_{x+t}$	$+ \dfrac{1}{\delta} \bar{P}(\bar{A}_x)[{}_tV(\bar{A}_x) - {}_tV_x]$	$+ {}_tV(\bar{A}_x) - {}_tV_x$	$= {}_tV(\bar{A}_x)$	Equation (2.9)
(2) Fully Continuous	$\bar{A}_{x+t} - \bar{P}(\bar{A}_x)\bar{a}_{x+t}$	$+0$	$+0$	$= {}_tV(\bar{A}_x)$	Equation (2.2)
(3) Discounted Continuous	$\bar{A}_{x+t} - \ddot{a}_{x+t}\bar{P}(\bar{A}_x)\bar{a}_{\overline{1}|}$	$+ \dfrac{\bar{P}(\bar{A}_x)}{\delta}(\bar{A}_{x+t} - A_{x+t})$	$+0$	$= {}_tV(\bar{A}_x)$	Equation (2.2)
(4) Semicontinuous	$\bar{A}_{x+t} - P(\bar{A}_x)\ddot{a}_{x+t}$	$+ \dfrac{1}{\delta} \bar{P}(\bar{A}_x)[{}_tV(\bar{A}_x) - {}_tV_x]$	$+0$	$= {}_tV(\bar{A}_x)$	Equation (2.6)

that of the Illustrative Life Table of Bowers et al. [2, p. 72]. Thus the q_x are calculated by integration of the Makeham law

$$\mu_x = A + B \, c^x \tag{2.11}$$

with constants $A=0.00078$, $B=0.00005$ and $c=10^{0.04}$. For the current purpose and to facilitate calculation of the continuous functions, a step form of the force of mortality was used. Thus the q_x, which agree with those of Bowers et al. [2], were used to calculate a force of mortality assumed constant within each year of age. Thus the force of mortality used to calculate the $\bar{A}_x$ and μ_x was slightly different from that given by (2.11) and indeed is a form of weighted average of (2.11) within each year of age.

TABLE 3

NUMERICAL EXAMPLES OF NET PREMIUMS

Type	Net Premium per Thousand (Issue Age 40)			
	Basic	Refund on Death	Immediate Payment of Claims	Corrected
(1) Curtate	10.8882	0.0649	0.3259	11.2789
(2) Fully Continuous	11.6107	+0	+0	11.6107
(3) Discounted Continuous	11.2789	+0	+0	11.2789
(4) Semicontinuous	11.2140	0.0649	+0	11.2789

Relevant Values:

$$1000A_{40} = 161.3242$$
$$1000\bar{A}_{40} = 166.1528$$
$$\ddot{a}_{40} = 14.81661$$
$$\bar{a}_{40} = 14.3103$$
$$1000\bar{P}(\bar{A}_{40}) = 11.6107$$
$$i = 0.06$$
$$\delta = 0.0582689$$

3. RESERVES AT DECEMBER 31 VALUATION

A. Accurate Reserve

Figure 1 illustrates the reserve of an annual premium policy. An accurate calculation could be made at any date of the discounted value of benefits less the discounted value of future premiums, where timings are treated exactly to the day. The solid line illustrates the path of an exact reserve so calculated. It shows jumps when premiums are payable, and it has a slight curve in the period between premiums. Whether the path rises or falls between premiums depends on the relative importance of interest and the cost of insurance.

TABLE 4

NUMERICAL EXAMPLES OF TERMINAL RESERVES

	Terminal Reserve per Thousand (Issue Age 40; Duration 10)			
Type	Basic	Refund on Death	Immediate Payment of Claims	Corrected
(1) Curtate	104.5974	0.6259	3.1411	108.3644
(2) Fully Continuous	108.3644	0	0	108.3644
(3) Discounted Continuous	106.8770	1.4874	0	108.3644
(4) Semicontinuous	107.7385	0.6259	0	108.3644

Relevant Values:

$1000A_{50}$ = 249.0475

$1000\bar{A}_{50}$ = 256.5122

$\ddot{a}_{50}$ = 13.2668

$\bar{a}_{50}$ = 12.7596

$1000\bar{P}(\bar{A}_{40})$ = 11.2139

$1000_{10}\bar{V}(\bar{A}_{40})$ = 108.3644

$1000_{10}V(\bar{A}_{40})$ = 107.7385

FIGURE 1

RESERVE AS A FUNCTION OF TIME

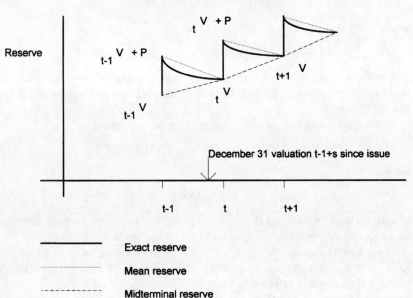

B. *Interpolated Reserve*

Generally the valuation will be at a date, typically December 31, between premium payment dates. In other words, as shown on Figure 1, we are required to calculate the reserve at a point on the curved path of the accurate reserve V_x^{ACC}. Assume that December 31 falls at time $t-1+u$ since policy issue at age x. In other words, valuation is a fractional year u after the start of the t-th policy year. Then the accurate reserve is given by:

$$_{t-1+u}V_x^{ACC} = \bar{A}_{x+t+u} - \frac{D_{x+t}\,P^{CU}}{D_{x+t-1+u}}\,\ddot{a}_{x+t} \tag{3.1}$$

To ease calculations, it has been traditional to perform a linear interpolation:

$$\begin{aligned}
_{t-1+u}V_x^{ACC} &\doteq (1 - u)\bar{A}_{x+t-1} + u\,\bar{A}_{x+t} \\
&\quad - P^{CU}\,[(1 - u)(\ddot{a}_{x+t-1} - 1) + u\ddot{a}_{x+t}] \\
&= (1 - u)[_{t-1}\bar{V}(\bar{A}_x) + P^{CU}] + u_t\bar{V}(\bar{A}_x) \tag{3.2} \\
&= MV_{t-1+u}
\end{aligned}$$

where

$$MV_{t-1+u} = (1 - u)[_{t-1}\bar{V}(\bar{A}_x) + P^{CU}] + u_t\,\bar{V}(\bar{A}_x) \tag{3.3}$$

is a mean reserve not necessarily with equal weights of one-half. This formula (3.2) corresponds to following the interpolation defined by the dotted line in Figure 1.

Alternatively the interpolated reserve can be expressed as:

$$_{t-1+u}V_x^{ACC} \doteq MTV_{t-1+u} + (1 - u)P^{CU} \tag{3.4}$$

where

$$MTV_{t-1+u} = (1 - u)_{t-1}\bar{V}(\bar{A}_x) + u_t\,\bar{V}(\bar{A}_x) \tag{3.5}$$

is a (weighted) midterminal reserve. The term $(1-u)P^{CU}$ is then identified as an unearned premium reserve addition to the midterminal reserve.

The assumption can be made of uniform distribution of policy anniversaries within the calendar year. Then at December 31, 1999, for example, policies then in their t-th policy year were issued between January 1, 1999$-t+1$ and December 31, 1999$-t+1$. If we make the assumption of uniform distribution of policy anniversaries within the calendar year, then we can approximate all the policies as having a June 30/July 1, 1999$-t+1$ issue date. Then $u = 1/2$ and we recover the familiar expressions for the mean and midterminal reserves

$$MV_{t-1+1/2} = \frac{1}{2}\left[_{t-1}\bar{V}(\bar{A}_x) + P^{CU}\right] + \frac{1}{2}{}_t\bar{V}(\bar{A}_x) \tag{3.6}$$

$$MTV_{t-1+1/2} = \frac{1}{2}{}_{t-1}\bar{V}(\bar{A}_x) + \frac{1}{2}{}_t\bar{V}(\bar{A}_x) \tag{3.7}$$

4. MODAL PREMIUMS

The intent of this paper was to illustrate the interrelationship of the various reserving methodologies and to highlight the steps used in deriving reserve values in practice. The discussion has been in terms of annual premiums. There is nothing in the early stages of the above analysis to prevent us from counting time in intervals $1/m$ rather than of one year. The annual premium $P^{CU} = \bar{P}(\bar{A}_x)\bar{a}_{\overline{1}|}$ would be replaced by $\bar{P}(\bar{A}_x)\bar{a}_{\overline{1/m}}$, and, for example, Equation (2.6) would be modified to give, for k integer,

$$_{t-1+k/m}V_x^{SC} = \bar{A}_{x+t-1+k/m} - P^{(m)}(\bar{A}_x)\ddot{a}_{x+t-1+k/m}^{(m)}$$

$$+ \frac{1}{\delta}\bar{P}(\bar{A}_x)\left[_{t-1+k/m}V(\bar{A}_x) - {}_{t-1+k/m}V_x\right]$$

$$= {}_{t-1+k/m}\bar{V}(\bar{A}_x). \tag{4.1}$$

Then the interpolation Equation (3.2) could be set up for $0 < w < 1$ and $0 \le k < m$ as

$$_{t-1+(k+w)/m}V_x^{ACC} \doteq (1 - w)\left[_{t-1+k/m}\bar{V}(\bar{A}_x)\right.$$

$$\left. + \bar{P}(\bar{A}_x)\bar{a}_{\overline{1/m}|}\right] + w\, _{t-1+(k+1)/m}\bar{V}(\bar{A}_x). \tag{4.2}$$

However, in practice, it is more common to interpolate between the annual values $_{t-1}\bar{V}(\bar{A}_x)$ and $_t\bar{V}(\bar{A}_x)$, even if premiums are modal. Thus we are led into discussion in a future paper of the treatment of deferred premiums and the nondeduction of deferred premium on death.

5. CONCLUSION

The accurate reserve held for a policy depends only on the future cash flows, their probabilities and the assumptions used. The various reserving methods lead to the same reserve if the appropriate adjustments are made.

The algebraic demonstrations of this paper and of Scher [3] can provide greater clarity when considering this intuitively reasonable equivalence of the reserving models.

REFERENCES

1. BOERMEESTER, J.M. "Actuarial Note: Certain Implications Which Arise When the Assumption Is Made that Premiums Are Paid Continuously and Death Benefits Are Paid at the Moment of Death," *TASA* L (1949): 71–5.
2. BOWERS, N.L., GERBER, H.U., HICKMAN, J.C., JONES, D.A., AND NESBITT, C.J. *Actuarial Mathematics*. Itasca, Ill.: Society of Actuaries, 1986.
3. SCHER, E. "Relationships among the Fully Continuous, the Discounted Continuous and the Semicontinuous Reserve Bases for Ordinary Life Insurance," *TSA* XXVI (1974): 597–606.
4. TULLIS, M.A., AND POLKINGHORN, P.K. *Valuation of Life Insurance Liabilities*. 2d ed. Winsted, Conn.: Actex Publications, 1992.

DISCUSSION OF PRECEDING PAPER

ELIAS S.W. SHIU AND SERENA TIONG:

Dr. Sharp is to be thanked for this paper, clarifying the equivalence of various reserve methodologies. The purpose of this discussion is to supplement this fine exposition using the notion of *apportionable annuity-due* and *apportionable premium* presented in the textbook *Actuarial Mathematics* [1]. We consider the case in which premiums are payable m times a year.

1. Integer Functions

For a real number t, let $\lfloor t \rfloor$ denote the *floor* of t, which is the greatest integer less than or equal to t, and let $\lceil t \rceil$ denote the *ceiling* of t, which is the least integer greater than or equal to t. If $T=T(x)$ denotes the random variable of the future lifetime of a life now aged x [1, p. 46], then $\lfloor T \rfloor$ is K, the curtate-future-lifetime of (x) [1, p. 48], and $\lceil T \rceil$ is the time until the end of the year of death of (x). Because $12T$ is the time, measured in months, until the death of (x), we see that $\lceil 12T \rceil$ is the time, measured in months, until the end of the month of death of (x), and hence $\lceil 12T \rceil/12$ is the time, measured in years, until the end of the month of death of (x). Similarly, $\lceil 52T \rceil/52$ gives the time, measured in years, until the end of the week of death of (x), and so on. See Figure 1. Thus we have, for each positive integer m,

$$A_x^{(m)} = E[v^{\lceil mT \rceil/m}], \tag{D.1.1}$$

$$\ddot{a}_x^{(m)} = E[\ddot{a}_{\overline{\lceil mT \rceil/m}}^{(m)}], \tag{D.1.2}$$

and

$$a_x^{(m)} = E[a_{\overline{\lfloor mT \rfloor/m}}^{(m)}]. \tag{D.1.3}$$

In Exercise 5.14 of *Actuarial Mathematics* [1], $\lceil mT \rceil/m$ is denoted as $K+J_m$. For two positive numbers s and t, we define

$$t \bmod s = t - s\lfloor t/s \rfloor \tag{D.1.4}$$

and

$$t \text{ pad } s = s\lceil t/s \rceil - t. \tag{D.1.5}$$

See Figure 2. The quantity "$t \bmod s$" is the (non-negative) remainder when t is divided by s, while "t pad s" is the least non-negative addition to t so

469

FIGURE 1
THE GRAPH OF THE FUNCTION $\lceil 2t \rceil / 2$

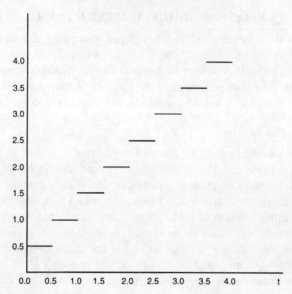

that the result is divisible by s. The term *mod*, short for *modulo*, is standard mathematical usage. In defining *pad*, we are "borrowing from computer science, in which the term *padding* means the adding of blanks or nonsignificant characters to the end of a block or record in order to bring it up to a certain fixed size" [4, p. 572]. Note that Graham, Knuth and Patashnik [2, p. 83] use the term "mumble" for our "pad," and they write: "But of course we'd need a better name than 'mumble.' If sufficient applications come along, an appropriate name will probably suggest itself."

Note that, if t is not divisible by s, that is, if

$$t \bmod s \neq 0,$$

then

$$t \bmod s + t \text{ pad } s = s. \tag{D.1.6}$$

FIGURE 2

THE GRAPH OF THE FUNCTION t pad $1/4$

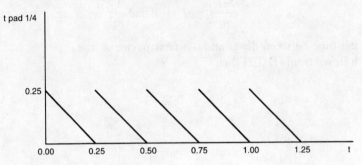

2. Apportionable Annuity-Due

Let s be a positive number, not necessarily an integer; we define

$$\ddot{a}_{\overline{s}|}^{(m)} = \frac{1 - v^s}{d^{(m)}}. \tag{D.2.1}$$

This definition extends the usual definition for $\ddot{a}_{\overline{s}|}^{(m)}$, where s is a positive integer; with $m=1$, (D.2.1) can be found in Exercise 5.32.a of *Actuarial Mathematics* [1]. Then

$$E[\ddot{a}_{\overline{T}|}^{(m)}] = \ddot{a}_x^{\{m\}} \tag{D.2.2}$$

is the single premium for an apportionable life annuity-due of 1 per year payable in installments of $1/m$ at the beginning of each m-th of a year while (x) survives (compare [1, Section 5.9]). It follows from (D.2.1) that

$$\ddot{a}_{\overline{\lceil mT \rceil/m}|}^{(m)} - \ddot{a}_{\overline{T}|}^{(m)} = v^T \, \ddot{a}_{\overline{(\lceil mT \rceil/m)-T}|}^{(m)}. \tag{D.2.3}$$

Taking expectations and applying (D.1.2) and (D.2.2) yields

$$\ddot{a}_x^{(m)} - \ddot{a}_x^{\{m\}} = E[v^T \, \ddot{a}_{\overline{(\lceil mT \rceil/m)-T}|}^{(m)}]. \tag{D.2.4}$$

The amount of refund at T, the time of death of (x), is

$$\ddot{a}_{\overline{(\lceil mT \rceil/m)-T}|}^{(m)}. \tag{D.2.5}$$

From (D.1.5), we have

$$\frac{\lceil mT \rceil}{m} - T = T \text{ pad } \frac{1}{m}; \tag{D.2.6}$$

it is the time between death and the next payment date.

It follows from (D.2.1) that

$$\ddot{a}_{\overline{s}|}^{(m)} = \frac{\delta}{d^{(m)}} \, \bar{a}_{\overline{s}|} \tag{D.2.7}$$

$$= \frac{1}{m\bar{a}_{\overline{1/m}|}} \, \bar{a}_{\overline{s}|}. \tag{D.2.8}$$

Hence expression (D.2.5), the amount of refund at the time of death, can be rewritten as

$$\frac{1}{m\bar{a}_{\overline{1/m}|}} \, \bar{a}_{\overline{(\lceil mT \rceil / m) - T}|}, \tag{D.2.9}$$

which is [1, (5.9.5)].

3. Apportionable Premium

Apportionable premiums are treated in Section 6.5 of *Actuarial Mathematics* [1]. Consider the *equivalence principle* [1, p. 162]:

E[present value of net premiums] = E[present value of benefits].   (D.3.1)

The provision for premium refund can be accounted for on the left-hand side of (D.3.1) or on its right-hand side. In the former approach, we have the equation

$$P^{\{m\}}(\bar{A}_x) \, \ddot{a}_x^{\{m\}} = \bar{A}_x, \tag{D.3.2}$$

while, in the latter,

$$P^{\{m\}}(\bar{A}_x) \, \ddot{a}_x^{(m)} = \bar{A}_x + \bar{A}_x^{PR,m}, \tag{D.3.3}$$

where $\bar{A}_x^{PR,m}$ denotes the single premium for the premium-refund benefit. The notation $\bar{A}_x^{PR,m}$ is due to Scher [3]; with $m=1$, it is written as $\bar{A}_x^{PR}$ in Scher [3] and in *Actuarial Mathematics* [1], and as $\bar{A}^{PR}$ in the paper. Because the amount of premium refund at the time of death is

$$P^{\{m\}}(\bar{A}_x) \; \ddot{a}^{(m)}_{\overline{(\lceil mT \rceil / m) - T}},$$ (D.3.4)

we have

$$\bar{A}^{PR,m}_x = P^{\{m\}}(\bar{A}_x) \; \mathrm{E}[v^T \; \ddot{a}^{(m)}_{\overline{(\lceil mT \rceil / m) - T}}].$$ (D.3.5)

Applying (D.2.4) to (D.3.5) yields

$$\bar{A}^{PR,m}_x = P^{\{m\}}(\bar{A}_x)[\ddot{a}^{(m)}_x - \ddot{a}^{\{m\}}_x],$$ (D.3.6)

verifying that equations (D.3.2) and (D.3.3) are equivalent.

Putting $s=T$ in (D.2.8) and taking expectations, we have

$$\ddot{a}^{\{m\}}_x = \frac{1}{m\bar{a}_{\overline{1/m}}} \; \bar{a}_x.$$ (D.3.7)

Substituting (D.3.7) into (D.3.2) yields

$$P^{\{m\}}(\bar{A}_x) = m\bar{a}_{\overline{1/m}} \; \bar{P}(\bar{A}_x).$$ (D.3.8)

With $m=1$, the right-hand side of (D.3.8) simplifies as

$$\bar{a}_{\overline{1}} \; \bar{P}(\bar{A}_x),$$ (D.3.9)

which is the "corrected" net premium in the paper. In other words, the "corrected" net premium in the paper is the apportionable premium $P^{\{1\}}(\bar{A}_x)$ in *Actuarial Mathematics* [1]. Substituting (D.3.8) and (D.2.8) (with $s=(\lceil mT \rceil / m) - T$) into (D.3.4) shows that the amount of premium refund can also be written as

$$\bar{P}(\bar{A}_x) \; \bar{a}_{\overline{(\lceil mT \rceil / m) - T}},$$ (D.3.10)

which, with $m=1$, is the "unearned premium"

$$\bar{P}(\bar{A}_x)\bar{a}_{\overline{1-s}}$$ (D.3.11)

in the paper.

It follows from (D.3.3) that

$$\bar{A}^{PR,m}_x = P^{\{m\}}(\bar{A}_x)\ddot{a}^{(m)}_x - \bar{A}_x$$

$$= [P^{\{m\}}(\bar{A}_x) - P^{(m)}(\bar{A}_x)]\ddot{a}^{(m)}_x.$$ (D.3.12)

Hence the net level annual premium for the premium-refund benefit, payable m times per year, is

$$P^{(m)}(\bar{A}_x^{PR,m}) = \frac{\bar{A}_x^{PR,m}}{\ddot{a}_x^{(m)}}$$

$$= P^{\{m\}}(\bar{A}_x) - P^{(m)}(\bar{A}_x), \tag{D.3.13}$$

which generalizes (6.5.9) of *Actuarial Mathematics* [1] and (2.4) in the paper.

Putting $s=T$ in (D.2.7) and taking expectations, we have

$$\ddot{a}_x^{\{m\}} = \frac{\delta}{d^{(m)}}\,\bar{a}_x, \tag{D.3.14}$$

which is [1, (5.9.7)]. Applying (D.3.14) to (D.3.2) and rearranging yields

$$P^{\{m\}}(\bar{A}_x) = \frac{d^{(m)}}{\delta}\,\bar{P}(\bar{A}_x). \tag{D.3.15}$$

Substituting (D.3.15) into the right-hand side of (D.3.13), we obtain

$$P^{(m)}(\bar{A}_x^{PR,m}) = \frac{d^{(m)}}{\delta}\,\bar{P}(\bar{A}_x) - P^{(m)}(\bar{A}_x)$$

$$= \bar{P}(\bar{A}_x)\left[\frac{d^{(m)}}{\delta} - \frac{\bar{a}_x}{\ddot{a}_x^{(m)}}\right]$$

$$= \bar{P}(\bar{A}_x)\frac{\bar{A}_x - A_x^{(m)}}{\delta\ddot{a}_x^{(m)}}, \tag{D.3.16}$$

which, for $m=1$, is (2.3) in the paper; see also Exercise 6.17 of *Actuarial Mathematics* [1].

4. Reserves

It follows from (D.3.14), (D.3.15), and a derivation similar to the one on page 207 of *Actuarial Mathematics* [1] that, if t is a positive number divisible by $1/m$, that is, if

$$t \bmod \frac{1}{m} = 0,$$

then

$${}_t V^{\{m\}}(\bar{A}_x) = {}_t\bar{V}(\bar{A}_x). \tag{D.4.1}$$

Also, extending the proof on page 208 of *Actuarial Mathematics* [1], we have

$$_tV^{(m)}(\bar{A}_x^{PR,m}) = {}_t\bar{V}(\bar{A}_x) - {}_tV^{(m)}(\bar{A}_x)$$

$$= {}_tV^{\{m\}}(\bar{A}_x) - {}_tV^{(m)}(\bar{A}_x). \qquad (D.4.2)$$

5. Interpolation

Let s be a positive number not divisible by $1/m$; suppose that we are to estimate the reserve at time s, $_sV^{\{m\}}(\bar{A}_x)$, by *linear interpolation*. The reserve at time $\lceil ms \rceil/m$ is

$$_{\lceil ms\rceil/m}V^{\{m\}}(\bar{A}_x) = {}_{\lceil ms\rceil/m}\bar{V}(\bar{A}_x) \qquad (D.5.1)$$

by (D.4.1). The reserve at a moment after time $\lfloor ms \rfloor/m$, that is, after the payment of $(1/m)P^{\{m\}}(\bar{A}_x)$, is

$$_{\lfloor ms\rfloor/m}V^{\{m\}}(\bar{A}_x) + \frac{1}{m}P^{\{m\}}(\bar{A}_x) = {}_{\lfloor ms\rfloor/m}\bar{V}(\bar{A}_x) + \bar{P}(\bar{A}_x)\bar{a}_{\overline{1/m}} \qquad (D.5.2)$$

by (D.4.1) and (D.3.8). Then

$$_sV^{\{m\}}(\bar{A}_x) \approx m \left\{ \left(s \text{ pad } \frac{1}{m} \right) [{}_{\lfloor ms\rfloor/m}\bar{V}(\bar{A}_x) + \bar{P}(\bar{A}_x)\bar{a}_{\overline{1/m}}] \right.$$

$$\left. + \left(s \text{ mod } \frac{1}{m} \right) {}_{\lceil ms\rceil/m}\bar{V}(\bar{A}_x) \right\}$$

$$= (\lceil ms \rceil - ms) [{}_{\lfloor ms\rfloor/m}\bar{V}(\bar{A}_x) + \bar{P}(\bar{A}_x)\bar{a}_{\overline{1/m}}]$$

$$+ (ms - \lfloor ms \rfloor) {}_{\lceil ms\rceil/m}\bar{V}(\bar{A}_x), \qquad (D.5.3)$$

which is (4.2) in the paper. An alternative linear-interpolation formula is:

$$_sV^{\{m\}}(\bar{A}_x) \approx (s \text{ pad } 1) {}_{\lfloor s\rfloor}V^{\{m\}}(\bar{A}_x) + (s \text{ mod } 1) {}_{\lceil s\rceil}V^{\{m\}}(\bar{A}_x)$$

$$+ \left(s \text{ pad } \frac{1}{m} \right) P^{\{m\}}(\bar{A}_x), \qquad (D.5.4)$$

which is Exercise 7.24.b of *Actuarial Mathematics* [1].

6. Endowment Insurance

For two real numbers s and t, let $s \wedge t$ denote the minimum of s and t. Replacing $\lceil mT \rceil/m$ by $(\lceil mT \rceil/m) \wedge n$ and T by $T \wedge n$, we can extend the analysis above from whole life insurance to n-year endowment insurance. For example, in place of (D.1.1), (D.1.2), and (D.1.3), we have

$$A_{x:\overline{n}|}^{(m)} = \mathrm{E}[v^{(\lceil mT \rceil / m) \wedge n}], \tag{D.6.1}$$

$$\ddot{a}_{x:\overline{n}|}^{(m)} = \mathrm{E}[\ddot{a}_{(\lceil mT \rceil / m) \wedge n}^{(m)}], \tag{D.6.2}$$

and

$$a_{x:\overline{n}|}^{(m)} = \mathrm{E}[a_{(\lfloor mT \rfloor / m) \wedge n}^{(m)}], \tag{D.6.3}$$

respectively.

7. Complete Annuities-Immediate

Parallel to the notion of the apportionable annuity-due is that of the *complete annuity-immediate*; see [1, Section 5.9]. Let t be a positive number, not necessarily an integer; we define

$$a_{\overline{t}|}^{(m)} = \frac{1 - v^t}{i^{(m)}} \tag{D.7.1}$$

and

$$s_{\overline{t}|}^{(m)} = \frac{(1 + i)^t - 1}{i^{(m)}}. \tag{D.7.2}$$

With $m = 1$, (D.7.1) can be found in Example 5.13.b and Exercise 5.31.a of *Actuarial Mathematics* [1]. Then

$$\mathring{a}_x^{(m)} = \mathrm{E}[a_{\overline{T}|}^{(m)}]. \tag{D.7.3}$$

It follows from (D.7.1) and (D.7.2) that

$$a_{\overline{T}|}^{(m)} - a_{\overline{\lfloor mT \rfloor / m}|}^{(m)} = v^T s_{\overline{T - (\lfloor mT \rfloor / m)}|}^{(m)}. \tag{D.7.4}$$

Taking expectations and applying (D.7.3) and (D.1.3) yields

$$\mathring{a}_x^{(m)} - a_x^{(m)} = \mathrm{E}[v^T s_{\overline{T - (\lfloor mT \rfloor / m)}|}^{(m)}]. \tag{D.7.5}$$

The adjustment payment at time T is $s_{\overline{T - \lfloor mT \rfloor / m}|}^{(m)}$. From (D.1.4), we have

$$T - \frac{\lfloor mT \rfloor}{m} = T \bmod \frac{1}{m}; \tag{D.7.6}$$

it is the time between the last payment date before death and the date of death.

Let n be a positive number divisible by $1/m$. Replacing T by $T \wedge n$ and $\lceil mT \rceil / m$ by $(\lceil mT \rceil / m) \wedge n$ in (D.7.3) and (D.7.4), we have

$$\overset{\circ}{a}{}^{(m)}_{x:\overline{n}|} = E[a^{(m)}_{\overline{T \wedge n}|}] \tag{D.7.7}$$

and

$$a^{(m)}_{\overline{T \wedge n}|} - a^{(m)}_{\overline{(\lfloor mT \rfloor / m) \wedge n}|} = v^{T \wedge n} s^{(m)}_{\overline{[(T \wedge n) - (\lfloor mT \rfloor) \wedge n]}|}. \tag{D.7.8}$$

Observe that

$$(T \wedge n) - [(\lfloor mT \rfloor / m) \wedge n] = \begin{cases} T - \lfloor mT \rfloor / m & \text{if } T < n \\ n - n = 0 & \text{if } T \geq n \end{cases}.$$

Let $I(\cdot)$ denote the indicator function,

$$I(A) = \begin{cases} 1 & \text{if } A \text{ is true} \\ 0 & \text{if } A \text{ is false}. \end{cases}$$

Since $s^{(m)}_{\overline{0}|} = 0$, the right-hand side of (D.7.8) can be simplified as

$$v^T s^{(m)}_{\overline{T - (\lfloor mT \rfloor / m)}|} I(T < n).$$

Hence it follows from (D.7.8), (D.7.7), and (D.6.3) that

$$\overset{\circ}{a}{}^{(m)}_{x:\overline{n}|} - a^{(m)}_{x:\overline{n}|} = E[v^T s^{(m)}_{\overline{T - (\lfloor mT \rfloor / m)}|} I(T < n)]. \tag{D.7.9}$$

Also, note that

$$\frac{\ddot{a}^{\{m\}}_{x:\overline{n}|}}{\overset{\circ}{a}{}^{(m)}_{x:\overline{n}|}} = \frac{i^{(m)}}{d^{(m)}}$$

$$= (1 + i)^{1/m}. \tag{D.7.10}$$

REFERENCES

1. BOWERS, N.L., JR., GERBER, H.U., HICKMAN, J.C., JONES, D.A., AND NESBITT, C.J. *Actuarial Mathematics.* Itasca, Ill.: Society of Actuaries, 1986.
2. GRAHAM, R.L., KNUTH, D.E., AND PATASHNIK, O. *Concrete Mathematics: A Foundation for Computer Science.* Reading, Mass.: Addison-Wesley, 1989.
3. SCHER, E. "Relationships between the Fully Continuous, the Discounted Continuous and the Semicontinuous Reserve Bases for Ordinary Life Insurance," *TSA* XXVI (1974): 597–606; Discussion 607–15.
4. SHIU, E.S.W. "Integer Functions and Life Contingencies," *TSA* XXXIV (1982): 571–90; Discussion 591–600.

(AUTHOR'S REVIEW OF DISCUSSION)

KEITH SHARP:

Dr. Shiu and Ms. Tiong are to be thanked for the useful extensions and alternative viewpoints given in their discussion. They were unaware of my unpublished paper on the case of modal premiums,* and there is some overlap. Their analysis, however, adds a thorough theoretical base to the development. The use of the pad and modulus terminology and the corresponding notation provides an elegant structure for their analysis. The apportionable annuity-due is indeed the concept corresponding to the "refund of unearned premium" practice. Clarification of the relationship between the underlying mathematics and the approximations used in practice will be a valuable outcome of this work.

*Sharp, K.P. "Reserves for Policies With Modal Premiums," *Research Report 95-15*. Waterloo, Ont.: University of Waterloo Institute of Insurance and Pension Research, 1995.

THE "PENSION MAX" ELECTION: AN INVESTIGATION OF THE STRUCTURAL AND ECONOMIC DIFFERENCES BETWEEN THE 100% CONTINGENT ANNUITY PENSION BENEFIT OPTION AND THE STRAIGHT LIFE BENEFIT OPTION USED IN CONJUNCTION WITH PENSION MAX

KLAUS O. SHIGLEY

ABSTRACT

The so-called "pension max" life insurance marketing concept is generating a great deal of excitement among life insurance marketers. It's also received some skeptical reviews in the popular news media, the most recent being a *Newsweek* article by Jane Bryant Quinn in the April 4, 1994 issue. The marketing concept calls for electing an unreduced pension, that is, *maximizing* the pension, in lieu of electing a reduced "contingent annuity" (CA) or "joint and survivor" (J&S) option. Further, the marketing concept calls for the purchase of life insurance on the employee to substitute for the economic exposure created by not electing the CA or J&S option. Although the marketing concept is clear and simple, its economics continue to generate a great deal of discussion. This paper attempts to add some clarity to this issue.

The differences between pension max and the CA option are examined in three parts:
- Differences in the funding pattern
- Differences in the benefit pattern
- Relative economics.

The paper concludes with some generalizations based on this analysis.

1. INTRODUCTION

We start with an immediate straight life annuity, of amount N, payable to an employee age X. The present value for this (in actuarial notation) is $N\ddot{a}_x$. The N stands for "normal" form. The pension plan benefit formula describes benefit accrual amounts in units of the normal form. The benefit amounts under other optional forms of payment are converted to different amounts, usually determined as the actuarial equivalent of the normal form.

All qualified pension plans must offer the option to receive benefits in a joint and survivor (J&S) or contingent annuity (CA) form. A $K\%$ J&S option refers to an optional annuity form whereby the annuity amount is reduced to $K\%$ of the initial annuity payment after the first death, regardless of whether the employee or the spouse dies first. This is similar to, but not the same as, the CA option. A $K\%$ CA option provides for a reduction to $K\%$ of the initial annuity amount only if the employee dies first. For $K\%$ equal to 100%, the CA option and the J&S option are the same.

For this discussion, we evaluate the trade-offs between the 100% CA (or J&S) annuity option and the straight-life normal form. An extension of the analysis to other percentages, such as a 50% CA or J&S option, is straight-forward [see Equation (3)]. We assume the employee is age X and has a spouse age Y.

The present value of the 100% CA benefit option, for an annuity amount of $(N-R)$, in actuarial notation, is:

$$(N - R)\ddot{a}_x + (N - R)\ddot{a}_{x|y}.$$

(The notation $\ddot{a}_{x|y}$ is used to denote a contingent annuity of \$1 per year payable to Y after the death of X.)

If R is the actuarial reduction, the expression for the 100% CA option says that the present value of an annuity of N payable in the straight-life normal form is equal to the present value of a reduced annuity of $(N-R)$ payable to X plus a contingent annuity of $(N-R)$ to Y if the employee, X, dies first.

In actuarial terms,

$$N\ddot{a}_x = (N - R)\ddot{a}_x + (N - R)\ddot{a}_{x|y}. \tag{1}$$

The left side of this equation can also be expressed as

$$N\ddot{a}_x = (N - R)\ddot{a}_x + R\ddot{a}_x. \tag{2}$$

Equation (2) says N dollars can be split into two pots, one pot having $(N-R)$ dollars and the other pot having R dollars. Equation (2) holds for all values of R. From (1) and (2), it follows that[1]:

$$R\ddot{a}_x = (N - R)\ddot{a}_{x|y}. \tag{3}$$

Finally, the normal form of the annuity can also be expressed as

---

[1]In order to generalize the discussion to other than 100% CA options, this expression can be interpreted as $R\ddot{a}_x = k(N-R)\ddot{a}_{x|y}$, with $k=1$. For $k=\frac{1}{2}$, this represents the familiar 50% CA option.

$$N\ddot{a}_x = (N - R)\ddot{a}_x + R\ddot{a}_{xy} + R\ddot{a}_{y|x}. \tag{4}$$

This expression is less obvious, but it follows from Equation (2) by substituting $(R\ddot{a}_{xy}+R\ddot{a}_{y|x})$ for the term $R\ddot{a}_x$. This substitution says that a life annuity of R dollars to X has the same value as an annuity of R while both X and Y are alive, plus a contingent annuity of R payable to X after Y dies. Equation (4) is true for any value of R.

From (1) and (2) it follows that:

$$(N - R)\ddot{a}_x + R\ddot{a}_x = (N - R)\ddot{a}_x + (N - R)\ddot{a}_{x|y}. \tag{5}$$

From (1) and (4) it follows that:

$$(N - R)\ddot{a}_x + R\ddot{a}_{xy} + R\ddot{a}_{y|x} = (N - R)\ddot{a}_x + (N - R)\ddot{a}_{x|y}. \tag{6}$$

If we clear out equal terms from both sides of Equations (5) and (6), we can see the idea behind pension max more clearly. Pension max is essentially an election to take $(R\ddot{a}_{xy}+R\ddot{a}_{y|x})$ instead of $(N-R)\ddot{a}_{x|y}$. That is, instead of $(N-R)$ payable to the spouse after the employee's death, the employee elects to receive the unreduced annuity N, which for simplicity we separate into $(N-R)$ and R. And R is then mathematically separable into two payment streams. The first payment stream is payable while both X and Y are alive, and the second payment stream is payable to the employee X after the death of the spouse Y. *The reduction, R, "pops up" again if the spouse dies first.* These two modes for receiving the pension benefit have the same value but very different characteristics.

2. DIFFERENCE IN THE FUNDING PATTERN BETWEEN PENSION MAX AND CA OPTION

One important reason for the appeal of the pension max election derives primarily from an unattractive aspect of the CA option. The election of a CA option involves a contract to purchase $(N-R)\ddot{a}_{x|y}$ in exchange for $R\ddot{a}_x$. This derives from Equation (5). *One problem with this election is that the obligation to fund the survivor benefit (that is, the reduction to the normal form N) often extends beyond the spouse's death.* This is similar to buying an expensive lottery ticket with a purchase price of $(N-R)\ddot{a}_{x|y}$ on the installment plan, with payments of R payable for life, but with the obligation to continue to make payments after the ticket has been declared a loser. That is, the funding obligation period could extend beyond the economic life of the benefit being purchased. The pension max election clearly avoids this problem.

On the other hand, the main problem with the pension max election is that if the employee dies first, the spouse has no retirement income. To cover this financial exposure, the reduction, R, is used to purchase life insurance on the employee. The use of life insurance instead of the CA option avoids the anomaly of funding the survivor annuity beyond the date of death of the spouse. If the spouse dies first, the employee merely lapses the life insurance policy, and the reduction, R, is effectively restored, or pops up again. This is the first importance difference between pension max and the CA or J&S option, although, as we shall see later, some pension plans have CA options with pop-ups that are designed to eliminate this problem.

Examining the trade-off between pension max and the CA option in the context of Equation (6), we note that Equation (6) provides a technique for quantifying the portion of the CA option purchase price that, on average, remains unpaid or unfunded after the spouse has died.

The contingent annuity of $(N-R)$ is purchased by $R\ddot{a}_x$. This purchase price, $R\ddot{a}_x$, as we saw above, equals the contingent piece of the annuity, $R\ddot{a}_{y|x}$, plus the joint life piece, $R\ddot{a}_{xy}$. The value of the contingent annuity, $R\ddot{a}_{y|x}$, relative to the total purchase price, $R\ddot{a}_x$, or relative to $(N-R)\ddot{a}_{x|y}$, which follows from Equation (3), is a measure of the proportion of the obligation remaining to be paid on the losing lottery ticket. Figure 1 gives some sample values for these pieces for a pair of age/sex combinations.

To help put these observations into better perspective, it is useful to compare the typical CA option with a true pop-up benefit option that is available in some pension plans. In a true pop-up benefit option, the contingent annuity option, $(N-R)\ddot{a}_x+(N-R)\ddot{a}_{x|y}$ from Equation (1), is modified by adding back the reduction R_p if Y dies first, that is, adding back $R_p\ddot{a}_{y|x}$. Thus R_p is calculated so that

$$N\ddot{a}_x = (N - R_p)\ddot{a}_x + (N - R_p)\ddot{a}_{x|y} + R_p\ddot{a}_{y|x}. \tag{7}$$

Recall from Equation (4) that, for all R,

$$N\ddot{a}_x = (N - R)\ddot{a}_x + R\ddot{a}_{y|x} + R\ddot{a}_{xy}.$$

It follows that in a true pop-up, reductions are calculated so that

$$(N - R_p)\ddot{a}_{x|y} = R_p\ddot{a}_{xy}. \tag{8}$$

Equation (8) states that the reduction, R_p, in the pop-up payment mode must be large enough so that, *during the joint lifetime of the employee and spouse*, it will fund the survivor annuity to the spouse. This of course makes

FIGURE 1

DECOMPOSITION OF THE CONTINGENT ANNUITY INTO JOINT LIFE PIECE
AND CONTINGENT PIECE FOR A 100% CA OPTION

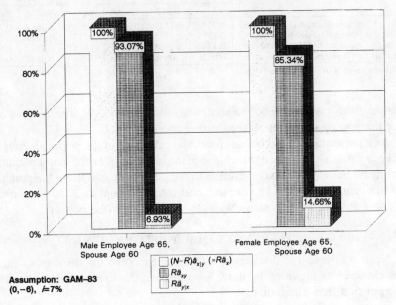

intuitive sense. The reduction can pop back up only if the contingent annuity has already been paid for at the first death. Because this funding period is shorter on average than the employee's lifetime, the reduction, R_p, to fund the pop-up must be bigger than the reduction to fund the conventional CA option. The reduction factor (that is, the ratio of R_p to N) for a 100% CA option with a true pop-up feature is given by the expression $\ddot{a}_{x|y} \div \ddot{a}_y$. This compares with a reduction factor of $\ddot{a}_{x|y} \div (\ddot{a}_x + \ddot{a}_y - \ddot{a}_{xy})$ for a standard 100% CA (or J&S) election. These ratios are derived from Equations (6) and (8). In the context of the preceding discussion, the election of a true pop-up CA option aligns the funding period with the economic life of the CA benefit option.

Table 1 compares the reductions for a true pop-up election with reductions for a conventional 100% CA option for a small sample of age and sex combinations. Reduction factors increase as the interest assumption decreases. The percentage *extra* cost for the pop-up (or increase to reductions)

TABLE 1

REDUCTION FACTORS FOR 100% CA OPTION*

	Interest = 7%		Interest = 6%		Interest = 5%	
	Regular	Pop-up	Regular	Pop-up	Regular	Pop-up
Male Employee 65/Female Spouse 60	0.2317	0.2447	0.2495	0.2643	0.2688	0.2857
Male Employee 60/Female Spouse 60	0.1591	0.1716	0.1728	0.1874	0.1879	0.2050
Female Employee 65/Male Spouse 60	0.1134	0.1304	0.1215	0.1412	0.1302	0.1532
Female Employee 60/Male Spouse 60	0.0726	0.0864	0.0777	0.0940	0.0832	0.1025

*Assumptions: GAM-83 $(0,-6)$, regular $= \ddot{a}_{x|y} \div (\ddot{a}_x + \ddot{a}_y - \ddot{a}_{xy})$; pop-up $= \ddot{a}_{x|y} \div \ddot{a}_y$; $N=1$.

ranges from just over 5.6% to somewhat more than 23%. The relative cost for the pop-up increases as the interest rate decreases.

As a percentage of the normal form, the extra cost of the pop-up is roughly 2%. In those situations in which the plan does not offer the pop-up annuity form and the CA option is preferred to the pension max option, the purchase of life insurance on the spouse, at a cost roughly equal to 2% of the normal form, would be an alternative way of manufacturing the pop-up.

3. DIFFERENCES IN BENEFIT PATTERNS

Next, we focus the discussion on a comparison of the differences in the benefit streams provided by the CA option and the life insurance benefit in the pension max alternative.

We start with the equivalence, $R\ddot{a}_x = (N-R)\ddot{a}_{x|y}$ from Equation (3). If we now take premium payments of R during the employee's life, with present value $R\ddot{a}_x$, to secure life insurance of F on the employee, with present value FA_x, then it follows from Equation (3) that $FA_x = (N-R)\ddot{a}_{x|y}$. This means that we are mathematically indifferent between the present values produced in the pension max option and the 100% CA option.

This conclusion, however, ignores the mismatch in timing between the benefit pattern provided by the pension plan and the benefit provided by life insurance. The plan provides for life income to the spouse of $(N-R)$, with a present value of $(N-R)\ddot{a}_{y+T}$, if the employee dies at duration T. The life insurance policy provides for level face amount F if the employee dies at duration T, where F is the insurance amount purchased by a premium of R. Figure 2 shows the relative values of these two liabilities at different times, for the special case of a male employee age 65 and a spouse age 60.

All things being equal, the contingent annuity is worth more in the early years, and the life insurance policy is worth more in the later years. The

FIGURE 2

RELATIVE BENEFIT LEVELS AT EMPLOYEE'S DEATH

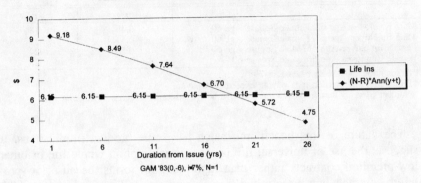

GAM '83(0,-6), i=7%, N=1

figure demonstrates that even though the present values are the same, the values are not the same at every time. This very crucial difference must be addressed. If this benefit mismatch is acceptable to the customer, then the choice between pension max and the CA comes down to a bet. Pension max wins the bet if the spouse predeceases the employee, *or* if the employee's death occurs after the time, T, when the face amount, F, first exceeds the present value of the surviving spouse's annuity, $(N-R)\ddot{a}_{y+T}$. Pension max loses the bet if the employee predeceases the spouse before time T. The expected value is equal on both sides of the bet. The odds or probability of winning the bet, however, do not have to be equal. The probability of winning the bet is measured by

$$1 - \sum_{t=0}^{T} {}_{t}p_{xy}q_{x+t}. \tag{9}$$

Table 2 gives some examples of probabilities and crossover years for sample ages. The odds of winning the bet are usually somewhat better than even for couples who are similar in age, and thus appear to be very favorable. To put this observation in perspective, note that for two lives with identical mortality expectations, the odds that one life predeceases the other approach $\frac{1}{2}$ as T in Equation (9) approaches the end of the mortality table. To the extent that the crossover point, T, occurs sooner than that, the probability that one life predeceases the other by time T will be less than $\frac{1}{2}$. The odds of winning the bet, which are equal to 1 minus this probability, thus tend to be better than even.

TABLE 2

100% CA Option*

	P†	T‡
Male Employee Age 65/Female Spouse Age 60	0.46	18
Male Employee Age 60/Female Spouse Age 60	0.51	22
Female Employee Age 65/Male Spouse Age 60	0.58	24
Female Employee Age 60/Male Spouse 60	0.66	28

*Assumptions: GAM-83 (0,−6), $i=7\%$.
†Probability that pension max payout exceeds CA payout.
‡Number of years that employee must survive before insurance exceeds CA payout.

The nature of this benefit mismatch has some product implications. It suggests the use of universal life or current assumption whole life or other low-premium contracts rather than high-premium forms, because low-premium contracts buy more initial face amount per dollar of premium, which minimizes the early-duration benefit mismatch. Furthermore, the risk that constant premium of R will ultimately purchase less insurance than initially illustrated is mitigated by the declining insurance need, measured as the present value of the survivor annuity, $(N-R)\ddot{a}_{y+t}$, as duration from issue goes up.

What happens if we want to reduce or eliminate the benefit mismatch and still elect the pension max option?

To eliminate the mismatch, it is necessary to buy decreasing term insurance on the employee's life for each year as long as both the employee and the spouse remain alive. The amount of term insurance purchased each year must be sufficient to purchase an annuity of $(N-R)$ for the surviving spouse, or $(N-R)\ddot{a}_{y+t}$. The present value of this series of annual term insurance purchases can be expressed as

$$(N - R) \sum_{t=1}^{\infty} v^t + p_{y\ t-1}p_x\ q_{x+t-1}\ \ddot{a}_{y+t}.$$

This present value[2] is precisely equal to $(N-R)\ddot{a}_{x|y}$, which is precisely equal to $R\ddot{a}_x$, which in turn is equal to FA_x. That is, the present value of the required sequence of decreasing-term insurance amounts is equal to the present value of the contingent annuity, is equal to the present value of the employee's annuity reduction, is equal to the present value of the level insurance amount, F. These equivalencies can be expressed as

---

[2]Jordan, C.W. *Life Contingencies*. Chicago, Ill.: Society of Actuaries, 1952, 231; see also the ensuing discussion by Elias Shiu.

$$R\ddot{a}_x = FA_x = (N - R)\ddot{a}_{x|y} = (N - R) \sum_{t=1}^{\infty} v^t + p_{y\ t-1}p_x\ q_{x+t-1}\ \ddot{a}_{y+t}. \quad (10)$$

We have demonstrated that the benefit pattern under a pension max election with the purchase of annual term insurance of $(N-R)\ddot{a}_{y+t}$ is identical to the benefit provided under the 100% CA option. However, differences in the funding pattern will continue. These funding patterns are illustrated in Figure 3.

FIGURE 3

RELATIVE FUNDING LEVELS BY YEAR FOR TERM COST VERSUS ANNUITY REDUCTION
100% CA OPTION

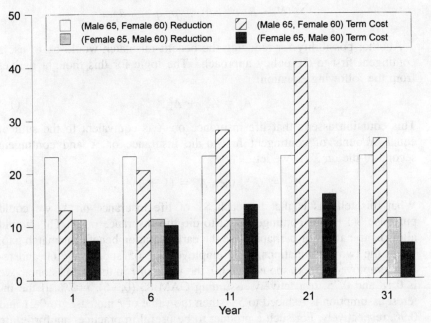

Assumptions: GAM-83 (0,6), $j = 7\%$, and $N = 100$

Figure 3 shows that, for these age/sex combinations, term costs start to exceed the reduction, R, in about the eighth year. Note that these term costs are for a decreasing insurance amount equal to $(N-R)\ddot{a}_{y+t}$. Term costs grow significantly higher until about year 20, at which point they decline. The *increase* in the term cost peaks at $1.76 \times R$ for the male employee and at

$1.43 \times R$ for the female employee. This could be problematical if R is the only financial resource available to fund the term insurance. The average outlays for the term insurance appear to be much higher than the reduction, R. A slightly different perspective emerges when the cumulative outlays for these two options are graphed with their associated discounts for mortality and interest.

In Figure 4 we compare the cumulative cost of the reduction R,

$$\sum_{t=0}^{T} R\, v^t\, {}_tp_x,$$

against the cumulative cost of the term insurance,

$$\sum_{t=1}^{T} (N - R)\, v^t + p_y\, {}_{t-1}p_x\, q_{x+t-1}\, \ddot{a}_{y+t}.$$

Another possibility for reducing the benefit mismatch would be to use a contingent first-to-die policy approach.[3] The logic for this thought derives from the following equation:

$$A_x = A_{xy}^1 + A_{xy}^2. \tag{11}$$

This equation asserts that life insurance on X is equivalent to the sum of equal amounts of contingent first-to-die insurance on X and contingent second-to-die on X. If we let:

$$A_{xy}^2 = rA_{xy}^1, \text{ then } A_x = (1 + r)A_{xy}^1.$$

What this tells us is that for each \$1 of life insurance on X, we could purchase \$$(1+r)$ of contingent first-to-die life insurance on X. This would allow us to narrow or perhaps close the early-duration benefit mismatch gap.

For the two combinations, male employee age 65/spouse age 60 and female employee age 60/spouse age 60, the value of r in the expression above is 0.18 and 0.75, respectively, assuming GAM-83 $(0,-6)$, $i=7\%$. If the interest assumption is reduced to 5%, then the value of r increases to 0.21 and 0.96, respectively. For such a product to be useful in practice, nonforfeiture laws might need to be modified to preclude the potential antiselection from selective lapsation in the event death is imminent. The factors above are calculated without regard to such antiselection.

---

[3]This idea was provided by Cary Lakenbach.

FIGURE 4

CUMULATIVE OUTLAYS FOR 100% CA OPTION, MALE EMPLOYEE AGE 65 SPOUSE AGE 60
DISCOUNTED FOR MORTALITY AND INTEREST

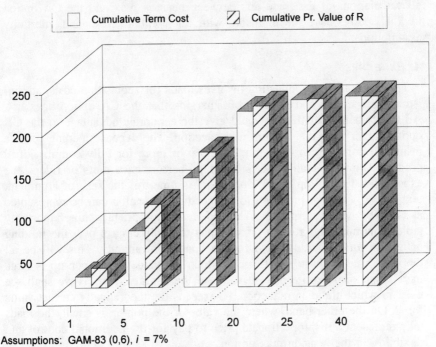

Assumptions: GAM-83 (0,6), i = 7%

Another approach to reducing the benefit mismatch, *often used in practice*,
involves the purchase of life insurance five years or more prior to retirement.
This allows for the purchase of higher face amounts for the same outlay, R,
from the retirement date forward. The increase in face amount that is
achieved through a prefunding program could be made sufficiently large to
close the benefit mismatch. For example, if a male age 65 (spouse age 60)
anticipates retirement at age 65 and uses the anticipated reduction
(R=\$23.17) to purchase and begin funding life insurance at age 60, the face
amount will be 49% greater than the face amount purchased at age 65 with
the same premium outlay from age 65 forward.[4]

---

[4]Assuming GAM-83 (0,−6), i=7%; 23.17 $\ddot{a}_{60}/A_{60}$=1.49(23.17 $\ddot{a}_{65}/A_{65}$).

4. DIFFERENCE IN ECONOMIC VALUE

The discussion to this point has ignored expenses and taxes. In addition, all calculations of the trade-offs between pension max and the CA option to this point have been made with identical interest and mortality assumptions.

A. Expenses

The pension max application involves loads for acquisition costs, administrative expenses, and issuer profit margins that the CA option does not. All things being equal, this would give the economic advantage to the CA option rather than the pension max election. The expense loading for life insurance policies can be as high as 35% or more for fully commissioned products. For low-load policies and high-performance units or riders, the expense load can drop to 10% or less.[5] Assume, for the sake of argument, that the fully loaded premium for a specific application can be represented as 110% of the net premiums calculated on an appropriately chosen mortality table. This might be a small price to pay to retain control over the funding pattern or amortization period for the contingent annuity. This will be all the more true in those situations in which the value of the pop-up is large in relation to the entire present value of the annuity R or, as we shall see next, in which the plan reduction, R, exceeds the theoretically correct value for R. On the other hand, where the value of the pop-up is small, the loads may represent a disproportionate price to pay for the additional control and flexibility in the pension max option.

B. Assumptions Used to Calculate Actuarial Equivalence

In practice, the relationship between R and N is governed by actuarial reduction factors defined in the retirement plan document. In qualified plans this relationship is typically independent of sex, health, or the current economic environment. In direct contrast, the insurance amount, F, which is purchased by premiums of R, as well as the present value of the contingent survivor annuity of $(N-R)$, will depend on *exact* age and sex characteristics, as well as prevailing interest rates and the health of the employee and spouse. Table 3 compares correct values for R with plan factors for R, which are

---

[5]Richard Schwartz estimated the expense component for a variable life policy (nonsmoker, age 45, 12% earned rate, retained for 20 years), as a 1.9% reduction to the earned rate ["The Scoop on Variable Life," *Probate & Property* (Jan.-Feb. 1993): 28].

TABLE 3

100% CA OPTION CALCULATION FOR *R* USING PLAN ASSUMPTIONS
VERSUS CORRECT ASSUMPTIONS*

	Correct *R*	Plan *R*
Male Employee 65/Female Spouse 60	0.2317	0.2142
Male Employee 60/Female Spouse 60	0.1591	0.1610
Female Employee 65/Male Spouse 60	0.1134	0.2142
Female Employee 60/Male Spouse 60	0.0726	0.1610

*Assumptions: Correct: GAM-83 $(0,-6)$; 7%; $N=1$
　　　　　　Plan: UP-84; 7%; $N=1$

derived from assumptions not too dissimilar from those used in a typical corporate plan. We use the GAM-83 $(0,-6)$ Table as a proxy for correct economic assumptions. Plan factors are calculated using the UP-84 Table.

In general, if the reduction *R* defined by the plan provisions is larger than the *R* that would be calculated under correct assumptions, then the pension max alternative becomes relatively more attractive, because the overstated reduction can be applied to purchase insurance at a fair price. An exception to this rule occurs if an employee is in bad health. In this case, paying a fair (that is, high) price for the life insurance will erode the advantage gained from using the overstated reduction *R* to fund the life insurance.

In practice, the variance between theoretically correct actuarial reductions and the actual reductions defined according to plan provisions is quite large. In the ten largest annuity contracts administered at John Hancock, plan reduction factors for a 100% CA option range from a high of 0.2796 to a low of 0.1277 for an employee age 65 and a CA age 60, and from 0.1959 to 0.1060 for an employee age 60 and a CA age 60. The interest assumption used to calculate the actuarially equivalent reductions in this sample varies from 5% to 8%. And *the most commonly used convention* for the mortality assumption is to use a larger setback for the CA than for the employee. This means that when the employee and the CA are equal in age, the CA is assumed to have better mortality than the employee. And, *in the special case where the spouse is the CA*, this is comparable to assuming that the spouse is longer-lived than the employee. Another common convention, used in three of the ten plans, is to assume the UP-84 Table, which makes no distinction between the employee and the CA.

In Table 4, we illustrate how differences between the plan *R* and the correct *R* can be used as a tool for choosing between pension max and the CA option.

TABLE 4

DECISION TOOL FOR MAKING A CHOICE BETWEEN THE 100% CA OPTION
AND THE PENSION MAX OPTION*

	(1) Plan R	(2) $R\ddot{a}_x$	(3) $(N-R)\ddot{a}_{x|y}$	(4) A_x	(5) $F=(3)/(4)$	(6) $R^1=(3)/\ddot{a}_x$
	Interest Rate = 7%					
Male Employee 65/Female Spouse 60	0.2142	2.0778	2.2985	0.3654	6.2907	0.2370
Male Employee 60/Female Spouse 60	0.1610	1.7450	1.7206	0.2909	5.9144	0.1587
Female Employee 65/Male Spouse 60	0.2142	2.3658	1.1103	0.2774	4.0019	0.1005
Female Employee 60/Male Spouse 60	0.1610	1.9245	0.7852	0.2180	3.6023	0.0657
	Interest Rate = 5%					
Male Employee 65/Female Spouse 60	0.2142	2.3869	3.2202	0.4694	6.8606	0.2890
Male Employee 60/Female Spouse 60	0.1610	2.0458	2.4671	0.3949	6.2473	0.1942
Female Employee 65/Male Spouse 60	0.2142	2.7847	1.5293	0.3809	4.0148	0.1176
Female Employee 60/Male Spouse 60	0.1610	2.3096	1.0927	0.3169	3.4482	0.0762
	i = 7%, Pref. Mort					
Male Employee 65/Female Spouse 60	0.2142	2.3217	1.9412	0.2909	6.6724	0.1791
Male Employee 60/Female Spouse 60	0.1610	1.8977	1.4507	0.2289	6.3380	0.1231
Female Employee 65/Male Spouse 60	0.2142	2.5605	0.9691	0.2180	4.4458	0.0811
Female Employee 60/Male Spouse 60	0.1610	2.0439	0.6891	0.1695	4.0655	0.0543

*Assumptions: Column (1) UP-84, i=7%; column (2)–column (6) first two blocks assume GAM-83 $(0,-6)$; column (2)–column (6) third block assumes GAM-83 $(-5,-11)$; N=1.

In column (1), the reduction R is calculated in accordance with gender-neutral (UP-84) plan provisions, as defined in Table 3. In columns (2) and (3), we use the R from column (1) in conjunction with correct economic assumptions to calculate the present value of the pension max election $(R\ddot{a}_x)$ and the CA option $(N-R)\ddot{a}_{x|y}$. (Recall that if we used "correct" economic assumptions to calculate the reduction R, then columns (2) and (3) would have the same values.) In column (4), we show the present value of $1 of life insurance. In column (5), we solve for the life insurance face amount, F, that is required to deliver the same economic benefit as would be provided by the plan if the CA option in column (3) had been selected. In column (6), we solve for the premium that will be required to buy F.

In general, if column (3) exceeds column (2), then the CA option is a better value than the pension max option, and vice versa. A good measure of the relative advantage or disadvantage between the CA option and pension max is to compare column (6) with column (1). Column (6) is the premium that is required to purchase life insurance with the same economic value as the CA annuity in column (3). *If column (6), after suitable adjustment for expenses and taxes, is less than column (1), then pension max is cheaper.*

The Table 4 calculation is developed for two different correct economic scenarios: 7% and 5%. In addition, a third scenario tests for the sensitivity in the results to lower mortality assumptions, in this case a five-year setback. The plan reduction factor, R, is the same for all three scenarios, UP-84 and $i=7\%$. *In practice, plan reduction factors do not change very often because it is administratively inconvenient and because the accrued benefit anticutback rules preclude reductions to accrued benefits, including optional forms.*

Table 4 allows us to make the following generalizations:

1. All things equal, pension max has a greater chance of success in a high-interest-rate scenario. This can be observed by noting the increase in the ratio of column (6) to column (1) as interest rates drop from 7% to 5%.

2. The tendency, or convention, in a qualified plan to assume that the CA has equal or better mortality experience than the employee will normally result in plan reductions for female employees being larger than the theoretically correct reduction calculation. In such a case, pension max will have a greater tendency to be a good value for female employees than for male employees.

3. All things equal, as mortality rates decline, the present value of $(N-R)\ddot{a}_{x|y}$ declines relative to $R\ddot{a}_x$. Thus, the relative economics of pension max will be improved to the extent that the employee qualifies for preferred underwriting.

C. Taxes

The present value analysis to this point has ignored taxes. To replicate the CA's annuity on a post-tax basis, we need to address three different tax considerations:

1. We need to ensure that the life insurance face amount, F, is not subject to estate or income taxes.

2. In practice, the option to receive the unreduced annuity subjects the entire pension payment, including R_1, to taxes. Thus only $(1-T)R$ is available to buy life insurance.

3. If we want to replicate the periodic income stream of the CA annuity, we need to *invest* the proceeds from the life insurance policy. The investment income that is generated from investing the proceeds may be taxable.

The first issue is easily taken care of. Life insurance proceeds are exempt from income taxes, and the ownership of a policy can be structured to avoid estate taxes.

The second issue is that we only have $(1-T)R$ to spend on life insurance. On the other hand, the contingent annuity, $N-R$, is also subject to taxes. If the tax rate for the contingent annuity, $N-R$, is also T, then the appropriate target amount of life insurance need only be sufficient to provide for an after-tax survivor annuity of $(1-T)(N-R)$. That is, on an after-tax basis, we need to provide $(1-T)(N-R)\ddot{a}_{x|y}$. Since

$$R\ddot{a}_x = (N - R)\ddot{a}_{x|y} = FA_x,$$

it follows that

$$(1 - T)R\ddot{a}_x = (1 - T)(N - R)\ddot{a}_{x|y} = (1 - T)FA_x.$$

This means that the conclusions drawn from the pre-tax analysis above will carry over for the post-tax scenario, provided that the tax rates before and after the employee's death are not too dissimilar.

To replicate the CA annuity, we need to *invest* the proceeds from the life insurance policy. While proceeds from life insurance are not subject to income tax, *the investment income* that is generated from investing the proceeds *is taxable*. Therefore, we need to find an investment with an after-tax rate of return equal to that assumed in the present-value calculation of the CA annuity. If we cannot find such an investment, we need to increase the premium commitment above, R, to maintain the target CA benefit amount. Stated a different way, to avoid increasing the premium commitment, proceeds would have to be invested aggressively. Conversely, a more conservative investment strategy will typically require a higher premium commitment or a lower target annuity amount.

We examine this issue by first looking at a special case with a very conservative investment policy. We assume that the proceeds from the life insurance are invested in tax-free municipal bonds, in which investment income is sheltered from further income taxes. We use Equation (10):

$$R\ddot{a}_x = (N - R)\ddot{a}_{x|y} = \sum_{t=1}^{\infty} v^t + p_{y\ t-1}p_x\ q_{x+t-1}\ (N - R)\ddot{a}_{y+t}.$$

In the pre-tax environment, all calculations are assumed to be done at 7%. If the term insurance proceeds of $(N-R)\ddot{a}_{y+t}$ in the expression above were invested in municipal bonds at 5%, then we would avoid income taxes, but we would need to reduce the CA benefit to maintain the equivalencies in Equation (10). We can see this if we rewrite the last expression in Equation (10) as follows:

$$\sum_{t=1}^{\infty} v_{(7\%)}^t + p_{y\ t-1}p_x\ q_{x+t-1} \left[(N - R) \frac{\ddot{a}_{y+t(7\%)}}{\ddot{a}_{y+t(5\%)}} \right] \ddot{a}_{y+t(5\%)}.$$

The reductions to the CA benefit will range from 15% (17%) for male (female) CAs if the employee's death occurs at the CA's age 60 to 8% (10%) for male (female) CAs if the employee's death occurs at the CA's age 80.

Alternatively, we could increase the funding levels to maintain the same benefit to the CA. If, in the expression above, we use a tax-free municipal bond investment rate of 5% to calculate the present value of an annuity of $(N-R)\ddot{a}_{y+t}$ to the spouse Y at every duration t, this defines a conservative estimate of the term insurance amount, F_t, that will be required at each of those durations to replicate the survivor annuity that would be provided by the plan. We use the expression,

$$\sum_{t=1}^{\infty} v_{(7\%)}^t + p_{y\ t-1}p_x\ q_{x+t-1}\ (N - R)\ddot{a}_{y+t(5\%)} = R^1 \ddot{a}_{x(7\%)},$$

to calculate the required premium, R^1, for this series of term insurance amounts. We compare this with the results of a similar calculation,

$$\sum_{t=1}^{\infty} v_{(7\%)}^t + p_{y\ t-1}p_x\ q_{x+t-1}\ (N - R)\ddot{a}_{y+t(7\%)} = R\ddot{a}_{x(7\%)},$$

where we use the pre-tax rate of 7% throughout, to calculate the required premium, R, for the term insurance of $(N-R)\ddot{a}_{y+t(7\%)}$. The ratio of these two calculations applied to R will give a conservative estimate of the additional percentage outlay required under pension max to replicate the qualified plan's benefits on an after-tax basis.

Similarly, we could apply this ratio to the face amount, F, previously calculated, if we wanted to adjust the level-target life insurance face amount to a tax-adjusted basis.

Table 5 quantifies this discussion with some examples. The 15% increase for the female spouse on account of the tax effect makes intuitive sense if we think of the average price sensitivity or duration of a straight-life annuity at these ages as approximately equal to 7.5. This combined with an assumed difference of 2% in the post-tax interest rate would suggest this additional cost and similarly for the male spouse at an average duration of 6.

The discussion above presumes that the employee's pre-tax hurdle rate is equal to the market-based fixed-income rate. This may not be true. To generalize the analysis of the after-tax effect, we need to consider the possibility

TABLE 5

ADJUSTMENT FOR TAXATION OF INVESTMENT INCOME ON LIFE INSURANCE PROCEEDS
SET ASIDE TO FUND THE SURVIVOR ANNUITY*

$$(N - R) \sum_{t=1}^{\infty} v^t + p_{y\,t-1} p_x\, q_{x+t-1}\, \ddot{a}_{y+t}$$

100% CA Option	(1) $v@7\%,\ \ddot{a}@5\%$	(2) $v@7\%,\ \ddot{a}@7\%$	(1)/(2)
Male Employee 65/Female Spouse 60	2.5925	2.2474	1.15
Male Employee 60/Female Spouse 60	1.9779	1.7245	1.15
Female Employee 65/Male Spouse 60	1.4088	1.2527	1.12
Female Employee 60/Male Spouse 60	0.9740	0.8680	1.12

*Assumptions: GAM-83 $(0, -6)$, $N=1$.

that the employee's pre-tax hurdle rate is different from the pre-tax fixed-income rates used in the analysis so far. The employee's after-tax rate is then determined as a function of this pre-tax hurdle rate. (In this discussion, the calculations have centered around 7%, where 7% is assumed to represent prevailing fixed-income returns.)

Selecting the employee's hurdle rate is not always an obvious exercise. Many individuals would prefer to have cash-in-hand (that is, the investable proceeds from life insurance) to the alternative of a greater present value, payable in periodic installments, as measured by the tax-adjusted market-based fixed-income rate. One reason for such a preference is the greater flexibility of cash-in-hand. Such flexibility could be manifested by investing the cash in opportunities such as a family business, at much higher rates than fixed-income rates, for example. The logic for selecting the employee's hurdle rate is beyond the scope of this paper.

In Table 6 we develop a generalized logic for making a decision on the relative merits of pension max versus the CA option on an after-tax basis. We start with the assumption that the employee's after-tax hurdle rate is 5% and market-based fixed-income returns are 7%. These rates are not necessarily linked, although they can and often will be linked.

R, in row (1), is calculated as before. The values in rows (2) and (3) are calculated at 5%, which is now meant to represent an arbitrary after-tax hurdle rate, specifically selected by our employee. *The ratio of rows (2) and (3) calculated at 5% is* entered in row (4). This ratio is *a measure of the relative value of the CA option and the pension max option on the after-tax basis selected by the employee.* For comparison, the results of a similar calculation at 7% (from Table 4) are entered in row (5). A quick comparison of rows (4) and (5) demonstrates that the use of lower discount rates (or

TABLE 6

DECISION TOOL FOR MAKING A CHOICE BETWEEN THE 100% CA OPTION AND THE PENSION MAX OPTION USING EMPLOYEE AFTER-TAX HURDLE RATES

	Assumption Key*	Male Employee 65 / Female Spouse 60	Male Employee 60 / Female Spouse 60	Female Employee 65 / Male Spouse 60	Female Employee 60 / Male Spouse 60
(1) Plan R	a	0.2142	0.1610	0.2142	0.1610
(2) R_{d_x}	b	2.3869	2.0458	2.7847	2.3096
(3) $(N-R)\ddot{a}_{x|y}$	b	3.2202	2.4671	1.5293	1.0927
(4) (2)/(3)	b	0.7412	0.8292	1.8208	2.1137
(5) (2)/(3)@7%	c	0.9040	1.0142	2.1307	2.4510
(6) $F=(3)/A_x$	b	6.8606	6.2473	4.0148	3.4482
(7) $R^1=(6)A_x/\ddot{a}_x$	d	0.2584	0.1677	0.1009	0.0629
(8) $R^2=(6)A_x/\ddot{a}_x$	e	0.1956	0.1298	0.0809	0.0515
(9) $R^3=F\dagger A_x/\ddot{a}_x$	d	0.2317	0.1519	0.1134	0.0726
(10) $R^4=R^1 1.2$	d	0.3101	0.2012	0.1210	0.0755

*Assumptions: $N=1$.
 a=UP-84; reduction factor as defined in the plan.
 b=GAM-83 $(0,-6)$, $i=5\%$; this represents the employee after-tax hurdle rate.
 c=GAM-83 $(0,-6)$, $i=7\%$; this represents the pre-tax fixed income rate.
 d=GAM-83 $(0,-6)$, $i=7\%$; this represents the insurer's assumptions.
 e=GAM-83 $(-5,-11)$, $i=7\%$; same as d with lower mortality assumption.
 †From Table 4, column (5).

497

hurdle rates) usually causes the present value of the CA benefit to increase by a greater amount than the present value of the annuity reduction, because lower discount rates give more weight to later cash flows. *This implies, all other things equal, that the higher the employee's after-tax hurdle rate, the more likely it is that pension max will be the more economically viable option.*

If $R\ddot{a}_x$ is still greater than $(N-R)\ddot{a}_{x|y}$, assuming the employee's individually selected after-tax hurdle rates, then the previous conclusions about the economic advantage of pension max over the CA annuity do not change. In Table 6, this occurs when the ratio in row (4) is greater than one and applies to the two scenarios in which the employees are female.

If $R\ddot{a}_x$ is less than $(N-R)\ddot{a}_{x|y}$, assuming the employee's after-tax hurdle rates, then a further determination needs to be made to determine whether premiums of R are sufficient to purchase an insurance amount, F, where F satisfies $(N-R)\ddot{a}_{x|y}=FA_x$, calculated using the *employee's hurdle rate.*[6] In other words, F is calculated to provide the same economic benefit as the CA option at the employee's after-tax hurdle rate. This value of F is entered in row (6).

In row (7), we solve for the value of the premium, R^1, which is required, using the *insurer's assumptions*, to purchase the insurance amount, F, which was calculated in row (6). Row (8) is similar to row (7), except that it tests for the premium required, R^2, to purchase F, assuming the insurer uses a better (preferred) mortality assumption. Row (8) is designed merely to test the sensitivity of R to the insurer's mortality assumption. *If R^1 (or R^2, if applicable) is less than R [from row (1)], then pension max is cheaper than the CA option on an after-tax basis, and vice versa.*

In row (7) the proxy for the insurer's assumptions is assumed to be GAM-83 $(0,-6)$, $i=7\%$.[7] Life insurance mortality assumptions are often based on multiples of the 1975–80 Basic Table. The GAM-83 $(0,-6)$ Table, which is used for most of this discussion, produces mortality rates roughly equivalent to the ultimate rates from the 1975–80 Basic Table at ages 60 and beyond. Policies sold with preferred mortality are commonly priced at less than 100% of the ultimate rates in the 1975–80 Basic Table. This logic would establish the GAM-83 $(0,-6)$ Table as a conservative standard for judging the relative

---

[6] Theoretically, this calculation of F also needs to reflect the customized mortality assumption for the employee and the CA, to the extent that it differed from the insurer's mortality assumption.

[7] To put this in perspective, these assumptions produce premiums of \$39.85, \$26.84, \$25.98, and \$18.24 per \$1,000 for insurances on a male 65, male 60, female 65, and female 60, respectively.

economics of pension max for individuals who qualify for preferred mortality rates.

Row (9) is similar to row (7) except that it tests for the required premium R^3 to purchase F assuming a higher employee after-tax hurdle rate (7%). Row (10) adds a 20% loading to the life insurance premiums calculated in row (7). The loading can be tailored to any specific situation.

Each of R^1, R^2, R^3, *and* R^4 *is designed to be tested against the R of row (1). The superscripted R's represent the premiums required to purchase life insurance for an amount that provides present value precisely equal to the present value of the CA annuity. As a general rule, when* R^n *is less than R, the employee is economically better off using the pension max approach.*

In practice, we would use an actual premium from an actual insurance illustration in making the pension max decision. This requires of course that we have some knowledge about the assumptions underlying the insurer's illustration. By choosing a set of calculation parameters from the illustration system that reflect the employee's (or an advisor's) view of the appropriate mortality, expense and interest assumptions, any desired degree of conservatism can be introduced into the algorithm. In this connection, most illustration systems calculate premiums to reflect any desired interest rate assumption. In the context of Table 6, if the reduction, R, from row (1) is sufficient to purchase, or fund, the equivalent insurance face amount, F, from row (6), as determined through such a unit cost calculation within the insurer's illustration system, then pension max is clearly a viable alternative.

We can also evaluate the tax effect in terms of Table 2, which was used to illustrate the benefit mismatch. The effect of the lower tax-adjusted discount rate is to increase the early-duration benefit mismatch and to extend the time before the face amount of insurance, F, exceeds the value of the survivor annuity. The results of a sample calculation are shown in Table 7.

For the Table 7 calculation, the target insurance amount is the survivor annuity, $(N-R)\ddot{a}_{y+r}$, calculated at the employee's after-tax hurdle rate. The face amount, F, is purchased by annual premiums of R. The reduction, R, is determined by the plan, and F is calculated by using the insurer's assumptions. The insurer's interest assumption in Table 7 is assumed to remain constant at 7%. The employee's hurdle rate is assumed to be 5% post-tax and 7% pre-tax. A comparison of the respective entries at 5% and 7% is a fair measure of the tax effect under these assumptions.

TABLE 7

Effect of Post-Tax Interest*

R		Insurer Interest Rate 7%; Employee Hurdle Rate 5%		Insurer Interest Rate 7%; Employee Hurdle Rate 7%	
		T†	P‡	T†	P‡
0.214	Male Employee 65/Female Spouse 60	24	0.31	21	0.38
0.161	Male Employee 60/Female Spouse 60	25	0.44	22	0.51
0.214	Female Employee 65/Male Spouse 60	6	0.92	1	0.98
0.161	Female Employee 60/Male Spouse 60	7	0.94	2	0.98

*Assumptions: The plan reduction factor, R, is calculated assuming UP-84, $i=7\%$, other entries assume GAM-83(0,−6)
†Number of years that employee must survive before insurance exceeds CA payout.
‡Probability that pension max payout exceeds CA payout.

5. WHAT CONCLUSIONS CAN WE DERIVE FROM THIS ANALYSIS?

Before we develop any conclusions, it is important to point out that this analysis has ignored certain other relevant factors that could influence the choice between pension max and the CA annuity option. Cost-of-living provisions were ignored. The analysis is easily extended to include them. Some plans extend eligibility for post-retirement health insurance to contingent annuitants, but do not extend eligibility to surviving spouses of employees who have elected an unreduced benefit. This factor is also ignored. Special plan provisions like these need to be analyzed separately before an informed decision on the pension max election can be made.

Other relevant factors were also deemed to be beyond the scope of this analysis, including the risk of changing tax rates and changing tax laws, as well as the investment risks associated with investing the proceeds of the life insurance policy.

The following conclusions are subject to the above-mentioned caveats:
1. The pension max application is a more flexible funding vehicle and does a better job of retaining control of the retirement annuity asset than the CA option. The design of the funding pattern as well as the benefit pattern can be fully controlled by the employee.
2. The present value of the life insurance purchased by annual premiums equal to the actuarial reduction, R, is equal to the present value of the CA benefit except for expenses and taxes. However, the expenses may be a small price to pay for the additional flexibility and control afforded by the pension max election.

3. There is a tax inefficiency in the pension max election. The inefficiency occurs because investment income from proceeds of life insurance is taxable. This inefficiency is measurable and is quantified in the text. Tax losses due to this inefficiency can be mitigated or eliminated by using aggressive investment policies. (See Tables 5 and 6.)

4. Close attention should be paid to the calculation of the actuarial reduction factors in the plan, to determine how the reduction compares with the correct actuarial reduction determined without regard to qualified-plan nondiscrimination rules, particularly those pertaining to unisex mortality rates. (See Table 4.) The unisex convention for calculating the plan reduction factors tends to make the pension max option more viable for female employees than male employees.

5. A good proxy for deciding whether the pension max election is a good bet or a bad bet is to use the ratio of the contingent annuity, $R\ddot{a}_{y|x}$, to the contingent annuity, $(N-R)\ddot{a}_{x|y}$. (See Figure 1.) This is a measure of the funding obligation that remains on average after the spouse has died. Another tool for deciding whether pension max is a good bet or a bad bet is to calculate probabilities directly from Formula (9). (See also Table 2.)

6. A fundamental challenge in implementing a successful pension max application is to determine how important it is to match the liability exposure created by opting out of the CA option. Decreasing term or universal life with target term capability is a better fit for solving this problem than high-premium/high-dividend policies. *It is fundamentally important, with regard to this objective, that the policy stays in force.*

In conclusion, the pension max option bears some additional costs, but these costs may be a fair price to pay for the additional advantages. One key driver of the relative economics of pension max versus the CA option is the set of actuarial assumptions that are used in the qualified plan to calculate the equivalencies between the benefit options. These assumptions can cause dramatic differences between the economic value of the pension max and the CA option, in both directions.

ACKNOWLEDGMENT

The author wishes to acknowledge the immense contributions of Susan Silverman and Sylvia Martin in the preparation of this paper, verifying formulas, calculating values, and correcting mistakes.

APPENDIX

1983 GAM MORTALITY TABLE

Age	Tabular Mortality	Scale H	Age	Tabular Mortality	Scale H
10	0.000293	0.00750	60	0.009158	0.01500
11	0.000298	0.00500	61	0.010064	0.01500
12	0.000304	0.00250	62	0.011133	0.01500
13	0.000310	0.00240	63	0.012391	0.01500
14	0.000317	0.00230	64	0.013868	0.01500
15	0.000325	0.00220	65	0.015592	0.01500
16	0.000333	0.00210	66	0.017579	0.01500
17	0.000343	0.00200	67	0.019804	0.01500
18	0.000353	0.00180	68	0.022229	0.01450
19	0.000365	0.00160	69	0.024817	0.01400
20	0.000377	0.00140	70	0.027530	0.01350
21	0.000392	0.00120	71	0.030354	0.01300
22	0.000408	0.00100	72	0.033370	0.01250
23	0.000424	0.00100	73	0.036680	0.01250
24	0.000444	0.00100	74	0.040388	0.01250
25	0.000464	0.00100	75	0.044597	0.01250
26	0.000488	0.00100	76	0.049388	0.01250
27	0.000513	0.00100	77	0.054758	0.01250
28	0.000542	0.00230	78	0.060678	0.01250
29	0.000572	0.00360	79	0.067125	0.01250
30	0.000607	0.00490	80	0.074070	0.01250
31	0.000645	0.00620	81	0.081484	0.01250
32	0.000687	0.00750	82	0.089320	0.01250
33	0.000734	0.01000	83	0.097525	0.01150
34	0.000785	0.01250	84	0.106047	0.01050
35	0.000860	0.01500	85	0.114836	0.00950
36	0.000907	0.01750	86	0.124170	0.00850
37	0.000966	0.02000	87	0.133870	0.00750
38	0.001039	0.02000	88	0.144073	0.00700
39	0.001128	0.02000	89	0.154859	0.00650
40	0.001238	0.02000	90	0.166307	0.00600
41	0.001370	0.02000	91	0.178214	0.00550
42	0.001527	0.02000	92	0.190460	0.00500
43	0.001715	0.01950	93	0.203007	0.00420
44	0.001932	0.01900	94	0.217904	0.00340
45	0.002183	0.01850	95	0.234086	0.00260
46	0.002471	0.01800	96	0.248436	0.00180
47	0.002790	0.01750	97	0.263954	0.00100
48	0.003138	0.01750	98	0.280803	0.00067
49	0.003513	0.01750	99	0.299154	0.00033
50	0.003909	0.01750	100	0.319185	0.00000
51	0.004324	0.01750	101	0.341086	0.00000
52	0.004755	0.01750	102	0.365052	0.00000
53	0.005200	0.01700	103	0.393102	0.00000
54	0.005660	0.01650	104	0.427255	0.00000
55	0.006131	0.01600	105	0.469531	0.00000
56	0.006618	0.01550	106	0.521945	0.00000
57	0.007139	0.01500	107	0.586518	0.00000
58	0.007719	0.01500	108	0.665268	0.00000
59	0.008384	0.01500	109	0.760215	0.00000
			110	1.000000	0.00000

DISCUSSION OF PRECEDING PAPER

CHARLES L. TROWBRIDGE:

Mr. Shigley brings to our attention some of the intricacies of the J&S and CA optional forms offered under most defined-benefit pension plans. He goes on to describe another way of accomplishing the same general purposes, through what he calls pension max.

Until 1980 I considered myself a pension, social security, and life insurance actuary, with a special knowledge of defined-benefit pension plans. Since then I have followed pension matters less closely, and Mr. Shigley's paper is my first exposure to the pension max concept. I hope readers view the following as comments from an intellectually interested retired actuary with adequate background but with no direct pension max experience.

There is general agreement among students of pensions that the election of some form of J&S annuity, to replace the normal single-life form, should be encouraged whenever the employee reaches retirement with a living spouse. As Mr. Shigley states in his second paragraph, all qualified pension plans must offer at least one J&S or CA alternative, and many offer several. There is no obligation on the retiring employee, however, to choose any such option. The normal form of straight life annuity may be more appropriate when the spouse has an adequate retirement income independent of that of the former employee.

The J&S and CA Options—How Alike and How Different?

As a starting point, consider the full J&S (or CA) option, whereby each $1 of the normal pension is replaced by a reduced pension of $(1-r)$, payable for as long as either x or y is alive; r is easily shown to be

$$r = \frac{\ddot{a}_{x|y}}{\ddot{a}_{xy} + \ddot{a}_{x|y} + \ddot{a}_{y|x}}.$$

Depending on the age and sex of x and y and on both the interest rate and the mortality tables assumed in the calculation of the annuities $\ddot{a}_x$, $\ddot{a}_y$, and $\ddot{a}_{xy}$, Mr. Shigley shows values of r as high as 0.27 and as low as 0.07. Of course the actual range is wider.

Next recognize that many married couples prefer that the pension benefit after the first death be a fraction ($\frac{3}{4}$, $\frac{2}{3}$, or $\frac{1}{2}$) of the pension during their joint lifetime. The pension while both are alive can be larger, and living

503

expenses for one person are presumably less than for two. This thinking gives rise to what Mr. Shigley calls the $X\%$ J&S option, of which the most popular is "joint and $\frac{2}{3}$." The single-life annuities after the death of either x or y are $\frac{2}{3}$ of the amount while both are alive.

Readers should be aware that OASI retirement benefits under present law are *exactly* joint and $\frac{2}{3}$ to a retiring couple, *if* the larger PIA is more than twice the smaller. If the PIAs are not that far apart, the result lies somewhere between joint and $\frac{2}{3}$ and joint and $\frac{1}{2}$. Note in particular that the benefit after the first death does not depend on which of the couple dies first. In either case it is the larger of the two PIAs.

Finally, there is the CA option, under which the percentage reduction on the first death occurs only if (x) dies first. Other things being equal, a $\frac{2}{3}$ CA option will require a greater reduction during y's lifetime, in exchange for a larger pension to the former employee after y has died.

The rationale for CA, rather than J&S, is that the normal single-life annuity (1) arose through the employment of (x) and hence (2) in some sense "belongs" to x, and (3) y should therefore be satisfied with a smaller after-the-first-death pension than x. Were the employee to take a community property view of the normal form pension, the choice would be expected to be J&S rather than CA. I have no information on the popularity of J&S versus CA, but I admit to a personal preference for the former. Of course Mr. Shigley is correct when he points out that the 100% CA and the 100% J&S are identical.

Actuarial Bases and Antiselection

The table of reductions when an optional form is elected can be found in the pension plan itself. It will invariably be based on some mortality table or tables and an interest rate. The mortality assumption will likely be conservative from an annuity point of view (such as GAM-83). The difference between male and female mortality may be recognized, likely through an age setback for females, but as Mr. Shigley has noted, some plans have chosen to use a sex-combined table such as UP-84.

The interest rate is theoretically the rate that the pension plan (or the insurance company if the retired life portion of the pension liability is insured) expects to earn on its investments. The higher the interest rate, the smaller the reduction factor r, and hence the cheaper the reversionary annuities, because the election of any of these options causes the pension to be paid later, and the value of this delay is greater when interest rates are high.

Note that mortality antiselection exists. Employees reaching retirement in poor health can be expected to maximize the pension payable to their spouses after their death. This antiselection is especially powerful if an employee, in poor health but not yet retired, simultaneously elects a 100% CA option and early retirement. At one time it was common to require any J&S or CA form to be elected at least three (or five) years prior to retirement to avoid some of the obvious antiselection. Despite such provisions, some antiselection must be expected. When the spouse is in poor health, as one example, it is very likely that the normal straight-life form will be the choice. Other than setting back the age for (y) and hence calculating the reduction on the assumption that y is in especially good health, there is no practical way of counteracting this less obvious form of antiselection.

The foregoing paragraphs suggest that there is no correct answer on the size of the reductions when an option is selected. The formulas are clear, but the assumptions behind them are not. The variations noted by Mr. Shigley (in Section 4-C) seem large, but they may be par for the course. We could wish that it were otherwise, but this is an imperfect world.

The Rationale behind Pension Max

Unacquainted as I am with the origin of pension max, I can only guess the motivation behind it. It seems to be based on the recognition that the conversion of a part of each r unit of straight-life pension ($_{x|y}\ddot{a}_x$) to a survivor income in reduced amount, $(1-r)\ddot{a}_{y+t}$, is technically the same as selling insurance on the life of (x) in a decreasing amount that will provide $(1-r)\ddot{a}_{y+t}$ where death occurs at age $x+t$. Perhaps one of the policies in the life insurance ratebook can be adapted to this use. If so, there is an additional opportunity to sell life insurance.

Two Important Differences between CA and Pension Max

In Sections 2 and 3 of the paper, Mr. Shigley tells us that CA and pension max, while similar in many ways, have important differences. He categorizes these as funding pattern differences and benefit pattern differences. The former revolve around the introduction of a "pop-up" option, the latter around the use of life insurance on x as a source for the reduced retirement income to y.

These two differences are only partially independent. The pop-up can exist outside of pension max, but pension max seems to be impossible without it. This discussion follows the order in which Mr. Shigley presents the two differences and hence treats the pop-up first.

Differences in Benefit Patterns

The formula for r, the dollar amount of reduction (for each \$1 of normal straight-life pension) required to provide a contingent annuity to y after the death of x, can be recast in the form

$$r(\ddot{a}_{xy} + \ddot{a}_{y|x}) = (1 - r)\ddot{a}_{x|y}.$$

In this form we see clearly that a reduction of r, imposed over the (xy) period and any period (y/x) will exactly fund $(1-r)\ddot{a}_{x|y}$, the reduced annuity to y after the death of x. In Shigley's Table 1, r turns out to be 0.2317 for the case of male employee 65/female spouse 60 and 7% interest.

Some of the rationale that Mr. Shigley presents for pension max revolves around the idea that there is something inherently defective with the traditional CA option *if* the contingent annuitant is the first to die. The reduction in pension during the joint life period (xy) continues for the period (y/x), leading Mr. Shigley to state, "One problem with this election is that the obligation to fund the survivor benefit (that is, the reduction to the normal form) often extends beyond the spouse's death." His facts are true enough—actually this will always occur whenever x lives longer than y. *Part of the reversionary annuity to y is being paid for by x's whose y's have already passed away.*

The question remains whether this is a real deficiency or simply one of the characteristics that needs to be recognized. It is true that the spouse annuity is being paid for throughout the life of x, not just the period (xy), and it is tempting to compare this with a losing wager whose loss is spread over a period after the die has been cast. It could just as well be argued that the pop-up feature (no reduction during the period when x is the survivor) is paid for (by the spouse) after x's death has made the pop-up valueless. There are other examples of this phenomenon that we take for granted. One that comes to mind is the loser of a political campaign, who has to pay campaign debts long after the election has been lost.

However one argues the desirability of the pop-up, one need not quarrel with the fact that some employees will prefer it. Any pension plan that chooses to do so can provide the pop-up among its range of options. There is a price, however. The formula for r', the reduction during the periods xy and $x|y$, but not during $y|x$, can be expressed as $r'\ddot{a}_{xy}=(1-r')\ddot{a}_{x|y}$. To avoid the reduction in the $y|x$ period, Mr. Shigley's Table 1 shows us that the reduction during y's lifetime must be 0.2447, instead of 0.2317. For a larger pension during the period $y|x$, the pension during xy and $x|y$ must be smaller.

Incidentally, the natural assumption that the pop-up will prove to pay out more dollars whenever y dies before x is not necessarily true. The critical factor is the ratio of the length of the period xy to the period $y|x$. If this ratio is as much as about 10, the r' modification to the CA option will pay less in total even if x dies first. As the extreme case, if x and y die in a common accident, the pop-up provision will prove to have been an unfortunate choice and especially so if the period xy is long.

There is another form of the pop-up, however, that ensures that if y dies first, the total payout will always be higher than under the usual form of the CA. Instead of a reduction of r' during the period xy, let it be r. The pop-up requires that the reduction during $y|x$ be zero. We can then calculate the necessary reduction r'' during $x|y$, such that $r\ddot{a}_{xy}=(1-r'')\ddot{a}_{x|y}$. As one would expect, r'' turns out to be greater than r', which in turn is greater than r. For the same example that we have illustrated before, $r=0.2317$, $r'=0.2447$, and $r''=0.2849$.

This third pattern of reductions is a continuation of the asymmetrical pattern seen before. With each step from J&S to CA and from r to r' to r'', the pattern is better for x, but worse for y. No pension plan of which I am aware provides a CA option in this r'' form, so why introduce it here? The reason becomes apparent by looking more carefully at how Mr. Shigley formulates pension max.

Differences in Benefit Patterns

Section 3 describes the second matter that distinguishes pension max. An insurance policy on the life of x, with premium r (per \$1 of normal annuity) payable throughout the life of x and with a level face amount F congruent with the insurer's premium structure, can substitute for the $(1-r)\ddot{a}_{x|y}$ that would have been provided under the CA. Presumably the contingent annuitant is the designated beneficiary, and a life income settlement option will be elected.

Mr. Shigley relies on Equation (10) when he states that "the benefit pattern under a pension max election ... is identical to the benefit provided under the 100% CA option." To paraphrase what Equation (10) tells us, "the death benefits from all of the insurance bought and maintained on the lives of all the x's are just sufficient to provide a $(1-r)$ contingent annuity for all the y's who survive their respective x's." Note that the insurance cannot lapse, even upon the death of y, and further that if x dies without a surviving y, the insurance proceeds must somehow be transferred to add to the CAs of those y's who have survived. This is clearly an impossible condition, but one that is necessary if the contingent annuities are to be in an amount $(1-r)$.

One quickly comes to the conclusion that pension max, as applied in the real world, *necessarily* incorporates a pop-up. The premium r may well be paid over the xy period but surely not over $y|x$. As shown earlier, if there is no premium over the $y|x$ period and if the premium during the xy period is r, the present value of the resulting CAs will be only $(1-r'')\ddot{a}_{x|y}$, not the $(1-r)\ddot{a}_{x|y}$ illustrated in Figure 2. If Mr. Shigley were to draw a graph of $(1-r'')\ddot{a}_{y+t}$, in addition to the annuity line that is already shown, we could tell at once how much of the gap between the insurance and annuity lines is caused by the fact that pension max is truly a pop-up coverage.

The rest of the gap between the insurance and annuity lines is simply the result of providing a level insurance coverage (F) to meet a decreasing need $(1-r'')\ddot{a}_{y+t}$. In the modern day of universal life and adjustable life coverages, one would think that a better fit could rather easily be attained. Under one of these flexible arrangements, with the premium r and the initial face set high, x could plan to reduce the face amount at intervals to better fit the value of the reversionary annuity.

Other Reasons for the Mismatch

To this point there has been an implicit assumption that the actuarial assumptions in the calculation of the reductions, and in the establishment of premiums and settlement options, are identical. Mr. Shigley reminds us that this assumption is untrue, for each of several reasons, among them the necessity for the insurance company to load the theoretical net premium for expenses, contingencies, and/or profit.

I have little to add, except to point out one matter that Mr. Shigley has not directly noted. The mortality assumptions underlying the reduction factors in the pension document will likely be those used in the calculation of annuities and hence conservative from an *annuity* point of view, but it would be an unusual insurer indeed who would price an *insurance* coverage on an annuity table.

The Effect of Federal Income Tax

I am not sure that I follow all that Mr. Shigley has to say about income tax effects, but I agree that pension max is tax-wise inefficient. During the xy period, taxable income seems to be increased by r; after a CA has commenced, it is presumably fully taxable under the usual form of CA, but may be only partially so under pension max. Whether these two effects are actuarial offsets or not, everybody I know, if given a choice, will opt for less tax early even if it means more tax later. The time value of money, in this case interest on the tax itself, is not to be ignored.

Conclusions

The main advantage of pension max, according to Mr. Shigley, is that the employee retains control of the retirement annuity asset, and the arrangement is more flexible. He tells us that the design of the funding pattern as well as the benefit pattern can be fully controlled by the employee. By funding pattern he seems to mean the use or disuse of the pop-up. In this respect I respectfully disagree. Under the usual arrangements included within a pension plan, there is no pop-up, but some plans provide a pop-up option, and others would if they saw a demand. But under pension max, the pop-up is inevitable, and its disadvantages, as well as its advantages, are built in. The most important disadvantage, not really discernible from the Shigley description, is that the CAs are necessarily lower, because the situation while x is alive is somewhat better.

Against the claimed advantages, there are (1) the higher "friction" loss under pension max, (2) the tax inefficiency, (3) the complicated mechanics, and (4) the lack of generality. Under (3) I note that pensions are normally payable monthly, so for consistency the insurance should be monthly as well; thus the offset of pension and insurance premium must happen twelve times a year. Under (4) I include (a) the fact that pension max is not applicable to what I consider the preferred form of retirment income, the J&S option of less than 100%, and (b) that when x is in poor health and needs the CA election most, pension max is not available because of insurer underwriting requirements.

After careful consideration of Mr. Shigley's presentation, I have one other concern. Will readers be led to the fallacious conclusion that pension max avoids the characteristic of traditional CA that Mr. Shigley finds offensive (which it does), but at the same time delivers the $(1-r)$ level of CA (which it does not)?

L. TIMOTHY GILES:

This is a fine paper dealing with an exciting topic.

I first encountered this challenge from a marketing department about 10 years ago. My solution was a reversionary annuity. Jordan's *Life Contingencies** devotes an entire chapter to it. I think it was approved in one state. I do not remember whether any were sold. The president of that company, not an actuary but quite astute nonetheless, rejected the possibility of a solution on the grounds that the pension plan factors were on a net basis, whereas any premiums in the company would most certainly be loaded for expenses. At that time I did not have access to the actual amount of typical reductions, an area that Mr. Shigley covers very convincingly. Clearly, any opinion of pension max ought to respond to a specific reduction.

One neat feature of a reversionary annuity is that it is exempt from non-forfeiture benefits. An unhealthy annuitant would choose cash surrender before the policy expires valueless at death. A possible disadvantage is that the annuity payments might be taxed with the investment in the contract being only the premiums paid, instead of the death benefit.

The particular aspects of a couple's situation are also very important. If you are not completely sure that this is the last spouse you will ever have, you will be more receptive to the purchase of pension max. You can always lapse it. Maybe the spouse has a pension and a partial replacement would suffice.

I do not know why reversionary annuities are not available today. The author's solution of decreasing term or level term with an annual partial lapse is more tailored than whole life, but requires researching the current market for annuities that fluctuate with interest rates. The designer of a reversionary annuity has to cast it into the form of annual renewable term with a life annuity as the death benefit. At what interest rates should these annuities be calculated?

I congratulate Mr. Shigley for rekindling an old flame and for providing an insightful analysis.

ELIAS S.W. SHIU:

This paper presents interesting applications of multiple life theory. I hope its results will be incorporated in the syllabus of the Life Contingencies Examination. I have one question. The paper seems to calculate insurance

---

*JORDAN, C.W. *Life Contingencies*. 2nd ed. Chicago, Ill.: Society of Actuaries, 1982.

values and annuity values with the same mortality table. When an annuitant elects the "pension max" option in the real world, is the *insurance* premium determined by an *annuity* mortality table?

The series expression in Equation (10) of the paper is incorrect because $_tp_x\,q_{x+t}$ is the probability that (x) will die in policy year $t+1$, while $\ddot{a}_{y+t}$ is the value of a life annuity starting at time t (which is the beginning of policy year $t+1$ and before the death occurs). It may be useful to point out that the reversionary annuity-due, $\ddot{a}_{x|y}$, is the same as the reversionary annuity-immediate, $a_{x|y}$. One way to see this relationship is as follows:

$$\ddot{a}_y - \ddot{a}_{xy} = (1 + a_y) - (1 + a_{xy})$$

$$= a_y - a_{xy}. \tag{D.1}$$

(Jordan [3], [4] seems to avoid using the reversionary annuity-due symbol.) If we can assume that (x) and (y) are independent lives (even though they are husband and wife), then

$$a_{x|y} = \sum_{j=0}^{\infty} {}_{j|}a_y\; {}_{j|}q_x.$$

Hence

$$\ddot{a}_{x|y} = a_{x|y}$$

$$= \sum_{j=0}^{\infty} {}_jE_y\; a_{y+j}\; {}_{j|}q_x$$

$$= \sum_{j=0}^{\infty} {}_{j+1}E_y\; \ddot{a}_{y+j+1}\; {}_{j|}q_x$$

$$= \sum_{j=0}^{\infty} v^{j+1}\; {}_jp_{xy}\; p_{y+j}\; q_{x+j}\; \ddot{a}_{y+j+1}, \tag{D.2}$$

which is the correct series expression for Equation (10). Unfortunately, the numerical values in the paper calculated according to Equation (10) need to be redone. Formula (D.2) is the same as Exercise 1 on page 231 of Jordan [3] and Exercise 1 on page 265 of Jordan [4].

Suppose that the pension max option is elected. The face amount of the whole life insurance on (x) purchased by an annual premium R is, of course, R/P_x. If (x) predeceases (y) *and* (y) survives to the end of the year of death of (x), then an annuity for (y) is purchased by the death benefit R/P_x paid at the end of the year of death of (x). Let T be the integer such that

$$(N - R)\ddot{a}_{y+T+1} > R/P_x \geq (N - R)\ddot{a}_{y+T+2}.$$

(The integer T here is not exactly the same as the one in the paper.) If (x) predeceases (y) before time $T+1$ *and* (y) survives to the end of the year of death of (x), then the annual payment of the annuity is less than $N-R$. The probability of this event of "losing the bet" is

$$\sum_{j=0}^{T} {}_{j}p_{xy}\, p_{y+j}\, q_{x+j}.$$ (D.3)

The sum (D.3) is not the same as the sum in Equation (9) in the paper; there is the extra term p_{y+j}, which gives the probability that the spouse survives to the end of the year of death of the employee.

Perhaps it is of pedagogical value to reformulate some of the results in the paper. Because the 100% CA option and the 100% J&S option are the same, Equation (1) in the paper can be written as

$$N\, \ddot{a}_x = (N - R)\ddot{a}_{\overline{xy}}.$$ (D.4)

Dividing (D.4) by N and rearranging yields

$$\frac{R}{N}\, \ddot{a}_{\overline{xy}} = \ddot{a}_{\overline{xy}} - \ddot{a}_x$$

$$= \ddot{a}_y - \ddot{a}_{xy}$$

$$= \ddot{a}_{x|y}.$$ (D.5)

Hence

$$\frac{R}{N} = \frac{\ddot{a}_{x|y}}{\ddot{a}_{\overline{xy}}},$$ (D.6)

numerical values of which can be found in Table 1 of the paper.

The formula corresponding to (D.4) for the true pop-up benefit option is

$$N\, \ddot{a}_x = (N - R_p)\ddot{a}_{\overline{xy}} + R_p\, \ddot{a}_{y|x}.$$ (D.7)

I think it is clearer to write R_p instead of R as in the paper, because we should distinguish it from the R in (D.4). Equation (D.7) is the same as (7) in the paper. Dividing (D.7) by N and rearranging yields

$$\frac{R_p}{N} (\ddot{a}_{\overline{xy}} - \ddot{a}_{y|x}) = \ddot{a}_{\overline{xy}} - \ddot{a}_x. \tag{D.8}$$

Because

$$\ddot{a}_{\overline{xy}} - \ddot{a}_{y|x} = \ddot{a}_y$$

and

$$\ddot{a}_{\overline{xy}} - \ddot{a}_x = \ddot{a}_{x|y},$$

we have

$$\frac{R_p}{N} = \frac{\ddot{a}_{x|y}}{\ddot{a}_y}, \tag{D.9}$$

numerical values of which can also be found in Table 1 of the paper.

On the other hand, if we formulate the equation for the true pop-up benefit option as

$$N \ddot{a}_x = (N - R_p)\ddot{a}_y + N \ddot{a}_{y|x}. \tag{D.10}$$

Then (D.9) follows from the identity

$$\ddot{a}_y - \ddot{a}_x + \ddot{a}_{y|x} = \ddot{a}_{x|y}. \tag{D.11}$$

My next remark is motivated by the expression

$$A_x = (1 + r)A_{xy}^1 \tag{D.12}$$

in the paper. In the very special situation where (x) and (y) are independent lives and each has a constant force of mortality,

$$\mu_{x+t} = \mu_x \tag{D.13}$$

and

$$\mu_{y+t} = \mu_y, \tag{D.14}$$

for all $t \geq 0$, one can show that in the continuous case

$$r = \frac{\mu_y}{\mu_x + \delta}. \tag{D.15}$$

Furthermore, suppose that we weaken conditions (D.13) and (D.14) as

$$\frac{\mu_{y+t}}{\mu_{x+t}} = \frac{\mu_y}{\mu_x} \tag{D.16}$$

for all $t \geq 0$. This condition is satisfied if the mortality for both lives follow Gompertz's law with the same parameters B and c. Under (D.16) and the independence assumption we have

$$A_{xy} = \left(1 + \frac{\mu_y}{\mu_x}\right) A_{xy}^1. \tag{D.17}$$

To verify (D.17), observe that (D.16) implies

$$\mu_{x+t} = \frac{\mu_x}{\mu_x + \mu_y} (\mu_{x+t} + \mu_{y+t}).$$

Hence

$$_tp_{xy}\, \mu_{x+t} = \frac{\mu_x}{\mu_x + \mu_y}\, _tp_{xy}(\mu_{x+t} + \mu_{y+t})$$

$$= \frac{\mu_x}{\mu_x + \mu_y}\, _tp_{xy}\, \mu_{x+t:y+t}$$

because of the independence assumption. Let $\lceil t \rceil$ denote the least integer greater than or equal to t. Then

$$A_{xy}^1 = \int_0^\infty v^{\lceil t \rceil}\, _tp_{xy}\, \mu_{x+t}\, dt$$

$$= \frac{\mu_x}{\mu_x + \mu_y} \int_0^\infty v^{\lceil t \rceil}\, _tp_{xy}\, \mu_{x+t:y+t}\, dt$$

$$= \frac{\mu_x}{\mu_x + \mu_y}\, A_{xy},$$

which is (D.17). Furthermore, replacing $\lceil t \rceil$ by $\lceil mt \rceil/m$ in the derivation above yields the more general formula

$$A_{xy}^{1(m)} = \frac{\mu_x}{\mu_x + \mu_y}\, A_{xy}^{(m)}$$

if (x) and (y) are independent lives and (D.16) holds.

I would like to point out a related paper by Jacka [2], who considers the problem of a trustee faced with investing a sum of money, the interest from which will be received by one party (the life-tenant) during his lifetime, while the capital will go to another party (the survivor) on the death of the life-tenant. Jacka assumes that there are $n+1$ assets in which the trustee may invest—n risky assets of geometric Brownian motion type and one nonrisky asset. Under assumptions about the utility functions of the two parties, he finds the collection of Pareto optimal investment strategies for the trustee together with the corresponding payoffs.

Let me conclude this discussion with an annuity story, as told by the late Dr. Bill Greenough, who was chairman and CEO of TIAA-CREF from 1963 to 1979. Below is from the section entitled "Actuarial Adversities" on pages 31 and 32 of his book [1].*

> A serious problem for the new company was that actuaries in 1918 did not know how long people were going to live in the 1920s, 1930s, and 1980s. Yet the fledgling association issued guarantees reaching that far ahead. It is hard to believe annuities were in their infancy in 1918 when TIAA started. President Pritchett selected, with the help of staff, the McClintock Annuity Mortality Table, 4 percent interest, and no provision for expenses, as the long-term actuarial assumption to calculate annuity rates on which to base guaranteed lifetime income payments.
>
> McClintock's table was the only major annuity mortality table available. Published in 1899, it was based on the annuity experience of 15 American companies before 1892. This table was retrospective in that it was not adjusted to reflect improved mortality rates for each succeeding generation. Actuaries had not yet begun to adjust mortality tables to project how long people were going to live decades in the future, as longevity increased because of such things as medical advances and improving sanitary conditions. And TIAA used the McClintock table from 1918 to 1928, 30 to 40 years after the experience on which it was based.
>
> The second factor of major financial importance was the guaranteed interest rate. TIAA's founders chose 4 percent because prevailing interest rates had always been above that level. And nothing had to be added to the rates for expenses; the Carnegie Foundation would pay all operating expenses.
>
> Pritchett then asked both existing actuarial societies to give advice as to the appropriateness of the new rates. The American Institute of Actuaries said the rates provided "ample financial security." The Actuarial

Society of America suggested the "mortality among college professors may be lower than the McClintock table, thereby creating a loss," but investment interest earnings above 4 percent would easily take care of any deficiency in mortality rates.

Were they ever wrong! Each of the actuarial factors chosen caused trouble, not immediately but within 20 to 30 years. Errors in annuities show up very slowly. The annuitants lived a good deal longer than the table said they would; interest rates fell to below 3 percent; and TIAA grew so rapidly the Carnegie Foundation could not forever pay all of its expenses.

The final result of the choice of inadequate annuity rates for the start of TIAA was unintended but not all that bad. What transpired was a gradual transition from wholly free to wholly financed pensions for the colleges, instead of the intended rapid change. As mentioned, Carnegie Corporation provided the initial capital of $1 million. In 1938, when TIAA and Carnegie Corporation separated, the corporation made additional grants of $6.7 million. And finally, from 1948 to 1958, Carnegie Corporation provided an additional $8.75 million to strengthen the longevity, interest, and expense provisions underlying the original contracts. Exit the free, enter the funded, but oh so slowly!

REFERENCES

1. GREENOUGH, W.C. *It's My Retirement Money—Take Good Care of It: The TIAA-CREF Story*. Homewood, Ill.: Irwin, 1990.
2. JACKA, S.D. "Optimal Investment of a Life Interest," *Mathematical Finance* 5 (1995): 279–96.
3. JORDAN, C.W., JR. *Life Contingencies*. Chicago, Ill.: Society of Actuaries, 1952.
4. JORDAN, C.W., JR. *Life Contingencies*, 2nd ed. Chicago, Ill.: Society of Actuaries, 1967.

ROBERT B. LIKINS:

I thank Mr. Shigley for this timely paper on an important subject. I have also been considering how a prospective buyer could make the choice between taking the higher single-life pension and buying life insurance for face amount L costing premium P on the pensioner's life (pension max) versus taking a lesser contingent spouse annuity (CA) to provide a continuing benefit for the pensioner's spouse. This discussion provides my own thoughts and suggests an analytical tool for evaluating these choices.

The analytical tool is useful for two reasons. First, the prospect here would be giving up the right for a CA, and this type of give-up is not a normal part of a life insurance purchase decision. Second, the pension max and the CA option are more complex to compare than they seem to be.

I simplify my discussion by considering only what the paper calls the $X\%$ CA. By doing this, R is the amount of the actuarial reduction that takes place at retirement for the life of the pensioner. I also assume that $X\%$ is 100%, so the pensioner's spouse gets just what the pensioner was getting before the pensioner died, that is, $N-R$.

This discussion covers the following:

- The comparison between the CA and pension max
- Pension max analysis
- Adequate pension max life insurance
- Margin in the analysis tool
- Additional intricacies of pension max
- Assumptions for use in pension max analysis
- Matrix analytical tool to select likely prospects for pension max
- Conclusion.

The Comparison

As the paper points out, pricing for the pensioner's CA option and the pension max life insurance is not done by using the same assumptions. And the life insurance face amount, L, that is bought does not precisely match the life insurance embodied in the CA option because it is not available as a policy. So the decision about the pension max approach is not as easy as just comparing the pension reduction, R, to the pension max life insurance premium, P.

A significant concern is the potential mismatch in benefits between what the spouse could have gotten with the CA and would get with the pension max life insurance. Mr. Shigley calls this "a bet," and I agree. If a pension max sale is for less than an adequate amount of life insurance (to fully replace the desired CA benefit of $N-R$) at some point after the pensioner starts his or her pension, then the pension max approach includes a bet.

The following is notation I have used:

CA = Spouse payments of $N-R$, for the 100% CA situation, beginning at the pensioner's death.

R = The reduction in the pensioner's annuity when he or she selects a CA for his or her spouse.

L = The face amount of life insurance needed to provide an after-tax spouse annuity equivalent to $(N-R)$ $(1-$postretirement tax rate) right after the pensioner retires, at the spouse's age y. This will be a larger face amount that F, which provides a spouse annuity less than this and more than zero if purchased at the spouse's age y. L would be $[(N-R)$ times (the current immediate annuity rate for a spouse age y) times $(1-$postretirement tax rate$)]$ plus (the taxes to be paid on the gross annuity payments to the spouse at the postretirement tax rate, but only on the nonexcluded part of the payments where the exclusion ratio is the cost of the payments, L, divided by the IRC expected amount of the payments).*

P = Premium for pension max life insurance of face amount L.

By establishing L in this way we eliminate the bet mentioned in the paper that exists if the pensioner dies too soon. L is conservative because it provides more than the needed funds for the spouse annuity once the pensioner survives for some time after retirement. This is shown graphically in Figure 1, where F is not sufficient to buy the full CA at retirement of $[(N-R)$ times (immediate annuity rate for spouse age y), adjusted for taxes].

Pension Max Analysis

One way to make the pension max decision is to compare the present values of the cash flows in each approach. This would provide a comparison of cash flows, after income taxes and the time value of money have been considered. We calculate and compare to find which has a larger value, (a) the pension plan's contingent spouse annuity (CA) option or (b) the pension max approach.

(a) The CA option contains: the smaller $N-R$ pension benefit plus the residual surviving spouse benefit of $N-R$

---

*Using actuarial notation and assuming the exclusion ratio applies to all the annuity payments:

$N-R$ = gross CA payments

TR = postretirement tax rate

$\ddot{e}_y$ = IRC expected number of annual payments

$\ddot{a}_y$ = Current immediate annuity cost for 1 per year

$$L = \frac{(N-R)(1-TR)}{\dfrac{1}{\ddot{a}_y} - TR\left(\dfrac{1}{\ddot{a}_y} - \dfrac{1}{\ddot{a}_y}\right)}$$

FIGURE 1
THE BET USING FACE AMOUNT F

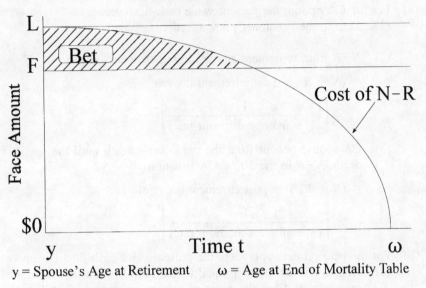

y = Spouse's Age at Retirement   ω = Age at End of Mortality Table

(b) The pension max approach contains: the larger N single-life pension
     benefit plus income from the life insurance death benefit, L, less the
     life insurance premium payments, P.

The analysis I describe here assumes that the pensioner lives until life
expectancy, determined at his or her retirement age, and that the spouse lives
that long and to her or his life expectancy determined at the end of the
retiree's life expectancy. The analysis covers the time from now until the
end of the spouse's life expectancy. Fixing the order of death dictates the
need for a spouse income for financial security.

When the pension max life insurance is purchased before retirement, life
insurance is bought for the face amount, L, from preretirement up to retirement. This benefit is not explicitly provided by the retiree's pension plan.
Therefore, even though it adds value, in this analytical tool it is not included
in the calculation comparing the pension max to the CA option, because the
pensioner can still make the CA selection at the pensioner's actual retirement
some years later, after this part of the death benefit coverage of the life
insurance has passed.

In each present value below, n is the number of years from the date of the valuation to the date of the cash flow payment.

(a) For the CA option, the present-value cash-flow stream is:

   (1) Zero to the pensioner prior to retirement age

      $= 0$

   (2) $N-R$ from retirement age until the pensioner's death

$$= (N - R)(1 - \text{postretirement tax rate})$$

$$\times \left[\frac{1}{(1 + \text{interest discount rate})} \right]^n$$

   (3) CA spouse benefit from the pensioner's death until the spouse's death, $N-R$ in the 100% CA situation

$$= (N - R)(1 - \text{postretirement tax rate})$$

$$\times \left[\frac{1}{(1 + \text{interest discount rate})} \right]^n$$

(b) For the pension max approach, the present-value cash-flow stream is:

   (1) Negative in an amount equal to the out-of-pocket life insurance premium, P, from the point of sale to retirement. This P is the premium that buys the needed amount of life insurance, L, so that the desired spouse annuity $N-R$, adjusted for taxes, can be purchased if the pensioner dies just after retiring. P can be reduced by policy dividends. If a COLI is involved, the L could be largest at a time several years after retirement

$$= - P \left[\frac{1}{(1 + \text{interest discount rate})} \right]^n$$

   (2) N, the single-life pension benefit, minus P, the premium for life insurance that must be paid out of pocket (P can be reduced by policy dividends) from retirement age until the pensioner's death.

$$= [N(1 - \text{postretirement tax rate}) - P]$$

$$\times \left[\frac{1}{(1 + \text{interest discount rate})} \right]^n$$

   (3) For consistency with the CA being given up, only an amount equal to that in (a)-(3) above. There is no comparable CA

pension benefit to the pension max additional spouse benefit that results from the excess postretirement death benefit coming from the decreasing cost of the spouse annuity as the surviving spouse ages. Note that getting (a)-(3) size annuity payment requires a smaller gross annuity payment than $N-R$ because tax is paid only on the nonexclusion ratio part of the annuity payment.

$$= (N - R)(1 - \text{postretirement tax rate})$$
$$\times \left[\frac{1}{(1 + \text{interest discount rate})} \right]^{n}$$

These cash flows can be valued for a variety of situations. If the purchase of life insurance is done at retirement rather than before retirement, then (b)-(1) is zero.

If the pension max is purchased before retirement but the policyowner wants to know the comparison at retirement age before making the CA decision, then in place of (b)-(1) the policy's cash surrender value is used as a negative amount (cost) because this value is left in the policy so that we can retain the policy's use in the pension max approach (something like a drop-in premium to get this policy to where it is). If the pension max approach is going to be used along with other, existing in-force policies, then the new policy's face amount is simply the amount needed, L, less the face amount(s) of the existing policy(ies); the cash flows (b)-(1) and (b)-(2) would be as follows.

(a) Negative in an amount equal to (i) the out-of-pocket life insurance premium for the new policy and for the in-force policy(ies) being considered in the pension max analysis, from the point of sale of the new policy to retirement and (ii) the in-force policy(ies)'s cash surrender value(s) at the point of sale of the new policy.

(b) Same as (b)-(2) above but including the out-of-pocket premiums for all new and in-force policies being considered in the pension max analysis.

Practical questions on using in-force policies in a pension max analysis are: Can it be economically built into the analysis tool/illustration system? Can another company's in-force policy be part of the analysis? Has the original need for the in-force policy been satisfied? Would an analysis using in-force policies inappropriately encourage the financing of one policy with the values of another?

The discount rate and other assumptions and techniques are described under "Assumptions."

Adequate Pension Max Life Insurance

There are several ways of providing an adequate Pension Max life insurance death benefit when the pensioner retires. First, whole life insurance can be purchased at retirement for premium P in an amount L large enough to fully replace what would have been provided to the spouse in the CA option immediately after the pensioner's retirement, at the spouse's age y. This option is shown in Figure 1.

The second option would be to provide term insurance in addition to a smaller amount of whole life insurance in such a way that their combination provides for an adequate spouse annuity. The term insurance can be reduced at several year intervals to somewhat follow the curve of the amount needed to purchase the contingent spouse annuity while always staying above that amount. This option is seen in Figure 2.

FIGURE 2

ADEQUATE TERM AND WHOLE LIFE INSURANCE

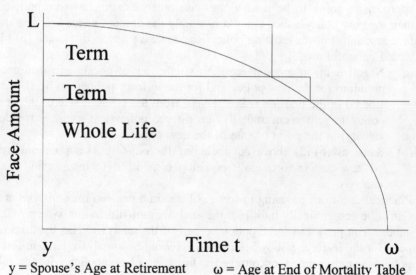

y = Spouse's Age at Retirement   ω = Age at End of Mortality Table

A third option is to have decreasing term insurance that closely follows the decrease in the contingent annuity purchase rate curve going down to a modest amount of whole life insurance; see Figure 3.

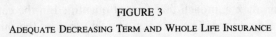

FIGURE 3

ADEQUATE DECREASING TERM AND WHOLE LIFE INSURANCE

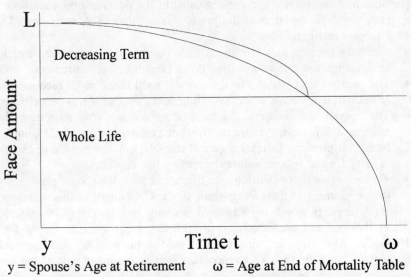

y = Spouse's Age at Retirement   ω = Age at End of Mortality Table

And finally, term insurance for precisely the face amount needed to buy the contingent annuity would be the most comparable amount to purchase, without excess, as described in the paper. This is simply the decreasing curve shown in the several previous figures.

And as Formula (11) points out, even this is more insurance than would be provided by the CA (assuming the pension plan does not provide a pop-up feature for the pensioner's reduced $N-R$ benefit, back up to N if the spouse predeceases the pensioner), because it provides A_{xy}^2 when the pensioner dies second, in addition to the CA benefit of A_{xy}^1, which pays off when $\ddot{a}_{x|y}$ starts paying and only pays when the pensioner dies first.

Margin in the Analysis Tool

I suggest that a margin be used in the CA versus pension max cash-flow comparison. The prospect might consider the economics of the pension max approach when the present values are close because there are benefits in the overall pension max approach that are not quantified in the cash-flow comparison I have described. The prospect should consider the purchase of the pension max approach if the present value of the pension max cash flow is at least, say, 90% as large as the present value of the CA cash flow. This 10% margin recognizes that:

- When the pension max life insurance is purchased before retirement, this analysis ignores the value of the death benefit before retirement.
- The pension max whole life insurance is used at its initial face amount, L, but will likely have a larger death benefit than that if it is participating.
- The pension max insurance is level or steps down after retirement, but as long as it provides insurance equal or greater than the decreasing CA benefit, it provides insurance greater than the amount needed to buy the annuity for the spouse with a decreasing life expectancy.
- There is value in the pension max life insurance if the spouse predeceases the pensioner and there is no value in the CA benefit in this situation.

Furthermore, it would be reasonable to vary the margin to be, say, 5% below the total CA cash flows for a 50% CA and, say, 10% below for a 100% CA. And when term insurance is used in the pension max approach, the margin could be reduced to recognize that a significant part of the non-required death benefit from level face amount whole life insurance will not be present and the term insurance has no cash value if the spouse predeceases the pensioner.

It would be possible to not use a simple margin but instead to value all the extra benefits that are not part of the CA option. Then the present value of the CA cash flow could be compared to (1) the present value of the pension max cash flow without the "extras" and to (2) the present value of the pension max cash flow with the "extras."

Additional Intricacies of Pension Max

Vanishing-Premium Payment Approach

An option in pension max is to buy a participating policy and accumulate the dividends as paid-up additions under the policy with the intent of discontinuing premium payments, P, in the future and letting those payments be made by the accumulated and future dividends. The vanishing-premium concept introduces a nonguaranteed element into the premium payment cash flow because dividends are not guaranteed.

Spouse Contingent Annuity Tied to Health Benefits

Another situation arises when health insurance for the spouse is provided only after the pensioner's death if the spouse is receiving a CA provided by the pension plan. If the pensioner can select the amount of the contingent annuity (100%, 75%, 50%, and so on), then the pensioner can select a CA, to allow the spouse to obtain the postretirement health insurance, but a smaller CA percentage than desired, with the remainder of the desired spouse annuity being provided by the pension max approach if it is more economical. In this case the pension max analysis would be done simply by using the amount of spouse annuity to be provided by life insurance rather than the entire desired CA benefit.

COLI Adjustment

While the paper mentions that it would not be particularly difficult to figure the cost-of-living increases (COLI) into the pension max comparison, this is likely to involve assumptions and risk. The comparison could require assumptions about (1) how often and (2) in what amounts the COLIs will occur. Several decades of COLIs could be provided after retirement to a pensioner and subsequently to a CA. If a sufficient amount of life insurance in the pension max approach is purchased to provide for the COLIs, which will depend upon the time of death, then the spouse will be left with an adequate annuity. But the spouse is unlikely to be able to buy an annuity that contains COLIs, so future increases would also need to be considered after the death of the pensioner if the CA is eligible for post-pensioner's death COLIs.

Possibly most of the COLIs can be covered in the pension max approach by purchasing level face amount insurance for the whole of life. If COLIs are provided only as long as the pensioner is alive, if the CA pension benefit is determined at the pensioner's death, and if the COLIs are 3% per year, then the decrease in the cost of the spouse's annuity is quite close to the 3% compound increases in the COLI pension benefit, so level whole life insurance of L provides good coverage. For larger COLIs or COLIs to the spouse after the pensioner's death, the life insurance face amount would need to be larger than the L described in this discussion.

Administrative Systems

It is helpful if the administrative systems are able to:
- Record the basis of sale as pension max.
- Record the basis of sale as vanishing premium, if applicable.
- Record the expected retirement date.
- If there is a change in underwriting class at issue from what was used in the analysis, request that a new analysis be performed.
- Implement communications for policy actions that will affect the policy's ability to fulfill its purpose, for example, for the vanishing premium life cycle (that is, the impact of loans, surrenders, and so on on the vanish date).
- Communicate the effect on pension max of transfer of ownership, beneficiary changes, policy face decreases/increases, other policy changes.
- Produce a "retirement approaching" letter to the agent and client before retirement and suggest that the CA-versus-pension max decision be reevaluated.

Assumptions for Use in Pension Max Analysis

Assumptions such as the following will be needed to prepare the analysis:
(1) *Dividend Scale*—Probably the current dividend scale, not guaranteed.
(2) *Settlement Option Rates*—Probably the current settlement option (immediate annuity) rates, not guaranteed.
(3) *Interest Discount Rate*—A 4%, 5%, or 6% rate could be justified based on historical inflation rates of 4% for the last 10 years, 6% the last 20 years, 5% the last 30 years, and 4% the last 40 years. This rate is not as high as an investment return rate, but, consistent with this, one might not want to reduce it for the effect of taxes.
(4) *Postretirement Tax Rate*—Analysis calculations might assume that the client is in the 25% tax bracket. This is used to compare the analysis calculations on an after-tax basis for all cash flows. A higher rate will disfavor the pension max sale.
(5) *Mortality Table Used for Life Expectancy*—The insurance company's single-premium immediate annuity mortality can be used to calculate life expectancy for the retiree at retirement age and for the spouse at the end of the retiree's life expectancy. *Tax Facts* Appendix A Table V ("Ordinary Life Annuity—One Life Expected Return Multiple") can be used to estimate the spouse's annuity taxation (exclusion ratio)

in determining the life insurance needed for pension max. It is on a unisex basis.

(6) *Pensioner's Death*—The pensioner and spouse are assumed to live to the year of the pensioner's life expectancy. Life expectancy of the pensioner is determined as of his or her retirement. For analysis calculations, the spouse's life expectancy is calculated as of the end of the pensioner's life expectancy. This provides a deterministic, not probabilistic, set of cash flows.

(7) *Preretirement Death Benefit*—This benefit has not been valued in my cash flows. It does help to support the use of a margin.

(8) *Postretirement Death Benefit*—This death benefit has three pieces:
   (a) That which is needed to provide the surviving spouse's income. This is a decreasing amount after retirement and it is used in the analysis calculation.
   (b) That which is more than (a) but not more than the guaranteed death benefit. This is an increasing amount after retirement, and it is not used in the analysis calculation because it is not required to replace the CA spouse's benefit.
   (c) That which is more than the guaranteed death benefit. This is a nonguaranteed amount, and it is not used in the analysis calculation because it is not required to replace the CA spouse's benefit and it is not guaranteed.

(9) *Pension Max Margin*—As described previously.

(10) *Premiums*—For the pension max cash flows, because the income to the pensioner from the pension benefit is stopped after the life expectancy of the pensioner (assumed time of death), we also assume no further premium payments after that time.

(11) *First Year of Retirement Death Benefit*—The analysis calculates a death benefit, L, so that the survivor will have at least as much after-tax income at the pensioner's retirement date, using the guaranteed face amount of the policy L and current settlement option rate, as would be provided to the spouse under the pension's CA option.

(12) *Policy Rating Classes*—Ratings above standard may nonqualify themselves based on their higher cost (greater negative cash flow for the pension max approach). A rated pensioner situation favors the CA option over the pension max approach because the pension plan would not normally change extra for the CA if the pensioner is sick at retirement.

(13) *Youngest Age*—Marketing of the pension max concept might be limited to prospects at some age (for example, 35 or 45) and above, because marketing the CA give-up and determining the pension benefits at younger ages is difficult.

(14) *Pension Pop-up*—This is an increase in the pensioner's benefit if the CA option is used and if the pensioner's spouse dies before the pensioner. It might be available in a pension. Our analysis assumes a scenario in which the pensioner dies before the spouse, so it does not add value to the pension max approach for the contingency in which the spouse dies before the pensioner. If the analysis includes both the pop-up's value in the CA cash flow and the policy's cash value at the spouse's death in the pension max cash flow, as the years pass after retirement the value to the pensioner of the pop-up benefit, in the year of the spouse's death, goes down and the value of the whole life policy's cash value goes up. Because this analysis uses fixed lifetimes for the pensioner and spouse, it would be difficult to bring in the value of this pop-up comparison. Leaving it out leaves the pension max approach with a bet if a pop-up is provided. Pension max results in less than full pop-up coverage when the spouse dies shortly after the pension max life insurance is purchased and the cash value is less than needed to replace the pop-up benefit.

Matrix Analytical Tool to Select Likely Prospects for Pension Max

For agents in the pension max market it can be particularly helpful if they have a tool for analyzing the likelihood of successfully selling the pension max approach to employees covered by a certain pension plan. A matrix display can be helpful; that is, general information on the pension plan is put into it, such as the reduction that will result when pensioners take the CA at various percentages of the pension benefit. The output is a matrix of pension max comparisons showing combinations of spouses' and pensioners' ages at retirement for a couple of spouse CA percentages (for example, 100% and 50%) and at several durations before retirement when the pension max approach is purchased (for example, 0, 5, and 10). By running large pension plans in an agent's territory through such a matrix, the agent can determine the likely candidates for a pension max sale based on where the sale provides the best deal for pensioners and their spouses. This can be seen in Table 1.

TABLE 1

Pension Max Plan Analysis Matrix for XYZ Pension Plan*

{(PV Pension Max divided by PV Pension CA Benefit) plus a 10% Margin}

Pensioner's Retirement Age	Spouse's Age versus Pensioner's	Purchased N Years before Retirement					
		N = 0		N = 5		N = 10	
		100% CA	50% CA	100% CA	50% CA	100% CA	50% CA
Male							
65	+5	92	97	91	98	89	97
	+0	95	98	94	99	92	98
	−5	98	100	97	101	95	100
60	+5	96	101	94	100	96	101
	+0	98	103	96	102	98	102
	−5	101	104	99	103	101	104
55	+5	97	103	99	103	99	103
	+0	100	104	101	104	101	104
	−5	102	105	104	105	104	105
Female							
65	+5	104	106	104	106	103	105
	+0	107	107	107	107	105	106
	−5	111	109	111	109	110	108
60	+5	106	107	104	106	104	106
	+0	108	108	107	108	107	107
	−5	112	110	110	109	110	109
55	+5	105	107	105	107	106	107
	+0	108	108	107	108	108	108
	−5	110	110	110	109	111	109

*Pension max sale looks most promising when ratio is 100 or more.

Some pension plans are potentially good ones to approach for the pension max sale, while others are more generous and a sale is not likely to look good economically. And even when the general plan matrix display described above is available, the specific pension max analysis tool is still helpful when approaching a particular pensioner.

Conclusion

Mr. Shigley's excellent paper points out the complexities of the pension max versus contingent spouse annuity (CA) decision. My discussion presents additional issues. The parties to the sale can benefit from a pension max analysis tool. The tool would use financial and demographic facts about the prospect, the pension and the spouse, combine them with assumptions and calculation techniques, and provide a comparison.

There is another view of the pension max decision. Some pensioners simply want to get the largest single-life pension possible. They may not want an analytical tool to justify their decision, and they may not want to buy all or any of the pension max life insurance called for to provide an annuity for their spouse at their death. That is reality, so the need for an analytical tool depends on how prospects view the pension max decision and the level of support the company and agent are able to provide prospects who are approaching this decision.

ROBERT T. McCRORY:

I enjoyed reading Mr. Shigley's paper on the pension max election. He has done a fine job of describing the election from the point of view of the member. It is also important to look at pension max from the point of view of the pension plan sponsor. In the presence of a significant number of pension max elections, the plan sponsor is confronted with a number of problems.

Antiselection

Mr. Shigley notes that pension max is likely to be most attractive to plan members who experience lower-than-average mortality. There are several reasons for this:

- The underlying structure of the pension max election favors members with low mortality rates, as shown in Table 4.
- By law, most pension plans offer unisex factors for converting from the normal form to one providing a death benefit. Such factors are usually based on combined male and female mortality rates, thus charging female pensioners more for the death benefit than they would pay under a female-only mortality table. As Mr. Shigley points out, this makes the pension max election more favorable than the plan death benefit for most females.
- The policies offered as part of the pension max election are individually underwritten. This means, of course, that the issuing insurance company can reject impaired lives. Therefore, pension max elections will be issued primarily to healthy retirees.

As a result, the healthiest members of the retiree population are those most likely to elect pension max and a life-only annuity form. The least healthy segment of the retiree population is left to elect a death benefit from the plan. The impact of such systematic, institutionalized antiselection on the plan's cost could be significant, depending on the aggressiveness with which pension max is marketed.

Incorrect Information

Sales of the pension max election are usually accompanied by a comparison of the benefits expected from the plan's death benefit election with those expected from pension max. I have reviewed a few such comparisons, and while my review is hardly exhaustive, I have yet to find one that I considered correct. A consistent problem is that cost-of-living adjustments (COLA) are seldom handled correctly, especially in the public sector.

The analysis of pension max is not easily extended to COLAs because COLAs may not be easy to compute. For example:

- In some cases, the annual COLA is equal to the increase in the Consumer Price Index (CPI), with no limit.
- Some COLAs are based on the earnings of an active member in the grade occupied by the retiree just before retirement.
- Many COLAs are driven by investment results: When earnings on plan assets exceed a certain level, a 13th monthly check may be issued or an increase in benefits may occur.
- Often, statutory minimum COLAs are accompanied by a program of regular, ad hoc benefit increases approved by the governing body.

In the above cases, projection of future COLAs may be difficult or impossible. Furthermore, the factors used by the pension plan for converting from the normal form to an annuity with a death benefit may totally or partially ignore the COLA. As a result, the sales illustrations accompanying pension max may misstate or omit projected COLAs. This means that the plan's death benefit may be significantly undervalued, and the member may be misinformed during the sales process.

Member Relations

Pension max is sometimes presented as a superior financial alternative to the plan's forms of benefit. In some cases, this may be correct, but probably not as often as portrayed during the sales process.

During the sales process, agents may sell against the plan sponsor, describing pension max as a better deal being offered by the insurance company than that offered by the inefficient pension plan. Often the sales literature is quite negative about the pension plan: One sales letter referred to the pension plan's election as a "no-win situation." This type of approach can be particularly effective against public sector plans, given the current bias against all things governmental.

Clearly, the plan sponsor has an interest in ensuring that the value of the plan is accurately appreciated by all active and retired members.

How should a plan sponsor react when confronted with numerous pension max elections? Here are some ideas:

1. The plan may offer more and better designed optional benefit forms, tailored to match some of the advantages of pension max. Such forms could include:
   - "Pop-up" annuity forms
   - Lump-sum death benefits
   - Preretirement savings for survivor annuities.
2. All benefit option factor tables should be reviewed for currency of interest rates and mortality tables.
3. Communication materials should be drafted to equip retirees with the information necessary to ask the right questions if approached for a pension max sale.
4. Incorrect or misleading sales literature or illustrations should be immediately brought to the attention of the state insurance commissioner.

I am certain that neither Mr. Shigley nor his company would engage in any intentionally deceptive practices. My concerns about the effect of pension max on the plan sponsor should not detract in any way from my regard for the high quality of Mr. Shigley's research and the fine paper that resulted from it.

CONRAD M. SIEGEL:

Mr. Shigley's paper represents a valuable addition to the pension actuarial literature because the subject of pension max has heretofore been discussed primarily in the press, such as Jane Bryant Quinn in *Newsweek* and periodic *Wall Street Journal* articles that have quoted actuaries. These articles have been largely negative to pension max. Mr. Shigley's conclusions in Section 5, on balance, seem positive, although he does attempt to provide suitable caveats.

I practice as a consulting actuary in Harrisburg, Pa., the capital city of Pennsylvania. The two major governmental plans in the state (state employees and public school employees) have a major influence on benefits of residents of our area, because they constitute a very large proportion of the pension dollars being paid to our area's retirees. The plans are generous: a 2% of final 3 years average pay for each year of service (including military service buyback options), not offset by Social Security. Member contributions are 5%–6.25% of pay. There is no lump-sum option, but member contribution accounts may be withdrawn at retirement with a reduction in benefits based on 4% actuarial factors.

The basic benefit is a modified cash refund pension (if member contributions have not been withdrawn, otherwise life only) and there are three principal options:

(1) Full cash refund
(2) 100% contingent annuity
(3) 50% contingent annuity

The attractiveness of this market is such that "free seminars" are available all year long, and especially in the heavy retirement months of June and December, at which insurance agents, banks, financial planners, and others give advice on investing the lump-sum refunds and on pension max.

From public sources I have attempted to gauge the effect of changes in election patterns over a six-year period in the public school system. The data, based on statewide dollars of annuity in force at each valuation date, are as follows:

	Males 1988	Males 1994	Females 1988	Females 1994
No option	49%	57%	81%	79%
Full CR	11	9	10	10
100% CA	11	12	3	4
50% CA	29	22	6	7

A reason suggesting *increased* use of the CA options was the decision by the governing board, after the Norris case, to "top-up" the factors to the best of any combination of sexes of the member and the contingent annuitant. During these six years there were two ad-hoc COLAs and some early retirement incentives, leading to an 88% increase in dollars of annuity in force with only a 23% increase in number of annuitants.

These data seem to indicate that CA options are more popular for male members than for females. The proportion of in-force male CA annuities dropped from 40% to 34%. The drop in male CA elections in 1988–94 *retirements* would be much greater. Pension max may have been responsible for some of this drop. Other reasons for the CA drop could be increased work force activity of spouses earning their own pensions.

I was particularly intrigued by Mr. Shigley's concern about antiselection against the insurance company in his description of a contingent first-to-die life insurance policy, leading him to suggest a change in nonforfeiture laws (Section 3). Of course the pension max proposal has, at its core, antiselection against the pension plan in which the plan's unisex actuarial factors vary from the "correct factors" (his conclusion 4 in Section 5).

This prompted me to revisit a paper written by the late John Hanson in 1961 entitled "What Is the Added Cost to Permit Unrestricted Election of Optional Forms of Retirement Income" [*TSA* XIII, Part I (1961): 169]. At that time the critical issue was whether pension plans would become "actuarially unsound" if the five-year election period requirement for CA options in group annuity plans was relaxed or eliminated! The actuaries employed by insurance companies were very concerned, and the consultants had solutions involving small-employer cost increases or factor changes. In the 1960s I wrote an article for Ralph Edward's newsletter (a homegrown predecessor to *The Actuary*), suggesting actuarial factors based on a linear formula involving the ages of the two persons. My suggestion was criticized by a giant of the profession as "unsound." My how things have changed!

The core idea of Mr. Shigley's paper is an economic justification of pension max to a prospective retiree. Our firm counsels many retirees of the major plans in retirement and divorce situations. Our experience is that the concepts of "economic value" and "expected value" as represented in his formulas are far too difficult for the typical retiree to understand. Further, the use of a single number to justify the purchase or to recommend against it is not sufficient, in my view.

The employee and spouse are interested in benefit levels. Mr. Shigley's Figure 2, while described as involving relative benefit levels, really involves relative *present value* of survivor's benefits. The graph would show a level line for the CA option and an increasing curve for the pension max option if dollars of annual income were graphed. While an insurance professional may look at CA as decreasing-face-amount whole life insurance, the retiree looks at it as income replacement after death.

Why do people select CA options? Very obviously to provide income to the surviving spouse. Since historically females have interrupted periods of employment with broken pension service and lower wages than males, the female dependent has a need for income after the death of the male employee. How much? Something less than the full income paid to both after retiring, since one can live less expensively than two, but not at 50% of the cost of two. Social security can be viewed as a 66.7% J&S annuity, if both persons retired after the early reduction ages.

Health is another reason for the CA election or lack thereof, or for the FCR election.

Since the intent is to enable the retiree to make a decision, I use a practical example of a reasonable comparison based on the state employees' plan. I find the paper's use of broad-brush assumptions for insurance policy costs not sufficiently rigorous.

I have set up a strawman comparison of equal after-tax income while both are alive and the use of insurance proceeds to buy an annuity to achieve some rigor in achieving a fair comparison. This precludes proposals of starting the policy before retirement or pouring in the proceeds of sale of another asset including the cash value of another insurance policy. While the use of insurance proceeds to invest in a business or to buy municipal bonds may be of interest, they do not facilitate an apples-to-apples comparison. They do point to added flexibility in dealing with insurance proceeds.

A male employee age 60 with a wife age 57 is entitled to a benefit of $2,000 per month for life, or $1,748 per month, for the 100% CA option. If he elects the no-refund annuity, he has $252 per month before tax, or $214 per month after 15% federal tax, to buy a life insurance policy to keep the gross pension income the same, $1,748 per month. I called the local agency of a major mutual company for values, both guaranteed and illustrated. The $214 premium would purchase a whole life policy in the face amount of $51,000+ for a male nonsmoker at age 60.

Because the policy is a whole life policy, it is participating in some form. There is no point to receiving dividends in cash each year, since the strawman comparison of equal income while both are alive must be maintained. The interest earned on dividend accumulations would also upset the tax comparison. The remaining possibility is paid-up additions or some form of supplemental term insurance. The result is that the insurance proceeds at death increase with duration since retirement. The resulting annuity from the proceeds will, if annuity rates do not change, increase with duration since annuity rates decrease with age. Since annuity rates change frequently, the actual annuity is not predictable except using settlement option rates in the policy, which are usually very unattractive.

Is an annuity that increases in initial amount with the age at death a desirable result? I do not think so. In the first five or ten years after retirement, the expenditures for travel and vacations are typically higher. When benefits commence at a very old age, the needs are less, yet that is the time when the largest initial annuity is payable to the surviving beneficiary.

The specific policy annuity proceeds are compared with the CA on an after-tax basis. The annuity payments are partially taxed, because some of the payments consist of a return of the basis. Nevertheless, Figure 1 shows the CA payment to be much superior to pension max, on both the guaranteed values and the illustrative dividends. At the time this illustration was done (December 1995), the low interest rates currently available provided unattractive illustrations.

I cannot get very concerned about the case in which the spouse dies first. The pop-up option makes no sense to me. Why would the employee want a larger pension after the death of the spouse (when he only has one person, himself, to support) than while two are alive? The cash value of the insurance policy could produce additional annuity income for the employee, again resulting in the same outcome: more income while one is alive than was received by two.

FIGURE 1

CA versus Pension Max

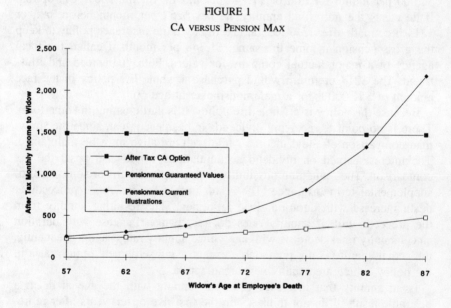

Two additional caveats should accompany the pension max proposal.

(1) The results illustrated are for a participating policy and are not guaranteed. In recent years insurance companies have failed to meet their illustrations at times, as interest rates have fallen. The benefits resulting from minimum guaranteed results are also shown.

(2) Major insurance companies have gotten into financial difficulties in recent years, and the state-operated system of guarantee programs has a very spotty record in terms of speed of reaction and extent of coverage.

An additional caveat applies in the two Pennsylvania plans.

The benefit is increased by an ad hoc COLA every five years, computed as some combination of flat dollars and percentages applied to some or all of current pension, years of service, years since retirement, and so on. There is a state constitutional prohibition against increasing the pension of a beneficiary after the death of an employee. The CA payment can be increased by a COLA after retirement but before the death of the employee. Thus the CA annuity will increase up to the date of death of the employee. Conversely the single-life annuity will be larger during the member's life under the pension max proposal, since some portion of the COLA is based on the current pension.

Mr. Shigley's paper stimulated my thinking, but has not changed my mind. If a friend asks for a one-word answer on pension max, the answer is "careful!" If a client wants a more extensive answer, we will do it based upon a comprehensive analysis specifically tailored to the client's income, assets, dependency, and tax position.

(AUTHOR'S REVIEW OF DISCUSSIONS)

KLAUS O. SHIGLEY:

I very much appreciate the six fine discussions of my paper. I reply to each discussant in turn.

Charles L. Trowbridge

Mr. Trowbridge's discussion adds some insights that I had not previously fully appreciated. Before commenting on these substantive insights, however, I believe it would be constructive to comment on some of the other issues he raises.

To begin, Mr. Trowbridge concludes that the main advantage for pension max, promoted within the paper, derives from an "inherent defect" in the CA approach. While the paper does not make this sufficiently clear, *the main advantage of pension max derives from the potential arbitrage between the qualified plan reduction factors and the true actuarial equivalents.* And it is not clear to me from reading Mr. Trowbridge's discussion that he appreciates this point. Because of the Supreme Court's *Norris* decision, a qualified plan must calculate identical reduction factors for a male employee age 65 with spouse age 60 and a female employee age 65 with spouse age 60. But obviously the same reduction cannot be correct for both scenarios. In the special case in which the plan uses the UP-84 7% Table to calculate these reductions and actual mortality is assumed to be GAM-83 (0, −6) 7%, the male employee is undercharged and the female is overcharged (see Table 3). The overcharge for the female is on the order of 89% of the correct charge.

Second, Mr. Trowbridge points out that insurers do not price life insurance on annuity tables. Page 498 deals with that issue:

> Life insurance mortality assumptions are often based on multiples of the 1975–80 Basic Table. The GAM-83 (0, −6) Table, which is used for most of this discussion, produces mortality rates roughly equivalent to the ultimate rates from the 1975–80 Basic Table at ages 60 and beyond. Policies sold with preferred mortality [*in practice*] are commonly priced at less than 100% of the ultimate rates in the 1975–80 Basic Table. This logic would establish the GAM-83 (0, −6) Table as a conservative standard for judging the relative economics of "pension max" for individuals who qualify for preferred mortality rates.

Mr. Trowbridge also points out, in his discussion of the tax effects, that the "time value of money is not to be ignored." Section 4-C states: "Since

$$R\ddot{a}_x = (N - R)\ddot{a}_{x|y} = FA_x$$

it follows that

$$(1 - T) R\ddot{a}_x = (1 - T)(N - R)\ddot{a}_{x|y} = (1 - T)FA_x.\text{"}$$

I believe this adequately covers the time value of money issue except for the caveat specifically noted thereafter.

Among the disadvantages, Mr. Trowbridge cites lack of generality. Although pension max is a natural fit for CA options, it is not obvious how to replicate J&S options of less than 100%. This is true. However, between the CA and the J&S option, the CA option is by far the more *prevalent option* within qualified plans. Among qualified annuities being paid at John Hancock, 97% of reversionary annuities are of the CA type and 3% are of the J&S type. Be that as it may, for individuals who prefer the J&S option (with continuance percentages less than 100%), a modification of Table 6 could be designed that would at least test the proposition that the reduction factor offered by the plan provides fair value at the "regulated unisex" assumptions. And if it does not, we could attempt to replicate the desired annuity flows by purchasing a sufficient amount of life insurance on the employee to provide the required reversionary annuity to the spouse. All things equal, the outlay for such insurance would need to be higher than the J&S reduction.

No doubt many other parameters could have been considered besides those above. In my view, however, these will have only second-order relevance when the "regulated unisex" plan reduction factors are clearly excessive compared with "free market" actuarial equivalents.

Moving forward to the heart of Mr. Trowbridge's discussion, I agree with most of what he says.

Fundamentally the paper deals with the following equality:

$$R\ddot{a}_x = (N - R)\ddot{a}_{x|y}$$

The left side represents the available funds; this is what we have to spend. The right side represents the benefit configuration that is offered by the qualified plan.

The basic premise of the paper is that participants are free to choose other benefit structures. The only constraint is that they must all have the same present value, that is, $R\ddot{a}_x$. For the sake of this discussion, let us assume the participant can select from any number of the following benefit structures: for simplicity, it is best to think of each of these structures as being fully paid up with purchase price equal to $R\ddot{a}_x$.

1. $(N-R)\ddot{a}_{x|y}$
2. $(N-R^{(2)})\ddot{a}_{x|y} + R\ddot{a}_{y|x}$
3. $F A_x$
4. $F(A_{xy}^1 + A_{xy}^2)$; since $A_{xy}^1 + A_{xy}^2 = A_x$
5. $F(A_{xy}^1) + R^{(3)} \ddot{a}_{y|x}$
6. $(1+r)F A_{xy}^1$; where r is defined on p. 488.
7. $(N-R) \sum\limits_{t=0}^{\infty} v^t \, {}_t p_{xy} \, q_{x+t} \, \ddot{a}_{y+t}.$

Benefit structure no. 1 is the CA option. Benefit structure no. 3 is the conventional pension max option. Benefit structure no. 7 is an alternative pension max formulation, presented on p. 486, which exactly replicates benefit structure no. 1. Benefit structure no. 6 is the level benefit equivalent of benefit structure no. 7. Mr. Trowbridge points out that for benefit structure no. 7 to replicate the reversionary annuity, the policy cannot be lapsed even if the spouse has died. Stated another way, if benefit structure no. 7 has been fully funded, the cash value remaining at the spouse's death must revert to the insurance company to fund CAs who outlive their spouses. Benefit structure no. 7 does not permit any money to pop up or revert to the participant. In other words, 100% of benefit structure no. 7 is allocated to the spouse. Mr. Trowbridge and I are in complete agreement on this point.

In the pension max alternative, we substitute benefit structure no. 3 for benefit structure no. 1. To the extent that benefit structure no. 3, that is, conventional life insurance in an amount, F, must comply with standard nonforfeiture laws, it must be presumed that the employee will lapse the policy if the spouse dies first. Thus the value of the benefit structure *must be split* between the spouse and the employee. The portion that reverts to the employee is the implicit pop-up. The balance of the benefit structure is all that is available to the spouse. Under pension max, therefore, the expected value of the spouse's portion will be smaller than that under the conventional CA. Thus, even though pension max and the CA option produce identical expected values for the entire family unit, the allocation between employee and spouse will be different. Mr. Trowbridge's discussion thus begs the question of how the present value of the pension max benefit structure is split between the employee and the spouse. This is an area that was not developed in the paper. Mr. Trowbridge's discussion provides the insight to answer this question.

Mr. Trowbridge argues that the relative shares to the spouse and the employee can be calculated with reference to benefit structure no. 2. I agree that if we fund for a reversionary annuity plus an *expectation* of a pop-up of R after the joint life period xy, then only $(N - R^{(2)})$ of reversionary annuity remains available. But this is *not* the benefit structure that is being purchased. Under pension max, we purchase benefit structure no. 3, which buys F amount of conventional insurance. If the spouse dies first, the employee takes the surrender value *and* stops future premiums. In practice, therefore, pension max is really an *implicit purchase of benefit structure no. 5* under which the employee buys contingent first-to-die insurance of F. And since premiums of R are more than sufficient to purchase this benefit, the redundant premium then pops up if y dies first. Thus the spouse's share of the pension max benefit would be calculated as the ratio of $F(A^1_{xy})$ to FA_x. Page 488 calculates this fraction as 85% for a male employee age 65/spouse age 60. Note, however, notwithstanding the fact that the spouse's share of FA_x is expected to be less than 100%, the probability that pension max is a winning bet is still correctly given in Table 2.

Mr. Trowbridge's discussion has thus served to define an algorithm to solve for the pension max outlay that preserves the *expected value* of the payout to the spouse at $(N-R)$ of reversionary annuity.

Mr. Trowbridge ends his discussion with a caution that readers should not conclude that with pension max it is possible to get *both* a pop-up *and* (on an expected value basis), to provide the full $(N-R)$ reversionary annuity to the spouse. I concur. Nevertheless, the entire family unit may be better off selecting the pension max approach because plan reduction factors often act more like "fixed exchange rates" than actuarial equivalents. This can and does happen because of the requirement to use unisex factors.

L. Timothy Giles

It had not occurred to me to develop a reversionary annuity to replicate the qualified annuity. This would certainly be practical in those situations in which the actuarial reductions calculated by the qualified plan are too high.

Note, however, all other things being equal, the calculated premium for a reversionary annuity would be higher than the reduction developed by the qualified plan, because the premiums for a commercial policy are uncollectible in the $y|x$ period. The qualified plan, on the other hand, in its calculation of the reversionary annuity reduction, does collect this premium. This is the point brought forth in Mr. Trowbridge's discussion. Thus it might be difficult to convince a potential customer that the commercial annuity is a better buy because the outlays are likely to be higher. In practice, this might restrict the applicability to those situations in which the plan's reduction factors are disproportionately large.

Elias S.W. Shiu

I am grateful to Dr. Shiu for pointing out his technical correction to Formula (10). The exhibits have been recalculated to reflect his correction. The resulting changes do not materially affect any of the conclusions.

Dr. Shiu raises the following question: "When an annuitant elects the "pension max" option in the real world, is the insurance premium determined by an annuity mortality table?" The paper attempts to capture this point in Table 6, in which an attempt is made to create an algorithm that solves for the "better" value between the plan's reversionary annuity and pension max. In Table 6, assumption set d is used as a proxy for the insurer's mortality and interest assumptions. As indicated in the paper, this is a reasonable proxy for individuals who qualify for preferred underwriting.

Robert B. Likins

Mr. Likins has given a great deal of thought to the practical implementation of pension max. My objectives, which were more limited, were to present a comparison between the reversionary annuity and pension max along two dimensions, the funding dimension and the benefit dimension, and then to develop a conceptually simple algorithm to test the relative economics of the two different benefit structures.

Mr. Likins' discussion adds a valuable practical dimension. Of particular significance, he starts from the premise that the insurance amount must be big enough to *eliminate* the financial exposure of the spouse. In addition, he assumes that life insurance will be used to purchase an annuity and he applies the tax mechanics for annuities. He also develops a decision matrix for screening specific applications. I think it would be worthwhile to try to investigate the characteristics of this decision matrix more fully. One way to do that would be to compare the results it produces against the algorithm presented in the paper.

Robert T. McCrory

I am in complete agreement with Mr. McCrory's comments on the importance of avoiding deceptive sales practices. This was certainly one of the objectives that motivated me to write this paper. Having once observed a sales seminar on this subject, I found that the cadence of the presentation soon outran my ability to keep pace with the supporting arguments. Subsequently, as I tried to confirm the representations made during this presentation, I ultimately concluded that the issue is more complex than it first appears. Furthermore, as Mr. McCrory's discussion points out, it seems that I have underestimated the complexity of extending the analysis to plans with COLAs.

Mr. McCrory's discussion also touches on some of the issues that pension max presents for the plan. My own reaction to these issues was to identify those demographic subgroups that are being severely overcharged for the CA election within my own company's plan.

Conrad M. Siegel

Mr. Siegel's observation that employees are more interested in benefit levels than "expected value" is a good one. And I agree that the use of a single "economic value" number may be insufficient to justify or recommend a purchase. But I also believe that a single measure of "economic value" is a valuable screening mechanism for false positives *as well as false negatives*. Moreover, I start from the premise that retirement annuities, like other financial assets, are fungible and they can be exchanged for similar goods with comparable value. If there is sufficient economic justification for selecting pension max, then it ought to be fairly evaluated. And in this connection, as several other discussants have pointed out, the use of universal life in conjunction with target term capabilities would be more appropriate than whole life.

For the record, I do not advocate a change in nonforfeiture laws. I merely state in Section 3 that it would be difficult in practice to develop a *contingent first-to-die policy* without relief from current nonforfeiture laws. This problem can be solved by using a reversionary annuity, which, as Mr. Giles points out, is exempt from a cash value nonforfeiture rule.

ANALYSIS OF HEALTH CARRIER INSOLVENCIES

JAMES B. ROSS AND CRISS WOODRUFF*

I. INTRODUCTION

This study was made possible by a grant from the Society of Actuaries, under the direction of William J. Bugg, Chairperson of the Project Oversight Group. This research had its genesis in the identification by the Health Financial Issues Task Force of "...the need to quantify the number of financial impairments that have occurred among health carriers and to identify the reasons for such situations."

Research objectives for the study were (1) to identify health carriers that became financially impaired because of the operation of their health business during a relatively long time and (2) to identify the reason(s) that each company became financially impaired. Health carriers specifically included were commercial insurance companies, Blue Cross/Blue Shield plans, and health maintenance organizations (HMOs).

The research was to include developing a meaningful definition of "financial impairment" (which might differ by type of health carrier), reviewing relevant studies, conducting necessary additional research, and presenting results and analysis in a written document.

This report presents the research results. Within each section we consider commercial insurers, Blue Cross/Blue Shield plans, and HMOs separately. The report is organized in the following sections:

- Section II explores relevant definitions of "financial distress" and allied terms. This part of the research looked at other studies, textbooks in insurance and finance, and articles in academic journals. Appendix A provides quotations directly from the source materials.
- Section III details the methodologies and presents the findings. Findings are displayed in Figures 1 through 10. Listings of commercial insurers identified are shown in Appendixes B through G. The listings are shown alphabetically (Appendix B), by assets (Appendix C), by percentage of health business (Appendix D), by year of insolvency (Appendix E), by reason for insolvency (Appendix F), and by state (Appendix G). The single insolvency for Blue Cross/Blue Shield is identified in the text.

---

*Dr. Woodruff, not a member of the Society, is Assistant Professor of Finance at the College of Business Administration, Texas A&M University, Corpus Christi.

Impaired HMOs could not be individually identified, but failed HMOs by year of insolvency had been *counted* in other research. Appendix H gives details on the approach to the counting of failed HMOs.

- Section IV comments on problems of definition, the difficulties in data collection, and the findings. Further, it contains our recommendations to the Oversight Group on how further research in this area might be carried forward.

II. MEANINGFUL DEFINITION OF FINANCIAL IMPAIRMENT

To inventory working definitions of "financial impairment" and allied terms, we reviewed copies of recent finance and insurance textbooks and conducted electronic searches of the academic literature in finance and insurance. ("Financial impairment" finds its chief expression in the A. M. Best studies.) Full quotations of definitions are given in the appendixes cited. We describe these definitions in the summary paragraphs below.

Appendix A, Section I, provides relevant quoted text from recent textbooks on some definitions of allied terms. "Financial distress" is the umbrella term applied to all types of business organizations; it encompasses "bankruptcy," "insolvency," "liquidation," "reorganization," "default," "failure," and other conditions. Marsh [22] and Van Horne and Wachowicz [42] provide typical definitions. Most texts go beyond these definitions to describe the legal procedures followed. Black and Skipper [8] address insurers directly. Their concept of "corrective orders" is linked to the A. M. Best application of the "financial impairment" concept.

Appendix A, Section II, contains relevant quotations from academic studies of "financial distress." Definitions are provided by Wruck [44], "...a situation where cash flow is insufficient to cover current obligations," and by Kose [20], "A firm is in financial distress at a given point in time when the liquid assets of the firm are not sufficient to meet the current requirements of its hard contracts."

Examples of financial distress are furnished by Gilson [16], large common stock price declines; DeAngelo and DeAngelo [13], multiple losses during 1980–1985; and by Gilbert, Menon, and Schwartz [15], negative cumulative earnings over any consecutive three-year period. Lau [21] identifies reducing dividend payments and defaulting on loan payments as intermediate states. BarNiv and Hershbarger [6] define "insolvent insurers" as those declared insolvent by their respective state insurance commissioners and reported by A. M. Best Company. BarNiv and McDonald [7] use financial distress and insolvency interchangeably to describe insurers experiencing liquidation, receivership, conservatorship, restraining orders, rehabilitation, and so on.

Looking at the definitions of "insolvency" and "financial distress" used in other studies shown in the references, we found the following.

A. Commercial Insurers

1. "Insurer Failures: Property/Casualty Insurer Insolvencies and State Guaranty Funds" [37]

This was a study of property/casualty insolvencies, 140 of them from 11/69 through 12/86, related to the state guaranty funds. The study's focus was on clear insolvencies; the data were obtained from the National Committee of Insurance Guaranty Funds (NCIGF); and the test was that the property/casualty guaranty fund was "triggered." The "triggering" event differs among states.

2. American Council of Life Insurance Task Force [5]

This was a study of both types of insurers, 68 of them from 1/85 through 9/89, for determining whether there was a solvency problem in the life insurance industry. Again, the Task Force's focus was on clear insolvencies; the data appear to have been obtained from the National Organization of Life & Health Guaranty Associations (NOLHGA); and the test was that the life/health guaranty fund was "triggered." An interesting footnote is that eight of the insolvencies were property/casualty carriers that wrote sufficient life or health business to trigger life/health guaranty fund assessments.

3. Failed Promises: Insurance Company Insolvencies [41]

This was a report by a House subcommittee that examined four specific instances of property/casualty failures (Mission, Integrity, Transit Casualty, and Anglo-American) plus two near-failures (Omaha Indemnity and Insurance Company of Ireland). The thrust of the inquiry was examination of common causes of property/casualty insurer failure. This particular case study approach is not helpful to us in inventorying failed or financially impaired health insurers, although it does provide excellent examples of the *multiple* reasons for these distressed insurers.

4. Best's Insolvency Study: Life/Health Insurers [2]

This was a report by A. M. Best, covering 290 "insolvencies" of life/health insurers in the period 1976–1991. These definitions are provided on page 87 of Best [2]:

> We dated a financially impaired company as of the first official action taken by the insurance department in its state of domicile. The reason for the state action may have been due to the company's insolvency or financial impairment. State actions included involuntary liquidation, receivership, conservatorship, cease-and-desist order, suspension, license revocation, administrative order, supervision or any other action which restricted a company's freedom to conduct business normally.
>
> We emphasize that a financially impaired company might not have been declared technically insolvent. Its capital and surplus simply could have been deemed inadequate to meet legal requirements, or there was concern regarding its general financial condition. The latter includes solvent companies against which actions were taken to protect them from financially weakened affiliates or a 'run-on-the-bank'.

To clarify the difference between "insolvency" and "financial impairment," in mid-1992 A. M. Best made these rough estimates for the financially impaired life/health carriers covered in its study: "50% have been or are being liquidated, 40% are still under some form of state supervision, 6% have resumed normal operations free from state supervision, and 4% have been merged into other companies."

5. Best's Insolvency Study: Property/Casualty Insurers [1]

Exactly the same definition of "financial impairment" was used by A. M. Best in its June 1991 property/casualty study, covering 372 "insolvencies" in the period 1969–1990. Best's own files on property/casualty insurers were augmented by additional material from the National Association of Insurance Commissioners (NAIC), the Insurance Information Institute (III), the NCIGF, and individual state departments.

B. Blue Cross and Blue Shield Plans

Blue Cross and Blue Shield plans present yet another problem for those who wish to construct a common definition of "financially impaired" entities. Extensive reading in the investigations of several large plans (including that of West Virginia, which was the only one that actually did become insolvent) suggests strongly that the kind of regulatory takeovers that comprise the bulk of "financially impaired" commercial insurers have no counterparts in practice in the regulation of Blue Cross and Blue Shield plans. Our Blue Cross and Blue Shield research sheds no useful light on the concept of "financial impairment" beyond the reasons for the insolvency of the West Virginia plan itself.

C. Health Maintenance Associations (HMOs)

HMOs are subject to the various degrees of financial distress outlined above; insolvencies in the classic sense do occur; and in addition, there are simple business closures due to the owners' strategic reasons that have nothing to do with financial distress—this last category appears relatively unique to HMOs in this study. Studies of financial distress among HMOs are rare. There are no focal points for the collection of data on distressed or failed HMOs, and there is no agreed-upon definition of "financial impairment" for HMOs (see Section III.C).

D. Conclusion

In this report on health insurance companies, we have chosen to utilize the approach defined by A. M. Best in its studies: we consider a commercial insurer "financially impaired" when the insurance department in its state of domicile takes official action with respect to it. Casey and Bartczak [11] provide two powerful reasons: comparability with prior research and the relative costs of alternative approaches. This approach permits building on the A. M. Best work. In the lone case in the Blue Cross/Blue Shield area, we have used genuine insolvency as the criterion, while for HMOs we have been forced by data limitations to back into a working definition that is insolvency-based.

III. IDENTIFYING THE POPULATION OF IMPAIRED HEALTH INSURERS

A. Commercial Carriers

Starting from lists of insolvent life/health or property/casualty carriers developed by A.M. Best, the NAIC, and NOLHGA, we first attempted to identify those companies that were primarily health carriers. As an operating definition endorsed by the Oversight Group, we categorized any company that derived more than 50% of its premium income from health business as a health carrier.

Because of the very low yield of financially impaired *health* carriers and because of the inability of the NAIC and the states to supply older data to us, it was decided *not* to pursue the identification of additional possible failed health insurers from the property/casualty data set. We estimate that thereby we may be missing another four health carriers.

Working back through the annual *Best's Reports, Life-Health Editions*, we calculated the percentage of health premiums for each company identified in the *Best's Insolvency Study* [2]. Where that calculation could be made and the percentage exceeded 50%, we classified the company as a health insurer. Completing that process left us with a number of companies known to be financially impaired (usually the reason therefor was also known), but the financial figures were not available to determine whether the company was a health insurer or not.

We sent to the NAIC's offices in Kansas City an extended list of impaired companies in the more recent years, for which figures were not available in the *Best's Reports*, asking that the annual statements from the companies be pulled and held for our visit. Results from the working visit were encouraging: most annual statements for that list were available, and the determination of "health insurer or not" from the annual statement figures was straightforward. Working simply with the annual statement figures on a sample of companies for which the primary reason for failure had been given by Best [2], we were able to replicate those reasons in nearly all cases, and we were able to use the same procedures to provide the "primary reason for failure" for most companies for which reasons were not available.

A longer list of impaired companies in earlier years, again those for which figures were not available in the Best's Reports, was prepared and sent to the NAIC offices to the people with whom we had worked on the visit. Two things quickly became clear:

1. The NAIC does not maintain its annual statement records for longer than 11 years. Earlier files are thrown away; no records of any sort for individual companies are kept.
2. Companies do not have to file annual statements with the NAIC, and many do not. The small, financially impaired carriers that are the principal objects of our study are especially apt not to file.

Still seeking financial information to determine the "health insurer" status of the 102 life/health companies known to have become financially impaired, we asked the Society of Actuaries to write to each state. The SOA's letter listed the companies domiciled in that state that had been identified as "financially impaired" and asked for specific data for each such company.

From the responses received, we determined that five of the 102 companies were primarily health companies, while 32 were primarily life carriers. Records were not available for 62 of the 102 companies. Two states, Idaho and Utah, and the Commonwealth of Puerto Rico failed to respond: each had one company on the list.

Because of the relatively high numbers of companies that were known to have been financially impaired but could not be identified as primarily health or primarily life, the totals for the health companies are probably substantially understated. In view of this, readers should use the listings and figures with caution, especially in the earlier years for which the relevant records have been discarded or destroyed.

Absent the information on the residuum of 65 companies, we have a list of 117 "financially impaired" commercial insurers over the period 1971 through 1993. For each firm we have listed the following five variables:
1. The size of the company in total assets just prior to financial impairment
2. The proportion of premium income derived from the health business
3. The year of financial impairment
4. The primary cause of financial impairment
5. The state of domicile.

Appendix B lists in alphabetical order the 117 commercial health insurers. Appendixes B–G list those same firms sorted according to the five variables shown above, in that same order. We have summarized the information in these listings of financially impaired health insurance companies in a series of figures, and they are discussed below.

Figures that show values other than years on the x-axis are self-explanatory. Except for the end bars, the figures that show numbers of insolvent companies (or FICs) show totals for three-year groupings. The high stress years of 1989, 1990, and 1991 are grouped together, and the other groupings follow. The end bars show data that may not comprise three-year groupings. The figures that show companies "in force" give the number of companies for the middle year of those three-year groupings. Again, the end bars are given to show all the data but may not be the centers of three-year groupings. The range of all data sets is the greatest available at this writing.

Figures 1–5 all refer to insolvencies of health insurance carriers. No count (on the 50%-of-premiums definition) is available for the number of health insurers, nor is there such a figure. Figures 6 and 7 show the life/health FICs and the life/health companies in force for comparison. These companies constituted the population underlying the A. M. Best study. Figure 8 gives the population of Blue Cross/Blue Shield companies; no figure is needed to display the single Blue Cross/Blue Shield insolvency in 1990. Figures 9 and 10 show the HMO FICs and the HMOs in force, again for comparison.

Figure 1 provides statistics on the size of the insolvent health companies by assets. The size of the companies in our sample (as measured by admitted assets in the year prior to impairment) ranges from $246,000 to $5,127,008,000; the average is $68,507,000. However, the median of $5,558,000 indicates that the distribution is skewed, with most cases to the left of the mean.

FIGURE 1

NUMBER OF INSOLVENCIES BY TOTAL ASSETS

in millions

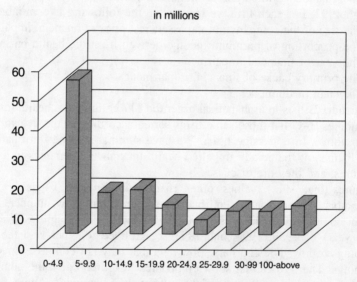

Figure 2 shows the financially impaired health companies by percentage of health business written. The proportion of premium income derived from health business varies from 50% to a full 100%; the average is 86%. However, the median of 87% indicates that, for most of the firms in the sample, health premiums provided the lion's share of premium income.

Figure 3 displays the data by year of financial distress for these failed health carriers. Distribution of the impairments across time shows that most

FIGURE 2

PERCENTAGE OF HEALTH BUSINESS OF INSOLVENT CARRIERS

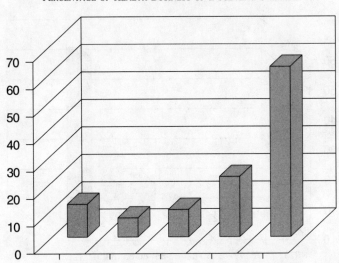

impairments were late in the sample period, with 23 impairments in 1989 and 16 each in 1990 and 1991. These figures highlight the surge in health insolvencies in the period 1989–1991, a period characterized by powerful competition in the health industry within an environment of sharply escalating costs for hospital and medical care.

Some 48 companies in our sample became financially impaired due to inadequate pricing and/or inadequate surplus, as Figure 4 indicates. The next most frequent reason for impairment was rapid growth ($n=29$), followed by affiliate problems ($n=9$), significant shift in business ($n=9$), overstated assets ($n=5$), fraud ($n=4$), and reinsurance failure ($n=3$). We are unable to determine the primary cause for impairment for the remaining 10 companies.

Consistent with Best [2], we define the primary causes (reasons) for financial impairment as the following:

1. *Inadequate pricing or inadequate surplus.* This typically involves product underpricing, leading to operating losses and declining surplus.
2. *Rapid growth.* This involves rapid expansion of the asset base beyond levels that can be supported by the existing capital/surplus base.

FIGURE 3

Number of Insolvent Carriers by Year in 1973–1992

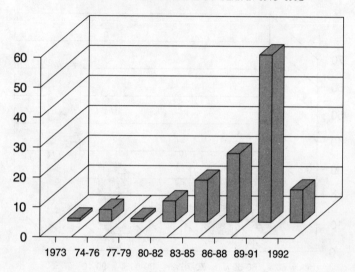

FIGURE 4

Causes of Insolvencies

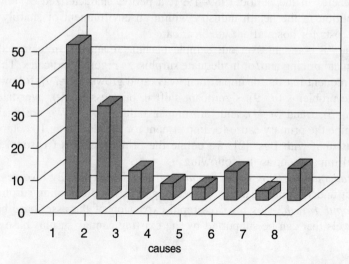

3. *Affiliate problems.* This involves investments in or affiliation with financially impaired companies such as S&Ls, real estate companies, or other insurers.
4. *Overstated assets.* This results from significant declines in the market value of assets held—declines that are not reflected in the book value of these assets. Thus, companies that appear solvent on the books may be insolvent in terms of market value. Insurer problems with investments in high yield bonds are a good case in point.
5. *Fraud.*
6. *Significant change in business, such as rapid expansion into new product lines or markets.*
7. *Reinsurance failure.*
8. *Cause undetermined.*

While mismanagement is not specifically cited as a reason for impairment, Best [2] reports that mismanagement was involved in nearly all cases of life/health insurer impairment. In addition, press coverage of commercial insurer failures, property/casualty and life/health, almost always identifies multiple reasons for failure. The same is true of the lone Blue Cross/Blue Shield failure and appears to be true in those HMO failures in which first-hand knowledge of the failure is available to the Oversight Group.

Figure 5 shows that, over the sample period, financial impairments of health insurers were domiciled in relatively few states. Texas, with 30 financially impaired companies, leads the list; followed by Arizona with 10; Florida, 8; California, 7; Louisiana and Oklahoma, 6 each; Illinois, 5; Pennsylvania, 4; and Alabama, Indiana, and Utah, 3 each. No other state of domicile accounted for more than two impaired companies.

To summarize, the financial impairments in our sample tended to be companies that had $5.6 million (median) in assets, derived 87% of premium income (median) from health business, and were domiciled in the Southwest, with the highest frequency of impairments over the period 1989 through 1991. These companies became financially impaired primarily because of some combination of inadequate pricing and rapid growth, with the caveat that other reasons are nearly always present.

Figures 6 and 7 refer to the life/health carriers analyzed in the A. M. Best study. Figure 6, which is similar to Figure 2, displays the number of those companies financially impaired in the periods shown, while Figure 7 gives the number of companies in business in the central years. (No such count is available for health carrers.) Figures 2 and 6 both demonstrate the stresses of the 1989–1991 period on health insurers.

FIGURE 5

NUMBER OF INSOLVENCIES BY STATE IN YEARS 1973–1992

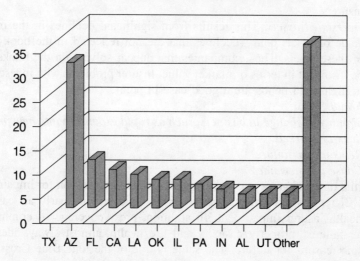

FIGURE 6

NUMBER OF LIFE/HEALTH FICs BY YEAR IN YEARS 1977–1991

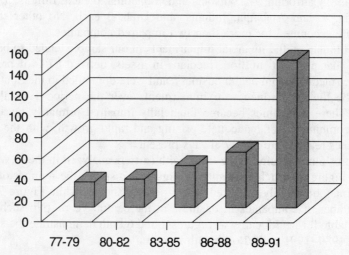

FIGURE 7

NUMBER OF LIFE/HEALTH COMPANIES IN BUSINESS IN YEARS 1978–1991

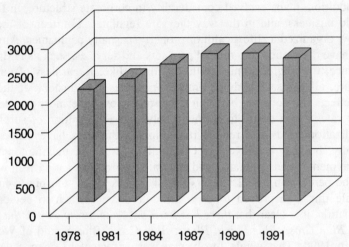

B. Blue Cross & Blue Shield Plans

Most Blue Cross and/or Blue Shield Plans were originally established under separate enabling legislation in a given state or area within a state, typically as hospital and medical service corporations. All were not-for-profit. Most were built around the notion of "prepayment" rather than insurance doctrines.

Blue Cross Plans can be traced back to the 1929 Baylor University Hospital Plan, which provided hospital "service" benefits. Blue Shield Plans developed in the 1938–1942 period, providing coverage of physician services. The Blue Shield medical-surgical service corporations were also a response to commercial insurer health care market penetration. Blue Cross organizations were legally separate from their Blue Shield counterparts even though they might have utilized a common staff and operations. There were several instances of multiple Blue Cross and/or Blue Shield Plans in a given state.

Over the past 25 years, the number of plans has been significantly reduced through mergers and consolidations into a single Blue Cross or Blue Shield Plan and/or into a combined Blue Cross and Blue Shield Plan. These affiliations were driven by management to realize economies, to make effective use of capital, and to take advantage of market synergies. In 1971 there were 138 plans. As of the end of 1994 there were 69.

In addition, plans evolved considerably in corporate structure, in the way they do business, and in the way they are regulated. Fourteen of the plans are now organized as life/health or property/casualty companies. Almost all plans have diversified into related products and services, such as HMOs, life insurance, third-party administration, and the like. Regardless of corporate structure, all plans embody insurance principles. The history of the plans also reflects the conflicts between a desire to cover the most people at the lowest rates and a desire to maintain solvency. Recognition of surplus and capitalization needs and related regulation in this area have evolved substantially, but not in all states. Originally it was not uncommon to find "prepayment" plans operated and regulated on more of a cash-flow basis, with the perception by all viewers that the plans were "too-big-to-fail."

While this area proved to be a difficult one in which to get database information, it is clear that *there has been only one insolvency in the history of the Blue Cross/Blue Shield Plans*: Blue Cross/Blue Shield of West Virginia in 1990. That single insolvency was sufficient to open a series of Congressional investigations by the Permanent Subcommittee on Investigations of the Senate's Committee on Governmental Affairs. Extensive testimony was taken (and published) in connection with subcommittee explorations of the difficulties of the Blue Cross/Blue Shield plans in West Virginia and several other jurisdictions.

Part of our charge in looking at financially distressed health insurers has been to find the reasons for failure. Unless unusual attention is paid to an insolvency, the reasons are seldom shown clearly for any kind of health insurer. The staff of the Investigating Committee (*Efforts to Combat Fraud and Abuse in the Insurance Industry*) lists [40, p. 210] the following reasons for the lone failure in West Virginia:

- Mismanagement by the senior officers of the plan
- Lax and inadequate oversight of management policies and activities by the Board of Directors
- Diversion of management and plan resources and attention to non-plan-related activities
- Conflicts of interest by senior management and the Chairman of the Board
- Creation of subsidiaries and affiliates for the personal gain of certain officers and members of the Board of Directors

- Inadequate state regulation of the plan by the Department of Insurance
- Increased health-care costs and cost-shifting to the plan.

Because of the single Blue Cross/Blue Shield insolvency in West Virginia in 1990, no figure has been prepared. Figure 8 shows the number of Blue Cross/Blue Shield plans in business at selected year-ends over the 1973–1994 period. The pattern for Blue Cross/Blue Shield plans has been one of consolidation, while both commercial life/health insurers and HMOs have grown in number over time and then topped out. Compare Figure 7 with Figure 10.

FIGURE 8

NUMBER OF BLUE CROSS/BLUE SHIELD COMPANIES IN YEARS 1973–1994

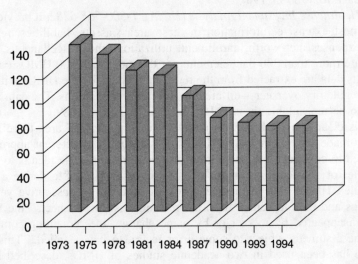

C. Health Maintenance Organizations

There is no central data-collecting body for gathering statistics on financially distressed or insolvent HMOs. They are neither uniformly regulated by the individual states nor covered by the state guaranty associations. We have found three organizations that regularly collect what might be called "in force" statistics on individual HMOs. In all three cases these sources provide a snapshot of data at December 31 of the calendar year.

1. *Best's Managed Care Reports, HMO* [3], [4]. It provides figures in these areas starting with 1990: assets, net worth, net premiums, total revenues, and net income. In addition, it shows enrollment data and ratios for liquidity, profitability, and leverage. It is prepared by A. M. Best from the HMO regulatory statement filings with the state insurance departments.

2. *National Directory of HMOs* [17]. It provides information on many facets of the HMO. The only figures provided are enrollment, operational date, number of physicians/hospitals/medical centers. It is prepared from data forms sent to HMOs directly by the Group Health Association of America (GHAA). Strong efforts are made to contact all HMOs, not just GHAA members. Compliance is voluntary. Data collection may go back to 1986 or 1987.

3. *Healthcare Investment Analysts (HCIA), 1-800-568-3282.* It provides the most extensive information in these areas: assets, liabilities, revenue, expenses, net worth, enrollment, utilization, and miscellaneous. There are more than 300 data elements for the more than 500 HMOs covered. Its data are extracted from the regulatory filings by the HMOs with their regulatory overseer—different in different jurisdictions. The data appear to be unavailable through HCIA for years before 1989.

It is clear that in the health maintenance organization area there are no ready-made lists of insolvent HMOs. A substantially different approach is needed to construct a population of insolvent insurers. The idea is to utilize a series of year-end inventories of "all" existing HMOs to derive a series of failed HMOs. The technique is to difference two consecutive year-end listings and then to screen from the resulting list of "suspects" the HMOs that disappeared by merger or by name change; the remaining companies can be assumed, subject to some error factor, to have "failed." This technique has been used in two academic studies of HMOs, described below. (Because obtaining the data is the real issue in the HMO area, we have included in Appendix H extended quotations from the data and methodology sections of the three academic studies involved.)

Christianson, Wholey, and Sanchez [12] use the differencing approach to construct charts that show the number of HMOs in operation (1978–1990); HMO failures, mergers, and acquisitions (1980–1990); HMO failures and mergers "by states" (1976–1990); HMO failures and mergers by HMO model type (1980–1990); and HMO failures and mergers (1980–1990), split by affiliation—local, national, Blue Cross/Blue Shield.

Wholey, Christianson, and Sanchez [43] process the data to show, for the lengthier period 1976–1991, charts of the numbers of both HMOs in force and HMO failures, split between groups and IPAs. Individual listings of failed HMOs are not given.

The following articles cited in the references provide commentary on reasons for HMO failure.

- Stone and Heffernan [39], drawing on their 1988 survey of HMO regulators for the GHAA, cite these reasons (in descending order of importance): too little initial capital and surplus, missing utilization controls, inadequate rates, inadequate permanent capital and surplus, and inadequate IBNR claim reserves.
- Boles [9] identifies the risks to which HMOs are exposed as these: revenue risk (variability and predictability of revenues), operating risk (nature and characteristics of the cost of operations), business risk (combination of revenue and operating risk), financing risk (use of debt and borrowed moneys), and total risk (variability in net income). He focuses on predictors of insolvency.
- Scheur [33] lists these causes of impaired plans: lack of operating capital, inability to deal effectively with competition, dissolution of the provider system, poor management, and shortcomings at the level of the Board of Directors.
- Christianson, Wholey, and Sanchez [12] tested affiliation status and found that local plans experienced higher rates of failure than national plans or those affiliated with Blue Cross/Blue Shield.
- Wholey, Christianson, and Sanchez [12], investigating the relationship between HMO size and HMO failure rates, found that the risk of failure is greatest for mid-sized groups. They found the following factors reduce failure rates:
  1. For individual practice associations: Blue Cross/Blue Shield affiliation, federal qualification, and national affiliation.
  2. For groups, national affiliation.
  3. More markets served.
  4. More physicians per capita.
  5. Low hospital utilization.

We have tested for ourselves the "differencing approach," working with members of the Oversight Group. Two computer runs were purchased from the HCIA data supplier in Baltimore: they compared the HMOs in force in 1991 with those in force in 1990, and similarly those in force in 1992 with those in 1991. The runs produced listings of HMOs that "fell out of force."

These listings have been reviewed by actuaries familiar with the HMO field. Here the idea has been that the Society of Actuaries has experts familiar with individual HMOs who can identify "failures" directly and can reduce the list by mergers, name changes, and so on to make a residual set of "likely failures." This process would replicate that described in Appendix H by Christianson, Wholey, and Sanchez [12].

The yield from repeated application of this process to past years would be a list of identified failed HMOs showing year of failure, size of assets, state of domicile, and percentage of A&H (usually 100%). The information on failed HMOs in such a list would track the information we have from other sources on the commercial health insurers. It would permit researchers to calculate numbers and rates of failure comparable to those of commercial health insurers, except that commercials are tracked on a regulatory intervention basis and HMOs would be tracked on an insolvency basis.

Society of Actuaries experts have examined several lists that represent products of the differencing approach. The opinion appears to be that the use of such lists for reconstructing the "failures" would not be very efficient this far after the fact. It is known, for example, that many of the plans identified in the differencing approach from 1989 are still operating.

The Seubold memorandum [35], provided by Harry Sutton, gives an analysis of 25 failed HMOs from a then population of 161 qualified by the Office of Health Maintenance Organizations (OHMO). Seven were taken over or merged;18 were not rescued. The conclusion by the OHMO director was: "The loss of these HMOs was brought about by the failure of management—administrative and medical—to control the utilization and costs of services; to react promptly and effectively when those problems were clearly identified. External factors did provide the last push in some instances, but only after the internal deficiencies had provided most of the momentum." To these causes of failure, Mr. Sutton adds inadequate initial financing, uncooperative medical providers, and poor utilization controls and fixed overhead costs for clinic plans. He suggests that the situation is different today, with much larger HMOs, more experienced managers, and more sophisticated management information systems.

Figure 9 shows the number of HMO FICs by the standard three-year periods; it exhibits the financial stress characteristic in an earlier period than do the health insurers and the Blue Cross/BlueShield plans. Figure 10 exhibits the number of HMOs in business in the selected years.

FIGURE 9
NUMBER OF HMO FICs BY YEAR IN YEARS 1977–1990

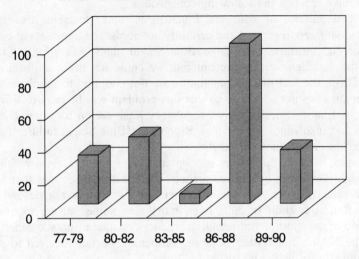

FIGURE 10
NUMBER OF HMOs IN YEARS 1979–1990

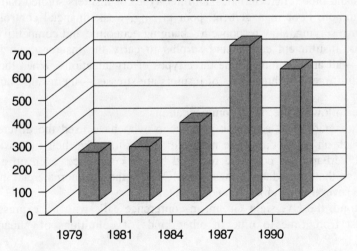

IV. CONCLUSIONS AND RECOMMENDATIONS

We have reached the following conclusions.

First, definitions of "financial impairment" and "financial distress" are not standardized in general and certainly not across the three sets of carriers: commercial insurers, Blue Cross/Blue Shield plans, and HMOs. Coupled with the data deficiencies encountered, we could not use a uniform definition. Given the fact that the regulators are not common to the three sets of carriers, it does not appear to us that this problem will be easy to solve. We have used, as mentioned above, regulatory intervention for commercial insurers and insolvency for the lone Blue Cross/Blue Shield failure and have backed into insolvency for HMOs.

Second, the data difficulties encountered were not foreseen by either the Oversight Group or by the researchers. The best data set was that for the commercial insurers, for whom earlier studies were available and upon which this study could be built. Even in that area, some data are not available because of the short record-retention practices of state insurance departments and the NAIC, and further because companies are not required to submit data directly to the NAIC (or A. M. Best).

The analysis of Blue Cross/Blue Shield plans was greatly simplified by using insolvency as the defining event of failure. Any other definition would create real data difficulties. HMO data can be put into usable form only in the most roundabout of ways.

Third, while there are great differences in the legal and organizational forms and other characteristics, all three types of insurers studied had much in common. Poor management, poor pricing, weak financial controls, improper reserving, slow response to changing economic and competitive conditions, insufficient capital and surplus to carry the insurer through lean times—all are common to the three types of organizations. When there are stressful times, all three types of insurers are stressed—the results show this clearly.

The following are our recommendations.

First, unaffiliated academic researchers who have used the differencing approach on HMO data have not been willing to make their files available to us. Perhaps this could be revisited by the committee, even on a grant basis, so that individual listings of HMOs, like those of commercial insurers in the several appendixes, could be obtained.

Second, the Oversight Group, in conference calls with us, expressed an interest from time to time in other kinds of definitions of "financially impaired," even for commercial insurers. We explored these briefly before settling on the ones we chose for practical reasons. It would be possible, but would take much larger budget allocations from the SOA, to explore the following alternative definitions of "distressed" or "impaired":

- Carriers with certain combinations of poor IRIS ratios
- Carriers that were merged or acquired by stronger market factors
- Carriers with below stipulated ratings from selected commercial ratings services.

We agree that such definitions would give rise to research whose findings would probably be more helpful in the prediction and avoidance of financial difficulty down the road. We think there are formidable problems with obtaining the data in many instances under these definitions, and the problem of comparability across the three kinds of carriers would still exist. On the other hand, some of the commercial ratings services do cover a number of Blue Cross/Blue Shield plans now and have begun to extend their ratings to selected HMOs.

ACKNOWLEDGMENTS

The authors acknowledge with appreciation the financial support of the Health Section of the Society of Actuaries and thank the following people for lending their guidance and support in the preparation of this report:

Society of Actuaries Project Oversight Group

William J. Bugg, Chairperson	Charles S. Fuhrer
Michael S. Abroe	Karl Madrecki
Darlene H. Davis	Harry L. Sutton, Jr.

Society of Actuaries Health Financial Issues Task Force

Burton D. Jay, Chairperson	Peter M. Muirhead
Michael S. Abroe	David V. Smith
William J. Bugg	Thomas J. Stoiber
Robert B. Cumming	Lynette L. Trygstad
Roy Goldman	Andrew B. Wang
Leonard Koloms	William C. Weller
Karl Madrecki	Ronald M. Wolf

Howard J. Bolnick, Vice-President, Health Benefit Systems Practice

Society of Actuaries Staff
Jeff Allen, Education Actuary
Ann Berg, Research Assistant
Tom Edwalds, Research Actuary
Joanne Temperly, Education Assistant

The authors further wish to thank Judy J. Suddarth and Daniel R. Bennett for their help on the typography and graphics of this study.

REFERENCES

1. A.M. BEST COMPANY. *Best's Insolvency Study: Property/Casualty Insurers 1969–90*. Oldwick, N.J.: June 1991.

2. A.M. BEST COMPANY. *Best's Insolvency Study: Life/Health Insurers 1976–91*. Oldwick, N.J.: June 1992.

3. A.M. BEST COMPANY. *Best's Managed Care Reports HMO*. Oldwick, N.J.: 1993.

4. A.M. BEST COMPANY. *Best's Managed Care Reports HMO*. Oldwick, N.J.: 1994.

5. AMERICAN COUNCIL OF LIFE INSURANCE. *Report of the ACLI Task Force on Solvency Concerns*. Washington, D.C.: ACLI, September 1990.

6. BARNIV, RAN, AND HERSHBARGER, ROBERT A. "Classifying Financial Distress in the Life Insurance Industry," *Journal of Risk and Insurance* 57, no. 1 (1990): 110–36.

7. BARNIV, RAN, AND MCDONALD, JAMES B. "Identifying Financial Distress in the Insurance Industry: A Synthesis of Methodological and Empirical Issues," *Journal of Risk and Insurance* 59, no. 4 (1992): 543–74.

8. BLACK, KENNETH, JR., AND SKIPPER, HAROLD D., JR. *Life Insurance*. 12th ed. Englewood Cliffs, N.J.: Prentice-Hall, 1994, pp. 1008–9.

9. BOLES, KEITH E. "Insolvency in Managed Care Organizations: Financial Indicators," *Topics in Health Care Financing* 19, no. 2 (Winter 1992): 40–57.

10. BREALEY, RICHARD A., MYERS, STEWART C., AND MARCUS, ALAN J. *Fundamentals of Corporate Finance*. New York, N.Y.: McGraw-Hill, 1995, pp. 393–400.

11. CASEY, CORNELIUS, AND BARTCZAK, NORMAN. "Using Operating Cash Flow Data to Predict Financial Distress: Some Extensions," *Journal of Accounting Research* 23, no. 1 (1985): 384–401.

12. CHRISTIANSON, JON B., WHOLEY, DOUGLAS R., AND SANCHEZ, SUSAN M. "State Responses to HMO Failures," *Health Affairs* (Winter 1991): 78–92.

13. DEANGELO, HARRY, AND DEANGELO, LINDA. "Dividend Policy and Financial Distress: An Empirical Investigation of Troubled NYSE Firms," *Journal of Finance* 45, no. 5 (1990): 1415–32.

14. EILERS, ROBERT D. *Regulation of Blue Cross and Blue Shield Plans*. Homewood, Ill.: Richard D. Irwin, Inc., 1963.

15. GILBERT, LISA R., MENON, KRISHNAGOPAL, AND SCHWARTZ, KENNETH B. "Predicting Bankruptcy for Firms in Financial Distress," *Journal of Business Finance and Accounting* 17, no. 1 (1990): 161–71.

16. GILSON, STUART C. "Management Turnover and Financial Distress," *Journal of Financial Economics* 25 (1989): 241–62.

17. GROUP HEALTH ASSOCIATION OF AMERICA, INC. *1994 National Directory of HMOs.* Washington, D.C.: 1994.

18. GRUBER, LYNN, SHADLE, MAUREEN, AND PION, KIRK. *The Interstudy Edge* 4 (1989): 1–65.

19. KEOWN, ARTHUR J., SCOTT, DAVID F., JR., MARTIN, JOHN D., AND PETTY, J. WILLIAM. "Determining the Financial Mix," in *Foundations of Finance—The Logic and Practice of Financial Management.* Englewood Cliffs, N.J.: Prentice Hall, 1994, p. 421.

20. KOSE, JOHN. "Managing Financial Distress and Valuing Distressed Securities: A Survey and a Research Agenda," *Financial Management* 22, no. 3 (1993): 60–78.

21. LAU, AMY HING-LING. "A Five-State Financial Distress Prediction Model," *Journal of Accounting Research* 25, no. 1 (1987): 127–38.

22. MARSH, WILLIAM H. *Basic Financial Management.* Cincinnati, Ohio: South-Western College Publishing, 1995, pp. 536–9.

23. MENSAH, YAW H., CONSIDINE, JUDITH M., AND OAKES, LESLIE. "Statutory Insolvency Regulations and Earnings Management in the Prepaid Health-Care Industry," *The Accounting Review* 69, no. 1 (January 1994): 70–95.

24. MOYER, R. CHARLES, MCGUIGAN, JAMES R., AND KRETLOW, WILLIAM J. *Contemporary Financial Management.* 6th ed. St. Paul, Minn.: West Publishing Company, 1995, p. 811.

25. NATIONAL ASSOCIATION OF INSURANCE COMMISSIONERS. *Status of Multistate Insurance Company Departmental Conservations, Rehabilitations, and Liquidations.* Kansas City, Mo.: (appropriate year).

26. NATIONAL ASSOCIATION OF INSURANCE COMMISSIONERS. *Status of Single State Insurance Company Departmental Conservations, Rehabilitations, and Liquidations.* Kansas City, Mo.: (appropriate year).

27. NATIONAL ORGANIZATION OF LIFE AND HEALTH INSURANCE GUARANTY ASSOCIATIONS. *Life and Health Insurance Company Impairments and Insolvencies 1983–93.* Herndon, Va.: 1993.

28. THE PACE GROUP. "Report on Status, Trends, Concerns," in *1993 Managed Care Regulatory Survey.* 1993, pp. 1–11.

29. PETTY, J. WILLIAM, KEOWN, ARTHUR J., SCOTT, DAVID F., JR., AND MARTIN, JOHN D. *Basic Financial Management.* 6th ed. Englewood Cliffs, N.J.: Prentice Hall, 1993, pp. 825–8.

30. RAO, RAMESH K.S. *Financial Management—Concepts and Applications*. 3rd ed. Cincinnati, Ohio: South-Western College Publishing, 1992, pp. 501–4.
31. ROSS, STEPHEN A., WESTERFIELD, RANDOLPH W., AND JORDAN, BRANFORD D. *Fundamentals of Corporate Finance*. 3rd ed. Homewood, Ill.: Irwin Publishers, 1995, pp. 391–3.
32. RUNDLE, RHONDA. "A. M. Best Launches Program to Assess the Strength of HMOs," *Wall Street Journal*, February 10, 1995, p. B2.
33. SCHEUR, BARRY. "Bankruptcy, Liquidation, and Rehabilitation," in Group Health Association of America (GHAA) Conference *Managed Care Law: New Risks, New Solutions*. New Orleans, La.: GHAA, September 16–18, 1990: 1–19.
34. SCHUYLER, W. THOMPSON. "Blue Cross/Blue Shield," Society of Actuaries Study Note, *Course G-320*. Itasca, Ill.: Society of Actuaries, 1987.
35. SEUBOLD, FRANK H. (Director OHMO, Department of Health and Human Services). "Summary Information on HMO Failures," Memorandum, June 15, 1982, 1–28.
36. SHARPE, WILLIAM F., ALEXANDER, GORDON J., AND BAILEY, JEFFERY V. *Investments*. 5th ed. Englewood Cliffs, N.J.: Prentice Hall, 1995, pp. 415–7.
37. SIMMONS, CRAIG A. "Insurer Failures: Property/Casualty Insurer Insolvencies and State Guaranty Funds," *Report to Congressional Requesters*. Washington, D.C.: GAO, 1987.
38. SIMMONS, CRAIG A. "Insurance Regulation: The Insurance Regulatory Information System Needs Improvement," *Report to the Chairman, Subcommittee on Commerce, Consumer Protection, and Competitiveness, Committee on Energy and Commerce, House of Representatives*. Washington, D.C.: General Accounting Office (GAO), 1990.
39. STONE, DIANE L., AND HEFFERNAN, SARI. "1988 Survey on Regulation of HMOs and HMO Solvency: Findings and Recommendations," *GHAA Journal* (May 1989): 28–39.
40. U.S. SENATE PERMANENT SUBCOMMITTEE ON INVESTIGATIONS OF THE COMMITTEE ON GOVERNMENTAL AFFAIRS. *Efforts to Combat Fraud and Abuse in the Insurance Industry*. Hearings, 102 Cong., 2nd sess., July 2, 29, and 30, 1992. Parts VI and VII. Washington, D.C.: General Printing Office (GPO), 1993.
41. U.S. HOUSE OF REPRESENTATIVES SUBCOMMITTEE ON OVERSIGHT AND INVESTIGATIONS OF THE COMMITTEE ON ENERGY AND COMMERCE. *Failed Promises—Insurance Company Insolvencies*. 101 Cong., 2nd sess., February 1990. Washington, D.C.: GPO, 1993.
42. VAN HORNE, JAMES C., AND WACHOWICZ, JOHN M., JR. *Fundamentals of Financial Management*. 9th ed. Englewood Cliffs, N.J.: Prentice Hall, 1995, p. 659.

43. WHOLEY, DOUGLAS R., CHRISTIANSON, JON B., AND SANCHEZ, SUSAN M. "Organization Size and Failure Among Health Maintenance Organizations," *American Sociological Review* 57 (December 1992): 829–42.
44. WRUCK, KAREN HOPPER. "Financial Distress, Reorganization, and Organizational Efficiency," *Journal of Financial Economics* 27, no. 2 (1990): 419–44.

APPENDIX A

QUOTATIONS ON FINANCIAL DISTRESS

In this appendix we show relevant quotations from (1) current finance and insurance textbooks and from (2) academic studies on financial distress from the finance and insurance literature.

1. Current Finance and Insurance Textbooks

29. Petty, J. William, Keown, Arthur J., Scott, David F., Jr., and Martin, John D. *Basic Financial Management.* 6th ed. Englewood Cliffs, N.J.: Prentice Hall, 1993, pp. 825–8.

"The term 'failure' is used in a variety of contexts. **Economic failure** suggests that a company's costs exceed its revenues. Stated differently, the internal rates of return on investments are less than a firm's cost of capital. **Insolvency** also is frequently used to specify serious financial problems. A firm is *technically insolvent* when it can no longer honor its financial obligations. Although the book value of assets may exceed total liabilities, indicating a positive net worth, the company simply does not have sufficient liquidity to pay its debts. This condition may be temporary, and reorganization may be possible, or irreversible. Another term used is *insolvency in bankruptcy.* In this case the company's liabilities are greater than the fair valuation of its assets, which means a negative net worth. Regardless of the liquidity of its assets, the company is completely and unquestionably unable to meet maturing obligations. This situation generally indicates that liquidation rather than a reorganization of the firm is necessary." (pp. 825–826)

8. Black, Kenneth, Jr., and Skipper, Harold D., Jr. *Life Insurance.* 12th ed. Englewood Cliffs, N.J.: Prentice-Hall, 1994, pp. 1008–9.

"**REHABILITATION AND LIQUIDATION.** A regulator's typical first responses to a troubled insurer are informal. The regulator may attempt to work with management to identify and deal with the sources of difficulty. A friendly merger or acquisition might be arranged. States also take formal actions—often in the form of so-called **corrective orders**—against financially troubled licensed insurers. ... The regulator may also revoke an insurer's license. All these actions are subject to court review.

"If the commissioner determines that reorganization, consolidation, conversion, reinsurance, merger, or other transformation is appropriate, a specific plan of rehabilitation may be prepared. Under an order of **rehabilitation**, the commissioner is granted title to the domestic insurance company's assets and is given the authority to carry on its business until the insurer either is returned to private management after the grounds for issuing the order have been removed or is liquidated.

"**Liquidation** of a domestic insurer is the ultimate power of the commissioner. When it is found not advisable to attempt rehabilitation, or if rehabilitation becomes impracticable, the commissioner must petition the proper court for a liquidation order." (pp. 1008–1009)

10. Brealey, Richard A., Myers, Stewart C., and Marcus, Alan J. *Fundamentals of Corporate Finance.* New York, N.Y.: McGraw-Hill, 1995, pp. 393–400.

"Financial distress occurs when promises to creditors are broken or honored with difficulty. Sometimes financial distress leads to bankruptcy. Sometimes it only means skating on thin ice." (p. 393)

22. Marsh, William H. *Basic Financial Management.* Cincinnati, Ohio: South-Western College Publishing, 1995, pp. 536–9.

"**Technical insolvency** occurs when a company is unable to meet its current obligations as they come due. Even though the value of assets is greater than the value of liabilities, the company is suffering from a liquidity crisis. ... If the conditions are temporary, it may be worked out with creditors. If the conditions are permanent, the company may become legally insolvent.

"**Legal insolvency** occurs when the total liabilities exceed the total assets, as recorded on the balance sheet. Absolute insolvency is similarly defined, but in this case, assets are shown at their fair market value. The latter suggests a more critical stage of financial difficulty, possibly leading to bankruptcy.

"**Bankruptcy** is a legal term indicating that the company has begun a legal proceeding under the control of a bankruptcy court. The Bankruptcy Act of 1938, amended in 1978 and 1984, allows a company to petition into bankruptcy using technical insolvency, legal insolvency, or absolute insolvency as a basis. This action leads to reorganization or liquidation." (pp. 536–537)

24. Moyer, R. Charles, McGuigan, James R., and Kretlow, William J. *Contemporary Financial Management*. 6th ed. St. Paul, Minn.: West Publishing Company, 1995, p. 811.

"It is ... common, however, for business failure to be viewed in a *financial context*, either as a *technical insolvency*, a *legal insolvency*, or a *bankruptcy*. A firm is said to be *technically insolvent* if it is unable to meet its current obligations as they become due, even though the value of its assets exceeds its liabilities. A firm is *legally insolvent* if the recorded value of its assets is less than the recorded value of its liabilities. A firm is *bankrupt* if it is unable to pay its debts and files a bankruptcy petition in accordance with the federal bankruptcy laws." (p. 811)

30. Rao, Ramesh K.S. *Financial Management—Concepts and Applications*. 3rd ed. Cincinnati, Ohio: South-Western College Publishing, 1992, pp. 501–4.

"A business is said to be experiencing **failure** when the realized rate of return on that business is consistently less than investors' opportunity costs. That is, the return provided by the firm is not adequate to offset the risk of the firm. Note that this definition says nothing about whether the firm can continue operations or will cease to exist. Corporate **financial distress**, however, threatens the viability of the firm.

"A firm is said to be experiencing financial distress if it faces **insolvency**. Insolvency implies that the firm is in default, and there are two variants. A financially distressed firm may be in **technical default** or in a more serious situation of **formal default**. Technical default arises when a firm violates a legally binding agreement with a creditor. ... The more serious formal default arises when the firm is unable to meet its interest obligations to the creditors." (pp. 501–502)

31. Ross, Stephen A., Westerfield, Randolph W., and Jordan, Bradford D. *Fundamentals of Corporate Finance*. 3rd ed. Homewood, Ill.: Irwin Publishers, 1995, pp. 391–3.

"One of the consequences of using debt is the possibility of financial distress, which can be defined in several ways:

1. *Business failure.* This is a term usually used to refer to a situation where a business has terminated with a loss to creditors, but even an all-equity firm can fail.

2. *Legal bankruptcy.* Firms bring petitions to a federal court for bankruptcy. *Bankruptcy* is a legal proceeding for liquidating or reorganizing a business.

3. *Technical insolvency.* Technical insolvency occurs when a firm defaults on a legal obligation; for example, it does not pay a bill.

4. *Accounting insolvency.* Firms with negative net worth are insolvent on the books. This happens when the total book liabilities exceed the book value of the total assets." (p. 391)

36. Sharpe, William F., Alexander, Gordon J., and Bailey, Jeffery V. *Investments.* 5th ed. Englewood Cliffs, N.J.: Prentice Hall, 1995, pp. 415–7.

"A corporation unable to meet its obligatory debt payments is said to be technically insolvent (or insolvent in the equity sense). If the value of the firm's assets falls below its liabilities, it is said to be insolvent (or insolvent in the bankruptcy sense)." (p. 415)

42. Van Horne, James C., and Wachowicz, John M., Jr. *Fundamentals of Financial Management.* 9th ed. Englewood Cliffs, N.J.: Prentice Hall, 1995, p. 659.

"Nevertheless, we must not lose sight of the fact that some firms fail. Internal management must keep this in mind, and so must a creditor who has amounts due from a company in financial distress. The word "failure" is vague, partly because there are varying degrees of failure. A company is regarded as *technically insolvent* if it is unable to meet its current obligations. However, such insolvency may be only temporary and subject to remedy. Technical insolvency, then, denotes only a lack of liquidity. *Insolvency in bankruptcy,* on the other hand, means that the liabilities of a company exceed its assets. In other words, the shareholders' equity of the company is negative. *Financial failure* includes that entire range of possibilities between these two extremes." (p. 659)

2. Academic Studies of Financial Distress

11. Casey, Cornelius, and Bartczak, Norman. "Using Operating Cash Flow Data to Predict Financial Distress: Some Extensions," *Journal of Accounting Research* 23, no. 1 (1985): 384–401.

Casey and Bartczak conducted their study "... to assess whether operating cash flow data and related measures lead to more accurate predictions of bankrupt and nonbankrupt firms. Bankruptcy was selected as the specific form of financial distress and as the criterion event for three primary reasons: (1) the direct and indirect costs of bankruptcy are significant in relation to the value of the firm (Altman [1983a]); (2) results from this study can be compared with previous studies of bankruptcy prediction; (3) the costs of data gathering and the problem of interpreting the economic significance of other events (e.g., loan default) were viewed as greater than the benefits of using events whose occurrences are arguably less subject to noneconomic factors than is bankruptcy." (pp. 384–385)

21. Lau, Amy Hing-Ling. "A Five-State Financial Distress Prediction Model," *Journal of Accounting Research* 25, no. 1 (1987): 127–38.

Lau "...extends previous corporate failure prediction models ... in two ways: (1) instead of the usual failing/nonfailing dichotomy, five financial states are used to approximate the continuum of corporate financial health ... The five financial states used in this study are: state 0: financial stability; state 1: omitting or reducing dividend payments; state 2: technical default and default on loan payments; state 3: protection under Chapter X or XI of the Bankruptcy Act; and state 4: bankruptcy and liquidation. States 1 to 4 are states of increasing severity of financial distress.

"Although a financially stable firm may reduce or omit dividends, say, to finance capital investments, empirical studies ... show that a firm that reduces dividends is typically encountering some financial distress. Therefore, this study uses 'dividend omission or reduction' to represent a financial condition between states 0 and 2." (pp. 127–128)

16. Gilson, Stuart C. "Management Turnover and Financial Distress," *Journal of Financial Economics* 25 (1989): 241–62.

"This study analyzes a sample of firms that experience large common stock price declines. This approach allows me to identify firms that have suffered an unexpectedly large decline in their cash flows. The incidence of default, bankruptcy, and debt restructuring is assumed to be relatively high for such firms ..." (pp. 242–243)

6. BarNiv, Ran, and Hershbarger, Robert A. "Classifying Financial Distress in the Life Insurance Industry," *Journal of Risk and Insurance* 57, no. 1 (1990): 110–36.

"In this study, insolvent insurers are defined as those companies which are declared insolvent by their respective state insurance commissioners and reported by A. M. Best Company ... Life insurance companies which were listed as "dissolved" are not included in this study since this term may include voluntary dissipation." (p. 114)

13. DeAngelo, Harry, and DeAngelo, Linda. "Dividend Policy and Financial Distress: An Empirical Investigation of Troubled NYSE Firms," *Journal of Finance* 45, no. 5 (1990): 1415–32.

DeAngelo and DeAngelo "...study the dividend policy adjustments of 80 NYSE firms to protracted financial distress as evidenced by multiple losses during 1980–1985." (p. 1415)

15. Gilbert, Lisa R., Menon, Krishnagopal, and Schwartz, Kenneth B. "Predicting Bankruptcy for Firms in Financial Distress," *Journal of Business Finance and Accounting* 17, no. 1 (1990): 161–71.

"Three groups of firms were used: (1) a bankrupt group, (2) a random group, and (3) a distressed group, i.e. firms which are identified as being financially weak but which did not go bankrupt. The bankrupt group consisted of US firms that filed a Chapter 11 bankruptcy petition between 1974 and 1983. ... The distressed group contained firms that had negative cumulative earnings (income from continuing operations) over any consecutive three year period between 1972 and 1983." (pp. 162–163)

44. Wruck, Karen Hopper. "Financial Distress, Reorganization, and Organizational Efficiency," *Journal of Financial Economics* 27, no. 2 (1990): 419–44.

"This paper defines financial distress as a situation where cash flow is insufficient to cover current obligations. These obligations can include unpaid debts to suppliers and employees, actual or potential damages from litigation, and missed principal and interest payments under borrowing agreements (default). Technical default, the violation of a debt covenant other than one specifying principal and interest payments (e.g. minimum-net-worth requirements or working-capital constraints), can be a warning that distress is imminent....

"Some confusion arises because the word insolvent is often used as a synonym for financial distress. Insolvency can be interpreted as pertaining to stocks or flows, and the two are often confused. ... A stock-based definition describes as insolvent a firm with a negative economic net worth: the present value of its cash flows is less that its total obligations. A firm in financial distress is insolvent on a flow basis if it is unable to meet current cash obligations.

"Bankruptcy and liquidation are also used as synonyms for financial distress. In this paper, bankruptcy refers to the court-supervised process for breaking and rewriting contracts. Liquidation refers to a sale of the firm's assets and distribution of proceeds to claimants." (pp. 421–422)

7. BarNiv, Ran, and McDonald, James B. "Identifying Financial Distress in the Insurance Industry: A Synthesis of Methodological and Empirical Issues," *Journal of Risk and Insurance* 59, no. 4 (1992): 543–74.

"This study presents a methodological approach for identifying insolvent insurance companies. In this article, financial distress and insolvency are used interchangeably to describe insurers experiencing liquidation, receivership, conservatorship, restraining orders, rehabilitation, etc." (p. 543)

20. Kose, John. "Managing Financial Distress and Valuing Distressed Securities: A Survey and a Research Agenda," *Financial Management* 22, no. 3 (1993): 60–78.

"The financial contracts of a firm can be loosely categorized into hard and soft contracts. An example of a hard contract is a coupon debt contract which specifies periodic payments by the firm to the bondholders. If these payments are not made on time, the firm is considered to be in violation of the contract and the claimholders have specified and unspecified legal recourse to enforce the contract. Contracts with suppliers and employees may be other examples of hard contracts. Common stock and preferred stock are examples of soft contracts. Here, even though its claimholders have expectations of receiving current payouts from the firm in addition to their ownership rights, the level and frequency of these payouts are often policy decisions made by the firm.

"The above categorization of the financing contracts of a firm ... gives rise to a natural definition of *financial distress*. A firm is in financial distress at a given point in time when the liquid assets of the firm are not sufficient to meet the current requirements of its hard contracts." (p. 61)

APPENDIX B

ALPHABETICAL LISTING OF COMMERCIAL HEALTH CARRIER INSOLVENCIES 1971–1993

Company	State	Date	Cause*	% A&H	Total Assets
Alpha Life Ins. Co.	TX	1991	1	78%	1,030
Amalgamated Labor Life Ins. Co.	IL	1989	3	92	17,164
American Financial Life Ins. Co.	FL	1991	4	81	9,478
American Protectors Ins. Co.	UT	1988	2	87	13,944
American Protectors Ins. Co.	UT	1990	1	84	13,473
American Standard Life & Accident Ins. Co.	OK	1988	5	54	82,121
American Sun Life Ins. Co.	FL	1989	1	87	17,287
American Teachers Life Ins. Co.	TX	1989	2	91	5,100
American Way General Ins. Co.	AZ	1990	1	100	28,354
American Way Life Ins. Co.	MI	1993	1	68	24,943
Associated Life Ins. Co.	IL	1989	1	55	15,820
Atlantic & Pacific Ins. Co.	CO	1983	1	92	1,426
Atlantic & Pacific Life Ins. Co. of America	GA	1991	1	74	13,667
Business Ins. Life of America	LA	1982	2	93	1,131
California Benefit Life Ins. Co.	CA	1989	2	98	2,522
California Life Ins. Co.	CA	1986	7	85	33,775
California Pacific Life Ins. Co.	CA	1989	1	96	4,848
Coastal Ins. Co.	CA	1989	6	93	34,813
Colombia Life Ins. Co.	PA	1991	4	84	23,266
Colony Charter Life Ins. Co.	CA	1987	1	95	10,023
Connecticut Commercial Travelers Mutual Life Ins. Co.	CT	1978	2	66	2,142
Consolidated Benefit Health Ins. Co.	TX	1989	1	99	878
Consolidated Savings Life Ins. Co.	TX	1987	8	95	2,687
Consumers United Ins. Co.	DE	1993	8	96	27,238
Continental Bankers Life Ins. Co. of the South	TN	1986	5	94	13,878
Continental Service Life & Health Ins. Co.	LA	1985	5	64	16,950
Diamond Benefits Life Ins. Co.	AZ	1988	6	73	7,853
Eagle Life Ins. Co.	TX	1986	2	90	18,302
Employers Equitable Life Ins. Co.	AR	1991	8	100	475
Employers Life Ins. Co.	AL	1992	8	93	4,013
Excalibur Life Ins. Co.	TX	1990	1	89	N/A
Farm & Home Life Ins. Co.	AZ	1990	1	87	211,829
Farmers National Life Ins. Co.	FL	1976	5	58	5,072
Farwest American Assurance Co.	OR	1989	3	90	25,926
Fidelity American Life Assurance Co.	AZ	1984	1	83	702
First Columbia Life Ins. Co.	LA	1988	6	91	N/A
First Farwest Life Ins. Co.	OR	1989	2	92	91,486
First Transcontinental Life Ins. Co.	WI	1988	6	94	N/A
First United Life Ins. Co. of America	TX	1981	2	74	1,425
Florida General Life Ins. Co.	FL	1983	1	82	5,839

APPENDIX B—*Continued*

Company	State	Date	Cause*	% A&H	Total Assets
Foundation Life Ins. Co.	NJ	1981	8	72	12,122
Galaxia Life Ins. Co.	LA	1989	6	100	1,924
General Life & Accident Ins. Co.	TX	1991	1	99	7,431
George Washington Life Ins. Co.	WV	1990	1	93	25,163
George Washington Life Ins. Co. of CA	CA	1990	3	92	4,301
Georgia Life and Health Ins. Co.	GA	1991	1	98	18,116
GIC Ins. Co.	TX	1989	2	98	5,558
Great Republic Ins. Co.	CA	1991	2	99	44,017
Guardian American Life Ins. Co.	OK	1989	1	100	489
Hermitage Health & Life Ins. Co.	TN	1986	2	67	22,993
Independent Bankers Life Ins. Co. of TX	TX	1984	1	98	8,584
Independent Liberty Life Ins. Co.	MI	1983	2	75	37,392
Independent Security Life Ins. Co.	TX	1993	1	53	598
Independent Standard Life Ins. Co.	TX	1984	1	57	N/A
International Fidelity Life Ins. Co.	TX	1987	2	97	N/A
International Life Ins. Co.	TX	1990	1	100	N/A
Iowa State Travelers Mutual Assurance Co.	IA	1983	1	85	10,638
Justice Life Ins. Co.	TX	1990	1	97	1,363
Key Life Ins. Co. of SC	SC	1983	1	99	753
Keystone Life Ins. Co.	TX	1987	2	90	17,082
L.A. Life Ins. Co.	FL	1988	1	91	1,782
Latin American Life Ins. Co.	FL	1987	1	96	2,307
Legacy Life Ins. Co.	NE	1991	1	92	14,700
Legal Protective Life Ins. Co.	TX	1991	1	97	N/A
Legal Security Life Ins. Co.	TX	1992	1	99	6,244
Life of Indiana Ins. Co.	IN	1989	2	87	27,770
Lumbermans Life Ins. Co.	IN	1988	6	84	22,344
Maine Ins. Co.	ME	1971	2	95	4,301
Maxicare Life & Health Ins. Co.	MO	1989	6	94	11,613
Merchants & Manufacturers Ins. Co.	OH	1986	2	54	4,258
Mid-Western Life Ins. Co.	OK	1989	4	90	10,054
Missouri National Life Ins. Co.	MO	1989	1	95	6,270
Modern Life & Accident Ins. Co.	IL	1982	1	91	1,138
Modern Pioneers Life Ins. Co.	AZ	1989	2	100	10,404
Monarch Life Ins. Co.	MA	1991	3	52	5,127,008
National American Life Ins. Co.	LA	1976	4	62	22,269
National Benefit Life Ins. Co.	TX	1990	1	97	5,435
National Society of Health	LA	1990	2	92	1,124
National Union Life Ins. Co.	AL	1986	4	100	2,008
Northeastern Life Ins. Co. of NY	NY	1976	1	88	31,162
Old Southern Life Ins. Co.	AL	1991	1	98	26,790
Parliament Life Ins. Co.	PA	1987	8	92	N/A
Paso Del Norte Life Ins. Co.	AZ	1991	8	81	825
Pilgrim Life Ins. Co.	PA	1993	1	80	11,604
Pioneer Annuity Life Ins. Co.	AZ	1984	6	59	11,403

APPENDIX B—*Continued*

Company	State	Date	Cause*	% A&H	Total Assets
Producers Ins. Co.	AR	1985	8	87	N/A
Professional Benefits Ins. Co.	TX	1990	8	99	6,872
Progress Life & Accident Ins. Co.	OK	1989	3	51	2,040
Progressive Mutual Life Ins. Co.	TX	1992	2	91	N/A
Regent Life Ins. Co.	TX	1989	1	80	246
Reliable Life & Casualty Co.	WI	1981	1	92	32,445
Republic American Life Ins. Co.	AZ	1991	2	99	2,824
Republic American Life Ins. Co.	AZ	1992	1	99	5,873
Rumford Life Ins. Co.	RI	1990	3	93	3,868
Seaboard Life Ins. Co.	FL	1975	1	62	41,980
Senior Security Life Ins. Co.	OK	1992	1	99	N/A
Southern General Life Ins. Co.	FL	1987	3	92	15,630
Southern General Life Ins. Co. of TX	TX	1989	2	91	2,444
Southern National Life Ins. Co.	TX	1989	7	100	1,648
Springfield Life Ins. Co.	VT	1991	3	76	161,782
State Security Life Ins. Co.	MS	1984	2	92	1,915
Tara Life Ins. Co. of America	DE	1983	1	100	13,987
Texas Consumer Life Ins. Co.	TX	1989	1	78	2,522
Texas Dealers Life Ins. Co.	TX	1990	8	52	479
Texas Fidelity Life Ins. Co.	TX	1986	2	84	1,338
Texas Investors Life Ins. Co.	TX	1989	1	94	4,539
UCSB Ins. Assoc.	UT	1981	1	100	946
Underwriters Life Ins. Co.	SD	1990	2	86	8,175
Underwriters National Assurance Co.	IN	1990	3	78	52,426
United Bankers Life Ins. Co.	TX	1982	2	80	12,785
United Equitable Life Ins. Co.	IL	1990	2	60	27,405
United Equity Life Ins. Co.	OK	1984	2	99	2,518
United Fire Ins. Co.	IL	1988	7	55	13,231
United Life of NA	AZ	1992	6	70	N/A
United Security Life Ins. Co.	TX	1992	1	82	N/A
US Bankers Life Ins. Co.	NM	1988	1	100	792
World Life & Health Ins. Co. of PA	PA	1991	2	90	28,446

*Cause:
1. Inadequate pricing or inadequate surplus
2. Rapid growth
3. Affiliate problems
4. Overstated assets
5. Fraud
6. Significant change in business, such as rapid expansion into new product lines or markets
7. Reinsurance failure
8. Cause undetermined.

APPENDIX C

LISTING IN DESCENDING ORDER BY TOTAL ASSETS
PRIOR TO FINANCIAL IMPAIRMENT
FOR COMMERCIAL HEALTH CARREIR INSOLVENCIES
1971–1993

Company	State	Date	Cause*	% A&H	Total Assets
Monarch Life Ins. Co.	MA	1991	3	52%	5,127,008
Farm & Home Life Ins. Co.	AZ	1990	1	87	211,829
Springfield Life Ins. Co.	VT	1991	3	76	161,782
First Farwest Life Ins. Co.	OR	1989	2	92	91,486
American Standard Life & Accident Ins. Co.	OK	1988	5	54	82,121
Underwriters National Assurance Co.	IN	1990	3	78	52,426
Great Republic Ins. Co.	CA	1991	2	99	44,017
Seaboard Life Ins. Co.	FL	1975	1	62	41,980
Independent Liberty Life Ins. Co.	MI	1983	2	75	37,392
Coastal Ins. Co.	CA	1989	6	93	34,813
California Life Ins. Co.	CA	1986	7	85	33,775
Reliable Life & Casualty Co.	WI	1981	1	92	32,445
Northeastern Life Ins. Co. of NY	NY	1976	1	88	31,162
World Life & Health Ins. Co. of PA	PA	1991	2	90	28,446
American Way General Ins. Co.	AZ	1990	1	100	28,354
Life of Indiana Ins. Co.	IN	1989	2	87	27,770
United Equitable Life Ins. Co.	IL	1990	2	60	27,405
Consumers United Ins. Co.	DE	1993	8	96	27,238
Old Southern Life Ins. Co.	AL	1991	1	98	26,790
Farwest American Assurance Co.	OR	1989	3	90	25,926
George Washington Life Ins. Co.	WV	1990	1	93	25,163
American Way Life Ins. Co.	MI	1993	1	68	24,943
Colombia Life Ins. Co.	PA	1991	4	84	23,266
Hermitage Health & Life Ins. Co.	TN	1986	2	67	22,993
Lumbermens Life Ins. Co.	IN	1988	6	84	22,344
National American Life Ins. Co.	LA	1976	4	62	22,269
Eagle Life Ins. Co.	TX	1986	2	90	18,302
Georgia Life and Health Ins. Co.	GA	1991	1	98	18,116
American Sun Life Ins. Co.	FL	1989	1	87	17,287
Amalgamated Labor Life Ins. Co.	IL	1989	3	92	17,164
Keystone Life Ins. Co.	TX	1987	2	90	17,082
Continental Service Life & Health Ins. Co.	LA	1985	5	64	16,950
Associated Life Ins. Co.	IL	1989	1	55	15,820
Southern General Life Ins. Co.	FL	1987	3	92	15,630
Legacy Life Ins. Co.	NE	1991	1	92	14,700
Tara Life Ins. Co. of America	DE	1983	1	100	13,987
American Protectors Ins. Co.	UT	1988	2	87	13,944
Continental Bankers Life Ins. Co. of the South	TN	1986	5	94	13,878
Atlantic & Pacific Life Ins. Co. of America	GA	1991	1	74	13,667
American Protectors Ins. Co.	UT	1990	1	84	13,473

APPENDIX C—*Continued*

Company	State	Date	Cause*	% A&H	Total Assets
United Fire Ins. Co.	IL	1988	7	55%	13,231
United Bankers Life Ins. Co.	TX	1982	2	80	12,785
Foundation Life Ins. Co.	NJ	1981	8	72	12,122
Maxicare Life & Health Ins. Co.	MO	1989	6	94	11,613
Pilgrim Life Ins. Co.	PA	1993	1	80	11,604
Pioneer Annuity Life Ins. Co.	AZ	1984	6	59	11,403
Iowa State Travelers Mutual Assurance Co.	IA	1983	1	85	10,638
Modern Pioneers Life Ins. Co.	AZ	1989	2	100	10,404
Mid-Western Life Ins. Co.	OK	1989	4	90	10,054
Colony Charter Life Ins. Co.	CA	1987	1	95	10,023
American Financial Life Ins. Co.	FL	1991	4	81	9,478
Independent Bankers Life Ins. Co. of TX	TX	1984	1	98	8,584
Underwriters Life Ins. Co.	SD	1990	2	86	8,175
Diamond Benefits Life Ins. Co.	AZ	1988	6	73	7,853
General Life & Accident Ins. Co.	TX	1991	1	99	7,431
Professional Benefits Ins. Co.	TX	1990	8	99	6,872
Missouri National Life Ins. Co.	MO	1989	1	95	6,270
Legal Security Life Ins. Co.	TX	1992	1	99	6,244
Republic American Life Ins. Co.	AZ	1992	1	99	5,873
Florida General Life Ins. Co.	FL	1983	1	82	5,839
GIC Ins. Co.	TX	1989	2	98	5,558
National Benefit Life Ins. Co.	TX	1990	1	97	5,435
American Teachers Life Ins. Co.	TX	1989	2	91	5,100
Farmers National Life Ins. Co.	FL	1976	5	58	5,072
California Pacific Life Ins. Co.	CA	1989	1	96	4,848
Texas Investors Life Ins. Co.	TX	1989	1	94	4,539
George Washington Life Ins. Co. of CA	CA	1990	3	92	4,301
Maine Ins. Co.	ME	1971	2	95	4,301
Merchants & Manufacturers Ins. Co.	OH	1986	2	54	4,258
Employers Life Ins. Co.	AL	1992	8	93	4,013
Rumford Life Ins. Co.	RI	1990	3	93	3,868
Republic American Life Ins. Co.	AZ	1991	2	99	2,824
Consolidated Savings Life Ins. Co.	TX	1987	8	95	2,687
California Benefit Life Ins. Co.	CA	1989	2	98	2,522
Texas Consumers Life Ins. Co.	TX	1989	1	78	2,522
United Equity Life Ins. Co.	OK	1984	2	99	2,518
Southern General Life Ins. Co. of TX	TX	1989	2	91	2,444
Latin American Life Ins. Co.	FL	1987	1	96	2,307
Connecticut Commercial Travelers Mutual Life Ins. Co.	CT	1978	2	66	2,142
Progress Life & Accident Ins. Co.	OK	1989	3	51	2,040
National Union Life Ins. Co.	AL	1986	4	100	2,008
Galaxia Life Ins. Co.	LA	1989	6	100	1,924
State Security Life Ins. Co.	MS	1984	2	92	1,915
L.A. Life Ins. Co.	FL	1988	1	91	1,782
Southern National Life Ins. Co.	TX	1989	7	100	1,648

APPENDIX C—*Continued*

Company	State	Date	Cause*	% A&H	Total Assets
Atlantic & Pacific Ins. Co.	CO	1983	1	92%	1,426
First United Life Ins. Co. of America	TX	1981	2	74	1,425
Justice Life Ins. Co.	TX	1990	1	97	1,363
Texas Fidelity Life Ins. Co.	TX	1986	2	84	1,338
Modern Life & Accident Ins. Co.	IL	1982	1	91	1,138
Business Ins. Life of America	LA	1982	2	93	1,131
National Society of Health	LA	1990	2	92	1,124
Alpha Life Ins. Co.	TX	1991	1	78	1,030
UCSB Ins. Assoc.	UT	1981	1	100	946
Consolidated Benefit Health Ins. Co.	TX	1989	1	99	878
Paso Del Norte Life Ins. Co.	AZ	1991	8	81	825
US Bankers Life Ins. Co.	NM	1988	1	100	792
Key Life Ins. Co. of SC	SC	1983	1	99	753
Fidelity American Life Assurance Co.	AZ	1984	1	83	702
Independent Security Life Ins. Co.	TX	1993	1	53	598
Guardian American Life Ins. Co.	OK	1989	1	100	489
Texas Dealers Life Ins. Co.	TX	1990	8	52	479
Employers Equitable Life Ins. Co.	AR	1991	8	100	475
Regent Life Ins. Co.	TX	1989	1	80	246
Excalibur Life Ins. Co.	TX	1990	1	89	N/A
First Columbia Life Ins. Co.	LA	1988	6	91	N/A
First Transcontinental Life Ins. Co.	WI	1988	6	94	N/A
Independent Standard Life Ins. Co.	TX	1984	1	57	N/A
International Fidelity Life Ins. Co.	TX	1987	2	97	N/A
International Life Ins. Co.	TX	1990	1	100	N/A
Legal Protective Life Ins. Co.	TX	1991	1	97	N/A
Parliament Life Ins. Co.	PA	1987	8	92	N/A
Producers Ins. Co.	AR	1985	8	87	N/A
Progressive Mutual Life Ins.	TX	1992	2	91	N/A
Senior Security Life Ins. Co.	OK	1992	1	99	N/A
United Life of NA	AZ	1992	6	70	N/A
United Security Life Ins. Co.	TX	1992	1	82	N/A

*Cause:
  1. Inadequate pricing or inadequate surplus
  2. Rapid growth
  3. Affiliate problems
  4. Overstated assets
  5. Fraud
  6. Significant change in business, such as rapid expansion into new product lines or markets
  7. Reinsurance failure
  8. Cause undetermined

APPENDIX D

LISTING IN DESCENDING ORDER BY PROPORTION OF BUSINESS DERIVED FROM HEALTH BUSINESS FOR COMMERCIAL HEALTH CARRIER INSOLVENCIES 1971–1993

Company	State	Date	Cause*	% A&H	Total Assets
American Way General Ins. Co.	AZ	1990	1	100%	28,354
Employers Equitable Life Ins. Co.	AR	1991	8	100	475
Galaxia Life Ins. Co.	LA	1989	6	100	1,924
Guardian American Life Ins. Co.	OK	1989	1	100	489
International Life Ins. Co.	TX	1990	1	100	N/A
Modern Pioneers Life Ins. Co.	AZ	1989	2	100	10,404
National Union Life Ins. Co.	AL	1986	4	100	2,008
Southern National Life Ins. Co.	TX	1989	7	100	1,648
Tara Life Ins. Co. of America	DE	1983	1	100	13,987
UCSB Ins. Assoc.	UT	1981	1	100	946
US Bankers Life Ins. Co.	NM	1988	1	100	792
Consolidated Benefit Health Ins. Co.	TX	1989	1	99	878
General Life & Accident Ins. Co.	TX	1991	1	99	7,431
Great Republic Ins. Co.	CA	1991	2	99	44,017
Key Life Ins. Co. of SC	SC	1983	1	99	753
Legal Security Life Ins. Co.	TX	1992	1	99	6,244
Professional Benefits Ins. Co.	TX	1990	8	99	6,872
Republic American Life Ins. Co.	AZ	1992	1	99	5,873
Republic American Life Ins. Co.	AZ	1991	2	99	2,824
Senior Security Life Ins. Co.	OK	1992	1	99	N/A
United Equity Life Ins. Co.	OK	1984	2	99	2,518
California Benefit Life Ins. Co.	CA	1989	2	98	2,522
Georgia Life and Health Ins. Co.	GA	1991	1	98	18,116
GIC Ins. Co.	TX	1989	2	98	5,558
Independent Bankers Life Ins. Co. of TX	TX	1984	1	98	8,584
Old Southern Life Ins. Co.	AL	1991	1	98	26,790
International Fidelity Life Ins. Co.	TX	1987	2	97	N/A
Justice Life Ins. Co.	TX	1990	1	97	1,363
Legal Protective Life Ins. Co.	TX	1991	1	97	N/A
National Benefit Life Ins. Co.	TX	1990	1	97	5,435
California Pacific Life Ins. Co.	CA	1989	1	96	4,848
Consumers United Ins. Co.	DE	1993	8	96	27,238
Latin American Life Ins. Co.	FL	1987	1	96	2,307
Colony Charter Life Ins. Co.	CA	1987	1	95	10,023
Consolidated Savings Life Ins. Co.	TX	1987	8	95	2,687
Maine Ins. Co.	ME	1971	2	95	4,301
Missouri National Life Ins. Co.	MO	1989	1	95	6,270
Continental Bankers Life Ins. Co. of the South	TN	1986	5	94	13,878
First Transcontinental Life Ins. Co.	WI	1988	6	94	N/A
Maxicare Life & Health Ins. Co.	MO	1989	6	94	11,613

APPENDIX D—*Continued*

Company	State	Date	Cause*	% A&H	Total Assets
Texas Investors Life Ins. Co.	TX	1989	1	94%	4,539
Business Ins. Life of America	LA	1982	2	93	1,131
Coastal Ins. Co.	CA	1989	6	93	34,813
Employers Life Ins. Co.	AL	1992	8	93	4,013
George Washington Life Ins. Co.	WV	1990	1	93	25,163
Rumford Life Ins. Co.	RI	1990	3	93	3,868
Amalgamated Labor Life Ins. Co.	IL	1989	3	92	17,164
Atlantic & Pacific Ins. Co.	CO	1983	1	92	1,426
First Farwest Life Ins. Co.	OR	1989	2	92	91,486
George Washington Life Ins. Co. of CA	CA	1990	3	92	4,301
Legacy Life Ins. Co.	NE	1991	1	92	14,700
National Society of Health	LA	1990	2	92	1,124
Parliament Life Ins. Co.	PA	1987	8	92	N/A
Reliable Life & Casualty Co.	WI	1981	1	92	32,445
Southern General Life Ins. Co.	FL	1987	3	92	15,630
State Security Life Ins. Co.	MS	1984	2	92	1,915
American Teachers Life Ins. Co.	TX	1989	2	91	5,100
First Columbia Life Ins. Co.	LA	1988	6	91	N/A
L.A. Life Ins. Co.	FL	1988	1	91	1,782
Modern Life & Accident Ins. Co.	IL	1982	1	91	1,138
Progressive Mutual Life Ins. Co.	TX	1992	2	91	N/A
Southern General Life Ins. Co. of TX	TX	1989	2	91	2,444
Eagle Life Ins. Co.	TX	1986	2	90	18,302
Farwest American Assurance Co.	OR	1989	3	90	25,926
Keystone Life Ins. Co.	TX	1987	2	90	17,082
Mid-Western Life Ins. Co.	OK	1989	4	90	10,054
World Life & Health Ins. Co. of PA	PA	1991	2	90	28,446
Excalibur Life Ins. Co.	TX	1990	1	89	N/A
Northeastern Life Ins. Co. of NY	NY	1976	1	88	31,162
American Protectors Ins. Co.	UT	1988	2	87	13,944
American Sun Life Ins. Co.	FL	1989	1	87	17,287
Farm & Home Life Ins. Co.	AZ	1990	1	87	211,829
Life of Indiana Ins. Co.	IN	1989	2	87	27,770
Producers Ins. Co.	AR	1985	8	87	N/A
Underwriters Life Ins. Co.	SD	1990	2	86	8,175
California Life Ins. Co.	CA	1986	7	85	33,775
Iowa State Travelers Mutual Assurance Co.	IA	1983	1	85	10,638
American Protectors Ins. Co.	UT	1990	1	84	13,473
Colombia Life Ins. Co.	PA	1991	4	84	23,266
Lumbermens Life Ins. Co.	IN	1988	6	84	22,344
Texas Fidelity Life Ins. Co.	TX	1986	2	84	1,338
Fidelity American Life Assurance Co.	AZ	1984	1	83	702
Florida General Life Ins. Co.	FL	1983	1	82	5,839
United Security Life Ins. Co.	TX	1992	1	82	N/A
American Financial Life Ins. Co.	FL	1991	4	81	9,478

APPENDIX D—*Continued*

Company	State	Date	Cause*	% A&H	Total Assets
Paso Del Norte Life Ins. Co.	AZ	1991	8	81%	825
Pilgrim Life Ins. Co.	PA	1993	1	80	11,604
Regent Life Ins. Co.	TX	1989	1	80	246
United Bankers Life Ins. Co.	TX	1982	2	80	12,785
Alpha Life Ins. Co.	TX	1991	1	78	1,030
Texas Consumers Life Ins. Co.	TX	1989	1	78	2,522
Underwriters National Assurance Co.	IN	1990	3	78	52,426
Springfield Life Ins. Co.	VT	1991	3	76	161,782
Independent Liberty Life Ins. Co.	MI	1983	2	75	37,392
Atlantic & Pacific Life Ins. Co. of America	GA	1991	1	74	13,667
First United Life Ins. Co. of America	TX	1981	2	74	1,425
Diamond Benefits Life Ins. Co.	AZ	1988	6	73	7,853
Foundation Life Ins. Co.	NJ	1981	8	72	12,122
United Life of NA	AZ	1992	6	70	N/A
American Way Life Ins. Co.	MI	1993	1	68	24,943
Hermitage Health & Life Ins. Co.	TN	1986	2	67	22,993
Connecticut Commercial Travelers Mutual Life Ins. Co.	CT	1978	2	66	2,142
Continental Service Life & Health Ins. Co.	LA	1985	5	64	16,950
National American Life Ins. Co.	LA	1976	4	62	22,269
Seaboard Life Ins. Co.	FL	1975	1	62	41,980
United Equitable Life Ins. Co.	IL	1990	2	60	27,405
Pioneer Annuity Life Ins. Co.	AZ	1984	6	59	11,403
Farmers National Life Ins. Co.	FL	1976	5	58	5,072
Independent Standard Life Ins. Co.	TX	1984	1	57	N/A
Associated Life Ins. Co.	IL	1989	1	55	15,820
United Fire Ins. Co.	IL	1988	7	55	13,231
American Standard Life & Accident Ins. Co.	OK	1988	5	54	82,121
Merchants & Manufacturers Ins. Co.	OH	1986	2	54	4,258
Independent Security Life Ins. Co.	TX	1993	1	53	598
Monarch Life Ins. Co.	MA	1991	3	52	5,127,008
Texas Dealers Life Ins. Co.	TX	1990	8	52	479
Progress Life & Accident Ins. Co.	OK	1989	3	51	2,040

*Cause:
1. Inadequate pricing or inadequate surplus
2. Rapid growth
3. Affiliate problems
4. Overstated assets
5. Fraud
6. Significant change in business, such as rapid expansion into new product lines or markets
7. Reinsurance failure
8. Cause undetermined.

APPENDIX E

LISTING IN CHRONOLOGICAL ORDER
BY YEAR OF FINANCIAL IMPAIRMENT
OF COMMERCIAL HEALTH CARRIER INSOLVENCIES
1971–1993

Company	State	Date	Cause*	% A&H	Total Assets
Maine Ins. Co.	ME	1971	2	95%	4,301
Seaboard Life Ins. Co.	FL	1975	1	62	41,980
Farmers National Life Ins. Co.	FL	1976	5	58	5,072
National American Life Ins. Co.	LA	1976	4	62	22,269
Northeastern Life Ins. Co. of NY	NY	1976	1	88	31,162
Connecticut Commercial Travelers Mutual Life Ins. Co.	CT	1978	2	66	2,142
First United Life Ins. Co. of America	TX	1981	2	74	1,425
Foundation Life Ins. Co.	NJ	1981	8	72	12,122
Reliable Life & Casualty Co.	WI	1981	1	92	32,445
UCSB Ins. Assoc.	UT	1981	1	100	946
Business Ins. Life of America	LA	1982	2	93	1,131
Modern Life & Accident Ins. Co.	IL	1982	1	91	1,138
United Bankers Life Ins. Co.	TX	1982	2	80	12,785
Atlantic & Pacific Ins. Co.	CO	1983	1	92	1,426
Florida General Life Ins. Co.	FL	1983	1	82	5,839
Independent Liberty Life Ins. Co.	MI	1983	2	75	37,392
Iowa State Travelers Mutual Assurance Co.	IA	1983	1	85	10,638
Key Life Ins. Co. of SC	SC	1983	1	99	753
Tara Life Ins. Co. of America	DE	1983	1	100	13,987
Fidelity American Life Assurance Co.	AZ	1984	1	83	702
Independent Bankers Life Ins. Co. of TX	TX	1984	1	98	8,584
Independent Standard Life Ins. Co.	TX	1984	1	57	N/A
Pioneer Annuity Life Ins. Co.	AZ	1984	6	59	11,403
State Security Life Ins. Co.	MS	1984	2	92	1,915
United Equity Life Ins. Co.	OK	1984	2	99	2,518
Continental Service Life & Health Ins. Co.	LA	1985	5	64	16,950
Producers Ins. Co.	AR	1985	8	87	N/A
California Life Ins. Co.	CA	1986	7	85	33,775
Continental Bankers Life Ins. Co. of the South	TN	1986	5	94	13,878
Eagle Life Ins. Co.	TX	1986	2	90	18,302
Hermitage Health & Life Ins.	TN	1986	2	67	22,993
Merchants & Manufacturers Ins. Co.	OH	1986	2	54	4,258
National Union Life Ins. Co.	AL	1986	4	100	2,008
Texas Fidelity Life Ins. Co.	TX	1986	2	84	1,338
Colony Charter Life Ins. Co.	CA	1987	1	95	10,023
Consolidated Savings Life Ins. Co.	TX	1987	8	95	2,687
International Fidelity Life Ins. Co.	TX	1987	2	97	N/A
Keystone Life Ins. Co.	TX	1987	2	90	17,082
Latin American Life Ins. Co.	FL	1987	1	96	2,307
Parliament Life Ins. Co.	PA	1987	8	92	N/A

APPENDIX E—*Continued*

Company	State	Date	Cause*	% A&H	Total Assets
Southern General Life Ins. Co.	FL	1987	3	92%	15,630
American Protectors Ins. Co.	UT	1988	2	87	13,944
American Standard Life & Accident Ins. Co.	OK	1988	5	54	82,121
Diamond Benefits Life Ins. Co.	AZ	1988	6	73	7,853
First Columbia Life Ins. Co.	LA	1988	6	91	N/A
First Transcontinental Life Ins. Co.	WI	1988	6	94	N/A
L.A. Life Ins. Co.	FL	1988	1	91	1,782
Lumbermens Life Ins. Co.	IN	1988	6	84	22,344
United Fire Ins. Co.	IL	1988	7	55	13,231
US Bankers Life Ins. Co.	NM	1988	1	100	792
Amalgamated Labor Life Ins. Co.	IL	1989	3	92	17,164
American Sun Life Ins. Co.	FL	1989	1	87	17,287
American Teachers Life Ins. Co.	TX	1989	2	91	5,100
Associated Life Ins. Co.	IL	1989	1	55	15,820
California Benefit Life Ins. Co.	CA	1989	2	98	2,522
California Pacific Life Ins. Co.	CA	1989	1	96	4,848
Coastal Ins. Co.	CA	1989	6	93	34,813
Consolidated Benefit Health Ins. Co.	TX	1989	1	99	878
Fawest American Assurance Co.	OR	1989	3	90	25,926
First Farwest Life Ins. Co.	OR	1989	2	92	91,486
Galaxia Life Ins. Co.	LA	1989	6	100	1,924
GIC Ins. Co.	TX	1989	2	98	5,558
Guardian American Life Ins. Co.	OK	1989	1	100	489
Life of Indiana Ins. Co.	IN	1989	2	87	27,770
Maxicare Life & Health Ins. Co.	MO	1989	6	94	11,613
Mid-Western Life Ins. Co.	OK	1989	4	90	10,054
Missouri National Life Ins. Co.	MO	1989	1	95	6,270
Modern Pioneers Life Ins. Co.	AZ	1989	2	100	10,404
Progress Life & Accident Ins.	OK	1989	3	51	2,040
Regent Life Ins. Co.	TX	1989	1	80	246
Southern General Life Ins. Co. of TX	TX	1989	2	91	2,444
Southern National Life Ins. Co.	TX	1989	7	100	1,648
Texas Consumers Life Ins. Co.	TX	1989	1	78	2,522
Texas Investors Life Ins. Co.	TX	1989	1	94	4,539
American Protectors Ins. Co.	UT	1990	1	84	13,473
American Way General Ins. Co.	AZ	1990	1	100	28,354
Excalibur Life Ins. Co.	TX	1990	1	89	N/A
Farm & Home Life Ins. Co.	AZ	1990	1	87	211,829
George Washington Life Ins. Co.	WV	1990	1	93	25,163
George Washington Life Ins. Co. of CA	CA	1990	3	92	4,301

APPENDIX E—*Continued*

Company	State	Date	Cause*	% A&H	Total Assets
International Life Ins. Co.	TX	1990	1	100%	N/A
Justice Life Ins. Co.	TX	1990	1	97	1,363
National Benefit Life Ins. Co.	TX	1990	1	97	5,435
National Society of Health	LA	1990	2	92	1,124
Professional Benefits Ins. Co.	TX	1990	8	99	6,872
Rumford Life Ins. Co.	RI	1990	3	93	3,868
Texas Dealers Life Ins. Co.	TX	1990	8	52	479
Underwriters Life Ins. Co.	SD	1990	2	86	8,175
Underwriters National Assurance Co.	IN	1990	3	78	52,426
United Equitable Life Ins. Co.	IL	1990	2	60	27,405
Alpha Life Ins. Co.	TX	1991	1	78	1,030
American Financial Life Ins. Co.	FL	1991	4	81	9,478
Atlantic & Pacific Life Ins. Co. of America	GA	1991	1	74	13,667
Colombia Life Ins. Co.	PA	1991	4	84	23,266
Employers Equitable Life Ins. Co.	AR	1991	8	100	475
General Life & Accident Ins. Co.	TX	1991	1	99	7,431
Georgia Life and Health Ins. Co.	GA	1991	1	98	18,116
Great Republic Ins. Co.	CA	1991	2	99	44,017
Legacy Life Ins. Co.	NE	1991	1	92	14,700
Legal Protective Life Ins. Co.	TX	1991	1	97	N/A
Monarch Life Ins. Co.	MA	1991	3	52	5,127,008
Old Southern Life Ins. Co.	AL	1991	1	98	26,790
Paso Del Norte Life Ins. Co.	AZ	1991	8	81	825
Republic American Life Ins. Co.	AZ	1991	2	99	2,824
Springfield Life Ins. Co.	VT	1991	3	76	161,782
World Life & Health Ins. Co. of PA	PA	1991	2	90	28,446
Employers Life Ins. Co.	AL	1992	8	93	4,013
Legal Security Life Ins. Co.	TX	1992	1	99	6,244
Progressive Mutual Life Ins. Co.	TX	1992	2	91	N/A
Republic American Life Ins. Co.	AZ	1992	1	99	5,873
Senior Security Life Ins. Co.	OK	1992	1	99	N/A
United Life of NA	AZ	1992	6	70	N/A
United Security Life Ins. Co.	TX	1992	1	82	N/A
American Way Life Ins. Co.	MI	1993	1	68	24,943
Consumers United Ins. Co.	DE	1993	8	96	27,238
Independent Security Life Ins. Co.	TX	1993	1	53	598
Pilgrim Life Ins. Co.	PA	1993	1	80	11,604

*Cause:
1. Inadequate pricing or inadequate surplus
2. Rapid growth
3. Affiliate problems
4. Overstated assets
5. Fraud
6. Significant change in business, such as rapid expansion into new product lines or markets
7. Reinsurance failure
8. Cause undetermined.

APPENDIX F

LISTING IN ASCENDING ORDER
BY PRIMARY CAUSE OF FINANCIAL IMPAIRMENT
OF COMMERCIAL HEALTH CARRIER INSOLVENCIES
1971–1993

Company	State	Date	Cause*	% A&H	Total Assets
Alpha Life Ins. Co.	TX	1991	1	78%	1,030
American Protectors Ins. Co.	UT	1990	1	84	13,473
American Sun Life Ins. Co.	FL	1989	1	87	17,287
American Way General Ins. Co.	AZ	1990	1	100	28,354
American Way Life Ins. Co.	MI	1993	1	68	24,943
Associated Life Ins. Co.	IL	1989	1	55	15,820
Atlantic & Pacific Ins. Co.	CO	1983	1	92	1,426
Atlantic & Pacific Life Ins. Co. of America	GA	1991	1	74	13,667
California Pacific Life Ins. Co.	CA	1989	1	96	4,848
Colony Charter Life Ins. Co.	CA	1987	1	95	10,023
Consolidated Benefit Health Ins. Co.	TX	1989	1	99	878
Excalibur Life Ins. Co.	TX	1990	1	89	N/A
Farm & Home Life Ins. Co.	AZ	1990	1	87	211,829
Fidelity American Life Assurance Co.	AZ	1984	1	83	702
Florida General Life Ins. Co.	FL	1983	1	82	5,839
General Life & Accident Ins. Co.	TX	1991	1	99	7,431
George Washington Life Ins. Co.	WV	1990	1	93	25,163
Georgia Life and Health Ins. Co.	GA	1991	1	98	18,116
Guardian American Life Ins. Co.	OK	1989	1	100	489
Independent Bankers Life Ins. Co. of TX	TX	1984	1	98	8,584
Independent Security Life Ins. Co.	TX	1993	1	53	598
Independent Standard Life Ins. Co.	TX	1984	1	57	N/A
International Life Ins. Co.	TX	1990	1	100	N/A
Iowa State Travelers Mutual Assurance Co.	IA	1983	1	85	10,638
Justice Life Ins. Co.	TX	1990	1	97	1,363
Key Life Ins. Co. of SC	SC	1983	1	99	753
L.A. Life Ins. Co.	FL	1988	1	91	1,782
Latin American Life Ins. Co.	FL	1987	1	96	2,307
Legacy Life Ins. Co.	NE	1991	1	92	14,700
Legal Protective Life Ins. Co.	TX	1991	1	97	N/A
Legal Security Life Ins. Co.	TX	1992	1	99	6,244
Missouri National Life Ins. Co.	MO	1989	1	95	6,270
Modern Life & Accident Ins. Co.	IL	1982	1	91	1,138
National Benefit Life Ins. Co.	TX	1990	1	97	5,435
Northeastern Life Ins. Co. of NY	NY	1976	1	88	31,162
Old Southern Life Ins. Co.	AL	1991	1	98	26,790
Pilgrim Life Ins. Co.	PA	1993	1	80	11,604
Regent Life Ins. Co.	TX	1989	1	80	246
Reliable Life & Casualty Co.	WI	1981	1	92	32,445
Republic American Life Ins. Co.	AZ	1992	1	99	5,873

APPENDIX F—*Continued*

Company	State	Date	Cause*	% A&H	Total Assets
Seaboard Life Ins. Co.	FL	1975	1	62%	41,980
Senior Security Life Ins. Co.	OK	1992	1	99	N/A
Tara Life Ins. Co. of America	DE	1983	1	100	13,987
Texas Consumers Life Ins. Co.	TX	1989	1	78	2,522
Texas Investors Life Ins. Co.	TX	1989	1	94	4,539
UCSB Ins. Assoc.	UT	1981	1	100	946
United Security Life Ins. Co.	TX	1992	1	82	N/A
US Bankers Life Ins. Co.	NM	1988	1	100	792
American Protectors Ins. Co.	UT	1988	2	87	13,944
American Teachers Life Ins. Co.	TX	1989	2	91	5,100
Business Ins. Life of America	LA	1982	2	93	1,131
California Benefit Life Ins. Co.	CA	1989	2	98	2,522
Connecticut Commercial Travelers Mutual Life Ins. Co.	CT	1978	2	66	2,142
Eagle Life Ins. Co.	TX	1986	2	90	18,302
First Farwest Life Ins. Co.	OR	1989	2	92	91,486
First United Life Ins. Co. of America	TX	1981	2	74	1,425
GIC Ins. Co.	TX	1989	2	98	5,558
Great Republic Ins. Co.	CA	1991	2	99	44,017
Hermitage Health & Life Ins. Co.	TN	1986	2	67	22,993
Independent Liberty Life Ins. Co.	MI	1983	2	75	37,392
International Fidelity Life Ins. Co.	TX	1987	2	97	N/A
Keystone Life Ins. Co.	TX	1987	2	90	17,082
Life of Indiana Ins. Co.	IN	1989	2	87	27,770
Maine Ins. Co.	ME	1971	2	95	4,301
Merchants & Manufacturers Ins. Co.	OH	1986	2	54	4,258
Modern Pioneers Life Ins. Co.	AZ	1989	2	100	10,404
National Society of Health	LA	1990	2	92	1,124
Progressive Mutual Life Ins. Co.	TX	1992	2	91	N/A
Republic American Life Ins. Co.	AZ	1991	2	99	2,824
Southern General Life Ins. Co. of TX	TX	1989	2	91	2,444
State Security Life Ins. Co.	MS	1984	2	92	1,915
Texas Fidelity Life Ins. Co.	TX	1986	2	84	1,338
Underwriters Life Ins. Co.	SD	1990	2	86	8,175
United Bankers Life Ins. Co.	TX	1982	2	80	12,785
United Equitable Life Ins. Co.	IL	1990	2	60	27,405
United Equity Life Ins. Co.	OK	1984	2	99	2,518
World Life & Health Ins. Co. of PA	PA	1991	2	90	28,446
Amalgamated Labor Life Ins. Co.	IL	1989	3	92	17,164
Farwest American Assurance Co.	OR	1989	3	90	25,926
George Washington Life Ins. Co. of CA	CA	1990	3	92	4,301

APPENDIX F—*Continued*

Company	State	Date	Cause*	% A&H	Total Assets
Monarch Life Ins. Co.	MA	1991	3	52%	5,127,008
Progress Life & Accident Ins. Co.	OK	1989	3	51	2,040
Rumford Life Ins. Co.	RI	1990	3	93	3,868
Southern General Life Ins. Co.	FL	1987	3	92	15,630
Springfield Life Ins. Co.	VT	1991	3	76	161,782
Underwriters National Assurance Co.	IN	1990	3	78	52,426
American Financial Life Ins. Co.	FL	1991	4	81	9,478
Colombia Life Ins. Co.	PA	1991	4	84	23,266
Mid-Western Life Ins. Co.	OK	1989	4	90	10,054
National American Life Ins. Co.	LA	1976	4	62	22,269
National Union Life Ins. Co.	AL	1986	4	100	2,008
American Standard Life & Accident Ins. Co.	OK	1988	5	54	82,121
Continental Bankers Life Ins. Co. of the South	TN	1986	5	94	13,878
Continental Service Life & Health Ins. Co.	LA	1985	5	64	16,950
Farmers National Life Ins. Co.	FL	1976	5	58	5,072
Coastal Ins. Co.	CA	1989	6	93	34,813
Diamond Benefits Life Ins. Co.	AZ	1988	6	73	7,853
First Columbia Life Ins. Co.	LA	1988	6	91	N/A
First Transcontinental Life Ins. Co.	WI	1988	6	94	N/A
Galaxia Life Ins. Co.	LA	1989	6	100	1,924
Lumbermens Life Ins. Co.	IN	1988	6	84	22,344
Maxicare Life & Health Ins. Co.	MO	1989	6	94	11,613
Pioneer Annuity Life Ins. Co.	AZ	1984	6	59	11,403
United Life of NA	AZ	1992	6	70	N/A
California Life Ins. Co.	CA	1986	7	85	33,775
Southern National Life Ins. Co.	TX	1989	7	100	1,648
United Fire Ins. Co.	IL	1988	7	55	13,231
Consolidated Savings Life Ins. Co.	TX	1987	8	95	2,687
Consumers United Ins. Co.	DE	1993	8	96	27,238
Employers Equitable Life Ins. Co.	AR	1991	8	100	475
Employers Life Ins. Co.	AL	1992	8	93	4,013
Foundation Life Ins. Co.	NJ	1981	8	72	12,122
Parliament Life Ins. Co.	PA	1987	8	92	N/A
Paso Del Norte Life Ins. Co.	AZ	1991	8	81	825
Producers Ins. Co.	AR	1985	8	87	N/A
Professional Benefits Ins. Co.	TX	1990	8	99	6,872
Texas Dealers Life Ins. Co.	TX	1990	8	52	479

*Cause:
1. Inadequate pricing or inadequate surplus
2. Rapid growth
3. Affiliate problems
4. Overstated assets
5. Fraud
6. Significant change in business, such as rapid expansion into new product lines or markets
7. Reinsurance failure
8. Cause undetermined

APPENDIX G

LISTING BY STATE OF COMMERCIAL HEALTH CARRIER INSOLVENCIES 1971–1993

Company	State	Date	Cause*	% A&H	Total Assets
Employers Life Ins. Co.	AL	1992	8	93%	4,013
National Union Life Ins. Co.	AL	1986	4	100	2,008
Old Southern Life Ins. Co.	AL	1991	1	98	26,790
Employers Equitable Life Ins. Co.	AR	1991	8	100	475
Producers Ins. Co.	AR	1985	8	87	N/A
American Way General Ins. Co.	AZ	1990	1	100	28,354
Diamond Benefits Life Ins. Co.	AZ	1988	6	73	7,853
Farm & Home Life Ins. Co.	AZ	1990	1	87	211,829
Fidelity American Life Assurance Co.	AZ	1984	1	83	702
Modern Pioneers Life Ins. Co.	AZ	1989	2	100	10,404
Paso Del Norte Life Ins. Co.	AZ	1991	8	81	825
Pioneer Annuity Life Ins. Co.	AZ	1984	6	59	11,403
Republic American Life Ins. Co.	AZ	1992	1	99	5,873
Republic American Life Ins. Co.	AZ	1991	2	99	2,824
United Life of NA	AZ	1992	6	70	N/A
California Benefit Life Ins. Co.	CA	1989	2	98	2,522
California Life Ins. Co.	CA	1986	7	85	33,775
California Pacific Life Ins. Co.	CA	1989	1	96	4,848
Coastal Ins. Co.	CA	1989	6	93	34,813
Colony Charter Life Ins. Co.	CA	1987	1	95	10,023
George Washington Life Ins. Co. of CA	CA	1990	3	92	4,301
Great Republic Ins. Co.	CA	1991	2	99	44,017
Atlantic & Pacific Ins. Co.	CO	1983	1	92	1,426
Connecticut Commercial Travelers Mutual Life Ins. Co.	CT	1978	2	66	2,142
Consumers United Ins. Co.	DE	1993	8	96	27,238
Tara Life Ins. Co. of America	DE	1983	1	100	13,987
American Financial Life Ins. Co.	FL	1991	4	81	9,478
American Sun Life Ins. Co.	FL	1989	1	87	17,287
Farmers National Life Ins. Co.	FL	1976	5	58	5,072
Florida General Life Ins. Co.	FL	1983	1	82	5,839
L.A. Life Ins. Co.	FL	1988	1	91	1,782
Latin American Life Ins. Co.	FL	1987	1	96	2,307
Seaboard Life Ins. Co.	FL	1975	1	62	41,980
Southern General Life Ins. Co.	FL	1987	3	92	15,630
Atlantic & Pacific Life Ins. Co. of America	GA	1991	1	74	13,667
Georgia Life and Health Ins. Co.	GA	1991	1	98	18,116
Iowa State Travelers Mutual Assurance Co.	IA	1983	1	85	10,638
Amalgamated Labor Life Ins. Co.	IL	1989	3	92	17,164
Associated Life Ins. Co.	IL	1989	1	55	15,820
Modern Life & Accident Ins. Co.	IL	1982	1	91	1,138

APPENDIX G—*Continued*

Company	State	Date	Cause*	% A&H	Total Assets
United Equitable Life Ins. Co.	IL	1990	2	60	27,405
United Fire Ins. Co.	IL	1988	7	55	13,231
Life of Indiana Ins. Co.	IN	1989	2	87	27,770
Lumbermens Life Ins. Co.	IN	1988	6	84	22,344
Underwriters National Assurance Co.	IN	1990	3	78	52,426
Business Ins. Life of America	LA	1982	2	93	1,131
Continental Service Life & Health Ins. Co.	LA	1985	5	64	16,950
First Columbia Life Ins. Co.	LA	1988	6	91	N/A
Galaxia Life Ins. Co.	LA	1989	6	100	1,924
National American Life Ins. Co.	LA	1976	4	62	22,269
National Society of Health	LA	1990	2	92	1,124
Monarch Life Ins. Co.	MA	1991	3	52	5,127,008
Maine Ins. Co.	ME	1971	2	95	4,301
American Way Life Ins. Co.	MI	1993	1	68	24,943
Independent Liberty Life Ins. Co.	MI	1983	2	75	37,392
Maxicare Life & Health Ins. Co.	MO	1989	6	94	11,613
Missouri National Life Ins. Co.	MO	1989	1	95	6,270
State Security Life Ins. Co.	MS	1984	2	92	1,915
Legacy Life Ins. Co.	NE	1991	1	92	14,700
Foundation Life Ins. Co.	NJ	1981	8	72	12,122
US Bankers Life Ins. Co.	NM	1988	1	100	792
Northeastern Life Ins. Co. of NY	NY	1976	1	88	31,162
Merchants & Manufacturers Ins. Co.	OH	1986	2	54	4,258
American Standard Life & Accident Ins. Co.	OK	1988	5	54	82,121
Guardian American Life Ins. Co.	OK	1989	1	100	489
Mid-Western Life Ins. Co.	OK	1989	4	90	10,054
Progress Life & Accident Ins. Co.	OK	1989	3	51	2,040
Senior Security Life Ins. Co.	OK	1992	1	99	N/A
United Equity Life Ins. Co.	OK	1984	2	99	2,518
Farwest American Assurance Co.	OR	1989	3	90	25,926
First Farwest Life Ins. Co.	OR	1989	2	92	91,486
Colombia Life Ins. Co.	PA	1991	4	84	23,266
Parliament Life Ins. Co.	PA	1987	8	92	N/A
Pilgrim Life Ins. Co.	PA	1993	1	80	11,604
World Life & Health Ins. Co. of PA	PA	1991	2	90	28,446
Rumford Life Ins. Co.	RI	1990	3	93	3,868
Key Life Ins. Co. of SC	SC	1983	1	99	753
Underwriters Life Ins. Co.	SD	1990	2	86	8,175
Continental Bankers Life Ins. Co. of the South	TN	1986	5	94	13,878
Hermitage Health & Life Ins. Co.	TN	1986	2	67	22,993

APPENDIX G—*Continued*

Company	State	Date	Cause*	% A&H	Total Assets
Alpha Life Ins. Co.	TX	1991	1	78	1,030
American Teachers Life Ins. Co.	TX	1989	2	91	5,100
Consolidated Benefit Health Ins. Co.	TX	1989	1	99	878
Consollidated Savings Life Ins. Co.	TX	1987	8	95	2,687
Eagle Life Ins. Co.	TX	1986	2	90	18,302
Excalibur Life Ins. Co.	TX	1990	1	89	N/A
First United Life Ins. Co. of America	TX	1981	2	74	1,425
General Life & Accident Ins. Co.	TX	1991	1	99	7,431
GIC Ins. Co.	TX	1989	2	98	5,558
Independent Bankers Life Ins. Co. of TX	TX	1984	1	98	8,584
Independent Security Life Ins. Co.	TX	1993	1	53	598
Independent Standard Life Ins. Co.	TX	1984	1	57	N/A
International Fidelity Life Ins. Co.	TX	1987	2	97	N/A
International Life Ins. Co.	TX	1990	1	100	N/A
Justice Life Ins. Co.	TX	1990	1	97	1,363
Keystone Life Ins. Co.	TX	1987	2	90	17,082
Legal Protective Life Ins. Co.	TX	1991	1	97	N/A
Legal Security Life Ins. Co.	TX	1992	1	99	6,244
National Benefit Life Ins. Co.	TX	1990	1	97	5,435
Professional Benefits Ins. Co.	TX	1990	8	99	6,872
Progressive Mutual Life Ins. Co.	TX	1992	2	91	N/A
Regent Life Ins. Co.	TX	1989	1	80	246
Southern General Life Ins. Co. of TX	TX	1989	2	91	2,444
Southern National Life Ins. Co.	TX	1989	7	100	1,648
Texas Consumers Life Ins. Co.	TX	1989	1	78	2,522
Texas Dealers Life Ins. Co.	TX	1990	8	52	479
Texas Fidelity Life Ins. Co.	TX	1986	2	84	1,338
Texas Investors Life Ins. Co.	TX	1989	1	94	4,539
United Bankers Life Ins. Co.	TX	1982	2	80	12,785
United Security Life Ins. Co.	TX	1992	1	82	N/A
American Protectors Ins. Co.	UT	1990	1	84	13,473
American Protectors Ins. Co.	UT	1988	2	87	13,944
UCSB Ins. Assoc.	UT	1981	1	100	946
Springfield Life Ins. Co.	VT	1991	3	76	161,782
First Transcontinental Life Ins. Co.	WI	1988	6	94	N/A
Reliable Life & Casualty Co.	WI	1981	1	92	32,445
George Washington Life Ins. Co.	WV	1990	1	93	25,163

*Cause:
  1. Inadequate pricing or inadequate surplus
  2. Rapid growth
  3. Affiliate problems
  4. Overstated assets
  5. Fraud
  6. Significant change in business, such as rapid expansion into new product lines or markets
  7. Reinsurance failure
  8. Cause undetermined

APPENDIX H

QUOTATIONS ON THE DIFFERENCING APPROACH TO HMOs

Because obtaining the data is the real issue in the HMO area, we quote liberally from the three academic studies involved.

Christiansen, Wholey and Sanchez [12] seek to establish the frequency of HMO failures and the types of HMOs that are likely to fail. The following quotations are from their section, "Sources of Data":

> "Reports of state regulators are one source of information about HMO failures. In 1988, state HMO regulators were surveyed to collect data to be used in crafting amendments to state HMO legislation. The survey, precipitated by the Maxicare bankruptcy, elicited responses from thirty-five states containing 92% of operational HMOs. It found only twelve states reporting HMO insolvencies (or "financial impairments") between 1982 and 1988. In total, respondents identified twenty-one HMO insolvencies, including three HMOs that ceased operations before enrolling any members. Almost all of these insolvent HMOs had adequate enrollee protection through insolvency insurance and "hold-harmless" contractual clauses that prohibited providers affiliated with the HMOs from billing enrollees directly for payment of services. Therefore, the researchers concluded that 'regulators' concern that many existing HMOs have a considerable likelihood of becoming insolvent and jeopardizing enrollee medical care and financial circumstances' is not supported by this survey.

> "This conclusion must be tempered by the nature of the survey, which focused on insolvencies and relied on regulators' recall over a seven-year period. HMOs may fail without becoming insolvent and still impose costs on involved parties.

> "The National HMO Census provides an alternative data source on HMO failures. As part of a larger study of organizational development within the HMO industry, we compiled National HMO Census data for the years 1978–1990. From the census, it is possible to obtain for all HMOs the HMO's name, headquarters, location, federal qualification status, the year founded, total enrollment in each year it was observed, and organizational form (staff, group, network, or IPA). From 1978 to 1980, the census was conducted by the federal government's Office of Health Maintenance Organizations (OHMO). Since 1981, InterStudy has conducted the census. From 1978 to 1984, there was no other major annual census of HMOs, but from 1985 to the present, the Group Health Association of America (GHAA) has also conducted an annual HMO

survey. A series of supplemental InterStudy reports, along with data supplied by Blue Cross and Blue Shield, permitted the identification of HMO mergers, acquisitions, and affiliations with national firms. We assumed that an HMO failed if it was not listed in the census after a specific year, after having been listed in previous years, and if it could not be identified as having been merged with or been acquired by another HMO. This process results in more HMO "failures" than identification of technically insolvent HMOs, since factors other than bankruptcy or financial insolvency can cause an existing HMO to close its doors. For instance, HMOs that foresee serious financial problems may terminate operations, even though they technically may not be insolvent."

Gruber, Shadle, and Pion [18] were the authors of the 1989, Volume 4, issue of *The InterStudy Edge* referred to in the text and appendix of this study. We include these brief statistics simply to provide an idea of the magnitude of the transactions with which researchers were dealing relative to the roughly 600 HMOs then in existence. With respect to transactions since the publication of Volume 2, Appendix B of this issue of *The InterStudy Edge* reports 18 name changes, 12 terminations ("plan ceases to enroll members"), 12 mergers, and three changes in reporting format.

Wholey, Christianson, and Sanchez [43] examine the relationship between HMO size, HMO type, and failure. They utilize the same data base used in Christianson, Wholey, and Sanchez [12], discussed above at length (in their own words.) They add these useful comments about the database:

> "We focus on HMO *failures*, although HMOs can exit a market by merging. We do not address mergers as they are a consequence of different processes and require at least two organizations deciding to combine operations. ... We also do not include acquisitions by a national firm in our analysis because acquisitions occur when a national firm chooses to enter a particular market. The acquisition decision is probably a function in part of how a particular market relates to other markets the national firm has already entered. Also an acquisition does not mean that an HMO failed—a strong HMO can be an attractive takeover target. Furthermore, after an HMO is acquired it still operates in the local community. Clearly the processes associated with acquisitions and mergers differ enough from failure processes to warrant separate analysis."

Mensah, Considine and Oakes [23] gather data on management behavior in setting HMO incurred but not reported claim reserves. These extended comments are taken from their section, *Source of Industry Data*:

"Given the relative lack of data on the HMO industry easily available to researchers, the source of the industry data used in this study and its possible limitations need to be discussed. The data were originally obtained from a database compiled by American International Healthcare (since acquired by Healthcare Investment Analysts) from several sources including state regulators and the Federal Health Care Financing Administration's Office of Prepaid Health Care.

"Although, according to American International Healthcare, the database covers all HMOs in the industry, HMO filings with the state regulatory agencies are sometimes incomplete. Thus, there are missing fields in the database for many HMOs who may have data in other fields for some years. Altogether there were 616, 698, 680, and 520 HMOs for the years 1986–1989 on the database. Of this total, however, only 455 HMOs had complete financial statement data over the years 1987 to 1989; the discontinuities presumably exist because of mergers, failures, and other sources of turnover.

...

"An analysis of the database provides adequate evidence of the financial pressures exerted on the HMOs in the 1986–1989 period. For example, 45 HMOs reported negative net worth in 1986, while 162 did in 1987. These figures dropped to zero in 1988, and then increased to 60 in 1989. ... Evidence of an intensive recapitalization effort in 1988 can be gathered from the fact that none of the financial statements filed with the state regulatory agencies showed negative net worth in that year. ... The re-emergence of HMOs with negative net worth in 1989 provides prima facie evidence of the continuing competitive turmoil in the industry even at that late date."

And from footnote 13: "Detailed analysis of the data for the states with minimum net worth standards in effect provides some additional insight. Seventy-five HMOs violated their respective net worth standards in 1987 only, one in both 1987 and 1988, 61 in both 1987 and 1989..., and three in both 1988 and 1989. However, 20 HMOs were in continuous violation from 1987 to 1989. Follow-up data on the fate of these HMOs after 1990 are not available, but the fact that they continued in existence suggests that state regulators in the eight states in which these 20 operated may have been rather lenient in enforcing the standards."

LONG-TERM CARE INSURANCE VALUATION METHODS

SOCIETY OF ACTUARIES LONG-TERM CARE INSURANCE VALUATION METHODS TASK FORCE[1]

EXECUTIVE SUMMARY

This final report is the culmination of the Society of Actuaries' response to the National Association of Insurance Commissioners (NAIC) 1991 request, and the general need felt, to develop valuation recommendations for long-term care (LTC) insurance. Specifically, the charge given the Task Force reads:

> This Task Force will develop recommendations for the valuation of long-term care insurance products, incorporating, as appropriate, an interim method, available data, the valuation actuary concept, and methodologies suitable for the type of product being valued and its underwriting characteristics.

This Executive Summary reviews the recommendations given in the various sections of the report—they are provided here only as an abbreviated snapshot. The spirit of the valuation actuary and this final report, for this sometimes elusive and always complex product, can be served only by carefully considering these recommendations in the context in which they are presented in the various sections.

The valuation recommendations in this final report apply to individual (or quasi-individual) insurance products. They include individual, association group, and group in which the employee pays all or nearly all of the premium.

Two basic sets of tables are provided: one for institutional benefits (nursing home) and one for noninstitutional benefits (home health care). The valuation actuary should use each of these with judgment and should blend/combine them if the insurance policy has both types of benefits. This final report provides guidance to the valuation actuary on how to adjust and use both of the basic tables. The tables and guidance for their usage are presented in this final report as well as on the companion valuation diskette, which is available from the SOA office.

The LTC morbidity tables of Section II, Institutional Tables, and Section III, Noninstitutional Tables, are to be combined for policies with elements of both institutional and noninstitutional LTC insurance.

---

[1]Task Force membership is given in Section XIX.

The valuation diskette provides guidance on the use of those basic tables. Areas in which assumptions are needed to be made are identified, and default assumptions are included to permit the programs to function while the valuation actuary considers the appropriate assumptions to make. This is described in Appendix D, Screens of Valuation Diskette with Users Manual, and Appendix E, Documentation of Valuation Diskette Program. The LTC valuation actuary will find it beneficial to become familiar with that valuation diskette.

Depending on the product being valued, the morbidity tables given in this report might have to be adjusted for such elements as product features, benefit triggers, spousal discount, geographic region, and various risk classes (Section IV, Application of Tables).

An appropriate mortality table is one piece of the overall termination assumption to be used in the valuation of LTC insurance (Section V, Mortality). Consideration was given to constructing a new mortality table by adding conservatism to the unloaded 1980 CSO mortality rates, which would be achieved by lowering them somewhat and extending the table beyond age 100. After making a number of attempts to construct such a modified table, we observed that the 1983 GAM table had characteristics very similar to those of the desired new table. The 1983 GAM table was chosen because it is an existing, recognized, publicly used table that has the appropriate characteristics.

It is appropriate to allow terminations in excess of mortality (Section VI, Voluntary Lapses). The proposed practice allows 80% of the voluntary lapse assumption used when the policy was filed and priced for state approval to market the product, not to exceed 8%. Lapse termination can be used in addition to the mortality decrement without limit on the combination.

Sound underwriting is critical to proper risk management of a block of LTC insurance (Section VII, Selection and Antiselection). At a minimum, reserves should be based on the morbidity tables prescribed without select adjustments. The valuation actuary should consider whether to include select morbidity adjustments used in pricing. However, in all cases selection factors should grade to an ultimate selection factor of at least 1.00 by duration 10.

Voluntary lapses will be more frequent on lower cost (healthier) individuals. As a result, voluntary lapses should be expected to increase claim costs per remaining individual. If lapses are included in the reserve calculation, the valuation actuary should recognize that lapses will have an impact on morbidity. The valuation diskette allows the valuation actuary to quantify the effect of assumed antiselective lapses.

Recognizing the time value of money is an important part of sound actuarial principles and commonly accepted *Actuarial Standards of Practice* (ASOP) (Section VIII, Interest Rate). The maximum allowable interest rate for active life reserves for LTC policies issued in a given year should be equal to the maximum allowable interest rate for calculating reserves for whole life insurance policies (with maturities 20 or more years after issue) issued in the same year. The maximum allowable interest rate for claim reserves incurred in a given year should be equal to the maximum allowable interest rate for calculating reserves for whole life insurance policies issued in the year of the claim.

Asset adequacy testing should be performed if the product is material to the insurer. Tests involving the sensitivity to declining interest rates are more important than disintermediation, unless significant nonforfeiture benefits payable in the form of cash are available.

Whether active life reserves should be calculated on the net level, one-year preliminary term or two-year preliminary term basis is of some considerable interest (Section IX, Method). Each method is used by insurers today, especially the two methods based on preliminary term. The Task Force believes that either the one-year or two-year preliminary term method can be an appropriate statutory reserve method. The method used should be tested by the valuation actuary and fit the circumstances. For pieces of additional coverage purchased periodically at attained age premiums, the reserve for such pieces should be calculated on the net level basis unless expenses for the purchased pieces are higher than normal renewal expenses.

It is important to understand the reserving implications of various nonforfeiture benefit options (Section X, Nonforfeiture Benefits). Actuaries should be very cautious about using intuition in trying to assess how to determine reserves for LTC nonforfeiture benefit options. Because of the variety and great number of possible nonforfeiture benefit forms, their amounts and patterns, and the developing nature and uncertainty of the subject, this final report does not prescribe precise applicability of its recommendations to this subject. Rather, it offers several components of possible reserves to be considered.

Unusual patterns of nonforfeiture benefits may cause reserves to be deficient if actual lapses and mortality do not follow assumptions. Testing for sensitivity to variations in mortality and lapses should be done when there is any doubt about reserve adequacy. The active life reserve should not be less than the net single premium for the nonforfeiture benefits at each policy duration.

Waiver of premium product features vary (Chapter XI, Premium Waiver). Waiver upon institutionalization is a common benefit in LTC insurance. Some policies also waive premiums if the insured is approved for home health care.

The approach used to compute active life reserves generally will determine which of two techniques should be employed to properly value waiver of premium benefits: (1) the active life reserve assumes future premiums are received from all in-force policies regardless of benefit status, or (2) the active life reserve omits premiums to be waived from the present value of future premiums. Note that the valuation diskette accompanying this final report assumes that no premiums are paid once under waiver due to claim status and therefore also does not include waived premiums as a benefit.

For claim reserves and those for reported claims:

- On nursing home (institutional) benefits, this recommendation uses the continuance tables based on utilization data from the 1985 National Nursing Home Survey (NNHS) as interpreted and developed by the Long-Term Care Experience Committee of the SOA (*TSA 1988-89-90 Reports*, 1992, pp. 101–164) (Section XII, Claim Reserves). Any generally accepted actuarial method can be used to calculate the liabilities, as long as the reserve aggregate exceeds the minimum.

- On home health care (noninstitutional) benefits, claims should be defined no more liberally than beginning on the first date of care after the elimination period and ending on the first date on which no covered home health care benefits have been received for the prior 14 days. For all home health care claims for which more than 180 days of service have been received, reserves should be set up on a case-by-case basis, with the reserve being the present value of future expected home health care benefits for each open claim. For open home health care claims for which less than 90 days of service has been received, reserves may be set up using any method in conformity with *ASOP No. 5*, "Incurred Health Claim Liabilities," and *ASOP No. 18*, "Long-Term Care Insurance."

Reserves for claims incurred but unreported can be established using any method in conformity with *ASOP No. 5*, "Incurred Health Claim Liabilities," and *ASOP No. 18*, "Long-Term Care Insurance."

Claim reserves are required to make good and sufficient provision for future expected claim payments on all claims that have been incurred prior to the valuation date. If such provision results in the need for reserves higher than the minimums described above, then such higher reserves should be held.

LTC insurance policies are issued, with very rare exceptions, on a guaranteed renewable basis. This, coupled with the structure of level premium by issue age for a benefit with substantially increasing claim costs by attained age, presents significant implications for LTC valuation requirements (Section XIII, Future Changes in Assumptions and Pricing). For existing business, the valuation actuary should consider whether changes in expected experience may indicate that current statutory reserves are no longer adequate on a gross premium valuation basis.

For GAAP purposes, original assumptions would be chosen by using the most likely realistic best estimates, with a provision for adverse deviation. Original GAAP assumptions would continue to be used unless a premium deficiency is recognized. When assumptions are adjusted corresponding to a change in premium scales, the effect should be prospective with no change in GAAP liability at the premium change date. If any change in reserve assumptions results in a material impact on the company financial statement, further disclosure in the annual report could be required.

For a product with so many varied features, so recently on the market, and evolving rapidly, there is increasing emphasis on upgrades, internal replacements, and other changes to existing business (Section XIV, Upgrades and Conversions). The pace of such changes to in-force business is expected to continue. When determining the proper level of reserves for the new policy resulting from an upgrade or a conversion, the valuation actuary must consider several elements. If the premiums under the new policy are not adequate to cover future claims and expenses, an initial reserve needs to be established, either from the reserves of the old policy or from surplus. Premiums under the old block of policies that do not upgrade or convert may not be adequate if only the best risks participate in the program. In such a case, reserves under the old block would have to be strengthened. In any event, appropriate gross premium valuation tests may be warranted.

There are several ASOPs under the auspices of the Actuarial Standards Board (ASB) that relate to the development and application of these proposals for LTC valuation (Section XV, Actuarial Standards of Practice). They are listed and their relevance to this final report is identified, for example:

- *ASOP No. 5*, "Incurred Health Claim Liabilities." Clearly, the standard applies fully to the valuation of LTC benefits. In fact, such benefits are directly referred to in the text of the standard.
- *ASOP No. 7*, "Performing Cash Flow Testing for Insurers." Cash flow testing would be useful if the assets purchased to back a stand-alone LTC policy do not produce future cash flows that closely match the

liability cash flows. Normally, in today's situation, it would appear that for LTC policies without surrender values, backed by reasonably well-matched assets, with reasonably predictable maturities, more simple sensitivity testing of the insurance risk assumptions would satisfy the standard.

- *ASOP No. 8*, "Regulatory Filings for Rates and Financial Projections for Health Plans." While LTC insurance is not specifically mentioned in the standard, it seems clear that it is directly included in the scope.
- *ASOP No. 10*, "Methods and Assumptions for Use in Stock Life Insurance Companies Financial Statements Prepared in Accordance with GAAP." Most LTC policies would be subject to *FAS 60* methodology, where the GAAP active life and claim reserves have a provision for adverse deviation and assumptions are "locked in" for the life of a policy, unless the loss recognition test is failed.
- *ASOP No. 11*, "The Treatment of Reinsurance Transactions in Life and Health Insurance Company Financial Statements." This standard applies fully to LTC coverage as it does to all health and life coverage.
- *ASOP No. 14*, "When To Do Cash Flow Testing for Life and Health Insurance Companies." Sensitivity and other testing for LTC insurance may be more useful for the C-2 (insurance) risk than cash flow testing for the C-3 (interest) risk.
- *ASOP No. 18*, "Long-Term Care Insurance." The last several pages provide sound basic instructions for valuing health insurance in general and LTC in particular. A revised and updated ASOP will be pursued beginning in late 1995, based in part on the content of this final report.

Currently, the Internal Revenue Code (IRC) has no specific language for LTC insurance (Section XVI, Tax Reserves). The basis is not clear and is fairly complex, as this final report summarizes. The basis for tax reserves may well be one of the areas in which significant change occurs soon.

The NAIC risk-based capital (RBC) formula gives instructions for the handling of LTC insurance related to the insurance risk (C-2) for health insurance but is silent elsewhere regarding LTC (Section XVII, Risk-Based Capital). Instructions for the treatment of LTC in the RBC formula provide little direct guidance. Until more is learned, the best course for developing RBC would be to apply the disability income factors to LTC earned premiums. In addition, the 5% of claim reserves component prescribed for all health insurance should apply to LTC.

With respect to deficiency reserves, the LTC valuation actuary should give appropriate consideration to the nature of the premium guarantees, other policy provisions constraining premium rate changes, premium rate regulations, the impact of premium rate changes on policy lapsation, and the level of benefit utilization of persisting policies (Section XVIII, Reserve Adequacy). For the valuation actuary to provide a clean opinion, the reserves held should not only satisfy the formulas and assumptions required by law but also, at a high probability level when combined with future expected premiums, be able to provide all benefits and expenses expected to be paid under the policies. The valuation actuary must ensure that reserves are adequate within the provisions of the LTC policies being valued and the environment within which that is done. Deviation from well-established or soundly emerging practices and standards should take place only when that deviation is necessary for the valuation actuary to be responsible in valuing LTC insurance. This means the LTC valuation actuary must become familiar with the current relevant environment, both within and outside of the actuarial profession.

A discussion in Appendix A, Product Features, highlights many of the features that must be considered for valuation, among the many that vary with this insurance product.

Appendix B, Mighty Fine Insurance Company: A Case Study, illustrates the thinking the valuation actuary should pursue in applying the recommendations of this final report and its companion valuation diskette to a specific LTC plan. It also serves to describe the default set of assumptions and resulting output, which are compared with illustrative variants in Appendix C, Input/Output of Some Cases Tested.

Appendix D, Screens of Diskette with Users Manual, and Appendix E, Documentation of Diskette Program, give assistance to the valuation actuary using the valuation diskette as a companion to this final report.

Appendix F, Current NAIC Models, gives the current valuation provisions for LTC insurance adopted by the NAIC.

I. INTRODUCTION

This final report of the Society of Actuaries Long-Term Care Insurance Valuation Methods Task Force presents the valuation recommendations for this product, as defined herein, to members of the actuarial profession, insurance regulators, and other interested parties.

A. The Charge

The NAIC requested the SOA to address the valuation needs for long-term care (LTC) insurance in a December 19, 1990 letter from John Montgomery, then Chair of the NAIC Life and Health Actuarial Task Force. The letter stated, in part, as follows:

> The NAIC Life and Health Actuarial Task Force requests that an appropriate committee of the Society of Actuaries undertake the following projects:
> 1. Develop a morbidity table, suitable for statutory valuation purposes, for long-term [sic] insurance. The valuation table should address the variety of product designs and "gatekeeper" mechanisms that exist in the market today.
> 2. Develop a mortality table. ...

As a result of that request, this Task Force was formed in the summer of 1991. Its charge reads as follows:

> This Task Force will develop recommendations for the valuation of long-term care insurance products, incorporating, as appropriate, an interim method, available data, the valuation actuary concept, and methodologies suitable for the type of product being valued and its underwriting characteristics.

B. United States Only

It is important to note this final report addresses the valuation actuary's environment only in the U.S.

C. The NAIC

From the very beginning it has been clear that one of the most important stakeholder groups for this venture is LTC insurance regulators. The regulators take somewhat diverse views in their several states on certain features of LTC insurance (for example, benefits to be provided, benefit triggers, and nonforfeiture benefits). However, they can be thought of, for the purpose of this final report, as the NAIC. The extent to which the NAIC may choose to adopt these valuation recommendations, and the timing of doing so, are of course beyond the purview of this Task Force. Even less certain is how these recommendations will play into those actually applied by the various states. The Task Force, or succeeding remnants thereof, stand ready to assist in those efforts, especially the interpretation and understanding of these recommendations, if requested.

The full relevant quotations from the current existing NAIC models are found in Appendix F.

It is clear that, to date, LTC insurance has been retrofitted for valuation purposes into a model regulation that generally does not apply to level premium (albeit guaranteed renewable) contracts with substantial prefunding and no available insured claim experience. There clearly is a regulatory need that the actuarial profession should address. This final report attempts to meet that need.

D. Products Addressed

The Task Force defined the LTC insurance products that it should address. The resulting definition, determined at the beginning of the Task Force's deliberations, remained through the preparation of this final report. The definition is specifically confined to stand-alone products but still covers the vast majority of LTC insurance products marketed.

1. Stand-Alone Long-Term Care Products

a. Individual (or Quasi-Individual) Products

It is clear that reserve standards for these coverages appropriately would be contained in any health valuation law or regulation. Available insured claim data, such as they are, are almost entirely from these products. Any methodologies developed for individual products may or may not be appropriate for other types of products. The valuation recommendations in this final report apply to these individual (or quasi-individual) insurance products. They include the following.

- *Individual.* Though there is substantial variation of product design (see Appendix A), these products all exist to pay benefits for LTC. Some pay benefits only for nursing home (institutional) stays; some pay only for home health care visits or other community services (noninstitutional); and some pay for both. Some pay regardless of whether LTC services are being provided from paid providers; most require paid services. These products are all individually underwritten, though the extent of underwriting varies considerably. Because of the sharply rising claim costs by attained age, any of these products will require policy reserves unless the premium structure is attained age (annual renewable term).

- *Association Group*. These products are very similar to individual LTC products. The association group contract is usually filed in one state, and certificates are issued much like individual contracts, perhaps in multiple states. The insured usually pays for the coverage from personal funds. Employment relationship or organization membership often is not required to be eligible for coverage. Reserve requirements should be the same as those for otherwise similar individual products.
- *Group (Employee Pays All)*. These products are also similar to individual LTC products. They are marketed most commonly to employee groups. Often spouses, parents, and other close relatives of the employee are also eligible for coverage. Premiums are usually level and based on issue age. After issue the coverage usually does not depend on continued employment. The extent of underwriting varies, even within a group, such as between employees and other covered lives; evidence of insurability is almost always required for nonemployees and may also be required for employees, because participation tends to be low. Reserve requirements should be the same as those for otherwise similar individual products.

b. True Group Products (Employer Pays a Substantial Portion of Premium)

This coverage would be true group insurance, in which full or nearly full participation is achieved because the employer pays much, even all, of the cost. There is little or no underwriting. The insured usually needs to stay with the employer to participate. Premiums tend to be based on annual cost of insurance. Pension-type funding and valuation would seem appropriate. This product was a low priority for the Task Force, because these products are not likely to develop very far without at least clarification of their tax status. They are not included in these valuation recommendations, though many elements appropriately could be applied.

2. Long-Term Care Riders on Life Insurance Products

These riders can be attached to life insurance products at issue or extended to in-force contracts. They grant the right to receive an LTC benefit.

- *Riders in Which the LTC Benefit Does Not Reduce the Death Benefit*. These riders provide an LTC benefit that is not integrated with the death benefit, and the premium is also separable. Thus, for reserve purposes these riders are independent of the base policy and are substantially similar to stand-alone products; methodologies developed for stand-alone

LTC products are likely to be transferrable to these products. The valuation recommendations of this final report should apply.

- *Riders in Which the LTC Benefit Reduces the Death Benefit and/or Cash Surrender Value.* These riders essentially begin payment of the death benefit while the insured is still alive. Usually nursing home (institutional) confinement is required for benefit eligibility. Typically the payment is 1%–2% per month of the original death benefit. Commonly, the death benefit is reduced by the LTC benefits received. The cost for the rider can vary from zero (when the LTC benefit is essentially a loan against the life insurance contract) to a significant amount (when there is substantial additional benefit). In some cases the reserve impact is minor, and in others the LTC benefit needs to be an integral part of the total reserve calculations (when the two benefits are significantly integrated). Developing reserve recommendations for these products is important, but it should be done by the actuarial profession after the stand-alone products addressed by this final report have been taken care of.

3. Long-Term Care Options on Annuity Products

These products provide additional annuity income benefits when LTC is received or provide LTC benefits packaged with an annuity. Because LTC benefits combined with annuities are not yet common in the market and because they raise unique complexities, they are not addressed by this final report.

4. Long-Term Care Insurability Guarantees Attached to Other Products

These provisions allow issue of an LTC product in the future without evidence of insurability. The feature may or may not have a separate premium. The reserve would simply be an accumulation for the inherent anti-selection. These provisions were not addressed by the Task Force.

E. General Valuation Approach

The following points summarize the basic characteristics of the valuation approach that is described in this final report.

- The work of the LTC valuation actuary must be consistent with the profession's general valuation actuary concepts. Any tables provided must be used with considerable judgment.
- Because of the many significant variations in products—how they are marketed, underwritten, and upgraded, and their claims adjudicated—it

is not possible to derive an adequate number of tables that can or should be applied simply by selecting from such a catalog.

- The practicing LTC valuation actuary, nonetheless, needs to be practical. True, the variations in certain product features (for example, benefit triggers) or underwriting standards (which are extremely important to LTC insurance) can have a direct and significant impact on LTC insurance risks. However, to some extent, that is also true for risks inherent in other products such as life insurance.
- Two basic sets of tables are provided: one for institutional benefits (nursing home) and one for noninstitutional benefits (home health care). The valuation actuary is to use each of these with judgment and should blend/combine them if the insurance policy has both types of benefits. This final report provides guidance to the valuation actuary on how to adjust and use both of the basic sets of tables.
- The tables and guidance for their usage are found in this final report as well as on the companion valuation diskette, available from the SOA office. This is much like the approach taken for disability income valuation, with the CIDA (Commissioners' Individual Disability Tables A) adopted in 1985 (*TSA*, Vol. XXXVII, pp. 449–601) and CGDT (Commissioners' Group Disability Tables) adopted in 1987 (*TSA*, Vol. XXXIX, pp. 393–458).

F. The Valuation Diskette

The diskette does not contain the actual set of recommendations the valuation actuary should follow (this final report does). Rather, the valuation diskette provides a useful tool for applying the guidance found herein, and it contains the morbidity tables the valuation actuary should employ as the underlying basis.

The use of the valuation diskette is fully described in Appendix D, and its programs are documented in Appendix E.

The valuation diskette contains the following features:

- It provides, as output, net premiums and reserves by issue age and duration for a chosen base policy.
- The valuation diskette permits use of net level, one-year preliminary term (1YPT) and two-year preliminary term (2YPT) valuation methods.
- The valuation diskette uses mortality, lapse, and interest rates, as described in other sections, with the ability for the user to vary those assumptions.

- It allows the user to make assumptions about: selection at issue and antiselection at lapse; inflation protection; daily benefit amounts; non-forfeiture benefits; length of the premium paying period; and mix by sex. These are fully documented in the appendixes of this final report.

The default assumptions are contained in the valuation diskette so that its programs will function as the valuation actuary explores what should be used. The insurer's tools are not intended to be supplanted by this tool. Rather, the valuation actuary may choose to develop tools other than this referenced companion valuation diskette or the insurer's current tools or to modify existing ones; information is provided to assist that process, if desired.

G. The Mighty Fine Insurance Company

This is described in Appendix B. The valuation actuary will find that this is helpful background for understanding the use of the valuation diskette and its default case.

II. INSTITUTIONAL TABLES

A. LTC Morbidity Data

As is generally known, there is very little LTC insured data upon which to base pricing or reserving of this product. Almost all data are from public sources (surveys, Medicare, state programs, etc.)—some from outside the U.S.—but most data that are particularly relevant are from within the U.S.

The SOA has pursued two activities to help address this problem:

- Since 1986 the SOA LTC Experience Task Force (now Committee) has pursued an intercompany study of LTC experience; this study is being made public for the first time in early 1995. Contributions from 10 companies covered exposure years 1984–91. Virtually no data for noninstitutional coverage were contributed. This Committee also has been pursuing other data sources.
- In 1991, in the *1988-89-90 TSA Reports* the SOA published an article on the 1985 National Nursing Home Survey (NNHS) Utilization Data (principal authors: John Wilkin, Gordon Trapnell, and Holen Chang), under the auspices of the SOA LTC Experience Committee. This 1985 NNHS is the principal data source used by actuaries for measuring nursing home (institutional) benefits. It serves as the basis of this final report's recommendations for nursing home claim costs.

In general, the difficulty in gathering and developing useful LTC morbidity data flows from three characteristics of the product:

- Only in recent years has it been marketed in any volume, so relatively little experience exists.
- The product has changed considerably in the last few years, in ways that have significant impact on claims—actual and anticipated.
- Little is known about future results due to antiselection, effects of lapsation, changes in underwriting awareness and claim adjudication, policy definitions (for example, activities of daily living), medical advances (for example, Alzheimer's), and other environmental impacts.

The insured claim data for institutional benefits are quite uncertain. They are even more uncertain for noninstitutional benefits.

B. Overview

The institutional tables are on the valuation diskette, as described in the appendixes of this final report. Examples from the tables are shown in this section. The valuation diskette provides continuance tables, which can be used appropriately by elimination period and maximum benefit period, in either days and years or in dollars.

The institutional tables are based on the 1985 NNHS, as interpreted and developed further in the *1988-89-90 TSA Reports*. The reader is referred to that source if additional details about the data are needed.

C. Standard Table and Adjustments

The reserves for institutional care are based on utilization data from the 1985 NNHS as interpreted and developed by the SOA LTC Experience Committee. In particular, this final report uses the rates from the *Reports* article for insurable stays, using the benefit period concept as explained therein. This concept combines nursing home stays that are interrupted by a hospital stay or transfers between nursing homes. The admission rates are from Tables 1 and 2 in the *Reports* article (for males and females, respectively), while the continuance table is from Table 17 in that report. (While the tables presented in this section correspond to the "insurable stays" basis described in the *Reports* article, both the "insurable stays" and "all stays" tables, both using the benefit period concept, are available for use with the valuation diskette. Case 11 of Appendix C demonstrates the impact of utilizing "all stays.")

As mentioned in that article, the SOA LTC Experience Committee did not develop these utilization rates from the point of view of a valuation actuary attempting to produce rates directly appropriate for the reserving of LTC insurance products. This Task Force believes, however, that the utilization rates from the 1985 NNHS are not too dissimilar from insured experience, although somewhat conservative. The degree of conservatism depends on many factors, including the strictness of the LTC product's underwriting criteria and benefit triggers. Some conservatism of course is considered appropriate for the purpose of establishing statutory reserves.

In addition, the Task Force has anticipated that the valuation actuary may wish to modify the utilization rates from the NNHS. Therefore, the companion valuation diskette produced by the Task Force contains a factor that multiplies each of the admission rates from the 1985 NNHS. The choice of the factor to be used in valuation is the responsibility of the valuation actuary. Considerations in this choice include the following:

- The 1985 NNHS is based on the general population instead of an insured population, although an attempt was made in the *Reports* to adjust the 1985 NNHS experience to be more applicable to an insured population.
- The environment in 1985 was one of very little insurance, so that nearly all nursing home residents had to pay for their care out-of-pocket or through Medicaid after depletion of nearly all their assets.
- In 1985, many states limited their nursing home bed supply in an effort to hold down Medicaid costs, yet individuals with private insurance might not have been as restricted in their access to nursing homes as the controls on the overall supply would suggest.
- The effects of selection at underwriting and antiselection at lapse (as discussed in Section VII) must be considered. The valuation diskette provides factors for both of these effects.
- The effects of product features (as discussed in Section IV and in Appendix A) must be considered.
- The 1985 NNHS admission rates do not reflect the effect of benefit triggers, such as activities of daily living (ADL), cognitive impairment (CI), or medical necessity.
- The effects of various premium classifications must be considered.

D. Method of Application of Rates

1. Admission Rates

There are two main considerations in applying the nursing home admission rates to calculate reserves: the exposure and the sex mix.

a. Exposure

The admission rates as published in the *Reports* were derived by dividing admissions by the noninstitutionalized population. Therefore, to be consistent, the admission rates to be used by the valuation actuary should be applied to an exposure calculated as the total number of policies in force less the number of policies for those residents in nursing homes. The valuation diskette applies the admission rates derived from Tables 1 and 2 in the *Reports* article to an estimate of this exposure, in order to calculate admissions in each policy year. That estimated exposure relies on the number of nursing home residents at the beginning of each policy year being estimated from the number of prior admissions and the probability of those admissions being still resident. Those probabilities of still being resident were obtained from continuance Table 11 in the *Reports* article.

Note that the continuance table used for estimating the number of nursing home residents is the "proportion of admissions still resident" table (which can be thought of as a "person" table, because it shows the distribution of persons by length of stay) as opposed to the "proportion of days after" table (which can be thought of as a "days" table, because it shows the distribution of days by length of stay). The estimate of the number of nursing home residents affects only the exposure and has a relatively minor effect on the reserve calculation.

The valuation diskette that is a companion to this final report uses a continuance function as an approximation to the actual person continuance Table 11 from the *Reports* article. The functional form is based on that presented in the 1959 *Transactions* article "Continuance Functions" by E. Paul Barnhart (Vol. XI, p. 649). The Barnhart function uses duration of stay as the only parameter; this was modified slightly in order to take into account that lengths of stay generally become shorter with higher admission ages. Table 1 compares the actual continuance table from the *Reports* article with the approximations derived by the continuance function approach, for admission ages 75–84 as an example. The table approach would more accurately model the effect of the elimination period and the maximum benefit amount, but results shown in Table 1 demonstrate the reasonableness of using the function approach.

b. Sex Mix

Even though LTC policies usually are priced on a unisex basis, nursing home admission rates vary significantly by sex. Therefore, the Task Force

TABLE 1

COMPARISON OF PROPORTION OF ADMISSIONS STILL RESIDENT
AT THE END OF THE PERIOD SHOWN
ADMISSION AGES 75–84; INSURABLE STAYS; BENEFIT PERIOD CONCEPT;
ADJUSTED TO MATCH THE 1985 NNHS RESIDENTS

Days from Admission (t)	Table 11 from 1988-89-90 Reports	Function = Formula Estimation	Function Less Table
0	1.0000	1.0000	0.0000
10	0.9212	0.9243	0.0031
20	0.8441	0.8485	0.0044
30	0.7728	0.7728	0.0000
60	0.6633	0.7102	0.0469
90	0.5858	0.6553	0.0695
121	0.5298	0.6052	0.0754
182	0.4570	0.5227	0.0657
365	0.3581	0.3581	0.0000
730	0.2497	0.2009	−0.0488
1095	0.1710	0.1292	−0.0418
1460	0.1185	0.0900	−0.0285
1825	0.0791	0.0661	−0.0130
2190	0.0504	0.0504	0.0000
2555	0.0306	0.0395	0.0089
2920	0.0179	0.0316	0.0137
3285	0.0103	0.0256	0.0153
3650	0.0059	0.0211	0.0152

thought it appropriate that the valuation actuary use sex-distinct tables to calculate reserves. However, unisex tables may be determined based on the sex mix at issue for each of the policies to be valued. If the sex mix is not known, the Task Force suggests that the mix be assumed to be 60% female and 40% male.

See test Cases 1 and 2 in Appendix C for the impact of differing assumptions about sex.

For unisex tables, the valuation diskette allows the valuation actuary to enter the proportion of policies sold that are female. From this proportion, a unique unisex table is created for each issue age. (The valuation actuary may choose to make sex-distinct tables by using factors of 0%/100% for female/male, or vice versa.) The valuation diskette first calculates a unisex mortality table by calculating the "l_x" for each age from issue until the end of life, separately for males and females. The radix for females is equal to 100,000 times the proportion female, while the radix for males is 100,000 less the female radix. The unisex "l_x" is calculated at each age as the sum of the sex-distinct l_x's, and then unisex mortality rates are calculated based on the ratio of succeeding unisex l_x's. Finally, unisex admission rates are calculated by weighing the sex-specific admission rates at each age by the l_x's. This results in a gradually increasing percentage female.

The admission rates and average lengths of stay used by the Task Force are shown in Table 2.

TABLE 2

ADMISSION RATE AND AVERAGE LENGTH OF STAY (ALOS)

Age	Males		Females	
	Admission Rate (%)	ALOS (Days)	Admission Rate (%)	ALOS (Days)
30	0.01	830	0.01	1,098
31	0.01	828	0.01	1,101
32	0.01	825	0.01	1,105
33	0.01	822	0.01	1,109
34	0.01	818	0.01	1,114
35	0.01	813	0.01	1,120
36	0.01	807	0.01	1,125
37	0.01	800	0.01	1,132
38	0.02	793	0.02	1,138
39	0.02	785	0.02	1,144
40	0.03	776	0.02	1,150
41	0.05	767	0.02	1,156
42	0.06	757	0.03	1,162
43	0.08	748	0.03	1,166
44	0.10	738	0.03	1,170
45	0.12	729	0.03	1,172
46	0.14	720	0.04	1,172
47	0.14	712	0.04	1,171
48	0.14	705	0.04	1,167
49	0.13	699	0.05	1,162
50	0.13	693	0.05	1,153
51	0.12	689	0.06	1,143
52	0.12	685	0.07	1,129
53	0.13	681	0.07	1,113
54	0.14	678	0.08	1,094
55	0.16	674	0.09	1,073
56	0.18	670	0.10	1,049
57	0.20	666	0.11	1,024
58	0.22	660	0.13	996
59	0.23	653	0.15	966
60	0.24	644	0.18	936
61	0.26	634	0.22	904
62	0.27	622	0.27	872
63	0.28	608	0.34	839
64	0.30	593	0.42	808

TABLE 2—*Continued*

Age	Males		Females	
	Admission Rate (%)	ALOS (Days)	Admission Rate (%)	ALOS (Days)
65	0.32	577	0.51	778
66	0.36	561	0.61	750
67	0.43	543	0.72	725
68	0.52	525	0.83	703
69	0.65	507	0.95	684
70	0.82	489	1.07	669
71	1.03	471	1.21	656
72	1.28	453	1.36	646
73	1.57	436	1.56	639
74	1.89	419	1.81	633
75	2.24	404	2.13	628
76	2.60	390	2.53	624
77	2.99	378	3.02	621
78	3.39	369	3.59	618
79	3.82	361	4.24	615
80	4.29	356	4.97	612
81	4.80	353	5.78	609
82	5.36	352	6.65	604
83	6.00	352	7.58	599
84	6.73	353	8.56	594
85	7.57	355	9.58	588
86	8.52	356	10.63	583
87	9.60	358	11.70	577
88	10.81	358	12.76	571
89	12.16	357	13.80	566
90	13.67	355	14.82	561
91	15.33	352	15.80	556
92	17.17	346	16.73	550
93	19.19	339	17.62	544
94	21.39	331	18.46	538
95	23.80	321	19.26	532
96	26.41	309	20.03	525
97	29.23	296	20.78	518
98	32.27	281	21.51	510
99	35.52	265	22.24	503
100	38.99	249	22.97	496
101	42.67	230	23.73	488
102	46.57	211	24.52	481
103	50.69	191	25.34	473
104	55.02	169	26.20	466
105	59.57	150	27.10	458
106	64.34	150	28.05	450
107	69.32	150	20.04	443
108	74.52	150	30.07	435
109	79.93	150	31.15	427
110	84.95	150	32.37	419

The Task Force notes that the admission rate for males crosses from below the female rate for ages 91 and younger to above the female rate for ages 92 and older. In addition, the male rates attain a rather high level after age 100. The Task Force tested the sensitivity of using unisex admission rates after age 91. The resulting reserves, assuming 60% female sales, were greater than those under the published admission rates, but by only a fraction of 1% for reserves at attained ages less than 95. Therefore, it was decided to use the published admission rates as the recommendation.

2. Continuance Table

The average length of stay (ALOS) is equal to the average number of days in a total stay, per admission. However, not all those days would generate a benefit payment because of the elimination period and maximum benefit period. In theory, using the "days" continuance table in order to estimate the proportion of a total stay that will fall within the benefit period (that is, after the elimination period and before the lifetime maximum) is relatively straightforward. There are a few decisions, however, that must be made in the detailed use of the table. These include the methods of interpolation between the discrete points in the table and the sex mix. The continuance table contains a set of probabilities for each sex separately for specific thresholds by age group. The valuation diskette does a two-way linear interpolation between age groups and thresholds. It is assumed that the continuance table for each age group represents the mid-age of the group. After the proportion of days within the maximum benefit period have been determined, these proportions are applied to the average length of stay in order to determine the average number of days per admission for which benefits are paid.

In order to handle the sex mix, a unisex continuance table is calculated from the sex-distinct tables in a manner similar to that used for calculating the unisex mortality table. The distributions of days for a cohort of male admissions and a cohort of female admissions are calculated separately and then combined in proportion to the sex distribution of the admissions, to create a unisex distribution. The continuance tables recommended by the Task Force are shown in Table 3, for males, and in Table 4, for females.

TABLE 3

PROPORTION OF DAYS AFTER THE PERIOD SHOWN; FOR MALES; INSURABLE STAYS;
BENEFIT PERIOD CONCEPT; ADJUSTED TO MATCH THE 1985 NNHS RESIDENTS

Days from Admission	Age at Admission						
	<45	45–54	55–64	65–74	75–84	85–94	95+
0	1.0000	1.0000	1.0000	1.0000	1.0000	1.0000	1.0000
10	0.9878	0.9844	0.9839	0.9786	0.9707	0.9711	0.9590
20	0.9773	0.9713	0.9705	0.9607	0.9470	0.9480	0.9243
30	0.9672	0.9589	0.9580	0.9442	0.9253	0.9270	0.8926
60	0.9396	0.9245	0.9243	0.9003	0.8689	0.8703	0.8092
90	0.9156	0.8949	0.8949	0.8626	0.8210	0.8208	0.7433
121	0.8937	0.8675	0.8678	0.8283	0.7776	0.7753	0.6878
151	0.8746	0.8432	0.8438	0.7985	0.7400	0.7357	0.6429
182	0.8565	0.8195	0.8208	0.7701	0.7044	0.6983	0.6033
212	0.8401	0.7976	0.7999	0.7444	0.6724	0.6648	0.5698
243	0.8242	0.7757	0.7795	0.7192	0.6413	0.6326	0.5391
273	0.8095	0.7551	0.7607	0.6959	0.6128	0.6032	0.5124
304	0.7949	0.7343	0.7420	0.6727	0.5848	0.5745	0.4872
334	0.7813	0.7147	0.7248	0.6509	0.5589	0.5480	0.4647
365	0.7678	0.6949	0.7077	0.6291	0.5333	0.5218	0.4430
547	0.6971	0.5925	0.6210	0.5134	0.4039	0.3856	0.3345
730	0.6395	0.5166	0.5530	0.4189	0.3044	0.2741	0.2393
912	0.5897	0.4583	0.4935	0.3408	0.2314	0.1906	0.1591
1095	0.5420	0.4063	0.4359	0.2721	0.1793	0.1328	0.1098
1277	0.4951	0.3609	0.3839	0.2148	0.1415	0.0931	0.0838
1460	0.4480	0.3209	0.3406	0.1683	0.1117	0.0640	0.0652
1642	0.4012	0.2829	0.3025	0.1290	0.0885	0.0427	0.0481
1825	0.3544	0.2490	0.2653	0.0941	0.0704	0.0269	0.0314
2190	0.2710	0.1988	0.2000	0.0474	0.0432	0.0069	0.0124
2555	0.2056	0.1561	0.1498	0.0245	0.0256	0.0006	0.0076
2920	0.1543	0.1204	0.1107	0.0131	0.0148	0.0000	0.0054
3285	0.1143	0.0914	0.0803	0.0073	0.0084	0.0000	0.0040
3650	0.0834	0.0682	0.0569	0.0042	0.0048	0.0000	0.0031
4015	0.0598	0.0502	0.0391	0.0026	0.0027	0.0000	0.0023
4380	0.0421	0.0364	0.0259	0.0016	0.0016	0.0000	0.0017
4745	0.0292	0.0261	0.0166	0.0011	0.0009	0.0000	0.0012
5110	0.0199	0.0185	0.0102	0.0007	0.0006	0.0000	0.0007
5475	0.0134	0.0131	0.0062	0.0005	0.0004	0.0000	0.0003
5840	0.0091	0.0092	0.0037	0.0003	0.0002	0.0000	0.0000
6205	0.0061	0.0064	0.0022	0.0002	0.0001	0.0000	0.0000
6570	0.0040	0.0045	0.0013	0.0001	0.0001	0.0000	0.0000
6935	0.0027	0.0030	0.0008	0.0001	0.0000	0.0000	0.0000
7300	0.0017	0.0020	0.0005	0.0001	0.0000	0.0000	0.0000
7665	0.0011	0.0013	0.0003	0.0000	0.0000	0.0000	0.0000
8030	0.0006	0.0008	0.0001	0.0000	0.0000	0.0000	0.0000
8395	0.0003	0.0004	0.0001	0.0000	0.0000	0.0000	0.0000
8760	0.0001	0.0002	0.0000	0.0000	0.0000	0.0000	0.0000
9125	0.0000	0.0000	0.0000	0.0000	0.0000	0.0000	0.0000
ALOS	820	667	669	488	355	361	258

TABLE 4

PROPORTION OF DAYS AFTER THE PERIOD SHOWN; FOR FEMALES; INSURABLE STAYS;
BENEFIT PERIOD CONCEPT; ADJUSTED TO MATCH THE 1985 NNHS RESIDENTS

Days from Admission	Age at Admission						
	<45	45–54	55–64	65–74	75–84	85–94	95+
0	1.0000	1.0000	1.0000	1.0000	1.0000	1.0000	1.0000
10	0.9905	0.9908	0.9889	0.9840	0.9826	0.9813	0.9789
20	0.9829	0.9828	0.9797	0.9706	0.9680	0.9657	0.9610
30	0.9758	0.9754	0.9711	0.9584	0.9546	0.9511	0.9441
60	0.9554	0.9556	0.9474	0.9257	0.9184	0.9115	0.8968
90	0.9356	0.9390	0.9268	0.8974	0.8865	0.8768	0.8538
121	0.9156	0.9238	0.9078	0.8714	0.8568	0.8445	0.8131
151	0.8968	0.9105	0.8908	0.8483	0.8303	0.8158	0.7770
182	0.8778	0.8974	0.8742	0.8259	0.8048	0.7879	0.7428
212	0.8598	0.8854	0.8589	0.8054	0.7814	0.7622	0.7121
243	0.8417	0.8733	0.8436	0.7849	0.7583	0.7368	0.6827
273	0.8245	0.8619	0.8292	0.7656	0.7369	0.7130	0.6561
304	0.8072	0.8504	0.8145	0.7462	0.7154	0.6892	0.6304
334	0.7908	0.8393	0.8006	0.7278	0.6953	0.6667	0.6069
365	0.7743	0.8281	0.7865	0.7091	0.6751	0.6441	0.5840
547	0.6841	0.7667	0.7098	0.6070	0.5665	0.5231	0.4710
730	0.5988	0.7166	0.6436	0.5199	0.4722	0.4210	0.3826
912	0.5206	0.6739	0.5862	0.4494	0.3908	0.3364	0.3119
1095	0.4580	0.6330	0.5358	0.3901	0.3200	0.2644	0.2540
1277	0.4068	0.5934	0.4906	0.3389	0.2601	0.2041	0.2068
1460	0.3587	0.5570	0.4470	0.2934	0.2091	0.1553	0.1676
1642	0.3164	0.5234	0.4047	0.2531	0.1665	0.1179	0.1335
1825	0.2833	0.4903	0.3627	0.2160	0.1313	0.0877	0.1032
2190	0.2290	0.4281	0.2906	0.1550	0.0795	0.0428	0.0554
2555	0.1813	0.3738	0.2380	0.1121	0.0474	0.0176	0.0217
2920	0.1400	0.3276	0.1986	0.0821	0.0283	0.0062	0.0049
3285	0.1050	0.2889	0.1684	0.0612	0.0172	0.0019	0.0004
3650	0.0759	0.2565	0.1446	0.0464	0.0109	0.0006	0.0000
4015	0.0527	0.2290	0.1254	0.0359	0.0072	0.0002	0.0000
4380	0.0350	0.2051	0.1095	0.0282	0.0050	0.0001	0.0000
4745	0.0221	0.1836	0.0958	0.0224	0.0036	0.0001	0.0000
5110	0.0134	0.1637	0.0838	0.0180	0.0026	0.0000	0.0000
5475	0.0079	0.1449	0.0728	0.0144	0.0019	0.0000	0.0000
5840	0.0047	0.1270	0.0626	0.0114	0.0014	0.0000	0.0000
6205	0.0027	0.1099	0.0533	0.0090	0.0011	0.0000	0.0000
6570	0.0016	0.0937	0.0446	0.0070	0.0008	0.0000	0.0000
6935	0.0009	0.0783	0.0366	0.0053	0.0005	0.0000	0.0000
7300	0.0005	0.0636	0.0293	0.0039	0.0004	0.0000	0.0000
7665	0.0003	0.0496	0.0225	0.0028	0.0003	0.0000	0.0000
8030	0.0002	0.0363	0.0162	0.0019	0.0002	0.0000	0.0000
8395	0.0001	0.0236	0.0103	0.0011	0.0001	0.0000	0.0000
8760	0.0000	0.0115	0.0050	0.0005	0.0000	0.0000	0.0000
9125	0.0000	0.0000	0.0000	0.0000	0.0000	0.0000	0.0000
ALOS	1107	1186	959	664	614	565	497

III. NONINSTITUTIONAL TABLE[2]

The limitations on LTC data in general and institutional data in particular, as expressed in Section II, apply even more strongly to noninstitutional data. Because of the absence of any publicly available noninstitutional data useful for valuation, this Task Force has undertaken a study of the 1982–84 National Long-Term Care Surveys (NLTCS). The results are prescribed here for valuation.

Proper valuation of noninstitutional benefits relies heavily upon the principles of the valuation actuary concept. Use of the tables presented in this chapter requires that valuation actuaries make explicit their aggregate assessment of the impact of such items as benefit triggers, underwriting standards, and claim administration practices. The section begins with a brief description of the data source and the methodology used to construct the tables. Next, the table values are presented and discussed. Finally, consideration is given to proper use of the tables.

A. Data Source: The National LTC Survey (NLTCS)

The NLTCS is a longitudinal survey of a random sample of Medicare enrollees exhibiting chronic ADL or instrumental activity of daily living (IADL) impairment. Screening interviews of 36,000 randomly selected Medicare enrollees in 1982 identified 6,393 community residents and 1,992 institutional residents with such impairments. Detailed interviews were obtained from 6,088 disabled community residents, while institutional residents were not questioned further. Follow-up surveys in 1984 and 1989 rescreened the surviving 1982 population, screened additional new Medicare enrollees, and conducted detailed interviews with both disabled community and institutional residents. The 1984 follow-up survey produced 5,934 community and 1,728 institutional questionnaires. The 1989 follow-up survey produced 4,463 community and 1,354 institutional questionnaires. Public use files containing the NLTCS screening and detailed interview results were used in the construction of the noninstitutional LTC tables of this section.

Unfortunately, the initial release of the 1989 NLTCS data was unusable, because there was no distinction between individuals screened out by reason of death and individuals screened out due to lack of chronic ADL/IADL impairment. A recent re-release of the 1989 survey results may provide this

[2] Much of the material of this section is based upon research conducted by Jim Robinson and funded, in part, by an award from the National Science Foundation (No. 9110891).

information. Rather than incorporate the revised information and further delay this final report, the Task Force constructed the noninstitutional table from the 1982 and 1984 survey responses alone.

The SOA LTC Experience Committee is currently analyzing insured data and the NLTCS data, including the revised 1989 survey results. Again, rather than wait for the Experience Committee's report, the Task Force decided to present its work without further delay.

Careful consideration should be given to whether the tables of this final report should be updated, whenever credible LTC experience becomes available, from whatever source.

B. Methodology

LTC claim incidence rates and claim costs are a function of the policyholder's health status (ADL and CI) and subsequent use of available services (institutional, noninstitutional, and informal). Health status, for whatever challenges it presents, is more easily studied and more reliably projected than service utilization. Health status is more likely to be out of the individual's control than is service use. Service utilization depends upon the individual's perceived service options, available financing, and disposition toward using LTC services, all subject to change over time. Consequently, the noninstitutional tables have been constructed to provide projections of future health status, but require that the valuation actuary determine the appropriate service utilization and frequency rates for each such health status.

The 1982 and 1984 NLTCSs include questions on the ADL and CI statuses of those questioned at both points in time. This information was analyzed in the following steps.

1. To simplify the analysis, ADL status alone was considered initially. Later, CI was conditionally examined based upon the individual's ADL status development.

   The 1982 and 1984 interviews were summarized by ADL status. Unless deceased, those screened out were assumed to be zero ADL-impaired. Detailed interviews were classified as 0, 1, 2, or 3+ ADL-impaired, requiring active human assistance, as opposed to supervision only. The six ADLs considered were eating, bathing, dressing, toileting, transference, and mobility. IADLs were not considered.

   The resulting 1982 and 1984 ADL status pairs were summarized by sex and 1982 age group to form six observed transition matrices, three each for males and females, for 1982 ages of below age 65, 65–74, and 75 and over for each sex. These matrices are shown in Table 5. As an example, the first section of the table shows the observed transition matrix for males age 65–74 in 1982. The table indicates, for example, that of 8,108 unimpaired individuals in 1982, 749 died by 1984, 7,165 remained unimpaired, and the remaining 194 became ADL-impaired and were still alive and impaired as shown in 1984. Despite the sparsity of data in some cells, the observed transition matrices provide some information about movement from one ADL status to another over the two years from 1982 to 1984.

2. Maximum likelihood estimation was used to fit a constant force of transition (CFT) model to the six observed sex/age group transition matrices. The CFT model assumes that the forces of transition from one ADL status to another are constant over time, at least over a two-year period. The constant transition forces may vary by sex, age group, starting ADL status, and destination ADL status (including death). The CFT model is similar to the constant force of mortality assumption frequently used within a year of age in mortality table analyses. In the CFT case, however, there are several statuses other than living or dead.

Note that many other model forms might also be fit to the observed transition matrices. Such alternative models might allow transition rates to vary through time or by duration in current status, both reasonable structures. However, because of the form of the data, the sparsity of the data, and a desire for model simplicity, the more restrictive CFT model was adopted for this analysis.

Table 6 displays, as an example, the estimated annual forces of transition for a 70-year-old male and a 70-year-old female. For example, the annual force of transition from 2 ADLs to 3 or more ADLs impaired is 11.79% for a male. The annual force of mortality for an individual with 3 or more ADLs impaired is 14.08% for a female. Notice that there is no force of remaining in the current status, just as there is no force of survival in the constant force of mortality counterpart to the CFT model.

TABLE 5

OBSERVED TRANSITION MATRIX FOR MALES AND FEMALES
AGED 65–74, 75–84 AND 85+ IN 1982

1982 Status	1984 Status					
	0 ADLs	1 ADL	2 ADLs	3+ ADLs	Dead	Total
Males, Age 65–74						
0 ADLs	7,165	73	43	78	740	8,108
1 ADL	44	24	13	9	35	125
2 ADLs	10	10	7	6	18	51
3+ ADLs	8	2	6	22	29	67
Total	7,227	109	69	115	831	8,351
Males, Age 75–84						
0 ADLs	2,834	87	34	66	566	3,587
1 ADL	29	12	13	14	64	132
2 ADLs	6	4	7	10	24	51
3+ ADLs	4	2	4	21	32	63
Total	2,873	105	58	111	686	3,833
Males, 85 and Up						
0 ADLs	386	28	18	22	161	615
1 ADL	9	12	3	13	26	63
2 ADLs	0	3	2	5	14	24
3+ ADLs	1	0	5	3	10	19
Total	396	43	28	43	211	721
Females, Age 65–74						
0 ADLs	9,854	141	41	64	468	10,568
1 ADL	61	41	15	15	28	160
2 ADLs	14	11	9	17	13	64
3+ ADLs	7	5	6	31	29	78
Total	9,936	198	71	127	538	10,870
Females, Age 75–84						
0 ADLs	4,881	265	77	109	653	5,985
1 ADL	69	51	13	34	46	213
2 ADLs	13	8	13	18	23	75
3+ ADLs	9	5	11	39	30	94
Total	4,972	329	114	200	752	6,367
Females, 85 and Up						
0 ADLs	955	145	48	72	299	1,519
1 ADL	30	37	10	22	44	143
2 ADLs	6	8	9	11	26	60
3+ ADLs	7	5	5	25	43	85
Total	998	195	72	130	412	1,807

TABLE 6

ANNUAL FORCES OF TRANSITION FOR MALE AND FEMALE AGE 70

Current Status	Destination Status				
	0 ADLs	1 ADL	2 ADLs	3+ ADLs	Dead
Male					
0 ADLs	—	0.0134	0.0030	0.0045	0.0453
1 ADL	0.3703	—	0.0557	0.0431	0.1721
2 ADLs	0.0832	0.3752	—	0.1179	0.1691
3+ ADLs	0.0552	0.0465	0.1723	—	0.2453
Female					
0 ADLs	—	0.0140	0.0032	0.0047	0.0260
1 ADL	0.4004	—	0.0580	0.0449	0.0988
2 ADLs	0.0899	0.4058	—	0.1227	0.0971
3+ ADLs	0.0596	0.0503	0.1863	—	0.1408

Transition forces for other ages are obtained from the forces at age 70 using the following adjustments. Forces of mortality, the right-most column, are multiplied (divided) by 1.0537 for each year of age beyond (before) age 70. Forces of impairment, the region above the diagonal, are multiplied (divided) by 1.0980 for each year of age beyond (before) age 70. Forces of recovery, the region below the diagonal, are multiplied (divided) by 0.9818 for each year of age beyond (before) age 70. For example, the annual force of transition from 1 ADL impaired to 3 or more ADLs impaired for a 90-year-old female is $0.0449 \times (1.0980)^{90-70} = 0.2913$.

Since the data provided no observations below age 65, transition forces for younger ages were further adjusted. Because of the lack of impairment data at younger ages, forces of impairment, including mortality, were related to the pattern of nursing home admission rates in the institutional tables from Section II. Forces of recovery were extended using the age adjustment from the previous paragraph.

3. Under the CFT model, the ADL transition process is completely specified. Forces of transition from the model were used to compute monthly probabilities of transition from one ADL status to another. In other words, the CFT model was used to extract expected monthly movement among the ADL statuses from the observed biannual movement.

Table 7 illustrates the resulting monthly probabilities of transition among the various ADL statuses, for males and females and for ages 70, 80 and 90. Note that the rows sum to one and there is a high probability of remaining in the same status.

TABLE 7

MONTHLY PROBABILITIES OF TRANSITION FOR MALES AND FEMALES AGE 70, 80, AND 90

Current Status	Destination Status				
	0 ADLs	1 ADL	2 ADLs	3+ ADLs	Dead
Males, Age 70					
0 ADLs	99.45%	0.11	0.03	0.04	0.38
1 ADL	3.00	94.81	0.44	0.35	1.41
2 ADLs	0.72	2.95	93.99	0.94	1.40
3+ ADLs	0.46	0.39	1.36	95.77	2.01
Males, Age 80					
0 ADLs	98.93%	0.27	0.06	0.10	0.64
1 ADL	2.47	93.18	1.10	0.88	2.37
2 ADLs	0.59	2.42	92.29	2.35	2.36
3+ ADLs	0.38	0.32	1.12	94.81	3.38
Males, Age 90					
0 ADLs	97.82%	0.68	0.16	0.25	1.09
1 ADL	2.01	89.12	2.67	2.21	3.99
2 ADLs	0.48	1.92	87.84	5.78	3.89
3+ ADLs	0.31	0.25	0.90	92.90	5.64
Females, Age 70					
0 ADLs	99.60%	0.11	0.03	0.04	0.22
1 ADL	3.25	95.12	0.46	0.36	0.81
2 ADLs	0.78	3.20	94.23	0.98	0.81
3+ ADLs	0.50	0.43	1.48	96.43	1.16
Females, Age 80					
0 ADLs	99.18%	0.29	0.07	0.10	0.37
1 ADL	2.69	93.87	1.15	0.92	1.37
2 ADLs	0.64	2.63	92.89	2.47	1.36
3+ ADLs	0.41	0.35	1.22	96.06	1.95
Females, Age 90					
0 ADLs	98.23%	0.71	0.17	0.26	0.63
1 ADL	2.19	90.34	2.82	2.35	2.31
2 ADLs	0.52	2.11	88.94	6.12	2.31
3+ ADLs	0.34	0.28	0.99	95.11	3.27

4. The monthly probabilities of transition were used to simulate 40,000 male and 40,000 female ADL status histories. Each simulated individual started at age 35, without ADL impairment, and progressed month by month according to the CFT monthly probabilities, until death. These simulation cohorts provide a convenient basis for determining ADL impairment incidence and continuation rates under various benefit trigger definitions.

5. CI statuses for the simulation cohorts were generated by a second-stage simulation based upon the known ADL status development of each individual. CI was defined as being unable to correctly answer five or

more of ten questions from the Short Portable Mental Status Questionnaire (SPMSQ), included in the NLTCS questionnaires. The NLTCS CI statuses were summarized by starting and ending ADL status and by age group. The observed conditional rates of CI and recovery were adjusted to a monthly basis and used to simulate the monthly CI status of the individuals in the simulation cohorts.

Table 8 shows summary characteristics of the two simulation cohorts. The second column shows the number of survivors to each quinquennial attained age. The third column is the annual mortality rate for the next five years of age. The remaining columns show the percentage allocation of the survivors among the various ADL/CI statuses. (Due to rounding, these values may not sum exactly to one across the last eight columns of each row.)

6. The simulated ADL/CI experience months were grouped into disability episodes, defined as a continuous sequence of months for which the individual was impaired cognitively or failed in at least one ADL. Episodes separated by no more than six unimpaired months were combined and treated as a single disability episode.

    Disability episodes were then classified by sex and quinquennial age at onset. The number of incurrals and the number of disability months were summarized for each such age group. Within each age of incurral, total disability months were summarized by ADL/CI status and duration from incurral.

7. Using the 1984 NLTCS, institutional prevalence rates were computed by sex, age, and ADL/CI status. A simple regression model was fit to smooth the results. These rates were applied to the disability episodes of the previous step to identify the remaining portion of disability months during which noninstitutional benefits might be generated.

8. The incidence rates, average number of noninstitutional days per episode, and ADL/CI-specific continuance tables were smoothed using a variety of graduation techniques. During this process, male and female incidence rates were set equal, and lengths of stay were graded together after age 93.

The next subsection displays the resulting incidence rates, average number of noninstitutional disability days per episode, and a breakdown of such days by ADL/CI status and duration since incurral.

TABLE 8

SUMMARY CHARACTERISTICS OF SIMULATION COHORTS

Attained Age	Survivors	Annual Mortality per 1,000	ADL/CI Status of Survivors (%)							
			No CI and No. of ADLs Failed				CI and No. of ADLs Failed			
			0	1	2	3+	0	1	2	3+
Male										
35	40,000	1	100.0	0.0	0.0	0.0	0.0	0.0	0.0	0.0
40	39,850	3	99.9	0.1	0.0	0.0	0.0	0.0	0.0	0.0
45	39,332	5	99.7	0.2	0.0	0.1	0.1	0.0	0.0	0.0
50	38,357	5	99.4	0.3	0.1	0.1	0.1	0.0	0.0	0.0
55	37,327	10	99.2	0.4	0.1	0.1	0.2	0.0	0.0	0.0
60	35,584	16	98.7	0.5	0.2	0.2	0.3	0.0	0.0	0.0
65	32,832	37	97.7	1.1	0.3	0.4	0.5	0.1	0.0	0.1
70	27,247	57	95.3	1.9	0.6	0.7	1.0	0.2	0.1	0.2
75	20,303	81	91.5	2.9	0.9	1.3	2.0	0.5	0.3	0.5
80	13,291	114	86.0	3.9	1.5	2.4	3.9	0.7	0.6	0.9
85	7,245	162	79.5	4.3	1.9	3.4	7.0	1.1	0.9	1.9
90	2,977	235	69.0	5.2	2.0	5.4	10.5	1.8	1.4	4.7
95	785	338	58.2	6.1	3.4	5.7	13.4	2.2	1.4	9.6
100	100	430	48.0	6.0	3.0	8.0	18.0	1.0	4.0	12.0
Female										
35	40,000	0	100.0	0.0	0.0	0.0	0.0	0.0	0.0	0.0
40	39,917	2	99.9	0.0	0.0	0.0	0.0	0.0	0.0	0.0
45	39,613	3	99.6	0.2	0.0	0.1	0.1	0.0	0.0	0.0
50	39,037	3	99.3	0.4	0.1	0.1	0.2	0.0	0.0	0.0
55	38,452	5	99.2	0.4	0.1	0.1	0.2	0.0	0.0	0.0
60	37,511	10	98.6	0.6	0.2	0.2	0.3	0.0	0.0	0.0
65	35,713	21	97.4	1.2	0.3	0.4	0.6	0.0	0.0	0.1
70	32,139	33	94.9	2.1	0.6	0.8	1.1	0.2	0.1	0.2
75	27,150	49	90.3	3.3	1.1	1.6	2.3	0.5	0.3	0.6
80	21,108	72	84.1	4.3	1.6	3.0	4.1	0.9	0.6	1.3
85	14,518	106	75.5	5.3	2.2	4.4	6.8	1.5	1.1	3.2
90	8,271	166	63.1	5.4	2.6	7.0	10.4	2.2	1.7	7.5
95	3,336	252	51.4	5.0	2.4	10.0	13.3	2.0	2.6	13.3
100	781	369	36.0	4.7	2.4	15.7	14.5	1.5	2.6	22.5

C. Noninstitutional Tables

Table 9 shows the incidence rate of disability episodes and the average number of noninstitutional days associated with each episode. The values are graduated.

TABLE 9

INCIDENCE RATES AND AVERAGE NUMBER OF NONINSTITUTIONAL IMPAIRMENT DAYS

Age	Male and Female Incidence per 1000 Survivors	Male Noninstitutional Days	Female Noninstitutional Days
37	0.47	1,652	2,111
42	0.88	1,339	1,624
47	1.63	1,133	1,337
52	2.96	1,001	1,178
57	5.26	923	1,111
62	9.18	882	1,110
67	15.35	824	1,065
72	24.45	742	961
77	37.15	644	813
82	53.80	538	646
87	74.28	434	483
92	97.77	337	338
97	122.68	237	237
102	146.76	160	160
107	167.38	103	103

Note that the incidence rates are per 1,000 survivors, not nondisabled survivors. Therefore, from a population of 1,000 72-year-old females of average disability, we expect to observe about 24 new disability episodes per year, each averaging 961 noninstitutional disability days.

Tables 10–25 allocate the noninstitutional disability days by ADL/CI status and duration from incurral. Again, the values are graduated.

As an example, a disability episode of a 72-year-old female is expected to average 961 noninstitutional days. According to the tables, 11.75% of these days, about 113 days, will arise after 3 months of disability and will be associated with 3 or more ADLs and no CI. We expect that 35.84% of the days, or 344 days, will correspond to CI without ADL impairment. About 59% of all noninstitutional days for such individuals will arise after 2 years of disability.

TABLE 10

NONINSTITUTIONAL DISABILITY DAYS BY ADL/CI STATUS AND DURATION FROM INCURRAL; ALL ADL/CI STATUSES; SEX: MALE

Percentage of Noninstitutional Disability Days beyond Duration

Duration (Months)	Incurral Age													
	37	42	47	52	57	62	67	72	77	82	87	92	97	102
0	100.00	100.00	100.00	100.00	100.00	100.00	100.00	100.00	100.00	100.00	100.00	100.00	100.00	100.00
1	98.55	98.16	97.92	97.72	97.55	97.40	97.25	97.07	96.73	96.11	94.99	93.44	92.12	90.18
2	97.14	96.38	95.91	95.51	95.18	94.90	94.61	94.25	93.61	92.42	90.33	87.46	85.05	81.59
3	95.78	94.66	93.96	93.38	92.90	92.49	92.06	91.55	90.62	88.93	85.98	82.01	78.70	74.06
4	94.46	92.99	92.07	91.31	90.69	90.16	89.61	88.95	87.77	85.61	81.92	77.03	72.97	67.44
5	93.18	91.37	90.24	89.31	88.55	87.91	87.25	86.46	85.04	82.46	78.13	72.47	67.80	61.59
6	91.93	89.81	88.47	87.37	86.49	85.74	84.98	84.07	82.43	79.47	74.58	68.28	63.11	56.41
7	90.73	88.29	86.75	85.50	84.50	83.65	82.79	81.77	79.93	76.63	71.26	64.44	58.86	51.82
8	89.56	86.81	85.09	83.68	82.57	81.63	80.68	79.55	77.54	73.93	68.15	60.90	55.00	47.72
9	88.42	85.39	83.48	81.92	80.71	79.69	78.65	77.43	75.25	71.36	65.23	57.64	51.48	44.05
10	87.32	84.00	81.92	80.22	78.91	77.81	76.69	75.39	73.05	68.91	62.50	54.63	48.26	40.76
11	86.25	82.66	80.41	78.56	77.17	75.99	74.81	73.42	70.95	66.59	59.93	51.84	45.31	37.79
12	85.22	81.36	78.95	76.97	75.49	74.24	72.99	71.53	68.94	64.37	57.51	49.26	42.60	35.12
15	81.93	77.24	74.32	71.94	70.19	68.72	67.25	65.53	62.67	57.56	50.30	41.94	34.49	26.78
18	78.95	73.53	70.16	67.42	65.47	63.81	62.16	60.24	57.21	51.72	44.32	36.08	28.17	20.64
21	76.26	70.18	66.43	63.37	61.25	59.44	57.65	55.57	52.42	46.69	39.31	31.32	23.18	16.06
24	73.81	67.16	63.06	59.72	57.47	55.54	53.64	51.44	48.22	42.33	35.08	27.41	19.20	12.58
27	71.59	64.42	60.03	56.43	54.08	52.06	50.06	47.76	44.52	38.53	31.49	24.14	15.99	9.92
30	69.57	61.95	57.29	53.47	51.04	48.94	46.87	44.49	41.24	35.21	28.40	21.39	13.37	7.87
33	67.72	59.70	54.81	50.79	48.31	46.14	44.01	41.56	38.33	32.29	25.73	19.05	11.23	6.27
36	66.04	57.66	52.57	48.37	45.85	43.63	41.44	38.94	35.73	29.71	23.41	17.05	9.46	5.01
48	59.96	50.43	44.74	39.78	37.16	34.40	32.13	29.35	26.15	20.31	15.22	10.66	4.36	1.91
60	55.61	45.45	39.47	33.98	31.39	28.22	25.90	22.94	19.82	14.35	10.25	6.96	2.07	0.76
72	52.33	41.84	35.76	29.89	27.37	23.85	21.49	18.40	15.41	10.37	7.07	4.67	0.99	0.30
84	49.70	39.07	33.00	26.85	24.41	20.60	18.21	15.05	12.19	7.61	4.94	3.18	0.48	0.12
96	47.49	36.82	30.83	24.47	22.11	18.06	15.65	12.47	9.76	5.65	3.49	2.19	0.24	0.05
108	45.55	34.92	29.04	22.52	20.23	16.00	13.58	10.43	7.88	4.22	2.48	1.51	0.12	0.02
120	43.79	33.24	27.50	20.86	18.63	14.26	11.87	8.77	6.40	3.17	1.77	1.05	0.06	0.01

TABLE 11

Noninstitutional Disability Days by ADL/CI Status and Duration from Incurral; ADLs: 0; CI: yes; Sex: Male

Percentage of Noninstitutional Disability Days beyond Duration

Duration (Months)	Incurral Age													
	37	42	47	52	57	62	67	72	77	82	87	92	97	102
0	59.34	48.23	40.45	35.43	32.63	31.49	31.49	32.05	32.64	32.71	31.71	29.10	24.31	16.81
1	59.20	48.10	40.32	35.29	32.50	31.36	31.32	31.83	32.35	32.29	31.20	28.42	23.51	16.13
2	59.06	47.97	40.20	35.14	32.38	31.22	31.15	31.62	32.05	31.87	30.70	27.75	22.74	15.48
3	58.92	47.83	40.08	35.00	32.26	31.08	30.98	31.40	31.76	31.46	30.20	27.10	21.99	14.85
4	58.78	47.70	39.96	34.86	32.14	30.95	30.81	31.19	31.47	31.05	29.71	26.47	21.27	14.25
5	58.65	47.57	39.83	34.72	32.02	30.81	30.65	30.98	31.19	30.65	29.23	25.85	20.57	13.67
6	58.51	47.43	39.71	34.58	31.89	30.67	30.48	30.77	30.91	30.26	28.76	25.24	19.90	13.12
7	58.37	47.30	39.59	34.44	31.77	30.54	30.32	30.56	30.63	29.87	28.29	24.65	19.24	12.59
8	58.24	47.17	39.47	34.31	31.65	30.40	30.16	30.35	30.35	29.48	27.84	24.08	18.61	12.08
9	58.10	47.04	39.35	34.17	31.54	30.27	29.99	30.15	30.07	29.10	27.39	23.51	18.00	11.59
10	57.97	46.91	39.23	34.03	31.42	30.14	29.83	29.94	29.80	28.72	26.94	22.96	17.41	11.12
11	57.83	46.78	39.11	33.90	31.30	30.01	29.67	29.74	29.53	28.35	26.51	22.43	16.83	10.67
12	57.70	46.65	38.99	33.76	31.18	29.87	29.51	29.54	29.26	27.98	26.08	21.90	16.28	10.23
15	57.26	46.22	38.61	33.35	30.79	29.41	28.92	28.76	28.32	26.70	24.60	20.30	14.06	7.95
18	56.84	45.80	38.24	32.95	30.41	28.95	28.34	28.00	27.41	25.47	23.20	18.81	12.15	6.17
21	56.41	45.39	37.87	32.55	30.03	28.50	27.77	27.26	26.52	24.31	21.88	17.43	10.49	4.80
24	55.99	44.97	37.50	32.16	29.66	28.06	27.21	26.54	25.67	23.19	20.64	16.16	9.06	3.73
27	55.57	44.56	37.14	31.77	29.29	27.62	26.66	25.84	24.84	22.13	19.47	14.97	7.83	2.89
30	55.15	44.16	36.78	31.39	28.92	27.19	26.12	25.16	24.04	21.11	18.36	13.88	6.76	2.25
33	54.74	43.76	36.42	31.01	28.56	26.77	25.60	24.49	23.27	20.14	17.32	12.86	5.84	1.75
36	54.33	43.36	36.07	30.63	28.21	26.35	25.08	23.85	22.52	19.22	16.33	11.92	5.05	1.36
48	52.48	41.56	34.45	28.75	26.37	23.89	22.31	20.45	18.63	14.70	11.82	8.38	2.52	0.49
60	50.70	39.82	32.91	26.98	24.65	21.67	19.85	17.53	15.41	11.25	8.55	5.89	1.26	0.18
72	48.97	38.17	31.43	25.32	23.05	19.65	17.65	15.04	12.74	8.60	6.19	4.15	0.63	0.07
84	47.30	36.58	30.02	23.76	21.54	17.82	15.70	12.89	10.54	6.58	4.48	2.92	0.32	0.02
96	45.70	35.05	28.68	22.30	20.14	16.16	13.97	11.06	8.72	5.04	3.24	2.05	0.16	0.01
108	44.14	33.59	27.39	20.92	18.83	14.65	12.42	9.48	7.21	3.85	2.35	1.44	0.08	0.00
120	42.64	32.19	26.16	19.64	17.60	13.28	11.05	8.13	5.96	2.95	1.70	1.01	0.04	0.00

631

TABLE 12

Noninstitutional Disability Days by ADL/CI Status and Duration from Incurral; ADLs: 1; CI: no; Sex: Male

Percentage of Noninstitutional Disability Days beyond Duration

Duration (Months)	Incurral Age													
	37	42	47	52	57	62	67	72	77	82	87	92	97	102
0	22.75	32.02	37.93	41.01	41.82	40.88	38.74	35.96	33.06	30.59	29.10	29.13	31.21	35.90
1	21.97	30.93	36.64	39.58	40.26	39.22	37.03	34.19	31.18	28.49	26.43	25.59	26.87	30.01
2	21.22	29.88	35.39	38.20	38.76	37.64	35.40	32.52	29.42	26.53	24.01	22.48	23.13	25.09
3	20.50	28.86	34.18	36.87	37.31	36.11	33.83	30.92	27.75	24.71	21.81	19.75	19.91	20.97
4	19.80	27.88	33.02	35.58	35.92	34.65	32.34	29.41	26.18	23.01	19.81	17.35	17.14	17.53
5	19.13	26.93	31.89	34.34	34.59	33.25	30.91	27.97	24.70	21.43	18.00	15.25	14.75	14.65
6	18.47	26.01	30.81	33.14	33.30	31.90	29.54	26.60	23.30	19.96	16.35	13.39	12.70	12.25
7	17.85	25.12	29.76	31.98	32.06	30.61	28.24	25.29	21.98	18.59	14.85	11.77	10.93	10.24
8	17.24	24.27	28.74	30.86	30.86	29.37	26.99	24.05	20.73	17.31	13.49	10.34	9.41	8.56
9	16.65	23.44	27.76	29.78	29.71	28.19	25.80	22.87	19.56	16.12	12.25	9.08	8.10	7.15
10	16.08	22.64	26.82	28.74	28.61	27.04	24.66	21.75	18.45	15.01	11.13	7.98	6.97	5.98
11	15.53	21.87	25.90	27.74	27.54	25.95	23.57	20.69	17.40	13.98	10.11	7.01	6.00	5.00
12	15.01	21.12	25.02	26.77	26.51	24.90	22.52	19.67	16.42	13.02	9.18	6.16	5.17	4.18
15	13.34	18.77	22.24	23.73	23.32	21.67	19.36	16.64	13.55	10.34	6.77	4.13	3.26	2.40
18	11.85	16.69	19.76	21.03	20.52	18.86	16.65	14.07	11.18	8.21	5.00	2.77	2.05	1.38
21	10.53	14.83	17.57	18.64	18.05	16.41	14.31	11.90	9.22	6.51	3.69	1.86	1.29	0.79
24	9.36	13.18	15.61	16.52	15.88	14.28	12.30	10.07	7.61	5.17	2.72	1.25	0.81	0.46
27	8.32	11.71	13.88	14.64	13.97	12.43	10.58	8.51	6.28	4.10	2.01	0.84	0.51	0.26
30	7.40	10.41	12.33	12.97	12.29	10.82	9.09	7.20	5.18	3.26	1.48	0.56	0.32	0.15
33	6.57	9.25	10.96	11.50	10.81	9.42	7.82	6.09	4.27	2.59	1.09	0.38	0.20	0.09
36	5.84	8.22	9.74	10.19	9.51	8.19	6.72	5.15	3.53	2.05	0.81	0.25	0.13	0.05
48	3.45	4.86	5.75	5.96	5.37	4.42	3.45	2.47	1.53	0.76	0.22	0.05	0.02	0.01
60	2.04	2.87	3.40	3.48	3.04	2.38	1.77	1.19	0.66	0.28	0.06	0.01	0.00	0.00
72	1.20	1.69	2.01	2.04	1.72	1.29	0.91	0.57	0.29	0.10	0.02	0.00	0.00	0.00
84	0.71	1.00	1.19	1.19	0.97	0.69	0.47	0.27	0.12	0.04	0.00	0.00	0.00	0.00
96	0.42	0.59	0.70	0.70	0.55	0.37	0.24	0.13	0.05	0.01	0.00	0.00	0.00	0.00
108	0.25	0.35	0.41	0.41	0.31	0.20	0.12	0.06	0.02	0.01	0.00	0.00	0.00	0.00
120	0.15	0.21	0.24	0.24	0.18	0.11	0.06	0.03	0.01	0.00	0.00	0.00	0.00	0.00

TABLE 13

NONINSTITUTIONAL DISABILITY DAYS BY ADL/CI STATUS AND DURATION FROM INCURRAL; ADLs: 1; CI: YES; SEX: MALE

Percentage of Noninstitutional Disability Days beyond Duration

Duration (Months)	Incurral Age													
	37	42	47	52	57	62	67	72	77	82	87	92	97	102
0	0.15	0.38	0.75	1.22	1.76	2.34	2.92	3.45	3.91	4.26	4.46	4.48	4.29	3.83
1	0.15	0.37	0.74	1.21	1.75	2.31	2.87	3.37	3.80	4.10	4.24	4.14	3.90	3.42
2	0.15	0.37	0.74	1.20	1.73	2.28	2.82	3.30	3.69	3.94	4.03	3.81	3.55	3.04
3	0.14	0.37	0.74	1.19	1.71	2.25	2.77	3.23	3.58	3.79	3.83	3.52	3.23	2.71
4	0.14	0.37	0.73	1.18	1.69	2.21	2.72	3.16	3.48	3.65	3.63	3.24	2.94	2.42
5	0.14	0.37	0.73	1.17	1.67	2.18	2.67	3.09	3.38	3.51	3.45	2.99	2.68	2.16
6	0.14	0.37	0.73	1.16	1.66	2.15	2.62	3.02	3.28	3.38	3.28	2.76	2.44	1.92
7	0.14	0.36	0.72	1.16	1.64	2.12	2.58	2.95	3.19	3.25	3.11	2.55	2.22	1.71
8	0.14	0.36	0.72	1.15	1.62	2.09	2.53	2.89	3.10	3.13	2.96	2.35	2.02	1.53
9	0.14	0.36	0.72	1.14	1.61	2.06	2.49	2.82	3.01	3.01	2.81	2.16	1.84	1.36
10	0.14	0.36	0.71	1.13	1.59	2.04	2.45	2.76	2.92	2.89	2.67	2.00	1.68	1.21
11	0.14	0.36	0.71	1.12	1.57	2.01	2.40	2.70	2.84	2.78	2.53	1.84	1.53	1.08
12	0.14	0.36	0.71	1.11	1.56	1.98	2.36	2.64	2.75	2.68	2.41	1.70	1.39	0.96
15	0.14	0.35	0.70	1.09	1.51	1.89	2.23	2.44	2.50	2.35	2.04	1.32	1.04	0.68
18	0.14	0.35	0.70	1.06	1.46	1.81	2.10	2.26	2.26	2.06	1.73	1.03	0.78	0.48
21	0.14	0.35	0.69	1.04	1.42	1.73	1.98	2.10	2.05	1.81	1.47	0.80	0.59	0.34
24	0.14	0.35	0.69	1.01	1.37	1.65	1.86	1.94	1.86	1.59	1.25	0.63	0.44	0.24
27	0.13	0.34	0.68	0.99	1.33	1.58	1.76	1.80	1.69	1.39	1.06	0.49	0.33	0.17
30	0.13	0.34	0.68	0.97	1.29	1.51	1.65	1.66	1.53	1.22	0.90	0.38	0.25	0.12
33	0.13	0.34	0.67	0.94	1.25	1.45	1.56	1.54	1.38	1.07	0.76	0.30	0.19	0.08
36	0.13	0.34	0.67	0.92	1.21	1.38	1.47	1.43	1.25	0.94	0.64	0.23	0.14	0.06
48	0.13	0.33	0.65	0.85	1.05	1.13	1.14	1.02	0.81	0.54	0.32	0.08	0.04	0.01
60	0.12	0.32	0.63	0.79	0.91	0.93	0.88	0.73	0.52	0.31	0.16	0.03	0.01	0.00
72	0.12	0.31	0.62	0.73	0.79	0.76	0.68	0.52	0.34	0.18	0.08	0.01	0.00	0.00
84	0.12	0.30	0.60	0.68	0.69	0.62	0.53	0.37	0.22	0.10	0.04	0.00	0.00	0.00
96	0.12	0.29	0.58	0.63	0.60	0.51	0.41	0.26	0.14	0.06	0.02	0.00	0.00	0.00
108	0.11	0.29	0.57	0.58	0.52	0.42	0.31	0.19	0.09	0.03	0.01	0.00	0.00	0.00
120	0.11	0.28	0.55	0.54	0.45	0.34	0.24	0.13	0.06	0.02	0.00	0.00	0.00	0.00

TABLE 14

NONINSTITUTIONAL DISABILITY DAYS BY ADL/CI STATUS AND DURATION FROM INCURRAL; ADLS: 2; CI: NO; SEX: MALE

Percentage of Noninstitutional Disability Days beyond Duration

Duration (Months)	Incurral Age													
	37	42	47	52	57	62	67	72	77	82	87	92	97	102
0	7.03	8.64	9.73	10.38	10.72	10.85	10.87	10.88	11.00	11.33	11.97	13.03	14.62	16.84
1	6.83	8.39	9.44	10.08	10.39	10.51	10.51	10.50	10.58	10.81	11.27	12.16	13.55	15.47
2	6.63	8.15	9.17	9.78	10.07	10.18	10.16	10.13	10.18	10.32	10.61	11.34	12.55	14.21
3	6.44	7.91	8.90	9.50	9.77	9.86	9.82	9.78	9.79	9.85	9.99	10.58	11.63	13.05
4	6.25	7.68	8.64	9.22	9.47	9.55	9.50	9.44	9.42	9.40	9.41	9.87	10.77	11.98
5	6.07	7.46	8.39	8.95	9.18	9.25	9.18	9.11	9.06	8.97	8.86	9.20	9.98	11.00
6	5.89	7.24	8.15	8.68	8.89	8.96	8.88	8.79	8.72	8.57	8.34	8.59	9.25	10.11
7	5.72	7.03	7.91	8.43	8.62	8.68	8.58	8.49	8.39	8.18	7.85	8.01	8.57	9.28
8	5.55	6.83	7.68	8.18	8.36	8.40	8.30	8.19	8.07	7.80	7.39	7.47	7.94	8.52
9	5.39	6.63	7.46	7.94	8.10	8.14	8.02	7.90	7.76	7.45	6.96	6.97	7.36	7.83
10	5.24	6.44	7.24	7.71	7.85	7.89	7.76	7.63	7.47	7.11	6.56	6.50	6.81	7.19
11	5.08	6.25	7.03	7.48	7.61	7.64	7.50	7.36	7.18	6.79	6.17	6.06	6.31	6.60
12	4.94	6.07	6.83	7.26	7.38	7.40	7.25	7.11	6.91	6.48	5.81	5.66	5.85	6.06
15	4.45	5.47	6.16	6.54	6.61	6.61	6.45	6.28	6.04	5.52	4.73	4.41	4.44	4.44
18	4.02	4.94	5.56	5.90	5.93	5.91	5.73	5.55	5.28	4.70	3.85	3.44	3.37	3.26
21	3.62	4.46	5.01	5.31	5.31	5.29	5.09	4.91	4.62	4.01	3.13	2.68	2.56	2.39
24	3.27	4.02	4.52	4.79	4.76	4.73	4.53	4.34	4.03	3.42	2.55	2.09	1.94	1.75
27	2.95	3.63	4.08	4.31	4.26	4.23	4.02	3.84	3.53	2.91	2.07	1.63	1.48	1.28
30	2.66	3.27	3.68	3.89	3.82	3.78	3.58	3.40	3.08	2.48	1.69	1.27	1.12	0.94
33	2.40	2.95	3.32	3.50	3.42	3.38	3.18	3.00	2.69	2.11	1.37	0.99	0.85	0.69
36	2.17	2.66	3.00	3.16	3.07	3.02	2.83	2.65	2.36	1.80	1.12	0.77	0.65	0.50
48	1.35	1.66	1.87	1.96	1.86	1.81	1.66	1.53	1.29	0.89	0.45	0.25	0.18	0.12
60	0.85	1.04	1.17	1.22	1.13	1.09	0.97	0.88	0.71	0.44	0.18	0.08	0.05	0.03
72	0.53	0.65	0.73	0.76	0.68	0.65	0.57	0.51	0.39	0.21	0.07	0.03	0.01	0.01
84	0.33	0.41	0.46	0.47	0.42	0.39	0.33	0.29	0.21	0.11	0.03	0.01	0.00	0.00
96	0.21	0.25	0.29	0.29	0.25	0.24	0.20	0.17	0.12	0.05	0.01	0.00	0.00	0.00
108	0.13	0.16	0.18	0.18	0.15	0.14	0.12	0.10	0.06	0.03	0.00	0.00	0.00	0.00
120	0.08	0.10	0.11	0.11	0.09	0.08	0.07	0.06	0.03	0.01	0.00	0.00	0.00	0.00

TABLE 15

Noninstitutional Disability Days by ADL/CI Status and Duration from Incurral; ADLs: 2; CI: Yes; Sex: Male

Percentage of Noninstitutional Disability Days beyond Duration

Duration (Months)	Incurral Age													
	37	42	47	52	57	62	67	72	77	82	87	92	97	102
0	0.37	0.32	0.41	0.63	0.93	1.28	1.66	2.04	2.37	2.64	2.81	2.86	2.74	2.44
1	0.36	0.32	0.41	0.62	0.92	1.27	1.64	2.00	2.32	2.57	2.70	2.67	2.53	2.20
2	0.36	0.31	0.41	0.62	0.90	1.25	1.61	1.97	2.27	2.50	2.59	2.50	2.34	1.99
3	0.36	0.31	0.41	0.61	0.89	1.23	1.59	1.93	2.22	2.43	2.49	2.33	2.16	1.80
4	0.36	0.31	0.41	0.61	0.88	1.21	1.56	1.90	2.17	2.36	2.39	2.18	1.99	1.62
5	0.36	0.31	0.41	0.60	0.87	1.20	1.54	1.86	2.13	2.30	2.29	2.04	1.84	1.47
6	0.36	0.31	0.41	0.60	0.86	1.18	1.51	1.83	2.08	2.23	2.20	1.91	1.70	1.32
7	0.36	0.31	0.40	0.59	0.84	1.16	1.49	1.80	2.04	2.17	2.11	1.78	1.56	1.20
8	0.36	0.31	0.40	0.59	0.83	1.15	1.47	1.77	1.99	2.11	2.03	1.66	1.44	1.08
9	0.35	0.31	0.40	0.58	0.82	1.13	1.45	1.74	1.95	2.05	1.95	1.56	1.33	0.98
10	0.35	0.31	0.40	0.58	0.81	1.11	1.42	1.71	1.91	2.00	1.87	1.45	1.23	0.88
11	0.35	0.30	0.40	0.57	0.80	1.10	1.40	1.68	1.87	1.94	1.79	1.36	1.14	0.80
12	0.35	0.30	0.40	0.57	0.79	1.08	1.38	1.65	1.83	1.89	1.72	1.27	1.05	0.72
15	0.35	0.30	0.39	0.55	0.76	1.04	1.31	1.56	1.71	1.72	1.51	1.03	0.81	0.52
18	0.34	0.30	0.39	0.53	0.73	0.99	1.25	1.47	1.60	1.57	1.32	0.83	0.63	0.37
21	0.33	0.29	0.38	0.51	0.70	0.95	1.19	1.39	1.49	1.44	1.16	0.67	0.49	0.27
24	0.33	0.29	0.38	0.49	0.67	0.91	1.13	1.31	1.40	1.31	1.01	0.55	0.38	0.20
27	0.33	0.29	0.38	0.47	0.64	0.87	1.07	1.24	1.31	1.20	0.89	0.44	0.30	0.14
30	0.32	0.28	0.37	0.46	0.62	0.84	1.02	1.17	1.22	1.09	0.78	0.36	0.23	0.10
33	0.32	0.28	0.37	0.44	0.59	0.80	0.97	1.11	1.14	1.00	0.68	0.29	0.18	0.07
36	0.31	0.27	0.36	0.42	0.57	0.77	0.92	1.05	1.07	0.91	0.59	0.23	0.14	0.05
48	0.31	0.27	0.35	0.37	0.47	0.62	0.71	0.78	0.75	0.58	0.32	0.09	0.05	0.01
60	0.29	0.25	0.33	0.32	0.39	0.51	0.55	0.58	0.53	0.37	0.17	0.04	0.02	0.00
72	0.28	0.24	0.32	0.27	0.32	0.41	0.43	0.43	0.37	0.24	0.09	0.01	0.01	0.00
84	0.27	0.23	0.31	0.24	0.26	0.33	0.33	0.32	0.26	0.15	0.05	0.01	0.00	0.00
96	0.26	0.22	0.29	0.20	0.22	0.27	0.26	0.24	0.18	0.10	0.03	0.00	0.00	0.00
108	0.25	0.21	0.28	0.18	0.18	0.22	0.20	0.18	0.13	0.06	0.01	0.00	0.00	0.00
120	0.24	0.20	0.27	0.15	0.15	0.18	0.15	0.13	0.09	0.04	0.01	0.00	0.00	0.00

635

TABLE 16

NONINSTITUTIONAL DISABILITY DAYS BY ADL/CI STATUS AND DURATION FROM INCURRAL; ADLS: 3+; CI: NO; SEX: MALE

Percentage of Noninstitutional Disability Days beyond Duration

Duration (Months)	Incurral Age													
	37	42	47	52	57	62	67	72	77	82	87	92	97	102
0	9.10	9.93	10.50	10.90	11.21	11.50	11.85	12.35	13.05	14.06	15.43	17.25	19.61	22.56
1	8.78	9.57	10.12	10.52	10.81	11.11	11.46	11.95	12.62	13.55	14.78	16.46	18.66	21.41
2	8.46	9.23	9.76	10.15	10.43	10.74	11.09	11.56	12.20	13.06	14.15	15.70	17.76	20.31
3	8.16	8.90	9.41	9.80	10.06	10.37	10.72	11.18	11.79	12.59	13.55	14.98	16.90	19.27
4	7.87	8.58	9.08	9.46	9.71	10.02	10.37	10.82	11.40	12.14	12.98	14.29	16.09	18.29
5	7.59	8.27	8.75	9.12	9.37	9.68	10.03	10.47	11.02	11.70	12.43	13.63	15.31	17.35
6	7.31	7.98	8.44	8.81	9.03	9.36	9.70	10.13	10.65	11.28	11.90	13.00	14.57	16.47
7	7.05	7.69	8.14	8.50	8.72	9.04	9.38	9.80	10.29	10.88	11.40	12.40	13.87	15.62
8	6.80	7.42	7.84	8.20	8.41	8.74	9.07	9.48	9.95	10.49	10.92	11.83	13.20	14.82
9	6.56	7.15	7.56	7.91	8.11	8.44	8.77	9.18	9.62	10.11	10.46	11.29	12.56	14.07
10	6.32	6.89	7.29	7.64	7.82	8.15	8.48	8.88	9.30	9.75	10.01	10.77	11.96	13.35
11	6.10	6.65	7.03	7.37	7.55	7.88	8.21	8.59	8.99	9.40	9.59	10.27	11.38	12.66
12	5.88	6.41	6.78	7.11	7.28	7.61	7.94	8.31	8.69	9.06	9.18	9.80	10.83	12.02
15	5.20	5.67	6.00	6.31	6.45	6.78	7.08	7.41	7.71	7.95	7.85	8.29	9.09	9.98
18	4.60	5.01	5.30	5.60	5.72	6.03	6.31	6.61	6.84	6.98	6.71	7.01	7.63	8.29
21	4.07	4.43	4.69	4.97	5.07	5.37	5.63	5.90	6.07	6.13	5.74	5.93	6.40	6.89
24	3.60	3.92	4.15	4.41	4.50	4.78	5.02	5.26	5.39	5.38	4.91	5.02	5.37	5.72
27	3.18	3.47	3.67	3.92	3.98	4.26	4.47	4.69	4.78	4.72	4.20	4.24	4.51	4.75
30	2.81	3.07	3.24	3.48	3.53	3.79	3.99	4.18	4.25	4.15	3.59	3.59	3.78	3.95
33	2.49	2.71	2.87	3.09	3.13	3.37	3.56	3.73	3.77	3.64	3.07	3.04	3.18	3.28
36	2.20	2.40	2.54	2.74	2.78	3.00	3.17	3.32	3.35	3.20	2.62	2.57	2.67	2.72
48	1.29	1.40	1.48	1.63	1.62	1.79	1.90	1.99	1.94	1.76	1.28	1.18	1.17	1.14
60	0.75	0.82	0.87	0.96	0.95	1.07	1.13	1.19	1.13	0.97	0.63	0.54	0.52	0.48
72	0.44	0.48	0.51	0.57	0.56	0.63	0.68	0.71	0.66	0.54	0.31	0.25	0.23	0.20
84	0.26	0.28	0.30	0.34	0.32	0.38	0.40	0.42	0.38	0.30	0.15	0.11	0.10	0.08
96	0.15	0.16	0.17	0.20	0.19	0.22	0.24	0.25	0.22	0.16	0.07	0.05	0.04	0.03
108	0.09	0.10	0.10	0.12	0.11	0.13	0.14	0.15	0.13	0.09	0.04	0.02	0.02	0.01
120	0.05	0.06	0.06	0.07	0.06	0.08	0.09	0.09	0.07	0.05	0.02	0.01	0.01	0.01

TABLE 17
Noninstitutional Disability Days by ADL/CI Status and Duration from Incurral; ADLs: 3+; CI: yes; Sex: Male

Percentage of Noninstitutional Disability Days beyond Duration

Duration (Months)	Incurral Age													
	37	42	47	52	57	62	67	72	77	82	87	92	97	102
0	1.27	0.48	0.24	0.42	0.93	1.65	2.47	3.28	3.96	4.41	4.51	4.15	3.22	1.61
1	1.27	0.48	0.23	0.42	0.92	1.63	2.43	3.22	3.88	4.30	4.37	4.01	3.10	1.54
2	1.26	0.48	0.23	0.42	0.91	1.61	2.39	3.16	3.80	4.19	4.24	3.88	2.98	1.47
3	1.26	0.47	0.23	0.41	0.89	1.58	2.35	3.10	3.72	4.09	4.11	3.75	2.87	1.41
4	1.25	0.47	0.23	0.41	0.88	1.56	2.31	3.04	3.64	3.99	3.99	3.63	2.76	1.34
5	1.25	0.47	0.23	0.41	0.87	1.54	2.28	2.98	3.57	3.89	3.87	3.51	2.66	1.29
6	1.24	0.47	0.23	0.40	0.86	1.52	2.24	2.93	3.49	3.79	3.75	3.39	2.56	1.23
7	1.24	0.47	0.23	0.40	0.85	1.50	2.20	2.87	3.42	3.70	3.64	3.28	2.46	1.18
8	1.23	0.47	0.23	0.40	0.83	1.48	2.16	2.82	3.35	3.61	3.53	3.17	2.37	1.12
9	1.23	0.46	0.23	0.39	0.82	1.45	2.13	2.77	3.28	3.52	3.42	3.07	2.28	1.08
10	1.22	0.46	0.23	0.39	0.81	1.43	2.09	2.71	3.21	3.43	3.32	2.97	2.20	1.03
11	1.22	0.46	0.22	0.39	0.80	1.41	2.06	2.66	3.14	3.34	3.22	2.87	2.12	0.98
12	1.21	0.46	0.22	0.38	0.79	1.39	2.03	2.61	3.08	3.26	3.12	2.77	2.04	0.94
15	1.19	0.45	0.22	0.37	0.75	1.32	1.91	2.44	2.85	2.98	2.79	2.46	1.78	0.80
18	1.17	0.44	0.22	0.36	0.71	1.25	1.80	2.27	2.64	2.72	2.50	2.18	1.55	0.69
21	1.15	0.43	0.21	0.35	0.67	1.19	1.69	2.12	2.44	2.49	2.24	1.94	1.36	0.58
24	1.13	0.43	0.21	0.34	0.64	1.13	1.59	1.98	2.26	2.27	2.01	1.72	1.19	0.50
27	1.11	0.42	0.20	0.33	0.61	1.07	1.50	1.84	2.09	2.08	1.80	1.53	1.04	0.43
30	1.09	0.41	0.20	0.32	0.57	1.02	1.41	1.72	1.94	1.90	1.61	1.35	0.91	0.36
33	1.07	0.40	0.20	0.31	0.54	0.96	1.33	1.60	1.79	1.73	1.44	1.20	0.79	0.31
36	1.05	0.40	0.19	0.30	0.52	0.91	1.25	1.49	1.66	1.58	1.29	1.07	0.69	0.26
48	0.95	0.36	0.18	0.26	0.41	0.73	0.97	1.12	1.20	1.07	0.80	0.63	0.38	0.13
60	0.86	0.33	0.16	0.22	0.32	0.58	0.75	0.84	0.87	0.73	0.49	0.37	0.21	0.06
72	0.78	0.30	0.14	0.19	0.26	0.46	0.58	0.63	0.63	0.49	0.30	0.22	0.11	0.03
84	0.71	0.27	0.13	0.17	0.20	0.37	0.45	0.47	0.46	0.33	0.19	0.13	0.06	0.02
96	0.64	0.24	0.12	0.14	0.16	0.29	0.35	0.36	0.33	0.22	0.12	0.08	0.03	0.01
108	0.58	0.22	0.11	0.12	0.13	0.23	0.27	0.27	0.24	0.15	0.07	0.05	0.02	0.00
120	0.53	0.20	0.10	0.11	0.10	0.19	0.21	0.20	0.17	0.10	0.04	0.03	0.01	0.00

637

TABLE 18

Noninstitutional Disability Days by ADL/CI Status and Duration from Incurral; All ADL/CI Statuses; Sex: Female

Percentage of Noninstitutional Disability Days beyond Duration

Duration (Months)	Incurral Age													
	37	42	47	52	57	62	67	72	77	82	87	92	97	102
0	100.00	100.00	100.00	100.00	100.00	100.00	100.00	100.00	100.00	100.00	100.00	100.00	100.00	100.00
1	98.88	98.41	98.10	97.95	97.86	97.82	97.78	97.67	97.42	96.94	96.14	94.98	93.06	91.36
2	97.79	96.87	96.26	95.97	95.80	95.72	95.64	95.41	94.94	94.02	92.50	90.32	86.82	83.73
3	96.73	95.39	94.48	94.05	93.80	93.68	93.57	93.24	92.55	91.23	89.05	85.99	81.18	76.99
4	95.71	93.95	92.76	92.20	91.87	91.71	91.56	91.13	90.25	88.56	85.79	81.95	76.09	71.01
5	94.72	92.56	91.11	90.41	90.00	89.80	89.62	89.10	88.04	86.00	82.71	78.19	71.47	65.69
6	93.76	91.22	89.50	88.67	88.19	87.95	87.74	87.14	85.91	83.56	79.79	74.69	67.28	60.95
7	92.82	89.92	87.96	87.00	86.44	86.17	85.92	85.24	83.85	81.22	77.03	71.41	63.46	56.71
8	91.92	88.66	86.46	85.38	84.75	84.44	84.16	83.41	81.87	78.98	74.40	68.35	59.98	52.91
9	91.04	87.44	85.02	83.81	83.11	82.76	82.46	81.63	79.96	76.83	71.92	65.48	56.79	49.49
10	90.19	86.27	83.62	82.29	81.52	81.14	80.81	79.92	78.12	74.77	69.55	62.79	53.87	46.40
11	89.36	85.13	82.28	80.83	79.99	79.57	79.21	78.26	76.34	72.80	67.30	60.27	51.19	43.61
12	88.55	84.02	80.97	79.41	78.50	78.05	77.66	76.66	74.63	70.91	65.17	57.90	48.72	41.07
15	85.99	80.54	76.88	74.93	73.80	73.23	72.73	71.54	69.18	64.97	58.64	50.88	41.73	34.07
18	83.66	77.42	73.22	70.92	69.58	68.90	68.30	66.96	64.33	59.75	53.04	45.03	36.15	28.66
21	81.53	74.61	69.94	67.32	65.79	64.99	64.31	62.83	59.99	55.15	48.19	40.11	31.61	24.41
24	79.58	72.07	67.00	64.08	62.38	61.48	60.70	59.12	56.10	51.08	43.98	35.93	27.87	20.99
27	77.80	69.78	64.37	61.17	59.30	58.30	57.45	55.77	52.60	47.45	40.29	32.35	24.73	18.20
30	76.16	67.71	62.00	58.54	56.52	55.43	54.49	52.73	49.44	44.20	37.04	29.25	22.07	15.88
33	74.64	65.82	59.86	56.17	54.01	52.82	51.81	49.98	46.57	41.29	34.16	26.55	19.80	13.94
36	73.24	64.10	57.93	54.02	51.73	50.45	49.37	47.47	43.97	38.66	31.59	24.18	17.83	12.29
48	67.95	57.97	51.20	46.52	43.72	41.99	40.55	38.41	34.61	29.30	22.71	16.32	11.44	7.15
60	63.87	53.61	46.64	41.42	38.26	36.16	34.40	32.04	28.04	22.87	16.85	11.42	7.65	4.36
72	60.52	50.31	43.35	37.77	34.35	31.94	29.89	27.33	23.20	18.21	12.77	8.18	5.26	2.76
84	57.64	47.63	40.80	34.99	31.38	28.72	26.43	23.71	19.48	14.71	9.82	5.96	3.68	1.79
96	55.06	45.35	38.70	32.76	29.02	26.16	23.66	20.80	16.54	12.00	7.63	4.39	2.61	1.19
108	52.69	43.32	36.89	30.87	27.04	24.03	21.36	18.40	14.16	9.86	5.97	3.26	1.88	0.80
120	50.49	41.47	35.27	29.21	25.32	22.20	19.41	16.37	12.19	8.15	4.70	2.44	1.35	0.54

638

TABLE 19

NONINSTITUTIONAL DISABILITY DAYS BY ADL/CI STATUS AND DURATION FROM INCURRAL; ADLS: 0; CI: YES; SEX: FEMALE

Percentage of Noninstitutional Disability Days beyond Duration

Duration (Months)	Incurral Age													
	37	42	47	52	57	62	67	72	77	82	87	92	97	102
0	70.94	58.74	49.85	43.70	39.77	37.51	36.38	35.84	35.36	34.39	32.39	28.83	23.16	12.86
1	70.76	58.60	49.72	43.57	39.64	37.36	36.21	35.63	35.09	34.04	31.95	28.32	22.71	12.57
2	70.58	58.45	49.59	43.45	39.51	37.21	36.04	35.43	34.82	33.69	31.51	27.82	22.26	12.28
3	70.40	58.30	49.47	43.32	39.38	37.07	35.87	35.22	34.55	33.35	31.08	27.32	21.82	12.00
4	70.22	58.15	49.34	43.20	39.25	36.92	35.70	35.02	34.28	33.01	30.65	26.84	21.39	11.73
5	70.04	58.00	49.22	43.07	39.12	36.78	35.54	34.81	34.02	32.68	30.23	26.36	20.97	11.47
6	69.86	57.86	49.09	42.95	38.99	36.64	35.37	34.61	33.76	32.35	29.81	25.90	20.56	11.21
7	69.69	57.71	48.97	42.82	38.86	36.49	35.21	34.41	33.50	32.02	29.40	25.44	20.16	10.95
8	69.51	57.57	48.85	42.70	38.73	36.35	35.04	34.21	33.24	31.69	29.00	24.99	19.76	10.71
9	69.33	57.42	48.72	42.57	38.61	36.21	34.88	34.01	32.99	31.37	28.60	24.54	19.37	10.46
10	69.16	57.27	48.60	42.45	38.48	36.07	34.72	33.81	32.73	31.05	28.20	24.11	18.99	10.23
11	68.98	57.13	48.48	42.33	38.35	35.93	34.55	33.62	32.48	30.74	27.82	23.68	18.62	10.00
12	68.81	56.98	48.35	42.20	38.23	35.79	34.39	33.42	32.23	30.42	27.43	23.26	18.25	9.77
15	68.21	56.49	47.93	41.77	37.79	35.31	33.84	32.75	31.36	29.33	26.13	21.86	17.04	9.04
18	67.61	55.99	47.51	41.35	37.35	34.84	33.31	32.10	30.51	28.28	24.88	20.54	15.91	8.36
21	67.02	55.50	47.09	40.92	36.91	34.38	32.77	31.46	29.68	27.27	23.70	19.30	14.85	7.74
24	66.43	55.02	46.68	40.50	36.49	33.92	32.25	30.83	28.88	26.29	22.57	18.14	13.86	7.16
27	65.85	54.53	46.27	40.09	36.06	33.47	31.74	30.21	28.10	25.35	21.50	17.05	12.94	6.62
30	65.28	54.06	45.87	39.68	35.65	33.03	31.23	29.60	27.34	24.44	20.47	16.02	12.08	6.13
33	64.70	53.58	45.47	39.27	35.23	32.59	30.74	29.01	26.60	23.56	19.50	15.05	11.28	5.67
36	64.14	53.12	45.07	38.87	34.83	32.15	30.25	28.43	25.88	22.71	18.57	14.15	10.53	5.25
48	61.63	51.04	43.31	37.10	33.00	30.18	27.99	25.82	22.76	19.15	14.82	10.66	7.70	3.68
60	59.22	49.04	41.61	35.41	31.27	28.32	25.90	23.45	20.02	16.15	11.83	8.04	5.63	2.59
72	56.90	47.12	39.98	33.80	29.63	26.58	23.97	21.30	17.60	13.62	9.44	6.06	4.11	1.82
84	54.68	45.28	38.42	32.26	28.08	24.95	22.18	19.35	15.48	11.48	7.54	4.56	3.01	1.28
96	52.54	43.51	36.92	30.80	26.60	23.41	20.53	17.57	13.61	9.68	6.02	3.44	2.20	0.90
108	50.48	41.81	35.47	29.39	25.21	21.97	19.00	15.96	11.97	8.16	4.80	2.59	1.61	0.63
120	48.51	40.17	34.09	28.06	23.89	20.62	17.58	14.50	10.53	6.88	3.83	1.95	1.17	0.44

TABLE 20

NONINSTITUTIONAL DISABILITY DAYS BY ADL/CI STATUS AND DURATION FROM INCURRAL; ADLS: 1; CI: NO; SEX: FEMALE

Percentage of Noninstitutional Disability Days beyond Duration

Duration (Months)	Incurral Age													
	37	42	47	52	57	62	67	72	77	82	87	92	97	102
0	17.77	26.79	32.63	35.81	36.85	36.27	34.60	32.36	30.08	28.27	27.46	28.18	30.95	36.29
1	17.11	25.80	31.42	34.50	35.50	34.90	33.24	30.96	28.58	26.55	25.37	25.44	26.88	30.85
2	16.47	24.84	30.25	33.24	34.20	33.59	31.94	29.62	27.15	24.94	23.43	22.96	23.34	26.23
3	15.86	23.92	29.13	32.02	32.95	32.33	30.69	28.34	25.80	23.42	21.64	20.72	20.27	22.30
4	15.27	23.03	28.05	30.85	31.75	31.11	29.48	27.12	24.52	22.00	19.98	18.70	17.60	18.96
5	14.70	22.17	27.00	29.72	30.58	29.94	28.33	25.94	23.30	20.66	18.46	16.88	15.29	16.12
6	14.16	21.35	26.00	28.63	29.47	28.81	27.21	24.82	22.14	19.40	17.05	15.23	13.27	13.71
7	13.63	20.55	25.03	27.58	28.39	27.73	26.15	23.75	21.03	18.22	15.75	13.75	11.53	11.66
8	13.12	19.79	24.10	26.57	27.35	26.69	25.12	22.72	19.99	17.12	14.54	12.41	10.01	9.91
9	12.64	19.06	23.21	25.60	26.35	25.68	24.14	21.74	18.99	16.08	13.43	11.20	8.69	8.43
10	12.17	18.35	22.35	24.66	25.39	24.72	23.19	20.80	18.05	15.10	12.41	10.11	7.55	7.16
11	11.71	17.67	21.52	23.76	24.46	23.79	22.28	19.90	17.15	14.18	11.46	9.12	6.56	6.09
12	11.28	17.01	20.72	22.89	23.56	22.89	21.41	19.04	16.29	13.32	10.58	8.23	5.69	5.18
15	9.92	14.97	18.23	20.18	20.78	20.11	18.70	16.40	13.75	10.85	8.22	5.99	3.72	3.18
18	8.73	13.17	16.04	17.79	18.32	17.66	16.33	14.13	11.61	8.83	6.38	4.36	2.43	1.95
21	7.68	11.58	14.11	15.69	16.16	15.51	14.26	12.18	9.79	7.19	4.95	3.17	1.59	1.20
24	6.76	10.19	12.41	13.83	14.25	13.63	12.46	10.49	8.27	5.86	3.84	2.31	1.04	0.73
27	5.95	8.97	10.92	12.19	12.56	11.97	10.88	9.04	6.98	4.77	2.98	1.68	0.68	0.45
30	5.23	7.89	9.61	10.75	11.08	10.51	9.50	7.79	5.89	3.88	2.32	1.22	0.44	0.28
33	4.60	6.94	8.46	9.48	9.77	9.23	8.30	6.71	4.97	3.16	1.80	0.89	0.29	0.17
36	4.05	6.11	7.44	8.35	8.61	8.11	7.25	5.78	4.19	2.58	1.40	0.65	0.19	0.10
48	2.29	3.45	4.20	4.77	4.92	4.56	3.99	3.01	2.00	1.06	0.48	0.17	0.03	0.01
60	1.29	1.95	2.37	2.72	2.81	2.56	2.19	1.56	0.96	0.44	0.16	0.05	0.01	0.00
72	0.73	1.10	1.34	1.55	1.61	1.44	1.21	0.81	0.46	0.18	0.06	0.01	0.00	0.00
84	0.41	0.62	0.76	0.89	0.92	0.81	0.66	0.42	0.22	0.07	0.02	0.00	0.00	0.00
96	0.23	0.35	0.43	0.51	0.52	0.46	0.37	0.22	0.10	0.03	0.01	0.00	0.00	0.00
108	0.13	0.20	0.24	0.29	0.30	0.26	0.20	0.11	0.05	0.01	0.00	0.00	0.00	0.00
120	0.07	0.11	0.14	0.17	0.17	0.14	0.11	0.06	0.02	0.01	0.00	0.00	0.00	0.00

TABLE 21

Noninstitutional Disability Days by ADL/CI Status and Duration from Incurral; ADLs: 1; CI: yes; Sex: Female

Percentage of Noninstitutional Disability Days beyond Duration

Duration (Months)	Incurral Age													
	37	42	47	52	57	62	67	72	77	82	87	92	97	102
0	1.54	1.07	1.00	1.24	1.72	2.33	2.99	3.61	4.12	4.40	4.39	3.99	3.12	1.68
1	1.54	1.07	1.00	1.24	1.70	2.30	2.95	3.56	4.03	4.28	4.23	3.80	2.88	1.53
2	1.53	1.06	0.99	1.23	1.69	2.28	2.92	3.51	3.95	4.16	4.08	3.62	2.66	1.39
3	1.53	1.06	0.99	1.22	1.68	2.26	2.88	3.46	3.88	4.05	3.93	3.45	2.46	1.26
4	1.52	1.06	0.99	1.22	1.67	2.24	2.85	3.41	3.80	3.93	3.79	3.29	2.28	1.15
5	1.52	1.05	0.98	1.21	1.66	2.22	2.82	3.36	3.73	3.82	3.65	3.13	2.10	1.04
6	1.51	1.05	0.98	1.20	1.65	2.20	2.78	3.31	3.65	3.72	3.52	2.98	1.94	0.95
7	1.51	1.05	0.98	1.20	1.64	2.18	2.75	3.27	3.58	3.61	3.39	2.84	1.80	0.86
8	1.51	1.04	0.98	1.19	1.63	2.16	2.72	3.22	3.51	3.51	3.26	2.71	1.66	0.78
9	1.50	1.04	0.97	1.19	1.62	2.13	2.69	3.17	3.44	3.41	3.15	2.58	1.53	0.71
10	1.50	1.04	0.97	1.18	1.61	2.11	2.66	3.13	3.37	3.32	3.03	2.46	1.42	0.64
11	1.49	1.04	0.97	1.17	1.60	2.09	2.62	3.08	3.31	3.23	2.92	2.34	1.31	0.59
12	1.49	1.03	0.96	1.17	1.59	2.07	2.59	3.04	3.24	3.13	2.81	2.23	1.21	0.53
15	1.48	1.02	0.96	1.15	1.56	2.01	2.48	2.88	3.02	2.85	2.50	1.92	0.96	0.40
18	1.46	1.01	0.95	1.13	1.53	1.94	2.38	2.73	2.82	2.59	2.22	1.65	0.77	0.31
21	1.45	1.01	0.94	1.11	1.49	1.88	2.28	2.59	2.63	2.36	1.97	1.43	0.61	0.23
24	1.44	1.00	0.93	1.10	1.46	1.82	2.18	2.45	2.45	2.14	1.75	1.23	0.48	0.18
27	1.43	0.99	0.92	1.08	1.43	1.76	2.09	2.33	2.29	1.95	1.55	1.06	0.39	0.13
30	1.41	0.98	0.92	1.06	1.40	1.70	2.00	2.21	2.13	1.77	1.38	0.91	0.31	0.10
33	1.40	0.97	0.91	1.05	1.37	1.64	1.92	2.09	1.99	1.61	1.22	0.79	0.24	0.08
36	1.39	0.96	0.90	1.03	1.34	1.59	1.84	1.98	1.86	1.46	1.09	0.68	0.19	0.06
48	1.32	0.91	0.85	0.93	1.20	1.35	1.51	1.57	1.37	0.96	0.64	0.35	0.07	0.02
60	1.25	0.87	0.81	0.85	1.08	1.15	1.24	1.24	1.01	0.63	0.38	0.18	0.03	0.01
72	1.19	0.82	0.77	0.77	0.97	0.98	1.02	0.98	0.75	0.42	0.23	0.09	0.01	0.01
84	1.13	0.78	0.73	0.70	0.87	0.83	0.84	0.77	0.55	0.27	0.13	0.05	0.00	0.00
96	1.07	0.74	0.69	0.64	0.78	0.71	0.69	0.61	0.41	0.18	0.08	0.02	0.00	0.00
108	1.01	0.70	0.66	0.58	0.70	0.60	0.56	0.48	0.30	0.12	0.05	0.01	0.00	0.00
120	0.96	0.67	0.62	0.53	0.63	0.51	0.46	0.38	0.22	0.08	0.03	0.01	0.00	0.00

641

TABLE 22

NONINSTITUTIONAL DISABILITY DAYS BY ADL/CI STATUS AND DURATION FROM INCURRAL; ADLS: 2; CI: NO; SEX: FEMALE

Percentage of Noninstitutional Disability Days beyond Duration

Duration (Months)	Incurral Age													
	37	42	47	52	57	62	67	72	77	82	87	92	97	102
0	3.57	5.96	7.64	8.75	9.42	9.79	10.00	10.18	10.47	11.00	11.91	13.34	15.42	18.28
1	3.44	5.75	7.37	8.45	9.11	9.48	9.70	9.87	10.14	10.59	11.34	12.54	14.22	16.69
2	3.32	5.55	7.12	8.17	8.81	9.19	9.40	9.58	9.82	10.20	10.81	11.79	13.12	15.24
3	3.21	5.36	6.87	7.90	8.52	8.90	9.12	9.29	9.51	9.83	10.29	11.09	12.10	13.91
4	3.10	5.17	6.64	7.63	8.24	8.62	8.84	9.01	9.21	9.46	9.80	10.43	11.16	12.70
5	2.99	5.00	6.41	7.38	7.96	8.35	8.57	8.74	8.92	9.11	9.34	9.80	10.30	11.59
6	2.89	4.82	6.19	7.13	7.70	8.09	8.31	8.47	8.64	8.78	8.90	9.22	9.50	10.58
7	2.79	4.66	5.97	6.89	7.45	7.83	8.06	8.22	8.37	8.45	8.47	8.67	8.76	9.66
8	2.69	4.50	5.77	6.66	7.20	7.59	7.82	7.97	8.11	8.14	8.07	8.15	8.08	8.82
9	2.60	4.34	5.57	6.44	6.97	7.35	7.58	7.73	7.86	7.84	7.69	7.67	7.46	8.05
10	2.51	4.19	5.37	6.22	6.74	7.12	7.35	7.50	7.61	7.55	7.33	7.21	6.88	7.35
11	2.42	4.05	5.19	6.01	6.51	6.90	7.13	7.28	7.37	7.28	6.98	6.78	6.34	6.71
12	2.34	3.91	5.01	5.81	6.30	6.68	6.91	7.06	7.14	7.01	6.65	6.37	5.85	6.13
15	2.08	3.47	4.45	5.19	5.63	5.99	6.22	6.35	6.39	6.15	5.62	5.17	4.50	4.57
18	1.85	3.09	3.96	4.63	5.03	5.38	5.60	5.72	5.71	5.40	4.76	4.20	3.46	3.41
21	1.64	2.75	3.52	4.13	4.49	4.83	5.04	5.15	5.11	4.74	4.03	3.41	2.67	2.54
24	1.46	2.44	3.13	3.69	4.01	4.34	4.53	4.63	4.57	4.16	3.41	2.76	2.05	1.89
27	1.30	2.17	2.78	3.29	3.59	3.89	4.08	4.17	4.09	3.65	2.88	2.24	1.58	1.41
30	1.15	1.93	2.47	2.94	3.20	3.49	3.67	3.75	3.66	3.21	2.44	1.82	1.21	1.05
33	1.03	1.72	2.20	2.62	2.86	3.14	3.30	3.38	3.27	2.81	2.07	1.48	0.93	0.79
36	0.91	1.52	1.96	2.34	2.56	2.81	2.97	3.04	2.93	2.47	1.75	1.20	0.72	0.59
48	0.54	0.90	1.15	1.40	1.55	1.73	1.85	1.89	1.77	1.37	0.83	0.47	0.23	0.16
60	0.32	0.53	0.67	0.84	0.93	1.06	1.16	1.17	1.07	0.76	0.39	0.19	0.07	0.04
72	0.19	0.31	0.40	0.50	0.56	0.65	0.72	0.73	0.65	0.42	0.19	0.07	0.02	0.01
84	0.11	0.18	0.23	0.30	0.34	0.40	0.45	0.45	0.39	0.23	0.09	0.03	0.01	0.01
96	0.06	0.11	0.14	0.18	0.21	0.25	0.28	0.28	0.24	0.13	0.04	0.01	0.00	0.00
108	0.04	0.06	0.08	0.11	0.12	0.15	0.18	0.17	0.14	0.07	0.02	0.00	0.00	0.00
120	0.02	0.04	0.05	0.06	0.08	0.09	0.11	0.11	0.09	0.04	0.01	0.00	0.00	0.00

TABLE 23

NONINSTITUTIONAL DISABILITY DAYS BY ADL/CI STATUS AND DURATION FROM INCURRAL; ADLS: 2; CI: YES; SEX: FEMALE

Percentage of Noninstitutional Disability Days beyond Duration

Duration (Months)	Incurral Age													
	37	42	47	52	57	62	67	72	77	82	87	92	97	102
0	0.88	0.38	0.21	0.32	0.62	1.06	1.57	2.06	2.49	2.77	2.84	2.63	2.07	1.10
1	0.88	0.38	0.21	0.31	0.62	1.05	1.55	2.04	2.45	2.72	2.77	2.54	1.98	1.04
2	0.87	0.37	0.21	0.31	0.61	1.05	1.54	2.02	2.42	2.67	2.70	2.46	1.90	0.98
3	0.87	0.37	0.21	0.31	0.61	1.04	1.52	2.00	2.39	2.63	2.63	2.38	1.82	0.93
4	0.87	0.37	0.21	0.31	0.61	1.03	1.51	1.98	2.36	2.58	2.56	2.30	1.74	0.88
5	0.86	0.37	0.21	0.31	0.60	1.02	1.50	1.96	2.32	2.53	2.50	2.22	1.67	0.83
6	0.86	0.37	0.20	0.31	0.60	1.02	1.48	1.94	2.29	2.49	2.43	2.15	1.60	0.79
7	0.85	0.36	0.20	0.30	0.60	1.01	1.47	1.92	2.26	2.44	2.37	2.07	1.53	0.74
8	0.85	0.36	0.20	0.30	0.59	1.00	1.46	1.89	2.23	2.40	2.31	2.00	1.46	0.70
9	0.84	0.36	0.20	0.30	0.59	0.99	1.45	1.87	2.20	2.36	2.25	1.94	1.40	0.67
10	0.84	0.36	0.20	0.30	0.58	0.99	1.43	1.85	2.17	2.32	2.20	1.87	1.34	0.63
11	0.84	0.36	0.20	0.29	0.58	0.98	1.42	1.84	2.14	2.27	2.14	1.81	1.28	0.60
12	0.83	0.35	0.20	0.29	0.58	0.97	1.41	1.82	2.11	2.23	2.09	1.75	1.23	0.56
15	0.82	0.35	0.19	0.28	0.56	0.94	1.36	1.74	2.01	2.09	1.91	1.56	1.06	0.47
18	0.80	0.34	0.19	0.28	0.55	0.92	1.32	1.67	1.91	1.96	1.75	1.39	0.92	0.39
21	0.79	0.34	0.18	0.27	0.53	0.89	1.27	1.61	1.82	1.83	1.60	1.24	0.80	0.33
24	0.77	0.33	0.18	0.27	0.52	0.86	1.23	1.54	1.73	1.71	1.46	1.11	0.69	0.27
27	0.76	0.32	0.18	0.26	0.51	0.84	1.19	1.48	1.64	1.60	1.34	0.99	0.60	0.23
30	0.74	0.31	0.17	0.26	0.50	0.81	1.15	1.42	1.56	1.50	1.22	0.88	0.52	0.19
33	0.73	0.30	0.17	0.24	0.48	0.79	1.11	1.37	1.48	1.40	1.12	0.79	0.45	0.16
36	0.71	0.27	0.15	0.23	0.47	0.76	1.08	1.31	1.41	1.31	1.02	0.70	0.39	0.13
48	0.63	0.24	0.13	0.20	0.40	0.64	0.89	1.07	1.09	0.96	0.68	0.43	0.21	0.06
60	0.56	0.21	0.12	0.18	0.35	0.53	0.74	0.87	0.85	0.71	0.46	0.26	0.11	0.03
72	0.50	0.19	0.11	0.16	0.30	0.45	0.61	0.70	0.66	0.52	0.30	0.16	0.06	0.01
84	0.45	0.17	0.10	0.14	0.25	0.37	0.51	0.57	0.51	0.38	0.20	0.10	0.03	0.01
96	0.40	0.15	0.09	0.13	0.22	0.31	0.42	0.46	0.40	0.28	0.13	0.06	0.02	0.00
108	0.35	0.14	0.08	0.12	0.19	0.26	0.35	0.38	0.31	0.21	0.09	0.04	0.01	0.00
120	0.31	0.13	0.07	0.11	0.16	0.22	0.29	0.31	0.24	0.15	0.06	0.02	0.01	0.00

TABLE 24

NONINSTITUTIONAL DISABILITY DAYS BY ADL/CI STATUS AND DURATION FROM INCURRAL; ADLS: 3+; CI: NO; SEX: FEMALE

Percentage of Noninstitutional Disability Days beyond Duration

Duration (Months)	Incurral Age													
	37	42	47	52	57	62	67	72	77	82	87	92	97	102
0	4.01	6.36	8.09	9.36	10.30	11.07	11.81	12.68	13.82	15.38	17.51	20.36	24.07	28.80
1	3.86	6.13	7.80	9.05	9.97	10.75	11.49	12.36	13.49	15.00	17.03	19.70	23.19	27.70
2	3.72	5.90	7.51	8.75	9.66	10.45	11.19	12.05	13.16	14.64	16.56	19.06	22.35	26.64
3	3.59	5.69	7.24	8.47	9.36	10.15	10.89	11.75	12.84	14.28	16.10	18.45	21.54	25.63
4	3.45	5.48	6.97	8.19	9.06	9.87	10.60	11.45	12.53	13.93	15.65	17.85	20.76	24.65
5	3.33	5.28	6.72	7.92	8.78	9.59	10.31	11.16	12.23	13.59	15.22	17.27	20.00	23.71
6	3.21	5.09	6.47	7.66	8.50	9.32	10.04	10.88	11.94	13.26	14.80	16.72	19.28	22.81
7	3.09	4.90	6.23	7.41	8.24	9.05	9.77	10.61	11.65	12.93	14.39	16.18	18.57	21.94
8	2.98	4.72	6.01	7.17	7.98	8.80	9.51	10.35	11.37	12.61	14.00	15.65	17.90	21.10
9	2.87	4.55	5.79	6.93	7.73	8.55	9.25	10.09	11.09	12.31	13.61	15.15	17.25	20.30
10	2.76	4.38	5.57	6.71	7.49	8.31	9.01	9.83	10.83	12.01	13.23	14.66	16.62	19.52
11	2.66	4.22	5.37	6.49	7.25	8.07	8.77	9.59	10.57	11.71	12.87	14.18	16.02	18.78
12	2.56	4.07	5.17	6.27	7.02	7.85	8.53	9.35	10.31	11.43	12.51	13.73	15.44	18.06
15	2.26	3.59	4.57	5.61	6.31	7.12	7.78	8.56	9.47	10.46	11.30	12.15	13.45	15.62
18	2.00	3.17	4.03	5.01	5.66	6.46	7.09	7.84	8.69	9.58	10.20	10.76	11.71	13.51
21	1.76	2.80	3.56	4.48	5.09	5.86	6.47	7.18	7.98	8.77	9.21	9.53	10.20	11.68
24	1.56	2.47	3.14	4.00	4.57	5.32	5.89	6.58	7.33	8.03	8.31	8.44	8.89	10.10
27	1.37	2.18	2.77	3.58	4.10	4.83	5.37	6.03	6.73	7.35	7.50	7.47	7.74	8.74
30	1.21	1.92	2.45	3.20	3.68	4.38	4.90	5.52	6.18	6.73	6.77	6.62	6.74	7.56
33	1.07	1.70	2.16	2.86	3.31	3.98	4.47	5.06	5.67	6.16	6.12	5.86	5.87	6.53
36	0.95	1.50	1.91	2.55	2.97	3.61	4.07	4.63	5.21	5.64	5.52	5.19	5.11	5.65
48	0.54	0.86	1.09	1.55	1.84	2.33	2.68	3.11	3.51	3.73	3.41	2.93	2.66	2.84
60	0.31	0.49	0.63	0.94	1.14	1.51	1.76	2.09	2.36	2.46	2.11	1.65	1.38	1.42
72	0.18	0.28	0.36	0.57	0.70	0.98	1.16	1.40	1.59	1.63	1.30	0.93	0.72	0.71
84	0.10	0.16	0.21	0.35	0.44	0.63	0.76	0.94	1.07	1.08	0.80	0.53	0.37	0.36
96	0.06	0.09	0.12	0.21	0.27	0.41	0.50	0.63	0.72	0.71	0.50	0.30	0.19	0.18
108	0.03	0.05	0.07	0.13	0.17	0.26	0.33	0.42	0.48	0.47	0.31	0.17	0.10	0.09
120	0.02	0.03	0.04	0.08	0.10	0.17	0.22	0.28	0.33	0.31	0.19	0.10	0.05	0.05

TABLE 25

NONINSTITUTIONAL DISABILITY DAYS BY ADL/CI STATUS AND DURATION FROM INCURRAL; ADLS: 3+; CI: YES; SEX: FEMALE

Percentage of Noninstitutional Disability Days beyond Duration

Duration (Months)	Incurral Age													
	37	42	47	52	57	62	67	72	77	82	87	92	97	102
0	1.30	0.70	0.58	0.83	1.33	1.98	2.66	3.26	3.68	3.79	3.49	2.67	1.21	1.00
1	1.29	0.70	0.58	0.82	1.32	1.96	2.64	3.24	3.65	3.75	3.46	2.64	1.20	0.99
2	1.29	0.70	0.58	0.82	1.31	1.95	2.62	3.21	3.61	3.72	3.42	2.61	1.18	0.97
3	1.28	0.69	0.57	0.81	1.30	1.93	2.60	3.18	3.58	3.68	3.39	2.58	1.17	0.96
4	1.28	0.69	0.57	0.81	1.29	1.92	2.58	3.15	3.55	3.64	3.35	2.55	1.15	0.94
5	1.27	0.69	0.57	0.80	1.28	1.90	2.56	3.12	3.52	3.61	3.32	2.52	1.14	0.93
6	1.27	0.69	0.57	0.79	1.27	1.89	2.54	3.10	3.48	3.57	3.29	2.49	1.13	0.91
7	1.27	0.68	0.57	0.79	1.26	1.87	2.51	3.07	3.45	3.54	3.25	2.47	1.11	0.90
8	1.26	0.68	0.56	0.78	1.25	1.86	2.49	3.04	3.42	3.50	3.22	2.44	1.10	0.89
9	1.26	0.68	0.56	0.78	1.25	1.84	2.47	3.02	3.39	3.47	3.19	2.41	1.09	0.87
10	1.25	0.68	0.56	0.77	1.24	1.83	2.45	2.99	3.36	3.43	3.16	2.38	1.07	0.86
11	1.25	0.67	0.56	0.77	1.23	1.81	2.43	2.96	3.33	3.40	3.13	2.36	1.06	0.85
12	1.24	0.67	0.56	0.76	1.22	1.80	2.41	2.94	3.30	3.36	3.09	2.33	1.05	0.83
15	1.22	0.66	0.55	0.74	1.18	1.74	2.35	2.85	3.19	3.24	2.97	2.23	0.99	0.78
18	1.20	0.65	0.54	0.72	1.15	1.69	2.28	2.76	3.08	3.12	2.86	2.13	0.94	0.74
21	1.18	0.64	0.53	0.70	1.11	1.64	2.22	2.67	2.97	3.00	2.74	2.04	0.90	0.69
24	1.16	0.63	0.52	0.68	1.08	1.59	2.15	2.59	2.87	2.89	2.64	1.95	0.85	0.65
27	1.15	0.62	0.51	0.66	1.05	1.55	2.09	2.51	2.77	2.78	2.53	1.86	0.81	0.61
30	1.13	0.61	0.50	0.65	1.02	1.50	2.03	2.43	2.68	2.68	2.43	1.78	0.77	0.58
33	1.11	0.60	0.50	0.63	0.98	1.46	1.98	2.36	2.59	2.58	2.34	1.70	0.73	0.54
36	1.09	0.59	0.49	0.61	0.96	1.41	1.92	2.28	2.50	2.49	2.24	1.63	0.69	0.51
48	1.00	0.54	0.45	0.53	0.81	1.20	1.64	1.94	2.11	2.07	1.85	1.31	0.54	0.37
60	0.92	0.49	0.41	0.45	0.68	1.02	1.40	1.66	1.78	1.72	1.52	1.06	0.42	0.27
72	0.84	0.45	0.38	0.39	0.58	0.86	1.20	1.41	1.50	1.43	1.25	0.85	0.33	0.20
84	0.77	0.41	0.34	0.33	0.49	0.73	1.02	1.20	1.27	1.19	1.03	0.69	0.26	0.14
96	0.70	0.38	0.32	0.28	0.41	0.62	0.87	1.02	1.07	0.99	0.85	0.56	0.20	0.11
108	0.64	0.35	0.29	0.24	0.35	0.52	0.75	0.87	0.90	0.82	0.70	0.45	0.16	0.08
120	0.59	0.32	0.26	0.21	0.29	0.45	0.64	0.74	0.76	0.68	0.58	0.36	0.12	0.06

645

D. Considerations in Using the Noninstitutional Tables

In order to use the tables to construct claim costs appropriate for the valuation of noninstitutional benefits, the valuation actuary should consider the following.

- How does the benefit trigger of the policy relate to the ADL/CI definitions used to construct the tables? Different ADL types and definitions of impairment may require translation to use the tables. For each tabular ADL/CI status, the valuation actuary must determine the probability of the policy's benefit trigger being met to the satisfaction of the those responsible for claim administration.
- The valuation actuary must further determine the rate of benefit utilization by the policyholder for each ADL/CI status. Such an assessment might consider the policyholder's perception of service options, available financing, disposition toward use of benefits, availability of spouse or family informal care, and possible interaction with institutional policy benefits. Absent any reasonable basis for determining the impact of such factors, the valuation actuary might conservatively assume that the policyholder will fully utilize policy benefits whenever the benefit trigger is satisfied.
- For examples of testing the valuation actuary may want to consider, see Cases 5, 6, 7, and 8 of Appendix C.
- What is the impact of underwriting, or lack thereof, on the incidence rates and average number of disability days? Similarly, what impact is associated with antiselective lapsation? These are discussed in Section VII.
- In what manner can episodic policy limits for noninstitutional benefits be reflected in the calculations? What is the impact of aggregate lifetime benefit limits for such a policy?
- The tables assume that the onset of a disability period is the point at which the individual failed in at least one ADL or was cognitively impaired, even if the benefit trigger is more restrictive. What adjustments are appropriate for the policy definition of claim incurral? While regroupings of disability months might significantly affect incidence rates and average disability days per episode, the quinquennial claims costs (the product) are not likely to change dramatically. These considerations may be more significant for claim reserve determination.

Claim costs by incurral age are obtained by multiplying the disability episode incidence rates by the corresponding average noninstitutional policy benefit. The latter is determined as the sum over all ADL/CI statuses and payment durations of the tabular percentage of disability days falling in that status/duration and the valuation actuary's estimate of noninstitutional benefits arising in that case.

For example, suppose the policy provides for a two-year home health care benefit of up to $50 per day after satisfying a three-month elimination period. The benefit trigger is 2 ADLs or CI. If we assume full utilization of benefits while the trigger is satisfied, the valuation actuary might proceed as follows. Assume again a 72-year-old female.

For each ADL/CI status, evaluate the percentage of disability days falling between 3 months and 27 months from incurral. If the actual elimination and benefit periods are measured in cumulative benefit (service) days rather than calendar days, a further adjustment would be necessary. That is, 24 benefit months would correspond to 48 calendar months if benefits were utilized only 15 days per month. This conversion rate would vary with ADL/CI status; that is, benefit utilization would be greater for more severe impairment. (The valuation diskette uses such a technique, allowing the calendar-to-service time conversion rate to vary by duration from incurral and ADL/CI status.) In this example, no adjustments are made.

$$\begin{array}{llll}
\text{ADL: } 0 & \text{CI: } & \text{yes} & 0.3522 - 0.3021 = 0.0501 \\
\text{ADL: } 1 & \text{CI: } & \text{no} & 0.2834 - 0.0904 = 0.1930 \\
\text{ADL: } 1 & \text{CI: } & \text{yes} & 0.0346 - 0.0233 = 0.0113 \\
\text{ADL: } 2 & \text{CI: } & \text{no} & 0.0929 - 0.0417 = 0.0512 \\
\text{ADL: } 2 & \text{CI: } & \text{yes} & 0.0200 - 0.0148 = 0.0052 \\
\text{ADL: } 3+ & \text{CI: } & \text{no} & 0.1175 - 0.0603 = 0.0572 \\
\text{ADL: } 3+ & \text{CI: } & \text{yes} & 0.0315 - 0.0251 = 0.0064
\end{array}$$

Excluding the portion associated with 1 ADL and no CI, the total is 18.14% of the 961 noninstitutional disability day average, about 174 days per episode. At $50 per day and with an incidence rate of 0.02445 per year, the claim cost is equal to $50 \times 0.02445 \times 174 = \$213$ per year.

No simple method can anticipate the many variations in policy specifications and other environmental factors encountered in practice. The valuation actuary must be relied upon to make appropriate adjustments to such baseline calculations.

IV. APPLICATION OF TABLES

Historically, many LTC policies provided only nursing home (institutional) coverage. In more recent years, home health care coverage has been provided. Some have provided home health care alone. Other LTC policies have been developed as what might be called comprehensive LTC policies, providing both basic types of coverage. These two basic types are included in a wide variety of combinations (such as different maximum benefit amounts, different daily benefit amounts, and different benefit triggers). Policies often provide a "pot of money" to be spent in any combination of nursing home and home health care that the eligible insured chooses.

It is clear that there are an unlimited number of ways in which institutional and noninstitutional benefits can be—and are—combined in LTC insurance policies. That presents very real challenges for developing valuation recommendations.

In some comments in other sections in this final report, reference is made to when and how the tables of Sections II and III are to be combined for policies with elements of both institutional and noninstitutional LTC insurance. For those and many other forms of variables to be recognized in the valuation, the valuation actuary should consider the assistance provided by the valuation diskette that is a companion to this final report, which is available from the SOA office. That valuation diskette provides guidance on the use of those basic tables. Assumptions needed to be made are identified, and default assumptions are provided. This is described in Appendixes D and E to this final report.

The LTC valuation actuary will find it beneficial to become familiar with that valuation diskette.

It is instructive to identify some of the LTC insurance product elements for which the valuation actuary may need to make adjustments to these valuation recommendations, including especially the morbidity tables that are found in Sections II and III.

A. Product Features

- Institutional policies may need morbidity adjustments for features of older generations of policies that define eligible benefits related to the requirements of a three-day hospital stay or the institution's levels of care (for example, skilled before lesser level).
- Noninstitutional benefits may require adjustment factors for various features that may not be included in the standard table, such as: respite care; adult day care; hospice care; various definitions of how the elimination period can be satisfied; and homemaker care services.
- All tables may need "integrated frequency adjustment factors" to account for the various combinations of institutional/noninstitutional LTC possibly provided in the policies. These may be:
  - An appropriate load for an institutional-only policy
  - An appropriate load for a noninstitutional-only policy
  - An appropriate reduction for comprehensive (that is, both institutional and noninstitutional) policies.

  The Task Force believes that the financial impact of separate elimination periods and benefit periods for institutional and noninstitutional portions of a plan is not significantly different from combined such limits.
- All tables may need an adjustment load for nonforfeiture benefits. (See Section X for discussion of this.)
- All tables may need an adjustment load for an indexed inflation protection feature.
- Some tables may need adjustment for indemnity versus expense-incurred benefit structures.
- All tables may need adjustment for claims-paying policies.
- All tables may need morbidity adjustment for alternative plans of care.
- All tables may need morbidity adjustment for variation in service utilization: noninstitutional for variation in service providers for which benefits would be paid (for example, licensure requirements) or institutional for variation in definition of types of institutions covered (for example, assisted-living facilities, Alzheimer's units).
- All tables may need adjustments for elimination period, maximum benefit amount, and daily benefit amount selection and antiselection (that is, loads or discounts beyond what the pure continuance tables would produce).

Illustrative of adjustments tested by the Task Force are Cases 9 and 10 of Appendix C.

B. Benefit Triggers

Many of today's LTC policies utilize ADLs as a trigger to determine an insured's eligibility for LTC benefits. While the use of ADLs has become very common, the specific ADLs used and the trigger points for benefits vary significantly by LTC product. In addition, some states regulate what ADLs can be used and what their trigger points are (for example, states such as Kansas, Texas, and California). The NAIC currently has a LTC Benefit Triggers Working Group studying the subject, intending some standardization, the outcome of which may lead to changes that the valuation actuary should take into consideration.

To merely illustrate the possible ADL variations, Table 26 shows some of the benefit triggers in use for each of a number of individual products for home health care.

TABLE 26

BENEFIT TRIGGERS USED BY SEVEN INSURERS FOR HOME HEALTH CARE

ADL	Insurer						
	A	B	C	D	E	F	G
Bathing					X		X
Dressing	X	X	X	X	X	X	X
Toileting	X	X	X	X	X	X	X
Transferring	X	X		X	X	X	X
Mobility			X				
Continence	X	X		X		X	X
Feeding	X	X	X	X	X	X	X
Taking Medication			X				
Trigger Number	1	2	2	2	2	2	2
Alternative Trigger(s)*	CI	MN	CI MN	—	CI MN	CI	CI

*CI = cognitive impairment; MN = medical necessity.

The impact of benefit triggers must be considered carefully. In particular, the valuation actuary should consider the following.

- Actual claim practices should be used in setting reserves. For example, an older policy that has a 3-day prior hospital stay trigger but is being administered as if that provision had been waived should be reserved accordingly. Likewise, a 3 ADL trigger that is being administered as if only 2 are required should be valued accordingly.
- The ADL and/or CI trigger is very much secondary to the nursing home placement in evaluating nursing facility utilization. Living in an institution may be presumptive evidence that the benefit trigger, however

defined, has been met. As a result, ADL adjustments may apply only, or to a much greater extent, to noninstitutional tables. (The resistance of the elderly to a nursing home placement may serve as self-policing risk management, although it is not always the elderly insured who makes the decision.)

- ADL adjustment for home health care benefits is more critical. The ADL trigger may be of primary significance in accurately predicting the population that will be eligible for services.
- There is no uniformly agreed-upon wording for any one ADL, and it is not likely that there will be soon. Also, they can be mixed and combined in various ways; this should be recognized.
- Agreement on a "hierarchy" to the ADL losses would be helpful to determine comparability of different triggers.
  - There is literature from research to support a definitive hierarchy to the 6-point Katz ADL scale: the ability to perform ADLs almost always (83%+) fails in the order, from first to last, of bathing, dressing, toileting, transferring, continence, and feeding.
  - Loss of continence often does not follow a predictable order.
  - It is not so clear where "taking medication" or "mobility" fall in the hierarchy.
- The degree of help needed to trigger benefits under an ADL definition is an important consideration. For example, the difference between "stand-by assistance" and "total dependence on human assistance" can be significant.
- Many policies include medical necessity and/or CI as an alternative trigger. This may significantly dampen the importance of the ADL trigger, because insureds will have alternative paths to qualifying for benefits.
- In the absence of any alternative triggers, the differences in the various ADL triggers still can be significant enough to warrant an adjustment in the standard tables.

C. Spousal Discount

Quite often, a discount in the premium is offered to an insured if the spouse of the insured is living or if the spouse of the insured is also insured. Some companies are more restrictive than others about the risk classification of the spouse and the continuation of the discount when the spouse dies. The amount of discount varies by company but is commonly 10% or 15% for both spouses insured.

General population statistics show that there are indeed differences in mortality and morbidity between married people and unmarried people. Lew and Garfinkel's paper, "Mortality at Ages 65 and Over" [*TSA* XXXVI (1984): 257–308], shows lower mortality for married people. The presence of a spouse as a caregiver is the obvious reason for the significantly smaller rate of institutionalization and the shorter length of stay of married people who are institutionalized in the 1985 NNHS. For example, the median duration of stay in the discharge portion of the 1985 NNHS is 41 days for married people, 107 days for widowed people, and 101 days for those who were never married. These are a function, probably, of a combination of both those less likely to be admitted if married, and thus more likely to be discharged dead, and those more likely to be discharged alive to an available spouse.

The presence of a caregiver, who may need help from time to time, may also be the reason for greater use of home health care by married people. Since a person who is married on the issue date of LTC insurance may later be unmarried, the claim cost curve for such a person is steeper than for a person unmarried at issue. Because of this, active life reserves reduced by the same percentage as may be used in discounting premiums may not produce adequate reserves.

Another factor for married couples is contagion. Often, the death or nursing home admission of one spouse is followed shortly by the death or admission of the other. This has been noted in the general population even when no contagious disease is involved.

When LTC insurance is introduced, a person's willingness to be a caregiver or to be the sole caregiver may diminish, because the insurance could be used to reduce the financial strain of having professional help. This situation would have a greater impact on the claim costs of products based on expense incurred—as opposed to disability—model policies, in which charges by professional caregivers do not have an impact on benefits payable.

Even if no premium discounts are offered to insureds with spouses, the valuation actuary ought to consider the impact of spouses, especially if the married versus unmarried mix is significantly different from the general population's distribution underlying the standard reserve tables. Such a distribution can be found in Trowbridge's paper, "Mortality Rates by Marital Status" [*TSA* XLVI (1994): 321–390].

D. Geographic Region

LTC costs and insurance claim costs do vary by the region of the country where the insured person resides. Some of the variation is due to different state regulations and related insurance policy content. Some of the variation is due to differences in the accessibility of services. For example, home health care service agencies are well established in Florida, which may reduce the rate of institutionalization, while the family is often the only source of home care in the rural Midwest. Also, the availability of nursing home beds as a percentage of the population varies significantly by region. Therefore, institutional benefits may need morbidity adjustments on a state-by-state or regional basis.

These possible geographic differences should be considered by the valuation actuary as related to the business being reserved.

E. Other Risk Classes

Some insurers classify LTC insureds as preferred, standard, and/or substandard or with several classes similar to disability income insurance. Related to these classifications, insureds can be identified as smokers versus nonsmokers. Variations among insurers are so widespread that no general statement about the impact of risk class on reserves can be made. Rather, the valuation actuary needs to consider the possible differences in incidence rates, length of claim, mortality, and voluntary lapse of the different risk classes that may be presented.

V. MORTALITY

An appropriate mortality table is one piece of the overall termination assumption to be used in the valuation of LTC insurance. The Task Force knows of no study of the mortality of LTC insurance contract-holders. Typically, insurers will find it impossible to distinguish between a death and a lapse, making such a study unusually difficult.

In the absence of good data, this final report's recommendations rely on Task Force judgment, guided by the following considerations:

- The Task Force judged LTC mortality to be antiselect. That is, lapses likely are to be from the more healthy lives, leaving a relatively higher mortality rate among persisters than would be experienced by lapsers.
- The Task Force believes LTC insurance underwriting is less selective on the basis of mortality than life insurance underwriting.

- The mortality basis should be conservative. That is, the mortality basis adopted for valuation should be lower than the mortality believed to be actually experienced. That is consistent with the conservative nature of statutory reserves, with relatively more insureds living to the higher claim older ages.
- The mortality basis of the valuation recommendation should extend beyond age 100.

The Task Force believed that unloaded life insurance mortality rates would be a good starting point for the recommendation. Consideration was given to constructing a new mortality table by adding conservatism to the unloaded 1980 CSO mortality rates, which would be achieved by lowering them somewhat and extending the table beyond age 100. After a number of attempts at constructing such a modified table had been made, the Task Force observed that the 1983 GAM table had the characteristics very similar to the desired new table. The 1983 GAM rates are a little lower than the unloaded 1980 CSO rates, and the 1983 GAM table extends to age 110. Some testing results are shown in Cases 15 and 16 in Appendix C.

It is important to note that the 1983 GAM table was *not* chosen because of any reasoning that LTC insured mortality was comparable, in principle, to group annuitant mortality. Rather, the 1983 GAM table was chosen because it is an existing, recognized, publicly used table that has the appropriate characteristics relative to the unloaded 1980 CSO rates.

A. Recommendation

The resulting mortality recommendation has the following elements:

- *Choice of Mortality Table.* Mortality is based on the 1983 GAM table.
- *Sex-Distinct Versus Unisex Mortality Rates.* The use of sex-distinct mortality and sex-distinct morbidity (see Sections II and III) is recommended. Sex-blended mortality (and morbidity) can be used if the result is not materially different from that using a sex-distinct calculation. The Task Force tested the sensitivity to blends by sex for mortality and morbidity; see Cases 1 and 2 in Appendix C as examples.
- *Age Basis.* The 1983 GAM mortality table, based on age nearest birthday (ANB), should be adjusted to an age last birthday (ALB) basis, if appropriate for a specific product.
- *Selection, Smoking/Nonsmoking, and the Like.* The effect of factors such as selection or a high prevalence of nonsmokers might make actual mortality less than aggregate mortality at the early policy durations or for

certain mixes of business. Conservatism in the total termination rates usually will be sufficient to provide for effects of mortality selection, even when unadjusted aggregate mortality rates are used for the mortality termination element. The testing done by the Task Force indicated that reserves are fairly insensitive to mortality selection factors. See Case 12 of Appendix C, for example.

B. Sensitivity

The Task Force tested the effect on the reserves of several different choices in the assumptions as compared to a typical average set of assumptions (identified as the "default").

Sensitivities tested included sex-blended versus sex-distinct mortality rates, different mortality tables, effects of mortality selection at issue, and antiselection on lapse. Some of the testing results are displayed in Cases 12, 13, and 14 in Appendix C.

There were no big surprises in the results. The results appear to be almost unaffected by the choice of mortality selection factors. The results with no antiselection on lapse were not very different from the default results, which included moderate antiselection on lapse. The most sensitivity was to the overall mortality and lapse assumptions.

The testing indicates that the valuation actuary should give particular care to ensure that the total termination assumptions are appropriate.

VI. VOLUNTARY LAPSES

It is appropriate to allow terminations in excess of mortality. The NAIC Model Minimum Reserve Standards for Individual and Group Health Insurance Contracts sets a ceiling of 8% on total terminations. (See Appendix F.) At the older issue ages at which much of this business is sold (above age 65 or 70) and for longer policy durations for which mortality is relatively high, the 8% global termination ceiling would significantly limit or even totally remove terminations for voluntary lapse from being allowed in addition to mortality. That is unduly restrictive.

However, morbidity probably will be affected by antiselection on lapses. That is, those who lapse probably are a better morbidity risk than those who do not lapse. (See Section VII.) Therefore, any allowance for lapses should be somewhat conservative (that is, lower than might be expected).

The effect of lapses on reserves was tested in various combinations of assumptions. Several illustrative test cases (Cases 17–21) are shown in Appendix C.

A. Recommendation

The proposed practice allows 80% of the voluntary lapse assumption used when the policy was filed and priced for state approval to market the product, with a ceiling of 8%. Lapse termination can be used in addition to the mortality decrement without a limit on the combination. If voluntary lapses are used in the valuation, an appropriate increase in morbidity due to the antiselection exhibited by persisters should be considered by the valuation actuary.

B. Treatment of Nonforfeiture Benefits

Reserves should be equal to at least the value of any nonforfeiture benefits. However, this level itself will be insufficient, in most cases, to provide an adequate reserve. (See Section X.)

VII. SELECTION AND ANTISELECTION

A. Selection

Sound underwriting is critical to proper risk management of a block of LTC insurance. Poor underwriting—whether inappropriate, not understood, or very little—leads to excessive early claims and an unstable block of business.

Underwriting must be done at issue, not at time of claim. Regulatory prohibitions against post-claims underwriting and "clean sheeting" of applications are widespread. These prohibitions are supported by consumers, regulators, and the insurance industry.

The impact of underwriting must be considered carefully. In particular, the valuation actuary should consider the following:

- *Select Period.* The impact of underwriting should be expected to level off after a period of time. Selection factors will vary by the degree of underwriting performed.
- *Age Variation.* Selection factors likely will vary by issue age; the effect of selection may be more significant at older issue ages. The select period may be longer for younger issue ages.

- *Rejection Rates.* The impact of underwriting might be considerable in situations in which a significant portion of applicants are rejected. However, if few applicants are rejected, positive selection will be less significant and antiselection by the consumer may be substantial.
- *Marketing Practices.* An insurer's marketing practices will cause rejection rates to vary and should be considered in establishing initial adjustments to claim costs.
- *Group Selection.* In the group market, morbidity can be affected by guaranteed issue provisions, participation rates, and requirements that employees be actively at work.
- *Substandard and Preferred Risk Classifications.* The impact of underwriting will vary by the risk classification system used by an insurer. Substandard risk morbidity may suggest an ultimate selection factor substantially greater than 1.00. Preferred risks likely will have a longer select period.
- *Ultimate or By Duration.* Positive selection during early durations will lower the valuation net premium and increase active life reserves. For statutory reserve purposes, the ultimate selection factor applied to the recommended morbidity basis should be at least 1.00.

B. Selection Recommendation

At a minimum, reserves should be based on the morbidity tables prescribed without select adjustments. The valuation actuary should consider including select morbidity adjustments used in pricing. However, selection factors should grade to an ultimate selection factor of at least 1.00 by duration 10.

The Task Force tested the impact on reserves from selection assumptions; see, for example, Cases 3 and 12 of Appendix C.

C. Antiselection

In the absence of nonforfeiture benefits, voluntary lapses will be more frequent on lower cost (healthier) individuals. As a result, voluntary lapses should be expected to increase claim costs per remaining individual. If lapses are included in the reserve calculation, the valuation actuary should recognize that lapses will have an impact on morbidity. In particular, the valuation actuary should consider the following:

- The level of antiselection should vary based on the level of lapse. For instance, a 10% lapse will produce higher antiselection than a 2% lapse.

- Statutory reserves will be based on lapse assumptions lower than those used in pricing. Therefore, the impact of antiselective lapses on reserve morbidity likely will be less than the impact on pricing morbidity.
- Antiselection on lapse may wear off after a period of time from lapse. In other words, although healthier individuals may lapse their policies while less healthy individuals persist, over time their morbidity may converge.
- In the absence of nonforfeiture benefits, it is clear that lapses will be for a healthier group of risks. The need to recognize antiselection on lapse may be less for policies with nonforfeiture benefits, depending on the richness of the nonforfeiture benefits.
- A minimum level of lapse, perhaps in the 2%–3% range, likely will not produce antiselection. This minimum level should be recognized when the level of antiselection is determined.

The valuation diskette provides the valuation actuary with one possible method for quantifying the effect of assumed antiselective lapses. The method is based on the theory that if insureds could *perfectly* select against the insurer, only individuals who will never require LTC services would lapse. The same number of future claims would be incurred but by a smaller group of insureds. Therefore, incidence rates would be greater. Conversely, if *no antiselective* lapse occurs, the number of claims decreases in the same proportion as the in-force policies and the incidence of claim does not change. In reality, experience will fall between the perfect and no antiselective lapse scenarios.

The valuation diskette allows users to input assumptions for two areas related to lapses: the basic lapse assumption (see Section VI) and factors to recognize the better health of lapsers by duration from lapse (up to 10 durations from lapse). The latter is the antiselective effect.

The valuation diskette calculates the morbidity load for antiselective lapses using the following formula, where A/S means antiselective:

$$
\begin{aligned}
\text{Morbidity Load}_t = 1 \ / \ [&(1 - \text{Lapse Rate}_{t-10} \times \text{A/S Lapse Factor}_{10}) \\
\times \ &(1 - \text{Lapse Rate}_{t-9} \times \text{A/S Lapse Factor}_9) \\
\times \ &(1 - \text{Lapse Rate}_{t-8} \times \text{A/S Lapse Factor}_8) \\
&\quad \cdot \\
&\quad \cdot \\
&\quad \cdot \\
\times \ &(1 - \text{Lapse Rate}_{t-1} \times \text{A/S Lapse Factor}_1 \ )]
\end{aligned}
$$

The A/S lapse factors reflect the level of antiselection or the proportion of claims retained even though premiums are lost due to lapse. These factors are input by duration from lapse and range between 0 (no antiselection) and 1 (perfect antiselection). The factors should decrease by duration from lapse, to recognize that antiselection wears off from the point of lapse.

See sample test Case 4 of Appendix C for the impact of antiselection.

D. Antiselection Recommendation

If lapses are included in the reserve calculation, the valuation actuary should recognize that lapses will increase the average morbidity for the persisting policyholders. That can be reflected through appropriate choice of A/S lapse factors in the valuation diskette.

VIII. INTEREST RATE

Recognizing the time value of money is an important part of sound actuarial principles and commonly accepted Actuarial Standards of Practice (ASOP). Two relevant references are *ASOP No. 18*, "Long-Term Care Insurance," and *ASOP No. 5*, "Insured Health Claim Liabilities." An interest rate is used to discount future paid premiums, paid claims, and paid expenses. This interest rate quantifies the time value of money and should be related to the projected investment income for related assets.

In LTC valuation, the effect of the discounting process is to give more weight to cash flows in the near future and less weight to the increasingly negative flows that are expected further in the future. Increasing the interest rate results in decreasing the significance of cash flows in the distant future.

Interest rates are given different considerations in three types of reserves. Relatively low interest rates are used for *statutory reserves* shown in the annual statement, because this is in line with the conservative approach used in statutory accounting. For GAAP (generally accepted accounting principles), the inclusion of reasonable provisions for adverse deviations typically results in interest rates for GAAP reserves higher than those used for statutory but somewhat lower than "best estimate" rates. However, using interest rates lower than those prescribed by the Internal Revenue Service for calculating *tax reserves* could disqualify the insurer's tax deductibility of such reserves.

A. *Issues to Consider*

- Substantial assets can build up under a typical LTC policy. Cash from these assets may not be needed for several years or even decades. Therefore, the investment income produced by these assets may be more comparable to that of pension funds, rather than life insurance products where nonforfeiture benefits are required. (Currently, very few LTC policies have nonforfeiture benefits, and the forms of nonforfeiture benefit that appear to be the most likely to be mandated by the NAIC model regulation do not produce a "cash on demand" through lapse.) This argues for generally higher interest assumptions.

- To the contrary, it can also be argued that disability income (DI) insurance is similar to LTC in the way assets are built up and in the nature of the benefits (for example, benefits are not certain as in life insurance, and DI policies rarely contain nonforfeiture benefits). There is no flexibility in model regulations or laws for assuming an interest rate higher for DI than the rate for life, and LTC ought to be consistent with DI in this regard.

- Because of the more limited availability of cash on demand, the C-3 (interest) risk is less with LTC than it is with annuities and life insurance.

- If conservative interest rates are recommended for valuation, it may be argued that higher interest rates should be allowed if adequate cash-flow testing by the valuation actuary demonstrates the adequacy of such reserves.

- One might argue that the interest rate should not be defined on the issue date of the policy. Rather, the time when the premiums are paid, or more specifically, when the cash flows are positive, ought to define the interest rate used. This is similar to the change in fund basis (versus issue-year basis) used in the valuation of annuities.

- The interest rate used in determining the present value of amounts not yet due on claims typically is the rate in effect for life insurance policies that are issued on the incurred date of the claim. Interest rates defined by the issue date of the policy rather than by incurred date of the claim may be more appropriate, because the assets supporting the claim reserves are not invested funds newly made at that time of claim but were generated by prior premiums.

- Some regulators may not approve premium rate increases if morbidity experience is as expected but returns from investments are much lower than expected.

• The discount rate used in determining anticipated loss ratios for premium rate filings need not be related to the investment income assumed in pricing. (Filing of premium rates is beyond the scope of this final report.)

Test cases 22 and 23 of Appendix C show the impact of the interest rate chosen on resulting reserves.

B. Recommendation

The Task Force considered the various issues that influence the potential choices of interest rate for LTC insurance valuation. It also considered the existence of the NAIC model regulation on valuation for health insurance products (see Appendix F). It recognized the significance of the role of interest in LTC insurance reserves and in gross premium valuations in which the valuation actuary tests their adequacy. The Task Force also acknowledges that the role of interest in approaches to valuation is under consideration for other products and valuation generally. On balance, the Task Force sees no reason to depart from the current guidance. Thus, the Task Force makes the following recommendation: The maximum allowable interest rate for active life reserves for LTC policies issued in a given year should be equal to the maximum allowable interest rate for calculating reserves for whole life insurance policies (with maturities 20 or more years after issue) issued in the same year.

The maximum allowable interest rate for claim reserves incurred in a given year should be equal to the maximum allowable interest rate for calculating reserves for whole life insurance policies issued in the year of the claim, for those policies requiring contract reserves. For LTC policies not requiring contract reserves, the interest rate should be equal to that for the valuation of single-premium immediate annuities issued in the same year as claim incurral, less 100 basis points. (See Appendix F.)

Asset adequacy testing should be performed if the product is material to the insurer. Tests involving the sensitivity to declining interest rates are more important than disintermediation, unless significant nonforfeiture benefits payable in the form of cash are available.

IX. METHOD

Whether active life reserves should be calculated on the net level, one-year preliminary term, or two-year preliminary term basis is of some considerable interest. Each method is used by insurers today. Both the one and two-year preliminary term methods are in common usage today. All three methods were tested by the Task Force; see, for example, Cases 24 and 25 of Appendix C.

In a June 1, 1990 statement to the NAIC Life and Health Actuarial Task Force (Statement No. PS-90H-7), the American Academy of Actuaries opined that the one-year preliminary term method was appropriate for LTC insurance policies. That opinion was somewhat softened by discussion in 1990, allowing two-year preliminary term for policies issued prior to 1990.

As described in Appendix F, the current NAIC Model Minimum Reserve Standards for Individual and Group Health Insurance Contracts, amended in 1991 to include LTC, requires the one-year preliminary term method.

As noted in Section XVI, the Internal Revenue Code (IRC), in the view of many, prescribes reserves according to the two-year preliminary term method as the maximum that may be deducted by insurers for tax purposes.

Although it is recognized that the insurer can be significantly negatively affected by a limitation on reserve deductibility by the IRC, which appears to recognize reserves only on a somewhat weaker basis, the LTC valuation actuary must focus on what is right and best for the financial solvency of the insuring enterprise. The valuation actuary must also serve the needs of statutory accounting.

A. Analysis

Considerable analysis was devoted to this matter by the Task Force. The following points are some of the considerations given to the subject.

- Many of the written comments received as a result of the exposure report commented on this issue. They were not unanimous.
- Oral input at meetings of the Society of Actuaries and at the Valuation Actuary Symposium also were not particularly conclusive.
- The Task Force conducted some analysis of the expenses related to placing LTC insurance in force. This, in turn, suggests some degree of statutory reserve relief in the first (and maybe second) policy year from the strain otherwise produced from net level reserves. Such expenses are the prime reason for using other than net level reserves. We recognized that expenses do vary considerably among insurers. The Task Force's charge did not include expense analysis.
- Several possible criteria for deciding the minimum reserve method were considered by the Task Force. None yielded a clear basis, but all agree that a gross premium test should not be violated.
- The Task Force did considerable analysis using gross premium valuation tests. Many assumptions necessarily were made (premiums, expenses,

lapse, mortality, morbidity, etc.), but differing benefits were not tested and a model office was not constructed (issue ages 45 and 70 for both male and female were calculated). In spite of considerable work, the analysis was, understandably, fairly well simplified. The numerous cash flows and resulting analyses did not lead the Task Force to a clear conclusion. Strain on assumed corporate surplus by using the one-year preliminary term method did not rule out that method. Neither did it seem that the two-year method produced excessive relief.

- The Task Force also reviewed statutory earnings resulting from such cash flow tests. They, too, were inconclusive.
- The results of cash flows in the gross premium reserve analysis are at least as much a function of other assumptions used, especially interest rates, as they are of the reserve method chosen. Any profit pattern that results is dependent upon the degree of conservatism in other assumptions, not just the implied expense allowance.
- The valuation actuary should give consideration to the overall level of reserves and margins. For example, the two-year preliminary term method is more likely to be reasonable if other assumptions are conservative and contribute small margins.

B. Recommendation

There was no clear consensus among Task Force members on the minimum basis. A majority thought that there was no convincing evidence that would support prohibition of the two-year preliminary term method. A sizable minority of the Task Force thought, nevertheless, that one-year preliminary term should be the minimum required.

On balance, the Task Force believes that the two-year preliminary term method is the appropriate statutory minimum reserve method. Allowing that method is not to be interpreted as a default assumption.

The valuation actuary should be satisfied that whatever method is used is appropriate to the circumstances. The valuation actuary also should establish a premium reserve and consider the implications of the current NAIC Model Minimum Reserve Standards for Individual and Group Health Insurance Contracts. This model states that the minimum reserve is the greater of (1) the sum of the unearned premium and active life reserves for all contracts of the insurer subject to contract reserve requirements, and (2) the gross modal unearned premium reserve on all such contracts. This test can be performed on an aggregate basis.

For pieces of additional coverage purchased periodically at attained age premiums, the reserve for such prices should be on the net level basis if only renewal expenses are incurred on the addition. If underwriting is done on additional pieces of coverage or if higher-than-renewal commissions or marketing expenses are incurred on the addition, preliminary term valuation may be appropriate.

X. NONFORFEITURE BENEFITS

It is important to understand the reserving implications of various non-forfeiture benefit options, due to recent and current state and federal legislative activities such as the following:

- The NAIC in 1993 voted to mandate that nonforfeiture benefit options be included in all newly issued LTC policies.
- President Clinton's Health Security Act introduced in late 1993 included a section mandating nonforfeiture benefits in LTC policies, as have some of the other federal LTC bills introduced.
- As this final report is being prepared, the NAIC is finalizing adoption of the model regulation that specifies use of the "benefit bank" form as the required nonforfeiture benefit.
- Certain states (for example, New York) require that LTC insurers offer policyholders the choice of electing or not electing to have a nonforfeiture benefit. It is possible that once the NAIC includes a specific mandated nonforfeiture benefit option in the LTC model regulation, some states will pass that model. Other states may choose their own version of nonforfeiture laws for LTC. In any event, varied state action in this subject can be expected.

Actuaries should be very cautious about using intuition in trying to assess how to determine reserves for LTC nonforfeiture benefit options. What seems to make sense for other products does not necessarily make sense for LTC, because LTC has some unique characteristics.

A. Description of Various Nonforfeiture Benefit Forms

The following are the various forms encountered.

- *Shortened Benefit Period.* Upon lapse an insured continues to remain covered for the same daily benefit as prior to lapse. However, the benefit period is reduced to a duration according to a scale in the policy that depends on the time the policy was in force as premium paying prior to lapse. A variation of the above option is the benefit bank approach.

Under this option, the full benefits continue to be payable while there are funds in the benefit bank. The bank includes all or some portion of the premiums paid to date of lapse less any claim payments already made. The valuation diskette handles the SBP form of nonforfeiture, for both its versions, as described in Appendix D, Screen 9.

- *Return of Premium.* Upon voluntary lapse, an insured or the beneficiary receives in cash all premiums paid less any claim payments received. Contrary to options not paid in cash, this must also be paid on death.
- *Extended Term Insurance.* Upon lapse, an insured remains covered for the same benefit period and daily benefit amount as prior to lapse. However, the period of coverage is reduced to reflect the insured's age and policy duration at lapse.
- *Reduced Paid-up Option.* Upon lapse, an insured remains insured for the same benefit period and coverage period as prior to lapse. However, the daily benefit amount is reduced to reflect the insured's age and policy duration at lapse.
- *Cash Value.* Upon lapse or death, an insured receives a cash value that is equal to an amount of cash defined in the policy. That amount can be determined by the policy drafter in any of a number of ways. Contrary to options not paid in cash, this must also be paid on death.
- *Life Annuity.* Upon lapse, an insured receives a life annuity, which theoretically can be determined in any number of ways.
- *Other.* Listed above are some of the more common nonforfeiture benefit options. There are others not listed here, some of which are variations of the above options.

B. Reserve Components

Because of the variety and great number of possible nonforfeiture benefit forms, their amounts and patterns and because of the developing nature and uncertainty of the subject, this final report does not prescribe precise applicability of its recommendations to this subject. Rather, it offers several components of possible reserves to be considered.

1. Active Life Reserve Prior to Lapsation

It is not clear what is a conservative lapse and mortality assumption. Zero lapsation may not produce the highest active life reserves, especially if the contract has rich nonforfeiture benefits. It is important to test the effect of zero lapsation.

2. Paid-up Nonforfeiture Benefit Reserve after Lapsation

- *Morbidity Assumption.* The valuation actuary needs to recognize a hierarchy of risks, from less risky to most risky. The forms of cash options present no reserving risk once lapsation occurs. Nonforfeiture benefits, where paid-up LTC benefits can be adjusted after lapse, present an increase in risk to the extent that such adjustments are constrained. Nonforfeiture benefits, where such benefits cannot be adjusted after lapse, present the greatest risk. It is important to set minimum loadings that vary by that hierarchy of risks. The valuation actuary needs to distinguish between two types of loadings, one for antiselection (expected extra morbidity) and the other for uncertainty of risk.
- *Expense Risk.* The valuation actuary must retain in the reserves a proper loading for expected future expenses. This can be set as additional claim expense reserves. Future maintenance expenses should have been loaded in the premium.
- *Mortality and Interest Assumptions.* These are not necessarily different from the base LTC reserving assumptions.
- *Interactions of Claim Reserve and Active Life.* It may be appropriately conservative to hold both claim and active life reserves in some cases. In others, it may be adequate to hold the greater of a nonforfeiture benefit reserve or the claim reserve.

3. Claim Reserves Arising from Paid-up Nonforfeiture Benefits

This is to be treated as other claim reserves. (See Section XII.)

C. General

When calculating reserves, the valuation actuary must be sure to include values of nonforfeiture benefits at death or lapse corresponding to assumed mortality and voluntary lapse assumptions, respectively.

Unusual patterns of nonforfeiture benefits may cause reserves to be deficient if actual lapses and mortality do not follow assumptions. Sensitivity testing for variations in mortality and lapses should be done when there is any doubt about reserve adequacy.

The active life reserve should not be less than the net single premium for the nonforfeiture benefits at each policy duration.

XI. PREMIUM WAIVER

Waiver of premium product features vary. Waiver upon institutionalization is a common benefit in LTC insurance. Some policies also waive premiums if the insured is approved for home health care.

As with other insurance products, treating the waived premium as a cash benefit when no cash transaction takes place can be confusing.

The approach used to compute active life reserves generally determines which of two techniques should be employed to properly value waiver of premium benefits.

If the active life reserves computation assumes future premiums are received from all in-force policies regardless of benefit status, then a correcting adjustment is necessary. This is commonly accomplished by explicitly recognizing future waived premium as an additional benefit amount. The adjusted benefit amount is applied to active life reserve and claim reserve factors.

If the active life reserves computation omits premiums to be waived from the present value of future premiums, then no additional adjustments may be required.

When properly constructed, either approach can be expected to produce equivalent aggregate reserves. Special consideration may be necessary if the elimination period for waiver differs from that for the policy benefit, for waiver of spousal premium, or for home health care episodes that require ongoing premium payments.

Note the valuation diskette accompanying this final report assumes no premiums are paid once under waiver due to claim status, and therefore it also does not include waived premiums as a benefit.

XII. CLAIM RESERVES

Although many adjustments to the claim costs are permitted in the calculation of active life reserves, most of these adjustments are judged to be applicable to incidence rates. Once someone has become a continuing LTC claimant, continuation in claim is unaffected by most of the factors that may be viewed as affecting the claim costs.

A. *Interest*

The interest rate to be used in discounting future claim payments for claim reserves should not exceed the maximum rate permitted in the calculation of active life reserves for a contract issued in the same year as the claim is incurred. (See Section VIII, especially for LTC policies not requiring contract reserves.)

B. Recommended Reserves for Reported Claims

1. Nursing Home (Institutional) LTC Claims

This recommendation uses the continuance tables based on utilization data from the 1985 NNHS as interpreted and developed by the LTC Experience Committee and published in the *TSA 1988-89-90 Reports*. In particular, the reserves for reported institutional claims that have been determined to be payable by the insurer will not be less than disabled life annuities, calculated using the claim termination rates implied in the continuance tables from the *Reports* using the benefit period concept for insurable stays as explained and shown in Table 11 therein. This table is reproduced here as Table 27.

The proportions of admissions still resident for each period can be treated in the same manner as the l_x column of a life table to calculate disabled life annuities.

Appropriate adjustments for claims with inflation protection after the incurred date of claim are to be made.

The valuation actuary can determine and use salvage values if they exist (that is, savings from paying an expense incurred amount lower than the maximum daily amount of benefit that may have been reflected in pricing).

Any generally accepted actuarial method can be used to calculate the liabilities, as long as the reserve aggregate exceeds the minimum.

2. Home Health Care (Noninstitutional) LTC Claims

For claim reserve purposes, any one home health care claim should be defined no more liberally than beginning on the first date of care after the elimination period and ending on the first date on which no covered home health care benefits have been received for the prior 14 days. If a contract provision calls for an earlier recognition of home health care claim incurral, the contract definition should be used. Even if strict contract liability is determined based on home health care service date, all home health care benefits continuing without a 14-day interruption should have incurred dates dated back to the first day of such benefits, and claim reserves should be established based on this incurred date definition.

For all home health care claims for which more than 180 days of service have been received, reserves should be set up on a case-by-case basis, with the reserve being the present value of future expected home health care

TABLE 27

Proportion of Admissions Still Resident at the End of the Period Shown
Insurable Stays; Benefit Period Concept;
Adjusted to Match the 1985 NNHS Residents

Days from Admission	Age at Admission						
	<45	45–54	55–64	65–74	75–84	85–94	95+
	Male						
0	1.0000	1.0000	1.0000	1.0000	1.0000	1.0000	1.0000
10	0.8701	0.9103	0.9456	0.9016	0.8915	0.8927	0.9348
20	0.8456	0.8408	0.8640	0.8477	0.8077	0.7950	0.8519
30	0.8160	0.8306	0.8122	0.7785	0.7319	0.7350	0.8088
60	0.6995	0.7017	0.6973	0.6570	0.6107	0.6362	0.6307
90	0.6130	0.6175	0.6163	0.5712	0.5273	0.5608	0.5074
121	0.5482	0.5613	0.5576	0.5095	0.4682	0.5022	0.4195
151	0.4992	0.5233	0.5137	0.4645	0.4250	0.4559	0.3552
182	0.4619	0.4970	0.4799	0.4311	0.3925	0.4190	0.3070
212	0.4333	0.4783	0.4528	0.4061	0.3671	0.3890	0.2702
243	0.4110	0.4641	0.4303	0.3871	0.3465	0.3645	0.2417
273	0.3931	0.4525	0.4109	0.3720	0.3291	0.3442	0.2191
304	0.3782	0.4419	0.3935	0.3597	0.3139	0.3271	0.2011
334	0.3650	0.4312	0.3774	0.3490	0.3001	0.3127	0.1866
365	0.3529	0.4198	0.3621	0.3392	0.2873	0.3002	0.1749
547	0.2856	0.3259	0.2784	0.2808	0.2213	0.2454	0.1405
730	0.2366	0.2355	0.2271	0.2270	0.1670	0.1946	0.1281
912	0.2163	0.1995	0.2141	0.1957	0.1200	0.1384	0.0940
1095	0.2121	0.1789	0.2051	0.1697	0.0852	0.0938	0.0487
1277	0.2113	0.1541	0.1745	0.1378	0.0648	0.0666	0.0290
1460	0.2110	0.1409	0.1456	0.1126	0.0514	0.0496	0.0247
1642	0.2102	0.1377	0.1370	0.0997	0.0396	0.0359	0.0240
1825	0.2100	0.0984	0.1356	0.0842	0.0319	0.0280	0.0221
2190	0.1647	0.0849	0.1039	0.0410	0.0211	0.0117	0.0049
2555	0.1293	0.0715	0.0806	0.0203	0.0132	0.0009	0.0020
2920	0.1012	0.0589	0.0627	0.0102	0.0079	0.0001	0.0011
3285	0.0786	0.0474	0.0487	0.0053	0.0045	0.0000	0.0008
3650	0.0604	0.0373	0.0373	0.0029	0.0026	0.0000	0.0006
4015	0.0457	0.0287	0.0280	0.0016	0.0014	0.0000	0.0005
4380	0.0338	0.0217	0.0203	0.0009	0.0008	0.0000	0.0004
4745	0.0245	0.0160	0.0141	0.0006	0.0005	0.0000	0.0004
5110	0.0172	0.0116	0.0092	0.0004	0.0003	0.0000	0.0003
5475	0.0117	0.0083	0.0056	0.0002	0.0002	0.0000	0.0003
5840	0.0080	0.0059	0.0034	0.0002	0.0001	0.0000	0.0000
6205	0.0054	0.0042	0.0021	0.0001	0.0001	0.0000	0.0000
6570	0.0037	0.0030	0.0012	0.0001	0.0001	0.0000	0.0000
6935	0.0025	0.0021	0.0008	0.0001	0.0000	0.0000	0.0000
7300	0.0017	0.0015	0.0005	0.0000	0.0000	0.0000	0.0000
7665	0.0012	0.0011	0.0003	0.0000	0.0000	0.0000	0.0000
8030	0.0008	0.0008	0.0002	0.0000	0.0000	0.0000	0.0000
8395	0.0005	0.0006	0.0001	0.0000	0.0000	0.0000	0.0000
8760	0.0004	0.0004	0.0001	0.0000	0.0000	0.0000	0.0000
9125	0.0003	0.0003	0.0000	0.0000	0.0000	0.0000	0.0000

TABLE 27—*Continued*

Days from Admission	Age at Admission						
	<45	45–54	55–64	65–74	75–84	85–94	95+
	Female						
0	1.0000	1.0000	1.0000	1.0000	1.0000	1.0000	1.0000
10	0.8969	0.9749	0.9289	0.9323	0.9374	0.9206	0.9162
20	0.8084	0.9193	0.8520	0.8509	0.8641	0.8522	0.8697
30	0.7636	0.8625	0.8185	0.7869	0.7952	0.8033	0.8200
60	0.7414	0.7078	0.6994	0.6676	0.6912	0.6931	0.7476
90	0.7215	0.6113	0.6189	0.5871	0.6167	0.6165	0.6821
121	0.7034	0.5500	0.5637	0.5317	0.5622	0.5622	0.6238
151	0.6866	0.5108	0.5257	0.4932	0.5217	0.5231	0.5724
182	0.6709	0.4860	0.4994	0.4660	0.4909	0.4943	0.5277
212	0.6557	0.4683	0.4807	0.4464	0.4669	0.4725	0.4890
243	0.6410	0.4555	0.4672	0.4320	0.4476	0.4554	0.4555
273	0.6263	0.4461	0.4573	0.4209	0.4317	0.4413	0.4265
304	0.6117	0.4393	0.4491	0.4119	0.4181	0.4291	0.4007
334	0.5971	0.4342	0.4415	0.4040	0.4060	0.4179	0.3779
365	0.5828	0.4293	0.4335	0.3966	0.3951	0.4072	0.3574
547	0.5251	0.3627	0.3737	0.3472	0.3401	0.3450	0.2690
730	0.5068	0.2947	0.3237	0.2854	0.2947	0.2870	0.2146
912	0.4319	0.2685	0.2827	0.2335	0.2560	0.2411	0.1737
1095	0.3336	0.2634	0.2481	0.1996	0.2195	0.2049	0.1425
1277	0.2983	0.2492	0.2322	0.1755	0.1862	0.1695	0.1164
1460	0.2805	0.2244	0.2256	0.1554	0.1570	0.1323	0.0983
1642	0.2298	0.2159	0.2211	0.1400	0.1306	0.1023	0.0890
1825	0.1753	0.2144	0.2199	0.1303	0.1068	0.0866	0.0727
2190	0.1543	0.1901	0.1590	0.0920	0.0675	0.0525	0.0576
2555	0.1347	0.1631	0.1178	0.0643	0.0406	0.0255	0.0342
2920	0.1157	0.1372	0.0894	0.0448	0.0237	0.0100	0.0115
3285	0.0972	0.1145	0.0695	0.0314	0.0136	0.0032	0.0009
3650	0.0790	0.0962	0.0555	0.0223	0.0078	0.0009	0.0001
4015	0.0618	0.0825	0.0455	0.0161	0.0046	0.0002	0.0000
4380	0.0459	0.0731	0.0384	0.0119	0.0029	0.0001	0.0000
4745	0.0321	0.0669	0.0334	0.0091	0.0019	0.0000	0.0000
5110	0.0208	0.0626	0.0300	0.0072	0.0013	0.0000	0.0000
5475	0.0123	0.0596	0.0277	0.0059	0.0010	0.0000	0.0000
5840	0.0073	0.0567	0.0256	0.0049	0.0007	0.0000	0.0000
6205	0.0043	0.0540	0.0236	0.0040	0.0006	0.0000	0.0000
6570	0.0026	0.0514	0.0218	0.0033	0.0004	0.0000	0.0000
6935	0.0015	0.0490	0.0202	0.0027	0.0003	0.0000	0.0000
7300	0.0009	0.0466	0.0186	0.0022	0.0002	0.0000	0.0000
7665	0.0005	0.0444	0.0172	0.0018	0.0002	0.0000	0.0000
8030	0.0003	0.0423	0.0159	0.0015	0.0001	0.0000	0.0000
8395	0.0002	0.0402	0.0147	0.0012	0.0001	0.0000	0.0000
8760	0.0001	0.0383	0.0136	0.0010	0.0001	0.0000	0.0000
9125	0.0001	0.0365	0.0125	0.0008	0.0001	0.0000	0.0000

benefits for each open claim. Explicit assumptions on termination rates from home health care status are to be established by the valuation actuary. Company experience should be the basis for these assumptions, if credible. The valuation actuary may determine salvage values and factors to adjust for intermittent care (covered home health care received for an average of less than seven days a week), as deemed appropriate.

For open home health care claims for which less than 90 days of service have been received, reserves can be set up using any method in conformity with *ASOP No. 5*, "Incurred Health Claim Liabilities," and *ASOP No. 18*, "Long-Term Care Insurance."

3. Ancillary Benefits

For benefits other than institutional LTC and home health care (such as respite care or wellness benefits), reserves should be established using any method in conformity with *ASOP No. 5*, "Incurred Health Claim Liabilities." Home health care benefits of a truly ancillary nature (for example, those with a very small calendar-year maximum) can be valued as ancillary benefits rather than being set up as disabled life reserves.

4. Premium Waiver Reserves

If active life reserves are calculated by assuming net premium funding from all in-force contracts, claim reserves are to be held to cover at least valuation net premiums corresponding to the gross premiums waived. (See Section XI.)

C. Recommended Reserves for Incurred But Not Reported Claims

Reserves for claims incurred but unreported can be established using any method in conformity with *ASOP No. 5*, "Incurred Health Claim Liabilities," and *ASOP No. 18*, "Long-Term Care Insurance."

D. Applicability of Minimum Standards

Claim reserves are required to make good and sufficient provision for future expected claim payments on all claims that have been incurred prior to the valuation date. If such provision results in the need for reserves higher than the minimums described above, then such higher reserves should be held. This provides, for example, for the possibility that an insurer may have only a few open claims for which the average claim termination rates are inappropriate. In some individual claim instances, straight life annuities might be a more appropriate indicator of liability. For an insurer with many open claims, the supposition is that such claims are offset by claims with higher-than-average expected claim termination rates, but in any particular instance, the use of aggregate termination rates could be inappropriate.

XIII. FUTURE CHANGES IN ASSUMPTIONS AND PRICING

LTC insurance policies are issued, with very rare exceptions, on a guaranteed renewable basis. Premiums on a block of in-force business can be changed on a class basis, either up or down, and usually only with approval of the appropriate regulatory authority. This, coupled with the structure of level premium by issue age for a benefit with substantially increasing claim costs by attained age, presents significant implications for LTC valuation requirements.

Questions have been raised about the manner of handling LTC active life reserves when premium rates are increased (or decreased) or when assumptions underlying existing reserves are materially different from those adopted by authorities as a new valuation standard basis. These questions have to be addressed separately for statutory and GAAP reserves.

A. Statutory Reserves

The needs for rate increases are usually due to claim experience diverging from original assumptions, but they may be caused by different persistency (or other experience) than expected. From a regulatory perspective, the ability of an insurer to increase rates due to changes in persistency or such factors as interest or expense assumptions is not clear. The effect of any rate stabilization regulations (that is, regulations that limit the rate increases permitted on existing policies) should be taken into account.

Claim costs or reserve factors adopted by regulatory authorities may be steeper, by attained age, than those used for existing LTC policies; lapse assumptions may be different; mortality may have different margins by attained ages; and the mortality table may have different terminal ages. New reserve standards are not made retroactive, but existing assumptions may be so far out of line that a prudent valuation actuary may wish to recalculate reserves or establish additional reserves.

For existing business, the valuation actuary should consider whether changes in expected experience may indicate that current reserves are no longer adequate on a gross premium valuation basis. (See Section XVIII.)

The adoption of new valuation standards could indicate that more experience is available now than when the current valuation basis was adopted. The assumptions included in a new standard may provide guidance for conducting gross premium valuations on business written before the new standard was adopted. These assumptions could also provide a basis for strengthening reserves where necessary, as identified by the gross premium tests.

For life insurers, statutory accounting requires that any changes in reserve basis be identified in the statutory annual statement's Exhibit 8A. The impact of the change in reserve basis, also shown in Exhibit 8A, does not affect the gain from operations but rather affects only the capital and surplus account.

For property/casualty insurers, a significant change in reserve basis would appear in the statutory statement as an adjustment to surplus on line 30 of the Underwriting and Investment Exhibit Statement of Income.

B. GAAP Reserves

For GAAP purposes, most LTC policies would fall under the *FAS 60* definition of a long-duration insurance contract. Under *FAS 60*, premium is included in revenues, and benefits and expenses are included in expenses. Original GAAP assumptions would be chosen by using the most likely realistic best estimates, with a provision for adverse deviation. *FAS 60* also includes the lock-in principle, under which original GAAP assumptions would continue to be used unless a premium deficiency is recognized. Given the uncertainty of future experience with LTC products, it is very possible that original GAAP assumptions will not be realized. When assumptions are adjusted corresponding to a change in premium scales, the effect should be prospective with no change in GAAP liability at the premium change date. If any change in reserve assumptions results in a material impact on the company financial statement, further disclosure in its annual report could be required. Actuarial aspects of GAAP for stock life insurers are discussed in *ASOP No. 10*, "Methods and Assumptions for Use in Stock Life Insurance Company Fiancial Statements Prepared in Accordance with GAAP."

XIV. UPGRADES AND CONVERSIONS

For a product with so many varied features, so recently on the market, and evolving rapidly, there is increasing emphasis on upgrades, internal replacements, and other changes to existing business. This is being increased by regulatory activities. The pace of such changes to in-force business is expected to continue.

Similarly, as true group LTC insurance (see Section I) begins to develop, through tax-clarified assistance to sales and as insurance on covered workers ages, the matter of conversion and portability of benefits will become more prominent.

In all such instances, the manner in which benefits and coverage are continued often will be unique to the specific insurer. Those insurers with internal upgrade or replacement programs to date exhibit no common approach.

When determining the proper level of reserves for the new policy resulting from an upgrade or a conversion, the valuation actuary must consider several elements:

- The difference in benefits in moving from the old policy to the new policy.
- Any nonforfeiture or upgrade or conversion benefits payable.
- The extent to which premiums under new policies issued through the upgrade or conversion differ from premiums under similar policies issued through direct means.
- Whether new premiums are based on (1) original issue age, (2) age at upgrade or conversion, or (3) some combination thereof.
- Whether the insurer employed proof of insurability or some other form of selecting insureds with a lower level of expected morbidity than otherwise might be expected from the original issue's risk pool.
- Expenses incurred due to upgrading or converting.
- Amount of reserves held under the old policy.

If the premiums under the new policy are not adequate to cover future claims and expenses, an initial reserve needs to be established, either from the reserves of the old policy or from surplus.

If an upgrade involves additional coverage that is rated separately (for instance, coverage in the form of an increase in daily benefit with premiums based on the insured's current age), reserves for the additional coverage often can be calculated separately as well. However, policy provisions (for instance, some nonforfeiture benefits earned) or actuarial assumptions (for instance, lapsation dependent on policy duration) may demand that these coverages be considered together for administration and for determining reserves.

Premiums under the old block of policies that do not upgrade or convert may not be adequate if only the best risks participate in the program. In such a case, reserves under the old block would have to be strengthened. If a disproportionate number of the best risks do not upgrade or convert, then reserves under the old block may be adequate while reserves for the new block may need to be strengthened.

If benefits between old and new are essentially the same, premiums are the same, and the upgrade or conversion is across the board, then reserve amounts may also continue as if there were no upgrade or conversion.

In any event, the ultimate adequacy of a gross premium valuation (see Section XVIII) is a test the valuation actuary should apply, as warranted, to changing blocks of LTC insurance business.

XV. ACTUARIAL STANDARDS OF PRACTICE

Several ASOPs under the auspices of the Actuarial Standards Board (ASB) relate to the development and application of these proposals for LTC valuation.

A. ASOP No. 5, *"Incurred Health Claim Liabilities"*

This standard is intended to apply broadly to the determination of claim liabilities for insured and noninsured health plans. A claim liability is defined as the actuarial present value, as of the valuation date, of future claim payments under the benefit plan for claims that have been incurred on or before the valuation date.

Recommended practices are described in *ASOP No. 5* for development, tabular and other methods of projecting the expected remaining claim payments. Clearly, *ASOP No. 5* applies fully to the valuation of LTC benefits. In fact, such benefits are directly referred to in the text of the standard.

B. ASOP No. 7, *"Performing Cash-Flow Testing for Insurers"*

In general, this standard also applies to LTC policies or riders. Extensive multiscenario cash-flow testing is most important when future flows of insurance liabilities and the related assets are not well matched or are interdependent or dependent (with different impacts) on the same external variable, such as prevailing interest rates.

Cash-flow testing would be useful if the assets purchased to back a standalone LTC policy do not produce future cash flows that closely match the liability cash flows. If assets mature after the insurance cash flows occur and interest rates have increased, fixed-income securities may have to be liquidated at a loss. On the other hand, if assets mature too early, the impact of reinvestment at lower interest rates should be examined.

If and as LTC plans are developed that offer competitive cash surrender values, especially if such values are credited with current interest rates, the products would assume characteristics similar to permanent interest-sensitive life insurance. In this case, the applicability of cash-flow testing would be the same as for those products.

Normally, in today's situation, it would appear that for LTC policies without surrender values, backed by reasonably well matched assets, with reasonably predictable maturities, simpler sensitivity testing of the insurance risk assumptions would satisfy *ASOP NO. 7.*

C. ASOP No. 8, *"Regulatory Filings for Rates and Financial Projections for Health Plans"*

This standard describes recommended practice related to the filing of rates and financial projections for health plans for which actuarial memoranda or similar documents are required. While LTC insurance is not specifically mentioned in the standard, it seems clear that it is directly included in the scope (along with medical, dental, vision, disability income, and accidental death and disability, which are mentioned).

D. ASOP No. 10, *"Methods and Assumptions for Use in Stock Life Insurance Companies Financial Statements Prepared in Accordance with GAAP"*

The original version of this standard was adopted in 1989. This current version, adopted by the ASB in October 1992, has been expanded to cover several of the American Academy of Actuaries recommendations and interpretations that are being phased out of other documents. This standard applies to all health insurance as well as life insurance.

Most LTC policies would be subject to *FAS 60* methodology, in which the GAAP active life and claim reserves have a provision for adverse deviation and assumptions are "locked in" for the life of a policy, unless the loss recognition test is failed. (See Section XIII.)

E. ASOP No. 11, *"The Treatment of Reinsurance Transactions in Life and Health Insurance Company Financial Statements"*

The reinsurance of LTC policies is becoming increasingly common. Insurers often wish to transfer a part of their LTC risk due, at least in part, to the scarcity of reliable insured experience for pricing and reserving.

ASOP No. 11 applies fully to LTC coverage as it does to all health and life coverage. Both the ceding and assuming insurers must establish net liabilities that consider all material cash flows, including contractual and contingent cash flows arising from reinsurance treaties.

F. ASOP No. 14, *"When To Do Cash Flow Testing for Life and Health Insurance Companies"*

Most of the comments for *ASOP No. 7* also apply for this standard. For most currently offered stand-alone LTC policies, backed by assets with reasonably predictable cash flows that closely match the liability cash flows, other types of sensitivity testing may be more appropriate. *ASOP No. 14* gives examples of situations in which cash flow testing may not be necessary:

> If the actuary can demonstrate that a block of business is relatively insensitive to influences such as changes in economic conditions, the actuary may determine that cash flow testing is not needed in order to support the opinion or recommendation given.

and

> Variation in benefit and expense experience for disability income and medical expense reimbursement policies may arise from secular uncertain trends in experience. These variations may appropriately be analyzed using statistical techniques applied to historical data to quantify the risk.

On the other hand, if the asset cash flows are not matched with the liability flows or are sensitive to differing dependent on economic conditions, multiscenario cash flow testing may be advisable to sign the Statement of Actuarial Opinion with respect to the related reserves.

Sensitivity and other testing for LTC insurance may be more useful for the C-2 (insurance) risk than cash flow testing for the C-3 (interest) risk.

G. ASOP No. 18, *"Long-Term Care Insurance"*

This standard is much more detailed and explicit than the others referenced in this final report. The last several pages of *ASOP No. 18* provide sound basic instructions for valuing health insurance in general and LTC in particular. Unique features of LTC that have an impact on the valuation process are the steep incurred claim cost curve, the scarcity of insured experience data, and the impact on cost of the many different benefit features and eligibility mechanisms.

The ASB has been advised that a revised and updated ASOP will be pursued beginning in late 1995, based in part on the content of this final report.

H. ASOP No. 22, *"Statutory Statements of Opinion by Appointed Actuaries for Life and Health Insurance"*

See Section XVIII.

XVI. TAX RESERVES

Currently, the Internal Revenue Code has no specific language for LTC insurance.

However, the code does provide guidelines for noncancelable accident and health insurance products. To the extent that LTC insurance is assumed to fall under this category, then the following are the elements that define the basis for tax reserves for LTC insurance.

A. *Morbidity and Mortality*

- ". . .the prevailing commissioners' standard tables for mortality and morbidity" (Section 807 (d)(2)(C) of the IRC).
- There are no prevailing tables (approved by 26 states) for accident and health insurance. Therefore, regulations have been issued by the Internal Revenue Service that define the table to be used. For "benefits issued after 1983 other than disability and accidental death," use the "tables used for NAIC statement reserves" (Reg. 1.807-1).
- Note that many actuaries are not entirely sure whether the IRC requires the use of 1980 CSO mortality, but that is the general belief. Something other than a life table ending at age 100 is appropriate. (See Section V.) The actuarial profession may eventually want to engage in dialogue with those determining the IRC.

B. *Interest Rate*

- For policies issued December 31, 1987 and after: Use the greater of the "state prevailing interest rate" and the "applicable Federal interest rate" (for whole life, "applicable Federal interest rate" is greater) (Section 807(d)(2)(B) of the IRC).
- However, there is no "state prevailing interest rate" for accident and health contracts. Therefore, the "applicable Federal interest rate" is used.

- For policies issued prior to January 1, 1988: Use "state prevailing interest rate" for whole life (Section 807(d)(4)(D) of the IRC).

C. Method

- "2-year full preliminary term method" (Section 807(d)(3)(A)(iii) of the IRC)

The language of the IRC requiring a two-year preliminary term method for noncancelable accident and health contracts is viewed by some as conflicting with the intent of the Senate Report from the 1984 Tax Act. Page 541 of that Senate Report makes the following statement:

> In general, the Federally Prescribed Reserve Method is the reserve method recommended by the NAIC for a particular type of contract. There is no requirement that the method required be based on the prevailing view of the states. As a general rule in computing any life reserves, a company should take into account any factors specifically recommended by the NAIC.

As noted in Appendix F, for LTC the method prescribed by the NAIC is the one-year preliminary term method.

This final report of course will become dated on many topics, at various paces. The basis for tax reserves well may be one of those areas in which significant change occurs soon. For example, an early bill (HR 8) introduced in Congress in 1995 addresses several aspects of LTC insurance. One was the matter of the method allowed for tax reserves, which it would explicitly make consistent with the NAIC prescribed method. The American Academy of Actuaries submitted a statement in support of such a change.

XVII. RISK-BASED CAPITAL

The NAIC risk-based capital formula gives the following instructions for the handling of LTC insurance related to the insurance risk (C-2) for health insurance (" NAIC Life Risk-Based Capital Report Including Overview and Instructions for Companies," July 27, 1994, p. 20):

> Premiums for Long-Term Care Insurance should be included for purposes of the RBC calculation with the line of business with which it is currently reported.

It is silent elsewhere regarding LTC.

The annual statement categories identified there are as follows:

Medical Insurance Premium
  Individual Morbidity
    Usual and Customary Major Med and Hospital
    Med Supp, Dental, and Other Limited Benefits Anticipating Rate
      Increases
    Hospital Indemnity, AD&D, and Other Limited Benefits Not Anticipating Rate Increases
  Group and Credit Morbidity
    Usual and Customary Major Med, Hospital and Dental
    Stop Loss and Minimum Premium
    Med Supp, and Other Limited Benefits Anticipating Rate
      Increases
    Hospital Indemnity, AD&D, and Other Limited Benefits Not Anticipating Rate Increases
Disability Income Premium
  Individual Morbidity
  Group and Credit Morbidity
Claim Reserves

LTC has been reported in several of these categories. It seems that the instructions for the treatment of LTC in the risk-based capital formula provide little direct guidance.

A small and informal survey indicates that companies have classified LTC insurance with disability income. The C-2 (insurance) risk component for disability income that is other than noncancellable of the risk-based capital formula is 25% of the first $50 million of earned premium and 15% of the excess. These two coverages, LTC and DI, would seem to have similar risk characteristics, being long term in nature and developing substantial active life reserves.

The NAIC's factors for DI were developed to provide the desired level of safety based on analysis of the variability of claim costs on large blocks of business in several companies. The experience of LTC claim costs reflects a much smaller data bank and may be changing due to innovations in methods of providing the care and new variations of the coverage being introduced. One may therefore argue that somewhat larger factors should be required for LTC in order to provide the same level of confidence. On the other hand, LTC claims could be more stable than DI claims during volatile economic periods.

As a global (not just LTC) observation, it would seem the required risk-based capital should be lower if a reserve is higher; the risk-based capital should not be independent of the reserve level.

The Health Organizations Risk-Based Capital effort by the American Academy of Actuaries for the NAIC has recently considered LTC insurance, though not as a primary focus of that large total effort. The work by the NAIC was still in progress when this final report was being written.

Until more is learned, the best course for developing LTC risk-based capital would be to apply the DI factors to LTC earned premiums. In addition, the 5% of claim reserves component prescribed for all health insurance should apply to LTC.

Separate explicit studies for LTC should be undertaken in the future, when the patterns of care and coverage have become more stabilized and the volume of available data provides greater credibility.

XVIII. RESERVE ADEQUACY

This subject generally refers to possible deficiency reserves and gross premium valuations.

The requirement for deficiency reserves in general is found in Section 8 of the NAIC Model Standard Valuation Law. Under this section, additional reserves may be required when

> ... in any contract year the gross premium charged by any life insurance company on any policy or contract is less than the valuation net premium for the policy or contract calculated by the method used in calculating the reserve thereon but using minimum standards of mortality and the rate of interest....

The section seems to apply to life insurance policies with guaranteed (as opposed to indeterminate) premiums.

Section 9 requires that for indeterminate premium life insurance plans reserves held must:

> ... be appropriate in relation to the benefits and the pattern of premiums for that plan;

and

> ... be computed by a method which is consistent with the principles of this Standard Valuation Law...

Section 10 states that

> ... the commissioner shall promulgate a regulation containing the minimum standards applicable to the valuation of health [disability, sickness and accident] plans.

There are no specific references to deficiency reserves in either the NAIC Model Minimum Reserve Standards for Individual and Group Health Insurance Contracts or the NAIC Model LTC Act or Model LTC Regulation.

The function of deficiency reserves is to capitalize anticipated losses under valuation assumptions. Expected profits are matched against future premium, while expected losses are recognized immediately. This approach is consistent with the conservative nature of statutory accounting. This principle is reasonable regardless of the form of premium guarantee.

Implementation of this principle is straightforward when policy features are fixed in advance. When premiums are not guaranteed, however, application of this principle is subject to interpretation.

The usual interpretation has been that a lack of premium guarantees eliminates the need for deficiency reserves. If conservative valuation assumptions prove correct, rather than the assumptions in pricing, the insurer simply increases gross premiums as needed.

There is nothing unique to LTC insurance with respect to the previous comments. The points are equally applicable to any insurance product.

However, with respect to deficiency reserves, the LTC valuation actuary should give appropriate consideration to the nature of the premium guarantees, other policy provisions constraining premium rate changes, premium rate regulations, the impact of premium rate changes on policy lapsation, and the level of benefit utilization of persisting policies.

Deficiency reserves are not necessarily needed when the gross premium is less than the net.

ASOP No. 22, "Statutory Statements of Opinion by Appointed Actuaries for Life or Health Insurance," provides guidance on when additional reserves are required due to deficiency situations:

> 5.5.3 Adequacy of Reserves and Related Items. In addition to meeting appropriate regulatory requirements, the appointed actuary should use professional judgment to be satisfied that the assets supporting the reserves and related items, plus related future revenues, are adequate to cover obligations under moderately adverse conditions. To hold reserves so great that a company could withstand any conceivable circumstances, no matter how adverse, would usually imply an excessive level of reserves.

The valuation actuary should keep in mind especially these portions of *ASOP No. 22*:

> 5.3 Statement of Opinion. The form, content, and recommended language of the statement of opinion are specified in Section 8 of the

Model Regulation (relevant to the Standard Valuation Law). The opinion must include a statement on reserve adequacy based on an asset adequacy analysis, the details of which are contained in the supporting memorandum to the company.

5.3.1. Asset Adequacy Analysis. Both the type and depth of asset adequacy analysis will vary with the nature and significance of the asset, obligation, and/or investment-rate-of-return risks. The appointed actuary may use a single analysis for reserves in aggregate or a number of analyses for each of several blocks of business. In either case, a number of considerations may bear on the actuary's work. The actuary should use professional judgment in determining which of the following, or other, considerations apply:

a.   Analysis Methods. A number of asset adequacy analysis methods are available to, and used by, actuaries. The most widely used method is cash flow testing (see *ASOP No. 7,* "Performing Cash Flow Testing for Insurers," and *ASOP No. 14,* "When To Do Cash Flow Testing for Life and Health Insurance Companies"). This method is generally appropriate for products and/or investment strategies where future cash flows may differ under different economic or interest-rate scenarios. Such differences are associated with, for example, call options and prepayment risk for assets, and with policyholder withdrawal rights in the case of products. Among other acceptable methods described in actuarial literature are:

   i.   Demonstration that a block of business being tested is highly risk-controlled or that the degree of conservatism in the reserve basis is so great that reasonably anticipated deviations from current assumptions are provided for. For example, such methods might be appropriate for a block of accidental death and dismemberment insurance.

   ii. Gross premium reserve tests, which may be appropriate when the business is not highly sensitive to economic or interest-rate risks, but is sensitive to obligation risk. If the reserve held is not materially greater than the gross premium reserve, sensitivity testing of variables such as expenses, mortality, morbidity, or lapse should be done to determine whether additional reserves are needed.

iii. Loss-ratio methods, development methods, or follow-
up studies as described in *ASOP No. 5,* "Incurred
Health Claim Liabilities."

The appointed actuary should be satisfied that the analysis methods
chosen are appropriate to support the opinion.

This indicates that, for the valuation actuary to provide a clean opinion,
the reserves held should not only satisfy the formulas and assumptions required by law but also, at a high probability level when combined with future
expected premiums, be able to provide all benefits and expenses expected
to be paid under the policies. This is applicable for LTC insurance.

Some LTC policies are issued with limited premium payment periods,
such as 10 or 20 years or even with a single premium. These present unique
future risks for the insurer. Similarly, policies may contain restraints on
when, how often, and to what extent the policy's guaranteed renewable premium may be changed after issue. The NAIC Model LTC Regulation and
various bills for federal LTC proposed legislation all currently propose versions of those restraints. The valuation actuary must assure that reserves are
adequate within the provisions of the LTC policies being valued and the
environment within which that is done.

In addition to the areas of advice and guidance identified in the sections
of this final report, the LTC valuation actuary should deviate from well-
established or soundly emerging practices and standards only when that deviation is necessary to be responsible in valuing LTC insurance.

This means the LTC valuation actuary must become familiar with the
current relevant environment, both within and outside of the actuarial
profession.

XIX. TASK FORCE MEMBERSHIP

Bartley L. Munson, FSA, Chair   William P. Bigelow, FSA
Coopers & Lybrand, LLP   Metropolitan Life Ins. Co.

Loida Rodis Abraham, FSA   Peggy L. Hauser, FSA
John Hancock Mutual Life Insurance   Milliman & Robertson, Inc.

Michael S. Abroe, FSA   Burton D. Jay, FSA
Milliman & Robertson, Inc.   United of Omaha Insurance Co.

Kenneth A. Klinger, FSA
CNA Insurance Companies

James M. Robinson, FSA
Coopers & Lybrand, L.L.P.

Frank E. Knorr, ASA
Duncanson & Holt, Inc.

Joyce A. Tollerud, FSA
Lutheran Brotherhood

Dennis M. O'Brien, FSA
Resource Deployment, Inc.

John C. Wilkin, FSA
Actuarial Research Corp.

Frederick J. Yosua, FSA
UNUM Life Insurance Co. of America

During the Task Force's existence, two members were added and four (Stephen R. Atkins, FSA, Mark E. Litow, FSA, Lew H. Nathan, FSA, and Morris Snow, FSA) were replaced by associates from their offices.

NAIC Liaison

Mark D. Peavy, FSA
National Association of Insurance Commissioners

SOA Staff Liaison

Jack A. Luff, FSA
Society of Actuaries

Jeff Allen, FSA
Society of Actuaries

Vice President—Health Benefit Systems Practice

Howard J. Bolnick, FSA (Current)
Celtic Life Insurance Co., Inc.

Sam Gutterman, FSA (Former)
Price Waterhouse L.L.P.

APPENDIX A

PRODUCT FEATURES

LTC insurance is varied, evolving, and complex, and thus it is difficult to accurately characterize product features. It is exactly those characteristics of the product that make this appendix a useful part of this final report.

I. Nursing Home (Institutional Care) Benefit

This is the cornerstone of most LTC policies. In general, a daily indemnity benefit is paid for each day of confinement in a licensed nursing facility. There is usually a secondary benefit trigger of either (1) a determination by a physician that the confinement is "medically necessary," (2) loss of a specified number of ADLs, and/or (3) some type of CI.

Early generations of LTC policies made distinctions on the level of care provided in the nursing home (skilled/intermediate/custodial) and whether the stay was preceded by a three-day hospital stay. These distinctions have essentially been eliminated for new policies now being issued.

II. Noninstitutional Care Benefits

A. Home Health Care (HHC) Benefit

This benefit is generally offered in conjunction with the nursing home benefit and typically (but not always) pays a daily indemnity amount equal to one-half of the nursing home benefit. Benefits are paid for each day the insured receives services from a licensed home health care agency. There is generally a requirement that the care be provided by a registered nurse (RN), licensed practical nurse (LPN), licensed therapist, or home health aide, and many policies now have ADL loss requirement as well.

A few insurers offer this as a stand-alone benefit, and benefit amounts are now offered for amounts other than 50% of the nursing home benefit.

B. Home Care (Personal) Benefit (Part of HHC)

This benefit is an extension of the benefit described above. The benefits provided under this coverage can range from limited homemaker services (laundry, cleaning) to a cash indemnity for insureds with a given ADL loss (for example, 2 of 5 or 2 of 6).

C. Adult Day Care Benefit (Part of HHC)

This benefit is generally an amount equal to or less than the home health care benefit and pays a daily benefit for each day the insured receives care in an adult day care (ADC) facility. The definition of what constitutes an ADC facility is fairly standard and generally includes requirements for the minimum and maximum hours a day that the facility operates and minimum staffing requirements (RNs, a physical therapist, a speech therapist, dietician, and so on).

D. Other Benefits

Benefits are also sometimes provided by a LTC policy for prescription drugs, ambulance, hospice services, and medical equipment usage.

III. Respite Care

This benefit is generally a daily indemnity in the same amount as the home health care benefit and is intended to provide short-term relief to a family member or other informal caregiver of the insured. The benefits provided under this type of coverage can range from professional home care services to unskilled homemaker services or short stays in institutional care settings. Benefits are usually limited to 15 or 20 days per year, maybe even less, and may be available prior to meeting the policy's elimination period requirement for other benefits.

IV. Elimination Period

An elimination period refers to the period after an insured has been deemed to have met the benefit eligibility criteria but prior to the inception of the period during which benefits become payable.

Policies tend to vary in their definition of elimination period in two major ways:

- Number of days after benefit eligibility met but without regard to services received (that is, by calendar days). For individual policies, this is often 20 days or 100 days; for group policies, this is often 30, 60, 90, or 120 days.
- Number of days after benefit eligibility met and during which services must be actually received.

Most individual policies tend to require that insureds receive LTC services during the elimination period. Such days of service, however, need not be consecutive. Some group policies, especially, do not require that actual services be received during the elimination period.

V. Benefit Period

The benefit period refers to the period during which benefits are payable. This period begins after the insured has met the elimination period requirement and lasts for as long as the insured receives LTC insurance benefits.

Note that this is not the same as the period of coverage. The period of coverage begins on the policy issue date and continues for as long as the insurance is in force (that is, for as long as the policy has not lapsed and benefits have not exceeded the policy's maximum benefit).

Benefit periods may apply separately to institutional and noninstitutional care, or there may be one combined benefit period for both.

Most policies prescribe maximum benefit periods of 3 years, 4 years, 5 years, or 6 years. Some have included lifetime benefits, thereby not limiting the policy to any prescribed period.

Most group plans as well as newer individual policies no longer use benefit periods expressed in time but instead use maximum benefit amounts in dollars. Such maximum benefit amounts are typically equal to a benefit period times a daily maximum. For example, a maximum benefit amount of $182,500 is calculated from a benefit period of 5 years and a daily maximum of $100. This plan design encourages insureds to use less expensive LTC services, thereby potentially increasing the period of time during which benefits are payable. It also eliminates the negative feelings that some insureds may have when they realize that they do not receive any "credit" for having a benefit payment that is actually less than the nursing home daily maximum.

VI. Nonforfeiture Benefits

Various types of nonforfeiture benefits have been offered to provide the insured a return of some of the prefunding that otherwise would be forfeited at time of voluntary lapsation (or, in some policies, death). See Section X of this final report for a description of these types and their relevance to reserves.

VII. Inflation Protection

Most LTC policies are available with some type of protection against the rising cost of LTC services due to "inflation." The NAIC Model Regulation requires an insurer to offer this at time of purchase. Two basically different types of inflation protection are as follows.

A. Option to Purchase Attained Age Increments

Under this option, the insured will be guaranteed the right to increase periodically both the nursing home maximum daily benefit and the home health care maximum daily benefit, where the premium for the increase is based on the insured's age at the time of increase. The right to purchase increases usually is restricted, for example, to the third policy anniversary and every third policy anniversary up to the insured's 85th birthday. If the insured declines the option, future offers sometimes may still be made. Offers may be withheld if a period of care was in effect any time during a certain period prior to the offer. The amount of the increase sometimes is based on the Consumer Price Index, or its medical component, and sometimes it is fixed at the time the policy is issued, to such as 5% per year.

B. Automatic Inflation Option

Under this option, the nursing home maximum daily benefit and home health care maximum daily benefit will increase by a fixed percentage (for example, 5%) on each policy anniversary. The percentage may be applied to the original benefit level (simple) or to the previous year's benefit level (compound). Increases may continue for a specified duration (for example, 20 years), up to a specified age (for example, 85), or for life. If expressed in dollars, the lifetime policy limit for nursing home care and/or home health care will be increased by the same percentage as the increase in the maximum daily benefit on each policy anniversary. The increase is automatic and will be made even if the insured is on claim. Premiums may remain level under this option or they may be increasing.

VIII. Benefit Triggers

The earlier generations of LTC policies used benefit triggers that were linked to "medical necessity." The more recently issued policies use a "functional necessity" type of benefit trigger and, often, CI, or some combination of these and medical necessity.

A. Medical Necessity

Some LTC policies require a certification from an attending physician to determine that the insured needs medically necessary care. The physician prescribes a diagnosis for a patient, which an insurer uses to determine the critical nature of the insured's ailment. In addition, the insurer may require a prior hospital stay (in earlier policies) or that the type of care required be of a skilled nature for at least the first 30 days (in earlier policies).

B. Functional Necessity

Today, many LTC policies use some type of ADL measurement to determine whether an insured needs help in performing the daily functions of life. Policies vary in their use of ADL criteria. Some require that the insured be dependent in at least 3 out of 6; others use 2 out of 5; and still others use 2 out of 6. The specific ADLs included among the 5 or 6 vary. They also vary in their exact definition of each of the ADLs. The definition of "inability to perform" varies by policy; some require assistance of mechanical devices, or standby or occasional human assistance, or full-time human assistance.

Below is an example of how one policy uses an ADL definition as a benefit trigger.

> An insured will be eligible for benefits under the LTC insurance policy if the insurer's LTC case manager certifies that the insured qualifies for benefits due to functional necessity. To qualify for functional necessity, an insured must be totally dependent on human assistance in performing at least three out of the following six activities of daily living.
> a. Bathing. Refers to the person's ability to get into and out of the tub or shower, turning on the water, getting the soap or other cleansing product, and bathing the entire body (including back and feet).
> b. Eating. Refers to the person's ability to bring food to his or her mouth (or to hold a glass to the mouth), and to be able to chew and swallow the food. (Eating does not include preparing or serving the food.)
> c. Dressing. Refers to a person's ability to get clothes from closets or drawers and putting them on or taking them off.
> d. Toileting. Refers to the person's ability to get to and from the toilet, onto and off the toilet, cleaning oneself after elimination, and adjusting his or her clothes after toileting.
> e. Transferring. Refers to a person's ability to get into or out of a bed or a chair.
> f. Continence. Refers to a person's ability to maintain control of urination and bowel movement.
> A person is generally considered to be totally dependent in an ADL if during the previous seven days, the person needed the help of another person to perform a major part of the activity.

C. Cognitive Impairment

An assessment is made, often using one of several recognized tests, whether the insured is cognitively impaired. If a certain number of wrong answers are experienced, the insured is assumed impaired and eligible for benefits. Some insurers look for certain behaviors as an indication of CI.

IX. Expense Incurred Versus Disability Income Products

An expense incurred product usually will pay actual expenses up to a specified limit in the policy. Sometimes actual expenses are reimbursed at 100%, other times at lower percentages, such as 80%.

The disability income policies typically pay benefits regardless of whether the insured is actually receiving LTC services. However, the insured must meet the benefit trigger, whether the trigger is medical necessity, ADL, and/or a CI trigger. In addition, the benefits payable may vary depending on whether the insured is in a nursing home or not.

The expense incurred approach and the disability income approach represent the two ends of a spectrum involving various methods of defining the amount of benefits payable. Somewhere in between the two are indemnity products. Some insurers define their indemnity approach as paying specified benefits as long as approved home health care services are provided; the specified benefit is not based on the actual cost of the service.

Note that if a policy pays 100% of actual costs up to a daily cap, and especially if it has no inflation rider, then over an extended period payments may end up at the cap and thus resemble an indemnity plan. Even though such payments may not directly be thought of as an indemnity benefit, such payments may still have very similar characteristics.

X. Limited Pay Policies

Policies can have premium payments limited to a predefined number of years (for example, 20 years, to age 65, or even single premium) or by a contingent event (for example, the policy is paid up upon the later of 10 years after issue and the first death of two jointly insured lives). These are not common.

XI. Alternative Plan of Care

Some policies provide for payment of services related to LTC outside of traditional covered services (for example, remodeling of the residence) if it is cost effective and of use to the insured, as jointly determined by the insured, the insured's physician, and the insurer.

XII. Bed Reservation Benefit

The policy will reserve a bed in the nursing facility if the insured is transferred to a hospital for care. The period of time for which it is reserved is usually measured in days and is limited to, at most, a few weeks.

While benefits are described here in isolation, it is important to realize that the morbidity experience for the benefits described above can be expected to vary significantly, depending on whether the benefits are offered alone or in conjunction with each other. For example, when the home health care benefits are offered as a stand-alone coverage separate from any nursing home coverage, a load should be applied to the morbidity costs to reflect the effects of substitution that can be expected to take place. A load also should be applied in the situation in which a policy is sold with nursing home coverage alone, because in some instances it could be expected that the nursing home utilization would be higher if the insured does not have coverage for home health care (again, due to substitution effects).

While the above only generally describes some of the more significant policy features that must be considered for appropriate LTC insurance valuation, it does provide some understanding of the complexities, possible variations, and the product issues the valuation actuary must consider.

APPENDIX B

MIGHTY FINE INSURANCE COMPANY: A CASE STUDY FOR APPLICATION OF THE TABLES

This appendix has two purposes:
- It illustrates the type of thinking the valuation actuary might go through in applying this final report and companion valuation diskette
- It describes as the case study the default set of assumptions contained in the valuation diskette. It is also the default or base case against which results for selective different sets of assumptions are displayed in Appendix C.

Mighty Fine Insurance Company markets an LTC insurance product. The product is marketed to individuals by the company's own agents and carefully selected brokers. Mighty Fine watches for sales abuses and removes an agent's writing privileges whenever there is good reason to believe the agent is placing business with a below-average number of good risks. Mighty Fine has strict underwriting standards. The agents frequently complain that Mighty Fine is too strict, but the company believes the careful underwriting is critical to its success.

The product is a daily indemnity, paying a specified amount for each day an insured qualifies for benefits and resides in a nursing home and 50% of the specified amount for each day the insured receives qualified home health care. Nursing home qualification is based on the inability to perform three of six specified ADLs without the assistance of another person. The ADLs used are eating, bathing, dressing, toileting, transference, and mobility. Home health care qualification is based on the inability to perform two of the six ADLs. In addition, insureds can qualify for either type of care if they have a CI requiring continual supervision.

The most common plan Mighty Fine sells has a four-year benefit period and a 100-day elimination period. The elimination period can be satisfied by either home care or nursing home days, or a combination. The insured must actually receive home health care or nursing home care to accrue a benefit day. This is also true for the benefit period. A home health care day counts as a full day, though the benefit is only 50%. The benefits are counted in service days and are accumulated regardless of where the care is received.

The following is a discussion of how a valuation actuary might use the new valuation tables from this final report to study the statutory reserves needed for this plan.

Insured

You decide to study reserves for females to simplify the study. You also decide to study issue age 70.

Morbidity

An insurance plan like this one is best modeled by insurable stays from the 1985 NNHS, so you select insurable stays. The plan is very carefully underwritten, and morbidity selection has yielded losses of 50% of the ultimate in the first duration, 60% in the second, 70% in the third, 80% in the fourth, 90% in the fifth, and 100% thereafter. No overall incidence rate adjustment is entered (1.0 is used), since the company has no compelling evidence from its own experience to justify any overall loading or reduction.

Mortality

You use the suggested 83 GAM table and no mortality adjustment (1.0 is used), since you have no compelling evidence Mighty Fine mortality is better or worse than the 83 GAM. You decide to use the same mortality selection factors as those you used for morbidity selection (50%, 60%, 70%, 80%, 90%, 100% thereafter).

Interest

You decide to use the reserve interest rate that is the statutory maximum (5%) for 1994 issues.

Method

You decide to use the minimum reserve method currently required by your state, one-year preliminary term.

Policy

You decide to define a unit as $100 daily benefit for nursing home and $50 for home health care. You conduct some studies of the impact of the integrated benefits. You discover that you have insufficient claim data to determine with confidence how the elimination period and benefit period should be adjusted. You also notice that any adjustment for the elimination period largely will be offset by any adjustment for the benefit period. (See Appendix C for information relating to such an analysis.) Thus, though the plan has elimination and benefit periods that are integrated between nursing home and home health care, you decide to determine reserves as if those periods apply separately to the two types of benefit coverage provided.

The premium is waived whenever the elimination period has been met and the insured resides in a nursing home. Therefore, zero days is entered as the base elimination period variable.

The plan is level premium and level benefit, so no inflation adjustment is needed.

Lapsation

Gross premiums were calculated assuming lapses of 15% in the first year, 9% in the second, 8% in the third, 7% in the fourth, and 5% thereafter. These are still reasonable in light of recent experience. Because lapses for valuation are limited to 80% of pricing assumptions, and you want to somewhat conservatively hold back from the limit, you use rates of 8% first year,

7% second year, 6% third year, 5% fourth year, and 4% thereafter. Your experience leads you to know that lapses are antiselective, and the higher the lapse rate the higher the antiselection. You decide that though lapsers take 100% of their future premiums with them, their departure reduces their otherwise future assumed claims by only 30% in the first year after lapse, 50% in the second, 70% in the third, 80% in the fourth, 90% in the fifth, and 100% by the sixth year after they lapse. Accordingly, you enter 70% in first-year antiselection, 50% in second, 30% in third, 20% in fourth, 10% in the fifth, and none thereafter. Finally, your state valuation law allows you to compute the reserves so that both mortality and voluntary lapses are counted as separate decrements, so you chose the option "Lapse rates exclude mortality."

Home Health Care Utilization

A study of your limited claims experience shows that when an insured has a single ADL and no CI, 10% of insureds will receive home health care services an average of two days per week; though your product has a two-ADL trigger, your experience shows some insureds with one ADL will be successful in applying for benefits. When there are two ADLs and no CI, 70% will receive services an average of four days per week. When there are three ADLs with no CI, 100% will use services an average of six days per week. When there are no ADLs but there is a CI, 30% use services an average of one day per week; one ADL and CI, 50% for three days; two ADLs and CI, 70% for five days; and three ADLs and CI, 100% for seven days.

Nonforfeiture

Since this product has no nonforfeiture values, zeros are entered in all fields.

Results

You compute the reserves on the valuation diskette and find the values shown in Table B-1.

TABLE B-1

MIGHTY FINE LTC RESERVE OUTPUT

Mighty Fine LTC Reserve Output

Default Specifications

Summary of 1-Year Preliminary Term Reserves at 5.000% for Issue Age 70 Assuming Females Are 100% of Sales

		NH	HC	Home Care EP/BP in Service Days
Net Premium: 1,641.93	Daily Benefit:	100.00	50.00	Inflation Protection: NONE
Lifetime Pay	Deductible Period:	100	100	
	Lifetime Maximum:	1460	1460	
	W/P Days in Ben:	0		

Mortality Table: 83 GAM
Adjustment Factor: 1.000
Mort. Selection Factors: (1) 0.500 (2) 0.600 (3) 0.700 (4) 0.800 (5) 0.900 (6) 1.000 (7) 1.000 (8) 1.000 (9) 1.000 (10) 1.000

Morbidity Table: 85 NNHS (Insurable Stays) and 82/84 NLTCS
Adjustment Factor: 1.000
Morb. Selection Factors: (1) 0.500 (2) 0.600 (3) 0.700 (4) 0.800 (5) 0.900 (6) 1.000 (7) 1.000 (8) 1.000 (9) 1.000 (10) 1.000
Antiselection Factors: 0.700 0.500 0.300 0.200 0.100 0.000 0.000 0.000 0.000 0.000

Home Care Service Utilization Rates by ADL/CI Status:
No Cognitive Impairment: (0 ADLs) 0.000 (1 ADLs) 0.100 (2 ADLs) 0.700 (3 ADLs) 1.000
Cognitively Impaired: 0.300 0.500 0.700 1.000

Home Care Service Frequency (per week) by ADL/CI Status:
No Cognitive Impairment: (0 ADLs) 0.000 (1 ADLs) 2.000 (2 ADLs) 4.000 (3 ADLs) 6.000
Cognitively Impaired: 1.000 3.000 5.000 7.000

Lapse rates are in addition to mortality - Maximum aggregate termination rate: 1.000
Lapse Rates: (1) 0.080 (2) 0.070 (3) 0.060 (4) 0.050 (5) 0.040 (6) 0.040 (7) 0.040 (8) 0.040 (9) 0.040 (10+) 0.040

Nonforfeiture benefits: SBP Cost Factor: 1.200   Reserves to exceed SBP cost per lapse
(3) .000 (4) .000 (5) .000 (10) .000 (15) .000 (20) .000 (25) .000 (30) .000 (35) .000 (40) .000 (45) .000 (50+) .000

t	BOY Inforce	Waiver Inforce	NH Inforce	NH Admiss.	HC Admiss.	EOY Lapses	Deaths	Net Prem. per Payor	NH Cost per Mid 1x	HC Cost per Mid 1x	NFO Cost per Lapse	Terminal Reserve	Mid-Term. Reserve
1	100,000	0	0	533	1,017	7,950	619	267.42	202.47	72.50	0.00	0.00	0.00
2	91,431	193	295	698	1,294	6,346	775	1,641.93	288.77	100.26	0.00	1,436.39	667.92
3	84,309	389	523	869	1,572	5,001	953	1,641.93	390.07	130.96	0.00	2,900.92	2,081.63
4	78,354	573	740	1,066	1,841	3,860	1,158	1,641.93	517.71	163.69	0.00	4,347.95	3,515.73
5	73,336	765	970	1,295	2,108	2,878	1,392	1,641.93	677.48	198.05	0.00	5,725.45	4,922.19
6	69,067	977	1,226	1,568	2,370	2,696	1,657	880.43	233.60	0.00		7,043.61	6,243.66
7	64,713	1,220	1,522	1,713	2,378	2,518	1,759	1,641.93	1,039.02	246.09	0.00	8,366.45	7,537.70
8	60,436	1,437	1,766	1,884	2,387	2,343	1,853	1,641.93	1,240.37	259.35	0.00	9,662.61	8,821.27
9	56,239	1,644	2,006	2,060	2,389	2,172	1,938	1,641.93	1,478.91	273.63	0.00	10,905.09	10,065.75
10	52,129	1,849	2,246	2,231	2,382	2,005	2,010	1,641.93	1,755.22	287.36	0.00	12,066.31	11,244.38
11	48,115	2,053	2,482	2,387	2,363	1,842	2,067	1,641.93	2,069.27	301.20	0.00	13,116.53	12,329.09
12	44,206	2,249	2,709	2,518	2,327	1,684	2,073	1,641.93	2,409.40	313.87	0.00	14,036.82	13,295.94
13	40,415	2,432	2,917	2,611	2,277	1,531	2,129	1,641.93	2,766.06	325.56	0.00	14,816.30	14,130.33
14	36,755	2,593	3,095	2,664	2,211	1,385	2,134	1,641.93	3,145.74	336.68	0.00	15,437.61	14,818.30
15	33,235	2,723	3,235	2,674	2,130	1,245	2,121	1,641.93	3,544.01	345.89	0.00	15,885.27	15,343.74
16	29,870	2,817	3,332	2,639	2,035	1,111	2,088	1,641.93	3,949.75	354.61	0.00	16,151.42	15,695.31
17	26,670	2,872	3,380	2,561	1,928	985	2,042	1,641.93	4,371.25	360.83	0.00	16,222.61	15,862.56
18	23,643	2,885	3,377	2,443	1,809	866	1,983	1,641.93	4,789.91	366.42	0.00	16,098.45	15,838.56
19	20,794	2,854	3,324	2,287	1,681	755	1,912	1,641.93	5,199.95	369.29	0.00	15,784.80	15,625.93
20	18,127	2,781	3,221	2,100	1,543	652	1,837	1,641.93	5,607.12	370.49	0.00	15,288.58	15,230.92
21	15,638	2,668	3,072	1,891	1,399	556	1,748	1,641.93	6,003.05	370.08	0.00	14,611.71	14,657.91
22	13,335	2,518	2,882	1,667	1,250	468	1,641	1,641.93	6,312.87	367.84	0.00	13,814.90	13,937.01
23	11,226	2,338	2,659	1,437	1,100	388	1,522	1,641.93	6,580.79	363.85	0.00	12,927.69	13,112.74
24	9,315	2,134	2,410	1,211	952	317	1,394	1,641.93	6,822.42	361.30	0.00	11,964.35	12,206.73
25	7,605	1,914	2,146	994	808	254	1,256	1,641.93	7,034.80	357.58	0.00	10,943.00	11,234.85
26	6,095	1,685	1,876	794	671	199	1,112	1,641.93	7,222.70	352.69	0.00	9,879.99	10,213.94
27	4,784	1,456	1,609	615	544	153	965	1,641.93	7,376.59	346.72	0.00	8,801.05	9,164.50
28	3,666	1,235	1,352	460	430	114	814	1,641.93	7,513.87	338.28	0.00	7,708.61	8,100.66
29	2,738	1,026	1,113	330	330	83	668	1,641.93	7,620.12	334.37	0.00	6,617.96	7,030.93
30	1,987	834	897	226	245	58	533	1,641.93	7,732.26	329.00	0.00	5,542.91	5,969.57
31	1,396	664	707	145	176	39	412	1,641.93	7,835.88	321.03	0.00	4,531.76	4,946.70
32	945	516	543	86	121	25	307	1,641.93	7,924.89	312.10	0.00	3,678.47	4,031.54
33	612	391	407	44	79	16	220	1,641.93	8,030.05	304.26	0.00	3,197.36	3,373.96
34	377	264	264	25	49	9	149	1,641.93	8,120.31	288.09	0.00	2,820.70	2,982.62
35	218	153	153	14	29	5	96	1,641.93	8,229.81	269.89	0.00	2,390.18	2,557.64
36	118	82	82	8	15	2	57	1,641.93	8,323.85	243.48	0.00	1,832.95	2,074.91
37	58	41	41	4	7	1	32	1,641.93	7,852.37	211.76	0.00	1,223.68	1,503.94
38	25	18	18	2	3	0	15	1,641.93	6,943.92	170.21	0.00	541.22	871.63
39	9	7	7	1	1	0	6	1,641.93	5,314.56	107.66	0.00	0.00	270.61
40	3	2	2	0	0	0	2	1,641.93	1,657.99	9.79	0.00	0.00	0.00

PREMIUM & BENEFIT TOTALS ($000)   1,630,490   2,102,167
PRESENT VALUES (5.00%) ($000)   1,136,343   1,136,343

SOCIETY OF ACTUARIES LONG TERM CARE VALUATION METHODS TASK FORCE - RESERVE PROGRAM TEST Version 1.3b

APPENDIX C

INPUT/OUTPUT OF SOME CASES TESTED

This appendix contains four tables of sample LTC reserve values. While the information is designed to support other parts of this final report, useful insights can be derived by studying this appendix apart from the references in the body of this final report. Of course, many other variations of assumptions are possible beyond those illustrated in this material. The reader is encouraged to use the valuation diskette software to explore further.

Table C-1 shows output from the valuation diskette software for the default case (see Appendix B) for issue ages 45 and 70. These values provide a comparison base for variations in assumptions.

Table C-2 provides selected output resulting from variations from the default elimination and benefit periods for issue ages 45 and 70.

Table C-3 summarizes the impact of home health care utilization assumptions on net premiums and mid-terminal reserves. The first two pages correspond to an integrated benefit plan (nursing home and home health care) and the last two pages assume home health care benefits only. The tables attempt to uncover the role of each ADL/CI status by setting the utilization rates to either zero or 100% in various combinations. For example, the entry labeled "2+ ADLs or CI" sets utilization rates for those with one ADL impaired and without CI to zero. Utilization rates for those with two *or more* ADLs impaired *or* who are cognitively impaired are set to 100%. Other combinations focus on specific cells, for example, "2 ADLs *and* CI." Output is provided assuming frequency of service use of 7 days per week (top of each page) and 3.5 days per week (bottom of each page) for those assumed to be using home health care services.

Table C-4 documents results of 25 cases with variations of assumptions from those of the default case. The variations range over a variety of assumptions. The first page of the table briefly describes each case. Each page that follows compares a case with the default. Mid-terminal reserves per surviving policy and per policy issued are graphically displayed on each page.

TABLE C-1

Default Case LTC Reserve Output

Summary of 1-Year Preliminary Term Reserves at 5.000% for Issue Age 45 Assuming Females Are 100% of Sales

			NH	**NC**	Home Care EP/BP in Service Days
Net Premium:	202.76	Daily Benefit:	100.00	50.00	Inflation Protection: **NONE**
Lifetime Pay		Deductible Period:	100	100	
		Lifetime Maximum:	1460	1460	
		W/P Days in Ben:	0		

Mortality Table: 83 GAM
Adjustment Factor: 1.000
Mort. Selection Factors: (1) 0.500 (2) 0.600 (3) 0.700 (4) 0.800 (5) 0.900 (6) 1.000 (7) 1.000 (8) 1.000 (9) 1.000 (10) 1.000

Morbidity Table: 85 NNHS (Insurable Stays) and 82/84 NLTCS
Adjustment Factor: 1.000
Morb. Selection Factors: (1) 0.500 (2) 0.600 (3) 0.700 (4) 0.800 (5) 0.900 (6) 1.000 (7) 1.000 (8) 1.000 (9) 1.000 (10) 1.000
Antiselection Factors: 0.700   0.500   0.300   0.200   0.100   0.000   0.000   0.000   0.000 (10) 0.000

Home Care Service Utilization Rates by ADL/CI Status:
No Cognitive Impairment: (0 ADLs) 0.000 (1 ADLs) 0.100 (2 ADLs) 0.700 (3 ADLs) 1.000
Cognitively Impaired: 0.300   0.500   0.700   1.000

Home Care Service Frequency (per week) by ADL/CI Status:
No Cognitive Impairment: (0 ADLs) 0.000 (1 ADLs) 2.000 (2 ADLs) 4.000 (3 ADLs) 6.000
Cognitively Impaired: 1.000   3.000   5.000   7.000

Lapse rates are in addition to mortality - Maximum aggregate termination rate: 1.000
Lapse Rates: (1) 0.080 (2) 0.070 (3) 0.060 (4) 0.050 (5) 0.040 (6) 0.040 (7) 0.040 (8) 0.040 (9) 0.040 (10+) 0.040

Nonforfeiture benefits: SBP Cost Factor: 1.200   Reserves to exceed SBP cost per lapser
(3) .000 (4) .000 (5) .000 (10) .000 (15) .000 (20) .000 (25) .000 (30) .000 (40) .000 (45) .000 (50+) .000

t	BOY Inforce	Waiver Inforce	NH Inforce	NH Admiss.	NC Admiss.	BOY Lapses	Deaths	Net Prem. per Payor	NH Cost per Mid 1x	NC Cost per Mid 1x	NFO Cost per Lapse	Terminal Reserve	Mid-Term. Reserve
1	100,000	0	0	15	64	7,996	51	10.61	7.13	3.75	0.00	0.00	0.00
2	91,954	5	8	23	94	6,432	62	202.76	11.81	5.36	0.00	210.15	97.72
3	85,459	12	16	26	107	5,123	74	202.76	13.91	7.32	0.00	438.46	311.15
4	80,262	18	22	28	131	4,009	88	202.76	15.65	9.56	0.00	682.24	543.29
5	76,165	22	27	38	157	3,042	103	202.76	21.40	12.14	0.00	933.40	789.15
6	73,020	28	35	40	187	2,916	121	202.76	22.80	15.11	0.00	1,204.17	1,044.71
7	69,983	33	41	46	200	2,784	126	202.76	27.51	16.95	0.00	1,494.02	1,319.22
8	67,063	39	47	51	214	2,677	131	202.76	32.31	19.10	0.00	1,804.46	1,613.15
9	64,255	44	54	48	229	2,565	137	202.76	32.53	21.48	0.00	2,142.26	1,930.81
10	61,554	47	56	53	247	2,456	142	202.76	37.38	24.31	0.00	2,504.76	2,273.42
11	58,955	51	61	57	265	2,352	150	202.76	42.21	27.57	0.00	2,894.20	2,641.89
12	56,453	55	66	61	285	2,252	158	202.76	46.89	31.31	0.00	3,313.09	3,037.39
13	54,043	59	70	66	305	2,155	167	202.76	51.48	35.56	0.00	3,764.22	3,463.37
14	51,721	63	75	72	328	2,062	178	202.76	60.46	40.49	0.00	4,245.79	3,920.09
15	49,481	69	83	80	351	1,972	189	202.76	69.11	46.10	0.00	4,760.88	4,408.11
16	47,321	76	91	91	375	1,885	201	202.76	82.03	52.56	0.00	5,307.99	4,928.27
17	45,235	85	102	107	400	1,801	212	202.76	99.25	59.83	0.00	5,885.50	5,479.04
18	43,222	96	114	125	426	1,720	225	202.76	120.36	67.80	0.00	6,492.45	6,089.13
19	41,277	111	134	150	452	1,642	238	202.76	149.29	76.39	0.00	7,123.79	6,668.65
20	39,397	129	158	177	479	1,566	252	202.76	181.72	85.75	0.00	7,778.69	7,295.67
21	37,580	152	185	204	506	1,493	265	202.76	217.29	95.78	0.00	8,456.76	7,948.59
22	35,822	177	215	233	533	1,422	280	202.76	256.09	106.50	0.00	9,158.15	8,624.29
23	34,120	204	248	261	561	1,353	296	202.76	298.54	117.78	0.00	9,882.96	9,322.90
24	32,471	232	282	286	588	1,286	315	202.76	340.79	129.97	0.00	10,636.11	10,046.81
25	30,869	260	315	310	614	1,221	337	202.76	387.41	142.72	0.00	11,419.38	10,799.36
26	29,311	288	347	331	639	1,158	363	202.76	435.47	155.94	0.00	12,239.31	11,584.56
27	27,790	315	378	354	664	1,096	393	202.76	488.59	169.65	0.00	13,100.66	12,407.97
28	26,302	341	409	376	686	1,035	425	202.76	547.11	183.68	0.00	14,009.62	13,274.95
29	24,842	367	439	406	706	975	459	202.76	627.95	198.54	0.00	14,955.93	14,183.65
30	23,407	396	473	442	724	917	494	202.76	729.98	213.40	0.00	15,931.66	15,125.16
31	21,997	429	513	486	739	859	528	202.76	861.88	228.68	0.00	16,920.10	16,087.48
32	20,610	467	561	538	750	802	560	202.76	1,028.58	243.62	0.00	17,900.11	17,052.10
33	19,248	513	616	596	757	746	590	202.76	1,235.38	258.31	0.00	18,844.18	17,995.26
34	17,912	564	678	654	760	692	617	202.76	1,477.42	273.35	0.00	19,728.21	18,891.63
35	16,602	620	745	709	759	638	640	202.76	1,755.22	287.36	0.00	20,527.52	19,717.32
36	15,324	678	814	759	752	587	658	202.76	2,069.27	301.20	0.00	21,214.69	20,446.81
37	14,079	735	880	801	741	536	671	202.76	2,409.40	313.87	0.00	21,771.53	21,067.68
38	12,872	789	942	831	725	488	678	202.76	2,766.06	325.54	0.00	22,188.06	21,536.03
39	11,706	836	995	848	704	441	680	202.76	3,145.74	336.68	0.00	22,446.38	21,868.29
40	10,585	875	1,037	851	678	396	675	202.76	3,544.01	345.89	0.00	22,532.22	22,038.66
41	9,513	903	1,066	840	648	354	665	202.76	3,949.75	354.61	0.00	22,437.34	22,036.03
42	8,494	918	1,079	815	614	314	650	202.76	4,371.25	360.83	0.00	22,148.05	21,849.74
43	7,530	921	1,077	778	576	276	631	202.76	4,789.91	366.42	0.00	21,666.83	21,473.14
44	6,623	910	1,060	728	535	241	609	202.76	5,199.95	369.29	0.00	20,995.11	20,910.07
45	5,773	886	1,026	669	491	208	585	202.76	5,607.12	370.49	0.00	20,147.14	20,160.18
50	2,422	609	683	317	257	81	400	202.76	7,034.80	357.58	0.00	14,120.79	14,512.10
55	633	266	285	72	78	19	170	202.76	7,732.26	329.00	0.00	7,141.84	7,692.67
60	70	49	49	5	9	2	31	202.76	8,229.81	269.89	0.00	3,143.36	3,327.54
65	1	1	1	0	0	0	1	202.76	1,637.99	9.79	0.00	0.00	121.83

PREMIUM & BENEFIT TOTALS ($000)   338,162   863,909
PRESENT VALUES (5.00%) ($000)   186,253   186,253

TABLE C-1—Continued

DEFAULT CASE LTC RESERVE OUTPUT

Summary of 1-Year Preliminary Term Reserves at 5.000% for Issue Age 70 Assuming Females Are 100% of Sales

			NH	HC	Home Care EP/BP in Service Days
Net Premium: 1,641.93		Daily Benefit:	100.00	50.00	Inflation Protection: NONE
Lifetime Pay		Deductible Period:	100	100	
		Lifetime Maximum:	1460	1460	
		W/P Days in Ben:	0		

Mortality Table: 83 GAM
  Adjustment Factor: 1.000
  Mort. Selection Factors: (1) 0.500 (2) 0.600 (3) 0.700 (4) 0.800 (5) 0.900 (6) 1.000 (7) 1.000 (8) 1.000 (9) 1.000 (10) 1.000

Morbidity Table: 85 NNHS (Insurable Stays) and 82/84 NLTCS
  Adjustment Factor: 1.000
  Morb. Selection Factors: (1) 0.500 (2) 0.600 (3) 0.700 (4) 0.800 (5) 0.900 (6) 1.000 (7) 1.000 (8) 1.000 (9) 1.000 (10) 1.000
  Antiselection Factors: 0.700   0.500   0.300   0.200   0.100   0.000   0.000   0.000   0.000   0.000

Home Care Service Utilization Rates by ADL/CI Status:
  No Cognitive Impairment: (0 ADLs) 0.000 (1 ADLs) 0.100 (2 ADLs) 0.700 (3 ADLs) 1.000
  Cognitively Impaired: 0.300   0.500   0.700   1.000

Home Care Service Frequency (per week) by ADL/CI Status:
  No Cognitive Impairment: (0 ADLs) 0.000 (1 ADLs) 2.000 (2 ADLs) 4.000 (3 ADLs) 6.000
  Cognitively Impaired: 1.000   3.000   5.000   7.000

Lapse rates are in addition to mortality - Maximum aggregate termination rate: 1.000
  Lapse Rates: (1) 0.080 (2) 0.070 (3) 0.060 (4) 0.050 (5) 0.040 (6) 0.040 (7) 0.040 (8) 0.040 (9) 0.040 (10+) 0.040

Nonforfeiture benefits: SBP Cost Factor: 1.200   Reserves to exceed SBP cost per lapser
  (3) .000 (4) .000 (5) .000 (10) .000 (15) .000 (20) .000 (25) .000 (30) .000 (35) .000 (40) .000 (45) .000 (50+) .000

t	BOY Inforce	Waiver Inforce	NH Inforce	NH Admiss.	HC Admiss.	BOY Lapses	Deaths	Net Prem. per Payor	NH Cost per Mid lx	HC Cost per Mid lx	NFO Cost per Lapse	Terminal Reserve	Mid-Term. Reserve
1	100,000	0	0	533	1,017	7,950	619	267.43	202.47	72.50	0.00	0.00	0.00
2	91,431	193	295	698	1,294	6,346	775	1,641.93	288.77	100.26	0.00	1,436.39	667.92
3	84,309	389	523	869	1,572	5,001	963	1,641.93	390.07	126.96	0.00	2,900.92	2,081.63
4	78,354	573	740	1,066	1,841	3,860	1,158	1,641.93	517.71	163.69	0.00	4,347.95	3,515.73
5	73,336	765	970	1,295	2,108	2,878	1,392	1,641.93	677.48	198.05	0.00	5,725.45	4,922.19
6	69,067	977	1,226	1,568	2,370	2,696	1,657	1,641.93	880.43	233.60	0.00	7,043.61	6,243.66
7	64,713	1,220	1,522	1,713	2,379	2,518	1,759	1,641.93	1,039.02	246.09	0.00	8,366.45	7,537.70
8	60,436	1,437	1,766	1,884	2,387	2,343	1,853	1,641.93	1,240.37	259.35	0.00	9,662.61	8,821.27
9	56,239	1,644	2,006	2,060	2,389	2,172	1,938	1,641.93	1,478.91	273.63	0.00	10,905.09	10,065.75
10	52,129	1,849	2,246	2,231	2,382	2,005	2,010	1,641.93	1,755.22	287.36	0.00	12,066.31	11,244.38
11	48,115	2,053	2,482	2,387	2,363	1,842	2,067	1,641.93	2,069.27	301.20	0.00	13,116.83	12,329.09
12	44,206	2,249	2,709	2,518	2,327	1,684	2,107	1,641.93	2,409.40	313.87	0.00	14,036.82	13,295.94
13	40,415	2,432	2,917	2,611	2,277	1,531	2,129	1,641.93	2,766.06	325.54	0.00	14,816.50	14,130.33
14	36,755	2,593	3,095	2,664	2,211	1,385	2,134	1,641.93	3,145.74	336.68	0.00	15,437.61	14,818.30
15	33,235	2,723	3,235	2,674	2,130	1,245	2,121	1,641.93	3,544.01	345.89	0.00	15,885.27	15,343.74
16	29,870	2,817	3,332	2,639	2,035	1,111	2,088	1,641.93	3,949.75	354.61	0.00	16,151.42	15,695.31
17	26,670	2,872	3,380	2,561	1,928	985	2,042	1,641.93	4,371.25	360.83	0.00	16,222.61	15,862.56
18	23,643	2,885	3,377	2,443	1,809	866	1,982	1,641.93	4,789.91	366.42	0.00	16,098.45	15,838.56
19	20,794	2,854	3,324	2,287	1,681	755	1,912	1,641.93	5,199.95	369.29	0.00	15,784.80	15,628.93
20	18,127	2,781	3,221	2,100	1,543	652	1,837	1,641.93	5,607.12	370.49	0.00	15,288.58	15,230.92
21	15,638	2,668	3,072	1,891	1,399	556	1,748	1,641.93	6,003.05	370.08	0.00	14,611.71	14,687.91
22	13,335	2,518	2,882	1,667	1,250	468	1,641	1,641.93	6,312.87	367.06	0.00	13,814.90	13,937.01
23	11,226	2,338	2,659	1,437	1,100	388	1,522	1,641.93	6,580.79	363.85	0.00	12,927.69	13,112.74
24	9,315	2,134	2,410	1,211	952	317	1,394	1,641.93	6,822.42	361.30	0.00	11,964.35	12,206.73
25	7,605	1,914	2,146	994	808	254	1,256	1,641.93	7,036.80	357.58	0.00	10,943.08	11,234.85
26	6,095	1,685	1,876	794	671	199	1,112	1,641.93	7,222.70	352.69	0.00	9,879.99	10,213.94
27	4,784	1,456	1,609	615	544	153	963	1,641.93	7,376.59	346.72	0.00	8,801.05	9,164.50
28	3,666	1,235	1,352	460	430	114	814	1,641.93	7,513.87	338.28	0.00	7,708.41	8,100.66
29	2,738	1,026	1,113	330	330	83	668	1,641.93	7,620.12	334.37	0.00	6,617.96	7,030.93
30	1,987	834	897	226	245	58	533	1,641.93	7,732.26	329.00	0.00	5,542.91	5,969.57
31	1,396	664	707	145	176	39	412	1,641.93	7,835.88	321.03	0.00	4,531.76	4,946.70
32	945	516	543	86	121	25	307	1,641.93	7,924.89	312.10	0.00	3,578.47	4,031.54
33	612	391	407	44	79	14	220	1,641.93	8,030.95	304.26	0.00	3,197.36	3,373.96
34	377	264	264	25	49	9	149	1,641.93	8,120.31	289.89	0.00	2,820.70	2,952.62
35	218	153	153	14	29	5	96	1,641.93	8,229.81	269.89	0.00	2,390.18	2,557.64
36	118	82	82	8	15	2	57	1,641.93	8,323.85	243.48	0.00	1,832.95	2,074.91
37	58	41	41	4	7	1	32	1,641.93	7,852.37	211.76	0.00	1,223.68	1,503.04
38	25	18	18	2	3	1	15	1,641.93	6,943.92	170.21	0.00	841.22	671.63
39	9	7	7	1	1	0	6	1,641.93	5,314.56	107.66	0.00	0.00	270.61
40	3	2	2	0	0	0	3	1,641.93	1,657.99	9.79	0.00	0.00	0.00

PREMIUM & BENEFIT TOTALS ($000)		1,630,490	2,102,167	
PRESENT VALUES (5.00%) ($000)		1,136,343	1,136,343	

SOCIETY OF ACTUARIES LONG TERM CARE VALUATION METHODS TASK FORCE - RESERVE PROGRAM TEST Version 1.3b

TABLE C-2

ELIMINATION AND BENEFIT PERIOD VARIATIONS

Daily Benefit NH/HC	Elim. Period NH/HC	Ben. Period NH/HC	Net Premium Age 45	Mid-Terminal Reserves Issue Age 45 by Duration from Issue			
				5	10	20	30
100/100	0/0	20/20	$359.40	$1,359.54	$3,838.02	$11,831.52	$23,168.29
100/100	0/0	4/0	182.23	724.70	2,125.47	7,141.96	15,678.41
100/100	0/0	4/2	263.73	1,015.57	2,903.11	9,185.27	18,766.99
100/100	0/0	4/3	280.64	1,078.49	3,074.23	9,639.92	19,414.25
100/100	0/0	4/4	289.69	1,113.01	3,169.04	9,894.07	19,764.85
100/100	0/100	20/20	342.12	1,298.76	3,676.46	11,407.28	22,503.95
100/100	0/100	4/0	182.23	724.70	2,125.47	7,141.96	15,678.41
100/100	0/100	4/2	252.09	975.74	2,798.43	8,911.65	18,319.15
100/100	0/100	4/3	266.53	1,029.85	2,945.92	9,303.29	18,871.14
100/100	0/100	4/4	274.02	1,058.38	3,024.48	9,514.56	19,159.58
100/100	100/0	20/20	328.86	1,237.14	3,478.79	10,614.03	20,485.67
100/100	100/0	4/0	156.90	622.46	1,824.33	6,110.79	13,387.77
100/100	100/0	4/2	238.34	913.09	2,601.23	8,151.57	16,470.67
100/100	100/0	4/3	255.24	975.95	2,772.19	8,605.71	17,116.76
100/100	100/0	4/4	264.28	1,010.45	2,866.92	8,859.56	17,466.73
100/100	100/100	20/20	311.59	1,176.40	3,317.38	10,190.33	19,822.52
100/100	100/100	4/0	156.90	622.46	1,824.33	6,110.79	13,387.77
100/100	100/100	4/2	226.71	873.29	2,496.64	7,878.31	16,023.65
100/100	100/100	4/3	241.14	927.35	2,644.02	8,269.52	16,574.63
100/100	100/100	4/4	248.62	955.86	2,722.51	8,480.55	16,862.56
100/100	50/50	20/20	333.43	1,259.71	3,553.63	10,929.07	21,319.38
100/100	50/50	4/0	167.53	665.43	1,951.16	6,545.69	14,359.71
100/100	50/50	4/2	243.49	937.46	2,679.20	8,458.34	17,232.58
100/100	50/50	4/3	258.87	994.77	2,835.02	8,873.12	17,819.39
100/100	50/50	4/4	267.12	1,026.26	2,921.87	9,105.85	18,138.78
100/50	0/0	20/20	299.35	1,142.03	3,251.99	10,285.71	20,913.50
100/50	0/0	4/0	182.23	724.70	2,125.47	7,141.96	15,678.41
100/50	0/0	4/2	222.98	870.14	2,514.29	8,163.62	17,222.70
100/50	0/0	4/3	231.43	901.59	2,599.85	8,390.94	17,546.33
100/50	0/0	4/4	235.96	918.85	2,647.25	8,518.01	17,721.64
100/50	0/100	20/20	290.71	1,111.63	3,171.20	10,073.58	20,581.33
100/50	0/100	4/0	182.23	724.70	2,125.47	7,141.96	15,678.41
100/50	0/100	4/2	217.16	850.21	2,461.95	8,026.80	16,998.79
100/50	0/100	4/3	224.38	877.27	2,535.69	8,222.62	17,274.78
100/50	0/100	4/4	228.12	891.54	2,574.98	8,328.26	17,419.00
100/50	100/0	20/20	268.85	1,019.81	2,893.30	9,070.08	18,235.05
100/50	100/0	4/0	156.90	622.46	1,824.33	6,110.79	13,387.77
100/50	100/0	4/2	197.62	767.77	2,212.77	7,131.18	14,929.22
100/50	100/0	4/3	206.07	799.20	2,298.26	7,358.25	15,252.27
100/50	100/0	4/4	210.59	816.45	2,345.61	7,485.18	15,427.25
100/50	100/100	20/20	260.22	989.44	2,812.59	8,858.23	17,903.48
100/50	100/100	4/0	156.90	622.46	1,824.33	6,110.79	13,387.77
100/50	100/100	4/2	191.80	747.87	2,160.48	6,994.55	14,705.70
100/50	100/100	4/3	199.02	774.90	2,234.17	7,190.16	14,981.20
100/50	100/100	4/4	202.76	789.15	2,273.42	7,295.67	15,125.16
100/50	50/50	20/20	277.73	1,057.52	3,008.33	9,490.51	19,233.37
100/50	50/50	4/0	167.53	665.43	1,951.16	6,545.69	14,359.71
100/50	50/50	4/2	205.51	801.46	2,315.18	7,502.02	15,796.15
100/50	50/50	4/3	213.20	830.10	2,393.09	7,709.41	16,089.55
100/50	50/50	4/4	217.32	845.85	2,436.52	7,825.77	16,249.24

TABLE C-2—*Continued*

ELIMINATION AND BENEFIT PERIOD VARIATIONS

Daily Benefit NH/HC	Elim. Period NH/HC	Ben. Period NH/HC	Net Premium Age 70	Mid-Terminal Reserves Issue Age 70 by Duration from Issue			
				5	10	20	30
100/100	0/0	20/20	$2,611.55	$7,365.55	$16,305.74	$21,737.18	$9,132.68
100/100	0/0	4/0	1,662.48	5,299.34	12,487.23	17,524.50	7,065.64
100/100	0/0	4/2	2,068.54	6,104.42	13,888.21	19,167.60	8,081.31
100/100	0/0	4/3	2,155.42	6,259.38	14,114.50	19,326.21	8,155.38
100/100	0/0	4/4	2,203.00	6,338.94	14,218.15	19,365.68	8,174.10
100/100	0/100	20/20	2,525.53	7,184.79	15,965.73	21,257.13	8,800.27
100/100	0/100	4/0	1,662.48	5,299.34	12,487.23	17,524.50	7,065.64
100/100	0/100	4/2	2,011.46	5,976.27	13,628.31	18,753.77	7,776.82
100/100	0/100	4/3	2,085.86	6,106.47	13,811.06	18,859.63	7,832.99
100/100	0/100	4/4	2,125.18	6,170.88	13,892.45	18,888.01	7,841.99
100/100	100/0	20/20	2,313.56	6,409.90	14,035.34	18,345.67	7,483.67
100/100	100/0	4/0	1,412.23	4,492.02	10,555.49	14,572.27	5,594.30
100/100	100/0	4/2	1,815.40	5,287.27	11,932.38	16,174.82	6,587.33
100/100	100/0	4/3	1,901.66	5,440.12	12,153.52	16,324.77	6,656.54
100/100	100/0	4/4	1,948.90	5,518.53	12,254.34	16,359.49	6,672.61
100/100	100/100	20/20	2,228.16	6,231.22	13,700.44	17,874.22	7,156.05
100/100	100/100	4/0	1,412.23	4,492.02	10,555.49	14,572.27	5,594.30
100/100	100/100	4/2	1,758.73	5,160.50	11,675.85	15,766.70	6,286.01
100/100	100/100	4/3	1,832.59	5,288.90	11,854.21	15,865.12	6,338.03
100/100	100/100	4/4	1,871.63	5,352.35	11,933.26	15,889.58	6,344.85
100/100	50/50	20/20	2,397.59	6,728.07	14,837.31	19,566.76	8,045.82
100/100	50/50	4/0	1,516.57	4,830.40	11,367.92	15,830.18	6,242.82
100/100	50/50	4/2	1,893.77	5,568.10	12,627.68	17,238.89	7,089.80
100/100	50/50	4/3	1,972.45	5,706.24	12,824.52	17,366.93	7,156.68
100/100	50/50	4/4	2,015.70	5,777.54	12,915.42	17,398.98	7,165.77
100/50	0/0	20/20	2,310.82	6,804.17	15,402.21	20,833.05	8,594.98
100/50	0/0	4/0	1,662.48	5,299.34	12,487.23	17,524.50	7,065.64
100/50	0/0	4/2	1,865.51	5,701.88	13,187.73	18,346.05	7,573.47
100/50	0/0	4/3	1,908.95	5,779.36	13,300.87	18,425.36	7,610.51
100/50	0/0	4/4	1,932.74	5,819.14	13,352.69	18,445.10	7,619.86
100/50	0/100	20/20	2,267.81	6,713.79	15,232.22	20,593.03	8,428.78
100/50	0/100	4/0	1,662.48	5,299.34	12,487.23	17,524.50	7,065.64
100/50	0/100	4/2	1,836.97	5,637.81	13,057.77	18,139.14	7,421.22
100/50	0/100	4/3	1,874.17	5,702.91	13,149.15	18,192.06	7,449.31
100/50	0/100	4/4	1,893.83	5,735.11	13,189.84	18,206.25	7,453.81
100/50	100/0	20/20	2,014.97	5,855.80	13,149.65	17,471.58	6,962.74
100/50	100/0	4/0	1,412.23	4,492.02	10,555.49	14,572.27	5,594.30
100/50	100/0	4/2	1,613.82	4,889.65	11,243.93	15,373.54	6,090.81
100/50	100/0	4/3	1,656.95	4,966.07	11,354.51	15,448.52	6,125.42
100/50	100/0	4/4	1,680.57	5,005.28	11,404.91	15,465.88	6,133.46
100/50	100/100	20/20	1,972.27	5,766.46	12,982.21	17,235.85	6,798.94
100/50	100/100	4/0	1,412.23	4,492.02	10,555.49	14,572.27	5,594.30
100/50	100/100	4/2	1,585.48	4,826.26	11,115.68	15,169.48	5,940.16
100/50	100/100	4/3	1,622.41	4,890.46	11,204.85	15,218.69	5,966.17
100/50	100/100	4/4	1,641.93	4,922.19	11,244.38	15,230.92	5,969.57
100/50	50/50	20/20	2,119.75	6,216.60	14,030.37	18,802.13	7,602.05
100/50	50/50	4/0	1,516.57	4,830.40	11,367.92	15,830.18	6,242.82
100/50	50/50	4/2	1,705.17	5,199.25	11,997.79	16,534.54	6,666.31
100/50	50/50	4/3	1,744.51	5,268.32	12,096.21	16,598.55	6,699.75
100/50	50/50	4/4	1,766.13	5,303.97	12,141.67	16,614.58	6,704.30

TABLE C-3

HOME HEALTH CARE UTILIZATION VARIATIONS FOR AN INTEGRATED BENEFIT PLAN

Integrated Benefit Plan		Net Premium Age 45	Mid-Terminal Reserves Issue Age 45 by Duration from Issue			
Frequency Per Week	Utilization 100% Use For		5	10	20	30
7 days	1+ADLs or CI	$330.86	$1,228.27	$3,418.55	$10,151.67	$19,090.67
	2+ADLs or CI	245.15	941.93	2,690.58	8,467.48	17,061.74
	3+ADLs or CI	221.43	858.66	2,471.85	7,918.36	16,282.23
	1+ADLs	302.53	1,127.01	3,141.20	9,362.05	17,782.87
	2+ADLs	212.58	822.78	2,360.44	7,512.24	15,471.65
	3+ADLs	186.77	730.60	2,114.98	6,877.09	14,537.33
	1 ADLs and no CI	242.61	908.80	2,552.29	7,794.97	15,416.70
	2 ADLs and no CI	180.62	705.73	2,043.06	6,659.91	14,167.27
	3 ADLs and no CI	183.97	718.91	2,081.19	6,778.92	14,387.47
	0 ADLs and CI	185.23	723.72	2,101.67	6,900.41	14,695.56
	1 ADLs and CI	161.13	640.35	1,877.11	6,276.41	13,670.05
	2 ADLs and CI	159.00	631.36	1,851.05	6,196.82	13,542.58
	3 ADLs and CI	159.70	634.14	1,858.11	6,208.96	13,537.63
3.5 days	1+ADLs or CI	252.70	956.38	2,703.85	8,332.20	16,429.25
	2+ADLs or CI	212.57	823.73	2,370.29	7,588.18	15,605.51
	3+ADLs or CI	200.62	781.65	2,259.73	7,312.58	15,231.46
	1+ADLs	229.66	875.61	2,485.02	7,727.59	15,490.81
	2+ADLs	186.81	731.63	2,118.47	6,884.48	14,513.46
	3+ADLs	173.41	683.44	1,989.70	6,552.04	14,044.79
	1 ADLs and no CI	197.03	755.11	2,157.89	6,854.81	14,211.50
	2 ADLs and no CI	168.85	664.54	1,934.89	6,386.38	13,761.81
	3 ADLs and no CI	171.28	674.60	1,964.22	6,478.66	13,935.58
	0 ADLs and CI	179.94	703.23	2,043.16	6,715.40	14,326.21
	1 ADLs and CI	159.62	633.79	1,857.30	6,209.89	13,541.37
	2 ADLs and CI	158.35	628.56	1,842.53	6,167.63	13,482.40
	3 ADLs and CI	159.03	631.30	1,849.80	6,184.18	13,496.96

TABLE C-3—*Continued*

HOME HEALTH CARE UTILIZATION VARIATIONS FOR AN INTEGRATED BENEFIT PLAN

Integrated Benefit Plan		Net Premium Age 70	Mid-Terminal Reserves Issue Age 70 by Duration from Issue			
Frequency Per Week	Utilization 100% Use For		5	10	20	30
7 days	1+ADLs or CI	$2,192.87	$5,880.30	$12,712.46	$16,517.48	$6,547.49
	2+ADLs or CI	1,882.45	5,450.41	12,183.00	16,157.20	6,294.34
	3+ADLs or CI	1,776.26	5,257.47	11,865.52	15,810.20	6,068.90
	1+ADLs	2,030.36	5,526.26	12,107.66	16,019.29	6,478.06
	2+ADLs	1,686.56	5,021.23	11,453.13	15,576.94	6,222.01
	3+ADLs	1,562.52	4,785.38	11,059.48	15,168.35	5,989.17
	1 ADLs and no CI	1,722.65	4,921.92	11,084.95	14,932.55	5,847.46
	2 ADLs and no CI	1,518.43	4,684.97	10,872.96	14,919.26	5,819.75
	3 ADLs and no CI	1,543.69	4,749.43	11,008.62	15,153.57	5,996.01
	0 ADLs and CI	1,574.74	4,846.06	11,160.29	15,070.46	5,663.73
	1 ADLs and CI	1,445.61	4,567.17	10,680.57	14,654.33	5,597.21
	2 ADLs and CI	1,430.08	4,534.93	10,631.66	14,633.85	5,601.70
	3 ADLs and CI	1,431.06	4,527.97	10,606.34	14,587.04	5,587.47
3.5 days	1+ADLs or CI	1,835.45	5,204.81	11,575.51	15,277.67	5,843.88
	2+ADLs or CI	1,701.83	5,046.53	11,423.98	15,250.48	5,831.12
	3+ADLs or CI	1,649.61	4,958.92	11,294.71	15,138.24	5,764.70
	1+ADLs	1,714.25	4,964.23	11,199.69	15,033.31	5,836.37
	2+ADLs	1,561.56	4,768.58	10,993.84	14,983.16	5,830.58
	3+ADLs	1,498.01	4,656.54	10,825.59	14,847.63	5,764.91
	1 ADLs and no CI	1,545.85	4,650.32	10,707.02	14,599.47	5,607.07
	2 ADLs and no CI	1,464.46	4,579.65	10,684.76	14,684.50	5,660.73
	3 ADLs and no CI	1,484.12	4,630.93	10,790.52	14,839.96	5,771.60
	0 ADLs and CI	1,533.43	4,732.62	10,931.31	14,816.64	5,601.81
	1 ADLs and CI	1,431.30	4,529.39	10,609.81	14,595.21	5,587.33
	2 ADLs and CI	1,423.56	4,516.44	10,594.46	14,595.56	5,593.55
	3 ADLs and CI	1,426.12	4,517.65	10,590.56	14,579.93	5,587.61

TABLE C-3—*Continued*

HOME HEALTH CARE UTILIZATION VARIATIONS FOR HOME HEALTH CARE ONLY PLAN

Home Health Care Only Plan		Net Premium Age 45	Mid-Terminal Reserves Issue Age 45 by Duration from Issue			
Frequency Per Week	Utilization 100% Use For		5	10	20	30
7 days	1+ADLs or CI	$173.96	$605.82	$1,594.22	$4,040.88	$5,702.91
	2+ADLs or CI	88.25	319.48	866.26	2,356.70	3,673.97
	3+ADLs or CI	64.53	236.20	647.52	1,807.58	2,894.47
	1+ADLs	145.63	504.55	1,316.88	3,251.26	4,395.10
	2+ADLs	55.69	200.32	536.12	1,401.46	2,083.89
	3+ADLs	29.87	108.15	290.65	766.31	1,149.57
	1 ADLs and no CI	85.71	286.34	727.96	1,684.18	2,028.94
	2 ADLs and no CI	23.72	83.27	218.74	549.11	779.51
	3 ADLs and no CI	27.07	96.46	256.87	668.13	999.71
	0 ADLs and CI	28.33	101.26	277.34	789.61	1,307.80
	1 ADLs and CI	4.23	17.89	52.80	165.62	282.29
	2 ADLs and CI	2.10	8.91	26.73	86.03	154.81
	3 ADLs and CI	2.80	11.69	33.78	98.17	149.87
3.5 days	1+ADLs or CI	95.80	333.93	879.54	2,221.41	3,041.49
	2+ADLs or CI	55.67	201.27	545.96	1,477.39	2,217.76
	3+ADLs or CI	43.72	159.19	435.40	1,201.79	1,843.70
	1+ADLs	72.76	253.16	660.70	1,616.80	2,103.04
	2+ADLs	29.91	109.17	294.14	773.68	1,125.70
	3+ADLs	16.52	60.99	165.38	441.26	657.02
	1 ADLs and no CI	40.13	132.66	333.57	744.02	823.73
	2 ADLs and no CI	11.95	42.08	110.56	275.59	374.06
	3 ADLs and no CI	14.38	52.14	139.90	367.87	547.82
	0 ADLs and CI	23.04	80.77	218.84	604.60	938.44
	1 ADLs and CI	2.72	11.33	32.98	99.09	153.61
	2 ADLs and CI	1.45	6.11	18.21	56.84	94.63
	3 ADLs and CI	2.13	8.84	25.48	73.40	109.20

TABLE C-3—*Continued*

HOME HEALTH CARE UTILIZATION VARIATIONS FOR HOME HEALTH CARE ONLY PLAN

Home Health Care Only Plan		Net Premium Age 70	Mid-Terminal Reserves Issue Age 70 by Duration from Issue			
Frequency Per Week	Utilization 100% Use For		5	10	20	30
7 days	1+ADLs or CI	$780.63	$1,388.27	$2,156.97	$1,945.21	$953.19
	2+ADLs or CI	470.21	958.38	1,627.51	1,584.93	700.03
	3+ADLs or CI	364.02	765.44	1,310.04	1,237.93	474.59
	1+ADLs	618.12	1,034.23	1,552.17	1,447.02	883.76
	2+ADLs	274.32	529.20	897.64	1,004.67	627.70
	3+ADLs	150.29	293.36	503.99	596.09	394.86
	1 ADLs and no CI	310.42	429.89	529.46	360.28	253.15
	2 ADLs and no CI	106.19	192.94	317.48	346.99	225.44
	3 ADLs and no CI	131.46	257.41	453.14	581.30	401.69
	0 ADLs and CI	162.51	354.04	604.80	498.20	69.43
	1 ADLs and CI	33.38	75.15	125.08	82.06	2.90
	2 ADLs and CI	17.85	42.90	76.17	61.59	7.40
	3 ADLs and CI	18.83	35.95	50.86	14.78	0.00
3.5 days	1+ADLs or CI	423.21	712.79	1,020.02	705.42	249.58
	2+ADLs or CI	289.60	554.51	868.49	678.21	236.82
	3+ADLs or CI	237.38	466.89	739.22	565.98	170.39
	1+ADLs	302.01	472.19	644.20	461.04	242.07
	2+ADLs	149.33	276.54	438.35	410.89	236.28
	3+ADLs	85.78	164.51	270.10	275.35	170.61
	1 ADLs and no CI	133.62	158.29	151.53	27.20	12.76
	2 ADLs and no CI	52.22	87.62	129.28	112.24	66.43
	3 ADLs and no CI	71.89	138.89	235.03	267.69	177.29
	0 ADLs and CI	121.20	240.59	375.82	244.38	7.51
	1 ADLs and CI	19.07	37.36	54.32	22.95	0.00
	2 ADLs and CI	11.33	24.42	38.97	23.30	0.00
	3 ADLs and CI	13.89	25.61	35.08	7.67	0.00

TABLE C-4

SAMPLE VARIATIONS FROM DEFAULT ASSUMPTIONS

Dimension	Default	Variation 1	Variation 2	Variation 3
Insured Sex	100% Female	(1) 100% Male	(2) 60% Female	
Morbidity				
Selection Factors	0.5, 0.6, 0.7, 0.8, 0.9, 1.0,...	(3) 1.0, 1.0,...		
Antiselection at Lapse Factors	0.7, 0.5, 0.3, 0.2, 0.1, 0.0,...	(4) 0.0, 0.0,...		
Home Care Utilization	0.0　0.3 0.1　0.5 0.7　0.7 1.0　1.0	(5) 0.0　1.0 0.0　1.0 1.0　1.0 1.0　1.0	(6) 0.0　0.1 0.0　0.3 0.5　0.5 0.7　0.7	
Home Care Frequency	0　1 2　3 4　5 6　7	(7) 7　7 7　7 7　7 7　7	(8) 0　1 1　2 3　4 5　6	
Incidence Adjustment Factor	1.0	(9) 0.8	(10) 1.2	
Type of NH Stays	Insurable Stays	(11) All Stays		
Mortality				
Selection Factors	0.5, 0.6, 0.7, 0.8, 0.9, 1.0,...	(12) 1.0, 1.0,...		
Adjustment Factor	1.0	(13) 0.8	(14) 1.2	
Mortality Table	83 GAM	(15) 80 CSO	(16) 80 Basic	
Lapsation				
Lapse Rates	8%, 7%, 6%, 5%, 4%,...	(17) Zero lapse	(18) 4.0%, 3.5%, 3.0%, 2.5%, 2.0%,...	(19) 12.0%, 10.5%, 9.0%, 7.5%, 6.0%,...
Coordination with Mortality	Lapse rates exclude mortality	(20) Lapse rates include mortality		
Maximum Total Termination Rate	100%	(21) 8%		
Interest	5%	(22) 4.5%	(23) 5.5%	
Reserve Method	One Year Preliminary Term	(24) Two Year Preliminary Term	(25) Full Net Level	

TABLE C-4—*Continued*

CASE 1

	Net Premiums						Default	Base Assumptions See Mighty Fine Description in Appendix B
	Default		Variant		Variant / Default			
Duration	Iss Age 45	Iss Age 70	Iss Age 45	Iss Age 70	Iss Age 45	Iss Age 70	Variant	Test Variations from Base Assumptions Sex: 100% Male at Issue
0	$11	$267	$26	$184	244%	69%		
1	203	1,642	138	901	68	55		
2	203	1,642	138	901	68	55		

Comparison of Mid-Terminal Reserves

	Per Policy In Force						Per Policy Issued					
	Default		Variant		Variant / Default		Default		Variant		Variant / Default	
Duration	Iss Age 45	Iss Age 70	Iss Age 45	Iss Age 70	Iss Age 45	Iss Age 70	Iss Age 45	Iss Age 70	Iss Age 45	Iss Age 70	Iss Age 45	Iss Age 70
1	$0	$0	$0	$0	NA	NA	$0	$0	$0	$0	NA	NA
2	98	668	52	334	54%	50%	83	560	45	274	53%	49%
5	789	4,922	395	2,273	50	46	576	3,359	286	1,442	50	43
10	2,273	11,244	1,103	4,697	49	42	1,339	5,294	635	1,800	47	34
15	4,408	15,344	2,051	7,166	47	47	2,082	4,423	928	1,369	45	31
20	7,296	15,231	3,542	8,680	46	57	2,732	2,249	1,161	639	42	28
25	10,799	11,235	5,125	7,259	47	65	3,146	622	1,304	145	41	23
30	15,125	5,970	6,948	3,832	46	64	3,287	71	1,204	13	37	18
35	19,717	2,558	8,504	2,087	43	82	2,957	2	890	1	30	22
40	22,039	0	10,139	21	46	NA	2,023	0	529	0	26	NA
45	20,168	0	10,846	0	54	NA	948	0	218	0	23	NA

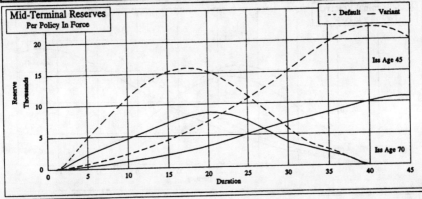

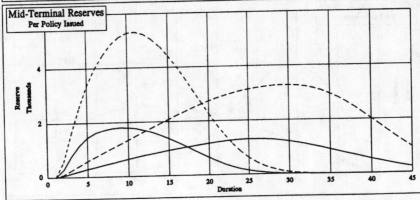

TABLE C-4—*Continued*
CASE 2

	Net Premiums						Default	Base Assumptions
	Default		Variant		Variant / Default			See Mighty Fine Description in Appendix B
Duration	Iss Age 45	Iss Age 70	Iss Age 45	Iss Age 70	Iss Age 45	Iss Age 70		
0	$11	$267	$19	$232	175%	87%	Variant	Test Variations from Base Assumptions
1	203	1,642	179	1,359	88	83		Sex: 60% Female at Issue
2	203	1,642	179	1,359	88	83		

	Comparison of Mid-Terminal Reserves											
	Per Policy In Force						Per Policy Issued					
	Default		Variant		Variant / Default		Default		Variant		Variant / Default	
Duration	Iss Age 45	Iss Age 70	Iss Age 45	Iss Age 70	Iss Age 45	Iss Age 70	Iss Age 45	Iss Age 70	Iss Age 45	Iss Age 70	Iss Age 45	Iss Age 70
1	$0	$0	$0	$0	NA	NA	$0	$0	$0	$0	NA	NA
2	98	668	79	544	81%	81%	83	560	68	452	81%	81%
5	789	4,922	627	3,948	79	80	576	3,359	456	2,619	79	78
10	2,273	11,244	1,790	8,967	79	80	1,359	5,294	1,045	3,912	78	74
15	4,408	15,344	3,443	12,946	78	84	2,082	4,423	1,598	3,236	77	73
20	7,296	15,231	5,710	13,930	78	91	2,732	2,249	2,077	1,650	76	73
25	10,799	11,235	8,614	10,964	80	98	3,146	622	2,383	454	76	73
30	15,125	5,970	12,143	5,993	80	100	3,287	71	2,426	51	74	72
35	19,717	2,558	15,887	2,894	81	113	2,957	2	2,095	2	71	81
40	22,039	0	18,498	0	84	NA	2,023	0	1,406	0	69	NA
45	20,168	0	18,028	0	89	NA	948	0	654	0	69	NA

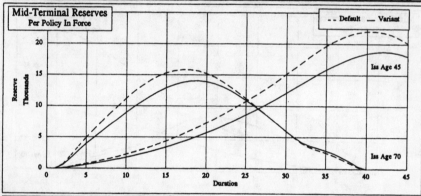

Mid-Terminal Reserves
Per Policy In Force

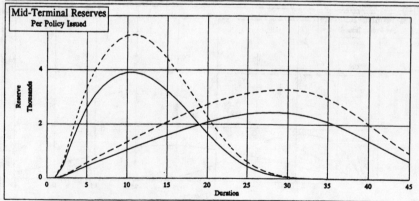

Mid-Terminal Reserves
Per Policy Issued

TABLE C-4—Continued
CASE 3

	Net Premiums						Default	Base Assumptions
	Default		Variant		Variant / Default			See Mighty Fine Description in Appendix B
Duration	Iss Age 45	Iss Age 70	Iss Age 45	Iss Age 70	Iss Age 45	Iss Age 70	Variant	Test Variations from Base Assumptions
0	$11	$267	$21	$535	200%	200%		Morbidity: No Selection at Issue
1	203	1,642	205	1,725	101	105		
2	203	1,642	205	1,725	101	105		

	Comparison of Mid-Terminal Reserves											
	Per Policy In Force						Per Policy Issued					
	Default		Variant		Variant / Default		Default		Variant		Variant / Default	
Duration	Iss Age 45	Iss Age 70	Iss Age 45	Iss Age 70	Iss Age 45	Iss Age 70	Iss Age 45	Iss Age 70	Iss Age 45	Iss Age 70	Iss Age 45	Iss Age 70
1	$0	$0	$0	$0	NA	NA	$0	$0	$0	$0	NA	NA
2	98	668	93	578	95%	86%	83	560	80	484	95%	86%
5	789	4,922	764	4,382	97	89	576	3,359	557	2,990	97	89
10	2,273	11,244	2,247	10,751	99	96	1,339	5,294	1,323	5,062	99	96
15	4,408	15,344	4,383	14,953	99	97	2,082	4,423	2,070	4,310	99	97
20	7,296	15,231	7,273	14,945	100	98	2,732	2,249	2,723	2,207	100	98
25	10,799	11,235	10,799	11,046	100	98	3,146	622	3,140	612	100	98
30	15,125	5,970	15,107	5,871	100	98	3,287	71	3,283	70	100	98
35	19,717	2,558	19,702	2,513	100	98	2,957	2	2,954	2	100	98
40	22,039	0	22,027	0	100	NA	2,023	0	2,022	0	100	NA
45	20,168	0	20,159	0	100	NA	948	0	948	0	100	NA

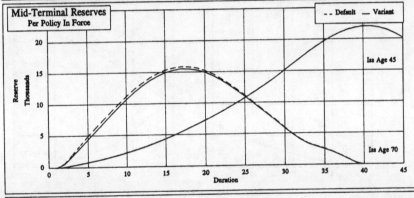

Mid-Terminal Reserves
Per Policy In Force

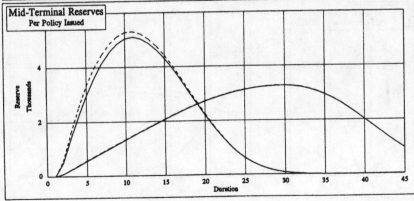

Mid-Terminal Reserves
Per Policy Issued

TABLE C-4—*Continued*

CASE 4

Net Premiums						Default	Base Assumptions
	Default		Variant		Variant / Default		See Mighty Fine Description in Appendix B
Duration	Iss Age 45	Iss Age 70	Iss Age 45	Iss Age 70	Iss Age 45	Iss Age 70	
0	$11	$267	$11	$267	100%	100%	Variant Test Variations from Base Assumptions
1	203	1,642	189	1,525	93	93	Morbidity: No Antiselection on Lapse
2	203	1,642	189	1,525	93	93	

Comparison of Mid-Terminal Reserves											
	Per Policy In Force						Per Policy Issued				
	Default		Variant		Variant / Default		Default		Variant		Variant / Default	
Duration	Iss Age 45	Iss Age 70	Iss Age 45	Iss Age 70	Iss Age 45	Iss Age 70	Iss Age 45	Iss Age 70	Iss Age 45	Iss Age 70	Iss Age 45	Iss Age 70
1	$0	$0	$0	$0	NA	NA	$0	$0	$0	$0	NA	NA
2	98	668	91	617	93%	92%	83	560	78	517	93%	92%
5	789	4,922	737	4,606	93	94	576	3,359	538	3,143	93	94
10	2,273	11,244	2,124	10,579	93	94	1,339	5,294	1,251	4,981	93	94
15	4,408	15,344	4,118	14,468	93	94	2,082	4,423	1,944	4,170	93	94
20	7,296	15,231	6,816	14,435	93	95	2,732	2,249	2,553	2,131	93	95
25	10,799	11,235	10,097	10,741	93	96	3,146	622	2,941	595	93	96
30	15,125	5,970	14,158	5,799	94	97	3,287	71	3,077	69	94	97
35	19,717	2,558	18,494	2,379	94	93	2,957	2	2,773	2	94	93
40	22,039	0	20,747	0	94	NA	2,023	0	1,905	0	94	NA
45	20,168	0	19,092	0	95	NA	948	0	898	0	95	NA

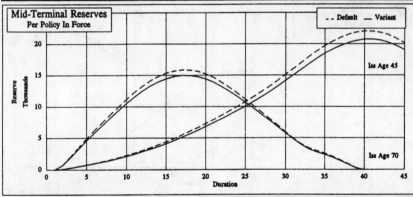

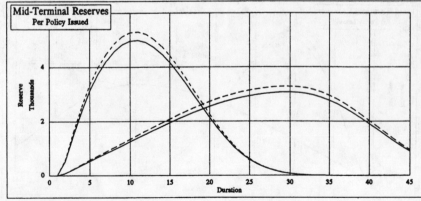

TABLE C-4—*Continued*

CASE 5

	Net Premiums						Default	Base Assumptions
	Default		Variant		Variant / Default			See Mighty Fine Description in Appendix B
Duration	Iss Age 45	Iss Age 70	Iss Age 45	Iss Age 70	Iss Age 45	Iss Age 70	Variant	Test Variations from Base Assumptions
0	$11	$267	$12	$285	110%	107%		Morbidity: Home Care Utilization
1	203	1,642	214	1,703	106	104		0%,0%,100%,100% 100%,100%,100%,100%
2	203	1,642	214	1,703	105	104		

	Comparison of Mid-Terminal Reserves											
	Per Policy In Force						Per Policy Issued					
	Default		Variant		Variant / Default		Default		Variant		Variant / Default	
Duration	Iss Age 45	Iss Age 70	Iss Age 45	Iss Age 70	Iss Age 45	Iss Age 70	Iss Age 45	Iss Age 70	Iss Age 45	Iss Age 70	Iss Age 45	Iss Age 70
1	$0	$0	$0	$0	NA	NA	$0	$0	$0	$0	NA	NA
2	98	668	103	687	105%	103%	83	560	88	576	105%	103%
5	789	4,922	830	5,036	105	102	576	3,359	605	3,436	105	102
10	2,273	11,244	2,385	11,408	105	101	1,339	5,294	1,404	5,371	105	101
15	4,408	15,344	4,612	15,489	105	101	2,082	4,423	2,178	4,465	105	101
20	7,296	15,231	7,606	15,318	104	101	2,732	2,249	2,848	2,262	104	101
25	10,799	11,235	11,207	11,273	104	100	3,146	622	3,265	624	104	100
30	15,125	5,970	15,590	5,988	103	100	3,287	71	3,388	71	103	100
35	19,717	2,558	20,173	2,559	102	100	2,957	2	3,025	2	102	100
40	22,039	0	22,414	0	102	NA	2,023	0	2,058	0	102	NA
45	20,168	0	20,425	0	101	NA	948	0	960	0	101	NA

Mid-Terminal Reserves
Per Policy In Force

- - Default — Variant

Iss Age 45

Iss Age 70

Reserve Thousands

Duration

Mid-Terminal Reserves
Per Policy Issued

Reserve Thousands

Duration

TABLE C-4—*Continued*

CASE 6

Net Premiums						Default	Base Assumptions
	Default		Variant		Variant / Default		See Mighty Fine Description in Appendix B
Duration	Iss Age 45	Iss Age 70	Iss Age 45	Iss Age 70	Iss Age 45	Iss Age 70	Variant Test Variations from Base Assumptions
0	$11	$267	$9	$242	87%	90%	Morbidity: Home Care Utilization
1	203	1,642	186	1,561	92	95	0%,0%,50%,70% 10%,30%,50%,70%
2	203	1,642	186	1,561	92	95	

Comparison of Mid-Terminal Reserves

	Per Policy In Force						Per Policy Issued					
	Default		Variant		Variant / Default		Default		Variant		Variant / Default	
Duration	Iss Age 45	Iss Age 70	Iss Age 45	Iss Age 70	Iss Age 45	Iss Age 70	Iss Age 45	Iss Age 70	Iss Age 45	Iss Age 70	Iss Age 45	Iss Age 70
1	$0	$0	$0	$0	NA	NA	$0	$0	$0	$0	NA	NA
2	98	668	90	644	92%	96%	83	560	77	540	92%	96%
5	789	4,922	729	4,777	92	97	576	3,359	532	3,260	92	97
10	2,273	11,244	2,113	11,022	93	98	1,339	5,294	1,244	5,190	93	98
15	4,408	15,344	4,123	15,111	94	98	2,082	4,423	1,947	4,356	94	98
20	7,296	15,231	6,877	15,041	94	99	2,732	2,249	2,575	2,221	94	99
25	10,799	11,235	10,266	11,100	95	99	3,146	622	2,990	615	95	99
30	15,125	5,970	14,526	5,870	96	98	3,287	71	3,157	70	96	98
35	19,717	2,558	19,119	2,511	97	98	2,957	2	2,867	2	97	98
40	22,039	0	21,509	0	98	NA	2,023	0	1,975	0	98	NA
45	20,168	0	19,759	0	98	NA	948	0	929	0	98	NA

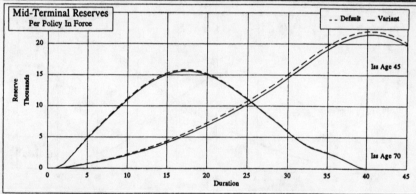

Mid-Terminal Reserves
Per Policy In Force

- - Default   — Variant

Iss Age 45

Iss Age 70

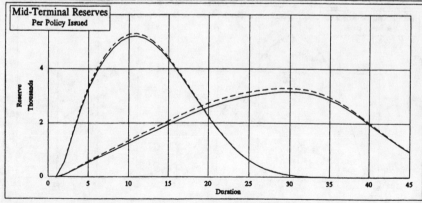

Mid-Terminal Reserves
Per Policy Issued

TABLE C-4—*Continued*

CASE 7

	Net Premiums						Default	Base Assumptions
	Default		Variant		Variant / Default			See Mighty Pine Description in Appendix B
Duration	Iss Age 45	Iss Age 70	Iss Age 45	Iss Age 70	Iss Age 45	Iss Age 70	Variant	Test Variations from Base Assumptions
0	$11	$267	$13	$297	120%	111%		Home Care Frequency
1	203	1,642	224	1,746	110	106		7.7.7.7 7.7.7.7 per week
2	203	1,642	224	1,746	110	106		

Comparison of Mid-Terminal Reserves

	Per Policy In Force						Per Policy Issued					
	Default		Variant		Variant / Default		Default		Variant		Variant / Default	
Duration	Iss Age 45	Iss Age 70	Iss Age 45	Iss Age 70	Iss Age 45	Iss Age 70	Iss Age 45	Iss Age 70	Iss Age 45	Iss Age 70	Iss Age 45	Iss Age 70
1	$0	$0	$0	$0	NA	NA	$0	$0	$0	$0	NA	NA
2	98	668	107	701	110%	105%	83	560	92	588	110%	105%
5	789	4,922	863	5,137	109	104	576	3,359	630	3,506	109	104
10	2,273	11,244	2,469	11,632	109	103	1,339	5,294	1,454	5,477	109	103
15	4,408	15,344	4,755	15,820	108	103	2,082	4,423	2,245	4,560	108	103
20	7,296	15,231	7,810	15,681	107	103	2,732	2,249	2,925	2,315	107	103
25	10,799	11,235	11,473	11,582	106	103	3,146	622	3,342	642	106	103
30	15,125	5,970	15,928	6,200	105	104	3,287	71	3,462	74	105	104
35	19,717	2,558	20,592	2,684	104	105	2,957	2	3,088	2	104	105
40	22,039	0	22,900	0	104	NA	2,023	0	2,102	0	104	NA
45	20,168	0	20,901	0	104	NA	948	0	983	0	104	NA

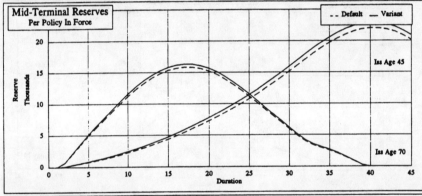

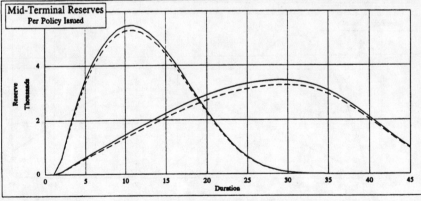

TABLE C-4—*Continued*

CASE 8

Net Premiums						Default	Base Assumptions
	Default		Variant		Variant / Default		See Mighty Fine Description in Appendix B
Duration	Iss Age 45	Iss Age 70	Iss Age 45	Iss Age 70	Iss Age 45	Iss Age 70	Variant	Test Variations from Base Assumptions
0	$11	$267	$10	$254	93%	95%		Home Care Frequency
1	203	1,642	194	1,599	96	97		0,1,3,5 1,2,4,6 per week
2	203	1,642	194	1,599	96	97		

Comparison of Mid-Terminal Reserves														
	Per Policy In Force						Per Policy Issued							
	Default		Variant		Variant / Default		Default		Variant		Variant / Default			
Duration	Iss Age 45	Iss Age 70	Iss Age 45	Iss Age 70	Iss Age 45	Iss Age 70	Iss Age 45	Iss Age 70	Iss Age 45	Iss Age 70	Iss Age 45	Iss Age 70		
1	$0	$0	$0	$0	NA	NA	$0	$0	$0	$0	NA	NA		
2	98	668	94	655	96%	98%	83	560	80	549	96%	98%		
5	789	4,922	757	4,839	96	98	576	3,359	552	3,302	96	98		
10	2,273	11,244	2,188	11,103	96	99	1,339	5,294	1,288	5,227	96	99		
15	4,408	15,344	4,258	15,175	97	99	2,082	4,423	2,011	4,374	97	99		
20	7,296	15,231	7,076	15,072	97	99	2,732	2,249	2,650	2,225	97	99		
25	10,799	11,235	10,517	11,105	97	99	3,146	622	3,063	615	97	99		
30	15,125	5,970	14,799	5,871	98	98	3,287	71	3,216	70	98	98		
35	19,717	2,558	19,374	2,504	98	98	2,957	2	2,905	2	98	98		
40	22,039	0	21,711	0	99	NA	2,023	0	1,993	0	99	NA		
45	20,168	0	19,892	0	99	NA	948	0	935	0	99	NA		

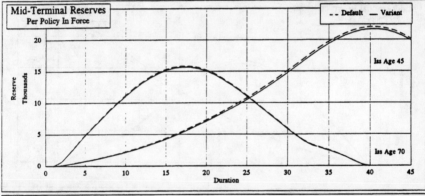

Mid-Terminal Reserves
Per Policy In Force

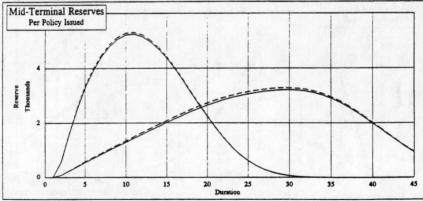

Mid-Terminal Reserves
Per Policy Issued

TABLE C-4—*Continued*

CASE 9

	Net Premiums						Default	Base Assumptions
	Default		Variant		Variant / Default			See Mighty Fine Description in Appendix B
Duration	Iss Age 45	Iss Age 70	Iss Age 45	Iss Age 70	Iss Age 45	Iss Age 70	Variant	Test Variations from Base Assumptions
0	$11	$267	$8	$214	80%	80%		Morbidity: 80% Incidence Factor
1	203	1,642	164	1,326	81	81		
2	203	1,642	164	1,326	81	81		

Comparison of Mid-Terminal Reserves

	Per Policy In Force						Per Policy Issued					
	Default		Variant		Variant / Default		Default		Variant		Variant / Default	
Duration	Iss Age 45	Iss Age 70	Iss Age 45	Iss Age 70	Iss Age 45	Iss Age 70	Iss Age 45	Iss Age 70	Iss Age 45	Iss Age 70	Iss Age 45	Iss Age 70
1	$0	$0	$0	$0	NA	NA	$0	$0	$0	$0	NA	NA
2	98	668	79	541	81%	81%	83	560	67	454	81%	81%
5	789	4,922	638	3,998	81	81	576	3,359	465	2,728	81	81
10	2,273	11,244	1,839	9,198	81	82	1,339	5,294	1,083	4,330	81	82
15	4,408	15,344	3,568	12,691	81	83	2,082	4,423	1,685	3,658	81	83
20	7,296	15,231	5,913	12,809	81	84	2,732	2,249	2,214	1,891	81	84
25	10,799	11,235	8,773	9,695	81	86	3,146	622	2,556	537	81	86
30	15,125	5,970	12,331	5,395	82	90	3,287	71	2,680	64	82	90
35	19,717	2,558	16,171	2,039	82	80	2,957	2	2,425	2	82	80
40	22,039	0	18,266	0	83	NA	2,023	0	1,677	0	83	NA
45	20,168	0	16,989	0	84	NA	948	0	799	0	84	NA

Mid-Terminal Reserves
Per Policy In Force

-- Default — Variant

Iss Age 45

Iss Age 70

Mid-Terminal Reserves
Per Policy Issued

TABLE C-4—*Continued*

CASE 10

	Net Premiums						Default	Base Assumptions
	Default		Variant		Variant / Default			See Mighty Fine Description in Appendix B
Duration	Iss Age 45	Iss Age 70	Iss Age 45	Iss Age 70	Iss Age 45	Iss Age 70		
0	$11	$267	$13	$321	120%	120%	Variant	Test Variations from Base Assumptions
1	203	1,642	241	1,952	119	119		Morbidity: 120% Incidence Factor
2	203	1,642	241	1,952	119	119		

Comparison of Mid-Terminal Reserves

	Per Policy In Force						Per Policy Issued					
	Default		Variant		Variant / Default		Default		Variant		Variant / Default	
Duration	Iss Age 45	Iss Age 70	Iss Age 45	Iss Age 70	Iss Age 45	Iss Age 70	Iss Age 45	Iss Age 70	Iss Age 45	Iss Age 70	Iss Age 45	Iss Age 70
1	$0	$0	$0	$0	NA	NA	$0	$0	$0	$0	NA	NA
2	98	668	116	792	119%	119%	83	560	99	664	119%	119%
5	789	4,922	938	5,821	119	118	576	3,359	684	3,972	119	118
10	2,273	11,244	2,700	13,206	119	117	1,339	5,294	1,590	6,218	119	117
15	4,408	15,344	5,231	17,828	119	116	2,082	4,423	2,470	5,139	119	116
20	7,296	15,231	8,646	17,422	119	114	2,732	2,249	3,238	2,572	119	114
25	10,799	11,235	12,769	12,553	118	112	3,146	622	3,720	695	118	112
30	15,125	5,970	17,822	6,461	118	108	3,287	71	3,873	77	118	108
35	19,717	2,558	23,099	3,079	117	120	2,957	2	3,464	3	117	120
40	22,039	0	25,558	0	116	NA	2,023	0	2,346	0	116	NA
45	20,168	0	23,033	0	114	NA	948	0	1,083	0	114	NA

Mid-Terminal Reserves — Per Policy In Force

Mid-Terminal Reserves — Per Policy Issued

TABLE C-4—*Continued*

CASE 11

	Net Premiums						Default	Base Assumptions
	Default		Variant		Variant / Default			See Mighty Fine Description in Appendix B
Duration	Iss Age 45	Iss Age 70	Iss Age 45	Iss Age 70	Iss Age 45	Iss Age 70		
0	$11	$267	$12	$291	112%	109%	Variant	Test Variations from Base Assumptions
1	203	1,642	217	1,726	107	105		Morbidity: All NH Stays
2	203	1,642	217	1,726	107	105		

	Comparison of Mid-Terminal Reserves											
	Per Policy In Force						Per Policy Issued					
	Default		Variant		Variant / Default		Default		Variant		Variant / Default	
Duration	Iss Age 45	Iss Age 70	Iss Age 45	Iss Age 70	Iss Age 45	Iss Age 70	Iss Age 45	Iss Age 70	Iss Age 45	Iss Age 70	Iss Age 45	Iss Age 70
1	$0	$0	$0	$0	NA	NA	$0	$0	$0	$0	NA	NA
2	98	668	106	698	108%	104%	83	560	90	585	108%	104%
5	789	4,922	845	5,136	107	104	576	3,359	616	3,505	107	104
10	2,273	11,244	2,413	11,686	106	104	1,339	5,294	1,421	5,502	106	104
15	4,408	15,344	4,659	15,835	106	103	2,082	4,423	2,200	4,565	106	103
20	7,296	15,231	7,701	15,708	106	103	2,732	2,249	2,884	2,319	106	103
25	10,799	11,235	11,341	11,655	105	104	3,146	622	3,304	646	105	104
30	15,125	5,970	15,811	6,231	105	104	3,287	71	3,436	74	105	104
35	19,717	2,558	20,537	2,819	104	110	2,957	2	3,079	3	104	110
40	22,039	0	22,811	0	104	NA	2,023	0	2,094	0	104	NA
45	20,168	0	20,830	0	103	NA	948	0	980	0	103	NA

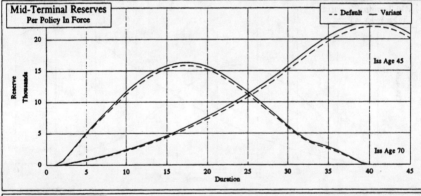

Mid-Terminal Reserves
Per Policy In Force

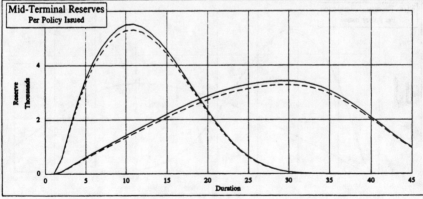

Mid-Terminal Reserves
Per Policy Issued

TABLE C-4—*Continued*

CASE 12

	Net Premiums						Default	Base Assumptions
	Default		Variant		Variant / Default			See Mighty Fine Description in Appendix B
Duration	Iss Age 45	Iss Age 70	Iss Age 45	Iss Age 70	Iss Age 45	Iss Age 70		
0	$11	$267	$11	$267	100%	100%	Variant	Test Variations from Base Assumptions
1	203	1,642	203	1,637	100	100		Mortality: No Selection at Issue
2	203	1,642	203	1,637	100	100		

Comparison of Mid-Terminal Reserves

	Per Policy In Force						Per Policy Issued					
	Default		Variant		Variant / Default		Default		Variant		Variant / Default	
Duration	Iss Age 45	Iss Age 70	Iss Age 45	Iss Age 70	Iss Age 45	Iss Age 70	Iss Age 45	Iss Age 70	Iss Age 45	Iss Age 70	Iss Age 45	Iss Age 70
1	$0	$0	$0	$0	NA	NA	$0	$0	$0	$0	NA	NA
2	98	668	98	670	100%	100%	83	560	83	553	100%	99%
5	789	4,922	790	4,954	100	101	576	3,359	575	3,304	100	98
10	2,273	11,244	2,274	11,275	100	100	1,339	5,294	1,336	5,189	100	98
15	4,408	15,344	4,408	15,368	100	100	2,082	4,423	2,078	4,330	100	98
20	7,296	15,231	7,296	15,249	100	100	2,732	2,249	2,727	2,201	100	98
25	10,799	11,235	10,800	11,247	100	100	3,146	622	3,140	609	100	98
30	15,125	5,970	15,125	5,974	100	100	3,287	71	3,281	70	100	98
35	19,717	2,558	19,717	2,560	100	100	2,957	2	2,951	2	100	98
40	22,039	0	22,038	0	100	NA	2,023	0	2,020	0	100	NA
45	20,168	0	20,167	0	100	NA	948	0	947	0	100	NA

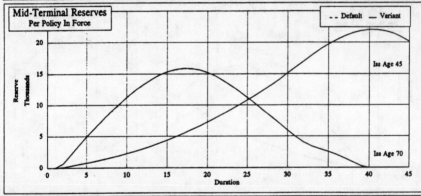

Mid-Terminal Reserves — Per Policy In Force (- - Default, — Variant; Iss Age 45, Iss Age 70)

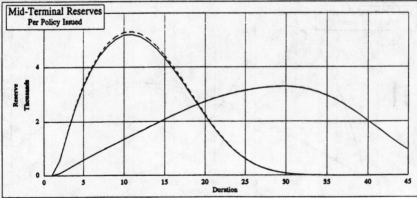

Mid-Terminal Reserves — Per Policy Issued

TABLE C-4—*Continued*

CASE 13

	Net Premiums						Default	Base Assumptions
	Default		Variant		Variant / Default			See Mighty Fine Description in Appendix B
Duration	Iss Age 45	Iss Age 70	Iss Age 45	Iss Age 70	Iss Age 45	Iss Age 70	Variant	Test Variations from Base Assumptions
0	$11	$267	$11	$268	100%	100%		Mortality: 80% Adjustment Factor
1	203	1,642	217	1,740	107	106		
2	203	1,642	217	1,740	107	106		

Comparison of Mid-Terminal Reserves

	Per Policy In Force						Per Policy Issued					
	Default		Variant		Variant / Default		Default		Variant		Variant / Default	
Duration	Iss Age 45	Iss Age 70	Iss Age 45	Iss Age 70	Iss Age 45	Iss Age 70	Iss Age 45	Iss Age 70	Iss Age 45	Iss Age 70	Iss Age 45	Iss Age 70
1	$0	$0	$0	$0	NA	NA	$0	$0	$0	$0	NA	NA
2	98	668	105	718	108%	108%	83	560	90	605	108%	108%
5	789	4,922	850	5,321	108	108	576	3,359	621	3,684	108	110
10	2,273	11,244	2,456	12,268	108	109	1,339	5,294	1,451	6,062	108	115
15	4,408	15,344	4,776	16,946	108	110	2,082	4,423	2,270	5,436	109	123
20	7,296	15,231	7,937	17,234	109	113	2,732	2,249	3,008	3,118	110	139
25	10,799	11,235	11,832	13,445	110	120	3,146	622	3,521	1,076	112	173
30	15,125	5,970	16,679	8,276	110	139	3,287	71	3,770	191	115	269
35	19,717	2,558	21,853	3,185	111	125	2,957	2	3,526	10	119	430
40	22,039	0	24,672	0	112	NA	2,023	0	2,584	0	128	NA
45	20,168	0	23,098	0	115	NA	948	0	1,365	0	144	NA

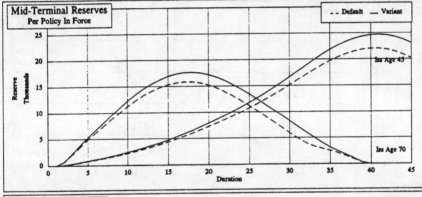

Mid-Terminal Reserves
Per Policy In Force

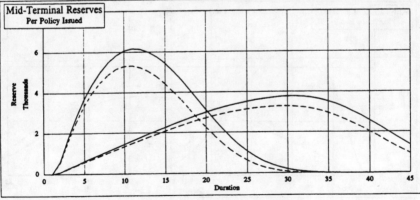

Mid-Terminal Reserves
Per Policy Issued

TABLE C-4—*Continued*

CASE 14

	Net Premiums						Default	Base Assumptions
	Default		Variant		Variant / Default			See Mighty Fine Description in Appendix B
Duration	Iss Age 45	Iss Age 70	Iss Age 45	Iss Age 70	Iss Age 45	Iss Age 70		
0	$11	$267	$11	$267	100%	100%	Variant	Test Variations from Base Assumptions
1	203	1,642	191	1,559	94	95		Mortality: 120% Adjustment Factor
2	203	1,642	191	1,559	94	95		

Comparison of Mid-Terminal Reserves

	Per Policy In Force						Per Policy Issued					
	Default		Variant		Variant / Default		Default		Variant		Variant / Default	
Duration	Iss Age 45	Iss Age 70	Iss Age 45	Iss Age 70	Iss Age 45	Iss Age 70	Iss Age 45	Iss Age 70	Iss Age 45	Iss Age 70	Iss Age 45	Iss Age 70
1	$0	$0	$0	$0	NA	NA	$0	$0	$0	$0	NA	NA
2	98	668	92	625	94%	94%	83	560	78	522	94%	93%
5	789	4,922	739	4,587	94	93	576	3,359	539	3,085	94	92
10	2,273	11,244	2,122	10,391	93	92	1,339	5,294	1,246	4,660	93	88
15	4,408	15,344	4,104	14,021	93	91	2,082	4,423	1,926	3,628	93	82
20	7,296	15,231	6,767	13,598	93	89	2,732	2,249	2,504	1,634	92	73
25	10,799	11,235	9,950	9,441	92	84	3,146	622	2,837	359	90	58
30	15,125	5,970	13,851	4,253	92	71	3,287	71	2,894	25	88	36
35	19,717	2,558	17,974	2,153	91	84	2,957	2	2,504	1	85	22
40	22,039	0	19,908	0	90	NA	2,023	0	1,600	0	79	NA
45	20,168	0	17,823	0	88	NA	948	0	665	0	70	NA

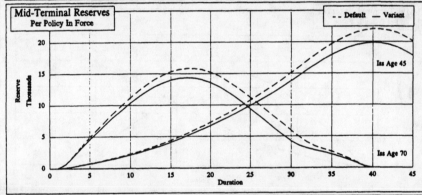

Mid-Terminal Reserves
Per Policy In Force
- - Default — Variant
Iss Age 45
Iss Age 70

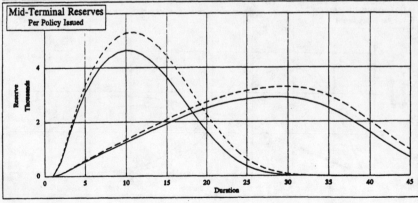

Mid-Terminal Reserves
Per Policy Issued

TABLE C-4—Continued
CASE 15

	Net Premiums						Default	Base Assumptions
	Default		Variant		Variant / Default			See Mighty Fine Description in Appendix B
Duration	Iss Age 45	Iss Age 70	Iss Age 45	Iss Age 70	Iss Age 45	Iss Age 70	Variant	Test Variations from Base Assumptions
0	$11	$267	$11	$267	100%	100%		Mortality: 80CSO Table
1	205	1,642	164	1,397	81	85		
2	205	1,642	164	1,397	81	85		

Comparison of Mid-Terminal Reserves

	Per Policy In Force						Per Policy Issued					
	Default		Variant		Variant / Default		Default		Variant		Variant / Default	
Duration	Iss Age 45	Iss Age 70	Iss Age 45	Iss Age 70	Iss Age 45	Iss Age 70	Iss Age 45	Iss Age 70	Iss Age 45	Iss Age 70	Iss Age 45	Iss Age 70
1	$0	$0	$0	$0	NA	NA	$0	$0	$0	$0	NA	NA
2	98	668	77	543	79%	81%	83	560	66	447	79%	80%
5	789	4,922	622	3,940	79	80	576	3,559	449	2,546	78	76
10	2,273	11,244	1,786	8,687	79	77	1,339	5,294	1,017	3,469	76	66
15	4,408	15,344	3,462	11,127	79	73	2,082	4,423	1,541	2,216	74	50
20	7,296	15,231	5,702	10,004	78	66	2,732	2,249	1,946	686	71	31
25	10,799	11,235	8,353	5,030	77	45	3,146	622	2,112	64	67	10
30	15,125	5,970	11,523	856	76	14	3,287	71	2,032	0	62	0
35	19,717	2,558	14,695	419	75	16	2,957	2	1,601	0	54	0
40	22,039	0	15,521	419	70	NA	2,023	0	844	0	42	NA
45	20,168	0	12,908	0	64	NA	948	0	242	0	25	NA

Mid-Terminal Reserves
Per Policy In Force

Mid-Terminal Reserves
Per Policy Issued

TABLE C-4—*Continued*
CASE 16

	Net Premiums						Default	Base Assumptions
	Default		Variant		Variant / Default			See Mighty Fine Description in Appendix B
Duration	Iss Age 45	Iss Age 70	Iss Age 45	Iss Age 70	Iss Age 45	Iss Age 70		
0	$11	$267	$11	$267	100%	100%	Variant	Test Variations from Base Assumptions
1	203	1,642	179	1,490	88	91		Mortality: 80 Basic Table
2	203	1,642	179	1,490	88	91		

Comparison of Mid-Terminal Reserves

	Per Policy In Force						Per Policy Issued					
	Default		Variant		Variant / Default		Default		Variant		Variant / Default	
Duration	Iss Age 45	Iss Age 70	Iss Age 45	Iss Age 70	Iss Age 45	Iss Age 70	Iss Age 45	Iss Age 70	Iss Age 45	Iss Age 70	Iss Age 45	Iss Age 70
1	$0	$0	$0	$0	NA	NA	$0	$0	$0	$0	NA	NA
2	98	668	85	590	87%	88%	83	560	73	491	87%	88%
5	789	4,922	688	4,302	87	87	576	3,359	499	2,861	87	85
10	2,273	11,244	1,979	9,566	87	85	1,339	5,294	1,145	4,154	86	78
15	4,408	15,344	3,838	12,443	87	81	2,082	4,423	1,755	2,957	84	67
20	7,296	15,291	6,328	11,673	87	77	2,732	2,249	2,255	1,115	83	50
25	10,799	11,235	9,310	7,135	86	64	3,146	622	2,515	173	80	28
30	15,125	5,970	12,875	1,199	85	20	3,287	71	2,514	1	76	1
35	19,717	2,558	16,452	411	83	16	2,957	2	2,097	0	71	0
40	22,039	0	17,583	411	80	NA	2,023	0	1,227	0	61	NA
45	20,168	0	15,221	0	75	NA	948	0	427	0	45	NA

Mid-Terminal Reserves — Per Policy In Force

Mid-Terminal Reserves — Per Policy Issued

TABLE C-4—*Continued*

CASE 17

	Net Premiums						Default	Base Assumptions
	Default		Variant		Variant / Default			See Mighty Fine Description in Appendix B
Duration	Iss Age 45	Iss Age 70	Iss Age 45	Iss Age 70	Iss Age 45	Iss Age 70		
0	$11	$267	$11	$267	100%	100%	Variant	Test Variations from Base Assumptions
1	203	1,642	408	1,881	201	115		Lapsation: No Lapsation
2	203	1,642	408	1,881	201	115		

Comparison of Mid-Terminal Reserves

	Per Policy In Force						Per Policy Issued					
	Default		Variant		Variant / Default		Default		Variant		Variant / Default	
Duration	Iss Age 45	Iss Age 70	Iss Age 45	Iss Age 70	Iss Age 45	Iss Age 70	Iss Age 45	Iss Age 70	Iss Age 45	Iss Age 70	Iss Age 45	Iss Age 70
1	$0	$0	$0	$0	NA	NA	$0	$0	$0	$0	NA	NA
2	98	668	206	805	211%	121%	83	560	205	789	246%	141%
5	789	4,922	1,521	5,545	193	113	576	3,359	1,513	5,158	263	154
10	2,273	11,244	4,093	12,323	180	110	1,339	5,294	4,030	9,701	301	183
15	4,408	15,344	7,244	16,262	164	106	2,082	4,423	7,015	9,613	337	217
20	7,296	15,231	10,940	15,803	150	104	2,732	2,249	10,303	5,868	377	261
25	10,799	11,235	14,911	11,669	138	104	3,146	622	13,398	1,994	426	320
30	15,125	5,970	19,231	6,570	127	110	3,287	71	15,810	296	481	416
35	19,717	2,558	23,265	2,281	118	89	2,957	2	16,185	9	547	414
40	22,039	0	24,670	0	112	NA	2,023	0	12,887	0	637	NA
45	20,168	0	21,891	0	109	NA	948	0	7,183	0	757	NA

Mid-Terminal Reserves
Per Policy In Force

-- Default — Variant

Mid-Terminal Reserves
Per Policy Issued

TABLE C-4—*Continued*
CASE 18

	Net Premiums						Default	Base Assumptions
	Default		Variant		Variant / Default			See Mighty Fine Description in Appendix B
Duration	Iss Age 45	Iss Age 70	Iss Age 45	Iss Age 70	Iss Age 45	Iss Age 70	Variant	Test Variations from Base Assumptions
0	$11	$267	$11	$267	100%	100%		Lapsation: 4%,3.5%,3%,2.5%,2%...
1	203	1,642	286	1,755	141	107		
2	203	1,642	286	1,755	141	107		

Comparison of Mid-Terminal Reserves

	Per Policy In Force						Per Policy Issued					
	Default		Variant		Variant / Default		Default		Variant		Variant / Default	
Duration	Iss Age 45	Iss Age 70	Iss Age 45	Iss Age 70	Iss Age 45	Iss Age 70	Iss Age 45	Iss Age 70	Iss Age 45	Iss Age 70	Iss Age 45	Iss Age 70
1	$0	$0	$0	$0	NA	NA	$0	$0	$0	$0	NA	NA
2	98	668	142	734	145%	110%	83	560	131	666	157%	119%
5	789	4,922	1,095	5,227	139	106	576	3,359	936	4,175	162	124
10	2,273	11,244	3,055	11,790	134	105	1,399	5,294	2,334	7,204	174	136
15	4,408	15,344	5,661	15,834	128	103	2,082	4,423	3,846	6,566	185	148
20	7,296	15,231	8,952	15,569	123	102	2,732	2,249	5,347	3,666	196	163
25	10,799	11,235	12,723	11,514	118	102	3,146	622	6,553	1,128	208	181
30	15,125	5,970	17,103	6,315	113	106	3,287	71	7,286	147	222	207
35	19,717	2,558	21,479	2,424	109	95	2,957	2	6,998	5	237	206
40	22,039	0	23,395	0	106	NA	2,023	0	5,174	0	256	NA
45	20,168	0	21,102	0	105	NA	948	0	2,650	0	279	NA

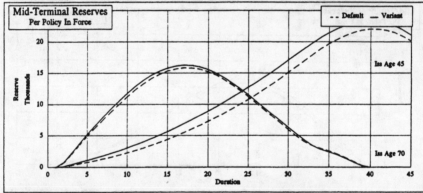

Mid-Terminal Reserves
Per Policy In Force

- - Default   — Variant

Iss Age 45

Iss Age 70

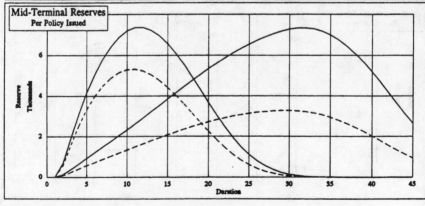

Mid-Terminal Reserves
Per Policy Issued

TABLE C-4—*Continued*

CASE 19

Net Premiums						Default	Base Assumptions
	Default		Variant		Variant / Default		See Mighty Fine Description in Appendix B
Duration	Iss Age 45	Iss Age 70	Iss Age 45	Iss Age 70	Iss Age 45	Iss Age 70	Variant Test Variations from Base Assumptions
0	$11	$267	$11	$267	100%	100%	Variant Test Variations from Base Assumptions
1	203	1,642	147	1,541	73	94	Lapsation: 12%,10.5%,9%,7.5%,6%,...
2	203	1,642	147	1,541	73	94	

Comparison of Mid-Terminal Reserves													
	Per Policy In Force						Per Policy Issued						
	Default		Variant		Variant / Default		Default		Variant		Variant / Default	
Duration	Iss Age 45	Iss Age 70	Iss Age 45	Iss Age 70	Iss Age 45	Iss Age 70	Iss Age 45	Iss Age 70	Iss Age 45	Iss Age 70	Iss Age 45	Iss Age 70
1	$0	$0	$0	$0	NA	NA	$0	$0	$0	$0	NA	NA
2	98	668	68	608	70%	91%	83	560	54	469	64%	84%
5	789	4,922	575	4,635	73	94	576	3,359	357	2,687	62	80
10	2,273	11,244	1,704	10,699	75	95	1,339	5,294	767	3,852	57	73
15	4,408	15,344	3,449	14,806	78	96	2,082	4,423	1,121	2,938	54	66
20	7,296	15,231	5,964	14,796	82	97	2,732	2,249	1,384	1,353	51	60
25	10,799	11,235	9,173	10,824	85	96	3,146	622	1,490	334	47	54
30	15,125	5,970	13,362	5,534	88	93	3,287	71	1,458	33	44	47
35	19,717	2,558	18,060	2,684	92	105	2,957	2	1,223	1	41	47
40	22,039	0	20,677	0	94	NA	2,023	0	772	0	38	NA
45	20,168	0	19,142	0	95	NA	948	0	329	0	35	NA

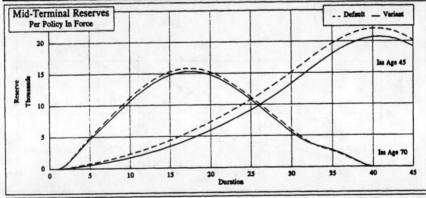

Mid-Terminal Reserves
Per Policy In Force

— — Default   —— Variant

Iss Age 45

Iss Age 70

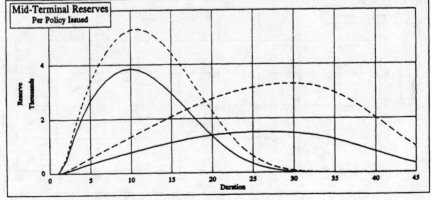

Mid-Terminal Reserves
Per Policy Issued

TABLE C-4—*Continued*

CASE 20

	Net Premiums						Default	Base Assumptions
	Default		Variant		Variant / Default			See Mighty Fine Description in Appendix B
Duration	Iss Age 45	Iss Age 70	Iss Age 45	Iss Age 70	Iss Age 45	Iss Age 70		
0	$11	$267	$11	$267	100%	100%	Variant	Test Variations from Base Assumptions
1	203	1,642	263	1,942	130	118		Lapsation: Lapse rates include mortality
2	203	1,642	263	1,942	130	118		

Comparison of Mid-Terminal Reserves

	Per Policy In Force						Per Policy Issued					
	Default		Variant		Variant / Default		Default		Variant		Variant / Default	
Duration	Iss Age 45	Iss Age 70	Iss Age 45	Iss Age 70	Iss Age 45	Iss Age 70	Iss Age 45	Iss Age 70	Iss Age 45	Iss Age 70	Iss Age 45	Iss Age 70
1	$0	$0	$0	$0	NA	NA	$0	$0	$0	$0	NA	NA
2	98	668	129	827	132%	124%	83	560	111	703	132%	126%
5	789	4,922	1,050	6,118	133	124	576	3,359	769	4,434	134	132
10	2,273	11,244	3,054	13,670	134	122	1,339	5,294	1,824	8,000	136	151
15	4,408	15,344	5,962	17,713	135	115	2,082	4,423	2,901	7,784	139	176
20	7,296	15,231	9,950	17,031	136	112	2,732	2,249	3,942	4,701	144	209
25	10,799	11,235	14,907	12,466	138	111	3,146	622	4,803	1,583	153	254
30	15,125	5,970	20,814	6,928	138	116	3,287	71	5,436	232	165	326
35	19,717	2,558	26,043	2,498	132	98	2,957	2	5,493	8	186	337
40	22,039	0	27,205	0	123	NA	2,023	0	4,309	0	213	NA
45	20,168	0	23,873	0	118	NA	948	0	2,375	0	250	NA

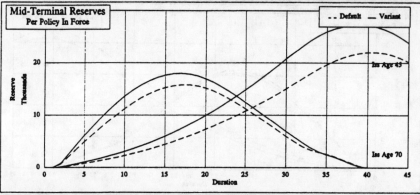

Mid-Terminal Reserves
Per Policy In Force

-- Default — Variant

Iss Age 45

Iss Age 70

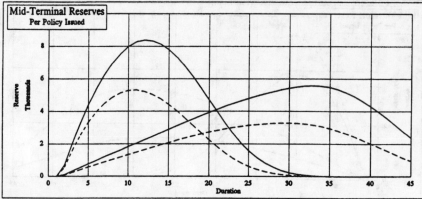

Mid-Terminal Reserves
Per Policy Issued

TABLE C-4—*Continued*

CASE 21

	Net Premiums						Default	Base Assumptions
	Default		Variant		Variant / Default			See Mighty Fine Description in Appendix B
Duration	Iss Age 45	Iss Age 70	Iss Age 45	Iss Age 70	Iss Age 45	Iss Age 70	Variant	Test Variations from Base Assumptions
0	$11	$267	$11	$267	100%	100%		Lapsation: Terminations less than 8%
1	203	1,642	212	1,739	105	106		
2	203	1,642	212	1,739	105	106		

Comparison of Mid-Terminal Reserves												
	Per Policy In Force						Per Policy Issued					
	Default		Variant		Variant / Default		Default		Variant		Variant / Default	
Duration	Iss Age 45	Iss Age 70	Iss Age 45	Iss Age 70	Iss Age 45	Iss Age 70	Iss Age 45	Iss Age 70	Iss Age 45	Iss Age 70	Iss Age 45	Iss Age 70
1	$0	$0	$0	$0	NA	NA	$0	$0	$0	$0	NA	NA
2	98	668	103	719	105%	108%	83	560	88	607	105%	108%
5	789	4,922	830	5,358	105	109	576	3,359	606	3,679	105	110
10	2,273	11,244	2,400	12,716	106	113	1,339	5,294	1,414	6,024	106	114
15	4,408	15,344	4,671	18,273	106	119	2,082	4,423	2,207	5,627	106	127
20	7,296	15,231	7,780	17,830	107	117	2,732	2,249	2,915	3,399	107	151
25	10,799	11,235	11,655	13,004	108	116	3,146	622	3,396	1,141	108	183
30	15,125	5,970	16,634	7,233	110	121	3,287	71	3,617	167	110	235
35	19,717	2,558	22,524	2,613	114	102	2,957	2	3,379	6	114	243
40	22,039	0	26,641	0	121	NA	2,023	0	2,598	0	128	NA
45	20,168	0	24,041	0	119	NA	948	0	1,451	0	153	NA

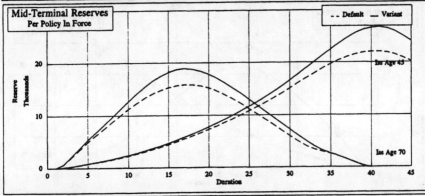

Mid-Terminal Reserves
Per Policy In Force

-- Default   — Variant

Iss Age 45

Iss Age 70

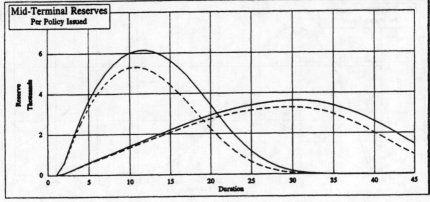

Mid-Terminal Reserves
Per Policy Issued

TABLE C-4—*Continued*

CASE 22

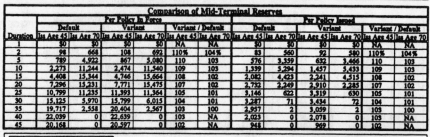

Duration	Net Premiums Default Iss Age 45	Default Iss Age 70	Variant Iss Age 45	Variant Iss Age 70	Variant/Default Iss Age 45	Variant/Default Iss Age 70
0	$11	$267	$11	$271	101%	101%
1	203	1,642	223	1,697	110	103
2	203	1,642	223	1,697	110	103

Default Base Assumptions
See Mighty Fine Description in Appendix B

Variant Test Variations from Base Assumptions
Interest: 4.5%

Comparison of Mid-Terminal Reserves

	Per Policy In Force						Per Policy Issued					
	Default		Variant		Variant/Default		Default		Variant		Variant/Default	
Duration	Iss Age 45	Iss Age 70	Iss Age 45	Iss Age 70	Iss Age 45	Iss Age 70	Iss Age 45	Iss Age 70	Iss Age 45	Iss Age 70	Iss Age 45	Iss Age 70
1	$0	$0	$0	$0	NA	NA	$0	$0	$0	$0	NA	NA
2	98	668	108	692	110%	104%	83	560	92	580	110%	104%
5	789	4,922	867	5,080	110	103	576	3,359	632	3,466	110	103
10	2,273	11,244	2,474	11,540	109	103	1,399	5,294	1,457	5,433	109	103
15	4,408	15,344	4,746	15,664	108	102	2,082	4,423	2,241	4,515	108	102
20	7,296	15,231	7,771	15,475	107	102	2,732	2,249	2,910	2,285	107	102
25	10,799	11,235	11,393	11,364	105	101	3,146	622	3,319	630	105	101
30	15,125	5,970	15,799	6,015	104	101	3,287	71	3,434	72	104	101
35	19,717	2,558	20,404	2,567	103	100	2,957	2	3,059	2	103	100
40	22,039	0	22,639	0	103	NA	2,023	0	2,078	0	103	NA
45	20,168	0	20,597	0	102	NA	948	0	969	0	102	NA

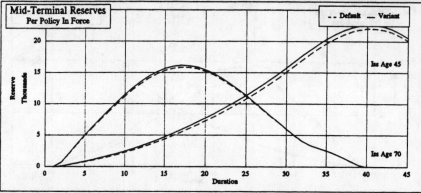

Mid-Terminal Reserves
Per Policy In Force

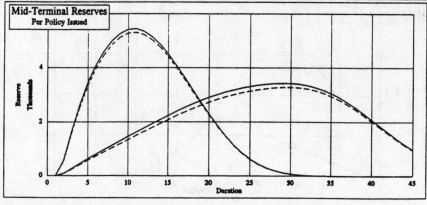

Mid-Terminal Reserves
Per Policy Issued

TABLE C-4—Continued

CASE 23

	Net Premiums						Default	Base Assumptions
	Default		Variant		Variant / Default			See Mighty Fine Description in Appendix B
Duration	Iss Age 45	Iss Age 70	Iss Age 45	Iss Age 70	Iss Age 45	Iss Age 70	Variant	Test Variations from Base Assumptions
0	$11	$267	$10	$264	99%	99%		Interest: 5.5%
1	203	1,642	185	1,589	91	97		
2	203	1,642	185	1,589	91	97		

	Comparison of Mid-Terminal Reserves											
	Per Policy In Force						Per Policy Issued					
	Default		Variant		Variant / Default		Default		Variant		Variant / Default	
Duration	Iss Age 45	Iss Age 70	Iss Age 45	Iss Age 70	Iss Age 45	Iss Age 70	Iss Age 45	Iss Age 70	Iss Age 45	Iss Age 70	Iss Age 45	Iss Age 70
1	$0	$0	$0	$0	NA	NA	$0	$0	$0	$0	NA	NA
2	98	668	89	645	91%	97%	83	560	76	541	91%	97%
5	789	4,922	720	4,771	91	97	576	3,359	525	3,255	91	97
10	2,273	11,244	2,091	10,958	92	97	1,339	5,294	1,231	5,159	92	97
15	4,408	15,344	4,097	15,030	93	98	2,082	4,423	1,935	4,333	93	98
20	7,296	15,291	6,854	14,990	94	98	2,732	2,249	2,566	2,213	94	98
25	10,799	11,235	10,241	11,105	95	99	3,146	622	2,983	615	95	99
30	15,125	5,970	14,484	5,923	96	99	3,287	71	3,148	70	96	99
35	19,717	2,558	19,057	2,548	97	100	2,957	2	2,858	2	97	100
40	22,039	0	21,456	0	97	NA	2,023	0	1,970	0	97	NA
45	20,168	0	19,748	0	98	NA	948	0	929	0	98	NA

Mid-Terminal Reserves
Per Policy In Force

-- Default — Variant

Iss Age 45

Iss Age 70

Mid-Terminal Reserves
Per Policy Issued

TABLE C-4—*Continued*

CASE 24

	Net Premiums						Default	Base Assumptions
	Default		Variant		Variant / Default			See Mighty Fine Description in Appendix B
Duration	Iss Age 45	Iss Age 70	Iss Age 45	Iss Age 70	Iss Age 45	Iss Age 70		
0	$11	$267	$184	$1,465	1732%	548%	Variant	Test Variations from Base Assumptions
1	203	1,642	184	1,465	91	89		Method: Net Level
2	203	1,642	184	1,465	91	89		

	Comparison of Mid-Terminal Reserves											
	Per Policy In Force						Per Policy Issued					
	Default		Variant		Variant / Default		Default		Variant		Variant / Default	
Duration	Iss Age 45	Iss Age 70	Iss Age 45	Iss Age 70	Iss Age 45	Iss Age 70	Iss Age 45	Iss Age 70	Iss Age 45	Iss Age 70	Iss Age 45	Iss Age 70
1	$0	$0	$91	$633	NA	NA	$0	$0	$84	$576	NA	NA
2	98	668	291	1,990	297%	298%	83	560	248	1,658	297%	298%
5	789	4,922	990	6,183	125	126	576	3,359	722	4,219	125	126
10	2,273	11,244	2,467	12,289	109	109	1,539	5,294	1,453	5,786	109	109
15	4,408	15,344	4,593	16,168	104	105	2,082	4,423	2,169	4,661	104	105
20	7,296	15,231	7,467	15,838	102	104	2,732	2,249	2,796	2,338	102	104
25	10,799	11,235	10,954	11,637	101	104	3,146	622	3,191	645	101	104
30	15,125	5,970	15,260	6,180	101	104	3,287	71	3,316	74	101	104
35	19,717	2,558	19,829	2,653	101	104	2,957	2	2,973	2	101	104
40	22,039	0	22,127	0	100	NA	2,023	0	2,031	0	100	NA
45	20,168	0	20,233	0	100	NA	948	0	951	0	100	NA

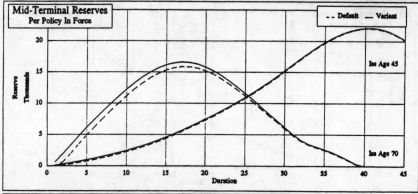

Mid-Terminal Reserves
Per Policy In Force

- - Default — Variant

Iss Age 45

Iss Age 70

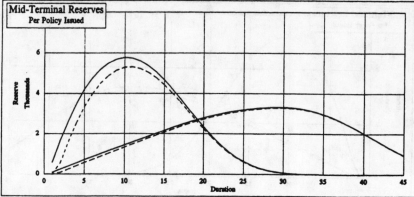

Mid-Terminal Reserves
Per Policy Issued

TABLE C-4—Continued

CASE 25

Net Premiums							Default	Base Assumptions See Mighty Pine Description in Appendix B
	Default		Variant		Variant / Default			
Duration	Iss Age 45	Iss Age 70	Iss Age 45	Iss Age 70	Iss Age 45	Iss Age 70		
0	$11	$267	$11	$267	100%	100%	Variant	Test Variations from Base Assumptions Method: 2 Year Preliminary Term
1	203	1,642	17	378	8	23		
2	203	1,642	222	1,828	110	111		

Comparison of Mid-Terminal Reserves

	Per Policy In Force						Per Policy Issued					
	Default		Variant		Variant / Default		Default		Variant		Variant / Default	
Duration	Iss Age 45	Iss Age 70	Iss Age 45	Iss Age 70	Iss Age 45	Iss Age 70	Iss Age 45	Iss Age 70	Iss Age 45	Iss Age 70	Iss Age 45	Iss Age 70
1	$0	$0	$0	$0	NA	NA	$0	$0	$0	$0	NA	NA
2	98	668	0	0	0%	0%	83	560	0	0	0%	0%
5	789	4,922	580	3,595	74	73	576	3,359	423	2,453	74	73
10	2,273	11,244	2,072	10,145	91	90	1,339	5,294	1,220	4,776	91	90
15	4,408	15,344	4,216	14,476	96	94	2,082	4,425	1,991	4,173	96	94
20	7,296	15,231	7,117	14,592	98	96	2,732	2,249	2,665	2,154	98	96
25	10,799	11,235	10,638	10,811	99	96	3,146	622	3,099	599	99	96
30	15,125	5,970	14,985	5,748	99	96	3,287	71	3,257	68	99	96
35	19,717	2,558	19,601	2,457	99	96	2,957	2	2,939	2	99	96
40	22,039	0	21,947	0	100	NA	2,023	0	2,015	0	100	NA
45	20,168	0	20,101	0	100	NA	948	0	945	0	100	NA

Mid-Terminal Reserves
Per Policy In Force

Mid-Terminal Reserves
Per Policy Issued

APPENDIX D

SCREENS OF VALUATION DISKETTE WITH USERS MANUAL

Reserve Program - Version 1.3b
March 20, 1995

Keep in mind that this software is only one reasonable implementation of the recommendations outlined in this final report. The software is not the set of recommendations to follow.

A. *Using the Program*

The LTC reserve program is executed by typing LTCRES at the DOS prompt.

The program consists of several input screens that are accessed from the main screen. Using a mouse, simply click on the appropriate button to activate an input screen. You may also use the TAB and arrow keys to position the button highlight and press the ENTER key if your computer lacks a mouse.

The input fields of each screen are intended to be largely self-explanatory. Nevertheless, a few comments are provided here. Once the input fields have been filled, the entries can be saved as a *.INP file using the SAVE button. Later, you can recall the entries using the RETRIEVE button. The input specifications are displayed later along with the output.

When the COMPUTE button is selected, you are asked to indicate the output destination. Choices include screen display, printer, text file, and Lotus worksheet (abbreviated output). The FILE VIEWER allows you to inspect the contents of any text file. Note that the screen display output option stores the program output temporarily in the file OUTPUT.SHL. You can view, rename, copy, etc. this file until the COMPUTE button is pressed again.

Batch processing is possible through optional command line parameters that indicate the names of input and output files. See Section 14 of this Appendix for more information.

B. Screen Images

Rough copies of the various input screens follow with comments where appropriate.

1. Opening Screen

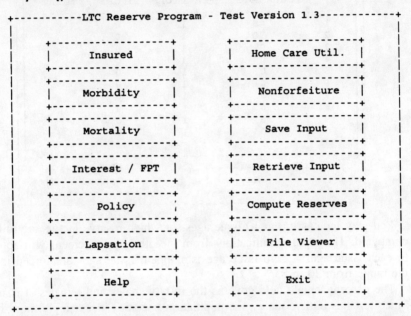

```
+-----------LTC Reserve Program - Test Version 1.3------------+
|                                                             |
|    +------------------+        +--------------------+       |
|    |     Insured      |        |  Home Care Util.   |       |
|    +------------------+        +--------------------+       |
|    +------------------+        +--------------------+       |
|    |    Morbidity     |        |    Nonforfeiture   |       |
|    +------------------+        +--------------------+       |
|    +------------------+        +--------------------+       |
|    |    Mortality     |        |    Save Input      |       |
|    +------------------+        +--------------------+       |
|    +------------------+        +--------------------+       |
|    |  Interest / FPT  |        |   Retrieve Input   |       |
|    +------------------+        +--------------------+       |
|    +------------------+        +--------------------+       |
|    |     Policy       |        |  Compute Reserves  |       |
|    +------------------+        +--------------------+       |
|    +------------------+        +--------------------+       |
|    |    Lapsation     |        |    File Viewer     |       |
|    +------------------+        +--------------------+       |
|    +------------------+        +--------------------+       |
|    |      Help        |        |      Exit          |       |
|    +------------------+        +--------------------+       |
|                                                             |
+-------------------------------------------------------------+
```

This is the main dialog screen from which you enter the other screens. The HELP button will allow you to view the file HELP.IN, which contains this introduction to the program.

2. Insured Ages and Percent Female Screen

```
+----------------------------Insured--------------------+
|                                                        |
| +----------------------------------------------------+ |
| |                                                    | |
| |                  Female      Benefit Bank          | |
| |       Issue Age  Fraction    Gross Premium         | |
| |       ---------  --------    -------------          | |
| |   1      45         1            0                 | |
| |   2      70         1            0                 | |
| |   3       0         1            0                 | |
| |   4       0         1            0                 | |
| |   5       0         1            0                 | |
| |   6       0         1            0                 | |
| |   7       0         1            0                 | |
| |   8       0         1            0                 | |
| |   9       0         1            0                 | |
| |  10       0         1            0                 | |
| |                                                    | |
| +----------------------------------------------------+ |
|                                                        |
|      +---------------+      +---------------+          |
|      |    Okay       |      |    Cancel     |          |
|      +---------------+      +---------------+          |
+--------------------------------------------------------+
```

You may indicate up to 10 issue ages for which reserve factors are to be computed. The input specifications from the other input screens will apply to each issue age. A zero issue age is skipped. Issue ages are forced into the range from 30 to 85.

The percent female field governs the mix of males and females at issue. Since females outlive males, the population becomes increasingly more female with time. Unisex morbidity assumptions are obtained by blending sex-distinct values using these mixed percentages.

The benefit bank gross premiums, if specified, are used to determine policy nonforfeiture benefit values at lapsation. See Section 9 of this Appendix.

3. Morbidity Screen

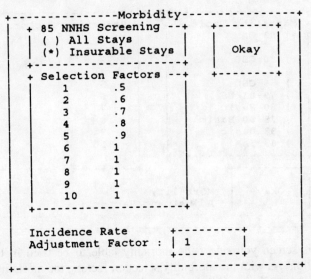

```
+---------------Morbidity----------------+
|  + 85 NNHS Screening --+   +---------+  |
|  | ( ) All Stays       |   |         |  |
|  | (*) Insurable Stays |   |  Okay   |  |
|  +---------------------+   |         |  |
|  + Selection Factors --+   +---------+  |
|  |     1       .5       |                |
|  |     2       .6       |                |
|  |     3       .7       |                |
|  |     4       .8       |                |
|  |     5       .9       |                |
|  |     6       1        |                |
|  |     7       1        |                |
|  |     8       1        |                |
|  |     9       1        |                |
|  |    10       1        |                |
|  +---------------------+                |
|                                          |
|  Incidence Rate      +---------+         |
|  Adjustment Factor : |   1     |         |
|                      +---------+         |
+-----------------------------------------+
```

On this screen you select the type of institutional experience, all stays or insurable stays, from the 1985 National Nursing Home Survey as reported by the SOA LTC Experience Committee in the *TSA 1988-89-90 Reports*.

The selection factors and incidence rate adjustment factors are applied to the policy year institutional and noninstitutional admission rates. The selection factors are forced to unity after 10 policy years. The incidence rate adjustment factor applies uniformly to all policy years.

4. Mortality Screen

```
+--------------------Mortality--------------------+
| + Mortality Table --+    + Selection Factors -+ |
| |(*)  83 GAM        |    |    1      .5       | |
| |                   |    |    2      .6       | |
| | ( )  80 CSO       |    |    3      .7       | |
| |                   |    |    4      .8       | |
| | ( )  58 CSO       |    |    5      .9       | |
| | ( )  79-81 US     |    |    6      1        | |
| | ( )  80 Basic     |    |    7      1        | |
| | ( )  75-80 Basic  |    |    8      1        | |
| | ( )  83 Basic     |    |    9      1        | |
| | ( )  83 IAM       |    |   10      1        | |
| +-------------------+    |                    | |
| +----------+             +--------------------+ |
| |          |                                    |
| |   Okay   | Mortality         +-----------+    |
| |          | Adjustment Factor : |  1      |    |
| +----------+             +-----------+         |
+-------------------------------------------------+
```

On this screen you select the mortality table to be used in the reserve computation. As with the morbidity selection factors, the mortality selection factors are forced to unity after 10 policy years. The mortality adjustment factor applies uniformly to all policy years.

5. Interest Rate and Preliminary Term Period Screen

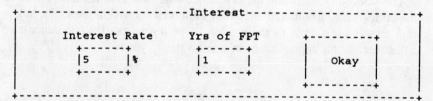

The annual effective interest rate is constant across all policy years. The years of full preliminary term may be zero, 1 or 2. The program computes and displays the annual claim cost as the net premium for each year of the preliminary term period.

6. Policy Specficiations Screen

```
+-------------------Policy Specifications-------------------+
|                          NH          HC                   |
|                      +---------++---------+               |
|  Max Daily Benefit ($) | 100    || 50     |               |
|                      +---------++---------+               |
|  Elimination Period  | 100     || 100     | days          |
|                      +---------++---------+               |
|  Max Benefit         | 4       || 4       | years/days/$  |
|                      +---------++---------+               |
|  Premium Period      | 0       | yrs/age                  |
|                      +---------+        +---------------+  |
| [X] Waiver of Premium                   |               |  |
|                      +---------+        |     Okay      |  |
|  W/P Waiting Period  | 0       | days    |               |  |
|                      +---------+        +---------------+  |
| [ ] Inflation Protection                +---------------+  |
|                      +---------+        |    Cancel     |  |
|  Inflation Period    | 0       | yrs/age +---------------+  |
|                      +---------+        +---------------+  |
|  Inflation Rate      | 5       | percent |   Compound    |  |
|                      +---------+        +---------------+  |
| [ ] Inflate Premium                                       |
+-----------------------------------------------------------+
```

The nursing home (NH) and home health care (HC) elimination period and maximum benefit are applied separately.

The home health care elimination and benefit periods are specified in terms of service time from disability onset. To translate from service time to calendar time, the program computes the average frequency of service (see Section 8 of this Appendix) for each policy year following disability onset. For example, if the service frequency is 3 days per week for the policy year of disability, then a 30-service-day elimination period requires 70 calendar days of disability before benefits are payable. The program subsequently accumulates service time year-by-year to determine when the service-time benefit period is exhausted.

The maximum benefit may be entered in years, days or dollars. Values less than 100 are treated as years, less than 7500 as days, and otherwise as dollars. The program translates the benefit period into days for the computation and displays the limit as days in the output. Note that the dollar limit is inflated with the daily benefit limit if you indicate inflation protection.

Premium and inflation protection periods of zero are treated as lifetime. Values less than 65 are interpreted as years, while larger values are treated as paid-to ages.

Waiver of premium, if indicated, applies only while institutionalized. The W/P waiting period is in addition to the elimination period for the NH benefits.

The type of inflation protection can be toggled between compound and simple.

7. Lapsation and Antiselection Screen

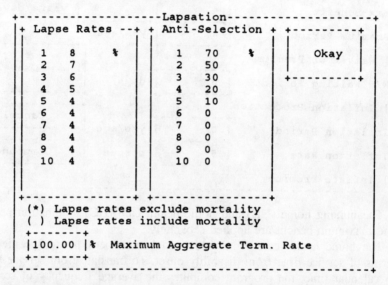

```
+----------------------Lapsation--------------------+
| + Lapse Rates --+ + Anti-Selection + +---------+ |
|                                                   |
|      1    8    %       1    70    %   |   Okay  | |
|      2    7             2    50       |         | |
|      3    6             3    30       +---------+ |
|      4    5             4    20                   |
|      5    4             5    10                   |
|      6    4             6     0                   |
|      7    4             7     0                   |
|      8    4             8     0                   |
|      9    4             9     0                   |
|     10    4            10     0                   |
|                                                   |
|                                                   |
| +---------------+ +---------------+               |
|  (*) Lapse rates exclude mortality                |
|  ( ) Lapse rates include mortality                |
| +-------+                                         |
| |100.00 |%  Maximum Aggregate Term. Rate          |
| +-------+                                         |
+---------------------------------------------------+
```

Policy-year lapse rates can be entered separately for the first nine years. The tenth entry is applied to all subsequent years.

You may elect to treat the values as voluntary lapse rates, which are added to the mortality rates, or as aggregate policy termination rates, which include mortality. If you indicate that the values include mortality, the program will use the greater of the specified value or the mortality rate for each policy year.

The antiselection factors are described in Section VII of this final report. Roughly speaking, if you enter 50% in the fifth position, the program will assume that 50% of the claim incurrals that would have been generated from each year's lapses five years after lapse will be retained, even though 100% of the premium is lost.

You may also specify a maximum aggregate (lapse plus mortality) termination rate. If the aggregate exceeds the limit, the voluntary lapse rate is reduced appropriately. If the mortality rate alone exceeds the limit, then the voluntary lapse rate is set to zero.

8. Home Care Utilization Rate Screen

```
+---------------Home Care Utilization----------------+
|                                                     |
|                  No CI              CI              |
|                                  +----+ +----+      |
|   No ADL's     No Utilization    |30  |% |1.0 |/wk  |
|                                  +----+ +----+      |
|                +----+ +----+     +----+ +----+      |
|   1 ADL        |10  |% |2.0 |/wk |50  |% |3.0 |/wk  |
|                +----+ +----+     +----+ +----+      |
|                +----+ +----+     +----+ +----+      |
|   2 ADL's      |70  |% |4.0 |/wk |70  |% |5.0 |/wk  |
|                +----+ +----+     +----+ +----+      |
|                +----+ +----+     +----+ +----+      |
|   3+ ADL's     |100 |% |6.0 |/wk |100 |% |7.0 |/wk  |
|                +----+ +----+     +----+ +----+      |
|            +----------------+ +----------------+    |
|            |     Cancel     | |     Okay       |    |
|            +----------------+ +----------------+    |
+-----------------------------------------------------+
```

This screen allows you to specify home care (HC) service utilization and frequency rates for noninstitutional disability days, by ADL/CI status. These rates apply uniformly to all issue ages, incurral ages, policy durations, and durations from incurral. The program estimates the number of noninstitutional disability days, policy year by policy year, for each year's incurrals, by ADL and CI status. You must indicate what portion of these days generate home care benefits and the frequency of use per week. For example, the sample screen above indicates that 70% of noninstitutionalized insureds with two ADL impairments and no CI use home care services. These individuals receive services 4 days per week. The program accumulates, by incurral year, the product of the disability days, the utilization rates, the frequency rates and the HC daily benefit, considering the HC elimination and benefit periods. These HC claim costs are displayed in the output per policy in force in the middle of each policy year. (See Section 15 of this Appendix.)

9. Nonforfeiture Benefits Screen

```
+----------------Nonforfeiture Values----------------+
|                                                     |
|    Dur   SBP%  Dur   SBP%          [ ] Benefit Bank |
|        +----+      +----+                           |
|     3  |0   |  25  |0   |           First Year       |
|        +----+      +----+        +------------+      |
|     4  |0   |  30  |0   |        |3           |      |
|        +----+      +----+        +------------+      |
|     5  |0   |  35  |0   |        Min NFO Ben Days     |
|        +----+      +----+        +------------+      |
|    10  |0   |  40  |0   |        |30          |      |
|        +----+      +----+        +------------+      |
|    15  |0   |  45  |0   |        +------------+      |
|        +----+      +----+                           |
|    20  |0   |  50  |0   |           Okay            |
|        +----+      +----+                           |
|    [X]  Post Lapse Inflation     +------------+      |
|    [X]  Reserve > SBP Cost                          |
|                           +----+ +------------+      |
|    NFO Loading Factor     |1.1 | |   Cancel   |      |
|                           +----+ +------------+      |
+-----------------------------------------------------+
```

Two forms of shortened benefit period (SBP) are supported by the program.

The first form expresses the paid-up benefit period after lapsation as a percentage of the premium-paying maximum benefit period. The same percentage is applied to both the nursing home and home care benefit periods. You enter SBP percentages at the indicated policy durations and the program interpolates to fill in the gaps. The entry for year 50 is applied to all subsequent years.

The second form limits the post-lapse benefit to the sum of gross premiums paid prior to lapse. The gross premiums used by the program exclusively for the benefit bank are entered on the insured screen described in Section 2 of this Appendix. You may specify the initial year of lapsation this benefit is available and impose a minimum value on the resulting shortened benefit period. Note that the benefit bank SBP as a percentage of the premium-paying benefit period may be different for nursing home and home health care benefits when the daily benefit amounts for these benefits differ.

You may indicate whether inflation protection, if present, continues after lapsation. If post-lapse inflation is elected, both the daily benefit amount and the benefit bank balance increase with inflation (that is, the benefit periods are frozen at lapse).

You may also indicate whether the terminal reserves must exceed the net single premium for the current SBP benefit. If you check this box, the displayed terminal reserve will be unaffected, but the mid-terminal will average the greater of the terminal reserve and the "cost per lapser" at the start and end of each policy year.

The NFO loading factor is applied to the net single premium for the SBP benefits associated with each year's lapsers. This provides a risk margin since the policy becomes noncancellable at lapse.

10. Save Specifications Screen

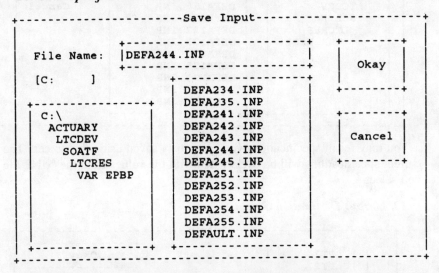

You can save the specifications to a *.INP file from this screen. To create a new file, simply type a new name in the FILE NAME box. You need not enter the .INP extension. To reuse an existing file, click on the filename in the listing below. The filename will be copied to the FILE NAME box.

11. Retrieve Specifications Screen

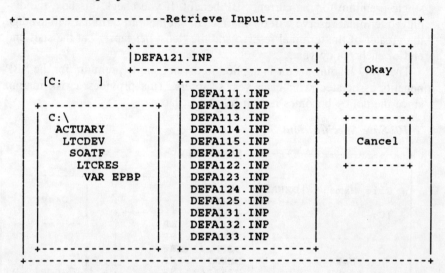

```
+---------------------Retrieve Input---------------------+
|                                                        |
|                   +------------------------+  +--------+|
|                   |DEFA121.INP             |  |        ||
|                   +------------------------+  | Okay   ||
|      [C:     ]     +------------------------+  |        ||
|                    |  DEFA111.INP          |  +--------+|
|   +----------------+  DEFA112.INP          |           |
|   |                |  DEFA113.INP          |  +--------+|
|   |  C:\           |  DEFA114.INP          |  |        ||
|   |  ACTUARY       |  DEFA115.INP          |  | Cancel ||
|   |   SOATF        |  DEFA121.INP          |  |        ||
|   |   LTCRES       |  DEFA122.INP          |  +--------+|
|   |    VAR EPBP    |  DEFA123.INP          |           |
|   |                |  DEFA124.INP          |           |
|   |                |  DEFA125.INP          |           |
|   |                |  DEFA131.INP          |           |
|   |                |  DEFA132.INP          |           |
|   |                |  DEFA133.INP          |           |
|   +----------------+  +-------------------+            |
+--------------------------------------------------------+
```

You may recall specifications you previously saved using this screen. The current specifications will be overwritten with the values from the *.INP file you select.

12. Output Destination Screen

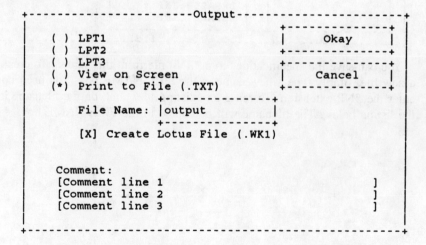

```
+----------------------Output----------------------+
|                       +---------------+          |
|    ( ) LPT1           |     Okay      |          |
|    ( ) LPT2           +---------------+          |
|    ( ) LPT3           +---------------+          |
|    ( ) View on Screen |    Cancel     |          |
|    (*) Print to File (.TXT)  +--------+          |
|            +----------------+                    |
|      File Name: |output          |               |
|            +----------------+                    |
|      [X] Create Lotus File (.WK1)                |
|                                                  |
|                                                  |
|      Comment:                                    |
|      [Comment line 1                       ]     |
|      [Comment line 2                       ]     |
|      [Comment line 3                       ]     |
|                                                  |
+--------------------------------------------------+
```

When you select the COMPUTE RESERVES button, this screen will allow you to specify the destination of the program output. If you elect to place the output in a text file, you may view it with the file viewer. (See Section 13 of this Appendix.) If you elect to display the output on the screen, the program will place the output in the file, OUTPUT.SHL, and automatically invoke the file viewer. This file will be overwritten the next time you compute reserves.

You may also save an abbreviated version of the output in a Lotus worksheet file (.WK1). The program places the output for each issue age in a separate worksheet column. This output includes the issue age, the first three policy year net premiums, the mid-terminal reserve factors for all durations and the mid-year in-force population for all policy years. The input specifications are shown at the bottom of the worksheet. Note that the program also produces a .TXT file with the standard output.

You may specify three comment lines that will be reproduced in the output and saved in subsequent .INP files.

13. File Viewer Screen

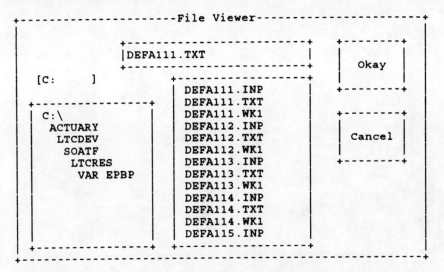

You can view the contents of any text (ASCII character based) file by selecting the file from this screen. In this way you can review output you previously save to *.TXT files. The program simply passes control to the BROWSE.COM utility program. Press {ESC} to return.

14. Batch Processing

You can create a DOS batch file (.BAT) to repeatedly execute the program with previously saved .INP files. Each line of the batch file would have the syntax,

LTCRES TESTIN TESTOUT.TXT

or

LTCRES TESTIN TESTOUT.WK1 .

The first form executes LTCRES, reads in TESTIN.INP and creates the output file TESTOUT.TXT. The second form does the same, but creates two output file, TESTOUT.TXT and TESTOUT.WK1. The program runs, unattended, once for each such line in the batch file.

15. Sample Program Output

Table D-1 is sample .TXT output from LTCRES.

TABLE D-1

SAMPLE .TXT OUTPUT FROM LTCRES

```
{Comment line 1}
{Comment line 2}
{Comment line 3}
Summary of 1-Year Preliminary Term Reserves at  5.000% for Issue Age 70 Assuming Females Are 100% of Sales
```

		NH	HC	Home Care EP/BP in Service Days
Net Premium: 1,641.93	Daily Benefit:	100.00	50.00	Inflation Protection: NONE
Lifetime Pay	Deductible Period:	100	100	
	Lifetime Maximum:	1460	1460	
	W/P Days in Ben:	0	0	

```
Mortality Table: 83 GAM
  Adjustment Factor: 1.000
  Mort. Selection Factors:   (1) 0.500 (2) 0.600 (3) 0.700 (4) 0.800 (5) 0.900 (6) 1.000 (7) 1.000 (8) 1.000 (9) 1.000 (10) 1.000

Morbidity Table: 85 NNHS (Insurable Stays) and 82/84 NLTCS
  Adjustment Factor: 1.000
  Morb. Selection Factors:   (1) 0.500 (2) 0.600 (3) 0.700 (4) 0.800 (5) 0.900 (6) 1.000 (7) 1.000 (8) 1.000 (9) 1.000 (10) 1.000
  Antiselection Factors:         0.700     0.500     0.300     0.200     0.100     0.000     0.000     0.000     0.000     0.000

Home Care Service Utilization Rates by ADL/CI Status:
  No Cognitive Impairment:  (0 ADLs) 0.000 (1 ADLs) 0.100 (2 ADLs) 0.700 (3 ADLs) 1.000
  Cognitively Impaired:             0.300         0.500         0.700         1.000

Home Care Service Frequency (per week) by ADL/CI Status:
  No Cognitive Impairment:  (0 ADLs) 0.000 (1 ADLs) 2.000 (2 ADLs) 4.000 (3 ADLs) 6.000
  Cognitively Impaired:             1.000         3.000         5.000         7.000

Lapse rates are in addition to mortality - Maximum aggregate termination rate: 1.000
  Lapse Rates:
          (1) 0.080 (2) 0.070 (3) 0.060 (4) 0.050 (5) 0.040 (6) 0.040 (7) 0.040 (8) 0.040 (9) 0.040 (10+) 0.040
    (15) .000 (20) .000 (25) .000 (30) .000 (35) .000 (40) .000 (45) .000 (50+) .000

Nonforfeiture benefits: SBP Cost Factor: 1.200   Reserves to exceed SBP cost per lapser
  (3) .000 ( 4) .000 ( 5) .000 (10) .000
```

745

TABLE D-1—Continued

t	BOY Inforce	Waiver Inforce	NH Inforce	NH Admiss.	HC Admiss.	BOY Lapses	Deaths	Net Prem. per Payor	NH Cost per Mid 1x	HC Cost per Mid 1x	NFO Cost per Lapses	Terminal Reserve	Mid-Term. Reserve
1	100,000	0	0	533	1,017	7,950	619	267.43	202.47	72.50	0.00	0.00	0.00
2	91,431	193	295	698	1,294	6,346	775	1,641.93	288.77	100.26	0.00	1,436.39	667.92
3	84,309	389	523	869	1,572	5,001	953	1,641.93	390.07	130.96	0.00	2,900.92	2,081.63
4	78,354	573	740	1,066	1,841	3,860	1,158	1,641.93	517.71	163.69	0.00	4,347.95	3,515.73
5	73,336	765	970	1,295	2,108	2,878	1,392	1,641.93	677.48	198.05	0.00	5,725.45	4,922.19
6	69,067	977	1,226	1,568	2,370	2,696	1,657	1,641.93	880.43	233.60	0.00	7,043.61	6,243.66
7	64,713	1,220	1,522	1,713	2,379	2,518	1,759	1,641.93	1,039.02	246.09	0.00	8,366.45	7,537.70
8	60,436	1,437	1,766	1,884	2,387	2,343	1,853	1,641.93	1,240.37	259.35	0.00	9,662.61	8,821.27
9	56,239	1,644	2,006	2,060	2,389	2,172	1,938	1,641.93	1,478.91	273.63	0.00	10,905.09	10,065.75
10	52,129	1,849	2,246	2,231	2,382	2,005	2,010	1,641.93	1,755.22	287.36	0.00	12,066.31	11,244.38
11	48,115	2,053	2,482	2,387	2,363	1,842	2,067	1,641.93	2,069.27	301.20	0.00	13,116.53	12,329.09
12	44,206	2,249	2,709	2,518	2,327	1,684	2,107	1,641.93	2,409.40	313.87	0.00	14,036.82	13,295.94
13	40,415	2,432	2,917	2,611	2,277	1,531	2,129	1,641.93	2,766.06	325.54	0.00	14,816.50	14,130.33
14	36,755	2,593	3,095	2,664	2,211	1,385	2,134	1,641.93	3,145.74	336.68	0.00	15,437.61	14,818.30
15	33,235	2,723	3,235	2,674	2,130	1,245	2,121	1,641.93	3,544.01	345.89	0.00	15,885.27	15,343.74
16	29,870	2,817	3,332	2,639	2,035	1,111	2,088	1,641.93	3,949.75	354.61	0.00	16,151.42	15,695.31
17	26,670	2,872	3,380	2,561	1,928	985	2,042	1,641.93	4,371.25	360.83	0.00	16,222.61	15,862.56
18	23,643	2,885	3,377	2,443	1,809	866	1,983	1,641.93	4,789.91	366.42	0.00	16,098.45	15,838.56
19	20,794	2,854	3,324	2,287	1,681	755	1,912	1,641.93	5,199.95	369.29	0.00	15,784.80	15,625.93
20	18,127	2,781	3,221	2,100	1,543	652	1,837	1,641.93	5,607.12	370.49	0.00	15,288.58	15,230.92
21	15,638	2,668	3,072	1,891	1,399	556	1,748	1,641.93	6,003.05	370.08	0.00	14,611.71	14,657.91
22	13,335	2,518	2,882	1,667	1,250	468	1,641	1,641.93	6,312.87	367.84	0.00	13,814.90	13,937.01
23	11,226	2,338	2,659	1,437	1,100	388	1,522	1,641.93	6,580.79	363.85	0.00	12,927.69	13,112.74
24	9,315	2,134	2,410	1,211	952	317	1,394	1,641.93	6,822.42	361.30	0.00	11,964.35	12,206.73
25	7,605	1,914	2,146	994	808	254	1,256	1,641.93	7,034.80	357.58	0.00	10,943.08	11,234.85
26	6,095	1,685	1,876	794	671	199	1,112	1,641.93	7,222.70	352.69	0.00	9,879.99	10,213.94
27	4,784	1,456	1,609	615	544	153	965	1,641.93	7,376.59	346.72	0.00	8,801.05	9,164.50
28	3,666	1,235	1,352	460	430	114	814	1,641.93	7,513.87	338.28	0.00	7,708.61	8,100.66
29	2,738	1,026	1,113	330	330	83	668	1,641.93	7,620.12	334.37	0.00	6,617.96	7,030.93
30	1,987	834	897	226	245	58	533	1,641.93	7,732.26	329.00	0.00	5,542.91	5,969.57
31	1,396	664	707	145	176	39	412	1,641.93	7,835.88	321.03	0.00	4,531.76	4,946.70
32	945	516	543	86	121	25	307	1,641.93	7,924.89	312.10	0.00	3,678.47	4,031.54
33	612	391	407	44	79	16	220	1,641.93	8,030.85	304.26	0.00	3,197.36	3,373.96
34	377	264	264	25	49	9	149	1,641.93	8,120.31	288.09	0.00	2,820.70	2,952.62
35	218	153	153	14	29	5	96	1,641.93	8,229.81	269.89	0.00	2,390.18	2,557.64
36	118	82	82	8	15	2	57	1,641.93	8,323.85	243.48	0.00	1,832.95	2,074.91
37	58	41	41	4	7	1	32	1,641.93	7,852.37	211.76	0.00	1,223.68	1,503.84
38	25	18	18	2	3	0	15	1,641.93	6,943.92	170.21	0.00	541.22	871.63
39	9	7	7	1	1	0	6	1,641.93	5,314.56	107.66	0.00	0.00	270.61
40	3	2	2	0	0	0	2	1,641.93	1,657.99	9.79	0.00	0.00	0.00

PREMIUM & BENEFIT TOTALS ($000)   1,630,490   2,102,167
PRESENT VALUES (5.00%) ($000)   1,136,343   1,136,343

SOCIETY OF ACTUARIES LONG TERM CARE VALUATION METHODS TASK FORCE - RESERVE PROGRAM TEST Version 1.3b

TABLE D-1—*Continued*

The top of the output displays the input assumptions.

The various columns of numeric data include:

(1) Policy year
(2) Beginning of year (BOY) number of policies
(3) Number of policies with waived premiums - BOY
(4) Number of policies institutionalized - BOY
(5) Mid-year nursing home admissions
(6) Mid-year ADL/CI disability episode incurrals
(7) End of year (EOY) lapses
(8) Policy year deaths
(9) Net premium per premium-paying policy - BOY
(10) Nursing home claim cost per mid-year noninstitutionalized policy
(11) Home care claim cost per mid-year policy (all)
(12) Loaded net single premium for SBP benefits per lapser - EOY
(13) Terminal reserve per EOY policy inforce
(14) Mid-terminal reserve

The mid-terminal is the average of the prior yearend's
post-lapse reserve factor and the next yearend's pre-lapse reserve factor.
At the user's option, each factor can be forced to be greater than the
net single premium for nonforfeiture benefits.

747

APPENDIX E

DOCUMENTATION OF VALUATION DISKETTE PROGRAMS

I. Overview

This appendix summarizes the major formulas used in the calculation of net premiums and reserve factors in the diskette developed by the SOA LTC Insurance Valuation Methods Task Force. This appendix is written for valuation actuaries who will be taking the responsibility for the adequacy of the reserve factors calculated.

The model is divided into three sections: (1) input files (which the computer program reads), (2) the computer program, and (3) output files (which the computer program generates). Each section is discussed below. In addition, the sample calculations of the default case nursing home and home health care admissions and claim costs are presented in Section V of this Appendix.

II. Input Files

There are seven input files. Each file is in ASCII format and can be edited with any DOS editor, as long as the exact position of the numbers is not changed. The input files and a brief description of the data in each file are summarized in Table E-1.

TABLE E-1

SUMMARY OF INPUT FILES

No.	DOS Name	Data
1	CONTIN.IN	Nursing home continuance tables from *TSA 1988-89-90 Reports* (Tables 16 and 17)
2	CONTINHC.IN	Home care continuance tables developed by the Task Force
3	HCRTALOS.IN	Home care incidence rates and average lengths of frailty (Task Force)
4	HCUTIL.IN	Utilization of home care disability days by ADL/CI status (default = 100%)
5	HELP.IN	Help information
6	MORTAL.IN	Mortality rates from 8 tables
7	NHRTALOS.IN	Nursing home admission rates and average lengths of stay from *Reports* (Tables 1 and 2)

III. Computer Program

The computer program, LTCRES, is written in Visual Basic for DOS and is divided into 12 "forms." A "form" in the parlance of Visual Basic refers to the program code that creates a screen image and the actions to be performed by the program in response to a user's interaction with the screen. Table E-2 summarizes the 12 forms. Although all these forms can be printed, all but the main form, LTCRES.FRM, contain limited information on understanding the equations used to calculate reserves. The information in these 11 forms consists of that necessary to produce the screen image and the code to store the input parameters into variable names. LTCRES.FRM contains the actual equations used to produce the reserve factors.

TABLE E-2

SUMMARY OF FORMS IN LTCRES COMPUTER PROGRAM

No.	Form	Description
1	COMPUTIN.FRM	Computer reserves screen
2	HC_UTIL.FRM	Home care utilization screen
3	INSURED.FRM	Issue age, % female screen, benefits bank gross premium screen
4	INTEREST.FRM	Interest rate, years of FPT screen
5	LAPSE.FRM	Lapse rate, antiselection on lapse screen
6	MORBID.FRM	Nursing home admission rates, morbidity selection factors, and morbidity adjustment factor
7	MORTAL.FRM	Mortality table, mortality selection factors, and mortality adjustment factor
8	NFO.FRM	Nonforfeiture value screen (SBP or benefits bank)
9	POLICY.FRM	Policy specification screen
10	PRNTVIEW.FRM	Output screen
11	SAVEFILE.FRM	Save input screen
12	LTCRES.FRM	Main screen and computation subroutines

A. Organization of the Main Form LTCRES.FRM

The main form of the computer program is LTCRES.FRM. It contains 26 subroutines and five functions. The 26 subroutines can be grouped as follows:
- One (Form_Load) starts the program
- 14 respond to a user's "click" on the main screen (Compute_bttn_Click starts the calculations)
- Eight perform the reserve calculations

- Two (lotlabel and lotnum) format output variables in the standard required to be recognized by spreadsheet software, such as LOTUS™
- 1 (comline) simply accesses a command line when the program is executed.

Of the five functions, two simply create the MAX and MIN functions. The other three perform calculations relevant to the determination of the reserve factors. The ten subroutines and the three functions that contain the important reserve calculations are summarized in Table E-3.

The premium is calculated with a present value formula that first accumulates the present value of benefit payments and $1 for each premium payment and then calculates the premium that will equate the two. The calculation flow through the most important subroutines is presented below.

B. Subroutine UNISQD

This subroutine opens "mortal.in" and skips all lines before the issue age (isag&). In order to calculate the unisex mortality table, it sets the radix of the unisex table to 100000 and splits this between females and males according to the user-defined percentage female (pfemale#).

lxa&(3)=100000
lxa&(2)=lxa&(3)*pfemale#
lxa&(1)=lxa&(3)−lxa&(2)

where

lxa(sx%)=number alive at the beginning of the year for sex sx%
sx%=1=male, 2=female, 3=total

The program then performs the following for each attained age (aa%) from the issue age until age 110. It reads the mortality rates per 1000, rqds#(sx%,itb%), for all the mortality tables in mortal.in, and then adjusts these rates by the mortality adjustment factor selected by the user (mort_adj#). It then uses the rates from the table selected by the user (istmt&) to calculate the number of lives at the end of the year separately for males and females. The total lives at the end of the year is obtained by summing the males and the females, and the unisex mortality rate is obtained as the complement of the probability of survival for all lives.

lxb&(sx%)=lxa&(sx%)*(1−rqds#(sx%, istmt&)/1000#)
lxb&(3)=lxb&(1)+lxb&(2)
qd#(aa%)=1#−lxb&(3)/lxa&(3)

TABLE E-3

SUMMARY OF MAIN SUBROUTINES AND FUNCTIONS IN LTCRES.FRM

No.	Subroutine / Function	Description
1	form_load	(1) Initializes variables, (2) reads "nhrtalos.in", "hcrtalso.in" and "contin.in", and (3) calls "readhc"
2	readhc	Reads "continhc.in" and "hcutil.in"
3	compute_bttn_click	Opens output files and calls calculation subroutines
4	unisqd	Reads "mortal.in" and projects the number of policies in force by sex and duration for the purpose of computing unisex admission rates, lengths of stay and continuance tables
5	factors	Projects the benefit and premium inflation factors, and, if applicable, determines the duration that the policy is paid up
6	demo	Projects the number of policies in force by duration using mortality and lapse assumptions and calculates the number of new claims (nursing home and home care separately), the number of active claims, and the number in premium waiver status for each duration
7	dayinh	Calculates the number of days qualifying for a nursing home benefit
8	dayihc	Calculates the number of days qualifying for a home care benefit
9	calc	(1) Determines the amount of benefit payments at each duration from days of benefit and policy specifications, (2) calculates the net premium necessary to match the present value of benefit payments, and (3) determines the reserve at each duration
10	outpt	Prints the output tables
11	sbp	Determines the value of nonforfeiture benefits in the form of a shortened benefit period or benefits bank
12	ftk	Interpolates between thresholds in the nursing home continuance table. This function is used in the "dayinh" subroutine
13	gtk	Interpolates between thresholds in the home care continuance table. This function is used in the "dayihc" subroutine

The unisex incidence rates and average lengths-of-stay are obtained by weighing the sex-distinct rates by the number alive at each attained age. For example, the unisex nursing home admission rate for insured stays at attained age aa% is calculated as follows:

$$nharis(aa\%,3)=(nharis(aa\%,1)*lxa\&(1)+nharis(aa\%,2)*lxa\&(2))/lxa\&(3)$$

The same calculation is performed for the average length-of-stay for insured stays [alosis(aa%,sx%)], the nursing home admission rate for all stays [nharas(aa%,sx%)], the average length-of-stay for all stays [alosas(aa%,sx%)], the home care incidence rate for all [hcar(aa%,sx%)], and the average length-of-stay in home care [aloshc(aa%,sx%)]. Each of the incidence rates are adjusted by a user-defined adjustment factor (inc_adj#).

Finally, a unisex continuance table is calculated by the weighted average of the days in disability status in each of the age groups for which the continuous tables apply. There are four continuance tables represented by the variables: (1) podis(k1, jage,sx) [percentage of days above threshold(k1) for insured stays in a nursing home by admission age group (jage) and sex (sx)], (2) podas(k1,jage,sx) [percentage of days above threshold in a nursing home for all stays], (3) podhc(k1,jage,sx) [percentage of service days (% using times frequency) above threshold in home care], and (4) podhct(k1,jage,sx) [percentage of impairment days (% using) above threshold in home care total].

C. Subroutine Factors

This subroutine sets the paid-up factors, inflation factors, and discount factors for each duration.

dr% = duration (1=first duration)

pdup(dr%) = 0 if paid-up,=1 if premium paying

fctb#(dr%) = inflation factor for daily benefits (indexed to the initial benefit level)

fctp#(dr%) = inflation factor for premiums (indexed to the initial premium level)

lip& = length of inflation protection. If < 65, then lip& is number of years of inflation protection. If=> 65, lip& is the attained age of the last increase.

tip$ = the type of inflation protection. S=simple, C=compound

rindb# = rate of increase in benefits.

If the type of inflation protection is simple, then

fctb#(dr%)=1+rindb#*(dr%−1).

If the type of inflation protection is compound, then

fctb#(dr%)=(1+rindb#)^(dr%−1).

If premiums inflate with benefits, then

fctp#(dr%)=fctb#(dr%);

otherwise all fctp#'s equal 1.0.

There are two sets of discount factors: vfy#(dr%) is a full year's discount for every duration (the first duration has no discount), and vhy#(dr%) is for one-half year additional discount.

D. Subroutine DEMO

This subroutine calculates the number of policies in force, the number paying premiums, the number of nursing home admissions, the number of home care incidences, and an estimate of the number of nursing home residents.

The subroutine initializes the number of policies in force at the issue age with a radix of 100,000 and the number of nursing home residents at 0.

lx(isag&)=100000
resnh(0)=0

The rest of the entire subroutine is in a FOR-NEXT loop that goes through all of the durations from the first through the duration at which age 110 is obtained (=mxdr). (mxdr=110−isag&, which was calculated in subroutine unisqd.) For each duration (dr%) the attained age (aa%) is calculated. Since the selection factors go for 10 years, the ultimate duration is 11. The variable "ldr," (which is limited to 11) is used as the subscript in variables that change during the first 10 years.

aa%=isag&+dr%−1

The number in force is projected by applying the double decrements of lapse (qw) and death (qdx). For each duration, the death rate is set to the total unisex death rate at the attained age times the mortality selection factor. The lapse rate is set to the user-defined lapse rate (stlr#), unless the user has indicated that the lapse rate includes the mortality rate. The variable "lpse%" equals 0 if lapses are in addition to mortality, and it equals 1 if lapses include mortality. Thus, if lpse% equals 1, then the "pure" lapse rate (qw) is calculated as the total lapse rate adjusted for deaths, but is not allowed to be negative. Also, if the total termination rate (lapses plus deaths) is greater than the user-defined maximum termination rate (maxterm#), then the lapse rate is adjusted again (but not below zero), so that the total termination rate is the greater of the maximum termination rate or the death rate. Finally, if the policy is fully paid-up (pdup=0), then no lapses are possible, and the lapse rate is set to 0.

qdx=qd#(aa%)*mtsf#(ldr)
qw=stlr#(dr%)

If lpse%=1, then

qw=max(0, 1−(1−qw)/(1−qdx))

If 1−(1−qw)*(1−qdx) > maxterm, then

qw=1−(1−maxterm)/(1−qdx)

If qw<0, then

qw=0

If pdup(dr%+1)=0, then

qw=0

The number of policies in force at the beginning of the next duration is then calculated.

lx(aa%+1)=lx(aa%)*(1−qw)*(1−qdx)

The terminations are split between the number of lapses (wx) and the number of deaths (dx).

ddqd=qdx
ddqw=(1−qdx)*qw
dx(aa%)=(lx(aa%)−lx(aa%+1))*ddqd/(ddqw+ddqd)
wx(aa%)=(lx(aa%)−lx(aa%+1))*ddqw/(ddqw+ddqd)

The number in force at midyear (la) is estimated by subtracting one-half the deaths during the year from the number in force at the beginning of the year. Premiums are assumed to be paid annually, so there are no midyear lapses. The active number (that is, not in a nursing home) at midyear (actla) is estimated by applying the percentage noninstitutionalized at the beginning of the year to the midyear in force.

la(aa%)=lx(aa%)−0.5*dx(aa%)
actla(aa%)=la(aa%)*(lx(aa%)−resnh(dr%−1))/lx(aa%)

To calculate the number of nursing home admissions during the year (nhadm), the admission rate is applied to the number in force at midyear. The admission rate is the base rate times the user-defined morbidity selection factor (mbsf) and the lapse antiselection factor (antilp). The base rate includes the user-defined adjustment factor and is either for insured stays (nharis) or for all stays (nharas) as specified by the user. The indicator "nhas&" is 0 if insured stays apply, and it is 1 if all stays apply. The antiselection-on-lapse factor is calculated as the compound effect of the number of lapses during the prior 10 years and the strength of the antiselection as specified by the user-defined antiselection-on-lapse factors (asolf#).

$$\text{antilp} = \prod_{t=1}^{10} 1/(1 - \text{stlp}(dr\% - t)*\text{asolf}(t))$$

$$\text{nhadm}(dr\%) = \text{actla}(aa\%)*\text{nharis}(aa\%,3)*\text{mbsf\#}(dr\%)*\text{antilp}$$

The number of new episodes of frailty for those at home (hcadm) is calculated in a similar manner. The home care probabilities are based on the number in force at the beginning of the year.

$$\text{hcadm}(dr\%) = \text{la}(aa\%)*\text{hcar}(aa\%,3)*\text{mbsf\#}(dr\%)*\text{antilp}$$

The final calculations in "subroutine demo" is to estimate the number of nursing home residents at the end of the year (nhres) and the number in premium waiver status. The number of residents is estimated by summing the product of the number of admissions during the prior 20 years and the probability of those admissions still being resident. The number in waiver status is estimated as the percentage of total residents that have been in the nursing home for durations greater than the waiver requirement. The waiver requirement is the sum of the elimination period (nhelpd) and the days of benefits required for waiver (wopdib).

E. Subroutine DAYINH and Subroutine DAYIHC

Subroutine "dayinh" determines the number of days in a nursing home that qualify for a benefit payment, that is, after the elimination period and before the lifetime maximum. The number of days for each admission age and each year in the length of stay (grouped by policy year) is calculated from the continuance table. The number of days is stored in the variable "days(los,adag)." The continuance table look-up procedure is performed by the function "ftk."

A similar process is performed for home care beneficiaries in the subroutine "dayihc." The number of days in benefit status is stored in the variable "dayshc(los,adag)" and the continuance table look-up is performed by the function "gtk."

For home care, days impaired in each policy year following impairment are available by ADL/CI status from the average number of noninstitutional days and the continuance tables in Section III of this final report. The user's utilization rates by ADL/CI status are applied and summed to obtain "home care utilization days" by duration from impairment. These values represent the portion of total noninstitutional impairment days associated with insureds electing to use home health care services at any non-zero level. The program also computes "home care service days" by duration from impairment. These are obtained by applying both utilization rates *and* frequency-of-use rates to noninstitutional impairment days by ADL/CI status and summing the results for each policy year following impairment. (To save space, some of these computations are applied as the home care continuance tables and are read in by the READHC subroutine.)

For each policy year following impairment, the program divides "home care service days" by "home care utilization days" to obtain weekly use rates. If the ratio is 40%, for example, the service use rate is 2.8 days per week. This ratio is used to convert calendar time to service time during that policy year. This translation is used to apply the policy home health care elimination and benefit periods, assumed to be expressed in service time.

F. Subroutine CALC

This subroutine calculates the net premium for the specified policy with the specified assumptions. It then calculates the terminal reserves at each duration. The first variable assigned a value is the number of years of full preliminary term (fpt&). This is set to the user-specified number of years (nyfptr&), but it is not allowed to be greater than two or greater than the number of years of premium payments (ppd&). The variable "pomit(dr%)" is then assigned the value of one (if past the preliminary term period) or zero (if in the preliminary term period).

The reserve at the end of each policy duration will be calculated with two variables. One of these, eoyrsv1d#(dr%), depends on the premium and, therefore, initially contains values per dollar of premium. The other, eoyrsv#(dr%), contains the full dollar amounts. Two variables are used to accumulate present values: pvbp# accumulates benefit payments and pvpm1d# accumulates the present value of premium payments based on a premium of $1. The variable "lfmx&" is the represents the nursing home lifetime maximum benefit in dollars, and "hclfmx&" represents the home care lifetime maximum benefit in dollars. The variable dr% is the policy year and aa% is the attained age in policy year dr%. This subroutine accumulates benefits and premiums for all durations from the issue age to age 110. The premiums paid in each year (if the full rate initial premium were \$1) are calculated in pp1d#(dr%). This is equal to the number of premium payers (prmpay) times the paid-up indicator (pdup(dr%)) times the premium inflation factor (fctp#(dr%)). The number of premium payers is equal to the number in force minus the number in premium waiver status.

prmpay=lx(aa%)−wopn(dr%−1)
pp1d#(dr%)=prmpay*pdup(dr%)*fctp#(dr%)

The nursing home benefit incurred in policy year dr% is the product of three factors:
(1) panhb#(dr%), which is the present value of nursing home days for admissions in year dr% (that is, with admission age aa%), increased for any applicable inflation protection benefits
(2) mxdb#, which is the user-specified maximum daily benefit
(3) nhadm(dr%), which is the number of nursing home admissions in year dr%.

$$panhb\#(dr\%)=mxdb\#*nhadm(dr\%)*\sum_{lyr\%=1}^{20}days(yr\%,aa\%)*fctb\#(lyr\%)$$
$$*(vhy\#(lyr\%)/vhy\#(dr\%))$$

A similar calculation is performed to determine the incurred home care benefits in policy year dr%, which is stored in the variable "pahcb#(dr%)."

The nonforfeiture benefit section uses several user-specified variables:

pli%   = indicates whether inflation protection continues after lapse (1=yes, 0=no)

sbpres%   = indicates whether terminal reserve (in the mid-terminal reserve calculation shown in the output) should be at least equal to the single premium value of the nonforfeiture benefit available at that duration (0=no, 1=yes)

bbfyr%   = indicates the end of the policy year in which nonforfeiture benefits are first available

bbmin%   = indicates the minimum number of days of a benefits bank nonforfeiture benefit

bb%   = indicates whether the nonforfeiture benefit is in the form of a benefits bank (BB) or shortened benefit period (SBP), 1=BB, 0=SBP nfofact   = the loading factor placed on nonforfeiture benefits

sbpscale(I%) = the shortened benefit period percentages by duration that specify the percentage of the original lifetime maximum benefit that a lapser receives. These percentages are not used for the benefit bank. The duration corresponding to the subscript I% is as follows:

Duration Corresponding to the Value
of Subscript for "sbpscale"

I%	Duration (policy year)
0	3
1	4
2	5
3	10
4	15
5	20
6	25
7	30
8	35
9	40
10	45
11	50+

If the policy has the SBP benefit, the "sbpscale(I%)" percentages are interpolated for each duration to obtain "sbpfact," which is applied to the original lifetime maximum to obtain the nonforfeiture benefit. If the policy has the BB benefit, "sbpfact" is calculated as the ratio of the accumulated past premiums divided by the original lifetime maximum, subject to the minimum value. Because the lifetime maximum benefit for nursing home and for home care may be different, under the BB option this ratio is calculated separately for nursing home and home care benefits ("sbpfactnh" and "sbpfacthc," respectively). Under the SBP option, both of these factors are set equal to "sbpfact." The present value of the nonforfeiture benefit per lapser (adjusted by the nonforfeiture factor, "nonfact") is then stored in "panfn#(dr%)."

panfb#(dr%)=sbp(aa%+1, dr%, sbpfactnh, sbpfacthc)*nonfact

The present value of the nonforfeiture benefit is calculated in the function "sbp," which depends on the attained age at lapse, the duration at lapse, and the SBP factors "sbpfactnh" and "sbpfacthc." This function is explained in the next section.

The present value of premiums (with a full-rate initial premium of $1) and the present value of benefits are accumulated, excluding those during the preliminary term period. The premiums are discounted by the factor applicable at the beginning of the policy year, full-rate benefits by the factor for midyear, and reduced nonforfeiture benefits by the factor for the end of the year. The dollar value of the nonforfeiture benefit is obtained by multiplying the value per lapser, "panfb," times the number of lapsers, "wx."

pvpm1d#=pvpm1d#+[pp1d#*vfy#(dr%)*pomit(dr%)]
pvbp#=pvbp#+{[panhb#(dr%)+pahcb#(dr%)]*vhy#(dr%)
    + [panfb#(dr%)*wx(dr%)*vfy#(dr%+1)]}*pomit(dr%)

The end-of-year reserve factors for each duration are:

eoyrsv1d#(dr%)=pvpm1d#/vfy#(dr%+1)
eoyrsv#(dr%)=pvbp#/vfy#(dr%+1)

After accumulating through all policy years up to age 110, the net premium can be calculated as follows:

pnetprm#=pvbp#/pvpm1d#

The preliminary term active life reserve and the dollar value of the premium payments for all durations after the preliminary term period can be calculated as follows:

pactrsv#(dr%)=[pnetprm#*eoyrsv1d#(dr%)]−eoyrsv#(dr%)
pp#(dr%)=pnetprm*pp1d#(dr%)

Finally the premium assumed to be paid during the preliminary term period (which matches the incurred benefits during that period) is determined for each duration that is applicable.

pp#(1)=pp1d#(1)*{[panhb#(1)+pahcb#(1)]*vhy#(1)
    + panfb#(1)*vfy(2)}/[pp1d#(1)*vfy#(1)]

pp#(2)=pp1d#(2)*{[panhb#(2)+pahcb#(2)]*vhy#(2)
+ panfb#(2)*vfy(3)}/[pp1d#(2)*vfy#(2)]

G. Function SBP

This function calculates the present value (at the time of lapse) per lapser of the nonforfeiture benefit for each cohort of lapsers. The function is transferred the attained age at lapse ("atage"), the duration at lapse ("t"), the fraction of the original lifetime maximum for nursing home benefits ("bpnh"), and the fraction of the original lifetime maximum for home care benefits ("bphc"). The function first determines the full-rate lifetime maximum in dollars for nursing home benefits ("lfmx&") and for home care benefits ("hclfmx&"). Then, for each duration from lapse ("jdur") until age 110, it projects the probability of survival ("lx"), the nursing home admissions, and the incidences of frailty in home care. For the year of lapse, lx=1. The midyear survivors ("midlx") are estimated by applying one-half year's mortality, taking into account mortality selection factor ("fct").

fct=mtsf#(t+jdur)
midlx=lx*[1−0.5*fct*qd#(atage+jdur−1)]

The number of nursing home admissions ("adnh") is calculated by applying the appropriate admission rate ("nharis" for insured stays or "nharas" for all stays) to the midyear survivors, taking into morbidity account selection ("fct"). The number of incidences of frailty in home care is calculated in a similar manner using the home care incidence rate ("hcar").

adnh=midlx*nharis(atage+jdur−1,3)*fct
adhc=midlx*hcar(atage+jdur−1,3)*fct

The number of days of benefit for these admissions is obtained from the "ftk" and "gtk" functions and the applicable benefit period. The benefit period starts after the elimination period ("lower") and ends after an additional number of days equal to the maximum number of days benefits can be paid ("upper"). The maximum number of days of benefit is the original lifetime maximum in dollars ("lfmx&") divided by the maximum daily benefit ("mxdb#") times the fraction of the original benefit applicable to the lapses in year "t."

lower=nhelpd&
upper=lower+(lfmx&/mxdb#)*bpnh

The function "ftk" is called to determine the days of benefit payments in each policy year so that the appropriate discount factor and benefit inflation factor can be applied. The sum is stored in the variable "bentot." The present value of all admissions in all years after lapse is accumulated in the variable "sp." For each year, the present value of the incurred benefit payments is equal to the number of admissions times the discounted days of benefit payments times the maximum daily benefit.

sp=sp+(adnh*bentot*mxdb#)

Similar calculations are performed for home care benefits that are accumulated in the same variable "sp." Finally the value calculated by the function "sbp" is equated to the accumulated "sp."

H. Subroutine OUTPT

While the primary purpose of this subroutine is to format the computations for output to the screen or to disk, some calculations are performed in this code. In particular, the mid-terminal reserve factors are derived from the terminal reserves obtained from CALC.

Since the program assumes annual premium mode, all lapsation occurs at the end of the policy year. This produces a jump in the terminal reserve factor at the point of lapsation. In computing the mid-terminal reserve factor, the program identifies a modified terminal reserve just prior to lapsation at the end of the policy year. This is accomplished by multiplying the conventional terminal reserve factor by the post-lapse in force, adding back in the net single premiums associated with the NFO benefits of those lapsing, and dividing by the pre-lapse in force. This modified terminal reserve is compared to the net single premium for the year end NFO benefit. If the user has indicated, the greater of these two values is used in the mid-terminal calculation.

The reserve at the start of the policy year is the post-lapse terminal reserve from the prior policy year. This value is compared to the NFO net single premium per lapser at the end of the prior year. If the user has indicated, the greater of these two values is used in the mid-terminal calculation.

IV. Output Files

The program produces three types of output files. When the user saves specifications, the program creates a file named filename.INP, where "filename" is provided by the user. The other two types of files created are associated with the output. The user may elect to store the program output in a text file, filename.TXT, and/or a spreadsheet file, filename.WK1.

V. Sample Calculations

Five values from the default case reserve onput (see Appendexes B and C) are rederived in this section to provide a "trail" from the tables in Sections II and III of this final report to the valuation diskette output. We consider the fifth policy year for females issued at age 70.

A. Nursing Home Admissions

(1) Start of year population	73,336
(2) Start of year NH population	970
(3) Difference	72,366
(4) Probability of surviving to mid-year $(1-1,392/2\times73,336)$	0.99051
(5) Product	71,679.2
(6) Admission rate (Section II)	0.0181
(7) Selection factor	0.9
(8) Antiselection factor $1/[(1-0.05\times0.7)(1-0.06\times0.5)$ $(1-0.07\times0.3)(1-0.08\times0.2)]=$	1.109
(9) Nursing home admissions $(5)\times(6)\times(7)\times(8)$	1,295

B. Nursing Home Cost per Mid-l_x

(1) Average number of NH days (Section II)   633

(2) Allocation of NH days by duration from admission

(1) Duration	(2) % Days Beyond	(3) Differences	(4) Days= $633\times(3)$	(5) Discount at 5%
100 days	88.417%	88.417%		
182.5	81.710	6.71	42.47	v^0
547.5	59.055	22.65	143.40	v^1
912.5	42.579	16.48	104.30	v^2
1,277.5	30.725	11.85	75.03	v^3
1,560	23.703	7.02	44.45	v^4

(3) NH days (discounted with interest) per admission
   $42.47 \times v^0 + ... + 44.45 \times v^4 =$ 375.03

(4) NH cost per mid-l_x
   $375.03 \times \$100 \times 0.181 \times 0.9 \times 1.109 =$ $677.51

C. Home Care Admissions

(1) Start-of-year population   73,336
(2) Half of deaths = 1,392/2   696
(3) Difference   72,640
(4) Impairment rate (Section III see input file to diskette
   for age-specific values)   0.02907
(5) Selection factor   0.9
(6) Antiselection factor   1.109
(7) HC admissions
   $(3) \times (4) \times (5) \times (6)$ 2,108

D. Home Care Cost per Mid -$\hbar_x$

(1) Average number of noninstitutional days impaired
   (Section III, see diskette input file for age-specific values.) 905 days
(2) Allocation of impairment days by duration from impairment.

Duration	(1) % Utilization Days	(2) % Service Days	(3) Service Days per User	(4) % Service Days in Benefit Period	(5) Benefit Days $905 \times (2) \times (4)$	(6) Discount at 5%
182.5	4.70%	2.87%	111.44	10.2%	2.7	v^0
547.5	7.93	4.90	225.54	100.0	44.3	v^1
912.5	6.09	3.77	225.95	↓	34.1	v^2
1,277.5	4.51	2.77	224.18	↓	25.1	v^3
1,642.5	3.67	2.21	219.80	↓	20.0	v^4
2,007.5	2.67	1.57	214.63	↓	14.2	v^5
2,372.5	2.00	1.13	206.23	100.0	10.2	v^6
2,737.5	1.53	.83	197.05	67.1	5.0	v^7

(3) HC benefit days (discounted with interest) per impairment
    $2.7 \times v^0 + ... + 5.0 \times v^7 =$ 136.52 days
(4) HC cost per mid-l_x
    $136.52 \times \$50 \times 0.02907 \times 0.9 \times 1.109 =$ $198.05

E. Mid-Terminal Reserve Factor

(1) EOY terminal reserve $ 5,725.45
(2) EOY post-lapse in force   69,067.00
(3) EOY pre-lapse in force
    $69,067 + 2,878 =$ 71,945.00
(4) EOY pre-lapse terminal reserve
    $(1) \times (2)/(3) =$ $ 5,496.42
(5) BOY reserve $ 4,347.95
(6) Mid-terminal reserve
    $[(4) + (5)]/2 =$ $ 4,922.19

APPENDIX F

CURRENT NAIC MODELS

There are two official groups within the NAIC that have adopted model regulations related to this final report: the NAIC LTC Senior Issues Task Force and the NAIC Life and Health Actuarial Task Force.

I. NAIC LTC Senior Issues Task Force

The NAIC LTC Senior Issues Task Force (in 1994 renamed from the NAIC LTC Insurance (B) Task Force) continues to develop the NAIC Model LTC Insurance Act and the Model LTC Insurance Regulation. These were first adopted in the mid-1980s and deal with all subjects pertaining to the product. However, the model act is silent on valuation, and the model regulation in its Section 15 (quoted in its entirety below) provides only very general guidance. It provides a lengthy Subsection A, describing how to value LTC benefits that are accelerated life insurance benefits and a much shorter Subsection B for other LTC benefits (that is, stand-alone) consisting of one sentence.

Section 15. Reserve Standards

A. When long-term care benefits are provided through the acceleration of benefits under group or individual life policies or riders to such policies, policy reserves for such benefits shall be determined in accordance with [cite the standard valuation law for life insurance, which contains a section referring to "special benefits" for which tables must be approved by the commissioner]. Claim reserves must also be established in the case when such policy or rider is in claim status.

Reserves for policies and riders subject to this subsection should be based on the multiple decrement model utilizing all relevant decrements except for voluntary termination rates. Single decrement approximations are acceptable if the calculation produces essentially similar reserves, if the reserve is clearly more conservative, or if the reserve is immaterial. The calculations may take into account the reduction in life insurance benefits due to the payment of long-term care benefits. However, in no event shall the reserves for the long-term care benefit and the life insurance benefit be less than the reserves for the life insurance benefit assuming no long-term care benefit.

In the development and calculation of reserves for policies and riders subject to this subsection, due regard shall be given to the applicable policy provisions, marketing methods, administrative procedures and all other considerations which have an impact on projected claim costs, including, but not limited to, the following:

(1) Definition of insured events;

(2) Covered long-term-care facilities;

(3) Existence of home convalescence care coverage;

(4) Definition of facilities;

(5) Existence or absence of barriers to eligibility;

(6) Premium waiver provision;

(7) Renewability;

(8) Ability to raise premiums;

(9) Marketing method;

(10) Underwriting procedures;

(11) Claims adjustment procedures;

(12) Waiting period;

(13) Maximum benefit;

(14) Availability of eligible facilities;

(15) Margins in claim costs;

(16) Optional nature of benefit;

(17) Delay in eligibility for benefit;

(18) Inflation protection provisions; and

(19) Guaranteed insurability option.

Any applicable valuation morbidity table shall be certified as appropriate as a statutory valuation table by a member of the American Academy of Actuaries.

B. When long-term care benefits are provided other than as in Subsection A above, reserves shall be determined in accordance with [cite law referring to minimum health insurance reserves, the NAIC version of which requires reserves "using a table established for reserve purposes by a qualified actuary and acceptable to the commissioner"].

Other than adopting this model regulation (and wishing there were some useful valuation standards to relate to as they develop regulations for LTC insurance nonforfeiture benefits), the NAIC Senior Issues (B) Task Force has deferred to the NAIC Life and Health Actuarial Task Force on valuation matters.

II. NAIC Life and Health Actuarial Task Force

This SOA Task Force has informed the regulators through the NAIC Life and Health Actuarial Task Force.

The current model regulation that pertains to LTC insurance statutory valuation is the NAIC Model Minimum Reserve Standards for Individual and Group Health Insurance Contracts. This was amended in June 1991 to include provisions specific to LTC. (Few states have officially adopted this model, although most states look to the NAIC model for guidance.) The following are the relevant provisions.

Morbidity

Since there is no morbidity standard for LTC, it

... shall be valued using tables established for reserve purposes by a qualified actuary and acceptable to the Commissioner. (Section 4.B.(1)(a))

Termination Rates

The NAIC model provides the following:

Termination Rates. Termination rates used in the computation of reserves shall be on the basis of a mortality table as specified in Appendix A except as noted in the following paragraph. (Section 4.B. (1)(c)).

That referenced Appendix A reads:

The mortality basis used shall be according to a table (but without use of selection factors) permitted by law for the valuation of whole life insurance issued on the same date as the health insurance contract. (Appendix A, Section III.)

The important exception cited above reads in whole as follows:

Under contracts for which premium rates are not guaranteed, and where the effects of insurer underwriting are specifically used by policy duration in the valuation morbidity standard, total termination rates may be used at ages and durations where these exceed specified mortality table rates, but not in excess of the lesser of:

(i) Eighty percent of the total termination rate used in the calculation of the gross premiums, or

(ii) Eight percent.

Where a morbidity standard specified in Appendix A is on an aggregate basis, such morbidity standard may be adjusted to reflect the effect of insurer underwriting by policy duration. The adjustments must be appropriate to the underwriting and be acceptable to the Commissioner. (Section 4.B.(1)(c))

Interest Rate

The maximum interest rate is specified in Appendix A. (Section 4.B.(1)(b))

The relevant section of Appendix A reads as follows:

II. Interest

A. For contract reserves the maximum interest rate is the maximum rate permitted by law in the valuation of whole life insurance issued on the same date as the health insurance contract.

B. For claim reserves on policies that require contract reserves, the maximum interest rate is the maximum rate permitted by law in the valuation of whole life insurance issued on the same date as the claim incurral date.

C. For claim reserves on policies not requiring contract reserves, the maximum interest rate is the maximum rate permitted by law in the valuation of single-premium immediate annuities issued on the same date as the claim incurral date, reduced by 100 basis points. (Appendix A, Section II.)

Method

For long-term care insurance, the minimum reserve is the reserve calculated on the one-year full preliminary term method. (Section 4.B.(1)(d)(ii))

DISCUSSION OF PRECEDING PAPER

DIANA S. WRIGHT:

The Society of Actuaries Long-Term Care Insurance Valuation Methods Task Force has done an excellent job of bringing together the complicated and diverse issues associated with long-term care (LTC) valuation. Also, I had an opportunity to use the diskette mentioned in the report when Bart Munson, Jim Robinson, and I provided some additional information to the Accident and Health Working Group of the National Association of Insurance Commissioners (NAIC) on the impact of one recommendation in the report. The working group was considering revising the NAIC Model on Minimum Reserve Standards for Individual and Group Health Insurance Contracts for LTC in light of recommendations in the Society's report. I found the diskette to be user-friendly and very helpful in the analysis of contract reserves. In these comments, I focus on the scope of the report as described in Section I, Introduction, and in Section IV, Application of Tables.

The Introduction states that the recommendations apply to individual (or quasi-individual) stand-alone insurance products or LTC riders attached to life insurance products in which the death benefits are not reduced. The report's recommendations do not address true group policies in which the employer pays a substantial portion of the premium, LTC riders on life insurance policies in which LTC benefit reduces the death benefit and/or cash surrender value, LTC options on annuity products, and LTC insurability guarantees attached to other products. The report indicates that many of its elements could appropriately be applied to employer-paid true-group policies. I agree with this approach and the reason for placing further consideration of this as a low priority. Also, because annuity products with LTC options are rare, I understand why this was not addressed, and as indicated, the reserve for LTC insurability guarantees would only be an accumulation of an antiselection risk. However, the report indicates that the recommendations for reduced-benefit LTC-ridered life policies should be generated after those for stand-alone products. I believe that it is desirable to generate recommendations on these products as soon as possible. The market is growing and changing, and this is an active part of that market. Everyone agrees that regulations should not suppress development; however, it is also important to not unduly influence the market through selective regulation and to keep a level playing field as much as possible.

769

The SOA LTC Insurance Valuation Methods Task Force faced many challenges in developing data. This was excellently summed up on page 611 of the report. One reason is that the product is relatively new, and I would like to add that the long duration before claim experience develops further complicates analysis. Also, as mentioned in the report, many significant benefit design changes have taken place, and little is known about the impact of antiselection, lapses, policy definitions, and medical advances. This made for a truly challenging assignment. Acknowledging that there are yet many unknowns, I direct the remainder of my comments to Section IV, Application of Tables.

Section IV-A, Product Features, indicates that "some tables may need adjustment for indemnity vs. expense incurred benefit structures." If this is done, then the adjustment needs to be based on more than whether the benefit structure is indemnity or expense incurred. The relativity of the allowable benefits to reasonable charges needs to be considered. Some expense-incurred policies also have maximum daily benefits, and those maximum daily benefits are at levels that are equal to or less than the reasonable charge level for that benefit. Such policies function the same as indemnity policies and should be reserved accordingly. Because currently there is no definitive source for reasonable charges, it would be a challenge to develop more specific factors for statutory regulations.

Section IV-B, Benefit Triggers, mentions that "there is no uniformly agreed wording for any one ADL." Note that since the release of the Society's report, the NAIC addressed this issue in the October 1995 revision of the Long-Term Care Insurance Model Regulation. A comment incorporated into the model regulation after the definitions states that "this section is intended to specify required definitional elements of several terms commonly found in long-term care insurance policies, while allowing some flexibility in the definitions themselves." The model contains definitions for bathing, cognitive impairment, continence, dressing, eating, hands-on assistance, toileting, and transferring.

The report addresses both the pros and cons of spousal discounts in Section IV-C. The report further states that "active life reserves reduced by the same percentage as may be used in discounting premiums may not produce adequate reserves." In spite of this statement, the final paragraph for this section recommends that if the married versus unmarried mix is significantly different from the general population, then an adjustment should be considered. There is no separate recommendation for statutory reserves. While it is desirable to make the reserves as accurate as possible, the primary focus for statutory purposes is financial adequacy. Because of this primary statutory purpose and because of the aforementioned statement in the report, unless statutory adjustments for spousal discounts are explicitly proposed, perhaps spousal discounts should not be allowed for statutory reserves.

Section IV-D pertains to geographic region. It indicates that institutional benefits may need morbidity adjustments on a state-by-state or regional basis, but no adjustment factors are recommended. No mention is made of whether this is for utilization or cost. Cost variation by state would be needed for incurred expense policies that did not behave as indemnity policies. Utilization variation, on the other hand, could be applicable to either indemnity or expense-incurred policies. I did a cursory review to determine the difficulty of locating institutional data by state/region that could be useful to indicate utilization variations. There are at least three sources. The sources that I found are as follows:

1. Table 5.18, "Nursing Care Facilities and Utilization, by State, 1991" from the *HIAA Source Book of Health Insurance Data, 1994*. The source data for this table are from the Health Care Financing Administration, unpublished data.

2. "Nursing Home Beds in 1991 and the Rate of Nursing Home Beds in 1991" from *Health Care State Rankings, 1995*. The source data are from the National Center for Health Statistics, unpublished data.

3. "Nursing Home Bed Distribution, 1986" from the *State-Level Data Book on Health Care Access and Financing* (1993). The source data are from the National Center for Health Statistics, 1986 Inventory of Long-Term Care Plans.

The table in the third source, "Nursing Home Bed Distribution," contains a column for which nursing home beds are expressed as per 1,000 population. This provides some indication of utilization; however, I prefer the ratio provided in the table of the second source entitled "Rate of Nursing Home Beds in 1991." The denominator in this ratio is not the entire state population; rather the denominator is the state population age 65 and older. Even though LTC policies are purchased by individuals younger than 65 and sometimes individuals younger than 65 are in nursing homes, the vast majority of nursing home care utilizers will be over age 65.

A complication develops when the data are examined more closely, however. The number of nursing home beds reported in the second source, which I believe is the basis for the associated Rate of Nursing Home Beds Table, is consistently less than the number of population in nursing care facilities reported in Table 5.18 of the first source. I am not sure whether the discrepancies are attributable to differences in definitions and/or estimation techniques. This might not be too bad if the relationships among the states stay consistent. Unfortunately this is not the case. When the nursing home population counts in the first source are divided by the state-specific over-65 population, the relativities between the states are different from those of the second source. Thus, further investigation into the development of the data for these tables is required, and there is no one easily obtainable definitive source. Medicare/Medicaid data would not be sufficient because they would exclude some nursing home utilization. For any statutory regulation to be more specific than requiring valuation actuarial judgment and to allow the reserves to reflect state variation, a definitive source would need to be developed.

I would also argue that there are probably state/regional differences for the utilization and cost of home health services. Data for this benefit are even more difficult to find than state institutional nursing home data.

In conclusion, the report of the SOA LTC Insurance Valuation Methods Task Force is a good first step toward developing statutory valuation methods, but many unknowns remain. I look forward to seeing future updates as the products and experience develop.

(AUTHORS' REVIEW OF DISCUSSION)

BARTLEY L. MUNSON:

We appreciate the generally kind words about both our final report and its companion valuation diskette. It was difficult to make both of them useful to valuation actuaries who must apply them to a wide variety of products.

It is good to hear from an actuary who understands those challenges and the regulators' needs for these tools to be user-friendly and helpful.

The actuarial profession seems to agree with the discussant's call for addressing non-stand-alone LTC products, especially accelerations in life insurance policies. While there are no plans to develop a successor LTC valuation report, the LTC Task Force of the Actuarial Standards Board has been resurrected to update *ASOP No. 18*, dated July 1991, among other changes, it will address the actuary's standards of practice for acceleration of life benefits, a subject largely omitted from *ASOP No. 18*.

The valuation actuary does indeed need to contemplate how a product's benefit limits work in relation to reasonable service charges. We, too, thought it is not reasonable to develop more specific guidelines for valuation regulations. For this and many other considerations, for a product without insured morbidity experience adequate to produce specific tables, and a product so varied and still evolving, we found no way to responsibly avoid relying on "the Valuation Actuary should consider. ..."

If in time benefit triggers, as defined in the NAIC's LTC Model Regulation subsequent to the release of our final report, are widely adopted, a successor report and even valuation requirements can address them. However, with state variations in benefit triggers to be expected even after they are specified by model regulation, it appears it will be some time before even that standardization finds its way into LTC insurance policies and thus might suggest some narrowing of specified valuation standards. Standard language will narrow but not eliminate differences in interpretation among carriers and jurisdictions.

Spousal discounts is a complex subject, sometimes deceivingly simple in appeal. It acts differently for institutional and noninstitutional products, for example. Our report intended to alert the valuation actuary to ponder the implications of this subject, if applicable. We did not intend to imply that reserves can be "discounted" similarly to premiums, without justification. If analysis of expenses and morbidity suggests some recognition in the reserves, that could be considered; more likely, as the discussant suggests, no reserve adjustment should be made. The overriding test for the primary goal of financial adequacy is a gross premium test, which we do comment upon later in the report. The valuation actuary's analysis may show the need for considering even a strengthening of reserves due to the steepening of the morbidity curve or the eventual absence of the spouse.

The discussant's research into regional LTC cost and utilization of services is a useful addition to our report. Regional differences, we thought, could be considered for a block of business that is geographically confined or for which demonstrable differences are available from or for the valuation actuary. However, in addition to the challenges the discussant observes, there are questions about the location of the insured when receiving services compared with the location at the time of the policy's purchase.

We appreciate the discussant's compliments on a "good first step." Undoubtedly, there is a need for our profession and the regulators to take future ones. We join the reviewer, and all LTC valuation actuaries and regulators, in looking forward to those times.

PRINCIPLES REGARDING PROVISIONS FOR LIFE RISKS

SOCIETY OF ACTUARIES COMMITTEE ON ACTUARIAL PRINCIPLES*

ABSTRACT

The Committee on Actuarial Principles is charged with identifying, circulating, and organizing actuarial principles (as distinct from standards) and recommending the resulting statements of principles to the Board of Governors for review and adoption. In October 1995, the Board accepted the Committee's statement entitled "Principles Regarding Provisions for Life Risks." This statement, which constitutes the following paper, is an expression of opinion by the Committee on Actuarial Principles and has been authorized by the Board of Governors. It has not been submitted to the vote of the membership and thus should not be construed as an expression of opinion by the Society of Actuaries.

BACKGROUND

The purpose of this statement is to describe principles and considerations regarding the provision made by insurance organizations relative to life actuarial risks. The terminology used to describe this provision is diverse and varies not only by jurisdiction but also in some cases by accounting purpose. For example, the provision is called a "reserve" in the U.S. and an "actuarial liability" in Canada. In addition, the provision sometimes consists of both an accounting liability item and a designated portion of accounting surplus. Some sense of adequacy or sufficiency adheres to each such provision but varies from system to system. This statement is intended to apply consistent notions of adequacy and sufficiency to provisions for life actuarial risks, however defined. It is hoped that the use of a neutral term ("provision") will permit a wide application of the principles without unnecessary confusion.

*Arnold A. Dicke, Chair, Allan Brender, Daniel F. Case, Carol Randolph Gramer, Stuart Klugman, Donald M. Peterson, Joseph H. Tan, and Warren R. Luckner, SOA Staff Liaison.

This statement may be regarded as an extension of "Principles of Actuarial Science," an earlier expression of opinions of the committee [*TSA* XLIV (1992) 565–628], which articulates general principles that apply to the areas of actuarial practice within the purview of the Society of Actuaries. The Glossary appended to this statement contains the Principles and Definitions originally set forth in "Principles of Actuarial Science."

This statement consists of three parts:

A. Definitions
B. Principles with Discussions
C. Considerations.

Clear and precise Definitions are essential for accurately articulating Principles. This statement uses terms defined in "Principles of Actuarial Science" and defines additional terms as needed.

Principles are defined in "Principles of Actuarial Science" as "statements grounded in observation and experience." The Principles presented in this document represent applications of the general principles to a defined area of practice. Brief Discussions explain and illustrate the Principles.

The Considerations provide a current context for application of the Principles and discuss areas in which Standards (defined in "Principles of Actuarial Science" as "rules of behavior, including, in particular, directives as to when and how professional judgment should be employed") may be needed.

A. DEFINITIONS

1. Terms Previously Defined

The following terms defined in "Principles of Actuarial Science" are used in this statement: *actuarial assumption, actuarial model, actuarial risk, actuarial value, asset, benefit, cash flow, consideration, degree of accuracy, degree of actuarial soundness, insurance system, obligation, potentially valid, premium structure, risk* (or *risk subject*), *scenario,* and *valid.* Definitions of these terms are found in the Glossary.

2. Additional Terms

A *life insurance and annuity system* is an insurance system in which the actuarial risks to be financed arise primarily from human mortality. The obligations related to the payment of benefits by a life insurance and annuity system are called *life risk obligations.*

An *accounting method* is a set of rules that assigns values (called *accounting values*) to the assets and obligations of a life insurance and annuity system. A *block* (or *block of life risk obligations*) is a subset of the life risk obligations of a life insurance and annuity system, together with the future considerations associated with these obligations.

The insurance subsystem consisting of a block and a collection of assets or portions of assets is called a *component* of the life insurance and annuity system. A component is said to be *in full compliance* if on a given date all applicable contractual, legal, and regulatory constraints that require or prohibit the assignment of specific assets to the block are satisfied.

The accounting value assigned to a block of life risk obligations on a given date (the *valuation date*) is called the *provision* for that block on that date. The sum of the provisions for all blocks of a life insurance and annuity system is called the (*aggregate*) *provision* for the system. A component of a life insurance and annuity system is said to achieve *accounting balance* on the valuation date if the total accounting value of the assets in the component equals the provision for the block of life risk obligations in the component on that date. An *allowable asset allocation* is an assignment or reassignment on the valuation date of assets or portions of assets to each block of a life insurance and annuity system, so that each of the resulting components is in full compliance and achieves accounting balance on that date.

A provision for a block of life risk obligations on a given valuation date will have been *ultimately sufficient* relative to an allowable asset allocation if, in the end, all benefits could have been paid as promised from the net cash flows generated directly or indirectly by the assets assigned to the block and by the considerations associated with the block. The likelihood on a given date, based on a valid actuarial model, that a provision will be ultimately sufficient relative to a specific allowable asset allocation is called the *indicated level of adequacy* of the provisions relative to the asset allocation. If the actuarial value calculated using a valid actuarial model of the system, or of a component consisting of a block of life risk obligations and the assets assigned to the block by an allowable asset allocation, is negative for a given scenario under that model, the absolute value of that actuarial value is called the *indicated current deficiency* of the system or of the block for that scenario.

B. PRINCIPLES

1. **PRINCIPLE (Likelihood of Ultimate Sufficiency).** The likelihood on a given valuation date that a provision for a block of life risk obligations will be ultimately sufficient relative to a specific allowable asset allocation depends upon:
   (a) the risk subjects covered,
   (b) the actuarial risks involved,
   (c) the future obligations and considerations arising from the financing of these risks,
   (d) the assets allocated to the block on the valuation date, and
   (e) the strategy for reinvesting or financing net future cash flows.

DISCUSSION. The likelihood of ultimate sufficiency for a block of life risk obligations depends on the enumerated factors, which represent aspects of the life insurance and annuity system. Each of these factors is in turn affected by external influences, such as the economic environment. The enumeration is not complete; for example, factors such as management capability may come into play. The actuarial risks may include risks besides those for which the financial security system was instituted. Some of the actuarial risks may involve events that fail to qualify as insurable events, for example, by being subject to control by an insured. Future obligations may include contractual benefits, such as withdrawal benefits and the payment of nonguaranteed elements, in addition to life insurance and annuity benefits. The premium structure of the life insurance and annuity system may also affect ultimate sufficiency. For example, if this structure involves broad groupings, ultimate sufficiency may be affected by adverse selection. The extent to which future obligations and considerations may be varied to reflect future circumstances will also affect ultimate sufficiency.

The ultimate sufficiency of the provision is affected by the cash flows generated by the assets allocated to the block and by investments of positive net cash flows and financing requirements for negative net cash flows. The cash flows, in turn, are not certain as to receipt or timing of receipt. Alternative sets of such assets may have the same accounting value but may generate significantly different cash flows and thus may have a different result as regards ultimate sufficiency. Constraints on allowable allocations will reduce the ways available to fund the obligations and thus may require a larger provision to achieve ultimate sufficiency. Conversely, the adoption of a strategy for reinvesting or financing net future cash flows that is capable of responding to potential changes in future obligations and considerations may reduce the provision that is required to achieve this goal.

The definition of ultimate sufficiency assumes that (a) the block of obligations is closed and (b) the net cash flows generated directly or indirectly from the initial assets and from subsequent considerations remain in the component until needed to fund the obligations. In theory, it is possible to track all cash flows deriving from the initial assets and subsequent considerations and reinvestments of cash flows. However, in real life applications, such investments may be in "assets" such as new business strain, which involve complex, hard-to-monitor cash flows.

Since ultimate sufficiency can be verified only in unrealistically simple situations, the ability to estimate the likelihood of ultimate sufficiency is of more theoretical than practical value. However, this theoretical possibility allows the use of actuarial models to test the choice of provisions (together with the choice of assets allocated to the block) and to determine relative likelihoods. As a practical matter, the model usually involves simplifying assumptions, such as a reinvestment assumption that ignores any use of future cash flows to fund new business.

2.   **PRINCIPLE (Estimation of the Likelihood of Ultimate Sufficiency). Any valid actuarial model that takes account of the dependencies enumerated in Principle 1 can be used to estimate the likelihood that a provision for a block of life risk obligations will be ultimately sufficient relative to a specific allowable asset allocation.**

DISCUSSION. Models used to estimate the likelihood of ultimate sufficiency may vary with respect to the degree of summarization of in-force data, the extent of refinement of the actuarial assumptions used, and the stochastic representation of various actuarial risks, among other factors. Among the models incorporating appropriate dependencies, no one unique model is selected by the validation process. It is not possible to state that the indicated level of adequacy from one such valid model represents a better estimate of the likelihood of ultimate sufficiency than the indicated level of adequacy from another such valid model.

The indicated level of adequacy depends on the assumptions inherent in the actuarial model, including aspects of the assumed future economic environment. The indicated level of adequacy is prospective, but the actuarial model is generally validated against past experience. It is incorrect to conclude on the basis of subsequent experience that the actuarial assumptions were inappropriate or that the indicated level of adequacy was overstated or understated.

Historical validation of economically sensitive elements, in particular, is useful only if the past period used for validation resembles the current period with respect to economic conditions.

If an actuarial risk variable is associated with events that do not qualify as insurable events, stochastic modeling may not result in useful estimates.

3. **PRINCIPLE (Changes in the Indicated Level of Adequacy). The indicated level of adequacy calculated on a date subsequent to an original valuation date can differ from the originally calculated indicated level of adequacy, even if the respective models have the same degree of accuracy and the assumptions regarding future events are unchanged and remain appropriate.**

DISCUSSION. Recalculation of the indicated level of adequacy after the passage of time will normally result in a changed value, even if the life insurance and annuity system appears unchanged. To begin with, the assumption set required to produce the estimate is reduced with the passage of time, especially for a closed block, that is, a block of life risk obligations into which no new business has been injected. This is true even if assumptions remain appropriate. Assumptions may be considered appropriate if deviations can be explained as random fluctuations and if no information is available indicating that changes in the assumptions should be made. While a later estimate may be considered to be a better estimate, this does not mean that the indicated level of adequacy will converge smoothly to a value. To be sure, for a closed block, as time passes, if the assets begin to exceed the expected value of future obligations, the indicated level of adequacy may approach one. Conversely, if the expected future obligations exceed the assets and all expected future investment income and considerations, the indicated level of adequacy will approach zero. However, there are many situations in which an intermediate value will remain appropriate until the cash flows and cash flow requirements of the block are nearly complete. Significant fluctuations may occur close to the end of this process.

Nevertheless, the indicated level of adequacy can be an important tool for managing a block of liabilities. For example, if the block is managed so that the indicated level of adequacy remains above a fixed level, possibly by injecting additional assets from time to time, the likelihood of fulfilling the obligations of the block may be enhanced.

4.   **PRINCIPLE (Aggregation). For some life insurance and annuity systems, the aggregate provision required to achieve a given indicated level of adequacy will be reduced if two or more selected blocks of life risk obligations are combined into a single block.**

DISCUSSION. Equivalently, for some blocks the indicated level of adequacy may be increased by combining the associated components without adding or substituting assets. This effect, sometimes referred to as "liability-side hedging," may arise from negative correlations between the risks in different blocks (for example, mortality improvement risks associated with life insurance and annuities) or from the fact that the combined block may require net cash flows that are easier to fund with the cash flows of available assets than would be the case for the blocks taken separately. An example of this latter situation is a combined block of deferred and immediate annuities. Note that this effect is distinct from the reduction in aggregate provision that occurs if provisions whose indicated levels of adequacy exceed the required level are reduced, provisions whose indicated levels of adequacy fall short of the required level are increased, and assets are appropriately reallocated.

5.   **PRINCIPLE (Current Deficiencies). Two or more blocks of life risk obligations with provisions having the same indicated level of adequacy relative to a valid actuarial model may have different indicated current deficiencies relative to a given scenario under the model.**

DISCUSSION. The indicated current deficiency for a given scenario can be determined as the amount of cash that must be added to the component to pay all obligations under that scenario. The likelihood that benefits will be paid (indicated level of adequacy) is distinct from the indicated current deficiencies for those scenarios under which benefits are not expected to be able to be paid. The actuarial values for a given scenario under a valid actuarial model of two components may differ, even if the provisions for the associated blocks of obligations have the same indicated levels of adequacy relative to that actuarial model when all tested scenarios are considered. This may be caused either by differences in the initial assets or differences in the actuarial risks, risk subjects, or obligations involved. Calculation of the indicated current deficiencies under various scenarios may be useful in surplus planning, solvency testing, and the management of industry guarantee associations.

C. CONSIDERATIONS

1. Provision Methodologies

One of the typical elements of an insurance accounting system is a methodology for establishing provisions for risk obligations.

Historically, the most common methodology involved formula reserves. A "formula reserve" is one of a set of values, assigned by a rule or formula, representing the provision to be established at each of a given set of future dates ("valuation dates") for the risk obligations remaining or projected to be remaining from a given block on that date. An "actuarial formula reserve" for a block as of a given valuation date relative to a given actuarial model is the formula reserve under which the provision at that valuation date equals the actuarial value at that date of the future cash flows arising from the obligations of the block less the actuarial value at that date of the future considerations payable to the block projected by the actuarial model. Statutory reserves and GAAP benefit reserves (under *SFAS 60*) in the U.S. are examples of an actuarial formula reserve. In both cases, calculated net premiums are used in place of actual gross premiums. This substitution represents an assumption in the actuarial model regarding expenses and profits. A desirable feature of actuarial formula reserves is the ability to calculate values as of future valuation dates.

An alternative approach is the "asset adequacy method," in which the provision for a block of risk obligations is taken to be the minimum aggregate accounting value of assets that allow the provision to attain a given indicated level of adequacy relative to an allowable asset allocation. The indicated level of adequacy for a provision calculated under the asset adequacy method is obviously predetermined, but, unlike the actuarial formula method, provisions as of future valuation dates are not easily projected.

When an accounting method includes a provision methodology that allows the projection of provisions required or desired as of future dates, another concept of adequacy may be of interest. The "indicated level of accounting adequacy" is an estimate of the likelihood as of a given valuation date that, in addition to paying all benefits as promised, the accounting values of the assets allocated to the block will exceed the projected provisions at each of a defined set of future dates. It is clear that the indicated level of accounting adequacy, if available, will always be less than or equal to the indicated level of ("economic") adequacy on the same valuation date. In other words, accounting adequacy is a stricter test because it does not allow shortfalls of assets relative to projected provisions for a block to be financed from possible future excesses.

2. Actuarial Submodels

Actuarial models used in developing or testing the provision made by life insurance and annuity systems relative to life actuarial risks usually involve several actuarial submodels. Typical submodels are associated with such actuarial risks as mortality, lapse, and investment default.

The validity of the actuarial model depends on which actuarial risks are represented by submodels and whether the submodels are valid or potentially valid. Among valid or potentially valid submodels, those which take account of "induced experience" (see Principle 4.4 in the Glossary) and future "antiselection" (see Principle 4.3 in the Glossary) are more likely to remain valid at future times.

3. Dependence on Status

The actuarial model used to calculate or test provisions may depend on the status of an insured event. For example, an actuarial model used in connection with provisions for obligations associated with events that have already occurred (for example, claim provisions for death benefits) or that are currently occurring (for example, provisions for annuities in payment status) may incorporate greater detail on the amount and timing of payments in progress, while a model used in connection with provisions for events that have yet to occur may incorporate greater detail on present-value assumptions.

4. Provision for Expenses

Normally, the expenses incurred in fulfilling the benefit obligations of a block are considered obligations of that block. If, as in the case of expenses related to claim payment, expected future expenses are provided for by considerations already received, an expense provision can be established. Conversely, if an expense that has been incurred is to be provided for by cash flows at one or more later dates, an offset to the provision can be used to defer recognition of the expense, or a portion thereof, until those dates.

5. Asset Allocation

The range of allowable asset allocations will affect the indicated level of adequacy of provisions. Variations in this range from year to year may affect comparability. Absent separate accounts or other contractual arrangements, the allocation of assets to a block creates no legal or contractual right to specific assets. Moreover, again absent separate account or other contractual arrangements, the loss associated with the default of an asset need not be charged solely to the component to which the asset has been assigned.

6. Experience Adjustment

Provisions may be based, in whole or part, on the experience of the life insurance and annuity system. Provisions may be adjusted if the experience of the life insurance and annuity system differs materially from that originally assumed. If the adjustment is made only if the new provision is larger than the old, the process is called "loss recognition." If periodic experience adjustments are required and if a pattern can be discerned, projected provisions at future valuation dates may be adjusted to reflect this pattern. This process is referred to as "trending."

7. Treatment of Profit Margins or Contributions to Surplus

The actuarial model associated with an actuarial formula reserve may specify the treatment of profit margins or contributions to surplus. Some models recognize these margins currently; others spread the margins over the life of the block of obligations, either explicitly or by the inclusion in assumptions of "provisions for adverse deviation."

8. Other Obligations

The term "other obligations" is used to indicate obligations of the life insurance and annuity system not arising from the actuarial risks assumed by the system. The existence of other obligations may limit the allowable asset allocations. For example, an obligation for incurred expense may need to be backed by cash, reducing the cash available for assignment to other blocks of obligations.

Note: The following glossary of Principles and Definitions was originally published as part of "Principles of Actuarial Science," by the Society of Actuaries Committee on Actuarial Principles, in *Transactions of the Society of Actuaries*, Volume XLIV, 1992, pp. 565–91.

GLOSSARY

PRINCIPLES OF ACTUARIAL SCIENCE

1.1   PRINCIPLE (Statistical Regularity). Phenomena exist such that, if a sequence of independent experiments is held under the same specified conditions, the proportion of occurrences of a given event stabilizes as the number of experiments becomes larger.

1.2   PRINCIPLE (Stochastic Modeling). A phenomenon displaying statistical regularity can be described by a mathematical model that can estimate within any desired degree of uncertainty the proportion of occurrences of a given event in a sufficiently long sequence of experiments.

2.1   PRINCIPLE (Diversity of Preferences). Different people may assign different current monetary values to the same economic good.

2.2   PRINCIPLE (Time Preference). Money has time value; that is, people tend to prefer receiving money in the present to receiving that same amount of money in the future.

2.3   PRINCIPLE (Present Value Modeling). For many persons, there exists a mathematical model that can estimate the current monetary value that the person would assign to any future cash flow.

3.1   PRINCIPLE (Modeling of Actuarial Risks). Actuarial risks can be stochastically modeled based on assumptions regarding the probabilities that will apply to the actuarial risk variables in the future, including assumptions regarding the future environment.

3.2   PRINCIPLE (Validity of Actuarial Models). The change over time in the degree of accuracy of an initially valid actuarial model depends upon changes in:

a. the nature of the right to receive or the duty to make a payment;

b. the various environments (regulatory, judicial, social, financial, economic, etc.) within which the modeled events occur; and

c. the sufficiency and quality of the data available to validate the model.

3.3 PRINCIPLE (Combinations of Cash Flows). The degree of uncertainty of the actuarial value of a combination of cash flows reflects both the uncertainties affecting each underlying actuarial risk variable and the process of combination.

4.1 PRINCIPLE (Risk Classification). For a group of risks associated with a given actuarial risk, it is possible to identify characteristics of the risks and to establish a set of classes based on these characteristics so that:
a. each risk is assigned to one and only one class; and
b. probabilities of occurrence, timing and/or severity may be associated with each class in a way that results in a actuarial model which, for some degree of accuracy, is:
   (1) valid relative to observed results for each class or group of classes having sufficient available data, and
   (2) potentially valid for every class.

4.2 PRINCIPLE (Pooling). If the actuarial risk associated with a risk classification system displays statistical regularity, it is possible to combine risk classes so as to ensure that there is an actuarial model associated with the new set of risk classes that is valid within a specified degree of accuracy.

4.3 PRINCIPLE (Antiselection). If the premium structure of a voluntary insurance system is based on a risk classification system such that a refinement of the system could result in significant differentials in considerations between risks originally assigned to the same class, there will be a tendency for relatively greater participation by those whose considerations would increase if the refinement were put in place.

4.4 PRINCIPLE (Induced Experience). The experience rates for events associated with a financial security system will tend to differ from those for the same events in the absence of any such system.

4.5 PRINCIPLE (Insured Experience). The experience rates for the insurable events of an insurance system will tend to differ from the overall rates of occurrence of the same events among all those subject to a given actuarial risk.

4.6   PRINCIPLE (Avoidance of Ruin). For most ruin criteria, there are combinations of values of the financial parameters that will reduce, below a given specified positive level, the ruin probability relative to an actuarial model.

4.7   PRINCIPLE (Actuarial Soundness). For most financial security systems, there are combinations of margins that will produce, relative to a valid actuarial model, a degree of actuarial soundness that exceeds a given specified level less than one.

DEFINITIONS

The assumptions upon which an actuarial model is based are called **actuarial assumptions.**

A model described by Principle 3.1, together with a present value model if applicable, is called an **actuarial model.**

An **actuarial risk** is a phenomenon that has economic consequences and that is subject to uncertainty with respect to one or more of the **actuarial risk variables:** occurrence, timing, and severity.

The **actuarial value** of a future cash flow that is contingent upon actuarial risk variables is the present value developed by an actuarial model associated with the actuarial risk variables.

The **actuarial value of a financial security system** relative to a given actuarial model is the actuarial value, developed by the model, of the combination of cash flows associated with assets, obligations, and considerations of the system.

An **asset** is money or economic goods held, or a right to receive future cash flows; an *obligation* is a duty to provide current or future cash flows.

A *financial security system* is an arrangement for risk financing in which one person assumes the obligation to make a payment (or series of payments), called a **benefit (benefits),** that offsets undesirable economic consequences that may be experienced by a second person in return for the payment, by or on behalf of the second person, of one or more amounts, called *considerations*.

A **cash flow** is the receipt or disbursement at a point in time of an amount of money (or of an economic good with a monetary value).

A *financial security system* is an arrangement for risk financing in which one person assumes the obligation to make a payment (or series of payments), called a *benefit (benefits)*, that offsets undesirable economic consequences that may be experienced by a second person in return for the payment, by or on behalf of the second person, of one or more amounts, called **considerations.**

A cash flow whose occurrence or amount depends on the occurrence of an event that is not certain to occur is said to be **contingent.**

Credibility is the importance assigned to the experience of a given risk class or group of risk classes relative to other information for the purpose of experience adjustment.

The amount of money a person is willing to trade for a good at a specific point in time is the good's **current monetary value** to that person.

A measure of the probability that a financial security system is likely to be able to pay all benefits as promised is called the **degree of actuarial soundness** of the financial security system.

A **deterministic model** is a simplified stochastic model in which the proportion of occurrences of a given event estimated by the stochastic model is assumed to occur with probability one.

An **economic good** is something which has value to a person and which the person may consider exchanging for something else.

The result of an experiment is called an *outcome*; an **event** is a set of one or more possible outcomes.

The probability-weighted average of the numerical values taken on by a random variable is called the **expected value** of the random variable.

The **experience** of a financial security system is the data obtained in the operation of the system.

An **experience adjustment** is a change in considerations or benefits applicable to the various risk classes to reflect the experience of the financial security system.

Estimates, based on such data, of rates of occurrence or amounts of payment related to an actuarial risk are called **experience rates.**

An **experiment** is an observation of a given phenomenon made under specified conditions.

If the actuarial value can be expressed as a function of any variable associated with the financial security system and independent of the actuarial model, that variable is called a **financial parameter** of the financial security system.

A **financial security system** is an arrangement for risk financing in which one person assumes the obligation to make a payment (or series of payments), called a *benefit (benefits)*, that offsets undesirable economic consequences that may be experienced by a second person in return for the payment, by or on behalf of the second person, of one or more amounts, called *considerations.*

An event is said to be **insurable** if:
   a. it is associated with a phenomenon that is expected to display statistical regularity;
   b. it is contingent with respect to number of occurrences, timing and/ or severity;
   c. the fact of its occurrence is definitely determinable;
   d. its occurrence results in undesirable economic consequences for one or more persons; and
   e. its future occurrence, timing and/or severity are neither precisely known nor controllable by these persons.

A person is said to have an **insurable interest** in an insurable event to the extent that the occurrence of the event creates an economic need involving that person.

An **insurance system** is a financial security system in which:
a. the actuarial risks to be financed arise from insurable events;
b. the risk subjects are grouped according to a risk classification system;
c. the benefits payable are related to an insurable interest;
d. the actuarial value of benefits payable, developed by an actuarial model associated with the risk classification system, is finite; and
e. considerations are consistent with the actuarial value of the associated benefits.

An insurance system is **mandatory** if all persons in a group or in society are required legally or otherwise to participate; otherwise, it is **voluntary.** It is a **personal insurance system** if the decision to participate is made by each insured individually; it is a **group insurance system** if the decision is made on behalf of a group, although participation may be mandatory or voluntary for the members of the group; and it is a **social insurance system** if all members of society (or a defined subgroup of society) are eligible to participate.

The entities to which actuarial risk is transferred in an insurance system (whether private or governmental) are called **insurers.**

The amounts by which the values of financial parameters can be changed without reducing the expected actuarial value of the financial security system below zero are called **margins.**

A **mathematical model** is a scientific model in which the representation is expressed in mathematical terms.

Money is a means of exchange which may be traded for economic goods.

A *refinement of a risk classification system* is a risk classification system formed from another by subdividing one or more classes. If there are actuarial models associated with the original risk classification system and with the refinement such that these models assign the same probabilities of occurrence, timing and/or severity to classes that were not subdivided, but they assign differing probabilities to one or more of the subdivisions of at least one class, the refinement is said to be **more homogeneous** than the original system.

An *asset* is money or economic goods held, or a right to receive future cash flows; an **obligation** is a duty to provide current or future cash flows.

The result of an experiment is called an **outcome;** an *event* is a set of one or more possible outcomes.

Phenomena are occurrences which can be observed.

The process of combining risk classes described in Principle 4.2 is called **pooling.**

A mathematical model is **potentially valid** if it produces results that are consistent with available observations of the modeled phenomena and of similar phenomena and is capable of being validated relative to the specified observed results when sufficient data are available.

The **premium structure** of an insurance system is a set of considerations that reflect the assignment of risks to various risk classes.

The estimate of the current monetary value of a future cash flow given by a present value model under a fixed assumption regarding future economic conditions is called the **present value** of the cash flow relative to that assumption.

A model described by Principle 2.3 is called a **present value model.**

Probability is a measure which takes on values from zero to one and gives the likelihood of occurrence of an event.

A rule which assigns a numerical value to every possible outcome is called a **random variable.**

A **refinement of a premium structure** is a premium structure based on a refinement of a risk classification system.

A **refinement of a risk classification system** is a risk classification system formed from another by subdividing one or more classes.

A set of classes, a set of characteristics and a set of rules for using the characteristics to assign each risk to a class in such a way that the conditions of Principle 4.1 are satisfied with respect to a given group of risks is called a **risk classification system.** These classes are called **risk classes,** and the rules used for assigning risks to risk classes are called *underwriting rules.*

Risk control is a process that reduces the impact of one or more of the actuarial risk variables associated with the actuarial risk.

Risk identification is a process for determining whether a given person or object is a risk subject for a given actuarial risk.

A **risk management system** is an arrangement involving one or more of risk identification, risk control, and risk transfer or risk financing.

A person or object involved in an event associated with an actuarial risk is called a **risk subject** or **risk.**

Risk transfer or **risk financing** is a mechanism that provides cash flows that are contingent upon the occurrence of an event associated with the actuarial risk and that tend to offset undesirable economic consequences.

Ruin occurs when a financial security system first fails to satisfy all conditions required to remain in operation.

The statement of the conditions under which ruin occurs is called the **ruin criterion.**

The probability that ruin will occur within a specified period of time, as calculated using an actuarial model, is called the **ruin probability** of the financial security system relative to that model within that period of time.

The estimate of the current monetary value of a future cash flow given by a present value model under a fixed assumption regarding future economic conditions is called the *present value* of the cash flow relative to that assumption. Such a fixed assumption regarding future economic conditions is called a **scenario.**

A **scientific model** is an abstract and simplified representation of a given phenomenon.

A phenomenon to which Principle 1.1 applies is said to display **statistical regularity.**

A model satisfying Principle 1.2 is called a **stochastic model.**

The rules used for assigning risks to risk classes are called **underwriting rules.**

A mathematical model is said to be **valid within a specified degree of accuracy** relative to certain observed results if it reproduces these results within that degree of accuracy.

The process of determining the actuarial value of a financial security system is called a **valuation.**

THE UP-94 AND GAR-94 TABLES: ISSUES IN CHOOSING THE APPROPRIATE TABLE

SOCIETY OF ACTUARIES COMMITTEE ON RETIREMENT SYSTEMS RESEARCH AND COMMITTEE ON RETIREMENT SYSTEMS PRACTICE EDUCATION*

I. INTRODUCTION

In 1993 and 1994, two Society of Actuaries task forces were at work examining the mortality of healthy retirees. One task force was working on an update to the group annuity reserve standard—the 1983 Group Annuity Mortality Table (GAM-83). The other task force was attempting to provide an update to uninsured pensioner mortality. It was anticipated that this second task force would produce a table that reflected recent uninsured mortality experience, and thus could serve as an update to the UP-1984 Table (UP-84), although not expressed on a unisex basis. As the task forces' work progressed, a convergence of the data at retirement ages was noted, and so the same underlying data were used as the basis for the mortality in each table. These underlying data were based on Civil Service Retirement System (CSRS) mortality for lives under age 66 and group annuity mortality at ages 66 and over. Even though the underlying data are the same, based on the different uses for the table, the task forces strongly believe it is appropriate for separate tables to be produced as insurance reserving standards and as a general uninsured pensioner mortality table.

Each of the task forces is publishing a paper† describing the development and appropriate uses of the table it produces. This paper is intended to summarize the differences in the tables and to review issues that arise for actuaries in choosing the appropriate mortality table. In essence, this paper addresses:

- How do the tables differ?
- Why do the tables differ?

---

*Members of the committees who were authors were: Christopher Bone, chairperson, Lindsay Malkiewich, Marilyn Oliver, Michael Virga, and Henry Winslow.

†See "The Uninsured Pensioner Mortality Table" by the Society of Actuaries UP-94 Task Force on page 819 and the "1994 Group Annuity Mortality Table and 1994 Group Annuity Reserving Table" by the Society of Actuaries Group Annuity Valuation Table Task Force on page 865.

795

- What should actuaries consider when using tables for uninsured plans?
- What should actuaries consider when using tables for insured plans?

This paper is intended to supplement the two task force papers on the individual mortality tables. As such, this paper focuses primarily on the choice between versions of the UP-94 and GAR-94 mortality tables; the appropriateness of other tables is not reviewed in detail. Certain areas that are only referenced here are addressed at greater length in those papers.

II. HOW DO THE TABLES DIFFER?

A. Definitions

In this paper, we use the following short-hand notation to refer to the proposed tables:

GAR-94 (The 1994 Group Annuity Reserving Table). This table is the product of the 1994 Group Annuity Valuation Table Task Force. For conservatism, because it is proposed as a reserve standard, the table includes a 7% reduction in q_x's at all but the oldest ages (this is referred to in general through the rest of the paper as the "7% margin"). Mortality is specifically projected using a generational approach through the use of a set of mortality improvement factors incorporated as part of the table.

UP-94 (The Uninsured Pensioner 1994 Table). This has the same underlying mortality as the GAR-94 Table, but does not include the 7% margin. There are a number of different ways in which the mortality rates in the UP-94 Table can be projected for use in a particular valuation. The use of the table with the full range of mortality factors and projection scale AA applied on a generational basis, including projection from 1994 to the valuation date, is referred to as UP-94G. Alternatively, actuaries may prefer to use the table projected for a certain number of years. We refer to a static table produced by projection of each mortality rate to a particular year as "UP-94 @ year" (for example, the table with rates projected to the year 2000 would be referred to as UP-94 @ 2000). This notation is extended for use with generational tables to indicate the point of initial projection, when different from the valuation date. (For example, UP-94G @ 2000 refers to a generational table of q_x's that has already been projected to 2000 and that will continue to be projected to each future year. This differs from UP-94 @ 2000, which refers to a table of mortality rates projected to the year 2000 but assumed to remain static thereafter.)

B. Differences

As can be seen from the above definitions, the two tables differ in two ways. First, GAR-94 reflects explicit margins for longer lifetimes than expected. Second, GAR-94 incorporates explicit projection of mortality decreases over time, while the UP-94 Table is designed to be projected in whatever fashion is most appropriate to the particular task at hand.

1. Margins

The GAR-94 Table reduces assumed mortality rates by an explicit margin of 7%. This margin is due to two adjustments:

(a) A 5% reduction in mortality rates to cover 95% of the random deviations in mortality for groups as small as 3000 lives. The size of the group chosen (3000 lives) was based on the numbers of lives covered by contracts at various insurers. It is anticipated that almost all carriers providing group annuity insurance will have at least this level of coverage in force.

(b) A 2% further reduction in mortality to cover the risk of non-homogeneous insured populations whose longevity is greater than the typical insured plan.

2. Projections

GAR-94 incorporates a defined projection of mortality improvements (that is, decreases in mortality rates) over time. Unlike GAR-94, a projection scale was not directly built into the UP-94 Table mortality rates. However, Scale AA, used to project the GAR-94 mortality rates beyond 1994, is included in the UP-94 Table Report, as are projections of UP-94 to sample future years using Scale AA. The purpose is to supply pension actuaries with tools to project the UP-94 Table based on their judgment about future general mortality trends and the nature and demographic attributes of particular retirement plans.

Scale AA is wholly based on the historic experience of the CSRS and of Social Security—1977 through 1993, by age and sex—with a minimum 0.5% per year improvement at ages under 85. The period 1977 through 1993 was considered a representative historical period on which to base future mortality projections.

The manner in which a scale is used in a particular retirement plan valuation will depend on the actuary's judgment, including:

- Future changes in overall mortality improvement trends
- Future changes in mortality improvement patterns by age and sex from the 1977–1993 period
- The appropriate time period for projecting future mortality improvement
- Particular workforce attributes and anticipated changes in a particular workforce's composition.

Though the incorporation of explicit projection scales has not previously been standard practice in the valuation of retirement plans, we believe that actuaries should carefully consider using mortality trend projection if adopting a version of the UP-94 Table. The argument for use of mortality improvement trends is bolstered by the following observations:

- The trend of mortality improvement has been a long and relatively consistent one in the U.S. throughout this century. The length and consistency of this trend separate it from trends affecting the other experience-related decremental assumptions.
- The preponderance of scientific and demographic literature foresees continued mortality improvement, at least at some level.
- Unlike the UP-84 Table, which was issued in 1975 and projected to a future date (1984), the UP-94 Table will be issued in 1994 and incorporates no margins for mortality improvement after that date except as explicitly projected by the actuary using the table.

However, the need to consider mortality improvement trends in setting assumptions should not be taken to imply that the only appropriate model is one in which mortality improvement trends explicitly appear. In determining liabilities, the actuary must also consider the actual population expected to retire under the plan, the interaction of assumptions, the relevance of various assumptions given alternate plan designs, and the significance of a particular assumption given the overall level of precision in the liability model. Thus the decision to project mortality trends explicitly or implicitly should reflect both the actuary's estimate of the magnitude of future trends and the limitations and approximations inherent in the interaction of these trends with the actuarial model of the benefit plan. Depending on the model, a static table that includes an appropriate degree of mortality projection may be most consistent with the plan benefit and actuarial model.

III. WHY DO THE TABLES DIFFER?

The tables differ because of their intended uses. GAR-94 is constructed for use as an annuity reserve standard to be applied within the constraints of insurance company reserve valuation laws promulgated by the states. As a reserve standard, it is designed to produce reasonably conservative estimates recognizing the statutory and business constraints of insurers. UP-94 is to be used as a tool to construct a table representing a best estimate of future mortality for a particular population under study. It is designed primarily for use by actuaries of uninsured plans. While the process for deriving a best estimate of future mortality may be difficult, the concept of best-estimate mortality is clear. A reserve mortality standard differs in a number of ways from this concept. The following section examines the differences between constraints on a reserve valuation standard and a best-estimate table.

A. GAR-94 and Reserving Standards

The GAR-94 Table would be used to compute statutory minimum reserves for group pension contracts for annuities established in the mid-1990s and later. For such uses, a mortality table must be consistent with both statutory constraints and actuarial standards of practice. Statutory constraints arise under Standard Valuation Laws (SVL) promulgated by the states. These define the use of a standard mortality component when reserves for a particular product or block of business are being established. Actuarial standards of practice include the following:

> *Adequacy of Reserves and Related Items.* In addition to meeting appropriate regulatory requirements, the appointed actuary should use professional judgment to be satisfied that the assets supporting the reserves and related items plus related future revenues, are adequate to cover obligations under moderately adverse conditions. To hold reserves so great that a company could withstand any conceivable circumstances, no matter how adverse, would usually imply an excessive level of reserves. [1]

While this paragraph explicitly discusses assets and related investment returns (whose performance is the most significant experience factor for annuities), it is reasonable to apply it to mortality tables as well. By focusing on the ability to withstand moderately adverse conditions, it seems clear that reserves, as with assets, should be determined on a basis that incorporates additional (but not excessive) conservatism.

Buyers of insurance policies and contracts expect their insurer to be able to deliver benefits many years after the insurer received premium payments. This expectation and contractual promise is helped in part by the insurer holding adequate reserves. These measure the present value of its benefit liabilities and, in the aggregate, are usually determined on a moderately conservative basis.

Based on historical trends in the U.S. and Canada, it seems reasonable that reserves anticipate a continued improvement in mortality. Beyond national trends, a mortality table used for reserves should also be adequate for companies whose customers exhibit lower-than-average mortality and to cover the statistical variations that different moderately sized in-forces may exhibit.

To cover these moderate adverse conditions, the GAR-94 Table incorporates both explicit projection of mortality trends and an explicit reduction in q_x's by a 7% margin. This type of explicit margin is not provided by a best-estimate table like UP-94. Explicit reasonable levels of additional security margin are characteristic of reserve standards. The following section summarizes briefly the need for security margins in developing insurer reserves.

B. Need for Security Margins

While insurer surplus may contain provision for extreme adversity, such as short-term mortality variations (for example, random or low rates of influenza during some year), the insurance company reserve is anticipated to be established using a mortality standard with sufficient security margins to cover most situations. These margins help to lessen the likelihood that additional surplus allocation will be required.

The determination of the size of the margin appropriate to cover potentially adverse experience varies by the type of business being reserved for. There are several reasons why variation may exist. Among them are the following:

1. Size of Annuity Business In Force

As a result of size variation, there is not always the same need to hold conservative reserves. Companies with sufficient contracts in force to absorb adverse experience, by sheer volume, may not require any margin. However, companies with smaller amounts of in-force contracts may not have the ability to absorb adverse experience. To be assured that sufficient reserves are held, a larger margin may be desired for these smaller books of business.

2. Nature of Industry

Depending on the type of business undertaken by the employer of a given contract's participants, anticipated mortality differs from a "typical" business group. Some businesses are inherently safer than other businesses (for example, desk jobs versus coal-mining) and would thus imply a longer life span for the employees being covered by the "safer" business group's contract. The "safer" businesses require a larger reserve be held to account for increased longevity, when compared to "less safe" businesses.

3. Other Demographic Factors

In addition to the type of employment, certain socioeconomic classes tend to experience different rates of mortality incidence. This inherent difference in mortality experience should be reflected in different reserve magnitudes. If we knew in advance which groups had higher or lower mortality and could hold an appropriate reserve, these different levels of experience would be properly addressed and sufficient assets would be allocated. Certainly, in some situations, the reserves should even be less extensive.

SVL requires that a minimum reserve be held by all companies based on standardized assumptions. If the reserve is to incorporate the ability to withstand the moderate adverse deviations anticipated under *ASOP No. 22,* margins must be built in to accommodate the types of variation above.

C. Why Should Future Mortality Improvement Be Incorporated?

Since SVL does not readily change over time, it is imperative that the SVL allow adequate group annuity reserves within the current framework of a given set of laws to minimize the need for future ad hoc reserve strengthening. Unfortunately, in the past, the SVL has not reflected the continuing improvement of mortality in reserve assumptions. While an adequate attempt has been made to modify the impact of artificially low interest rates (which produce unreasonably high reserves), there has been no effort to address the continued improvement in mortality. Since longer lifetimes produce a larger outflow of funds, the reserves allocated for any longer lived groups lose their adequacy over time. Future projection as part of an ongoing Valuation Standard helps to address this concern without resorting to the more difficult task of frequent SVL changes.

Improving mortality can easily erode a given reserve's sufficiency since the ultimate gain or loss of a contract is reflected in payments actually made under it to participants (in addition to what the underlying funds actually earn relative to the interest assumption). The inclusion of mortality improvement in a new Valuation Standard allows the allocated reserve to keep pace with this potentially increasing liability.

Should the rate of mortality improvement change, reflection of recent improvements should at least make the resulting difference in liabilities less important, than had a static table been used.

Larger reserves produced by using mortality improvement factors may still be inadequate, if mortality improves greatly, but they would be less so than if mortality followed the pattern implied from the reserve assumptions. Furthermore, the reserve would undoubtedly be sufficient should mortality improvement slow down or even reverse.

By allowing for such improvement, the new Reserve Standard addresses a need that is not adequately accounted for with the current SVL. By reflecting improved mortality in the SVL, the laws would be better prepared to respond to changes in the likely lengthening of payout period that results from the mortality improvement. It better matches a rapidly improving mortality trend when compared to the current SVL, which does not allow for such mortality improvement. As an example, future mortality improvement shifts could be incorporated more readily by a simple change to the projection scale alone. This obviates the need for a new mortality table while simplifying the updating process.

D. Insurer Business Environment

There are other significant differences in the use of mortality assumptions when contemplating pension funding versus establishing group annuity reserves. The differences relate to timing and the desire to universally apply a set of assumptions as required values. They also relate to the inability for an insurer to request additional premium as initial estimates are revised in light of experience.

1. Reserve Assumptions Are Not Changed Annually

When an insurance company establishes a reserve, the mortality assumption is set by SVL. This SVL prescribes the use of a given interest rate, or set of rates, as well as the mortality table. For any company doing business within any given state, the reserves established for filing purposes must follow the SVL of that particular state. Since most states have adopted the Dynamic Valuation Law, these reserves are based on standard assumptions, which are not frequently modified. The process of changing statutes is typically a multiyear process.

While individual insurance companies may strengthen reserves as needed, there are significant financial and other hurdles in so doing. These include public relations effects, tax deferrals and surplus concerns. Thus it is preferable that reserves be initially established on a somewhat conservative basis.

2. Comparability

Reserves are also important components of insurer Annual Statements. There are many users of insurance company Annual Statements. A critical goal of an Annual Statement is to enable users to compare and evaluate general solvency and strength of a given group of insurers. The reserves shown in the Annual Statement are determined under the same minimum basis for all insurers. By applying a minimum reserve mortality standard, users can be assured that reported liabilities are not distorted, at least on a minimum basis. Of course, to the extent that a standard assumption does not represent the true underlying liabilities, comparability of the strength of given corporate entities is impaired.

3. Inability to Demand Additional Premium

An insurer's need for reserve adequacy is further caused by an inability to demand additional premium under many types of contracts, even if it is suffering losses. This is in direct contrast to the situation for uninsured plans, which are typically funded on an annual basis.

E. How Do Uninsured Plans Address Issues Such as Mortality Projection?

Unlike insurance company reserves, which must comply with SVL and other related laws, the adequacy of an uninsured pension plan's funding program is related to the plan-specific assumptions. These plan assumptions are based on an actuary's best estimate of each specific assumption employed in the funding process. Since the actuary has the opportunity to address and modify these assumptions on an annual basis, if necessary, the accuracy of each individual assumption can be addressed and consequently updated within a reasonable period.

1. Overall Adequacy of Funding Is the Primary Concern

The primary concern of pension funding is that adequate funds exist over the lifetime of a plan to satisfy the liabilities. The plan itself is an ongoing entity with generally a greater portion of liabilities dependent on a number of future contingencies: future hires, salary increases, benefit accruals, turn-over, and a wider variation of investment returns. In fact, these other as-sumptions may have a larger impact on the adequacy of the funding process than the ongoing mortality assumption. Therefore, while mortality improve-ment is as much of a concern to the uninsured pension plan sponsors as it is with an insurance company, there are other assumptions that must be addressed in conjunction with it.

2. Annual Observation Affects Future Funding Assumptions

By doing an annual gain or loss analysis, a pension plan actuary monitors results on an ongoing basis. Through this monitoring process, actuaries can modify the specific assumptions that are proving inadequate. Given the on-going nature of an uninsured plan, it is likely that these assumptions will include more than just the mortality component. Of course, identification of mortality changes may be long deferred, particularly for a relatively young pension plan.

3. Practicality

The relative degree of uncertainty in significantly more important as-sumptions leads to a desire to keep the degree of complexity in the mortality assumption to a minimum. This may argue for the use of a static projected table as an approximation.

IV. WHAT SHOULD ACTUARIES CONSIDER WHEN USING TABLES FOR UNINSURED PLANS?

The role of mortality in determining liabilities for uninsured plans is dif-ferent than the role of a reserve standard for insured plans. Typically, for financial reporting, for determining funding requirements and for calculating tax deductions, the uninsured pension plan actuary is focused on a best estimate of future experience under the plan. We believe that actuaries should directly consider trends in mortality improvement in setting such a best estimate. However, it is also important to recognize that the relevance of the mortality assumption can only be determined by reference to the total environment in which the plan is designed and operates.

Projection of future mortality trends is an issue that should be considered in setting up a best estimate of future experience. A considerable body of evidence has accumulated showing that continuous mortality improvements have occurred throughout most of this century. In our opinion, the continuing pace of medical discovery presents a strong argument that provision should be made for mortality improvement in setting a best estimate—unless significant factors can be demonstrated that would justify not using an improvement trend for current and future retirees under a particular pension plan.

However, the need to consider mortality improvement trends in setting assumptions should not be taken to imply that the only appropriate model is one in which mortality improvement trends explicitly appear. In determining liabilities, actuaries must be concerned with a variety of issues. These include the actual population expected to retire under the plan, the interaction of assumptions, the relevance of various assumptions given alternate plan designs, and the significance of a particular assumption given the overall level of precision in the liability model. In the following sections we consider both the setting of the mortality trend and these other factors as they affect the choice of mortality tables.

A. Projection Scales

Table 1 illustrates the effect of mortality improvement Scale AA when applied to the UP-94 mortality table on a generation basis for a few sample calculations of the present value of an annuity. It shows the present value of benefits for a deferred annuity issued at age 32 and at age 47 with the annuity starting at age 62 and for an immediate annuity issued at age 62, assuming 7% interest. It shows the present values assuming that (1) there is no mortality improvement (UP-94 @ 1994), (2) Scale AA is applied on a generation basis starting in 1994 (UP-94G @ 1994), and (3) Scale AA is applied on a generation basis assuming that mortality rates have already been projected to 2004 (UP-94G @ 2004). It also shows the ratio of the latter two values to the present value assuming no mortality improvement.

TABLE 1

MORTALITY IMPROVEMENT ASSUMPTION ANNUITY FACTORS DEFERRED TO AGE 62

Issue Age	Sex	(1) UP-94 @ 1994	(2) UP-94G @ 1994	(3) (2)/(1)	(4) UP-94G @ 2004	(5) (4)/(1)
32	Male	1.209	1.360	1.125	1.397	1.156
	Female	1.378	1.442	1.046	1.459	1.059
47	Male	3.396	3.646	1.074	3.761	1.107
	Female	3.844	3.950	1.028	3.995	1.039
62	Male	10.081	10.335	1.025	10.591	1.051
	Female	11.036	11.167	1.012	11.266	1.021

For a deferred annuity issued to a male age 32, the mortality improvement scale applied on a generation basis starting in 1994 causes the present value to increase by 12.5%, but the present value of an immediate annuity at age 62 increases by only 2.5%. Thus the use of generational mortality improvement is much more significant for uninsured pension valuations involving active lives than for valuations for retired lives only.

Because of the discount for interest, the present values for deferred annuities are significantly less than those for immediate annuities, but this difference would be reduced if a salary increase assumption were used during the deferral period. Nevertheless, the full impact of the long-term mortality improvement is somewhat lessened because of the discount for interest. In contrast, the mortality improvement assumption would have the greatest impact in long-term open group projections, such as are used for Social Security, because the future payments to beneficiaries are not discounted.

Some actuaries may wish to apply a different scale for projecting trend. Issues in choosing trend are more fully discussed in the UP-94 paper. However, given the relative scarcity of published material evaluating alternative methods of mortality trend projection, we encourage further research into this area.

B. Population Factors

The GAR-94 Table mortality table is unlikely to reflect a best estimate for current uninsured plan populations. This is, in part, because of the inherent conservatism in the table. First, rates are purposely reduced by 5% to ensure that annuity values will be sufficient to cover 95% of random variations in mortality assuming a group of as small as 3000 lives. Margins to cover random variation may lead to systematic overstatement of the expected value of liabilities. Also, when margins for future deviation from expected results are being set, mortality may well be among the least of the uninsured pension actuary's worries. Random deviations due to turnover, retirement, form of benefit distribution, salary scale, and particularly the asset earnings rate may all show more deviation than mortality.

In addition, the GAR-94 Table is loaded by an extra 2% to adjust for groups with better-than-expected mortality. For an uninsured plan, it is anticipated that any adjustment for better or worse mortality for certain groups will only be incorporated based on the experience of that particular group. Thus the *general* margin in the GAR-94 Table for the possibility of having a better-than-average group should be replaced by an adjustment to reflect the likely ratio of experience for the *actual* group covered by the plan who are expected to retire and will elect an annuity form of benefit. The Retirement Plans Experience Committee report [2] demonstrates how mortality may vary for certain groups of average employees that share a particular characteristic.

But more importantly, actuaries should use a table that reflects anticipated experience of the population covered under the plan. Some considerations that may apply include industry, bargained status, and geographic region. Plans with sizable populations should be able to directly compare actual to expected rates.

C. Interaction of Assumptions

The impact of increases in longevity on other assumptions should also be considered. Longer life expectancies may delay retirements for economic reasons. In addition, if the increased longevity is accompanied by increased health, retirements may be further delayed, and disability and termination rates decreased. However, other factors will also affect these rates, including the economy, labor supply and demand, and changes in societal values.

Actuaries must take care to evaluate the significance of mortality improvements in setting other assumptions. Under the UP-94G @ 1994, life expectancies at age 60 for a male employee currently age 35 are approximately 3.5 years longer than under a static version of the table UP-94 @ 1994. This increase in life expectancy may have an impact on a participant's desire and ability to continue working as the cohort of younger workers nears retirement, compared to current workers near retirement. The Appendix demonstrates some simple examples of the effect on plan cost if the participant is assumed to spend some of the extra years of life employed at the same company. Depending on the degree of early-retirement subsidy, the use of projection and retirement at age 62 may provide very similar results to no projection and retirement at age 60 for certain active employees. Of course, the effect of projected longevity on a current retiree population will not be offset by changes in future retirement patterns, and the actuary must determine the extent to which perceived mortality improvement is already embedded in current retirement behavior. Further, the degree to which the extra life expectancy reflects greater health and ability to work must be considered, as must the other pressures urging work or retirement. However, participants' realization of additional life expectancies may well affect retirement and turnover patterns.

D. Plan Design

1. Forms of Benefit

It is not enough to consider the actual plan population and the interaction of longevity with other assumptions. An actuary must also consider the terms that govern payment of benefits under the plan. Most importantly, the actuary must consider the likelihood and value of alternative forms of payment under the plan.

Actual experience under the plan will reflect not only the mortality of annuitants but also the cost associated with election of non-annuity forms. If, for instance, lump sums are calculated on a basis only vaguely related to life expectancy (for example, a cash balance plan), annuitant mortality will matter only to the extent that annuity forms of benefit are elected. For a plan that aggressively communicates the lump-sum value of benefits, annuity forms of payment may be relatively rare. If the actuary does not explicitly model election rates for different forms of benefit, it is important that the mortality table chosen correctly reflect the mortality of future annuitants who will elect an annuity and reflect the implicit mortality of forms of benefit that are not annuity-based. Thus, in general, the annuity table chosen should reflect not just mortality experience but also the interaction of plan terms and participant election of alternative forms of benefit.

2. Postretirement Benefits Other Than Pensions

The actuary must also consider the effect of mortality trend projection on postretirement benefits other than pensions that are provided to pensioners and sometimes to pensioner dependents. These benefits include life insurance, medical benefits, and extension of employee discounts and other fringe benefits. In evaluating the effect of longer lifetimes on a life insurance benefit, it appears that lower liabilities should result. However, the effect of longer lifetimes on medical benefits should be very carefully evaluated in the context of the actual benefits provided under the plan and the assumed linkage (if any) between decreases in mortality and decreases in morbidity.

Current U.S. accounting guidelines, particularly *FAS 106*, appear to assume that the postretirement medical benefit liability can be evaluated as an annuity for an average claim amount at each age. However, it is rare that a medical benefit plan performs precisely as does an annuity. Some plans (for example, pure catastrophic coverage plans with very high deductibles) may function more like life insurance benefits than annuities, whereas other plans (for example, Medicare Part B premium reimbursement programs) may replicate a pure annuity. Actuaries will need to carefully review the use of mortality projection against the methodology for claim projection in evaluating these liabilities. Introduction of a mortality improvement trend into the mortality rates without corresponding changes to the age-related pattern of medical costs could significantly overstate liabilities in certain types of plans. This issue is further complicated by the lack of a consensus on the effects of improved longevity on morbidity patterns.

E. Model Sophistication Issues

The particular choice of mortality trend factors in the GAR-94 Table reflects both the underlying experience of the source pool of data and a desire for a fairly simple model. More complicated projections of mortality trends have been used for some purposes. For instance, Social Security uses a curve to represent mortality trends over the short-term, intermediate and long-term future.

The complications inherent in projecting mortality will interact with the intended use of the table. Social Security is concerned with a very long duration of benefit payout, in part because of issues surrounding the decision to discount or not to discount ultimate cash flows. Uninsured pension plans may be expected to have more interest in the long-term trend than would insured plans, since uninsured plans are more likely to have significant portions of the liability due to benefits yet to be earned.

Practicality issues interact with relative importance of longer term payout periods. To reflect a trend that changes over time requires a significantly greater amount of computer resources. Computer resources are cheap and getting cheaper; however, testing the correctness of increasingly complicated models does not appear to be realizing comparable decreases in cost.

The UP-94 Table paper illustrates how to approximate a fully projected table with a static table. Actuaries will want to consider the importance of the precision of the mortality assumption. As discussed above in the section on interaction of assumptions, in some situations a two-year difference in retirement age appears to be roughly equivalent to the difference between projecting mortality and assuming no mortality improvement. Relatively small changes in assumed rates of return on assets may also overwhelm the mortality projection. Using the same simplified plan and assumptions as in the Appendix, retiree mortality projection has approximately the same effect as a 0.2% to 0.3% change in rate of return assumption. Thus, approximation by a static table may often prove to provide reasonably accurate results.

V. WHAT SHOULD ACTUARIES CONSIDER WHEN USING TABLES FOR INSURED PLANS AND CONTRACTS?

Insurers use mortality tables for a number of purposes in addition to, or in conjunction with, valuing reserves in compliance with SVL. These include:

- Pricing
- Cash-flow testing
- Internal financial projections.

Tables selected by an insurer for these purposes would probably range from the UP-94 Table to the GAR-94 Table, as tempered by company experience and the need for approximations. It is possible that margins for poor experience or further improvement will be supplied by setbacks to static tables, higher profit charges (reduced interest assumption) or loading (a percentage increase to the premium).

A. Pricing

Many mortality patterns selected for nonparticipating annuities are likely to closely approximate the GAR-94 Table. Perhaps the pattern would be slightly less conservative than used for reserving, but still a nonparticipating premium basis should be expected to be adequate more often than not. However, overall company experience from its group annuities, any credible experience from the group being priced, and/or mortality applicable to a dominant socioeconomic group may influence the pattern.

Again, while pricing is likely to employ mortality improvement and contain margins, this may be accomplished using lower interest assumptions with approximately the same price impact, or by using a static table projected several years beyond the current year or by using set of static tables with the same price impact, or by using a series of age setbacks to a static table (the younger the annuitant, the greater the setback). Whatever method selected, females have traditionally been priced with a male table with a six-year setback. Actuaries may wish to reconsider this issue based on the mortality and improvements thereon that are incorporated in the GAR-94 Table, which shows this setback as age-dependent and decreasing over time.

It is assumed that the insurer cannot require additional premium if the mortality assumption or other pricing bases prove inadequate. However, in the case of participating purchase rates, it is possible that retention of gains or margins in the premiums can partially offset this inability. Nonetheless, with participating business, the value of participation rights and the risk the insurer may distribute gains, but later face losses can lead to premiums in excess of nonparticipating levels. While such excesses implicitly consider mortality, they are quite likely to be developed with lower interest assumptions or higher loading (for example, the buyer must contribute the premium plus 10%).

B. Cash-Flow Testing

Often cash-flow projections are associated with tests of reserve adequacy. The conservatism of assumptions in a projection should not be inconsistent with the general philosophy of reserves quoted earlier in this paper.

Thus, a base case might employ a mortality table slightly less conservative but nonetheless similar to the GAR-94 Table. However, where extreme variations of other assumptions are being tested, it might be reasonable to be more liberal with the mortality to avoid the combination of assumptions tested being too extreme. Such tests should somehow consider mortality improvement and of course must utilize any tables required by statute or regulation.

Cash-flow projections are also utilized to measure the Macaulay duration of liability, measuring the extent of cash-flow mismatches, convexity risks, and investment planning. Here mortality tables without margins like UP-94, but with improvement factors, would seem most appropriate. Indeed, improvement may be most important if each year's cash flow is considered crucial, as opposed to approximating the dynamic table with a projected static one. Of course, static table approximations will be closer for immediate annuities than for deferred annuities.

C. Internal Financial Projections

For these purposes we again assume a "base case" projection, not one designed to measure the impact of adverse mortality. The longer the term of the projection, the more mortality improvement assumptions seem needed. However, for one- to five-year projections, a static table and/or UP-94 would probably produce reasonable results. Also, to the extent company experience differs from national levels, that might properly influence short-term projections.

VI. CONCLUSION

We believe that the explicit incorporation of mortality improvement in the GAR-94 Table represents an improvement in the overall level of actuarial practice, made possible by the advent of less expensive computing resources. Actuaries should, in general, consider explicit inclusion of mortality trend in evaluating liabilities. In particular, the inclusion of mortality projection for the purposes of a standard reserving table appears to produce appropriate results, viewed over the duration of benefits covered by the reserving standard and in conjunction with the purposes of the Standard Valuation Laws.

As indicated in the above, however, the GAR-94 Table should not be blindly applied in all circumstances. Instead actuaries must carefully consider the interaction of mortality trend and other assumptions to ensure that the model of future liabilities is appropriately true to the actual liabilities in question. All modeling involves some simplification of underlying realities. It is important that appropriate care be taken in changing a basic feature of a model, to ensure that the model remains true to the underlying realities. Thus, actuaries incorporating an explicit mortality trend should also review models to ensure the model is consistent with an explicit trend.

Finally, it is anticipated that GAR-94 will not be used for projecting realistic best-estimate projections of mortality for most current populations, since—as a reserve standard—it is adjusted to cover the risk of additional longevity for *all* groups, including groups that may have significantly better longevity than the particular group under study. Of course, to the extent that the particular group under study is expected to be particularly long-lived, or if current projections of longevity turn out to be understated, the GAR-94 Table may become appropriate as a best-estimate table. The UP-94 Table differs from the GAR-94 Table by removing the additional explicit margins for conservatism in the GAR-94 Table, and by leaving the degree and duration of mortality projection to the actuary's judgment. Thus, with modification to reflect the underlying population, plan and model limitations, it is designed to be useful in projecting best-estimate liabilities.

ACKNOWLEDGMENTS

The authors acknowledge the significant assistance of other members of the UP-94 Task Force, the Group Annuity Valuation Table Task Force, Committee on Retirement Systems Research, and Committee on Retirement Systems Practice Education and those who provided written comments to the exposure draft of this paper, as well as other individual actuaries. In particular, we thank Judy Anderson, William Crosson, Jeffrey Groves, Edwin Hustead, Michael Johnston, Ethan Kra, Rita Lawlor, Walter McLaughlin, Richard Moody, Michael Mudry, Laurence Pinzur, Kurt Piper, Jeff

Schwartzman, Michael Sze, and Zenaida Samaniego for their written comments.

REFERENCES

1. ACTUARIAL STANDARDS BOARD. "Statutory Statements of Opinion Based on Asset Adequacy Analysis by Appointed Actuaries for Life or Health Insurers," *Actuarial Standard of Practice No. 22.* Washington, D.C., American Academy of Actuaries, April 1993.
2. RETIREMENT PLANS EXPERIENCE COMMITTEE. "Mortality Among Members of Uninsured Pension Systems," *Transactions of the Society of Actuaries 1991-92 Reports of Mortality, Morbidity, and Other Experience* (1993): 45–64

APPENDIX

TABLE A-1

VALUATION AT JANUARY 1, 1994
ENTRY AGE NORMAL COST METHOD

MORTALITY BASED ON THE STATIC UP-94 TABLE WITH NO PROJECTION (UP-94) AND A RETIREMENT AGE OF 60

Other Assumptions

Age	35
Service	10
Pay	$ 35,000
Salary Scale Increase	5%
Interest rate	8%

Results

Normal Cost	$2,560
Accrued Actuarial Liability	$29,985

Year	Age	Service	Pay	1.5% of FAP5	PVPAY	Ret date	Ret PVB
1984	25	0	21,487	0	484,947	0	35,467
1985	26	1	22,561	293	500,537	0	38,304
1986	27	2	23,689	615	516,214	0	41,369
1987	28	3	24,874	969	531,926	0	44,678
1988	29	4	26,118	1,357	547,617	0	48,252
1989	30	5	27,423	1,781	563,219	0	52,112
1990	31	6	28,795	2,244	578,659	0	56,281
1991	32	7	30,234	2,749	593,854	0	60,784
1992	33	8	31,746	3,299	608,709	0	65,647
1993	34	9	33,333	3,897	623,120	0	70,898
1994	35	10	35,000	4,546	636,970	0	76,570
1995	36	11	36,750	5,251	650,127	0	82,696
1996	37	12	38,588	6,014	662,448	0	89,312
1997	38	13	40,517	6,841	673,769	0	96,456
1998	39	14	42,543	7,736	683,912	0	104,173
1999	40	15	44,670	8,703	692,679	0	112,507
2000	41	16	46,903	9,747	699,850	0	121,507

TABLE A-1—*Continued*

Year	Age	Service	Pay	1.5% of FAP5	PVPAY	Ret date	Ret PVB
2001	42	17	49,249	10,874	705,182	0	131,228
2002	43	18	51,711	12,090	708,408	0	141,726
2003	44	19	54,296	13,399	709,233	0	153,064
2004	45	20	57,011	14,810	707,332	0	165,309
2005	46	21	59,862	16,328	702,346	0	178,534
2006	47	22	62,855	17,961	693,883	0	192,817
2007	48	23	65,998	19,716	681,510	0	208,242
2008	49	24	69,298	21,602	664,753	0	224,902
2009	50	25	72,762	23,627	643,092	0	242,894
2010	51	26	76,401	25,800	615,956	0	262,325
2011	52	27	80,221	28,132	582,720	0	283,311
2012	53	28	84,232	30,633	542,699	0	305,976
2013	54	29	88,443	33,313	495,145	0	330,454
2014	55	30	92,865	36,185	439,238	0	356,891
2015	56	31	97,509	39,261	374,082	0	385,442
2016	57	32	102,384	42,554	298,699	0	416,277
2017	58	33	107,503	46,078	212,020	0	449,579
2018	59	34	112,878	49,848	112,878	0	485,546
2019	60	35	118,522	53,880	0	1	524,389
2020	61	36	124,449	58,190	0	0	0
2021	62	37	130,671	62,797	0	0	0
2022	63	38	137,205	67,719	0	0	0
2023	64	39	144,065	72,976	0	0	0

TABLE A-2

VALUATION AT JANUARY 1, 1994
ENTRY AGE NORMAL COST METHOD

MORTALITY BASED ON A FULLY GENERATIONAL VERSION OF THE UP-94 TABLE (UP-94G @ 1994)
BUT WITH A RETIREMENT AGE OF 60

Other Assumptions		Results	
Age	35	Normal Cost	$2,580
Service	10	Accrued Actuarial Liability	$30,219
Pay	$35,000		
Salary Scale Increase	5%		
Interest rate	8%		

Year	Age	Service	Pay	1.5% of FAP5	PVPAY	Ret date	Ret PVB
1984	25	0	21,487	0	500,757	0	36,908
1985	26	1	22,561	293	517,612	0	39,861
1986	27	2	23,689	615	534,654	0	43,050
1987	28	3	24,874	969	551,842	0	46,494
1988	29	4	26,118	1,357	569,126	0	50,213
1989	30	5	27,423	1,781	586,449	0	54,230
1990	31	6	28,795	2,244	603,747	0	58,569
1991	32	7	30,234	2,749	620,949	0	63,254
1992	33	8	31,746	3,299	637,972	0	68,315
1993	34	9	33,333	3,897	654,724	0	73,780
1994	35	10	35,000	4,546	671,102	0	79,682
1995	36	11	36,750	5,251	686,990	0	86,057
1996	37	12	38,588	6,014	702,259	0	92,942
1997	38	13	40,517	6,841	716,765	0	100,377
1998	39	14	42,543	7,736	730,348	0	108,407
1999	40	15	44,670	8,703	742,830	0	117,080
2000	41	16	46,903	9,747	754,013	0	126,446

TABLE A-2—*Continued*

Year	Age	Service	Pay	1.5% of FAP5	PVPAY	Ret date	Ret PVB
2001	42	17	49,249	10,874	763,679	0	136,562
2002	43	18	51,711	12,090	771,584	0	147,487
2003	44	19	54,296	13,399	777,463	0	159,285
2004	45	20	57,011	14,810	781,020	0	172,028
2005	46	21	59,862	16,328	781,930	0	185,791
2006	47	22	62,855	17,961	779,833	0	200,654
2007	48	23	65,998	19,716	774,336	0	216,706
2008	49	24	69,298	21,602	765,006	0	234,043
2009	50	25	72,762	23,627	751,365	0	252,766
2010	51	26	76,401	25,800	732,891	0	272,987
2011	52	27	80,221	28,132	709,009	0	294,826
2012	53	28	84,232	30,633	679,092	0	318,412
2013	54	29	88,443	33,313	642,449	0	343,885
2014	55	30	92,865	36,185	598,326	0	371,396
2015	56	31	97,509	39,261	545,897	0	401,108
2016	57	32	102,384	42,554	484,260	0	433,196
2017	58	33	107,503	46,078	412,426	0	467,852
2018	59	34	112,878	49,848	329,316	0	505,280
2019	60	35	118,522	53,880	233,753	0	545,703
2020	61	36	124,449	58,190	124,449	0	589,359
2021	62	37	130,671	62,797	0	1	636,508
2022	63	38	137,205	67,719	0	0	0
2023	64	39	144,065	72,976	0	0	0

THE 1994 UNINSURED PENSIONER MORTALITY TABLE

SOCIETY OF ACTUARIES UP-94 TASK FORCE[1]

1. EXPERIENCE DATA

The Uninsured Pensioner Mortality Subcommittee[2] was established under the Retirement Plans Experience Committee to develop a recommendation for an uninsured pensioner mortality table, which would thus serve as an update to the UP-1984 Mortality Table (the UP-84 Table).[3]

The Retirement Plans Experience Committee issued a report entitled "Mortality among Members of Uninsured Pension Systems," which appears in the *Transactions of the Society of Actuaries, 1991-92 Reports*. This report compares recent mortality experience for 29 retirement systems with the UP-84 and the 1983 Group Annuity Mortality Table (GAM-83).[4] These systems included the following: Medicare participants in Social Security, the U.S. Federal Civil Service Retirement System (CSRS), the U.S. Military Retirement System, Public Service of Canada, and a combination of 24 private sector systems together with one state system, which is referred to as the private sector uninsured pension plan mortality experience. This report shows that current uninsured pensioner mortality, based on experience from 1985 through 1989, was generally in the range of 82% to 86% of the mortality expected under the UP-84 Table.

When the Uninsured Pensioner Mortality Subcommittee was established, the Group Annuity Valuation Table Task Force was developing a new Group Annuity Mortality Valuation Standard. This standard is based primarily on group annuity mortality experience at ages 66 and older and on CSRS mortality experience for ages under 66. Age is defined as age nearest birthday at the beginning of the year.

The Subcommittee compared the recent experience for uninsured pensioner mortality that had been collected by the Retirement Plans Experience

---

[1]Michael Virga, chairperson, Mark Hanrahan, Ed Hustead, Lindsay Malkevich, Walter Mc-Laughlin, Marilyn Oliver, Thomas Sloan, and Diane Storm.

[2]This subcommittee was set up as a Task Force in the fall of 1994.

[3]The UP-1984 Mortality Table was promulgated in the *Proceedings of the Conference of Actuaries in Public Practice* XXV (1975): 456–507.

[4]The 1983 Group Annuity Mortality Table was promulgated in the *Transactions of the Society of Actuaries* XXXV (1983): 859–900.

Committee with this group annuity mortality experience and concluded that the uninsured experience was sufficiently close to the insured experience, so that it would be reasonable to use the same underlying data as a basis for both tables.

A comparison of the mortality experience for group annuities, CSRS, uninsured pension plans, and the Railroad Retirement System is displayed in Figures 1 (male) and 2 (female). Experience rates for the Railroad Retirement System are included as an example of how the experience for a particular group, which is predominantly blue collar, can differ from the experience used for the proposed table. As presented in Figures 1 and 2, the mortality rates under Railroad Retirement are considerably higher than the other rates shown, at all ages. The mortality rates cover ages 66 through 95 because the group annuity experience was limited to these ages. All these experience rates were first graduated using a Whittaker-Henderson type B formula to simplify the presentation.

The Group Annuity Mortality Experience (GAM-88) covers years 1986 through 1990, as does the CSRS experience (CSRS-88). The private sector uninsured pension plan experience (UPP-88), which was collected by the Retirement Plans Experience Committee, covers years 1985 through 1989, but was adjusted to central year 1988 based on the ratio of CSRS experience for 1986–1990 to the CSRS experience for 1985–1989. The mortality experience for nondisabled retired lives under the Railroad Retirement System (RRR-88) covers policy anniversaries in years 1988–1991 and was adjusted to a central year 1988 based on the ratio of CSRS experience for the respective years.

Table 1 lists these graduated mortality experience rates, and Table 2 shows the ratios of the rates for CSRS, private sector uninsured private pension plans, and Railroad Retirement to the group annuity rates.

2. PROPOSED UP-94 TABLE

The Subcommittee worked closely with the GAM Task Force to develop a common set of mortality improvement trend factors to be used to project the group annuity mortality experience rates from 1988 to 1994 and to

FIGURE 1

GRADUATED MORTALITY EXPERIENCE FOR MALES FOR GROUP ANNUITIES, CIVIL SERVICE RETIREMENT, UNINSURED PENSION PLANS, AND RAILROAD RETIREMENT

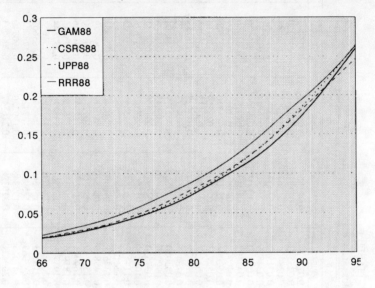

FIGURE 2

GRADUATED MORTALITY EXPERIENCE FOR FEMALES FOR GROUP ANNUITIES, CIVIL SERVICE RETIREMENT, UNINSURED PENSION PLANS, AND RAILROAD RETIREMENT

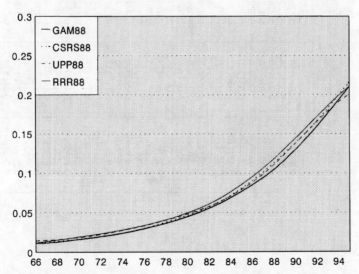

TABLE 1

GRADUATED MORTALITY EXPERIENCE RATES

Age	Male				Female			
	GAM-88	CSRS-88	UPP-88	RRR-88	GAM-88	CSRS-88	UPP-88	RRR-88
66	0.019291	0.019830	0.019690	0.022714	0.011357	0.011772	0.014495	0.012028
67	0.020619	0.021725	0.021895	0.025513	0.011919	0.012814	0.015220	0.013784
68	0.022490	0.023950	0.024532	0.028435	0.013031	0.013965	0.016185	0.015641
69	0.024923	0.026466	0.027113	0.031532	0.014571	0.015303	0.017362	0.017536
70	0.027709	0.029092	0.029575	0.034835	0.016312	0.016824	0.018781	0.019450
71	0.030760	0.031790	0.032285	0.038430	0.018092	0.018469	0.020500	0.021404
72	0.034110	0.034641	0.035674	0.042407	0.019892	0.020205	0.022586	0.023462
73	0.037710	0.038010	0.039812	0.046932	0.021834	0.022075	0.025009	0.025683
74	0.041568	0.041987	0.044323	0.052094	0.024079	0.024230	0.027626	0.028134
75	0.045732	0.046488	0.049067	0.057733	0.026783	0.026869	0.030418	0.030865
76	0.050289	0.051509	0.054302	0.063757	0.029864	0.030113	0.033486	0.033906
77	0.055296	0.057105	0.060363	0.070022	0.033131	0.033928	0.036883	0.037251
78	0.060818	0.063258	0.067107	0.076435	0.036630	0.038073	0.040519	0.040921
79	0.067025	0.069873	0.073933	0.083080	0.040560	0.042379	0.044304	0.044981
80	0.074043	0.076735	0.080648	0.090060	0.045010	0.046843	0.048306	0.049572
81	0.081723	0.084014	0.087512	0.097550	0.049983	0.051736	0.052741	0.054864
82	0.089667	0.092009	0.094918	0.105694	0.055564	0.057343	0.057879	0.061014
83	0.097668	0.100840	0.103074	0.114527	0.061849	0.063855	0.063903	0.068123
84	0.105614	0.110353	0.111850	0.124107	0.068821	0.071462	0.070865	0.076207
85	0.113911	0.120469	0.121186	0.134522	0.076497	0.080246	0.078883	0.085281
86	0.123225	0.131355	0.131299	0.145810	0.084879	0.090212	0.088129	0.095286
87	0.133824	0.143214	0.142430	0.157769	0.094169	0.101211	0.098740	0.106188
88	0.145520	0.156060	0.154600	0.169944	0.104594	0.112951	0.110726	0.117985
89	0.158288	0.169753	0.167461	0.181926	0.116356	0.125226	0.123786	0.130652
90	0.172483	0.184011	0.180597	0.193738	0.129563	0.138110	0.137544	0.144032
91	0.188231	0.198749	0.193776	0.205721	0.144091	0.151794	0.151638	0.157910
92	0.205217	0.214056	0.206887	0.218363	0.159660	0.166536	0.165602	0.171988
93	0.223081	0.230100	0.219987	0.232065	0.175982	0.182425	0.178864	0.185799
94	0.241380	0.246814	0.233184	0.247075	0.192948	0.199250	0.190740	0.198816
95	0.259812	0.263772	0.246742	0.263421	0.210728	0.216547	0.200693	0.210670

TABLE 2

RATIO OF GRADUATED MORTALITY EXPERIENCE RATES
TO GAM-88 GRADUATED MORTALITY RATES

	Male			Female		
Age	CSRS-88/ GAM-88	UPP-88/ GAM-88	RRR-88/ GAM-88	CSRS-88/ GAM-88	UPP-88/ GAM-88	RRR-88/ GAM-88
66	1.028	1.021	1.177	1.037	1.276	1.059
67	1.054	1.062	1.237	1.075	1.277	1.156
68	1.065	1.091	1.264	1.072	1.242	1.200
69	1.062	1.088	1.265	1.050	1.192	1.204
70	1.050	1.067	1.257	1.031	1.151	1.192
71	1.034	1.050	1.249	1.021	1.133	1.183
72	1.016	1.046	1.243	1.016	1.135	1.179
73	1.008	1.056	1.245	1.011	1.145	1.176
74	1.010	1.066	1.253	1.006	1.147	1.168
75	1.017	1.073	1.262	1.003	1.136	1.152
76	1.024	1.080	1.268	1.008	1.121	1.135
77	1.033	1.092	1.266	1.024	1.113	1.124
78	1.040	1.103	1.257	1.039	1.106	1.117
79	1.043	1.103	1.240	1.045	1.092	1.109
80	1.036	1.089	1.216	1.041	1.073	1.101
81	1.028	1.071	1.194	1.035	1.055	1.098
82	1.026	1.059	1.179	1.032	1.042	1.098
83	1.032	1.055	1.173	1.032	1.033	1.101
84	1.045	1.059	1.175	1.038	1.030	1.107
85	1.058	1.064	1.181	1.049	1.031	1.115
86	1.066	1.066	1.183	1.063	1.038	1.123
87	1.070	1.064	1.179	1.075	1.049	1.128
88	1.072	1.062	1.168	1.080	1.059	1.128
89	1.072	1.058	1.149	1.076	1.064	1.123
90	1.067	1.047	1.123	1.066	1.062	1.112
91	1.056	1.029	1.093	1.053	1.052	1.096
92	1.043	1.008	1.064	1.043	1.037	1.077
93	1.031	0.986	1.040	1.037	1.016	1.056
94	1.023	0.966	1.024	1.033	0.989	1.030
95	1.015	0.950	1.014	1.028	0.952	1.000

develop another set of factors to project mortality improvements for years beyond 1994. The factors for projecting mortality improvement from 1988 to 1994 are based on the CSRS mortality experience from 1987 to 1993. The factors for projecting improvement beyond 1994 are based on the average of the CSRS and Social Security mortality improvement trends from 1977 to 1993, with a minimum of 0.5% for ages under 85, and are referred to as Scale AA.

The proposed UP-94 Mortality Table, along with Scale AA, is shown in Table 3.

TABLE 3

UP-94 MORTALITY RATES AND SCALE AA

Age	UP-94 Rates		Scale AA	
	Male	Female	Male	Female
1	0.000637	0.000571	0.020	0.020
2	0.000430	0.000372	0.020	0.020
3	0.000357	0.000278	0.020	0.020
4	0.000278	0.000208	0.020	0.020
5	0.000255	0.000188	0.020	0.020
6	0.000244	0.000176	0.020	0.020
7	0.000234	0.000165	0.020	0.020
8	0.000216	0.000147	0.020	0.020
9	0.000209	0.000140	0.020	0.020
10	0.000212	0.000141	0.020	0.020
11	0.000223	0.000148	0.020	0.020
12	0.000243	0.000159	0.020	0.020
13	0.000275	0.000177	0.020	0.020
14	0.000320	0.000203	0.019	0.018
15	0.000371	0.000233	0.019	0.016
16	0.000421	0.000261	0.019	0.015
17	0.000463	0.000281	0.019	0.014
18	0.000495	0.000293	0.019	0.014
19	0.000521	0.000301	0.019	0.015
20	0.000545	0.000305	0.019	0.016
21	0.000570	0.000308	0.018	0.017
22	0.000598	0.000311	0.017	0.017
23	0.000633	0.000313	0.015	0.016
24	0.000671	0.000313	0.013	0.015
25	0.000711	0.000313	0.010	0.014
26	0.000749	0.000316	0.006	0.012
27	0.000782	0.000324	0.005	0.012
28	0.000811	0.000338	0.005	0.012
29	0.000838	0.000356	0.005	0.012
30	0.000862	0.000377	0.005	0.010
31	0.000883	0.000401	0.005	0.008
32	0.000902	0.000427	0.005	0.008
33	0.000912	0.000454	0.005	0.009
34	0.000913	0.000482	0.005	0.010
35	0.000915	0.000514	0.005	0.011
36	0.000927	0.000550	0.005	0.012
37	0.000958	0.000593	0.005	0.013
38	0.001010	0.000643	0.006	0.014
39	0.001075	0.000701	0.007	0.015
40	0.001153	0.000763	0.008	0.015
41	0.001243	0.000826	0.009	0.015
42	0.001346	0.000888	0.010	0.015
43	0.001454	0.000943	0.011	0.015
44	0.001568	0.000992	0.012	0.015
45	0.001697	0.001046	0.013	0.016
46	0.001852	0.001111	0.014	0.017
47	0.002042	0.001196	0.015	0.018
48	0.002260	0.001297	0.016	0.018
49	0.002501	0.001408	0.017	0.018
50	0.002773	0.001536	0.018	0.017

TABLE 3—*Continued*

Age	UP-94 Rates		Scale AA	
	Male	Female	Male	Female
51	0.003088	0.001686	0.019	0.016
52	0.003455	0.001864	0.020	0.014
53	0.003854	0.002051	0.020	0.012
54	0.004278	0.002241	0.020	0.010
55	0.004758	0.002466	0.019	0.008
56	0.005322	0.002755	0.018	0.006
57	0.006001	0.003139	0.017	0.005
58	0.006774	0.003612	0.016	0.005
59	0.007623	0.004154	0.016	0.005
60	0.008576	0.004773	0.016	0.005
61	0.009663	0.005476	0.015	0.005
62	0.010911	0.006271	0.015	0.005
63	0.012335	0.007179	0.014	0.005
64	0.013914	0.008194	0.014	0.005
65	0.015629	0.009286	0.014	0.005
66	0.017462	0.010423	0.013	0.005
67	0.019391	0.011574	0.013	0.005
68	0.021354	0.012648	0.014	0.005
69	0.023364	0.013665	0.014	0.005
70	0.025516	0.014763	0.015	0.005
71	0.027905	0.016079	0.015	0.006
72	0.030625	0.017748	0.015	0.006
73	0.033549	0.019724	0.015	0.007
74	0.036614	0.021915	0.015	0.007
75	0.040012	0.024393	0.014	0.008
76	0.043933	0.027231	0.014	0.008
77	0.048570	0.030501	0.013	0.007
78	0.053991	0.034115	0.012	0.007
79	0.060066	0.038024	0.011	0.007
80	0.066696	0.042361	0.010	0.007
81	0.073780	0.047260	0.009	0.007
82	0.081217	0.052853	0.008	0.007
83	0.088721	0.058986	0.008	0.007
84	0.096358	0.065569	0.007	0.007
85	0.104559	0.072836	0.007	0.006
86	0.113755	0.081018	0.007	0.005
87	0.124377	0.090348	0.006	0.004
88	0.136537	0.100882	0.005	0.004
89	0.149949	0.112467	0.005	0.003
90	0.164442	0.125016	0.004	0.003
91	0.179849	0.138442	0.004	0.003
92	0.196001	0.152660	0.003	0.003
93	0.213325	0.167668	0.003	0.002
94	0.231936	0.183524	0.003	0.002
95	0.251189	0.200229	0.002	0.002
96	0.270441	0.217783	0.002	0.002
97	0.289048	0.236188	0.002	0.001
98	0.306750	0.255605	0.001	0.001
99	0.323976	0.276035	0.001	0.001

TABLE 3—*Continued*

Age	UP-94 Rates		Scale AA	
	Male	Female	Male	Female
100	0.341116	0.297233	0.001	0.001
101	0.358560	0.318956	0.000	0.000
102	0.376699	0.340960	0.000	0.000
103	0.396884	0.364586	0.000	0.000
104	0.418855	0.389996	0.000	0.000
105	0.440585	0.415180	0.000	0.000
106	0.460043	0.438126	0.000	0.000
107	0.475200	0.456824	0.000	0.000
108	0.485670	0.471493	0.000	0.000
109	0.492807	0.483473	0.000	0.000
110	0.497189	0.492436	0.000	0.000
111	0.499394	0.498054	0.000	0.000
112	0.500000	0.500000	0.000	0.000
113	0.500000	0.500000	0.000	0.000
114	0.500000	0.500000	0.000	0.000
115	0.500000	0.500000	0.000	0.000
116	0.500000	0.500000	0.000	0.000
117	0.500000	0.500000	0.000	0.000
118	0.500000	0.500000	0.000	0.000
119	0.500000	0.500000	0.000	0.000
120	1.000000	1.000000	0.000	0.000

3. COMPARISON WITH OTHER TABLES

The table and scale are intended to provide actuaries with a standard for measuring and projecting the underlying mortality of pension plans, subject to the actuary's judgment on the mortality for the particular group being valued. The UP-94 Mortality Table is the same as the 1994 Group Annuity Mortality Basic Table. It does not include the 7% margin that was included in the 1994 Group Annuity Mortality Static Table (GAM-94 Static). This 7% margin comprises a 5% margin for random variation in mortality rates and a 2% margin for other contingencies.

Although the UP-84 table was primarily designed to be a unisex table, the Subcommittee believes that sex-distinct tables are more appropriate for actuarial valuations, and since sufficient experience is now available to accurately determine female mortality rates, separate tables should be used whenever feasible. In cases in which unisex factors are required, the actuary can combine the results for male and female in a way that would be most appropriate in that particular situation.

Figures 3 and 4 show a comparison of the mortality rates for the UP-94, GAM-94 Static, GAM-83, and UP-84 Tables. For the UP-84 Table, the rates by sex are based on the recommended four-year age setback for males and the one-year age set-forward for females. The actual mortality rates are listed in Appendix A. The ratios of the UP-94 rates to the GAM-83 rates, and the ratios of the UP-94 rates to the UP-84 rates, are shown in Table 4.

4. USE OF PROJECTION SCALE AA

The use of Scale AA to project mortality improvement on a generational basis was not directly incorporated in the UP-94 Mortality Table as it was for the 1994 Group Annuity Reserving Table (GAR-94), which is a combination of the GAM-94 Static Table and Scale AA. Use of the 1994 Group Annuity Reserving Table implies that the GAM-94 Static mortality has been improved on a generational basis using Scale AA.

However, the Subcommittee believes that projection of future mortality trends is an issue that should be considered in setting up a best estimate of future experience for uninsured pension plans. A considerable body of evidence has accumulated showing that continuous mortality improvements have occurred throughout most of this century. We think that the continuing pace of medical discovery presents a strong argument that provision should be made for mortality improvement in setting a best estimate. In other words, the actuary would have to demonstrate significant factors that would justify not using an improvement trend for current and future retirees under a particular pension plan.

The need to consider the mortality improvement trend in setting assumptions should not be taken to imply that the only appropriate model is one in which mortality improvement trends explicitly appear. In determining liabilities, actuaries must be concerned with a variety of issues. These include the actual population expected to retire under the plan, the interaction of assumptions, the relevance of various assumptions given alternate plan designs, and the significance of a particular assumption given the overall level of precision in the liability model.

Scale AA is included to provide actuaries with a tool for projecting the UP-94 Mortality Table, to be applied in accordance with the actuary's

FIGURE 3

COMPARISON OF MORTALITY TABLES FOR MALES

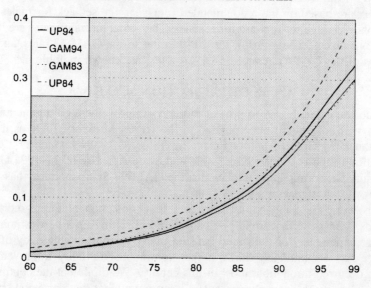

FIGURE 4

COMPARISON OF MORTALITY TABLES FOR FEMALES

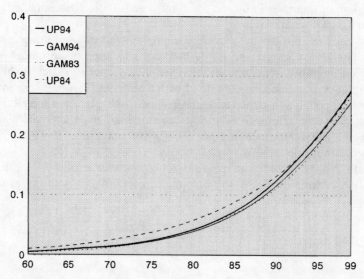

TABLE 4

COMPARISON OF MORTALITY TABLES: RATIOS OF THE UP-94 RATES
TO THE GAM-83 RATES AND TO THE UP-84 RATES

Age	Male		Female	
	UP-94/GAM-83	UP-94/UP-84	UP-94/GAM-83	UP-94/UP-84
1				
2				
3				
4				
5	0.746		1.099	
6	0.767		1.257	
7	0.775		1.398	
8	0.735		1.413	
9	0.716		1.443	
10	0.724		1.469	
11	0.748		1.423	
12	0.799		1.407	
13	0.887		1.451	
14	1.009	0.220	1.550	
15	1.142	0.258	1.664	
16	1.264	0.298	1.752	
17	1.350	0.334	1.767	
18	1.402	0.366	1.744	
19	1.427	0.397	1.682	0.207
20	1.446	0.430	1.614	0.212
21	1.454	0.468	1.532	0.218
22	1.466	0.512	1.467	0.225
23	1.493	0.551	1.391	0.232
24	1.511	0.594	1.310	0.239
25	1.532	0.642	1.237	0.247
26	1.535	0.692	1.179	0.259
27	1.524	0.739	1.141	0.278
28	1.496	0.749	1.119	0.294
29	1.465	0.754	1.113	0.315
30	1.420	0.755	1.102	0.341
31	1.369	0.753	1.102	0.370
32	1.313	0.747	1.101	0.404
33	1.243	0.703	1.097	0.419
34	1.163	0.653	1.088	0.434
35	1.064	0.605	1.080	0.450
36	1.022	0.564	1.096	0.469
37	0.992	0.535	1.106	0.491
38	0.972	0.518	1.122	0.496
39	0.953	0.506	1.136	0.501
40	0.931	0.495	1.147	0.504
41	0.907	0.486	1.154	0.503
42	0.881	0.478	1.146	0.496
43	0.848	0.470	1.120	0.484
44	0.812	0.460	1.079	0.467
45	0.777	0.450	1.036	0.450
46	0.749	0.443	0.995	0.435
47	0.732	0.441	0.967	0.424
48	0.720	0.443	0.949	0.419
49	0.712	0.445	0.936	0.413
50	0.709	0.448	0.933	0.408

TABLE 4—*Continued*

Age	Male		Female	
	UP-94/GAM-83	UP-94/UP-84	UP-94/GAM-83	UP-94/UP-84
51	0.714	0.451	0.940	0.403
52	0.727	0.458	0.956	0.402
53	0.741	0.466	0.967	0.402
54	0.756	0.474	0.968	0.399
55	0.776	0.482	0.970	0.398
56	0.804	0.492	0.983	0.402
57	0.841	0.506	1.012	0.416
58	0.878	0.523	1.049	0.436
59	0.909	0.538	1.087	0.460
60	0.936	0.553	1.125	0.483
61	0.960	0.568	1.164	0.506
62	0.980	0.584	1.204	0.529
63	0.995	0.601	1.244	0.554
64	1.003	0.617	1.283	0.579
65	1.002	0.629	1.315	0.599
66	0.993	0.641	1.333	0.613
67	0.979	0.654	1.333	0.619
68	0.961	0.666	1.304	0.616
69	0.941	0.672	1.251	0.606
70	0.927	0.677	1.192	0.594
71	0.919	0.683	1.138	0.590
72	0.918	0.688	1.098	0.599
73	0.915	0.692	1.067	0.615
74	0.907	0.692	1.039	0.631
75	0.897	0.693	1.017	0.648
76	0.890	0.696	1.002	0.666
77	0.887	0.708	0.994	0.685
78	0.890	0.723	0.990	0.703
79	0.895	0.739	0.986	0.719
80	0.900	0.753	0.986	0.733
81	0.905	0.767	0.992	0.748
82	0.909	0.779	1.003	0.770
83	0.910	0.786	1.016	0.790
84	0.909	0.789	1.028	0.807
85	0.911	0.791	1.042	0.823
86	0.916	0.794	1.058	0.842
87	0.929	0.802	1.077	0.866
88	0.948	0.812	1.097	0.894
89	0.968	0.822	1.110	0.921
90	0.989	0.830	1.119	0.946
91	1.009	0.836	1.125	0.967
92	1.029	0.841	1.126	0.984
93	1.051	0.845	1.121	0.997
94	1.064	0.847	1.112	1.006
95	1.073	0.845	1.098	1.011

TABLE 4—*Continued*

Age	Male		Female	
	UP-94/GAM-83	UP-94/UP-84	UP-94/GAM-83	UP-94/UP-84
96	1.089	0.838	1.079	1.013
97	1.095	0.827	1.064	1.014
98	1.092	0.810	1.048	1.012
99	1.083	0.789	1.029	1.008
100	1.069	0.765	1.007	1.000
101	1.051	0.741	0.981	0.989
102	1.032	0.718	0.950	0.976
103	1.010	0.698	0.921	0.962
104	0.980	0.680	0.890	0.949
105	0.938	0.659	0.851	0.931
106	0.881	0.634	0.803	0.906
107	0.810	0.604	0.744	0.871
108	0.730	0.570	0.679	0.830
109	0.648	0.533	0.612	0.784
110	0.497		0.492	0.736
111				0.686
112				0.636
113				0.586
114				0.541

judgment on future general mortality trends and the nature and demographic attributes of particular retirement plans.

Some actuaries may wish to project the table for a fixed number of years on a static basis, rather than apply mortality improvement on a generational basis. If the mortality rates are projected on a static basis to a specific year, for example, 2004, the projected mortality rate at each age would be given by the following formula:

$$q_x^{2004} = q_x^{1994} \times (1 - AA_x)^{2004-1994}$$

When mortality improvement is applied on a generational basis, the mortality rate for an individual who is age y in the year the decrement is assumed to apply (denoted CYD or calendar year of death) and who was age x in the year of the valuation (denoted CYV or calendar year of valuation) is defined as follows:

$$q_y^{CYV+y-x} = q_y^{1994} \times (1 - AA_y)^{(CYV-1994)+(y-x)}$$

In this formula, the mortality is projected from 1994 to the calendar year of valuation and is also projected from the start of the valuation to the year in which the death is assumed to occur, which is given by the expression

$CYV+y-x$ (and which can also be denoted CYD). Thus, with generational mortality improvement, mortality is projected from 1994 to the calendar year of death, and the formula above can be expressed as follows:

$$q_y^{CYD} = q_y^{1994} \times (1 - AA_y)^{CYD-1994}$$

In some cases, such as a long-term, open-group projection, an actuary may wish to phase Scale AA into a postulated ultimate long-term mortality improvement trend. A phase-in such as this is used in the projections of Social Security benefits that are done by the Office of the Actuary at the Social Security Administration. See Appendix B for further details.

When the UP-94 Mortality Table is projected on a static basis for a fixed number of years, say, to 2004, it can be referred to as the UP-94 @ 2004. (When the UP-94 Mortality Table is not projected, it is not necessary to append @ 1994 to the title.) The mortality rates that are obtained by projecting the UP-94 Mortality Table on a static basis to the year 1999, and to every fifth year thereafter, through the year 2024, are listed in Appendixes E and F.

The UP-94 Mortality Table with full generational mortality improvement, that is, with mortality projected from 1994 to the calendar year of death, can be referred to as the UP-94G. For a valuation year of, say, 1997, the projection of mortality improvement can be thought of as a two-step process: first, the mortality table is projected three years on a static basis from 1994 to the valuation year of 1997, and then it is projected from 1997 to the calendar year of death. With this interpretation in mind, the mortality table for a valuation year 1997 could also be referred to as the UP-94G @ 1997. However, with full generational mortality improvement, it is understood that mortality is first projected to the valuation year, and the designation @ 1997 is not necessary.[5]

In some cases, an actuary may wish to approximate the effect of using full generational mortality improvement by using the UP-94 Mortality Table projected on a static basis for a fixed number of years. The Subcommittee has found an empirical rule of thumb that can be helpful in this respect. The

---

[5]In some cases, an actuary may wish to use a modified version of generational mortality improvement in which the mortality rates would, for example, be the same as for the UP-94G @1997, with the mortality improvement trends applied in exactly the same way, but would be used for a valuation year of, say, 2002. This version of the table could still be referred to as the UP-94G @1997, but in this case the designation @1997 is necessary.

valuation results using the UP-94 Mortality Table with mortality improvement applied on a generational basis turn out to be very close to the results that are obtained by using the UP-94 Mortality Table projected on a static basis for n years, where n is equal to the duration of the liabilities being valued. The "duration" of a liability is the negative of the first derivative of the liability with respect to the change in the valuation interest rate, divided by the liability. For this discussion, the duration is approximated by the following formula:

$$\text{Duration} = \frac{pvb(i) - pvb(i + 0.001)}{pvb(i) \times 0.001}$$

where $pvb(i)$ is the present value of benefits at the valuation interest rate i, and $pvb(i+0.001)$ is the present value of benefits determined with the interest rate increased by one-tenth of one percentage point, that is, by ten basis points.

When the valuation is being performed as of a year that is after 1994, the number of years the static table should be projected should be equal to the duration of the liabilities plus the number of years elapsed between the calendar year of valuation (denoted CYV) and 1994. Thus the mortality rate for each age x is given by the following formula:

$$q_x^{CYV+\text{Duration}} = q_x^{1994} \times (1 - AA_x)^{CYV+\text{Duration}-1994}$$

This formula was tested for deferred and immediate annuities at various issue ages, and for hypothetical populations of active and retired employees, using valuation interest rates of 3%, 7%, and 11%. It was also tested for valuations of the Civil Service Retirement System. The error in using this rule of thumb is generally less than one-half of one percent. See Appendix G for further details.

5. EFFECT OF PROJECTION SCALE AA

To compare the UP-94 Mortality Table with other mortality tables, and to compare the effect of different ways of projecting mortality improvement for the UP-94 Mortality Table, it is helpful to compare the annuity values based on these different tables. Such comparisons can be seen most easily by examining the ratios of the annuity values based on each of the different mortality tables to the values based on the UP-94 Mortality Table.

In Table 5 and Appendix C, the annuity values for the UP-94 Mortality Table are compared with the annuity values for the following mortality

TABLE 5

RATIO OF THE NET SINGLE PREMIUM FOR A LIFE ANNUITY TO THE PREMIUM BASED ON THE UP-94 TABLE, ASSUMING 7% INTEREST (DEFERRED TO AGE 62 FOR AGES UNDER 62, IMMEDIATE FOR AGES OVER 62)

Age	UP-94 @2004	UP-94 @2014	UP-94 @2024	UP-94G @1994	GAM-94 Static	GAR-94	GAM-83	UP-84
Male								
20	1.041	1.078	1.113	1.162	1.023	1.179	0.972	0.828
25	1.040	1.077	1.112	1.147	1.023	1.165	0.971	0.830
30	1.040	1.077	1.111	1.131	1.022	1.149	0.970	0.831
35	1.040	1.077	1.110	1.115	1.022	1.133	0.969	0.833
40	1.040	1.076	1.109	1.098	1.022	1.117	0.969	0.836
45	1.039	1.075	1.107	1.081	1.021	1.100	0.970	0.842
50	1.037	1.072	1.103	1.063	1.020	1.082	0.974	0.853
55	1.034	1.066	1.095	1.046	1.019	1.064	0.980	0.871
60	1.029	1.056	1.081	1.031	1.017	1.047	0.985	0.897
65	1.030	1.058	1.084	1.025	1.018	1.043	0.982	0.904
70	1.036	1.069	1.100	1.022	1.023	1.045	0.971	0.894
75	1.037	1.073	1.106	1.017	1.029	1.046	0.963	0.885
80	1.034	1.067	1.100	1.012	1.035	1.048	0.964	0.885
85	1.030	1.060	1.089	1.008	1.043	1.051	0.977	0.880
90	1.022	1.044	1.066	1.004	1.052	1.056	1.022	0.878
95	1.014	1.027	1.041	1.002	1.062	1.063	1.064	0.848

TABLE 5—Continued

Age	UP-94 @2004	UP-94 @2014	UP-94 @2024	UP-94G @1994	GAM-94 Static	GAR-94	GAM-83	UP-84
				Female				
20	1.014	1.028	1.041	1.061	1.016	1.075	1.020	0.859
25	1.014	1.028	1.041	1.055	1.016	1.069	1.019	0.863
30	1.014	1.027	1.040	1.049	1.015	1.063	1.019	0.867
35	1.014	1.027	1.039	1.042	1.015	1.056	1.019	0.870
40	1.013	1.026	1.038	1.036	1.015	1.050	1.019	0.873
45	1.013	1.025	1.037	1.030	1.015	1.044	1.018	0.877
50	1.012	1.023	1.034	1.024	1.014	1.038	1.018	0.884
55	1.011	1.021	1.031	1.019	1.014	1.032	1.019	0.896
60	1.010	1.019	1.028	1.014	1.012	1.026	1.018	0.916
65	1.011	1.022	1.032	1.012	1.014	1.026	1.018	0.920
70	1.015	1.029	1.042	1.012	1.018	1.030	1.012	0.911
75	1.019	1.037	1.054	1.011	1.023	1.034	1.009	0.914
80	1.021	1.041	1.060	1.009	1.029	1.038	1.018	0.926
85	1.018	1.036	1.054	1.006	1.037	1.042	1.041	0.951
90	1.015	1.029	1.044	1.003	1.046	1.049	1.060	0.989
95	1.010	1.021	1.031	1.001	1.055	1.057	1.039	1.005

tables: UP-94 @ 2004, UP-94 @ 2014, UP-94 @ 2024, UP-94G @ 1994, GAM-94 Static, GAR-94, GAM-83, and UP-84. The annuity values based on the GAM-94 Static Table are based on the mortality table for 1994 and do not reflect any mortality improvement for years beyond 1994. For ages under 62, the annuity being valued is a deferred annuity payable at the beginning of each month, commencing at age 62 and issued at five-year age intervals, from age 20 through 60. For ages over 62, it is an immediate annuity payable at the beginning of each month, issued at five-year age intervals, from age 65 through 95. These annuity values are based on 7% interest. The ratios of the annuity values for each of these tables to the annuity values for the UP-94 Mortality Table are shown in Table 5, while the actual annuity values are listed in Appendix C.

6. OTHER COMPARISONS

It may also be helpful to compare the effect on the annuity values of using different interest rates with the effect of using different mortality tables or different mortality improvement trends. These comparisons can be facilitated by examining the ratios of the annuity values based on certain alternative interest rates to the annuity values based on the 7% interest rate. Table 6

TABLE 6

COMPARISON OF NET SINGLE PREMIUMS FOR LIFE ANUITIES FOR THE UP-94 TABLE
(DEFERRED TO AGE 62 FOR AGES UNDER 62; IMMEDIATE FOR AGES OVER 62)

| | Ratio of the Premiums Assuming 8% and 9% Interest to the Premium Assuming 7% Interest | | | |
| | Male | | Female | |
Age	8%	9%	8%	9%
20	0.629	0.399	0.624	0.393
25	0.659	0.437	0.654	0.431
30	0.690	0.480	0.685	0.473
35	0.723	0.526	0.718	0.519
40	0.757	0.577	0.752	0.569
45	0.793	0.633	0.788	0.625
50	0.831	0.695	0.825	0.685
55	0.871	0.762	0.865	0.752
60	0.912	0.836	0.906	0.825
65	0.934	0.876	0.927	0.864
70	0.942	0.891	0.936	0.879
75	0.951	0.906	0.945	0.895
80	0.959	0.922	0.954	0.911
85	0.967	0.937	0.963	0.928
90	0.975	0.951	0.971	0.943
95	0.981	0.962	0.978	0.957

shows these ratios for alternative interest assumptions of 8% and 9%. The actual annuity values are shown in Appendix D.

Table 7 shows a comparison of the expected age at death for each of these mortality tables. It is equal to the current age plus the life expectancy at that age.

ACKNOWLEDGMENT

The Subcommittee expresses its special appreciation to Christopher Bone for his many helpful comments and suggestions, and also thanks the following persons who provided written comments on the UP-94 Exposure Draft: Robert L. Brown, William H. Crosson, Gene B. Fife, Ed Hustead, Harvey Fishman, Zachary Granovetter, Paul H. Jackson, G. Thomas Mitchell, Richard L. Moody, Michael Mudry, John Nader, Donald W. Parkyn, Kurt F. Piper, Owen A. Reed, Joe Sullivan, Shaun Wang, David A. Wiener, and William S. Wright.

TABLE 7

COMPARISON OF EXPECTED AGE AT DEATH
(CURRENT AGE PLUS LIFE EXPECTANCY)

Age	UP-94	UP-94 @2004	UP-94 @2014	UP-94 @2024	UP-94G @1994	GAM-94 Static	GAR-94	GAM-83	UP-84
				Male					
20	78.6	79.9	81.0	82.1	83.9	79.4	84.6	77.9	73.8
25	78.8	80.0	81.1	82.2	83.6	79.6	84.3	78.0	74.1
30	79.0	80.2	81.3	82.4	83.3	79.7	84.0	78.1	74.3
35	79.2	80.4	81.5	82.6	83.0	79.9	83.7	78.3	74.6
40	79.4	80.6	81.7	82.7	82.7	80.1	83.4	78.5	74.9
45	79.7	80.8	81.9	82.9	82.4	80.4	83.1	78.7	75.4
50	80.0	81.1	82.2	83.2	82.2	80.7	82.9	79.2	76.0
55	80.5	81.5	82.5	83.5	82.2	81.1	82.9	79.8	76.9
60	81.2	82.2	83.1	83.9	82.5	81.8	83.1	80.6	78.1
65	82.3	83.1	83.9	84.7	83.1	82.8	83.7	81.7	79.7
70	83.8	84.5	85.2	85.9	84.3	84.3	84.9	83.2	81.7
75	85.7	86.2	86.7	87.2	86.0	86.1	86.4	85.2	84.0
80	88.0	88.3	88.7	89.0	88.1	88.4	88.5	87.6	86.8
85	90.9	91.1	91.3	91.5	90.9	91.2	91.3	90.7	90.0
90	94.2	94.3	94.4	94.5	94.2	94.4	94.4	94.3	93.5
95	97.9	98.0	98.0	98.1	98.0	98.2	98.2	98.2	97.4

TABLE 7—*Continued*

Age	UP-94	UP-94 @2004	UP-94 @2014	UP-94 @2024	UP-94G @1994	GAM-94 Static	GAR-94	GAM-83	UP-84
Female									
20	83.4	84.0	84.6	85.1	86.2	84.1	86.9	84.1	78.4
25	83.5	84.1	84.7	85.2	86.0	84.2	86.7	84.2	78.8
30	83.6	84.2	84.7	85.3	85.9	84.3	86.5	84.3	79.1
35	83.7	84.3	84.8	85.4	85.7	84.4	86.4	84.4	79.3
40	83.8	84.4	84.9	85.5	85.6	84.5	86.2	84.5	79.6
45	84.0	84.6	85.1	85.6	85.5	84.7	86.2	84.7	79.9
50	84.2	84.7	85.2	85.7	85.5	84.9	86.1	84.9	80.4
55	84.5	85.0	85.5	85.9	85.5	85.2	86.2	85.2	81.0
60	85.0	85.4	85.9	86.3	85.8	85.6	86.4	85.7	81.9
65	85.7	86.1	86.5	87.0	86.3	86.3	86.9	86.3	83.1
70	86.8	87.2	87.6	87.9	87.2	87.3	87.7	87.1	84.7
75	88.1	88.5	88.8	89.1	88.4	88.6	88.9	88.4	86.7
80	89.9	90.2	90.4	90.7	90.0	90.3	90.5	90.2	89.0
85	92.2	92.3	92.5	92.7	92.2	92.5	92.6	92.6	91.8
90	95.0	95.1	95.2	95.3	95.1	95.3	95.4	95.4	95.0
95	98.5	98.6	98.6	98.6	98.5	98.8	98.8	98.7	98.5

839

APPENDIX A

COMPARISON OF MORTALITY RATES FOR VARIOUS MORTALITY TABLES

Age	Male				Female			
	UP-94	GAM-94 Static	GAM-83	UP-84	UP-94	GAM-94 Static	GAM-83	UP-84
1	0.000637	0.000592			0.000571	0.000531		
2	0.000430	0.000400			0.000372	0.000346		
3	0.000357	0.000332			0.000278	0.000258		
4	0.000278	0.000259			0.000208	0.000194		
5	0.000255	0.000237	0.000342		0.000188	0.000175	0.000171	
6	0.000244	0.000227	0.000318		0.000176	0.000163	0.000140	
7	0.000234	0.000217	0.000302		0.000165	0.000153	0.000118	
8	0.000216	0.000201	0.000294		0.000147	0.000137	0.000104	
9	0.000209	0.000194	0.000292		0.000140	0.000130	0.000097	
10	0.000212	0.000197	0.000293		0.000141	0.000131	0.000096	
11	0.000223	0.000208	0.000298		0.000148	0.000138	0.000104	
12	0.000243	0.000226	0.000304		0.000159	0.000148	0.000113	
13	0.000275	0.000255	0.000310		0.000177	0.000164	0.000122	
14	0.000320	0.000297	0.000317	0.001453	0.000203	0.000189	0.000131	
15	0.000371	0.000345	0.000325	0.001437	0.000233	0.000216	0.000140	
16	0.000421	0.000391	0.000333	0.001414	0.000261	0.000242	0.000149	
17	0.000463	0.000430	0.000343	0.001385	0.000281	0.000262	0.000159	
18	0.000495	0.000460	0.000353	0.001351	0.000293	0.000273	0.000168	
19	0.000521	0.000484	0.000365	0.001311	0.000301	0.000280	0.000179	0.001453
20	0.000545	0.000507	0.000377	0.001267	0.000305	0.000284	0.000189	0.001437

APPENDIX A—*Continued*

	Male				Female			
Age	UP-94	GAM-94 STATIC	GAM-83	UP-84	UP-94	GAM-94 STATIC	GAM-83	UP-84
21	0.000570	0.000530	0.000392	0.001219	0.000308	0.000286	0.000201	0.001414
22	0.000598	0.000556	0.000408	0.001167	0.000311	0.000289	0.000212	0.001385
23	0.000633	0.000589	0.000424	0.001149	0.000313	0.000292	0.000225	0.001351
24	0.000671	0.000624	0.000444	0.001107	0.000313	0.000291	0.000239	0.001311
25	0.000711	0.000661	0.000464	0.001107	0.000313	0.000291	0.000253	0.001267
26	0.000749	0.000696	0.000488	0.001083	0.000316	0.000294	0.000268	0.001219
27	0.000782	0.000727	0.000513	0.001058	0.000324	0.000302	0.000284	0.001167
28	0.000811	0.000754	0.000542	0.001083	0.000338	0.000314	0.000302	0.001149
29	0.000838	0.000779	0.000572	0.001111	0.000356	0.000331	0.000320	0.001129
30	0.000862	0.000801	0.000607	0.001141	0.000377	0.000351	0.000342	0.001107
31	0.000883	0.000821	0.000645	0.001173	0.000401	0.000373	0.000364	0.001083
32	0.000902	0.000839	0.000687	0.001208	0.000427	0.000397	0.000388	0.001058
33	0.000912	0.000848	0.000734	0.001297	0.000454	0.000422	0.000414	0.001083
34	0.000913	0.000849	0.000785	0.001398	0.000482	0.000449	0.000443	0.001111
35	0.000915	0.000851	0.000860	0.001513	0.000514	0.000478	0.000476	0.001141
36	0.000927	0.000862	0.000907	0.001643	0.000550	0.000512	0.000502	0.001173
37	0.000958	0.000891	0.000966	0.001792	0.000593	0.000551	0.000536	0.001208
38	0.001010	0.000939	0.001039	0.001948	0.000643	0.000598	0.000573	0.001297
39	0.001075	0.000999	0.001128	0.002125	0.000701	0.000652	0.000617	0.001398
40	0.001153	0.001072	0.001238	0.002327	0.000763	0.000709	0.000665	0.001513

APPENDIX A—*Continued*

Age	Male				Female			
	UP-94	GAM-94 Static	GAM-83	UP-84	UP-94	GAM-94 Static	GAM-83	UP-84
41	0.001243	0.001156	0.001370	0.002556	0.000826	0.000768	0.000716	0.001643
42	0.001346	0.001252	0.001527	0.002818	0.000888	0.000825	0.000775	0.001792
43	0.001454	0.001352	0.001715	0.003095	0.000943	0.000877	0.000842	0.001948
44	0.001568	0.001458	0.001932	0.003410	0.000992	0.000923	0.000919	0.002125
45	0.001697	0.001578	0.002183	0.003769	0.001046	0.000973	0.001010	0.002327
46	0.001852	0.001722	0.002471	0.004180	0.001111	0.001033	0.001117	0.002556
47	0.002042	0.001899	0.002790	0.004635	0.001196	0.001112	0.001237	0.002818
48	0.002260	0.002102	0.003138	0.005103	0.001297	0.001206	0.001366	0.003095
49	0.002501	0.002326	0.003513	0.005616	0.001408	0.001310	0.001505	0.003410
50	0.002773	0.002579	0.003909	0.006196	0.001536	0.001428	0.001647	0.003769
51	0.003088	0.002872	0.004324	0.006853	0.001686	0.001568	0.001793	0.004180
52	0.003455	0.003213	0.004755	0.007543	0.001864	0.001734	0.001949	0.004635
53	0.003854	0.003584	0.005200	0.008278	0.002051	0.001907	0.002120	0.005103
54	0.004278	0.003979	0.005660	0.009033	0.002241	0.002084	0.002315	0.005616
55	0.004758	0.004425	0.006131	0.009875	0.002466	0.002294	0.002541	0.006196
56	0.005322	0.004949	0.006618	0.010814	0.002755	0.002563	0.002803	0.006853
57	0.006001	0.005581	0.007139	0.011863	0.003139	0.002919	0.003103	0.007543
58	0.006774	0.006300	0.007719	0.012952	0.003612	0.003359	0.003443	0.008278
59	0.007623	0.007090	0.008384	0.014162	0.004154	0.003863	0.003821	0.009033
60	0.008576	0.007976	0.009158	0.015509	0.004773	0.004439	0.004241	0.009875

APPENDIX A—*Continued*

Age	Male				Female			
	UP-94	GAM-94 Static	GAM-83	UP-84	UP-94	GAM-94 Static	GAM-83	UP-84
61	0.009663	0.008986	0.010064	0.017010	0.005476	0.005093	0.004703	0.010814
62	0.010911	0.010147	0.011133	0.018685	0.006271	0.005832	0.005210	0.011863
63	0.012335	0.011471	0.012391	0.020517	0.007179	0.006677	0.005769	0.012952
64	0.013914	0.012940	0.013868	0.022562	0.008194	0.007621	0.006386	0.014162
65	0.015629	0.014535	0.015592	0.024847	0.009286	0.008636	0.007064	0.015509
66	0.017462	0.016239	0.017579	0.027232	0.010423	0.009694	0.007817	0.017010
67	0.019391	0.018034	0.019804	0.029634	0.011574	0.010764	0.008681	0.018685
68	0.021354	0.019859	0.022229	0.032073	0.012648	0.011763	0.009702	0.020517
69	0.023364	0.021729	0.024817	0.034743	0.013665	0.012709	0.010922	0.022562
70	0.025516	0.023730	0.027530	0.037667	0.014763	0.013730	0.012385	0.024847
71	0.027905	0.025951	0.030354	0.040871	0.016079	0.014953	0.014128	0.027232
72	0.030625	0.028481	0.033370	0.044504	0.017748	0.016506	0.016160	0.029634
73	0.033549	0.031201	0.036680	0.048504	0.019724	0.018344	0.018481	0.032073
74	0.036614	0.034051	0.040388	0.052913	0.021915	0.020381	0.021092	0.034743
75	0.040012	0.037211	0.044597	0.057775	0.024393	0.022686	0.023992	0.037667
76	0.043933	0.040858	0.049388	0.063142	0.027231	0.025325	0.027185	0.040871
77	0.048570	0.045171	0.054758	0.068628	0.030501	0.028366	0.030672	0.044504
78	0.053991	0.050211	0.060678	0.074648	0.034115	0.031727	0.034459	0.048504
79	0.060066	0.055861	0.067125	0.081256	0.038024	0.035362	0.038549	0.052913
80	0.066696	0.062027	0.074070	0.088518	0.042361	0.039396	0.042945	0.057775

APPENDIX A—*Continued*

Age	Male				Female			
	UP-94	GAM-94 Static	GAM-83	UP-84	UP-94	GAM-94 Static	GAM-83	UP-84
81	0.073780	0.068615	0.081484	0.096218	0.047260	0.043952	0.047655	0.063142
82	0.081217	0.075532	0.089320	0.104310	0.052853	0.049153	0.052691	0.068628
83	0.088721	0.082510	0.097525	0.112816	0.058986	0.054857	0.058071	0.074648
84	0.096358	0.089613	0.106047	0.122079	0.065569	0.060979	0.063807	0.081256
85	0.104559	0.097240	0.114836	0.132174	0.072836	0.067738	0.069918	0.088518
86	0.113755	0.105792	0.124170	0.143179	0.081018	0.075347	0.076570	0.096218
87	0.124377	0.115671	0.133870	0.155147	0.090348	0.084023	0.083870	0.104310
88	0.136537	0.126980	0.144073	0.168208	0.100882	0.093820	0.091935	0.112816
89	0.149949	0.139452	0.154859	0.182461	0.112467	0.104594	0.101354	0.122079
90	0.164442	0.152931	0.166307	0.198030	0.125016	0.116265	0.111750	0.132174
91	0.179849	0.167260	0.178214	0.215035	0.138442	0.128751	0.123076	0.143179
92	0.196001	0.182281	0.190460	0.232983	0.152660	0.141973	0.135630	0.155147
93	0.213325	0.198392	0.203007	0.252545	0.167668	0.155931	0.149577	0.168208
94	0.231936	0.215700	0.217904	0.273878	0.183524	0.170677	0.165103	0.182461
95	0.251189	0.233606	0.234086	0.297152	0.200229	0.186213	0.182419	0.198030
96	0.270441	0.251510	0.248436	0.322553	0.217783	0.202538	0.201757	0.215035
97	0.289048	0.268815	0.263954	0.349505	0.236188	0.219655	0.222044	0.232983
98	0.306750	0.285277	0.280803	0.378865	0.255605	0.237713	0.243899	0.252545
99	0.323976	0.301298	0.299154	0.410875	0.276035	0.256712	0.268185	0.273878
100	0.341116	0.317238	0.319185	0.445768	0.297233	0.276427	0.295187	0.297152

APPENDIX A—Continued

Age	Male				Female			
	UP-94	GAM-94 Static	GAM-83	UP-84	UP-94	GAM-94 Static	GAM-83	UP-84
101	0.358560	0.333461	0.341086	0.483830	0.318956	0.296629	0.325225	0.322553
102	0.376699	0.350330	0.365052	0.524301	0.340960	0.317093	0.358897	0.349505
103	0.396884	0.368542	0.393102	0.568365	0.364586	0.338505	0.395843	0.378865
104	0.418855	0.387855	0.427255	0.616382	0.389996	0.361016	0.438360	0.410875
105	0.440585	0.407224	0.469531	0.668696	0.415180	0.383597	0.487816	0.445768
106	0.460043	0.425599	0.521945	0.725745	0.438126	0.405217	0.545886	0.483830
107	0.475200	0.441935	0.586518	0.786495	0.456824	0.424846	0.614309	0.524301
108	0.485670	0.457553	0.665268	0.852659	0.471493	0.444368	0.694885	0.568365
109	0.492807	0.473150	0.760215	0.924666	0.483473	0.464469	0.789474	0.616382
110	0.497189	0.486745	1.000000		0.492436	0.482325	1.000000	0.668696
111	0.499394	0.496356			0.498054	0.495110		0.725745
112	0.500000	0.500000			0.500000	0.500000		0.786495
113	0.500000	0.500000			0.500000	0.500000		0.852659
114	0.500000	0.500000			0.500000	0.500000		0.924666
115	0.500000	0.500000			0.500000	0.500000		
116	0.500000	0.500000			0.500000	0.500000		
117	0.500000	0.500000			0.500000	0.500000		
118	0.500000	0.500000			0.500000	0.500000		
119	0.500000	0.500000			0.500000	0.500000		
120	1.000000	1.000000			1.000000	1.000000		

APPENDIX B

ISSUES IN CHOOSING A MORTALITY IMPROVEMENT TREND

Social Security Trends

The methods and assumptions used in determining the mortality improvement trends for Social Security are summarized in *Actuarial Study No. 107*. As part of this process, the long-term trends in age-adjusted central death rates were first examined. The average annual rates of improvement, which appear in Table 4 on page 9 of *Actuarial Study No. 107*, are summarized below. The data reveal several distinct periods of mortality improvement since 1900.

AVERAGE ANNUAL REDUCTIONS IN AGE-ADJUSTED CENTRAL DEATH RATES

Age	1900–36	1936–54	1954–68	1968–82	1982–88	1900–88
			Male			
25–64	0.87%	1.69%	−0.18%	2.27%	0.79%	1.09%
65+	0.21	1.15	−0.32	1.49	0.23	0.52
			Female			
25–64	1.07	3.30	0.62	2.13	0.61	1.59
65+	0.33	1.84	0.79	2.01	−0.17	0.95

Because the reduction in mortality has varied greatly by cause of death, for purposes of determining the Social Security mortality improvement trend assumptions, mortality rates were also calculated and analyzed by age group and sex for ten different groups of causes of death.

After these past trends had been examined, ultimate annual percentage reductions in central death rates were postulated for years after 2016, by age, sex, and cause of death, after considering such factors as: the development and application of new diagnostic, surgical and life sustaining techniques; the presence of environmental pollutants; improvements in exercise and nutrition; the incidence of violence; the isolation and treatment of causes of disease; the emergence of new forms of disease; improvements in prenatal care; the prevalence of cigarette smoking; the misuse of drugs (including alcohol); the extent to which people assume responsibility for their own health; education on health; and changes in our conception of the value of life.

For years after 1990, the reductions in mortality were assumed to gradually change from an initial rate of 100% of the average annual reductions observed for the 1968–88 period to the postulated ultimate percentage reductions, which were assumed to apply after the year 2016. These ultimate trend rates are generally in the range of 0.5% to 0.6% per year, depending on age.

Use of an Ultimate Trend

Scale AA is based on an average of Social Security and Civil Service overall mortality improvement trends, based on experience for the years 1977 through 1993, and it applies to all future years and does not phase into a different long-term ultimate trend. However, for some applications, such as a long-term open group projection, an actuary may prefer to phase Scale AA into some ultimate trend, which can be denoted "Scale AB." For example, Scale AB may be 0.005 (that is, 0.5%) for all ages, or it might be the lesser of 0.005 and Scale AA. First, we shall assume that the phase-in is over 30 years, from 1994 to 2024.

If a linear interpolation is used, for a person age y, the mortality improvement factor in calendar year CY would be:

$$1 - AA_y \times (2024 - CY)/30 - AB_y \times (CY - 1994)/30$$

However, when using a linear interpolation formula such as this, it is not possible to come up with a simple mathematical expression for the cumulative improvement for each year in the future, and a geometric interpolation formula works better, where the mortality improvement factor in the year CY would be:

$$(1 - AA_y)^{(2024-CY)/30} \times (1 - AB_y)^{(CY-1994)/30}$$

When generational mortality improvement is applied, the mortality rate is projected to the year in which the decrement is assumed to occur, which we denote CYD, or calendar year of death. Using geometric interpolation (and assuming the 30-year phase-in), it can be shown that if the mortality rate in 1994 at age y is q_y^{1994}, then the mortality rate in the year CYD is:

$$q_y^{CYD} = q_y^{1994} \times (1 - AA_y)^{(CYD-1994)(2053-CYD)/60}$$
$$\times (1 - AB_y)^{(CYD-1994)(CYD-1993)/60}$$

This formula would be true for CYD less than or equal 2024. For years greater than 2024, the formula would be:

$$q_y^{CYD} = q_y^{1994} \times (1 - AA_y)^{14.5} \times (1 - AB_y)^{CYD-1994-14.5}$$

In the more general case, in which the mortality improvement is being phased from Scale AA to Scale AB over N years (rather than 30 years in the example shown above), the mortality rate in year CYD would be:

$$q_y^{CYD} = q_y^{1994} \times (1 - AA_y)^{(CYD-1994)(1993+2N-CYD)/2N}$$
$$\times (1 - AB_y)^{(CYD-1994)(CYD-1993)/2N}$$

This formula would be true for a CYD less than or equal 1994+N. For years greater than 1994+N, the formula would be:

$$q_y^{CYD} = q_y^{1994} \times (1 - AA_y)^{(N-1)/2} \times (1 - AB_y)^{CYD-1994-(N-1)/2}$$

Note that if the Scale AB were equal to Scale AA at a particular age, the above formulas would simplify to the following at that age:

$$q_y^{CYD} = q_y^{1994} \times (1 - AA_y)^{(CYD-1994)}.$$

APPENDIX C

COMPARISON OF NET SINGLE PREMIUMS FOR LIFE ANNUITIES ASSUMING 7% INTEREST
(DEFERRED TO AGE 62 FOR AGES UNDER 62, IMMEDIATE FOR AGES OVER 62)

Age	UP-94	UP-94 @2004	UP-94 @2014	UP-94 @2024	UP-94G 1994	GAM-94 Static	GAR-94	GAM-83	UP-84
					Male				
20	0.532	0.554	0.574	0.592	0.618	0.544	0.628	0.517	0.440
25	0.749	0.779	0.807	0.832	0.859	0.766	0.872	0.727	0.621
30	1.054	1.096	1.135	1.171	1.192	1.078	1.212	1.023	0.876
35	1.485	1.544	1.599	1.649	1.656	1.518	1.683	1.439	1.237
40	2.093	2.176	2.252	2.322	2.298	2.138	2.338	2.029	1.750
45	2.956	3.071	3.176	3.273	3.194	3.018	3.250	2.867	2.490
50	4.189	4.345	4.489	4.621	4.452	4.274	4.531	4.079	3.575
55	5.979	6.183	6.371	6.544	6.253	6.093	6.362	5.859	5.209
60	8.646	8.898	9.131	9.347	8.910	8.792	9.052	8.520	7.758
65	9.413	9.695	9.958	10.203	9.645	9.584	9.814	9.242	8.512
70	8.243	8.538	8.814	9.071	8.425	8.432	8.613	8.006	7.368
75	6.984	7.244	7.491	7.726	7.105	7.183	7.306	6.729	6.179
80	5.684	5.878	6.067	6.251	5.755	5.886	5.958	5.480	5.028
85	4.506	4.641	4.775	4.906	4.542	4.698	4.735	4.401	3.968
90	3.418	3.493	3.568	3.643	3.432	3.594	3.609	3.493	3.002
95	2.560	2.595	2.630	2.664	2.564	2.718	2.722	2.723	2.171

APPENDIX C—Continued

Age	UP-94	UP-94 @2004	UP-94 @2014	UP-94 @2024	UP-94G @1994	GAM-94 Static	GAR-94	GAM-83	UP-84
Female									
20	0.610	0.618	0.627	0.635	0.647	0.619	0.655	0.622	0.523
25	0.856	0.868	0.880	0.891	0.903	0.870	0.915	0.873	0.739
30	1.203	1.220	1.236	1.251	1.262	1.221	1.278	1.226	1.043
35	1.691	1.714	1.736	1.757	1.762	1.716	1.786	1.723	1.470
40	2.378	2.410	2.441	2.470	2.464	2.414	2.498	2.423	2.075
45	3.351	3.394	3.435	3.474	3.451	3.400	3.498	3.412	2.937
50	4.728	4.784	4.838	4.889	4.842	4.796	4.906	4.815	4.178
55	6.694	6.765	6.834	6.901	6.818	6.785	6.907	6.820	5.999
60	9.541	9.634	9.724	9.812	9.672	9.660	9.789	9.717	8.740
65	10.439	10.554	10.665	10.773	10.567	10.583	10.710	10.623	9.607
70	9.342	9.478	9.610	9.738	9.458	9.507	9.622	9.451	8.512
75	8.058	8.207	8.352	8.492	8.148	8.241	8.331	8.131	7.368
80	6.672	6.809	6.943	7.073	6.731	6.867	6.926	6.795	6.179
85	5.288	5.384	5.478	5.571	5.317	5.482	5.512	5.505	5.028
90	4.011	4.070	4.128	4.186	4.024	4.195	4.209	4.252	3.968
95	2.987	3.018	3.049	3.080	2.991	3.153	3.157	3.103	3.002

APPENDIX D

COMPARISON OF NET SINGLE PREMIUMS
FOR LIFE ANNUITIES FOR THE UP-94 TABLE,
ASSUMING INTEREST RATES OF 7%, 8%, AND 9%
(DEFERRED TO AGE 62 FOR AGES UNDER 62,
IMMEDIATE FOR AGES OVER 62)

Age	Male			Female		
	7%	8%	9%	7%	8%	9%
20	0.532	0.335	0.212	0.610	0.381	0.240
25	0.749	0.493	0.327	0.856	0.560	0.369
30	1.054	0.728	0.506	1.203	0.824	0.569
35	1.485	1.074	0.781	1.691	1.213	0.877
40	2.093	1.585	1.208	2.378	1.788	1.354
45	2.956	2.345	1.872	3.351	2.639	2.093
50	4.189	3.482	2.910	4.728	3.902	3.239
55	5.979	5.206	4.556	6.694	5.787	5.031
60	8.646	7.887	7.227	9.541	8.641	7.867
65	9.413	8.793	8.245	10.439	9.681	9.017
70	8.243	7.769	7.343	9.342	8.741	8.208
75	6.984	6.642	6.331	8.058	7.612	7.209
80	5.684	5.454	5.241	6.672	6.364	6.081
85	4.506	4.359	4.222	5.288	5.090	4.907
90	3.418	3.331	3.249	4.011	3.894	3.784
95	2.560	2.510	2.463	2.987	2.921	2.858

APPENDIX E

UP-94 PROJECTED MALE MORTALITY RATES

Age	Projected to Year					
	1999	2004	2009	2014	2019	2024
1	.000576	.000520	.000470	.000425	.000384	.000347
2	.000389	.000351	.000318	.000287	.000259	.000235
3	.000323	.000292	.000264	.000238	.000215	.000195
4	.000251	.000227	.000205	.000186	.000168	.000152
5	.000230	.000208	.000188	.000170	.000154	.000139
6	.000221	.000199	.000180	.000163	.000147	.000133
7	.000212	.000191	.000173	.000156	.000141	.000128
8	.000195	.000176	.000160	.000144	.000130	.000118
9	.000189	.000171	.000154	.000140	.000126	.000114
10	.000192	.000173	.000157	.000142	.000128	.000116
11	.000202	.000182	.000165	.000149	.000135	.000122
12	.000220	.000199	.000179	.000162	.000147	.000133
13	.000249	.000225	.000203	.000184	.000166	.000150
14	.000291	.000264	.000240	.000218	.000198	.000180
15	.000337	.000306	.000278	.000253	.000230	.000209
16	.000382	.000348	.000316	.000287	.000261	.000237
17	.000421	.000382	.000347	.000315	.000287	.000260
18	.000450	.000409	.000371	.000337	.000306	.000278
19	.000473	.000430	.000391	.000355	.000323	.000293
20	.000495	.000450	.000409	.000371	.000337	.000307
21	.000521	.000475	.000434	.000396	.000362	.000331
22	.000549	.000504	.000462	.000424	.000390	.000358
23	.000587	.000544	.000505	.000468	.000434	.000402
24	.000629	.000589	.000551	.000516	.000484	.000453
25	.000676	.000643	.000612	.000582	.000553	.000526
26	.000727	.000705	.000684	.000664	.000644	.000625
27	.000763	.000744	.000725	.000707	.000690	.000673
28	.000791	.000771	.000752	.000734	.000715	.000698
29	.000817	.000797	.000777	.000758	.000739	.000721
30	.000841	.000820	.000800	.000780	.000760	.000742
31	.000861	.000840	.000819	.000799	.000779	.000760
32	.000880	.000858	.000837	.000816	.000796	.000776
33	.000889	.000867	.000846	.000825	.000805	.000785
34	.000890	.000868	.000847	.000826	.000805	.000786
35	.000892	.000870	.000849	.000828	.000807	.000787
36	.000904	.000882	.000860	.000839	.000818	.000798
37	.000934	.000911	.000889	.000867	.000845	.000824
38	.000980	.000951	.000923	.000895	.000869	.000843
39	.001038	.001002	.000967	.000934	.000902	.000871
40	.001108	.001064	.001022	.000982	.000943	.000906

APPENDIX E—*Continued*

Age	Projected to Year					
	1999	2004	2009	2014	2019	2024
41	.001188	.001136	.001085	.001037	.000992	.000948
42	.001280	.001217	.001158	.001101	.001047	.000996
43	.001376	.001302	.001232	.001165	.001103	.001043
44	.001476	.001390	.001308	.001232	.001159	.001092
45	.001590	.001489	.001395	.001306	.001224	.001146
46	.001726	.001608	.001499	.001397	.001302	.001213
47	.001893	.001756	.001628	.001509	.001399	.001298
48	.002085	.001923	.001774	.001637	.001510	.001393
49	.002296	.002107	.001934	.001775	.001629	.001495
50	.002532	.002312	.002112	.001928	.001761	.001608
51	.002806	.002549	.002316	.002104	.001912	.001737
52	.003123	.002823	.002552	.002307	.002085	.001885
53	.003484	.003149	.002846	.002573	.002326	.002102
54	.003867	.003495	.003160	.002856	.002582	.002334
55	.004323	.003927	.003568	.003242	.002945	.002676
56	.004860	.004438	.004053	.003701	.003380	.003086
57	.005508	.005055	.004640	.004259	.003909	.003588
58	.006249	.005765	.005318	.004906	.004526	.004175
59	.007032	.006487	.005985	.005521	.005093	.004699
60	.007912	.007299	.006733	.006211	.005730	.005286
61	.008960	.008308	.007703	.007142	.006622	.006140
62	.010117	.009381	.008698	.008065	.007478	.006933
63	.011495	.010713	.009984	.009304	.008671	.008081
64	.012967	.012084	.011262	.010495	.009781	.009115
65	.014565	.013574	.012650	.011789	.010986	.010239
66	.016356	.015320	.014350	.013441	.012590	.011793
67	.018163	.017013	.015935	.014926	.013981	.013095
68	.019900	.018546	.017284	.016107	.015011	.013989
69	.021774	.020292	.018910	.017623	.016424	.015306
70	.023659	.021937	.020340	.018860	.017487	.016214
71	.025874	.023991	.022245	.020626	.019124	.017732
72	.028396	.026329	.024413	.022636	.020989	.019461
73	.031107	.028843	.026744	.024797	.022992	.021319
74	.033949	.031478	.029187	.027063	.025093	.023267
75	.037288	.034750	.032385	.030181	.028126	.026212
76	.040943	.038156	.035559	.033138	.030883	.028780
77	.045494	.042613	.039914	.037386	.035018	.032801
78	.050828	.047851	.045048	.042409	.039925	.037586
79	.056834	.053776	.050883	.048145	.045555	.043104
80	.063427	.060319	.057362	.054551	.051878	.049335

APPENDIX E—*Continued*

Age	Projected to Year					
	1999	2004	2009	2014	2019	2024
81	.070519	.067402	.064423	.061576	.058855	.056253
82	.078020	.074949	.071998	.069164	.066441	.063826
83	.085228	.081873	.078650	.075554	.072580	.069723
84	.093032	.089821	.086721	.083728	.080839	.078049
85	.100950	.097466	.094102	.090854	.087719	.084691
86	.109829	.106038	.102379	.098845	.095434	.092140
87	.120690	.117113	.113641	.110273	.107004	.103832
88	.133157	.129862	.126647	.123513	.120456	.117474
89	.146237	.142618	.139088	.135645	.132288	.129014
90	.161179	.157981	.154847	.151775	.148763	.145812
91	.176281	.172783	.169355	.165995	.162701	.159473
92	.193079	.190200	.187364	.184570	.181818	.179107
93	.210144	.207011	.203924	.200884	.197888	.194938
94	.228478	.225071	.221715	.218409	.215153	.211945
95	.248687	.246210	.243758	.241330	.238926	.236547
96	.267747	.265081	.262440	.259826	.257239	.254677
97	.286169	.283319	.280497	.277703	.274937	.272199
98	.305219	.303696	.302181	.300673	.299172	.297679
99	.322359	.320751	.319150	.317558	.315973	.314396
100	.339414	.337720	.336035	.334358	.332689	.331029
101	.358560	.358560	.358560	.358560	.358560	.358560
102	.376699	.376699	.376699	.376699	.376699	.376699
103	.396884	.396884	.396884	.396884	.396884	.396884
104	.418855	.418855	.418855	.418855	.418855	.418855
105	.440585	.440585	.440585	.440585	.440585	.440585
106	.460043	.460043	.460043	.460043	.460043	.460043
107	.475200	.475200	.475200	.475200	.475200	.475200
108	.485670	.485670	.485670	.485670	.485670	.485670
109	.492807	.492807	.492807	.492807	.492807	.492807
110	.497189	.497189	.497189	.497189	.497189	.497189
111	.499394	.499394	.499394	.499394	.499394	.499394
112	.500000	.500000	.500000	.500000	.500000	.500000
113	.500000	.500000	.500000	.500000	.500000	.500000
114	.500000	.500000	.500000	.500000	.500000	.500000
115	.500000	.500000	.500000	.500000	.500000	.500000
116	.500000	.500000	.500000	.500000	.500000	.500000
117	.500000	.500000	.500000	.500000	.500000	.500000
118	.500000	.500000	.500000	.500000	.500000	.500000
119	.500000	.500000	.500000	.500000	.500000	.500000
120	1.000000	1.000000	1.000000	1.000000	1.000000	1.000000

APPENDIX F

UP-94 PROJECTED FEMALE MORTALITY RATES

Age	Projected to Year					
	1999	2004	2009	2014	2019	2024
1	.000516	.000467	.000422	.000381	.000345	.000311
2	.000336	.000304	.000275	.000248	.000224	.000203
3	.000251	.000227	.000205	.000186	.000168	.000152
4	.000188	.000170	.000154	.000139	.000126	.000113
5	.000170	.000154	.000139	.000126	.000113	.000103
6	.000159	.000144	.000130	.000117	.000106	.000096
7	.000149	.000135	.000122	.000110	.000100	.000090
8	.000133	.000120	.000109	.000098	.000089	.000080
9	.000127	.000114	.000103	.000093	.000084	.000076
10	.000127	.000115	.000104	.000094	.000085	.000077
11	.000134	.000121	.000109	.000099	.000089	.000081
12	.000144	.000130	.000117	.000106	.000096	.000087
13	.000160	.000145	.000131	.000118	.000107	.000097
14	.000185	.000169	.000155	.000141	.000129	.000118
15	.000215	.000198	.000183	.000169	.000156	.000144
16	.000242	.000224	.000208	.000193	.000179	.000166
17	.000262	.000244	.000227	.000212	.000198	.000184
18	.000273	.000254	.000237	.000221	.000206	.000192
19	.000279	.000259	.000240	.000222	.000206	.000191
20	.000281	.000260	.000239	.000221	.000204	.000188
21	.000283	.000259	.000238	.000219	.000201	.000184
22	.000285	.000262	.000240	.000221	.000203	.000186
23	.000289	.000266	.000246	.000227	.000209	.000193
24	.000290	.000269	.000250	.000231	.000215	.000199
25	.000292	.000272	.000253	.000236	.000220	.000205
26	.000297	.000280	.000264	.000248	.000234	.000220
27	.000305	.000287	.000270	.000254	.000240	.000226
28	.000318	.000300	.000282	.000265	.000250	.000235
29	.000335	.000316	.000297	.000280	.000263	.000248
30	.000359	.000341	.000324	.000308	.000293	.000279
31	.000385	.000370	.000355	.000341	.000328	.000315
32	.000410	.000394	.000379	.000364	.000349	.000336
33	.000434	.000415	.000396	.000379	.000362	.000346
34	.000458	.000436	.000415	.000394	.000375	.000357
35	.000486	.000460	.000435	.000412	.000390	.000369
36	.000518	.000487	.000459	.000432	.000407	.000383
37	.000555	.000520	.000487	.000456	.000428	.000400
38	.000599	.000558	.000520	.000485	.000452	.000421
39	.000650	.000603	.000559	.000518	.000480	.000445
40	.000707	.000656	.000608	.000564	.000523	.000485

APPENDIX F—*Continued*

Age	Projected to Year					
	1999	2004	2009	2014	2019	2024
41	.000766	.000710	.000658	.000611	.000566	.000525
42	.000823	.000763	.000708	.000656	.000609	.000564
43	.000874	.000811	.000752	.000697	.000646	.000599
44	.000920	.000853	.000791	.000733	.000680	.000630
45	.000965	.000890	.000821	.000758	.000699	.000645
46	.001020	.000936	.000859	.000788	.000724	.000664
47	.001092	.000997	.000911	.000832	.000759	.000694
48	.001184	.001082	.000988	.000902	.000824	.000752
49	.001286	.001174	.001072	.000979	.000894	.000816
50	.001410	.001294	.001188	.001090	.001001	.000918
51	.001555	.001435	.001324	.001221	.001127	.001039
52	.001737	.001619	.001509	.001406	.001310	.001221
53	.001931	.001818	.001711	.001611	.001517	.001428
54	.002131	.002027	.001927	.001833	.001743	.001658
55	.002369	.002276	.002186	.002100	.002017	.001938
56	.002673	.002594	.002517	.002443	.002370	.002300
57	.003061	.002986	.002912	.002840	.002769	.002701
58	.003523	.003435	.003350	.003267	.003187	.003108
59	.004051	.003951	.003853	.003758	.003665	.003574
60	.004655	.004540	.004427	.004318	.004211	.004107
61	.005340	.005208	.005079	.004954	.004831	.004711
62	.006116	.005964	.005817	.005673	.005532	.005395
63	.007001	.006828	.006659	.006494	.006333	.006177
64	.007991	.007793	.007600	.007412	.007229	.007050
65	.009056	.008832	.008613	.008400	.008192	.007990
66	.010165	.009913	.009668	.009429	.009195	.008968
67	.011288	.011008	.010736	.010470	.010211	.009958
68	.012335	.012030	.011732	.011442	.011158	.010882
69	.013327	.012997	.012675	.012361	.012056	.011757
70	.014398	.014041	.013694	.013355	.013024	.012702
71	.015602	.015140	.014691	.014256	.013833	.013423
72	.017222	.016711	.016216	.015735	.015269	.014816
73	.019043	.018386	.017751	.017139	.016547	.015976
74	.021159	.020428	.019723	.019043	.018385	.017751
75	.023433	.022510	.021624	.020773	.019955	.019170
76	.026159	.025129	.024140	.023190	.022277	.021400
77	.029448	.028432	.027451	.026503	.025589	.024705
78	.032938	.031801	.030703	.029644	.028620	.027633
79	.036712	.035445	.034221	.033040	.031900	.030799
80	.040899	.039487	.038125	.036809	.035538	.034312

APPENDIX F—*Continued*

Age	Projected to Year					
	1999	2004	2009	2014	2019	2024
81	.045629	.044054	.042534	.041066	.039648	.038280
82	.051029	.049268	.047567	.045926	.044341	.042810
83	.056950	.054985	.053087	.051255	.049486	.047778
84	.063306	.061121	.059012	.056975	.055008	.053110
85	.070677	.068582	.066549	.064576	.062662	.060805
86	.079013	.077057	.075150	.073290	.071476	.069706
87	.088555	.086798	.085076	.083388	.081734	.080112
88	.098880	.096919	.094996	.093111	.091264	.089453
89	.110790	.109138	.107511	.105908	.104329	.102773
90	.123152	.121316	.119507	.117725	.115970	.114241
91	.136378	.134344	.132341	.130368	.128424	.126509
92	.150384	.148141	.145933	.143757	.141613	.139502
93	.165998	.164345	.162708	.161087	.159483	.157894
94	.181696	.179886	.178095	.176321	.174565	.172826
95	.198235	.196260	.194305	.192370	.190454	.188557
96	.215614	.213466	.211340	.209235	.207151	.205088
97	.235009	.233837	.232670	.231509	.230353	.229204
98	.254330	.253060	.251798	.250541	.249291	.248047
99	.274657	.273287	.271923	.270566	.269216	.267873
100	.295750	.294274	.292805	.291344	.289890	.288444
101	.318956	.318956	.318956	.318956	.318956	.318956
102	.340960	.340960	.340960	.340960	.340960	.340960
103	.364586	.364586	.364586	.364586	.364586	.364586
104	.389996	.389996	.389996	.389996	.389996	.389996
105	.415180	.415180	.415180	.415180	.415180	.415180
106	.438126	.438126	.438126	.438126	.438126	.438126
107	.456824	.456824	.456824	.456824	.456824	.456824
108	.471493	.471493	.471493	.471493	.471493	.471493
109	.483473	.483473	.483473	.483473	.483473	.483473
110	.492436	.492436	.492436	.492436	.492436	.492436
111	.498054	.498054	.498054	.498054	.498054	.498054
112	.500000	.500000	.500000	.500000	.500000	.500000
113	.500000	.500000	.500000	.500000	.500000	.500000
114	.500000	.500000	.500000	.500000	.500000	.500000
115	.500000	.500000	.500000	.500000	.500000	.500000
116	.500000	.500000	.500000	.500000	.500000	.500000
117	.500000	.500000	.500000	.500000	.500000	.500000
118	.500000	.500000	.500000	.500000	.500000	.500000
119	.500000	.500000	.500000	.500000	.500000	.500000
120	1.000000	1.000000	1.000000	1.000000	1.000000	1.000000

APPENDIX G

APPROXIMATING THE EFFECT OF FULL GENERATIONAL MORTALITY IMPROVEMENT BY USING A STATIC TABLE PROJECTED *N* YEARS BEYOND 1994

For uninsured pension plans, actuaries may wish to use the UP-94 Mortality Table with mortality rates at each age projected a fixed number of years using Scale AA, rather than to apply the mortality improvement on a generational basis, as in the Group Annuity Reserving valuation standard.

The valuation results that are obtained using the UP-94 Mortality Table projected *N* years are very close to the results using the UP-94 with full generational mortality improvement if *N* is equal to the duration of the liabilities being valued, where the "duration" of a liability is the negative of the first derivative of the liability with respect to the change in the valuation interest rate, divided by the liability. (See "An Introduction to Duration for Pension Actuaries" by Richard Daskais and David LeSueur in *The Pension Forum* for June 1993.) For this discussion, the duration is approximated by the following formula:

$$\text{Duration} = \frac{pvb(i) - pvb(i + 0.001)}{pvb(i) \times 0.001}$$

where $pvb(i)$ is the present value of benefits at the valuation interest rate i, and $pvb(i+0.001)$ is the present value of benefits determined with the interest rate increased by one-tenth of one percentage point, that is, by ten basis points.

When the valuation is being performed as of a year (denoted *CYV*) that is after 1994, the number of years the static table should be projected should be equal to the duration of the liabilities plus the number of years elapsed between the valuation year and 1994 *(CYV*+duration− 1994)*.

This formula was tested for the following cases: for deferred annuities issued at ages 35 through 60 (at five-year age intervals) and commencing at age 62; for immediate annuities issued at ages 65 through 90 (at five-year age intervals); for a hypothetical population of active employees; for a hypothetical population of retired employees; and for these active and retired employee populations combined. Each of these cases was valued for male and female separately, using valuation interest rates of 3%, 7%, and 11%, for valuation year 1994.

The error from using this rule of thumb was less than one-half of 1% in most of the cases tested. The hypothetical population of retired employees was based on the population of CSRS annuitants who are age 62 and older. The hypothetical population of active employees was assumed to comprise an equal number of employees at each age from age 35 through 61, where the number at each age was set equal to the number of CSRS annuitants at age 61.

Finally, the rule of thumb was tested using the valuation program for civil service retirement for federal employees for valuation year 1994. An average duration was determined for both sexes combined, and both male and female mortality rates were projected using this average duration. There are two tiers of benefits for federal employees: one for pre-1984 hires, which is referred to as the Civil Service Retirement System, or CSRS, and one for post-1983 hires, which is referred to as the Federal Employees Retirement System, or FERS. The valuation assumptions include: 7% interest, 4.5% inflation, and 4.5% general salary increases. CSRS has a COLA equal to inflation, and FERS has a COLA of inflation minus 1%. In determining the duration for CSRS and FERS, the ten-basis-point increase in the interest rates was not assumed to imply a corresponding increase in the inflation assumption.

The results of these tests are shown in Tables G-1 through G-4, where the numbers in the columns are defined as follows:

A *For 35–60.* This is the issue age of a deferred annuity commencing at age 62.

A *For 65–90.* The issue age of an immediate annuity.

A *For Active.* Results are for the hypothetical population of active employees.

A *For Retired.* Results are for the hypothetical population of retired employees.

A *For Combined.* Results are for the hypothetical population of active and retired employees combined.

B Ratio of present value of benefits based on the UP-94 table with full generational mortality improvement, that is, the UP-94G @1994, to the present value of benefits based on UP-94 static table with no projection.

C Exact number of years the UP-94 table must be projected on a static basis to give the same present value of benefits as for the UP-94G @1994.

TABLE G-1

ANALYSIS OF THE ACCURACY OF RULE OF THUMB FOR APPROXIMATING FULL GENERATIONAL
MORTALITY IMPROVEMENT WITH A STATIC TABLE PROJECTED TO *CYV*+DURATION
ASSUMING AN INTEREST RATE OF 3%

(A) Age	(B) UP-94G @1994/UP-94	(C) Exact N	(D) Duration of Liabilities	(E) UP-94 @1994+Duration/ UP-94G @1994
		Male		
35	1.157	34.0	35.3	1.004
40	1.135	28.9	30.6	1.006
45	1.112	24.1	25.8	1.007
50	1.090	19.5	21.1	1.006
55	1.068	15.6	16.3	1.003
60	1.047	12.1	11.6	0.998
65	1.037	9.4	8.8	0.998
70	1.031	6.9	7.5	1.002
75	1.023	5.2	6.2	1.004
80	1.016	4.0	5.0	1.004
85	1.010	2.8	3.9	1.003
90	1.005	2.0	3.0	1.002
Active	1.091	20.5	21.1	1.002
Retired	1.031	7.6	7.7	1.001
Combined	1.061	14.3	14.5	1.001
		Female		
35	1.064	36.0	36.4	1.001
40	1.055	31.5	31.7	1.000
45	1.046	27.2	27.0	1.000
50	1.038	23.5	22.3	0.998
55	1.030	20.0	17.5	0.996
60	1.023	16.1	12.7	0.995
65	1.020	12.7	9.9	0.996
70	1.018	9.5	8.5	0.998
75	1.015	6.7	7.1	1.001
80	1.011	4.7	5.7	1.003
85	1.007	3.3	4.5	1.002
90	1.004	2.4	3.4	1.002
Active	1.039	24.2	22.4	0.997
Retired	1.018	9.7	8.7	0.998
Combined	1.028	16.6	15.6	0.998

D   Duration of liabilities, using the approximate formula described above.
E   Ratio of present value of benefits based on the UP-94 table projected N years, where N is equal to the duration of the liabilities, that is the UP-94 @(1994+duration), to the present value of benefits based on the UP-94G @1994.

TABLE G-2

ANALYSIS OF THE ACCURACY OF RULE OF THUMB FOR APPROXIMATING FULL GENERATIONAL
MORTALITY IMPROVEMENT WITH A STATIC TABLE PROJECTED TO $CYV+$DURATION
ASSUMING AN INTEREST RATE OF 7%

(A) Age	(B) UP-94G @1994 / UP-94	(C) Exact N	(D) Duration of Liabilities	(E) UP-94 @1994 + Duration / UP-94G @1994
Male				
35	1.115	31.5	32.2	1.002
40	1.098	26.5	27.7	1.003
45	1.081	21.8	23.1	1.004
50	1.063	17.4	18.6	1.004
55	1.046	13.6	14.0	1.001
60	1.031	10.5	9.3	0.997
65	1.025	8.2	7.0	0.996
70	1.022	6.1	6.0	1.000
75	1.017	4.6	5.1	1.002
80	1.012	3.6	4.2	1.002
85	1.008	2.6	3.4	1.002
90	1.004	1.9	2.6	1.002
Active	1.057	16.8	16.6	1.000
Retired	1.021	6.5	6.1	0.999
Combined	1.035	10.5	10.2	0.999
Female				
35	1.042	32.5	32.9	1.001
40	1.036	28.1	28.4	1.000
45	1.030	24.1	23.9	1.000
50	1.024	20.7	19.3	0.998
55	1.019	17.7	14.7	0.997
60	1.014	14.1	10.1	0.996
65	1.012	11.2	7.7	0.996
70	1.012	8.5	6.8	0.998
75	1.011	6.0	5.8	1.000
80	1.009	4.2	4.8	1.001
85	1.006	3.0	3.9	1.001
90	1.003	2.2	3.0	1.001
Active	1.022	20.1	17.5	0.997
Retired	1.012	8.3	6.8	0.998
Combined	1.016	12.2	10.9	0.998

TABLE G-3

ANALYSIS OF THE ACCURACY OF RULE OF THUMB FOR APPROXIMATING FULL GENERATIONAL
MORTALITY IMPROVEMENT WITH A STATIC TABLE PROJECTED TO *CYV*+DURATION
ASSUMING AN INTEREST RATE OF 11%

(A) Age	(B) UP-94G @1994/UP-94	(C) Exact N	(D) Duration of Liabilities	(E) UP-94 @1994+Duration/ UP-94G @1994
Male				
35	1.088	29.3	29.8	1.001
40	1.075	24.4	25.4	1.003
45	1.060	19.7	21.0	1.003
50	1.046	15.5	16.6	1.003
55	1.032	11.9	12.2	1.001
60	1.020	9.0	7.7	0.997
65	1.017	7.1	5.6	0.997
70	1.016	5.4	5.0	0.999
75	1.013	4.1	4.3	1.001
80	1.010	3.3	3.6	1.001
85	1.007	2.4	2.9	1.001
90	1.004	1.8	2.3	1.001
Active	1.036	13.7	13.3	0.999
Retired	1.015	5.5	5.0	0.999
Combined	1.021	8.0	7.5	0.999
Female				
35	1.030	29.1	30.3	1.001
40	1.025	24.9	25.9	1.001
45	1.020	21.1	21.5	1.000
50	1.016	18.0	17.1	0.999
55	1.012	15.4	12.7	0.998
60	1.008	12.2	8.2	0.997
65	1.008	9.8	6.1	0.997
70	1.009	7.6	5.5	0.998
75	1.008	5.4	4.8	0.999
80	1.007	3.8	4.1	1.000
85	1.005	2.8	3.3	1.001
90	1.003	2.1	2.6	1.001
Active	1.013	16.6	13.8	0.998
Retired	1.008	7.0	5.5	0.998
Combined	1.009	9.2	8.0	0.999

TABLE G-4

ANALYSIS OF THE ACCURACY OF RULE OF THUMB FOR APPROXIMATING FULL GENERATIONAL
MORTALITY IMPROVEMENT WITH A STATIC TABLE PROJECTED TO CYV+DURATION
FOR VALUATIONS OF CIVIL SERVICE RETIREMENT

	(B) UP-94G @1994 / UP-94	(C) Exact N	(D) Duration of Liabilities	(E) UP-94 @1994+Duration / UP-94G @1994
CSRS active	1.052	23.9	21.8	.996
CSRS retired	1.023	9.8	9.5	.999
CSRS total	1.038	16.7	15.9	.998
FERS active	1.063	33.5	30.4	.995

1994 GROUP ANNUITY MORTALITY TABLE
AND 1994 GROUP ANNUITY RESERVING TABLE

SOCIETY OF ACTUARIES GROUP ANNUITY VALUATION TABLE TASK FORCE*

EXECUTIVE SUMMARY

The Society of Actuaries Group Annuity Valuation Table Task Force has completed its research and has developed a table that it recommends as suitable for a new Group Annuity Reserve Valuation Standard.

The proposed new table, recommended as suitable for a new Group Annuity Reserve Valuation Standard, if accepted and adopted by regulators, would incorporate the use of generational mortality into statutory reserving requirements for group annuities for the first time. Generational mortality allows for the recognition of explicit assumptions for future mortality improvement in the calculation of reserve values.

The Task Force strongly believes that the use of generational mortality in group annuity reserving is appropriate given the trends in mortality improvement that have been observed in the past and the continued improvement expected to occur in the foreseeable future. Modern systems capabilities are sufficient to allow for the increased refinement and computation intensity that generational mortality requires.

The 1994 Group Annuity Reserving Table

The 1994 Group Annuity Reserving Table appears in Table 1. This table includes q_x values on an age nearest birthday basis for each age in 1994 and projection factors to be used in generating q_x values in years beyond 1994.

Use of the Values in the Table To Produce Projected Mortality Rates

The values in the 1994 Group Annuity Reserving Table are as follows:

q_x^{1994} = the mortality rate for a person age x in 1994.

*Lindsay J. Malkiewich, Chairperson, David B. Berg, Neil J. Broderick, John B. Gould, Edwin C. Hustead, Naftali Teitelbaum, Charles N. Vest, Michael R. Virga, and John A. Luff, SOA Staff Liaison.

TABLE 1

1994 Group Annuity Reserving Table

Age (x)	Male q_x^{1994}	Male AA_x	Female q_x^{1994}	Female AA_x	Age (x)	Male q_x^{1994}	Male AA_x	Female q_x^{1994}	Female AA_x
1	0.000592	0.020	0.000531	0.020	31	0.000821	0.005	0.000373	0.008
2	0.000400	0.020	0.000346	0.020	32	0.000839	0.005	0.000397	0.008
3	0.000332	0.020	0.000258	0.020	33	0.000848	0.005	0.000422	0.009
4	0.000259	0.020	0.000194	0.020	34	0.000849	0.005	0.000449	0.010
5	0.000237	0.020	0.000175	0.020	35	0.000851	0.005	0.000478	0.011
6	0.000227	0.020	0.000163	0.020	36	0.000862	0.005	0.000512	0.012
7	0.000217	0.020	0.000153	0.020	37	0.000891	0.005	0.000551	0.013
8	0.000201	0.020	0.000137	0.020	38	0.000939	0.006	0.000598	0.014
9	0.000194	0.020	0.000130	0.020	39	0.000999	0.007	0.000652	0.015
10	0.000197	0.020	0.000131	0.020	40	0.001072	0.008	0.000709	0.015
11	0.000208	0.020	0.000138	0.020	41	0.001156	0.009	0.000768	0.015
12	0.000226	0.020	0.000148	0.020	42	0.001252	0.010	0.000825	0.015
13	0.000255	0.020	0.000164	0.020	43	0.001352	0.011	0.000877	0.015
14	0.000297	0.019	0.000189	0.018	44	0.001458	0.012	0.000923	0.015
15	0.000345	0.019	0.000216	0.016	45	0.001578	0.013	0.000973	0.016
16	0.000391	0.019	0.000242	0.015	46	0.001722	0.014	0.001033	0.017
17	0.000430	0.019	0.000262	0.014	47	0.001899	0.015	0.001112	0.018
18	0.000460	0.019	0.000273	0.014	48	0.002102	0.016	0.001206	0.018
19	0.000484	0.019	0.000280	0.015	49	0.002326	0.017	0.001310	0.018
20	0.000507	0.019	0.000284	0.016	50	0.002579	0.018	0.001428	0.017
21	0.000530	0.018	0.000286	0.017	51	0.002872	0.019	0.001568	0.016
22	0.000556	0.017	0.000289	0.017	52	0.003213	0.020	0.001734	0.014
23	0.000589	0.015	0.000292	0.016	53	0.003584	0.020	0.001907	0.012
24	0.000624	0.013	0.000291	0.015	54	0.003979	0.020	0.002084	0.010
25	0.000661	0.010	0.000291	0.014	55	0.04425	0.019	0.002294	0.008
26	0.000696	0.006	0.000294	0.012	56	0.004949	0.018	0.002563	0.006
27	0.000727	0.005	0.000302	0.012	57	0.005581	0.017	0.002919	0.005
28	0.000754	0.005	0.000314	0.012	58	0.006300	0.016	0.003359	0.005
29	0.000779	0.005	0.000331	0.012	59	0.007090	0.016	0.003863	0.005
30	0.000801	0.005	0.000351	0.010	60	0.007976	0.016	0.004439	0.005

TABLE 1—Continued

Age (x)	Male q_x^{1994}	AA_x	Female q_x^{1994}	AA_x
61	0.008986	0.015	0.005093	0.005
62	0.010147	0.015	0.005832	0.005
63	0.011471	0.014	0.006677	0.005
64	0.012940	0.014	0.007621	0.005
65	0.014535	0.014	0.008636	0.005
66	0.016239	0.013	0.009694	0.005
67	0.018034	0.013	0.010764	0.005
68	0.019859	0.014	0.011763	0.005
69	0.021729	0.014	0.012709	0.005
70	0.023730	0.015	0.013730	0.005
71	0.025951	0.015	0.014953	0.006
72	0.028481	0.015	0.016506	0.006
73	0.031201	0.015	0.018344	0.007
74	0.034051	0.015	0.020381	0.007
75	0.037211	0.014	0.022686	0.008
76	0.040858	0.014	0.025325	0.008
77	0.045171	0.013	0.028366	0.007
78	0.050211	0.012	0.031727	0.007
79	0.055861	0.011	0.035362	0.007
80	0.062027	0.010	0.039396	0.007
81	0.068615	0.009	0.043952	0.007
82	0.075532	0.008	0.049153	0.007
83	0.082510	0.008	0.054857	0.007
84	0.089613	0.007	0.060979	0.007
85	0.097240	0.007	0.067738	0.006
86	0.105792	0.007	0.075347	0.005
87	0.115671	0.006	0.084023	0.004
88	0.126980	0.005	0.093820	0.004
89	0.139452	0.005	0.104594	0.003
90	0.152931	0.004	0.116265	0.003
91	0.167260	0.004	0.128751	0.003
92	0.182281	0.003	0.141973	0.003
93	0.198392	0.003	0.155931	0.002
94	0.215700	0.003	0.170677	0.002
95	0.233606	0.002	0.186213	0.002
96	0.251510	0.002	0.202538	0.002
97	0.268815	0.002	0.219655	0.001
98	0.285277	0.001	0.237713	0.001
99	0.301298	0.001	0.256712	0.001
100	0.317238	0.001	0.276427	0.001
101	0.333461	0.000	0.296629	0.000
102	0.350330	0.000	0.317093	0.000
103	0.368542	0.000	0.338505	0.000
104	0.387885	0.000	0.361016	0.000
105	0.407224	0.000	0.383597	0.000
106	0.425599	0.000	0.405217	0.000
107	0.441935	0.000	0.424846	0.000
108	0.457553	0.000	0.444368	0.000
109	0.473150	0.000	0.464469	0.000
110	0.486745	0.000	0.482325	0.000
111	0.496356	0.000	0.495110	0.000
112	0.500000	0.000	0.500000	0.000
113	0.500000	0.000	0.500000	0.000
114	0.500000	0.000	0.500000	0.000
115	0.500000	0.000	0.500000	0.000
116	0.500000	0.000	0.500000	0.000
117	0.500000	0.000	0.500000	0.000
118	0.500000	0.000	0.500000	0.000
119	0.500000	0.000	0.500000	0.000
120	1.000000	0.000	1.000000	0.000

867

AA_x = the annual improvement factor in the mortality rate for age x.

To produce the mortality rate for a person age x in year $(1994+n)$, the following formula would be used:

$$q_x^{1994+n} = q_x^{1994} (1 - AA_x)^n$$

The application of generational mortality techniques to produce reserve values is described in this report.

Standard Table Names

Several tables are presented in this report. To avoid confusion about what each of these tables represents, the following standard table names are used:

1. The 1994 Group Annuity Mortality Basic (or GAM-94 Basic) Table, which is presented as Table 13, is a static mortality table containing unloaded mortality rates for calendar year 1994.
2. The 1994 Group Annuity Mortality Static (or GAM-94 Static) Table, which is presented as Table 18, is a static mortality table containing loaded mortality rates for calendar year 1994.
3. Projection Scale AA (or Scale AA), which is presented as Table 15, represents the annual rates of mortality improvement by age for projecting future mortality rates beyond calendar year 1994.
4. The 1994 Group Annuity Reserving (or GAR-94) Table, which is presented as Table 1, is a combination of the GAM-94 Static Table and Projection Scale AA. Whenever reference is made to the use of this table, it implies that generational mortality derived from static mortality rates and projection scale factors has been used.

I. INTRODUCTION

A. Charge of The Task Force

The Group Annuity Valuation Table Task Force has been charged by the Society of Actuaries Board of Governors with developing a new Group Annuity Mortality Valuation Standard that would be suitable as a replacement for the current standard, which is based upon the 1983 Group Annuity Mortality Table (GAM-83).

B. New Standard To Replace GAM-83

The Society of Actuaries committee that published the GAM-83 Table recommended that a new mortality table be developed when credible annuitant experience became available, since the GAM-83 was only an update of prior data. The Task Force examined the annuitant experience from 1986 through 1990 and found that this was a sufficient basis for a new mortality table.

Further, that experience shows that mortality improvement has resulted in male actual-to-expected mortality ratios near 1.00, as shown in Table 2. Therefore, the margin included in the male rates in the GAM-83 no longer exists, and a new table with a sufficient margin is warranted.

TABLE 2
RETIRED EXPERIENCE BY ANNUITY INCOME
ACTUAL-TO-EXPECTED MORTALITY RATIOS BY EXPERIENCE YEAR

	Experience Year				
	1986	1987	1988	1989	1990
Males	1.05	1.08	1.06	1.03	1.01
Females	1.21	1.26	1.22	1.18	1.14

Finally, because the data, especially for female annuitants, are much more extensive than those used in the development of previous tables, the results produced in this report are more representative of current mortality.

For these reasons, the Task Force recommends that the new standard, as described in this report, be adopted as a replacement for the GAM-83.

C. Intended Form of the New Standard

The Task Force strongly believes that the new standard should accomplish the goals of:
1. Recognizing mortality improvement
2. Serving for at least 15 years.

As shown in this report, while analyzing the data collected through 1990 and comparing them to GAM-83, the Task Force recognized that the trend in mortality improvement had not abated. Consequently, the Task Force decided that the observed mortality improvement trend should be explicitly recognized in this recommended new standard.

This decision to explicitly recognize mortality improvement was discussed in a 1992 position paper [1]. This position paper generated several very worthwhile suggestions and comments. Many of these suggestions were considered in the development of this recommended new standard.

The Task Force further believes that the new standard should be appropriately designed so that it will be useful for a reasonable time and not need as frequent an update as some of the more traditional standards.

To achieve these two results, the Task Force decided that a generational mortality approach, which is more fully discussed later in this report, would be appropriate. Note also that the great majority of input received by the Task Force in response to the position paper supported such a decision. Thus, the Task Force has proceeded with a recommendation that incorporates a generational approach as part of the new standard. This is the first time that projection scales are being recommended as suitable for a new standard for statutory reserving purposes.

The Task Force further recognizes that this approach departs from the traditional one of solely publishing a static table. Prior papers have published projection scales, but these projection scales were not recommended to be part of the statutory reserving standards. While the implementation of this approach is somewhat more complex than that of previous standards, modern systems capabilities facilitate implementation of this new standard. It is also intended that if and when the new standard is adopted for statutory reserving, insurers should be allowed sufficient time to incorporate this generational approach.

The various sections of this report discuss the development and application of this new standard. Note that additional report(s) will discuss how an adaptation of the new standard also serves as an update to the UP–84 Mortality Table and other related issues.

II. DEVELOPMENT OF 1988 BASE YEAR GROUP ANNUITY MORTALITY TABLE

A. 1988 Base Year Core Experience

Our objective was to develop a 1994 base year mortality table for males and females on an age-nearest-birthday basis based on credible group annuity mortality experience. The core mortality information for ages 66–95 was derived from group annuity mortality experience for retired lives for the 1986–1990 experience years. These data were obtained from the Society of Actuaries Group Annuity Experience Committee. In turn, their data were based upon the collective experience of annuitants in payment status for insured contracts from 11 large insurance companies. Data from contributors that were excluded in reports published by this committee were also excluded from our data. The experience we used was examined for data integrity, and where clearly appropriate, data were excluded when determined to be erroneous.

All experience from the 1986–1990 group annuity mortality studies for the younger ages and for the very old ages were excluded from the experience committee data because of a lack of sufficient exposure at these ages. Mortality rates for these young and old ages were derived using the processes discussed later in this report.

Table 3 presents the crude mortality rates resulting from the income-based experience initially gathered by the committee for these ages. Table 3 forms the core of the initial 1988 base table prior to extensions for younger and older ages.

TABLE 3

GROUP ANNUITY MORTALITY EXPERIENCE
UNADJUSTED, UNGRADUATED, BEFORE MARGINS
YEARS 1986–1990
1988 BASE YEAR

Age	Values of q_x		Age	Values of q_x	
	Male	Female		Male	Female
66	0.019269	0.011659	81	0.083702	0.050633
67	0.020827	0.011558	82	0.087230	0.053618
68	0.021989	0.012648	83	0.100734	0.062886
69	0.025223	0.014816	84	0.108259	0.067163
70	0.027970	0.016470	85	0.109440	0.079880
71	0.030305	0.018468	86	0.118562	0.083499
72	0.034400	0.019646	87	0.137411	0.093969
73	0.037566	0.022562	88	0.151901	0.106342
74	0.041715	0.022690	89	0.156454	0.112547
75	0.045670	0.026181	90	0.161550	0.127477
76	0.049899	0.031442	91	0.199729	0.144480
77	0.055961	0.033878	92	0.194778	0.161609
78	0.060834	0.035267	93	0.234746	0.193206
79	0.066465	0.040115	94	0.232451	0.178502
80	0.072808	0.045878	95	0.267373	0.199738

B. Ages 25–65

The first extension of Table 3 was for ages 25 through 65. These mortality rates were derived from Civil Service Retirement System (CSRS) mortality experience by lives for the years 1985–1989 for retired annuitants and 1983–1986 (trending to 1985–1989) for active annuitants. Specifically, experience for active annuitants was used to derive mortality rates for ages 25–50. A blend of experience for active and retired annuitants was used for ages 51–65, based on active/retired distributions of civil service annuitants as shown in Table 4.

TABLE 4

ASSUMED ACTIVE/RETIRED SPLIT OF CIVIL SERVICE ANNUITANTS
USED TO DERIVE EXPERIENCE MORTALITY FOR AGES 51–65

Age	Male Annuitants		Female Annuitants	
	Active	Retired	Active	Retired
51	0.96	0.04	0.98	0.02
52	0.95	0.05	0.97	0.03
53	0.93	0.07	0.96	0.04
54	0.92	0.08	0.95	0.05
55	0.84	0.16	0.93	0.07
56	0.68	0.32	0.85	0.15
57	0.63	0.37	0.82	0.18
58	0.57	0.43	0.78	0.22
59	0.53	0.47	0.74	0.26
60	0.45	0.55	0.66	0.34
61	0.37	0.63	0.53	0.47
62	0.29	0.71	0.42	0.58
63	0.21	0.79	0.29	0.71
64	0.17	0.83	0.22	0.78
65	0.13	0.87	0.17	0.83

Because the rates from CSRS based upon number of lives closely matched the rates from 1986–1990 group annuity mortality experience based upon annual income as shown in Table 5, the Task Force concluded that the CSRS experience was a reasonable basis for extension of the initial 1988 base table for ages below 66.

TABLE 5

COMPARISON OF MORTALITY RATES FOR BLENDED CSRS
AND 1986–1990 GROUP ANNUITY EXPERIENCE

Age	Blended CSRS Experience		Group Annuity Experience		Ratios	
	Male	Female	Male	Female	Male	Female
65	0.017188	0.009975	0.016831	0.009770	0.97923	0.97945
66	0.019160	0.010456	0.019269	0.011659	1.00569	1.11505
67	0.021456	0.012152	0.020827	0.011558	0.97068	0.95112
68	0.023483	0.012638	0.021989	0.012648	0.93638	1.00079
69	0.026761	0.014862	0.025223	0.014816	0.94253	0.99690
70	0.029621	0.017459	0.027970	0.016470	0.94426	0.94335

The blended mortality rates from the CSRS experience for ages 25–65 were then combined with the Table 3 group annuity experience for ages 66–95. An adjustment of the blended CSRS experience for ages 25–65 to reflect group annuity experience at age 65 was *not* needed, because the mortality rates for the blended CSRS experience were quite similar to the mortality rates for the group annuity experience at ages following age 64, as shown in Table 5.

Table 6 shows the crude mortality rates derived for ages 25 through 65 from the blended CSRS experience.

TABLE 6

BLENDED CSRS EXPERIENCE
UNADJUSTED, UNGRADUATED, BEFORE MARGINS
YEARS 1985–1989

	Values of q_x			Values of q_x	
Age	Male	Female	Age	Male	Female
25	0.000684	0.000365	46	0.002060	0.001202
26	0.000804	0.000280	47	0.002124	0.001232
27	0.000665	0.000369	48	0.002596	0.001387
28	0.000848	0.000324	49	0.002754	0.001763
29	0.000867	0.000375	50	0.003070	0.001540
30	0.000863	0.000414	51	0.003447	0.001766
31	0.000850	0.000411	52	0.003698	0.002068
32	0.000821	0.000381	53	0.004081	0.002153
33	0.000813	0.000438	54	0.004963	0.002313
34	0.000939	0.000555	55	0.004763	0.002522
35	0.001009	0.000539	56	0.005751	0.002669
36	0.000880	0.000585	57	0.007180	0.003222
37	0.000976	0.000620	58	0.007569	0.003703
38	0.000987	0.000568	59	0.008356	0.004186
39	0.001149	0.000810	60	0.009165	0.004759
40	0.001219	0.000701	61	0.010456	0.004990
41	0.001202	0.000991	62	0.011893	0.005865
42	0.001491	0.000861	63	0.013728	0.007110
43	0.001683	0.001265	64	0.015347	0.008633
44	0.001925	0.000993	65	0.017188	0.009975
45	0.001792	0.001065			

C. Extreme Ages (Ages 1–24 and 96–120)

Mortality rates for ages 1–24 and ages 96–120 were developed based on mortality rates from the Life Tables for calendar year 1990 and published in *Actuarial Study No. 107* (*SSA 107*) [2]. U.S. Census statistics, information compiled by the National Center for Health Statistics and published in the volumes of *Vital Statistics of the United States*, and Medicare data are the underlying data sources for *SSA 107*.

The Life Tables were combined with the group annuity experience and the blended CSRS experience as follows:

1. For ages 1–24, mortality rates from the *SSA 107* Life Tables were used with modifications to the rates above age 12. The mortality rates for ages 12–24 were obtained by adjusting the *SSA 107* rates by a formula designed to replicate the *SSA 107* age 12 rate and the age 25 rate from the blended CSRS experience. These values are shown in Table 7.

TABLE 7

SSA 107 LIFE TABLES FOR 1990
MORTALITY RATES BEFORE AND AFTER ADJUSTMENT
TO GROUP ANNUITY EXPERIENCE LEVELS
AGES 1–25

	Before Adjustment		After Adjustment	
Age	Male	Female	Male	Female
1	0.000736	0.000647	0.000736	0.000647
2	0.000497	0.000422	0.000497	0.000422
3	0.000413	0.000315	0.000413	0.000315
4	0.000322	0.000236	0.000322	0.000236
5	0.000295	0.000213	0.000295	0.000213
6	0.000282	0.000199	0.000282	0.000199
7	0.000270	0.000187	0.000270	0.000187
8	0.000249	0.000173	0.000249	0.000173
9	0.000222	0.000159	0.000222	0.000159
10	0.000200	0.000148	0.000200	0.000148
11	0.000209	0.000149	0.000209	0.000149
12	0.000276	0.000172	0.000276	0.000172
13	0.000416	0.000221	0.000314	0.000194
14	0.000608	0.000289	0.000367	0.000226
15	0.000823	0.000368	0.000426	0.000262
16	0.001026	0.000441	0.000481	0.000295
17	0.001203	0.000495	0.000530	0.000320
18	0.001336	0.000520	0.000566	0.000331
19	0.001435	0.000524	0.000593	0.000333
20	0.001533	0.000524	0.000620	0.000333
21	0.001634	0.000530	0.000648	0.000336
22	0.001708	0.000539	0.000668	0.000340
23	0.001747	0.000554	0.000679	0.000347
24	0.001764	0.000574	0.000683	0.000356
25	0.001767	0.000594	0.000684	0.000365

2. For ages 96–119, mortality rates from the *SSA 107* Life Tables were appended to the experience table. The resulting mortality rates were then set at a maximum rate of 0.5. No adjustment was required because the age 95 mortality rates in the experience table and the Life Tables were similar. These values are shown in Table 8.

TABLE 8

SSA LIFE TABLES FOR 1990 MORTALITY RATES
(MODIFIED ABOVE AGE 107)
AGES 96–119

Age	Male	Female	Age	Male	Female
96	0.278505	0.237204	111	0.500000	0.500000
97	0.294423	0.254388	112	0.500000	0.500000
98	0.310198	0.271234	113	0.500000	0.500000
99	0.325708	0.287508	114	0.500000	0.500000
100	0.341993	0.304758	115	0.500000	0.500000
101	0.359093	0.323044	116	0.500000	0.500000
102	0.377047	0.342426	117	0.500000	0.500000
103	0.395900	0.362972	118	0.500000	0.500000
104	0.415695	0.384750	119	0.500000	0.500000
105	0.436479	0.407835			
106	0.458303	0.432305			
107	0.481218	0.458243			
108	0.500000	0.485738			
109	0.500000	0.500000			
110	0.500000	0.500000			

Strong consideration was given to setting an ultimate value equal to 0.5. Setting the highest mortality rate at a value of 0.5 instead of 1.0 would mean that there is no theoretical end to the mortality table. Such a proposed table would depart from past practice by not setting the mortality rate to 1.0 at some ultimate age. This change from tradition could be proposed for two reasons:
1. A number of studies have shown that the ultimate mortality rate peaks at a rate of less than 500 per 1,000, so that a rate of 1.0 is not supported by the facts.
2. Current methods of constructing annuity tables do not require an ultimate value of 1.0.

The mortality curve has long been known to bend upwards during the middle ages, and that is a feature of the proposed new standard table as well as all past tables. Studies of mortality at the very old ages have shown that the mortality rate has a second bendpoint in the 80s or 90s, which reflects a deceleration in the rate of increase. The rate then proceeds to an approximately level ultimate rate after age 100. For example, Bayo and Faber [3] conducted a detailed study of the first OASDI beneficiaries who have now all died. They concluded that the mortality rates began to decelerate at about age 85. Lew and Garfinckel [4] found that the mortality rate first exceeded 0.33 in the late 90s and fluctuated between 0.28 and 0.44 after that point.

The ungraduated group annuity experience is sparse after age 95, but the data show the second bendpoint and the peaking of the rate of mortality. The male rates rise to about 0.25 in the mid-90s and then fluctuate around that point. The female rates also seem to peak at about 0.25 at those ages.

The use of such a mortality table without a final value could be implemented as follows:
1. Add an ultimate value to the annuity
2. Stop the table with a value of 1.0 at a certain age
3. Stop the table at a certain age but use 0.5 as the ultimate rate.

While the Task Force strongly believes an ultimate value of 0.5 is appropriate and could be properly programmed, there are some inconsistencies that could result without an assumed actual "end to the table." To avoid these inconsistent practical applications, the ultimate value is set equal to 1.0 at age 120.

Combining Tables 3, 6, 7, 8 and the ultimate rate of 1.0 at age 120 produces Table 9. This represents ungraduated mortality rates (adjusted for CSRS mortality for ages 25–65 and *SSA 107* Life Tables for ages 1–24 and 96–119), as limited to a maximum rate of 0.5, at all ages except the ultimate age of 120, assuming a base year of 1988. Note that Table 9 does not include any margins.

III. PROJECTION SCALES DECISION-MAKING

The central calendar year of the modified mortality experience shown in Table 9 is 1988. The development of the new standard requires two projections of this 1988 base year mortality experience:
1. To project the mortality experience from the central experience year of 1988 to central year 1994, to produce a 1994 Basic Table
2. To develop the mortality projection scale used to project mortality into the future, after calendar year 1994, for the generational mortality table process.

TABLE 9

MORTALITY EXPERIENCE UNGRADUATED BEFORE MARGINS
1988 BASE YEAR

Age	Values of q_x Male	Values of q_x Female	Age	Values of q_x Male	Values of q_x Female	Age	Values of q_x Male	Values of q_x Female
1	0.000736	0.000647	21	0.000648	0.000336	41	0.001202	0.000991
2	0.000497	0.000422	22	0.000668	0.000340	42	0.001491	0.000861
3	0.000413	0.000315	23	0.000679	0.000347	43	0.001683	0.001265
4	0.000322	0.000236	24	0.000683	0.000356	44	0.001925	0.000993
5	0.000295	0.000213	25	0.000684	0.000365	45	0.001792	0.001065
6	0.000282	0.000199	26	0.000804	0.000280	46	0.002060	0.001202
7	0.000270	0.000187	27	0.000665	0.000369	47	0.002124	0.001232
8	0.000249	0.000173	28	0.000848	0.000324	48	0.002596	0.001387
9	0.000222	0.000159	29	0.000867	0.000375	49	0.002754	0.001763
10	0.000200	0.000148	30	0.000863	0.000414	50	0.003070	0.001540
11	0.000209	0.000149	31	0.000850	0.000411	51	0.003447	0.001766
12	0.000276	0.000172	32	0.000821	0.000381	52	0.003698	0.002068
13	0.000314	0.000194	33	0.000813	0.000438	53	0.004081	0.002153
14	0.000367	0.000226	34	0.000939	0.000555	54	0.004963	0.002313
15	0.000426	0.000262	35	0.001009	0.000539	55	0.004763	0.002522
16	0.000481	0.000295	36	0.000880	0.000585	56	0.005751	0.002669
17	0.000530	0.000320	37	0.000976	0.000620	57	0.007180	0.003222
18	0.000566	0.000331	38	0.000987	0.000568	58	0.007569	0.003703
19	0.000593	0.000333	39	0.001149	0.000810	59	0.008356	0.004186
20	0.000620	0.000333	40	0.001219	0.000701	60	0.009165	0.004759

TABLE 9—Continued

Age	Values of q_x Male	Female	Age	Values of q_x Male	Female	Age	Values of q_x Male	Female
61	0.010456	0.004990	81	0.083702	0.050633	101	0.359093	0.323044
62	0.011893	0.005865	82	0.087230	0.053618	102	0.377047	0.342426
63	0.013728	0.007110	83	0.100734	0.062886	103	0.395900	0.362972
64	0.015347	0.008633	84	0.108259	0.067163	104	0.415695	0.384750
65	0.017188	0.009975	85	0.109440	0.079880	105	0.436479	0.407835
66	0.019269	0.011659	86	0.118562	0.083499	106	0.458303	0.432305
67	0.020827	0.011558	87	0.137411	0.093969	107	0.481218	0.458243
68	0.021989	0.012648	88	0.151901	0.106342	108	0.500000	0.485738
69	0.025223	0.014816	89	0.156454	0.112547	109	0.500000	0.500000
70	0.027970	0.016470	90	0.161550	0.127477	110	0.500000	0.500000
71	0.030305	0.018468	91	0.199729	0.144480	111	0.500000	0.500000
72	0.034400	0.019646	92	0.194778	0.161609	112	0.500000	0.500000
73	0.037566	0.022562	93	0.234746	0.193206	113	0.500000	0.500000
74	0.041715	0.022690	94	0.232451	0.178502	114	0.500000	0.500000
75	0.045670	0.026181	95	0.267373	0.199738	115	0.500000	0.500000
76	0.049899	0.031442	96	0.278505	0.237204	116	0.500000	0.500000
77	0.055961	0.033878	97	0.294423	0.254388	117	0.500000	0.500000
78	0.060834	0.035267	98	0.310198	0.271234	118	0.500000	0.500000
79	0.066465	0.040115	99	0.325708	0.287508	119	0.500000	0.500000
80	0.072808	0.045878	100	0.341993	0.304758	120	1.000000	1.000000

A. *Projection of Mortality Rates to 1994*

For the 1988–1994 projection of mortality reduction, the Task Force considered mortality improvements from the following sources:

1. Projections of mortality improvement in the general population presented in *SSA 107*, with further detail covering the periods 1988–1994 and 1986–1992, from the *1992 Trustees Report* Intermediate Alternative II Assumptions, which are consistent with *SSA 107*
2. CSRS mortality improvement experience
3. Scale H, which was presented with the development of the GAM-83.
4. The Society of Actuaries Group Annuity Mortality Study covering the period 1985–1990.

Comparisons of mortality improvement rates at quinquennial age groups from these studies appear in Table 10.

After much discussion, including interaction with the UP-94 Table Task Force, the Group Annuity Valuation Table Task Force concluded that the CSRS data would provide the most meaningful projection, because they were produced from a large database and also used directly to extend the mortality table for active lives.

This conclusion was arrived at after examining the *SSA 107* experience and the age-by-age trends of the CSRS experience without modification. The *SSA 107* experience did not include actual experience past calendar year 1988, whereas the CSRS data included experience through 1993. The CSRS data would therefore provide the better projection for all ages, even though some slight modification and smoothing were required.

The scale of mortality improvement factors for projecting the mortality rates shown in Table 9 from 1988 to 1994 was based on the average trends for CSRS over the period 1987–1993. A mortality table based on CSRS experience was constructed for each year over this period and graduated by using a Whittaker-Henderson type B method. Then a mortality improvement rate for each age was determined based on a least-squares best fit trend line through logarithms of the death rates for that age. The resulting scale of mortality improvement trends for each age was then itself graduated using the same method and rounded to the nearest one-tenth of one percentage point. However, the trends for females at ages 60–65 were changed from negative to zero, because the group annuity trend experience for these ages was slightly positive. A trend of 2% was used at the younger ages.

Table 11 shows the final mortality improvement factors compared to the actual CSRS 1987–1993 trends.

TABLE 10

ANNUAL MORTALITY IMPROVEMENT RATES FROM VARIOUS STUDIES
RATES IN PERCENTAGE PER YEAR

Ages	SSA 88–94	SSA 86–92	CSRS 86–92	Scale H	SOA 85–90	CSRS Nondisability
Male Lives						
25–29	−2.13	−1.67	0.97	0.10		
30–34	−3.34	−3.04	−1.24	0.75		
35–39	−2.98	−3.51	−0.69	2.00		
40–44	−2.21	−1.39	−0.68	2.00		
45–49	0.64	0.62	1.35	1.75		
50–54	0.91	1.25	2.19	1.75		
55–59	1.41	1.40	2.53	1.50	3.90	2.70
60–64	1.60	1.57	1.78	1.50	2.30	1.77
65–69	1.52	1.08	1.29	1.50	3.00	1.23
70–74	1.03	1.24	1.90	1.25	3.40	1.88
75–79	0.79	0.89	2.18	1.25	2.90	2.18
80–84	0.68	0.57	1.70	1.25	1.00	1.69
85–89	0.73	0.22	1.04	0.75	0.70	1.08
90–94	1.00	−0.23	0.16	0.75	0.30	0.17
Female Lives						
25–29	−0.05	−0.73	3.40	0.75		
30–34	−1.68	−1.47	0.21	1.25		
35–39	0.00	−0.68	2.13	2.25		
40–44	1.29	1.78	3.00	2.25		
45–49	1.81	1.77	0.97	2.00		
50–54	1.39	1.50	1.66	2.00		
55–59	1.20	0.65	−0.26	1.75	0.60	3.06
60–64	0.69	0.74	−0.07	1.75	1.80	−0.44
65–69	0.45	0.35	0.50	1.75	2.60	0.54
70–74	0.54	0.64	1.20	1.75	3.90	1.22
75–79	0.87	0.74	1.20	1.50	2.50	1.19
80–84	1.22	0.86	1.16	1.50	0.70	1.17
85–89	1.19	0.66	1.15	1.00	2.00	1.14
90–94	0.93	0.18	0.85	0.50	2.10	0.81

Table 12 shows the ungraduated base year 1994 mortality table rates before margins. The rates in Table 12 were obtained by taking the 1988 base year mortality rates from Table 9 and projecting them to 1994 using the GAM 88–94 mortality improvement factors in Table 11. The following formula was used to project the mortality rates:

$$q_x^{1994} = q_x^{1988} \times (1 - scale_x)^{(1994-1988)} \tag{A}$$

TABLE 11

Annual Mortality Improvement Factors for Use in Projecting Mortality Rates from 1988 to 1994 (GAM 88-94 Column)
Rates in Percentage per Year

Age	Male CSRS 87–93	Male GAM 88–94	Female CSRS 87–93	Female GAM 88–94
1	2.0	2.0	2.0	2.0
2	2.0	2.0	2.0	2.0
3	2.0	2.0	2.0	2.0
4	2.0	2.0	2.0	2.0
5	2.0	2.0	2.0	2.0
6	2.0	2.0	2.0	2.0
7	2.0	2.0	2.0	2.0
8	2.0	2.0	2.0	2.0
9	2.0	2.0	2.0	2.0
10	2.0	2.0	2.0	2.0
11	2.0	2.0	2.0	2.0
12	2.0	2.0	2.0	1.9
13	2.0	1.9	2.0	1.8
14	1.9	1.9	1.8	1.7
15	1.9	1.9	1.6	1.6
16	1.9	1.9	1.5	1.5
17	1.9	1.9	1.4	1.5
18	1.9	1.9	1.4	1.5
19	1.9	1.9	1.5	1.5
20	1.9	1.9	1.6	1.6
21	1.8	1.8	1.7	1.6
22	1.7	1.7	1.7	1.6
23	1.5	1.5	1.6	1.6
24	1.3	1.2	1.5	1.5
25	1.0	0.8	1.4	1.3
26	0.6	0.3	1.2	1.1
27	−0.4	−0.1	0.9	0.9
28	−0.6	−0.6	0.5	0.7
29	−0.9	−1.0	0.3	0.6
30	−1.3	−1.2	0.4	0.5

Age	Male CSRS 87–93	Male GAM 88–94	Female CSRS 87–93	Female GAM 88–94
31	−1.5	−1.2	0.8	0.5
32	−1.3	−1.0	0.9	0.5
33	−0.8	−0.7	0.6	0.5
34	−0.1	−0.2	0.3	0.5
35	0.6	0.1	0.1	0.6
36	1.0	0.5	0.4	0.7
37	0.9	0.7	0.9	0.8
38	0.7	1.0	1.3	1.0
39	0.7	1.2	1.4	1.1
40	1.0	1.4	1.2	1.1
41	1.6	1.7	1.0	1.2
42	2.1	1.9	1.0	1.3
43	2.3	2.0	1.2	1.4
44	2.4	2.0	1.5	1.6
45	2.2	2.0	1.8	1.8
46	1.8	1.8	2.2	1.9
47	1.4	1.7	2.3	1.9
48	1.2	1.6	2.1	1.9
49	1.3	1.6	1.6	1.5
50	1.5	1.6	1.0	1.2
51	1.9	1.7	0.7	1.0
52	2.2	1.8	0.6	0.8
53	2.2	1.9	0.6	0.8
54	2.0	1.9	0.8	0.8
55	1.7	1.9	0.9	0.9
56	1.6	1.9	1.0	0.9
57	1.7	1.8	1.0	0.8
58	1.8	1.9	0.9	0.6
59	1.9	1.9	0.4	0.2
60	2.0	1.9	−0.1	0.0

TABLE 11—*Continued*

Age	Male CSRS 87–93	Male GAM 88–94	Female CSRS 87–93	Female GAM 88–94
61	1.9	1.9	−0.6	0.0
62	1.9	1.8	−0.8	0.0
63	1.8	1.7	−0.8	0.0
64	1.6	1.5	−0.6	0.0
65	1.3	1.3	−0.2	0.0
66	1.1	1.2	0.2	0.2
67	1.0	1.2	0.8	0.7
68	1.0	1.2	1.3	1.2
69	1.3	1.3	1.7	1.5
70	1.6	1.5	1.9	1.8
71	1.9	1.7	2.0	2.0
72	2.0	1.9	2.0	2.0
73	2.0	2.1	1.9	2.0
74	2.1	2.2	1.8	1.9
75	2.2	2.3	1.8	1.8
76	2.3	2.3	1.7	1.7
77	2.4	2.3	1.6	1.5
78	2.4	2.3	1.4	1.4
79	2.3	2.2	1.2	1.2
80	2.2	2.1	1.1	1.1
81	1.9	1.9	1.0	1.0
82	1.7	1.8	0.9	1.0
83	1.6	1.7	0.9	0.9
84	1.5	1.6	1.0	0.9
85	1.4	1.5	1.0	0.9
86	1.4	1.4	1.0	0.9
87	1.4	1.4	1.0	0.9
88	1.3	1.3	1.0	0.9
89	1.2	1.3	0.8	0.8
90	1.1	1.2	0.8	0.8

Age	Male CSRS 87–93	Male GAM 88–94	Female CSRS 87–93	Female GAM 88–94
91	0.9	0.9	0.8	0.8
92	0.7	0.7	0.8	0.9
93	0.6	0.6	0.9	0.9
94	0.5	0.5	1.0	1.0
95	0.4	0.5	1.1	1.1
96	0.4	0.4	1.1	1.1
97	0.4	0.4	1.1	1.0
98	0.5	0.3	1.1	0.9
99	0.5	0.2	1.0	0.7
100	0.0	0.2	0.0	0.4
101	0.0	0.1	0.0	0.2
102	0.0	0.0	0.0	0.1
103	0.0	0.0	0.0	0.0
104	0.0	0.0	0.0	0.0
105	0.0	0.0	0.0	0.0
106	0.0	0.0	0.0	0.0
107	0.0	0.0	0.0	0.0
108	0.0	0.0	0.0	0.0
109	0.0	0.0	0.0	0.0
110	0.0	0.0	0.0	0.0
111	0.0	0.0	0.0	0.0
112	0.0	0.0	0.0	0.0
113	0.0	0.0	0.0	0.0
114	0.0	0.0	0.0	0.0
115	0.0	0.0	0.0	0.0
116	0.0	0.0	0.0	0.0
117	0.0	0.0	0.0	0.0
118	0.0	0.0	0.0	0.0
119	0.0	0.0	0.0	0.0
120	0.0	0.0	0.0	0.0

TABLE 12
GROUP ANNUITY MORTALITY RATES UNGRADUATED—NO MARGIN
1994 BASE YEAR

Age	Male	Female	Age	Male	Female	Age	Male	Female
1	0.000652	0.000573	21	0.000581	0.000305	41	0.001084	0.000922
2	0.000440	0.000374	22	0.000603	0.000309	42	0.001329	0.000796
3	0.000366	0.000279	23	0.000620	0.000315	43	0.001491	0.001162
4	0.000285	0.000209	24	0.000635	0.000325	44	0.001705	0.000901
5	0.000261	0.000189	25	0.000652	0.000337	45	0.001587	0.000955
6	0.000250	0.000176	26	0.000790	0.000262	46	0.001847	0.001071
7	0.000239	0.000166	27	0.000669	0.000350	47	0.001916	0.001098
8	0.000221	0.000153	28	0.000879	0.000311	48	0.002357	0.001244
9	0.000197	0.000141	29	0.000920	0.000362	49	0.002500	0.001610
10	0.000177	0.000131	30	0.000927	0.000402	50	0.002787	0.001432
11	0.000185	0.000132	31	0.000913	0.000399	51	0.003110	0.001663
12	0.000244	0.000153	32	0.000872	0.000370	52	0.003316	0.001971
13	0.000280	0.000174	33	0.000848	0.000425	53	0.003637	0.002052
14	0.000327	0.000204	34	0.000950	0.000539	54	0.004423	0.002204
15	0.000380	0.000238	35	0.001003	0.000520	55	0.004245	0.002389
16	0.000429	0.000269	36	0.000854	0.000561	56	0.005126	0.002528
17	0.000472	0.000292	37	0.000936	0.000591	57	0.006439	0.003070
18	0.000504	0.000302	38	0.000929	0.000535	58	0.006746	0.003572
19	0.000529	0.000304	39	0.001069	0.000758	59	0.007448	0.004136
20	0.000553	0.000302	40	0.001120	0.000656	60	0.008169	0.004759

TABLE 12—Continued

Age	Male	Female	Age	Male	Female	Age	Male	Female
61	0.009319	0.004900	81	0.074602	0.047670	101	0.356944	0.319187
62	0.010665	0.005865	82	0.078223	0.050480	102	0.377047	0.340376
63	0.012386	0.007110	83	0.090886	0.059566	103	0.395900	0.362972
64	0.014017	0.008633	84	0.098273	0.063617	104	0.415695	0.384750
65	0.015890	0.009975	85	0.099952	0.075662	105	0.436479	0.407835
66	0.017923	0.011520	86	0.108945	0.079090	106	0.458303	0.432305
67	0.019372	0.011081	87	0.127035	0.089007	107	0.481218	0.458243
68	0.020453	0.011764	88	0.140431	0.100727	108	0.500000	0.485738
69	0.023318	0.013532	89	0.145522	0.107252	109	0.500000	0.500000
70	0.025545	0.014769	90	0.152096	0.121479	110	0.500000	0.500000
71	0.027342	0.016360	91	0.189183	0.137682	111	0.500000	0.500000
72	0.030660	0.017403	92	0.186739	0.153076	112	0.500000	0.500000
73	0.033074	0.019986	93	0.226421	0.183005	113	0.500000	0.500000
74	0.036503	0.020223	94	0.225564	0.168056	114	0.500000	0.500000
75	0.039719	0.023478	95	0.259451	0.186913	115	0.500000	0.500000
76	0.043397	0.028368	96	0.271887	0.221973	116	0.500000	0.500000
77	0.048669	0.030941	97	0.287427	0.239501	117	0.500000	0.500000
78	0.052907	0.032406	98	0.304656	0.256913	118	0.500000	0.500000
79	0.058160	0.037312	99	0.321819	0.275642	119	0.500000	0.500000
80	0.064102	0.042932	100	0.337910	0.297517	120	1.000000	1.000000

where

q_x^y = mortality rate in calendar year y at attained age x

$scale_x$ = mortality improvement factor for attained age x.

The resulting rates are an ungraduated set of mortality rates for ages 1–120, by sex, with a base experience year of 1994.

B. Graduated Mortality Rates

The resulting set of mortality rates in Table 12 was then graduated by using the Karup-King four point graduation formula, as follows. Mortality rates were averaged by quinquennial age groups q_n, q_n, q_n, q_n, ... Graduated mortality rates $q_{n\,t}$ were derived based on the following formula:

$$q_{n+t} = A_1 \times q_{n-5} + A_2 \times q_n + A_3 \times q_{n+5} + A_4 \times q_{n+10} \qquad (B)$$

where

$A_1 = -0.5 \times S_1 \times (1 - S_1)^2$

$A_2 = 1.5 \times S_1^3 - 2.5 \times S_1^2 + 1$

$A_3 = -1.5 \times S_1^3 + 2 \times S_1^2 + 0.5 \times S_1$

$A_4 = 0.5 \times S_1^2 \times (S_1 - 1)$

$S_1 = t/5$

At the extreme ages (under age 7 and over age 102), minor adjustments were made.

The adjusted mortality rates with a base year of 1994 of Table 12 *after graduation* are shown in Table 13. Table 13 is the 1994 Group Annuity Mortality Basic (GAM–94 Basic) Table.

C. Projection of Mortality Rates beyond 1994

For the projection of mortality reduction beyond 1994, the Task Force decided to use a blend of the CSRS and *SSA 107* mortality reduction trends based upon experience between years 1977 through 1993, with adjustments. A mortality improvement scale based entirely on CSRS data over the period 1977–1993 was constructed. The starting point was a mortality table for each year 1977 through 1993, graduated by Whittaker-Henderson type B. Then a mortality improvement trend for each age was determined based on

TABLE 13
1994 GROUP ANNUITY MORTALITY TABLE
GRADUATED—NO MARGIN
1994 BASE YEAR

Age	Male	Female	Age	Male	Female	Age	Male	Female
1	0.000637	0.000571	21	0.000570	0.000308	41	0.001243	0.000826
2	0.000430	0.000372	22	0.000598	0.000311	42	0.001346	0.000888
3	0.000357	0.000278	23	0.000633	0.000313	43	0.001454	0.000943
4	0.000278	0.000208	24	0.000671	0.000313	44	0.001568	0.000992
5	0.000255	0.000188	25	0.000711	0.000313	45	0.001697	0.001046
6	0.000244	0.000176	26	0.000749	0.000316	46	0.001852	0.001111
7	0.000234	0.000165	27	0.000782	0.000324	47	0.002042	0.001196
8	0.000216	0.000147	28	0.000811	0.000338	48	0.002260	0.001297
9	0.000209	0.000140	29	0.000838	0.000356	49	0.002501	0.001408
10	0.000212	0.000141	30	0.000862	0.000377	50	0.002773	0.001536
11	0.000223	0.000148	31	0.000883	0.000401	51	0.003088	0.001686
12	0.000243	0.000159	32	0.000902	0.000427	52	0.003455	0.001864
13	0.000275	0.000177	33	0.000912	0.000454	53	0.003854	0.002051
14	0.000320	0.000203	34	0.000913	0.000482	54	0.004278	0.002241
15	0.000371	0.000233	35	0.000915	0.000514	55	0.004758	0.002466
16	0.000421	0.000261	36	0.000927	0.000550	56	0.005322	0.002755
17	0.000463	0.000281	37	0.000958	0.000593	57	0.006001	0.003139
18	0.000495	0.000293	38	0.001010	0.000643	58	0.006774	0.003612
19	0.000521	0.000301	39	0.001075	0.000701	59	0.007623	0.004154
20	0.000545	0.000305	40	0.001153	0.000763	60	0.008576	0.004773

TABLE 13—*Continued*

Age	Male	Female	Age	Male	Female	Age	Male	Female
61	0.009663	0.005476	81	0.073780	0.047260	101	0.358560	0.318956
62	0.010911	0.006271	82	0.081217	0.052853	102	0.376699	0.340960
63	0.012335	0.007179	83	0.088721	0.058986	103	0.396884	0.364586
64	0.013914	0.008194	84	0.096358	0.065569	104	0.418855	0.389996
65	0.015629	0.009286	85	0.104559	0.072836	105	0.440585	0.415180
66	0.017462	0.010423	86	0.113755	0.081018	106	0.460043	0.438126
67	0.019391	0.011574	87	0.124377	0.090348	107	0.475200	0.456824
68	0.021354	0.012648	88	0.136537	0.100882	108	0.485670	0.471493
69	0.023364	0.013665	89	0.149949	0.112467	109	0.492807	0.483473
70	0.025516	0.014763	90	0.164442	0.125016	110	0.497189	0.492436
71	0.027905	0.016079	91	0.179849	0.138442	111	0.499394	0.498054
72	0.030625	0.017748	92	0.196001	0.152660	112	0.500000	0.500000
73	0.033549	0.019724	93	0.213325	0.167668	113	0.500000	0.500000
74	0.036614	0.021915	94	0.231936	0.183524	114	0.500000	0.500000
75	0.040012	0.024393	95	0.251189	0.200229	115	0.500000	0.500000
76	0.043933	0.027231	96	0.270441	0.217783	116	0.500000	0.500000
77	0.048570	0.030501	97	0.289048	0.236188	117	0.500000	0.500000
78	0.053991	0.034115	98	0.306750	0.255605	118	0.500000	0.500000
79	0.060066	0.038024	99	0.323976	0.276035	119	0.500000	0.500000
80	0.066696	0.042361	100	0.341116	0.297233	120	1.000000	1.000000

a least-squares best-fit trend line through the logarithms of the rates for that age. The opening year of 1977 was chosen because it provided a reasonable representation of anticipated trends in the future and, properly, did not reflect more rapid mortality improvement rates found in the experience of prior periods.

The trends for Social Security are based on data from *SSA 107* along with additional data used in this study, which were provided by the Office of the Actuary at the Social Security Administration. These additional data included central death rates for five-year age groups for each calendar year over the period 1960–1988. Before the Social Security trends for 1977–1988 could be blended with the CSRS trends for 1977–1993, it was necessary to extend the Social Security trends up through 1993. This extension was based on mortality improvement trends for the CSRS from 1988 through 1993. The *SSA 107* extended central death rates for each year 1989 through 1993 were obtained by multiplying the SSA central death rate for 1988 by the ratio of the CSRS central death rate for the corresponding year to the CSRS central death rate for 1988. Then the average trend for each central age over the entire 1977–1993 period was determined based on a least-squares best-fit trend line through the logarithms of these central death rates. The Social Security data did not cover central ages beyond age 92, and the CSRS data at these older ages were limited. The mortality improvement trends for individual ages were interpolated from the trends for the central ages by using the Karup-King four-point interpolation formula.

The trends at ages 1–25 were based on Social Security data and on the Social Security assumptions for future trends listed in *SSA 107* and start out at a rate of improvement of 2% per year. Then the CSRS mortality improvement trend for each age was averaged with the corresponding trend for Social Security. These average trends were then rounded to the nearest one-tenth of one percentage point. The resulting mortality improvement factors are shown in Table 14.

To obtain the mortality improvement factors for projecting mortality beyond 1994, the following modifications were made in this scale:
1. Any mortality improvement factors that were less than 0.5% for ages under 85 were changed to 0.5%, because the Task Force thought that the use of lower factors would result in excessive mortality rates in the future.
2. A maximum mortality improvement rate of 2.0% was set for ages under 60. This reduced the highest rate of 2.3% to 2.0% at male ages 52–54 and provided a smoother progression of rates around these ages.

TABLE 14

ANNUAL MORTALITY IMPROVEMENT FACTORS FROM THE *SSA* 107 AND CSRS STUDIES
BASED UPON 1977–1993 EXPERIENCE RATES IN PERCENTAGE PER YEAR

	Male			Female		
Age	SS 77–93	CSRS 77–93	Average	SS 77–93	CSRS 77–93	Average
1	2.0	2.0	2.0	2.0	2.0	2.0
2	2.0	2.0	2.0	2.0	2.0	2.0
3	2.0	2.0	2.0	2.0	2.0	2.0
4	2.0	2.0	2.0	2.0	2.0	2.0
5	2.0	2.0	2.0	2.0	2.0	2.0
6	2.0	2.0	2.0	2.0	2.0	2.0
7	2.0	2.0	2.0	2.0	2.0	2.0
8	2.0	2.0	2.0	2.0	2.0	2.0
9	2.0	2.0	2.0	2.0	2.0	2.0
10	2.0	2.0	2.0	2.0	2.0	2.0
11	2.0	2.0	2.0	2.0	2.0	2.0
12	2.0	2.0	2.0	2.0	2.0	2.0
13	2.0	2.0	2.0	2.0	2.0	2.0
14	1.9	1.9	1.9	1.8	1.8	1.8
15	1.9	1.9	1.9	1.6	1.6	1.6
16	1.9	1.9	1.9	1.5	1.5	1.5
17	1.9	1.9	1.9	1.4	1.4	1.4
18	1.9	1.9	1.9	1.4	1.4	1.4
19	1.9	1.9	1.9	1.5	1.5	1.5
20	1.9	1.9	1.9	1.6	1.6	1.6
21	1.8	1.8	1.8	1.7	1.7	1.7
22	1.7	1.7	1.7	1.7	1.7	1.7
23	1.5	1.5	1.6	1.6	1.6	1.6
24	1.3	1.3	1.3	1.5	1.5	1.5
25	1.0	1.0	1.0	1.4	1.4	1.4
26	0.6	0.6	0.6	1.2	1.2	1.2
27	0.3	0.4	0.3	1.1	0.9	1.0
28	0.0	−0.4	−0.2	0.9	1.4	1.2
29	−0.5	−1.0	−0.8	0.8	1.6	1.2
30	−1.0	−1.4	−1.2	0.6	1.5	1.0
31	−1.4	−1.6	−1.5	0.5	1.1	0.8
32	−1.7	−1.5	−1.6	0.5	0.6	0.6
33	−1.7	−1.2	−1.4	0.7	0.2	0.4
34	−1.5	−0.9	−1.2	1.0	0.0	0.5
35	−1.2	−0.5	−0.9	1.3	0.1	0.7
36	−0.9	−0.3	−0.6	1.6	0.4	1.0
37	−0.6	−0.1	−0.4	1.8	0.8	1.3
38	−0.3	0.0	−0.2	1.9	1.0	1.5
39	0.0	0.0	0.0	2.0	1.1	1.5
40	0.3	0.2	0.2	2.0	1.0	1.5
41	0.6	0.4	0.5	2.0	0.8	1.4
42	0.9	0.7	0.8	2.0	0.7	1.3
43	1.1	1.0	1.1	2.0	0.7	1.4
44	1.3	1.3	1.3	2.0	0.9	1.4
45	1.5	1.6	1.5	2.0	1.2	1.6

TABLE 14—*Continued*

	Male			Female		
Age	SS 77–93	CSRS 77–93	Average	SS 77–93	CSRS 77–93	Average
46	1.6	1.8	1.7	1.9	1.4	1.7
47	1.7	2.1	1.9	1.9	1.6	1.8
48	1.8	2.3	2.0	1.9	1.6	1.8
49	1.8	2.5	2.2	1.9	1.6	1.8
50	1.9	2.7	2.3	1.9	1.5	1.7
51	1.9	2.8	2.3	1.9	1.3	1.6
52	1.9	2.7	2.3	1.9	1.0	1.4
53	1.8	2.6	2.2	1.7	0.8	1.2
54	1.8	2.4	2.1	1.5	0.6	1.0
55	1.7	2.2	1.9	1.3	0.4	0.8
56	1.6	2.0	1.8	1.0	0.2	0.6
57	1.6	1.8	1.7	0.8	0.1	0.5
58	1.6	1.7	1.6	0.6	0.0	0.3
59	1.6	1.5	1.6	0.4	−0.2	0.1
60	1.7	1.4	1.6	0.2	−0.4	0.0
61	1.8	1.3	1.5	0.0	−0.5	−0.2
62	1.8	1.2	1.5	0.0	−0.5	−0.2
63	1.7	1.2	1.4	0.0	−0.5	−0.2
64	1.6	1.2	1.4	0.0	−0.4	−0.1
65	1.5	1.2	1.4	0.1	−0.2	0.0
66	1.4	1.3	1.3	0.2	0.0	0.1
67	1.3	1.4	1.3	0.3	0.1	0.2
68	1.3	1.5	1.4	0.4	0.3	0.3
69	1.3	1.5	1.4	0.5	0.3	0.4
70	1.3	1.6	1.5	0.7	0.4	0.5
71	1.4	1.6	1.5	0.8	0.4	0.6
72	1.4	1.6	1.5	0.9	0.4	0.6
73	1.3	1.6	1.5	0.9	0.5	0.7
74	1.3	1.6	1.5	0.9	0.5	0.7
75	1.3	1.6	1.4	1.0	0.6	0.8
76	1.2	1.5	1.4	0.9	0.6	0.8
77	1.2	1.4	1.3	0.9	0.5	0.7
78	1.1	1.3	1.2	0.9	0.5	0.7
79	1.0	1.2	1.1	0.9	0.5	0.7
80	0.9	1.0	1.0	0.9	0.5	0.7
81	0.9	0.9	0.9	0.9	0.5	0.7
82	0.8	0.8	0.8	0.9	0.6	0.7
83	0.8	0.8	0.8	0.9	0.5	0.7
84	0.8	0.7	0.7	0.8	0.5	0.7
85	0.8	0.6	0.7	0.8	0.4	0.6
86	0.8	0.6	0.7	0.8	0.3	0.5
87	0.7	0.5	0.6	0.7	0.2	0.4
88	0.6	0.5	0.5	0.7	0.1	0.4
89	0.5	0.4	0.5	0.7	0.0	0.3
90	0.4	0.3	0.4	0.7	0.0	0.3
91	0.3	0.2	0.3	0.6	0.0	0.3
92	0.2	0.2	0.2	0.6	0.0	0.3

3. At the higher ages the mortality improvement rates were graded to a value of 0.1% at age 100 and set to 0 for all ages greater than 100.
4. Other minor adjustments were made as described below.

After age 37, the factors for males start to increase fairly rapidly from one age to the next, going from a factor of 0.2% (before change) at age 38 to 2.3% at age 50.

When there are large mortality improvement factor increases from one age to the next like this, it is possible that, after the mortality improvement scale has been applied for a number of years, the mortality rate for a particular age could become lower than the rate for an age one year younger. To minimize this possibility, it was decided to limit the increase in the factor from one age to the next to one-tenth of one percentage point. As a result, the mortality improvement factors for males were modified so that they increase from 0.5% at age 37 to 2.0% at age 52. The factors for some ages were increased by this process, and factors for other ages were reduced.

There are also significant age-to-age increases for females in the factors from ages 33 through 38. The factors for females for ages 32 through 38 were therefore also modified, as were the factors at female ages 41 to 44.

Mortality improvement factors to be used in the new Group Annuity Mortality Table when projecting mortality rates beyond 1994 are shown in Table 15 and are referred to as the Projection Scale AA. Figure 1 displays a graph of the Projection Scale AA factors for males. Figure 2 displays a graph of the Projection Scale AA factors for females.

IV. MARGINS

Consistent with accepted actuarial practice and precedent set in the development of existing mortality tables used in reserving, the Task Force deemed it necessary and appropriate to add margins to the q_x values of the 1994 Group Annuity Mortality Basic Table. The overall margin comprises two components:
1. Margins for random variation in mortality rates
2. Margins for other contingencies.

A. *Margins for Random Variation in Mortality Rates*

The unloaded 1994 Group Annuity Mortality Basic Table q_x values shown in Table 13 represent expected values. Considering current reserving theory, the Task Force decided to incorporate margins to produce annuity reserve

TABLE 15

Projection Scale AA
Mortality Improvement Factors To Be Used in the New Table When Projecting Mortality Rates beyond 1994
Factors Are Shown as Percentage per Year

Attained Age	Male Factor	Female Factor	Attained Age	Male Factor	Female Factor	Attained Age	Male Factor	Female Factor
1	2.0	2.0	21	1.8	1.7	41	0.9	1.5
2	2.0	2.0	22	1.7	1.7	42	1.0	1.5
3	2.0	2.0	23	1.5	1.6	43	1.1	1.5
4	2.0	2.0	24	1.3	1.5	44	1.2	1.5
5	2.0	2.0	25	1.0	1.4	45	1.3	1.6
6	2.0	2.0	26	0.6	1.2	46	1.4	1.7
7	2.0	2.0	27	0.5	1.2	47	1.5	1.8
8	2.0	2.0	28	0.5	1.2	48	1.6	1.8
9	2.0	2.0	29	0.5	1.2	49	1.7	1.8
10	2.0	2.0	30	0.5	1.0	50	1.8	1.7
11	2.0	2.0	31	0.5	0.8	51	1.9	1.6
12	2.0	2.0	32	0.5	0.8	52	2.0	1.4
13	2.0	2.0	33	0.5	0.9	53	2.0	1.2
14	1.9	1.8	34	0.5	1.0	54	2.0	1.0
15	1.9	1.6	35	0.5	1.1	55	1.9	0.8
16	1.9	1.5	36	0.5	1.2	56	1.8	0.6
17	1.9	1.4	37	0.5	1.3	57	1.7	0.5
18	1.9	1.4	38	0.6	1.4	58	1.6	0.5
19	1.9	1.5	39	0.7	1.5	59	1.6	0.5
20	1.9	1.6	40	0.8	1.5	60	1.6	0.5

TABLE 15—Continued

Attained Age	Male Factor	Female Factor	Attained Age	Male Factor	Female Factor	Attained Age	Male Factor	Female Factor
61	1.5	0.5	81	0.9	0.7	101	0.0	0.0
62	1.5	0.5	82	0.8	0.7	102	0.0	0.0
63	1.4	0.5	83	0.8	0.7	103	0.0	0.0
64	1.4	0.5	84	0.7	0.7	104	0.0	0.0
65	1.4	0.5	85	0.7	0.6	105	0.0	0.0
66	1.3	0.5	86	0.7	0.5	106	0.0	0.0
67	1.3	0.5	87	0.6	0.4	107	0.0	0.0
68	1.4	0.5	88	0.5	0.4	108	0.0	0.0
69	1.4	0.5	89	0.5	0.3	109	0.0	0.0
70	1.5	0.5	90	0.4	0.3	110	0.0	0.0
71	1.5	0.6	91	0.4	0.3	111	0.0	0.0
72	1.5	0.6	92	0.3	0.3	112	0.0	0.0
73	1.5	0.7	93	0.3	0.2	113	0.0	0.0
74	1.5	0.7	94	0.3	0.2	114	0.0	0.0
75	1.4	0.8	95	0.2	0.2	115	0.0	0.0
76	1.4	0.8	96	0.2	0.2	116	0.0	0.0
77	1.3	0.7	97	0.2	0.1	117	0.0	0.0
78	1.2	0.7	98	0.1	0.1	118	0.0	0.0
79	1.1	0.7	99	0.1	0.1	119	0.0	0.0
80	1.0	0.7	100	0.1	0.1	120	0.0	0.0

FIGURE 1

MORTALITY IMPROVEMENT FACTORS—MALE
SCALE AA

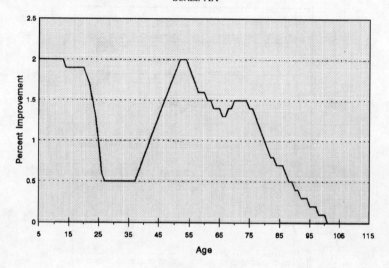

FIGURE 2

MORTALITY IMPROVEMENT FACTORS—FEMALE
SCALE AA

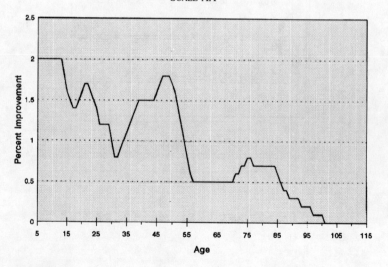

values that would be adequate for random variation of two standard deviations from expected mortality.

Probability theory was used to develop variances of distributions of annuity values as indicated below.

For a single life age x, assume Y is a random variable representing the present value of annuity payments received. Y would have the following probability distribution:

Y	$Pr\,(Y = y)$
0	$1 - p$
$a_{\overline{1}\rceil}$	$_{1\mid}q_y \; [= p_y\,(1 - p_{y+1})]$
$a_{\overline{2}\rceil}$	$_{2\mid}q_y$
$a_{\overline{3}\rceil}$	$_{3\mid}q_y$
$\cdot$	$\cdot$
$\cdot$	$\cdot$
$\cdot$	$\cdot$

The mean, variance, and standard deviation of this distribution would be determined as follows:

$$\mu = E[Y] = \sum_{t=0}^{\infty} a_{\overline{t}\rceil} \times Pr\,(Y = a_{\overline{t}\rceil}) \tag{C}$$

$$E[Y^2] = \sum_{t=0}^{\infty} a_{\overline{t}\rceil}^2 \times Pr(Y = a_{\overline{t}\rceil}) \tag{D}$$

$$\sigma^2 = E[Y^2] - (E[Y])^2 \tag{E}$$

$$\sigma = \sqrt{\sigma^2} \tag{F}$$

For a distribution of annuity values for N lives age x, assumed to be independent, the mean, variance and standard deviations would be calculated as follows:

$$\mu_N = N \times \mu \tag{G}$$

$$\sigma_N^2 = N \times \sigma^2 \tag{H}$$

$$\sigma_N = \sqrt{N} \times \sigma \tag{I}$$

As the size of a company's group annuity block of business increases, the required margins for random variations decrease. The Task Force reviewed recent statutory annual statement data on group annuity business to determine an appropriate company block of business volume assumption to use in calculating the random variation margin component. To ensure that the new standard would provide at least a two-standard-deviation margin for the vast majority of companies (more than 95%) having insured group annuity business, the Task Force decided that a 3,000-life block of business would be appropriate for computing margins for random variation.

Tables 16 and 17 show the results of applying these concepts and the determination of required margins to be built into the GAM-94 Basic Table q_x values shown in Table 13. Expected values and standard deviations were calculated by using the formulas presented in this section with a value of N 3,000. The interest rate used in the analysis was 6%. Note that use of other interest assumptions and forms of annuity did not significantly change the level of required margins.

TABLE 16

RANDOM VARIATION ANALYSIS OF REQUIRED MARGINS FOR MALES
GAM-94 BASIC TABLE EXPECTED MORTALITY
3,000-LIFE GROUP, INTEREST AT 6%

Annuity Type	Age	Expected Value	Standard Deviation	Required Margins	
				1 Standard Deviation	2 Standard Deviations
Immediate Life	45	41,400	128	3.0%	6.0%
Annuities	50	38,987	148	2.8	5.6
	55	36,043	167	2.6	5.2
	60	32,574	184	2.5	4.9
	65	28,724	194	2.3	4.6
	70	24,697	195	2.2	4.3
	75	20,459	188	2.0	4.0
	80	16,180	175	1.9	3.8
Deferred to Age	30	3,281	33	2.3%	4.6%
65 Life Annuity	35	4,410	43	2.3	4.6
	40	5,931	58	2.3	4.6
	45	7,990	76	2.3	4.6
	50	10,804	101	2.3	4.7
	55	14,713	132	2.4	4.7
	60	20,301	167	2.4	4.7

Based on these results, the Task Force concluded that a 5% margin would make adequate provision for random variations in mortality for reserving purposes.

TABLE 17

RANDOM VARIATION ANALYSIS OF REQUIRED MARGINS FOR FEMALES
GAM-94 BASIC TABLE EXPECTED MORTALITY
3,000-LIFE GROUP, INTEREST AT 6%

| | | | | Required Margins | |
| | | Expected | Standard | 1 Standard | 2 Standard |
Annuity Type	Age	Value	Deviation	Deviation	Deviations
Immediate Life	45	43,301	107	3.3%	6.5%
Annuities	50	41,342	125	3.0	6.0
	55	38,861	145	2.8	5.6
	60	35,810	165	2.7	5.3
	65	32,307	180	2.5	4.9
	70	28,439	186	2.3	4.6
	75	24,039	187	2.1	4.3
	80	19,406	180	2.0	4.0
Deferred to Age	30	3,907	30	2.6%	5.1%
65 Life Annuity	35	5,239	40	2.6	5.1
	40	7,032	53	2.6	5.1
	45	9,453	70	2.6	5.1
	50	12,727	92	2.6	5.1
	55	17,192	120	2.6	5.1
	60	23,381	153	2.6	5.1

B. Margins for Other Contingencies

The Task Force thought that the 5% margin was adequate for random variation for most insurance companies. However, blocks of business of less than 3,000 lives would have a greater standard deviation than shown above. Also, variations in the mix of business that companies write may cause the underlying mortality for a given company to differ from the underlying mortality in the valuation standard. Examples of business characteristics that could affect the underlying mortality averages include:

1. The mix of white-collar and blue-collar workers
2. The mix of higher-income and lower-income annuitants
3. Degree of concentration by geographic area.

For these reasons, the Task Force decided to recommend a specific margin to be added to the 5% statistical margin. The conclusion was to add 2% to the 5% statistical margin to produce a total 7% margin. It is anticipated that this margin produces reserves that are adequate to cover various business characteristics and random variations.

The resulting q_x values, including the 7% margin, comprise the 1994 Group Annuity Mortality Static Table and are presented in Table 18. Table 18 is calculated as 93% of the corresponding Table 13 values, with modification after age 102. No margin was applied to the mortality rates of 0.5

TABLE 18
1994 GROUP ANNUITY MORTALITY STATIC TABLE
1994 BASE YEAR

Age	Values of q_x		Age	Values of q_x		Age	Values of q_x	
	Male	Female		Male	Female		Male	Female
1	0.000592	0.000531	21	0.000530	0.000286	41	0.001156	0.000768
2	0.000400	0.000346	22	0.000556	0.000289	42	0.001252	0.000825
3	0.000332	0.000258	23	0.000589	0.000292	43	0.001352	0.000877
4	0.000259	0.000194	24	0.000624	0.000291	44	0.001458	0.000923
5	0.000237	0.000175	25	0.000661	0.000291	45	0.001578	0.000973
6	0.000227	0.000163	26	0.000696	0.000294	46	0.001722	0.001033
7	0.000217	0.000153	27	0.000727	0.000302	47	0.001899	0.001112
8	0.000201	0.000137	28	0.000754	0.000314	48	0.002102	0.001206
9	0.000194	0.000130	29	0.000779	0.000331	49	0.002326	0.001310
10	0.000197	0.000131	30	0.000801	0.000351	50	0.002579	0.001428
11	0.000208	0.000138	31	0.000821	0.000373	51	0.002872	0.001568
12	0.000226	0.000148	32	0.000839	0.000397	52	0.003213	0.001734
13	0.000255	0.000164	33	0.000848	0.000422	53	0.003584	0.001907
14	0.000297	0.000189	34	0.000849	0.000449	54	0.003979	0.002084
15	0.000345	0.000216	35	0.000851	0.000478	55	0.004425	0.002294
16	0.000391	0.000242	36	0.000862	0.000512	56	0.004949	0.002563
17	0.000430	0.000262	37	0.000891	0.000551	57	0.005581	0.002919
18	0.000460	0.000273	38	0.000939	0.000598	58	0.006300	0.003359
19	0.000484	0.000280	39	0.000999	0.000652	59	0.007090	0.003863
20	0.000507	0.000284	40	0.001072	0.000709	60	0.007976	0.004439

898

TABLE 18—Continued

Age	Values of q_x Male	Female	Age	Values of q_x Male	Female	Age	Values of q_x Male	Female
61	0.008986	0.005093	81	0.068615	0.043952	101	0.333461	0.296629
62	0.010147	0.005832	82	0.075532	0.049153	102	0.350330	0.317093
63	0.011471	0.006677	83	0.082510	0.054847	103	0.368542	0.338505
64	0.012940	0.007621	84	0.089613	0.060979	104	0.387855	0.361016
65	0.014535	0.008636	85	0.097240	0.067738	105	0.407224	0.383597
66	0.016239	0.009694	86	0.105792	0.075347	106	0.425599	0.405217
67	0.018034	0.010764	87	0.115671	0.084023	107	0.441935	0.424846
68	0.019859	0.011763	88	0.126980	0.093820	108	0.457553	0.444368
69	0.021729	0.012709	89	0.139452	0.104594	109	0.473150	0.464469
70	0.023730	0.013730	90	0.152931	0.116265	110	0.486745	0.482325
71	0.025951	0.014953	91	0.167260	0.128751	111	0.496356	0.495110
72	0.028481	0.016506	92	0.182281	0.141973	112	0.500000	0.500000
73	0.031201	0.018344	93	0.198392	0.155931	113	0.500000	0.500000
74	0.034051	0.020381	94	0.215700	0.170677	114	0.500000	0.500000
75	0.037211	0.022686	95	0.233606	0.186213	115	0.500000	0.500000
76	0.040858	0.025325	96	0.251510	0.202538	116	0.500000	0.500000
77	0.045171	0.028366	97	0.268815	0.219655	117	0.500000	0.500000
78	0.050211	0.031727	98	0.285277	0.237713	118	0.500000	0.500000
79	0.055861	0.035362	99	0.301298	0.256712	119	0.500000	0.500000
80	0.062027	0.039396	100	0.317238	0.274427	120	1.000000	1.000000

899

at ages 112 and older. A modified Karup-King graduation process was used
to obtain a smooth transition from the rates under age 103 to the rates at
age 112 and above. Figure 3 displays a graph of the mortality rates for male
and female ages 1–119 shown in Table 18. Figures 4, 5 and 6 display those
rates by the age categories of 1–40, 40–70, and 70–119, respectively.

FIGURE 3

1994 GROUP ANNUITY MORTALITY STATIC TABLE RATES
1994 BASE YEAR
AGES 1–119

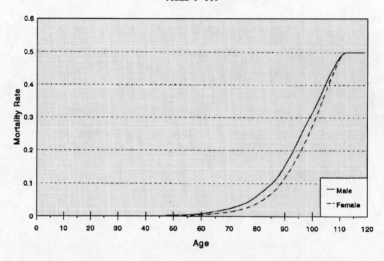

V. THE GENERATION MORTALITY TABLE

A. Development of Generation Mortality Tables

The Task Force was now in a position to produce the generation mortality
tables for males and females.

Prior mortality table generation methodologies included mortality tables
produced from projection scales. Thus, if we have a static mortality table
that is appropriate for 1994, together with mortality improvement factors
that are assumed to apply in the calendar years 1995 and later, we can
produce a static mortality table for each calendar year 1995 and later.

FIGURE 4

1994 GROUP ANNUITY MORTALITY STATIC TABLE RATES
1994 BASE YEAR
AGES 1–40

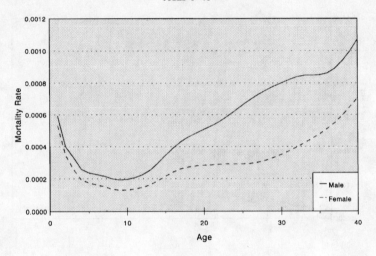

FIGURE 5

1994 GROUP ANNUITY MORTALITY STATIC TABLE RATES
1994 BASE YEAR
AGES 40–70

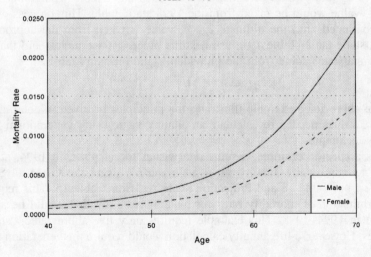

FIGURE 6

1994 GROUP ANNUITY MORTALITY STATIC TABLE RATES
1994 BASE YEAR
AGES 70–119

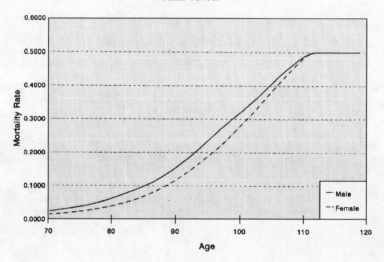

For example, assume a set of generation mortality rates is required to calculate annuity values for issue age 65 in calendar year 1997. The attained age 65 q_x value would be taken from the 1997 static table. The attained age 66 q_x value would be taken from the 1998 static table. This process would be continued until the ultimate age q_x value is taken from the appropriate final static table. Table 19 illustrates this process if we understand that the columnar rates come from the individual static mortality tables.

$$q_x^y = q_x^{1994} (1 - AA_x)^{y-1994} \tag{J}$$

An abbreviated example illustrates the principles involved in determining the q_x values needed to calculate an annuity value using generational mortality techniques.

As a specific example, assume one wishes to calculate, in 1994, a five-year temporary life annuity for a male age 63, using the GAM-94 Static Table from Table 18 and Projection Scale AA from Table 15. This requires determination of mortality rates for male ages 63–67 that would be applicable in 1994–1998. This example requires only five abbreviated "static" tables. However, a life annuity calculation would require the generation table

TABLE 19

ILLUSTRATION OF THE DEVELOPMENT OF A GENERATION MORTALITY TABLE FROM STATIC MORTALITY TABLES

Age	1994	1995	1996	1997	1998	1999	2000	2001	...	2052
65	q^{1994}_{65}	q^{1995}_{65}	q^{1996}_{65}	q^{1997}_{65}	q^{1998}_{65}	q^{1999}_{65}	q^{2000}_{65}	q^{2001}_{65}	...	q^{2052}_{65}
66	q^{1994}_{66}	q^{1995}_{66}	q^{1996}_{66}	q^{1997}_{66}	q^{1998}_{66}	q^{1999}_{66}	q^{2000}_{66}	q^{2001}_{66}	...	q^{2052}_{66}
67	q^{1994}_{67}	q^{1995}_{67}	q^{1996}_{67}	q^{1997}_{67}	q^{1998}_{67}	q^{1999}_{67}	q^{2000}_{67}	q^{2001}_{67}	...	q^{2052}_{67}
68	q^{1994}_{68}	q^{1995}_{68}	q^{1996}_{68}	q^{1997}_{68}	q^{1998}_{68}	q^{1999}_{68}	q^{2000}_{68}	q^{2001}_{68}	...	q^{2052}_{68}
69	q^{1994}_{69}	q^{1995}_{69}	q^{1996}_{69}	q^{1997}_{69}	q^{1998}_{69}	q^{1999}_{69}	q^{2000}_{69}	q^{2001}_{69}	...	q^{2052}_{69}
.				.	.	.	.	.	⋮	.
.				.	.	.	.	.	⋮	.
.				.	.	.	.	.	⋮	.
120	q^{1994}_{120}	q^{1995}_{120}	q^{1996}_{120}	q^{1997}_{120}	q^{1998}_{120}	q^{1999}_{120}	q^{2000}_{120}	q^{2001}_{120}	...	q^{2052}_{120}

to comprise 57 "static" tables, using age 120 as the last attained age in the calculations.

Table 20 shows our assumptions of mortality improvement factors and $1000q_x$ values in columns (1) and (2), respectively, and the resulting calculated values for future years in columns (3) to (6). Column (1) shows the final male mortality improvement factors from Table 15 by attained age, ages 63–67 in our example. Column (2) shows the GAM-94 Static Table of death rates in 1994 for attained ages 63–67 from Table 18. Columns (3) to (6) show calculated generation table death rates during the calendar years 1995–1998.

TABLE 20

GENERATION MORTALITY TABLE FOR THE YEARS 1994–1998 BASED ON GAM-94 STATIC TABLE
FOR MALES WITH FULL GENERATION USING PROJECTION SCALE AA
SPECIMEN $1000q_x$ MORTALITY RATES FOR ISSUE YEAR 1994

Attained Age	(1) Mortality Improvement Factor	Values of $1000q_x$				
		(2) 1994	(3) 1995	(4) 1996	(5) 1997	(6) 1998
63	1.4%	11.471	11.310	11.152	10.996	10.842
64	1.4	12.940	12.759	12.580	12.404	12.230
65	1.4	14.535	14.332	14.131	13.933	13.738
66	1.3	16.239	16.028	15.820	15.614	15.411
67	1.3	18.034	17.800	17.568	17.340	17.114

The values in columns (3) to (6) for age 63 are calculated as 11.471 multiplied successively by (1–0.014). For age 65 values under columns (3) to (6), 14.535 would be multiplied successively by (1–0.014).

Our required mortality rates are therefore found along the diagonal beginning with 11.471, followed by 12.759, 14.131, 15.614, and 17.114.

Generation mortality rates from the GAM-94 Static Table for males and females at *issue age 65* until attained age 120 are shown in Table 21 and Table 22, respectively. These tables compare the rates of mortality for issues of 1994, 1999, 2004, and 2009. A similar set of tabular rates applies to each issue age, for each issue year. Note that the mortality rates by issue year are the same for attained ages 101 and older because no mortality improvement is assumed at these advanced ages.

Note that the generation tables shown for each issue year in Table 21 (male) and Table 22 (female) reflect projected mortality using the general formula on page 909:

TABLE 21

GENERATION MORTALITY RATES PER 1,000 FOR ISSUES OF 1994, 1999, 2004, AND 2009
AT MALE ISSUE AGE 65 IN THE INDICATED YEAR
BASED UPON GAM-94 STATIC TABLE WITH FULL GENERATION AND PROJECTION SCALE AA

| | Male Issue Age 65 in the Year | | | |
Age	1994	1999	2004	2009
65	14.535	13.546	12.624	11.764
66	16.028	15.013	14.062	13.171
67	17.568	16.456	15.413	14.437
68	19.037	17.741	16.533	15.408
69	20.537	19.140	17.837	16.623
70	22.003	20.401	18.917	17.540
71	23.701	21.976	20.377	18.894
72	25.622	23.757	22.028	20.425
73	27.648	25.635	23.770	22.040
74	29.720	27.557	25.552	23.692
75	32.318	30.118	28.068	26.157
76	34.988	32.607	30.387	28.319
77	38.607	36.162	33.872	31.727
78	42.918	40.404	38.037	35.809
79	47.847	45.273	42.837	40.532
80	53.347	50.732	48.246	45.881
81	59.374	56.750	54.242	51.844
82	65.892	63.298	60.806	58.412
83	71.403	68.592	65.892	63.298
84	78.416	75.710	73.097	70.574
85	84.495	81.579	78.763	76.045
86	91.282	88.132	85.090	82.153
87	101.327	98.323	95.409	92.581
88	113.153	110.352	107.621	104.957
89	123.646	120.585	117.601	114.690
90	138.350	135.605	132.915	130.277

TABLE 21—*Continued*

Age	Male Issue Age 65 in the Year			
	1994	1999	2004	2009
91	150.708	147.717	144.787	141.914
92	168.078	165.572	163.103	160.671
93	182.385	179.665	176.987	174.348
94	197.701	194.754	191.850	188.989
95	219.989	217.798	215.628	213.481
96	236.375	234.021	231.690	229.382
97	252.134	249.622	247.136	244.675
98	276.012	274.635	273.265	271.901
99	291.221	289.768	288.322	286.883
100	306.321	304.793	303.272	301.759
101	333.461	333.461	333.461	333.461
102	350.330	350.330	350.330	350.330
103	368.542	368.542	368.542	368.542
104	387.855	387.855	387.855	387.855
105	407.224	407.224	407.224	407.224
106	425.599	425.599	425.599	425.599
107	441.935	441.935	441.935	441.935
108	457.553	457.553	457.553	457.553
109	473.150	473.150	473.150	473.150
110	486.745	486.745	486.745	486.745
111	496.356	496.356	496.356	496.356
112	500.000	500.000	500.000	500.000
113	500.000	500.000	500.000	500.000
114	500.000	500.000	500.000	500.000
115	500.000	500.000	500.000	500.000
116	500.000	500.000	500.000	500.000
117	500.000	500.000	500.000	500.000
118	500.000	500.000	500.000	500.000
119	500.000	500.000	500.000	500.000
120	1000.000	1000.000	1000.000	1000.000

TABLE 22

GENERATION MORTALITY RATES PER 1,000 FOR ISSUES OF 1994, 1999, 2004, AND 2009
AT FEMALE ISSUE AGE 65 IN THE INDICATED YEAR
BASED UPON GAM-94 STATIC TABLE WITH FULL GENERATION AND PROJECTION SCALE AA

| | Female Issue Age 65 in the Year | | | |
Age	1994	1999	2004	2009
65	8.636	8.422	8.214	8.010
66	9.646	9.407	9.174	8.947
67	10.657	10.393	10.136	9.885
68	11.587	11.301	11.021	10.748
69	12.457	12.148	11.848	11.554
70	13.390	13.059	12.736	12.420
71	14.423	13.995	13.580	13.178
72	15.825	15.356	14.901	14.459
73	17.342	16.743	16.165	15.607
74	19.132	18.472	17.835	17.219
75	20.935	20.111	19.319	18.559
76	23.183	22.271	21.394	20.552
77	26.073	25.173	24.304	23.465
78	28.958	27.959	26.994	26.062
79	32.050	30.944	29.876	28.845
80	35.456	34.232	33.051	31.910
81	39.280	37.924	36.615	35.351
82	43.620	42.115	40.661	39.258
83	48.341	46.673	45.062	43.507
84	53.360	51.518	49.740	48.024
85	60.057	58.276	56.549	54.873
86	67.819	66.140	64.503	62.907
87	76.931	75.405	73.909	72.443
88	85.558	83.860	82.197	80.566
89	97.317	95.866	94.437	93.029
90	107.852	106.244	104.660	103.099

TABLE 22—*Continued*

Age	Female Issue Age 65 in the Year			
	1994	1999	2004	2009
91	119.076	117.301	115.552	113.829
92	130.911	128.959	127.036	125.142
93	147.431	145.962	144.508	143.069
94	161.050	159.446	157.858	156.286
95	175.358	173.612	171.882	170.171
96	190.350	188.454	186.577	184.719
97	212.734	211.672	210.616	209.565
98	229.993	223.845	227.703	226.567
99	248.126	246.888	245.656	244.430
100	266.915	265.583	264.258	262.339
101	296.629	296.629	296.629	296.629
102	317.093	317.093	317.093	317.093
103	338.505	338.505	338.505	338.505
104	361.016	361.016	361.016	361.016
105	383.597	383.597	383.597	383.597
106	405.217	405.217	405.217	405.217
107	424.846	424.846	424.846	424.846
108	444.368	444.368	444.368	444.368
109	464.469	464.469	464.469	464.469
110	482.325	482.325	482.325	482.325
111	495.110	495.110	495.110	495.110
112	500.000	500.000	500.000	500.000
113	500.000	500.000	500.000	500.000
114	500.000	500.000	500.000	500.000
115	500.000	500.000	500.000	500.000
116	500.000	500.000	500.000	500.000
117	500.000	500.000	500.000	500.000
118	500.000	500.000	500.000	500.000
119	500.000	500.000	500.000	500.000
120	1000.000	1000.000	1000.000	1000.000

$$q_{65+n}^{1994+n+t} = q_{65+n}^{1994} \times (1 - AA_{65+n})^{n+t} \tag{K}$$

where

n attained age less 65

t issue year less 1994.

B. The 1994 Group Annuity Reserving Table

As initially indicated, the Task Force was charged with recommending a new Group Annuity Mortality Valuation Standard that would be suitable for calculating group annuity valuation reserves. By definition, this new standard shall be known as the 1994 Group Annuity Reserving (GAR-94) Table.

The GAR-94 Table combines three components:

1. Projection Scale AA, whose mortality improvement factors are shown in Table 15, for projecting mortality beyond the year 1994
2. The GAM-94 Static Table, whose q_x values are shown in Table 18
3. All the generation tables produced by multiplying the Projection Scale AA mortality improvement factors by the respective GAM-94 Static Table q_x values (of which examples for *issue age 65* and certain issue years are shown in Table 21 and Table 22).

The complete GAR-94 Table appears as Table 1 in the Executive Summary.

Note that this approach implies that a different set of mortality rates should be used for each different issue year for a specific issue age. However, it also implies that the same mortality rate should be used when the attained age and issue year offsets are the same. Thus, the mortality rate for issue age 65 in 1994 five years after issue is the same as that for issue age 70 in 1999 (and issue age 67 in 1996 two years after issue).

C. Financial Values Using the GAR-94 Tables

Table 23 shows and compares the life annuity net single premiums for an annuity due of $1 per year, payable monthly, for various issue ages based upon GAM-83 mortality and 7% level interest and for various issue ages and issue years based upon GAR-94 mortality and the same interest rate. In this table, on the GAR-94 basis, the net single premiums are significantly greater (at least 3%) for male issue ages 40–90 in 1994, 1999 and 2004, and 35–90 in 2009. At male issue age 65, for these issue years, the percentages are 6.2%, 7.7%, 9.1%, and 10.4%, respectively. Female issue ages show no significantly greater net single premiums in 1994 and only for issue age 75 in 1999. Because of the improving mortality, issues in 2004 show

TABLE 23

LIFE ANNUITY NET SINGLE PREMIUMS ASSUMING 7% LEVEL INTEREST RATE AND MORTALITY FROM GAR-94 TABLE VERSUS MORTALITY FROM GAM-83 TABLE

Value of $\ddot{a}_x^{(12)}$

				Issue Year				
	(1)	(2)	(3)	(4)	(5)	(6)	(7)	(8)	(9)
		1994		1999		2004		2009	
Issue Age	GAM-83	GAR-94	(2)/(1)	GAR-94	(4)/(1)	GAR-94	(6)/(1)	GAR-94	(8)/(1)
					Male				
20	14.334	14.463	1.009	14.477	1.010	14.490	1.011	14.502	1.012
25	14.169	14.346	1.012	14.363	1.014	14.378	1.015	14.393	1.016
30	13.947	14.190	1.017	14.213	1.019	14.234	1.021	14.255	1.022
35	13.649	13.970	1.024	14.002	1.026	14.032	1.028	14.061	1.030
40	13.252	13.653	1.030	13.699	1.034	13.741	1.037	13.782	1.040
45	12.737	13.215	1.038	13.278	1.042	13.337	1.047	13.393	1.052
50	12.099	12.625	1.043	12.708	1.050	12.786	1.057	12.860	1.063
55	11.329	11.861	1.047	11.963	1.056	12.059	1.064	12.151	1.073
60	10.380	10.915	1.052	11.034	1.063	11.149	1.074	11.259	1.085
65	9.242	9.814	1.062	9.950	1.077	10.080	1.091	10.206	1.104
70	8.006	8.613	1.076	8.757	1.094	8.896	1.111	9.031	1.128
75	6.729	7.306	1.086	7.434	1.105	7.560	1.123	7.682	1.142
80	5.480	5.958	1.087	6.055	1.105	6.150	1.122	6.244	1.139
85	4.401	4.735	1.076	4.803	1.091	4.870	1.107	4.937	1.122
90	3.493	3.609	1.033	3.647	1.044	3.685	1.055	3.723	1.066
95	2.723	2.722	1.000	2.740	1.006	2.757	1.012	2.775	1.019

TABLE 23—Continued

Value of $\ddot{a}_x^{(12)}$

		1994		1999		2004		2009	
						Issue Year			
	(1)	(2)	(3)	(4)	(5)	(6)	(7)	(8)	(9)
Issue Age	GAM-83	GAR-94	(2)/(1)	GAR-94	(4)/(1)	GAR-94	(6)/(1)	GAR-94	(8)/(1)
				Female					
20	14.510	14.552	1.003	14.560	1.003	14.567	1.004	14.574	1.004
25	14.400	14.456	1.004	14.466	1.005	14.475	1.005	14.483	1.006
30	14.253	14.320	1.005	14.333	1.006	14.344	1.006	14.355	1.007
35	14.054	14.133	1.006	14.149	1.007	14.165	1.008	14.180	1.009
40	13.786	13.877	1.007	13.898	1.008	13.918	1.010	13.937	1.011
45	13.430	13.532	1.008	13.553	1.009	13.583	1.011	13.607	1.013
50	12.964	13.066	1.008	13.096	1.010	13.125	1.012	13.154	1.015
55	12.359	12.450	1.007	12.484	1.010	12.518	1.013	12.552	1.016
60	11.586	11.657	1.006	11.701	1.010	11.745	1.014	11.787	1.017
65	10.623	10.710	1.008	10.764	1.013	10.818	1.018	10.871	1.023
70	9.451	9.622	1.018	9.688	1.025	9.752	1.032	9.816	1.039
75	8.131	8.331	1.025	8.404	1.034	8.476	1.042	8.547	1.051
80	6.795	6.926	1.019	6.993	1.029	7.060	1.039	7.126	1.049
85	5.505	5.512	1.001	5.560	1.010	5.607	1.019	5.654	1.027
90	4.252	4.209	0.990	4.288	0.997	4.268	1.004	4.297	1.011
95	3.103	3.157	1.017	3.172	1.022	3.188	1.027	3.203	1.032

significantly greater net single premiums for ages 70–80. At female issue age 65, for these issue years, the percentages are 0.8%, 1.3%, 1.8%, and 2.3%, respectively. The progression of ratios of GAR-94 net single premiums for males to those of the GAM-83 is relatively smooth and increasing until issue age 80 and then proceeds to decrease. Such ratios for females begin to materially decrease starting at issue age 80 but then show a sharp increase at issue age 95.

The mortality rate equivalence under GAR-94 mortality outlined above implies the same equivalence between net single premiums and reserves. Thus the net single premium for issue age 70 in 1999 is the same as the fifth-year reserve for issue age 65 in 1994, while the net single premium for issue age 75 in 2004 is the same as the tenth year reserve for issue age 65 in 1994 (and the fifth-year reserve for issue age 70 in 1999). Thus, for male issue age 65 in 1994, the percentage increases of the initial and fifth-, tenth-, and fifteenth-year reserves relative to the GAM-83 values are 6.2, 9.4, 12.3, and 13.9, respectively. For female issue age 65, the values are 0.8, 2.5, 4.2, and 4.9.

This analysis further confirms the need for a new reserve valuation standard to replace the GAM-83.

7. CONCLUSION

Present-day mortality levels have eroded the margins built into the 1983 Group Annuity Mortality Tables. They are no longer adequate for valuation purposes. Therefore, the Task Force has developed the 1994 Group Annuity Reserving Table presented in this report. The Task Force recommends that this new table replace the 1983 Group Annuity Mortality Table for use as a Valuation Mortality Standard.

A. Potential Uses of the New Standard

This report does not preclude other uses of the new standard, as long as the user clearly understands the development and coinciding limitations (margins, annual mortality improvement, and so on) of this new standard. Other reports that will be released will discuss additional uses of the tables presented in this report.

B. Acknowledgment

The Chair would like to thank each Task Force member as well as their employers for the time and unceasing effort devoted to this endeavor. This report and incorporated recommendation would not be as complete or as well-defined without the effort extended by each of these Task Force members. In addition, the Society of Actuaries staff and especially our assigned actuarial liaison's support have been invaluable throughout the process.

The Task Force thanks the following individuals for their written comments on the Exposure Draft of this report: Robert L. Brown and Shaun Wang, William H. Crosson, Harvey Fishman and Zachary Granovetter, G. Thomas Mitchell, Michael Mudry, Bruce E. Nickerson, Owen A. Reed, Robert Stalzer, David A. Wiener, William S. Wright, and especially Walter J. McLaughlin. Their comments only served to improve the final report.

Special thanks go to Charles F. Brown and Marian Rivera from Bankers Security Life for their tireless assistance in developing the Exposure Draft and presenting it in its final format. To try and name each and every individual who helped the Task Force would be to forget someone who should not be forgotten. However, we want to acknowledge the many helpful suggestions we received during the development of the tables. Thus, our appreciation to all, even those not named, is total.

REFERENCES

1. ANNUITY VALUATION TABLE COMMITTEE. "Position Paper." Schaumburg, IL.: Society of Actuaries, August 1992.
2. BELL, FELCITE, WADE, ALICE, AND GASS, STEPHEN. "Life Tables for the United States Social Security Area 1900–2080," *Actuarial Study No. 107, SSA Publication No. 11–11536*, Washington, D.C.: U.S. Department of Health and Human Services, August 1992, 34–35, Table 5.
3. BAYO, FRANCISCO R., AND FABER, JOSEPH F., "Mortality Experience around Age 100," *Transactions of the Society of Actuaries* XXXV (1983): 37–64.
4. LEW, EDWARD A., AND GARFINCKEL, LAURENCE, "Mortality at Ages 65 and Over in a Middle-Class Population," *Transactions of the Society of Actuaries* XXXVI (1984): 257–308.

DISCUSSION OF PRECEDING PAPER

JACQUES F. CARRIERE:

The purpose of this discussion is to present a parametric model or mathematical formula that will explain the pattern of mortality for the male and female GAM-94 tables. In my opinion, parametric formulas for mortality rates are always preferable to tabular rates, if the formula gives a good fit. Generally, the parametric approach always yields very smooth rates.

Before proceeding, it is instructive to plot the crude and graduated rates and examine the pattern of mortality in the GAM-94 tables. Consider the function

$$y_x = \log_e\{-\log_e(1 - q_x)\}$$

where q_x is the mortality rate for a life aged x. Remember that $\mu_{x+0.5} \approx \exp(y_x)$, where $\mu_{x+0.5}$ is a force of mortality. Let y_x^{crude} be the value based on the crude or ungraduated rates found in Table 12 and let y_x^{grad} be the value based on the graduated rates found in Table 13. Figure 1 presents plots of y_x^{crude}, y_x^{grad}, and $y_x^{crude} - y_x^{grad}$ versus $x=1, 2, \ldots, 108$ for both the female and male rates. The graduated values y_x^{grad} are based on the classical Karup-King method, which did an excellent job.

The parametric models for the male and female rates have nine parameters, denoted as $\theta = (\psi_1, m_1, \sigma_1, m_2, \sigma_2, \psi_3, m_3, \sigma_3)$. The parametric formula for the *male* rates is

$$y_x^{form}(\theta) = \psi_1 \times r_x(m_1, \sigma_1) + \psi_2 + s_x(m_2, \sigma_2) + \psi_3 \times t_x(m_3, \sigma_3),$$

while the formula for the *female* rates is

$$y_x^{form}(\theta) = \psi_1 \times r_x(m_1, \sigma_1) + \psi_2 \times r_x(m_2, \sigma_2) + \psi_3 \times t_x(m_3, \sigma_3),$$

where

$$r_x(m, \sigma) = \exp\left\{-\left(\frac{x}{m}\right)^{m/\sigma}\right\},$$

$$s_x(m, \sigma) = 1 - \exp\left\{-\left(\frac{x}{m}\right)^{-m/\sigma}\right\},$$

$$t_x(m, \sigma) = \frac{1}{\sigma}\left(\frac{x}{m}\right)^{(m/\sigma)-1}\exp\left\{-\left(\frac{x}{m}\right)^{m/\sigma}\right\}.$$

915

FIGURE 1

A Comparison of the Crude and Graduated Rates from the GAM-94.
The Horizontal Axis on All Graphs is the Attained Age x.
The First Column of Graphs Gives $y_x = \log_e\{-\log_e(1-q_x)\}$ Versus x.
The Second Column Shows $y_x^{crude} - y_x^{grad}$, the Difference in Crude and Graduated Rates.

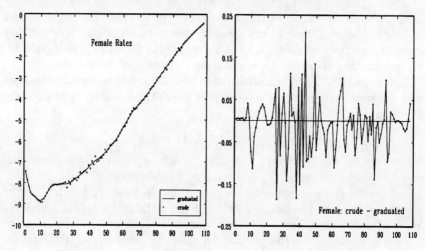

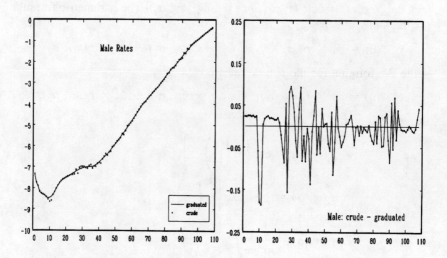

Notice that the male formula is a function of r_x, s_x, and t_x, while the female formula is a function of r_x, r_x, and t_x, so the male and female formulas are different. Both the male and female formulas were specifically created for the GAM-94 tables. Thus, applying these formulas on other tables may or may not yield good results. To estimate the parameters θ, we minimized the loss function

$$L(\theta) = \sum_{x=1}^{108} [y_x^{form}(\theta) - y_x^{crude}]^2.$$

The parameter estimates are shown in Table 1. Figure 2 presents plots of y_x^{crude}, y_x^{form}, and $y_x^{crude} - y_x^{form}$ versus $x = 1, 2, \ldots, 108$ for both the female and male rates. The graduated values, y_x^{form}, based on our formulas did an excellent job. Comparison of Figure 1 and Figure 2 shows y_x^{form} is smoother than y_x^{grad}, but the Karup-King values, y_x^{grad}, are slightly better fitting than y_x^{form}.

TABLE 1

PARAMETER ESTIMATES FOR THE PARAMETRIC MODELS

Model	ψ_1	m_1	σ_1	ψ_2	m_2	σ_2	ψ_3	m_3	σ_3
Male	9.800	82.09	22.15	-2.428	75.88	11.67	13.82	11.20	4.882
Female	188.3	96.59	59.35	-180.9	97.84	62.85	12.10	9.973	4.459

FIGURE 2

A COMPARISON OF THE CRUDE AND GRADUATED RATES FROM THE FORMULAS.
THE HORIZONTAL AXIS ON ALL GRAPHS IS THE ATTAINED AGE x.
THE FIRST COLUMN OF GRAPHS GIVES $y_x = \log_e\{-\log_e(1-q_x)\}$ VERSUS x.
THE SECOND COLUMN SHOWS $y_x^{crude} - y_x^{form}$, THE DIFFERENCE IN CRUDE AND FORMULA RATES.

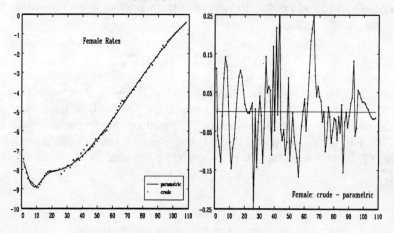

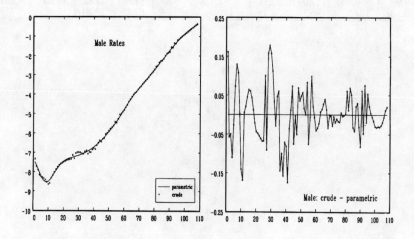

(AUTHOR'S REVIEW OF DISCUSSION)

LINDSAY J. MALKIEWICH:

The Task Force thanks Dr. Carriere for his thought-provoking discussion on a possible parametric model for explaining mortality patterns. While it is interesting to note that such a model can help to explain some of the GAR-94 results, it seems that an exploration of the model's computational viability would enhance the discussion. In other words, whereas the solution to a one-parameter model is readily developed, additional parameters will surely increase the difficulty of finding such a solution.

In addition to the increased difficulty of solving a multiple-parameter problem, the issue of parameter sensitivity should be addressed. Small changes in the provided formula's coefficients can cause drastic changes in the estimates of the given parameters. Therefore, an easy solution for a model making use of nine parameters would, logically, be quite difficult to find. It would be an interesting addition if the discussion explored various methods that would be used to discover such solutions.

In a related observation, a range of choices was shown for these parameter estimates in Table 1. Some of the differences between a given male versus female parameter are quite large. Therefore, it follows that small changes in the formula's coefficients may yield very different results, given the same parameters or even slightly different ones. Is this situation intended? Based on the discussion alone, it is unclear.

While the above concerns suggest areas in which additional demonstrations and more research could enhance the model, this discussion does serve as a worthwhile start. As stated, the model as presented does help to explain some of the GAR-94 results. The Task Force is, of course, pleased that such a model could do so. Perhaps, additional research could be that much more enlightening.

ABOUT THE AUTHORS

Patrick L. Brockett, not a member of the Society, is the Director of the Risk Management and Insurance Program and holds the Gus S. Wortham Memorial Chair in Risk Management and Insurance in the College and Graduate School of Business at the University of Texas at Austin. He is the former Director of the Center for Cybernetic Studies and former Director of the Actuarial Science Program in the Graduate School of Business. He is a Fellow of the Institute of Mathematical Statistics, the American Statistical Association, the Royal Statistical Society, and the American Association for the Advancement of Science; a Chartered Statistician by the Royal Statistical Society; and a Full Member of the Operations Research Society (now INFORMS). He is a member of the American Risk and Insurance Association, the Western Risk and Insurance Association, the International Actuarial Association (ASTIN section), and the Casualty Actuarial Society (Academic Corresponding Member). In addition to refereeing for numerous academic journals, he has published two books or monographs and more than 100 journal articles and is an Associate Editor of the journal *Insurance: Mathematics and Economics* and of the *North American Actuarial Journal.* Papers published in the *Transactions* include "Optimal Ruin Calculations Using Partial Stochastic Information" and "Statistical Adjustments of Mortality Tables to Reflect Known Information," both with Samuel H. Cox, Jr. (Volume XXXVI, 1984) and "Information Theoretic Approach to Actuarial Science: A Unification and Extension of Relevant Theory and Application" (Volume XLIII, 1991).

Robert L. Brown, F.S.A. 1976, F.C.I.A. 1977, and A.C.A.S. 1980, is Professor in the Department of Statistics and Actuarial Science and Director of the Institute of Insurance and Pension Research at the University of Waterloo, Ontario. He received an Hons.B.Math degree and an M.A. (gerontology) from the University of Waterloo. He has served as President of the Canadian Institute of Actuaries, was a member of the Board of Governors (1992–95), and Director of Publications

(1994–96) of the Society of Actuaries. He is the author of five books, including *Economic Security in an Aging Population* (Toronto, Ont.: Butterworths Canada, 1991) and *Introduction to the Mathematics of Demography*, 2nd edition (Winsted and Avon, Conn.: Actex Publications, 1993). He has published several papers in scientific and technical journals, including "Actuarial Aspects of the Changing Canadian Demographic Profile" (*TSA* Volume XXXIV, 1982), "Future of Group Insurance: Demographic Aspects" with Ben W. Lutek (*TSA* Volume XXXV, 1983), and "Toward Computerized Underwriting—A Biological Age Model" with K.S. Brown (*TSA* Volume XXV, 1983).

Samuel H. Cox, Jr., F.S.A. 1980, is Professor of Actuarial Science at Georgia State University. He earned B.A. and M.S. degrees at Texas Christian University and a Ph.D. at Louisiana State University, all in mathematics. Dr. Cox is a Chartered Property and Casualty Underwriter (1996). He is Editor of the Society of Actuaries-sponsored *North American Actuarial Journal*. Dr. Cox is a contributing author to several textbooks and has published scholarly papers in mathematics, actuarial science, insurance, and finance.

Niels H. Fischer, F.S.A. 1953, is a consultant with Bay State Actuaries in Needham, Mass. His practice is principally in accident and health special risks and international reinsurance. Following U.S. Navy service in World War II and graduation from Middlebury College, he was employed by Aetna from 1949 to 1976, where he was Vice President heading individual, special risk, and small-group health insurance operations, and introduced the industry's first cash-value disability policy. He was later Vice President, group staff, at Metropolitan Life, and a consulting actuary with Milliman & Robertson, where he formed the firm's Boston health practice. He has authored articles in publications including *Best's Review*, *Insurance Advocate*, and *Money Magazine*. He was a contributor to *Life Insurance* (Heubner & Black) and was co-author of the Society's textbook: *Health Insurance through Individual Policies*. Mr. Fischer served the Society as chairperson of an examination committee. He has made numerous presentations at meetings of the Society and at meetings of civic groups, senior living groups, the Association of Life Insurance Medical Doctors of America, and the Health Insurance Association of America (HIAA); he also chaired an annual HIAA Forum. He was a member of the committees on Continuing Care Retirement Communities of the Academy of Actuaries and of the National Association of Insurance Commissioners.

John Gavin, not a member of the Society, graduated in mathematics from University College, Cork, in 1987 and received a diploma and a master's degree in actuarial science from The City University, London, in 1988 and 1992, respectively. He is currently studying for a Ph.D. in statistics at the University of Bath. His work experience includes four years service with the Sun Alliance Insurance Group. He has published papers in *Insurance*: *Mathematics and Economics* and *The Journal of the Institute of Actuaries*. His research interests focus on computational statistics, nonparametric statistics, and data visualization.

Steven Haberman, F.I.A. 1975, A.S.A. 1976, is Professor of Actuarial Science at City University and Dean of the School of Mathematics. He is founding director of the Actuarial Research Centre at the University. He graduated from Cambridge University in mathematics in 1972 and received a Ph.D. in 1982 from City University. After graduation, he joined the Prudential Assurance Company before joining City in 1974 as a Lecturer. He has also worked part-time for the Government Actuary's Department and served as a consultant to a number of insurance companies. He is currently in his second term on the Council of the Institute of Actuaries and has served on several committees, including the CMI AIDS subcommittee. He is the co-author of *Pensions*: *The Problems of Today and Tomorrow* (Allen and Unwin: 1987), *Actuarial Mathematics* (Institute and Faculty of Actuaries: 1993), and *The History of Actuarial Science* (Pickering and Chatts: 1995). He has published more than 60 papers, which have appeared in the *Journal of the Institute of Actuaries, Insurance: Mathematics and Economics, Transactions of the International Congress of Actuaries, Journal of Actuarial Practice, Geneva Papers on Risk and Insurance, Journal of Royal Statistical Society, Social Science and Medicine*, and the *Actuarial Research Clearing House*. He has won two Research Prizes from the

Institute of Actuaries. His research interest focuses on graduation methods, pension fund models, motor insurance premium rating, and mortality and morbidity.

Boaz Golany, not a member of the Society, is the Associate Dean of the Industrial Engineering and Management Faculty at the Technion-Israel Institute of Technology. He has a B.Sc. (summa cum laude) in industrial engineering and management from the Technion (1982) and an interdisciplinary Ph.D. from the Business School of the University of Texas at Austin (1985). Dr. Golany has published over 40 papers in academic and professional journals and books. His publications are mostly in the areas of industrial engineering, operations research, and management science.

Robert J. Johansen, F.S.A. 1954, retired MetLife vice president and actuary, is currently a consulting actuary. He received an M.A. in mathematics/statistics from Columbia in 1974. He has served on the SOA Board of Governors and numerous SOA committees. He has held various positions on the E&E Committee, including General Chairperson. In addition to chairing the industry committee that designed the Separate Accounts Annual Statement Blank in 1977, he chaired SOA committees that produced the 1983 Table *a* (IAM) and the Blended 1980 CSO tables for life insurance policies affected by the Norris decision. He is currently Vice-Chair of the Life Practice Research Committee and chairs several of its Project Oversight Groups; he is also a member of the Life Practice Advancement Committee and chairs the SOA Task Force on Mortality Guarantees in Variable Products; and he is a member of the American Academy of Actuaries Work Group on Reserving for Minimum Guaranteed Death Benefits in Variable Annuities. His publications have appeared in the *Transactions, The Actuary, Best's Review* (P&C Edition), and the *Proceedings of the ASA Social Statistics Section.*

Bertram M. Kestenbaum, A.S.A. 1985, is an actuary in the Office of the Actuary of the Social Security Administration. He graduated summa cum laude from Brooklyn College with a bachelor's degree in mathematics and received a master's degree in biostatistics from the Johns Hopkins University School of Hygiene and Public Health. His papers have appeared in *Transactions* ("The Birthday Rule and the Difference in Spouses' Ages" (XLIV, 1992), the *Journal of the American Statistical Association, Demography,* and other journals. He serves on the Society's Course 161 (demography) Examination Committee.

Kevin Law, F.S.A. 1977, is Vice President and Group Actuary at Pan-American Life Insurance Company in New Orleans, La. His field of specialization is group life and health insurance, with current responsibilities for portfolios in the U.S. and in eight Latin American countries. Previously, he was employed by Aetna Life and Casualty and Phoenix Mutual (now Phoenix Home Life) in Hartford, Conn. Law received a B.A. in mathematics from the University of California at Santa Barbara. He is the 1995–96 Chairperson of the International Section Council. He was the Chairperson of the Organizing Committee for the International Section when it was formed in 1991–92; he served as the 1993–95 editor of the section's newsletter, the *International Section News* and as Associate Editor during 1992–93. He is a member of the Society's Committee on International Relations and the American Academy of Actuaries Committee on International Issues. He has participated in Society Spring and Annual meetings as a panelist and as a moderator and has made presentations at meetings of the Latin American insurance industry organization El Instituto de Estudios e Investigaciones del Seguro de Centro América, Panamá, y el Caribe (ISCAPC).

Ernest J. (Jack) Moorhead, F.S.A. 1938 and A.I.A., began his actuarial career at Great-West Life in 1929; from 1945 until 1948, he was with a predecessor of the Life Insurance Marketing and Research Association (LIMRA, at that time LISRB and then LIAMA); from 1948 to 1952, at United States Life in New York City; from 1952 to 1967, at New England Mutual Life; and from 1967 until his retirement in 1972, at Integon in Winston-Salem, N.C. Since 1972, he has participated in public interest activities, including advisory work for the U.S. Senate Subcommittee on Antitrust and Monopoly and two studies of the financial problems of the Social Security system. He served the Society of Actuaries as chairperson of the Committee on Papers, President (1969–70), and editor of *The Actuary*, and is currently chairperson of the Committee on Memorials. He served the American Academy of Actuaries as President (1973–74). He is the author of *Our Yesterdays: the History of the Actuarial Professional in North America, 1809–1979*, which was published by the Society as part of the profession's Centennial Celebration in 1989. He has published several papers, discussions, and book reviews in the *Transactions*, including "The Construction of Persistency Tables" (Volume XII, 1960), "Mortality Investigation with Expected Mortality Estimated at Issue by Use of Persistency Factors" (Volume XIII, 1961), "Valuation of Nonvested Renewal Commissions" (XV, 1963), "Report on the Forthcoming Sequel to the 1966–67 Future Outlook Study of the Institute of Life Insurance" (XXIV, 1972), "Unresolved OASDI Decoupling Issue," with C.L. Trowbridge (XXIX, 1977), "Sketches of Early North American Actuaries" (XXXVI, 1984), and "Mortality Experience of Fellows of the Actuarial Society of America and the American Institute of Actuaries" with John H. Cook (XLII, 1990). He resides in a CCRC.

Fred Phillips, not a member of the Society, is Professor of Management and Head of the Department of Management in Science and Technology at the Oregon Graduate Institute of Science and Technology. Dr. Phillips attended The University of Texas and Tokyo Institute of Technology, earning a Ph.D. at Texas (1978) in mathematics and management science. He has held teaching and research positions at the Universities of Aston and Birmingham in England, the General Motors Research

Laboratories, and St. Edward's University. Until 1995, he was at The University of Texas at Austin, where he held the titles of Director of Research and Academic Programs and Judson Neff Centennial Fellow at the IC² Institute, associate director of the Center for Cybernetic Studies, and Senior Lecturer on the faculties of marketing, economics, and Asian studies. Until 1989, he was a vice president at MRCA Information Services. Dr. Phillips is a member of The Institute of Management Sciences, the Information Industries Association, the Western Regional Science Association, and the American Marketing Association (Executive Member). He is the author or co-author of many publications in operations research and marketing, and editor of two recent books for managers: *Thinkwork*: *Working, Learning, and Managing in a Computer-Interactive Society* (Praeger, 1992) and *Concurrent Life Cycle Management*: *Manufacturing, MIS, and Marketing Perspectives* (IC² Institute of the University of Texas at Austin, 1990). He is a founder and member of the Advisory Board of the Austin Software Council.

Stephen Reddy, F.S.A. 1983, is a vice president at Morgan Stanley & Co. in New York, doing consulting on asset-liability management issues. He received a B.A. in mathematics from Bucknell University. Prior to joining Morgan Stanley in 1992, he worked at three large mutual life insurers, concentrating on the areas of life and annuity product development. He is currently on the SOA's Investment Section Council and is a member of the American Academy of Actuaries. Mr. Reddy's research activities have included the development of an interactive asset-liability computer model, co-authoring a LOMA research study "Asset Liability Management in the Life Insurance Industry" (1993), co-authoring a paper "Market Valuation of Liabilities" (1995), and co-editing the SOA's *Dynamic Financial Condition Analysis Handbook* (1995).

James B. Ross, F.S.A. 1954, is Associate Professor of Finance in the College of Business and Economics at Radford University in Radford, Va. His business experience includes service with Connecticut General Life, CIGNA, Insurance Company of North America, Continental Corp., and Metropolitan Life. He received an A.B. in mathematics from Harvard College, an M.B.A. from the University of Rhode Island, and a Ph.D. in finance from the University of Connecticut. His papers have appeared in the *Transactions, Journal of Actuarial Practice, Journal of Economics and Finance,* and the *Journal of Financial Services Research.*

David P.M. Scollnik, A.S.A. 1988, is an associate professor in the department of mathematics and statistics at the University of Calgary, where he teaches actuarial science and statistics. He has also lectured in actuarial science at the University of Toronto. He received a combined Honors B.Sc. in pure mathematics and actuarial science from the University of Western Ontario and both an M.Sc. and a Ph.D. in statistics from the University of Toronto. His doctoral research was partially supported by a SOA Ph.D. grant in 1991–92. Dr. Scollnik's professional actuarial experience includes service with Towers Perrin and Canada Life. He is a member of the American Risk and Insurance Association, the American Statistical Association, and the Statistical Society of Canada. He is also an academic correspondent with the Casualty Actuarial Society. His papers have appeared in *Insurance: Mathematics and Economics, ARCH, Biometrics, Communications in Statistics,* and the Proceedings of the Casualty Actuarial Society.

Keith P. Sharp, F.S.A. 1990, F.C.I.A. 1983, F.I.A. 1982, F.I.A.A. 1981, is an Associate Professor and Associate Director of the Institute of Insurance and Pension Research at the University of Waterloo. His business experience includes periods with Commercial Union Assurance in London, PTOW (now Towers Perrin) in Melbourne, and Towers Perrin in Toronto. He received a bachelor's degree in mathematics from Cambridge University, a master's degree in statistics from the University of California at Berkeley, and a doctorate in finance from the University of Waterloo. Dr. Sharp's papers have appeared in various journals, including *Review of Economics and Statistics*, *Insurance*: *Mathematics and Economics*, *Journal of Actuarial Practice*, and *Journal of Insurance Regulations*.

Klaus O. Shigley, F.S.A. 1976, is a vice president in John Hancock's Guaranteed and Stable Value Products division. He has responsibility for the pricing, underwriting, and financial reporting functions for guaranteed group pension products, primarily GICs and group annuities. From 1988 through 1993, he was responsible for the pricing and product development of retail life insurance products. Mr. Shigley currently serves as a member of the SOA's Investment Section Council and the Committee on Life Practice Research. He is a former Chairperson of the Committee on Papers for the *Transactions* and is past president of the Boston Actuaries Club and is a former member of the Product Development Section Council. He is a frequent speaker at SOA Meetings ("Pricing and Profit Testing," San Francisco, 1994; "Impact of Low Interest Rates," Boston, 1993; "Capital Management," Quebec, 1993; "Pricing on a Unisex Basis," Vancouver, 1989; and "Matching Insurance Company Pension Assets and Liabilities," San Diego, 1986). He was a participating faculty member of the "GIC Product Management" seminar sponsored by the Society in 1986. He is also a frequent speaker at GIC conferences. His published papers include "Guaranteed Investment Contracts" in *The Handbook of Fixed Income Securities* (Fabozzi, 3rd ed.), and "Unit Expense Factors for Risk Based Capital Requirements" (*Product Development News* 1992). Mr. Shigley is an Enrolled Actuary and a Chartered Life Underwriter. He holds a B.A. in mathematics from the University of California at Berkeley and an M.A. in mathematics from the University of Massachusetts.

Yun Song is currently on the actuarial staff of the National Actuarial Services Group, Ernst & Young, LLP. She received a Ph.D. in management science and information systems from The University of Texas at Austin in May 1996. Her research has been conducted mainly in the area of actuarial science. Prior to joining Ernst & Young, she was an actuarial intern with Texas Department of Insurance and the United Teacher Associates Insurance Company in Austin, Texas. She published a paper in *Journal of Actuarial Practice*, "Obtaining a Life Table for Spinal Cord Injury Patients Using Medical Study."

Richard Verrall, not a member of the Society, is a Reader in the Department of Actuarial Science and Statistics at City University. He graduated in mathematics from St. John's College, Cambridge in 1981 and received an M.Sc. in statistics from University College, London in 1982. In 1989, he received his Ph.D. from City University for a dissertation on aspects of claims reserving. He has published papers on claims reserving, graduation, motor premium rating, and excess mortality rating in *Insurance: Mathematics and Economics*, *ASTIN Bulletin*, *Journal of the Institute of Actuaries*, and the *Scandinavian Actuarial Journal*. In 1993, he was awarded first prize in the Casualty Actuarial Society's prize competition on the variability of loss reserves. He is director of the M.Sc. program in actuarial science at City University and is an examiner in Statistics for the Institute of Actuaries.

Criss G. Woodruff, not a member of the Society, is Assistant Professor of Finance at Texas A&M University in Corpus Christi, Tx. He earned a B.A. degree from Centenary College of Louisiana and M.Ed., M.B.A., and D.B.A. degrees from Mississippi State University. Prior to joining the faculty at Texas A&M, Dr. Woodruff was Assistant Professor of Finance at Radford University in Radford, Va. He has also worked in retail management and state government. Dr. Woodruff's research has recently appeared in the *Journal of Economics and Finance* and the *Journal of Actuarial Practice*. He is a member of several professional organizations, including the International Financial Management Association and Decision Sciences International.

Xiaohua Xia, not a member of the Society, is the Manager of Management Information Services for AutoBond Acceptance Corporation, a consumer finance company in Austin, Texas. He graduated with a B.S. degree in computer science from Zhejiang University, Hangzhou, People's Republic of China, in 1983, and received a Ph.D. in management science and information systems from the University of Texas at Austin. Mr. Xia has coauthored two other papers, which will appear in *Insurance: Mathematics and Economics* and *IMPACT* (W.W. Cooper and S. Thore, eds., Greenwood Publishing Group, Inc.). He is a member of the American Risk and Insurance Association.

INDEPENDENT AUDITOR'S REPORT

We have audited the accompanying statement of financial condition of the Society of Actuaries as of July 31, 1995 and 1994, and the related statements of revenues and expenses and changes in membership equity, and cash flows for the years then ended. These financial statements are the responsibility of the Society's management. Our responsibility is to express an opinion on these financial statements based on our audits.

We conducted our audits in accordance with generally accepted auditing standards. Those standards require that we plan and perform the audits to obtain reasonable assurance about whether the financial statements are free of material misstatement. An audit includes examining, on a test basis, evidence supporting the amounts and disclosures in the financial statements. An audit also includes assessing the accounting principles used and significant estimates made by management, as well as evaluating the overall financial statement presentation. We believe that our audits provide a reasonable basis for our opinion.

In our opinion, the financial statements referred to above present fairly, in all material respects, the financial position of the Society of Actuaries as of July 31, 1995 and 1994, and the results of its operations and cash flows for the years then ended in conformity with generally accepted accounting principles.

> [*Signed*] SELDEN, FOX AND ASSOCIATES, LTD.
> Certified Public Accountants

September 15, 1995

FINANCIAL REPORT

STATEMENT OF FINANCIAL CONDITION

ASSETS

| | July 31, 1995 | | | July 31, 1994 | | |
---	General Fund	Restricted Fund	Total	General Fund	Restricted Fund	Total
Current Assets:						
Cash and cash equivalents	$ 996,265	$1,222,107	$ 2,218,372	$ 239,386	$1,143,829	$ 1,383,215
Investments	1,602,873		1,602,873	3,719,023		3,719,023
Accounts receivable, less allowance for doubtful						
accounts of $35,000 for 1995 and 1994	775,891		775,891	373,806		373,806
Inventories	304,685		304,685	213,134		213,134
Prepaid experience studies expense	158,836		158,836	177,013		177,013
Other	282,984		282,984	228,107		228,107
Total Current Assets	4,121,534	1,222,107	5,343,641	4,950,469	1,143,829	6,094,298
Equipment and leasehold improvements, at cost, less						
allowance for depreciation and amortization of						
$520,038 ($514,195 in 1994)	442,508		442,508	349,631		349,631
Long-term investments	5,819,876		5,819,876	5,106,689		5,106,689
Total Assets	$10,383,918	$1,222,107	$11,606,025	$10,406,789	$1,143,829	$11,550,618

934

STATEMENT OF FINANCIAL CONDITION—*Continued*

LIABILITIES AND MEMBERSHIP EQUITY

| | July 31, 1995 | | | July 31, 1994 | | |
	General Fund	Restricted Fund	Total	General Fund	Restricted Fund	Total
Current Liabilities:						
Accounts payable and accrued expenses	$ 2,069,612	$ 98,567	$ 2,168,179	$ 1,622,806	$ 99,297	$ 1,722,103
Deferred revenues	2,009,294		2,009,294	1,818,729		1,818,729
Accrued contribution to Society of Actuaries Foundation	500,000		500,000	500,000		500,000
Total current liabilities	4,078,906	98,567	4,177,473	3,941,535	99,297	4,040,832
Membership equity	6,305,012	1,123,540	7,428,552	6,465,254	1,044,552	7,509,786
Total Liabilities and Membership Equity	$10,383,918	$1,222,107	$11,606,025	$10,406,789	$1,143,829	$11,550,618

See accompanying notes.

935

STATEMENT OF REVENUES AND EXPENSES AND CHANGES IN MEMBERSHIP EQUITY

	For the Year Ended July 31, 1995			For the Year Ended July 31, 1994		
	General Fund	Restricted Fund	Total	General Fund	Restricted Fund	Total
Revenues:						
Membership dues	$ 3,265,679	$346,828	$ 3,612,507	$ 2,940,323	$320,416	$ 3,260,739
Continuing education fees	2,545,602	127,686	2,673,288	2,487,619	111,455	2,599,074
Education and examination fees	6,635,025		6,635,025	6,318,608		6,318,608
Sale of publications	70,678	5,251	75,929	88,718	5,576	94,294
Experience studies	577,363		577,363	594,451		594,451
Income from allied organizations	261,923		261,923	305,432		305,432
Investment income	532,636	43,115	575,751	461,081	27,953	489,034
Contributions		62,865	62,865		55,325	55,325
Other	115,690		115,690	104,259		104,259
Total Revenues	14,004,596	585,745	14,590,341	13,300,491	520,725	13,821,216
Operating expenses:						
Salaries and related expenses	4,791,661		4,791,661	4,386,447		4,386,447
Printing	1,394,993	70,074	1,465,067	1,392,665	71,318	1,463,983
Travel and honoraria	2,154,781	106,409	2,261,190	2,207,025	115,140	2,322,165
Postage and mailing	1,139,778	88,343	1,228,121	1,191,743	75,497	1,267,240
Grading services/course development	533,200		533,200	512,744		512,744
Exam Centers	144,855		144,855	141,313		141,313
Fellowship Admission Course and intensive seminars	435,919		435,919	458,749		458,749
Cost of calculators sold	108,898		108,898	115,230		115,230
Rent	648,582		648,582	605,978		605,978
Office stationery, supplies and maintenance	143,729	7,282	151,011	96,400		96,400
Program supplies and services	326,976	9,993	336,969	312,824	6,731	319,555
Computer	136,214		136,214	100,496		100,496
Public relations/strengthening profession	46,905		46,905	101,658		101,658
Telephone	143,194	7,831	151,025	129,941	8,210	138,151
Professional fees	167,561		167,561	257,234		257,234
Depreciation—books	40,778		40,778	44,988		44,988
Depreciation—equipment	52,303		52,303	49,758		49,758
Insurance	59,931		59,931	44,343		44,343
Wharton seminar	104,183		104,183			
Research projects	262,261	70,583	332,844	212,217	63,592	275,809

STATEMENT OF REVENUES AND EXPENSES AND CHANGES IN MEMBERSHIP EQUITY—Continued

	For the Year Ended July 31, 1995			For the Year Ended July 31, 1994		
	General Fund	Restricted Fund	Total	General Fund	Restricted Fund	Total
Experience studies	$ 474,935	$	$ 474,935	$ 538,351	$	$ 538,351
Other research expenses	12,500		12,500	12,000		12,000
College/university initiative	72,628	100,049	172,677	70,758	81,732	152,490
Government employee travel	6,911		6,911	7,766		7,766
Library	42,305		42,305	49,899		49,899
Student Newsletter	25,734		25,734	35,321		35,321
Bulletin Board	12,693	3,750	16,443	15,880		15,880
Actuarial Standards Board/Actuarial Board for Counseling and Discipline courses	(475)		(475)	5,698		5,698
International relations	22,674		22,674	23,121	16,864	39,985
SOA Foundation expenses	269,226		269,226			
Administration fee		42,057	42,057			
Miscellaneous	165,342	366	165,708	128,569	1,040	129,609
Total operating expenses	13,941,175	506,737	14,447,912	13,249,116	440,124	13,689,240
Revenues over operating expenses	63,421	79,008	142,429	51,375	80,601	131,976
Other income (expense):						
Contribution to Society of Actuaries Foundation	(53,663)		(53,663)	(500,000)		(500,000)
Sales tax assessment	(170,000)		(170,000)			
Recognition of deferred rent				824,944		824,944
Deferred rent shared with CCA and AAA				(55,912)		(55,912)
Revenues over (under) expenses	(160,242)	79,008	(81,234)	320,407	80,601	401,008
Membership equity, beginning of the year	6,465,254	1,044,532	7,509,786	6,144,847	963,931	7,108,778
Membership equity, end of the year	$ 6,305,012	$1,123,540	$ 7,428,552	$ 6,465,254	$1,044,532	$ 7,509,786

See accompanying notes.

STATEMENT OF CASH FLOWS

	For the Year Ended July 31, 1995			For the Year Ended July 31, 1994		
	General Fund	Restricted Fund	Total	General Fund	Restricted Fund	Total
Cash flows from Operating Activities:						
Revenue over (under) expenses	$ (160,242)	$ 79,008	$ (81,234)	$ 320,407	$ 80,601	$ 401,008
Adjustments to reconcile revenue over (under) expenses to net cash provided by operating activities:						
Depreciation and amortization	99,695		99,695	83,172		83,172
Accrued rent				(942,796)		(942,796)
Loss on sale of equipment	1,184		1,184			
Amortization and accretion of investment discounts and premiums	46,369		46,369	79,755		79,755
Changes in certain working capital items:						
Net accounts receivable	(402,085)		(402,085)	(190,943)		(190,943)
Inventory	(91,551)		(91,551)	(16,138)		(16,138)
Prepaid experience studies	18,177		18,177	79,139		79,139
Other current assets	(54,877)		(54,877)	132,877		132,877
Accounts payable and accrued expenses	(53,194)	(730)	(53,924)	244,624	78,941	323,565
Deferred revenues and advances	190,565		190,565	(28,466)		(28,466)
Net cash provided by (used in) operating activities	(405,959)	78,278	(327,681)	(238,369)	159,542	(78,827)
Cash flows from Investing Activities:						
Purchase of property and equipment	(195,641)		(195,641)	(156,389)		(156,389)
Proceeds from sale of equipment	1,885		1,885			
Investment purchases	(2,343,406)		(2,343,406)	(2,477,885)		(2,477,885)
Proceeds from maturity of investments	3,700,000		3,700,000	1,100,000		1,100,000
Net cash provided by (used in) investing activities	1,162,838		1,162,838	(1,534,274)		(1,534,274)
Net increase (decrease)	756,879	78,278	835,157	(1,772,643)	159,542	(1,613,101)
Cash and cash equivalents, beginning of the year	239,386	1,143,829	1,383,215	2,012,029	984,287	2,996,316
Cash and cash equivalents, end of the year	$ 996,265	$1,222,107	$ 2,218,372	$ 239,386	$1,143,829	$ 1,383,215

See accompanying notes.

938

NOTES TO THE FINANCIAL STATEMENTS

NOTE 1. SUMMARY OF SIGNIFICANT ACCOUNTING POLICIES

Organization and Purpose. The Society of Actuaries is an educational, research, and professional membership organization primarily for actuaries in Canada and the United States. Its objectives are to advance the knowledge of actuarial science and to promote the maintenance of high standards of competence and conduct within the actuarial profession.

Cash and Cash Equivalents. The Society considers all highly liquid investments with an original maturity of three months or less to be cash equivalents.

Inventories. Inventories are stated at the lower of cost, determined on the first-in, first-out method, or market.

Experience Studies. Approximately annually, the Society conducts various experience studies for use by its members. Expenses in connection with the compilation of these studies are charged to a prepaid account. The following fiscal year insurance companies and other commercial employers of actuaries are assessed for these and other related expenses, at which time the prepaid account is relieved by charging expense.

Property and Equipment. Acquisitions, improvements and replacements of major assets are capitalized at cost. Depreciation and amortization are computed on the straight-line method based on the estimated useful lives of the assets or the terms of the leases.

Membership Dues. Dues are deferred and recognized as income on a pro rata basis over the Society's membership period.

NOTE 2. INVESTMENTS

Investments, which are stated at amortized cost, consist of the following:

	1995		1994	
	Amortized Cost	Market Value	Amortized Cost	Market Value
Short-term:				
United States Treasury notes	$1,600,873	$1,629,733	$3,719,023	$3,731,950
Corporate bond	2,000	2,000		
	1,602,873	1,631,733	3,719,023	3,731,950
Long-term:				
United States Treasury notes	$5,457,810	$5,507,758	$4,966,889	$4,887,799
Corporate bond	9,948	9,450	11,945	11,463
S&P Depository Receipts	292,609	347,975	109,266	110,100
Toronto 35 Index Fund	59,509	63,450	18,589	19,050
	5,819,876	5,928,633	5,106,689	5,028,412
	$7,422,749	$7,560,366	$8,825,712	$8,760,362

NOTE 3. MEMBERSHIP EQUITY

General Fund. General Fund membership equity at July 31, 1995 and 1994 is as follows:

	JULY 31,	
	1995	1994
General Fund:		
Board designated for research development	$ 93,112	$ 93,112
Unrestricted, undesignated	6,211,900	6,372,142
	$6,305,012	$6,465,254

Restricted Fund. The Society has restricted funds for contributions for educational awards, a minority recruitment program and Special Interest Sections. Disbursements to support these programs are made upon the authorization of the committee or section chairperson. The fund balances at July 31, 1995 and 1994 of the various restricted funds are as follows:

Educational Award Fund	$ 15,076	$ 15,476
Minority recruitment	28,240	47,984
	43,316	63,460
Special interest sections:		
Actuary of the Future	19,939	12,623
Computer science	64,360	57,243
Education and research	7,391	5,934
Financial reporting	169,714	114,609
Futurism	24,779	19,299
Health insurance	188,243	184,536
International	21,584	22,125
Investment	146,380	145,208
Nontraditional marketing	35,036	35,051
Pension	151,799	131,283
Product development	172,457	164,165
Reinsurance	66,337	79,535
Smaller Insurance Company	12,205	9,461
	1,080,224	981,072
Total	$1,123,540	$1,044,532

NOTE 4. EQUIPMENT AND LEASEHOLD IMPROVEMENTS

A summary of equipment and leasehold improvements at July 31 follows:

	1995	1994
Office equipment	$491,471	$465,724
Computer equipment	394,972	321,999
Truck	20,165	20,165
Leasehold improvements	55,938	55,938
	962,546	863,826
Less accumulated depreciation and amortization	520,038	514,195
	$442,508	$349,631

NOTE 5. LEASE COMMITMENTS

The Society occupies office space under a renegotiated lease agreement through 2008 that includes an agreed-upon 2.7% increase per year and escalation clauses to cover future increases in operating costs above base year costs. The Society also leases warehouse space under a lease agreement through 1998 that includes an agreed-upon 2% increase per year.

As of July 31, 1995, future minimum rental commitments, exclusive of executory costs such as real estate taxes and operating expenses, for these noncancelable leases are as follows:

1996	$ 394,000
1997	405,000
1998	416,000
1999	400,000
2000	411,000
2001–2008	3,726,000
	$5,752,000

The prior lease provided for a period of free rent through 1993, the effects of which were recognized over the lease term on a straight-line basis. Effective with the signing of the new lease, the balance of the deferred rent ($824,944) was taken into income in 1994, and $55,912 was returned to the Conference of Consulting Actuaries (CCA) and the American Academy of Actuaries (AAA) that utilize space within the Society's office.

NOTE 6. RETIREMENT PLAN

All employees of the Society, subject to minimum eligibility requirements, are covered by a tax deferred annuity program. The Society contributes 10% of the employees' basic salaries, up to the maximum allowable under IRS guidelines. The employees may contribute amounts up to the limitation as defined in the Internal Revenue Code. Contributions are applied to purchase tax deferred annuity contracts from insurance companies. The Society's policy is to fund retirement costs accrued. Pension expense for the years ended July 31, 1995 and 1994 was $349,172 and $303,719, respectively.

NOTE 7. INCOME TAXES

The Society is qualified as a tax-exempt organization under Section 501(c)(3) of the Internal Revenue Code. During 1995, the Society paid and expensed $12,429 for unrelated business income taxes. The income tax liability for 1994 amounted to $3,429 and was paid during 1995.

NOTE 8. RESEARCH COMMITMENTS

The Society has outstanding commitments of $469,300 to outside individuals or organizations for research projects in progress or about to begin. Of this amount, various Sections of the Society have agreed to contribute up to $100,900 toward these projects.

NOTE 9. SOCIETY OF ACTUARIES FOUNDATION
AND ACTUARIAL EDUCATION AND RESEARCH FUND (AERF)

The Society of Actuaries Foundation (Foundation) was created July 25, 1994. During the fiscal year ending July 31, 1994, the Society had approved and accrued an unconditional contribution of $500,000 as seed money for the Foundation as a pledge of support towards continuing education and research. The Society has also made a commitment to provide a dollar-for-dollar matching funds challenge up to an additional $500,000. During 1995, the Society matched $53,663 in contributions to the Foundation.

All administrative costs of the Foundation are currently provided for in the Society's budget. In 1995, the Society paid direct expenses of $269,226 on behalf of the Foundation and allocated expenses of $179,700.

The Society also allocated expenses of $21,300 for staff efforts to support AERF. Allocated expenses, in both cases, consist mostly of salary, fringe benefits and occupancy costs. The Society did not allocate any expenses to the Foundation or AERF in 1994.

NOTE 10. SALES TAX AUDIT

The Illinois Department of Revenue has completed a sales and use tax audit of the Society for the period July 1981 through December 1994. As a consequence of this audit, the Department has proposed a deficiency against the Society for its sales of publications and other items. The Society disagrees with the deficiency findings and intends to contest the proposed assessment with the Department. If the maximum deficiency, which has been accrued, is upheld, the tax liability, together with interest and penalties, would total approximately $170,000.

At this time, it is impossible to predict whether a negotiated settlement will occur, or the likelihood of success if there is an appeal to the state courts.

NOTE 11. NEW ACCOUNTING PRONOUNCEMENTS

The Financial Accounting Standards Board has issued *Statements Number 116 and 117. Statement 116* is entitled "Accounting for Contributions Received and Contributions Made" and will require that contributions received, including unconditional promises to give, are recognized on the accrual basis of accounting. *Statement 117* is entitled "Financial Statements of Not-for-Profit Organizations" and will require the financial statements to be reformatted to focus on the entity as a whole, rather than by funds; and to present balances and transactions according to the existence or absence of donor-imposed restrictions. The requirements of these statements will need to be applied no later than fiscal year July 31, 1996. The effects of adopting these statements have not yet been determined.

NOTE 12. RECLASSIFICATIONS

Certain items in the prior-year financial statements have been reclassified to conform with the current-year presentation. These reclassifications had no effect on net income or membership equity.

BOOK REVIEWS AND NOTICES

Edward I. Altman and Irwin T. Vanderhoof, editors, *The Financial Dynamics of the Insurance Industry*, 512 pp., published by Irwin Professional Publishing, New York, N.Y., 1995.

The Financial Dynamics of the Insurance Industry is a collection of papers presented in 1993 at a conference on the dynamics of the insurance industry organized by the Salomon Center of New York University, in cooperation with the Stern School of Business. The 23 papers cover solvency issues for life and property and casualty insurance companies as well as the management of assets and liabilities, analysis of asset performance, and performance measurement. The book is a valuable collection of papers with a good mix of theory and practical applications.

The papers are written to address issues primarily from a U.S. perspective, but the issues raised and the approaches discussed will be of interest to managers in other countries.

The book will be of particular interest to those in the insurance business with asset-liability management and reporting responsibilities. The papers bring together viewpoints from practitioners, regulators and academics. Many insurance managers need to keep themselves aware of emerging theories of financial management in the industry as well as the complex regulatory climate. For example, the theory of risk-based capital, which has become an important part of financial management and regulation, is also a useful tool for assessing the appropriate asset mix to meet corporate objectives.

Several papers consider some of the practical issues surrounding the matching of assets and liabilities for life and P&C insurance organizations. These papers provide a useful perspective to supplement some of the theoretical considerations of asset-liability matching. The papers on performance measurement address issues that have challenged insurance company management for some time.

Although it has been a few years since I was in the insurance industry, I believe the papers offer practical and useful advice for managers. As the editors note, the industry is facing financial challenges—and public perception challenges. Regulators, investors and customers are increasingly questioning the actions of management—in some cases, with justification. Most managers and professionals will want to read selectively and focus on the issues important to their responsibilities. However, *Financial Dynamics of the Insurance Industry* also provides a valuable resource to assess trends, theories and concerns that were important to the industry in 1993 and in most cases, remain valid in 1996.

ROBERT H. STAPLEFORD

Bruce S. Pyenson, editor, *Calculated Risk: A Provider's Guide to Assessing and Controlling the Financial Risk of Managed Care*, 67 pp., published by American Hospital Publishing, Inc., Chicago, Illinois, 1995.

Calculated Risk is intended to provide hospitals and provider organizations with guidance in managing financial risk under the many managed care arrangements that integrate provider services with financial risk for the cost of care. Developing integrated networks and successfully managing capitated arrangements will require that providers learn many risk management functions similar to those used by insurers and managed care organizations (for example, HMOs). The publication outlines steps to help hospitals develop risk management strategies wherever the hospital lies on the managed care continuum.

Chapter 1 identifies the new elements of provider risk, including underpricing risk, fluctuation risk, and business and administrative risk. Chapter 2 deals with how risk is measured and evaluated. It defines the basic elements of the actuarial cost model and defines a methodology for assessing the degree of health care management for a hospital. The various approaches used by HMOs, PPOs, insurance carriers, and employers for shifting risk to providers are reviewed in Chapter 3. Valuable guidance for evaluating a capitated proposal and a managed care partner is included in Chapter 4. This chapter also discusses the keys to success under capitation contracts. While the first four chapters are written by actuaries, the last two chapters are written by physicians. Chapter 5 discusses how to align clinical practice with aggregate managed care goals for a hospital or integrated system. Chapter 6 discusses the role and risk assumed by partners in a provider network, integrators of a full-service provider network, and owner/operators of a provider/insurer organization.

Calculated Risk does not offer to hospitals any easy solution for surviving under managed care, but it does provide valuable advice and insight for hospitals from an actuarial perspective. The publication should not replace the need to seek competent design, legal, medical, and actuarial assistance once a hospital or provider organization decides to assume financial risk. *Calculated Risk* would be more valuable if it included contributions by a wider range of consultants and dealt with a broader array of critical issues. For example, how much risk-taking by providers is allowed under state insurance law before the organization needs an HMO license?

This book is recommended as a primer for students who want a quick introduction to the strategies of health care capitation. The importance of the book arises from its strategic perspective of the issues facing providers that assume financial risk.

THOMAS J. LIVORSI

Phelim P. Boyle, *Options and the Management of Financial Risk*, 223 pp., published by the Society of Actuaries, Schaumburg, Illinois, 1994, $25.00.

The introduction states: "The aim of this text is to communicate concepts and models from modern financial economics and investment theory that are useful in actuarial science." Investors and insurance policy-owners have become increasingly knowledgeable over the past two decades. In that span, the conceptual framework of financial economics has replaced the traditional actuarial models of classic compound interest as the preferred tool for managing interest rate spreads. With this book, Dr. Boyle creates the bridge from the deterministic to the stochastic approach to dealing with interest rate uncertainty.

The book is targeted to a wide audience of both actuaries and nonactuaries who seek an introduction to the concepts of finance without immediately committing to a 400-page or more text. I would recommend the text for students of the Fellowship Syllabus as they commence the Finance Track. Senior actuaries whose duties are no longer primarily technical will find the text helpful in facilitating discussions with investment and actuarial technicians.

Given the great breadth of subjects encompassed in the economics of finance, a 220-page text simply cannot address any one subject with great rigor. For example, the subject of interest rate swaps merited a two and one-half page treatment. The math background assumed is suggested by the statistical material presented in Chapter 6, "Models of Uncertainty": the central limit theorem, the normal and lognormal distributions, the random walk, arithmetic and geometric Brownian motion, Wiener processes, and Ito's lemma. Given the compactness of the book, many conclusions are merely stated and not demonstrated.

Consistent with the goal of brevity, the book contains no index, no appendices, and no exercises. Nonetheless, the examples work effectively, in that all instruments are discussed from the common initial premise of a defined term structure of interest rates. Conclusions are clearly set out in bold, with ample white space to ease the reader's way.

The author's approach is to concentrate on the underlying theory and concepts, with only limited institutional detail. Assumptions are idealized; financial markets are assumed to be frictionless; transaction costs are ignored.

The most effective approach to grasping the material is to follow the chapters in order, given the abundant references to preceding material. The format is an integrated progression from the building blocks of term structure of interest rates to pricing by stochastic methods.

To provide a flavor of the material, herewith is a nibbler's taste of what piqued this reviewer's interest:

Chapter 1, "Introduction," presents a fundamental contrast between financial risks and insurance risks. Financial risks are statistically correlated, so that the risk reduction accruing from pooling of assets is limited: more assets means more risk. Hence, the use of derivative assets to hedge financial risk has grown rapidly in the past two decades. In contrast, insurance risks are assumed to be independent, that is, not correlated. Hence, pooling risks provides the primary tool for reducing risk from insurance liabilities.

In sum, increasing the volume of assets merely increases risk, while increasing the volume of insurance liabilities greatly reduces risk. The stochastic model of risk management, with its capacity to measure correlation of risks, is the preferable tool for managing the balance sheet. The deterministic model fails utterly, in the era of tight profit margins and the advanced level of financial knowledge of investors and policyholders. It cannot measure the costs of exercising options.

Chapter 2, "The Term Structure of Interest Rates," creates the basic vocabulary of financial economics at its elemental level: spot rates and forward rates build the transition from the limiting notion of force of interest to stochastic term structure models.

With the discussion of duration in Chapter 3, the book is off to a strong start. The foundation is laid for the discussion of derivative assets to follow.

Chapter 4, "Options, Forwards and Futures," introduces the purposes, the pricing and the terminology for the most common types of derivative financial instruments: American options, European options, forward contracts, futures contracts, futures options, and interest rate swaps. Though this list hardly defines the universe of derivative instruments, the discussion of their features successfully illustrates the concepts of the economics of finance.

Chapter 5 presents "General No-Arbitrage Relationships" that hold among the prices of various derivative securities. A fundamental defect of the deterministic classical compound interest rate model is that arbitrage profits are indeed possible. The stochastic model solves that defect and thus realistically portrays the efficiency of the market in trading out any apparent gains at no risk.

Chapter 6, "Models of Uncertainty," outlines the fundamental statistical concepts supporting pricing models based on stochastic processes. The author faces a tremendous challenge in the attempt to set these out in a mere 23 pages. In unfortunate consequence, so does the reader, in the attempt to comprehend it. Of course, the material is readily available from other sources.

Chapter 7, "The Pricing of Stock Options," discusses the properties of the Black-Scholes solution and illustrates conclusions with numerical examples. The starting point is a discrete time binomial model, followed by the continuous-time option-pricing model. Once the Black-Scholes formula has been developed, it becomes possible to analyze the sensitivity of stock option prices to five underlying parameters. This is quite an elegant tool for risk analysis.

Chapter 8, "Scholastic Interest Rate Models," addresses the fundamental problem of how to develop future interest rate scenarios for calculating bond prices. Bond prices depend on an entire term structure of interest rates, both currently and at future dates. Accordingly, constructing a valid model for pricing bonds is much more complex than that for pricing stock options. Dimensions of the problem include reasonability of scenarios, plausibility (that is, probability) of scenarios occurring, and prevention of arbitrage profits. Numerous solutions exist, of varying complexity. The author outlines one successful approach.

My final observations are twofold: first, financial modeling software is viewed by many as a black box of indeterminate calculations, particularly for market values. For some, the problem is lack of familiarity with the software. For others, the problem is also lack of familiarity with the *theory*. Dr. Boyle's text goes far in removing the latter concern. Second, the emergence of modeling software and the cash-flow-testing requirements have created deep problems of resources for smaller companies, which lack the critical mass to effectively exploit these capital investments. The same might also be said for the *intellectual* capital required to manage financial risk in today's world. Not surprisingly, asset management consulting services are enjoying tremendous growth these days.

Dr. Boyle has done a great service to the actuarial community in introducing many to the economics of finance. Whether you "just want to know something about the subject" or you ultimately plan to attack the subject in depth, my judgment is that the time invested in reading this book is well spent.

RICHARD J. JUNKER

Obituary

WARREN ROLLAND ADAMS
LAWRENCE ALPERN
JOSEPHINE WAKEMAN BEERS
KAREN M. CHALK
WILLIAM THOMAS CHAMBERS
MILTON F. CHAUNER
FRANK DOMINIC CUBELLO
EUGENE FREDERICK DORFMAN
JACK M. ELKIN
EDMUND DEAN FORBES
HERBERT SYMONDS GARDNER
DAVID LAWRENCE GILBERT
A. ALLAN GRUSON
THOMAS CHARLES HARDING
RICHARD FRASER STAPLES HAZLETT
JAMES HUNTER
WILLIAM WARD KEFFER
LARRY LANG
BEN ZIJON LIPSHITZ
ARTHUR EARL LOADMAN
RALPH HAYNES MAGLATHLIN
KEITH LESLIE MCCOMB
ALEXANDER MARSHALL
LAURENCE HARDING MIGOTTI
MORTON DAVID MILLER
ZEHMAN IRVING MOSESSON
CHARLES EDWIN RICKARDS
ALEXANDER CAMPBELL MACINTOSH ROBERTSON
JOSEPH F. SAULON
EDWARD GLADSTONE SCHAFER
PHILIP D. SLATER
ANATASE EUGENE STATIUS
TERENCE NORMAN TOWRY
PAUL FRANKLIN WEBER
WILLIAM RULON WILLIAMSON, JR.

1931   Warren Rolland Adams   1995

Warren R. Adams, a Fellow of the Society, died in Des Moines, Iowa on November 29, 1995. He was 64 years old.

Born in Blockton, Iowa on February 11, 1931, Mr. Adams served in the U.S. Air Force Security Service with the rank of Master Sergeant during the Korean War, 1951 to 1954. During those years, he studied Russian and was for some time stationed in Japan. Upon returning home, he entered the State University of Iowa, graduating in 1956.

In 1957, he joined the actuarial staff at Bankers Life Company (now Principal Financial Group) in Des Moines, where he was appointed assistant actuary after earning his Society Fellowship in 1964. In 1967 he entered the teaching profession at Drake University for a 20-year career that included a leave of absence in 1978–1979 to serve as the first Society of Actuaries Director of Education. From 1987 until his untimely death, he was back at Principal Financial Group as Director, Actuarial Education and Research.

Mr. Adams contributed substantially to the Society's literature. Apart from much material arising from his office duties, he authored a paper, "The Effect of Interest on Pension Contributions" (*TSA* XIX, 170), as well as several discussions and a book review. He helped to establish the direction of numerous research activities and, as a consequence of his facility with the Russian language, was of great value as a member of a 1994 Society delegation to Moscow to start developing a branch of our profession in Russia.

An active volunteer in the Alliance for the Mentally Ill (AMI), he served as President of the Iowa chapter and was elected to the Board of Directors of the National AMI, serving as President for two terms.

Mr. Adams will be remembered for his friendliness, sense of humor and warm, caring personality. He was an active member of the Society of Actuaries, having served in both staff and volunteer capacities. In his professional career, Warren freely offered suggestions, shared his perspective, and provided input on a multitude of issues, displaying a strong commitment to improving the actuarial profession and the ability to turn plans into action.

He is survived by his wife, Vicki, two sons, a daughter, and a grandson.

1909   Lawrence Alpern   1995

Lawrence Alpern, an Associate of the Society, died in Glen Burnie, Maryland on September 17, 1995. He was 86 years old.

Born in New York City on April 15, 1909, Mr. Alpern graduated from New York University in 1929 and was employed in 1930 by the New Jersey Insurance Department. In 1941 he joined the Social Security Administration in Baltimore for a distinguished 34-year career. He earned his Associateship in 1945 and retired in 1975.

At the Social Security Administration Mr. Alpern became the Chief of the Actuarial Section in 1946, with responsibility for short-range (5 to 10 years) cost estimates. In 1963 he became the Deputy Chief Actuary for Short-Range Estimates in the Office of the Actuary.

He always exhibited high levels of professionalism and excellence. His example inspired and motivated many other actuaries to exert their best professional efforts. His dedication, energy, and high-quality actuarial services earned the admiration and respect of his colleagues.

He is survived by his wife, Esther, a daughter, a granddaughter, and two great-grandchildren.

1908   Josephine Wakeman Beers   1994

Josephine W. Beers, a Fellow of the Society, died in Hermosa Beach, California on October 25, 1994. She was 86 years old.

Born in Guilford, Connecticut on June 24, 1908, a sister of the famous actuary Henry S. Beers (remembered in *TSA* XXXIII, 798), Miss Beers graduated from Wellesley College in 1929 and joined the actuarial staff at Travelers Insurance Company. In 1935 she moved to New Mexico as actuary of Western American Life and in 1938 to Occidental Life, Los Angeles. She served in the U.S. Navy from 1943 to 1946, then returned to Occidental Life for the rest of her career, earning her Society Fellowship in 1951.

At Occidental Miss Beers was head of the mathematical department and then specialized in group insurance. She retired in 1973 from the post of Group Actuary.

She was active in Society affairs, contributing to discussions and serving two three-year terms on the Board of Governors, 1962–1965 and 1967–1970.

She was a thoughtful, private, widely respected lady whose close friendship one had to earn. Her retirement years, afflicted by emphysema, were in seclusion. She is believed to have left no close family survivors.

1963   Karen D.M. Chalk   1995

Karen D.M. Chalk, an Associate of the Society, died from cancer in Tillsonburg, Ontario on September 26, 1995. She was 32 years old.

Born in the same city on August 29, 1963, Miss Chalk graduated from the University of Western Ontario in 1986 and was first employed as an actuarial student at the Equitable Life Insurance Company of Canada. Subsequently she worked at The Citadel Assurance Company in Toronto. In 1990 she earned her Associateship and joined Sun Life of Canada in Toronto.

At Sun Life she became a manager in the actuarial department responsible for annuity valuation and cash-flow testing, while continuing her actuarial studies and also working toward a professional accounting designation.

She was a lover of musical theatre and enjoyed ballroom dancing. She will be remembered as a very warm person liked and respected by her colleagues. She is survived by her parents, a sister, and a brother.

1928   William Thomas Chambers   1995

William T. Chambers, an Associate of the Society, died in Milwaukee, Wisconsin on October 16, 1995. He was 67 years old.

Born in Kalamazoo, Michigan on July 17, 1928, Mr. Chambers graduated from Kalamazoo College in 1950. After joining the U.S. Army and doing overseas duty in Korea, he earned his master's degree in the University of Michigan actuarial program in 1954 and joined Northwestern Mutual Life for a 34-year career, earning his Society Associateship in 1956. He performed extensive work with agents' compensation, the company retirement plan and development of the 1955 American Annuity Table and then transferred to underwriting, where he directed and performed research in that field. Shortly before retiring in 1988, he returned to the actuarial department with the title of actuary.

He was an avid bridge player and loved traveling, and will be remembered for his keen mathematical mind, his quick wit, and warm personality. He is survived by his mother and two sisters.

1917   Milton F. Chauner   1995

Milton (Milt) F. Chauner, a Fellow of the Society, died in Wayne, Pennsylvania on January 20, 1995. He was 77 years old.

Born in Bozeman, Montana on July 18, 1917, Mr. Chauner graduated from Montana State College in 1938 and completed advanced studies at University of Michigan's actuarial course and at Harvard Business School. After service at Connecticut General and in the U.S. Army and then at Standard Oil of California, he joined California Western States Life in 1950, becoming group actuary there and earning his Society Fellowship in 1953. After a period as vice president of Life Insurance Company of North America in Philadelphia, he entered the consulting field with Milliman & Robertson in 1964, his first assignment being to establish that firm's Philadelphia office.

In his 20 years at M&R, Mr. Chauner established or was closely involved in its offices at New York, Toronto, and Gainesville, Florida. One measure of his contribution is the number, 13, of principals and associate members of his firm whom he recruited and developed. He became primarily responsible for his company's rise to a leading position in health consulting and served as the first chairman of its professional development committee. For 18 years he was a member of its board and also was active in international actuarial affairs for the profession.

After retirement in 1984, Milt added poetry to his list of interests. He was a good and gentle man with many appreciative friends. He is survived by his wife, Helen, two sons, and five grandchildren.

1907   Frank Dominic Cubello   1995

Frank D. Cubello, a 1949 Fellow of the Society, died in Livingston, New Jersey on January 18, 1995. He was 87 years old.

Born in Niagara Falls, New York on May 18, 1907, Mr. Cubello graduated from Rensselaer Polytechnic Institute in 1929. After earning his master's degree at Princeton University in 1933, he immediately joined Prudential

Insurance Company's Actuarial Student Training Program and made his career with that company until retiring from the post of vice president and assistant actuary in the group pension department in 1972. After retirement, he established and operated his own pension consulting firm in Short Hills, New Jersey.

As well as being a good actuary, he was exceptionally companiable with and considerate to his colleagues. And he was active in a great variety of community programs including the local Hospital Center and the Easter Seal Society. He was a member of the Knights of Columbus Council and an Oblate of St. Benedict.

Surviving are his wife, Marion, a son, and a brother.

1913   Eugene Frederick Dorfman   1995

Eugene F. Dorfman, a Fellow of the Society, died in Boca Raton, Florida on November 23, 1995. He was 82 years old.

Born in Pittsfield, Massachusetts on May 20, 1913, Mr. Dorfman graduated from Williams College in 1936. After brief employment outside life insurance, he joined Guardian Life in New York City in 1937 for a career that was to last 41 years, though interrupted by U.S. Army service, partly as a medic in the European theater, from 1941 to 1945. He earned his Fellowship in 1948 and was a company actuary with an unusually agile brain and lifelong advocacy of sound actuarial principles until his retirement in 1978. He continued to live in New York City until shortly before his death.

In a sense Mr. Dorfman wrote his own obituary in advance with these 1987 words: "As you can see, a life without distinction, yet of some use." He was quiet, yet earned warm affection and esteem from those few who knew him well. Although living alone after a very early divorce, he loved children and people needing help to cope with life's problems. And he possessed fine appreciation of good music and literature. He is survived by cousins and nieces.

1913   Jack M. Elkin   1995

Jack M. Elkin, an Associate of the Society, died in New York City on June 29, 1995. He was 82 years old.

Born in the same city on January 26, 1913, Mr. Elkin graduated from the College of the City of New York in 1931 and a year later at age 19 earned his master's in mathematics from Columbia University. He entered federal employment and without keen interest in an actuarial career did not achieve Associateship until after leaving the Railroad Retirement Board to found the Martin E. Segal Company's actuarial department in 1954. He became an authority on funding of multi-employer pension plans, writing articles on that subject and on funding of the Railroad Retirement System. He retired from the post of Segal's Senior Vice President & Chief Actuary in 1979.

He then continued independently in the consulting field. He also taught mathematics, especially calculus and analytical geometry, at both the Illinois Institute of Technology and Long Island University, proving himself a superb teacher.

A man of wide interests, Mr. Elkin loved the English language and was adamant about expressing himself clearly and economically; it was hard to find a word with whose etymology he was unacquainted. And he was also concerned about the world's political, economic, and social condition. He was a frequent respondent to the puzzle columns of actuarial magazines.

He was active in charitable organizations, particularly the American Jewish Congress of which he was Executive Vice President for several years. He is survived by his wife, Lillian, and a daughter.

1920   Edmund Dean Forbes   1995

E. Dean Forbes, an Associate of the Society, died in Mesa, Arizona on August 10, 1995. He was 75 years old.

Born in Kingsley, Iowa on April 7, 1920, Mr. Forbes graduated from Morningside College in 1941. He had been a star fullback and had given inspiration to many hometown youngsters in counseling them on football. Entering the U.S. Army in 1942, he served in a field artillery unit and was promoted in the battlefield. In November 1944 he was listed as missing in action; in fact, he was a prisoner of war, during which confinement he studied bridge and remained a keen bridge player all his life. In May 1945 his family first learned that he was alive. Upon return to civilian life he took and in 1946 passed the actuarial course at State University of Iowa.

He was first employed by United Benefit Life of Omaha, where he earned his Society Associateship in 1954. Then in August 1955 he entered the consulting field with Nelson & Warren in St. Louis, where he remained until his retirement in 1978. He specialized in working with new and small life insurance companies then springing up all over the Midwest and needing guidance in every phase of their operations.

Mr. Forbes' family life was a test that clearly showed his strength of character. His father having died when he was twelve, he became the man of the house and set a stellar example to his much younger brother. He is survived by his wife, Jan, a son, a daughter, a stepdaughter, his brother Leon who is a Fellow of the Society, and a sister.

1903   Herbert Symonds Gardner   1995

Herbert S. Gardner, a Fellow of the Society, died in Hancock, New Hampshire on July 1, 1995. He was 91 years old.

Born in Hancock on August 1, 1903, Mr. Gardner graduated cum laude from Harvard College in 1924. After nine years in the Boston branch office of Equitable Life Assurance Society, he joined New England Mutual Life Insurance Company in 1934 for a career that was to last 34 years. He earned his Society Fellowship in 1941 and retired in 1968 from the post of Actuary.

Known by many friends as Larry, Mr. Gardner was an actuary of keen judgment and unfailingly cordial disposition with a talent for accepting life as he found it. His sense of humor was penetrating yet gentle, making him a highly valued colleague and companion. Among his lifelong interests were sports, particularly baseball. He is survived by his wife, Sophia, two sons, and six grandchildren.

1960   David Lawrence Gilbert   1995

David L. Gilbert, a Fellow of the Society, died in Philadelphia on March 17, 1995 after an extended illness.

Born in that city on December 9, 1960, Mr. Gilbert graduated from Temple University with a major in actuarial science in 1982. He then joined Life Insurance Company of North America in Philadelphia while continuing his studies at Villanova University. In 1986 he joined the group pension department at Provident Mutual Life, where his contributions included development and pricing as well as client consultation in that young department. He did not permit a serious ailment to defeat his efforts and earned his

Fellowship in 1993. But in December 1994 his condition forced him into disability retirement.

He will be remembered for his dedication, outgoing nature, and a hint of flamboyance. He loved to travel and to share his experiences with friends and coworkers. He is survived by his father, stepmother and several siblings.

1911   A. Allan Gruson   1995

A. Allan Gruson, a 1948 Associate of the Society, died in Freehold, New Jersey on January 8, 1995. He was 83 years old.

Born in Dublin, Ireland on November 6, 1911, Mr. Gruson moved to Canada after high school and graduated from the University of Toronto in 1934. From 1935 to 1941 he was employed at Berkshire Life in Pittsfield, Massachusetts and then joined the actuarial staff at Metropolitan Life, New York. He retired in 1976 from the post of Senior Research Assistant.

He was active and interested in a wide range of community affairs and enjoyed bridge and studying world affairs. He is survived by his wife, Frances, three daughters, and four grandchildren.

1947   Thomas Charles Harding   1995

Thomas C. Harding, an Associate of the Society, died of cancer in Allen, Texas on March 25, 1995. He was 47 years old.

Born in Austell, Georgia on September 19, 1947, Mr. Harding graduated in 1969 from West Georgia College and was employed at Protective Life in Birmingham, Alabama, where he earned his Associateship in 1978. In 1980 he joined American Family Life in Columbus, Georgia, where he was Second Vice President & Assistant Actuary until 1991. He was then employed as an assistant actuary at National Financial Insurance Company in Dallas until an ownership change terminated his as well as other positions.

While actively seeking a new post, his ailment was diagnosed, forcing him into retirement as totally disabled. In August 1994 he married Allison Kelt, who survives him. His other survivors are his mother, a brother, two nephews, and a niece.

1912   Richard Fraser Staples Hazlett   1995

Richard F.S. Hazlett, a Fellow of the Society and of the Canadian Institute of Actuaries, died in Fredericton, New Brunswick on December 5, 1995. He was 83 years old.

Born in that city on February 15, 1912, Mr. Hazlett graduated from the University of New Brunswick in 1932 and was employed in the Dominion Department of Insurance until 1940 and then briefly at Massachusetts Mutual Life and then Maritime Life until his career was interrupted by war service in the Royal Canadian Air Force. In 1945 he returned to Maritime Life in Halifax and in 1947 accepted a post at Shenandoah Life in Roanoke, Virginia, where he earned his Society Fellowship in 1951. In 1958 he became actuary of Peoples Life in Frankfort, Indiana and then entered the consulting field with Connell Company in Wellesley, Massachusetts. From 1974 until his retirement in 1983, he was in private consulting, first in Boston and then back in Fredericton, Canada.

Mr. Hazlett, a lifelong bachelor, left no immediate survivors.

1904   James Hunter   1995

James Hunter, a Fellow of the Society and of the Faculty of Actuaries, died in Toronto, Ontario on December 8, 1995, He was 91 years old.

Born on the Isle of Bute, Scotland on April 27, 1904, Mr. Hunter graduated from Rothesay Academy and earned his diploma in actuarial mathematics at Edinburgh University. He came to Canada in 1927 after three years service at Scottish Life Assurance Company, Edinburgh, to accept the post of assistant actuary at Continental Life Insurance Company in Toronto, where he achieved his Society Fellowship in 1933.

At Continental Life Mr. Hunter had a 40-year career, reaching the post of vice president and general manager. In 1967 he went to Zurich Life of Canada in Toronto, which had been merged with his company before his retirement in 1970.

Mr. Hunter was a quiet gentleman, always a credit to the profession and active in Society affairs. In 1939 he and Benjamin T. Holmes submitted an influential paper recommending revision of the Society's educational system. He is survived by his wife, Phyllis, three sons, four grandchildren, and two great-grandchildren.

1922   William Ward Keffer   1995

William W. Keffer, a Fellow of the Society, died in Littleton, Colorado on May 2, 1995. He was 73 years old.

Born in Hartford, Connecticut on March 19, 1922, son of the distinguished actuary Ralph Keffer, he graduated from Brown University in 1943 and served in the Army Air Corps as a first lieutenant in World War II. In 1946 he joined Connecticut General in Hartford, earning his Society Fellowship in 1950 and achieving vice president rank. Although quiet by nature, he was active in discussion at Society meetings and on education and examination committees.

In 1973 he moved to Colorado to accept responsibility for group insurance operations at the U.S. headquarters of Great-West Life of Winnipeg. After 1982 until his retirement in 1987, he was executive vice president successively of Phoenix Mutual in Hartford and Benetech in Colorado.

Mr. Keffer was a man of many talents and church and community interests. He enjoyed hiking and collecting Native American art, was a licensed amateur radio operator, and engaged enthusiastically in carpentry and reading. He is survived by his wife, Kathleen, six daughters, a son, and three grandchildren.

1952   Larry Lang   1995

Larry Lang, a Fellow of the Society, died suddenly in Brooksville, Florida on April 5, 1995. He was 42 years old.

Born in Savannah, Georgia on May 9, 1952, Mr. Lang excelled scholastically in high school and graduated summa cum laude in mechanical engineering from Stevens Institute of Technology in 1974 after having passed some Society examinations. He immediately joined Prudential Insurance Company as an actuarial trainee and earned his Fellowship in 1977 at age 25.

He thereupon entered the consulting field with The Wyatt Company in Dallas, where he demonstrated high ethical standards and great energy. In 1994 he moved to the post of vice president and actuary at Pan-American Life in New Orleans, but after a few months returned to consulting in Texas and Florida.

Mr. Lang was a man of extraordinary talents, particularly in music. At age 15 he was playing in the Valley Forge (Pa.) Orchestra for gifted students, and he played both violin and clarinet in high school and college orchestras. He was also active and proficient in tennis and marathon running.

A devoted husband and father, he is survived by his wife, Joyce, and a daughter, as well as by his parents and a sister.

1940   Ben Zijon Lipshitz   1995

Ben Z. Lipshitz, a Fellow of the Institute of Actuaries and an Associate of the Society, died suddenly from a heart attack in Johannesburg, South Africa on July 6, 1995. He was 55 years old.

Born in Johannesburg on February 29, 1940, Mr. Lipshitz graduated from the London School of Economics in 1964 and immediately began actuarial work at Liberty Life Association of Africa in Johannesburg. He earned his Institute Fellowship in 1967 and his Society Associateship by waiver the following year.

He was with Liberty Life Association in the post of Senior General Manager at the time of his untoward death.

1908   Arthur Earl Loadman   1995

A. Earl Loadman, a 1933 Fellow of the Society, died in Winnipeg, Canada on October 8, 1995. He was 87 years old.

Born in Winnipeg on July 28, 1908. Mr. Loadman graduated from University of Manitoba's actuarial course in 1928 and in 1929 joined the actuarial department of Manufacturers Life for two separate terms in 1929 and in 1930–1931. He moved to Great-West Life in Winnipeg in 1931 for a career there that was to last almost 40 years, his ultimate post being vice-president and senior actuary. He retired in 1970.

Mr. Loadman had a brilliant mind and high ethical standards. His personality was gentle and his sense of humor apt, dry, and thoroughly engaging. He is survived by his wife, Rita.

1914   Ralph Haynes Maglathlin   1995

Ralph H. Maglathlin, a Fellow of the Society, died in West Hartford, Connecticut on September 14, 1995. He was 81 years old.

Born in Springfield, Massachusetts on August 29, 1914, Mr. Maglathlin graduated from Williams College in 1935 and joined Travelers Insurance Company the next year for a career that was to last 40 years. From 1942 to 1946 he served in the U.S. Navy with rank of lieutenant. He earned his Fellowship in 1950.

At Travelers he rose to the post of Vice President and Actuary in the group pension and asset management fields. He served on several actuarial committees involved with group underwriting, accounting and federal legislation and contributed substantially to Society discussions for a number of years.

Mr. Maglathlin was a gentle man whose civic and community activities were extensive in such fields as municipal finance, ski and yacht clubs, and alumni and church bodies. His first wife, Beverly, and second wife, Hilda, having both long predeceased him, he is survived by two daughters, a stepdaughter, and five grandchildren.

1940   Keith Leslie McComb   1995

Keith L. McComb, a Fellow of the Society, died in Calgary, Alberta on August 18, 1995. He was 55 years old.

Born in Dauphin, Manitoba on May 24, 1940, Mr. McComb after high school began teaching and then entered life insurance, selling with Sun Life of Canada and then Canadian Premier Life. In 1966 he enrolled at University of Manitoba, where, learning of the actuarial profession from Professor E.R. Vogt, he took the actuarial course, graduating in 1970. He earned his Society Fellowship in 1976 while employed at Monarch Life and in 1978 entered the consulting field, first with Turnbull & Turnbull, Winnipeg and then in 1980 with Reed Stenhouse in Calgary. From 1982 until his death he was consulting for the Wyatt Company in Calgary. From time to time he lectured at the Universities of Manitoba and Calgary.

He was active in Freemasonry in Winnipeg and Calgary and also in Scottish Rite and the Shrine.

Mr. McComb was a good person with a big heart and was known for his generous hospitality, booming infectious laugh, and tremendous sense of humor. Devoted to his family, friends, profession, and Lodge, he was also an avid soccer fan and a gourmet cook. He is survived by his wife, Heather, two sons, his mother, and a sister.

1923　　　Alexander Marshall　　　1995

Alexander Marshall, a Fellow of the Society, died in Tucson, Arizona on April 17, 1995. He was 71 years old.

Born in Winnipeg, Canada on September 12, 1923, Mr. Marshall graduated from the University of Manitoba in 1945. Shortly afterwards he moved to Kentucky as an actuarial clerk at Commonwealth Life. In 1949 he joined the actuarial staff at Occidental Life of California, where he earned his Society Fellowship in 1958. He later moved to West Coast Life, first as Associate Actuary and then as Vice President. His final move was to Metropolitan Life in New York City, where in due course he reached the post of Vice President. Unfortunately his health was poor, and in September 1986 he retired on permanent total disability.

Despite his health problem he was an avid traveler by recreational vehicle; friends recall that he continued this activity even when he had to take along a dialysis machine. He is survived by his wife, Alberta, and a son.

1924　　Laurence Harding Migotti　　1994

L. Harding Migotti, an Associate of the Society, died in Calgary, Alberta on July 17, 1994. He was 69 years old.

Born in La Plata, Argentina on October 23, 1924, Mr. Migotti graduated from Cambridge University in 1949 after serving in the Royal Navy from 1943 to 1946. From 1950 to 1953 he taught at St. George's College in Argentina and then went to Canada and taught briefly at Trinity College School in Port Hope, Ontario. He earned his Society Associateship in 1957.

Successfully combining business and teaching careers, Mr. Migotti worked first at William M. Mercer in Montreal, then at Equitable Life Assurance Society in New York, Tomenson-Alexander in Calgary, and finally at Alexander Consulting Group in Calgary until retiring from the post of vice president in 1987. Meanwhile he taught mathematics at Concordia University in Montreal from 1963 to 1975 and at University of Calgary as adjunct associate professor from 1987 until his death.

His colleagues at the University of Calgary describe him as a scholar and a gentleman and credit him with having helped to establish its actuarial department. They are establishing a scholarship for actuarial students in his name. He is survived by his wife, Jean, a son, a daughter, and two grandchildren.

1915   Morton David Miller   1995

Morton D. Miller, a Fellow and a Past President of the Society, and also of the American Academy of Actuaries, died in New York City on July 8, 1995 after a long illness. He was 80 years old.

Born in New York City on January 4, 1915, Mr. Miller graduated from the College of the City of New York in 1937 and immediately joined the actuarial staff of Equitable Life Assurance Society for a distinguished career that was to last for 43 years. He retired in 1980 from the post of Vice Chairman of his company's Board.

Mr. Miller achieved his Society Fellowship in 1941. He was elected to our Board of Governors in 1956, as Vice President in 1959, for a second Board term in 1961, again as Vice President in 1964, and became our President in 1967.

His contributions to our profession's literature were many and diverse. A major and eminently successful task was his authorship in 1946 of *Elements of Graduation*, the first American text on its subject, relieving generations of students from seeking enlightenment by plowing through original papers; in this he was assisted by Henry S. Beers, Charles A. Spoerl, and Hugh H. Wolfenden. Mr. Miller wrote three papers early in his career on group health insurance topics, and through the years contributed discussions on a wide range of subjects, notably in 1964 (*TSA* XVI, D332) on the birth of the Medicare program. A fourth formal paper in 1961 (*TSA* XIII, 586) reported on the Commissioners 1960 Standard Group Mortality Table and resulting group life premium rates, which had been constructed under his chairmanship of the Industry Advisory Committee to the National Association of Insurance Commissioners.

Mr. Miller devoted most of his Society Presidential Address (*TSA* XX, 309) to appraising the Society's ability to cope with an era of increasingly complex actuarial responsibilities. Applying to our organization several tests of viability offered in John W. Gardner's book *Self-Renewal*, Mr. Miller concluded that we could feel "secure in the knowledge that the Society has prepared well for what the future may bring."

He was a studious, friendly, and utterly determined actuary who accomplished his full share in assuring that our profession would continue to make its worthy contribution to the welfare of mankind. He did this by personal example much more than by injunction. Active also in industry and community affairs, he gave leadership and wise counsel in national health insurance and social security fields.

Mr. Miller is remembered by his many friends for his modesty, his devotion to high standards, and his gentle humor. His wife, Florence, having predeceased him in 1980, he is survived by a son, Jonathan.

1911   Zehman Irving Mosesson   1995

Zehman (Z) I. Mosesson, a Fellow of the Society, died in Union, New Jersey, on August 1, 1995 after a brief illness. He was 83 years old.

Born in Brownsville, Pennsylvania of Russian parentage on October 11, 1911, Mr. Mosesson graduated from Harvard University in 1931 and by 1937 had earned his M.A. and Ph.D. from that institution. He then joined the actuarial staff at Prudential Insurance Company out of, he said, desperation; he doubted that he would be a brilliant research mathematician and saw no prospect of a good college teaching post in that depression era. Completion of his Society Fellowship, in 1948, had been delayed by World War II service in the Coast Artillery 1941–1946 as one of several actuaries chosen for their mathematical expertise.

In his company he became, for most of his career, a vice president in charge of valuation and drafting policies for individual life, health, and pension coverages. He retired in 1972 and for several subsequent years taught at the College of Insurance in New York.

A ranking authority on actuarial mathematics, Mr. Mosesson contributed substantially to the education, indeed to the inspiration, of several generations of our students, particularly as longtime member, chairman, and consultant on life contingencies to the Society's Education and Examination Committee. Professor C. Wallace Jordan cited him for countless improvements throughout the 1967 edition of Jordan's *Life Contingencies*, the Society's textbook. But his enthusiasm for Jordan's treatment did not prevent Mr. Mosesson from mastering its successor *Actuarial Mathematics*, published in 1986. He had, remarked one student, the patience of Job and, when he finally gave up helping students, wanted to make sure that life contingencies would be as readily taught as it had been when he first proofread Jordan's text.

Early in his career, Mr. Mosesson wrote a Society paper, "Prudential 1946–1948 Disability Experience" (*TSA* I, 499) and several discussions. He also contributed the section labeled "Actuarial Opportunities" to the Mathematical Association of America's 1949 pamphlet informing college students of available mathematical careers.

Apart from his professional and business accomplishments, Mr. Mosesson was well-known and admired for his cheerful good nature, keen wit, and his wide-ranging store of general knowledge. His hobby was classical music, particularly Wagnerian opera. He was regularly a Metropolitan Opera patron and frequently attended the Wagner festivals at Bayreuth. He even instructed that his ashes be scattered in that German city. He is survived by a sister in Florida.

1906 Charles Edwin Rickards 1995

Charles E. Rickards, a Fellow of the Society, died in Gladwyne, Pennsylvania on June 20, 1995. He was 88 years old.

Born in Philadelphia on September 23, 1906, Mr. Rickards graduated from Swarthmore College in 1927 and earned his master's degree in mathematics there in 1928. He then joined the actuarial staff of Penn Mutual Life in Philadelphia for a career that was to continue for 43 years of steadily increasing responsibility followed by 5 years as a consultant. His Society Fellowship was achieved with unusual speed in 1932.

In his company he was promoted to Vice President and Actuary in 1950 and to Senior Vice President and Chief Actuary in 1961. He gained a reputation for brilliance in problem-solving, exemplified by his pioneering his company's early entry into the computer field in the mid-1950s. He retired in 1971.

Although of a naturally quiet disposition, Mr. Rickards was active in Society discussions and in committee work. He was proud of his profession's ethical standing, serving as a model in good practices to his colleagues. Likewise he was diligent in good works on behalf of his community and his college. His wife, Dorothy, having predeceased him in 1993, he is survived by three daughters and four grandchildren.

1923 Alexander Campbell Macintosh Robertson 1995

Alexander C.M. Robertson, a Fellow of the Faculty of Actuaries and an Associate of the Society, died in Toronto, Canada on March 11, 1995 after a courageous battle with cancer. He was 71 years old.

Born in Glasgow, Scotland on May 26, 1923, Mr. Robertson entered Aberdeen University in 1941 from Gordon's College, Aberdeen. His studies were in abeyance from 1942 to 1945 by service in the Royal Air Force as a pilot with the rank of flight lieutenant. After graduation in 1947 he joined Sun Life of Canada at its London, England headquarters, moving in 1952 to his company's Montreal head office. He earned his Faculty Fellowship in 1954 and obtained his Society Associateship by waiver that year.

Blessed with a keen mind and an outgoing personality, Mr. Robertson was rapidly promoted to positions of increasing company responsibility, particularly in its Group Division, which he ultimately headed several years before being appointed Chief Actuary and Chief Financial Officer in 1973. He was an executive officer from 1965 until his retirement in 1983.

Mr. Robertson became well-known in the Society for his spirited part in its discussions and for his role as a popular host at its meetings, where he was frequently seen with the late Andrew C. Webster, a fellow Aberdonian. In Montreal and Toronto he was a keen competitor in badminton, golf, and curling. His many other interests included stamp and coin collecting, serious reading, theatre, and symphony. He is remembered also for his helpfulness and his infectious sense of humor.

He is survived by his wife, Joyce, a son, and a daughter.

1921   Joseph F. Saulon   1995

Joseph F. Saulon, a 1965 Associate of the Society, died in Wayzata, Minnesota on February 3, 1995. He was 74 years old.

Born in Lowell, Massachusetts on January 12, 1921, Mr. Saulon graduated from the University of Iowa in 1947 after World War II service in the Army Air Corps and earned his master's at the same university in 1948. His entire actuarial career from 1948 until his retirement in 1981 was in the consulting field with Marsh & MacLennan and William M. Mercer in Chicago and Minneapolis.

Joe is survived by his wife, Gloria, a son, two daughters, and a granddaughter.

1906   Edward Gladstone Schafer   1995

Edward G. Schafer, a Fellow of the Society, died in Waterloo, Ontario on February 4, 1995 following a heart attack. He was 88 years old.

Born in Erbsville, Ontario on July 9, 1906, Mr. Schafer graduated from Waterloo College in 1923 and then, after brief employment as a clerk in Dominion Life Assurance Company in Waterloo, took a leave of absence to enter the University of Toronto, graduating in 1929. He then returned to his company, earning his Society Fellowship in 1934. In World War II he served with the Adjutant General's Branch of the Canadian Army with the rank of Major.

Mr. Schafer served Dominion Life in increasingly responsible posts, culminating in seven years as President and C.E.O. In 1969 he was President of the Canadian Life Insurance Association. After retirement from his company in 1971, he joined Lutheran Life in the formation of that Canadian company.

Mr. Schafer was notably active in community affairs, particularly in the arts and his church. He was elected to and rose to become Vice Chairman of the Waterloo Public School Board and served on the Board of Governors of then Waterloo Lutheran, now Wilfred Laurier, University.

He is survived by his wife, Geraldine, and by two sons.

1915   Philip D. Slater   1995

Philip D. Slater, a Fellow of the Society, died in Nyack, New York on July 26, 1995. He was 79 years old.

Born Philip Di Salvatore in Newark, New Jersey on October 19, 1915, Mr. Slater graduated from the Massachusetts Institute of Technology in 1936 and earned his master's degree at Princeton University in 1938. Among his memories of Princeton was studying under Albert Einstein and playing the viola in that great man's string quartet.

In 1939 Mr. Slater entered the actuarial program at Guardian Life in New York City. He transferred to the Equitable Society in 1942, qualifying as a Fellow of the Actuarial Society in 1948 and continuing with that company as an assistant actuary until 1966. For the next three years he was Executive Director of the Federation Pension Bureau in New York City and from 1969 till his retirement in 1982 was in the consulting field in his firm, Woodward & Slater.

Philip is remembered as a very private person. He is survived by his wife, Cecile, two daughters, and four grandchildren.

1905   Anastase Eugene Statius   1994

Anastase (Stacey) E. Statius, an Associate of the Society, died in Fort Lee, New Jersey on August 26, 1994. He was a few days short of his 89th birthday.

Born in Greece on September 1, 1905, Mr. Statius graduated from the University of Rochester in 1927 and joined the actuarial staff of Guardian Life Insurance Company in New York City. He earned his Society Associateship in 1936 and entered the consulting field with George B. Buck Company. He remained with that firm until his retirement from the post of vice president in the early 1970s. He remained in consulting work on his own for several years afterward.

His friends remember him for his lighthearted sense of humor. He is survived by his wife, Ellen, a daughter, and two grandchildren.

1939   Terence Norman Towry   1995

Terence (Terry) N. Towry, a Fellow of the Society, died in Glastonbury, Connecticut on July 30, 1995 after a long illness. He was 55 years old.

Born in Tulsa, Oklahoma on November 29, 1939, Mr. Towry graduated from Tulsa University in 1963. From then until 1967 he was an actuarial student at U.S. Fidelity & Guaranty in Baltimore. In 1958 he joined Phoenix Mutual Life and earned his Society Fellowship in 1973. He was appointed reinsurance vice president in 1979 and six years later senior vice president responsible for administration and support services and for developing his company's international operations. He had retired shortly before his death.

Mr. Towry had a quiet and easy-going manner and enjoyed the respect and confidence of his colleagues. He was an ardent golfer, and he had served as a deacon of his church and on the board of Church Homes, Inc. in the Hartford area. He is survived by his wife, Susan, three daughters, and a sister.

1946   Paul Franklin Weber   1995

Paul F. Weber, a Fellow of the Society, died suddenly while driving on a highway near New York City on August 8, 1995, apparently of a heart attack. He was 49 years old.

Born in Paterson, New Jersey on February 24, 1946, Mr. Weber graduated from Carnegie-Mellon University in 1968. He then spent several years in the U.S. Army, which included time in Vietnam. He joined the staff of Travelers Insurance Company in Hartford, achieving his Society Fellowship in 1976. Subsequently he was with American Life in Delaware, moving to Metropolitan Life in 1986. At the time of his death he held the post of Assistant Vice President and Actuary in that company's Financial Management Section.

He had a lifelong interest in the external world of mountains, national parks, animals, and astronomy and was an active contributor to charitable and religious activities. He is survived by his father, Joseph, and three brothers.

1918   William Rulon Williamson, Jr.   1994

William (Bill) R. Williamson, Jr., an Associate of the Society, died in Santa Rosa, California on December 5, 1994. He was 76 years old.

Born in Hartford, Connecticut on October 2, 1918, son of the famous actuary whose obituary is printed in *TSA* XXXII, 698, Mr. Williamson graduated from Wesleyan University, Middletown, Connecticut in 1940 and immediately joined the actuarial staff of Metropolitan Life Insurance Company for a 40-year career. From 1942 to 1946 he served in the U.S. Air Force, reaching the rank of captain. He earned his Society Associateship in 1950 and retired in 1980 from the post of Manager in the Group Life Actuarial Division. Afterward he enjoyed tutoring young people in mathematics and doing volunteer work for the Audubon Society.

He was a quiet and faithful member of his company's actuarial contingent, respected and esteemed by his colleagues. An ardent family man, he bestowed loves for nature, for hiking, and for appreciative sightseeing. He is survived by his wife, Elizabeth, two daughters, and two grandchildren.